CONCRETE TECHNOLOGY

B.L. Gupta
M.E. Civil Engg. (Roorkee)
Formerly Head of Civil Engg. Dept. & Principal

and

Amit Gupta
B.E. (Hons) I.R.S.E.

STANDARD PUBLISHERS DISTRIBUTORS

1705-B, NAI SARAK, POST BOX No.: 1066, DELHI-110006
Phones : 3262700, 3285798, Fax: 3243180
email: stpub@vsnl.com www.standardpublishers.com

Published by :
A. K. Jain
For Standard Publishers Distributors
1705-B, Nai Sarak, Delhi-110006.

First Edition : 1989
Third Edition : 2004
Reprint : 2008
Fourth Edition : 2010
Reprint : 2012
Reprint : 2014
Reprint : 2018

Price Rs. 275-00

ISBN : 978-81-8014-170-6

Laser Typesetting by : Bhargave Laser Printers, Delhi.
Printed by : Prabhat Offset Press, Delhi.

PREFACE

Cement mortar and cement concrete are the most widely used in construction materials. Technological advancement is taking place at a much faster rate in all fields through out the world. During last two decades much technological advancement in the production of cement and construction activities have taken place through out the world. Cement production is India in 2002 has crossed 100 million tones.

Concrete technology is getting momentum every day and has become a major branch of Civil Engineering now. Thus to keep the development in the field of cement and concrete technology authors have tried to consolidate the available new material on the subject in a consize form in the lucid language useful for students preparing for degree, diploma and competitive examinations.

All chapters have been fully revised and chapters have been increased from 18 to 28 to accommodate new materials. At the end of each chapter objective type questions have been added to enhance the knowledge of the students. In all about 550 objective type questions have been added. We hope this book will prove useful not only to students preparing for examinations but to Practicing Engineers also.

Authors are thankful to all those, who helped in any form in preparing this book. Though every effort has been made to eliminate errors, yet some printing errors might have been left unnoticed. Authors sincerely request the readers to bring any mistake noticed by them to the notice of publisher or authors for the improvement of the text. Any constructive criticism for the improvement of the book will be welcome.

At the end we express our thanks to the M/s Standard Publishers Distributors to bring out this book in so nice a get up in a very short period.

B.L. GUPTA
AMIT GUPTA

CONTENTS

1
Introduction

1.1. GENERAL

Cement concrete is an important construction material. Its importance is increasing every day. It is a composite material consisting a binding material, which is essentially cement, inert mineral filler, known as aggregates and water. Thus cement concrete can be prepared by mixing above ingredients in a fixed proportion. Green concrete is a plastic mass, which can be moulded into any desired shape. This is its main advantage as a construction material.

Aggregate, coarse and fine combined occupy about 75% space with in a given mass of concrete and the rest of 25% space is filled by water, cement and air voids.

1.2. FUNCTIONS OF AGGREGATE AND CEMENT PASTE

The aggregate has following three main functions:

1. It provides a mass of particles, which resists the action of applied loads, abrasion, percolation of moisture and the action of the weather.
2. It reduces the volume changes resulting from setting and hardening process and from moisture changes in the cement paste.
3. It provides a relatively cheap filler for the cementing material.

The properties of concrete resulting from the use of a particular aggregate depend upon the following factors:

1. **The mineral characteristics of the aggregate particles.** It influences particularly strength, durability and elasticity of concrete.
2. **Surface characteristics of the particles.** It has a marked influence on the workability of fresh concrete and bond in the hardened concrete.
3. **Grading of aggregate.** It has a marked influence on the workability, density and economy of concrete.
4. **Amount of aggregate per unit-volume of concrete.** It has a marked influence on the cost and volume changes due to drying.

1.3. CEMENT PASTE

It is a binder material, which is formed by the hydration of cement. After adding water to the cement, it begins to hydrate and forms a gel. Cement needs 23% water of its weight for hydration and 15% for filling the space or voids of gel. Thus for complete hydration of cement 38% of water of weight of cement is required. If more water is added to cement paste, it will evaporate forming capillary voids, resulting honey combed structure of the paste. This will reduce the strength and other properties of concrete. The gel occupies about 2.1 times the volume of dry cement and forms cement paste with fine aggregate. The strength of concrete depends upon the physical characteristics of this gel.

1.3.1. Functions of Cement paste

Folowings are the main functions of the cement paste:

1. It provides lubrication to the coarse aggregate and helps in compaction of the green concrete.
2. It fills the voids in between the inert-aggregates.
3. It provides a plastic mass, which can be moulded in any shape.
4. It provides strength and water tightness to the concrete in the hardened state.

The properties of hardened paste depend upon the following factors.

(*a*) Characteristics of cement

(*b*) Water-cement ratio and

(*c*) Completeness of hydration of cement.

1.4. GENERAL PROPORTION OF ORDINARY CONCRETE

The properties of green *i.e.* freshly prepared concrete and hardened concrete depend upon the relative proportions of the component ingredients. In fresh concrete the coarse aggregate is suspended in the cement paste. In this state the cement paste should not only coat the aggregate, but also should fill the voids between them. The consistency of the mass is controlled by the fluidity of the paste and gradation and shape of aggregate particles. For almost all works, plastic consistency is desirable as too wet or too harsh a mixture will produce defective products.

In case of hardened concrete, strength and porosity is one function of the density of paste, which in turn is controlled by water-cement ratio in the mix. Thus there are practical limits to the proportions of cement, water and aggregate (coarse as well as fine aggregate) in normal concrete. The general proportions of practical mixes are shown in the lower diagram of Fig. 1.1. All mixes are of the same consistency. In this figure, the ratio of cement to combined aggregate varies from 1:3 to 1:9. From the figure it will be seen that the volume of aggregate varies from 66% for 1:3 ratio to 76% for 1:9 cement aggregate ratio and the cement ratio varies from 16% to 7% making cement and aggregate as 82% to 83% of the volume of concrete. Thus in lean mixes the quantity of cement is even less than 50% than in the rich mixes.

The water content varies from 16% to 18% of the total volume of concrete. The amount of water for 1:3 mix is 18%, 16% for 1:6 mix and 17.3% for 1:9 mix. Thus it is clear from the above that water content is practically constant for all mixes while the cement content varies considerably. Hence in lean mixes greater water cement ratio is used. Thus for the same consistency an intimate relation exists between the richness of mix and water cement ratio.

The upper diagram of Fig. 1.1 shows the relative proportion of cement, combined water and free water in the total volume of paste of the mixes represented by the lower diagram. From the diagram it will be seen that per unit of paste, the amount of combined water practically remains the same for all mixes. Also to produce a workable mix about 70% more water is required to be added than is necessary for the hydration of

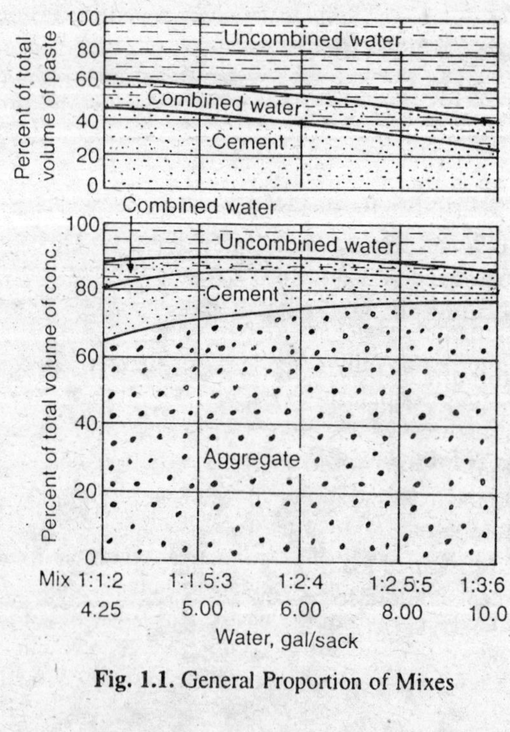

Fig. 1.1. General Proportion of Mixes

cement. Actually about 25% to 30% water is required for hydration of cement, which is added to a workable mix. Thus pastes having high water cement ratios contain more free or uncombined water than those having low water-cement-ratios. As free water occupies effective pore space, the paste in lean mixes has more porous structure than rich mixes. Actually the properties of the concrete are governed by the physical structure of the gel, discussed in chapter 7 (properties of fresh concrete).

1.5. ADVANTAGES OF CONCRETE

Concrete is considered superior than other construction materials due to the following reasons:

1. Green or freshly prepared concrete can be moulded in any desired shape easily.
2. Concrete can be mixed at places many kilometer away from the actual site of work and used without any loss of property of the good concrete.
3. Concrete of any desired compressive strength can be prepared.
4. Using steel along with concrete any type of structure can be built.
5. Almost all types of structures can be built with R.C.C.
6. As concrete has high compressive strength, it can be used economically.
7. Light weight and fire resistant concrete can also be prepared. Light weight concrete is useful for partition work.
8. Materials used in the production of concrete are easily available.
9. It can be pumped and placed even in very difficult locations.
10. It can be sprayed and can be used to rectify small cracks and repair work by gunitting or shot creting.
11. It provides quickness and ease in the construction of monolithic members of the structures.
12. It provides good architectural look to the structure.
13. It is quite durable and not liable to be attacked by white ants or termite.
14. The maintenance cost of structure made of concrete is less.
15. It is fire resistant and can also be used as sound proof by replacing the coarse aggregate either by light weight aggregate or using foam concrete.

1.6. DISADVANTAGES OF CONCRETE

Concrete has following disadvantages:

1. It's tensile strength is very low of the order of 10% of the compressive strength. Thus it develops cracks. To avoid the development of cracks, steel is used as reinforcement.
2. Due to rise in temperature, concrete expands and due to fall in temperature it shrinks. Thus to avoid the development of deformation in concrete structures, expansion joints are provided at suitable locations and interval discussed later in chapter 27.
3. The fresh concrete shrinks very much on drying and hardened concrete expands on getting moisture, and again shrinks on drying.
4. Concrete is not fully impermeable material. Hence to store salty water, special treatment of the surface is essential, more specially at joints.
5. For structures which come in contact with alkaline and sulphate mixed water, special cement should be used as ordinary cement will disintegrate easily.
6. Due to the more weight of concrete, more reinforcement is needed, which increases the cost of the structure.
7. Due to sustained load, more creep develops in the concrete. Hence at the time of design, provision for creep should also be kept.

QUESTIONS

1. Discuss the functions of aggregate and cement paste in concrete.
2. Why cement concrete is considered superior to other constructional materials.
3. Give advantages and disadvantages of concrete.
4. Write a note on general proportion of ordinary concrete.
5. Write a note on cement paste.
6. What are the harmful effects of more water in cement paste.

OBJECTIVE TYPE QUESTIONS

1. Cement is an essential ingredient of concrete due to
   (*a*) It is an active ingredient
   (*b*) It is a binding medium for other ingredients
   (*c*) It is an delicate link of the chain
   (*d*) It is the only scientifically controlled ingredient
   (*e*) Any of above
2. Which of the following statements is not fully correct
   (*a*) Coarse aggregate provides mass to the concrete
   (*b*) It controls the volume changes in the cement paste of the concrete
   (*c*) It is fully inert ingredient of the concrete.
   (*d*) It provides relatively cheap filler for the cementing material
3. Which of the following statements is not correct
   (*a*) The cement paste provides lubrication to the coarse aggregate and helps in the compaction of green concrete
   (*b*) It provides a plastic mass to the concrete, which can be moulded in any shape
   (*c*) It provides strength and impermeability to the concrete
   (*d*) It does not fills the voids in between the aggregate particles
   (*e*) It does not provides durability to the concrete
4. Which of the following statements is incorrect
   (*a*) The properties of hardened paste depend upon the water/cement ratio
   (*b*) The properties of hardened paste depend upon the heat of hydration
   (*c*) The properties of hardened paste depend upon the completeness of hydration of cement
   (*d*) The properties of hardened paste depend upon the characteristics of cement
5. In an ordinary concrete the ratio of cement to combined aggregate 1:3 to 1:9 varies as
   (*a*) 60 to 70% (*b*) 55 to 65% (*c*) 66 to 76% (*d*) 57 to 75%
6. In an ordinary concrete the cement ratio varies
   (*a*) 16 to 7% (*b*) 19 to 10% (*c*) 17 to 11% (*d*) 21 to 5%
7. The water content in an ordinary concrete varies
   (*a*) 16 to 18% (*b*) 15 to 20% (*c*) 12 to 20% (*d*) 20 o 25%
8. Identify the true or false statements
   (*a*) Green Concrete can not be moulded in the desired shape.
   (*b*) Concrete can be pumped and placed in congested places.
   (*c*) Concrete of any desired strength can not be prepared.
   (*d*) For the production of high strength concrete w/c ratio less than 0.33 can be used usefully with out any other aid.
   (*e*) Concrete can be mixed far away from the site of work and used with out any loss of its property.
   (*f*) Concrete can not be used in all types of structures.
   (*g*) The maintenance cost of concrete structures is less.
   (*h*) Concrete is fully impermeable material.
   (*i*) The tensile strength of concrete is about 10% of its compressive strength.
   (*j*) Due to the rise in temperature concrete expands and due to the fall in temperature it shrinks.

Answers

1. (*e*)
2. (*c*)
3. (*d, e*)
4. (*b*)
5. (*c*)
6. (*a*)
7. (*a*)
8. *False:* (*a, c, d, f, h*)

2
Cement

2.1. INTRODUCTION

Cement is the main constituent of concrete. It can be defined as a material having adhesive and cohesive properties which make it capable of bonding mineral fragments into a compact mass. Actually this definition covers a large variety of cementing materials. For constructional purposes, the meaning of the term cement is restricted to the bonding materials used with stones, bricks, and sand etc. The principal constituents of this type of cement are compounds of lime. On adding water to cement a chemical reaction known as *hydration* of cement takes place and a large quantity of heat-liberates. On hydration of cement, gel is formed which binds the aggregate particles together and provides strength and water tightness to concrete on hardening. Thus cement has the property of setting and hardening under water by virtue of a chemical reaction with it. Such cements are called hydraulic cements. They consist mainly of aluminates and silicates of lime.

2.2. EARLY HISTORY OF CEMENT

The history of cementing material is as old as that of Engineering Construction. In ancient times Romans, Egyptians and Indians used some kind of cementing materials in their constructions. It is believed that Egyptians used burnt gypsum ($CaSo_4$) as cementing material in their constructions. Not much is known about the cementing material used by Indians in the construction of the cities of Harrapa and Mohenjadaro.

The analysis of mortar used in the construction of Great Pyramid showed that it contained 81.5 percent of calcium sulphate and about 9.5 percent calcium carbonate only. It is believed that early Romans and Greeks used cementing materials obtained by calcination (burning), of lime stone. The remarkable hardness of the mortars used by early Romans in their constructions obtained from some of the existing works provides sufficient evidence of the perfection of art of preparing cementing materials in ancient times. The superiority of Roman mortar is attributed to the thorough mixing and continued ramming for a long period.

Latter Romans and Greeks learnt that better cementing material may be obtained by mixing certain volcanic ash and tuff with lime stone, sand and water. This mixture produced a cementing material of superior strength and durability. The tuff used in the mix was found near the village Pozzuoli near mount vesuvius in Italy. The tuff or ash mostly is siliceous in nature. This type of tuff or ash was given the name of Pozzolana. After wards any material natural or artificial having the same properties as those of tuff or ash found near Pozzuoli was called pozzolana. In the absence of natural volcanic ash, Romans used powdered pottery or tiles as Pozzolana. In India surkhi (brick powder) has been used as Pozzolana in the mortar. In India the thorough mixing and long continuous ramming of lime mortar with or with out the use of surkhi yielded strong and imperious mortar which confirmed the secret of Roman mortar superiority.

Latter it is learnt that in order to improve the workability of mortar and concrete Romans added milk, blood and lard in the mix. The blood Haemoglobin is a powerful air entraining agent and plasticizer, which increases the workability, resulting the increase in the durability of their structures.

After 1756 John Smeaton carried out extensive experiments and made enquires to find out the best material to withstand severe action of sea water. On the basis of his experiments he concluded that lime stones containing considerable proportion of clayey matter produced better lime possessing superior hydraulic properties. However the findings of John Smeaton made little advancement and the old practice of a mixture of lime and Pozzolana remained in use for a long time.

In 1796 hydraulic cement was produced by burning the nodules of argillaceous lime stones. Four years latter in 1800 this product was given the name as Roman cement. This cement remained in use till 1850. After 1850 this cement was outdated and new product named portland cement was introduced.

2.3. CLASSIFICATION OF CEMENTS

Cements mainly can be classified into two groups, *viz.*

1. Natural cement
2. Artificial cement or portland cement.

1. Natural Cement. This type of cement can be obtained by burning lime stone containing 20-40% clay and crushing it to powder. It is brown in colour and sets very quickly when mixed with water. It is very akin to eminent hydraulic lime. The only difference between hydraulic lime and natural cement is that lime starts to slake on mixing water with it and natural cement sets immediately after adding water to it.

2. Artificial Cement. It can be classified as follows:

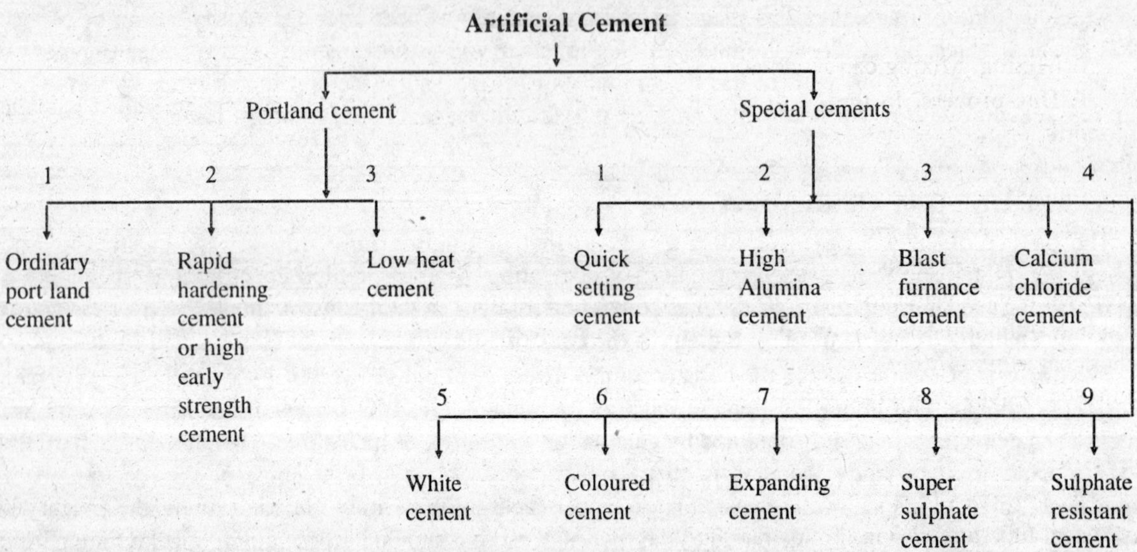

2.4. PORTLAND CEMENT

Portland cement was invented in 1824 by Joseph Aspdin, a brick layer of Leeds (Yorkshire) England. He obtained the patent of portland cement on 21st October 1824. This cement was prepared by heating a mixture of finely divided clay and hard lime stone in furnace until calcium dioxide (CO_2) had been driven off. This resulted at much lower temperature than that necessary for clinkering. The prototype of modern cement was made by Isaac Johnson, burning a mixture of clay and lime or chalk at clinkering temperature in 1845.

Originally, the name "Portland Cement" was given due to the fact that the mortar made with this cement resembled in appearance, colour and hardness to the stone which was quarried on the Isle of

Portland, U.K. The German standard specifications for portland cement were drawn in 1877, while British and American standard specifications were drawn in 1904.

In India, the portland cement was first manufactured in 1904 near madras, but the venture failed. Between 1912 and 1913, the Indian Cement Company Ltd. was established at Porbander (Gujrat) and by 1914 this company produced about 1000 tons of portland cement. By 1918 three more cement factories were established in India and all the factories produced about 85000 tons of cement every year.

After independence during 1951-56 cement production rose from 2.69 million tons to 4.6 million tons. By 1969 the production of cement in India was 13.2 million tons occupying the 9th place in the world, USSR being the highest cement producing country with the production of 89.4 million tons. In 2002 the production of cement in India crossed 100 million tons mark and we attained second position after China in the production of cement in the world.

2.5. MANUFACTURE OF PORTLAND CEMENT

As stated above portland cement can be manufactured by intimately mixing together calcareous and argillaceous stones containing silica, alumina, and iron oxide etc. and burning it in large rotary kilns at a temperature of approximately 1400°C to 1500°C. At his temperature the materials partially fuse, forming clinker. This clinker is cooled and ground to fine power. Usually it is gray or brownish in colour.

Manufacture

The manufacture of portland cement consists of the following three distinct processes.

1. Mixing
2. Burning
3. Grinding

1. Mixing. Mixing can be done either by dry process or wet-process.

1. Dry-process. In this process, the raw materials, lime stone and clay etc. are mixed in calculated proportions, crushed and ground in tube mills. The finely ground mixture is stored in silos and burnt as per need in the kiln and ground. Some times the crushed power is mixed with water and balls are prepared of the crushed material. Then these balls are burnt at clinker temperature in suitable hearths. The clinker formed is cooled and ground to specified fineness. This process has proved costlier.

2. (*a*) Wet-process. In this process the raw materials are crushed in roll mills and mixed in proper proportion with water to form slurry. The slurry is ground to form a smooth liquid in a huge horizontal rotating cylindrical mill. This slurry is stored in silos and proportion of materials checked. The correct chemical composition is adjusted by adding pure slurry of different materials prepared separately. The adjusted slurry is stored in silos to be fed into rotary kiln as and when required. This process ensures better control on chemical composition of slurry. The slurry is of creamy consistency having 35 to 50% water content.

2. (*b*) Burning. The fine slurry or dry mixture is burnt in rotary kilns shown in Fig. 2.1. A rotary kiln is a steel tube upto 7.5 m in diameter and 230 m long. usually the dimensions of a rotary kiln vary from 2 to 3 m in diameter and 30 to 100 m in length. It is kept inclined at a gradient of 1 in 25 to 1 in 30 with the horizontal rotating once every minute. This kiln is lined from inside with refractory material.

The slurry is fed at the upper end of the kiln and it gradually descends towards the flame burners at the lower end of the kiln. As the slurry descends, it comes in contact with hot gases and dries up forming small lumps or "nodules". These nodules gradually move downwards through rising temperature till they reach burning zone at a temperature of 1500°C to 1700°C. At this

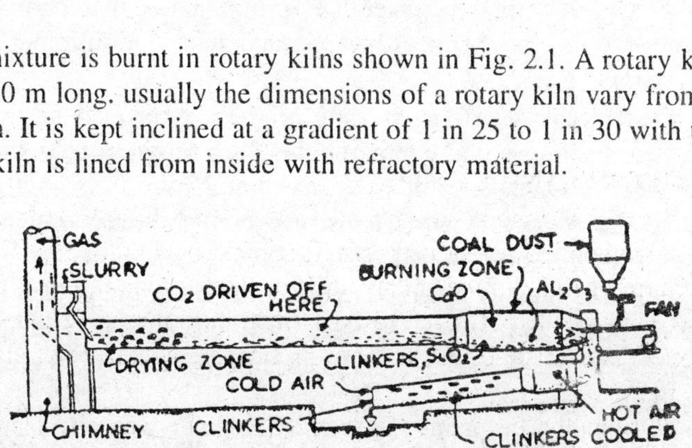

Fig. 2.1. Rotary kiln

temperature about 20-30% of the constituents of slurry become liquid and recombination of lime-silica-alumina mixture takes place, and the resulting mass fuses into balls known as clinker. At this temperature, the clinker is red hot emitting white rays of light. The flame is produced by burning pulverised coal or oil.

Now the clinker is discharged into another rotary tube which resembles the rotary kiln, but shorter in length having about 12 coolers. Various types of coolers are used in these tubes. The air sent by coolers become hot by exchanging heat from clinker. This hot-air is allowed to pass through the rotary kiln, which helps to heat the clinker. The largest existing capacity rotary kiln produces 3600 tonnes clinker per day. The cool clinker characteristically is black, glistening (shining brightly) and hard. The density of clinker is about 1100 to 1300 kg/per m^3.

2. (*c*) Effect of rate of cooling of clinker on strength of cement. It has been observed that the rate of cooling of clinker affects considerably the strength properties of cement. It has been observed that a moderate rate of cooling of clinker in the rotary cooler gives about 3.7% higher strength of cement at 28 days than quick cooling and about 11.1% less strength at slow cooling. The results based on the experiments carriedout by ENKEGAARD are shown in Table 2.1.

Table 2.1. Influence of rate of cooling of clinker on cement strength

Type of Cement	*Cooling Conditions*	*Compressive strength of Cement in (MPa)*		
		3 days	*7 days*	*28 days*
Normal cement	Quick	9.9	15.3	26
	Moderate	9.7	21.0	27
	Slow	9.7	19.3	24
	Very slow	8.7	18.7	23
High early strength cement	Quick	10.2	18.8	29
	Moderate	14.2	26.7	33
	Slow	10.2	21.0	29
	Very slow	9.1	18.1	28

From table 2.1, it can be seen that the moderate rate of cooling of clinker in the rotary cooler results in higher strength of cement.

Moderate rate of cooling may be taken that rate at which the clinker temperature from 1200°C to 500°C is reduced in about 15 minutes and from 500°C to normal atmospheric temperature in about 10 minutes.

The rate of cooling of the clinker influences the degree of crystallisation, size of the crystal and the quantity of amorphous materials present in the clinker. The properties of this amorphous material for similar chemical composition are found different from a crystalined one.

2. (*d*) Grinding. The grinding of the clinker is done in ball mills, consisting several compartments with progressively smaller steel balls. The diameter of balls may vary from 5 cm to 13 cm. Due to the impact of steel balls, the clinker breaks into small pieces. Fig. 2.2 shows a ball mill, while Fig. 2.3 shows a roll and ring mill. The product obtained in ball mills is ground in tube mills. The diameter and length of tube mill are 2-5 m and 10 m respectively. The diameter of balls used in this mill is 2.5 cm. Fig. 2.4 shows a tube mill.

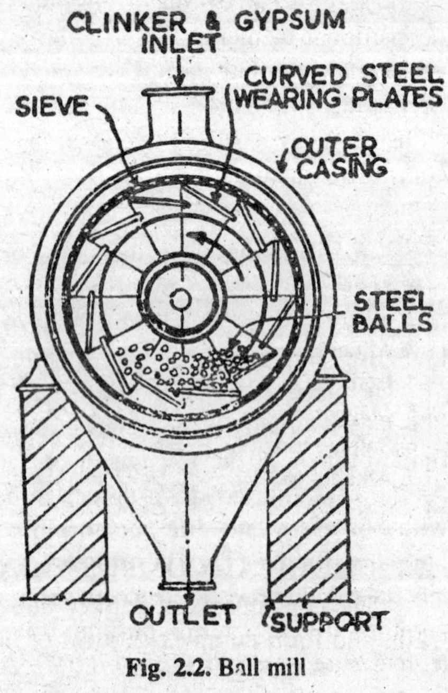

Fig. 2.2. Ball mill

At the time of grinding a small quantity of gypsum ($CaSo_4 2H_2O$) is added to the clinker to prevent flash setting of the

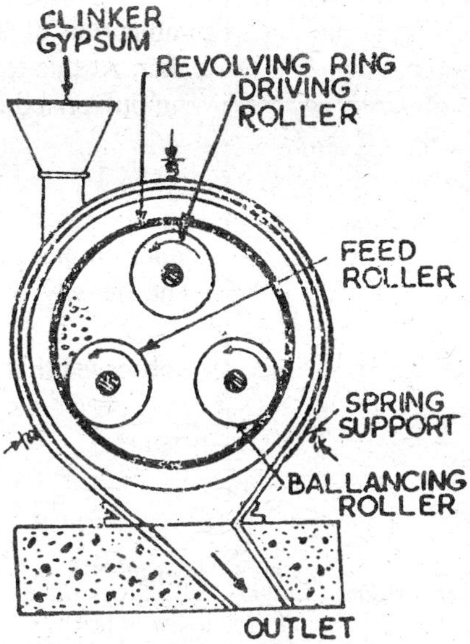

Fig. 2.3. Roll & Ring Mill

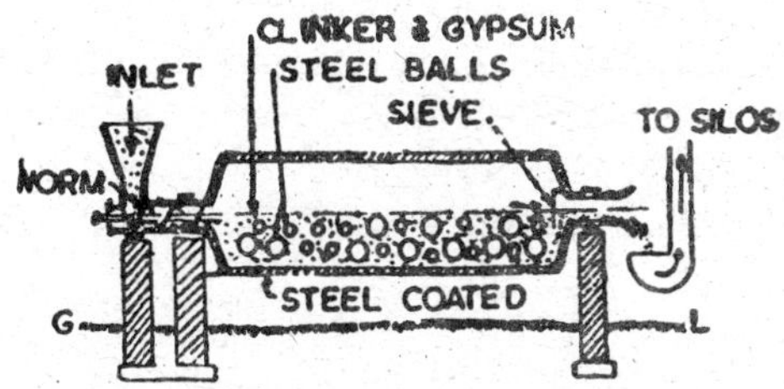

Fig. 2.4. Tube mill

cement. Usually gypsum is added from 2 to 4% by weight of clinker depending upon the quantity of C_3A and alkali content of cement. If the quantity of C_3A is not more than 5% then gypsum should not be added more than 2.5%, if C_3A is more than 5%, then 3% gypsum should be added, but in no case it should be more than 4%. The flow diagram of cement manufacture is a shown on page 10.

Coal requirement. In dry process 100 kg coal is required per ton of cement, while in wet process 350 kg coal is required for the same quantity of cement. In 1998 there were 173 large cement plants in India. Out of 173 plants 49 operated on wet-process, while 115 operated on dry process and 9 on semi dry process.

2.6. ELEMENTARY COMPOSITION OF CEMENT

The results of chemical analysis of cement have shown the percentage of oxides of principal constituent elements. The oxide composition of cement is shown in Table 2.2 Though variation range is fairly narrow, but it may result in an appreciable change in the proportion of the components actually present.

Table 2.2. Typical oxide composition of portland cement

Oxide		*Percent by weight*		
		Range	*Average*	*Value of compounds in %*
1. Lime	CaO	60 — 67	63	C_3S = 54.1
2. Silica	SiO_2	18 — 25	20	C_2S = 16.6
3. Alumina	Al_2O_3	3 — 8	6	C_3A = 10.8
4. Iron	Fe_2O_2	0.5 — 6	3	C_4AF = 9.1
5. Magnesesia	Mgo	0.1 — 4	1,5	
6. Sulpher trioxide	SO_3	1 — 3	2	
7. Alkalies etc.	K_2O and Na_2O	0.2 — 1.3	1	

2.7. CHEMICAL COMPOSITION OF CEMENT

The constituents of cement mainly lime, silica, alumina, and iron oxide interact with each other in the kiln and form complex product of definite molecular structure. The principal reactive compounds present

FLOW DIAGRAM OF CEMENT MANUFACTURE

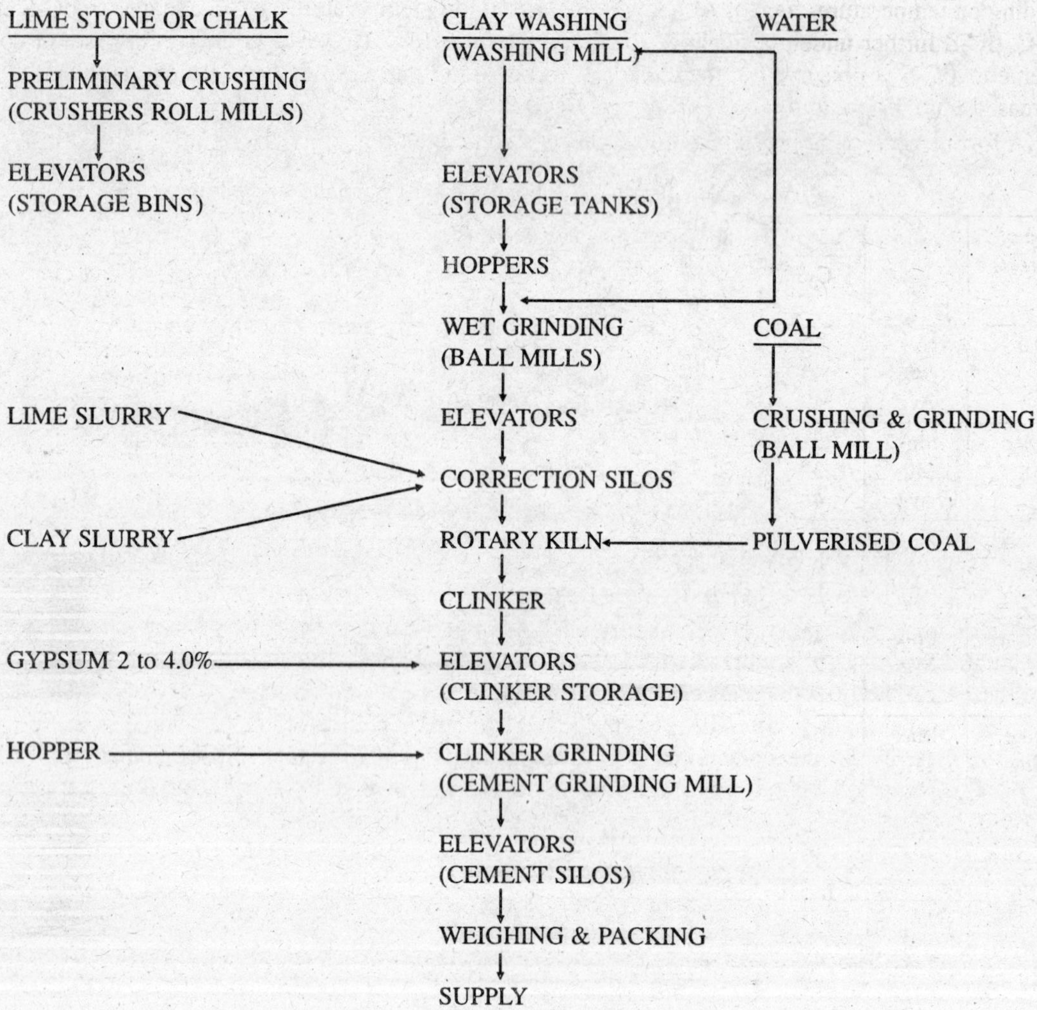

in the clinker as shown in Table 2.3 are known as Bogue's compounds.

Table 2.3. Principal compounds in Portland cement

Name of compoun	*Oxide composition*	*Abbreviation*
Tricalcium silicate	$3CaO.SiO_2$	C_3S
Dicalcium silicate	$2CaO.SiO_2$	C_2S
Tricalcium aluminate	$3CaO.Al_2O_3$	C_3A
Tetra calcium alumino ferite	$4CaO.Al_2O_3.Fe_2O_3$	C_4AF

The percentage of the compounds noted above depends upon the oxide percentage in the clinker and vary considerably from cement to cement as shown in table 2.4. In a well burnt modern clinker the amount of C_3S is about 40% and that of C_2S 25%. The sum total of C_3S and C_2S in most cements varies from 70-74%. Normally C_3S is found in largest quantity in any cement. It occurs as small equi-dimensional colourless grains. However the sum of the contents of C_3A and C_4AF has decreased slightly in modern cements. On cooling below 1250°C C_3S decomposes slowly, but if cooling is not very slow, C_3S remains unchanged and relatively is stable at ordinary temperatures. C_2S is found to have three or even four forms, depending on temperature, such as αC_2S, which exists at high temperatures, αC_2S changes to βC_2S at about 1450°C, βC_2S further undergoes change to γC_2S at about 670°C. However at the cooling rate of commercial cements βC_2S is preserved in the clinker. It forms round grains. In modern cement the quantity of C_3S is increased upto 45% and total of C_3S & C_2S to 70-80%.

C_3A forms rectangular crystals, while C_4AF is a solid solution.

Table 2.4. Compound composition of portland cement

Type of cement		*Compound composition %*								*Remarks*
		C_3S	C_2S	C_3A	C_4AF	$CaSO_4$	Free lime (CaO)	MgO	Ignition loss	
Normal	Max	67	31	14	12	3.4	1.5	3.8	2.3	
	Min	42	8	5	6	2.6	0.0	0.7	0.6	
	Avg	49	25	12	8	2.9	0.8	2.4	1.2	
Modified	Max	55	39	8	16	3.4	1.8	4.4	2.0	
	Min	37	19	4	6	2.1	0.1	1.5	0.5	
	Avg	46	29	6	12	2.8	0.6	3.0	1.0	
High early strength	Max	70	38	17	10	4.6	4.2	4.8	2.7	
	Min	34	0	7	6	2.2	0.1	1.0	1.1	
	Avg	56	15	12	8	3.9	1.3	2.6	1.9	
Low heat	Max	44	57	7	18	3.5	0.9	4.1	1.9	
	Min	21	34	3	6	2.6	0.0	1.0	0.6	
	Avg	30	46	5	13	2.9	0.3	2.7	1.0	
Sulphate resisting	Max	54	49	5	15	3.9	0.6	2.3	1.2	
	Min	35	24	1	6	2.4	0.1	0.7	0.8	
	Avg	43	36	4	12	2.7	0.4	1.6	1.0	

2.8. CALCULATION OF PERCENTAGE OF MAJOR COMPOUNDS

The percentage of major compounds in a clinker may be found from the Bogue's equations given below:

$$C_3S = 4.07\,(CaO) - 7.60(SiO_2) - 6.72\,(Al_2O_3) - 1.43\,(Fe_2O_3) - 2.85\,(SO_3)$$

$$C_2S = 2.87\,(SiO_2) - 0.754\,(3\,CaO.SiO_2)$$

$$C_3A = 2.65\,(Al_2O_3) - 1.69\,(Fe_2O_3)$$

$$C_4AF = 3.04\,(Fe_2O_3)$$

The oxide shown in brackets represent the percentage of the same in the raw material.

The method of calculation is illustrated by Example 2.1 below.

Example 2.1. *From Bogue equations, calculate the different compounds of the three cements, whose oxide composition is given below in table 2.5.*

Table 2.5

Oxide	*Content %*		
	A	*B*	*C*
CaO	68.2	61.0	64.2
SiO_2	22.4	25.0	20.7
Fe_2O_3	0.3	3.0	5.3
Al_2O_3	4.6	4.0	3.9
SO_3	2.4	2.5	2.0
Free lime	3.3	1.0	1.5

Solution. From Bogue equation the C_3S, C_2S, C_3A & C_4AF are given as follows:

$$C_3S = 4.07\,(CaO) - 7.6(SiO_2) - 6.72\,(Al_2O_3) - 1.43\,(Fe_2O_3) - 2.85\,(SO_3)$$

$$C_2S = 2.87\,(SiO_2) - 0.754\,(3\,CaO.SiO_2)\ \textit{i.e.}\ C_3S$$

$$C_3A = 2.65\,(Al_2O_3) - 1.69\,(Fe_2O_3)$$

$$C_4AF = 3.04\,(Fe_2O_3)$$

For cement A,

$$C_3S = 4.07(68.2) - 7.6(22.4) - 6.72(4.6) - 1.43\,(0.3) - 2.85\,(2.4)$$
$$= 277.574 - 170.24 - 30.96 - 0.429 - 6.84$$
$$= 277.574 - 208.469 = 69.1\%$$

$$C_2S = 2.87\,(22.4) - 0.754\,(69.1)$$
$$= 64.288 - 52.305 = 11.983 = 12\%$$

$$C_3A = 2.65\,(4.6) - 1.69\,(0.3)$$
$$= 12.19 - 0.507 = 11.69 \approx 11.7$$

$$C_4AF = 3.04\,(0.3) = 0.912 \approx 0.91$$

For cement B,

$$C_3S = 4.07\,(61.0) - 7.6\,(25.0) - 6.72\,(4.0) - 1.43\,(3.0) - 2.85\,(2.5)$$
$$= 248.27 - 190.0 - 26.88 - 4.29 - 7.125$$
$$= 248.27 - 228.295 = 19.975 \approx 20.0\%$$

$$C_2S = 2.87\,(25) - 0.754\,(20.0)$$
$$= 71.75 - 15.08 = 56.67\%$$

$$C_3A = 2.65\,(4.0) - 1.69\,(3) = 10.60 - 5.07 = 5.53\%$$

$$C_4AF = 3.04 \times 3 = 9.12\%$$

For cement C,

$$C_3S = 4.07\,(64.2) - 7.6\,(20.7) - 6.72\,(3.9) - 1.43\,(5.3) - 2.85\,(2.0)$$
$$= 261.294 - 157.32 - 26.608 - 7.579 - 5.70$$
$$= 261.294 - 196.808 = 64.486 \approx 64.5\%$$

$$C_2S = 2.87\,(20.7) - 0.754\,(64.5)$$
$$= 59.41 - 48.63 = 10.78 \approx 10.8\%$$

$$C_3A = 2.65\,(3.9) - 1.69\,(5.3)$$
$$= 10.335 - 8.957 = 1.378 \approx 1.4$$

$$C_4AF = 3.04 \times 5.3 = 16.1\%$$

Ans.

Cement	*Compound %*			
	C_3S	C_2S	C_3A	C_4AF
A	69.1	12	11.7	0.91
B	20.0	56.67	5.53	9.12
C	64.5	10.8	1.4	16.1

2.9. INFLUENCE OF CHANGE IN OXIDE COMPOSITION ON THE COMPOSITION OF CEMENT

It is interesting to note, the large influence of the change in the oxide composition on the compound composition of cement. In general a small increase in the total lime content of the raw materials appreciably increases the percentage of C_3S and decreases $C_2{\cdot}S$. An increase in the iron oxide content decreases the percentage of C_3A by causing formation of C_4AF·W. Czernin has shown that if lime content is decreased by 3% and other oxides increased as shown in column (2) of table 2.6 in the raw materials of a rapid hardening cement, the value of C_3S decreases from 65% to 33% and that of C_2S increases from 8% to 38%. Similarly if alumina is reduced from 7% to 5.5%, ironoxide increases from 3.0% to 4.5% (lime and silica contents being kept constant) the value of C_3S increases from 65% to 73% and that of C_2S decreases from 8% to 2%, while C_3A and C_4AF are also affected greatly. This data has been presented in table 2.6. Column (1) of table 2.6 shows the typical data of a rapid hardening cement, column (2) shows the change in other oxides when 3% lime is decreased. Column (3), shows a change of 1.5% in alumina and iron contents compared with the content of column (1). Thus the variation in composition depends largely on the ratio of CaO to SiO_2 in the raw materials.

Table 2.6. Influence of change in oxide composition of the compound composition of rapid hardening cement

Oxide	*Percentage in cement*			*Compounds*	*Percentage of compounds*		
	(1)	(2)	(3)		(1)	(2)	(3)
CaO	66.0	63.0	66.0	C_3S	65.0	33.0	73.0
SiO_2	20.0	22.0	20.0	C_2S	8.0	38.0	2.0
Al_2O_3	7.0	7.7	5.5	C_3A	14.0	15.0	7.0
Fe_2O_3	3.0	3.3	4.5	C_4AF	9.0	10.0	14.0
Others	4.0	4.0	4.0				

Thus the pattern of formation and hydration of cement can be shown schematically as follow:

Component elements

Ca	Si	O_2	Al	Fe

↓

Component oxide

CaO	SiO_2	Al_2O_3	Fe_2O_3

↓

Cement compounds (On burning)

C_3S	β C_2S	C_3A	C_4AF

↓

Portland cement

Various types of portland cements

↓

On-hydration of cement

GEL	$Ca(OH)_2$

↓

Products of Hydration

C-S-H Gel	$Ca(OH)_2$

Both Le Chateliar and Tornebohm observed four different kinds of crystals in thin sections of cement clinkers. Tornebohm named them as Alite, Belite, Celite and Felite. This description of minerals in cement was found similar to that of Bogue's description of compounds C_3S, C_2S, C_3A and C_4AF. Hence Bogue's compounds some times are also called as Alite, Belite, Celite and Felite.

2.10. HYDRATION OF CEMENT

On Adding water to the cement, the silicates and aluminates present in the cement start a chemical reaction and form a spongy mass known as gel. During this process a large quantity of heat is liberated. The quantity of heat liberated depends upon the amount of different constituents in the cement. In other words, hydration of cement can be defined as the reaction taking place in water and cement paste by virtue of which portland cement becomes a bonding agent. There are two ways in which the compounds present in the cement may react with water. In the first case, on addition of water, the cement compounds dissolve to produce a super saturated solution from which different hydrated products are precipated, this is a true reaction of hydration. In the second type of reaction the water is hydrolysed. Actually the term hydration is applied to both true hydration and hydrolysis.

The products of hydration of cement chemically are the same as the products of hydration of individual compounds under similar conditions. This fact was stated for the first time by Le Chateliar. Main hydrates can be classified as calcium silicate hydrates and tri-calcium aluminate hydrate. The two calcium silicates are the main cementitious compounds in cement. The physical behaviour of cement during hydration is similar to that of these compounds alone. C_4AF is supposed to hydrate into tri-calcium aluminate hydrate and $CaO.Fe_2O_3$ aqueous.

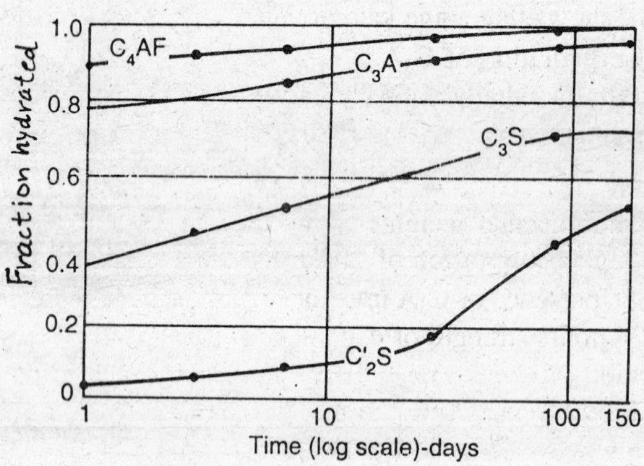

Fig. 2.5. Rate of hydration of pure compounds

(*a*) Calcium silicate hydrates

As already stated, in modern cements the total amount of calcium silicate hydrate varies from 70-80%. The rates of hydration of C_3S and C_2S in pure state differ considerably as shown in Fig. 2.5.

When water is added in a limited quantity as in the case of cement paste or cement concrete, C_3S undergoes hydrolysis first, producing calcium silicate of lower basicity. Ultimately $C_3S_2H_3$ is formed and lime as $Ca(OH)_2$ is released. Then hydrates C_2S. Making the approximate assumption that both C_3S and C_2S produce $C_3S_2H_3$ as the final product of hydration, their equations of hydration can be written as follows:

(*i*) For C_3S

$$\underset{(100)}{2C_3S} + \underset{(24)}{6H} \rightarrow \underset{(75)}{C_3S_2H_3} + \underset{+(49)}{3Ca(OH)_2}$$

(*ii*) For C_2S

$$\underset{(100)}{2C_2S} + \underset{(21)}{4H} \rightarrow \underset{(99)}{C_3S_2H_3} + \underset{+(22)}{Ca(OH)_2}$$

From the above equations it is clear, that on weight basis both silicate require approximately the same amount of water for their hydration, but C_3S produces more than two times the $Ca(OH)_2$ as is formed by hydration of C_2S. The amount of $Ca(OH)_2$ is not a desirable product in the concrete mass as it is soluble in water and may get leached out making the concrete porous. Thus in hydraulic structures cement with higher percentage of C_2S should be used. The physical properties of calcium silicate hydrates are useful in connection with setting and hardening properties of cement discussed in succeeding paragraphs.

It has been observed that the hydration of C_3S does not take place at a constant rate. The initial rapid release of calcium hydroxide into the solution leaves an outer layer about 10^{-6} cms thick of calcium silicate hydrate. After this, for some time very little reaction takes place. This period of little reaction is called as *dormant period.* After some time, the coating on unhydrated cement grain ruptures due to the pressure beneath it and hydration proceeds again. Further it has been observed that calcium silicate hydrates show strength development similar to that of portland cement. A considerable strength is developed before the process of hydration is complete and a small amount of hydrate binds together the unhydrated remaining particles.

(*b*) Tri-calcium aluminate hydrate

The amount of C_3A in most cements is comparatively small, but its behaviour is very important. The reaction of pure C_3A with water is very violent and leads immediate stiffening of paste. The immediate stiffening of paste is called *flash-set.* To prevent flash set 2-3% by weight of clinker, gypsum is added to the cement clinker. Gypsum ($CaSO_4.2H_2O$) reacts with C_3A and forms insoluble calcium sulpho-aluminate ($3CaO$, Al_2O_3, $3CaSO_4$, $31H_2O$) and ultimately a tri-calcium aluminate hydrate is formed. As more C_3A comes into solution, the composition changes, the sulphate content decreases continuously. The rate of reaction of the aluminate is high, and if this readjustment in composition is not rapid enough direct hydration of C_3A may take place. The peak rate of heat development within 5 minutes of adding water to cement shows that some calcium aluminate hydrate is formed directly during this period.

The hydration of C_3A is retarted by $Ca(OH)_2$, which is liberated by the hydrolysis of C_3S. It happens due to the fact that $Ca\ (OH)_2$ reacts with C_3A and water to form C_4AH_{12}, which form a protective layer or coating on the surface of unhydrated grain of C_3A. The equation can be written as:

$$C_3A + 6H = C_3AH_6$$

The molecular weights show that 100 parts of C_3A react with 40 parts of water by weight, which is a much higher proportion of water than that required by the silicates.

The presence of C_3A in cement is undesirable. It contributes to strength upto 3 days and more specially upto 24 hours strength of cement or concrete. When hardended, cement paste is attacked by sulphates, and disruption of cement paste takes place due to the formation of sulpho aluminate from C_3A. The high rate of heat development also causes cracks in the concrete which is not desirable.

However C_3A acts as flux, reducing the burning temperature of clinker which results in saving of fuel. It also facilitates the combinations of lime and silica. For these reasons C_3A is useful in the manufacture of cement.

(*c*) C_4AF

It also acts as a flux. If C_4AF is not present, the reaction in the kiln would progress much more slowly and would probably be incomplete. Gypsum with C_4AF forms calcium sulpho ferrite as well as calcium sulpho aluminate and its presence accelerates the hydration of silicates. Gypsum reacts both with C_3A and C_4AF.

The amount of gypsum to be added to the cement clinker should be decided very carefully as excess amount of gypsum would lead to an expansion and consequent disruption of the set cement paste. The optimum content of gypsum is determined by observing the generation of heat of hydration. If the amount of gypsum is more, immediately after adding water a second peak in the rate of heat evolution would take place after 4 to 8 hours of the first peak of rate of heat evolution Fig. 2.8. If the amount of gypsum is correct, there will be little C_3A left to react after all the gypsum has combined and no second peak of rate of heat of hydration will occur. The amount of gypsum required increases with the C_3A content and also alkali contents in the cement. Increasing the fineness of cement has the effect of increasing the quantity of C_3A available at early ages and this increases the gypsum requirements. If C_3A present is not more than 5%, then, 2.5% gypsum is sufficient, but if C_3A is more than 5%, then 3% gypsum should be added.

(*d*) Calcium hydroxide $Ca(OH)_2$

As stated above, calcium hydroxide is produced during the hydration of C_3S and C_2S. It constitutes 20 to 25% of the volume of solids in the hydrated paste and makes the concrete porous, weak and undurable. $Ca(OH)_2$ also reacts with sulphates present in water or soil to form calcium sulphates which further reacts with C_3A and causes deterioration of concrete. The effect of calcium hydroxide can be reduced by using pozzolanic materials. The only advantage of $Ca(OH)_2$ is that it being alkaline in nature, maintains the p_H value of water around 13 in the concrete which reduces the corrosion of reinforcement.

2.11. WATER REQUIREMENT FOR HYDRATION OF CEMENT

For fully hydration of portland cement on an average 23% of water by weight is required, where as C_3S requires 24% of water by weight of cement and C_2S requires 21%. This 23% of water chemically combines with cement and is called *bound water.* A certain amount of water is filled with in the pores of the gel and is known as *gel water.* The *bound water* and *gel water* are complimentary to each other. If the quantity of water is inadequate to fill the gel pores, the gel formation will stop. If the gel formation stops, there is no question of the gel pores presence. It has been estimated that about 15% water by weight of cement is required to fill up the gel pores. Thus for the complete chemical reaction and to fill up the gel pore space, a total 23% + 15% = 38% of water by weight of cement is required.

Thus it will be seen if only 38% by weight of cement water is used, the resultant paste will go full hydration and no extra water will be available for the formation of undesirable capillary cavities. On the other hand if more than 38% of water is used, then the excess water will form undesirable capillary cavities. Thus greater the amount of water above 38%, larger the undesirable capillary cavities.

On hydration the volume of cement particles increases to 2.06 to 2.1 times of its unhydrated volume. Upto water cement ratio of about 0.6, the gel fully fills up the space occupied by water and the structure is homogeneous. If the cement ratio is more than 0.7, the increase in volume of hydrated product will not be sufficient to fill up the voids produced by water in the paste, resulting porous mass.

2.12. STRUCTURE OF HYDRATED CEMENT

Many of the mechanical properties of hardened cement and concrete depend not so much on the chemical composition of the hydrated cement but on the physical structure of the product of hydration known as 'gel'. Fresh cement paste is a plastic net work of particles of cement in water as shown in Fig. 2.6. After setting of the paste, its gross volume remains approximately constant. At any stage of hydration, the hardened paste consists of hydrates of the various compounds known as gel, crystals of $Ca(OH)_2$, unhydrated cement and some other minor compounds and the residue of the water filled in the spaces of the fresh paste. In hydrated paste two distinct classes of pores exist, one of them is known as *capillary pores* shown by letter C in the Fig. 2.6 and other as *interstitial pores* which exist within the gel itself.

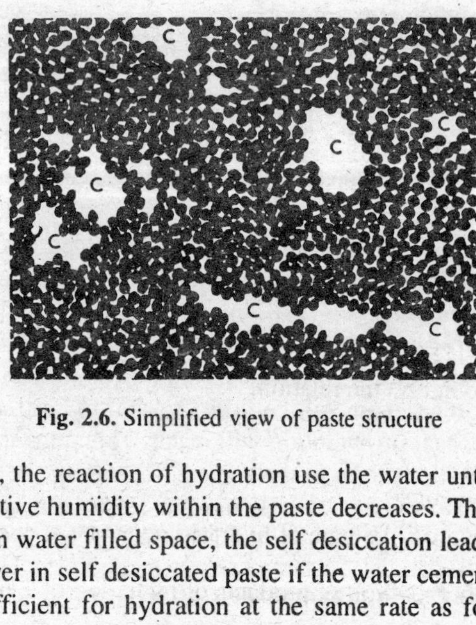

Fig. 2.6. Simplified view of paste structure

Most of the products of hydration are colloidal and the surface area of the solid phase increases more than twice its original volume and large amount of free water becomes adsorbed on this surface. If no movement of water neither from outside to inside nor from inside to outside is permitted, the reaction of hydration use the water until very little water is left to saturate the solid surface and the relative humidity within the paste decreases. This condition is known as *self desiccation.* as gel can form only in water filled space, the self desiccation leads to lower hydration compared with a moist cured paste. However in self desiccated paste if the water cement ratio is in excess of 0.5, the amount of mixing water is sufficient for hydration at the same rate as for moist-cured paste.

For hydration of all particles of cement, about 23% water of weight of dry cement is required to form gel. The hydrated product of cement or gel consists of solid products and water held physically or adsorbed on the large surface area of the hydrates. This water is called gel water. The amount of this water is about 15% of the weight of the dry cement. The volume of this gel water is about 28% of the gel of cement. Thus if the water/cement ratio is less than 0.38 or 0.40, there is no extra water in the cement to provide workability to the concrete. If the water/cement ratio is more than 0.4, then this additional water forms capillary channels and can be evaporated.

In fully hydrated cement the water is held very firmally and can not be evaporated. This water is known as combined water. The amount of this water is about 23% of the weight of the dry cement.

Capillary water. The solid products of hydration occupy a volume less than the sum of absolute volumes of the original dry cement and the combined water by about 18.5%. This residue space for a fully hydrated cement with no excess water required for hydration is known as *capillary pores.* Water present in these pores is called *capillary water.*

Thus the total water added to cement can be classified into three groups:

1. Gel water
2. Capillary water and
3. Combined water

2.13. VOLUME OF PRODUCT OF HYDRATION

The gross space available for the products of hydration consists of the absolute volume of the dry cement together with the volume of water added to the mix. The small losses of water due to bleeding etc. have been neglected. It has been observed that the four compounds of cement namely C_3S, C_2S, C_3A and C_4AF need 24%, 21%, 40% and 37% water by weight for their chemical reaction respectively. The non evaporable water in cement is found by experiment as 23% of the weight of unhydrous cement.

Further it has been observed that the specific gravity of the products of hydration of cement is such that they occupy a greater volume than the absolute volume of unhydrated cement, but smaller than the sums of volumes of the dry cement and the non evaporable water by approximately 0.254 of the volume of non evaporable water. The average value of specific gravity of the products of hydration in a saturated state is assumed as 2.16. The procedure of determining the volumes of different components is illustrated by the following example.

Let us consider the hydration of 100 gram of cement for simplicity in calculation.

Let

The specific gravity of dry cement be 3.15

Then absolute volume of unhydrated cement $= \dfrac{100}{3.15} = 31.8$ ml (c.c.)

Non evaporable water as assumed above $= 23\% = 23$ ml (c.c.)

$\therefore$ Solid products of hydration will occupy a volume $= 31.8 + 0.23 \times 100\,(1 - 0.254)$

$= 48.96$ ml app.

It has been found that paste in this condition contains 28% porosity, then volume of gel water Wg is found by the relation,

$$\frac{Wg}{48.96 + Wg} = 0.28$$

or $\quad Wg = 19.0$ ml.

$\therefore$ Volume of hydrated cement $= 48.96 + 19 = 67.96$ml.

$\therefore$ Vol. of products of hydration of 1 ml of dry cement $= \dfrac{67.96}{31.8} = 2.14$

In the above case hydration is considered in a sealed tube. It has been observed that hydration in a sealed specimen can progress to a stage till the combined water becomes about half of the original water content. After this stage no hydration is possible. Thus full hydration in a sealed specimen is possible only when the mixing water is atleast twice the water required for chemical reaction, *i.e.* the mix has a water-cement-ratio of about 0.5 by weight. Actually full hydration is possible when for gel formation, sufficient water is available both for chemical reaction and for filling the pores of gel formed.

2.14. HYDRATION OF PASTE CURED UNDER WATER

In this case water can be imbibed through capillaries. Let us consider hydration of 100 gram of cement. The specific gravity of cement being 3.15, the volume occupied by 100 gram of cement will be 31.8 ml. As shown in the above example this volume of dry cement will occupy a volume of 67.96 ml app. on full hydration. Thus original mixing water will be (67.96 – 31.8) = 36.15 ml. This corresponds to a water cement ratio of 0.36 by weight. But by actual experiments it has been observed, (if water is also allowed for bleeding) that for water cement ratio less than 0.38 by weight, complete hydration is not possible as the volume of water and cement available is insufficient to accommodate all the products of hydration. Further if the water/cement ratio is reduced to 0.3 about 19% of the original weight of cement will remain unhydrated and will never be able to hydrate as gel has occupied all available space. Further it may be stated that this unhydrated cement will not prove detrimental to the strength. Actually by water cement ratio law it has been found that lower the water/cement ratio, higher the strength, this is probably due to the fact that in such cases the layers of hydrated paste surrounding the unhydrated grains are thinner.

On the other hand, if the water/cement ratio is higher than about 0.38 or 0.4, all the cement particles can hydrate but capillary pores will also be present. Some of the capillaries will contain excess water from the mix and the others will be filled by imbibing water from outside.

2.15. CAPILLARY PORES

At any stage of hydration the capillary pores represent that part of the gross volume which has not been filled by the products of hydration. As stated earlier that hydrated products occupy more than two times the volume of dry cement alone, thus the volume of the capillary system is reduced with the progress of hydration. Capillary pores are much larger than gel pores.

The capillary porosity of paste depends upon the water/cement ratio of the mix and degree of hydration. Actually the type of cement has more influence on the degree of hydration than water/cement ratio. As stated above, water cement ratios higher than 0.38, the volume of gel is unable to fill all the space available in the mix and capillary pores are left even for complete hydration of cement.

In a good concrete, however continuous capillaries are not desirable. It has been seen that in mature and dense pastes, the capillaries are blocked by gel, Table 2.7 shows age required to produce maturity at which capillaries becomes blocked or segmented.

Table 2.7.

S. No.	*Water/cement ratio by weight*	*Degree of hydration %*	*Time required (Curing period)*
1.	0.4	50	3 days
2.	0.45	60	7 days
3.	0.50	70	14 days
4.	0.60	92	180 days
5.	0.70	100	365 days
6.	Above 0.70	100	impossible

2.16. GEL PORES

As already discussed that the products, of hydration of cement is called gel, which is porous in structure. The gel pores are inter-connected forming interstitial spaces between its particles. By experiments the space occupied by gel pores is found about 28%. In other words gel pores occupy space equal to about one third of the vol. of the gel solids.

2.17. HEAT OF HYDRATION OF CEMENT

The hydration of cement is accompanied by liberation of heat. Such a chemical reaction is known as exothermic and there are many exothermic chemical reactions. Normal cement generally produces heat of hydration about 90 cal/gram in 7 days and 90 to 120 cal/gram in 28 days (360 to 500 joules/gram (as 1 cal/g = 4.2 joul/g). As the conductivity of concrete is very low it acts as an insulator and in the interior of a large mass of concrete such as a dam, hydration of cement can develop very high temperature. At the same time heat dissipation takes place from the exterior surface of the concrete and a steep temperature gradient develops. During further cooling of interior, causes serious cracking of the concrete. It has been fully discussed in chapter 18 (concreting under extreme conditions). In cold climate, heat produced by hydration of cement prevents freezing of water in the capillaries of the fresh concrete. In such situations high evolution of heat is advantageous.

The heat of hydration is the quantity of heat in calories/gram or jouls/gram of unhydrated cement developed on complete hydration of cement at a given temperature. The temperature at which the hydration takes place affects the rate of heat development as shown in the following Table 2.8.

Table 2.8. Development of heat of hydration

Type of cement	*Heat of hydration developed at the temperature shown*							
	4°C (40°F)		24°C (75°F)		32°C (90°F)		41°C (105°F)	
	Cal/g	*J/g*	*Cal/g*	*J/g*	*Cal/g*	*J/g*	*Cal/g*	*J/g*
Ordinary portland cement	36.9	154	68.0	285	73.9	399	80.0	335
Rapid hardening cement	52.9	221	83.2	348	85.3	357	93.2	390
Low heat cement	25.7	108	46.6	195	45.8	192	51.2	214

Strictly speaking heat of hydration is a composite quantity, consisting of chemical heat of reaction of hydration and heat of adsorption of water on the surface of the gel formed by the process of hydration. The heat of adsorption being about 25% of the total heat of hydration. From practical considerations, total heat of hydration is not important, but the rate of heat evolution is important.

C_3A hydrates most rapidly and liberates heat at a very high rate at the early age as shown in Fig. 2.7 (*a*). 7% C_3A lbterates about 35 Cal/g heat at the age of 12 hours and 53 Cal/g at the age of 24 hours. In this Fig. the C_3S contents are assumed as constant.

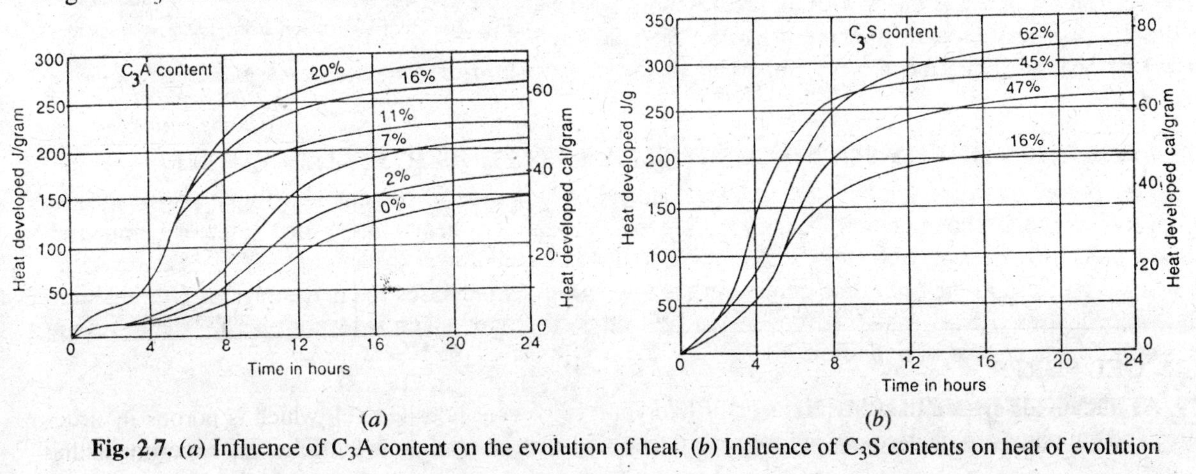

(*a*) (*b*)

Fig. 2.7. (*a*) Influence of C_3A content on the evolution of heat, (*b*) Influence of C_3S contents on heat of evolution

Fig. 2.7 (*b*) shows the influence of C_3S contents on the evolution of heat while C_3A contents are considered constant.

As per Bogue, for usual range of portland cements, about 50% of the total heat is liberated between 1 and 3 days, about 75% in 7 days and from 83 to 91% of the total heat in 180 days. In fact the heat of hydration depends on the chemical composition of cement and the heat of hydration of cement is very nearly equal to sum of the heats of hydration of individual compounds when hydrated separately. The heat of hydration of main compounds of cement based on the study of VERBECK and C.W. FOSTER are given in Table 2.9 below:

Table 2.9. Heat of Hydration

Compounds	*Heat of Hydration at the given age in cal/gram*		
	3 days	*90 days*	*13 years*
C_3S	58	104	122
C_2S	12	42	59
C_3A	212	311	324
C_4AF	69	98	102

The influence of C_3A and C_3S on the development of heat of hydration is shown in Fig. 2.7 (*a, b*). The quantity of cement in a mix also will affect the total heat development. Thus by adjusting or reducing the quantity of C_3A and C_3S in a cement, heat of hydration can be controlled.

2.17.1. Heat liberation pattern from setting cement

Heat liberation from setting cement after adding water to the cement is shown in Fig. 2.8 based on the work of W. Lerch. As already discussed, the reaction of water with cement is exothermic. The liberation of heat is known as heat of hydration. On mixing water with the cement, a rapid heat evolution occurs, which lasts for few minutes. This heat of evolution is due to aluminates and sulphates (C_3A). This is shown by ascending peak A. On adding gypsum, the solubility of aluminate is depressed and the initial heat evolution eases quickly in about 2 hours time.

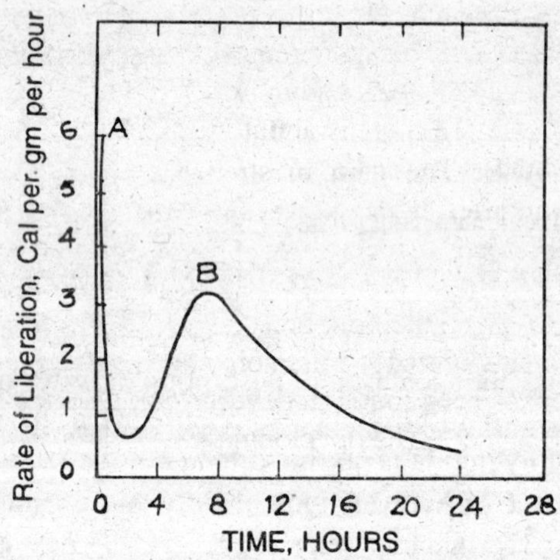

Fig. 2.8. Heat Liberation from a setting cement

Next heat evolution is due to C_3S and represented by B on the graph. This peak reaches in about 8 hours. The study and control of heat of hydration is very important in the construction of concrete dams and other massive structures.

2.18. INFLUENCE OF COMPOUND COMPOSITION ON PROPERTIES OF CEMENT

In the preceding section, it has been shown that heat of hydration of cement is a simple additive function of the compound composition of cement. In general in modern cements the lime silicates compound C_3S and C_2S on an average vary from 70% to 80%. In a well burnt clinker the amount of C_3S is about 45%, but a small increase in the total lime content in the raw materials increases the percentage of C_3S appreciably and decreases C_2S. C_3A varies from 1% to 12% on an average, which is responsible for the development of high rate of heat of hydration.

2.19. STRENGTH DEVELOPMENT

On adding water to the cement, C_3A is the earliest to hydrate and contributes to the strength of the cement paste at one to three days age but at the advanced age it causes retrogression in the development of strength, particularly in cements with high contents of C_3A or (C_3A + C_4AF) both. Due to the development of large amount of heat of hydration, it causes cracks in the paste and disintegrates the hardened paste or concrete. Although C_3A is least desirable in cement, but it acts as flux for the fusion of clinker and reduces the temperature of fusion, resulting in saving of fuel. It also facilitates the combination of lime and silica. An increase in iron content decreases the percentage of C_3A, but is causes higher formation of C_4AF. A low C_3A cement generates less heat and develops higher ultimate strength and exhibits greater resistance to the destructive elements than cements containing higher percentage of C_3A. For these reasons C_3A is useful in the manufacture of cement.

C_4AF: It is considered as a inert material, but it also acts as a flux for clinker fusing at lower temperature, resulting in the saving of fuel. Practically it does not contribute any strength.

C_3S: After adding water to the cement, C_3S hydrates immediately next to C_3A and contributes, early strength to the cement paste or concrete. In general the early strength of portland cement will be higher with higher percentage of C_3S. Many researchers have found that C_3S contributes most to the strength development during the first four weaks. The 7 days strength of neat C_3S has been found about 400 kg/cm^2 or 40 Newton per mm^2 and after 18 months about 700 kg/cm^2.

C_2S: The gain in strength of C_2S has been found after 28 days on wards after adding water to the cement. At seven days no strength develops in C_2S. At the age of 1 year, weight for weight C_3S and C_2S both compounds contribute equally to the ultimate strength. For moist curing after 180 days C_2S has been found to develop greater strength, after about 18 months C_2S has been found to develop about 700 kg/cm^2. The development of strength of different compounds has been shown in Fig. 2.9.

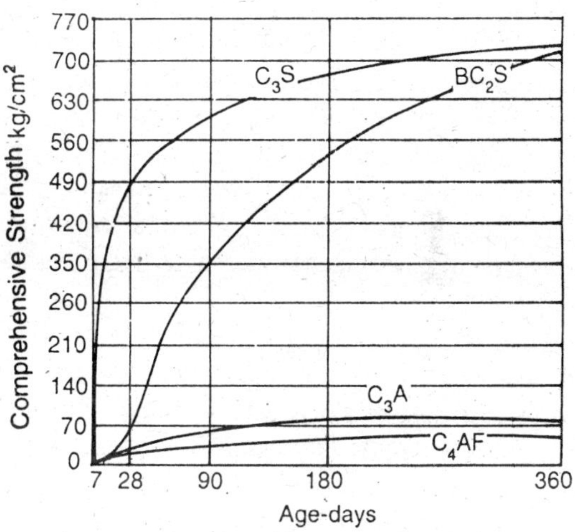

Fig. 2.9. Development of strength of pure compounds

2.20. EFFECT OF IMPURITIES IN CALCIUM SILICATE ON STRENGTH

The impurities in calcium silicate strongly affect the rate of reaction and strength development of the hydrates. Al_2O_3 has a marked effect on the strength development of C_3S. It has been observed that 1% addition of Al_2O_3 to pure C_3S increases the early strength of the paste very much upto about 35 days as shown in Fig. 2.10.

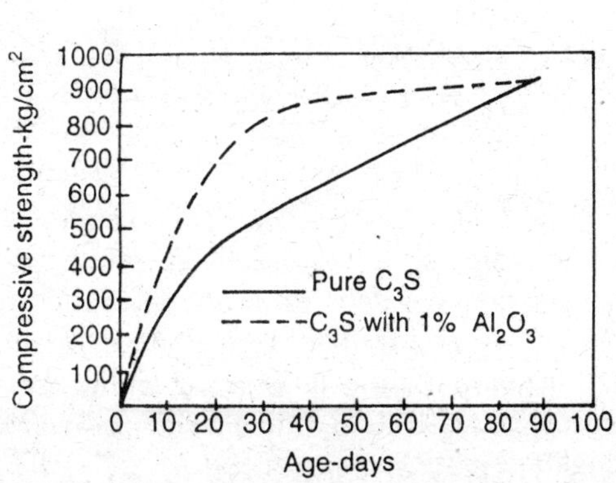

Fig. 2.10. Effect of AL_2O_3 on the development of strength of pure C_3S

2.21. EFFECT OF ALKALIES ON THE STRENGTH OF CEMENT

Test results have shown that the increase in strength beyond the age of 28 days is strongly affected by the alkali contents. The greater the amount of alkali present, lower the gain in strength. Thus the amount of alkalies should not be more than 0.4%. Table 2.10 shows the effect of principal compounds of cement on its properties.

Table 2.10. Effect of compounds on the properties of cement

Property	*Relative behaviour of each compound*			
	C_3S	C_2S	C_3A	C_4AF
Rate of reaction	Medium	Slow	Fast	Slow
Heat librated per unit weight of compound	Medium	Small	Large	Small
Cementing value per unit weight of compound. Early	Good	Poor	Good	Poor
Ultimate	Good	Good	Poor	Poor

2.22. SETTING AND HARDENING OF CEMENT

Term setting is used to describe the stiffening of the cement paste. Broadly speaking setting refers to a change from a fluid to a rigid state. On adding sufficient amount of water to cement, a paste is formed, which gradually becomes less plastic and finally becomes stiff and hard. When the paste has lost its plasticity and becomes sufficient rigid to withstand an arbitrarily defined pressure, then the paste is said to have set. The setting period has been divided into two groups known as *initial set* and *final set.* After the final set, the cement paste further increases in strength and rigidity. This state of paste is called as *hardening of* cement paste.

The setting process is accompanied by temperature changes in the cement paste. The initial set corresponds to a rapid rise in temperature and the final set to the peak temperature. The setting time of cement is found to decrease with the rise in temperature, but at 30°C (85°F) the reverse effect is observed. At low temperatures setting is retarted. Further cement set can be divided into the following two groups.

1. Flash set 2. False set

1. **Flash set.** If on adding water to the cement a very violent reaction takes place with the evolution of large amount of heat of hydration and cement sets with in five minutes after adding water to it; then this set is known as *flash set.* After flash set the restoration of plasticity of paste is not possible.
2. **False set.** If the abnormal premature stiffening of cement paste takes place in few minutes after mixing water with the cement then it is called false set. In the case of false set no appreciable heat is evolved and remixing of the cement paste with out adding any water and restoring plasticity of the paste is possible until it sets in the normal manner and without any loss of strength.

2.22.1. Causes of false set

1. If gypsum is added and inter ground in a very hot clinker, the dehydration of gypsum takes place and lime-hydrate ($CaSO_4$, $0.5H_2O$) or anhydrite ($CaSO_4$) are formed. When water is added to such cements, these hydrates form gypsum and the plaster set takes place resulting stiffening of paste.
2. If alkalies are present in the cement, during storage period they form alkali carbonates. These alkali carbonates react with calcium hydroxide $Ca(OH)_2$ liberated by the hydrolysis of C_3S to form $CaCO_3$. This $CaCO_3$ precipitates and produces rigidity in the paste.
3. At moderately high temperature, the aeration of C_3S also can cause false set in the cement. In this condition water is adsorbed on the grains of the cement and these freshly activated surfaces can combine very rapidly with more water during mixing. This rapid hydration will cause false set.

If false set is found to occur in any cement, it can be dealt with by remixing the concrete with out adding any water to it. By this process, workability will also increase and concrete can be laid in the normal way with out any difficulty.

2.23. TESTS AND SPECIFICATIONS OF PHYSICAL PROPERTIES OF CEMENT

The manufacture of cement requires strict control on its quality. Therefore following tests and specifications have been laid as per I.S.I. 269-1967 and 1976.

1. Chemical composition
2. Fineness
3. Soundness
4. Consistency test
5. Setting time
6. Compressive strength
7. Tensile strength
8. Heat of hydration

1. Chemical composition. The ordinary and rapid hardening portland cements can be tested in accordance with the methods given in I.S. 4032. The results of tests should comply with the following chemical requirements.

(*a*) Ratio of percentage of lime to percentage of silica, alumina, and iron oxide when calculated by the following formula,

$$\frac{CaO - 0.7\,SO_3}{2.8\,SiO_2 + 1.2\,Al_2O_3 + 0.65\,Fe_2O_3}$$

should not be greater than 1.02 and less than. 0.66.

(*b*) Ratio of percentage of alumina to iron oxide should not be less than 0.66.

(*c*) Weight of insoluble residue should not be more than 2%.

(*d*) Weight of magnesia should not exceed 6%.

(*e*) Total sulphur content calculated as sulphuric anhydride (SO_3) should not exceed 2.75 or 3.0%. When C_3A by mass is 7% or less and greater than 7% respectively. C_3A is calculated by the formula,

$$C_3A = 2.65\,(Al_2O) - 1.69\,(Fe_2O_3)$$

(*f*) Total loss on ignition should not be more than 5%.

Test procedure

(*a*) *Loss on ignition.* Take 1.0 gram sample of cement and weigh it carefully. Heat this cement in weighed and covered platinum crucible for 15 minutes at about 900°C to 1000°C and cool. On cooling weigh again. Total loss on ignition should not exceed 4%. If the porcelain crucible is used, then heating should be done for about 1 hour. The loss on ignition shows the extent of carbonation and hydration of free lime and free magnesia due to exposure of cement to the atmosphere. Usually in a freshly ground normal cement, the free lime is less than 1%, but total uncombined free lime should not be allowed greater than 3% as it will cause unsoundness in the cement due to slow hydration of this free lime.

(*b*) *Sulphuric anhydride (SO_3).* Weigh 1.0 gram cement carefully and add 25 ml (c.c.) cold water to it and stirred vigorously. While stirring 5 ml HCl (hydrochloric acid) may be added to the mixture. If necessary the solution may be heated and the cement is ground well with a flattened end of a glass rod. The process of grinding the cement should be continued till the decomposition of cement is complete.

Now dilute the solution to 50 ml and allow to remain in this condition for 15 minutes. Filter the solution and wash the residue thoroughly with hot water. Leave the filtre paper and residue. Dilute the filtrate to 250 ml and heat to boiling. To this solution add drop by drop 10 ml of hot barrium chloride solution and continue the boiling till precipitate is well formed and heat it on steam bath atleast for 4 hours. Now filtre the precipitate and wash it thoroughly. Place the filtre paper with residue in a crucible and incinerate the paper slowly and then ignite the product at 800°C to 900°C. Now cool it in a desicator and weigh the barrium sulphate. From this weight calculate the weight of SO_3. It should not exceed 2.75% as excess of SO_3 will cause unsoundness of cement.

(*c*) *Weight of magnesiun.* Magnesium oxide (MgO) reacts with water very slowly that is the hydration of MgO is very slow. On hydration after the cement paste has set, MgO also swells in volume and causes cracks in the structure. Thus excessive MgO causes unsoundness in the cement. Thus as per I.S. 269-1967, the amount of MgO in cement should not be more than 6% by weight. It can be determined as per I.S. 269.

(*d*) *Insoluble residue.* It is a measure of adulteration of cement largely arising from the impurities in gypsum. As per I.S. 269-1967 it should not exceed more than 2%. The test can be carried out as per I.S. 269.

2. Fineness of cement

Regardless of composition, fineness is a vital property of cement, which influences the rate of reaction of cement with water. For a given weight of a finely ground cement, the surface area of the particles is greater than for a coarsely ground cement. For a satisfactorily ground cement, usually there should be 1.1×10^{12} particles per kg of cement. However if the cement is ground too finely, the extremely fine particles may become pre-hydrated by moisture present as vapour in the grinding mills or during storage etc. and thus no cementing value can be derived from such particles. If the particles are coarser than normal, the rate of hydration of cement will be slower. The advantages of finer cements can be summarized as follows:

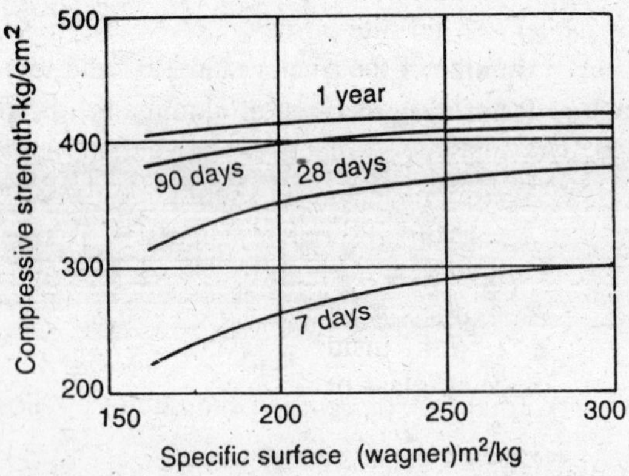

Fig. 2.11. Relation between strength of concrete and fineness of cement at different ages

Advantages

(*a*) The finer the cement, greater the rate of hydration.

(*b*) Finer the cement, rapid and greater the strength development as shown in Fig. 2.11.

(*c*) Coarser the cement, greater the period of hydration and complete hydration is not possible.

(*d*) Finer the cement, lesser they bleed.

(*e*) Finer the cement, better the workability.

Disadvantage

(*a*) Finer the cement, higher the cost of grinding.

(*b*) Finer the cement, more rapidly it deteriorates on exposure to atmosphere.

(*c*) Finer the cement, stronger the reaction with alkali reactive aggregates.

(*d*) Finer the cement, greater the shrinkage and the proneness to cracking.

(*e*) Finer the cement, greater amount of C_3A they possess and more amount of gypsum they require for proper retardation of setting time.

(*f*) For a standard consistency pastes, finer the cement, greater the amount of water needed.

Methods of determining of fineness of cement

(*a*) *By sieve analysis.* Weigh 100 grams of cement accurately and place it in a standard I.S. Sieve No. 9 (90 micron) and break lumps if any by pressing with fingers. In no case it should be rubbed on the sieve. Holding sieve in both hands sieve for 15 minutes continuously with a gentle motion of wrist, so that no cement spills out. After 15 minutes sieving, weight the residue left on the sieve.

In case of ordinary portland cement and rapid hardening cement it should not be more than 10% and 5% respectively.

(*b*) *Specific surface area method.* Fineness of cement can be tested by BLAINE'S air permeability method.

(*c*) By LEA & NURSE METHOD.

(*a*) Determination of fineness of Cement by specific surface by Blaine air permeability method (as per IS 4031-1958)

The determination of specific surface of cement is a recent development. It is a very accurate method of determining the fireness of cement, which affects the hydration and strength development of cement.

Apparatus.

The Blaine air permeability apparatus consists essentially of a means of drawing a definite quantity of air through a prepared bed of cement of definite porosity. The number and size of the pores in a prepared bed of cement of definite porosity is a function of the size of the particles and determines the rate of air flow through the bed. The apparatus consists mainly of the following parts as shown in Fig. 2.12.

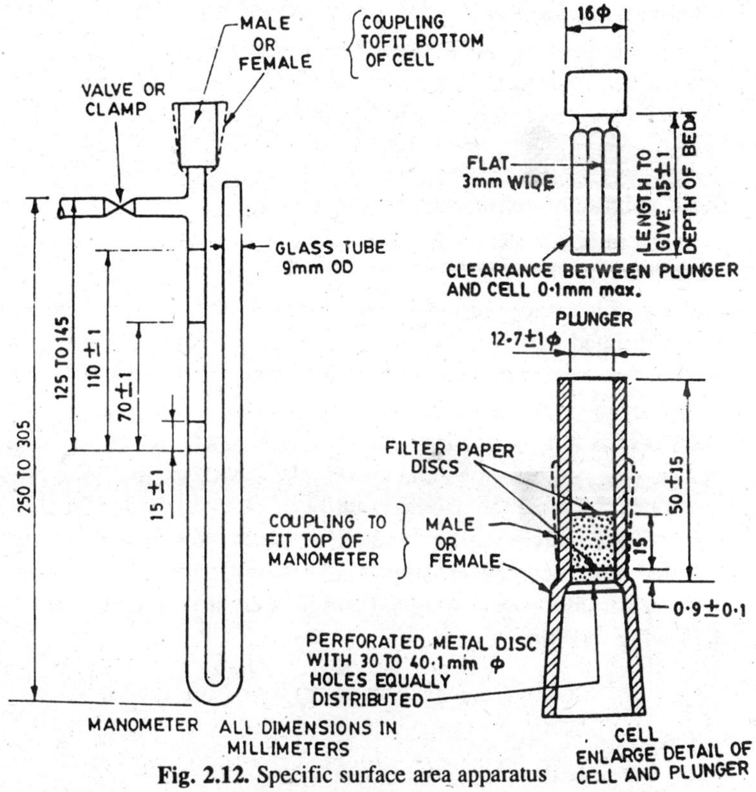

Fig. 2.12. Specific surface area apparatus

(*a*) *Permeability Cell.* It consists of a rigid Cylinder 12.7 ± 1 mm inside diameter made of glass or non-corroding metal. The bottom of the cell shall form an air tight connection with the top of the manometer. A ledge of 0.5 to 1.0 mm in width shall be an integral part of the cell for support of the perforated metal disc Fig. 2.12 (*b*).

(*b*) *Disc.* It is made of non-corroding metal 0.9 ± 0.1 mm in thickness having 30 to 40 perforations of 1 mm diameter holes equally distributed over its whole area. This will be fitted in the inside of the cell snugly as shown in Fig. 2.12 (*b*).

(*c*) *Plunger.* The plunger fits into the cell with a clearance of not more than 0.1 mm. The bottom of the plunger has sharp square edges at right angle to the principal axis. An air vent is provided either in the centre or on one side of the plunger. The top of the plunger is provided with a collar such that when the plunger is placed in the cell and the collar is brought in contact with the top of the cell, the distance between the bottom of the plunger and the top of the perforated disc should remain 15.0 ± 1.0 mm.

(*d*) *Filtre paper.* It is the medium of retention. This should be equivalent to No 40 whatman filtre paper.

(*e*) *Manometer.* The manometer of standard wall glass tube of outside diameter of 9 mm is made in U shape as shown in Fig. 2.12 (*a*). The top of one arm of the manometer forms an air tight connection with the permeability cell. On the manometer arm connected with permeability cell a line is engraved around the tube at 125 to 145 mm below the top of the side outlet and also others at distances of 15 ± 1 mm, 70 ± 1 mm and 110 ± 1 mm above that line. A side outlet is provided at 250 mm to 305 mm above the bottom of the manometer. This outlet is used to evacuate the manometer arm connected to the permeability cell. A positive air tight valve or clamp is provided on the out-side out let not more than 50 mm from the arm of the manometer. The manometer is mounted firmly in such a way that its arms are always vertical. It is filled up to the mid-point with a non-volatile and non-hydroscopic liquid of low density and viscosity, such as light grade mineral oil, dibutylphthalate etc.

Timer. The stop watch should be capable to read to the nearest 0.5 sec. or less. It should be accurate to 0.5 sec or less for time intervals upto 60 sec and to 1% or less upto 60 to 300 seconds.

Calibration of apparatus

Before starting the test, the calibration of the equipment is very essential. The calibration should be made using *National Bureau of standards, standard sample No. 114* or *Indian Cements having specific surface equivalent to NBS standard sample 114.* The samples should be at room temperature at the time of test.

Bulk volume of compacted bed of powder

The bulk volume of the compacted bed of powder is determined by the mercury displacement method as follows:

Two filtre paper discs are placed in the permeability cell in such a way that the filtre discs are flat on the perforated metal disc and then the cell is filled with mercury. Any air bubbles adhering both walls of the cell are removed. The mercury is levelled with the top of the cell with the help of a small glass plate.

Now the mercury is removed from the cell, weighed and its weight recorded. At this stage one of the filtre disc is removed and a trial sample quantity of cement of about 2.8 grams is compressed in the cell. At this trial stage use of standard sample is not essential. The prepared bed should be firm. It should not be too loose. In case, the above quantity of cement cannot be compressed to the desired volume, adjust the weight. After compressing the cement, place the second filtre disc over it. The remaining space of the cell is filled with mercury, entrapped air removed, and top of it is levelled off as before. Now the mercury is removed from the cell, weighed and its weight recorded. The bulk volume of cement is then given by the following relation.

$$V = \frac{Wa - Wb}{D}$$

where,

V = bulk volume of cement in cm^3

Wa = weight of mercury in grams required to fill the cell without cement

Wb = weight of mercury in grams required to fill the top portion of cell not occupied by the prepared bed of cement in the cell.

D = density of mercury at temperature of test in g/cm^3. (Table 2.11 shows the relation of temperature, density of mercury, viscosity of air etc.)

At least two determinations of bulk volume of cement should be made using separate compactions for each determination. The bulk volume value to be used for subsequent calculations will be the average of the above two values. The difference acceptable is ± 0.005 cm^3. The temperature at the beginning and end of determination should be noted.

Preparation of sample

The sample of cement is enclosed in a 125 gram jar and shaken vigorously for two minutes to make it soft (stuff) and break lumps if any.

Weight of sample

The weight of standard sample should be sufficient to produce a bed of cement having a porosity of 0.500 ± 0.005 and is calculated as

$$w = V \cdot \rho\ (1 - e)$$

where,

w = weight of sample required in grams
ρ = specific gravity of cement usually taken as 3.15 for portland cement
v = bulk volume of bed of cement in cm^3 as determined above
e = desired porosity of bed of cement (0.500 ± 0.005).

Preparation of bed

The perforated disc is seated on the ledge in the permeability cell and a filtre paper disc is placed in the metalic cell and the edges pressed down with a rod slightly smaller than the cell diameter. The quantity of cement determined as above is placed in the cell. The weight of the cement should be correct upto 0.001 gram. To level the cement upto the bed, the side of the cell is tapped slightly. A filtre paper disc is placed on the top of the cement and the cement is compressed with the plunger till the plunger collar is in contact with the top of the cell. The plunger is then removed slowly. For each determination fresh filtre paper disc should be used.

Permeability test

The permeability cell is attached to the manometer. Care should be taken that the prepared bed is not disturbed and air tight connection is obtained. The air in the one arm of the U tube manometer is slowly evacuated until the liquid in the manometer reaches the top mark. At this stage the valve is closed tightly. The stop watch or timer is started as soon as the meniscus of the manometer liquid reaches the second (*i.e.* next to the top) mark and stopped as soon as the bottom of the meniscus of liquid reaches the third next to the bottom mark. The time interval is measured in seconds and noted. The temperature of test also is noted and recorded in degree centigrade.

Procedure of test sample

Same as for standard sample for calibration of apparatus.

Calculation

Calculations of specific surfaces are made by the following equations

$$S = \frac{S_s \sqrt{T}}{\sqrt{T_s}} \quad \text{...(1)}$$

$$S = \frac{S_s \sqrt{n_s}}{\sqrt{T_s}} \times \frac{\sqrt{T}}{\sqrt{n}} \quad \text{...(2)}$$

$$S = \frac{S_s\,(1 - e_s) \sqrt{e^3} \times \sqrt{T}}{\sqrt{e_s^3} \times \sqrt{S_s} \times (1 - e)} \quad \text{...(3)}$$

$$S = \frac{S_s\,(1 - e_s)\ \sqrt{e^3}\ \sqrt{n_s}\ \sqrt{T}}{\sqrt{e_s^3}\ \sqrt{T_s}\ \sqrt{n}\ (1 - e)} \quad \text{...(4)}$$

$$S = \frac{S_s \rho_s (1 - e_s) \sqrt{e^3} \sqrt{T}}{\rho (1 - e) \sqrt{e_s^3} \sqrt{T_s}} \quad \text{...(5)}$$

$$S = \frac{S_s \rho_s (1 - e_s) \sqrt{n_s} \sqrt{e^3} \sqrt{T}}{\rho (1 - e) \sqrt{e_s^3} \sqrt{T_s} \sqrt{N}} \quad \text{...(6)}$$

where,

S = specific surface in sq cm per gram of the test sample.

S_s = specific surface in sq cm per gram of the standard sample used in calibration of the apparatus.

T = measured true interval in seconds of manometer drop for test sample.

T_s = measured true interval in seconds of manometer drop for standard sample used in calibration of the apparatus.

n_s = viscosity of air in poise at the temperature of test of the standard sample used in calibration of the apparatus

n = viscosity of air in poise at the temperature of the test sample

e_s = porosity of prepared bed of standard sample used in calibration of apparatus.

e = porosity of prepared bed of test sample.

ρ_s = specific gravity of standard sample used in calibration of apparatus (assumed as 3.15).

ρ = specific gravity of test sample (3.15).

Note: 1. Equations (5) and (6) are used for materials other than portland cement. Equation 5 is used when the temperature of the test of the sample is with in ± 3°C of the temperature of calibration test of the standard fineness sample and equation 6 is used if the temperature of test is out side of this range.

2. Equations (1) and (2) are used in calculation if fineness of portland cements compacted to the same porosity as the standard fineness sample. Equation (1) is used if the temp. of test sample is within ± 3°C of the temperature of calibration test of the standard fineness and equation 2 is used if the temperature range is outside this range.

3. Equations (3) and (4) are used if the portland cement is compacted to other porosity than that of the standard fineness sample used in the calibration test. Rest same:

Table 2.11 Showing density of mercury, viscosity of air etc. at a given temperature

Table 2.11

Room temperature in°C	*Density of mercury gram/cm³*	*Viscosity of air in poise, n*	$\sqrt{n}$
16	13.56	1.788×10^{-4}	0.01337
18	13.55	1.798×10^{-4}	0.01341
20	13.55	1.808×10^{-4}	0.01344
22	13.54	1.818×10^{-4}	0.01348
24	13.54	1.828×10^{-4}	0.01352
26	13.53	1.837×10^{-4}	0.01355
28	13.53	1.847×10^{-4}	0.01359
30	13.52	1.857×10^{-4}	0.01362
32	13.52	1.867×10^{-4}	0.01366
34	13.51	1.876×10^{-4}	0.01369

Porosity of bed (e)	$\sqrt{e^3}$	T	$\sqrt{T}$
0.495	0.348	26.0	5.10
0.496	0.349	26.5	5.15
0.497	0.350	27.0	5.20
0.498	0.351	27.5	5.25
0.499	0.352	28.0	5.29
0.500	0.354	28.5	5.34
0.501	0.355	29.0	5.39
0.502	0.356	29.5	5.44
0.503	0.357	30.0	5.48
0.504	0.358	30.5	5.52

C. FINENESS OF CEMENT BY LEA & NURSE AIR PERMEABILITY METHOD

The apparatus used in this method is shown in Fig. 2.13. The specific surface is expressed as total surface area in square cm per gram or square metre per kg of cement. The principle of the method is based on the relation between the flow of air through the cement bed and the surface area of the particles consisting the cement bed. From this, the surface area per unit weight of the body material can be related to the permeability of a bed of a given porosity. The cement bed in the permeability cell is 2.5 cm in diameter and 1 cm depth knowing the density of cement the weight required to make a cement bed of porosity of 0.475 can be calculated. This quantity of cement is placed in the permeability cell.

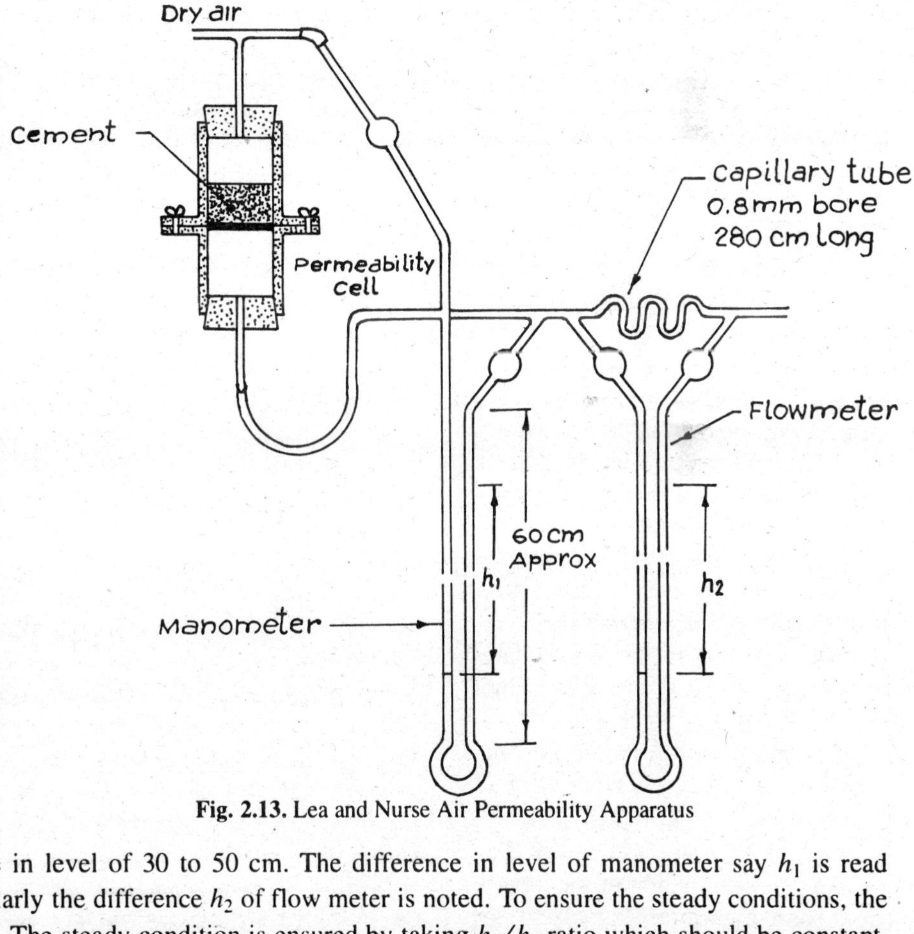

Fig. 2.13. Lea and Nurse Air Permeability Apparatus

Now the air is passed through the cement bed at a constant velocity. The rate of flow of air is adjusted till the flow meter shows a difference in level of 30 to 50 cm. The difference in level of manometer say h_1 is read carefully and noted. Similarly the difference h_2 of flow meter is noted. To ensure the steady conditions, the observations are repeated. The steady condition is ensured by taking h_1/h_2 ratio which should be constant. Then specific surface area Sw is calculated from the following relation.

$$Sw = \sqrt{h_1/h_2}$$

and $$K = \frac{14}{d(1-n)} \sqrt{\frac{n^3 A}{CL}}$$

where,

n = porosity of cement taken as 0.475
A = area of cement bed in cm^2
L = length of cement bed in cm
d = density of cement
C = flow meter constant.

Cements should comply with the following requirements.

	Type of cement	*Specific surface area cm²/gram*
1.	Ordinary	Not less than 2250
2.	Rapid hardening	Not less than 3250
3.	Low heat	Not less than 3200

3. Standard consistency test

Standard consistency of a cement paste can be defined as that consistency which will permit the vicat plunger as shown in Fig. 2.14 to penetrate to a point 5 ± 2 mm from the bottom of the vicat mould when the cement paste is tested by this apparatus. The water content of the standard paste is expressed as a percentage by weight of the dry cement. Usually this percentage varies from 26% to 33%.

Vicat apparatus

As shown in Fig. 2.14 vicate apparatus consists of a frame bearing a movable rod of weight 300 grams. At the upper end of this rod a cap is provided, while at the lower end there is arrangement to attach either the 1.13 mm needle or plunger of 10 mm diameter as shown in the Fig. This Fig. shows a side view as well as front view. In the front view a indicator and graduated scale attached to the frame is also shown.

The needle C is of 1 mm square in section or 1.13 mm dia round needle. There is another needle with a metal attachment at the end of the needle projecting 5 mm from the end of the needle.

Mould E. As shown in the Fig. the diameter and height of the mould are 80 and 40 mm respectively.

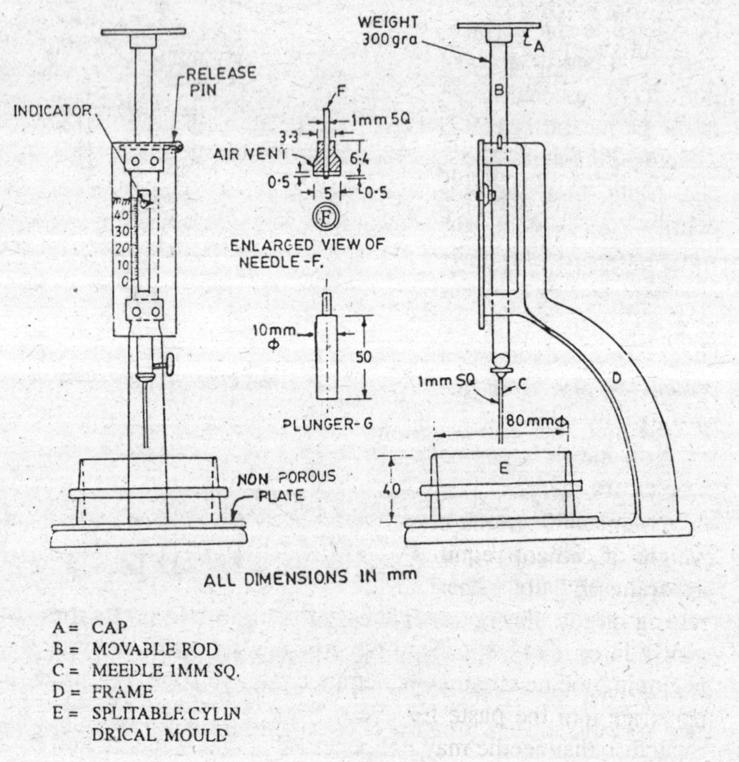

Fig. 2.14. Vicat apparatus

Procedure

Weigh about 300 gram cement carefully and put it in a clean crucible and add about 25% water of the weight of cement to the cement and mix it thoroughly with a standard spatula. Care should be taken that gauging (mixing) time should not be less than 3 min. and not more than 5 min. Gauging shall be counted from the time of adding water to the dry cement upto starting filling the paste in the mould.

The paste should be filled in the mould from bigger end to the smaller end. Now wipe out the excess paste from the bigger end and put it on the glass plate and put the mould with plate on the base of the frame of the apparatus. If paste is in excess on the upper end, then remove it with the help of a trowel. In the entire process of filling paste in the mould, no pressure should be exerted on the paste.

Now fix the 10 mm dia plunger in the moving rod and bring it in touch with the paste and note down the indicator's reading on the scale. Now release the plunger to penetrate it in the paste and find out its depth of penetration.

Repeat the procedure till the plunger is able to penetrate upto 5 ± 2 mm from the bottom of the mould. The temperature of experiment should be 27 ± 2°C (25 – 29°C). Express the amount of water used in the paste as the percentage by weight of the dry cement. Usually this percentage varies from 26% to 33%.

4. Determination of Setting time

Broadly speaking setting refers to a change from a fluid to a rigid state. During setting, the paste also acquires some strength, while hardening refers to the gain of strength of a set cement paste. Setting of cement may also be defined as when the cement paste has lost its plasticity and becomes sufficient rigid to with-stand an arbitrarily defined pressure then it is said to have set. The period of setting is divided into two parts as follows:

(*a*) Initial setting period (*b*) Final setting period

(*a*) Initial setting

Initial setting period is defined as the time from mixing water to the cement till the cement paste is unable to fill the cracks developed in it by itself. Initial setting period of cement is very important as it affects the durability and strength of cement concrete. If the setting period is too short, it will be impossible to transport and place the concrete at the site of work before it becomes too rigid to compact. On the other hand if the setting period is too long, it would tend to slow down the progress of work unduly as adequate strength will not develop at the desired age.

(*b*) Final setting time

This is the stage of setting of cement paste or cement concrete at which it has gained sufficient strength.

Determination of setting time

Setting time also is determined with the help of vicat's apparatus shown in Fig. 2.14.

Procedure

Weigh 400 grams cement carefully and prepare neat cement paste by adding 0.85 times water by weight of cement required to give a paste of standard consistency. Fill this paste into the mould of the apparatus and attach the 1.13 mm diameter needle in the moving rod of the apparatus. Now place the mould resting on the non-porous plate under the needle on the base plate of the apparatus and lower the needle gently in contact with the surface of the paste and release, allowing it to penetrate into the paste. In the beginning the needle may penetrate completely into the paste. Repeat this procedure till the needle fails to penetrate into the paste for about 5 mm above the bottom of the mould. Each time the mould should be rotated so that needle may not penetrate at one point only all the time. The period elapsing between the time when water added to the cement and the time at which the needle fails to pierce the paste by 5 mm from the bottom is known as *initial setting time.*

Final setting time

Now replace the 1.13 mm diameter needle of the vicat apparatus by the needle with an annular attachment shown in the Fig. 2.14. The cement shall be considered as finally set when applying gently 1.13 mm diameter needle to the surface of the paste may make an impression on it, where as the attachment fails to do so.

The temperature of the test should be 27 ± 2°C and relative humidity as 90%. As per I.S. 4031-1968 the setting times of different cements should be as follows:

S. No.	*Type of cement*	*Initial setting time in minutes not less than*	*Final setting time in minutes not less than*
1.	Ordinary	30	600
2.	Rapid hardening	30	600
3.	Low heat	60	600
4.	Portland pozzolana	30	600 max.

5. Determination of compressive strength

For determining the compressive strength of cement, cubes 50 cm^2 in surface area having a length of 7.06 cms are prepared of cement and standard sand and compacted by means of a standard vibration machine.

Standard sand

As per I.S. 650-1966, standard sand should have the following composition:

S. NO.	*Particle size*	*Percent*
1.	Greater than 1 mm	33.33
2.	Smaller than 1 mm and greater than 500 micron	33.33
3.	Below 500 microns	33.33

Thus this sand when sieved through 2 mm I.S. sieve, it passes through it 100% and when sieved on 90 micron sieve, 100% will be retained on it. Further it should be free from organic impurities.

Preparation of mix

For each cube of 7.06 cm length, 185 gram cement is needed. The ratio of cement and standard sand should be as 1:3 by weight. Weigh the materials separately for each cube and place them on a non-porous plate. Now mix the cement and sand dry for one minute with trowel. Now add water given by the following relation, and mix it till the colour is uniform. After adding water, mix should be mixed for not less than 3 minutes. If it takes more than 4 minutes to obtain a uniform colour, the mix should be rejected and the operation should be repeated with a fresh quantity of cement, sand and water.

For each cube, material required shall be as follows when the cement is tested with single graded sand:

Cement 185 gram

Standard sand 555 gram

Water $P = \left(\frac{P_n}{4} + 3.5\right.$ percent of combined wt. of cement & sand)

Where P_n is percentage of water required to produce a paste of standard consistency.

When graded sand is to be used, the material for each cube should be as follows:

Cement 200 gram

Standard sand 600 gram

Water $\left(\frac{P_n}{4} + 3.0\right.$ percent of combined weight of cement & sand)

Where P_n is same as above.

Moulding of specimens

Clean the dust of the mould and apply a thin film of oil or grease on inside of it. Now place the mould in a vibrating machine, having a vibrating frequency of 12000 ± 400 per minute and pour mixture of cement, sand and water prepared as above in the mould and vibrate at least for 2 minutes. Wipe out the excess mortar from the mould and make the surface smooth with the help of trowel.

Curing

The cubes should be cured after vibration for 24 hours at a temperature of 27 ± 2°C and at a relative humidity of 90%. After 24 hours, remove the mould and immerse the specimens in fresh water and keep them there till testing. Before testing the specimen should be taken out of water and wipe out excess water with jute or cloth.

Test. For compressive strength, cement cube can be tested at the age of, 7 and 28 days and the average of at least three cubes should be taken at each age. The difference between the average of three cube's strength and individual strength should not be more than 15%. The specimen should be put in the centre of the testing machine on the face other than the face cast. The rate of loading should not be more than 140 kg/cm^2 per minute. As per I.S. 269-1967, the compressive strength of cement should be as follows:

S. No.	*Time of testing*	*Type of cement*			
		Ordinary kg/cm^2	*Rapid hardening* kg/cm^2	*Low heat* kg/cm^2	*Pozzolana cement* kg/cm^2
1.	24 hours ± 30 minutes, not less than	—	160	—	—
2.	72 ± 1 hour, not less than	160	275	100	—
3.	168 ± 2 hour, not less than	220	—	160	175
4.	336 ± 4 hour, not less than	—	—	—	250
5.	672 ± 1 hour, not less than	—	—	350	—

6. Determination of tensile strength

Cement is very weak in tensile strength. Its tensile strength is determined with the help of briquettes shown in Fig. 2.15. As shown in Fig. 2.15 the thickness of the briquettes is 25.4 mm and the minimum area of its cross section is 645 mm^2. For preparing briquettes cement sand mortar of 1:3 ratio is used. For each briquette 250 gram cement and 750 gram sand is used. The amount of water to be used in the mortar is given by the relation:

$$P = \left(\frac{P_n}{5} + 2.5\% \text{ combined weight of cement and sand}\right)$$

Preparation of specimen

The sand cement mixture is prepared as for cubes with the proper quantities of cement, sand, and water as explained above. The mould is cleaned and oiled. It is now put on a steel plate and the mixture of sand and cement is filled in it and compacted with the help of a standard spatula and finished plane. Now it is put on up side down and finished as

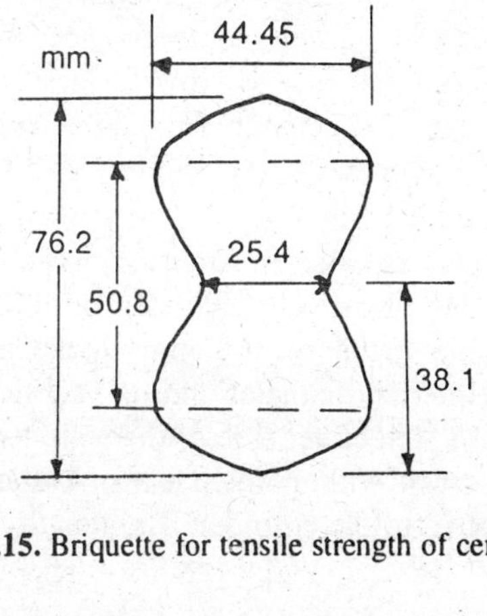

Fig. 2.15. Briquette for tensile strength of cement

explained above. Now the mould is kept for 24 hours at 27 ± 2°C and 90% relative humidity. After 24 hours, the mould is removed and the specimen is put in fresh water for curing. Curing water should be changed every week. As far as possible the curing temperature should be kept at 27 ± 2°C.

Test. The tensile strength test of cement should be done at 3 and 7 days age. For testing, the briquette is taken out of curing water and excessive water wiped out and fixed into the clamp as shown in Fig. 2.16.

This machine works on the principle of compound lever. Before starting the test, the jaws D-D of the machine are greased and the briquette is fixed and the lead shot are allowed to fall in container B from container A. The change of shots from A to B should be so regulated that the rate of increase in load on briquette should increase at the rate of 35 kg/cm^2 per minute or 7 kg/cm^2 per 12 seconds. The breaking stress of briquette can be obtained by dividing the weight of lead shots in chamber B at the time of breaking by the area of cross section.

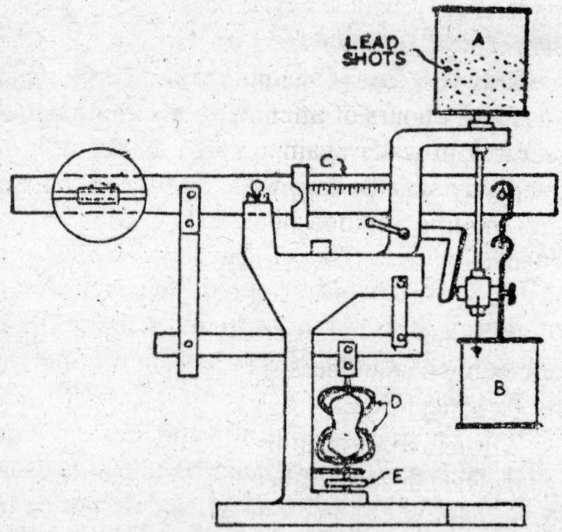

Fig. 2.16. Cement tensile strength testing machine

Result. For one age, the average of six briquette strength should be taken. The individual strength of any briquette should not differ by 15% from the average value. For different cements as per I.S. 269-1958, the tensile strength should be as follows:

Time	*Ordinary Cement kg/cm^2*	*RAPD Hardening Cement Kg/cm^2*
24h ± 30 min	—	20.0
72 h ± 60 min	20.0	30.0
168 h ± 120 min	25.0	—

7. Determination of soundness of Cement

Cements which exhibit expansions due to delayed or slow hydration of free lime, magnesia and calcium sulphate are known as unsound cements. As unsoundness of cement is not apparent for months together after adding water to cement, therefore it is essential to test the soundness of cement in accelerated manner. Le Chatelier was first to provide a test for soundness of cement. He used a very simple apparatus as shown in Fig. 2.17.

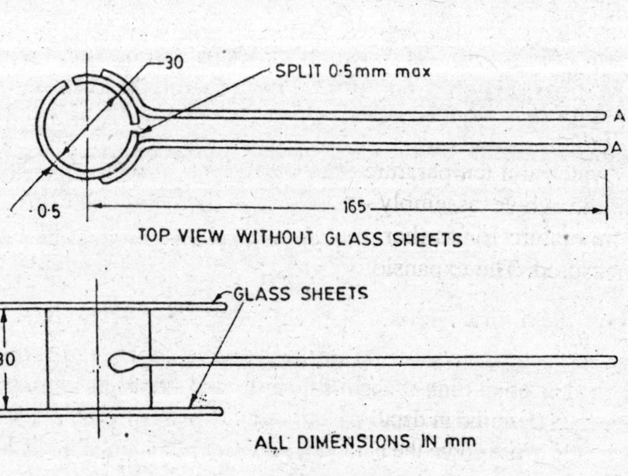

Fig. 2.17. Le Chatelier apparatus

Le Chatelier apparatus consists of a small brass split cylinder or other suitable metal of 0.5 mm thickness. The internal diameter and its height is 30 mm. On either side of the split, two indicators with pointed ends AA are attached to the cylinder. The length of these pointers from the centre of the cylinder is 165 mm. The split of the cylinder should not be more than 0.5 mm.

Test. Weigh 100 grams of cement carefully and add 0.78 times water needed for preparing a paste of standard consistency. Now place the cylinder on a glass plate and fill it with the cement paste prepared and cover it with an other glass plate and put a small weight on this covering sheet or plate. Immerse the whole assembly in water at a temperature of 27°C to 32°C and keep it there for 24 hours. At the end of this period *i.e.* after 24 hours of immersion, measure the distance between the indicator points and submerge the whole assembly in water again at the temperature as above (27°C- 32°C). Now heat the water in such a way that water may start boiling within 25 to 30 minutes. Keep the mould assembly in boiling water for one hour. After boiling for one hour, the assembly is taken out of water and allowed to cool. After cooling the distance between the indicators is measured again. The increase in this distance represents the expansion of the cement. The expansion of aerated cement should not exceed more than 5 mm.

Le Chatelier test detects unsoundness due to free lime only; but if magnesia is also present in the cement, then soundness should be tested with the help of *autoclave* test, which is sensitive to both free lime and free magnesia.

Autoclave. It is an high pressure steam boiler, equipped with an automatic pressure control and safety valve. The capacity of heating unit should be such that with the maximum load (water plus specimen etc.) the pressure of the saturated steam in the autoclave may be raised to a gauge pressure of 21 kg/cm^2 in about 60 ± 15 minutes time from the start of heating. It should be capable of maintaining the pressure of 21 ± 1 kg/cm^2 corresponding to a temperature of 215.7°C. Further it should be capable to drop pressure from 21 kg/cm^2 to 0.7 kg/cm^2 in 60 minutes after shutting off the supply of heat. The pressure gauge has a dial diameter of about 11.5 cms and graduated from zero to 42 kg/cm^2. The least count of the gauge is 0.4 kg/cm^2. The error in the gauge should not be more than 0.2 kg/cm^2.

Test. 500 gram of cement is weighed carefully and sufficient water is mixed to make a paste of standard consistency. The paste is filled in the mould of cross section 25 × 25 mm and 250 mm length. The mortar is filled in the mould by pressing it with thumb or fore finger in on or two layers. After compacting the mortar, the surface is flushed with the help of trowel.

After moulding, the specimens are stored in a moist room. After 24 ± 1/2 hours of moulding, the mould is removed and the length of the specimen measured carefully, and placed in the autoclave at room temperature and about 7 to 10% volume of autoclave is filled with water.

To permit air to escape from the autoclave during the early portion of heating period, the vent valve is left open till the steam begins to escape. Now the valve is closed and the temperature of the autoclave is raised in such a way that a pressure of 21 kg/cm^2 is developed in the autoclave at a temperature of 216°C in about 60 ± 15 min. from the start of heating and this pressure is maintained for 3 hours. At the end of 3 hours, heat supply is stopped and autoclave is allowed to cool at a rate such that the pressure falls less than 1 kg/cm^2 at the end of one hour. Now the autoclave is opened and test specimens are immediately placed in water at a temperature above 90°C and cooled by adding cold water in such a way that the temperature of the whole assembly including water falls down to 27 ± 2°C in 15 minutes. After maintaining this temperature for further 15 minutes, the specimens are taken out of water, surface dried and their lengths measured. The expansion of the bar should not be more than 0.8% but preferablly 0.5%.

QUESTIONS

1. Define cement and distinguish between natural and artificial cement.
2. Describe in detail the process of manufacture of cement by wet process.
3. Write down the names of important compounds of cement and explain the influence of each on the properties of cement.
4. Write down the specifications and test to be carried out to determine the quality of cement.

5. Explain the procedure of the following tests carried out in the laboratory:
   (*a*) Soundness of cement
   (*b*) Standard consistency of cement
   (*c*) Initial and final setting time of cement
   (*d*) Compressive strength of portland cement
6. Define hydration of cement in detail.
7. Define heat of hydration of cement. How it can be reduced?
8. Describe the important effects of C_3A on the properties of concrete.
9. Why is the C_3A content in cement of interest?
10. Discuss the effects of C_3S on the properties of concrete.
11. How does gypsum influence the hydration of C_3A?
12. Compare the contribution of various compounds in cement to its heat of hydration.
13. How is fineness of cement in measured?
14. Differentiate between false set and flash set.
15. Discuss the reaction of hydration of the main compounds in the portland cement.
16. Name the compounds of portland cement and discuss their roles.
17. What is meant by loss on ignition?
18. What is the difference between false set, initial set and final set?
19. Compare the contributions of C_3S and C_2S to the 7 day and 28 day strength of concrete.
20. Why is C_3A undesirable in cement.
21. How does the gypsum content in ordinary portland cement specified?

OBJECTIVE TYPE QUESTIONS

1. Cement is an essential ingredient of concrete due to..
   (*a*) It is an active ingredient
   (*b*) It is a binding medium for other ingredients
   (*c*) It is the only scientifically controlled ingredient
   (*d*) It is an delicate link of the chain
   (*e*) Any of the above
2. In the manufacture of portland cement, the mixture of argillacious and calcareous materials is heated upto a temperature.
   (*a*) 750 to 850°C (*b*) 375°C to 475°C
   (*c*) 1400°C to 1500°C (*d*) 1650°C to 1850°C
3. During the manufacturing process, gypsum is added..
   (*a*) To reduce the generation of heat of hydration
   (*b*) To increase the strength of cement
   (*c*) To impart colour to the cement
   (*d*) To retard initial setting time of cement
4. The percentage of gypsum added to cement clinker is
   (*a*) 0.35 to 0.55 (*b*) 0.55 to 0.75
   (*c*) 2.5 to 3.0 (*d*) 7.5 to 9.5
   (*e*) 10 to 15%
5. The setting and hardening of cement after addition of water is due to
   (*a*) Evaporation of water (*b*) Binding actin of water
   (*c*) Hydration of cement (*d*) Presence of gypsum
   (*e*) none of the above
6. In a cement, the maximum percentage of oxide is that of..
   (*a*) Alumina (*b*) Silica
   (*c*) Magnesium (*d*) Lime
   (*e*) iron
7. In a cement, the minimum percentage of oxide is that of..
   (*a*) Iron (*b*) Magnesium

(*c*) Lime (*d*) Alumina
(*e*) Silica

8. Which of the following effects have oxide composition of cement
(*a*) The presence of iron oxide gives grey colour to the cement
(*b*) The presence of unburnt lime and magnesia cause unsoundness in cement
(*c*) High silica content retards the setting time resulting in more strength
(*d*) High lime content increases the setting time resulting in more strength
(*e*) All of the above

9. The presence of tricalcium aluminate (C_3A) in cement causes..
(*a*) It produces highest heat of hydration
(*b*) It reacts characteristically fast with water
(*c*) It develops least resistance to sulphate attack
(*d*) All the above

10. Which of the following compounds of cement act as binder
(*a*) C_3S, C_2S and So_3 (*b*) C_3S, C_2S and C_3A
(*c*) C_3S and C_4AF (*d*) C_2S, C_4AF, C_3A

11. Which of the following statements is incorrect?
(*a*) C_3S and C_2S together constitute about 70 to 85% of cement
(*b*) C_3S and C_2S produce the same product on hydration
(*c*) C_2S hydrates slowly resulting-high later strength
(*d*) C_3S hydrates faster and produces greater heat of hydration
(*e*) C_3S is more resistant to chemical attack

12. Which of the following statements is incorrect?
(*a*) C_3A reacts fast resulting in immediate stiffening of the paste
(*b*) C_3A is responsible for the production of the highest heat of hydration
(*c*) C_3A is more resistant to sulphate attack
(*d*) The flash set action of C_3A is prevented by the addition of gypsum

13. The decreasing order of rate of hydration of cement constituents is..
(*a*) C_3S, C_2S and C_3A (*b*) C_2S, C_3A, C_3S
(*c*) C_3A, C_2S and C_3S (*d*) C_3A, C_3S, C_2S

14. The decreasing order of strength development of cement constituents is
(*a*) C_2S, C_3S, C_3A and C_4AF (*b*) C_3S, C_2S, C_3A and C_4AF
(*c*) C_2S, C_4AF, C_3A and C_3S (*d*) C_3S, C_3A, C_2S and C_4AF

15. Which of the cement compounds sets and hardens first
(*a*) C_2S (*b*) C_3S
(*c*) C_3A (*d*) C_4AF

16. The dicalcium silicate adds to the strength of cement after..days
(*a*) 1-5 (*b*) 7-10
(*c*) 10-18 (*d*) 28-30
(*e*) 40-50

17. What happens after adding water to the cement?
(*a*) Heat is generated (*b*) Chemical reaction starts
(*c*) Heat is absorbed (*d*) All of the above

18. Dicalcium silicates (C_2S) acts as..
(*a*) Hydrates immediately (*b*) Hardens rapidly
(*c*) More resistant to chemical attack (*d*) Generates less heat of hydration
(*e*) Has no reaction with water

19. For the loss on ignition test the cement sample is heated upto..
(*a*) 175°C (*b*) 250°C
(*c*) 900-1000°C (*d*) 1250-1350°C

20. For portland cement the loss on ignition should not exceed
(*a*) 5% (*b*) 7%

(*c*) 9% (*d*) 4%

21. In the ignition test for ordinary portland cement the loss in weight is due to..
(*a*) Chemical reaction (*b*) Evaporation of moisture and carbon dioxide
(*c*) Melting of C_3A (*d*) Decomposition of silicates
22. The insoluble residue in cement should be less than...
(*a*)1.5 to 2.5% (*b*) 0.85 to 0.9%
(*c*) 5.0 to 6.5% (*d*) 10 to 15%
23. The total quantity of heat of hydration of cement is independent of
(*a*) Chemical composition of cement (*b*) Fineness of cement
(*c*) Ambient temperature (*d*) Quantity of water added to the cement
24. About 90% heat of hydration is liberated in...
(*a*) 7 days (*b*) 15 days
(*c*) 28 days (*d*) 180 days
25. About 50% heat of hydration is liberated in
(*a*) 1 to 3 days (*b*) 5 to 7 days
(*c*) 7 to 10 days (*d*) 28 to 35 days
26. The duration in which the concrete mixture remains in plastic state depends upon
(*a*) Amount of mixing water (*b*) Setting time of cement
(*c*) Ambient temperature (*d*) Amount of cement
(*e*) On all the above factors
27. The initial setting time is maximum for
(*a*) Portland slag cement (*b*) Low heat portland cement
(*c*) High strength portland cement (*d*) Portland pozzolanic cement
28. The setting time of cement is influenced by
(*a*) Temperature and humidity (*b*) Amount of water and its temperature
(*c*) Time of mixing (*d*) By all the above factors
29. For medium strength concrete, the water/cement ratio should not be less than
(*a*) 0.55 (*b*) 0.4
(*c*) 0.45 (*d*) 0.5
30. State whether the following statements are true or false
(*a*) The hydrated crystals of cement form an inter locking random three dimensional net work called gel
(*b*) The micro structure of hydrated cement governs the physical properties of concrete
(*c*) The hydrated paste has a porous structure
(*d*) The size of the gel pore is less than 4×10^{-4} micron
(*e*) White cement is unsuitable for ordinary concrete work
(*f*) The colour of pozzolana cement is white
(*g*) The high alumina cement is a rapid setting cement
(*h*) In normal concrete construction ordinary portland cement and high alumina cement may be mixed with advantage
(*i*) The term strength of cement implies compressive strength.
(*j*) Tricalcium silicate may be written as C_3S.
(*k*) Properly stored cement should not be disturbed till it is to be used. [**Ans.** *false*. (*d*), (*e*), (*g*), (*h*)]
31. The compressive strength of concrete basically is related to
(*a*) Hydrate space ratio (*b*) Water cement ratio
(*c*) Specific surface area of cement (*d*) Amount of gypsum
32. In cement the insoluble material is
(*a*) The inactive part of cement which should be kept at the maximum permissible limit
(*b*) The inactive part of cement which should be kept at the minimum level
(*c*) The active part of cement which should be kept at the maximum permissible limit
(*d*) The active part of cement which should be kept at the minimum level
33. Finer the cement higher is..
(*a*) Rate of hydration

(*b*) The surface area
(*c*) The possibility of prehydration by atmospheric moisture
(*d*) Lesser amount of water required for constant slump
(*d*) All are correct

34. The quantity of free magnesia in ordinary portland should be
(*a*) Between 5 to 10% (*b*) Between 10 to 15%
(*c*) Less than 5% (*d*) Less than 0.5%

35. In portland cement the excess amount of free lime results in
(*a*) Increased initial setting time
(*b*) Development of unsoundness in the product
(*c*) Increased strength
(*d*) Improvement in the quality of concrete

36. The specific surface area obtained by air permeability method is (in cm^2/g)
(*a*) 200 to 250 (*b*) 2250 to 3500
(*c*) 400 to 4500 (*d*) 5000 to 7000

37. In consistency test, the paste is said of normal consistency if the rod penetrates upto from top
(*a*) 5 to 10 mm (*b*) 15 to 18 mm
(*c*) 33 to 37 mm (*d*) 45 to 48 mm

38. To check the large changes in volume after setting add...
(*a*) Maximum quantity of water to the mix
(*b*) Minimum quantity of water to the mix
(*c*) Excess quantity of fine aggregate
(*d*) Provide proper curing
(*e*) Limit the quantities of free lime and magnesia in the cement

39. For the production of medium strength concrete the absolute minimum water/cement ratio should be
(*a*) 0.30 (*b*) 0.32 to 0.35
(*c*) 0.42 to 0.45 (*d*) 0.36 to 0.4
(*e*) 0.5 to 0.55

40. For hydration of 100 kg of cement the minimum amount of water required is...
(*a*) 20 kg (*b*) 30 kg
(*c*) 45 kg (*d*) 25 kg
(*e*) 42 kg

41. For testing cement cubes they should be kept at
(*a*) 17 ± 2°C and 100% humidity (*b*) 27 ± 2°C and 90% humidity
(*c*) 37 ± 2°C and 80% humidity (*d*) 47 ± 2°C with 70% humidity

42. The three day compressive strength of ordinary portland cement should be more than
(*a*) 150 kg/cm^2 (15 MPa) (*b*) 160 kg/cm^2 (16 MPa)
(*c*) 220 kg/cm^2 (22 MPa) (*d*) 255 kg/cm^2 (25.5 MPa)
(*e*) 350 kg/cm^2 (35 MPa)

Answers

1. (*e*)	8. (*e*)	15. (*c*)	22. (*b*)	29. (*b*)	37. (*c*)
2. (*c*)	9. (*d*)	16. (*d*)	23. (*b*)	31. (*a*)	38. (*e*)
3. (*d*)	10. (*b*)	17. (*a*)	24. (*d*)	32. (*a*)	39. (*d*)
4. (*c*)	11. (*e*)	18. (*d*)	25. (*a*)	33. (*e*)	40. (*d*)
5. (*c*)	12. (*c*)	19. (*c*)	26. (*a*)	34. (*d*)	41. (*b*)
6. (*d*)	13. (*d*)	20. (*d*)	27. (*b*)	35. (*b*)	42. (*b*)
7. (*b*)	14. (*b*)	21. (*b*)	28. (*d*)	36. (*b*)	

3

Cements of Different Types

3.1. INTRODUCTION

In the previous chapter, the properties of portland cement have been discussed. It has been seen in the last chapter that cements differing in chemical composition and physical characteristics exhibit different properties on hydration. Thus cements of desired properties can be produced by selecting suitable mixtures of raw materials. The various types of portland cements and some special cements have been discussed in this chapter.

3.2. TYPES OF PORTLAND CEMENT

Main types of portland cements are as follows:

1. Ordinary portland cement—High strength ordinary portland cement
2. Modified portland cement
3. Rapid hardening or high early strength portland cement
4. Low heat portland cement
5. Sulphate resisting portland cement
6. Blast furnance portland cement
7. White cement
8. Coloured cement
9. Portland pozzolana cement
10. Slag cement etc.

The chemical composition of first five types of cements has been shown in table 2.3. In order to ensure good durability of concrete under different conditions, various types of cements have been developed. Though the chemical composition of cement determines to a large degree the rate of gain of strength, but the principal mechanical properties of hardened cement concrete, such as strength, permeability, shrinkage, resistance to weathering, creep etc. are also affected by factors other than cement composition. Fig. 3.1 shows the rate of development of strength of different portland cements. While the rate of development of strength at the early age say about 28 days varies very much but after 90 days the strength of the cements practically is same.

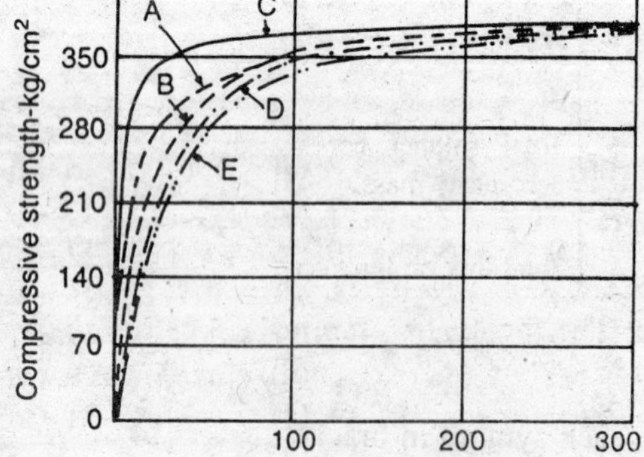

Fig. 3.1. Strength development of different cements at different ages

From the Fig. 3.1, it will be seen that slower the rate of development of strength at the early age, higher the ultimate strength. In other words denser the gel, greater the ultimate strength.

1. Ordinary portland cement. This type of cement is suitable for use in general concrete construction wherever it is not exposed to sulphates in the soil or in ground water. The modern portland cements have higher C_3S contents and are of greater fineness than cements about 50 years back. Thus modern cements exhibit higher 28 days strength than cements in 1920-25. Fig. 3.2 shows strength development of cement between 1915 & 1970 etc. (Other details have been discussed in chapter 2). Fig. 3.2 shows the rate of gain of strength since 1916 of 1970.

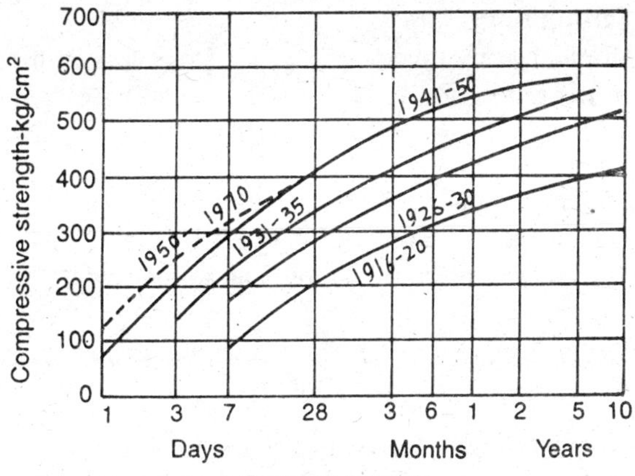

Fig. 3.2. Rate of gain of strength of portland cement between 1916-70

The German classification of cements is based on the 28 days strength of 1:3 mortars with a water cement ratio of 0.5 as 350, 450 & 550 kg/cm^2 etc.

3.2.1. High Strength ordinary Portland Cement

High Strength ordinary portland cement. This cement also is manufactured as ordinary portland cement. This cements is useful where high strength at eary age is required. In other details it is similar to ordinary portland cement, but its chemical and physical requirements should be as follows as per I.S. 8112-1976.

Table 3.1. Physical requirements of (OPC)

S. No.		*Requirements*
1.	Ratio of percentages of lime to percentage of silica, alumina, and iron oxide when calculated by the formula, $\dfrac{Cao - 0.7\ So_3}{2.85\ SiO_2 + 1.2\ Al_2O_3 + 0.65\ Fe_2O_3}$	Not greater than 1.02 and not less than 0.66
2.	Ratio of percentage of alumina to that of iron oxide	not less than 0.66
3.	Insoluble residue percent by mass	not more than 2.0%
4.	Magnesia percent by mass	not more than 6.0%
5.	Total sulpher content calculated as sulphuric anhydride (SO_3) percent by mass.	not more than 2.75 and 3.0 when C_3A is 7% or less and greater than 7% respectively.
6.	Total loss on ignition.	not more than 4.0%.

***Note:** The tricalcium aluminate is calculated by the formula,

$$C_3A = 2.65\ (Al_2O_3) - 1.69(Fe_2O_3),$$

where each symbol in brackets refers to the percent (by mass of total cement) of the oxide excluding any contained in insoluble residue referred at serial No. 3.

Physical Requirements

1. Fineness. It's specific surface area should not be less than 3500 cm^2/gram.

2. Soundness. When tested by the Le Chateliar method, un-aerated cement should not have an expansion more than 10 mm.

3. Setting time

(*a*) Initial setting time	not less than 30 minutes
(*b*) Final setting time	not more than 600 minutes

Compressive strength

The average compressive strength of at least three mortar cubes (area of face 50 cm^2) composed of one part of cement and three parts of standard sand and ($P/4$ + 3.1 percent of combined mass of sand and cement) water, and prepared, stored and tested under standard conditions should be as follows:

Time	*Compressive strength*
72 ± 1 hours	230 kg/cm^2
168 ± 2 hours	300 kg/cm^2
672 ± 4 hours	430 kg/cm^2

After 1987 higher grade cements have been introduced in India. The original ordinary portland cement (OPC) has been divided into three grades, namely 33 grade, 43 grade and 53 grade. These grades indicate the compressive strength at 28 days when tested as per IS 4031-1988. The compressive strength of cement should not be less than 33 N/mm^2 (330 kg/cm^2), 43 N/mm^2 (430 kg/cm^2) and 53 N/mm^2 (530 kg/cm^2) at 28 days. The physical properties of these cements are shown in Table 3.2.

Table 3.2

	Type of cement	*Fineness cm^2/gram*	*Soundness by Le-Chatelier mm*	*Auto Clave (% max.)*	*Initial setting time min.*	*Final setting time in min.*	*Compressive strength in MPa*		
							3 days	*7 days*	*28 days*
1.	33 grade OPC (IS 269-1989)	2250	10	0.8	30	600	16	22	33
2.	43 grade OPC (IS 8112-1989)	2250	10	0.8	30	600	23	33	43
3.	53 grade OPC (IS 1269-1987)	2250	10	0.8	30	600	27	37	53

* MPa is strength of cement/concrete in N/mm^2. 1 kg = 9.8 Newton (N) and 1 kg/cm^2 $\frac{0.1N}{(mm)^2}$ called (MPa) (Mega Pascal). Thus 1 MPa = 10 kg/cm^2.

The production of high quality cement could be possible by using high quality lime stone, modern equipment and close control on lime constituents, finer grinding, better packing and maintaining better particle size distribution.

3.2.2. Advantages of high grade cements

Following advantages of high grade cements have been observed:

1. They offer 10-20% saving in the consumption of cement.
2. They develop strength at faster rate. Thus saving time in construction. The formwork may be released at earlier time and can be reused on other works, resulting in saving of time and money both.

The production of ordinary portland cement is decreasing through out the world due to the popularity of blended cement on account of lower energy consumption, environmental, economic and other technical reasons.

In advanced countries, the consumption of OPC has come down to about 40% of the total cement production. In India in the year 1998-99 the production of OPC has come down to 70% *i.e.* from 79 million tones to 57 million tones. The production of pozzolana portland cement to 19% and slag cement to 10% of the total cement production. In times to come its use is expected to decline further, how ever it will remain an important type of cement for general use.

3.2.3. Rapid hardening cement

This cement is very similar to the ordinary portland cement. As the name implies, it develops strength more rapidly. Therefore it is also known as high early strength cement. Its setting time is similar to that of ordinary portland cement. Its chemical requirements are same as that of ordinary portland cement.

The strength developed by the rapid hardening cement at the age of 24 hours is of the order as that of 3 days strength of ordinary portland cement and 3 day strength of rapid hardening cement is of the order of 7 day strength of portland cement with the same water cement ratio. The increased rate of gain of strength of the rapid hardening cement is achieved by a higher C_3S content of the order of about 56%. Some times C_3S Content in rapid hardening cement is 70%. It is finer than ordinary portland cement. It's specific surface area is 3250 cm^2/gm of cement.

The requirement of chemical composition and soundness for rapid hardening cement are same as those for ordinary portland cement; discussed in the last chapter. The density of this cement is 1280 kg per cubic metre.

Use of Rapid hardening cement

The use of rapid hardening cement is recommended in the following situations:

1. Where form work is required to be removed early for re-use else where.
2. For road, air strip and bridge repairs etc.
3. In cold weather concreting.
4. In prefabricated concrete construction.

The rapid hardening cement being more fine than ordinary portland cement needs more water for the same workability. Its shrinkage is also more than ordinary portland cement. The rapid gain of strength means a high rate of heat development. The rate of heat development varies from 53 Cal/g to 93.2 Cal/g at 4°C to 41°C. As the rate of heat development is high, this cement should not be used for mass concrete construction as large quantity of heat will cause cracks in the structure. On the other hand at places of low temperatures, the use of this cement is found useful, as the high rate of heat liberation will prove a satisfactory safeguard against frost damage at early age.

3.2.4. Extra rapid hardening portland cement

This cement is useful for cold weather concreting or when a very high early strength is required, but it should not be used with reinforcement due to the risk of corrosion. The strength of this cement is about 25% higher than that of rapid hardening cement at 1 or 2 days and 10 to 20% higher at 7 days but the gain in strength disappears at the age of 90 days. The setting time also of this cement is short from 5 minutes to 30 minutes depending upon the temperature at the time of placement. Hence it should be finished with in 20 minutes. It's shrinkage is also higher than rapid hardening cement. It should not be stored for more than a month.

This cement can be obtained by intergrinding calcium chloride with rapid hardening portland cement. The quantity of calcium chloride should not exceed 2%. As calcium chloride is deliquescent, this cement should be stored under dry conditions and generally should be used with in one month of dispatch from cement plant.

3.2.5. Ultra high early strength portland cement

This cement is manufactured by separating fines from rapid hardening portland cement by a cyclone air elutriator. This cement is more fine than ordinary rapid hardening portland cement. It's specific surface area is of the order of 7000 cm^2/g to 9000 cm^2/gram. Due to its high fineness, it has low bulk density and deteriorates rapidly on exposure. It's high degree of fineness leads to a rapid hydration, which leads to high rate of heat generation at early ages and to a rapid development of strength. This cement develops strength at 16 hours of the same order as 3 days strength of rapid hardening portland cement and at 24 hours as 7 days strength of rapid hardening portland cement. However after 28 days, the gain in strength is very little.

As this cement contains no admixtures, therefor it is suitable for use in reinforced and pre stressed concrete. The creep and shrinkage are more or less same as those of other portland cements. The ultra high early strength portland cement has its trade name as *Swift Crete*. This cement is used in great Britain. However for the same mix proportion this cement results in lower workability. Gypsum content is 4%.

3.2.6. Very high strength cement

For rapid repair of damaged concrete roads and air field pavements very high strength cements have been developed. Some of them are as follows:

1. **Magnesium phosphate cement (MPC).** This cement has been developed by Central Road Research Institute Delhi. This is an important development for emergency repair of airfields, launching pads, hard surface road pavements suffering damage due to enemy bombing and missile attack etc. This cement can be used for such emergency repairs.

   This cement has been found to possess unique hydraulic properties, particularly a controlled rapid set and early strength development. It is a prepacked mixture of dead burnt magnesite with fine aggregate mixed with phosphate. It sets rapidly and yields durable high strength cement mortar.
2. **Pyrament cement.** It is the trade name of a super high early strength Cement developed by cement industries in U.S.A. It is a blended hydraulic cement. This cement produces a high and very early strength of mortar and concrete which can be used for emergency repair works. No chlorides are added to this cement. The typical properties of concrete and mortar of these cements are shown in Table 3.3 below.

Table 3.3

Material	*Compressive strength in MPa*	*Flexural strength in MPa*
Hardened Mortar		
2 hour	17 (170 kg/cm^2)	—
3 hour	24 (240 kg/cm^2)	4.1 (41 kg/cm^2)
24 hour	41 (410 kg/cm^2)	6.9 (69 kg/cm^2)
7 Days	69 (690 kg/cm^2)	10.3 (103 kg/cm^2)
Hardened Concrete		
4 hour	17 (170 kg/cm^2)	3.45 (34.5 kg/cm^2)
1 Day	34 (340 kg/cm^2)	5.52 (55.2 kg/cm^2)
28 Days	69 (690 kg/cm^2)	8.27 (82.7 kg/cm^2)

3.2.7. Speed Cement

This cement is used in Belgium. It is some what less fine than ultra high early strength portland cement. It has specific surface area of the order of 4590 cm^2/g. The compressive strength of standard vibrated 1:3 mortar cubes is 280 kg/cm^2 at one day, 480 kg/cm^2 at 3 days and 680 kg/cm^3 at 28 days. This cement is suitable for winter concreting or for urgent jobs as well sealing or repair of roads etc.

3.2.8. Regulated set cement or jet cement

This cement consists essentially of a mixture of portland cement and calcium fluoro-aluminate ($C_{11}A_7CaF_2$) with an appropriate retarder (usually citric acid). The setting time of this cement can vary between 1 and 30 min. The setting time is controlled at the time of manufacture of cement as the raw materials are inter-ground and burnt together. The strength development is slower with slower setting.

The early strength development is controlled by the content of calcium fluoro-aluminate. 5% calcium fluoro-aluminates develops a strength of 60 kg/cm^2 at 1 hour where as 50% of this material will produce a strength of 200 kg/cm^2 at the same time *i.e.* 1 hour. After wards the strength development is similar to that of parent portland cement. This cement is widely used in Japan, Austria, and Germany.

3.2.9. Low heat portland cement (IS 12600-1989)

As stated in the previous chapter, cement generates heat during hydration. Heat generated during hydration raises the temperature in the interior of a large concrete mass. In case the heat generated is not lost quickly, it will cause serious cracks in the concrete mass as the outer layers will cool and contract, while the inner mass is still at higher temperature. For this reason, it is necessary to limit the rate of heat evalution of cement used for mass concrete. The rate of heat evaluation of this cement is limited to 65 cal/g at the age of 7 days and 75 cal/gram at the age of 28 days. The limits of lime contents of this cement after correction should be as shown below.

$$\frac{CaO}{2.4\,(SiO_2) + 1.2\,(Al_2O_3) + 0.65\,(Fe_2O_3)} \leq 1 \text{ and}$$

$$\frac{CaO}{1.9\,(SiO_2) + 1.2\,(Al_2O_3) + 0.65\,(Fe_2O_3)} \geq 1$$

In this cement the more rapidly hydrating components tri-cal-aluminate C_3A and tri-calcium silicate C_3S are kept low at 5% and 13% respectively by weight resulting increase in C_2S. The rate of strength development of this cement is lower initially, but the ultimate strength is unaffected *i.e.* it is same as that of ordinary portland cement. In any case to ensure a sufficient rate of gain of strength, specific surface area of this cement should not be less than 3200 cm^2/g. The setting and hardening times of this cement are nearly the same as those of ordinary portland cement. Its strength after 7 days is 50% that of portland cement and 66% after 28 days. Its strength becomes more or less equal to that of portland cement after 90 days.

Hence this cement is unsuitable for ordinary work as it will require prolonged curing and keeping the form works in position. However it is very useful for mass concrete work as dams, bridges etc. This cement was developed in USA during 1930.

3.2.10. Modified cement

This cement contains about 6% C_3A and 46% C_3S. This cement generates heat at some what higher rate than that of low heat cement with a rate of gain of strength similar to that of portland cement. This cement is recommended for use in structures where a moderately low heat generation is desirable or where moderate sulpher attack may occur. This cement is extensively used in U.S.A.

3.2.11. Portland Blast-furnace Cement or Slag Cement (IS 455-1989)

This type of cement is made by intergrinding the portland cement clinker and granulated slag. The quantity of slag should not exceed 65% of the weight of the mixture. It may vary from 25 to 65%.

The slag is a waste product of the manufacture of pig iron. To utilize this slag which is a waste product the manufacture of this cement has been started. The development of this cement has considerably increased in recent times. Its production in 1998-99 was about 8 million tones *i.e.* 10% of the total production of all cements.

The slag is a mixture of lime, silica and alumina, that is, it contains same oxides that make up portland cement, but not in the same proportions. A slag is considered satisfactory if it contains 42% lime, 30% silica, 19% alumina, 5% magnesia and 1% alkalies. Blast furnace slag varies greatly in composition and physical structure depending on the process used and on the method of cooling of the slag. Slag to be used in the cement has to be quenched (rapid cooling by water) in such a way that it solidifies as a glassy granulated slag and its crystallization is prevented. The rapid cooling by water results also in the fragmentation of the material into the granulated form.

As per I.S. 12089-1987 the portland slag cement should have the following chemical requirements.

Table 3.4. Chemical requirements of PBC

Oxide	*Max. percentage*
Manganes oxide	5.5
Magnesium oxide %	17.0
Sulpher triodixe (So_3)	3.0
Sulphide sulpher (S)	2.0
Loss on ignition	4.0
Glass content %	85% min.

The composition of granulated slag should comply to one of the following requirements:

$$\frac{CaO + MgO + 1/3\ Al_2O_3}{SiO_3 + 2/3\ Al_2O_3} \geq 1$$

or

$$\frac{CaO + Mgo + Al_2O_3}{SiO_2} \geq 1$$

or

$$\frac{CaO + C_2S + 1/2\ MgO + Al_2O_3}{SiO_2 + MnO} \geq 1.5$$

Generally following composition meets the above requirements of the granulated blast furnace slag.

Sillicon dioxide (SiO_2)	30.0–38%
Aluminium oxide (Al_2O_3)	15–25%
Ferrous oxide (FeO)	0.5–2%
Calcium oxide (CaO)	30–45%
Magnessium oxide (MgO)	4–17%
MnO_2	1.0–5.0%

The chemical composition of Blast Furnace slag (BFS) and cement clinker are similar. The approximate chemical composition of cement-clinker, blast-furnace slag (BFS) and fly ash are shown in Table 3.5 below.

Table 3.5. Approximate chemical composition of cement-clinker, BFS and Flyash

S. No.	*Constituents*	*% Contents*		
		Cement clinker	*Blast furnace slag*	*Fly ash*
1.	CaO	60 – 67	30 – 45	1.0 – 3.0
2	SiO_2	17 – 25	30 – 38	35 – 60
3.	Al_2O_3	3.0 – 8.0	15 – 25	10 – 30
4.	Fe_2O_3	0.5 – 6.0	0.5 – 2.0	4 – 10
5.	Mgo	0.1 – 4.0	4.0 – 17.0	0.2 – 5.0
6.	Mno_2		1.0 – 5.0	—
7.	Glass		85 – 98	20 – 30
8.	Sp. gravty	3.15	2.9	2.1– 2.6

Manufacture of slag cement

Slag can be used in different ways to manufacture blast furnance slag cement. In the first case, slag can be used together with lime stone as a raw material for the conventional manufacture of portland cement. Clinker obtained from these materials often used in the manufacture of blast furnance cement. Secondly the dry granulated slag is fed with portland cement clinker into a grinding mill for grinding. At this time, a measured quantity of gypsum is also added in order to control its setting time. Slag being harder than clinker presents some difficulties in grinding.

Blast furnance cement has been used in many countries for a number of years such as Scotland, U.S.A., Germany, France, Belgium, and Netherland. In different countries different percentage of slag has been used. In Netherland slag quantity upto 85% has been used.

Belgians have developed a new process in which wet ground granulated slag is fed in the form of a slurry direct into the concrete mixer, together with portland cement and aggregates. In this process the cost of drying the slag is saved and slag could be ground finer in wet state, resulting in saving of energy.

Portland blast furnace cement is similar in many respects to ordinary portland cement. The requirements for setting times, soundness and compressive strength of portland cement and blast furnance cement are same. The rate of hardening of portland blast furnance cement is some what slower during the first 28 days and proper curing is essential. Thus its 28 days strength is lower than ordinary portland cement. The standard mortar cube 28 days strength is of the order of 340 kg/cm^2 & for concrete cubes 220 kg/cm^2. However after 90 days there is practically no difference in their strengths. However the exact nature of hydration of portland blast furnance cement is not quite clear.

Fineness. Its specific surface area should not be less than 2250 cm^2/gram.

Compressive strength

At

72 ± 1h not less than 150 kg/cm^2

168 ± 2 h not less than 220 kg/cm^2

The heat of hydration of portland blast furnance cement is lower than that of ordinary portland cement. Thus it can be used in mass concrete works with advantage. However in cold weather, the low heat of hydration and low rate of strength development can lead to frost damage. Further this cement is fairly sulphate and alkali resistant as the C_3A contents in this cement is low and as such it can be used in sea water construction with advantage. The shrinkage and modulus of elasticity of concrete made with this cement are same as those of ordinary portland cement concrete. Fig. 3.3 shows strength development of concrete made with portland blast furnance cement. Recently for laying 3.5 m dia sewer line 40 m below mean sea level, in Bombay cement made out from a mixture of 70% ground granulated blast furnance slag and 30% ordinary cement clinker was used with advantage.

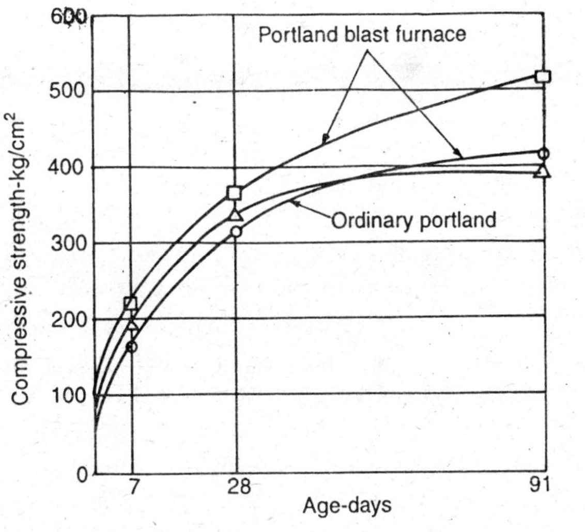

Fig. 3.3. Strength development of concrete made with PSC

The recent extensive research has shown that the presence of ground granulated furnance slag (GGBS) increases the intrinsic properties of fresh as well as hardened concrete. Recently following advantages of GGBS have been recognised.

1 Increased resistance to chemical attack.

2. Reduced generation of heat of hydration.

3. Reduced permeability.
4. Refinement of pore structure.

Application of GGBS concrete

Recent studies have shown that combining the ground granulated blast-furnance slag (GGBS) and ordinary portland cement at mixer gives the equivalent factory made portland slag cement. Concrete of different properties can be made by varying the proportion of GGBS.

1. For use in mass concrete works, where the risk of early age thermal cracking is important, concrete containing 50% to 90% of GGBS can be used. Generally 70% GGBS and 30% ordinary portland cement (OPC) may be used.
2. Resistance to chemical attack may be increased by using GGBS in concrete. The resistance to acid attack may be increased by using 70% GGBS in concrete.
3. To counter the sulphate and chloride attack 40% to 70% GGBS may be used.
4. In foundation concrete and water retaining structures the effect of aggressive water can be reduced by using GGBS.
5. The risk of ASR (alkali-salt reaction) can be minimised by the use of 50% GGBS.

3.2.12. Sulphate Resisting cement (IS 12330-1988)

The reaction of C_3A with gypsum ($CaSo_42H_2O$) forms calcium sulpho-aluminate and causes expansion or soundness in cement. This is more prominent during setting process of cement. Similarly in hardened concrete, calcium aluminate hydrate can react with a sulphate salt from out side the concrete in a similar manner as above, forming calcium sulpho-aluminate. In this case the increase in the volume of solid phase is 227%, hence disintegration of concrete takes place. This reaction or expansion in volume of concrete is known as *sulphate attack.*

A second type of reaction is that of base exchange between calcium hydroxide and sulphates, resulting in the formation of gypsum with an increase in the volume of solid phase by 124%.

The increase in volume by any type of reaction is called sulphate attack. Magnesium and sodium sulphates are more active salts. Sulphate attack is accelerated in alternate wetting and drying conditions such as in marine structures.

The sulphate attack can be minimised by keeping the C_3A in cement as low as possible. The C_3A content may be allowed upto 3.5%, but in no case more than 5%. The minimum fineness should be 2200 cm^2/g. In other respects it is similar to ordinary portland cement.

In portland cement C_4AF varies between 6 to 12%. As often it is not feasible to reduce the Al_2O_3 content of the raw material, Fe_2O_3 may be added to reduce the C_3A content. However the addition of Fe_2O_3 increases the contents of C_4AF. To limit the C_3A and C_4AF contents, IS code has suggested that the total content of C_4AF and C_3A should be as follows:

$$2\ C_3A + C_4AF \text{ should not exceed } 25\%.$$

The low C_3A and comparatively low C_4AF contents of sulphate resisting cement mean that it has a high silicate content, which gives the cement a high strength. However in this cement C_2S is quite high of the order of 36%, thus its early strength is low. The rate of heat development of sulphate resisting cement is of the same order as that of low heat cement. Thus this cement is ideal one, but due to special requirements for the composition of the raw materials it can not be manufactured at low cost.

Use of Sulphate resisting cement

The use of sulphate resisting cement is recommended under the following conditions:

1. Concrete to be used in marine conditions.
2. Concrete to be used in foundations and basements. where soil is infested with sulphates.
3. Concrete to be used in sewage treatment works constructions.

4. Concrete to be used for the fabrication of pipes to be used under sulphate bearing soils or in marshy regions.

3.2.13. Super Sulphate cement

It is not a portland cement. It is made by intergrinding a mixture of 80 to 85% of granulated slag with 10 to 15% of calcium sulphate (in the form of dead burnt gypsum) and about 5% of portland cement clinker. It is ground very fine. Usually its fineness is of the order of 4000 cm^2/g to 5000 cm^2/g. This cement deteriorates very rapidly in moist conditions, therefore it should be stored under very dry conditions.

The heat of hydration of this cement is low about 40 to 45 cal/g at 7 days and 45 to 50 cal/g at 28 days. Thus it is very suitable for mass concrete work, but care must be taken if used in cold weather as the rate of strength development reduces considerably at low temperatures. The rate of hardening of super sulphated cement increases with temperature upto about 50°C, but at higher temperatures abnormal behaviour has been observed. Therefore, steam curing above 50°C should not be done with out proper prior tests. Further this cement should not be mixed with portland cement, because the lime liberated by the hydration of an excessive amount of the portland cement will interfere with the reaction between the slag and calcium sulphate.

Wet curing for at least 95 hours after casting is essential as premature drying will result in powdery surface layer, specially in hot weather.

Super sulphated cement needs more water for hydration than ordinary portland cement. Therefore concrete with a water/cement ratio less than 0.4 should not be made. Mixes leaner than 1:6 should not be used. The water/cement ratio law has less effect on this cement than other cements *i.e.* the decrease in strength with an increase in water/cement ratio has been observed less than other cements. However its early strength development depends on the type of slag used in the manufacture of cement, therefore it is advisable to determine actual strength characteristics prior to use.

This cement is highly resistant to sea water and can withstand the higher concentration of sulphates normally found in soil or ground water. It is also resistant to oils and peaty acids. Concrete with water/cement ratio upto 0.45 has been found not to be affected in contact with weak solutions of mineral acids of PH value below 3.5. Due to these reasons this cement can be used in construction of sewers and in contaminated ground. However it has been suggested that this cement is less resistant than sulphate resisting portland cement when the sulphate concentration is more than 1%. Super sulphated cement has been used extensively in Belgium, France, U.K., Germany etc. The strength at different ages of mortar cubes and concrete cubes is shown in Table 3.6 below:

Table 3.6

Age in days	*Compressive strength*	
	Standard vibrated mortar test cube kg/cm^2	*Standard concrete cubes* kg/cm^2
1	70	50 – 100
3	280	170 – 280
7	350 – 480	280 – 350
28	380 – 660	350 – 450
6 months	-	520

3.2.14. Portland-Pozzolana cement (IS 1484-1991)

An inter ground or blended mixture of portland cement and pozzolana is called portland pozzolana cement. This cement can be manufactured either by intimately inter grinding portland cement clinker and Pozzolana or by intimately and uniformly blending portland cement and fine Pozzolana. If portland-Pozzolana cement is manufactured by inter grinding portland cement clinker and Pozzolana, then gypsum or calcium sulphate should be added to regulate its setting time. Grinding of the two materials together presents no difficulty, but mixing of dry powders intimately is extremely difficult. Therefore blending method should only be adopted, when grinding method is impossible or uneconomical in a particular case.

As per I.S. 1489-1976, the pozzolana constituent should not be less than 10% and not more than 25% by weight of the cement. ASTM has recommended the limits of pozzolana between 15% and 40% of the weight of the portland-Pozzolana cement, while in U.K. the maximum limit of pozzolana has been fixed as 35%.

Chemical requirements

Portland-Pozzolana cement should comply with the following chemical and physical properties

(*a*) Loss on ignition 5.0% max.

(*b*) Weight of magnesia (Mgo) 6.0% max.

(*c*) Sulphuric anhydide (So_3) 2.75% max

and 3.0% when C_3A is 7% or less and greater than 7% respectively.

Tri-calcium aluminate C_3A is calculated by the formula.

$$C_3A = 2.65\ (Al_2o_2) - 1.69\ (Fe_2o_3)$$

where each symbol in brackets refers to the percentage (by mass of total cement) of oxide, excluding any contained in the insoluble residue referred at S.No. (*d*) below.

(*d*) Insoluble material $= x + \dfrac{2.0\ (100 - x)}{100}$ per cent max.

where x is the declared percentage of pozzolana in the given cement.

Physical requirement

(*a*) **Fineness.** Specific surface area should not be less than 3000 cm^2/g

(*b*) **Soundness.** When tested with Le Chatelier method, expansion should not be more than 10 mm.

(*c*) **Setting time:**

(*i*) Initial setting time 30 min.

(*ii*) Final setting time 600 min. max.

Compressive strength

The average strength of not less than three mortar cubes of surface area 50 cm^2 composed of 1:3 cement and standard sand by weight and $\left(\dfrac{P}{4}\right.$ + 3.0 percent of combined mass of cement and sand) water should be as follows:

At 168 ± 2 h 220 kg/cm^2 min.

At 672 ± 4 h 310 kg/cm^2 min.

The portland Pozzolana cement produces less heat of hydration and offers greater resistance to the attack of aggressive waters than normal portland cement. It also reduces the leaching of calcium hydroxide liberated during the setting and hydration of cement and also reduces the permeability of concrete. It is particularly useful in marine and hydraulic constructions and other mass concrete structures. The addition of pozzolana does not contribute to strength at early age. Generally this cement can be used where ever ordinary portland cement is usable under normal conditions.

3.3. POZZOLANA

The history of pozzolanic materials goes back to Roman time. It is a natural or artificial material containing silica in a reactive form. As per ASTM specifications, a pozzolana is a silicious or silicious and aluminous material which itself possesses little or no cementitious properties, but in finely divided form and in the presence of moisture, it chemically reacts with calcium hydroxide at ordinary temperatures to form compounds possessing cementitious properties. It is essential that a pozzolana should be in a finely divided state, only then silica can combine with calcium hydroxide (liberated by hydrating portland cement) in the presence of water to form stable calcium silicates which have cementitious properties. Following materials may be used as pozzolana.

1. Calcined dictomaceous earths 2. Pumicite 3. Opaline, shales and cherts
4. Burnt clay 5. Volcanic ash. 6. Fly ash etc.

While considering pozzolanas in general, it should be noted that the silica should be amorphous as crystalline silica has very low reactivity.

The pozzolanic activity with cement is determined either by the measurement of a pozzolanic activity index. The pozzolanic activity index is the ratio of compressive strength of the mixture with a specified replacement of cement by pozzolana to the strength of a mix without replacement. There is also a pozzolanic activity index with lime, which determines the total activity of a pozzolana. Pozzolanic activity is assessed by comparing the quantity of calcium hydroxide $Ca(OH)_2$ present in a liquid phase in contact with the hydrated pozzolanic cement, with the quantity of calcium hydroxide $Ca(OH)_2$ capable of saturating a medium of the same alkalinity. The underlying principle is that the pozzolanic activity consists of fixing $Ca(OH)_2$ by the pozzolana, so that lower the resulting quantity of $Ca(OH)_2$, the higher the pozzolanacity.

3.3.1. Fly ash

It is a waste product from coal fired power stations and Railway locomotives etc. It is the most common artificial pozzolana. The fly ash particles are spherical and of the same fineness as cement such that silica is always readily available for reaction.

The pozzolanic activity of fly ash is good, but it is essential that it has a constant fineness and constant carbon content. These two requirements are often inter dependent, since the carbon particles tend to be coarser. In fly ash usually loss on ignition should not be greater than 7%, however carbon content upto 12% is acceptable. Actually carbon is not pozzolanic, but a filler only. To maintain the uniformity of the resulting concrete, it is essential to maintain the uniformity in the properties of fly ash. A good pozzolanic fly ash should contain the following percentages of different constituents as per I.S. 3812-1981.

Table 3.7

Chemical requirements of fly ash

S. No.	*Characteristics*	*Requirement*
1.	Silicon dioxide (SiO_2) plus aluminium oxide (Al_2O_3) plus iron oxide (Fe_2O_3) by mass minimum	70%
2.	Silicon dioxide (SiO_2) by mass minimum	35%
3.	Mgnessium oxide (MgO) by mass minimum	5%
4.	Total sulphur as sulphur trioxide (SO_3) by mass minimum)	2.75%
5.	Available alkali as sodium oxide (Na_2O) by mass minimum	1.5%
6.	Loss on ignition percent by mass	12%

Physical requirements of fly ash

S. No.	*Characteristics*	*Requirement*	
		Grade I	*Grade II*
1.	Fineness, specific surface area in cm^2/gram	3200	2500
2.	Lime reactivity average compessive strength in kg/cm^2	40	30
3.	Compressive strength at 28 days in kg/cm^2	Not less than 80% of the corresponding plain cement mortar	
4.	Drying shrinkage percent max.	0.15	1.0
5.	Soundness by autoclave test, expansion of specimen percent max.	0.8	0.8

It has been observed that the colour of concrete is affected by the use of fly ash.

As stated earlier also, portland pozzolana cement gains strength very slowly and thus curing is required for a longer period, but their ultimate strength is approximately the same as that of ordinary portland cement. It has been observed that after about four months time the strength of fly ash pozzolanic concrete is same as that of ordinary cement concrete and after wards it is higher than that of ordinary cement concrete strength. A typical strength curve is shown in Fig. 3.4.

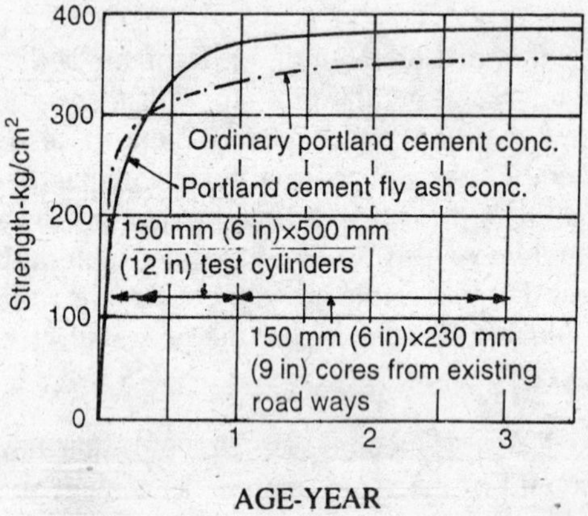

Fig. 3.4. Strength development of concrete made with cement mixed with fly ash

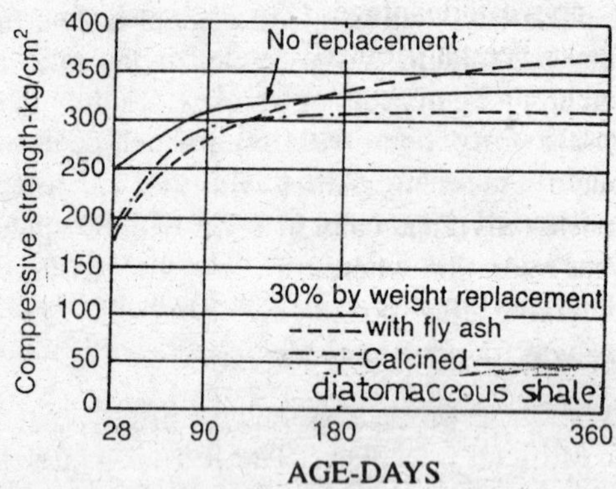

Fig. 3.5. Effect of addition of pozzolana on the strength of concrete

Pozzolanas are often cheaper than portland cement that they replace, but their main advantage lies in slow hydration and thus low rate of heat development. This property is of great importance in mass concrete construction, that is why portland pozzolana cement or a partial replacement of portland cement by the pozzolana is mostly used When pozzolanas are used as a partial replacement for cement, the cement and pozzolanas should be batched separately and mixed with the other ingredients in the mixer.

Partial replacement of portland cement by pozzolana has to be carefully defined, as the specific gravity of pozzolanas is much lower than that of cement. The specific gravity of fly ash varies from 1.9 to 2.4 where as the specific gravity of cement is 3.15. With replacement the concrete mixes have a lower early strength than when only portland cement is used, but beyond about three months age, there is no loss of strength. With lean mixes there may even be a long term gain of strength due to the replacement as shown in Fig. 3.5. In case equal early strength is required and pozzolana is to be used, then addition of pozzolana rather than partial replacement of cement is essential. Partial replacement of portland cement by pozzolana reduces the permeability of concrete to a great extent due to continued filling of pores by formation of hydrates and absence of free lime, which could be leahed out.

3.4. ADVANTAGES OF PORTLAND POZZOLANA CEMENT (PPC)

If the right quality fly ash is used in optimum percentage, the following advantages of portland pozzolana cement (PPC) have been observed over ordinary portland cement.

1. It is economical as in PPC a part (25%) of costly clinker of OPC is replaced by cheaper pozzolanic material.
2. Improvement in permeability as soluble calcium hydroxide is converted into insoluble cementitious product. Hence it offers all-round durability characteristics, specially in the construction of hydraulic and marine structures.
3. Reduction in the production of calcium hydroxide as PPC consumes calcium hydroxide. Thus the calcium hydroxide is not produced as much as in the case of ordinary portland cement.
4. It generates less heat of hydration at a low rate than ordinary portland cement.

5. Reduction in permeability of PPC offers many other advantages, such as durability.
6. Portland pozzolana cement improves pore size distribution and also reduces the micro cracks in the cement paste at the transition zone due to pozzolanic action and being finer than OPC.
7. A 50 kg bag of the portland pozzolana cement gives more volume of mortar than ordinary portland cement as the fly ash is finer and of lower density.
8. If enough moisture is available for continued pozzolanic action the long term strength of portland pozzolana cement beyond 90 days is higher than ordinary portland cement.

The above advantages of portland pozzolana cement have been attributed due to the slow conversion of calcium hydroxide $Ca(OH)_2$ in the hydrated cement paste into cementitious product.

In one of the recent studies in a ordinary portland cement paste only 20% calcium hydroxide was found after 1 year hydration where as in a similarly hydrated paste containing 30% pozzolana, only 8.8% calcium hydroxide was found. It may be noted that due to leaching and dilution certain reduction in calcium hydroxide may have taken place. Considering this loss also, the amount of calcium hydroxide should have been 14%. The difference in calcium hydroxide (14.0 – 8.4) = 5.6 proves that 5.6% calcium hydroxide was converted due to pozzolanic activity. A typical hydroxide $Ca(OH)_2$ reduction is shown in Fig. 3.6.

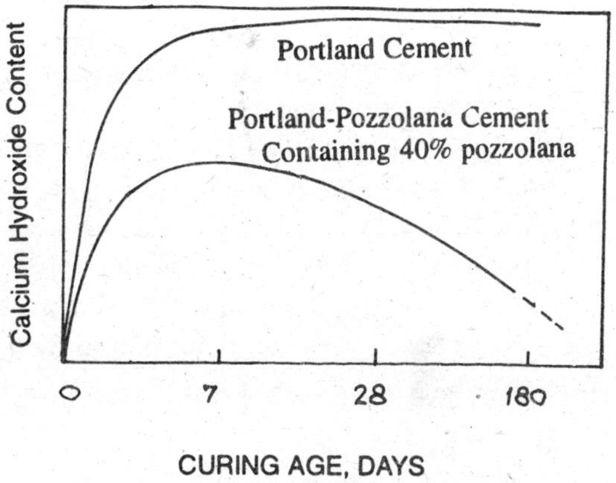

Fig. 3.6. Typical Reduction of $Ca(OH)_2$

Disadvantages

Following disadvantages have been observed of portland pozzolana cement.

1. Less rate of development of strength initially than ordinary Portland cement.
2. It reduces the resistance to corrosion of steel reinforcement due to alkalinity reduction. But it improves permeability of concrete considerably.
3. Setting time is longer.

Use

The portland pozzolana cement has been found useful under the following conditions:

1. For the construction of hydraulic structures.
2. For the construction of massive structures as dams, thick foundations, bridge piers etc.
3. For marine structures.
4. For the construction of sewers and sewage disposal works etc.

3.5. WHITE CEMENT

For architectural purposes white concrete is required. To achieve best results, it is advisable to use white cement with suitable fine and coarse aggregates. Further as this cement contains low contents of alkalies it is not liable to cause staining. A typical compound composition of white cement is shown in Table 3.7.

White portland cement is manufactured from raw materials containing no iron oxide or very little iron oxide and manganese oxide. Generally China clay is used together with lime stone or chalk free from impurities. Further to avoid contamination with coal ash in kiln, oil is used as fuel in place of pulverised coal. The elimination of iron oxide needs higher temperature in kiln to fuse the raw materials as iron oxide acts as a flux. To obtain higher temperature in kiln needs more fuel which is not economical. Hence to lower down the fusing temperature, sometimes cryolite (sodium aluminum fluoride) is added as a flux.

Table 3.8. Chemical composition of white cement

S. No.	*Compound*	*Content percent*	*Remark*
1.	C_3S	51	The percentage of C_3S and C_2S may vary considerably
2.	C_2S	26	
3.	C_3A	11	
4.	C_4AF	1.0	
5.	SO_3	2.6	
6.	Alkalies	0.25	

To prevent contamination of the cement with iron during grinding, nickel and molybdenum alloy balls are used in place of ordinary iron grinding balls. Thus the cost of grinding is higher. Due to higher grinding cost and expensive raw materials, make this cement about 3 times costlier than ordinary portland cement.

To obtain good colour, usually white concrete of rich proportions is used. The water cement ratio usually is not adopted higher than 0.4. White cement has slightly lower specific gravity than ordinary portland cement, generally between 3.05 to 3.10. Strength of white cement also is lower than ordinary portland cement.

3.5.1. Birla White Cement

Birla white and J.K. white cements are manufactured around Jodhpur in Rajasthan. The suitable raw material used for white cement is only available around Jodhpur in Rajasthan. The raw material used for white cement should be of high purity. Lime stone having 96% $CaCO_3$, and iron oxide less than 0.07% is the best. Other raw materials are China clay with iron content about 0.72 to 0.8%, silica (sand) flouspar as flux and selenite as retarder. The fuels used are refined furnance oil or gas. Sea shells and coral can also be used as raw material for the production of white cement. The white cement is ground finer than ordinary portland cement. The whiteness of white cement measured by ISI scale should not be less than 70%, while measured by Hunter's scale, it should not be less than 90%. The strength of Birla white cement is much higher than given in IS Code 8042-1989. Typical test results of Birla white cement are shown in Table 3.9 below.

Table 3.9. Properties of Birla white cement

Characteristics	*IS 8042–1989*	*Birla White*
1. Physical		
(a) Degree of whiteness %		
(*i*) ISI scale	min 70	88
(*ii*) Hunter's scale	min 90	91
(*b*) Fineness (Blainé method) cm^2/gram	min 2250	4500
(*c*) Setting time		
(*i*) Initial in minutes	min 30	80
(*ii*) Final in minutes	max 600	120
(*d*) Compressive strength (1:3 cement and standard sand)		
(*i*) 3 days (MPa)	min 14.4 (144 kg/cm^2)	45 (450 kg/cm^2)
(*ii*) 7 days (MPa)	min 19.8 (198 kg/cm^2)	55 (550 kg/cm^2)
(*iii*) 28 days (MPa)	min 29.7 (297 kg/cm^2)	67 (670 kg/cm^2)

Characteristics	*IS 8042–1989*	*Birla White*
(*e*) Soundness		
(*i*) Lechateliar method in (mm)	max 10 mm	1.0mm
(*ii*) Autoclave expension %	max 0.8%	Negligible
(*f*) Rentension on 63 micron sieve %	—	1.00
2. Chemical		
(*a*) Insoluble residue %	max 2.0	0.60
(*b*) Iron oxide %	max 1.0	0.20
(*c*) Magnesium oxide %	max 6.0	0.80
(*d*) Sulphur trioxide %	max 3.0	2.90
(*e*) Aluminium/Iron oxide	min 0.66	9.00
(*f*) Lime saturation factor	0.66 – 1.09	0.90
(*g*) Loss on ignition	—	< 3.0 %

These values are based on product literature of Birla white.

3.5.2. Coloured cements

For the manufacture of coloured cements either gray or white portland cement is used as base. With grey cement only red or brown colour can be given successfully, for other colours white cement clinker is used. Usually 5 to 10% pigment by weight is intimately grounded with the portland cement clinker. The pigment used should be chemically inert with cement and should have fast colour. Some times a film of free calcium hydroxide deposits on the surface of the concrete and covers the effect of pigment. It can be removed by washing the surface with dilute hydrochloric acid (HCl, 1:10) and then with plain water. The surface should be wetted with water before applying HCl. HCl should not be allowed to stay in contact with concrete surface for long.

3.6. OTHER PORTLAND CEMENTS

Numerous cements have been developed for special uses. Some of them have been discussed in the following paragraphs in short.

3.6.1. Hydrophobic portland cement

This cement is obtained by grinding ordinary portland cement clinker with 0.1 to 0.5% by weight of an additive called hydrophobic agent. This additive imparts an water repelling property to ground cement by forming a water repellant film around each particle of cement which shall be destroyed only by wet attrition such as in a concrete mixer. The hydrophobic property of cement facilitates its storage for longer periods in extremely wet climatic conditions. Some of the hydrophobic agents are Oleic acid, Naphthenic acid, stearic acid, and Pentachlorophenol etc.

The addition of these substances increases the grindability of the clinker, probably due to electrostatic forces resulting from a polar orientation of the acid molecules on the surface of the cement particles.

Oleic acid reacts with alkalies in cement to form calcium and sodium oleates which foam, resulting in production of air entraining. If the production of air entraining is not desired, a de-entraining agent such as tri-n-butyl phosphate has to be added during grinding.

This cement deteriorates very little during prolonged storage under unfavorable conditions. The hydrophobic properties are produced due to the formation of a water repellent film around each particle of the cement. This film is broken during the mixing of concrete in the mixer and normal hydration takes place. The early strength of this cement is low. In appearance this cement is similar to that of ordinary portland cement, but has a characteristic musty smell. In handling this cement seems more fluid than other portland cements. The hardened concrete also retains the water repellant characteristics of the cement. The properties of hydrophobic cement are nearly the same as that of ordinary portland cement, but its cost is a little more than the ordinary portland cement.

Physical requirements

As per I.S. 8043-1978.

1. **Soundness.** Same as for ordinary portland cement.
2. **Fineness.** Specific surface area should not be less than 3500 cm^2/gram.
3. **Compressive strength.** The average compressive strength of three cubes of face area 50 cm^2 made of one part of cement and three parts of standard sand and water given by the relation,

$$\text{Water} = \left(\frac{P}{4} + 3.0 \text{ percent of combined mass of cement and sand}\right).$$

Prepared, stored and tested as per I.S. 4031-1968 should be as follows:

72 ± 1 hour	Not less than 156.9 kg/cm^2
168 ± 2 hour	Not less than 215.7 kg/cm^2
672 ± 4 hour	Not less than 304.0 kg/cm^2

Chemical requirement

As for ordinary portland cement I.S. 260-1976.

3.6.2. Masonry cement (IS 3466-1988)

Ordinary cement, when used in masonry gives a harsh mortar and water is sucked by the masonry, which results in poor bond The mortar made of ordinary cement is inferior than lime mortar in respect of workability, water retentivity, shrinkage and extensibility. Hence to over come this disadvantage masonry cement has been developed. Masonry cement is made by inter-grinding very finely ground portland cement, white lime stone and air entraining agent or alternatively portland cement and hydrated lime, granulated slag, or an inert filler and an air entraining agent.

Masonry cement is mainly used for mortar in brick work. This cement produces a more plastic mortar than ordinary portland cement. This mortar also has a greater water retaining power and lower shrinkage. The strength of masonry cement is lower than that of ordinary portland cement, particularly if a high air content is introduced. However the low strength of masonry cement has been found advantageous in brick construction, but this cement should not be used in structural concrete.

3.6.3. Anti-bacterial cement

It is a portland cement inter-ground with an anti-bacterial agent, which prevents microbiological fermentation. This bacterial action is encountered in concrete floors of food processing plants where fermentation is caused by bacteria in the presence of moisture after the cement has been leached out by the action of acids. Anti-bacterial cement can also be used successfully in swimming pools, public baths or similar places where bacteria or fungii are present.

3.6.4. Expansive Cement

The cement which does not suffer over all change in volume on drying is known as expansive cement. This type of cement has been developed after long experimentation by using an expanding agent and a stabilizer very carefully. In order to obtain the desired expansion proper material and controlled proportioning is very necessary.

Need of expansive cement

Concrete made with ordinary portland cement shrinks during setting period due to loss of free water. Shrinkage of concrete continues for long, which is known as dry shrinkage. Cement used for grouting pre-stressed concrete ducks, for grouting anchor bolts or grouting machine foundations, if shrinks, the purpose for which the grout is used will be defeated to some extent. Hence to over come this short coming of cement the necessity of expanding cement is felt. At present there are many types of expansive cements available in the market. Here only few of them are discussed.

Generally mixing about 8 to 20 parts of the sulpho-aluminate clinker with 100 parts of the ordinary portland cement and 15 parts of the stabilizer, a expansive cement may be obtained. As the expansion takes place in the presence of moisture, curing of concrete should be carefully controlled. The use of expanding cement requires skill and experience.

One type of expansive cement is known as self stressing cement. When this cement is used in concrete, it induces significant compressive stresses after the drying shrinkage has occurred. The induced compressive stresses not only compensate the shrinkage, but also give some sort of pre-stressing effect in the tensile zone of a flexural member. An other type of expansive cement is known as shrinkage compensating cement. When this cement is used in concrete, it induces compressive stresses which approximately off set the tensile stresses induced by shrinkage.

H. LOSSIER expansive cement

This type of cement for the first time was developed by H. LOSSIER in France. He used a mixture of portland cement, an expanding agent, and a stabilizer.

Expanding agent

The expanding agent is obtained by burning a mixture of gypsum, bauxite and chalk, which form calcium sulphate and calcium aluminate (mainly C_5A_3). In the presence of water, these compounds react to form calcium sulpho-aluminate hydrate and the expansion of the paste takes place.

Stabilizer

It is a blast furnance slag. It consumes the excess calcium sulphate slowly and neutralizes the expansion.

Thus in order to get a desired expansion, the proportioning of the cement ingredients should be done very carefully. Generally about 8 to 20 parts of the sulpho-aluminate clinker are mixed with 100 parts of portland cement and 15 parts of stabi-lizer.

3.6.5. High energy expanding cement

It is made by inter-grinding portland cement clinker, high alumina clinker and gypsum approximately in the proportions of 65:20:15. Expansion in this cement also takes place due to the formation of sulpho-aluminate as in LOSSIER'S cement with in two or three days after casting.

This cement is quick setting and rapid hardening. It develops a strength of about 70 kg/cm^2 in 6 hours and 500 kg/cm^2 in 28 days. This cement has a high resistance to sulphate attack also.

Thus expansive cements are used for the following purposes.

(*a*) To neutralise the shrinkage of concrete made from ordinary cement in order to eliminate cracks. A small percentage of this cement in the concrete will not allow it to crack. This treatment is specially essential for hydraulic structures.

(*b*) In repair work, to keep the new concrete tight fit in the old concrete, expansive cement is used. Usually it takes about 15 days to expand fully, but the time can be controlled by curing. The upper limit of expansion is upto 1% but it can be adjusted to any lower value by decreasing the quantity of this cement. However this cement will not do well in contact with sea water.

3.6.6. High alumina cement

This cement is quite different from ordinary portland cement in its composition and also in some properties. Hence its structural use is very limited. The search for a solution to the attack of gypsum bearing waters on portland cement concrete structures led Jules Bied of France to the discovery of the high alumina cement. As its name suggests it contains about 40% alumina 40% lime, and upto 8% silica with some ferous and ferric oxides. The oxide composition is shown in table 3.10 below. However alumina should be less than 32% by weight and Alumina/Lime ratio between 0.85 and 1.3.

Table 3.10. Typical oxide composition of high alumina cement

S. No.	*Name*	*Oxide*	*Content percentage*
1.	Silica	SiO_2	3 – 8
2.	Alumina	Al_2O_3	37 – 41
3.	Lime	CaO	36 – 40
4.	Iron oxide	Fe_2O_3	9 – 10
		FeO	5 – 6
	Titanium	TiO_2	1.5 – 2
5.	Magnessium	MgO	1.0
6.	Insoluble residue		1.0

The knowledge of compound composition of high alumina cement is very little in comparison to portland cement and no simple method of calculation is available. The main cementitious compounds are calcium aluminates of low basicity; CA and C_5A_3. Other compounds are present in few percent, but no free lime exists. Hence there is no problem of unsoundness in high alumina cement.

Manufacture

The raw materials used are lime stone or chalk and bauxite. Bauxite is a residual deposit formed by weathering under tropical conditions of rocks containing aluminium. It consists of hydrated alumina, oxides of iron and titanium, with small amounts of silica.

The two materials *i.e.* bauxite and lime are crushed into lumps not larger than 100 mm. Dust and small particles of bauxite formed during crushing are cemented into briquettes of smaller size as dust would damp the furnace. The crushed materials in the required proportions are fed into an open hearth furnance which is a combination of the cupola (vertical stack) and reverberatory (horizontal type) furnance. Pulverized coal is used for firing. The weight of coal is about 22% by weight of the cement produced. The moisture and carbon dioxide in the furnance are driven off and the materials are heated by the hot gases of the furnance at about 1600°C, which is the fusion point of the materials. The fusion takes place at the lower end of the stack and the molten material falls in the reverberatory furnace and from there through a spout into steel pans. The molten material solidifies in steel pans in the form of pigs. It is fragmented in a rotary cooler and ground in a tube mill.

During grinding all particles of iron are separated by magnetic separators. The fineness of this cement is kept of the order of 2500 cm^2/gram to 3200 cm^2/gram, but in no case its specific surface area should be less than 2250 cm^2/gram.

The hardness of high alumina cement clinker is very high. Hence the power consumption and wear of the grinding mill is more than ordinary portland cement. Hence due to high cost of power for grinding, bauxite high cost of fuel for firing materials upto high tempeature, the cost of this cement is very high (about three times) in comparision of ordinary portland cement.

As stated earlier, the materials used in the manufacture of high alumina cement are fused completely in the kiln. Due to this fact the properties of ordinary portland cement and high alumina cement are quite different. While discussing ordinary portland cement, it was stated that the alumina compounds in ordinary portland cement are mainly responsible for the attack of sulphate solutions, but high alumina cement containing 40% alumina is free from such a attack. It is due to the fact that in high alumina cement all materials are fused and no free lime is available, while it is not so in the case of ordinary portland cement *i.e.* in ordinary portland cement free lime is available.

The high alumina cement should never be mixed or stored together with ordinary portland cement as the combination of high alumina cement, will cause flash set of the ordinary cement. The free lime of ordinary cement combines with the aluminates of high alumina cement, forming calcium aluminate. This compound expands and causes cracks in the concrete. This cement is known by different names in different countries as Fondu in France, lightening in U.K. and Lumonite in U.S.A.

3.6.6.1. Hydration of high alumina cement (HAC)

During the setting of the high alumina cement (HAC) the important reaction is the formation of mono-calcium aluminate deca-hydrate (CAH_{10}), dicalcium aluminate octa-hydrate (C_2AH_8) and alumina gel (AHn). These aluminates develop high strength in the high alumina cement concrete but these aluminates are unstable and convert gradually to tri-calcium alumina hexa-hydrate (C_3AH_6) and gibbsite, which are more stable. The change in composition of high alumina cements results in loss of strength. The change in crystal form from hexagonal to cubical form releases much water, resulting in increased porosity of concrete. The manner in which these changes take place depends on water/cement ratio, temperature and chemical environment. The process of change in composition resulting in loss of strength and change in crystal form from hexagonal to cubical form in called as CONVERSION.

The decomposition in chemical reaction of conversion from CAH_{10} to C_3AH_6 and alumina hydrate is affected by temperature. The higher the temperature, faster the rate of conversion. It is also affected by higher concentration of lime or rise in alkalinity. Further, higher the water/cement ratio, greater the rate of conversion. It is shown as

$$CA + 10H \rightarrow CAH_{10}$$

$$3CAH_{10} \rightarrow C_3AH_6 + 2AH_3 + 18H$$

This reaction liberates the water required for the conversion process to continue. Thus conversion is a function of temperature and water/cement ratio both. The conversion reaction results in the reduction of volume of solids and an increase in the porosity as the overall dimensions of specimens of cement paste or concrete remain constant.

3.6.6.2. Effect of conversion of high alumina cement

The conversion of high alumina cement leads to loss of strength due to the fact that converted cubic tri-calcium alumina hexa-hydrate (C_3AH_6) has a higher density than the un-converted mono calcium aluminate deca-hydrate (CAH_{10}). Thus, if the over all volume of the body remains constant, then conversion results in an increased porosity of the paste, which has an tremendous effect on the strength of cement paste or cement concrete. The effect of conversion on strength has been shown in Fig. 3.7. Fig. 3.8 shows the influence of w/c ratio on the conversion of HAC cured at 18°C and 40°C. The loss of strength due to conversion is a function of temperature and water/cement ratio both. At moderate and high *w/c* ratio, the residual strength is so low which can not be accepted for most of the structural purposes. Even with low w/c ratio, conversion increases the porosity so much that chemical attack may take place easily. Thus due to conversion effects HAC is no longer used for structural concrete above or below ground level, but it is useful material for repair work of limited life and for temporary works.

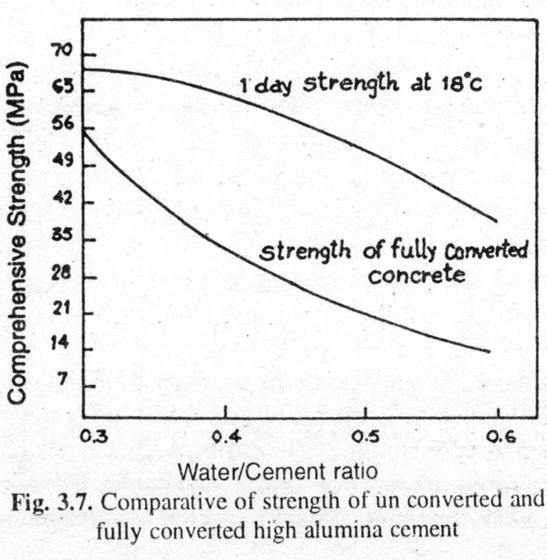

Fig. 3.7. Comparative of strength of un converted and fully converted high alumina cement

The water of hydration of high alumina cement is

about 50% of the weight of the dry cement, which is about twice the water required for the hydration of ordinary portland cement, but with high alumina cement low water cement ratio of the order of 0.35 are practical and indeed desirable.

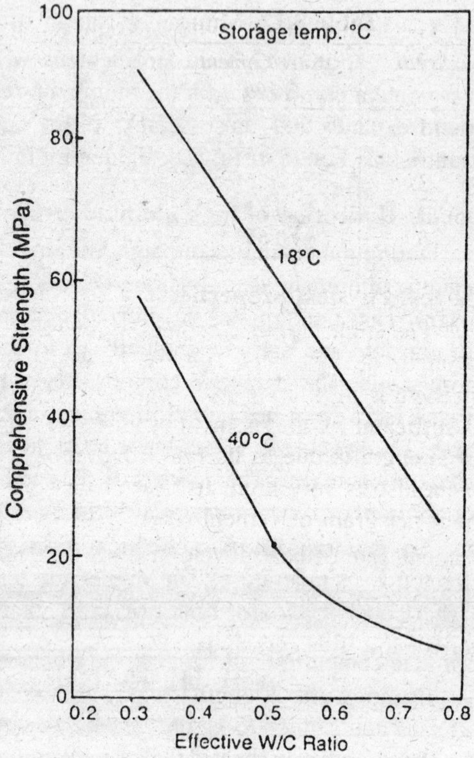

Fig. 3.8. Effect of curing temp on conversion

3.6.6.3. Effect of curing temperature on the strength development

Long term field studies and experiments carried at the laboratory have shown that:

(*a*) Concrete made with HAC with a free water/cement ratio less than 0.4 and stored in water at 18°C throughout its initial period of curing and its subsequent life, a minimum strength will be reached after about 5 years. However this minimum strength will not be appreciably less than the one day strength.

(*b*) If concrete made with HAC is stored in water at 18°C for 24 hours and then stored in water at 38°C, it converts rapidly to high limit and reaches a minimum strength in about 90 days. However this strength is very substantially less than 1 day strength.

(*c*) If concrete made with HAC is stored in water at 18°C for a long period say upto about $8\frac{1}{2}$ years and then immersed in water at 38°C, it will convert rapidly and loose strength to the minimum reached for continuous storage at 38°C.

(*d*) The 38°C temperature is the upper limit of temperature likely to be developed during curing or normally heated buildings. Hence it is recommended that the design of high alumina concrete should be based on the minimum strength at 38°C temperature.

(*e*) Highly converted high alumina cement concrete is prone to chemical attack in the presence of long term wetness and a chemically aggressive agent. This risk may be more serious for concrete with higher water/cement ratio.

The influence of w/c ratio on loss of strength on conversion in shown in the following Table 3.11.

Table 3.11.

Cement	*Water/cement ratio*	*Aggregate/cement ratio*	*1 Day strength MPa*	*Strength of converted concrete as a% of strength of 18°C*
A.	0.29	2.0	91.0	62
	0.35	3.0	84.4	61
	0.45	4.0	72.1	26
	0.65	6.2	42.8	12
B.	0.3	2.1	92.4	63
	0.35	3.0	80.7	60
	0.45	4.0	68.6	43
	0.65	6.2	37.2	30
	0.75	7.2	24.5	29

The minimum strength value after conversion may be adopted as shown in the following Table 3.12.

Table 3.12. Minimum strength after conversion

S. No.	*Water/Cement ratio*	*Converted strength as a percentage of initial unconverted strength*
1.	0.30	56 — 63
2.	0.35	55 — 61
3.	0.45	26 — 43
4.	0.55	20 — 35
5.	0.65	12 — 30

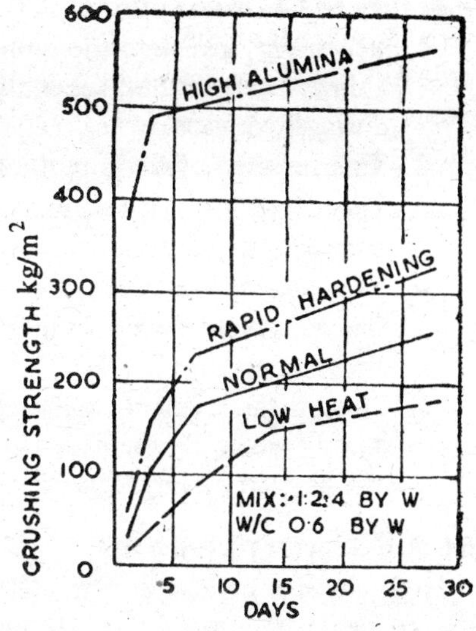

Fig. 3.9. Strength development of concrete made with different cements

3.6.6.4. Physical properties

The high alumina cement is black in colour and its rate of strength development is very high. About 80% of its ultimate strength is developed at the age of 24 hours Even 8 hours strength is sufficient for the removal of the form work. The high rate of gain of strength is due to its rapid hydration. Its rate of heat development also is very high. Its rate of heat development is 9 calories/hour per gram of cement (9 cal/g/h), whereas for rapid hardening cement, rate of heat development is (3.5 cal/g/h) *i.e.* it is $2\frac{1}{2}$ times that of rapid hardening portland cement. However total heat of hydration is of the same order for both the cements. For ordinary portland cement rate of heat development is 1.6 cal/h per gram.

Compressive strength of 1:2:4 concrete prepared with high alumina cement gives about 420 kg/cm^2 after 24 hours and 490 kg/cm^2 after 3 days. Its ultimate strength is also higher than that of ordinary cement. As stated above its heat development is very rapid and takes place, about in the first 10 hours. The high rate of heat development makes this cement unfit for mass concrete work, but rapid rate of heat development is of great advantage when concrete is placed in freezing weather. Fig. 3.9 shows strength development of concretes made with different cements.

Setting time

High alumina cement is slow setting cement. It's initial setting time is 4 to 5 hours and final setting time about 30 minutes later after initial setting. The setting time of high alumina cement is greatly affected by the addition of plaster of paris, lime, portland cement, and organic matter. Thus no additives should be used. To lower down the setting time of this cement 1 to 2% hydrated lime may be added to it. When rapid setting is of vital importance *i.e.* for stopping the ingress of water or temporary construction between the tides etc. mixtures of ordinary portland cement and high alumina cement in suitable proportions are used, but the ultimate strength of such pastes is quite low.

In normal concrete construction, the two cements should not be allowed to come in contact with each other as in such cases flash set will occur. The flash set or accelerated setting time is due to the formation of a hydrate of C_4A by the addition of lime from the ordinary portland cement to calcium aluminate from the high alumina cement. Also gypsum contained in portland cement may react with hydrated calcium aluminates and cause flesh set.

If the layers of two cements are to be placed, then they should be laid at different times. If the first layer is laid of high alumina cement, then the layer of portland cement should be laid at least 24 hours later. In case first layer is made with portland cement, then the concrete made with high alumina cement should be laid after 3 to 7 days. Contamination through plant or tools should also be avoided. For the same water/cement ratio and equal mix proportions concrete made with high alumina cement exhibits more workability than portland cement concrete due to the fact that particles of high alumina cement have smoother surface than portland cement particles, as the raw materials of high alumina cement fuse fully in the hearth. Secondly high alumina cement has lower total surface area 2500 cm^2/to 3200 cm^2/g.

Resistance to Chemical attack

1. It is highly resistant to sulphate attack. This is due to the absence of $Ca(OH)_2$ in hydrated high alumina cement and secondly due to the protective influence of the relatively inert gel, formed during hydration.
2. This cement is free from the attack of CO_2 dissolved in pure water.
3. This cement is not acid resistant, but can withstand well very dilute solutions of acids (PH value greater than 3.5 to 4.0) found in industrial effluents.
4. This cement is attacked readily by nitric, hydrochloric, or hydrofluoric acids.
5. Caustic alkalies even in dilute solutions attack this cement with great vigour by dissolving the alumina gel.
6. Though this cement stands extremely well to sea water, but sea water should never be used as mixing water. By the use of sea water as mixing water, the setting and hardening of the cement are affected very badly. Similarly calcium chloride should never be added to this cement.

3.6.6.5. Refractory properties

High alumina cement concrete is one of the foremost refractory materials but its performance varies with the range of temperature. Between room temperature and about 500°C, concrete made with high alumina cement loses strength more than concrete made with portland cement, then upto 800°C the two concretes are comparable but above 1000°C, high alumina cement gives excellent performance. Between 700°C to 1000°C, solid reactions between the cement and fine aggregate take place. This reaction is known as *ceramic bond,* which is responsible for the increase in the strength of high alumina cement concrete between 800°C to 1000°C. The rate of reaction increases with rise of temperature.

Thus concrete made with high alumina cement and crushed fired brick as aggregate can with stand very high temperatures say upto 1350°C. Temperatures above 1350°C upto 1500°C can be withstood by using special aggregates such as fused alumina or Carborundum. Temperature upto 1800°C can be with stood over a prolonged period of time by concrete made from special white calcium aluminate cement with fused alumina aggregate. This cement contains 70-80%. Al_2o_3, (Alumina) 20-25% lime and about 1.0% iron and silica. Its composition reaches to C_3A_5. However its price is very high.

Refractory concrete made with high alumina cement has a good resistance to acid attack. The chemical resistance increases by firing at 900°C to 1000°C. As soon as the concrete hardens, it can be put to use, that is it should not be pre fired. The refractory brick work expands on heating thus it needs provision of expansion joints, while high alumina cement concrete can be cast monolithically or with but joints only exactly to the required size and shape. Thus refractory high alumina cement concrete can withstand considerable thermal shocks. Refractory linings can be made by shot creting high alumina cement mortar.

For insulation purposes when temperature rise is expected upto 950°C, light weight concrete made with high alumina cement and light weight aggregates can be used with advantage. The density and thermal conductivity of this concrete are of the order 500 to 1000 kg/m^3 and 0.21 to 0.29 j/m^{2}s.°C/m.

3.6.6. IRST 40 special grade cement

For the gauge conversion, Indian Railways needed large number of sleepers. The non availability of high quality timber sleepers at reasonable rates, choice fell on concrete sleepers. For the manufacture of these sleepers Ministry of Railways laid down specification for the developments of cement vide its letter no IRS-T40-1985. The main requirement was the development of high early strength. This objective is achieved by increasing the C_3S content in the ordinary cement clinker and grounding the clinker very fine *i.e.* by increasing the fineness of cement. This cement can also be used for high rise buildings, pre-stressed concrete and for other purposes where high early strength is required.

3.6.7. Oil well cement (IS 8229-1986)

The oil wells are drilled to a great depth, some times upto 6000 m through stratified sedimentary rocks.

Oil or gas may escape through the annular space between the steel casing and the rock formation. To safe guard against this possibility cement slurry is injected to seal off the annular space between the steel casing and rock formation and also to seal off the cavities or fissures in the sedimentary rock layers at considerable depth, where the prevailing temperature may vary from 175°C to 200°C. To inject the cement slurry or grout at such depths, the pressure required may go upto 1300 kg/cm^2. Thus under these conditions cement slurry or grout should remain in fluid condition for 3 to 4 hours and then harden fairly rapidly *i.e.* its initial setting time should be sufficiently more *i.e.* cement slurry should not set for several hours. In addition to above, the cement slurry should be corrosive resistant due to sulpher gases or salts dissolved in water. Thus cement suitable for such conditions *i.e.* cement having high initial setting time, and corrosive resistant properties is known as *oil well cement.*

The cement suitable for above conditions may be obtained either by adjusting the compound composition of cement or adding retarders to ordinary portland cement.

For this purpose the most commonly used retarder is calcium sulphate. In addition to gypsum, sugar, salts of acids, starches, cellulose products may be used. The quantity of sugar added for retarding purposes should be kept from 0.05 to 0.15% by weight of cement. Addition of 0.05% sugar by weight of cement retards setting time by 4 hours and 0.2% cement upto 72 hours. The use of 0.2% to 1.0% of sugar will virtually prevent the setting of cement. Some authrs have suggested that the quantity of sugar more than 0.15% increases the process of setting while others have recommended this amount more than 0.2% by weight of cement.

The exact effect of sugar depends on the chemical composition of cement. Hence quantity of sugar as a retarder should be determined by trial mixes.

3.6.8. Rediset Cement

For the rapid rapair of air strips *i.e.* airport runways, cement concrete roads and pavements, slip forming and in the precast concrete industry an early setting and hardening cement is needed. Though high alumina cement is good for early strength, but when this cement is exposed to hot and humid conditions, it starts loosing its strength. Thus to over come this short coming experimentation started to develop a cement which could yield high strength during few hours after adding water to it, with out showing any retrogression. Investigation carried out in U.S.A developed such a cement and it was given the name as *Regset* where as associated cement company of India developed an equivalent cement and it was named *Rediset* cement.

Properties of Rediset-Cement

Following properties have been found of this cement:

1. This cement sets very early and gives only 8 to 10 minutes for its handling *i.e.* it should be finished with in 10 minutes after adding water to it.
2. The strength developed in Rediset-cement concrete in 3 to 6 hours is equal to that of 7 days strength of ordinary cement concrete.
3. The rate of release of heat of hydration of Rediset-Cement is very high which is advantageous in winter concreting, but excess heat liberation is harmful to mass concrete.
4. Though the rate of shrinkage of Rediset is fast, but the total shrinkage is similar to that of ordinary portland cement.
5. The sulphate resistance of this cement is very poor.
6. The comparative strength pattern of REDISET and REGSET cement is shown below in table 3.13.

Uses of RESET Cement

It can be used for the following purposes:

1. For very high early (3 to 4 hours) strength mortar or concrete.
2. For emergency and patch repairs.

Table 3.13. Comparative strength in MPa

Cement	Strength in MPa		
	4 hours	24 hours	28 days
ACC REDISET mortar 1:3	20 (200)	42 (420)	42 actual test (420)
ACC REDISET 1:5.5	21 (210)	25 (250)	32 actual test (320)
USA REGSET mortar 1:2.75 mix	7.0 (70)	18 (180)	42 Fram literature (420)
USA REGSET concrete 1:6	9.0 (90)	16 (160)	— do —

Figures in bracket show strength in kg/cm². (1 MPa = $\frac{0.1\,N}{mm^2}$ = 10 kg/cm²).

3. In the precast concrete product industry for early release of form work.
4. Construction between tides.
5. Slip formed concrete construction.
6. Palletisation of iron ore dust etc.

3.7. STORING OF CEMENT

Modern Portland cement and other cements being very finely ground are highly hygroscopic, that is they absorb moisture readily from air. Therefore it is essential to protect them from dampness before they are used, so that they may fulfill their intended functions. Thus following precautions should be observed while storing cement.

1. The floor level of the ware house should be at least 1.2 m higher than the general ground level, so that any water collected nearby may not seep by capillary action.
2. The wails of the ware house should be made of water proof concrete masonry or brick work plastered with cement mortar on both faces.
3. The roof should be made of reinforced cement concrete and should be provided with waterproof treatment, so that no leakage or seepage of water may take place.
4. The floor thickness should not be less than 15 cm. Preferablly the floor should be made of cement concrete laid on a dry course of brick soling.
5. The plinth level of the ware house should be such that a truck can back conveniently to the door for loading and unloading the cement.
6. If a newly built ware house is to be used for storing cement, it should be fully ensured that it is thoroughly dry from interior at the time of storing cement in it.
7. Cement bags should not be piled touching the walls, but a 30 cm space between the wall and cement bags pile should be left all round.
8. Cement bags should not be directly placed on the floor, but on wooden planks. However if the floor is made of concrete and is fully dry, then cement bags may be placed directly on it.
9. In order to reduce the air circulation in the store, space between cement bags stacks should not be left.
10. Not more than 15 bags should be

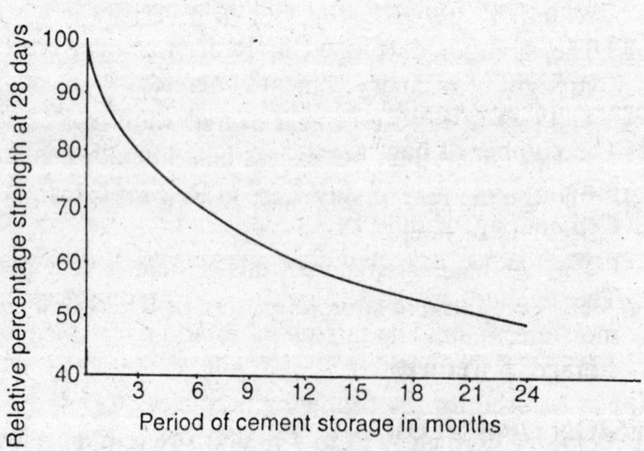

Fig. 3.10. Effect of storage of cement on its strength

piled in a stack. The maximum width of a stak should not be more than 3 m.

11. If more than 7 bags are to be put in a stack, then they should be arranged alternately as header and stretcher.
12. During monsoon, the cement bag's pile should be enclosed completely in 700 gauge polythene sheet.
13. Due to the weight on the lower layer of bags, the cement becomes some what hard which is known as *ware house pack.* This can be removed by rolling the bags when cement is taken out. If the cement does not become in powder form as used, then it should be rejected. Due to warehouse pack restacking is not required.
14. When removing cement bags from the store, bags should be removed from two or three stacks rather all from one tier or stack.
15. At the time of taking out cement, 'first in, first out' rule should be adopted, that is oldest stored cement should be taken out first. For this purpose each consignment as it comes should be stacked separately and a placard bearing the date of arrival should be placed on the pile. The storage of cement affects its strength considerably as shown in table 3.13, Fig. 3.14, also shows the effect of storage on the strength of cement.
16. The cement store should have minimum no of doors and windows, so that air circulation should be minimum. A 1.2 m wide passage should be provided so that a labour can take out a cement bag putting on his back easily.

Table 3.14. Showing the effect of storage time on strength of the Cement

S. No.	*Duration of cement storage*	*Relative strength of cement at 28 days*
1.	Fresh cement	100%
2.	3 months storage	80%
3.	6 months storage	70%
4.	12 months storage	60%
5.	24 months storage	50%

Further experiments carried out about the effect of storing period on the strength of concrete, it is observed that though initial strength obtained is lower but it improves with wet-curing for longer period. The rate of hardening of concrete is found as given below in Table 3.15.

Table 3.15. Showing rate of hardening of 1:5 concrete made with stored and fresh cement

Age at the testing time	*Concrete made with fresh cement*	*Concrete made with cement stored for 6 months*
7 days	100%	73%
28 days	100%	75%
6 months	100%	84%

Temporary storage at site

1. The number of bags should be kept to a minimum, preferably just sufficient for the day's consumption.
2. Cement bags should be stored on a dry platform made of wooden planks resting on a brick masonry, concrete, dry sand or, aggregate platform about 15 cm above the ground.
3. The cement bags should be fully covered by tarpaulin or polythene sheet and protected against the moisture in air. The tarpaulins should overlap each other properly. However temporary method of storage in wet weather should not be adopted.

3.8. DESIGN OF A STORAGE BUILDING

Design a ware house to store 2500 bags in it. Assume weight of 1 bag of cement as 50 kg.

Solution.

1. The height of a cement bag = 0.18 m.
2. The number of cement bags in a pile should not be more than 15 Nos.

$\therefore$ Maximum height of the ware house = $15 \times 0.18 = 2.70$ m

The floor area occupied by one cement bag = $0.3\ m^2$

Volume occupied by one cement bag $= 0.3 \times 0.18$

$= 0.054\ m^3$

Volume required to store 2500 bags $= 0.054 \times 2500$

$= 135.0\ m^3$

Area required to store 2500 cement bags $= \dfrac{135}{2.7} = 50\ m^2$

Assuming the ratio of breadth to length as 1:1.25,

then breadth = 6.4 m and length = 8.0 m.

But cement bags are to be stored at a distance of 30 cm from walls,

then length = 8 + 0.6 = 8.6 m and breadth = 6.4 + 0.6 = 7.0 m

Provide passage 1.2 m wide for the movement of labour at the time of taking cement out or storing it;

then total length $= 8.0 + 1.2 \times 2 = 10.4$ m

Width of store $= 7 + 2.4 = 9.4$ m

Height of store $= 2.7 + .10 = 2.8$ m (adding 10 cm height for ease in placing cement bags)

The floor should be made of 15 cm thick cement concrete over laid on 22.5 cm compact soling.

3.9. COMPARATIVE STUDY OF DIFFERENT CEMENTS

Table 3.16. Proportions of basic oxides

Type of Cement	*Oxide Composition %*			
	Lime CaO	*Silica* SiO_4	*Alumina* Al_2O_3	*Iron oxide* Fe_2O_3
Ordinary cement	63.1	20.6	6.3	3.6
Rapid hardening cement	64.5	20.7	5.2	2.9
Low heat cement	60.0	22.5	6.2	4.6
Sulphate resisting cement	64.0	25.4	3.7	3.0
High alumina cement	37.5	3.8	43.5	13.1

Table 3.17. Compound Composition

Type of Cement	*Average Compound Composition %*			
	C_3S	C_2S	C_3A	C_4AF
Normal cement	49	25	12	2.9
Modified cement	46	29	5	12
High early strength cement	56	15	12	8
Low heat cement	30	46	5	13
Sulphate resistant cement	43	36	4	12

Table 3.18. Showing heat of hydration of various cements

Type of Cement	*Heat of Hydration in calories per gram of cement at different age in days*							
	1	3	7	14	28	90	180	365
Normal cement	51	80	87	90	92	96	100	103
Modified cement	42	63	75	79	82	88	92	94
High early strength cement	77	103	108	112	114	115	—	—
Low heat cement	28	46	52 – 65	59	66 – 76	77	81	86
Sulphate resistant cement	32	49	56	62	69	80	84	89

Table 3.19. Rise in temperature of concrete made with different cements at the different age in days

Type of Cement	*Temperature °C rise after days*				
	1	3	7	14	28
Normal	20.5	31.0	35	35	36
Modified	16.7	25.0	30	32	32
High early strength	31.0	40.0	44	44	44
Low heat	11.0	18.5	21	23.5	66
Sulphate resistant	15.5	20	23	15.5	27.5

Table 3.20. Relative strength of concrete made with different cements

Type of Cement	*Compressive strength % strength of normal portland cement at age shown in days*		
	3 days	*28 days*	*90 days*
Normal	100	100	100
Modified	80	85	100
High early strength	190	130	115
Low heat	50	65	90
Sulphate resistant	65	65	85

3.10. FIELD TEST OF CEMENT

If the cement supply is doubtfull and it is not possible to conduct laboratory test, it's purity and quality can be judged by the following tests;

1. The colour of pure cement should be uniformly greenish gray.
2. When rubbed in between thumb and fore finger, it should feel smooth. Grittiness shows adulteration.
3. A small quantity of cement thrown into a bucket of water, should float, in case it is of good quality. If it sinks it contains impurities.
4. It should not be felt oily when touched.
5. Any lump of cement should break when pressed between thumb and fore finger. If it does not break, the cement has developed air set.
6. If hand put into a cement bag, it should feel cool and not warm.

Table 3.20. Physical properties of various types of cement

S. No.	*Type of Cement*	*Fineness cm^2/g minimum*	*Soundness*		*Setting time*		*Compressive strength (minimum)*			
			Le-Chateliar (mm) max	*Auto clave (%) max*	*Initial in (mts) min*	*Final (mts) max*	*1 day MPa*	*3 day MPa*	*7 day MPa*	*28 day MPa*
1.	*Ordinary portland cement* 33 grade (IS 269-1989)	2250	10	0.8	30	600	N.S.	16 (160 kg/cm^2)	22 (220 kg/cm^2)	33 (330 kg/cm^2)
2.	43 grade (IS 8112-1989)	2250	10	0.8	30	600	N.S.	23 (230 kg/cm^2)	33 (330 kg/cm^2)	43 (430 kg/cm^2)
3.	53 grade (IS 12269-1989	2250	10	0.8	30	600	N.S.	27 (270 kg/cm^2)	37 (370 kg/cm^2)	53 (530 kg/cm^2)
4.	Sulphate resisting cement (IS 12330-1988)	2250	10	0.8	30	600	N.S.	10 (100 kg/cm^2)	16 (160 kg/cm^2)	33 (330 kg/cm^2)
5.	Portland pozzolana cement (IS 1489-1991) part 1	3000	10	0.8	30	600	N.S.	16 (160 kg/cm^2)	22 (220 kg/cm^2)	33 (330 kg/cm^2)
6.	Rapid Hardening cement (IS 8041-1990)	3250	10	0.8	30	600	16 (160 kg/cm^2)	27 (270 kg/cm^2)	N.S.	N.S.
7.	Slag cement (IS 455-1989)	2250	10	0.8	30	600	N.S.	16 (160 kg/cm^2)	22 (220 kg/cm^2)	33 (330 kg/cm^2)
8.	High Alumina cement (IS 6452-1989)	2250	5	N.S.	30	600	30 (300 kg/cm^2)	35 (350 kg/cm^2)	N.S.	N.S.
9.	Super sulphated cement (IS 6909-1990)	4000	5	N.S.	30	600	N.S.	15 (150 kg/cm^2)	22 (220 kg/cm^2)	30 (300 kg/cm^2)
10.	Low Heat cement (IS 12600-1989)	3200	10	0.8	60	600	N.S.	10 (100 kg/cm^2)	16 (160 kg/cm^2)	35 (350 kg/cm^2)
11.	Masonary cement (IS 3466-1988)	N.S.	10	1.0	90	1440	N.S.	N.S.	2.5 (25 kg/cm^2)	5 (50 kg/cm^2)
12.	IRS-T-40	3700	5	0.8	60	600	N.S.	N.S.	37.5 (375kg/cm^2)	N.S.

N.S. = Not Specified

Table 3.21. Chemical characteristics of various types of cement

S. No.	*Type of Cement*	*Lime saturation factor (%)*	*Sulphuric anhydride (So_3)*	*Alumina iron ratio (%) min.*	*Insolable residuce (%) max.*	*Magnesia (%) max.*	*Loss on ignition (%) max.*
1.	*Ordinary Cement* 33 grade (IS 269-1989)	0.66 min 1.02 max	2.5% max when C_3A is 5% or less 3.5% when C_3A is greater than 5%	0.66	4	6	5
2.	43 grade (IS 8112-1989)	0.8 min 1.02 max	2.5% max when C_3A is 5% or less 3.0% when C_3A is greater than 5%	0.66	2	6	5
3.	53 grade (IS 12269-1989)	0.8 min 1.02 max	— do —	0.66	2	6	4
4.	Sulphate resisting cement (IS 12330-1988)	0.66 min 1.02 max	2.5% max	N.S.	4	6	5
5.	Portland pozzolana cement (IS 1489-1991) part 7	N.S.	3% max	N.S.	$x+\frac{4(100-x)}{100}$	6	5
6.	Rapid Hardening cement (IS 8041-1990)	0.66 min 1.02 max	2.5% max when C_3A is 5% or less 3.0% when C_3A is greater than 5%	0.66	4	6	5
7.	Slag cement (IS 455-1989)	N.S.	3.0% max	N.S.	4	8	5
8.	High Alumina cement (IS 6452-1989)	N.S.	N.S.	N.S.	N.S.	N.S.	N.S.
9.	Super sulphated cement (IS 6909-1990)	N.S.	6.0% min	N.S.	4	10	N.S.
10.	Low Heat cement (IS 12600-1989)	N.S.	2.5% max when C_3A is 5% or less 3.0% when C_3A is greater than 5%	0.66	4	6	5
11.	IRST-40	0.5 min 1.02 max	3.5% max.	0.66	2	5	4

N.S. = Not Specified

QUESTIONS

1. Name the principal compounds of ordinary portland cement and mention the approximate percentage of each. Also explain their functions in detail.
2. How does high early strength cement differ from normal portland cement?
3. Explain the properties and uses of the following cements
   (*a*) Hydrophobic cement
   (*b*) Masonry cement
   (*c*) Anti-bacterial cement
   (*d*) Expansive cement
4. Describe the manufacture, properties and uses of high alumina cement.
5. Define pozzolana, why it is some times used with portland cement.
6. What is a white cement? Explain it's manufacture giving its typical oxide composition.
7. Differentiate between low heat cement, sulphur resistant cement, and portland blast furnace cement.
8. What is meant by total heat of hydration?
9. What is meant by conversion of high alumina cement? What factors influence the rate of conversion?
10. How does the conversion of high alumina cement affect its properties. Would you recommend the high alumina cement for structural purposes?
11. What would happen of high alumina and ordinary portland cements are blended in the construction work.
12. What is the pozzolanic actively index?

OBJECTIVE TYPE QUESTIONS

1. State which of the following statement is correct
   (*a*) The initial setting time of rapid hardening cement should not be less than 5 minutes and final setting time not more than 30 minutes.
   (*b*) The initial setting time of rapid hardening cement should not be less than 30 minutes and final setting time not more than 600 minutes.
   (*c*) The initial setting time of rapid hardening cement should not be less than 60 minutes and final setting time not more than 240 minutes.
   (*d*) The initial setting time of rapid hardening cement should not be less than 15 minutes and final setting time not more than 60 minutes.
2. Heat of hydration of cement is expressed as
   (*a*) Calories
   (*b*) Grams
   (*c*) Farads
   (*d*) Calories/gram
   (*e*) Calories/cm^3
3. The heat generated during the process of setting and hardening of cement is called
   (*a*) Latent heat
   (*b*) Heat of hydration
   (*c*) Sensible heat
   (*d*) Heat of evaporation
   (*e*) Heat of setting
4. The apparatus from which heat of hydration determined is called...
   (*a*) Calorimeter
   (*b*) Hygrometer
   (*c*) Hydrometer
   (*d*) Photometer
   (*e*) Pedometer
5. The warehouse cement set is caused due to
   (*a*) The moisture in the ware house
   (*b*) storing cement adjacent to walls
   (*c*) The load of the cement bags placed above
   (*d*) No such setting occurs
6. An ideal ware house should have...
   (*a*) No windows and minimum number of doors
   (*b*) Water proof masonry walls
   (*c*) Water proof roof
   (*d*) 150 mm thick cement concrete floor
   (*e*) All the above

7. From the ware house the cement should be taken out on the basis of
   (*a*) First in, last out
   (*b*) Last in, first out
   (*c*) First in, First out
   (*d*) Any of the above
8. In fineness test of rapid hardening cement, the residue on 1*S* sieve 9 should not be more than
   (*a*) 3.5%
   (*b*) 7.5%
   (*c*) 10%
   (*d*) 5%
   (*e*) Any of the above
9. State which of the following statements is false
   (*a*) White cement usually is used for normal construction work
   (*b*) White cement is used mostly for decorative works
   (*c*) Portland pozzolana cement produces less heat of hydration
   (*d*) Expanding cement is used for filling the cracks
   (*e*) High strength portland cement is produced from special materials
   (*f*) By varying the basic compounds of cement clinker several types of cements can be produced
   (*g*) The good quality cement dissolves in water immediately
   (*h*) The good quality cement floats on the surface of the water
   (*i*) The good quality cement sinks to the bottom of the container
   (*j*) The good quality cement when sprinkled on water gets evaporated
   (*k*) The good quality cement when sprinkled on water produces bubbles.

   [**Ans.** *false.* (*a*), (*e*), (*g*), (*i*), (*j*), (*k*)]
10. State whether the following statements are true or false
   (*a*) Argillacious materials have alumina as the main constituent
   (*b*) Argillacious materials have lime as the main constituent
   (*c*) Argillacious materials evolve heat on addition of water
   (*d*) Argillacious materials break easily when hammered
   (*e*) Calcium chloride should not be used in reinforced and pre stressed concrete
   (*f*) The strength of concrete increases below freezing point of water
   (*g*) The ingredient of concrete should be mixed with in three minutes
   (*h*) In hot weather the hardening of concrete takes place rapidly

   [**Ans.** *true.* (*a*), (*e*), (*g*), (*h*), *false.* (*b*), (*c*), (*d*), (*f*)]
11. How many bags can be stored in a pile of 4 × 3 × 0.9 m high store
   (*a*) 250
   (*b*) 200
   (*c*) 150
   (*d*) 175
   (*d*) 100
12. Cement bags stored for 24 months are likely to result...
   (*a*) Formation of lumps
   (*b*) Loss of strength by 50%
   (*c*) Changé in colour of cement
   (*d*) Swelling by 17%
13. In ordinary portland cement the magnesia content is restricted to
   (*a*) 2.5%
   (*b*) 1.5%
   (*c*) 5%
   (*d*) 1.0%
14. The total sulphar content in cement should be less than
   (*a*) 2.5%
   (*b*) 5%
   (*c*) 10%
   (*d*) 0.25%
15. Low heat cement is used for
   (*a*) Twin structures
   (*b*) Massive or thick structures
   (*c*) Under water construction
   (*d*) Repair of roads etc.
16. For the repair of roads works which cement is used
   (*a*) Rapid hardening cement
   (*b*) Low heat cement
   (*c*) High alumina cement
   (*d*) Sulphate resisting cement
   (*e*) Ordinary portland cement
17. For the construction of docks and harbours cement used is
   (*a*) Hydrophobic cement
   (*b*) Blast furnace slag cement

(*c*) Water proof cement (*d*) High strength portland cement
(*e*) Sulphate resisting cement

18. For lining of a sulphuric acid plant, cement used is
(*a*) Portland slag cement (*b*) Super sulphate cement
(*c*) High alumina cement (*d*) Rapid hardening portland cement
(*e*) Portland pozzolana cement

19. For lining deep wells, cement used is
(*a*) Oil well cement (*b*) Sulphate resisting portland cement
(*c*) Portland pozzolana cement (*d*) High alumina cement
(*e*) Blast furnance slag cement

20. For the repair of canal banks during rainey season cement used is
(*a*) Portland slag cement (*b*) Ordinary portland cement
(*c*) Rapid hardening portland cement (*d*) High alumina cement
(*e*) Portland pozzolana cement

21. For the construction of road pavements cement used is
(*a*) Low heat cement (*b*) Ordinary portland cement
(*c*) Rapid hardening cement (*d*) Blast furnance slag cement

22. Lechatelier's method is used to determine...
(*a*) Fineness of cement (*b*) Sulpher content of cement
(*c*) Soundness of cement (*d*) Iron content of cement

23. The specific surface area of ordinary portland cement is determined by
(*a*) Air permeability method (*b*) Sieve analysis
(*c*) Autoclave method (*d*) Photo calorimeter method
(*e*) Lechateliar apparatus

24. The specific surface of cement is expressed as
(*a*) mm^3/g (*b*) g/mm^3
(*c*) mm^2/g (*d*) g/mm^2

25. Hydration of cement-concrete ceases at a temperature of
(*a*) 0°C (*b*) 0°F
(*c*) 11°C (*d*) 11°F

26. For the test of fineness of cement IS sieve used is...
(*a*) 300 micron (*b*) 150 micron
(*c*) 90 micron (*d*) 9 micron

27. Fill up the blanks from the correct groups given below of each question

A. While.........is a calcareous material and.........is a argillaceous material
(*a*) Lime stone, shale (*b*) Clay, lime stone
(*c*) Shale, lime stone (*d*) Slate, laterite
(*e*) Marl, chalk

B. The colour of portland pozzolana cement is .... and that of ordinary portland cement.........
(*a*) Brown, grey (*b*) White, grey
(*c*) Grey, black (*d*) White, black
(*e*) Grey, white

C. Low heat cement is used in.........structures while white cement is used in......
(*a*) Thin, costliest (*b*) Thick, costliest
(*c*) Thick, chepest (*d*) Chepest, thin

[Ans. A. (*a*), B. (*b*), C. (*b*)]

28. Which of the following group of portland cement has specific surface area in the descending order
(*a*) Rapid hardening, high strength, low heat, ordinary portland
(*b*) Ordinary portland, Rapid hardening, high strength and low heat cement
(*c*) High strength, Rapid hardening, low heat, and ordinary portland
(*d*) Low heat, ordinary portland, Rapid hardening, and high strength

29. State which of the following statement is correct

(*a*) Hydrophotic portland cement is an ordinary cement having 0.1 to 0.5% by weight of an additive called hydrophobic agent.
(*b*) It contains about 35% alumina by weight.
(*c*) The additive imparts an water repellent film to the cement.
(*d*) The additive increases the setting time of the cement.
(*e*) This cement deteriorates to a great extent during prolonged storage.
(*f*) This cement deteriorates very little during the prolonged storage.
(*g*) The water repellent film of the cement is broken during the mixing of cement with aggregate in the mixer.

[**Ans.** *True*. (*a*), (*c*), (*f*), (*g*)]

30. State which of the following statements is true
(*a*) High alumina cement suffers by unsoundness to a great extent.
(*b*) It contains lime and alumina approximately equally about 40%.
(*c*) The silica content in high alumina cement is of the order of 20 to 25%.
(*d*) The surface area of high alumina cement varies from 2500 to 3200 cm^2/gram.
(*e*) The conversion reaction in high alumina cement results in the reduction of volume of solids and increase in porosity.

[**Ans.** *false*. (*a*), (*d*)]

31. State which of the following statements is false
(*a*) Curing of high alumina cement concrete above 18°C reduces its strength.
(*b*) The increase in water/cement ratio of high alumina cement concrete from 0.3 to 0.45 reduces its strength from 60 to 35% of unconverted strength.
(*c*) About 80% strength of high alumina cement develops in 24 hours.
(*d*) The rate of strength development of high alumina cement is very low.
(*e*) The rate of heat development of high alumina cement is $2\frac{1}{2}$ times that of rapid hardening cement.
(*f*) The colour of high alumina cement is brown.
(*g*) The rediset cement sets in about 8 to 10 minutes after adding water to it.
(*h*) The strength after 3 to 6 hours of rediset cement is equal to 7 days strength of ordinary portland cement.
(*i*) The rate of hydration of rediset cement is very low.

[**Ans.** *false*. (*d*) , (*f*), (*i*)]

32. State which of the following statements is true
(*a*) The expansive cement is called self stressing cement
(*b*) Anti-bacterial cement is one type of high alumina cement
(*c*) The colour of high alumina cement is pure white.
(*d*) Free lime is in excess in high alumina cement.
(*e*) High alumina cement strength increases on conversion.

[**Ans.** (*a*)]

33. In a oil well cement the percentage of sugar should be added
(*a*) 5.0 to 7.0% (*b*) 2.0 to 5.0%
(*c*) 1.0 to 3.0% (*d*) 0.05 to 0.2%

Answers

1. (*a*)	7. (*c*)	15. (*b*)	21. (*c*)	28. (*c*)
2. (*d*)	8. (*d*)	16. (*a*)	22. (*c*)	33. (*d*)
3. (*b*)	11. (*b*)	17. (*e*)	23. (*a*)	
4. (*a*)	12. (*b*)	18. (*c*)	24. (*c*)	
5. (*c*)	13. (*c*)	19. (*a*)	25. (*d*)	
6. (*e*)	14. (*a*)	20. (*c*)	26. (*c*)	

4

Aggregates

4.1. GENERAL

Originally mineral aggregate was used as an inert filler in the cement concrete. In fact the aggregate is not an inert filler and its physical, thermal and chemical properties influence the performance of the concrete to a great extent. Further the aggregate is cheaper than cement and thus it is cheaper to use as much quantity of aggregate and as little of cement as possible, but economy alone is not the reason for using aggregate in the concrete. Aggregate provides better strength, stability and durability to the structure made out of the cement concrete than cement paste alone.

In any concrete, usually aggregate occupies about 70 to 75% of the total volume of the concrete mass. The selection and proportioning of aggregate should be given due attention as it not only affects the strength, but durability and structural performance of the concrete also. While selecting aggregate for a particular concrete, following requirements should be kept in mind.

(*a*) Economy of the mixture (*b*) Strength of the hardened mass and

(*c*) Durability of the structure

4.2. CLASSIFICATION OF AGGREGATE

Generally aggregates may be classified as follows:

1. According to source
2. According to mineralogical composition
3. According to mode of preparation
4. According to size

1. According to source. According to this classification aggregates may further be classified as

(*a*) Natural aggregates

(*b*) Artificial aggregates

(*a*) **Natural aggregates.** These aggregates are formed from naturally occurring material. The natural aggregates such as gravel and sand are the product of weathering and action of running water. Natural aggregates may be derived from any rock as igneous, sedimentary or metamor- phic rock. The classification of aggregates according to rock has been shown in Table 4.1.

(*b*) **Artificial aggregates.** These aggregates are usually produced for some special purpose as burned clay aggregates for making light weight concrete. Some artificial aggregates are the byproduct of an unrelated industrial process as blast furnance slag, cinder etc. Some times crushing of rock may also be adopted to produce a desired sized aggregate.

2. According to mineralogical composition. According to this classification aggregates may be classified as silicous or calcareous etc.

Table 4.1. Rocks used for the manufacture of aggregates

Igneous Rocks			
Granite group	*Basalt group*	*Gabbro group*	*Aplite group*
1. Granite 2. Gneiss 3. Granodiorite 4. Granulite 5. Quartz-diorite	1. Basalt 2. Andesite 3. Diabese 4. Dolerites 5. Quartz-dolerite	1. Gabbro 2. Norite 3. Peridotite 4. Pyroxenite 5. Epidiorite 6. Anorthosite	1. Aplite 2. Porphyry 3. Quartz-reef
Rocks			
Delerite group	*Rhyolite group*		
1. Dolerite 2. Lamprophyre	1. Rhyolite 2. Trachyte 3. Felsite 4. Pumicite etc.		
Sedimentary Rocks			
Sand stone group	*Lime stone group*		
1. Sand stone 2. Quartzite 3. Arkose 4. Grit 5. Gray wacke	1. Lime stone 2. Dolomite 3. Marble		
Metamorphic Rocks			
Schist group	*Marble group*	*Granulite Gneiss group*	
1. Slate 2. Phyllite 3. Schist	1. Marble 2. Crystalline lime stone	1. Granite gneiss 2. Composite gneiss 3. Amphibolite 4. Granulite	

Note: All rocks are not equally good for the manufacture of aggregate for a particular type of construction. Hence before use, the suitability of rock should be tested.

3. According to mode of preparation. According to this classification distinction is made between aggregates reduced to its present size by natural agents and crushed aggregate obtained by a deliberate fragmentation of rock.

4. According to size of aggregate particle. According to this classification the aggregate is further sub-divided as

(*a*) coarse aggregate and

(*b*) Find aggregate

(*a*) Coarse aggregates. It is defined as the aggregate most of which is retained on 4.75 mm I.S. sieve and containing only so much finer material as is permitted for various types described in I.S. 383-1970 in Table 4.2.

(*b*) Fine aggregates. Aggregates most of which passes through 4.75 mm I.S. sieve is called fine aggregate. The four zones of fine aggregates are shown in Table 4.3.

Table 4.2. Showing percentage passing of different sizes of aggregates

I.S. Sieve Designation	*Percentage passing for single sized aggregate of nominal size*						*Percentage passing for graded aggregate of nominal size*			
	63 mm	40 mm	20 mm	16 mm	12.5 mm	10 mm	40 mm	20 mm	16 mm	12.5 mm
1	2	3	4	5	6	7	8	9	10	11
80 mm	100	—	—	—	—	—	100	—	—	—
63 mm	85 to 100	100	—	—	—	—	—	—	—	—
40 mm	0 to 30	85 to 100	100	—	—	—	95 to 100	100	—	—
20 mm	0 to 5	0 to 20	85 to 100	100	—	—	30 to 70	95 to 100	100	100
16 mm	—	—	—	85 to 100	100	—	—	—	90 to 100	—
12.5 mm	—	—	—	—	85 to 100	100	—	—	—	90 to 100
10 mm	0 to 5	0 to 5	0 to 20	0 to 30	0 to 45	85 to 100	10 to 35	25 to 55	30 to 70	40 to 85
4.75 mm	—	—	0 to 5	0 to 5	0 to 10	0 to 20	0 to 5	0 to 10	0 to 10	0 to 10
2.36 mm	—	—	—	—	—	0 to 5	—	—	—	—

Table 4.3. Showing grading zones of the fine aggregates

S. No.	*I.S. Sieve Designation*	*Grading zone 1 %age passing*	*Grading zone 2 %age passing*	*Grading zone 3 %age passing*	*Grading zone 4 %age passing*	*Remarks*
1.	10 mm	100	100	100	100	**Note 1.** For crushed stone sand, the permissible limit on 150 micron I.S. SIEVE is increased to 20%. **Note 2.** Fine aggregate of any zone is suitable for concrete, but the concrete mix should be properly designed for high strength concrete. **Note 3.** Fine aggregate of zone 4 should not be used in reinforced concrete. If to be used, it should be tested fully.
2.	4.75 mm	90 — 100	90 — 100	90 — 100	95 — 100	
3.	2.36 mm	60 — 95	75 — 100	85 — 100	95 — 100	
4.	1.18 mm	30 — 70	55 — 90	75 — 100	90 — 100	
5.	600 micron	15 — 34	35 — 59	60 — 79	80 — 100	
6.	300 micron	5 — 20	8 — 30	12 — 40	15 — 50	
7.	150 micron	0 — 10	0 — 10	0 — 10	0 — 15	

4.3. EFFECT OF AGGREGATE ON THE PROPERTIES OF CONCRETE

In addition to the petro-logical (rock structure etc.) character of aggregate, its external characteristics also are of importance which have marked influence on the properties of concrete. Following characteristics are of importance.

1. Shape and texture of particle
2. Size of particles
3. Quantities of impurities in aggregate
4. Crushing strength of aggregate
5. Grading of aggregate.

1. Shape of particles. The shape of the particles depends upon the source of aggregate. The different shapes of particles are discussed in Table 4.4.

Table 4.4. Shape of particles

S. No.	*Classification*	*Description*	*Example*	*Fig. No.*
1.	Rounded	Fully water worn or completely shaped by attrition	River or sea shore gravel, desert, sea shore and wind blown sand	Fig. 4.1
2.	Irregular	Naturally irregular, or partly shaped by attrition and having rounded edges	Pit sand and gravel or dug flints, cuboid rocks	Fig. 4.2
3.	Angular	Possessing well defined edges formed at the intersection of roughly plane faces.	Crushed rocks of all types, talus crushed slag etc.	Fig. 4.3
4.	Flaky	Materials of which the thickness is small relative to other two dimensions usually they are angular	Laminated rocks as slate	Fig. 4.4
5.	Elongated	Material usually angular in which the length is considerably larger than other two dimensions		
6.	Flaky and elongated	Material having the length considerably larger than the width and the width considerably larger than the thickness.		

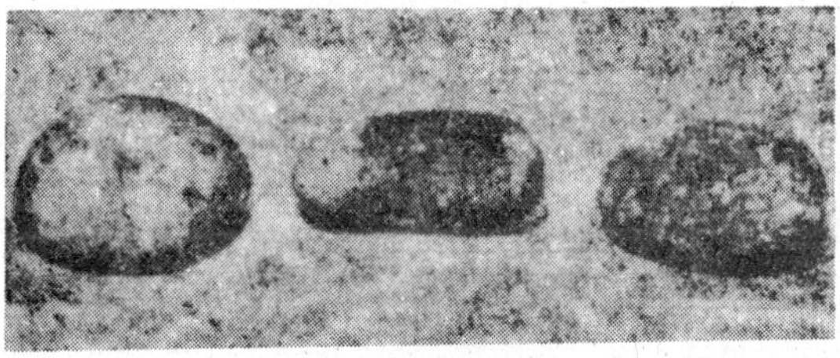

Fig. 4.1. Rounded Particles

Fig. 4.2. Irregular particles

Angularity. It can be expressed qualitatively by a figure called angularity number as suggested by F.A. **Shergold**. It is based on the percentage voids in the aggregate after compaction as per IS 2386-1963 part-1. This test gives a value called as angularity number. The percentage voids are calculated as follows:

A single sized aggregate is filled in a metallic cylinder of three litre capacity. The aggregate is compacted in a standard manner and percentage voids calculated. The voids can be found out by filling water in the cylinder till the water level reaches upto the brim or top edge of the cylinder or by knowing the specific gravity and bulk density of the aggregate. If the calculated value of voids is 33%, it is assumed that angularity is zero and solid volume of aggregate is 67% and the angularity is zero. If the voids are 44%, then it is assumed that angularity number is 11 and the solid volume of aggregate is 56%. An aggregate having angularity number between zero to 11 is considered suitable for making concrete. Zero angularity represents the most suitable rounded aggregate and angularity number 11 indicates the most angular aggregate that can be tolerated for making concrete not unduly harsh and uneconomical. Murdok has suggested the following relation for expressing the shape of the aggregate. This relation is called as angularity index f_A.

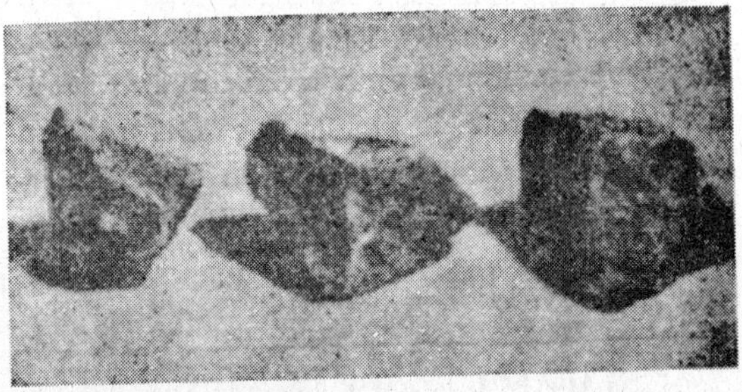

Fig. 4.3. Angular particles

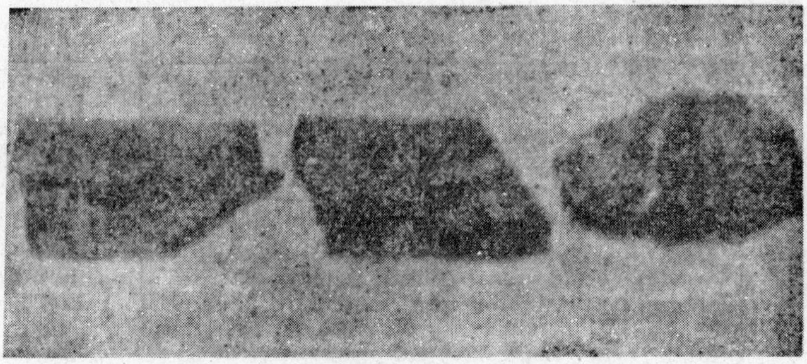

Fig. 4.4. Flaky particles

$\therefore$ Angularity index $f_A = \dfrac{3 \cdot f_H}{20} + 1.0$ where f_H is angularity number.

The shape of aggregate affects the workability of the concrete to a great extent, hence its strength and durability. Shape affects compressive strength by 22% and flexure strength by 30%.

Flaky particle

A particle is said to be flaky, if its least dimension (thickness) is less than 0.6 times the mean sieve size. The mean size is determined by passing and retained of particle on the sieve. If a particle passes through a 25 mm sieve and retained on a 20 mm sieve, then mean size is $\dfrac{25 + 20}{2} = 22.5$ mm.

Thus if the least dimension of any particle is $22.5 \times 0.6 = 13.50$ mm, then it is known as flaky particle. They orient in one particular plane forming water and air voids under neath. Thus flaky particles in the concrete should not be more than 10 to 15% of the weight of the coarse aggregate.

Elongated particles

If the largest dimension (length) of a particle is 1.8 times the mean sieve size, then this particle is called as elongated particle. In any concrete the quantity of flaky and elongated particles should not be much as they affect the workability of concrete.

As the surface area of such particles is greater, they need more water for wetting their surface, leaving smaller quantity of water for workability and produce porous concrete and thus the strength and durability of concrete is reduced. Therefore the quantity of such particles combined should not be more than 35% to 40% of the weight of coarse aggregate. Thus as per I.S. 2386 part I, the dimensions of the coarse aggregate particles should be as shown in Table 4.5.

Table 4.5.

Size of aggregate		*Thickness gauge mm*	*Length gauge mm*
Passing through I.S. Sieve	*Retained on I.S. Sieve*		
63 mm	50 mm	33.9	—
50 mm	40 mm	27.0	81.0
40 mm	35 mm	19.5	58.5
31.5 mm	25 mm	16.95	—
25 mm	20 mm	13.50	40.5
20 mm	16 mm	10.80	32.4
16 mm	12.5 mm	8.55	25.6
12.5 mm	10.0 mm	6.75	20.2
10.0 mm	6.0	4.89	14.7

Surface texture

The classification of surface texture is based on the degree to which the particle surfaces are polished or dull, smooth or rough etc. Surface texture depends on the hardness, grain-size, and pore characteristics of the parent rock. Visual estimation of roughness is quite reliable. Though there is no recognised method of measuring the surface roughness, but surface texture shown in Table 4.6 is a good indication.

Table 4.6. Showing Surface Texture of Aggregates

Group	*Surface texture*	*Characteristic*	*Example*
1.	Glassy	Conchoidal fracture (Sea shell)	Black flint vitreous slag
2.	Smooth	Water worn or smooth due to fracture of laminated or fine grained rock	Gravel, chert, slate, marble, and some rhyolites
3.	Granular	Fracture showing more or less uniform rounded grain	Sand stone, oolite
4.	Rough	Rough fracture of fine or medium grained rock containing no easily visible crystalline constituents	Basalt, felsite, lime stone
5.	Crystal-line	Containing easily visible crystalline constituents	Granite, gabbro, gneiss, dolerite, lime stone
6.	Honey combed	With visibly pores and cavities	Brick, pumice foamed slag, clinker, expanded clay

The shape and texture of aggregate influence the concrete strength considerably. The flexure strength is more affected than the compressive strength. These factors are more significant in the case of high strength concrete. Surface texture affects compressive strength by 44% and flexture strength by 26%.

4.4. BOND STRENGTH OF AGGREGATE

The resistance developed to shear the aggregate particles from the hardened cement paste is called bond strength of aggregate. The bond between the cement paste and aggregate is an important factor in the strength of concrete, specially the flexural strength. Bond is partly due to the interlocking of the aggregate and the paste owing to the roughness of the surface of the aggregate particles. Thus rougher the surface as that of a crushed stone, better the bond. Secondly bond is also affected by other physical and chemical properties of aggregate.

The determination of bond strength of aggregate is difficult and no accepted test exists. It is judged by the surface of a crushed concrete. If in a crushed concrete specimen, larger number of aggregate particles are seen pulled out from their sockets and some of them seen fractured or broken right through, then the bond is called good. Greater number of crushed aggregate particle suggest weaker aggregate. Usually a aggregate used in cement concrete is considered at least 10 times stronger than hardened cement paste. Hence the strength of concrete depends upon its bond strength. The bond strength depends upon the strength of cement paste and on the properties of aggregate surface as well. Bond strength is found to increase with the age of concrete.

4.5. CRUSHING STRENGTH OF AGGREGATE

The compressive strength of concrete can not exceed that of the aggregate used therein. Actually it is not easy to determine the crushing strength of individual particles. It is the bulk aggregate crushing strength which is determined. As stated above, usually aggregate is considered ten times stronger than crushing strength of concrete, but some particles break also and influence its strength. Therefore aggregate to be used in cement concrete should not be weaker than the strength of hardened cement paste.

4.5.1. Determination of Crushing Strength of aggregate

Material for the standard crushing test should pass through 12.5 mm I.S. sieve and retained on 10 mm I.S. sieve. The aggregate shall be thoroughly sieved on the above sieves before test. It should be surface dried at the time of test. If it is to be dried by heating, the period of drying should not be more than four hours. The aggregate should be heated to bone dry at 100°C to 110°C for four hours and then cooled to room temperature before use.

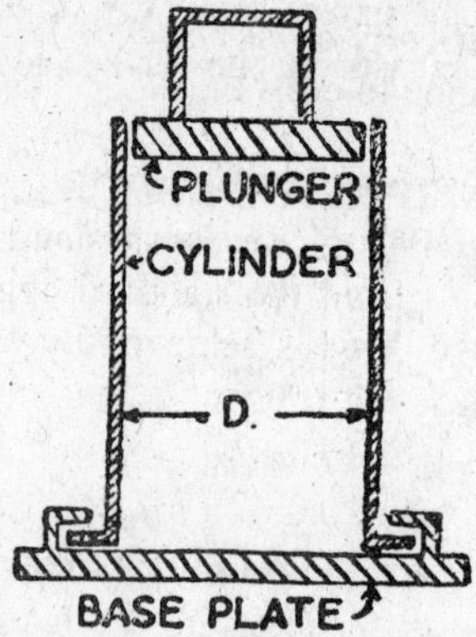

Fig. 4.5. Apparatus for crushing strength of aggregate

Apparatus

(*a*) Apparatus used for standard test consists of a 15 cm diameter open ended steel cylinder of height 13.0 to 14 cm; with plunger and base plate.

(*b*) A 60 cm long steel rod of 1.6 cm diameter and rounded at one end.

4.5.2. Test Procedure

The cylinder of the test apparatus is filled upto 1/3rd of its height with the prepared aggregate and tamped with 25 strokes by the tamping rod. In this way the next 1/3rd height of cylinder is filled and tamped again by 25 strokes with the tamping rod. Finally the cylinder is filled to its full height and subjected to 25 strokes by the tamping rod.

Now the plunger is inserted in such a way that it rests horizontally on this surface. Care is taken that plunger does not jam in the cylinder. The whole assembly is now placed in a compression testing machine. The load should be applied at a uniform rate in such a way that the total 40 tonne load is applied in 10 minutes or rate of loading should be 22.7 kg/cm^2 per minute. Now the load is released and the whole aggregate in the cylinder is sieved on a 2.26 mm I.S. sieve for the standard test and fraction passing through the sieve weighed. The ratio of the passing fraction should not be more than 45% for all types of concrete and 30% for wearing surfaces.

In case standard size aggregate *i.e.*, aggregate particles passing 12.5 mm sieve and retained on 10 mm sieve is not available, then available aggregate upto 25 mm size can be tested. In this case material should be sieved on sieves shown in Table 4.7. For measuring the sample, cylinder of 11.5 cm diameter and 18 cm height may be used.

Details of aggregate crushing test for non standard sizes of aggregates are shown in Table 4.7.

Table 4.7.

Nominal I.S. sieve sizes		*Diameter of cylinder to be used mm*	*Height of cylinder to be used mm*	*Size of sieve to be used for seperating fines mm*	*Remark*
Passing through mm	*Retained on mm*				
25	20	150.0	130 – 140	4.75	**Note: 1.** In general, larger sizes of aggregate than standard give higher values of aggregate crushing strength. 2. Smaller sizes of aggregate than standard give lower values of crushing strength. 3. If 75 mm diameter cylinder is used, this gives slightly higher value of crushing strength of aggregate.
20	12.5	150.0	130 – 140	3.35	
10	6.3	150.0 or 75	For 75 cm dia	1.70	
6.3	4.75	150.0 or 75	cylinder height varies from	1.18	
4.75	3.35	150.0 or 75	70 to 80	800 micron	
3.35	2.36	150.0 or 75	– do –	600 micron	
Note: About 6.5 kg. of natural aggregate is required to provide two test samples for the 150 mm cylinder and about 1 kg. for 75 mm cylinder.					

The crushing strength test discussed above has been found insensitive to the variation in strength of weaker aggregates. Therefore when such aggregates are tested by this method, they do not give true picture, because they get crushed before the full load of 40 tonne has been applied and get compacted causing the plunger to jam. Thus the amount of crushing during later stages of the test is reduced. To over come this difficulty a *ten per cent fine value* test has been developed. This test is a measure of resistance of an aggregate to crushing.

Resistance to Crushing

For this test also standard crushing apparatus is used. In this case a load which could produce 10% fines from the standard aggregate *i.e.* aggregate passing 12.5 mm sieve and retained on 10 mm sieve is used. This is achieved by applying a progressively increasing load on the plunger so that this load could cause the following penetration of the plunger in 10 minutes.

(*a*) 15.0 mm for rounded or partially rounded aggregates.

(*b*) 20.0 mm for normal crushed aggregate.

(*c*) 24.0 mm for honeycombed aggregate.

After reaching the required maximum penetration, the load is released and the whole material in the cylinder is sieved on 2.36 mm I.S. sieve. The percentage of passing material through the sieve should be between 7.5% and 12.5%. If the above percentage is not met, the test is repeated. The value of load to give the 10% fines can be obtained as follows.

If y is the actual percentage of fines due to a maximum load of x tonnes, then load required to give 10% fines is given by the relation $\frac{14x}{y+4}$ tonnes.

The ten percent fine value test shows a fairly good correlation with the standard crushing value test for strong aggregates, while for weaker aggregates the ten percent fines value test is more sensitive and gives a truer picture of differences between more or less weak aggregates. For this reason, this test is usually used for light weight aggregate, but there is no simple relation between the test result and the upper limit of strength of concrete made with the given aggregate.

4.6. OTHER MECHANICAL PROPERTIES OF AGGREGATE

Several mechanical properties of aggregate are of interest for the manufacture of concrete, specially high strength concrete subjected to high wear. Some of them are discussed here in brief.

1. Toughness
2. hardness
3. Specific gravity
4. Density of aggregate
5. Moisture content of aggregate-free surface moisture and absorption
6. Porosity of aggregate
7. Bulking of sand
8. Soundness of aggregate.

1. Toughness. It is defined as the resistance of aggregate to failure by impact. The impact value of bulk aggregate can be determined as per I.S. 2386 (Part-IV) 1963. The test procedure is as follows:

The aggregate shall be taken as in the case of crushing strength value test *i.e.* the aggregate should pass through 12.5 mm I.S. sieve and retained on 10 mm I.S. sieve. It should be oven dried at 100°C to 110°C for four hours and then air cooled before test.

Now the prepared aggregate is filled upto 1/3rd height of the cylindrical cup of the equipment. The diameter and depth of the cup are 102 mm and 50 mm respectively. After filling the cup upto 1/3rd of its height, the aggregate is tamped with 25 strokes of the rounded end of the tamping rod.

After this operation the cup shall be further filled upto 2/3rd of its height and a further tamping of 25 strokes given. The cup finally shall be filled to over flowing and tamped with 25 strokes and surplus aggregate removed and the weight of aggregate noted. The value of weight will be useful to repeat the experiment.

Now the hammer of the equipment weighting 14.0 kg or 13.5 kg is raised till its lower face is 380 mm above the upper surface of the aggregate and allowed to fall freely on the aggregate and the process is repeated for 15 times.

The crushed aggregate is now removed from the cup and sieved through 2.36 mm I.S. sieve. The fraction passing through the sieve is weighed accurately.

Let the weight of oven dry sample in the cup = W kg.

Weight of aggregate passing 2.36 mm sieve = W_1 kg.

$$\text{Then impact value} = \frac{W_1}{W} \times 100$$

This value should not be more 30% for aggregate to be used in concrete for wearing surfaces as road and 45% for other type of concrete.

2. Hardness. It is defined as the resistance to wear by abrasion, and the aggregate abrasion value is defined as the percentage loss in weight on abrasion. For testing hardness of aggregate following three methods can be used.

(*a*) Deval Attrition test (*b*) Dorry abrasion test

(*c*) Los Angeles test

Deval Attrition test. This test has been covered by IS 2386 Part (IV)-1963. In this test particles of known weight are subjected to wear in an iron cylinder rotated 10,000 (ten thousand) times at the rate of 30 to 33 revolutions per minute. After the specified revolution of the cylinder the material is taken out and sieved on 1.7 mm sieve and the percentage of material finer than 1.7mm is determined. This percentage is taken as the attrition value of the aggregate. The attrition value of about 7 to 8 usually is considered as permissible.

Dorry Abrasion test. This test has not been covered by Indian standard specifications. In this test a cylindrical specimen having its diameter and height of 25 cm is subjected to abrasion against a rotating metal disk sprinkled with quartz sand. The loss in weight of the cylinder after 1000 (one thousand) revolutions is determined. Then the hardness of rock sample is expressed by an empirical relation as follows:

$$\text{Hardness of sample} = 20 - \frac{\text{Loss in weight in gram}}{3}$$

For good rock this value should not be less the 17. The rock having this value of 14 is considered poor.

Los-Angeles test. This test has been covered by IS 2386 (Part-IV) 1963. In this test aggregate of the specified grading is placed in a cylindrical drum of inside length and diameter of 500 mm and 700 mm respectively. This cylinder is mounted horizontally on stub shafts. For abrasive charge, steel balls or cast iron balls of approximately 48 mm diameter and each weighting 390 grams to 445 gram are used. The number of balls used vary from 6 to 12 depending upon the grading of the aggregate. For 10 mm size aggregate 6 balls are used and for aggregates bigger than 20 mm size usually 12 balls are used.

Procedure. For the conduct of test, the sample and the abrasive charge is placed in the Los-Angeles testing machine and it is rotated at a speed of 20 to 33 revolution per minute. For aggregates upto 40 mm size the machine is rotated for 500 revolutions and for bigger size aggregate 1000 revolutions. The charge is taken out from the machine and sieved on 1.7 mm sieve.

Let the weight of oven dry sample put in the drum = W Kg.

Weight of aggregate passing through 1.7 sieve = W_1 Kg.

$$\text{Then abrasion value} = \frac{W_1}{W} \times 100$$

The abrasion value should not be more then 30% for wearing surfaces and not more than 50% for concrete used for other than wearing surface. The results of Los Angeles test show good correlation not only the actual wear of aggregate when used in concrete, but also with the compression and flexural strength of concrete made with the given aggregate.

Table 4.8 gives an idea of toughness, hardness, crushing strength etc. of different rocks.

Table 4.8. Average test values for Rocks of different Groups

S. No.	*Rock Group*	*Crushing strength MPa*		*Abrasion value*	*Impact value*	*Attrition value*		*Specific gravity*
		Rock	*Aggregate*			*Dry*	*Wet*	
1.	Basalt	207	12	17.6	16	3.3	5.5	2.85
2.	Flint	214	17	19.2	17	3.1	2.5	2.55
3.	Granite	193	20	18.7	13	2.9	3.2	2.69
4.	Gristone	229	12	18.1	15	3.0	5.3	2.67
5.	Lime stone	171	24	16.5	9	4.3	7.8	2.69
6.	Quartizite	339	16	18.9	16	2.5	3.0	2.62
7.	Schist	254	—	18.7	13	3.7	4.3	2.76
8.	Gabbro	204	—	18.7	19	2.5	3.2	2.95
9.	Homfels	354	11	18.8	17	2.7	3.8	2.88
10.	Porphyry	239	12	19.0	20	2.6	2.6	2.66

3. Specific gravity. The specific gravity of a substance is the ratio of the weight of unit volume of the substance to the unit volume of water at the stated temp. In concrete making, aggregates generally contain pores, both permeable and impermeable, hence the term specific gravity has to be defined carefully. Actually there are several types of specific gravity. Here only absolute, and apparent specific gravity has been discussed. In concrete technology specific gravity is used for the calculation of quantities of ingredients. Usually the specific gravity of most aggregates varies between 2.6 and 2.8.

Specific gravity of certain materials as per concrete hand book CA-1 Bombay may be assumed as shown in Table 4.9.

Table 4.9. Specific gravity of cement and aggregate

Material	*Specific gravity*
Cement	3.15
Average sand	2.00
Granite	2.80
Gravel	2.66
Sand	2.65

Method of determination of specific Gravity of aggregate

IS-2386-Part-III-1963 describes various procedures to find out the specific gravity of aggregates of different sizes. Here the method applicable to aggregates larger than 10 mm in size has been described as follows:

A sample of aggregate not less than 2 kg in weight is taken and washed thoroughly to remove dust, and silt particles etc. The washed sample is placed in a wire basket and immersed in distilled water at a temperature of 27 ± 5°C.

Immediately after immersion, the entrapped air is removed from the sample by lifting the basket containing sample 25 mm above the bottom of the jar or tank and allow it drop 25 times at the rate of 1 mm per sec. During this operation, care should be taken that basket and aggregate remain fully immersed in water. After this, the sample is kept in water for about $24 \pm \frac{1}{2}$ hour.

After this period the basket and aggregate is given a jerk to remove the air etc. and weighed in water at the temperature of 27 ± 5°C. Let the weight of basket and aggregate be A_1. The basket and sample of aggregate is removed from the water and allowed to drain for a few minutes. Then the aggregate is taken out from the basket and placed on a dry cloth and dried further. The empty basket is again immersed in water and weighed in water after giving 25 jolts. Let this weight be A_2. The aggregate is surface dried in shade for not more than 10 minutes and the aggregate is weighed in air. Let this weight be B. Now the aggregate is oven dried for $24 \pm \frac{1}{2}$ hour at a temperature of 100 to 110°C. It is then cooled in air tight container and weighed. Let this weight be C. Thus

Weight of sample in water $= (A_1 - A_2) = A$

Weight of saturated surface dry in air sample $= B$

Weight of oven dry sample $= C$

(*a*) Then specific gravity $= \dfrac{C}{B - A}$

(*b*) Apparent specific gravity $= \dfrac{C}{C - A}$

(*c*) Water absorption $= 100\,(B - C)$

(*d*) Bulk density $= \dfrac{\text{Net weight of the aggregate in kg.}}{\text{capacity of the container in litres}}$

Example 4.1. *Find the value of (i) Specific gravity, (ii) Apparent specific gravity, (iii) Apparent particle density, (iv) Bulk particle density.*

(i) Mass of oven dry sample C = 480 gram

(ii) Mass of saturated surface dried sample in air B = 490 gram

(iii) Weight of vessel with water = 1400 gram

(iv) Weight of vessel + water + sample = 1695 gram.

Solution.

(*i*) Specific gravity $= \dfrac{\text{mass of oven dry sample}}{\text{mass of saturated surface sample} - \text{sample weight in water}}$

$$= \frac{C}{B - A} = \frac{480}{490 - 295}$$

$$= \frac{480}{195} = 2.50$$

(*ii*) Apparent specific gravity $= \dfrac{C}{C - A} = \dfrac{480}{480 - 295}$

$$= \frac{480}{185} = 2.59$$

(*iii*) Apparent particle density $= 1000 \times$ Apparent specific gravity $= 2.59 \times 1000$

$= 2590\ \text{kg/m}^3$

(*iv*) Bulk Particle density $=$ Bulk specific gravity $\times$ 1000

$= 2.50 \times 1000 = 2500\ \text{kg/m}^3$

Absolute specific gravity. It can be defined as the ratio of the weight of the solid, referred to vacuum, to the weight of an equal volume of gas free distilled water both taken at the standard or a stated temperature, usually it is not required in concrete technology. Actually the absolute specific gravity and particle density refer to the volume of solid material excluding all pores, while apparent specific gravity and apparent particle density refer to the value of solid material including impermeable pores, but not the capillary pores. In concrete technology apparent specific gravity is required.

Apparent specific gravity. It can be defined as the ratio of the weight of the aggregate dried in an oven at 100°C to 110°C for 24 hours to the weight of water occupying a volume equal to that of the solid including the impermeable pores. This can be determined by using pycno-meter for solids less than 10 mm in size *i.e.* sand.

Bulk specific gravity. It can be defined as the ratio of the weight in air of a given volume of material (including both permeable and impermeable voids) at the standard temperature to the weight in air of an equal volume of distilled water at the same standard temperature (20°C). The specific gravity of a material multiplied by the unit weight of water gives the weight of 1 cubic metre of that substance. Some times this weight is known as *solid unit weight.* The weight of a given quantity of particles divided by the solid unit weight gives the *solid volume* of the particles.

$$\text{Solid vol. in m}^3 = \frac{\text{wt. of substance in kg}}{\text{specific gravity} \times 1000}$$

Bulk density. The weight of aggregate that would fill a container of unit volume is known as *bulk density* of aggregate. Its value for different materials as per concrete hand book CIA Bombay is shown in Table 4.10.

Table 4.10. Bulk density kg/lit. (concrete hand book CA-1 Bombay)

Material	*Specific gravity*
Cement	1.44
River sand fine	1.44
Medium	1.52
Coarse	1.60
River shingle	1.60
Broken stone	1.60
Stone screaning	1.44
Broken Granite	1.68

Voids. With respect to a mass of aggregate, the term *voids* refers to the space between the aggregate particles. Numerically this voids space is the difference between the gross volume of aggregate mass and the space occupied by the particles alone. The knowledge of voids of coarse and fine aggregate is useful in the mix design of concrete.

$$\text{Percentage voids} = \frac{G_s - \gamma}{G_s} \times 100$$

where G_s = specific gravity of aggregate and γ is bulk density in kg/litre.

Unit weight. The weight of a unit volume of aggregate is called as *unit weight.* For a given specific gravity, greater the unit weight, the smaller the percentage of voids and better the gradation of the particles, which affects the strength of concrete to a great extent.

Porosity and absorption of water by aggregate. As shown in Fig. 4.6, all aggregates. particles have pores with in their body. The characteristics of these pores are very important in the study of the properties of aggregate. The porosity, permeability, and absorption of aggregates influence the resistance of concrete to freezing and thawing, bond strength between aggregate and cement paste, resistance to abrasion of concrete etc.

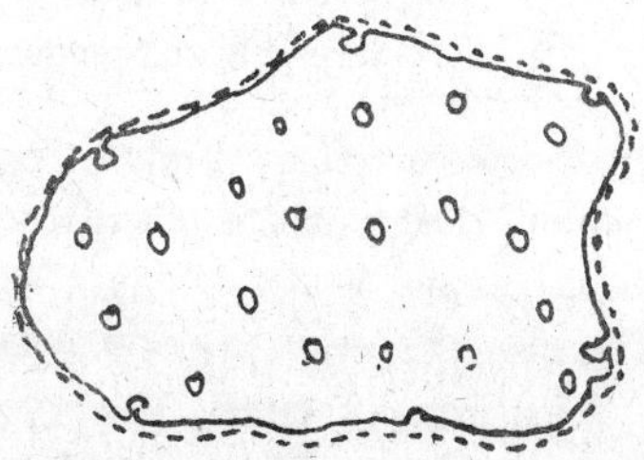

Fig. 4.6. Pores in the body of aggregate

The size of pores in the aggregate varies over a wide range, some being very large, which could be seen even with naked eye. The smallest pore of aggregate is generally larger than the gel pores in the cement paste. Pores smaller than 4 microns are of special interest as they are believed to affect the durability of aggregates subjected to alternate freezing and thawing. As shown in Fig. 4.6, some of the pores are wholly within the body of the aggregate particles and some of them are open upto the surface of the particle. The cement paste due to its viscosity can not penetrate to a great depth into the pores except the largest of the aggregate pores. Therefore, for the purpose of calculating the aggregate content in concrete, the gross volume of the aggregate particles is considered solid. However water can enter these pores, the amount and rate of penetration depends upon the size, continuity and total volume of pores.

When all the pores in the aggregate are full with water, then the aggregate is said to be saturated and surface dry. If this aggregate is allowed to stand in the laboratory, some of the moisture will evaporate and the aggregate will be known as air dry aggregate. If aggregate is dried in oven and no moisture is left in it, then it is known as *bone dry* aggregate. Thus the ratio of the increase in weight to the dry weight of the sample, expressed as a percentage is known as *absorption*. The knowledge of absorption of aggregate is important in adjusting water-cement ratio of the concrete. If water available in the aggregate is such that it contributes some water to the dilution of cement paste, in that case the water-cement ratio will be more than the required and the strength will go down. On the other hand, if the aggregate is so dry that it will absorb some of the mixing water, in that case the mix will have lower water-cement ratio and the mix may become unworkable. Hence, while deciding the water-cement ratio, it is assumed that the aggregate is in saturated but surface dry condition, *i.e.* neither it will add water to cement paste, nor it will absorb water from the mix. Fig. 4.7 shows aggregate and cement paste particles etc.

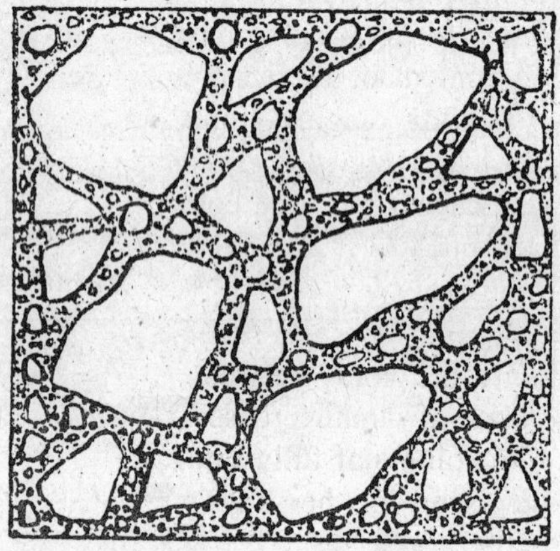

Fig. 4.7. General Structure of Concrete

It has been observed that absorption of water by dry aggregate slows down due to the coating of particles with cement paste. The water absorption by aggregate should be determined for 10 to 30 minutes instead of total water absorption. The value of absorption of water may be taken as follows as recommended by concrete hand book CAI Bombay in Table 4.11.

Table 4.11. Water absorption by aggregates

S. No.	*Aggregate*	*Moisture absorbed by wt of aggregate*
1.	Average sand	1.0 %
2.	Pebbles and crushed lime stone	1.0 %
3.	Granite and trap rock	0.5 %
4.	Porous sand stone	7.0 %
5.	Very light and porous aggregate	25.0 %

Surface water. While using aggregate in the concrete, water on the surface of the aggregate should be taken into account, as it will contribute to the water in the mix and will affect the water-cement ratio of the mix, causing lower strength of the concrete. It is difficult to measure surface water of the aggregate. Therefore its value may be assumed according to I.S. 456, 1964 given in Table 4.12.

Bulking of sand. The moisture present in fine aggregate causes increase in its volume, known as *bulking of sand.* The moisture in the fine aggregate develops a film of moisture around the particles of sand and due to surface tension push apart the sand particles, occupying greater volume. The bulking of the sand affects the mix proportion, if mix is designed b volume batching. Bulking results in smaller weight of sand

Table 4.12. Surface water carried by average aggregate

S. No.	*Aggregate*	*App. quantity of surface water in lit/m^3*
1.	Very wet sand	120.0
2.	Moderately wet sand	80.0
3.	Moist sand	40.0
4.	Moist gravel or crushed rock (as coarser the aggregate, lesser the surface water)	20 to 40

occupying the fixed volume of the measuring box, and the mix becomes deficient in sand and the resulting concrete becomes honeycombed and its yield is also reduced.

The extent of bulking depends upon the percentage of moisture present in sand and its fineness. The increase in volume relative to that occupied by a saturated and surface dry sand increases with an increase in the moisture content of the sand upto a value of 5 to 8%, causing bulking ranging from 20 to 40% as shown in Table 4.13. and Fig. 4.8. Table 4.13 shows bulking of sand with various moisture contents as suggested by concrete hand book CAI, Bombay.

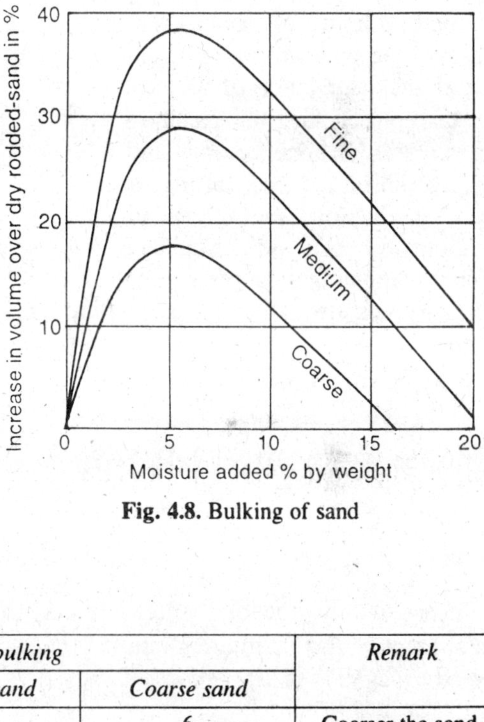

Fig. 4.8. Bulking of sand

As the moisture content increases, the film of water formed around the sand particles merge and the water moves into the voids between the particles so that the total volume of sand decreases, till the sand is fully saturated. The volume of fully saturated sand is same as that of the dry sand for the same method of filling the container.

Determination of bulking of sand. Since the volume of saturated sand is same as that of dry sand, the most convenient way of determining bulking of sand is by measuring the decrease in volume of the given sand on saturation. For the measurement of bulking of sand, usually a container of known volume, a 30 cm long steel rule, and a 6 mm iron rod is required.

Table 4.13.

S. No.	*Moisture percent*	*Percentage bulking*			*Remark*
		Fine sand	*Medium sand*	*Coarse sand*	
1.	1	16	8	6	Coarser the sand, lesser the bulking
2.	2	26	16	12	
3.	3	32	22	15	
4.	4	36	27	17	
5.	5	38.5	29	18	
6.	6	37	28	18	
7.	8	35	26	16	
8.	10	32	22	12	
9.	12	28	19		
10.	15	22	12	8	
11.	17	10	7	0	
12.	20	0	0	0	
13.	27	0	0	0	

Procedure. Put sufficient quantity of sand loosely into the container, till it is about two-thirds full. Level off the top of the sand with steel rule, and push this rule at the middle of the surface to the bottom of the container and measure its height. Let the height be h cm.

Now empty this sand into another container. While emptying, care should be taken that no sand particles are lost. Take about 1/3rd to half-full the first container with water and add about half the sand to it and rod it with 6 mm diameter steel rod. The sand should be roded till the air bubbles cease to come out. At this stage the volume of sand is minimum. At this stage add the remaining sand and rod it also till air bubbles cease to come out. Smooth and level the top surface of the saturated sand and measure its height by pushing the steel rule at the middle of the surface to the bottom of the container. Let this height be h_1 cm.

$$\text{Then \% bulking} = \frac{h - h_1}{h_1} \times 100 \qquad \ldots(4.1)$$

Effect of bulking of sand

For volume batching, bulking has to be allowed for by increasing the total volume of sand used, otherwise the mix will be deficient in sand and segregation of the mix may take place. Also the resulting concrete will be honeycombed and its yield will be reduced, raising its cost of production. The volume to be increased can be calculated either by knowing this percentage of bulking as shown above or by bulking factor.

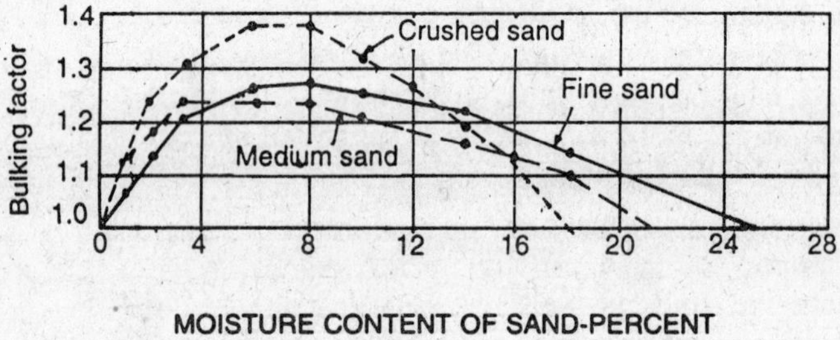

Fig. 4.9. Bulking factor for sand with different moisture contents

If,

V_m = vol. of moist sand

V_s = vol. of saturated sand

$$\text{then bulking} = \frac{V_m - V_s}{V_s}$$

$$\text{and bulking factor} = 1 + \frac{V_m - V_s}{V_s} = \frac{V_m}{V_s}$$

Hence to know the total volume of sand to be used can be calculated by multiplying the vol. V_s by the bulking factor. The value of bulking factor can be determined by the curves of Fig. 4.9. Fig. 4.9 gives bulking factor against moisture content upto 20% for three types of sands.

4.7. DELETERIOUS SUBSTANCE IN AGGREGATE

Deleterious substances can be classified into the following three categories.

1. Impurities which interfere with the process of hydration of cement.
2. Coatings on aggregates which prevent the development of good bond between aggregate and the cement paste.
3. Unsound or weak particle.

Organic impurities

Natural aggregates may be sufficiently strong and wear resistant, even then they may not be satisfactory for concrete making if they contain organic impurities which interfere with the hydration of cement. The organic matter found in aggregate usual.v is vegetable matter (mainly tanic acid and its derivatives) which appear in the form of humus or organic loam. Such materials are more likely to be present in fine aggregate (sand) than in coarse aggregate which is easily washed.

All organic matter is not found harmful and it is best to check the harmful effects by making actual test cubes. However it is time saving to ascertain first whether the amount of organic matter is sufficient to cause harmful effect to the concrete. The amount of organic matter can be determined as per I.S. 2386 part-II.

Test. The sand is taken as delivered at site without drying 3 percent solution of sodium hydroxide (NaOH) in water is filled in a 350 cc graduated clear bottle upto 75 cc mark. Now the given sample of sand is poured in this bottle gradually till the sand reaches upto 125 cc mark. The volume in the bottle is made upto 200 cc mark by adding more solution of 3% sodium hydroxide. The bottle is stoppered and shaken vigorously and then allowed to stand for 24 hours. The organic content can be judged by the colour of the solution above the sand. It has been found that greater the organic matter darker the colour of the solution.

The colour of the solution can be compared with a freshly prepared standard solution. This solution is prepared by adding 2.5 cc of 2 percent solution of tanic acid in 10% alcohol, to 97.5 cc of 3 percent sodium hydroxide solution. This solution is filled in a 350 cc bottle, stoppered and shaken vigorously and allowed to stand for 24 hours before comparision with the above solution.

If the observed colour is darker than the standard solution *i.e.* if the colour of the solution appears brownish or brown, then aggregate has a rather high quantity of organic matter and the further tests are necessary. Concrete cubes are made using the suspected aggregate and their strength is compared with concrete of the same mix proportions but made with aggregate of known quality.

Coatings on aggregates

Clay, silt and crusher dust etc. may be present in aggregate. Silt may be present in aggregate in the form of surface coatings and may interfere with the bond between the aggregate and cement paste. To have a good strength and durability concrete, it is essential to ensure a good bond between aggregate and cement paste. The problem of silt coating is important.

Silt and crusher dust also may form similar coatings as those of clay. These materials should not be present in excessive quantity as due to their fineness and large surface area, they need more water for wetting their surface and consequently need more water for a fixed water-cement ratio, to produce a concrete of a definite workability. The quantities of these materials may be determined by sedimentation method as per I.S. 2386 (Part-II)-1963 or B.S. 812 Part-I 1975. As per B.S. 882-1975, the quantities of all the three materials together should not be more than the following quantities:

1. 15% by weight in crushed stone sand.
2. 3% by weight in natural or crushed gravel sand.
3. 1% by weight in coarse aggregate.

Test. The quantities of three materials may be determined by sedimentation method. The sand sample is placed in a sodium oxalate solution (containing 8 gram sodium oxalate per lit of distilled water) in a stoppered jar and rotated with the axis of the jar horizontal for 15 minutes at approximately 10 revolutions per minute. The fine solids become dispersed and the amount of suspended material is then measured by means of Anderson pipette. The percentage of clay and fine dust is given by the relation.

$$\text{percentage of silt, clay or fine dust} = \frac{1000}{w_1}\left[\frac{100\, w_2}{v} - 0.8\right]$$

where,

w_1 = weight in gram of the original sample

w_2 = weight in gram of the dried residue

v = volume in cc or ml of the pipette

0.8 is the weight in gram of sodium oxalate in one lit. of dilute solution.

The result should be correct upto 0.1%.

Salt contamination

Sand excavated from sea shore or from the bed of river contains salt. If salt is not removed, it will absorb moisture from the air and cause efflorescence (unsightly) white deposits on the surface of concrete) and a slight corrosion of reinforcement may also result. However the danger of corrosion in good quality concrete with adequate cover to reinforcement is not of dangerous degree. These salts may be removed by washing sand with fresh water.

Sea bed sands may contain large quantity of shell contents. Though shell content is not found to have adverse effect on the strength of concrete but workability of concrete is reduced if aggregate having large content of shell is used.

Unsound particles. The unsound particles of aggregate may be classified into two categories as follows:

1. Those particles which fail to maintain their integrity.
2. Those particles that lead to disruptive expansion on freezing or even exposure to water. The disruptive properties are characteristics of certain rock groups.

Non durable impurities

Shale, clay lumps, wood, coal etc. and other particles of low density are regarded as unsound. If these particles used in concrete they may lead to pitting and scaling. If present more than 2 to 5% of the weight of aggregate, these particles may adversely affect the strength of concrete. Thus they should not be used in concrete which is exposed to abrasion.

Coal in addition to being soft material, is undesirable for other reasons as well. Coal swells very much, causing disruption of concrete. If present in large quantities in finely divided form, it can disturb the process of hardening of the cement paste. However discrete particles of hard coal amounting to not more than 0.5% of the weight of aggregate have no adverse effect on the strength of concrete.

The presence of coal and other low density materials can be determined by flotation in a liquid of suitable specific gravity.

Mica. The presence of mica in fine aggregate even by few percent of the weight of the aggregate affects adversely the water requirement and consequently the strength of the concrete. The presence of mica in the fine aggregate has been found to reduce considerably the durability and compressive strength of concrete. Hence its effects on the concrete should be determined. Thus before using a aggregate, its mica contents should be determined and an allowance is made for the possible reduction in the strength.

Iron pyrites. It is the most expansive material in the aggregate. This sulphide reacts with water and oxygen in the air to form ferrous sulphate which subsequently decomposes to form hydroxide, and the sulphate ions react with the calcium aluminate in the cement. Due to this chain reaction, surface staining of the concrete and disruption of the cement paste may result, particularly under warm and humid conditions.

Gypsum and other sulphates also should not be present in the aggregate. The permissible quantities of deleterious substances is shown in Table 4.14 as per I.S. 384-1970.

Soundness of aggregates

The ability of aggregate to resist excessive changes in volume due to the changes in physical conditions is known as soundness of aggregate. The physical causes of permanent volume changes of aggregate are freezing and thawing, thermal changes at temperatures above freezing, and alternate wetting and drying.

A aggregate is said to be unsound when volume changes induced by the above causes, results in deterioration of concrete. This may range from local scaling to extensive surface cracking and to disintegration

Table 4.14. Showing limits of deterious substances

Deleterious substance	*Fine aggregate*		*Coarse aggregate*		*Method of test*
	Uncrushed	*Crushed*	*Uncrushed*	*Crushed*	
Coal and lignite	1.00	1.00	1.00	1.00	IS-2386 1963 part II
Clay lumps	1.00	1.0	1.00	1.00	– do –
Soft fragnents	—	—	3.00	—	– do –
Materials passing 75 micron sieve	3.00	1.5	3.00	1.00	Part I
Shale	1.00	—	—	—	do Part II
Total	5.00	2.50	8.00	3.00	

over considerable depth and can thus vary from impaired surface to structurally dangerous situation.

Test. A test for soundness of aggregate can be performed as described in I.S. 2386 Part-V-1963. In this test the sample of graded aggregate is subjected alternately to immersion in the saturated solution of sodium or magnesium sulphate for not less than 16 hours and not more than 18 hours in such a manner that the solution covers the aggregate to a depth of at least 15 mm. The evaporation of solution is checked by covering the container. The temperature of the test is maintained at 27± 1°C.

After immersion, the aggregate is removed from the solution and allowed to be drained for 15 ± 5 minutes and placed in the oven at temperature of 105°C to 110°C. The sample is dried to constant weight at this temperature. The formation of salt crystals in the pores of aggregate tend to disrupt the aggregate particles in a similar manner as the action of ice. The reduction in size of the particles as shown by sieve analysis, after a number of cycles of exposure denotes the degree of unsoundness. No. of cycles of exposure depends upon the mutual agreement of the supplier and the purchaser.

4.8. ALKALI AGGREGATE REACTION

Till 1940, aggregates were considered as inert materials, but after 1940, it has been clearly established that aggregates are not fully inert. Some of the aggregates contain reactive silica which react with the alkalis (Sodium oxide Na_2O and potassium oxide K_2o) present in cement.

For the first time in U.S.A. it was observed that many failures of concrete structures as sea walls, piers and pavements occurred due to the alkali-aggregate reaction. On the basis of systematic study since these failure now it has been established beyond doubt that certain type of reactive aggregates are responsible for promoting alkali-aggregate reaction.

The rocks which contain reactive constituents are siliceous lime stones, trap, andesite and certain types of sand stones. The reactive constituents may be in the form of volcanic glass, zeolites, opals, charts etc. The reaction starts with the attack on the reactive siliceous minerals in the aggregate by the alkaline hydroxide formed by the alkaline hydroxide (K_2o and Na_2o) present in the cement. As a result of this reaction the alkali silicate gel of unlimited swelling property is formed and the alteration of boarders of the aggregates take place. This gel swells if favourable conditions for its swelling are met. The gel swells by absorbing water. As this gel is confined by the surrounding cement paste, internal pressure increases resulting disruption of concrete by expansion, and cracking of concrete and eventually failure of concrete structures takes place. The rate of deterioration may be fast or slow depending upon the conditions.

The expansion may be due to hydraulic pressure generated by the process of osmosis but it can also be caused by the swelling pressure of the still solid products of the alkali silica reaction. It is believed that the swelling of the hard aggregate particles is most harmful to the concrete. Some of the relatively soft gel latter is leached out by water and deposited in the cracks already formed by the swelling of the aggregate. The size of siliceous particles controls the speed with which reaction takes place. Fine particles of 20 to 30 microns lead to expansion with in a month or two, while larger particles cause expansion only after some years.

4.9. FACTORS EFFECTING THE REACTIVITY OF AGGREGATES

Following factors affect the reactivity of aggregates

(*a*) *Particle size and its porosity.* These factors influence the surface area over which the reaction takes place.

(*b*) *Quantity of cement.* The quantity of alkalies depends on the quantity of cement. The minimum quantity of alkali in cement at which expansive reaction may take place is 0.6 percent of the soda equivalent ($Na_2o + 0.658\ K_2o$). The quantity ($Na_2o + 0.658\ K_2o$) is known as soda equivalent.

(*c*) Availability of non evaporable water in the paste.

(*d*) Permeability of paste.

(*e*) Type of aggregate.

(*f*) Optimum temperature conditions.

The reaction is accelerated under conditions of alternate wetting any drying. Moisture is necessary for the reaction to take place. The necessity of the presence of $Ca(OH)_2$ also has been suggested. The ideal condition of temperature for the promotion of alkali aggregate reaction is the range of 10 to 38°C. The temperature above or below this range is not ideal for this reaction. Thus various physical and chemical factors make the problems of alkali aggregate reaction complex. In particular the gel can change its constitution by absorption and thus exerts a considerable pressure, while at other times diffusion of the gel out of the confined area takes place. It may be noted that as the hydration of cement progresses, much of the alkali concentrates in the aqueous phase raising PH value and all silica minerals become soluble.

Though it can be predicted that with the given materials an alkali aggregate reaction will take place, but generally it is not possible to estimate the extent of deleterious effects from the knowledge of the quantities of the reactive materials alone.

The potential reactivity of aggregate can be determined as suggested by I.S. 2386 Part VII-1963.

The aggregate is pulverized and treated for 24 hours with a normal solution of sodium hydroxide (NaOH) at 80°C. The degree of reactivity is determined from the amount of silica dissolved by the solution and reduction in alkalinity of the solution. The aggregate is pulverized and sieved to pass a 300 micron sieve and retained on a 150 micron sieve. The finer material than 50 micron is removed and the sample washed and dried at 100°C to 105°C for 20 ± 4 hours. This sample is now cooled and sieved on 150 micron sieve again.

Now weigh three samples of 25 grams each from the prepared sample as described above. Each of the three sample is put into three separate reaction containers and 25 c.c. solution of 1 N (normality) of sodium hydroxide (NaOH) is added to each container. In a fourth container only sodium hydroxide solution of the same consistency is taken. All the four containers are sealed and gently shaken to liberate trapped air. After sealing these containers they are put in liquid bath at 80 ± 1°C for 24 hours. After $24 \pm \frac{1}{4}$ hours the containers are removed from the water bath and çooled for 15 ± 2 minutes under flowing water till the temperature falls below 30°C.

After cooling, the containers are opened and their solutions filtered and the filtrate is collected in flasks. After the completion of filtration, the filtrate is stirred. Now take about 10 c.c. of filtrate and dilute it with water to 200 c.c. in a volumetric flask. This dilute is used for the determination of dissolved silica and reduction in alkalinity.

4.9.1. Determination of dissolved silica

The quantity of dissolved silica can be determined either by gravimetric method or by the photometric method. Here only gravi-metric method has been discussed. In this method 100 c.c. dilute filtrate as prepared above is transferred to an evaporating dish and 5 to 10 c.c. of hydrochloric acid (HCl of Sp. gr. 1.19) is added and the dilute is evaporated to dryness on a steam bath. Now without further heating of the residue, it is treated with 5 to 10 c.c. of HCl (Sp. gr. 1.19), and again evaporated to dryness on the steam bath. Now the 10 c.c. to 20 c.c. of HCl (1:1) is poured on this residue, covered and left for 10 minutes on a hot-plate. Now the solution is diluted with hot water and filtered. The separated silica is washed with hot water and the residue is kept reserved.

Again this filtrate is evaporated to dryness by heating in a oven for one hour at 105°C to 110°C. The residue is treated with 10 c.c. to 15 c.c. HCl (1:1) and heated on a hot plate. The solution is diluted with hot water and filtered to separate any silica particles left. The filter paper along with the silica particle is put in a platinum crucible and ignited. When the filter paper is completely burnt, then it is heated upto 1100°C to 1200°C till the weight becomes constant. The results obtained are plotted as shown in Fig. 4.10. The degree of alkali reactivity is indicated if the plotted data falls to the right of the boundary line shown in the above figure. If the test results fall on right side of the curve of Fig. 4.10 then the aggregate is reactive and not suitable for concrete. If the results fall on left of the curve, the aggregates may be used in the concrete. For further details refer I.S. 2386 part VII-1963,

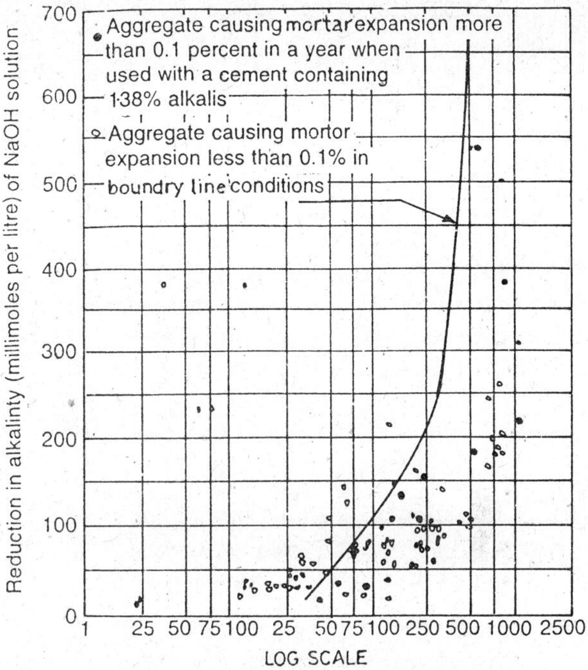

SILLICA DISSOLVED FROM 300 μm TO 150 μm AGGREGATE MATI (MILLIMOLES PER LITRE) BY NaOH SOLUTION

Fig. 4.10.

Mortar bar expansion test

As suggested by STANTON this test has proved to be very reliable for determining the reactivity of the aggregate. The test is carried out as per IS 2386-1963 Part VII. A specimen of size 25 mm × 25 mm and 250 mm length is cast. cured and stored as per IS 2386 part-VII. The length of the specimen is measured periodically at the age of 1, 2, 3, 5, 9 and 12 months The difference in length of the specimen is observed nearest to 0.001% and the expansion of the specimen is noted. If the expansion after 3 months is found more than 0.05% and after 6 months more than 0.1%, then the aggregate tested is harmful and should be rejected.

4.9.3. High Alkali content in Cement

As stated above high alkali content in cement is the most important factors contributing to the alkali aggregate reaction. As per standard specification the contents of alkali in the cement should be less than 0.6%. A cement containing total alkali (Na_2o + 0.658 K_20) known as soda equivalent as 0.6% is called low alkali cement. Generally Indian cements do not contain high alkalies as that of U.K. and U.S.A cements. The results of investigations on Indian cements for alkali contents are shown in the table 4.15 below. From the table it will be seen that out of 26 samples only 11 showed more than 0.6 alkali content. These results are based on cements manufactured before 1975. The present day modern cements have even lower alkali contents.

Table 4.15

No. of samples	*Alkali content %*	*% of No. of samples to the total*
1	2	3
8	Below 0.40	30.0
7	0.40 – 0.60	26.9
5	0.60 – 0.80	19.2
6	0.60 – 1.0	23.1
NIL	Above 1.0	NIL

Reduction in alkalinity

20 c.c. out of 200 c.c. of dilute prepared for the test in a flask is taken and 2 or 3 drops of Phenolphthalein, solution is added to it. Now this solution is titrated with 0.1 N HCl to the end point of the Phenophihalein, then reduction in alkalinity is given:

$$\text{Re} = \frac{20\,N}{V_1}(V_3 - V_2) \times 1000$$

where,

Re = Reduction in alkalinity in milimoles per litre.

N = Normality of HCl used for titration.

V_1 = Vol. in ml (c.c.) of dilute solution used.

V_2 = Vol. of HCl used to attain the end point of phenolphthalein in the test.

V_3 = Vol. of HCl used to attain the end point of phenolphthalein with the blank.

4.10. CONTROL OF ALKALI AGGREGATE REACTION

The alkali aggregate reaction can be controlled by the following methods

1. By the selection of non reactive aggregates.
2. By the use of low alkali cement 0.6 to 0.4 alkali content cement.
3. By the use of admixtures such as pozzolana.
4. By controlling void space in concrete.
5. By controlling moisture and temperature.

Presence of water or moisture is necessary for the development of alkali-aggregate reaction. It has been observed experimentally that lack of water greatly reduces this reaction. This deterioration will not occur in the interior of mass concrete, but will be more on the surface. The deterioration of surface may be controlled by the application of some water proofing agents on the surface of the concrete which will prevent the in gress of water into the structure.

Temp Conditions. As stated above the ideal range of temperature for the promotion of alkali-aggregate reaction is 10°C to 38°C. If the temperature condition is less or more than this, it will not provide an ideal condition for the promotion of alkali-aggregate reaction.

4.11. THERMAL PROPERTIES OF AGGREGATE

Following thermal properties of aggregate are significant in the performance of concrete:

1. Coefficient of thermal expansion.
2. Specific heat and
3. Conductivity

1. Coefficient of thermal expansion of aggregate. It influences the value of the coefficient of thermal expansion of concrete containing the given aggregate. Higher the coefficient of expansion of the aggregate, higher the coefficient of expansion of the concrete. However the coefficient of thermal expansion of concrete also depends upon the aggregate content in the mix and the mix proportions as well. However it has been seen that changes in temperature upto 60°C have no large difference between the coefficients of aggregate and concrete. Thermal coefficients of linear expansion of some rocks are shown in Table 4.16. Specific heat and conductivity will be discussed along with mass concrete.

Table 4.16. Showing value of coefficient of thermal expansion

S. No.	*Type of rock*	*Thermal coefficient of linear expansion 10^{-6} per°C*	*Remark*
1.	Granite	1.8 to 11.9	
2.	Diorite	4.1 to 10.3	
3.	Basalt, Gabbro	3.6 to 9.7	
4.	Sand stone	4.3 to 13.9	
5.	Dolomite	6.7 to 8.6	
6.	Lime stone	0.9 to 12.2	
7.	Marble	1.1 to 16.0	

4.12. SIEVE ANALYSIS

The operation of dividing a sample of aggregate into fractions, each fraction consisting particles of the same size is called sieve analysis. In practice each fraction contains particles between the openings of the standard test sieves. Test sieves used for concrete aggregates have square openings and described by the size of the openings in mm for larger sizes and by the number of openings per lineal cm for sieves smaller than about 3 mm. Coarser test sieves (4 mm and larger) are made of perforated mild steel plate with a screening area of 44 to 65 percent, where as smaller sieves (less than 4 mm) are made of wire cloth. The screening area in this case varies between 34 to 53 percent of the gross area of the sieve.

The sieves used for concrete aggregate consist of a series in which the clear opening of any sieve is approximately one half of the opening of the next larger sieve sizes. Usually sieve sizes used for concrete aggregate as per I.S. 383-1970 are as follows:

80.0, 63.0, 40.0, 20.0, 16.0, 12.5, 10.0, 4.75, 2.36 and 1.18 mm, 600 micron, 300 micron, and 150 micron. In U.K. as per B.S. 812. Part-I, for grading aggregate following sieves are used:

75.0, 50.0, 37.5, 20.0, 10.0, 5.0, 2.36, 1.18 mm and 600, 300 and 150 micron. The standard British and American sieve sizes are shown in Table 4.17.

Table 4.17. Showing Aperture sizes of I.S., B.S. and ASTM Sieves

I.S. 460-1962		*B.S. 410-1962*		*ASTM 11-1961*	
Sieve designation	*Width of aperture mm*	*Width of aperture mm*	*Mesh No.*	*Sieve designation (standard)*	*Width of aperture mm*
5.60 mm	5.6	—	—	5.66 mm	5.66
4.75 mm	4.75	—	—	4.76 mm	4.76
4.00 mm	4.00	—	—	4.00 mm	4.00
3.35 mm	3.35	3.35	5	3.36 mm	3.36
2.80 mm	2.80	2.8	6	2.83 mm	2.83
2.36 mm	2.36	2.40	7	2.38 mm	2.38
2.00 mm	2.00	2.00	8	2.00 mm	2.00
1.70 mm	1.70	1.68	10	1.68 mm	1.68
1.40 mm	1.40	1.40	12	1.41 mm	1.41

I.S. 460-1962		*B.S. 410-1962*		*ASTM 11-1961*	
Sieve designation	*Width of aperture mm*	*Width of aperture mm*	*Mesh No.*	*Sieve designation (standard)*	*Width of aperture mm*
1.18 mm	1.18	1.20	14	1.19 mm	1.19
1.00 mm	1.00	1.00	16	1.00 mm	1.00
850 μ (micron)	0.850	850 μ (micron)	18	841 μ (micron)	0.841
710 μ (micron)	0.710	710 μ (micron)	22	707 μ (micron)	0.707
600 μ (micron)	0.600	600 μ (micron)	25	595 μ (micron)	0.595
500 μ (micron)	0.500	500 μ (micron)	30	500 μ (micron)	0.500
425 μ (micron)	0.425	420 μ (micron)	36	420 μ (micron)	0.420
355 μ (micron)	0.355	355 μ (micron)	44	354 μ (micron)	0.354
300 μ (micron)	0.300	300 μ (micron)	52	297 μ (micron)	0.297
250 μ (micron)	0.250	250 μ (micron)	60	250 μ (micron)	0.250
212 μ (micron)	0.212	210 μ (micron)	72	210 μ (micron)	0.210
180 μ (micron)	0.180	180 μ (micron)	85	177 μ (micron)	0.177
150 μ (micron)	0.150	150 μ (micron)	100	149 μ (micron)	0.149
125 μ (micron)	0.125	125 μ (micron)	120	125 μ (micron)	0.125
106 μ (micron)	0.106	105 μ (micron)	150	105 μ (micron)	0.105
90 μ (micron)	0.090	90 μ (micron)	170	88 μ (micron)	0.088
75 μ (micron)	0.075	75 μ (micron)	200	74 μ (micron)	0.074
63 μ (micron)	0.063	63 μ (micron)	240	63 μ (micron)	0.063
53 μ (micron)	0.053	53 μ (micron)	300	53 μ (micron)	0.053
45 μ (micron)	0.045	45 μ (micron)	350	44 μ (micron)	0.040

In order to obtain satisfactory and comparable results from sieve analysis sample of the aggregate must be representative of the lot. To reduce a large sample to the size of the test, quartering of the aggregate is advocated. Before resorting to quartering, sampling of the aggregate is essential. The lot of the aggregate should be divided into the sub-lots depending upon the volume or size of the lot as shown in Table 4.18.

Table 4.18.

Size of lot in m^3	*No. of sub-lot*
101 – 500	3 No
501 – 1500	5 No
1500 – 5000	7 No

After dividing the aggregate into sub-lots, the representative gross sample should be taken from each sub-lot from the full cross section and thickness of the sub-lot and should be kept separate for each sub-lot. Scoop may be used for sampling as shown in Fig. 4.11.

It's dimensions vary according to its capacity as shown in table 4.19 The number of increment to be taken and weight of gross sample are shown in Table 4.19.

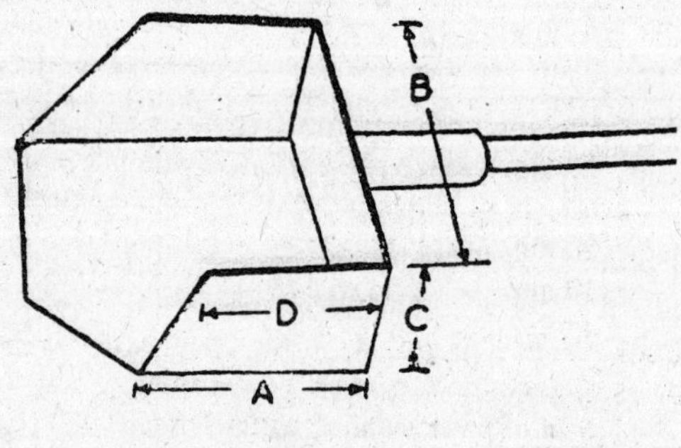

Fig. 4.11. Scoop for taking samples

Table. 4.19.

S. No.	Capacity of scoop in kg.	Dimensions of the scoop in mm			
		A	B	C	D
1.	10	250	250	120	200
2.	5	200	200	90	175
3.	2	150	150	75	125

Table 4.20. Minimum weights of the gross sample and minimum No. of increments

S. No.	Max. size present in substantial proportion	Weight of gross sample minimum in kg	Weight of increment kg (app.)	No. of increments minimum
1.	Coarse and all in aggregate (Nominal size more than 20 mm)	300	10	30
2.	Coarse and all in aggregate (Upto 20 mm nominal size)	200	5	40
3.	Fine aggregate	100	2	50

After drawing the sample, it should be spread on a clean surface and divided into four quarters, discart two diametrically opposite quarters and combine the remaining two quarters The process should be repeated till the size of sample is reduced to the required quantity.

Before the sieve analysis is performed, the aggregate sample should be air dried to avoid lumps of fine particles and also to prevent clogging of the finer sieves. The weights of the reduced samples for sieving as per I.S. 2386-1963 is shown in Table 4.21.

Table 4.21. Sizes of samples required for various Tests.

	Test	Minimum sample size	
		To be available in the laboratory	To be tested
A.	**Sieve analysis**		
	Maximum size present in substantial proportions		
	63 mm	150	50
	50 mm	150	35
	40 mm to 31.5 mm	50	15
	25 mm	15	5
	20 mm to 16 mm	10	2
	12.5 mm	5	1
	10.0 mm	2	0.5
	6.3 mm	2	0.2
	4.75 mm	2	0.2
	2.36 mm	2	0.1
B.	**Determination of material finer than 75 micron**		
	Maximum size present in substantial proportions		
	40 mm or above	20	5.0
	20 mm	10	2.5
	10 mm	10	2.0
	4.75 mm	5	0.5
C.	**Determination of clay lumps**		
	Size of particles making up sample		
	40 mm or above	20	5
	40 mm to 20 mm	15	3
	20 mm to 10 mm	10	2
	10 mm to 4.75 mm	5	1

	Test	Minimum sample size	
		To be available in the laboratory	*To be tested*
D.	**Determination of clay, fine silt and fine dust**		
	Maximum size present in substantial proportions		
	63 mm to 25 mm	30	6
	20 mm to 12.5 mm	20	1
	10 mm to 6.3 mm	10	0.5
	4.7 mm and smaller	10	0.3
E.	**Determination of light weight pieces (coal and lignite etc.)**		
	80 mm	50	10
	40 mm	25	5
	20 mm	15	3
	6.3 mm	5	0.2
F.	**Determination of soft particles**		
	Maximum size of aggregate		
	63 mm to 40 mm	60	12
	40 mm to 25 mm	30	4.5
	25 mm to 20 mm	10	1.5
	20 mm to 12.5 mm	5	0.6
	12.5 mm to 10 mm	5	0.2
G.	**Determinaton of fineness**		
	Coarse Agg.	60	10
	Fine Agg.	10	1
H.	**Determination of abrasion value by**		
	(*a*) Los Angeles test	300	50
	(*b*) By DEVAL machine	30	6
I.	**Determination of impact value by**	5	1
J.	**Determination of**		
	(a) Ten percent value	30	7
	(b) Crushing value	30	7
K.	**Determination of bulk density of voids**		
	Maximum size of aggregate.		
	Over 40 mm	150	60
	40 mm to 4.75 mm	100	30
	Less than 4.75 mm	20	6
L.	**Determination of Sp. gr. and water absorption**		
	Aggregate larger than 10 mm	10	2
	10 mm to 4.75 mm	5	1
	Less than 4.75 mm	3	0.5
M.	**Determination of organic impurities**	5	0.5

4.13. GRADING CURVES

The graphical representation of the results of sieve analysis is called grading curves. By using grading curves it is possible to see at a glance whether the grading of a given sample confirms to that specified or is too coarse, or too fine or deficient or in excess in a particular size. In the grading curves usually ordinates represent cumulative percentage passing and abscissa the sieve opening plotted to a logarithmic scale. A logarithmic plot shows these openings at a constant spacing as the openings of sieves in a standard series are in the ratio of 1/2.

Requirements of Grading curves

The grading of the aggregate should be such that mix prepared by it could be compacted to a maximum density with a reasonable amount of work for a given water cement ratio. It means that the grading should be such that the voids of the larger particles are filled by the next lower fraction and so on and the voids of fine aggregate are filled by cement. The strength of a fully compacted concrete with a given water/cement ratio is independent of the grading of the aggregate. Grading only affects the workability of the mix and the development of strength corresponding to a given water/cement ratio requires full compaction, which can be achieved only with the sufficiently workable mix. In actual practice there is no ideal grading curve, but a compromise is aimed at.

4.14. FACTORS AFFECTING THE GRADING OF AGGREGATE

Following factors affect the grading of aggregate:

1. Surface area of the aggregate
2. Relative volume occupied by the aggregate
3. Workability of the mix
4. Segregation of the mix.

1. Surface area of the aggregate

For a given maximum size of aggregate, larger the size of aggregate particles, lesser the surface area of aggregate in a given mix, which will require lesser amount of water to wet its surface and greater portion of the water will be available for imparting workability to the mix for a particular water-cement ratio.

The water/cement ratio of the mix is generally fixed from strength Consideration, but at the same time, the amount of cement paste should be sufficient to cover the surface of all the particles so that lower the surface area of the aggregate, the less paste and thus less water is required. Assuming the aggregate particle as spherical of diameter D, the ratio of the surface area to volume comes out to be 6/D. This ratio of the surface of the particle to their volume is called *specific surface*, which is inversely proportional to the particle size, but the coefficient of 6/D will be different for different shape of particles. It is also defined as the surface area per unit weight.

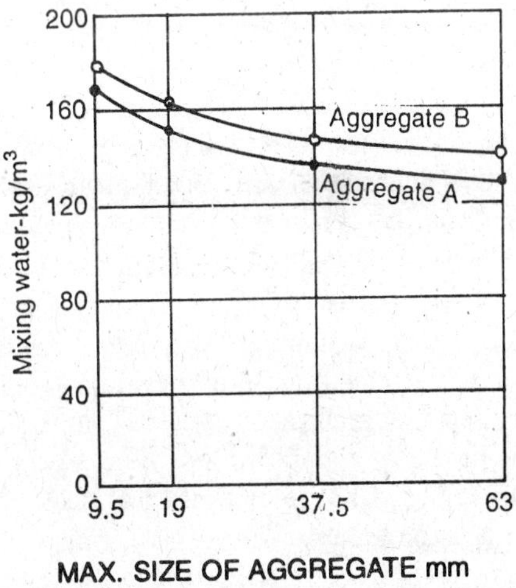

Fig. 4.12. Influence of Max. size of aggregate on mixing water required for a constant slump.

In case of graded aggregate, the grading and the over all specific surface is related to one another. If the grading extends to a larger maximum aggregate size, the over all specific surface is reduced and the water requirement decreases, but the relation is not linear.

For example if the size of aggregate is increased from 10 mm to 63 mm, under certain conditions, the water/cement ratio can be decreased by 0.15. Variation of water reduction with the increase in the aggregate size is shown in Fig. 4.12. From the study of the Fig. 4.12 it will be clear that by the increase of particle size about 50 kg. water per cubic metre of concrete can be reduced.

The specific surface is found to give some what misleading picture of the workability to be expected. An increase in the specific surface of the aggregate for a constant water/cement ratio has been found to lead to a lower strength of concrete. The reasons for this are not quite clear. It may be possible that a reduction in density of the concrete consequent upon an increase in fineness of the aggregate is instrumental in lowering the strength. Though it seems that the surface area of the aggregate is an important factor in determining the workability of the mix, but the exact role played by the finer particles has not been ascertained.

2. Relative volume occupied by the aggregate

For a mix to be satisfactorily workable, it must contain a sufficient amount of material smaller than 300 micron size including cement particles. Thus a richer mix requires a lower content of fine aggregate than a lean mix. If the grading of fine aggregate (sand) is such that it is deficient in finer particles, in that case increase in fine/coarse aggregate ratio will not prove useful as it may lead to an excess of middle sizes resulting in harshness of the mix. (A mix is said to be harsh when one size fraction present is in excess, as shown by steep step in the middle of grading curve so that particle interference results). For this reason the minimum contents of particles passing 300 and 150 micron are laid down. Some times particles passing through 150 micron are suggested as shown in Table 4.22.

Table 4.22. Vol. of fine aggregate

Maximum aggregate size in mm	*Absolute volume of fines as a fraction of volume of concrete*
63.0	0.110
32.0	0.125
16.0	0.140
8.0	0.165

The volume of entrained air can be taken as equivalent to one half of the volume of fines and should be included in the above figures. This approach has been adopted by the Germans and Dutch for the mix design.

The requirement that the aggregate should occupy as large a relative volume as possible is due to economic considerations, as aggregate is cheaper than the cement paste. Technically also, too rich mixes are undesirable, as they suffer from the defect of excessive shrinkage.

Further it has also been assumed that greater the amount of solid particles that can be packed into a volume of concrete higher the strength. Thus the maximum density theory has suggested the grading curves as parabolic in shape or partly parabolic and then straight as shown in Fig. 4.13. However it has been observed that aggregate graded to give maximum density produce a harsh and unworkable mix.

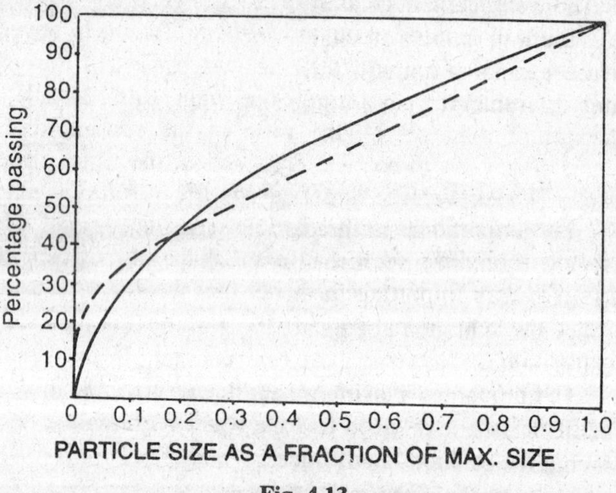

Fig. 4.13

3. Workability of the mix

The workability is improved when there is an excess of paste above that required to fill the voids in the fine aggregate, and also an excess of mortar above that required to fill the voids in the coarse aggregate.

4. Segregation

It can be defined as separation of the constituents of a heterogeneous mixture so that their distribution is no longer uniform. In the case of concrete the difference in the size of particles and in the specific gravity of the mix constituents is the main cause of segregation, but its extent can be controlled by the choice of suitable grading and by care in handling.

Types of segregation

Segregation can be divided into two categories as follows:

1. The coarser particles tend to separate. In this case the coarser particles tend to travel further along a slope or to settle more than finer particles. This type of segregation occurs in lean mixes when with some gradings too dry mix is prepared. Addition of water will improve workability.

2. Grout separates out from the mix. This type of segregation occurs in wet mixes. The grout (cement slurry) separates out from the rest of the mix. If in a lean mix, excessive water is used, this type of segregation will occur.

Segregation is affected by grading of aggregate. The grading should be such that the mortar should be prevented from passing freely out of the voids in the coarse aggregate. It is also essential for the voids in the combined aggregate to be sufficiently small to prevent the cement paste from passing through and separating out.

The actual extent of segregation depends on the method of handling and placing of concrete. While handling concrete it should not be allowed to drop from a height of more than 1 m. Dropping of concrete from a considerable height, passing along a chute, particularly with changes of direction and discharging against an obstacle lead to segregation. Hence by adopting correct method of handling and placing, segregation of concrete can be checked.

Thus there is no doubt that the grading of aggregate is a major factor in the workability of a concrete mix. Workability in turn affects the water and cement requirements, controls segregation and bleeding and influences the placing and finishing of concrete. These factors influence the properties of green as well as hardened concrete such as strength, shrinkage and durability.

Grading is thus of vital importance in proportioning of concrete mixes, but its exact role in mathematical terms is not still fully known. Finally it can be said that ensuring a constant grading is far more important than devising a good grading, otherwise variable workability will produce concrete of variable strength.

4.15. PRACTICAL GRADINGS

The importance of grading of aggregate has already been discussed in the previous section. The grading should be such that it could give a reasonable workability with minimum segregation. Segregation is very important in the production of good concrete. A workable mixture which could produce a strong and economical concrete will result in honey combed, weak, undurable and variable end product if segregation takes place.

The process of calculation of the proportions of aggregates of different sizes to achieve the desired grading comes within the scope of mix design and is discussed in chapter 20 on mix design. Here properties of some good grading curves have been discussed. Usually aggregate available locally or within an economic distance has to be used. It can produce satisfactory concrete, if sufficient care and intelligent approach is adopted. In India no ideal grading curves have been prepared. However Road Research Institute U.K. has prepared some curves using 19.0 mm and 38 mm maximum size aggregates. These curves are shown in Fig. 4.14 and 4.15 respectively.

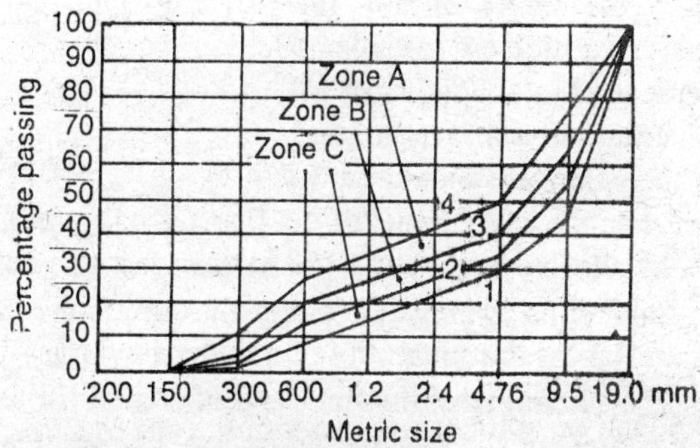

Fig. 4.14. Grading curves–Max size 19.0 mm

Four curves are shown for each maximum size of aggregate, but due to the presence of over and under size aggregate and also due to variation within any fraction size, practical gradings may be in the vicinity of these curves than to follow them exactly. Therefore it is convenient to specify grading zones rather than a single curve. These zones are marked on the curves.

Curve No. 1 represents the coarsest grading in each set of curves. These gradings are comparatively workable and can be used for mixes with low water/cement ratio or for rich mixes. How ever it should be ensured that no segregation takes place. At the other extreme, curve No. 4 represents a fine grading. It will be cohesive, but not very workable. In particular, an excess of material between 1.20 and 4.75 mm test sieves will produce a harsh concrete, which may be compacted by vibration, but difficult to place by hand. If the same workability is to be obtained using aggregates with grading curve No. 4 and 1, the latter would require a considerably higher water content. This means a lower strength if both concretes are to have the same aggregate/cement ratio or if the same strength is required, the concrete made with fine aggregate would have to be considerably richer. The change between the extreme gradings should be progressive. In case of gradings lying partly in one zone and partly in another, there is likely hood of segregation if too many intermediate sizes are missing. If on the other hand there is an excess of middle sized aggregate, the mix will be harsh and difficult to compact with hand and possibly even by vibration. Therefore it is preferable to use aggregate with grading similar to type rather than totally dissimilar ones.

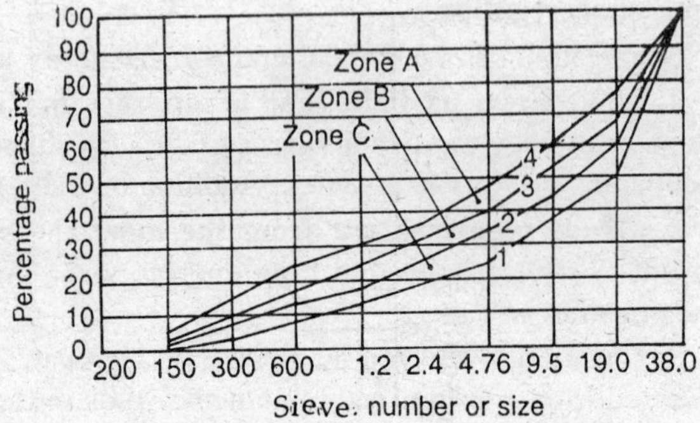

Fig. 4.15. Grading curves–Max size 38 mm

4.16. GRADING OF FINE AND COARSE AGGREGATES

For all important works coarse and fine aggregates are batched separately, hence their grading should be known and controlled. Grading curves of the four zones of fine sand of table 4.3 as per I.S. 386 Part-I 1963 are shown in Fig. 4.16 to 4.19. The grading curve of any fine aggregate falling wholly within the limits of any one zone is considered suitable. A tolerance of total amount of 5% on certain sieves is permitted, but the aggregate should not be finer than the exact limits of the finest grading or coarser than the coarset grading. In case of crushed stone 20% is allowed to pass the 150 micron test sieve in all zones.

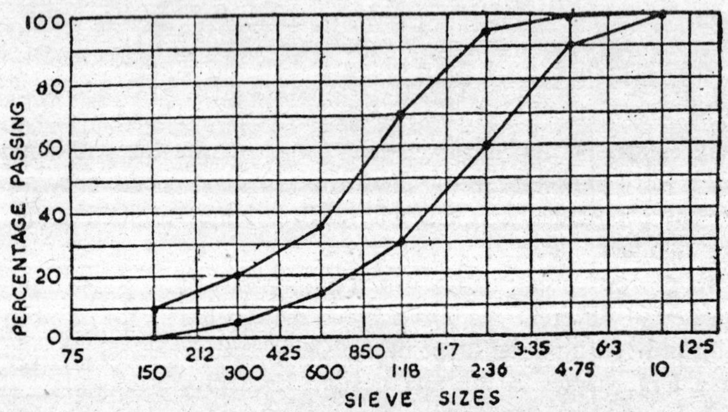

Fig. 4.16. Grading limits for zone no. I of fine aggregate

Sand (fine aggregate) falling into any zone can be generally used in concrete, although under some circumstances the suitability of a given sand may depend on the grading and shape of the coarse aggregate.

The suitability of the fine sand of zone 4 for use in reinforced concrete should be tested. For sands, the sand content of the mix should be low whose greater part is smaller than 600 micron. In general, finer the grading of the fine aggregate, higher should be the coarse/fine aggregate ratio. Typical values are shown in Table 4.23.

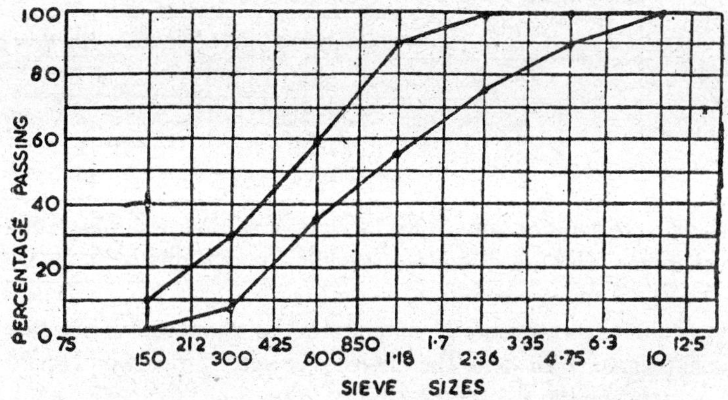

Fig 4.17. Grading limits for zone no. II of fine aggregate

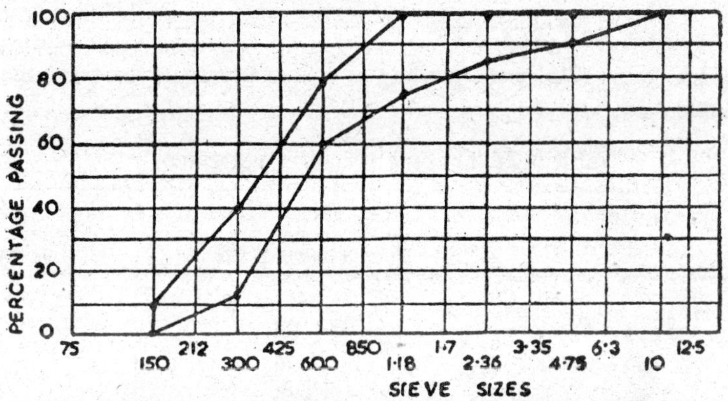

Fig. 4.18. Grading limits for zone no. III of fine aggregate

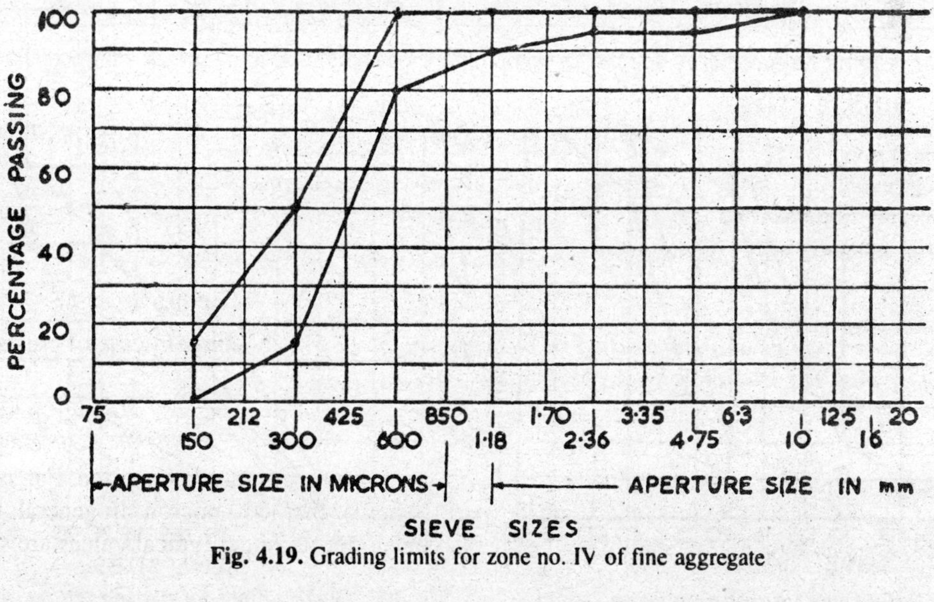

Fig. 4.19. Grading limits for zone no. IV of fine aggregate

Table 4.23. Ratio of fine and coarse aggregate

S. No.	Maximum size of coarse aggregate in mm	Coarse/fine aggregate ratio for sand of zone			
		1	2	3	4
1.	10.0	1 : 1	1 : 1.5	1 : 2	1 : 3.0
2.	19.0	1 : 1.5	1 : 2	1 : 3	1 : 3.5
3.	38.0	1 : 2	1 : 3	1 : 3.5	—

On the other hand the coarse sand of zone I produces a harsh mix and a high content of sand may be necessary for higher workability. This sand is more suitable for rich mixes or for use in concrete of low workability.

Zone II represents a medium sand, generally suitable for the standard 1:2 fine to coarse mix, when the maximum size of coarse aggregate is 20 mm. The choice of correct proportion is particularly important as the grading of the sand approaches the fine outer limit of zone 4 or the coarse outer limit of zone I. It is worth noting that if proportioned correctly, fine sand can be utilized with success and its use is economical as it is available locally in desired quantity.

4.17. GRADING OF COARSE AGGREGATE

The requirements of I.S. 383-1970 for the grading of coarse aggregate are reproduced in Table 4.2 and for all in aggregate in Table 4.24.

Table 4.24. Grading for all in aggregate

S. No.	I.S. sieve designation	Percentage passing for all in aggregate of	
		40 mm nominal size	20 mm nominal size
1.	80 mm	100	—
2.	40 mm	95 – 100	100
3.	20 mm	45 – 75	95 – 100
4.	4.75 mm	25 – 45	30 – 50
5.	600 micron	8 – 30	10 – 35
6.	150 micron	0 – 6	0 – 6

The actual grading requirements depend to some extent on the shape and surface characteristics of the

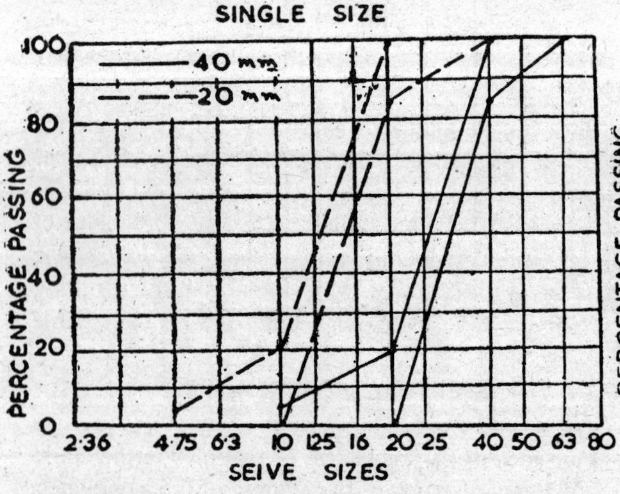

Fig. 4.20. Grading limit for coarse aggregate 40 mm and 20 mm single size

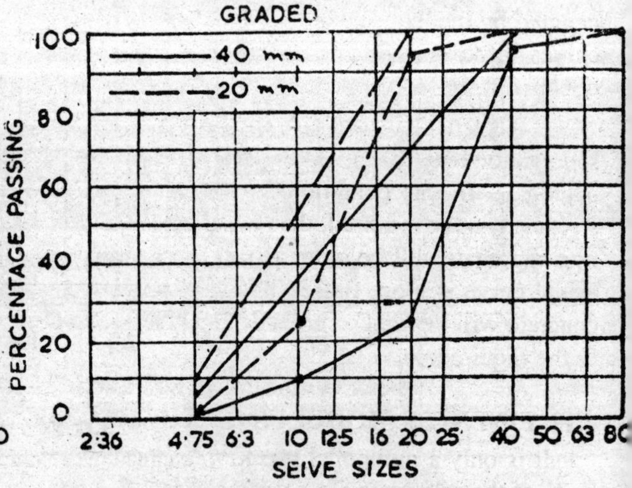

Fig. 4.21. Grading limits for coarse aggregate 40 mm and 20 mm graded

particles. For example, sharp, angular particles with rough surfaces should have a slightly finer grading in order to reduce the possibility of interlocking and to compensate for the high friction between the particles. Some of the gradings for single size and for all in aggregate are shown in Fig. 4.20 to 4.21. Curve 4.22 shows the grading limits for all in aggregates.

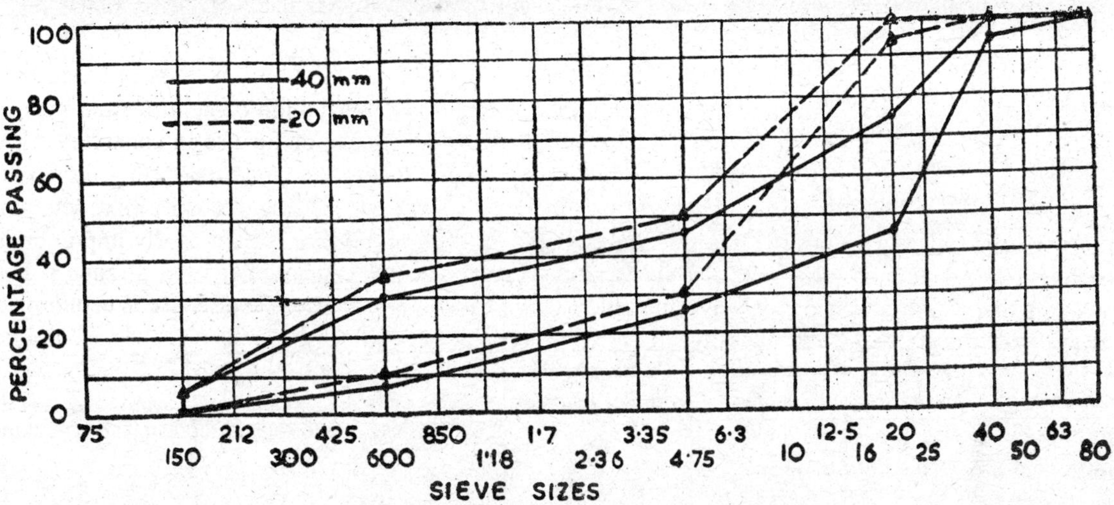

Fig. 4.22. Grading limits for all in aggregates

Oversize and undersize

Strict adherence to size limits of aggregate is not possible. Breakage during handling will produce some undersize material and wear of screen in the quarry or at the crusher will result in oversize particles being present. As per I.S. 383-1970, the limit for oversize is permitted between 5% to 15%. However no aggregate must be retained on a sieve one size larger than the nominal maximum size. The allowable limit of undersize material is 5 to 10%. For fine aggregate a total departure of 5% from zone limits is allowed, but not beyond the coarser limit of zone I or finer limit of zone IV.

4.18. INTERPRETATION OF GRADING CURVES

From the study of the grading curve say for zone I sand, it will be seen that higher percentage of passing material represents upper curve and lesser passing percentage lower curve. These curve may be denoted by the letter U and L respectively. The upper curve represent grading of finer material while lower curves those of coarser material. The desired grading curve of a mixed aggregate can also be similarly obtained.

If the actual curve is lower than the desired curve, then it is an indication of coarser aggregate and the segregation may result. On the other hand if the actual curve is higher than the required, then it shows finer aggregate. In this condition for the same workability more water will be needed. If the actual curve is steeper than the required, then it indicates that the average particles are more. In this case the percentage of fine aggregate will be more and its workability for a fixed water/cement ratio will not be good. In case the actual curve is more flat, it indicates the deficiency of average particles, in which condition the resulting concrete will be honey combed. Thus the grading curve should be smooth, parallel and as near as possible to the required curve.

4.19. FINENESS MODULUS OF AGGREGATE

It is only a numerical index of fineness. It gives some idea of the mean size of particles in the entire body of the aggregate. To a certain extent it is a method of standardization of the grading of the aggregates. It is obtained by adding the cumulative percentages of weights retained on the sieves of the standard series

150, 300, 600 micron and 1.18, 2.36, 4.75 or 5 mm and upto the largest sieve size to be used and dividing the sum by 100. It should be remembered that when all particles in a sample are Coarser than say 600 micron, then the cumulative percentage retained on 300 micron should be entered as 100. Same value also would be entered for 150 micron. Coarser the aggregate, higher the value of fineness modulus. Fine aggregate having fineness modulus less than 1.0 should not be used. Higher the F.M., harsher the mix, lower F.M. gives an uneconomical mix.

Generally the fineness modulus for fine aggregates varies from 2.0 to 3.5, and for coarse aggregate between the 5.5 and 8.0 and for all in aggregate between 3.5 to 6.5. Following example of table 4.25 will illustrate the method of determining the fineness modulus of aggregate.

Example 4.1. *Find the fineness modulus of fine and Coarse aggregate for which the sieve analysis is given in the following Table 4.25.*

Table 4.25.

	Weight of sample 10 kg (Coarse Agg.)			*Weight of sample 1 kg (Fine agg.)*		
I.S. sieve	*Weight retanined*	*Total weight retained*	*Cumulative percentage retained*	*Weight retained*	*Total weight retained*	*Cumulative percentage retained*
75 mm	0	0	0	0		
40 mm	0	0	0	0		
20 mm	2.5	2.5	25	0		
10 mm	4.5	7.5	75	0		
4.75 or 5 mm	2	9.0	90	0		
2.36 mm	1	10.0	100	0.15	0.15	15
1.18 mm		10.0	100	0.15	0.30	30
600 micron		10.0	100	0.20	0.5	50
300 micron		10.0	100	0.25	0.75	75
150 micron		10.0	100	0.25	0.95	95
Total			690			265
F.M.			6.90			2.65

4.20. SURFACE INDEX

In order to get good workability of mix, the importance of a good grading of coarse and fine aggregate already has been discussed. The quantity of water required to get a given workability of the mix depends to a large extent on the surface area of the aggregate.

As already discussed under head, factors affecting the grading of aggregates, the concept of specific surface gives some what misleading picture of the workability to be expected. To over come this difficulty *Murdock* suggested the use of *surface index*. Surface index is an empirical number related to the specific surface of the particles. More weightage has been given to the finer particles. The empirical numbers representing the surface index of aggregate particles with in a set of sieve size are shown in Table 4.26. below as suggested by *Murdock.*

Table 4.26. Surface index of aggregate particles

S. No.	*Sieve size with in which particles lie.*	*Surface index for particles with in seive size indicated*
1.	80 – 40 mm	– 2.5
2.	40 – 20 mm	– 2.0
3.	20 – 10 mm	– 1.0

S. No.	*Sieve size with in which particles lie.*	*Surface index for particles with in seive size indicated*
4.	10 – 4.75 mm	+ 1.0
5.	4.75 – 2.36 mm	4
6.	2.36 – 1.18 mm	7
7.	1.18 – 600 micron	9
8.	600 – 300 micron	9
9.	300 – 150 micron	7
10.	Smaller than 150 micron	2

Calculation of surface index

The total surface index (fx) of a mixture of aggregate may be determined by multiplying the percentage of material retained on its sieve by the corresponding index shown in Table 4.26. The product of all particles is added. To this sum an empirical constant of 330 is added and the result is divided by 1000. The method of calculation is illustrated by the following example.

Example 4.2. *Find out the surface index of a combined grading shown in the following table 4.27.*

Table 4.27

S. No.	*Sieve size with in which particle lie*	*Percentage of particles with in sieve size*	*Surface index for particles with in sieve size*	*Surface index (fx)*
1.	20 – 10 mm	53	– 1	– 53
2.	10 – 4.75 mm	13	+ 1	13
3.	4.75 – 2.36 mm	9	4	36
4.	2.36 – 1.18 mm	8	7	56
5.	1.18 – 600 micron	8	9	72
6.	600 – 300 micron	7	9	63
7.	300 – 150 micron	2	7	14
				Total = 201 add constant 330 531

$$\therefore \text{ Surface index} = \frac{531}{1000} = 0.531$$

Similarly the surface index can be calculated for standard curve and the value of surface index can be taken as desirable for combined aggregate.

The values of surface index can be used for finding out the proportion of fine to coarse aggregate as follows:

Let,

x = surface index of fine aggregate
y = surface index of coarse aggregate
z = surface index of combined aggregate
p = proportion of fine to coarse aggregate

Then
$$p = \frac{(z - y)}{(x - z)}$$

The procedure is illustrated by the following example.

Example 4.3. *Find the proportion of fine to coarse aggregate from the sieve analysis shown in Table 4.28*

Table 4.28

Sieve size with in which particle lie	*Percentage of particles with in sieve size*	*Surface index for particles with in sieve size*	*Surface index (fx)*
20 – 10 mm	62	– 1	– 62
10 – 4.75 mm	38	+ 1	+ 38
			Total = – 24
			add constant 330
			306
			$\therefore fx = \frac{306}{1000} = 0.306$
Fine aggregate			
4.75 – 2.36 mm	15	4	60
2.36 – 1.18 mm	18	7	126
1.18 – 600 micron	17	9	153
600 – 300 micron	30	9	270
300 – 150 micron	15	7	105
			Total = 714
			add constant 330
			1044

$\therefore$ Surface index fx of fine aggregate $= \frac{1044}{1000} = 1.044$

Let,

Surface index of combined aggregate = 0.62

x = Surface index of F.A. = 1.044

y = Surface index of C.A. = 0.306

z = Surface index of combined aggregate as assumed = 0.62

$$\therefore \text{ Proportion of fine to coarse aggregate} = \frac{z-y}{x-z} = \frac{0.62 - 0.306}{1.044 - 0.62}$$

$$= \frac{0.314}{0.424} = 0.74$$

Hence the ratio of F.A.:C.A. = 1 : 1.35

≈ **1 : 1.35 Ans.**

4.21. GAP GRADING OF AGGREGATE

The aggregate particles of a given size pack in such a way to form voids, that can be penetrated only if the next smaller size of particles is sufficiently small. This means that there must be a minimum difference between the sizes of any two adjacent particle fractions. In other words sizes of aggregate differing only very little can not be used side by side. This fact has led to the advocacy of gap grading of aggregates. Thus gap grading of aggregates can be defined as a grading in which one or more intermediate size fractions are omitted. The term continuously graded is used to describe conventional grading when it is necessary to distinguish it from gap grading. On a grading curve, gap grading is represented by a horizontal line over the range of sizes omitted as shown in Fig. 4.23.

Advantages of gap grading

Some researchers as *Shack-lock* have advocated that for a given aggregate/cement ratio and water/cement ratio, a higher workability can be obtained with a lower sand content in case of gap graded

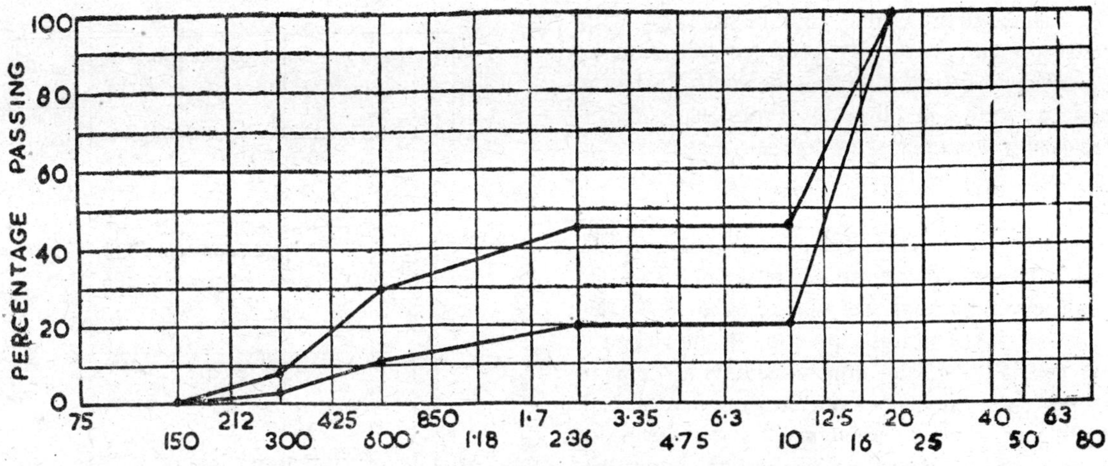

Fig. 4.23. Typical gap gradings

aggregate than continuously graded aggregate. However mixes, for the more workable range of gap graded aggregate showed more likelihood of segregation. For this reason gap grading is recommended for mixes of relatively low workability that are to be compacted by vibration. In this case good control, and care is essential in handling to avoid segregation.

Though from time to time various claims of superior properties of concrete made with gap graded aggregate have been made, but neither compressive nor tensile strength appears to be affected by the gap grading. The shrinkage also is found unaffected by gap grading. On the other hand resistance of concrete to freezing and thawing is found lower with gap graded aggregate.

4.22. MAXIMUM SIZE OF AGGREGATE

As stated earlier, the larger the aggregate particle, the smaller the surface area to be wetted per unit weight of aggregate. Thus extending the grading of aggregate to a larger maximum size, lowers the water requirement of the mix, such that for a specified workability and richness, the water/cement ratio can be reduced resulting increase in the strength of the concrete. This fact has been verified by some researchers with aggregates upto 38.1 mm maximum size and assumed to extend to larger sizes as well. Recent experimental results have shown that above 38.1 mm maximum size of aggregate the gain in strength due to the reduced water requirement is off set by the detrimental effects of lower bond area and of discontinuities introduced by the very large particles particularly in rich mixes. Concrete becomes grossly heterogeneous and results in lower strength.

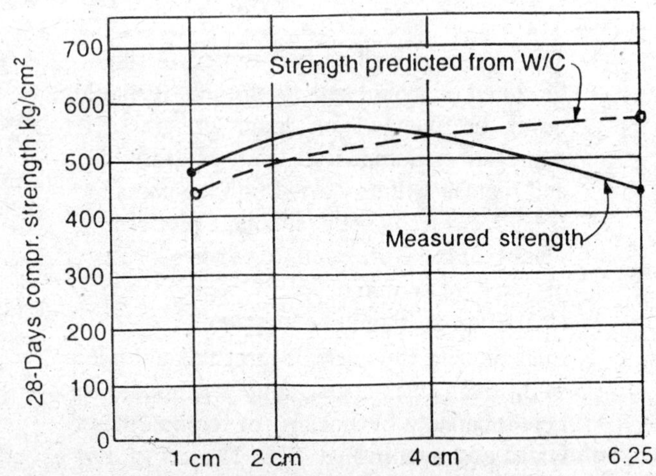

Fig. 4.24. Effect of max. size of coarse aggregate on the compressive strength of concrete

The adverse effect of increase in the size of the largest aggregate particles in the mix exists through out the ranges of sizes, but below 38.1 mm, the effect of size on the decrease in the water requirement is dominant.

Bloem has compared the actual strength with expected strength on the basis of the variation in water/cement ratio from that required with 38.1 mm aggregate as shown in Fig. 4.24. From the study of the Fig. 4.24 it would be seen that actual decrease of strength starts with 25 mm maximum size of aggregate.

For larger sizes, the balance of two effects depends on richness of the mix as shown in Fig. 4.25. Thus the best maximum size of aggregate from the point of view of strength is a function of the richness of mix, specially in lean concretes having cement 170 kg per cubic metre of concrete, the use of 150 mm aggregate is most advantageous. However in structural concrete of usual proportions, from the strength point of view, use of greater size aggregate than 25 mm or 38 mm has not been found advantageous. There are structural limitations also on the size of the aggregate. As per I.S. 416-1964 the maximum size should not be greater than 1/5 to 1/4 of the thickness of concrete section. Secondly the maximum size of aggregate should be at least 5 mm smaller than the spacing of reinforcement. Thirdly the maximum size should be at least 5 mm smaller than the cover given to the concrete reinforcement. Thus looking to these limitations and *Bloem* experimental results, the maximum size of aggregate for structural concrete should be limited to 25 mm preferably 20 mm. However for mass concrete aggregate sizes upto 150 mm can be used. However the decision would also be influenced by the cost and availability of different sizes of fractions.

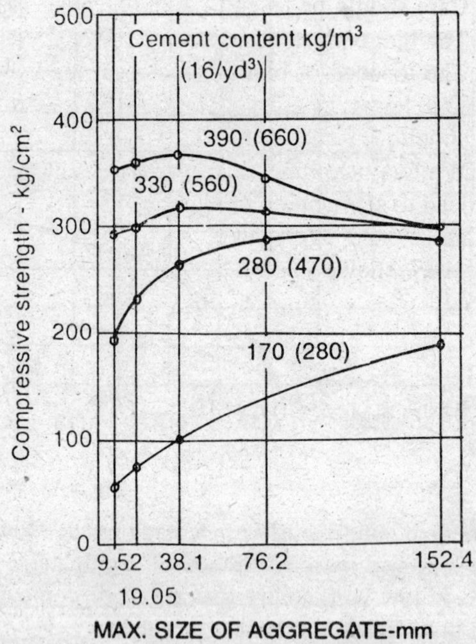

Fig. 4.25. Influence of max. size of aggregate on the 28 day compressive strength of concrete of different richness

4.23. HANDLING OF AGGREGATE

Handling and stock piling of coarse aggregate can easily lead to segregation, more specially when the aggregate has to roll down a slope. While stockpiling aggregate at site following precautions should be adopted.

1. The coarse as well as fine aggregate should be stored on a hard and dry ground. It should never be dumped on loam or grass. If aggregate is dumped on loam or grass, dirt and rubbish will be carried into the concrete. If hard surface is not available, a platform of planks, or old corrugated iron sheets, or floor of brick or a thin layer of weak concrete (1:5:10) or so should be prepared.
2. Piles of sand and coarse aggregate, and piles of different sized coarse aggregate should be kept separately by means of compartment walls as shown in Fig. 4.26. These fractions should be remixed in the desired proportion at the time of feeding them into the mixer.

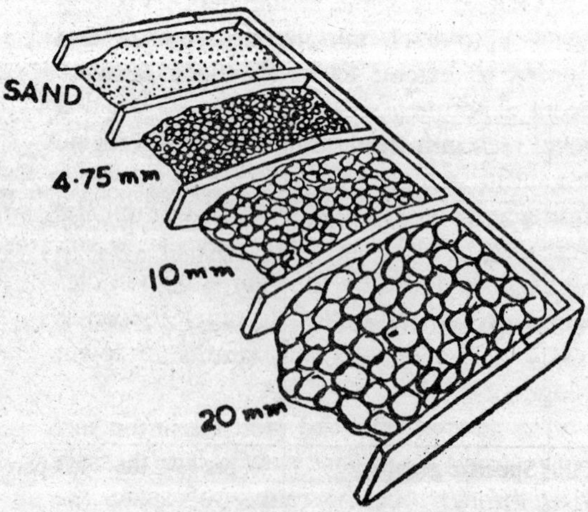

Fig. 4.26. Storage of different fractions of coarse aggregate

3. Care should be taken to avoid breakage of the aggregate.
4. The bidi ends, tea leaves or sugar etc. should not be allowed to be thrown into the aggregate piles. The tobacco of bidi or nicoten of tea leaves or sugar will slow down the setting of the concrete. Tree leaves or grass root etc. will also damage the binding properties of concrete. Hence aggregate should be kept clean.
5. While stockpiling, successive consignments should not be dropped at the same place. This will lead to segregation of aggregate Fig. 4.27-4.30 show the correct and incorrect methods of handling and storing aggregates.

Fig. 4.27 shows correct and incorrect method of storing aggregate falling from the end of belt conveyer.

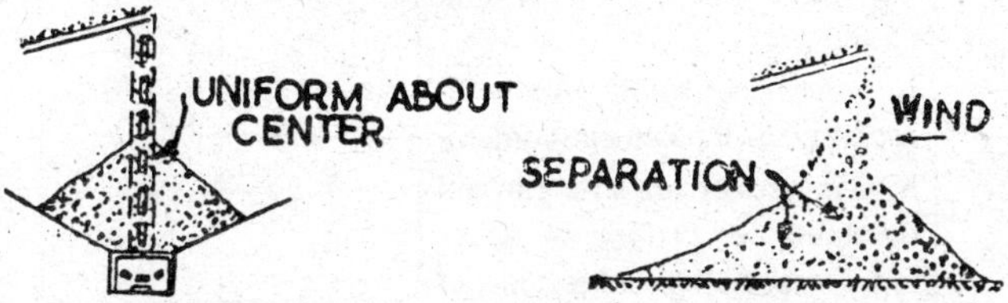

CORRECT INCORRECT

Fig. 4.27

CORRECT INCORRECT

Fig. 4.28

Fig. 4.28 shows correct and incorrect method while aggregate is brought by trucks and stored at site.
Fig. 4.29 shows the correct and incorrect methods of filling in the bins.

CORRECT INCORRECT

Fig. 4.29

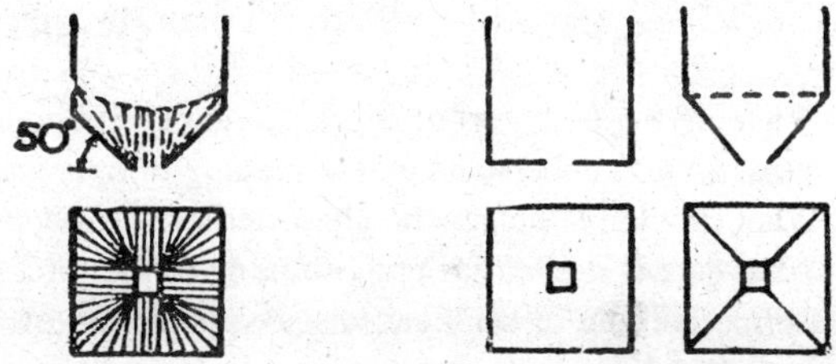

CORRECT INCORRECT

Fig. 4.30

Fig. 4.30 shows correct and incorrect method of stock piling the screened material.

Table 4.29. Summery of aggregate properties

S. No.	*Characteristics*	*Test*	*Significance*	*Specifications*
1.	Particle shape and texture	Visual inspection. Flakiness and elongation test as per IS 2386 1963 part-I	It affects workability of a fresh concrete	Flakiness index should not be greater than 30 to 40%
2.	Resistance to crushing	Aggregate crushing value test as per IS 2386-1963 part-IV	For high strength concrete low crushing strength aggregate will not give proper strength as it will get crushed earlier.	30% impact value for pavements and 45% for other purposes.
3.	Specific gravity	As per IS 2386-1963 part-III	It is used in mixdesign calculations, unit weight and yield of concrete	—

S. No.	*Characteristics*	*Test*	*Significance*	*Specifications*
4.	Bulk density	As per IS 2386-1963 part-III	Roded bulk density is used to check the uniformity of aggregate grading, loose bulk density is useful to convert mass into bulk volume or vice versa	—
5.	Absorption and surface moisture	— do —	It is used to maintain w/c ratio constant as it affects mix proportion	—
6.	Deleterious substances	— do —	Surface coating and organic impurities affect the hydration of cement	Limts should be as per IS 383-1970
7.	Grading	As per IS 2386-1963 part-I	It improves workability and economizes the cement content.	As per IS 383-1970
8.	Chemical stability	As per IS 2386-1963 part-VII	It is important for strength and durability of all type of structures, specially subjected to chemical attack.	—
9.	Resistance to freezing and thawing	— do —	It is significant in cold countries where frost action deteriorates the concrete due to alternate freezing and thawing	—

QUESTIONS

1. What are the functions of aggregate in cement concrete? How aggregate can be classified? Explain fully.
2. What do you understand by the grading of aggregate? How it affects the strength of concrete?
3. What should be the general characteristics of good aggregate?
4. What data is needed for proportioning of mixtures of concrete?
5. Define bulking of sand and discuss its effects on the properties of concrete. How its value is determined? Explain fully.
6. Define fineness modulus. What is its importance in mix design?
7. Discuss the effects of maximum size of aggregate on the placement, workability and economy of the concrete with a given w/c ratio.
8. What is grading of aggregate? How does the grading of aggregate affects the properties of concrete?
9. What precautions should be taken while stockpiling and storing the aggregate?
10. What is meant by surface texture of aggregate?
11. Why elongation and flakiness index determined?
12. What may be the consequences of impurities in aggregate?
13. Define soundness, elongation and flakiness of aggregate.
14. How does the shape of aggregate particles influence the properties of fresh concrete?
15. What is a gap grading? Discuss its advantages.
16. What are the common deleterious materials found in aggregates.
17. What is the maximum size of fine aggregate?
18. Define over size and under size aggregate.
19. How does the grading of aggregate affects the water requirement of the mix?
20. Explain the following terms:
    (*a*) Apparent specific gravity (*b*) Bulk specific gravity
    (*c*) Bulk density (*d*) Toughness of aggregate (*e*) Void ratio
21. What are the effects of clay and very fine materials on the properties of concrete.

OBJECTIVE TYPE QUESTIONS

1. Which of the following statements incorrect
   (*a*) Aggregate is cheaper than cement and is relatively is inert material
   (*b*) It imparts volume, stability and durability to the concrete
   (*c*) It increases the density of the concrete
   (*d*) Aggregates occupy about 75% space in a given mass of concrete
   (*e*) All the above
2. The functions of fine aggregate in concrete are
   (*a*) It helps in providing uniformity and workability to the concrete mixture
   (*b*) It helps the cement paste to hold the coarse aggregate
   (*c*) It provides plasticity to the mixture
   (*d*) It helps in preventing segregation of the paste and coarse aggregate
   (*e*) All the above
3. An aggregate should be
   (*a*) Hard, clean and well graded (*b*) It should be of proper size and shape
   (*c*) It should be chemically inert (*d*) It should be resistant to abrasion
   (*e*) All the above
4. Which of the following textured coarse aggregate is not suitable for concrete work
   (*a*) Rough (*b*) Glassy
   (*c*) Granular (*d*) Honey combed
   (*e*) Smooth
5. Coarse aggregate can be classified according to
   (*a*) Size (*b*) Shape
   (*c*) Unit weight (*d*) Geological origin
   (*e*) Any of the above
6. The minimal size of graded particles is said 20 mm, when most the of it pass through.... mm IS sieve and retained on IS sieve....
   (*a*) 20, 4.75 (*b*) 12.5, 4.75
   (*c*) 20, 10 (*d*) 25, 12.5
7. According to size, the classification is called
   (*a*) Crushed stone sand, natural sand and crushed gravel sand
   (*b*) Fine aggregate, coarse aggregate, and all in aggregate
   (*c*) Fine, medium and coarse aggregate
   (*d*) Coarse aggregate, single sized aggregate, and all in aggregate
   (*e*) Any of the above
8. The sand whose fineness modulus is 2.5 is classified as
   (*a*) Coarse sand (*b*) Medium sand
   (*c*) Very fine sand (*d*) Fine sand
   (*e*) Very coarse sand
9. Bulking of sand is the phenomenon of...
   (*a*) Segregation of sand particles of a particular size
   (*b*) Compaction of sand particles
   (*c*) Increase in volume of sand due to surface tension which keeps them apart
   (*d*) Reduction of sand volume to the minimum
10. Addition of 5% moisture content to fine sand causes bulking of the order
    (*a*) 35 to 40% (*b*) 25 to 30%
    (*c*) 30 to 35% (*d*) 10 to 15%
11. Addition of 4% moisture content to fine sand, causes bulking of the order of
    (*a*) 25 to 30% (*b*) 15 to 25%
    (*c*) 10 to 15% (*d*) 5 to 10%
12. Bulking of coarse aggregate in comparison to fine aggregate is
    (*a*) Less than sand (*b*) More than sand

(*c*) 40% at 8% moisture (*d*) Negligible
(*d*) 15% at 4% moisture content

13. Which of the following materials is/are deleterious materials in aggregate?
 (*a*) Shale (*b*) Coal
 (*c*) Clay lumps (*d*) Soft fragments
 (*e*) All of the above
14. Deleterious materials are undesirable in aggregates as they many...
 (*a*) Interfere in the chemical reaction of hydration
 (*b*) Affect the workability, strength and long term performance of concrete
 (*c*) Cause softness, fineness and have intrinsic weakness
 (*d*) Interference with the bond between cement paste and aggregate
 (*e*) Any of the above
15. Grading of the aggregate affects
 (*a*) Strength of concrete (*b*) Workability of concrete
 (*c*) Water/cement ratio (*d*) Non of the above
16. Which of the following statements is false?
 (*a*) The fineness modulus of aggregate is a numerical index of fineness of aggregate.
 (*b*) It is a index of compressive strength of concrete
 (*c*) It gives some idea of the mean size of particles present in the aggregate body
 (*d*) It is regarded as weighted average size of sieve on which material is retained
17. Which one of the following statements is true
 (*a*) In the gap grading one or more intermediate fractions of particles are absent
 (*b*) In the grading the particles fall with in a narrow limit of size fractions
 (*c*) In the gap grading all the particles are of uniform size
 (*d*) In the gap grading the grading curve is smooth
18. State which of the following statements are false
 (*a*) The alkali aggregate reaction takes place between the active silica constituent of the aggregate and alkalis in cement
 (*b*) The durability of concrete is affected by the thermal properties of the aggregate
 (*c*) The empty spaces between aggregate particles are known as voids
 (*d*) The surface moisture of aggregates expressed as a percentage of the weight of saturated surface dry aggregate is known as moisture content
 (*e*) An aggregate particle is said flaky when its mean dimension is less than 0.9 times the mean sieve size
 (*f*) Higher the glassy surface textured particles, more the bond strength
 (*g*) Irregular shaped aggregate require less cement paste to make a workable concrete

 [Ans. *false.* (*e*), (*f*), (*g*)]
19. Which of the following statements are true
 (*a*) Round aggregate require minimum cement paste to make good concrete
 (*b*) Irregular shaped aggregate need more cement paste to make a workable concrete
 (*c*) The shape and surface texture of the aggregate does not influence the workability of fresh concrete
 (*d*) Higher the angularity number, the less angular is the aggregate
 (*e*) The higher modulus of elasticity of concrete is obtained by the use of aggregate of higher modulus of elasticity
 (*f*) The bond strength between the aggregate and cement paste depends on the surface texture of the aggregate
 (*g*) The bulk density of aggregate is not affected by the particle shape, size and grading of aggregate
 (*h*) The sintered fly ash aggregate produces concrete of 12 to 14 kN/m^3

 [Ans. *false.* (*c*), (*d*) (*g*)]

Answers

1. (*e*)	4. (*b*)	7. (*b*)	10. (*a*)	13. (*e*)	16. (*b*)
2. (*e*)	5. (*e*)	8. (*d*)	11. (*b*)	14. (*e*)	17. (*a*)
3. (*e*)	6. (*a*)	9. (*c*)	12. (*d*)	15. (*b*)	

5

Water

5.1. INTRODUCTION

For the production of cement concrete, water is one of the most important ingredient as hydration of cement is possible only in the presence of water. The hydration of cement forms gel, which on hardening gives strength to the concrete. Thus concrete of any type can not be prepared with out water. The properties of water have been found to influence the properties of concrete to a great extent. For concrete production water is used for the following purposes.

1. Water for preparing concrete *i.e.* for mixing concrete ingredients.
2. Water for curing concrete.
3. Water for washing aggregates.

5.2. QUALITY OF WATER FOR PREPARING CONCRETE (Mixing water)

The common criteria or yard stick to the suitability of water for preparing concrete is that water fit for human consumption (drinking) is fit for concrete making also. But this yard stick is not true for all conditions. Water containing 0.05% sugar by weight of cement is quite fit for drinking, but it retards cement's initial setting time by 4 hours. Thus water to be used for concrete production should not contain substances which may have appreciable harmful effect on the initial setting time, strength, and durability of the concrete. Substances like oils, acids, carbonates and bi-carbonates, alkalis, sugar, silt and organic materials have been found to have harmful effect on the properties of the fresh and hardened concrete. Hence concrete mixing water should be free from these impurities. The p_H value of concrete mixing water should be between 6 and 8.

Streams carrying large concentration of suspended solids, industrial and domestic waste, streams and wells in mining and arid alkali areas should be viewed with suspension and the effect of such waters should be determined before the use in actual construction. The effluents from paint, textile, fertilizer, and sugar factories, sewage works, gas works have been found to have harmful effect on concrete.

5.3. EFFECT OF WATER IMPURITIES ON PROPERTIES OF CONCRETE

1. Carbonates and bicarbonates of potassium and sodium. The carbonates and bicarbonates of potassium and sodium affect the setting time of cement. The presence of sodium carbonate accelerates the setting time, while bicarbonate may either accelerate or retard the setting of the cement. The higher concentrations of these salts will reduce the concrete strength sufficiently. Salts of Mangnese, Tin, Zinc, Copper and lead reduce the concrete strength to a great extent. Sodium iodate, sodium borate, sodium posphate reduce the initial strength of concrete to an extra ordinarily high degree. Sodium sulphide also deteoriates the strength of concrete. Even very small quantity of sodium sulphide of the order of 100 ppm needs testing. Brackish water contains chlorides and sulphates. Chlorides upto 10,000 ppm and sulphates upto 3000 ppm are harm less.

The presence of zinc chloride retards the rate of setting to such an extent that strength does not develop upto 72 hours. The effect of lead nitrate is completely destructive. Carbonates of sodium and potassium may cause very high rapid setting and if present in large concentration, reduce the strength of concrete. The presence of calcium chloride accelerates the setting and hardening of concrete. The quantity of calcium chloride is restricted to 1.5% by weight of cement.

Algee. It may be present on the surface of aggregate or in mixing or washing water. It combines with cement forming a layer on the surface of aggregate and reduces the bond between the cement paste and aggregate. Algee also has the air entraining effect in large quantities in the concrete, resulting in lowering the strength of concrete.

Mineral oils. Mineral oils not mixed with vegetable or animal oils have no adverse effect on the concrete strength. Concentration of mineral oils upto 2% by weight of cement have been found to increase the strength of concrete. 8% Concentration of mineral oil reduces the strength slightly. The vegetable oils have adverse effect on the strength of concrete at later ages.

The tolerance of concentration of some impurites and their effect is shown in following Table 5.1.

Table 5.1. Permissible concentration of impurities

S. No.	*Imperities*	*Tolerable Concentration*
1.	Chlorides	10,000 ppm
2.	Calcium chloride	2% by weight of cement in non pre-stressed concrete
3.	Sodium and potassium carbonates and bicarbonates	1000 ppm (total). If this limit exceeds, test for initial and setting time and 28 days strength should be carriedout
4.	Sulphuric anhydride	3000 ppm
5.	Sodium sulphide	less than 100 ppm, even for 100 ppm test should be carriedout
6.	Sodium hydoxide	0.5% by weight of cement. If quick setting is not induced
7.	Sodium iodates, sodium sulphate, sodium borate and arsenate	very low
8.	Salts and suspended particles	2,000 ppm, With high contents of suspended solids the mixing water should be allowed to stand in a setling tank before use.
9.	Total dissolved salts	15,000 ppm
10.	Organic material	3,000 ppm. The presence of humic acid or such other organic acids affect the hardening of concrete adversely
11.	PH	it should be less than 6. Praferably between 6 and 8

5.4. PRACTICAL APPROACH

The practical recourse for evaluating the effect of use of doubtful quality water is to carry out comparative test for setting time and soundness of cement and for strength and durability of concrete.

For comparing the compressive strength of concrete at least three 15 cms cubes be prepared using the available water at site and three cubes using distilled water and cured for 28 days under similar conditions. The cubes should be prepared and tested as per IS 516-1959. The average compressive strength of 3 cubes prepared with available water should not be less than 90% of the average compressive strength of similar cubes prepared with distilled water. Tests have shown that water containing excessive amount of dissolved salts reduces the compressive strength from 10 to 30% of that obtained using fresh or distilled water. The effects on compressive strength of concrete due to various dissolved salts are shown in Table 5.2. below.

Table 5.2. Effect of dissolved salts in water on compressive strength

S. No.	*% of salt in water*	*% reduction in compressive strength*
1.	0.50 SO_4 (Sulphate)	4
2.	1.0 SO_4 (Sulphate)	10
3.	5.0 NaCl (Chlorides)	30
4.	1.5 Co_3 (Carbonates)	20

The initial setting time of test samples made with appropriate cement and water proposed to be used should not be less than 30 minutes and should not differ by ± .30 minutes from the initial setting time of controlled samples prepared with the same cement and distilled water. The test should be carried as per IS 4031-1961.The permissible limits of solids in water as per revised IS 456-2000 should be as shown in Table 5.3 below.

Table 5.3. Permissible limits for solids as per IS 456-2000

S. No.	*Matter*	*Tested as per IS*	*Permessible limit*	
			Parts	*%*
1.	Organic	IS 3025 part 18	200 mg/lit	0.02%
2.	Inorganic	IS 3025 part 18	3000 mg/lit	3.0%
3.	Sulphate (So_4)	IS 3025 part 24	400 mg/lit	0.04%
4.	Suspended matter	IS 3025 part 17	2000 mg/lit	2.0%
5.	Chlorides (Cl)	IS 3025 part 32	2000 mg/lit	2.0% For plain cement concrete work
			500 mg/lit	0.05% For reinforce concrete work

5.5. EFFECT OF ACIDS AND ALKALIS

The effect of acidity in water as gauged on the basis of total acidity, the extent of which should satisfy the following requirements.

To neutratize 100 ml (c.c.) sample of water using phenolphthalein as an indicator, it should not require more than 1 ml (c.c.) of 0.1 normal NaOH. This acidity is equivalent to 49 ppm of H_2So_4 or 36 ppm of HCl.

The limit of alkalinity is guided on the basis of total alkalinity, the extent of which should satisfy the following requirement.

To neutratize 100 ml of sample of water using methyl orange as an indicator it should not require more than 5 ml (c.c.) of 0.1 normal HCl. This alkalinity is equivalent to 265 ppm as carbonate (Na_2Co_3), 420 ppm as bicarbonate ($NaHCo_3$) and 685 ppm as the sum of both carbonates and bicarbonates. (Both the tests should be carried out as per IS 3025).

5.6. USE OF SEA WATER FOR MIXING CONCRETE

Sea water contains about 3.5% salinity. This salinity contains about 78% sodium chloride and 15% chlorides and sulphates of magnesium. Sea water also contains small quantities of sodium and potassium salts as shown in table 5.4. These salts can react with reactive aggregates in the same way as alkalies in the cement. Thus if aggregates are found alkali reactive, then sea water should not be used even for the production of plain cement concrete. It has been reported that the use of sea water for mixing concrete does not reduce the strength of concrete appreciably, but it may lead to corrosion of reinforcement in certain conditions. Researchers are unanimous in their opinion about the use of sea water in plain cement concrete or mass concrete. Sea water has been found to accelerate the early strength of concrete slightly, but it reduces the 28 days strength by 10 to 15%.

Sea water containing large quantities of chlorides may cause efflorescence and constant dampness in the structure. Thus where appearance is important, sea water should not be used for concrete mixing. The use of sea water is also not advisable in plaster work, where the surface is likely to be painted on a later date.

Researchers differ in their opinions about the corrosion of reinforcement by the use of sea water. Some researchers have expressed concern about the risk of corrosion of reinforcement specially in tropical climatic regions, where as others did not find any risk of corrosion due to the use of sea water.

Experiments have shown that corrosion of reinforcement occurred even when concrete was made and cured immersed in pure water but the concrete was comparatively porous. On the other side no corrosion of reinforcement was observed when concrete was made and cured immersed in sea or salty water, but the concrete was dense with adequate provision of cover to the reinforcement. From this fact it can be concluded that the cause of corrosion of reinforcement is not the use of sea water or the quality of water where concrete is placed. The reason of reinforcement corrosion is the permeability of concrete and lack of proper cover to the reinforcement. However, it will be wise to avoid the use of sea water for the production of reinforced concrete. For economical or other reasons if sea water has to be used then the concrete should be made dense using low water/cement ratio, and vibration for compaction with the provision of 7.5 cm cover to the reinforcement.

The IS 456-2000 totally prohibits the use of sea water for mixing and curing reinforced and pre-stressed concrete works. However the specifications of this code permit the use of sea water for the production and curing of plain cement concrete under unavoidable circumstances. Sea water contains following salts. The salt composition of different sea waters in gram/lit. is shown in Table 5.4.

Table 5.4. Composition of sea water (gram/lit.)

S. No.	*Constituent salt*	*Indian sea*	*Mediterranean sea*	*Atlantic sea*	*Mean value of salts in sea water*
1.	Chloride (Cl)	19.00	21.38	17.83	19.4
2.	Sulphate (So_4)	3.65	3.06	2.54	3.08
3.	Calcium (Ca)	0.40	0.47	0.41	0.43
4.	Bromide (Br)	0.07	0.07	0.06	0.07
5.	Sodium (Na)	10.56	11.56	9.95	10.67
6.	Potassium (K)	0.38	0.42	0.33	0.376
7.	Magnessium (Mg)	1.27	1.78	1.50	1.52
8.	Bicarbonate (HCo_3)	0.14	—	—	0.05
Total		35.47	38.74	32.63	35.62

5.7. EFFECT OF SUGAR ON THE PROPERTIES OF CONCRETE

Sugar has a marked effect on setting of cement. 0.05% sugar by weight of cement retards the setting time by 4 hours. The quantity of sugar upto 0.1% at normal temperature has little adverse effect on the rate of hydration, but 0.2% sugar by weight has been found to retard the final setting time upto 72 hours or more. Sugar more than 1% by weight of cement has very destructive effect on setting and strength of concrete. While some researchers say that sugar upto 0.15% by weight of cement retard setting time of cement and reduce carly strength, while 28 days strength improves. 0.2% sugar by weight of cement accelerate the setting of cement. If the percentage of sugar is increased more than 0.2%, very rapid setting may occur and the 28 days strength reduces. Thus before use, test should be carried out to find out the effect of sugar contents on the properties of concrete.

5.8. WATER FOR WASHING OF AGGREGATES

The most important effect of the use of impure water for wasing aggregate is the deposition of coating of salts and silt, organic matter etc. on the surface of the aggregate particles. The coating of the impurities form a layer between the gel and aggregate surface resulting poor bond between them, poor bond between aggregate and cement paste reduces the compressive strength of concrete to a great extent. Thus the concentration of impurities in water which cause deleterious coatings on particles are more harmful than those present in mixing water. However no limits have been laid. Thus to judge the harmful effect, a comparative study has to be made. However water used to wash the truck mixer is satisfactory as mixing water as the solids in this water are proper cement ingredients.

5.9. WATER FOR CURING OF CONCRETE

Generally water suitable for mixing concrete, is also suitable for curing of concrete. However following points should be noted regarding the use of water for curing of concrete. Generally curing water should be free from following impurities.

1. **Iron or organic matter.** The presence of these matters may cause staining of concrete particularly if the flow of water over the concrete is slow and evaporation is rapid.
2. Water should be free from carbon dioxide (Co_2) as it attacks hardened concrete.
3. Water formed by melting ice or by condensation should not be used for curing as it contains little Co_2. This Co_2 in water dissolves forming $Ca(OH)_2$ and cause surface erosion. Sea water also is prohibited for curing purposes.

5.10. EFFECT OF SOME OTHER IMPURITIES

1. **Pure water.** Pure water has been found to dissolve free lime from cement concrete. This reaction accelerates in the presence of Co_2 as it forms calcium bicarbonate, which is soluble. Thus concrete deteriorate, if pure water is used with ordinary portland cement. However this reaction does not take place if pure water is used with high alumina cement.
2. **Marshy water.** This water contains free carbonic acid or humic acid. Hence it is not good for good concrete production.
3. **Water having tanic acid.** Tanic acid retards the setting time of cement as 0.05% of sugar.

QUESTIONS

1. Discuss the use of water in cement concrete.
2. What should be the qualities of water to be used in concrete making.
3. What are the common impurities in water? State the limits of impurities.
4. Specify the water for use in concrete mix.
5. Can wash water from concrete mixer be used as mix water, if so why?
6. State the requirements of water to be used for curing the concrete.
7. Is drinking water always suitable for concrete making.
8. Discuss the effects of solid contents in the mix water on the properties of concrete.
9. Write detailed note on the followings:
   (*a*) Use of sea water for concrete making
   (*b*) Use of brackish water for various types of construction
   (*c*) Tests to determine the suitability of water to be used in concrete.

OBJECTIVE TYPE QUESTIONS

1. State which of the following statements are false.
   (*a*) Water is the most important and less expensive ingredient of concrete
   (*b*) Mixing water of concrete is consumed in the hydration of cement and in lubrication of aggregate
   (*c*) Excess water does not form laitance on the free surface
   (*d*) Excess water does not make concrete honeycombed
   (*e*) The presence of iron compounds and tanic acid is not objectionable
   (*f*) Water which is suitable for mixing is not suitable for curing

(*g*) Curing water should not produce objectionable stains on the surface of concrete
(*h*) Water which is suitable for drinking may not be suitable for mixing

2. Which of the following statements are true
   (*a*) In concrete mixing water, the quantity of calcium chloride should not be more than 1.5%
   (*b*) The suspended particles of silt and clay should be less than 0.02%
   (*c*) The PH value generally should be between 6 and 8
   (*d*) Free vegetable oil is harmful but mineral oil upto 2% is beneficial
   (*e*) All the above
3. Which of the following statement is false
   (*a*) The use of sea water for preparing the concrete will cause efflorescence
   (*b*) The use of sea water for preparing the concrete will not corrode the reinforcement
   (*c*) The use of sea water for preparing concrete will reduce its ultimate strength
   (*d*) The use of sea water for preparing concrete may cause dampness in the structure
   (*e*) Sea water can be safely used for prestressed concrete works.
   (*f*) Use of sea water in the concrete does not affect surface finish of the structure
4. Which of the following statement is true
   (*a*) The vegetable oil present in mixing water will increase the strength of concrete
   (*b*) The vegetable oil present in the mixing water will reduce its strength
   (*c*) The vegetable oil present in mixing water will produce more slump
   (*d*) The presence of vegetable oil in mixing water will improve its workability
   (*e*) The presence of vegetable oil in mixing water will give smooth surface to the concrete
5. Which of the following statements is true
   (*a*) The concentration of mineral oil upto 8% in mixing water will reduce the strength of the concrete.
   (*b*) The concentration of mineral oil upto 2% in mixing water will increase the strength of concrete.
   (*c*) The presence of mineral oil in water reduces the strength of concrete for all concentrations
   (*d*) The presence of mineral oil in mixing water increases strength for all concentrations beyond 8%
   (*e*) The presence of mineral oil in mixing water does not affect the strength of concrete at all.
6. The presence of sugar in mixing water for concrete work...% will not have adverse effect on the strength of concrete
   (*a*) less than 0.05% (*b*) upto 0.15%
   (*c*) 0.2% (*d*) 1.0%
   (*e*) 1.5%
7. Which of the following impurities in the mixing water is destructive?
   (*a*) Sugar (*b*) Alkalis
   (*c*) Algae (*d*) Lead nitrate
   (*e*) Calcium chloride
8. The presence of 0.20% of sugar by weight in mixing water may cause
   (*a*) Reduction in early strength of concrete
   (*b*) Acceleration in the setting time of concrete
   (*c*) Retardation in the setting time of concrete
   (*d*) Reduction in the final workability of concrete

Answers

1. (*c, d, e, f*) 2. *e* (All) 3. (*b, e, f*) 4. (*b*) 5. (*b*) 6. (*a*)
7. (*d*) 8. (*b*)

6

Admixtures

6.1. INTRODUCTION

Admixtures may be defined as the materials other than the basic ingredients of concrete *i.e.* cement, aggregates and water added to the concrete mix immediately before or during the mixing process to modify one or more specific properties of concrete in fresh or hardened state. Where as an additive is a material which is added at the time of grinding cement clinker in the cement factory.

The use of admixture should offer improvement in the properties of concrete by adjusting the proportions of cement and aggregates. How ever it should not affect adversely any property of concrete. An admixture should be used only after assessing its effects on the concrete to be used under a intended situation. It should be kept in mind that admixtures are no substitute for good workmanship *i.e.* the effects of bad workmanship can not be improved by the use of admixtures.

6.2. HISTORY OF ADMIXTURES

The history of admixtures goes with the history of cement Concrete, *i.e.* it is as old as that of concrete. But a few types of admixtures called as plasticizers and super plasticizer have been developed recently. They are developed in Japan and Germany around 1970. Later on they found use in U.S.A., Europe, middle east and far east etc. However in India they became popular around 1985. They are discussed later in this chapter.

6.3. FUNCTIONS OF ADMIXTURES

Admixtures are used for the following purposes

1. To accelerate the initial setting and hardening of concrete.
2. To retard the initial setting of concrete.
3. To increase the strength of concrete.
4. To improve the workability of fresh concrete.
5. To improve the durability of concrete.
6. To reduce the heat of evaluation.
7. To control the alkali aggregate expansion.
8. To promote pozzolanic properties in concrete.
9. To aid in curing of concrete.
10. To improve wear resistance to concrete.
11. To reduce shrinkage during setting of concrete.
12. To reduce bleeding of concrete.
13. To impart colour to concrete.
14. To aerate concrete or mortar to produce light weight concrete.

15. To reduce segregation in grout mixes.
16. To increase the bond between old and new concrete surfaces and also between concrete and reinforcement.
17. To produce fungal, insects etc. resistant concrete.
18. To produce non skid surface of concrete.
19. To increase the resistance to chemical attack.
20. To decrease the permeability of concrete.
21. To check the corrosion of concrete reinforcement.

Many admixtures have been found useful and effective in accomplishing their intended use but some of them are not found as useful as advocated. While taking a decision regarding the use of a substance as admixture following points should be kept in mind.

1. The possibility of achieving the desired results by a small modification in the basic mix.
2. Justification of additional cost of admixture against benefits obtained by the modified basic mix.
3. Possible adverse effects on properties other than that which the admixture is intended to improve.

Some admixtures serve more than one purpose. Calcium chloride is one of them. Due to its hygroscopic properties calcium chloride under some conditions improves the workability, acts as an antifreezing agent by accelerating setting and hardening of concrete and also tends to aid in curing. Where as some admixtures, specially finely powdered substances, though improve the workability of concrete, but on the other hand increase drying shrinkage. Thus an admixture should be judged by its over all effects upon the serviceability of concrete. Further the number of admixtures proposed for use in concrete is quite large and the popularity of a particular admixture changes with time. Therefore the selection of a particular admixture should be made after due consideration.

6.4. CLASSIFICATION OF ADMIXTURES

The admixtures can be broadly classified according to their characteristic effect as follows:

1. Accelerating admixtures.
2. Retarding admixtures
3. Grouting admixtures.
4. Air entraining admixtures.
5. Pozzolanic or mineral admixtures
6. Air detraining admixtures
7. Gas forming admixtures
8. Workability admixtures
9. Alkali aggregate expansion inhibiting admixtures
10. Damp proofing admixtures
11. Corrosion inhibiting admixtures
12. Bonding admixtures
13. Fungicidal, Germicidal, and insectidal admixtures
14. Colouring admixtures
15. Plasticizers
16. Super plasticizers.

6.4.1. Accelerating admixtures

Sometimes conditions require to shorten the time of set and to increase the rate of hardening for early strength development in concrete. This effect can be obtained by using certain substance in the concrete known as *accelerator*. An accelerator also serves as an antifreeze agent by increasing the rate of heat evaluation and causing concrete to set before frost-damage could occur. Accelerators are used to increase the rate of early hardening for the following purposes.

1. Permitting earlier removal of form work.
2. Shortening the curing period.
3. Opening the structure for use at the earliest opportunity.
4. Off setting the retarding effects of low temperatures.
5. For compensating the retarding effects of some other admixtures.

Accelerating agents

Usually chlorides of calcium, aluminium and sodium, the sulphates of sodium and potassium, caustic soda, caustic potash, certain silicates, carbonates, triethanolamine and fluosilicates etc. are used for accelerating and hardening agents in concrete. Out of the above substances calcium chloride is the most commonly used accelerating and antifreeze admixture It has also been found that the use of $CaCl_2$ increases the resistance of concrete to erosion and abrasion and improvement persists at all ages.

Calcium chloride may be added to rapid hardening as well as ordinary portland cement. The more rapid the natural rate of hardening of the cement, the greater is the action of the accelerator. However calcium chloride should not be used with high alumina cement. Most probably the action of calcium chloride is that of a catalyst in the reactions of hydration of C_3S and C_2S. The reduction in the alkalinity of the solution promotes the hydration of the silicates. By the addition of calcium chloride the hydration of C_3A is delayed some what, but the normal process of hydration of cement is not changed.

As per IS 456-1964, $1\frac{1}{2}$ % of calcium chloride by weight of cement is sufficient to increase the hardness of concrete, but many other researchers have advocated the use upto 2 % of calcium chloride to produce the desired results. Although 2% is a conservative maximum value, but during freezing weather with cold materials, calcium chloride upto 4% has been used. However more than 4% of calcium chloride has been found to have adverse effect on the properties of concrete. The maximum amount of calcium chloride in relation to temperature is suggested as follows Table 6.1.

Table 6.1. Relation between temperature and weight of $CaCl_2$ to be used

S. No.	*Prevailing temperature in °F*	*Maximum weight of calcium chloride in gram per bag of cement (50 kg)*
1.	70°F or less	900 gram
2.	70°F to 90°F	675 gram
3.	Above 90°F	450 gram

The most effective amount of calcium chloride was found 2 percent at 40 to70°F and $1\frac{1}{2}$ percent at 90°F. Further increase in workability was found with the addition of calcium chloride upto 3 percent.

By the use of 2% calcium chloride increase in compressive strength of concrete was found 17% at 1 day, 30% at 7 days and about 10% at 28 days. The increase of about 10% in compressive strength is found at all ages (upto 2 years). The increase in cement mortar of 1:2.6 mortar mix was found as shown in the following Table 6.2.

Table 6.2. Increase in compressive strength of mortar at curing temperature indicated % over plain mortar

Age at test days	*40°F*	*70°F*	*90°F*
1	300	145	90
3	117	68	41
7	75	32	23
28	20	12	15
90	10	14	16

Fig. 6.1 shows the effect of adding 2% calcium chloride on the compressive strength of concrete for two different curing conditions.

Further it has been observed that the use of 2% calcium chloride increases the rate of heat evolution at early ages and reduces the setting time to about $\frac{1}{3}$rd of the normal setting time of cement. The addition of each 1% anhydrous calcium chloride affects the rate of hardening as much as a rise of 6°C (11°F) temperature. Fig. 6.2 shows the relation between the setting time of portland cement and calcium chloride content (percentage by weight of cement).

Some researchers have suggested the acceleration in setting time of cement by the use of $CaCl_2$ as shown in Table 6.3.

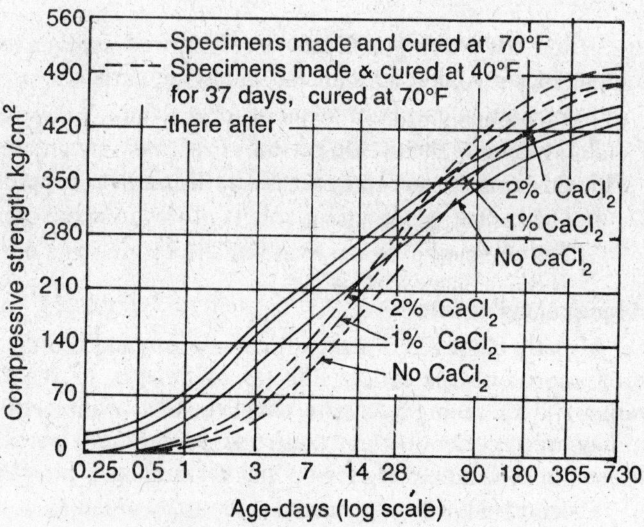

Fig. 6.1. Effect of adding 2% calcium chloride on the strength of concrete

Table 6.3. Influence of calcium chloride on setting time

S. No.	*Weight of calcium chloride as percentage of weight of cement*	*Acceleration of set in minutes*
1.	0.1	25
2.	0.5	45
3.	1.0	85

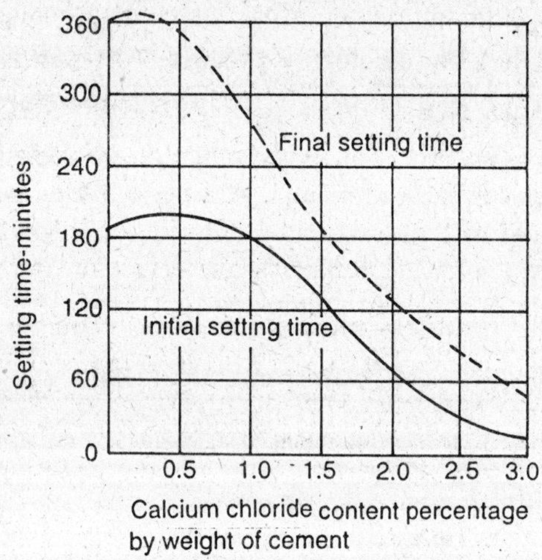

Fig. 6.2. Effect of calcium chlorid content on setting time of cement

Using 2% calcium chloride at 20°C or high early strength cement, concrete roads can be opened for traffic after 1 day curing, while under normal conditions they cannot be opened before 4 days curing. Raising temperature higher than 20°C, the reduction in duration of curing can further be reduced, which is more important in the case of aerodrome and bridges. The effect of temperature on the compressive strength of concrete has been shown in Fig. 12.2.

Calcium chloride can be used most advantageously in cold weather to reduce the time of wet curing at normal temperatures. However concrete with calcium chloride should not be used during hot weather as rapid evaporation at exposed surfaces may cause shrinkage and cracking. Hence it is essential to protect the surface with in first few hours. Later when concrete cools, larger thermal tensile stresses develop due to the contraction of concrete and cause rupture in the body of the structure. Further the use of calcium chloride has been found to increase the corrosion of reinforcing steel and increase of drying shrinkage upto 40% of normal concrete. It may also increase the efflorescence on the surface of the concrete. Resistance to sulphate attack is also found to be reduced by the addition of calcium chloride.

Thus $CaCl_2$ should not be used in the following situations:

1. In prestresing concrete specially concrete in contact with pre-stressing wires.
2. Reinforced concrete to be steam cured, as the use of calcium chloride has been found to have severe corrosion of reinforcement steel.

3. Concrete having alkali reactive aggregate.

Thus it is advised that test should be carriedout on concrete before use.

Calcium chloride is available in anhydrous (water free) form or in a hydrated form ($CaCl_2$ $2H_2O$), containing 67 to 72% of calcium chloride by weight and the remaining 33 to 28% water. The amount of water should be taken into account while using it in concrete. It should be remembered that $CaCl_2$ should be uniformly distributed throughout the mix. It can be achieved by dissolving it in the mixing water before use in the mixer. $CaCl_2$ being hygroscopic should be stored in dry place.

R.S. Varshaney has suggested the setting time of cement by the use of different chemicals as shown in Table 6.4.

Table 6.4

S. No.	*Materials*	*Setting time in minutes*	
		Initial	*Final*
1.	Neat cement	85	217
2.	Cement with calcium chloride ($CaCl_2$)		
	(*a*) 3%	22	52
	(*b*) 4%	3	6
	(*c*) 5%	3	4
	(*d*) 6%	3	4
3.	Cement with calcium carbonate ($CaCO_3$)		
	(*a*) 3%	24	112
	(*b*) 4%	11	34
	(*c*) 5%	4	22
	(*d*) 6%	3	8
4.	Cement with sodium carbonate ($NaCO_3$)		
	(*a*) 3%	10	21
	(*b*) 4%	9	18
	(*c*) 5%	3	9
	(*d*) 6%	1.5	5
5.	Cement with alum $(NH_4)_2SO_4Al_2(SO_4)_3$ $24H_2O$		
	(*a*) 3%	15	42
	(*b*) 4%	2	7
	(*c*) 5%	1.5	5.5
	(*d*) 6%	1.0	3.5
6.	Cement with ammonium chloride (NH_4Cl)		
	(*a*) 3%	—	—
	(*b*) 4%	2	5
	(*c*) 5%	2	5
	(*d*) 6%	1	3
7.	Cement with sodium hydroxide ($NaOH$)		
	(*a*) 3%	11	27
	(*b*) 4%	5.5	12
	(*c*) 5%	3.5	10
	(*d*) 6%	2.4	8
8.	Cement with aluminium nitrate [$Al_3(NO_3)_2$]		
	(*a*) 3%	24	90
	(*b*) 4%	6.5	30
	(*c*) 5%	5.5	15
	(*d*) 6%	4	6

S. No.	Materials	Setting time in minutes	
		Initial	Final
9.	Cement with plaster of paris		
	(*a*) 3%	11	20
	(*b*) 4%	7.5	17
	(*c*) 5%	7	14
	(*d*) 6%	7	9.5
10.	Cement with Feric chloride ($FeCl_3$)		
	(*a*) 6%	3	5
11.	Cement with ammonium sulphate [$(NH_4)_2SO_4$)		
	(*a*) 6%	2.5	9
12.	Cement with sodium aluminate		
	(*a*) 1%	—	3
	(*b*) 2%	—	2
13.	Cement with sodium silicate		
	(*a*) 10%	36	4
	(*b*) 15%	6	2
	(*c*) 20%	1	1

6.4.2. Accelerator plasticizer

To accelerate the strength development of concrete some ingredients are added to the plasti- cizers or super plasticizers. Such admixtures are known as accelerator plastecizers. The addition of such accelerator plasticizers to the concrete results in the development of strength in the concrete at a faster rate. The accelerating materials added to plasticizers or super plasticizers are as follows:

1. Calcium nitrite
2. Nitrates and flousilicate
3. Triethenolamine chloride

The accelerating plasticizers or super plasticizers manufactured by reputed firms are chloride free.

The physical requirements of accelerators and retarders are shown in Table 6.5.

Till recent past calcium chloride ($CaCl_2$) was one of the commonly used material as accelerator. Now a days it is not used and some of the soluble carbonates, silicates, flousilicate and some organic compounds such as triethenolamine are used. Flousilicates and triethenolamine are comparatively costly accelerators.

The recent studies have shown that calcium chloride ($CaCl_2$) as accelerators is harmful to the rein- forced and pre stressed concrete. However it can be used for plain cement concrete in comparatively high dose.

Some of the new accelerators produced are so powerful that with the use of these accelerators it is possible to get the cement set as hard as a stone with in 5 minutes or less. With the availability of such powerful accelerates concreting under following situations has become very easy, as

1. Concreting under water
2. Repair work to the water front structures in the region of tidal variations
3. Basement water proofing operations
4. In fabricating factories
5. Concreting in cold weather conditions, as such accelerators can be used upto – 10°C temperatures.

6.4.3. Retarders

Admixtures capable of delaying or prolonging the setting of cement paste in concrete are called retarders. The use of retarders slows down the chemical process of hydration, so that concrete may remain in plastic state and workable for longer period. Retarders are used primarily to offset the accelerating and

Table 6.5. Physical requirements According to IS 1903-1999

S. No.	Requirements	Accelerating Admixture	Retarding Admixture	Water reducing Admixture	Air entraining Admixture	Super plasticizing admixtures for water reduced concrete mix.		Test reference of IS 1903-1999 clause
						Normal	Retarding type	
1	2	3	4	5	6	7	8	9
1.	Water content, percent of control sample, max	—	—	95	—	80	80	7.25
2.	Slump	—	—	—	—	Not more then 15 mm below that of the control mix concrete		7-2.1 & 7-2.1
3.	Time of setting, allowable deviation from control sample hours							
	Initial							
	Max	– 3	+ 3	± 1	–	–	+ 4	
	Min.	– 1	+ 1	+ 1	–	+ 1.5	+ 1	
	Final							
	Max.	– 2	+ 3	± 1	–	± 1.5	± 3	
	Min.	– 1	+ 1	–	–	–	–	8-2-1
4.	Compressive strength percent of control sample minimum							
	1 days	–	–	–	–	140	–	
	3 days	125	90	110	0	125	125	
	7 days	100	90	110	90	125	125	
	28 days	100	90	110	90	115	115	
	6 months	90	90	100	90	100	100	
	1 year	90	90	100	90	100	100	8-2-2
5.	Flextural strength percent of control sample minimum							
	3 days	110	90	100	90	110	110	
	7 dyas	100	90	100	90	100	100	
	28 days	90	90	100	90	100	100	8-2-3
6.	Length change percent increase over control sample max.							
	28 days	0.01	0.01	0.01	0.01	0.01	0.01	
	6 months	0.01	0.01	0.01	0.01	0.01	0.01	
	1 year	0.01	0.01	0.01	0.01	0.01	0.01	8-7-4

S. No.	*Requirements*	*Accelerating Admixture*	*Retarding Admixture*	*Water reducing Admixture*	*Air entraining Admixture*	*Super plasticizing admixtures for water reduced concrete mix.*		*Test reference of IS 1903-1999 clause*
						Normal	*Retarding type*	
1	2	3	4	5	6	7	8	9
7.	Bleeding percent increase over control sample mix	5	5	5	5	5	5	8-2-4
8.	Loss of workability	—	—	—	—	At 45 min the slump should not be less than that of control mix concrete at 15 min.	At 2 hours the slump should not be less than that of control mix concrete at 15 min	
9.	Air content % max over control concrete					1.5	1.5	7.2-1.2

damaging effect of high temperature and keep concrete workable during the whole period of placing so that construction joints may not develop. Retarder are used usually in the following situations.

1. In situations where concreting is to be done in large number of lifts with out development of construction joints.
2. Pumping cement grouts in oil wells.
3. In situations where concrete has to be hauled for long distances and it is required to keep concrete in plastic and placeable condition.
4. To eliminate the tendency of some cements to develop false set.
5. To obtain aggregate look on the exposed face of the concrete.

6.4.3.1. MATERIALS USED AS RETARDER

A number of substances can be used as retarders. Perhaps the most common retarder is calcium sulphate. It is inter ground to retard the setting of cement. The use of gypsum for retarding setting time should only be recommended when adequate control and inspection is available. The quantity of gypsum to be used should be determined carefully for the given job, other wise it may cause undesirable expansion and undue delay in setting of concrete.

Another most effective retarding agent is common sugar. It can be used for delaying the setting time of concrete with out any harmful effect on the ultimate strength of concrete. Some researchers say that at normal temperature addition of 0.05% sugar by weight of cement retards the setting time up to 4 hours and 0.2% sugar by weight of cement hydration is retarted to such an extent that final set may not take place even within 72 hours. While some other researchers say that sugar from 0.05% to 0.15% by weight of cement retard the setting time of cement and early strength of concrete also is reduced but the 28 days strength improves. According to them the use of 0.2% sugar by weight setting is accelerated. Further increase in sugar quantity results in rapid setting and reduction in 28 days strength.

6.4.4. OIL WELLS

Some times oil wells are drilled upto a depth of 6 kilometer (6000 m) depth, where the temperature may be about 205°C. Some times through this depth stratified, fissured or porous strata may be encountered, which needs to be cement grouted.

In addition to this, annular spacing between the tube and the walls of the well will have to be sealed with cement grout to prevent the entry of oil and gas into some strata. For all these works cement grout should remain in fluid or mobile condition for about 3 to 4 hours even at high temperature with out getting set. For this purpose sugar is one of the good retarder.

Other materials used successfully as retarding agents are as follows:

1. Ligno-sulphonic acids and their salts.
2. Hydroxylated carboxylic acids and their salts.

These agents in addition to the retarding effect also reduce the water quantity required for a given workability, which increases the 28 days compressive strength of concrete by 10 to 20%. In addition, materials like calcium acetate, Mucic acid, starches, carbohydrate derivaties, soluble Zinc salts and borates ammonia, sodium bicarbonate and some commercial products are used as retarding agents. These days admixtures are manufactured to combine set retarding and water reducing properties These admixtures are the combination of conventional water reducing agents and sugar or hydroxylated carboxylic acids or their salts. These materials affect both setting time and rate of development of strength. These are shown in Table 6.6 below.

6.4.5. Retarding plasticizer (Water reducing admixtures)

All the plasticizers and super plasticizer developed show retardation to some extent by themselves.

Table 6.6. Effect of retarding/water reducing admixtures on setting time & strength

S. No.	*Admixture added lit/50 kg bag*	*Setting time in hours*		*Water/cement ratio*	*Comp. Strength MPa*		
		Initial	*Find*		*3 days*	*7 days*	*28 days*
1.	0	4.5	9	0.68	20 (200)	28 (280)	37 (370)*
2.	0.14	8.0	13	0.61	28 (280)	36 (360)	47 (470)
3.	0.21	11.5	16	0.58	30 (300)	40 (400)	50 (500)
4.	0.28	16.0	21	0.58	30 (300)	42 (420)	54 (540)

*Figures in bracket show strength in kg/cm^2.

Many a times the extent of reduction of setting time developed by admixtures is found inadequate. In stead of adding retarders separately, they are mixed with plasticizers or super plasticizers at the time of commercial production. Such productions are known as retarding plasticizers (ASTM Type-D) or retarding super plasticizers (ASTM Type-G).

Retarding plasticizers or super plasticizers are used in the ready mixed concrete industry for retaining the slump loss during high temperatures and along transportation to avoid construction joint, regulation of heat of hydration and slip form construction etc.

The selection of such ready made retarding admixtures should be done very carefully. Due to the heterogeneous nature and different molecular weight of different retarders used with plasticizers they tend to separate out or settle down. Generally it happens when sugar solution is used as retarder, but when gluconate is used as retarder, such separation or settlement does not take place. Thus such retarding plasticizers should be well shaken or stirred before use. There are cases when settlement of retarders from the rest of the ingredients have caused excessive retardation resulting failure of the structure.

Further it has been observed that the effectiveness of an admixture depends on the time when it is added to the mix. A delay of even 2 minutes after water has come into contact with the cement increases the retardation. The increased retardation occurs specially with cements which have a high C_3A content, because once some C_3A has hydrated, it does not absorb the admixture and the more of it is left to retard the hydration of the calcium silicates (C_3S and C_2S). Retarders tend to increase the plastic shrinkage due to extended plastic stage, but drying shrinkage is not affected.

Certain materials are also available as surface retardants. These are applied as a liquid to the inside of the form work. When the shuttering is stripped, the soft surface of the cement is brushed to give the exposed aggregate surface. Thus an architectural finish of exposed aggregate surface can be obtained. The main difficulty in this method is to produce uniformity over the surface and the effect is often patchy. Great care must be exercised while using such materials and advance experiments must be conducted before using them.

6.5. AIR ENTRAINMENT

Since 1930, one of the most advancement made in concrete technology is the discovery of air entrained concrete. Since then there has been an increasing use of air entrained concrete all over the world, especially in U.S.A. and Canada. Due to the merits of air entrained concrete, about 85%. Concrete manufactured in U.S.A. contains air entraining agent. Now air entraining agent is considered as a fifth ingredient of concrete.

Air entrainment in concrete can be defined as the deliberate incorporation of air by means of a suitable air entraing agent. The entrained air should be clearly distinguished from accidentally entrapped air. The difference between the entrained air and entrapped air can be recognised from the difference in the size of their bubbles. The size of the entrained air varies from 5 micron to 80 micron while the size of entrapped air may vary from 10 to 1000 micron.

Secondly the entrained air is delilerably incorporated in the concrete in the shape of spherical bubbles distributed evenly in the entire mass of the concrete, while entrapped air is present in the voids of concrete due to insufficient compaction. The entrapped air voids may be of any shape and size. Normally they are formed in between aggregate surfaces. Also they are not uniformly distributed through out the concrete mass.

6.6. FACTORS AFFECTING THE AMOUNT OF AIR ENTRAINMENT

Following factors influence the air entrainment:

1. **Type and amount of air entraing agent.** It has been observed that different air entraining agents produce diferent amount of air entrainment depending upon the elasticity of film of bubbles produced and the extent to which the surface tension is reduced. Similarly different quantities of air entraining agents produce different air entrainment. Hence the production of air entrained concrete is very difficult.
2. **Water Cement ratio of the mix.** It is one of the most important factors which affects the quantity of air produced. At very low w/c ratio *i.e.* about (0.35 to 0.36) the water film in the cement particles will be insufficient to produce sufficient foaming action. At water/cement ratio 0.4 to 0.6 abundant air bubbles will be produced. At more than 0.6 water/cement ratio large amount of air bubbles will be produced in the beginning but large proportion of these bubbles will be lost progressively with time. A more workable mix holds more air than dry mix.
3. **Type and Grading of aggregates.** It has been observed that grading of aggregates has a marked influence on the quantity of air entrainment. It has been established that the quantity of air increase from the lowest fineness modulus of sand and attains the peak value at fineness modulus (F.M) of about 2.5 and afterwards decreases sharply. The sand fraction of 300 and 150 micron has shown a marked effect on the quantity of air entrainment. Higher the quantities of 300 and 150 micron fractions more will be the air entrainment. Excess of very fine particles reduces the amount of air entrained.
4. **Mixing time.** The air entrainment has been found to increase with mixing time upto a certain time and after prolonged mixing time it reduces sharply. Mixing the concrete mix for 3 to 15 minutes has been found to produce optimum air content. A very fast rotation of the mixer increases the amount of air entrained. Agitating of the mix upto 300 revolution seems to decrease the loss of air entrained but after 2 hours a loss upto 20% of the original air content has been found.
5. **Temperature at the time of mixing.** The temperature at the time of concrete mixing has been found to have a significant effect on the air entrainment. It has been found that with the increase in temperature, the amount of air entrainment decreases. At normal temperature the reaction starts at the time of mixing and may continue for 1.5 to 4.0 hours. At temperature above 38°C the reaction may be completed with in 30 minutes and at 4°C the reaction may not even start for several hours. An increase in temperature from 10°C to 32°C may result in the loss of about 50% air entrained.
6. **Type of cement.** The type of cement, *i.e.* the constituents of cement, especially the alkali content has a marked influence on the entrainment of air in concrete. Alkali content more than 0.8% increases the amount of entrained air. Similarly fineness of cement also influences the air entrainment in concrete. An increase in fineness of cement decreases the effectiveness of air entraing. For example if the surface area of cement is increased from 3000 cm^2/g to 5000 cm^2/g the amount of air entraing agent will be required double of the quantity for the same amount of air entrained.
7. **Compaction.** Compaction of concrete reduces the air entrainment. During the process of compaction the bubbles move to the surface and also get destroyed resulting in the decrease of air entrainment. It has been found the $2\frac{1}{2}$ minute vibration of concrete, air entrainment is lost by 50 percent and 9 minutes vibration of concrete resulted in 80% loss of air entrainment. Experiments

carried out at Hirakund dam showed that 10.5% air contents reduced to 6% after 30 sec vibration.

8. **Influence of other admixtures.** The use of other admixtures along with air entraining agents also has been found to have significant effect on the air entrainment. The use of fly ash and calcium chlorides have been found to reduce the amount of air entrainment i.e. the increase in carbon content decreases the amount of air entraned. The increase of carbon content of fly ash from 1 to 12% needs the air entraing agents 3 times more of the original.
9. Hard mixing water reduces the entrained air content.
10. Very fast rotation of mixer increases the amount of entrained air.

6.7. EFFECT OF AIR ENTRAINMENT ON THE PROPERTIES OF CONCRETE

Air entrainment has direct effect on the following properties:

1. Resistance to freezing and thawing
2. Improvement in workability
3. Reduction in strength

6.7.1. RESISTANCE TO FREEZING AND THAWING

The high resistance developed in the hardened concrete to scaling due to freezing and thawing is the greatest advantage of air entrained concrete. It is observed that when an ordinary concrete is subjected to a temperature below freezing point, the water present in the pores of the concrete freezes and swells to a volume of 1.1 times of the original volume *i.e.* volume of ice is found 10% more than original volume of water. Thus the ice formed in the pores of hardened concrete exerts considerable pressure on the hardened concrete, resulting scaling of the surface and disruption of the concrete at the weaker sections. Similar phenomen of surface scaling and disruption of concrete takes place in plain concrete, when salts used for removing the ice from the concrete. Similar failure pattern is also observed in concrete structures at tidal and spray zones. Now it has been established that air entrainment increases the resistances to freezing and thawing about 3 to 7%.

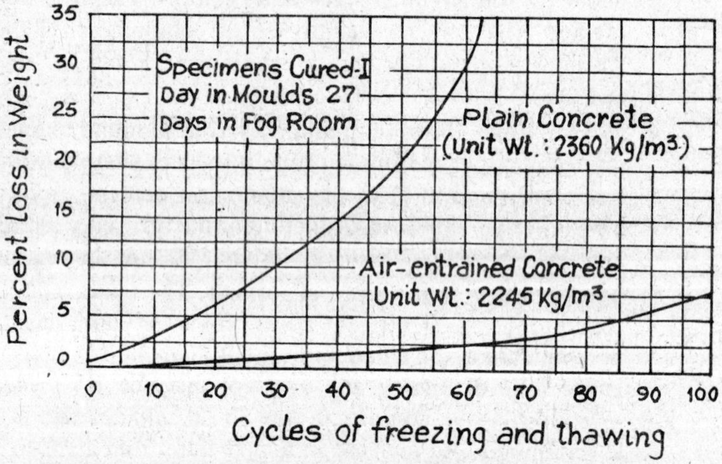

Fig. 6.3. Durability of plain and air entrained concrete frozen and thawing in 10%, Calcium chloride solution

The probable reason for the increased resistance to freezing and thawing seems to be the modification in pore structure of air entrained concrete. In ordinary concrete bigger voids interconnected by capillaries exist. The capillaries are formed due to bleeding. In case of air entrained concrete, though the total number of air voids is more, but the voids are minute. The bubbles are comparatively of uniform size and regular spherical shape. This air void system reduces the tendency for the development of large size ice crystals in concrete. Secondly the interconnected air voids system works as a buffer zone to relieve internal pressure. Fig. 6.3 shows the relative durability of plain and air entrained concrete .

The resistance of concrete to freezing and thawing was measured by "Blanks" by means of durability factor. He defined durability factor as the number of cycles of freezing and thawing till the failure of concrete divided by 100. Curves produced by Blanks are reproduced in the following Fig. 6.4. From the curves it can be seen that good quality concrete with 4% air entrainment withstood 2000 cycles of freezing and thawing where as poor quality concrete need about 14% air contents and disintegrated at about 200 cycles.

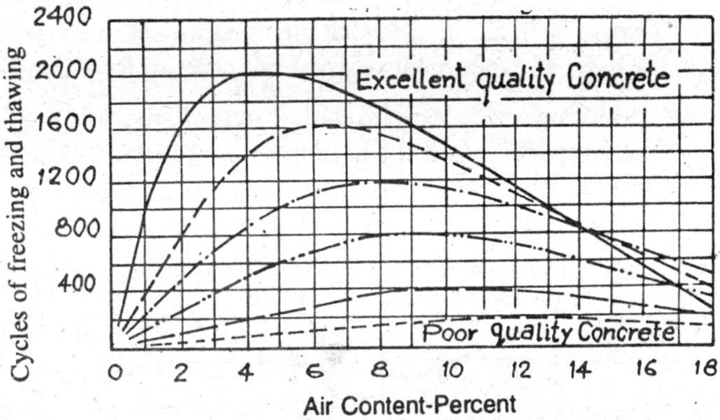

Fig. 6.4. Relation between optimum air content and durability of concrete

6.7.2. Effect on Workability

The entrainment of air in fresh concrete improves its workability. The placeability of an air entrained concrete having 7.5 cm slump was found better than a non air entrained concrete having a slump of 12.5 cms. Better place-ability of air entrained concrete results in more homogeneous concrete with least segregation, bleeding and honeycombing.

The air entrained concrete is more plastic and can be handled more easily than ordinary concrete. Air entrainment also increases the pumpability of the concrete to a great extent.

For better workability of concrete, the aggregate particles should be spaced in such a way that they can move one over the other with ease during mixing and placing. In ordinary non air entrained concrete better workability can be achieved by including sufficient fine sand, cement and water to separate the particles of coarse aggregate and supply of matrix. In this condition the movement of particles may take place with minimum interference.

Improvement in workability by air entrainment may also be explained as follows.

The proportioning of concrete mixes involves compromise between the requirements of workability, strength, durability and other properties of the hardened concrete. Workability requires that the voids in between the particles of coarse aggregates be more than which could be filled by cement paste, while the good quality hardened concrete needs that these voids should be such which just could be filled by cement paste. The entrained air increases the effective volume of cement paste during mixing and placing eliminating the need for extra cement paste to improve workability. During the process of compaction the extra air will escape resulting hardened concrete of desired density. During compaction 50 to 66% of air may excape from the fresh concrete depending upon the water cement ratio and duration of compaction.

As a matter of fact the minute air bubbles introduced in the concrete by the use of air entraining agents behave as ball bearing over which the particles of aggregates slide easily. This is called an lubricating effect of air bubbles. They also provide a cushioning effect between the sand grains, reducing particle interference to a minimum. The increase in workability by the use of air entrained agents is found more in the following type of concretes:

1. The increase in workability is found more in concretes made with angular aggregates than rounded aggregates.
2. The increase in workability is found greater for wetter mixes than drier ones.
3. The increase in workability is found more in leaner mixes than richer ones.

The effect of air entrainment on compacting factor for different water cement ratios and different mixes is shown in Fig. 6.5 based on the results of experiments carried by "WRIGHT". Road research Laboratory U.K. It is found that 5% air entrainment increases the compacting factor by 0.07, which would be equal to an increase in slump from 1.2 cm to 5.0 cms.

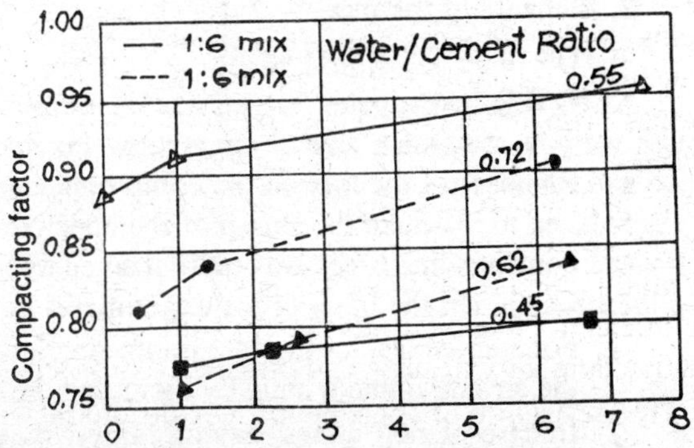

Fig. 6.5. Effect of Entrained air on the compacting factor of concrete

6.7.3. Effect of air entrainment on the strength of concrete

Generally it can be said that air entrainment in concrete reduces the compressive strength of concrete. On the basis of experiments carried out at Road Research Laboratory U.K., 'WRIGHT' has stated that each

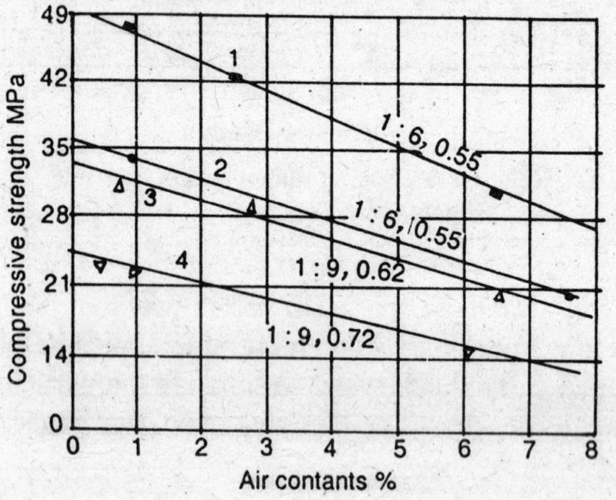

Fig. 6.6. Effect of entrained air on compressive strength

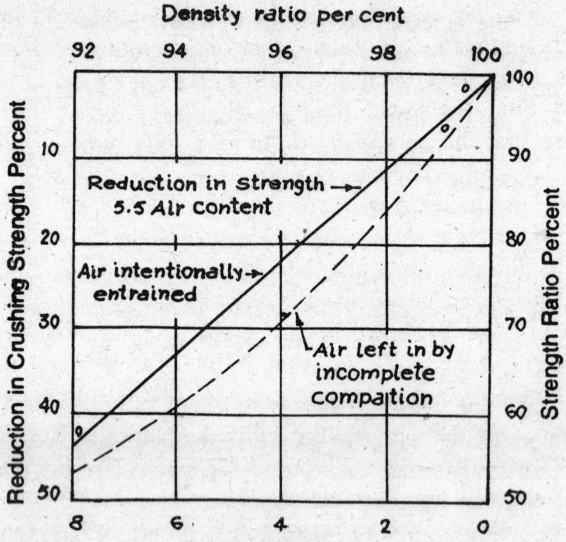

Air Content %

Fig. 6.7. Effect of entroped air on compressive strength

1% of air entrained results in the loss of 5.5% in compressive strength of concrete. The actual strength obtained is shown in Fig. 6.6. The mix proportion and water-cement ratio is shown on the curves on the right hand side. From the curves it will be seen that strength decreases with the increase in air content. Some results have been expressed as a percentage of the strength of concrete without air. These results form a single straight line as shown in Fig. 6.7. This represents a decrease in strength of 5.5% per each 1% air entrained. He further states that entrapped air effects the compressive strength of concrete slightly more than the entrained air as shown in Fig. 6.7. However the air voids caused by in complete compaction do not contribute other advantages of entrained air such as better workability and increased durability.

It has been observed that the effect of air entrainment on strength depends upon the following three factors:

1. The amount of air entrained
2. Richness of the mix
3. Type of air entraining agent

KLIEGER investigated the effects of entraining air on the strength and durability of concrete made with various, maximum size of aggregates. He made extensive study on the effect of amount of air entrained and Richness of the mix on the compressive as well as flexural strength of concrete. The water content was reduced to maintain the slump of the concrete constant as the air content was increased. The reduction in water content some times was more than compensated due to the increase in air content for the reduction in the strength. On the basis of his experiments he stated as under:

1. For lean mixes, having maximum smaller size aggregate, when the reduction in water was greatest, the air entrainment actually increased the strength of concrete both in compression and bending.
2. In case of rich mixes, having largest maximum size aggregate, where greater reduction in water content could not be effected, there was reduction in both compressive as well as flexural strengths of concrete.

3. Between these two extremities the strength varied from an increase of about 10% in bending and about 17.5% in compression and a reduction of about 24% in bending and about 46% in compression. Thus the effect of air entrainment on flexural strength is less than the effect on compressive strength. The effect of air entrainment is more on compressive strength.

The above facts also have been confirmed by CORDON and BLANKS. CORDON carried out experiments to study the effect of air entrainment on the compressive strength of concrete. The results of his study have been shown in Fig. 6.8. From the above graph it can be seen that the compressive strength of concrete decreases uniformly with the increase in air content of fresh concrete. At a constant water/cement ratio each one percent of entrained air resulted decrease of about 5% on average in the compressive strength of concrete.

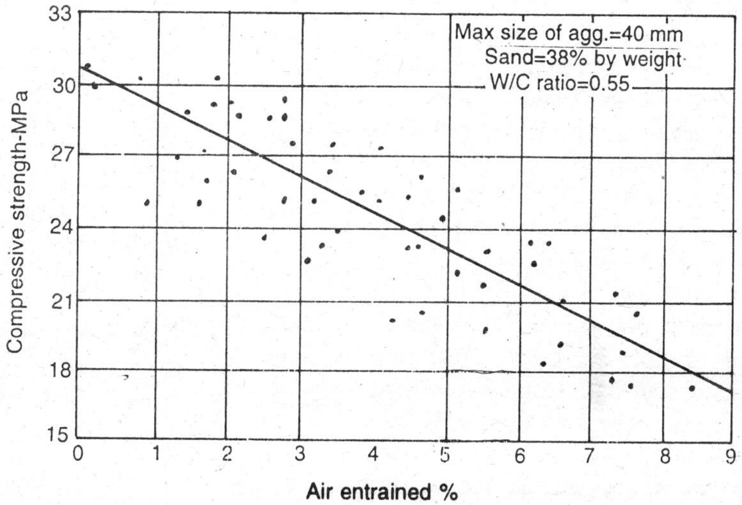

Fig. 6.8. Effect of air entrainment on the strength of concrete

On the other hand, experiments carried out at the Military Engineering College, Pune using RITHA powder as an air entraining agent, show average reduction in compressive strength of about 2% for each 1% air entrained. In addition to the above main effects, following effects have also been found useful.

6.7.4. Effect on Segregation, Bleeding and Laitance

The bleeding and segregation of concrete are different processes of loss of homogeneity. Segregation is defined as separation of cement paste from aggregates while bleeding is the emergence of water to the surface from freshly placed concrete. Usually bleeding results due to the sedimentation of the solid particles due to compaction and self weight of the solids. Due to the bleeding phenomenon, a series of water channels are formed and some of them extend upto the surface. The channel of water emerging at the surface of concrete, often brings some quantity of cement with it and forms a layer of cement on the surface of concrete. This layer of cement formed on the surface is called laitance.

Air entrainment has been found effective in reducing segregation, bleeding and laitance formation. These actions probably result from physical phenomenon due to the introduction of minute air bubbles in the fresh concrete. Air bubbles act as follows:

1. Air bubbles buoy up the aggregates and cement, resulting in the reduction of rate of sedimentation of these particles in the fresh concrete.
2. The bubbles decrease the effective area through which the differential movement of water takes place.
3. The bubbles increase the mutual adhesion between cement and aggregate particles.
4. The surface area of voids in the plastic concrete is sufficiently large to retard the rate of separation of water from the paste by drainage.

All researchers are unanimous regarding the reduction in bleeding by the use of entrained air, but they are divided about the role played by entrained air in reducing segregation.

RITHA Powder has been found an efficient air entraining agent in reducing the bleeding in cement concrete and cement mortars. Experiments have been carried out at the Military Engineering College, Pune to find the effect of vinsol resin and RITHA Powder on the reduction of bleeding in cement concrete and mortars. The test results have been shown in Fig. 6.9. From the curves it can be seen that plain mortar *i.e.* with out entrained air bled 15% of the mixing water in about 3 hours times where as mortars containing RITHA Powder bled 7.5% of the mixing water and the mortars containing vinsol resin bled 11% of the mixing water, both RITHA Powder and vinsol resin were mixed 0.1% by weight of cement.

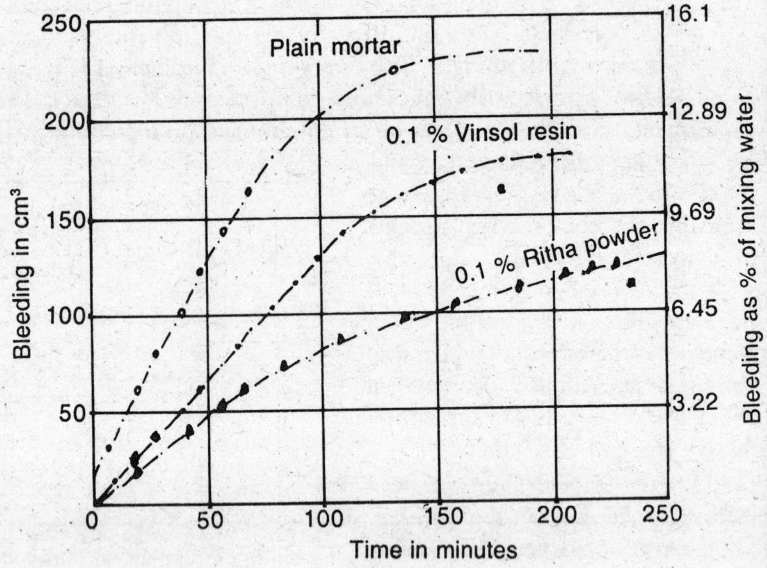

Fig. 6.9. Effect of air entrainment on bleeding

The reduction in bleeding automatically reduces the formation of laitance as these two are interrelated. The reduced bleeding of concrete permits the early finishing of the concrete surface reducing the waiting period for the commencement of trowelling. Reduction in bleeding also improves the wearing quality of the concrete surface. If the bleeding does not reduce, the masons are in the habit of sprinkling of dry cement over the concrete surface to reduce the waiting period for troweling. The finished surface scales off after some time, rendering the surface unpleasant.

6.7.5. Effect on permeability

Air entrainment has been found to have much effect on the permeability of concrete due to the following reasons.

1. The entrained air increases the workability of concrete resulting in its greater uniformity.
2. The entrained air also modifies the pore structure of the concrete.
3. The entrained air also reduces the bleeding of concrete resulting in reduction of water channels.
4. The reduction of water/cement ratio also reduces the permeability of concrete.

6.7.6. Effect on chemical resistance

Experiments conducted at Road Research Laboratory U.K. showed that air entrained concrete has greater chemical resistance than ordinary concrete.

6.7.7. Effect on sand, water and cement contents

It has been observed that minute spherical air bubbles formed due to air entrainment act as fine aggregate and enable the reduction of sand (fine aggregates). The reduction of fine aggregate results in the reduction of water requirement without any ill effect on the workability and slump. On the basis of experiments, researchers have found that the sand content by weight of total aggregate may be reduced by one percent for each percent increase in air entrainment upto about 8% with out any appreciable change in workability or slump.

Cordon on the basis of his experiments, has shown that water requirement of an average concrete mix is reduced approximately 3.5 kg/m^3 of concrete with rounded aggregates and 4.8 kg/m^3 with angular aggregates for each percent air entrained. His results are shown in Fig. 6.10. The advantages of air entrained concrete regarding reduction of sand and water requirements are shown in Table 6.7 below.

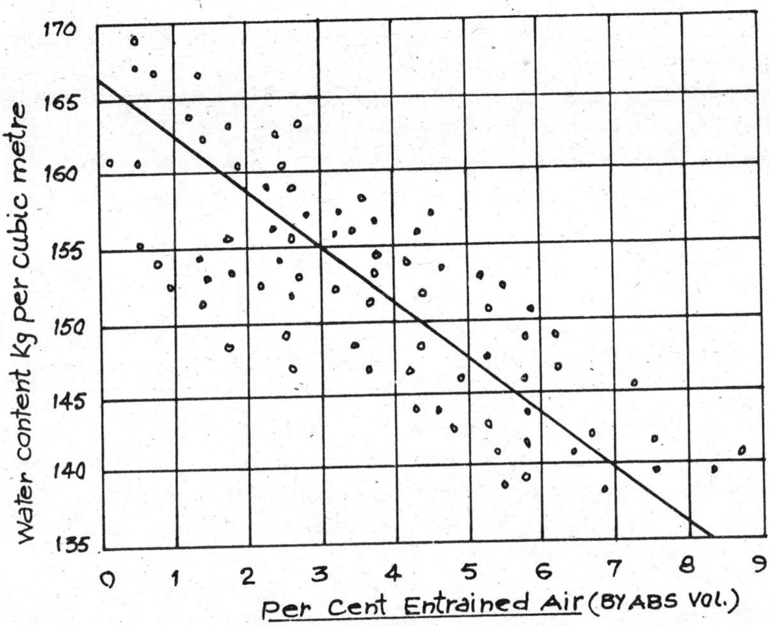

Legend:
Maximum size aggregate: 40mm constant slump within each series of 6 mixes. Slump range between 25 to 125 mm Average 75 mm

Fig. 6.10. An average reduction of 3.9kg of water per cubic metre of concrete results from each one percent increase in air content

Table 6.7. Approximate sand and water content per m^3 of plain and air entrained concrete

S. No.	*Plain concrete*			*Air entrained Concrete*		
	Max. size of coorse aggregate in mm	*Sand % of total aggregate (Absolute vol.)*	*Net water content per m^3 conc in kg*	*Recommended air content %*	*Sand % of total agg. (absolute vol.)*	*Net water content per m^3 conc in kg*
Rounded Aggregate						
1.	12.5	51	152	6 ± 1	47	132
2.	20	46	141	5 ± 1	42	122
3.	25	41	136	4.5 ± 1	37	118
4.	40	37	127	4.0 ± 1	34	112
5.	50	34	120	4.0 ± 1	31	107
6.	80	31	114	3.5 ± 1	28	100
7.	160	26	100	3.0 ± 1	24	89
Angular Aggregate						
1.	12.5	55	164	6 ± 1	51	141
2.	20	50	152	5 ± 1	46	132
3.	25	45	147	4.5 ± 1	42	127
4.	40	41	139	4.0 ± 1	38	120
5.	50	38	132	4.0 ± 1	35	118
6.	80	35	125	3.5 ± 1	32	110
7.	160	30	112	3.0 ± 1	27	98

Entrainment of air has been found useful in case of lean mixes. In lean mixes many a time increase in strength has been observed. In such cases for the given strength, a reduction in cement content may be effected. Blanks and Cordon found that concrete made with 160 mm maximum size aggregate gave satisfactory strength for mass concrete work using only 106 kg cement/m^3 concrete with air entrainment, resulting in lower production of heat of hydration and lower rise of temperature. The lower rise in temperature resulted in reduced cracking and undesirable internal stresses in mass concrete.

Effect on Unit weight. Air entrained concrete of the same workability and strength was found to have 5% less solid materials. Hence of lower weight. This will result in an economy of about 5% in the cost of cement and aggregate.

Effect on Alkali-Aggregate reaction. Air entrained concrete is found more resistant to alkali-aggregate reaction.

Effect on modulus of elasticity. With the same water/cement ratio and the same aggregate the reduction in modulus of elasticity of air entrained concrete is found 2 to 3% for each percent of air entrainment.

Abrasion resistance. It has been observed that concrete with air entrainment less than 6% has the same resistance to abrasion as that of ordinary concrete with out air entrainment. If the air entrainment is increased beyond 6%, then abrasion resistance decreases. When the air content is about 10%, the abrasion resistance decreases greatly. For satisfactory abrasion resistance generally air entrainment for pavement concrete is specified not more than 3 to 6%.

6.8. AIR CONTENTS

For each mix there must be a minimum volume of voids required for protection from frost. On the basis of his experiments, KLIEGER found that the minimum volume of voids should be 9 percent of the volume of mortar and the air must be distributed uniformly through out the cement paste. The actual controlling factor is the spacing of air bubbles *i.e.* the thickness of cement paste between adjacent air voids. A spacing of 0.25 mm between the voids is found satisfactory for full protection from frost damage. In Germany it is taken as 0.2 mm.

To be more effective against frost damage, the air bubbles should be as small as possible. Their size depends to a large degree on the foaming process. Also the voids are not all of one size, therefore it is convenient to express their size in terms of specific surface. For air entrained concrete of satisfactory quality the specific surface (square mm per cubic mm) of voids may vary from 15 to 24 mm^{-1} and the specific surface of accidental air is less than 12 mm^{-1}. The size of entrained air bubbles varies from 0.05 mm to 1.25 mm. For a given air content of the concrete, the spacing of air bubbles depends on water/cement ratio of the mix. Typical values of the amount of air required for a 0.25 mm spacing for different mixes are given in the following table based on *powers* results.

Table 6.8. Air content required for a void spacing of 0.25 mm

Approximate cement content of concrete kg/m^3	*Water/cement ratio*	*Air requirement as a percentage of volume of concrete for specific surface of voids mm^{-1}*				
		14	18	20	24	31
445		8.5	6.4	5.0	3.4	1.8
390	0.35	7.5	5.6	4.4	3.0	1.6
330		6.4	4.8	3.8	2.5	1.3
445		10.2	7.6	6.0	4.0	2.1
390	0.49	8.9	6.7	5.3	3.5	1.9
330		7.6	5.7	4.5	3.0	1.6
280		6.4	4.8	3.8	2.5	1.3
445		12.4	9.4	7.4	5.0	2.6
390		10.9	8.2	6.4	4.3	2.3

Approximate cement content of concrete kg/m³	*Water/cement ratio*	*Air requirement as a percentage of volume of concrete for specific surface of voids mm⁻¹*				
		14	18	20	24	31
330	0.66	9.3	7.0	5.5	3.7	1.9
280		7.8	5.8	4.6	3.1	1.6
225		6.2	4.7	3.7	2.5	1.3

6.8.1. Optimum Air Content in Concrete

The air content in a given concrete has been found a function of the following factors:

1. The purpose for which concrete is used.
2. The location and climatic conditions of the area.
3. Maximum size of aggregate used in concrete
4. Richness of the mix.

Usually the desirable limit of air content is between 3 to 6%. Ti s range constitute reasonable specifications covering all conditions. Below 3% air entrainment maynot provide the advantage of air entrained concrete.

6.8.2. Air Entraining Agents

The main types of air entraining agents are as follows:

1. Animal and vegetable fats and oils and their fatty acids such as beef stearic and oleic acids.
2. Natural wood resins which react with lime in the cement to form a soluble resinate. The resin may be pre-neutralized with NaOH, so that a water soluble soap of a resin acid is formed. Vinsol resin is a good example of this group.
3. Wetting agents such as alkali salts of sulphated and sulphonated organic compounds. Their trade names being Darex and Cormix etc.
4. Water soluble soaps of resin acids, animal and vegetable fatty acids.
5. Miscellaneous materials such as sodium salts of petroleum sulphonic acids, hydrogen peroxide and aluminum powder.

Though there are numerous air entraing agents available in the market. In U.S.A. vinsol resin, Darex, Airalon, Teepol, Petrosan etc. are available as air entraining agents. Out of these materials vinsol resin and Darex are most-popular through out the world.

In India till 1950 no air entraining agent was developed. However in the construction of Hirakud dam, Koyana dam, Rihand dam air entrained concrete was used. In these dams American air entraing agents such as vinsol resin and DAREX etc. were used. Later in 1950. Certain air entraing agents were developed. They are RITHA Power, HICO, KOYNAEA, RIHAND AEA and Aerosin-HRS. Now numerous commercial brand air entraing agents are available in the market. They are MICHOEL AEA, COMPLAST AEA 215, ROFF AEA 330, MC MISCHOEL AEA etc.

Though numerous proprietary brands of air entraining agents are available commercially, but the performance of the unknown admixture should be checked by trial mixes. The essential requirements of an air entraining agent are that it should rapidly produce a system of finely divided and stable form of the individual bubbles which resist coalescence (merger). The foam should have no harmful chemical effect on the cement paste.

6.9. MEASUREMENT OF AIR CONTENTS IN AIR ENTRAINED CONCRETE

Mainly there are three methods of measuring air contents of fresh concrete.

1. Gravimetric method
2. Volumetric method
3. Pressure method

1. Gravimetric method

This method is simple and does not require any special equipment as such it is the first method used for calculating the air contents in concrete. The method principally comprises in the determination of density of fresh concrete compacted by a standard method. This density is then compared with the theoretical density of air free concrete calculated from mix proportions and specific gravities of the constituent materials of the concrete.

Let the density of air free concrete $= 2380 \text{ kg/m}^3$

Measured density of concrete $= 2220 \text{ kg/m}^3$

Then 1 m^3 concrete will contain solid & liquid matter $= \dfrac{2220}{2380} \text{ m}^3$

$= 0.924 \, m^3$

$\therefore$ Air content $= 1 - 0.924 = .076$ or 7.6%

This method is found useful for laboratory use. It is not well suited for field use as it requires knowledge of mix proportion of concrete.

2. Volumetric method

This method aims at measuring the volume of air in the sample of fresh concrete directly. The sample of known volume of concrete is taken and all air is removed from it by any method and then amount of water required to restore the original volume is determined. This method is tedious and time consuming.

3. Pressure method of air measurement

This is the most popular and best suited method for site use. It is based on the relation between the volume of air and the applied pressure (at a constant temperature) given by Boyle's law. This meter is directly graduated for percentage of air and proportions or properties of materials need not be known. This meter is not suitable for use with porous aggregates and need calibration if used at high attitude.

A simple meter is shown in Fig. 6.11. The procedure of the test consists of observing the decrease in the volume of a sample of compacted concrete when subjected to a known pressure. The pressure is applied with a small pump as that of bicycle pump and measured by a pressure gauge. Due to the increase in pressure over atmospheric the volume of air in the concrete decreases and this causes a fall in the level of the water above the concrete. By arranging the level of the water to vary within a calibrated tube, the air content can be read even by an unskilled operator.

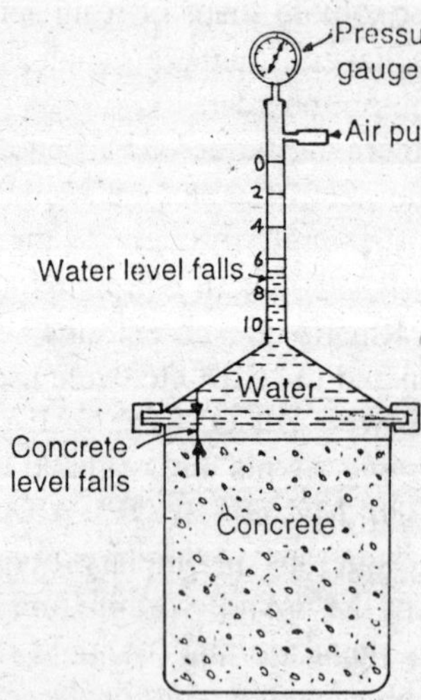

Fig. 6.11. Pressure type air meter

Methods of air entraining

Air entrainment can be effected by adding finely divided aluminium powder to the cement. By the addition of this powder a chemical reaction takes place and hydrogen is librated. The addition of 0.1% to 0.2% of aluminium powder of the weight of the cement produces sufficient gas to form a cellular structure in the cement paste producing a light weight concrete on hardening. This method however is not found suitable for air entraining as the bubbles produced are relatively large and the process is effective when cement with little sand or neat cement is used.

Therefore the best method of air entrainment is, to use surface active agents, which can be used from 0.025 to 0.1% by weight of the cement.

6.10. GAS FORMING AGENTS

Gas forming agent in concrete is a chemical admixture. Aluminium powder, Zinc, magnesium powder and hydrogen peroxide may be used as gas forming agents in concrete. Generally aluminium powder is used as a gas forming agent in concrete. Aluminium powder reacts with hydroxide produced during the process of hydration of cement resulting in the production of minute hydrogen gas bubbles through out the cement paste. The extent of gas production depends upon the following factors.

1. Type and amount of aluminium powder
2. Chemical composition and fineness of cement
3. Mix proportion
4. Temperature

The amount of aluminium powder usually added varies from 0.005 to 0.02% by weight of cement *i.e.* one tea spoonful powder per bag of cement.

Properly controlled action of aluminium powder causes slight expansion in plastic concrete or mortar. The expansion of plastic concrete has the following effects on the concrete properties.

1. It reduces the settlement of concrete ingredients.
2. It increases the bond of cement paste with reinforcing bars.
3. It improves effectiveness of cement grout filling in joints.

It is particularly useful for grouting under machine bases. The effect on strength depends whether or not the concrete is restrained from expansion. If it is restrained, the effect on strength is negligible and if not restrained the loss of strength is considerable. Thus to get good results it is important that form work be tight and the grout confined completely.

In hot-weather, the action of aluminium powder is very quick and its beneficial effect is lost, where as in cold weather the action is very slow and desired results may not be produced before the concrete has set.

To produce the same amount of expansion at 4°C as at 21°C, twice the amount of aluminium powder is required. As the very small quantity of aluminium powder is used, and it has a tendency to float on water, it should be pre mixed with sand and then this mix should be added to the mixer.

Aluminium powder is also used for the production of light weight concrete. For this purpose about 100 gram of aluminium powder is used per bag of cement. Some times Sodium hydroxide or tri sodium phosphate is used to accelerate the reaction.

By varying the proportion of aluminium powder depending upon the temperature and controlling the gas formation, light weight concrete in a wide range of density, may be produced.

6.11. DAMP AND WATER PROOFING ADMIXTURES

In practice one of the most important requirements of concrete is that it must be impervious to water under the following conditions.

1. When concrete surface is subjected to water pressure on one side.
2. The concrete should be impervious to the absorption of surface water by capillary action.

To achieve the above objectives, the use of well chosen admixtures has been accepted. Here it is to be noted that the use of admixture is not the substitute for bad materials, bad design or workman ship. An admixture can not compensate for cracks or large voids in concrete causing permeability.

Water proofing agents may be obtained in liquid, paste or powder form and may consist of water repellent or pore filling materials.

6.11.1. Pore filling materials

Following are the main pore filling materials:

(*a*) Silicates of soda

(*b*) Aluminium and Zinc sulphates

(*c*) Calcium and aluminium chlorides.

These materials are chemically active pore fillers. In addition to this, they also act to accelerate the setting time of concrete, rendering the concrete more impervious at early age.

The chemically inactive pore filling materials are earth fullers, chalk and talc etc. These materials are ground very finely. Their main action is:

1. To improve the workability
2. To reduce the water requirement for the given workability
3. To make the concrete dense which is basically impervious

6.11.2. Water repelling materials

In this group of admixtures, following materials are included.

Resins, fats, waxes, soda, potash and calcium soaps and coaltar residue etc.

Some times in some of the water proofing admixtures inorganic salts of fatty acids usually ammonium or calcium stearate or oleate along with lime and calcium chloride are added. Calcium or ammonium stearate or oleate act mainly as water repelling material, lime as pore filling material while calcium chloride acts as an accelerator for the development of early strength and also helps in efficient curing of concrete. All these factors contribute for the development or making concrete imperious.

Heavy mineral oil free from fatty or vegetable oil has been found to be effective in making concrete water proof. The use of asphalt cut back has been tried in quantities of 2.5, 5 and 10% of the weight of cement. The strength and workability has not been found affected.

6.12. WORKABILITY AGENTS

Workability of concrete is one of the most important characteristics. The improvement of workability has two distinct aspects as follows:

1. It makes the mix more fluid.
2. It improves the character of the mix, so that it becomes more cohessive.

Workability is most important under the following situations.

1. If the concrete is to be placed in deep beams, thin sections and closely spaced reinforcement.
2. If the concrete is harsh due to poor grading or poor characteristics of aggregates.
3. For making high strength concrete with low water/cement ratio.
4. Under special circumstances where special means of placement are required as tremie, chute or pumping equipment etc.

There are many materials available which can improve the workability of concrete. They can be divided into the following groups:

1. Finely divided materials or powders.
2. Surface active materials including air entraining agents.
3. Plasticizers and super plasticizers.

1. Finely divided materials. These materials are chemically inert. Their main function is to increase the cohesiveness of concrete, if used in appropriate quantity. If used excessively they will stiffen the mix, resulting in lowering the strength. The use of these materials improves the workability, reduces the bleeding, increases the strength of lean concrete and may not increase water requirement and drying shrinkage.

Under this category many materials can be used. The common materials used are bentonite, Kaolite, hydrated lime, fly ash, talc, finely divided silica, diatomaceous earth etc. The use of these admixtures is desirable under the following conditions:

(*a*) The aggregate is deficient in grading *i.e.* deficient in fine material.

(*b*) The cement has a marked tendency to bleed.

These admixtures are often added to the concrete at the mixer. Hydrated lime usually is used in mortars for brick work. Hydrated lime is also used if the sand is more coarse or sharp.

2. Surface active materials. Surface active materials are of greater importance in practice as they have better effects on the other properties of concrete also. These materials are similar to detergents. These materials reduce the surface tension of water and behave as surface wetting agents. Along with wetting the surfaces of the solid particles more easily, they also produce lathering effect, resulting in the production of minute air bubbles ranging from 0.05 mm to 1.55 mm diameter in the cement paste. Air bubbles make the mix more cohessive and more fluid. Air entrainment has been discussed separately in this chapter.

The surface active admixtures are used in small quantities and usually ground with cement or some times dissolved in the mixing water for the batch. Usually calcium chloride, some oils, stearates are used as surface active agents. Some proprietary products are also used as wetting agents.

3. Plasticizer and super plasticizers. Almost in all the situations the use of these admixtures is for improving the workability of concrete. These admixtures are discussed in detail separately.

6.13. GROUTING AGENTS

Grouting under different situations needs different qualities of grout mix. Some times the grout mixture will be required to set quickly as in situations where the plugging effect is desired. On the other hand as in the case of oil wells, grout mixtures should be in fluid state over a long period, so that it may flow into all cavities and fissure. Following admixtures are used for grouting mixtures.

(*a*) Accelerates

(*b*) Retarders

(*c*) Gas forming agents

(*d*) Workability agents

(*e*) Plasticizers

(*a*) *Materials to be used.* For accelerators calcium chloride or tri-ethanolamine can be used. Accelerators are used where a plugging effect is desired.

(*b*) *For Retarders.* Gypsum, mucic acid and RDA (Ray Lig Binder) may be used. They are used where grout is required in fluid state for longer time.

(*c*) *Gas forming agents.* Gas forming admixture are used in grout while grouting is to be done in completely confined areas, such as under machine bases. For gas formation agent, Aluminium powder is the most commonly used material, which chemically reacts to form small bubbles of hydrogen and produces expansion of the grout. This expansion eliminates the shrinkage and settlement.

Plasticizers and super plasticizers in powder form have been always used as one of the ingredients of the grout mixture for effective flowability and obtaining high strength.

6.14. CORROSION PREVENTIVE AGENTS

Though the problem of corrosion of reinforcing steel in concrete is universal, but it is more acute when the concrete is exposed to saline water or to industrial corrosive fumes. Dougill of U.K. got a patent for the use of sodium benzoate as a corrosion preventive agent. In this process 2% sodium benzoate can be added in the mixing water or 10% benzoate cement slurry may be used to paint the reinforcement or both may be applied at a time. Sodium benzoate is also found as an accelerator of compressive strength. Different agents have been found useful for the prevention of corrosion of concrete reinforcing steel as follows:

1. When the steel reinforcement in concrete is subjected to direct or alternating current, the use of calcium lignosulphonate is found to decrease the rate of corrosion of steel embedded in the concrete.
2. For autoclave products, the use of sodium and calcium nitrate have been found effective to prevent the corrosion of steel of concrete. 2 to 3% of sodium nitrate by weight of cement is found to be

quite effective for the prevention of corrosion of reinforcing steel of concrete. There are many commercial admixtures available to prevent the corrosion of steel in the market.

6.15. BONDING ADMIXTURES

These admixtures are water emulsion of many organic materials. These admixtures are mixed with cement or mortar grout to be applied to an old concrete surface just before the patching with concrete or mortar to be done. The function of bonding admixtures is to increase the bond strength between the old and new concrete. This procedure is applied for patching up spalled or eroded concrete or for adding thin layers of resurfacing.

The commonly used bonding admixtures are made from natural or synthetic rubber or from organic polymers. Polyvinyl chloride and polyvinyl acetate are important polymers used in the manufacture of bonding admixtures.

Bonding admixtures can be divided into the two groups as follows:

1. Re emulsifiable type
2. Non re-emulsifiable type. This class of bonding admixtures is better suited for external use as it is water resistant.

These emulsions generally are added to the mixtures in proportion of 5 to 20% by weight of cement. Usually bonding admixtures cause entrainment of air and sticky consistency in a grout mixture. The bonding admixtures are effective on sound and clean surfaces.

6.16. POZZOLANIC MATERIALS

There are siliceous and aluminous materials, possessing little or no cementitious value by themselves, but in finely divided form and in the presence of moisture react chemically with calcium hydroxide librated on hydration of cement at ordinary temperature to form compounds, possessing cementitious properties.

The Silicious or aluminious compounds in a finely divided form react with calcium hydroxide to form highly stable, cementitious substances of complex composition involving calcium, silica and water. Generally amorphous silicate reacts much more rapidly than the crystalline form. The calcium hydroxide a water soluble material is converted into insoluble cementitious material by the reaction of pozzolanic materials.

Initially the pozzolanic reaction is slow and thus the production of heat of hydration and development of strength is also slow. The reaction involves the consumption of $Ca(OH)_2$ and thus there is no production of $Ca(OH)_2$. The reduction of $Ca(OH)_2$ increases the durability of cement paste by making the cement paste dense and impervious.

Materials. Pozzolanic materials may be divided into two groups.

Natural pozzolanic materials

Under this group following materials can be grouped:

1. Calcined diatomaceous earths
2. Volcanic ash, tuffs and pumicites
3. Opaline cherts
4. Clay and shales

Natural pozzolans need further grinding and calcining to activate them. Now a days they have lost their popularity due to the availability of more active artificial pozzolans. Hence they have not been discussed here.

Artificial pozzolanas

Under this group following substances are grouped:

1. Silica fume
2. Fly ash
3. Blast furnace slag
4. Rice husk
5. Surkhi
5. Meta kaoline etc.

Out of these materials here only some of them have been discussed in some details.

6.17. SILICA FUME

It is an artificial pozzolanic material. It is produced by the reduction of high quality quartz with coal in an electric arc furnance in the manufacture of silicon or ferro silicon alloy. In the process silica fume rises as oxidised vapour. It cools, condenses and collected in cloth bags. The silica fume so collected is further processed to remove impurities and to control particle size. The condensed silica fume is essentially silicon dioxide (SiO_2) more than 90% in non crystalline form. Its shape is spherical and extremely fine in size less than 1 micron. Its average diameter is about 0.1 micron. It is about 100 times smaller than average cement particles. The specific surface area of silica fume is about 200000 cm^2/gram as against 2300 to 3000 cm^2/gram that of cement.

The use of silica fume along with super plasticizers has been found very effective in the high performance of concrete. About twenty five years ago perhaps no one would have imagined that the production of concrete of 1200 kg/cm^2 compressive strength could be achieved, which is possible now with the use of silica fume with super Plasticizers.

As a matter of fact silica fume by it self does not contribute to the strength dramatically. It contributes to the strength property as a very fine pozzolanic material and creating a dense packing pore filler of cement paste. Really speaking the high strength of the high performance concrete containing silica fume is attributed to a larger extent to the reduction in water content which is possible in the presence of high dose of super plasticizers and dense packing of cement paste.

6.17.1. Some information about silica fume

Silica fume is also called micro silica. It is an very important new material. Some details about this material are as follows:

(*a*) Initially it was produced as an ultra fine un densified powder.

(*b*) It contained at least 85% SiO_2

(*c*) The mean size of diameter is between 0.1 to 0.2 micron.

(*d*) Its minimum specific surface area is 150000 cm^2/gram.

(*e*) The shape of its particles is spherical.

Available form

It is available in the following forms:

(*a*) Undensified form with bulk density of 200 to 300 kg/m^3

(*b*) Densified form with bulk density of 500 to 600 kg/m^3.

(*c*) Micro pellitised form with bulk density of 600 to 800 kg/m^3.

(*d*) Slurry form with density 1400 kg/m^3.

(*e*) Slurry of silica fume is the easiest and most practical to use in the concrete mix. The slurry is produced by mixing undensified silica fume powder and water in equal proportion by weight usually 50:50.

(*f*) Its surface area is 15 to 20 × 10^4 cm^2/gram.

(*g*) The p_H value of standard slurry is 4.7, specific gravity 1.3 to 1.4, dry content of silica fume 48 to 52%.

Pozzolanic action

Silica fume or micro silica is much more reactive than fly ash or any other natural pozzolana. The reactivity of a pozzolana can be quantified by measuring the amount of calcium hydroxide in the cement paste at different times. Most of the researchers agree that the C-S-H formed by the reaction between the silica fume and $Ca(OH)_2$ appears dense and amorphous. The 15% silica fume has been found to reduce the quantity of $Ca(OH)_2$ of samples of cement from 24% to 12% in 90 days and from 25% to 11% in 180 days.

6.17.2. Influence of silica fume on fresh concrete

The demand of water in concrete increases in proportion to the amount of silica fume added to it. The increase in water demand of concrete having silica fume will be about 1% for every 1%. cement substituted. It has been observed that 20 mm maximum sized aggregate concrete having 10% silica fume will need an increased water content of about 20 litres/m^3. Thus steps should be taken to avoid this increase in water by adjusting the grading and using some plasticizers. The addition of silica fume to concrete has the following effects.

1. It lowers the slump of the mix, but increases its cohesiveness to a great extent.
2. It makes the fresh concrete sticky in nature and hard to handle.
3. It reduces the bleeding of the concrete. Hence the concrete can be handled and transported without segregation.
4. It introduces piastic shrinkage cracking in the concrete.
5. Silica fume produces more heat of hydration at the initial stages, but total generation of heat will be less than that of concrete without silica fume.

6.17.3. INFLUENCE ON HARDENED CONCRETE

Silica fume has the following effects on the hardened concrete.

(*a*) With the use of silica fume, concrete of 60 to 80 MPa strength can be obtained easily.

(*b*) The modulus of elasticity of silica fume concrete is less than that of ordinary concrete with out silica fume.

(*c*) It increases the durability of concrete, but its frost resistance has been found less.

(*d*) It has been found effective in reducing the alkali-aggregate reaction, but some researchers are of the view that addition of silica fume even in small quantities actually increases the expansion in concrete.

Mixing

The silica fume should be added to concrete mix in the 50:50 slurry as it is easy to store and to mix. The use of slurry has been found to produce significantly higher compressive and tensile strength than in other forms. However to avoid gelling and sedimentation of slurry it is to be kept agitated for few hours in a day.

Curing

Curing of a silica fume concrete is very important. If the rate of evaporation from the surface is faster than the rate of migration of water from the interior to the surface, plastic shrinkage will take place. In the absence of bleeding and slow movement of water from the interior to the surface, early curing is essential.

6.18. FLY ASH

As stated on page 47 also, it is a finely divided residue from the combustion of powdered coal. It is a waste product from coal fired power stations and Railway locomotive etc. It is the most common artificial pozzolana material. The fly ash particles are spherical and of the same fineness as that of cement. Thus silica is alway readily available for reaction.

The pozzolanic activity of fly ash is good but it is essential that it has constant carbon content and constant fineness. The use of fly ash in concrete as an admixture not only extends the technical advantage to the properties of concrete, but it also contributes to the environmental pollution control. For physical & chemical requirements of fly ash please refer page 47.

6.18.1. Effect of Fly ash on fresh Concrete

The use of right quntity of fly ash is found in the reduction of water content required for the production of desired slump. With the reduction of water content in concrete, bleeding and drying shrinkage is also reduced. As fly ash is not highly reactive, the heat of hydration can also be reduced by the replacement of a part of cement with fly ash. 30% replacement of cement by fly ash has been found to reduce the rise of temperature by about 6°C as shown in Fig. 6.12.

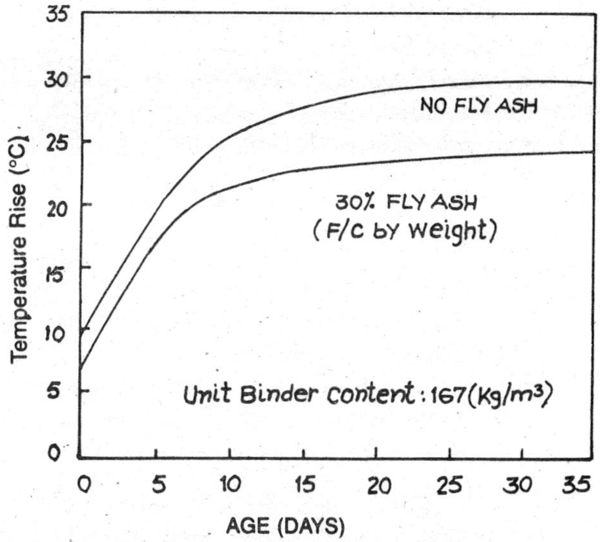

Fig. 6.12. Change in rate of the heat evolution of concrete with and without fly ash

6.18.2. Effect of fly ash on hardened concrete

Fly ash is an industrial waste, but the use of good quality fly ash in concrete has shown following effects on the concrete properties.

1. Fly ash being a pozzolanic material, its reaction takes place slowly. The initial strength of fly ash concrete is less than that of concrete without fly ash sufficiently but the strength at the later age is much greater than that of concrete with out fly ash.
2. Fly ash also develops dense texture of concrete, resulting in the decrease of permeability of concrete.
3. As pozzolanic reaction can take place only in the presence of water, thus fly ash concrete needs long curing period for the development of strength. Thus it should be cured for longer period.
4. The use of good quality fly ash reduces the heat of hydration.
5. It also increases the durability of concrete.

6.19. HIGH VOLUME FLY ASH CONCRETE (HVFA)

At present India generates about 100×10^6 tones of fly ash and out of which about 5% is utilised in making blended or pozzolanic cement, in which 10 to 30% addition of fly ash of the cement content is permissible. Thus the disposal of fly ash has become a serious problem. One of the practical approach to reduce the disposal problem of fly ash is to popularise the use of high volume fly ash concrete.

The high volume fly ash concrete is a concrete in which 50 to 60% fly ash is incorporated. First it was developed for use for the mass concrete structures as dams where the development of low heat of hydration is the main consideration. Later on the use of this concrete showed excellent durability and mechanical properties required for structural and pavement constructions. It is also found useful for light weight concrete, shot creating and roller compacted concrete.

6.19.1. Properties of high volume fly ash concrete

Experiments carried out at Canada centre for Mineral and Energy Technology with more fluid concrete having 18.0 to 20 cm slump have been observed as follows:

1. **Bleeding and setting time.** Due to the low water content in high volume fly ash concrete, bleeding also is very low. The setting time is little longer than that of conventional concrete. Its use in cold weather concreting should be done with great care. The form work can not be removed early as in the case of ordinary cement concrete.
2. **Heat of hydration.** Due to low contents of cement, its heat of hydration is low. Experiments have shown that the heat of hydration of high volume fly ash is 15 to 25% less than ordinary concrete with out fly ash.
3. **Curing period.** The high volume fly ash concrete has to be cured effectively for longer period than ordinary as well as normal fly ash concrete to obtain the continued pozzolanic reaction for the

development of strength. It should be properly protected from pre-matured drying by covering the surface properly.

4. **Durability of (HVFA) concrete.** Investigations carried out in Canada & U.S.A. have shown that high volume fly ash concrete has excellent durability.

Mechanical properties. Its mechanical properties also have been found excellent.

6.19.2. Use of high volume fly ash

Laboratory and field experiments have shown that concrete containing 55 to 60% high volume fly ash has excellent structural and durability characteristics. Hence after 1985, high volume fly ash has been used in the construction of many high rise buildings, industrial structures, concrete roads and Roller Compacted Concrete dams etc. There is bright future for this material due to sound economy and usefulness to utilize the large waste and harmful material.

Slag is a waste product of the manufacture of pig iron. It is a non metallic product consisting essentially of silicates and aluminates of calcium and other bases. The molten slag is rapidly chilled by quenching it in water to form a glassy and granulated material like sand. For further details please refer page 41-42.

6.20. PERFORMANCE OF BLAST FURNANCE SLAG IN CONCRETE

Fresh concrete. The replacement of cement with ground granulated blast furnance slag has been found to reduce the amount of water in the fresh concrete to obtain the same slump. The reduction in water content will be more with the increase of slag content and fineness of the slag. This is due to the different configurations and shape of slag and cement particles. Further the water added for mixing is not immediately lost due to the slight lower surface hydration of slag than cement. The reduction of water with the amount of slag and its fineness is shown in Fig. 6.13. Reduction in bleeding has not been found significant with slag having fireness of 4000 cm^2/gram. However significant benificial effect has been observed with fineness of 6000 cm^2/gram and above of the slag. Fig. 6.14 shows the relation between fineness of Blast furnace slag and unit water content. (Courtsy TAKATO et-al and ENDO. H.et al)

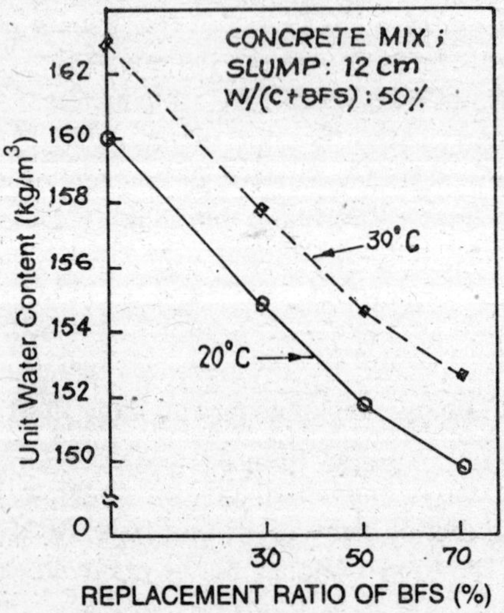

Fig. 6.13. Relationship between replacement ratio of slag and water content

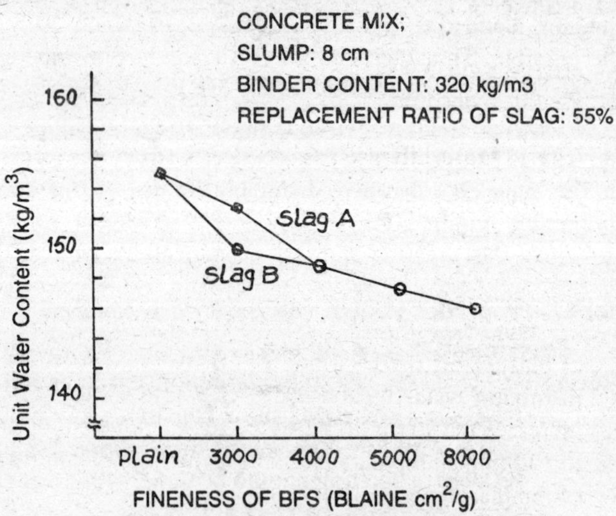

Fig. 2.14. Relationship between fineness of BFS and unit water content

Hardened Concrete. Experiments carried out on the use of slag have shown that the use of slag in concrete enhances the intrinsic properties of fresh as well as of hardened concrete. Following advantage have been noted.

1. Reduction in the evaluation of heat of hydration.

2. Refinement of pore structures.
3. Increased resistance to the chemical attack.
4. Reduction in the permeability of concrete.

6.21. PLASTICIZERS (WATER REDUCING AGENTS)

The essence of good quality concrete is the requirement of right workability. Under different situations concrete of different degree of workability is needed. A high degree of workability is required in situations like deep beams, thin sections with high percentage of reinforcement, beam and column junctions, pumping of concrete, tremie concreting, hot weather concreting etc. The conventional methods of improving workability are by improving the gradation or increasing the quantity of fine aggregate or by increasing the cement quantity. In the field there are limitations and difficulties to obtain high workability under the given set of conditions. In the field in most of the cases generally extra water is added to the concrete unmindful of its ill effects on the properties of the concrete. The use of extra water is very harmful and should never be used. The use of extra water will not improve the inherent good quality such as cohesiveness and homogeneity of the mix, which reduces the bleeding and segregation of the concrete. Now a days many water reducing admixtures are available in the market. These admixtures are known as plasticizers and super plasticizers. The combination of organic substances or combinations of organic and inorganic substances which cause reduction in water content for a given workability or give a higher workability at the same water content are known or termed as plasticizer admixtures. These are used for the following proposes.

1. To achieve a higher strength by decreasing the water/cement ratio at the same workability as that of an admixture free mix.
2. To achieve the same workability by decreasing the cement and to reduce the heat of hydration in the mass concrete.
3. To increase the workability to provide ease in placing concrete in inaccessible locations.

The use of plasticizer is found to improve the desirable qualities of the plastic or green concrete. For making reinforced concrete or mass concrete of higher workability now a days it has become an standard practice to use plasticizer or super plasticizer. Now a days the use of super plasticizer has become an universal practice to reduce the water/cement ratio for the given workability. The reduction in water/cement ratio increases the strength and improves durability of the concrete. Some times plasticizers are used to reduce the cement content and heat of hydration in mass concrete.

6.21.1. Materials used as plasticizers

Generally following materials are used as plasticizers

1. Ligno sulphates and their derivatives and modifications, salts of sulphonates hydrocarbons.
2. Polyglycol esters, acid of hydroxylated carboxylic acids and their derivaties and modifications.
3. Carbohydrates.

Out of these materials, sodium, calcium and ammonium ligno sulphates are most popular. The amount of plasticizers used varies from 0.1% to 0.4% by weight of cement. At constant workability, the reduction in mixing water by the use of 0.1 to 0.4% of plasticizer is expected from 5% to 15%, which naturally increases the strength. At the same water/cement ratio, the increase in workability may range from 30 mm to 150 mm slump depending upon the initial slump of concrete, type of cement, content of cement and dose of the plasticizer.

A gouu plasticizer produces fluidity in concrete or mortar in a different way than that of an air entraining agent. However some plasticizers also entrain some air along with improving the workability. A good plasticizer should not entrain air in concrete more than 1 to 2% as air entrainment reduces the strength of concrete.

Generally one of the most common chemical used as plasticizer is ligno sulphonic acid in the form of its calcium or sodium salt. This chemical is a natural product derived from wood processing industries. It has been observed that a normal recommended dose of plasticizer does not affect the setting time significantly, but higher dose than prescribed may cause excessive retardation.

6.21.2. Action of plasticizers

The main action of plasticizers is to produce fluidity in the mix and improve the workability of concrete, mortar or grout. The mechanism of the process may be explained as follows:

(*i*) Dispersion

Portland cement being very fine, its particles have a tendency to move and collect in pockets of the wet concrete forming bunch of particles. In other words cement has a tendency to flocculate in wet concrete. These bunch of cement particles or flocculations entrap certain amount of water used in the mix. Thus the total water used in the mix is not available for producing fluidity in the mix.

The principal active components of water reducing admixtures are surface active agents which concentrate at the interface between two emmiscible phases, which alter the physico-chemical forces at the interface.

When plasticizers are used, their surface active agents are attracted and hold at the surface of cement particles *i.e.* the surface active agents are adsorbed on the cement particles. Due to this adsorption the cement particles get negatively charged and produce repulsive force on the particles, which repulse the particles away from each other and neutratize the force of attraction of the particles resulting in stabilizing their dispersion.

This repulsive force is called Zeta potential, which depends on base, solid contents and the quantity of plasticizer used. The over all effect of adsorbtion of plasticizer is that cement particles get deflocculated and dispersed. On the deflocculation of cement particles the water trapped inside the flocs, gets released and is available to produce fluidity in the mix. The mechanism is shown in Fig. 6.15.

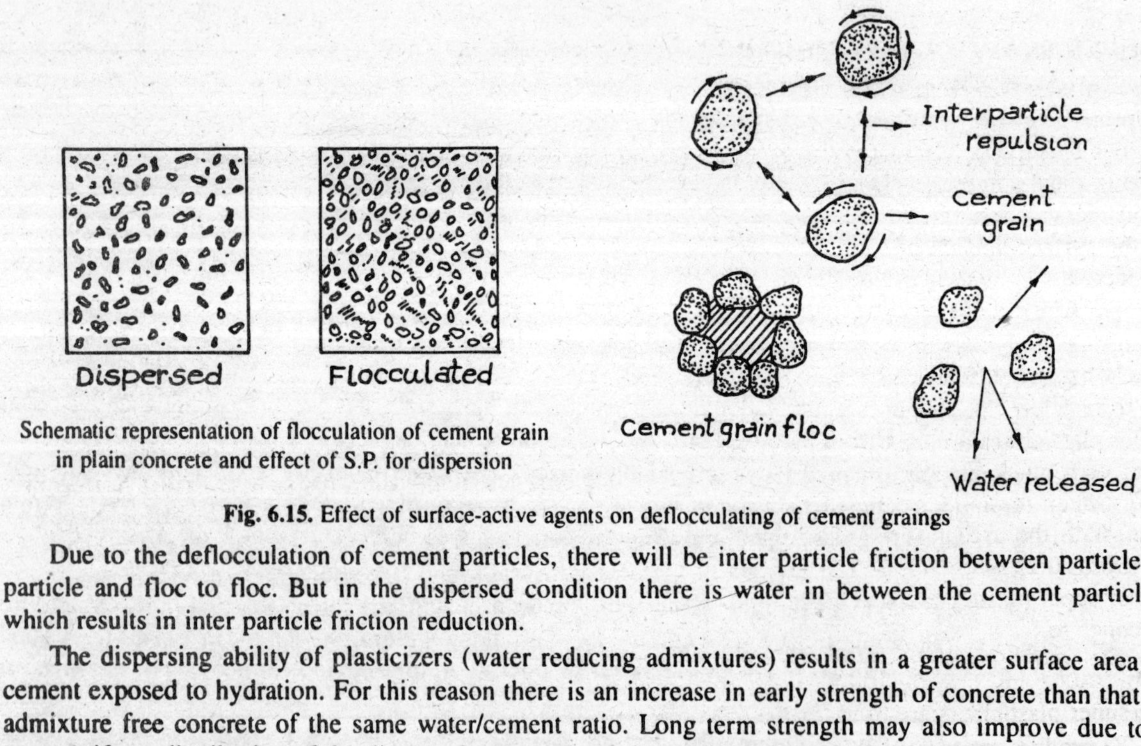

Fig. 6.15. Effect of surface-active agents on deflocculating of cement graings

Due to the deflocculation of cement particles, there will be inter particle friction between particle to particle and floc to floc. But in the dispersed condition there is water in between the cement particles, which results in inter particle friction reduction.

The dispersing ability of plasticizers (water reducing admixtures) results in a greater surface area of cement exposed to hydration. For this reason there is an increase in early strength of concrete than that of admixture free concrete of the same water/cement ratio. Long term strength may also improve due to a more uniform distribution of the dispersed cement through out the concrete.

In general terms, these plasticizers are effective with all types of cements, though their influence on strength is more with cements of low C_3A or low alkali content. No detrimental effects on other long term properties of concrete are observed. However if admixture is used correctly, the improved durability of concrete is found.

(ii) Retarding effect

As mentioned above the plasticizer gets adsorbed on the surface of cement particles and form a thin film. This film prevents the surface hydration reaction between the water and cement particles as long as sufficient molecules of Plasticizer are available at the particle or solution interface. The quantity of available plasticizer will decrease progressively as the polymers become entrapped in hydration products.

Many researchers have stated that one or more than one mechanism of the following may take place simultaneously:

1. Reduction in the surface tension of water.
2. Development of electrostatic repulsion between cement particles.
3. Development of lubricating film between cement particles.
4. Dispersion of cement grains and release of entrapped water with in cement flocs.
5. Prevention of surface hydration reaction of the cement particles, leaving more water for the fluidity of the mix.
6. Change in the form and structure (morphology) of the products of hydration.
7. Prevention of particle to particle contact.

It may be noted that all plasticizers are set retarders to some extent depending upon the base of plasticizers, dose and concentration etc. Hence it is advised that users should follow the instructions of the manufactures fully.

6.22. SUPER PLASTICIZERS (HIGH RANGE WATER REDUCERS)

Super plasticizers are also called high range water reducers. They are of recent origin and relatively are more effective type water reducing admixtures. They were developed in Japan and Germany during 1960 and 1970 respectively. Chemically they are different from normal plasticizers. The dose levels of super plasticizers usually is higher than that of (0.5 to 3.0%) conventional water reducers and (0.18 to 0.47) they have considerably less undesirable side effects on the properties of concrete. As super plasticizers do not reduce the surface tension of water to a great extent, they have not found to entrain significant amount of air in concrete.

The use of super plasticizers can permit the reduction of water in the concrete mix upto 30% with out producing any ill effect on the workability of the concrete *i.e.* with out reduction in the workability of concrete, where as normal plasticizers with doses upto 0.1 to 0.4% by weight of cement can reduce water content from 5 to 15%.

Super plasticizers are used for producing flowing concrete to be used in inaccessible locations, floors or where very quick placing is required. A self levelling and self compacting concrete is called *flowing* concrete. Super plasticizers are also used for the production of high strength and high performance concrete. With the use of super plasticizers, flowing concrete could be produced with the water/cement ratio as low as 0.25 or even less. The strength of such concrete was found 120 MPa (1200 kg/cm^2) or more. The use of super plasticizers also made it possible to use the fly ash, slag and silica fume to produce high quality concrete.

Use

The super plasticizers are used for the following purposes:

1. To produce more workable concrete than the concrete with out the use of super Plasticizer at the same water/cement ratio.
2. For the same workability, the use of super plasticizer permits the use of lower water/cement ratio.

3. The use of super plasticizer also permits the reduction in cement content due to the increase in strength.
4. The use of plasticizers also produce a homogeneous and cohessive concrete with out any tendency of segregation and bleeding.

Action

Same as that of ordinary plasticizers.

6.23. CLASSIFICATION OF SUPER PLASTICIZERS

Following polymers are commonly used as base for super plasticizers:

1. Sulphonated melamine formaldehyde condensate (SMF)
2. Sulphonated naphthalene formaldehyde condensate (SNE)
3. Modified Lignosulphonates (MLS)
4. Other types.

In addition to the above, following new generation super plasticizers are also used in other countries.

(*a*) Multi-carboxylatethers (MCE)
(*b*) Copolymer of carboxylic acrylic acid with acrylic ester (CAE)
(*c*) Poly carboxylate ester (PC)
(*d*) Cross linked acrylic polymer (CLAP)
(*e*) Acrylic polymer based (AP)
(*f*) Combination of the above.

The first-four super Plasticizers differ from one another due to the base component or due to different molecular weight. Probably the Sulphonated napthalene formaldehyde condensate (SNF) is more effective in dispersing the cement. It is also found to have some retaining properties. The dispersing action mainly is developed by the sulphonic acid. The sulphonic acid gets adsorbed on the surface of cement particles, making them negatively charged and mutually repulsive. This action increases the workability at a given water/cement ratio, increasing the slump from 75 mm to 200 mm. The resulting concrete is cohesive and not subjected to excessive bleeding and segregation. The cohesiveness is found if fine aggregate is increased by 4 to 5% and very angular and flaky coarse aggregate is avoided.

Each commercial product has been found to have different action on cements. The dosage of conventional plasticizers do not exceed 0.25% by weight of cement in case of ligno-sulphanates and 0.1% in case of carboxylic acids. The dosages of super plasticizers like SMF and NSF are used as high as 0.5 to 3.0% as they do not entrain air, but at the relatively high dosage they can produce undesirable effects as acceleration or retardation in setting time. However they increase the air entrainment in concrete.

Plasticizers and super plasticizers are water based. The solid contents may vary to any extent in a product manufactured by different firms.

6.24. EFFECTS OF SUPER PLASTICIZERS ON FRESH CONCRETE

By nominal dosages of plasticizers or super plasticizers the improvement in the workability of very stiff or zero slump concrete has not been observed. A mix having 20 mm to 30 mm initial slump can only be fluidised by the use of plasticizers or super plasticizers. To fluidify a no slump concrete a high dosage is required. An improvement in slump may be obtained upto the extent of 250 mm depending upon the initial slump of the mix, dosage and cement content. It has been observed that slump increases with the dosage. but after a certain limit of the dosage, slump starts decreasing. After about 1.0% dosage by weight of cement, slump starts decreasing. A typical curve showing the effect of dosage of super plasticizer on slump is shown in Fig. 6.16.

The improved workability developed due to the use of super plasticizers lasts only for a short duration. It has been observed that this improvement in workability lasts only from 30 minutes to 90 minutes. Some researchers have found this period from 30 minutes to 120 minutes. Hence the rate of loss of slump is very steep. After this period of 90 to 120 minutes the workability returns to normal. Hence it is recommended that Plasticizers or super plasticizers should be added to concrete just prior to placing. The slump loss with time is shown in Fig. 6.17.

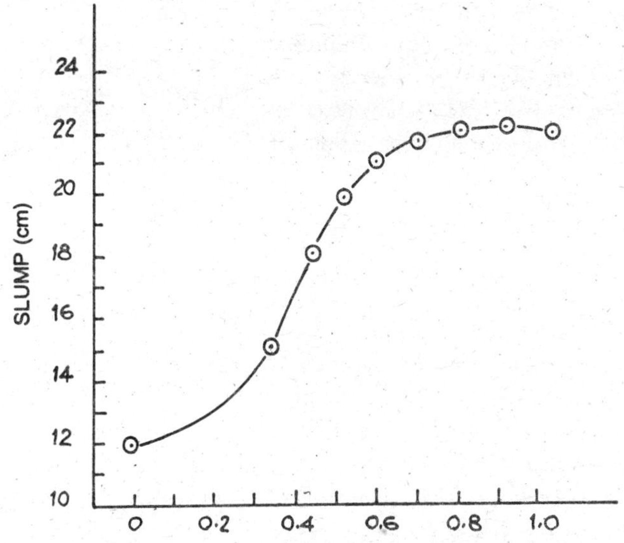

Fig. 6.16. Effect of additions of superplasticizer (Alklaryl sulphonate-formal dehyde condensates) on the workability of a concrete. Cement content 300 kg/m^3, w/c ratio = 0.6

6.25. FACTORS AFFECTING THE WORKABILITY

Following factors have been found affecting the workability of concrete

1. Type of super plasticizer
2. Dosage
3. Mix composition
4. Variation in cement composition and properties
5. Mixing procedure
6. Equipment
7. Others

1. Type of super plasticizer. It has been well established that efficiency of a super plasticizer is the function of its molecular weight (molecular weight of plasticizer). Higher the molecular weight, the higher is the efficiency. However beyond a maximum value of molecular weight, the efficiency starts to decline. Further it has also been noticed that some intrinsic properties of the super plasticizers also influence the performance.

2. Dosages. It has been established that the dosage of a super plasticizer influence the viscosity of the mix and hence the workability of the concrete. For a given brand of cement, water/cement ratio and plasticizer, the dosage or quantity of super plasticizer may be decided by MARSH CONE TEST.

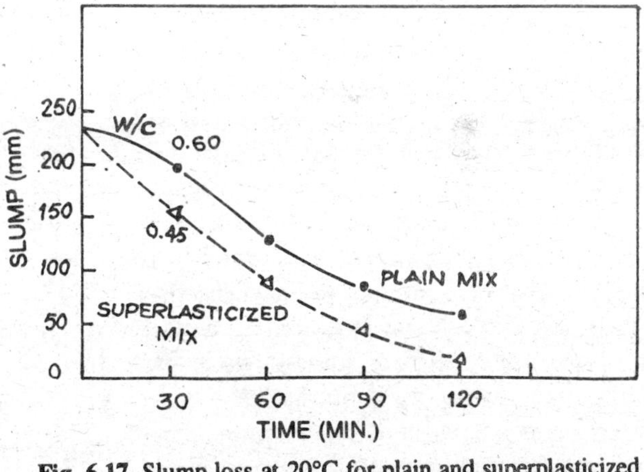

Fig. 6.17. Slump loss at 20°C for plain and superplasticized mix. at the same initial slump. Superplasticizer 0.4 percent as dry NSF polymer by weight of cement

For normal concrete work, the dosage in India generally is adopted low. A dosage more than 2.5% by weight of cement is rarely used, where as in other countries 4 to 5% dosages are used. Some researchers have advocated the use of super plasticizers upto a dosage of 3.0% with out any adverse effect on the properties of hardened concrete. Higher dosages than 3.0% have been reported to affect the shrinkage and creep properties of concrete.

3. Mix composition. The aggregate/cement ratio, or richness of the mix, water/cement ratio and the use of other suplimentry cementing materials like fly ash or Silica fume have been found to affect the workability of the mix. Wetter the mix, better the dispersion of cement particles, resulting in better workability. Sand grading, size and shape of aggregate also influence the workability.

4. Variation in cement composition. The variation in compound composition of cement, such as C_3A content, C_3S/C_2S ratio, fineness of cement, alkali and gypsum contents have been found to have different effects with different super plasticizers, especially the C_3A content has been found to have more influence on the performance of the super plasticizer. The workability of a cement mortar containing 2% calcium lignosulphonate has been found to decrease sharply from 27 mm to 5 mm as the C_3A content increases from 3% to 14% as shown in Fig. 6.18.

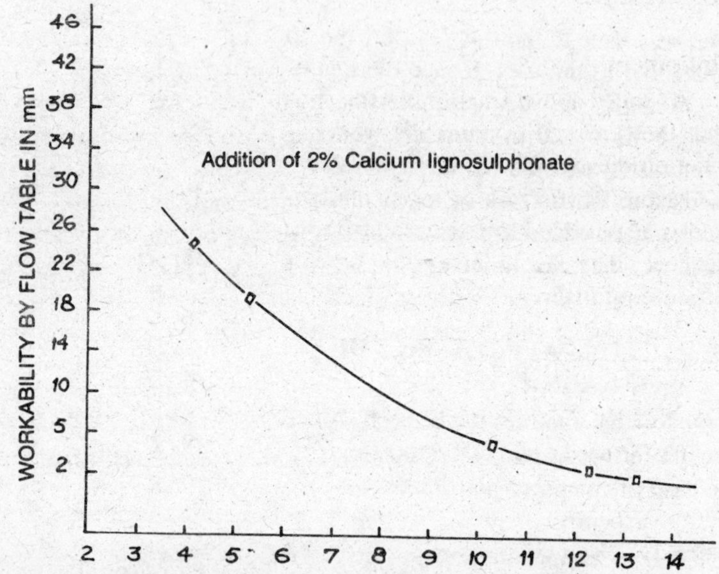

Fig. 6.18. Effect of calcium lignosulphonate on C_3A

5. Mixing procedure. The sequence of putting materials into the mixer has been found to influence the workability of the concrete to a great extent. When super plasticizers are to be used in the concrete, hand mixing is not permitted. In case the concrete mixer is used, following sequence of putting the materials in the drum of the mixer has been found to give better results.

Add all water, in the drum holding back one litre of water. The exact quantity of super plasticizer is added to this one litre of water to have well stirred solution and other materials loaded into the drum and mixed well. Now the solution of super plasticizer is added into the drum in two or three installments over the well mixed concrete. After adding super plasticizer to the mix, it is further mixed in the mixer for about one minute before discharging. This method has proved to produce better dispersion of super plasticizer. The practice of adding super plasticizer with bulk mixing water has not been found giving good results.

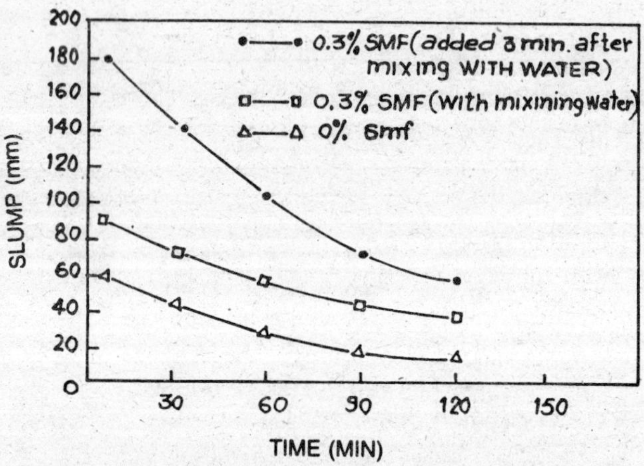

Fig. 6.19. Effect of delayed addition of sulphonated malamine formaldehyde condensate on slump and slump loss

Experiments have shown that adding super plasticizer after three minutes of mixing ingredients has yielded better results. Fig. 6.19 shows the effect of adding superplasticizer in water three minutes after mixing with the water.

It has been found that through out India for conducting laboratory trials, small electrically operated laboratory mixers are used. Using laboratory small mixers have not yielded satis- factory results. In such situations, following sequence of putting materials should be adopted.

All the quantity of calculated water is put in the drum. Then all the quantity of cement and sand is put in the drum and ingredients mixed well. After mixing the sand and cement well, the calculated quantity of super plasticizer is added to the mix and mixed thoroughly in the mixer. Then coarse aggregate is added and mixed for one minute more. This procedure is found to give good results.

Equipment

As stated above small mixers have not been found efficient to mix the concrete uniformly and properly. Thus they are unable to exploit the action of super plasticizers fully. Generally pan type mixers have shown better efficiency.

Mixers of pan type of half a cubic metre capacity or more have been found very efficient. The mixing time is about 20 seconds and in this short period, the mixing is very intimate. It is observed that for identical parameters concrete mixing in batching plant give about 20 to 30 mm more slump than mix trials carried out in laboratory using small mixers.

Others. The slump value of a super plasticizer concrete is also found affected due to the use of other admixtures along with super plasticizers such as fly ash, slag, silica fume and air entraining agents etc.

6.26. EFFECT OF SUPER PLASTICIZERS ON SETTING OF CONCRETE

The effect of the use of super plasticizers on the setting of concrete is not found significant except in the case of cements having very low contents of C_3A. If the C_3A contents are very low the retardation of setting of cement may be very significant. However the other long term properties are not appreciably affected.

The only real disadvantage of super plasticizers is the relatively high cost due to the expenses of manufacturing a product of a high molecular mass.

6.27. EFFECT OF SUPER PLASTICIZERS ON THE PROPERTIES OF CONCRETE

The super plasticizers or plasticizers do not take part in any chemical reaction with cement or blending material such as fly ash used in concrete. The action of plasticizers or super plasticizers in fluidizing the mix is only physical made even with low water content. Their fluidifying action lasts only as long as the mix is in plastic condition. Once the effect of adsorption layer is lost, the hydration process continues normally. It has been proved experimentally that the right quality of plasticizers or super plasticizers used upto 3.0% by weight of cement produces no bad effect on the properties of hardened concrete. However the bad quality ligno sulphate based plasticizers have resulted in the air entrainment, there by reducing the strength of concrete. As the plasticizers and super plasticizers improve workability, and compactability results in the reduction of water/cement ratio, there by increasing the strength of concrete. It results in the alround improvement in the properties of the hardened concrete. Now a days the use of plasticizers or super plasticizers has become a practice to obtain high performance concrete.

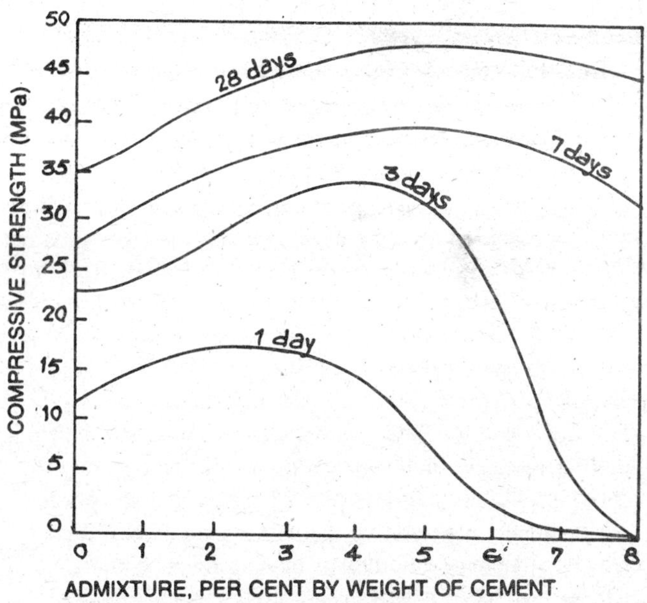

Fig. 6.20. Effect of overdose of water-reducing admixture on the compressive strength of concrete

When the plasticizers or super plasticizers are used in higher dose, the strength development is reduced significantly beyond one day upto 7 days. However seven day strength and beyond, the reduction will not be appreciable. The effect of ligno-sulphonate type of super plasticizers on strength development is shown in Fig. 6.20.

When it is desired to achieve the high strength of concrete with a given water/cement ratio, the water content may be reduced by 25 to 35% by weight of cement by the use of super plasticizers, where as with the use of conventional water reducing admixture the reduction of water may be about one half of the above value. The effect of the use of super plasticizers on the early strength of concrete (3 days) is shown in Fig. 6.20.

Further following points should be remembered:

1. At the same water/cement ratio, naphthalene or melamine based super plasticizers have not been found to modify the drying shrinkage of concrete considerably. Some times at the same consistency they have been found to reduce the drying shrinkage appreciably.
2. At high water/cement ratio of the order of 0.64, the total creep is found higher with the use of naphthalene sulphonates where as at low water/cement ratio the difference in creep between with and with out plasticizers is insignificant.
3. Durability of concrete is the function of its impermeability, which depends on water/cement ratio. Hence super plasticizers enhance the durability of concrete. Super plasticizers due to the reduction in water/cement ratio, reduce the penetration of chlorides and sulphates into the concrete and thus improve the resistance to the sea water or deicing effect. The resistance to sulphate attack also has increased due to the same reason. Thus it can be concluded that with the use of plasticizers or super plasticizers reduction in water/cement ratio of concrete can be effected with out effecting the workability of concrete, and producing stronger concrete. Thus the use of super plasticizers will contribute to the alround improvement in the properties of concrete.

6.28. NEW GENERATION SUPER PLASTICIZERS

As already discussed the super plasticizers are used for the following purposes:

1. To increase the workability of concrete with out any change in the composition of the mix.
2. To reduce the water content of mixing water, to reduce the water/cement ratio resulting in increase of strength and durability of concrete.
3. To reduce cement and water contents in the concrete to reduce the cost of production of concrete. The reduction in cement and water contents reduce the creep, shrinkage and heat of hydration.

One of the most important draw backs of the traditional super plasticizers as sulphonated melamine formaldehyde condensates (SMF) or Sulphonated naphthalene formaldehyde Condensates (SNF) and Modified ligno-sulphate (MLS) is the slump loss. The slump loss with time presents a serious limitations on the advantages of these super plasticizers. To over come this limitation, experiments were conducted in Europe and Japan and they discovered new generation of super plasticizers recently. The more recently developed all new generation super plasticizers are based on the family of acrylic polymers (A, P). These new super plasticizers are listed on page 152 under the head of classification of super plasticizers. Out of these super plasticizers, the properties of the following two super plasticizers namely carboxylated acrylic ester (CAE) Copolymer and multi-carboxylatether (MCE) are discussed here.

The carboxylated Acrylic Ester Contains Carboxylic (COO) instead of sulphoric (SO_3) groups present in the SNF and SMF. In the case of SNF and SMF dispersion of cement grain was considered to be caused by the electrostatic repulsion, but the recent experiments carried out by M. Collpardi et al and Y-O Tanaka et al did not confirm the above hypothesis for the mechanism of plasticizing

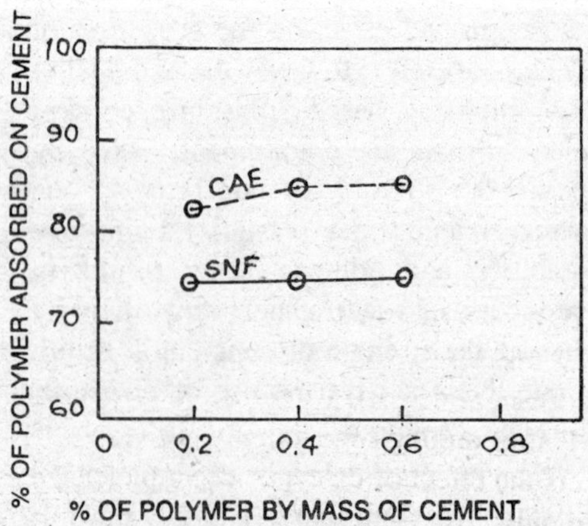

Fig. 6.21. Adsorption of CAE or SNF on cement as a function of polymer dosage

action of the acrylic polymers. The production of repulsive force known as zeta potential produced by acrylic polymers (AP) and in SNF based super plasticizers is shown in Table 6.9. From the table it will be seen that AP based super plasticizers produce negligible zeta potential change (0.3 to 5 mv) in contrast to SNF based super plasticizers (23.0-28.0 mv) in aqueous suspension of cement particles as reported by Sakai E and Daiman M. in 1997.

Table 6.9. Zeta potential of cement particles in suspension with super plasticizers

Super plasticizers	*Main component*	*Zeta potential (– mV)*
A	AP*	5.0
B	AP	0.30
C	AP	1.0
D	AP	4.0
E	AP	4.0
F	AP	2.0
G	SNF	23.0
H	SNF	28.0

AP*-Polycarboxylate type

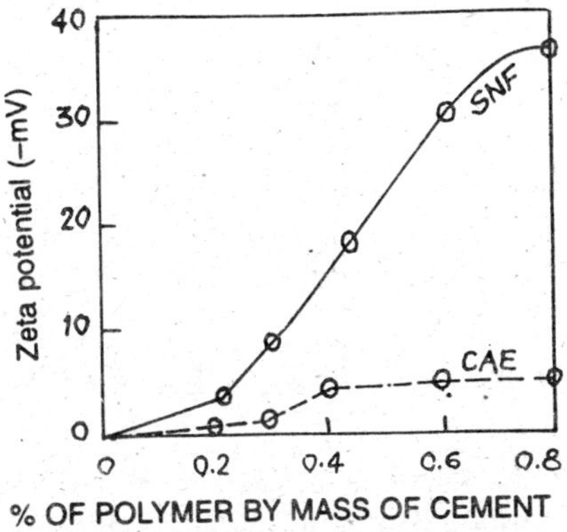

Fig. 6.22. Zeta potential of CAE or SNF cement pastes as a function of polymer dosage

Fig. 6.21 shows the adsorption of CAE and SNF on cement as a function of polymer dose, as reported by Collpardi M. From the Fig. 6.21 it will be seen that the adsorption of CAE is about 85% and that of SNF as 75% *i.e.* the adsorption of CAE is much more than SNF. Fig. 6.22 shows the zeta potential of CAE and SNF on cement particles as a function of polymer dose. From this Fig. 6.22 it will be seen that the zeta potential of cement particles mixed with CAE is much lower than SNF.

Super plasticizers based on acrylic polymers show the following characteristics:

1. Flowing concrete can be produced at lower water/cement ratio.
2. The effectiveness of super plasticizer does not depend on the addition procedure (immediate or delayed) as shown in Table 6.10 below.
3. The slump loss is much reduced in comparison of trational sulphonated super plasticizers.

Table 6.10. Effect of method of addition of super plasticizer on the slump of concrete mix

Type	*Admixture*		*Water/cement*	*Slump (mm)*
	Dosage %*	*Method of addition***		
CAE	0.3	immediate	0.39	230
CAE	0.3	delayed	0.39	235
NSF	0.48	immediate	0.4	100
NSF	0.48	delayed	0.4	230

* As dry polymer by weight of cement

** Immediate *i.e.* admixture is mixed with mixing water, delayed *i.e.* admixture is added after mixing the mix for 1 minute.

From table 6.10 it will be seen that slump *i.e.* workability of concrete increases markedly by adding NSF after mixing for 1 minute. Slump increase is found from 100 to 230 mm, while in cae of CAE plasticizers the effect of delayed addition of super plasticizer is inappreciable *i.e.* the increase is from 230 to 235 mm only.

Fig. 6.23 shows the slump loss of CAE and NSF family super plasticizers. From this Fig. 6.23 it will be seen that with the use of (0.3%) CAE plasticizers the loss in slump is negligible for agitating mix for

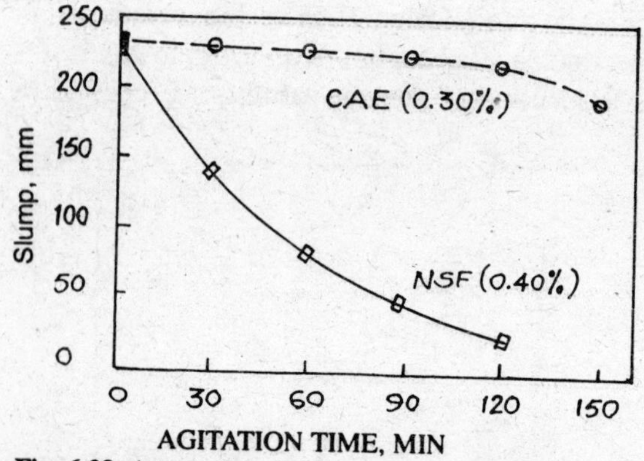

Fig. 6.23. A typical slump loss of CAE and NSF

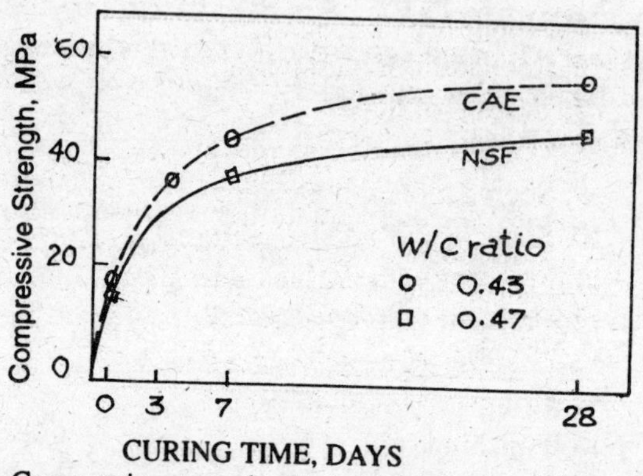

Fig. 6.24. Compressive strength of superplasticized concrete with OPC cement and CAE or NSF polymer based admixtures

150 minute where as in case of (0.4%) NSF slump reduces from 230 mm to about 25 mm for agitating about 120 minutes.

Fig. 6.24 shows the effect of curing time on the 28 days compressive strength of concrete. It wil be seen from the Fig. 6.24 that in case of CAE super plasticizers the gain in strength is more even with reduced water/cement ratio than the NSF family super plasticizers. Thus it can be said that the increase in compresive strength is due to the ability of CAE to reduce more water content for the same workability. The effect of super plasticizers is shown with different water/cemnt ratio on 1 to 3 days strength in Fig. 6.25.

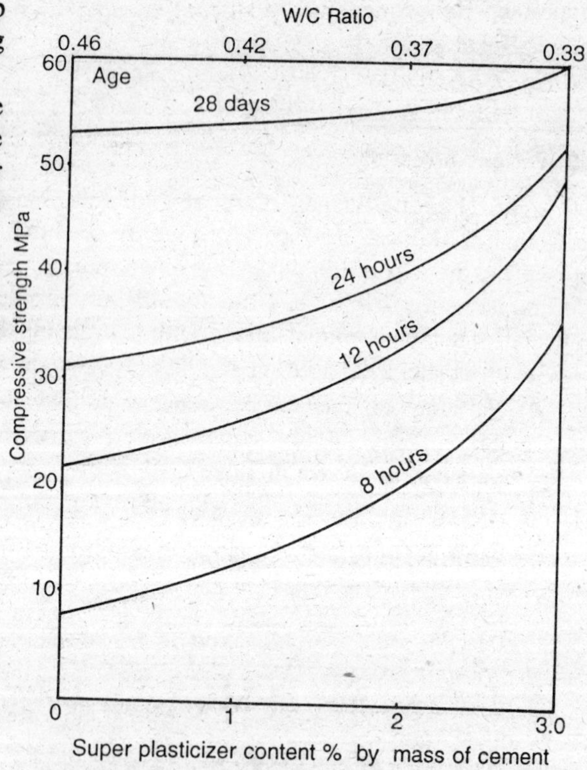

Fig. 6.25. Effect of adding super plasticizers on the strength of concrete

Multicarboxylatether

For the production of high performance concrete new generation super plasticizer named multicarboxylatether (MCE) is found more effective. The properties of these super plasticizers are found as follows:

1. The water reduction is found high.
2. At low water/cement ratio their flowability is found excellent.
3. Lower slump loss with time is observed.
4. Shorter retardation time is observed.
5. Early strength is found very high.
6. The quantity of dose is low.

6.29. PROBLEMS ENCOUNTERED AT SITE IN THE USE OF SUPER PLASTICIZERS

Some of the practical problems encountered at site in the use of super plasticizers are as follows:

1. Slump of concrete with out plasticizer is known as reference mix.
2. Inefficient laboratory mixer used for trial.

3. Selection of plastizer and super plasticizer.
4. Determination of dosage.
5. Slump loss
6. Reduction of slump loss.
7. Casting of cubes
8. Compaction of concrete at site
9. Segregation and bleeding
10. Sequence of adding plasticizer
11. Problem with crushed dust
12. Problem with crushed sand
13. Grading of coarse aggregate
14. Compatibility with cement
15. Finishing
16. Removal of form work etc.

Out of the above problems maintenance of proper slump at the point of placing concrete is very important. Hence reduction in slump may be checked by taking any one or more of the following steps:

1. Keeping initial slump high.
2. Using retarders.
3. Keeping low temperature.
4. By using retarder plasticizers or super plasticizers.
5. By using super plasticizer at final point.
6. By repetitive dose etc.

QUESTIONS

1. What is an admixture? Name the principal purposes for which admixtures are used.
2. What is flowing concrete?
3. What is the difference between an additive and an admixture?
4. Which cement should not be used with calcium chloride?
5. Should calcium chloride be used for R.C.C. work in the interior of a building? Give your reasons.
6. What are the uses of plasticizers? Discuss the mechanism of action of plasticizers.
7. Discuss the advantages and disadvantages of "accelerator". In what way they serve as antifreeze agents.
8. Explain the effect of calcium chloride when used as a admixture.
9. Discuss the advantages and disadvantages of calcium chloride used in portland cement concrete with out and with reinforcement.
10. Describe some workability admixtures. What other effects they have on concrete.
11. What are retarders? Under what circumstances they are usually used. Name some of the principal retarders.
12. What is air entrainment? What materials are used for air entrainment? Describe their effects on the properties of concrete.
13. What is pozzolanic action? Name few artificial pozzolanic materials and write their effects on the properties of concrete.
14. Under what conditions the use of gas producing agents is desirable?
15. Explain pressure method of air entrainment.
16. What are super plasticizers? Discuss their effects on the properties of concrete.
17. Describe the mechanism of action of plasticizers.
18. What are the main differences between plasticizers and super plasticizers?
19. What are the disadvantages of plasticizers.
20. State the advantages and disadvantages of plasticizers and super plasticizers.
21. Discuss surface active materials including wetting agents.

OBJECTIVE TYPE QUESTIONS

1. Which of the following statements is true
   (*a*) An admixture is a basic ingredient of concrete
   (*b*) An admixture is a substitute for the bad practice of concreting
   (*c*) An excess quantity of admixture is beneficial to the properties of concrete
   (*d*) It improves the workability of the mix but not economically
2. Which of the following statements is false
   (*a*) The use of admixtures decrease the permeability of concrete
   (*b*) The use of admixtures check the corrosion of reinforcement of concrete
   (*c*) The use of admixture produces celluor concrete
   (*d*) The use of admixtures does not produce non skid surface of the concrete
3. Admixture accelerators can be used to
   (*a*) Increase the strength of concrete
   (*b*) Improve the workability of concrete
   (*c*) Accelerate the initial setting of concrete
   (*d*) Increase the heat of evolution
   (*e*) Reduce the freezing effect on the concrete
   (*f*) Any of the above
4. Admixtures can be used to
   (*a*) Retard the initial set of concrete
   (*b*) Increase the durability of concrete
   (*c*) Improve pumpability of concrete
   (*d*) Controls alkali aggregate reaction
   (*e*) Any of the above
5. Which of the following statement is false
   (*a*) Adding an accelerator to the concrete increases its alkali aggregate reaction resistance
   (*b*) Addition of an accelerator increases the rate of hydration of cement
   (*c*) Addition of an accelerator increases the shrinkage of concrete
   (*d*) Addition of an accelerator increases the rate of evolution of heat
6. Which of the following statements is false
   (*a*) Addition of an accelerator shortens the setting time
   (*b*) Addition of an accelerator shortens the curing period
   (*c*) Addition of an accelerator shortens the strength of concrete
   (*d*) Addition of an accelerator shortens the period of form work removal
7. Out of the following compounds which can not be used as an accelerator
   (*a*) $CaSo_4$
   (*b*) $CaCl_2$
   (*c*) $NaSO_4$
   (*d*) K_2SO_4
   (*e*) Nacl
8. Which of the following statements is false
   (*a*) Addition of a retarder to concrete decreases the rate of hydration
   (*b*) Addition of a retarder to concrete decreases the water/cement ratio
   (*c*) Addition of a retarder to concrete decreases the rate of evolution of heat
   (*d*) Addition of a retarder to concrete decreases the rate of development of strength
   (*e*) Addition of a retarder to concrete decreases the workability and compressive strength of concrete
9. Which of the following statements is false
   (*a*) Addition of air entraining agents to concrete increases the workability of concrete
   (*b*) Addition of air entraining agents increases the strength of concrete
   (*c*) Addition of air entraining agents increases the durability of concrete
   (*d*) Addition of air entraining agents increases the uniformity of concrete
   (*e*) Addition of air entraining agents increases the impermeability of concrete
10. Addition of pozzolana admixtures results in
    (*a*) Reduction in heat of hydration
    (*b*) Increased resistance to attack of sulphate
    (*c*) Reduced leaching of calcium hydroxide

(*d*) Improve workability
(*e*) All of the above

11. Which of the following statements are true
(*a*) Flyash may be used as a part replacement of cement in concrete
(*b*) Flyash consists of spherical glassy particles
(*c*) Flyaash may be used as a part replacement of fine aggregate
(*d*) Specific surface area of fly ash is about 35000 to 50000 cm^2/gram
(*e*) Flyash may be used as a part placement of cement and fine aggregate simultaneously
(*f*) Flyash contains like portland cement oxide of calcium, aluminium and silicon
(*g*) Flyash can be used as an admixture
(*h*) Flyash is a residual from the combustion of pulverised coal collected by electrostatic separators from fuel gases of thermal power plants

12. The addition of super plasticizers in concrete result in
(*a*) Greatly increased workability
(*b*) Production of flowing concrete
(*c*) An increased tendency of segregation
(*d*) Produce increased compressive strength
(*e*) All the above

13. Air entraing agents can be used for
(*a*) Increasing the frost resistance of concrete
(*b*) For entraining air in concrete.
(*c*) For producing discrete cavities in the cement paste
(*d*) To check the increase in permeability of concrete
(*e*) All of the above

14. Which of the following materials can be used as water proofing materials
(*a*) Petroletum waxes
(*b*) Potash soaps
(*c*) Butyl stearate
(*d*) All of them

Answers

1. (*d*)
2. (*d*)
3. (*f*)
4. (*e*)
5. (*a*)
6. (*c*)
7. (*a*)
8. (*e*)
9. (*b*)
10. (*e*)
11. (*a, c, e, g*)
12. All
13. (*e*)
14. (*d*)

7

Properties of Fresh Concrete

7.1. INTRODUCTION

Fresh or plastic concrete is a freshly mixed material which can be moulded into any shape. The relative quantities of its ingredients such as cement, fine and coarse aggregates and water mixed together control its properties in wet or green state as well as in hardened state. In this chapter workability of fresh concrete will be discussed in detail.

7.2. WORKABILITY

The strength of concrete of a given proportion is affected very much by the degree of its compaction. Therefore it is desirable that the fresh concrete can be transported and placed without segregation and bleeding, compacted and finished easily. This property of concrete is known as *workability*. The workability of concrete depends upon a number of properties of concrete, which can not be satisfactorily measured. Further more, workability is a relative thing, a workability of concrete suitable for mass concrete is not necessarily sufficient for thin or heavily reinforced or inaccessible sections. Therefore workability should be defined as a physical property of concrete alone without reference to the circumstances of a particular type of construction. To obtain such a definition, it is necessary to consider the phenomenon while compacting the concrete. Whatever may be the mode of compaction, whether it is achieved by ramming or vibration, the essential feature of the process is to eliminate the entrapped air from the concrete until it has achieved as close a configuration as possible for a given mix. Thus the work done in compaction can be divided in the following three parts.

1. To overcome the friction between the individual particles in the concrete. This is called internal friction.
2. To overcome the friction between the concrete and the surface of the mould or the reinforcement. This is called surface friction.
3. In addition to the above two works, some work done is used in vibrating the mould or in shock or vibrating those parts of concrete which have already been fully compacted. Actually this work done is a waste.

Thus the work done in over coming the friction of individual particles in the concrete is called internal friction and surface friction *i.e.* work done in (1) and (2) is useful work. As the internal friction is an intrinsic property of the mix, the workability can be best defined *as the amount of useful internal work necessary to produce the full compaction.* In other words the property of concrete which determines the amount of useful internal work necessary to produce complete compaction is called workability of concrete.

7.2.1. Consistency

It relates to the degree of wetness of concrete within limits. Wet concretes are more workable than dry concretes, but concretes of the same wetness (consistency) may vary in workability.

7.3. FACTORS AFFECTING THE WORKABILITY

Following factors affect the Workability of concrete:

1. Water content
2. Size of aggregate particles
3. Coarse and fine aggregate ratio
4. Particle interference
5. Particle interlocking
6. Admixtures.

1. Water content

It is the main factor which influences the workability of concrete. More the water content, higher the water/cement ratio, resulting in better workability, but the strength of concrete is reduced. Further approximately it can he assumed that for a given type and grading of aggregate and workability of concrete, the water content is independent of the aggregate/cement ratio.

On the basis of this assumption, the mix proportions of concrete of different richness can be determined. Typical values of water content for different slumps and maximum sizes of aggregate are shown in Table 7.1. These values are applicable only for non-air entrained concretes. For air entrained concrete the reduction of water content may be done according to the amount of air entrained as shown in Fig. 7.1. The effect of air entrainment have been discussed in chapter 6.

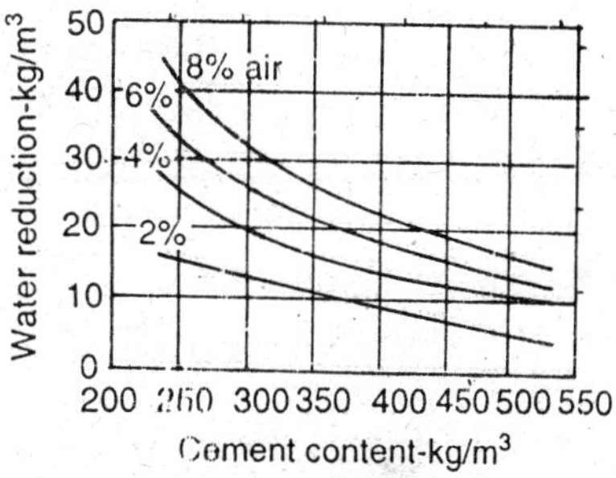

Fig. 7.1. Relation between reduction in water due to air entrainment

Table 7.1. Approximate water content for different slumps and max. size of aggregate

Maximum size of aggregate in mm	*Water content of concrete*					
	Slump 25-50 mm		*Slump 75-100 mm*		*Slump 150-175 mm*	
	Rounded aggregate kg/m³	*Angular aggregate kg/m³*	*Rounded aggregate kg/m3*	*Angular aggregate kg/m³*	*Rounded aggregate kg/m3*	*Angular aggregate kg/m³*
9.5	190	210	200	225	230	255
19.0	170	195	190	210	210	225
38.1	160	170	170	190	190	210
50.8	150	165	165	180	180	195
76.2	135	155	155	165	160	185

Note: These values are based on the work of National Ready Mixed Concrete Association, Washington.

2. Size of aggregate particles

Increase in the maximum sizes of aggregate, without any change in the mix, improves the workability of mix as smaller quantity of water is needed to wet the surface area of the aggregate particles and more water is available to act as lubricant in the mortar. Further as the size of aggregate particles increases, voids decrease and require less mortar to fill the voids. Thus more mortar is available to cause lubrication of the particles.

3. Coarse and fine aggregate ratio

For a constant aggregate/cement ratio, if the quantity of coarse aggregate is increased and fine aggregate decreased to maintain the total aggregate/cement ratio constant, the total surface area of the aggregate is reduced. Thus for a constant water/cement ratio the quantity of water available per unit, area of aggregate surface is increased resulting in improvement of the workability.

4. Relative quantities of paste and aggregate

For any given paste (a quantity of cement with its definite proportion of water) decreasing the amount of paste with respect to the quantity of aggregate stiffens the mixture and increasing the amount of paste makes the mix more fluid. Further if the quantity of the paste is reduced to such an extent that there is not enough paste to fill the voids and actually float the aggregate Particles, then the mix becomes granular or harsh and its placement will be impossible.

5. Particle interference

Particle interference occurs when the aggregate particles of one size are present in excess in the mix. and the average clear space between the particles is less than the diameter of the particles in the size group next lower to it. Where there is no particle interference, smaller grains can pass freely between the large particles to distribute themselves evenly in the mass.

When grains of one size are in excess they form bunches and the lower size particles can not pass through them. This causes local voids in the concrete from which water can leak. The mixing water will fill up these voids and quantity of water needed for lubrication of aggregate particles will decrease, resulting in lower workability as well as density. Thus the aggregate should be so graded in descending order of size and in quantity that the voids in coarse aggregate in its coarser fraction is filled up by finer coarse fraction, this in turn leaving individual void of sufficient size to accept the coarse particles of the fine aggregate and still leave room necessary for the cement paste and fine sand.

6. Particles interlock

The surface texture of the aggregate also affects the workability. Smoothed surfaced round aggregate have higher workability for the same water/cement ratio than crushed aggregate due to the mechanical interlock between the crushed aggregate particles and their relatively high coefficient of friction.

7. Grading of aggregates

A well graded aggregate is one, which has least voids in a given volume. Other factors being the same, when the total voids are less, more paste is available to produce better lubricating effect. With excess amount of paste, the mix becomes cohesive which prevents segregation of particles and aggregate particles will slide over each other with minimum compaction. The better the grading, the less is the void content, and higher the workability. Thus it is one of the factors which has the maximum influences on the workability.

8. Use of admixtures

As explained in chapter 6, use of certain admixtures improves the workability of concrete.

7.4. MEASUREMENT OF WORKABILITY

Truly speaking there is no acceptable test which can measure directly the workability as defined earlier. Numerous attempts have been made to correlate workability with some easily determinable physical measurements, but none is found fully satisfactory. However they may provide useful information with in a range of variation in workability.

7.5. TESTS FOR WORKABILITY

Usually following tests can be adopted to determine the workability of concrete.

1. Slump test
2. K. slump test
3. Kelly Ball test
4. Compacting factor test
5. Flow test
6. Determination of consistency by Vee. Bee Consisto-meter etc.

7.5.1. Slump test

This test is used extensively at the site of work all over the world. Actually this test does not measure the workability of concrete but is useful for finding the variations in the uniformity of a mix of given nominal proportions and specifies procedure for determining the consistency of concrete where the nominal maximum size of the aggregate does not exceed 38.0 mm.

Apparatus. The mould for the slump test is a frustum of a Cone having internal diameters of bottom and top as 20 cms & 10 cms respectively and 30 cms height. The mould will be made of metal of at least 1.6 mm thickness, having smooth internal surface. To facilitale in lifting the mould in the vertical direction, suitable guide attachment should be provided in the mould. (2) Tamping rod of steel 60 cms long and 1.6 cms in diameter and round at one end.

Test Procedure. The internal surface of the mould is cleaned thoroughly and oiled or greased. Then this mould is placed on a smooth; horizontal, rigid and non-absorbent surface, such as a carefully levelled metal plate with the smaller opening at the top. The mould should be held firmly in place while filling it with concrete. It is filled in four layers, each approximately 7.5 cms in thickness and each layer is tamped with twenty five strokes of the rounded end of the tamping rod. The strokes should be distributed uniformly over the whole area of cross section of the mould and for the second and subsequent layers should penetrate into the underlying layer. The bottom layer should be tamped throughout its depth. After tamping the top layer, the top surface is struck off level with a trowel or rolling motion of tamping rod such that the mould is exactly filled. Any mortar leaked out between the mould and its base should be wiped out immediately. Now the mould should he lifted up vertically slowly and carefully. This will allow the unsupported concrete to subside or slump, hence the name of the test. The decrease in the height of the centre of the slumped concrete is called *slump* and is measured to the nearest of 5 mm. Thus slump is the difference between the original height of concrete in the mould and the highest part of concrete in subsided position. The experiment should be conducted at a place which is free from vibration or shock and within a period of 2 minutes after taking sample from the mix.

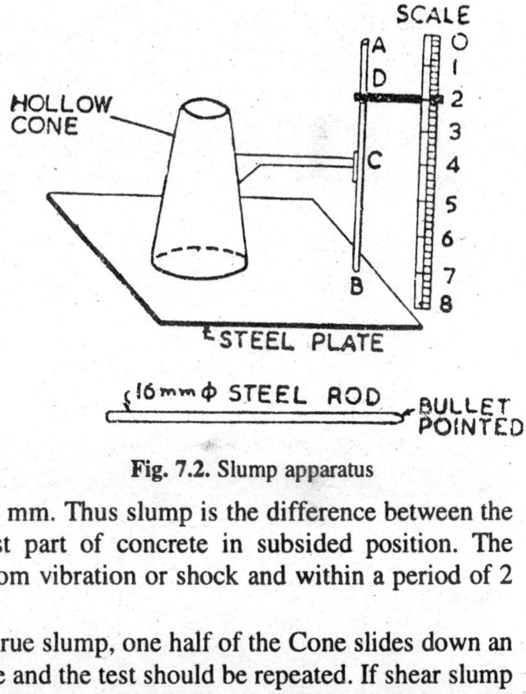

Fig. 7.2. Slump apparatus

If instead of slumping evenly alround as in the case of true slump, one half of the Cone slides down an inclined plane, then a shear slump is said to have taken place and the test should be repeated. If shear slump persists as in the case of harsh mixes, then it is an indication of non cohessive mix. Mixes of stiff consistency have zero slump and in the dry range of mixes no variation can be detected between mixes of different workability. Rich mixes behave satisfactorily, their slump being sensitive to variations in workability. However in a lean mix with a tendency to harshness a true slump can change easily to the shear type slump and widely different values of slumps can be obtained in different samples for the same mix. Refer exp. No. 18.

Thus this test is not a true guide to workability. Essentially it is a measure of consistency or wetness of the mix. This test is suitable for concrete having 25 to 125 mm of slump *i.e.* for medium to high workability. For example a harsh mix can not be said to have the same workability as one with a large proportion of sand even though they have the same slump. Similarly 12.5 mm slump in concrete made with 75 mm maximum size crushed aggregate will not necessarily give the same workability as that given by 20 mm maximum size gravel concrete.

The recommended values of slump for different works are shown in Table 7.2, These values depend upon the method of compaction possible at the site in each case. Smaller slump values are required where concrete can be rammed hard or where there is no obstruction like reinforcement etc.

Table 7.2

S. No.	*Type of work*	*Recommended slump in cms*
1.	Road work	2.5 to 5.0
2.	Foundation of reinforced concrete walls, footings, slabs on ground, side walls etc.	5.0 to 10.0
3.	Footing without reinforcement, sub-structure walls, cassion etc.	2.5 to 7.5
4.	Reinforced ordinary slab; beams etc.	5.0 to 12.5
5.	Columns, thin vertical sections and retaining walls	7.5 to 12.5
6.	Bridge deck etc.	5.0 to 7.5
7.	Mass concrete	2.5 to 5.0

The patterns of slump is shown in Fig. 7.3. It indicates the characteristics of concrete in addition to the slump value. If the concrete slumps evenly, then it is called true slump. If one half of the cone slides down, then it is called shear slump. In this case the slump value is measured as the difference in heights of mould and the average value of subsidence. It also shows that the concrete is non cohesive and indicates segregation characteristics. If concrete spreads then it is called collapse.

Slump test gives fairly good results for a plastic mix. This test is not sensitive for a stiff mix or zero slump mix. In case of dry mix, no variation can be detected between mixes of different workability. In case of rich mixes, the value is satisfactory, their slump being sensitive to variations in workability. IS 456-2000 suggests that in the "very low" category of workability, where strict control is necessary as for pavement quality concrete, workability should be determined by compacting factor apparatus. A value of 0.75 to 0.80 of compacting factor should be adopted.

In case of very high category of workability, measurement of workability by flow test will be more appropriate. In case of a lean mix with a tendency of harshness a true slump can easily change to shear slump and widely different values of slump can be obtained in different samples from the same mix. Thus the slump test is unreliable for lean mixes.

Despite the above limitations, slump test is very useful on the site to check the day to day variations in the materials being fed into the mixer. An increase in slump may mean either moisture content of aggregate has increased unexpectedly or grading of aggregate has changed (deficiency in sand). Thus too high or too low a slump gives a warning to the mixer operator to remedy the situation. Simplicity of this test is an other reason of its popularity inspite of the fact that many other workability tests are in vogue. In the past IS adopted compacting factor test values for denoting the workability of concrete. Even IS 10262-1982 recommended the use of compacting factor values for denoting workability of the mix., but IS 456-2000 reverted back to slump values to denote workability.

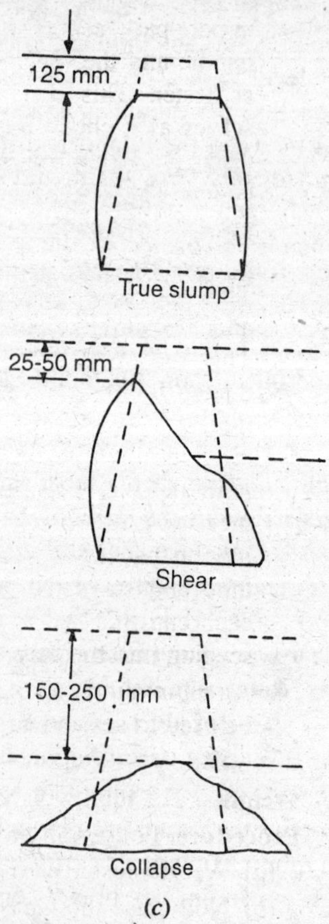

(c)

Fig. 7.3. Various types of slumps

7.5.2. K. Slump test

Very recently a new apparatus known as K. slump tester has been developed. It can be used to measure the slump directly in one minute after it has been inserted into the fresh concrete to the level of the floater disc. The K-slump tester can be used to measure the slump of the concrete in one minute in cylinders, buckets, wheel barrows, slabs or in any desired location where the fresh concrete is placed. Thus K-slump tester is very simple, practical, handy, and economical to use both in the laboratory and field. It has been found on the basis of about 500 tests carried out with K-slump tester, that it has a good correlation with slump cone apparatus results.

Apparatus

The apparatus is consisted of the following four parts.

1. **A chrome plated steel tube.** The external and internal diameters of this tube are 1.9 and 1.6 cms respectively. The length of the tube is 25 cms. The lower part of the tube is used to measure the slump of the concrete. The length of this part is 15.5 cms including the length of lower solid cone which facilitates the insertion of the tube into the concrete. In this lower tube fallowing types of openings are provided.
   (*a*) 4 slots of 5.1 cms length and 0.8 cm width marked A-A.
   (*b*) 22 round openings of 0.64 cm diameter shown as B-B. All these openings are distributed uniformly in the lower part as shown in Fig. 7.4.
2. A disc floater, 0.24 cm thick and 6 cm in diameter. This disc divides the tube into two parts as upper and lower. The upper part serves as a handle and the lower one as tester. This disc also serves as a check for the tester to sink into the concrete upto a correct pre-determined level.
3. **A hollow plastic rod.** This rod is 25 cm long and 1.3 cm in diameter. This rod contains a graduated scale in centimeters. This rod can move freely in side the tube and can be used to measure the height of mortar that flows into the tube and stays there. At each end this rod is plugged with a plastic cap to prevent cement paste or other material from seeping into the tube.

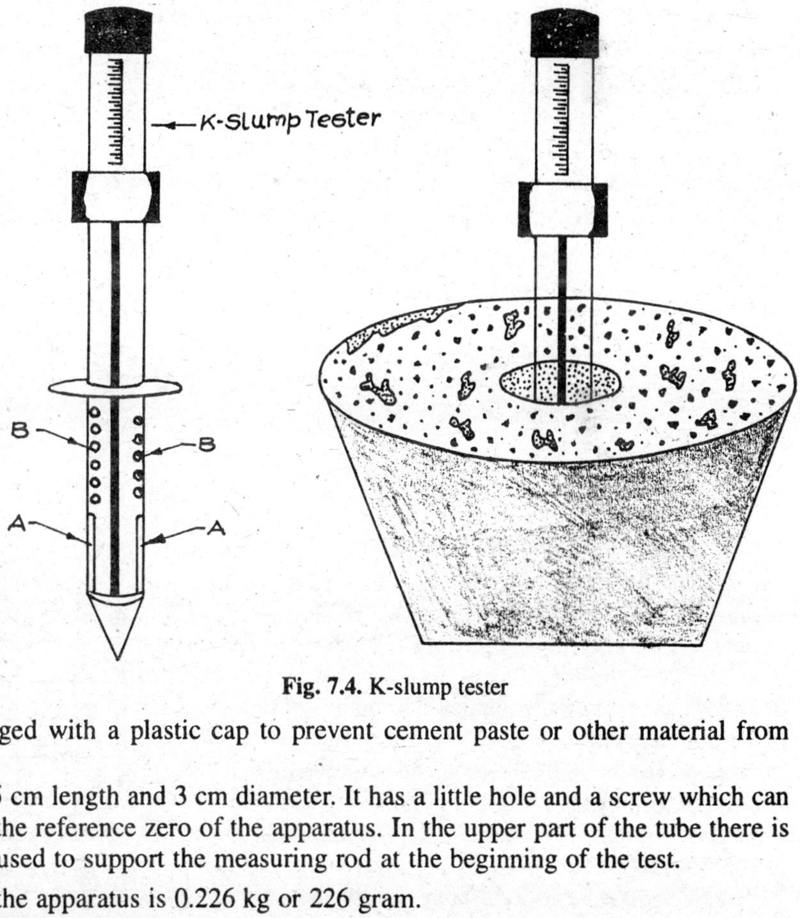

Fig. 7.4. K-slump tester

4. An aluminium cap of 2.25 cm length and 3 cm diameter. It has a little hole and a screw which can be used to set and adjust the reference zero of the apparatus. In the upper part of the tube there is also a small pin which is used to support the measuring rod at the beginning of the test.

Weights. The total weight of the apparatus is 0.226 kg or 226 gram.

Procedure. Following procedure is adopted:

(*a*) Wet the tester with clean water before use and shake off the excess water.

(*b*) Now raise the measuring rod of the tester and tilt it slightly so that the measuring rod may rest on the pin located inside the tester for this purpose.

(*c*) Level the surface of concrete to be tested. Insert the tester in the levelled concrete surface vertically down wards until the disc floater comes in contact with the concrete surface. The tester should not be rotated while inserting or removing.

(*d*) After 1 minute, lower the measuring rod slowly till it rests on the surface of the concrete that has entered into the tube. Now read the K-slump directly on the scale of the measuring rod.

(*e*) Raise the measuring rod again and let it rest on the pin.

(*f*) Remove the tester from the concrete vertically up wards and again lower the measuring rod slowly till it touches the surface of the concrete retained in the tube and read workability (W) directly on the scale of measuring rod.

7.5.3. Ball penetration test

This is a simple field test devised by J.W. Kelly and is known as kelly ball test after the name of its inventor Kelly. This test has not been covered by Indian standard specifications, but it has been covered by ASTM standard 360-92.

Apparatus. The apparatus is consisted of 15.2 cm diameter spherical metal ball weighing 14 kg (30 lbs) with a measuring scale on the stem (vertical rod) of the handle.

Principle. In this test, the penetration of the ball of the apparatus in the fresh concrete is measured. The depth of penetration gives an idea of the fluidity of concrete. Actually it works on the same principle as that of slump test. It is also used for routine checking of consistency for control purposes.

Procedure of test. The surface of the concrete is levelled, avoiding excess working. On the levelled concrete surface the ball of the apparatus is lowered gradually. The depth of penetration of the ball in the concrete is read from the scale of its stem to the nearest 6 mm. The test can be performed with in about 15 seconds.

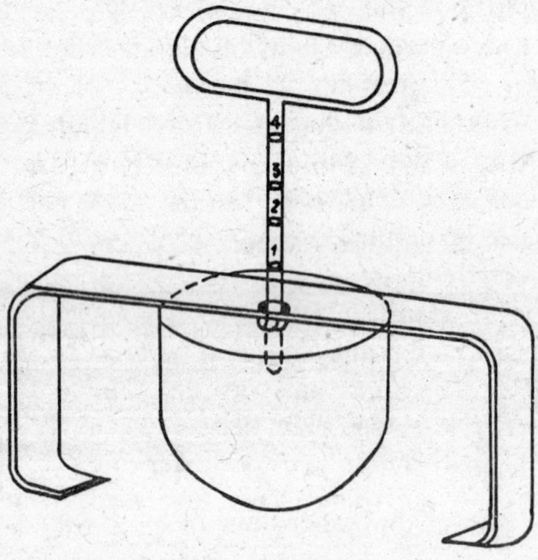

Fig. 7.5. Kelly Ball

Advantages

Following advantages have been observed of the test

1. This test is simpler and quicker than slump test.
2. It can be applied to the surface of concrete in the actual form work or in a wheel barrow.
3. This test can be performed with greater precision.
4. This test can be used as an alternative of slump test.

Disadvantages

1. This test requires a large sample of concrete and it can not be carried out in case the concrete is placed in a thin section.
2. The minimum depth of concrete must be at least 20 cm and the minimum distance

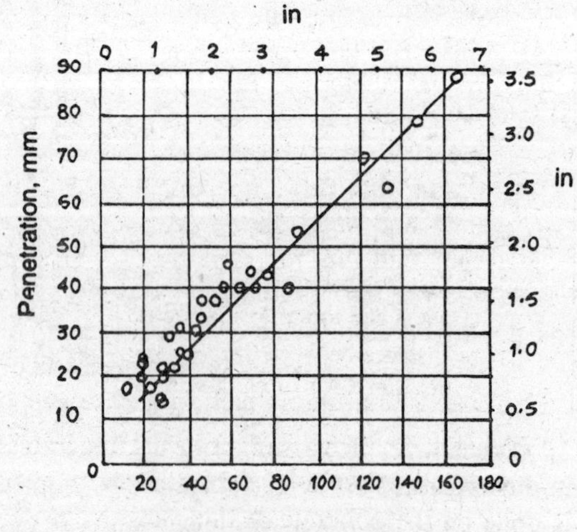

Fig. 7.6. Relation between penetration and slump

from the centre of the ball to the nearest edge of concrete should be 23 cms or the least lateral dimension of the concrete should be 460 mm.

Remark. Actually there is no simple correlation between penetration and slump test. They are used to measure specific condition. In practice the ball penetration test is used essentially to measure the variation in the mix., such as those of a variation in the moisture content of the aggregate. When a particular mix is used, correlation can be found as shown in Fig. 7.6.

7.5.4. Compacting factor test

This test is designed primarily to determine the workability of concrete in the laboratory where maximum size of aggregate does not exceed 38 mm, however it may also be used in the field. It is more sensitive and precise than slump test and is particularly useful for concrete mixes of very low workability as are normally used for concrete to be compacted by vibration, such concrete may fail to slump.

This test known as compacting factor test was developed at Road Research Laboratory England. The workability is defined as the amount of work required to place and compact concrete fully. The degree of compaction, called compacting factor is measured by the density ratio. It is the ratio of the actually achieved density in the test to the density of the same fully compacted concrete. Thus compacting factor can be defined *as the ratio of the actual density obtained during the test to the density of fully compacted concrete.*

Apparatus. The apparatus consists essentionally of two hoppers, each of the shape of a frustum of a cone and one cylinder. The hoppers are hinged on a vertical frame one above the other as shown in Fig. 7.7. The hoppers have hinged doors at their bottoms. The inside surfaces of the hoppers are polished to reduce friction. The dimensions of the hoppers, mould and distances between them are shown in table 7.3 below.

Table 7.3. Dimensions of the compacting factor apparatus for use with aggregate not exceeding 38 mm,

S. No.	*Details*	*Dimensions in cms.*
Upper hopper A		
1.	Top internal diameter	25.4
2.	Bottom internal diameter	12.7
3.	Internal height	27.9 – 28.0
Lower hopper B		
1.	Top internal diameter	22.9
2.	Bottom internal diameter	12.7
3.	Internal height	22.9
Cylinder C		
1.	Internal diameter	15.2
2.	Internal height	30.5
3.	Distance between the bottom of upper hopper A and top of lower hopper B	20.3
4.	Distance between the bottom of lower hopper B and top of cylinder C	20.3

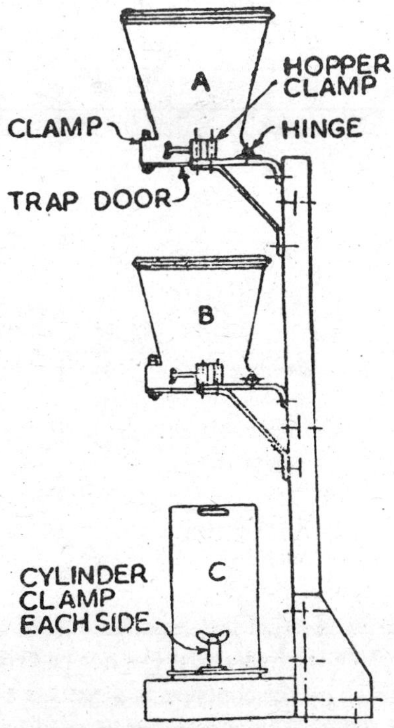

Fig. 7.7. Compacting factor apparatus

Procedure. The sample of concrete to be tested is placed gently in the upper hopper A by the hand scoop in such a way that no work is done on the concrete at this stage to produce compaction. While filling concrete in the upper hopper A, hopper B and cylinder C should be covered, so that no concrete should fall into them. After filling the concrete in hopper A, the cover from hopper B is removed and the hinged bottom door of hopper A is released and the concrete is allowed to fall into the lower hopper B. The hopper B being smaller than upper hopper A is filled to over flowing state. Thus it always contains approximately the same amount of concrete in a standard state. This reduces the influence of the personal factor in filling the top hopper. Now the cover from the cylinder is removed and the bottom door of the lower hopper B is released and concrete is allowed to fall into the cylinder. The excess concrete in the cylinder is cut off by the help of two trowels sliding across the top of the cylinder. The outside of the cylinder is wiped clean and cylinder weighed. The net weight of the concrete in the cylinder is called as weight of partially compacted concrete and dividing it by the volume of cylinder, its density is determined. Now the concrete in the cylinder is filled in four layers & fully compacted and the density of the fully compacted concrete is obtained. The ratio of the two densities or weights of partially compacted concrete & fully compacted concrete will give its compacting factor.

i.e. $\text{Compacting factor} = \dfrac{\text{Weight of partially compacted concrete}}{\text{Weight of fully compacted concrete}}$

The value of compacting factor varies from 0.78 to 1.0.

The apparatus shown above in Fig. 7.7 is 1.2 m high. For concrete with a maximum size of over 20mm & upto 40 mm a large apparatus of height 1.8 m may be employed. For the same concrete higher apparatus gives from 1.0% to 2.65% higher values of compacting factor than smaller apparatus, for very high to very low degree of workability. For this reason usually bigger apparatus is not used. The values of compacting factors for different workability are shown in Table 7.4 below.

Table 7.4. Workability, slump and compacting factor of concrete with 19.0 or 38.0 mm max. size aggregate

S. No.	*Degree of workability*	*Slump in cms*	*Compacing factor*		*Use for which concrete is suitable*
			Small apparatus	*Large* apparatus*	
1.	Very low	0 – 2.5	0.78	0.80	This class of concrete is suitable for roads vibrated with power operated machines. Concrete at the more workable end can be compacted by hand operated machines.
2.	Low	2.5 – 5.0	0.85	0.87	This class of concrete is suitable for roads vibrated by hand operated machines. More workable concrete can be manually compacted in roads using round or irregular aggregate. This concrete can also be used for mass concrete work in foundations without vibrations and lightly reinforced sections with vibration.
3.	Medium	5.0 – 10.0	0.92	0.935	This class of concrete is suitable for normal reinforced concrete work manually compacted and heavily reinforced sections with vibration. Less workable concrete can be used for flat slabs using crushed aggregate and manually compacted.
4.	High	10.0 – 17.5	0.95	0.96	This group of concrete is used for sections with congested reinforcement. Normally it is not suitable for vibration.

* Normally bigger apparatus is not used.

Note : For comparable results each test should be carried out at a constant time interval after mixing of concrete is complete. A convenient time for releasing concrete from the upper hopper has been found to be two minutes after the completion of mixing.

Limitation of compaction factor method

1. This method is not very good for dry mixes.
2. Coarse and dry mixes are unduly favoured as the initial compaction of such mixes is greater for a given quantum of work than that in latter stages when full compaction can be attained by the reorientation of the particles in the mix.
3. In case, the maximum size of aggregate is very large than the mean size of aggregate particles, the drop into the lower hopper will produce segregation and will give unreliable comparision of weights with other mixes of small maximum aggregate size.
4. The method of introducing concrete into cylinder does not bear any relation to any method of placing and compacting high quality concrete.
5. This method does not indicate any tendency of segregation of fine and coarse materials. It also does not indicate the ease with which the concrete can be finished and smooth surface obtained.
6. This method is more accurate for medium to low workability *i.e.* for compacting factor 0.9 to 0.8. For concrete having compacting factor 0.7 or less, the test is not suitable. The relationship between slump and compacting factor is shown in Fig. 7.8.

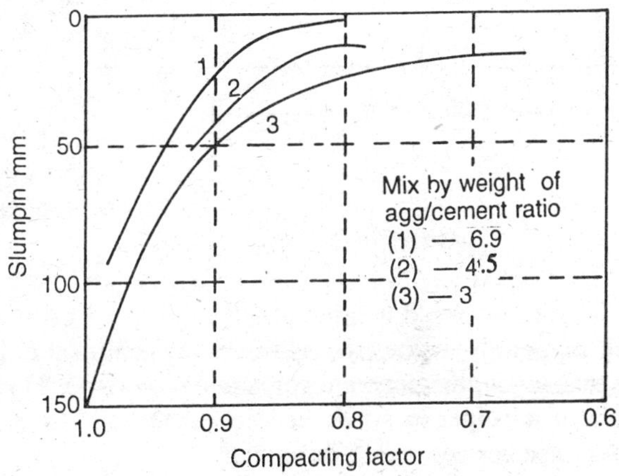

Fig. 7.8. Relation between slump and compacting factor

7.5.5. Measurement of consistency or flow of cement concrete by the use of flow table

This method gives an indication of the consistency and cohesiveness of concrete and also proneness to segregation by measuring the spread of a pile of concrete subjected to jolting. This test is of greatest value with regard to segregation. However it also gives a good assessment of consistency of stiff, rich and cohesive concrete mixes. Normally this method is used for concrete, where nominal size of aggregate does not exceed 38 mm. The flow test gives satisfactory results for concrete of the consistencies for which slump test may be used.

Apparatus. The test requires two apparatus as follows :

1. **Mould.** A mould in the form of a frustum of cone of base diameter 25 cm, top diameter 17 cm and height 12 cm is used. The internal surface of the mould should be smooth. It should also be provided with two handles. A tamping rod 61 cm long and 1.6 cm in diameter having one end rounded is also needed for rodding the concrete.
2. **Flow table.** It is a 76.0 cm diameter brass top table. It is mounted in such a way that it can be jolted by a drop of 13 mm. This table is bolted to a concrete base having a height of 40 cm to 50 cm and weighing not less than 140 kg.

Procedure. Just before the test, the top of table and inside surface of the mould is wetted and cleaned of all gritty material and excess water removed. The mould is placed at the centre of the table and held firmly in place and filled with concrete in two equal layers and each layer is rodded with 25 strokes of a straight 1.6 cm diameter and 61cm long rod, having one end rounded as in case of slump test.

The strokes should be uniformly distributed over the full cross- section of the mould and should penetrate into the underlying layer. The bottom layer should be rodded throughout its depth. After rodding the top layer, the top surface should be struck off with a trowel, filling the mould exactly upto its top, *i.e.*, the top surface of concrete should be horizontal and the excess concrete should be removed and table cleaned.

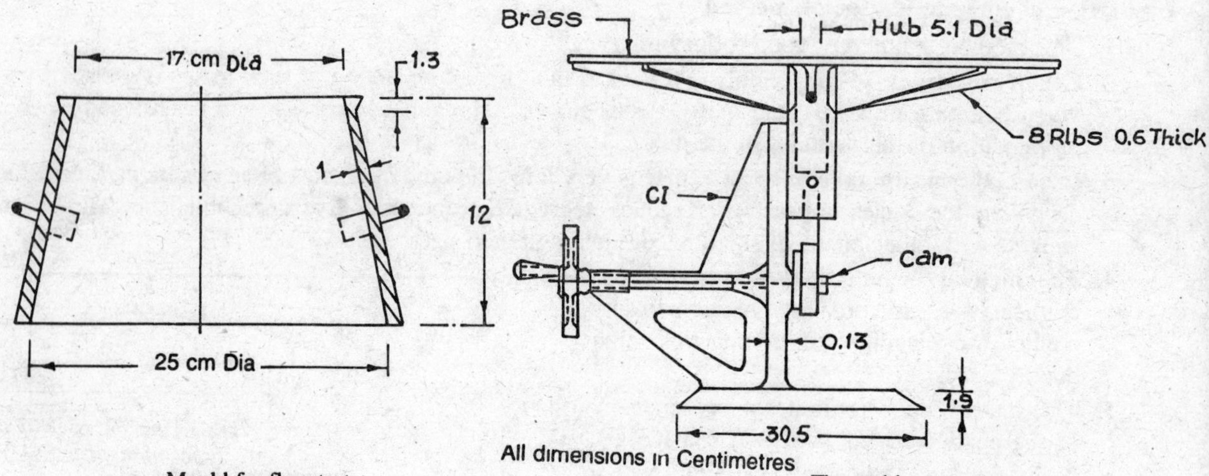

Mould for flow test

Flow table apparatus

Fig. 7.9. Flow Table

Now the mould is lifted up vertically by a gradual upward pull and the concrete stands on its own with out support. Now the table is raised and dropped through a height of 13 mm, 15 times in 15 seconds. Due to this action, the concrete spreads on the table. The diameter of the spread concrete is measured with the help of a caliper in six derections nearest to 5 mm and the average diameter is determined. The reading should be correct upto 5 mm, then

$$\text{Flow percent} = \frac{\text{spread diameter in cms.} - 25}{25} \times 100$$

The value of flow percentage varies from 0 to 150. The jolting during the test encourages the segregation. Further it should be noted that this test does not measure the workability as concretes having the same flow may differ in their workability considerably. It gives good indication of segregation of concrete.

7.5.6. Determination of consistency of concrete by Vee-Bee consisto-meter method

In this method, the consistency of concrete is determined by Vee-Bee Consisto-meter, which determines the time required to transform by vibration a concrete specimen in the shape of a conical frustum into a cylinder.

This is a very good laboratory test, particularly for dry mixes. In case of compacting factor test, some of the concrete may remain sticking with the hopper if the concrete is dry, which may affect the results. Further this test has the advantage that the treatment of concrete during the test is comparatively closely related to the method of placing concrete in practice. The name Vee-Bee has been derived from the initials of V. Bahrner of Sweeden who developed this test.

This test is not suitable for concrete having slump 75 mm or more. This test gives satisfactory performance of concrete of consistencies for which slump can not be measured.

Apparatus

The apparatus is shown diagramatically in Fig. 7.10 and a line diagram in Fig. 7.11. A Vee-Bee consisto-meter consist of the followings.

(*a*) A vibrating table resting on elastic supports [I.S. 1199-1959]

(*b*) A metal pot

(*c*) A sheet metal cone, open at both ends as slump test apparatus

(*d*) A standard iron rod 20 mm in diameter and 500 mm long.

The vibrating table (G) Fig. 7.11, is 380 mm long and 260 mm wide. It is supported on rubber shock

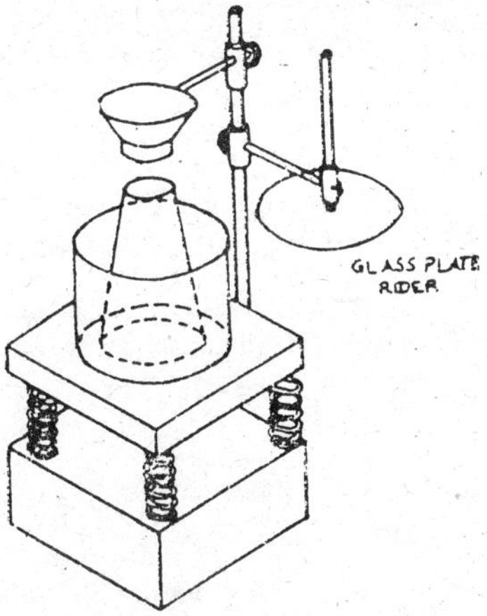

Fig. 7.10. Vee-Bee Consistometer

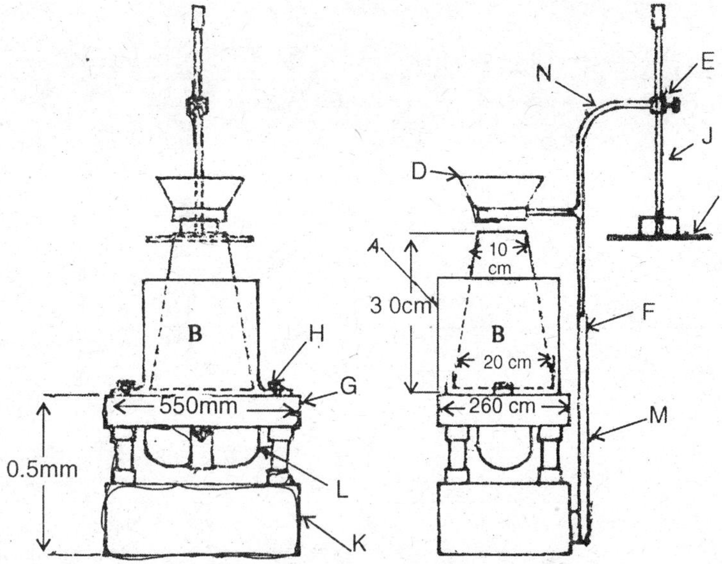

Fig. 7.11

absorbers at a height of about 305 mm above the floor level. The table is mounted on a base (K) which rests on three rubber feet and is fitted with an electrically operated vibrator mounted under it. A sheet metal cone (B) open at both ends is placed in a metal pot (A) and the pot is fixed on the vibrating table by means of two wing nuts (H). The sheet metal cone is 30 cm high, having bottom and top diameters as 20 cm and 10 cm respectively. A swivel arm holder (M) is fixed to the base and into this is telescoped another swivel arm (N) with funnel (D) and guide sleeve (E) The swivel arm can be readily detached from the vibrating table. The graduated rod (J) is fixed on to the swivel arm and at the end of graduated arm a glass disc (C) is screwed. The division of the scale on the rod records the slump of the concrete cone in Centimeters and the volume of concrete after vibration of the concrete in the pot.

Procedure. First of all slump of the concrete is determined by putting the metal cone B in the sheet metal cylinder 'A' of the consistometer. The glass disc 'C' is placed on the top of the slump cone in the cylinder before lifting the cone by moving the swivel arm and the position of concrete cone noted by adjusting the glass disc. Now the cone is lifted up and the slump is read on the graduated rod by lowering the glass disc on the top of concrete cone. The electric vibrator is now switched on and the concrete is allowed to spread in the cylinder. The vibration is continued until the whole concrete surface uniformly adheres to the glass disc and time taken in this operation noted with the help of a stop watch. The time is recorded in seconds. The consistency of concrete is expressed in Vee-Bee seconds or (Vee-Bee degrees) which are equal to the time in seconds as recorded above. The required slump is obtained by the Table 7.5. The curve of Fig. 7.11 shows a relationship between slump in cms and consistency. Vee-Bee seconds.

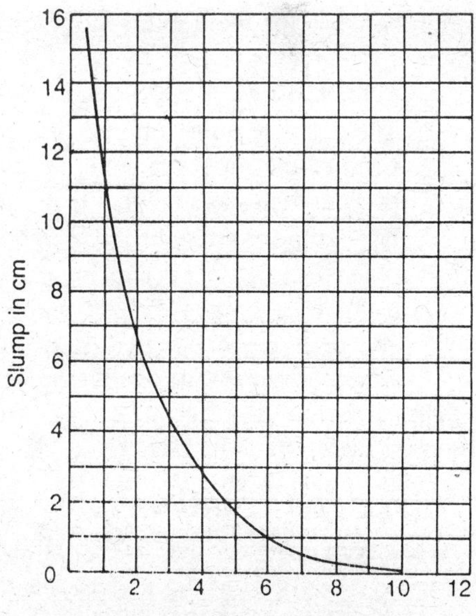

Fig. 7.12. Relation between slump and Vee-Bee seconds

Thus the time required for complete re-moulding of concrete in seconds is nearest of workability and expressed in number as Vee bee second.

Table 7.5. Consistency scale

S. No.	*Consistency*	*No. of Vee-Bee degree*	*Characteristics*
1.	Moist earth	40 to 25 — 20	Particles of coarse aggregate in the concrete are adhessive, but concrete does not clot. Risk of segregation.
2.	Very dry	20 to 15 — 10	Concrete has the consistency of very stiff porridge (soft food of oat), forms a mound when dumped, and barely tends to shake or roll itself to form an almost horizontal surface when conveyed for a long time in a wheel barrow.
3.	Dry	10 to 7 — 5	Concrete has the consistency of a stiff porridge, forms a mound when dumped, and shakes or rolls itself to form a horizontal surface when conveyed for a long time in a wheel barrow.
4.	Plastic	5 to 4 — 3	Concrete can be shaped into a ball between the palms of the hands and adheres to the skin.
5.	Semi fluid	3 to 2 — 1	Concrete can not be rolled into a ball between the palms of hands, but spreads out even though slowly and without affecting the cohesion and the segregation does not occur.
6.	Fluid	More fluid than 1	Concrete spreads out rapidly and segregation takes place.

From the above table it will be seen that for dry mixes where slump test is less sensitive, Vee-Bee test gives reliable results. All concretes intended to be vibrated lie between the range of 40 to 25 Vee-Bee degrees. For this range this test is very sensitive and accurate. The variation of $\frac{1}{2}$ Vee-Bee degree corresponds to a change of 0.004 in water/cement ratio or a change in strength of about 0.8%. This is a great sensitivity for concrete. A concrete having V-B degree equal to 4, correspond to a slump of 3 cm, and is plastic enough to be shaped into a ball between the palms of hands.

Remarks. As all these tests measure only a particular aspect of workability, hence there is no rigid correlation between the workabilities of concrete measured by different test methods. Hence it is recommended that for a given concrete, the appropriate test method be decided before hand to decide the workability. The major draw backs of the above methods are summarised below:

1. The tests are quite arbitrary and empirical as far as the measurement of workability is concerned. Each of these tests is a single point test measuring a single quantity, which at times may classify two concretes as identical that may behave quite differently on the job or site.
2. Even minor variations in techniques of conducting the test, may vary the results of tests.
3. Non of these tests is capable of covering the whole range of workabilities of concrete. The slump test is incapable of differenciating between concretes of very low (zero slump) workability or two concretes of very high workability (collapse slump). More over the test results may be used as simple statement of qualitative behaviour of concrete under specific conditions.

The expected range of values of workability obtained by different test methods are shown in the following Table 7.6.

7.6. EFFECT OF TIME AND TEMPERATURE ON WORKABILITY

It has been observed that freshly mixed concrete stiffens with time due to the fact that some water from the mix is absorbed by the aggregates and some is lost by evaporation, particularly if the concrete is exposed directly to the sun or wind and some water is consumed by initial chemical reactions. The compacting factor has been found decreasing upto 0.1 during a period of one hour from mixing. However the exact value of the loss of workability depends upon the following factors.

Table 7.6. Suggested values of workability of concrete for different placing conditions

S. No.	*Placing condition*	*Degree of workability*	*Compacting factor for using of different size of aggregate*			*Vee-Bee time in sec and slump for 20 mm size aggregate*
			40 mm	*20 mm*	*10 mm*	
1.	Hand compaction of heavy reinforced sections	Flowing type (High)	0.95	0.95	0.95	Vee Bee method not possible 125-150 mm slump
2.	Hand compaction of lightly reinforced sections or vibration compaction for heavily reinforced sections. as concreting of lightly reinforced sections.	Medium (plastic)	0.92	0.90	0.88	5-2 Sec Vee Bee time 25-75 mm slump
3.	Road pavements and slabs etc compacted with hand operated vibrators and mass concrete with vibrations.	Low (Stiff plastic)	0.85	0.84	0.82	10-5 sec Vee Bee time 5-50 mm slump
4.	Concreting in shallow sections with vibrations	Very low (Stiff)	0.80	0.78	0.75	20-10 see Vee Bee time 0-25 mm slump
5.	Concreting with intensive vibrations	Extremely low very stiff	Not used	0.68	0.65	30-20 see Vee Bee time No slump test possible

1. Richness of the mix
2. Type of cement
3. Temperature of concrete
4. Ambient temperature
5. Initial workability of concrete
6. Moisture condition of aggregate. (Loss being greater for dry aggregate owing to absorption of water by aggregate) and grading of aggregate.

Evans has suggested the following curve correlating slump with time. From the laboratory tests it has been found that on a hot day the water content of the mix would have to be increased for a constant workability to be maintained as shown in Fig. 7.13, Fig. 7.14 shows the effect of temperature on the slump of concrete made with different sized aggregate. Thus it is evident that on a hot day the water content of

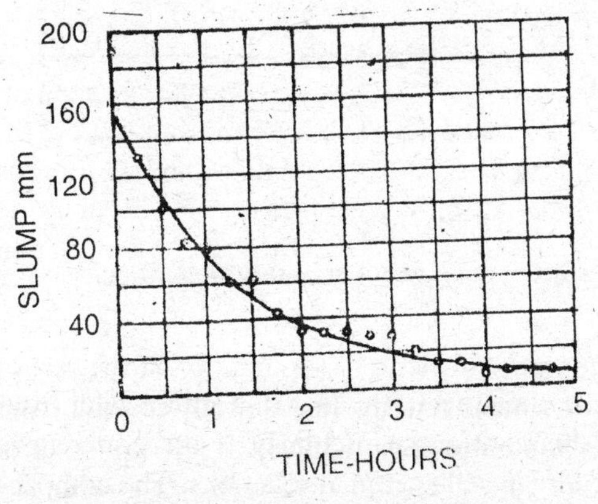

Fig. 7.13. Relation between slump and time

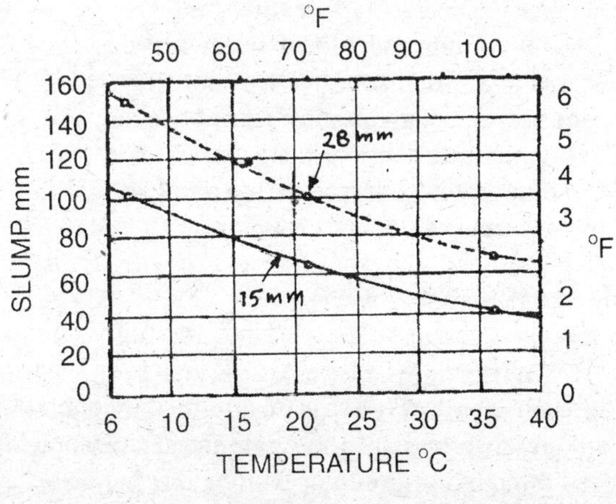

Fig. 7.14. Influence of temperature on slump of concrete with different max., aggregate size

the mix would have to be increased for a constant workability to be maintained. Fig. 7.15 shows that as the concrete temperature increases the percentage increase in water required to effect a 2.5 cm change in slump also increases.

However *Shalon* did not observe any loss of workability with increase in temperature in a hot climate by site tests. Upto a temperature of 104°F (40°C) and a relative humidity between the range of 20% to 70%, no effect of temperature on slump was observed. Only above 122°F (50°C) effect of temperature or below 20% humidities, the slump falls off rapidly. Actually full phenomenon is not known as yet and it is recommended that for any new conditions actual site tests should be made. Further it has also been observed that if the temperature rises from 40°F to 100°F, the slump falls from 16 cm to 7.0 cm as shown in Fig. 7.16.

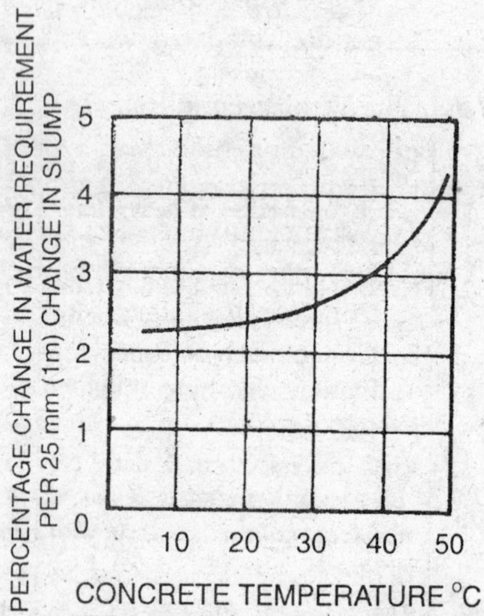

Fig. 7.15. Influence of temperature on amount of water required to change slump

7.7. SEGREGATION

Segregation can be defined as the separation of the constituent materials of concrete of a heterogeneous mixture so that their distribution is no longer uniform. In a good concrete all the ingredients should be properly distributed to make it a homogeneous mixture. The concrete which shows the tendency of separation say coarse aggregate separates from rest of the ingredients, such a concrete is said to be showing the tendency of segregation. The segregation of concrete will not only produce weak, but also non homogeneous concrete which would develop undesirable properties in the hardened concrete. The difference in the size of aggregate particles and the specific gravity of the mix constituents are the main cause of segregation, but the extent can be controlled by the choice of suitable grading and by careful handling.

A well made concrete taking various parameters into consideration such as grading, size, shape and surface texture of aggregate with optimum quantity of water makes a cohesive mix. Such concrete will not show any tendency of segregation. The cohesive and fatty characteristics of matrix do not allow the different constituents to fall apart, causing segregation.

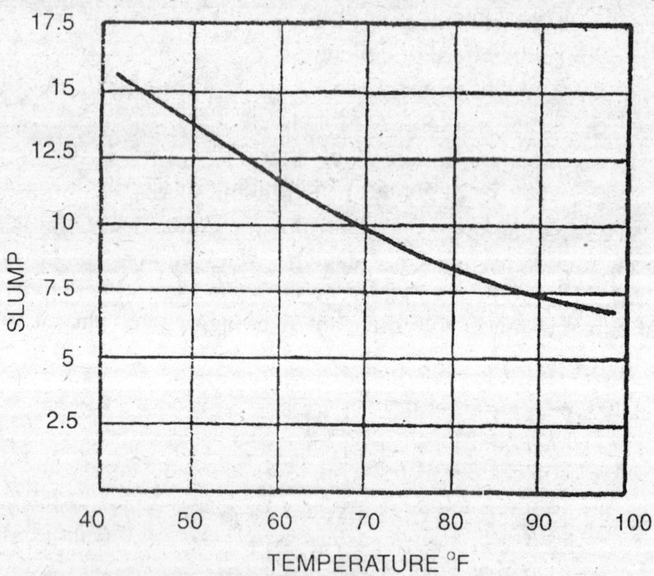

Fig. 7.16. Effect of temperature on slump of concrete

7.7.1. Types of segregation

Segregation can be divided into the following groups:

1. **Coarse aggregate segregation.** In this case, the coarser particles tend to separate from the rest of the matrix. This type of segregation occurs in lean mixes when a too dry mix is prepared with same grading of aggregate. Addition of water will improve the workability.
2. **Paste or matrix separating out from the mix.** This type of segregation occurs in wet-mixes. The paste separates out from the rest of the mix. This type of segregation occurs, if excessive water is used in lean mixes.

3. **Water separation.** When water separates out from the rest of the mix, then it is called water segregation. This is known as bleeding.

7.7.2. Favourable conditions for segregation

Following conditions are favourable for segregation to occur:

1. Badly proportioned mix, where sufficient matrix is not there to bind and contain the aggregates.
2. Insufficiently mixed concrete with more water content.
3. Dropping of concrete from a height more than one metre.
4. Concrete discharged from a badly designed mixer or from a mixer of worn out blades.
5. Conveyance of concrete by conveyer belts, wheel barrow, long distance haul by dampers, long lift by skip and hoist etc.
6. Excessive vibration used for spreading concrete.

7.7.3. Remedial measures

The tendency of segregation can bc checked by the following measures:

1. By correctly proportioning the mix 2. Proper handling
3. Proper transporting 4. Proper placing
5. By proper compacting and finishing

7.8. BLEEDING

It is also known as *water gain.* It is a form of segregation in which some of the water in the mix tends to rise to the surface of the freshly placed concrete, being of the lowest specific gravity of the all ingredients of the concrete. The phenomenon of bleeding is caused due to the inability of the solid materials of the mix to hold the mixing water when they settle down.

7.8.1. Causes of Bleeding

Bleeding is observed under the following conditions:

1. In highly wet mixes
2. Badly proportioned mixes
3. Insufficiently mixed concrete
4. In thin members like roof slab or road slab etc.
5. When concrete is placed in sunny weather.

7.8.2. Effects of Bleeding

Due to bleeding following effects are observed:

1. Due to bleeding, water comes up and accumulates at the surface. Along this water certain quantity of cement also comes to the surface. When the surface is worked up with a trovel and floats, the aggregate and cement go down and water comes up on the surface, forming a cement paste at the surface, known as *'Laitence'*. In such cases the top surface of slab and pavement will be of poor wearing quality. The laitence formed on the pavement will form dust in summer and mud in rainy season. This can be avoided by delaying the finishing operations till the bleeding water has evaporated and avoiding over working on the surface and using wooden floats.
2. As the top surface of the slab has higher water content and less aggregate matter, develops higher shrinkage cracks.
3. Due to bleeding, the top of every lift *i.e.* layer of concrete placed may become too wet and if this water is trapped by placing an other layer over it a porous and weak layer of non durable concrete will result. The bond with the next lift or layer will be poor due to the formation of a plane of weakness. This can be avoided by removing the laitence fully before pouring the next lift or layer.

4. If the rate of evaporation from the surface of bleeding water is faster than the bleeding rate, the plastic shrinkage cracks would develop.
5. Water rising from bottom to top makes continuous capillary channels. If the water/cement ratio used is more than 0.7, the bleeding channels remain as such and do not get filled by the development of cement 'gel'. These capillary channels are responsible for the development of impermeable concrete structure.
6. The bleeding water in the process of coming up may be intercepted or blocked by aggregate particles and reinforcement. In such situations water is likely to accumulate below aggregate and reinforcement. This accumulation of water produces water voids below aggregates and reinforcement and reduces the bond between cement paste and aggregate and also between cement paste and reinforcing bars. The ill effect of poor bond between cement paste and aggregate or cement pate and reinforcement may be remedied by revibration of concrete.

7.8.3. PREVENTION OF BLEEDING

The amount of bleeding depends largely on the properties of cement. It can be decreased by the following measures:

1. It can be reduced by increasing the fineness of cement.
2. It can be reduced by adding high contents of C_3A in the cement.
3. It can also be reduced by adding calcium chloride to the cement.
4. Rich mixes are less prone to bleeding than lean mixes.
5. Addition of pozzolanic or air entrainment admixture reduces the bleeding of concrete.

7.8.4. Determination of bleeding water content

The amount of bleeding water is determined by the following method.

Equipment

Following equipments are used for this test.

(*a*) Cylindrical container of inside diameter of 250 mm and inside height 280 mm. The capacity of the container is about 0.01 m^3.

(*b*) Tamping rod of steel 600 mm long and 16 mm in diameter having one end round as a bullet.

(*c*) A pipette for drawing free water from the surface of the concrete.

(*d*) A graduated jar of 100 cm^3 capacity.

Test Procedure

A sample of freshly mixed concrete is taken and filled in the cylindrical container upto a height of about 50 mm layer and tamped by the tamping rod 25 times. In this way 5 layers in all giving a total depth of concrete 250 ± 3 mm are filled and each layer is tamped before adding the next layer. After filling the concrete upto 250 ± 3 mm depth the top layer is made smooth by trowelling.

Now the test specimen is weighed and its weight is noted.

Let the weight of empty container $= w_1$

the weight of container + concrete $= w_2$

∴ weight of concrete $= w_2 - w_1$

Now the cylindrical container is placed on a level surface free from vibrations at a temperature of 27°C ± 2°C and covered with a lid. Water accumulated at the levelled surface of the concrete is withdrawn with the help of pipette at 10 minutes interval for the first 40 minutes and at 30 minutes interval after wards till the bleeding ceases. All the water is collected in the 100 c.c. capacity jar. To facilitate the collection of bleeding water, the container may be tilted slightly. Knowing the total water content in 1 m^3 of concrete, the water content in the cylindrical container may also be calculated.

$$\text{Thus bleeding water percentage} = \frac{\text{Total quantity of bleeding water collected}}{\text{Total quantity of water in the sample of concrete}} \times 100$$

7.9. ANALYSIS OF FRESH CONCRETE

Some times it is essential to determine the proportions of various constituents of concrete. This can be done easily in the field if the concrete is fresh and analysis is done within five minutes of discharge of the concrete mix from the mixer or agitator. If it is not possible to start the test within five minutes after discharge of concrete from the mixer, the concrete is taken from the charge of the mixer within five minutes and placed in a air tight container till the commencement of the analysis. The analysis of such concrete should be commenced within two hours from the time of addition of water to the solid ingredients. This analysis can be done with the help of Dunagon Buoyency apparatus as shown in Fig. 7.17. Before commencement of analysis of the fresh concrete samples of coarse and fine aggregates used in concrete should also be taken to determine their specific gravities, water absorption and for sieve analysis etc.

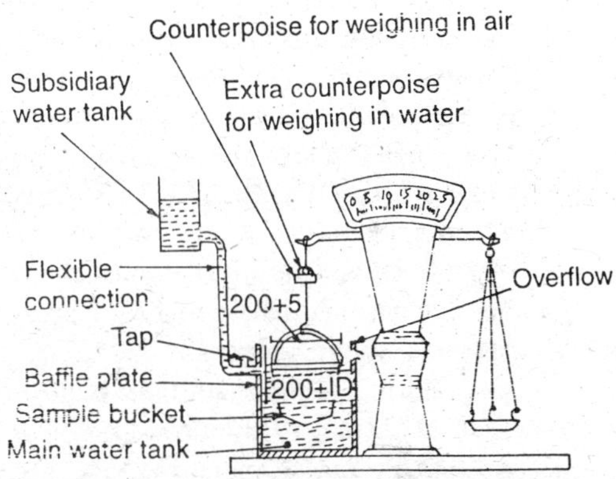

Fig. 7.17. Dunagon Buoyency apparatus

Apparatus

One form of the apparatus consists of the following parts.

A. Balance. A semi-automatic balance capable of weighing upto 5 kg to an accuracy of 0.5 gram. The balance is provided with two counter poises to obtain equilibrium, one for when an empty bucket is being weighed in air and the other, when the bucket is being weighed whilst immersed in water. If the sample is to be weighed in air and covered with water at site before transporting it to a laboratory for analysis, then the balance capable of weighing upto 5 kg to an accuracy of 1 gram should be available at site.

B. At least eight seamless bucket shaped containers of corrosion resisting metal, such as stainless steel, chromium or nickle plated steel sheet 2.0 mm thick, each 200 ± 5 mm diameter at top (internal) and 180± 5 mm deep having smooth sloping side and a rounded bottom to prevent trapping of air when it is immersed. All the containers should be of the same weight in air correct up to ± 0.25 gram and each should be clearly marked with the necessary correction figure to allow for the difference between its loss in weight when immersed in water and weight of second counterpoise Fig. 7.18.

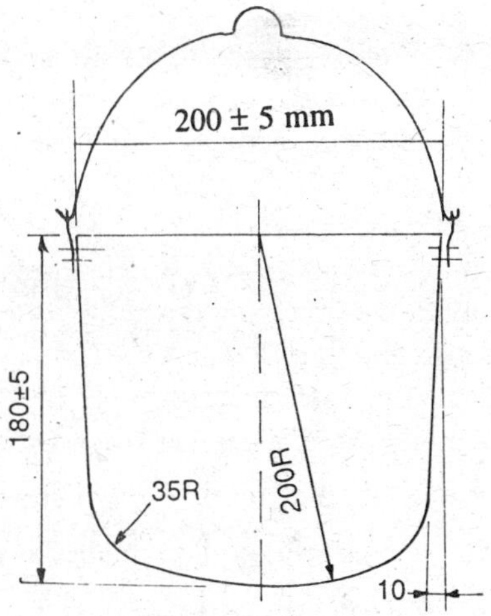

Fig. 7.18. Seamless Bucket

C. Tank. The tank should be large enough to receive the bucket-shaped container easily and made of corrosion resisting metal such as stainless steel or chromium or nickel plated steel sheet 2.0mm thick. The internal diameter of the tank should be of the order of 500 mm and 300 mm deep as shown in Fig. 7.19. The tank is provided with an overflow spout in such a position that the rim of the bucket hung from the balance should remain completely immersed when the tank is full. The spout should preferably be 5 mm below the tap of the tank. The tank should be connected by a tap and flexible pipe to a subsidiary tank, so that the water level in the main tank can be raised or lowered without disturbance by altering the level of the subsidiary tank. The tap should preferably be at a distance of 20 mm from the top of the tank, so that in the lowest position of the subsidiary tank when the tap is open the level of water is below the lip of the bucket hanging on the balance. A baffle plate of corrosion less metal as above (approximately 1.7 mm thick and 70 mm deep and 100 mm long) should be provided inside the main tank opposite the inlet of the tap extending from the tap of the tank to a position 50 mm below the centre of connection of the tap as shown in Fig. 7.19.

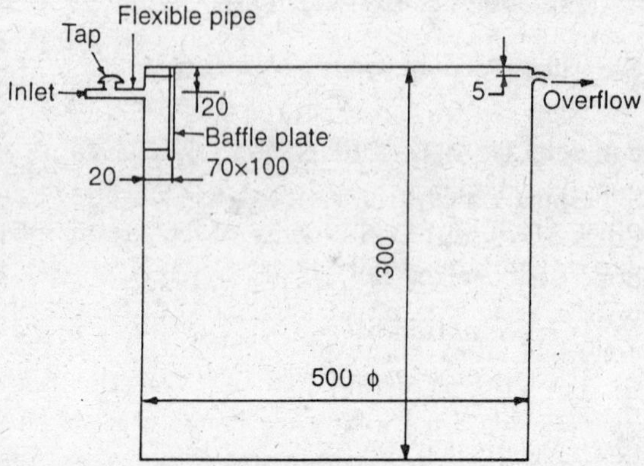

Fig. 7.19. Tank

D. Subsidiary tank. The subsidiary tank should be of suitable size and made of corrosion resisting metal as above. The bottom of this tank is connected to the top of the main tank by a flexible pipe. The position of the subsidiary tank should be movable, so that it can be raised or lowered from the position of the tap on the main tank as necessity arises.

E. Sieves. Two nesting sieves 450 mm diameter are used. One I.S. sieve 4.75 mm (100 mm in depth) and the other I.S. sieve 150 micron (300 mm in depth) supported in the sieve frame by an adequately rigid spider of brass as shown in Fig. 7.20. The plan of spider is shown in Fig. 7.21.

F. Funnel. A funnel approximately 500 mm in diameter at top, 150 mm diameter at the bottom and 250 mm deep made of 1.6 mm thick corrosion resistant metal as shown in Fig. 7.22. is provided to facilitate the washing of materials from the large sieves into the buckets without loss of any material.

G. Hose. A hose fitted with nozzle capable of giving a fairly fine and strong spray of water should be provided.

H. Stirring rod. A 15 mm diameter and 300 mm long mild steel rod is used for stirring purposes.

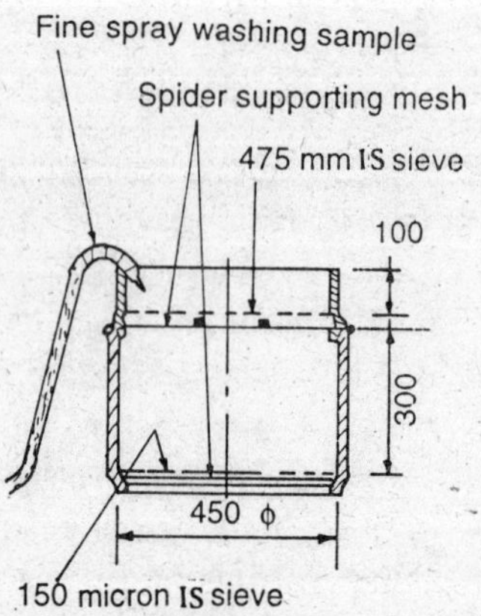

Fig. 7.20

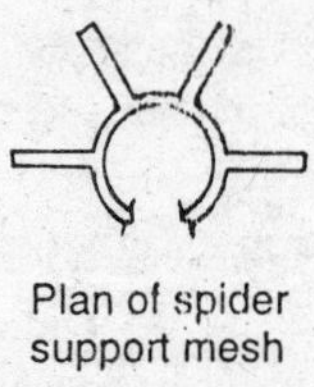

Fig. 7.21

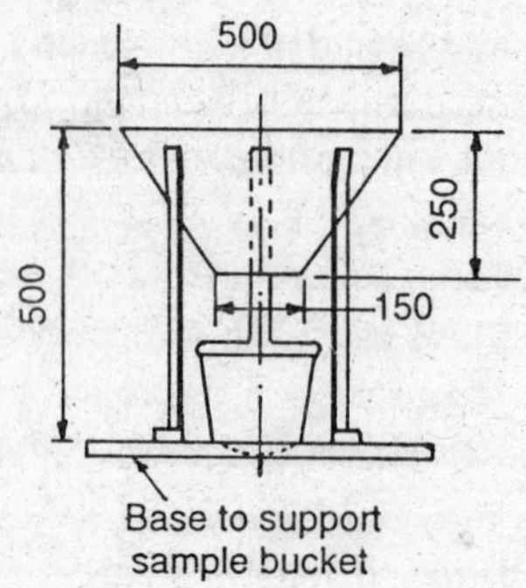

Fig. 7.22

I. Weight box. A standard weight box of capacity 5 kg should be provided.

Samples

Samples from each of the various sizes of aggregates in the same nominal proportions as used in the concrete are taken. The weight of the samples should be approximately 3.5 kg. The weight of sample of concrete should be about 4 kg if the maximum nominal size of aggregate used does not exceed 19mm, otherwise 8 kg weight of concrete sample should be taken and analysed in two parts, each of 4 kg. Before carrying out the actual analysis, the determination of specific gravities of aggregate and cement is essential.

(*a*) Determination of specific gravity of aggregate

The specific gravities of the aggregates should be determined under identical conditions under which the analysis of the concrete is to be carried out. Temperature variation during the test should not be more than 2°C. Each sample of coarse and fine aggregate should be dried in a ventilated oven at a temperature of 100°C to 110°C for 24 hours, cooled and weighed. The weights of coarse and fine aggregate in gram should be denoted by A_a and A_s as per I.S.1199-1959.

Now each sample is placed in a clean bucket shaped container and filled with water upto within 25 mm of the lip. To remove any entrapped air from the sample, it is stirred for one minute and the bucket shaped container or bucket is hung in the water tank from the balance. The water level in the tank should then be raised steadily by raising the subsidiary tank till the water starts over-flowing through the spout. The weight of sample is taken at this situation in water. During weighing to get accurate results, maximum movement of the bucket should be limited upto 6.5 mm.

Now the sample is left under water for 20 minutes, then stirred, reimmersed, and reweighed. This procedure is repeated till the variation in weight between two consecutive weighing is less than 0.5 gram, but in no case the period of immersion should exceed 8 hours. The final weights of coarse and fine aggregate should be recorded as B_a and B_s respectively. Time required to get constant weights should also be noted.

Calculations

$$\text{Specific gravity of coarse aggregate} = \frac{A_a}{A_a - B_a}$$

$$\text{Specific gravity of fine aggregate} = \frac{A_s}{A_s - B_s}$$

Note. Average specific gravity for each of them should be calculated. The maximum time required for any sample to attain the constant weight, shall be taken as the time required for absorption of water by the aggregates as a whole.

7.10. SPECIFIC GRAVITY OF THE CEMENT

For the purpose of this test, the specific gravity of portland cement can be taken as 3.15. For other cements, the value of specific gravity should be determined with the help of specific gravity bottle using an inert liquid.

Procedure. The specific gravity bottle is first weighed in air. Let its weight be W_1 gram. Now the bottle is filled with water and wiped dry from out side and weighed. Let this weight of bottle filled with water be W_2 gram.

Then the bottle is emptied and dried by rinsing it with alcohol. About 20 grams of cement is then placed in the bottle and weighed. Let this weight be W_3 grams. Now kerosene oil or benzene is filled upto about half the capacity of the bottle and shaken thoroughly to expell all the air from the cement. When air bubbles cease coming out and cement is fully dispersed in the liquid, then the bottle is fully filled with the liquid and weighed. Let this weight be W_4 gram. The bottle is emptied again and washed thoroughly with the liquid to clean it of all cement. Now it is filled with this liquid and weighed. Let this weight be W_5 grams,

$$\text{then sp. gr. of liquid} = \frac{W_5 - W_1}{W_2 - W_1} = d_1 \text{ (say)}$$

$$\text{weight of cement in the bottle} = (W_3 - W_1) \text{ gram}$$

$$\text{weight of an equal volume of liquid} = [(W_5 - W_1) - (W_4 - W_3)] \text{ grams}$$

$$\text{vol. of this weight of liquids} = \frac{(W_5 - W_1) - (W_4 - W_3)}{d_1}$$

$$\text{density of cement} = \frac{(W_3 - W_1)\, d_1}{(W_5 - W_1) - (W_4 - W_3)} \text{ gr/c.c.}$$

which is also equal to sp. gr. of cement.

Sieve Analysis

Each of the samples used to determine the specific gravity of the aggregate should be used for its sieve analysis.

One sample of the coarse aggregate should be put on 4.75 mm I.S. sieve placed over I.S. 150 micron sieve and washed for two minutes under the spray of water, the aggregate being stirred during the washing. The material retained on I.S. sieve 4.75 mm is then washed into a clean bucket by means of the funnel, stirred, immersed in water and weighed. Let the weight be D_a.

One sample of fine aggregate is then added to the material retained on I.S. 150 micron sieve and washed under spray of water for atleast ten minutes, continuing till the water is clear. The residue retained on the sieve is washed into a clean bucket, stirred, immersed and weighed. Let the weight be D_s. Care should be taken that no material is wasted while transferring the sample to the sieve and back to the bucket. Correction factor then shall be calculated as follows:

$$\text{Correction factor for coarse aggregate } C_a = \frac{B_a}{D_a}$$

$$\text{Correction factor for fine aggregate } C_s = \frac{B_s}{D_s}$$

The correction factor is used to make allowance for the amount of coarse aggregate passing I.S. sieve 4.75 mm and the amount of total aggregate passing 150 micron sieve. B_a and B_s same as determined in the sp. gr. determination.

7.11. ANALYSIS OF CONCRETE

1. The sample of concrete is put in a clean bucket and its weight is taken in air. Let the weight of concrete in air be Wkg.
2. Now the bucket is filled with water upto within 25 mm of the lip and the contents stirred thoroughly for one minute to remove any entrapped air.
3. The sample is left immersed in water for a period of time not less than that required for absorption of water by the aggregate as determined above, but not longer than 8 hours in any case. After this period the concrete is again thoroughly stirred for one minute to remove air expelled from the aggregates.
4. The bucket is hung in the water tank from the balance with the water level in the tank below the top of the bucket. The bucket then is carefully filled with water up to the lip and the sample left to settle for five minutes.

5. The water level in the tank is now raised steadily by raising the subsidiary tank. When water begins to overflow from the spout in the main tank, the tap is closed and the weight of sample is taken in water. Let it be w_s. During the process, care is taken that sample is not shaken and the maximum movement of bucket is not allowed more than 6.5 mm to avoid inaccuracy. Less cement particles will flow out of the bucket, if the water level is raised steadily. If the water in the tank becomes dis-coloured, it should be changed between weighing to avoid any change in the specific gravity of the aggregates.
6. Now the concrete of the bucket is washed on to the I.S. sieve 4.75 mm placed over 150 micron sieve. No particles should remain in the bucket. After this, the sample is washed in the sieve under spray of water at least for two minutes continuously till the coarse aggregate is clean. During washing process, the material is kept stirred.
7. The clean coarse aggregate retained on I.S. sieve 4.75 mm is then washed into a clean bucket with the help of funnel and spray of water. The spray is used to remove any small particles from the mesh. The washing should be repeated till the water becomes clear ,before the aggregate is placed in the bucket.
8. The coarse aggregate in the bucket is covered with water and stirred thoroughly for one minute. The bucket is immersed in water in the tank and the aggregate weighed as before. Let the weight of coarse aggregate be W_a.
9. Fine aggregate retained on sieve 150 micron is also washed under spray. The clean fine aggregate also is washed clean into a clean bucket, stirred, immersed in water and weighed as before. Let the weight be W_s.

Calculations of proportions

1. The weight of coarse aggregate in the sample $W_a = w_a C_a F_a$
2. The weight of fine aggregate in the sample $W_s = w_s C_s F_s$
3. The weight of cement in the sample $W_c = [w - (w_a C_a + w_s C_s)] F_c$
4. The weight of water in the sample $W_w = W - (w_a + w_s + w_c)$

where,

$$F_a = \frac{\text{specific gravity}}{\text{specific gravity} - 1} \text{ for the coarse aggregate}$$

$$F_s = \frac{\text{specific gravity}}{\text{specific gravity} - 1} \text{ for the fine aggregate}$$

$$F_c = \frac{\text{specific gravity}}{\text{specific gravity} - 1} \text{ for the cement}$$

W = the weight of concrete in air
w = the weight of concrete in water
W_c = the weight of coarse aggregate in water
W_s = the weight of fine aggregate in water
C_a = the correction factor for coarse aggregate
C_s = the correction factor for fine aggregate.

Determination of weight per cubic metre of concrete, yield, cement factor and air content of freshly mixed concrete are carriedout as follows.

1. Weight per cubic metre of concrete. Following apparatus is needed to measure the weight of the freshly prepared concrete.

(*a*) **Measure.** The measure should be strong enough with handles usually 4 mm to 5.5 m thick. Its dimension may be as follows:

Table 7.7.

S. No.	*Nominal size of coarse aggregate in mm*	*Nominal capacity in* m^3	*Inside diameter mm*	*Inside height mm*
1.	upto 38 mm	0.01	250	280
2.	over 38 mm	0.02	350	285

(*b*) **Tamping bar.** It is a steel bar 38 cm long, having ramming face square. It's weight is 1.8 kg.

Procedure. The prepared concrete to be tested is taken and filled in the measure selected from the above table and compacted fully either by hand or by vibration. It should be compacted in such a way that neither it results in segregation nor in excessive laitance. While compacting with hand, the number of strokes per layer required to produce the specified condition vary according to the consistency of concrete but in no case the number of strokes shuld be less than 60 per layer for 0.01 m^3 measure or 120 strokes per layer for 0.02 m^3 measure. The strokes should be distributed uniformly over the whole surface.

To remove the air from the concrete, the exterior surface should be tapped 1 to 15 tims and then top surface struck off and finished smoothly. Care should be taken to see that measure remains full. The excess concrete from the exterior is wipped off and cleaned. Now the measure is weighed.

Calculations

The weight of concrete per cubic metre is calculated by dividing the weight of fully compacted concrete of the measure by its volume. Let the weight of concrete be *W* kg, then

$$\textit{Weight per cubic metre} = \frac{W}{0.01} = 100\text{ W kg/m}^3$$

Volume of concrete per batch V. The volume of concrete per batch is given by the relation.

$$V = \frac{(N \times 50) + w_f + w_c + w_w}{W} \qquad \text{...(7.1)}$$

where,

V = volume of concrete produced per batch

N = No. of 50 kg cement bags used per batch

w_f = total weight of fine aggregate used per batch in kg

w_c = total weight of coarse aggregate used per batch in kg

w_w = total weight of water used per batch in kg

W = weight of concrete in kg/m^3.

Yield per bag of cement

It is given as $$Y = \frac{V}{N} \qquad \text{...(7.2)}$$

where,

Y = yield of concrete per 50 kg bag of cement in m^3

V = volume of concrete produced per batch in m^3

N = number of 50 kg bags of cement used per batch.

Cement factor $$N_1 = \frac{N}{V} \qquad \text{...(7.3)}$$

Air content A. Air content is given as

$$A = \frac{T - W}{T} \times 100 \qquad \text{...(7.4)}$$

where,

A = air content (% voids) in the concrete
T = theoretical weight of concrete in kg/m^3
W = actual weight of concrete in kg/m^3.

Example 7.1. *Find out the yield of concrete per bag of cement from the following data by thumb rule and by specific gravity method.*

Data:

(*a*) *Mix proportions by weight* = *1:2:4*
(*b*) *Water cement ratio* = *0.65*
(*c*) *Air content* = *1%*
(*d*) *Specific gravity of cement* = *3.15*
(*e*) *Specific gravity of fine aggregate* = *2.60*
(*f*) *Specific gravity of coarse aggregate* = *2.65*

Solution.

Total volume of compacted concrete per bag of cement

V = Absolute volume of cement + Absolute volume of fine aggregate + Absolute volume of coarse aggregate

or
$$V = \frac{\text{weight of cement}}{\text{sp. gr. of cement}} + \frac{\text{weight of F.A.}}{\text{sp. gr. of F.A.}} + \frac{\text{weight of C.A.}}{\text{sp. gr. of C.A.}} + \frac{\text{weight of water}}{\text{sp. gr. of water}} + \text{vol. of air.}$$

Taking weight of cement per bag as 50 kg. and volume 35 litres, we get,

$$V = \frac{50}{3.15} + \frac{50 \times 2}{2.6} + \frac{50 \times 4}{2.65} + \frac{50 \times 0.65}{1} + 0.01\,V$$

or
$$0.99\,V = 15.88 + 38.46 + 75.50 + 32.50 = 158.34 \text{ lit.}$$

or
$$V = \frac{158.34}{0.99} = 160 \text{ litres}$$

(*ii*) By thumb rule method

Volume of compacted concrete = $\frac{2}{3}$ (vol. of cement + vol. of combined dry aggregate used for the concrete).

∴ Vol. of concrete per bag of cement for 1:2:4 mix.

$$= \frac{2}{3}(35 + 70 + 140)$$

$$= \frac{245 \times 2}{3} = 163.4 \text{ litres} \approx 164 \text{ litres.}$$ **Ans.**

Example 7.2. *Find out the yield of concrete per bag of cement from the following data.*

Data:

(*a*) *Mix proportion by volume* = *1:2:4*
(*b*) *Water cement ratio by weight* = *0.65*
(*c*) *Air entrained* = *1%*

(*d*) *Specific gravities*

(*i*) *Cement* = *3.15*

(*ii*) *F.A.* = *2.60*

(*iii*) *C.A.* = *2.65*

Bulk densities F.A. = *1.5 kg./lit.*

C.A. = *1.6 kg./lit.*

Solution. The solution of this problem differs from the above problem. In this case the proportions are given in volume so they have to be converted into weight before proceeding further.

$$\therefore \quad V = \frac{50}{3.15} + \frac{35 \times 2.0 \times 1.5}{2.60} + \frac{35 \times 4 \times 1.6}{2.65} + \frac{50 \times 0.65}{1} + 0.01\,V$$

$$\therefore \quad V = 15.88 + 40.4 + 84.5 + 32.5 + 0.01\,V$$

or $\quad 0.99\,V = 173.28$ lit.

or $\quad V = \frac{173.28}{0.99} = 175$ litres. **Ans.**

Example 7.3. *Find out quantities of ingredients required per cubic metre (m^3) of compacted concrete using the data of example 7.1.*

Solution.

(*a*) Cement in bags $= \frac{1000}{160} = 6.25$ bags.

(*b*) Fine aggregate $= 6.25 \times 50 \times 2 = 312.5$ kg.

(*c*) Coarse aggregate $= 6.25 \times 50 \times 4 = 625$ kg.

(*d*) Water $= 32.5 \times 6.25 = 203.725$ kg.

Example 7.4. *Find out approximate yield of concrete for the mixes by thumb rule and also suggest the capacity of mixer to be used per bag of cement per batch.*

Mix proportions 1:1:2, 1:1 $\frac{1}{2}$: 3, 1:2:4, 1:3:6.

Solution. It is shown in tabular from below:

Table 7.8.

S. No.	Nominal mix by Vol.	Vol. of dry materials per bag of cement			Yield per bag of cement	min. capacity of mixer in litres
		C	F.A.	C.A.		
1.	1 : 1 : 2	35	35	70	$\frac{2}{3}(35 + 35 + 70) = 93.33$ lit.	100
2.	$1 : 1\frac{1}{2} : 3$	35	52.5	105	$\frac{2}{3}(35 + 52.5 + 105) = \frac{192.5}{3} \times \frac{2}{3}$ $= 128.4$ lit.	140
3.	1 : 2 : 4	35	70	140	$\frac{2}{3}(35 + 70 + 140) = \frac{245 \times 2}{3}$ $= 163.33$ lit.	200
4.	1 : 3 : 6	35	105	210	$\frac{2}{3}(35 + 105 + 210) = \frac{350 \times 2}{3}$ $= 233.33$ lit.	400

Example 7.5. *Find out the yield of concrete per bag of cement if the unit weight of concrete is 2400 kg/m^3 with the following data.*

Mix. proportions by weight $= 1:1\frac{1}{2}:3$

Water cement ratio $= 0.6$

Air content $= 1\%$

Solution. Volume of compacted concrete per bag of cement

$$V = \frac{\text{total weight of ingredients per bag of cement used}}{\text{unit weight of concrete}}$$

Weights:

(*a*) Weight of cement per bag = 50 kg.

Weight of fine aggregate $= 50 \times 1.5 = 75$ kg.

Weight of coarse aggregate $= 50 \times 3 = 150$ kg.

Water $= 50 \times 0.6 = 30$ kg.

Total weight = 305 kg.

Unit weight of concrete $= \frac{2400}{1000} = 2.4$ kg./lit.

$\therefore$ Yield of concrete per bag of cement $Y = \frac{305}{2.4} = 127$ litres.

$\therefore$ No. of cement bags required to produce 1 m^3 concrete

$$N = \frac{1000}{Y} = \frac{1000}{127}$$

$$= 7.87 \approx 8 \text{ bags.}$$

$\therefore$ Quantity of each material of concrete for $1:1\frac{1}{2}:3$ proportion by weight.

Cement $= 50 \times 8 = 400$ kg.

Fine aggregate $= 75 \times 8 = 600$ kg.

Coarse aggregate $= 150 \times 8 = 1200$ kg.

Water $= 8 \times 30 = 240$ kg. **Ans.**

Example 7.6. *At a particular site cement used per batch is 5 bags. Calculate yield of concrete per batch with the following data.*

Proportions of mix by weight $= 1:2:4$

Water cement ratio $= 0.65$

Unit weight of concrete $= 2400$ kg/m^3

Solution.

Yield
$$Y = \frac{N \times 50 + W_f + W_c + W_w}{W}$$

$$= \frac{5 \times 50 + 2 \times 5 \times 50 + 4 \times 5 \times 50 + 0.65 \times 5 \times 50}{2400}$$

$$= \frac{250 + 500 + 1000 + 162.5}{2400} = \frac{1912.5}{2400} \text{ m}^3$$

$$= 0.797 \text{ m}^3 \text{ or } 797 \text{ litres. say } 800 \text{ lit.}$$

Note. Terms used in formula convey their meaning as discussed on page 184.

QUESTIONS

1. Discuss the use of flow table for determining the workability of concrete.
2. For what mixes the following tests are not suitable?
   (*a*) Slump test (*b*) Vee-Bee test
   (*c*) Flow table test (*d*) Compacting factor test
3. What is meant by consistency of a mix?
4. What is meant by segregation and bleeding of concrete? Explain fully.
5. What is the relation between cohesiveness of mix and (*a*) Segregation, (*b*) Bleeding.
6. What is the significance of bleeding in construction which proceeds in several lifts?
7. Discuss the factors affecting the followings
   (*a*) Cohesion of concrete (*b*) Bleeding of concrete
   (*c*) Segregation of concrete (*d*) Consistency of concrete
8. What is the relation between bleeding and plastic settlement?
9. Why is slump not a direct measure of workability?
10. What type of slump in a slump test is un satisfactory?
11. Why the absence of segregation from concrete is important?
12. What are the requirements of concrete to be used with congested reinforcement.
13. What factors govern the plasticity of concrete? Discuss.
14. Define workability of concrete. How it is determined by slump cone apparatus?
15. Describe the compacting factor method of determining the workability of concrete.
16. Describe the Vee-Bee method of determining the workability of concrete.
17. What is bleeding or water gain? Discuss its undesirable effects.
18. Discuss the effects of different factors on the value of workability of concrete.
19. Discuss the limitations of compacting factor method for determining the workability of concrete.
20. Compare the slump and compacting factor method for determining the workability of concrete.
21. Find the yield per batch of concrete with the following data:
    1. Proportion of mix by weight = 1:1.5:3
    2. Water/cement ratio = 0.6
    3. Unit weight of concrete = 2350 kg/m^3
    4. Air content = 1.0%

[**Ans.** Cement 400 kg, F.A. 600 kg, C.A. 1200 kg, Water 240 kg.]

OBJECTIVE TYPE QUESTIONS

1. The workability of fresh concrete can be most appropriately defined by
   (*a*) Its slump and compaction factor values
   (*b*) Its consistency and plasticity
   (*c*) The composite property satisfying the requirements of stability, mixability, transportability, placeability, compactability and finishability
   (*d*) Homogeneity and case with which it can be mixed, placed, compacted and finished
2. By which of the following tests the workability of fresh concrete can be assessed
   (*a*) Compacting factor test (*b*) Slump test
   (*c*) Flow test (*d*) Vee Bee consistency test
   (*e*) All the above
3. For assessing the workability of fresh concrete the conventional empirical tests suffer from the draw backs as
   (*a*) They measure only a particular aspect of workability *i.e.* they are single point tests
   (*b*) None of these tests is capable of dealing the whole range of workability
   (*c*) They are not amenable to physical idelised modelling
   (*d*) They are operator sensitive
   (*e*) All the above
4. Which of the following statements are true?
   (*a*) The fresh concrete should be mixable, *i.e.* it should be homogeneous

(*b*) The fresh concrete should be stable *i.e.* neither it should segregate nor bleed during transportation and placing
(*c*) The fresh concrete should be flowable *i.e.* it should be cohesive and sufficiently mobile
(*d*) The fresh concrete should be compactable and finishable
(*e*) All of the above

5. Which of the following statements is false?
(*a*) The mixability of a concrete mix governs the power requirement in the mixing plant
(*b*) The mixability of a concrete mix governs the time of mixing
(*c*) The mixability of a concrete mix governs the homogeneity of fresh concrete
(*d*) The mixability of a concrete mix governs the reproducibility of concrete batches
(*d*) None of above

6. Which of the following statements is false?
(*a*) A high water content may result in segregation and bleeding in concrete
(*b*) Water content in concrete is limited to the given water/cement ratio value
(*c*) The change in workability due to a relative change in the water content in concrete is dependent on the mix ratio
(*d*) An increase in water content may result increase in workability
(*e*) The use of rounded or large sized aggregate gives higher workability
(*f*) The use of finer sand increases the workability for the same water content
(*g*) For workability the grading of fine aggregate is more critical than the grading of coarse aggregate
(*h*) Fineness of cement has an influence on the bleeding
(*i*) For the production of high strength concrete a coarser grading is preferred

7. Which of the following statements is false?
(*a*) The segregation of coarse particles in a lean dry mix may be checked by adding small quantity of water to the mix
(*b*) The tendency of segregation may be minimized by reducing the height of dropping of concrete
(*c*) The separation of cement paste from the concrete mix is not known as segregation
(*d*) The aim is to have minimum possible workability consistent with satisfactory placement and compaction of concrete
(*e*) All of the above

8. The slump test is most widely used field test due to
(*a*) The simplicity of test procedure and apparatus
(*b*) It measures wetness or consistency of the mix
(*c*) It measures uniformity of many different batches of similar concrete
(*d*) It indicates the behavior of fresh concrete under the influence of gravitational forces

9. The workability of concrete by slump test is expressed as
(*a*) mm (*b*) mm^2/h
(*c*) mm^3/h (*d*) metres
(*e*) hours (*f*) mm/h

10. A concrete having a slump of 75 mm is known as
(*a*) Dry (*b*) Semi plastic
(*c*) Plastic (*d*) flowing
(*e*) All of the above

11. The concrete to be transported by pumping, its slump should be
(*a*) Between 25-50 mm (*b*) more than 100 mm
(*c*) Between 50-75 mm (*d*) more then 30 mm
(*e*) more than 15 mm

12. A concrete having a slump of 75-80 mm is called of workability
(*a*) Very high (*b*) High
(*c*) Medium (*d*) Low
(*e*) Very low

13. The slump test of concrete is carried out to measure its

(*a*) Consistency (*b*) Mobility
(*c*) Homogeneity (*d*) compaction under gravitational force
(*e*) All of the above

14. For the construction of a R.C.C. slab the slump of concrete should be
(*a*) 25-100 mm (*b*) 50-125 mm
(*c*) 25-50 mm (*d*) 100-150 mm
(*e*) 0-25 mm

15. The concrete to be transported by belt conveyers should have a slump of
(*a*) 25-50 mm (*b*) 50-75 mm
(*c*) 75-100 mm (*d*) 100-125 mm

16. The finishing of concrete surface is found difficult if the slump exceeds
(*a*) 25 mm (*b*) 40 mm
(*c*) 50 mm (*d*) 75 mm
(*e*) 100 mm

17. For mass concrete work, the slump of concrete should be
(*a*) 50-75 mm (*b*) 75-100 mm
(*c*) 25-50 mm (*d*) 0-25 mm

18. The compacting factor test is considered superior to slump test due to
(*a*) It measures compactability of concrete
(*b*) It exhibits behaviour of fresh concrete under the action of external forces
(*c*) It is more accurate than slump test for medium and low workability concrete mixes
(*d*) It is more sensitive and gives more consistent results

19. Which of the following statements is true
(*a*) Compacting factor test for fresh concrete is adopted when the nominal size of coarse aggregate does not exceed 20 mm
(*b*) Compacting factor test is adopted to measure the relative effort required to change a mass of concrete from one definite shape to another
(*c*) Compaction factor test is adopted as it gives an indication of mobility of fresh concrete
(*d*) Compaction factor test is adopted as it measures the compaction obtained by a standard amount of work applied to a standard quantity of concrete

20. If the compacting factor of a concrete is 0.88, it indicates
(*a*) High workability (*b*) Medium workability
(*c*) Low workability (*d*) Very low workability

21. Concrete is considered unsuitable for compaction by vibration if
(*a*) The compacting factor is more than 0.9 (*b*) The workability is low
(*c*) The concrete is very stiff (*d*) Slump is between 40-50 mm

22. Which of the following statements is true?
(*a*) The workability of concrete is high if it has a compacting factor 0.65 and slump 125-150 mm
(*b*) The workability of concrete is medium if it has a compacting factor 0.78 and slump 25-75 mm
(*c*) The workability of concrete is low if it has a compacting factor 0.84 and slump 10-50 mm
(*d*) The workability of concrete is very low having a compacting factor 0.9 having no slump
(*e*) The concrete is suitable for normal R.C.C. work having compacting factor 0.92 and slump 50-100 mm

23. A concrete is said workable if
(*a*) It is almost fluid (*b*) It can be easily mixed, placed and compacted
(*c*) It is of uniform colour (*d*) It has a tendency of segration and bleeding

24. Which of the following statements is false?
(*a*) Vee Bee test is suitable for concrete mixes of low workabilities
(*b*) It is a remoulding test
(*c*) It is unsuitable for concrete having slump of 75 mm or more
(*d*) It is suitable as the concrete receives a similar treatment in the test as that of in actual practice
(*e*) Any of the above

25. Which of the following statements is true

(*a*) The bleeding of concrete is said to occur when the coarser particles get separated
(*b*) The bleeding of concrete is said to occur when the finer particles settle down at the bottom
(*c*) The bleeding of concrete is said to occur when the cement paste rises to the surface of the concrete
(*d*) The bleeding of concrete is said to occur when finer particles collect in isolated pockets
(*e*) None of the above

26. Which of the statement is false?
(*a*) Bleeding of concrete causes laitance on the surface of concrete
(*b*) Bleeding of concrete increases its permeability
(*c*) Bleeding of concrete reduces its durability
(*d*) Bleeding of concrete can be checked by adding small quantity of water in the concrete

27. During transportation the separation of coarse aggregate from cement paste is called
(*a*) Flow of concrete (*b*) Cohesion of concrete
(*c*) Segregation of concrete (*d*) Bleeding of concrete
(*e*) Creeping of concrete

28. The workability of concrete is independent of
(*a*) Water content (*b*) Environment conditions
(*c*) Mix proportion (*d*) Size, shape and texture of aggregate

29. Which of the statements is false?
(*a*) The workability of concrete can be improved by adding copper sulphate
(*b*) The workability of concrete can be improved by adding fly ash
(*c*) The workability of concrete can be improved by adding calcium chloride
(*d*) The workability of concrete can be improved by adding plasticizer or super plasticizers

30. The segregation of concrete causes
(*a*) Honey combing of concrete (*b*) Porous layers in concrete
(*c*) Surface scaling of concrete (*d*) Sand streaks in concrete
(*e*) All of the above

31. The retarder plasticizer reduces the workability loss due to
(*a*) Hydrophobic action (*b*) The process of flocculation
(*c*) Air entrainment (*d*) slowing down the process of setting

Answers

1. (*c*)	8. (*a*)	15. (*b*)	22. (*c*)	29. (*a*)
2. (*e*)	9. (*a*)	16. (*e*)	23. (*b*)	30. (*e*)
3. (*e*)	10. (*c*)	17. (*c*)	24. (*e*)	31. (*d*)
4. (*e*)	11. (*c*)	18. (*d*)	25. (*e*)	
5. (*e*)	12. (*c*)	19. (*d*)	26. (*d*)	
6. (*c*, *f*.)	13. (*b*)	20. (*b*)	27. (*c*)	
7. (*c*)	14. (*b*)	21. (*a*)	28. (*c*)	

8

Strength of Hardened Concrete

8.1. INTRODUCTION

The compressive strength of hardened concrete is one of the most important and useful properties of concrete. In most of the structural uses, the concrete is used mainly to resist the compressive stresses. In situations where the shear or tension strength is of importance, the compressive strength is usually used as a measure of these properties. Thus the concrete making properties of ingredients of the mix are usually measured in terms of the compressive strength. It is also used as a qualitative measure of other properties of hardened concrete.

No exact qualitative relation ship between the compressive strength and other properties like tensile strength, flexural strength, modulus of elasticity, wear resistance, permeability and fire resistance exists. However some statistical or empirical relations have been established between them to be used in the field work. These relations give only approximate value of these properties. It should be noted that the indicated strength of concrete increases as the size of specimen decreases, where as modulus of elasticity decreases. Thus modulus of elasticity does not follow the compressive strength. In situations where concrete is subjected to freezing and thawing, the compressive strength does not indicate the other useful properties of the concrete. As stated in chapter 6, that concrete containing about 6% air entrainment is relatively weaker in compressive strength, but on the other hand it has been found to be more durable than dense and strong concrete.

The strength of concrete is the measure of its resistance to rupture. As stated above strength of concrete may be measured as strength in tension, strength in compression, in flexural or in shear. All these strengths, indicate a particular method of testing. When concrete fails under compressive load, the failure is essentially a mixture of crushing and shear failure. The mechanics of failure resisting concrete, generates cohesion and internal friction both. The development of cohesion and internal friction in concrete simultaneously is a function of single parameter water/cement ratio.

For a given cement and aggregate the strength developed by workable, properly placed mix of ingredients is affected by the following factors:

(*a*) Water/cement ratio

(*b*) Cement/aggregate ratio

(*c*) Maximum size of aggregate

(*d*) Surface texture, shape, grading, strength etc. of aggregate particles.

Out of the above factors, water/cement ratio is the prime factor affecting the strength of concrete. The other factors influence the water/cement ratio, thus influencing the strength indirectly.

8.2. WATER/CEMENT RATIO

Water/cement ratio can be expressed in terms of weight and volume too. In terms of weight, the quantity of water to be used per unit weight of cement (1 kg) is known as water/cement ratio. If 500 grams of water is used per kg of cement then the water/cement ratio will be 0.5. Normally water/cement ratio more than 1.0 is not used. In terms of volume water used in liters per bag of cement (50 kg) is taken as water/cement ratio by volume. Suppose 25 liters of water is used per bag of cement, then again water/cement ratio will be 0.5. Actually water/cement. ratio is an index of the strength of concrete. The strength of concrete mainly depends upon the strength of the cement paste, and the cement paste strength depends upon the dilution of cement pate. In other words the strength of cement paste increases with cement content and decreases with water and air content.

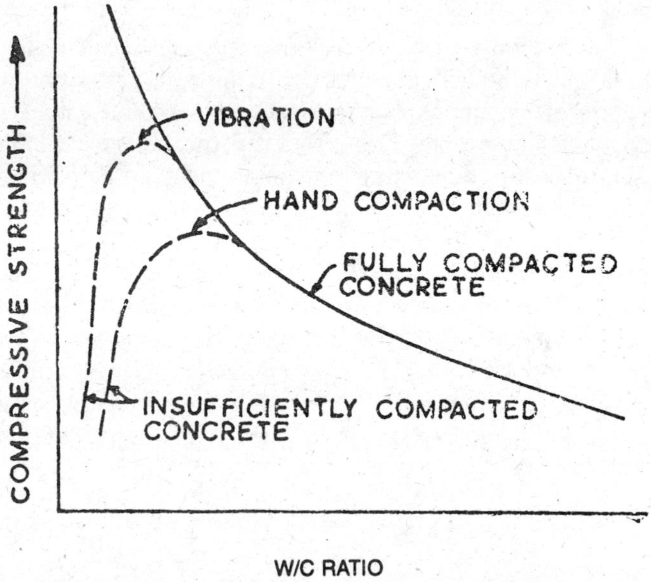

Fig. 8.1. Relation between w/c ratio and compressive strength of concrete

For a fully compacted concrete, its strength is taken to be inversely proportional to the water/cement ratio. A typical curve of strength versus water/cement ratio is shown in Fig. 8.1.

8.3. ABRAM'S WATER/CEMENT LAW

More importance to concrete properties was attached after the first world war and more stress was given for the development of cheap construction materials. Keeping this aim in view Duff Abram carried out extensive experiments and on the basis of his experimental results he proposed a relation between the compressive strength of concrete and water/cement ratio in 1919, which is known as water/cement ratio law, which is reproduced below as

$$f_c = \frac{K_1}{(K_2)^x} \quad \ldots(8.1)$$

where,

f_c = concrete cylinder (15 × 30 cm) strength at 28 days after proper curing

K_1 & K_2 = constants

x = water/cement ratio.

He suggested empirically the values for K_1 as 984 and for K_2 as 7 in M.K.S. units

thus
$$f_c = \frac{984}{(7)^x} \quad \ldots(8.2)$$

ABRAM'S water/cement ratio law states that the strength of concrete is only dependent on water/cement ratio provided the mix is workable.

The numerical values for K_1 and K_2 may vary with the type of cement and aggregate, method of curing, age of concrete at which strength is desired, and mode of testing etc. Thus these values are variable. Due to the advancement in cement technology, the better quality cement is available now. Hence the compressive strength given by equation 8.2 can be assumed as 7 days strength and 28 days strength can be assumed as

$$f_c = \frac{984}{(4)^x} \quad \ldots(8.3)$$

This relation was found true for a fully compacted concrete. Later it has been found that water/cement ratio law holds equally good for tensile strength, resistance of concrete to wear, bond between concrete and steel, resistance to weather influence and water tightness etc. *i.e.* the decrease in water/cement ratio improves the above properties. This is particularly more important in respect of water tightness. To obtain plastic mixtures, more water is required than can be permanently combined with cement even on longer curing. Some water remains uncombined and leaves voids after it evaporates. Thus the quantity of water and the extent of curing both affect the water tightness of concrete. After ABRAM many researchers put forth their theories, but non of them could stand the test of time and disappeared slowly. However ABRAM'S water/cement ratio law stood the test of time and is held valid even today. Though some modifications have been suggested but the truth of statement remains unchanged.

Although Abram established his law independently, but it is a special case of a general rule formulated by Ferret in 1896. He expressed the compressive strength of concrete as,

$$f_c = K\left[\frac{c}{c + w + a}\right]$$

where f_c is strength of concrete, c, w and a are absolute volumes of cement, water, and air respectively and K is a constant.

Further as stated in Chapter 2, the water/cement ratio determines the porosity of the hardened cement paste at any stage of hydration. Thus the water/cement ratio and the degree of compaction both affect the volume of voids in concrete and that is why volume of air in concrete has been included in Ferret's eqaution.

The relation between strength of concrete and total volume of voids is not a unique property of concrete, but in other brittle material also in which water leaves pores behind in the same way. For example the strength of plaster also is a direct function of its voids. If the strength of different materials is expressed as a fraction of the strength at a zero porosity, many materials such as steel, iron, alumina etc. Confirm the same relation between the relative strength and porosity Fig. 8.2.

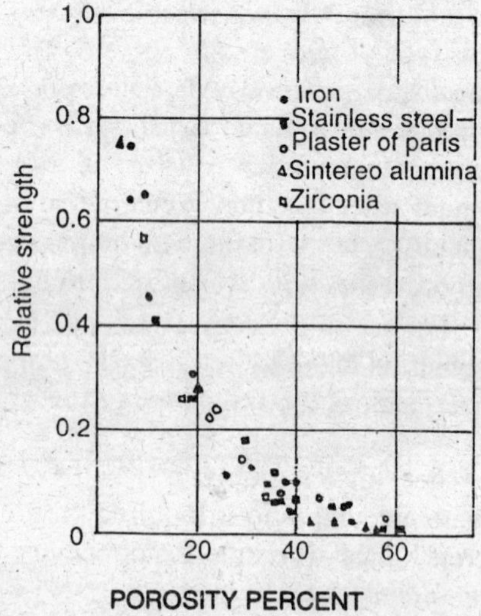

Fig. 8.2. Influence of porosity on relative strength of materials

8.4. TYPE OF POROSITY

Porosity may be divided into the following groups:

1. Gel porosity
2. Capillary porosity
3. Total porosity
4. Concrete porosity.

1. **Gel porosity.** It is the ratio of the volume of gel pores to the total volume of hydrated cement paste.
2. **Capillary porosity.** It is the ratio of the volume of the capillary pores to the total volume of hydrated cement paste. Capillary pores are much larger than gel pores.
3. **Total porosity of cement paste.** It is the ratio of the sum of volumes of gel pores and capillary pores to the total volume of cement paste.
4. **Concrete porosity.** It is independent of whether the capillary pores are full of water or empty and has some entrapped air in it.

The influence of volume of pores on strength can be expressed as $f_c = f_{co}(1-p)^n$ where f_c is strength of concrete at porosity p, while f_{co} denotes concrete strength at zero porosity and 'n' is a coefficient which need not be a constant. From test-results it has been observed that there is a direct relation between strength and porosity of concrete, but the exact form of this relation has not yet been established. Fig. 8.3 shows a straight line relation between the strength and log of porosity.

Fig. 8.1 shows that the range of validity of the water/cement ratio law is limited. At the lower water/cement ratio, when full compaction is no longer possible, the curve ceases to be followed. The actual position of the point of departure depends on the means of compaction available. It is also evident that mixes with very low water/cement ratios and with extremely high cement content exhibit retrogression of strength, particularly when large size aggregate is used. Thus in this type of mix, at later ages a lower water/cement ratio would not produce higher strength. This may be due to the stresses induced by shrinkage, whose restraint by aggregate particles causes loss of bond between the aggregate and cement paste. Theoretically the lesser the water/cement ratio, higher should be the strength, but as stated above it is not true, below a certain water/cement ratio, full compaction of concrete is not possible. It has been shown by broken lines in Fig. 8.1. In practice water/cement ratio is the largest single factor which influence the strength of fully compacted concrete.

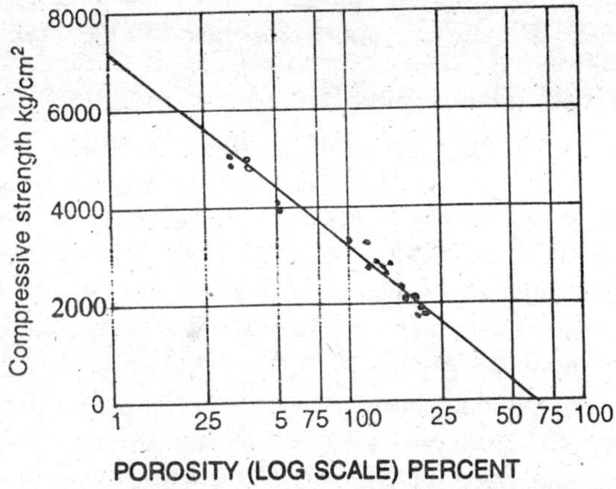

Fig. 8.3. Relation between compressive strength and logarithm of porosity of cement paste

From Fig. 8.1 it can also be seen that lower water/cement ratio can be used when the concrete is vibrated to get higher strength, where comparatively higher water/cement ratio is required than hand competed concrete. Thus when the water/cement ratio is lower than the practical limit, the strength of concrete falls rapidly due to introduction of air voids.

Fig. 8.4 shows a relation between compressive strength and cement/water ratio which gives a straight-line in the range of cement/water ratio between about 1.2 and 2.5. Whose equation may be as

$$S = A + B\,\frac{C}{W}$$

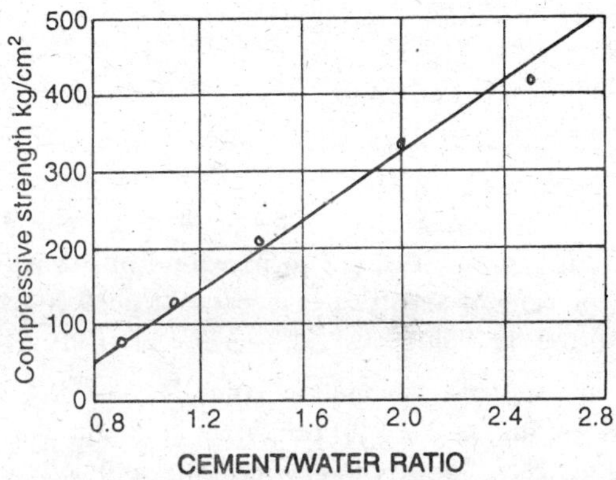

Fig. 8.4. Relation between c/w ratio and strength of concrete

where,

S = compressive strength in kg/cm^2

A = constant value = – 24

B = constant value = 267

C/W = cement/water ratio by weight

However this relation is true for a particular given cement only and in any practical case the actual relation between the strength and cement/water ratio should be determined. However according to Gilkey, the strength developed by a workable and properly placed concrete is influenced by the following factors.

1. Ratio of cement to mixing water
2. Ratio of cement to aggregate
3. Grading, surface texture, shape, strength and stiffness of aggregate particles
4. Maximum size of aggregate.

However factors (2) to (4) are of lesser importance than factor (1) for aggregates upto 38 mm in size. The plot of strength of concrete and water/cement ratio is approximately a hyperbola. This relation is true for concrete made with any given type of aggregate and at any age, while the relation between strength and cement/water ratio is approximately linear (straight line) in the range of cement/water ratios between about 1.2 and 2.5, which is more convenient to use than water/cement ratio curve.

8.5. GEL/SPACE RATIO

According to T.C. Powers the influence of water/cement ratio on strength does not truly constitute a law as the water/cement rule does not include many necessary conditions for its validity. In particular, strength at any water/cement ratio depends on the degree of hydration of cement, its chemical and physical properties, temperature at which hydration takes place, air content of concrete, change in effective water/cement ratio and formation of capillaries or fissures formed due to bleeding etc. Thus it will be more correct to correlate strength to the concentration of the solid products of hydration of cement in the space available for these products.

Powers and Brownyard have established the relation between the strength development and the gel/space ratio. This ratio is defined as the ratio of the volume of hydrated cement paste to the sum of the volumes of hydrated cement and the capillary pores.

In Chapter 2, it has been shown that hydrated cement occupies about 2.15 times its original volume *i.e.* more than twice its original volume. In the following calculations the increase of volume is assumed as 2.06. Though all the hydrated material is not gel, yet as a approximation it is considered as such.

Power's experiments showed that a relationship of the type $f_c = Ax^b$ could be established, where f_c is concrete strength and x is gel/space ratio where A and b are constants which depend on the type of cement. The constant A represents the intrinsic or maximum strength of gel in Newton/mm^2 when x = 1, for the type of cement and type of specimen used. From his study he suggested the value of A as 240. b = 3. Thus strength f_c = 240 x^3. The strength calculated from the power's equation holds good for an Idial case for the type of cement and specimen used by him. The relationship between strength and gel/space ratio is shown in Fig. 8.5.

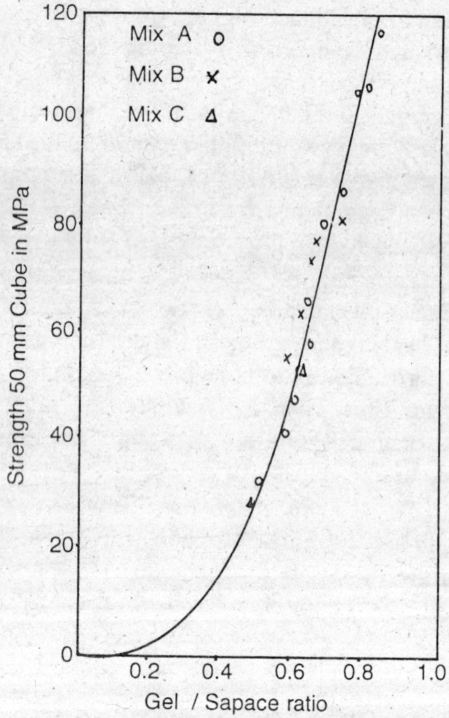

Fig. 8.5. Relation between compressive strength of mortar and gel/space ratio

It may be pointed out here that the relationship between the strength and water/cement ratio holds good primarily for 28 days strength for fully compacted concrete, where as the relation ship between the strength of concrete and gel/space ratio is independent of age. Gel/space ratio can be calculated at any age for any degree or fraction of hydration of cement as follows:

Case I. *Calculations for gel/space ratio for complete hydration*

Let

C = weight of cement in grams

V_c = specific volume of cement = 0.319 ml/gram

w_0 = volume of water mixed in ml (c.c.)

Assuming that on hydration 1 ml cement will produce 2.06 ml of gel.

Then volume of gel $= C \times 0.319 \times 2.06$

$= 0.657\ C$

$$\text{Total space available} = \text{vol. of gel} + \text{vol. of water}$$
$$= 0.319\,C + w_0$$

$$\therefore \text{ Gel/space ratio} \quad x = \frac{\text{volume of gel}}{\text{vol. of space}} = \frac{0.657\,C}{0.319\,C + w_0} \qquad \ldots(1)$$

CASE II. *Calculation of gel/space ratio for partial hydration*

Let

α = fraction of hydrated cement

$$\text{Volume of gel} = \alpha \times C \times 0.319 \times 2.06 = 0.657\;\alpha\,C$$

$$\text{Total space available} = C \cdot V_c \cdot \alpha + w_0 = C \times 0.319 \cdot \alpha + w_0$$

$$\therefore \text{ Gal/space ratio} \quad x = \frac{0.319 \times 2.06 \times C \times \alpha}{0.319\,C \cdot \alpha + w_0}$$

Example 8.1. *Calculate the gel/space ratio and theoretical strength of a concrete sample made with 600 gram of cement with 0.5 water/cement ratio on full hydration and at 70% hydration.*

Solution. (*i*) *for full hydration*

(*a*) Weight of cement = 600 gram

For 0.5 water/cement ratio, weight of water = 300 gram

$\therefore$ Vol. of mixing water w_0 = 300 m.l.

$$\therefore \text{ Gel/space ratio} = \frac{0.657\,C}{0.319\,C + w_0}$$

$$= \frac{0.657 \times 600}{0.319 \times 600 + 300}$$

$$= \frac{394.2}{191.4 + 300} = \frac{394.2}{491.4} = 0.8$$

$\therefore$ Theoretical strength of concrete = $240\,(0.8)^3$ = 123 MPa

(*ii*) Gel space ratio for 70% hydration

$$x = \frac{0.657\;C \times \alpha}{0.319\,C \times \alpha + w_0} = \frac{0.657 \times 600 \times 0.7}{0.319 \times 600 \times 0.7 + 300}$$

$$= \frac{275.94}{133.98 + 300} = \frac{275.94}{433.98} = 0.636$$

say 0.64

$\therefore$ Theoretical strength = $240\,(0.64)^3$

$= 240 \times 0.2624 = 62.98$ say 63.0 MPa. **Ans.**

Earlier IS Code 456-1978 considered age factor and allowed the design stress in lower columns in multi-story buildings. Earlier only type of cement governed by IS 269-1976 was used in which after 28 days appreciable increase in strength was considered. After gradation of ordinary portland cement, the present day cements particularly 53 grade cement is grounds very fine. Thus the increase in strength after 28 days is nominal. In well cured concrete, the development of strength will take place with in 28 days. Thus the allowance of age factor generally is not necessary. Thus IS 456-2000 has revised this clause The revised clause states that normally the gain in strength beyond 28 days depends upon grade, type of cement, curing and environmental conditions. Thus the design should be based on 28 days characteristic strength of concrete, unless there is an evidence to justify a higher strength for a particular structure due to age. However British Code has suggested the age factor for permissible compressive stress in concrete as shown in Table 8.1.

Table 8.1. Age factor for permissible compressive stress in concrete as per British Code

S. No.	*Minimum age of member when ful design load is applied in months*	*Age factor for lower strength concrete*	*Additional strength for high strength concrete in MPa.*
1.	1	1.0	0
2.	2	1.1	4.2
3.	3	1.16	5.5
4.	6	1.20	7.7
5.	12	1.24	10.2

The grade of concrete as per IS 456-2000 are shown in Table 8.2 below.

Table 8.2. Grade of concrete as per IS 456-2000

Groups	*Grade designation*	*Specified characteristic comp. strength of 150 mm cube at 28 days in N/mm²*	*Remark*
Ordinary Concrete	M 10 M 15 M 20	10 (100 kg/cm²) 15 (150 kg/cm²) 20 (200 kg/cm²)	1 N/mm² = 10 kg/cm² Permissible stress in concrete is given in chapter 14, page 285-286.
Standard Concrete	M 25 M 30 M 35 M 40 M 45 M 50 M 55	25 30 35 40 45 50 55	
High Strength Concrete	M 60 M 65 M 70 M 75 M 80	60 65 70 75 80	

Many a times the knowledge of strength of concrete becomes necessary to forecast the strength of the structure and it may prove futile to wait for 28 days. In this direction many researchers have attempted to forecast or corelated 28 days strength from 1, 3 or 7 days strength. The relationship between the strength at lower age and 28 days strength depends upon the following factors:

1. Compound composition of cement 2. Fineness of cement
3. Temperature of curing etc.

Further, mixes with low water/cement ratio gain strength more rapidly than that of higher water/ cement ratio concrete. This may happen presumably due to the fact that in low water/cement ratio concrete, the voids in between cement particles are less or they are held closer than that of higher water/ cement ratio concrete, forming thicker gel, which results in more strength.

As stated earlier, capillary pores are much larger than gel pores. In partially hydrated cement, the paste contains an interconnected system of capillary pores, resulting in increased permeability, lower strength and more prone to freezing and thawing and chemical attack. These problems are avoided if the hydration of cement is high as the capillary pore system would be segmented by higher hydration. The minimum period of curing required for the segmentation of capillary pores is shown in Table 2.6.

Researchers in Germany have suggested following relations between 7 and 28 days compressive strength of concrete.

1. $\sigma_{28} = 1.4\,\sigma_7 + 150$ and $\sigma_{28} = 1.7\,\sigma_7 + 850$

where σ is expressed in lbs/cm² (1 lbs/cm² = 0.0727 kg/cm²)

2. This relation is of the type $f_{28} = K_2 (f_1)^{K_1}$ where f_{28} and f_7 are the concrete strength at 28 and 7 days respectively and K_1 and K_2 are coefficients which are different for different cements and curing conditions. The value of K_1 varies from 0.3 to 0.8 and that of K_2 from 3 to 6.

Prof. King suggested a quick method of estimating 28 days strength after its cast. This method gives results which have a good correlation with field results. This method is known as *Accelerated curing test method.*

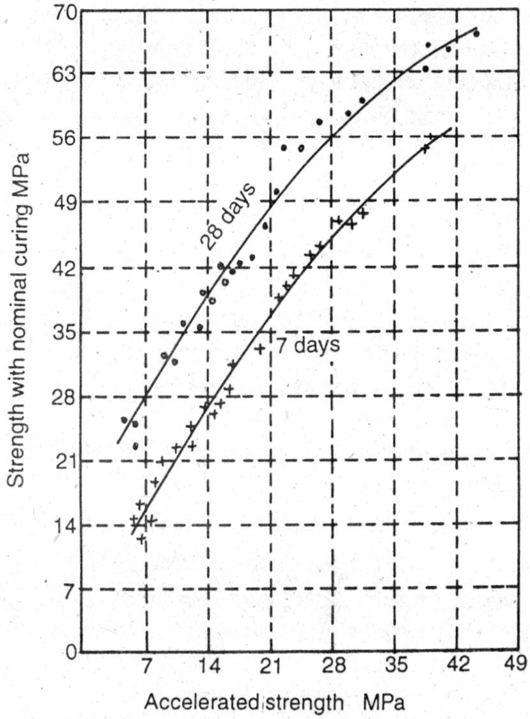

Fig. 8.6. Relation between accelerated strength and 7 and 28 days strength

8.6. ACCELERATED CURING TEST

In this test the standard cubes of 15 cm × 15 cm × 15cm are cast and covered at top with plates. To prevent drying of concrete, the joints are sealed with special grease. With in 30 minutes of adding water, the effectively sealed cubes are placed in an air tight oven. The oven now is switched on. The temperature of the oven is brought to 93°C in about 60 minutes. The temperature of the oven is maintained at 93°C for 5 hours. After 5 hours curing at 93°C temperature, the cubes are removed from oven, mould removed, cooled to room temperature and tested. The test should be completed with in 30 minutes.

The strength of concrete is determined by this method with in 7 hours of casting. This accelerated strength shows good relationship with normally cured concrete at 7 days and 28 days. This relationship is shown in Fig. 8.6.

8.6.1. Factors affecting the results

One of the main factors that affects the rate of gain of strength is the fineness of cement. It has been observed that particles of cements over 40 micron in size contribute to the compressive strength of concrete only over long periods, while particles lower than 25 to 30 micron contribute to 28 days strength. The particles smaller than 20 to 25 micron contribute to 7 days strength. The particles smaller than 5 to 7 micron contribute to 1 to 2 days strength. The relative gain of strength with time of concrete prepared with different water/cement ratio using ordinary portland cement is shown in Fig. 8.7.

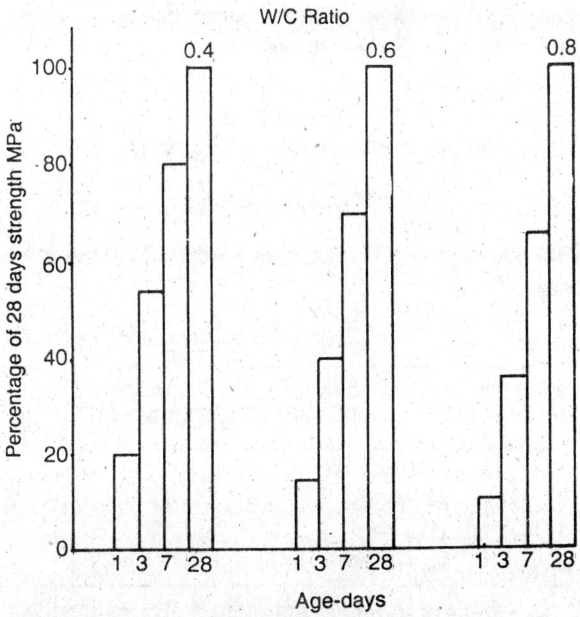

Fig. 8.7. Relative gain of strength at different age with different w/c ratios

8.7. MATURITY CONCEPT OF CONCRETE

As pointed out earlier also that temperature during the early period of hydration also influences the rate of gain of strength of concrete. As the strength development of concrete depends on time and temperature both, it can be said that the strength of concrete is a function of summation of product of time and temperature. This summation is called the *maturity* of concrete. Thus

Maturity of concrete = Σ (time × temperature)

The temperature is reckoned from an origin lying between – 12 and – 10°C. Experimentally it has been observed that hydration of concrete continues to take place upto about – 11°C, Thus – 11°C is taken as the datum time for computing maturity.

Maturity is measured in degree centigrade hours (°C hours) or degree centigrade day (°C day). If the graph between the strength of concrete and logathirum of maturity is drawn, it will be a straight line as shown in Fig. 8.8.

A sample of concrete cured at 18°C for 28 days is assumed as fully matured concrete. Its maturity would be

$$= 28 \times 24\,[18 - (-11)]$$

$$= 28 \times 24 \times 29 = 19480°\text{C h}$$

However in standard calculations of maturity of fully cured concrete is taken as 19800°C h. This discrepancy is due to the fact that the exact value of datum is not known.

If the period is broken into smaller intervals and the corresponding temperature is recorded for each small interval of time, the summation of the product of time and temperature will give an accurate result.

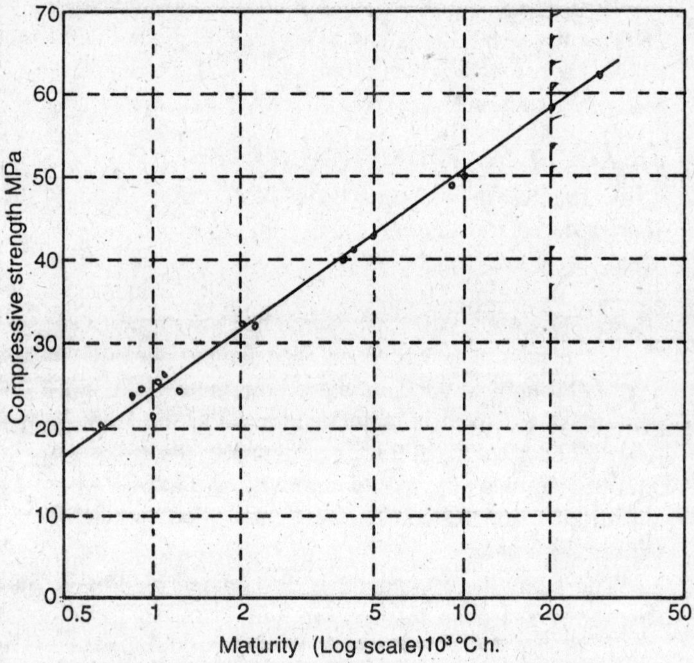

Fig. 8.8. Relation between maturity of concrete and its strength

Maturity concept is useful for estimating the strength of concrete at any other maturity as a percentage of strength of concrete of known maturity. For the calculation of concrete at any maturity as a percentage of fully matured concrete *plowman* has suggested the following relation.

Strength at any maturity as a % of strength at a maturity of.

$$19800°\text{Ch} = A + B \log_{10} \frac{\text{maturity}}{1000}$$

The values of coefficient A & B depend on the strength of concrete. These values are shown in Table 8.3 below

Table 8.3. Plowman's coefficients for maturity equation

S. No.	*Strength at 28 days at 18°C (Meturity of 19800°C h, MPa*	*Coefficients*	
		A	*B*
1.	Less then 17.5	10	68
2.	17.5 to 35	21	61
3.	35 to 52.5	32	54
4.	52.5 to 70.0	42	46.5

If the values of A and B are plotted against the cube strength at the maturity of 19800°C h, a straight line relationship will be obtained as shown in Fig. 8.8 indicating that they are directly proportional to the strength. Plowman has divided the length into four zones as shown in the above table 8.3 and has assigned the values of A and B for each zone. From the Fig. 8.8 it will be noted that the maturity equation holds good for initial temperature of concrete less than 38°C.

Example 8.2. *The strength of a sample of fully matured concrete is found to be 44.0 MPa. Find the strength of identical concrete at 7 days when cured at an overage temperature during day time at 23°C and at night at a temperature of 9°C.*

Solution.

The maturity equation = Σ (time × temperature)

∴ Maturity strength of concrete at 7 days

$$= \Sigma \text{ time} \times \text{temperature}$$
$$= 7 \times 12\ [23 - (-11) + 7 \times 12\,(9 - (-11)]$$
$$= 7 \times 12 \times 34 + 7 \times 12 \times 20$$
$$= 7 \times 12 \times 54 = 4536°\text{Ch}$$

The range of this concrete falls in III zone for which the values of A and B are 32 and 54, respectively.

∴ The percentage strength at maturity of 4536°C h $= A + B \log_{10} \dfrac{4536}{1000}$

$$= 32 + 54 \log_{10} 4.536 = 32 + 54 \times 0.6567$$
$$= 32 + 35.462$$
$$= 32 + 35.62 = 67.462$$

∴ The strength at 7 days $= \dfrac{44 \times 67.462}{100} = 29.68$

$$\approx 29.7 \text{ MPa}$$ **Ans.**

Example 8.3. *Experiments carried out in the laboratory on a particular mix showed a strength of 34.0 MPa for a fully matured concrete. If an identical concrete is placed at a location whose mean temperature is 7°C. Can the form work be removed at the age of 20 days if the concrete is likely to be subjected to a stripping stress of 29.0 MPa.*

Solution. The strength of fully matured concrete = 34.0 MPa (Given)

The maturity of identical concrete at 20 days when cured at average temperature of 7°C

$$= 20 \times 24 \times [7 - (-11)]$$
$$= 20 \times 24 \times 18 = 8640°\text{Ch}$$

As the maturity strength is 34 MPa, this concrete falls is zone II for which the value for A = 21 and B = 61

∴ Percentage of strength $= A + B \log_{10} \dfrac{\text{Moturity}}{1000}$

$$= 21 + 61 \log_{10} \frac{8640}{1000}$$
$$= 21 + 61 \log_{10} 8.64$$
$$= 21 + 61\,(0.9365)$$
$$= 21 + 57.13 = 78.13$$

The strength of concrete at 20 days $= 34 \times \dfrac{78.13}{100} = 34 \times 0.7813$

$$= 26.56 \text{ MPa.}$$

As the stress of concrete is less than the stress to which it is likely to be subjected while removing the form work, the concrete may fail. Hence form work can not be removed at 20 days time.

If the strength at a given maturity is known then the number of days required to reach the same strength at any other temperature can be calculated as

$$\frac{M}{24\ [t - (-11)]}$$

where M is the maturity for the given strength, t the alternate temperature in °C.

In the above example for reaching the same strength.

$$= \frac{M}{24\ [t - (-11)]} = \frac{19800}{24\ [7 - (-11)]}$$

$$= \frac{19800}{24 \times 18} = \frac{1100}{24} = 45.83 \approx 46 \text{ days } \textbf{Ans.}$$

8.8. FACTORS AFFECTING THE STRENGTH OF CONCRETE

Generally following factors affect the strength of concrete.

1. Age of concrete
2. Coarse aggregate used
3. Richness of the mix
4. Curing of concrete
5. Temperature of concrete.

1. Age of concrete. The relation between the water/cement ratio and strength of concrete applies to one type of cement at one age only. As already discussed in Chapters 3, different types of cements require different length of time to produce the same quantity of gel. It is assumed that 90% hydration is complete with in 28 days. Actually there are many variables which influence the intrinsic rate of hardening of commercial cements. Mixes with low water/cement ratio gain strength more rapidly than with higher water/cement ratio. It is because in the first case the cement grains are closer to one another and a continuous system of gel is formed more rapidly. For this reason a general rule connecting 7 day strength to 28 days strength is not easy. However when no specific data on the materials used is available, the 7 days strength may be assumed as 60-67% of the 28 days strength as per Indian code of practice. In general it is taken 2/3 at 7 days and 75 to 80% at 14 days of 28 days strength. Fig. 8.9 shows the develop- ment of strength of moist cured concrete with age. From the Fig. 8.9 it will be seen that hydration is far more rapid at early ages than at later ages.

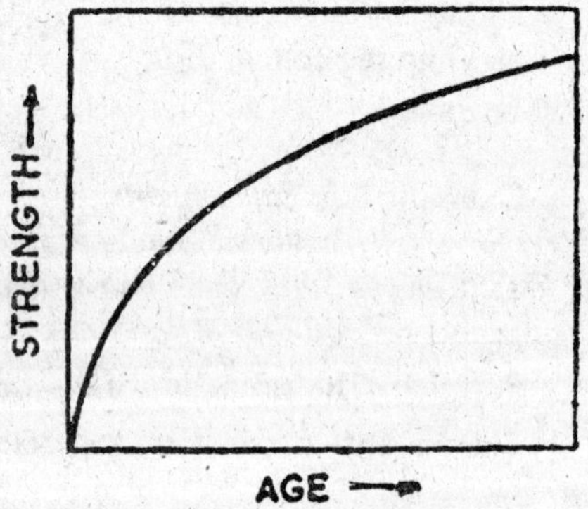

Fig. 8.9. Relation between age and strength

2. Coarse aggregate. The shape and surface texture of coarse aggregate have been found to affect the strength of concrete to a great extent. The influence of the type of coarse aggregate on the strength of concrete varies in magnitude and depends upon water/cement ratio of the mix. For water/ratio less than 0.40, the use of crushed aggregate has been found to give higher strengths by more than 38% than when gravel is used. With the increase in water/cement ratio, the influence of aggregate has been found to decrease, presumably because the strength of paste itself becomes paramount (superior) and at a water/cement ratio of 0.65, the influence of type of aggregate does not exists, and no difference is found in strengths made with crushed stone aggregate and gravel.

3. Richness of the mix. As stated earlier also, mixes with a very low water/cement ratio and an extremely high cement content (470 to 530 kg/m^3) exhibit retrogression of strength, particularly when large size aggregate is used. But the aggregate/cement ratio has been found to affect the strength of all medium and high strength concrete *i.e.* concrete having strength 350 kg/cm^2 and above. However aggregate/cement ratio is a secondary factor in the strength of concrete, but it has been found that for a constant water/cement ratio a leaner mix leads to a higher strength. This behaviour is probably due to the absorption of water by aggregate as larger quantity of aggregate absorbs greater quantity of water, reducing the effective water/ cement ratio. Thus total water content per cubic metre of concrete is lower in a leaner mix than in a rich mix. As a consequence in a leaner mix the voids form a smaller fraction of the total volume of concrete, resulting in higher strength. The effect of cement content is shown in Fig. 14.8.

Effect of size of aggregate and cement content on the strength of concrete is shown in Fig. 4.25. Concrete strength is found to increase with the size of aggregate upto 38 to 40 mm as shown in Fig. 4.25 Fig. 8.10 shows the influence of maximum size of aggregate on compressive strength of concrete made with different w/c ratio.

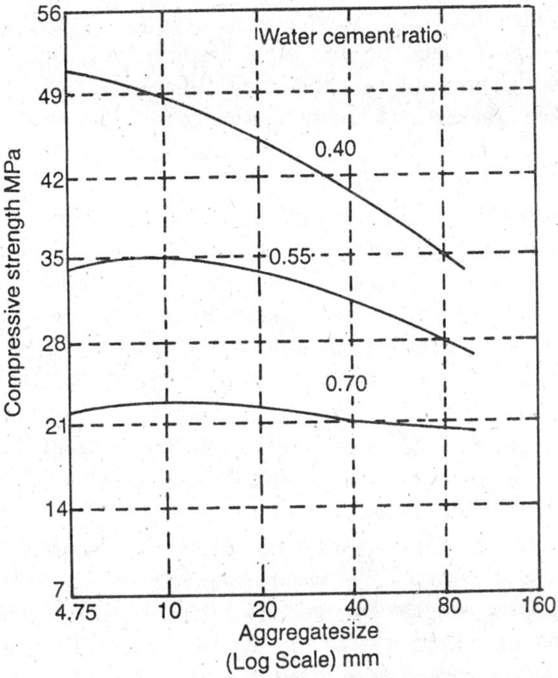

Fig. 8.10. Relation between size of aggregate w/c ratio and strength

4. Effect of curing on strength of concrete. Curing is the name given to the procedure used for promoting the hydration of cement. It controls the temperature of concrete and moisture movement from and into the concrete.

The object of curing is to keep the concrete saturated or as nearly saturated as possible, till the originally water filled space in the fresh cement paste has been filled to the desired extent by the products of hydration of cement. In case of site concrete, it has been observed that active curing stops long before the maximum possible hydration could take place.

The study of Fig 8.11 will show that longer the period of moist storage, greater the strength. Exposure to air, with consequent drying, arrests hydration. The rate and extent of drying depends on the mass of the concrete relative to the exposed surface area as well as on the humidity of the surrounding air. During testing it was observed that specimens exposed to air and tested in air dry condition gave 25% to 33% higher strengths than corresponding specimens exposed to air for the same period, but saturated just before the test. Resumption of moist curing after a period of air drying results in resumption of hydration, though at a slower rate than that in progress when drying was begun. The loss of strength due to inadequate curing is more pronounced in thinner sections.

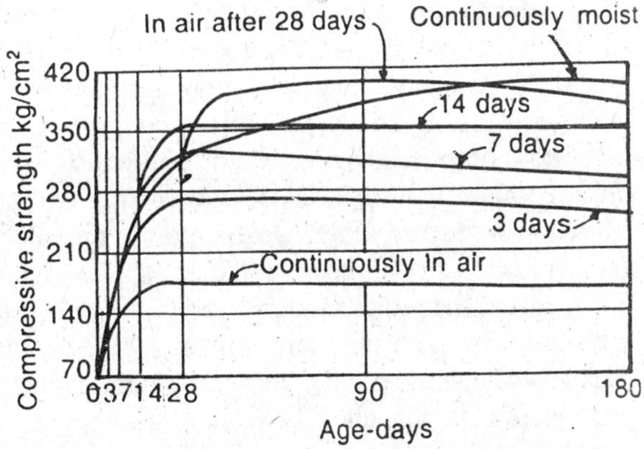

Fig. 8.11. Influence of curing temp on strength of concrete

The necessity of curing arises due to the fact that hydration of cement can take place only in water filled capillaries. That is why a loss of water by evaporation from capillaries should be prevented. Further, water lost internally by self drying up (desiccation) has to be replaced by water from out side *i.e.* the ingress of water in concrete should be made possible.

In case of sealed specimen, hydration can proceed only if the amount of water present in the paste is at least twice that of the water already combined. Thus self desiccation is of importance in mixes with water/cement ratio below 0.5. For higher water/cement ratios the rate of hydration of a sealed specimen is equal to that of a saturated specimen. Further it should be remembered that only half the water present in the paste can be used for chemical combination. This is true even if the total amount of water present is less than the water required for combination. The recent studies have shown that hydration can take place only when the vapour pressure in the capillaries is sufficiently high about 0.8 times of the saturation pressure. Below 0.8 times of saturation pressure is low and below 0.3 it is negligible. Thus hydration at a maximum rate can proceed only under saturation Conditions.

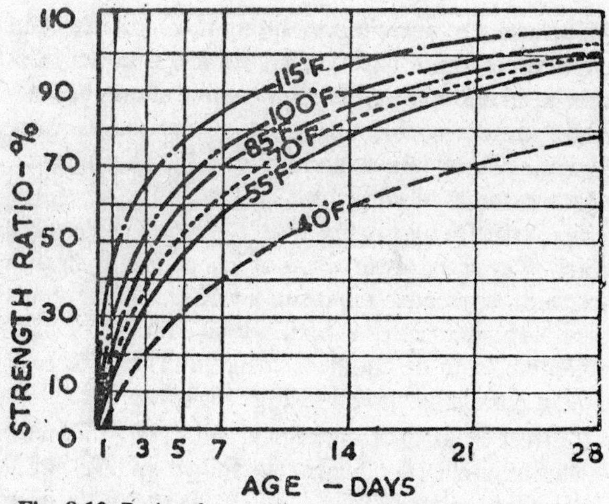

Fig. 8.12. Ratio of strength cured at different temperature

Recent studies also showed that for a satisfactory development of strength, the hydration of total cement is not necessary, nor it is achieved in practice at site. The quality of concrete depends mainly on the gel/space ratio of the paste. However if the water filled space in fresh concrete is greater than the volume that can be filled by the products of hydration, greater hydration will take place resulting in higher strength and lower permeability of concrete. The evaporation of water from concrete just after its placement depends on the temperature, relative humidity of the surrounding air and the velocity of wind.

5. Effect of temperature. The influence of temperature of moist curing on concrete strength depends on the time-temperature history. The strength of concrete is a function of Σ (time interval × temperature). This summation is known as maturity. Thus a rise in temperature accelerates the chemical reactions of hydration and affects the early strength of concrete. A higher temperature during placing and setting though increases the early strength of concrete, but affects adversely later strengths from about 7 days on wards. The reason of this is that a rapid initial hydration appears to form products of a poor physical structure, probably more porous, such that a large proportion of pores always remains unfilled. *Helmuth* on the basis of his experimental results has suggested that the rapid initial rate of hydration at higher temperatures retards the subsequent hydration and produces a non-uniform distribution of the products of hydration in the paste. The probable reason for this is that at high initial rate of hydration there is insufficient time available for the diffusion of the products of hydration away from the cement grain and for a uniform precipitation in the interstitial space resulting building up a high concentration of the products of hydration in the vicinity of hydrating grain. This retards subsequent hydration and adversely affects the long term strength of concrete. Fig. 8.12 shows the ratio of strength of concrete cured at different temperatures as shown on the Fig. to the 28 days strength of concrete cursed at 76°F for a particular concrete.

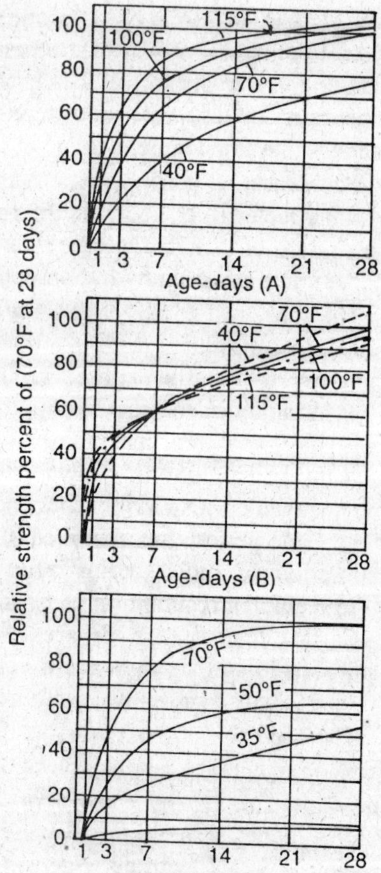

Fig. 8.13. Strength of concrete cured at different temperature

The effect of temperature on the strength of concrete is shown in Fig. 8.13 (*a*). Fig. 8.13 (*a*) shows the strength of concrete cast and cured at the, constant indicated temperatures on the curve. From the Fig. it will be seen that higher the temperature within limits, the more rapid the hydration and higher the resulting strength at ages upto 28 days. At later ages, higher the temperature, lower the strength obtained. The decrease in strength is found to vary from 25% to 35%.

Fig. 8.13 (*b*) shows the effect of temperature during the first two hours after mixing on the development of strength of concrete. The temperature was varied from 4°C to 46°C (40°F to 115°F). The specimens cast and maintained for two hours at the indicated temperature and after two hours they all were cured at 21°C (70°F. From the Fig. it will be seen that higher the initial temperature, lower the strength at 28 days. However upto the age of 7 days higher temperature results higher strength. Further cylinders moist cured during the first 24 hours at 2°C (36°F) and 18°C (64°F) and after 24 hours all cylinders were cured at 18°C (64°F). Test results have shown that cylinders cured at 2°C (36°F) gave 10% higher strength.

Fig. 8.13 (*c*) shows the effect of temperature on strength when concrete cast and maintained at 70°F for 6 hours and then cured at temperature indicated on the diagram. From the Fig. it will be seen that lower the curing temperature within limits, lower the strength. At a temperature of 33°F the strength is found only 47% of the continuously cured concrete at 70°F and at 16°F (below freezing point) only 9% strength was obtained.

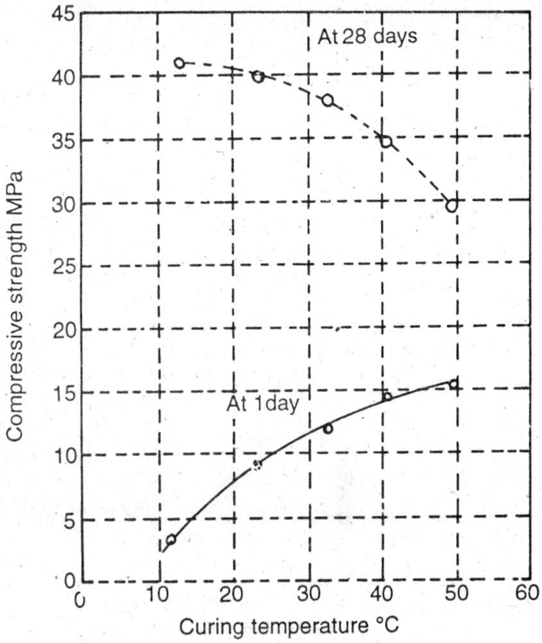

Fig. 8.14. Influence of curing temperature on strength of concrete

The temperature at the time of placement also affects the strength of concrete. Some field tests have confirmed that an increase of 5°C (9°F) in temperature decreases the strength of concrete by 19 kg/cm^2.

Fig. 8.14 shows the influence of curing temperature on the strength of concrete tested after 1 and 28 days curing. From the curve it will be seen that strength after 1 day curing increases upto the maximum range of temperature, while the strength at 28 days curing decreases considerably at high temperature at 50°C (122°F).

At 122°F the strength decreases from 400 kg/cm^2 to 300 kg/cm^2 *i.e.* a decrease of about 25% occurred.

8.9. EFFECT OF DIFFERENT WATER/CEMENT RATIOS ON STRENGTH

From experimental data it has been found that for no un-hydrated cement to be left and no capillary pores to be left there should be sufficient water in the mix. The least quantity of this water corresponds to 0.38 water/cement ratio by weight. Thus for water/cement ratio less than 0.38 complete hydration is not possible. From workability consideration this water/cement ration is found as 0.4. At a water/cement ratio of 0.4, mix has

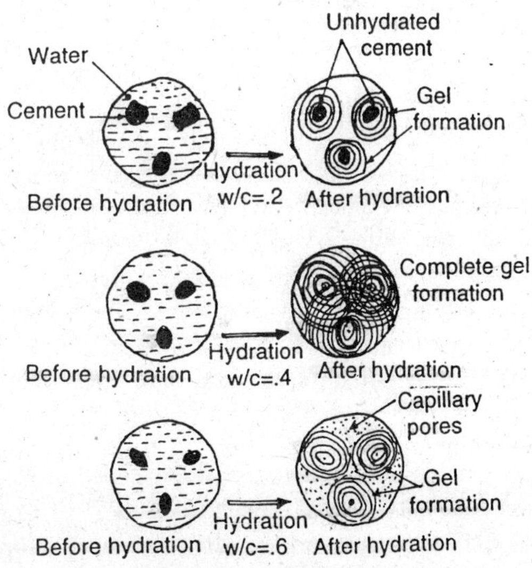

Fig. 8.15. Effect of different w/c ratio on strength of concrete

sufficient water for hydration as well as for providing ease in compaction. At this water/cement the 'gel' formed is of good physical structure being dense. At higher water/cement ratio the 'gel' is formed of poor physical structure probably more porous resulting in lower strength of concrete. The effect of water/cement ratio on compressive strength of concrete at different age is shown in Fig. 8.15.

8.10. CONDITIONS OF APPLICATION OF WATER CEMENT LAW

Water-cement law is applicable under the following conditions.

1. Internal moisture condition of hydration of cement should continue till the concrete gains full strength.
2. Concrete should be cured under standard temperature.
3. Size of concrete specimen should be same.
4. Test should be done at the same age.

The effects of these factors have already been discussed.

8.11. HIGH STRENGTH CONCRETE

Generally concrete is classified as Normal strength Concrete (NSC), High strength Concrete (HSC) and ultra high strength concrete (UHSC). However there is no clear cut boundary for the above classification. Indian Standard for mix design has suggested the boundary at 35 MPa (350 kg/cm^2) between Normal and High strength concretes. However no boundary has been fixed between High strength concrete and ultra high strength concrete. In international forum about in 1970, High strength label was applied to concrete having compressive strength of about 40 MPa (400 kg/cm^2). However recently this limit has been raised to 50 to 60 MPa. Since about 1985 in the world concrete having compressive strength of 90 to 120 MPa has been used in the construction of long span bridges and high rise buildings.

The advent of pre-stressed concrete Technique has given the impetus for the production of high strength concrete. In India the first pre-stressed concrete bridge was built in 1949 for the Assam Rail Link bridge at Siliguri. In fifty's a number of pre-stressed concrete structures were constructed using concrete of compressive strength of 35 to 45 MPa. For the construction of pre-stressed concrete bridge over Ram Ganga near Moradabad, Central Building Research Institute* had developed a Mix Proportion for the production of 50 MPa concrete. However in general construction works, concrete having strength more than 35 MPa was not used. In the construction of Konkan Railway project and Mumbai Municipal Corporation Roads Construction probably concrete of strength more than 35 MPa was used. In Indian Construction scenario only during 90's high strength concrete has stepped in. Later on concrete of strength varying from 45 to 60 MPa has been used in high rise buildings in Mumbai, Delhi and other Metropolitan cities. High strength concrete was also employed in the construction of bridges and fly-overs. Recently in the year 2000 in Mumbai concrete having strength 75 MPa was used in the construction of fly-over. In India high strength concrete has also been used at Kaiga power project. Here high performance concrete of 60 MPa with silica fume has been used.

For the obvious benefits of high strength concrete, the manufacture of high strength concrete will grow and find its due place in concrete construction. Thus the ready mixed concrete is developing fast in India. In the modern batching plants high strength concrete is produced in a mechanical manner. However one has to take care about mix proportioning, shape and kind of aggregates, use of supplementary cementitious materials as silica fumes and super plasticizers. Now with the use of modern equipments and under standing of the role of the constituent materials etc. the production of high strength concrete has become a routine matter.

8.12. METHODS OF PRODUCTION OF HIGH STRENGTH CONCRETE

There are many special methods of making high strength concrete. Some of them are as follows:

1. Use of admixtures
2. Re-vibration

*Senior author worked on this project.

3. High speed slurry mixing
4. Prevention of cracks
5. Sulphur impregnation or Sulphur filling
6. Use of cementitious aggregates
7. Seeding.

1. **Use of admixture.** Substances used for reducing water contents are known as admixtures. They are discussed in detail in chapter 6.
2. **Revibration.** The mixing water in concrete creates continuous capillary channels, Bleeding and water accumulation at certain selected places. All these factors reduce the strength of concrete. Thus concrete undergoes plastic shrinkage. The controlled revibration controls all these defects and increases the strength of the concrete.
3. **High speed slurry mixing.** In this process, first cement and water mixture is prepared and then aggregate is blended to produce concrete. The development of higher compressive strength is attributed to the more efficient hydration of cement particles and water saved in the vigorous blending of cement paste.
4. **Inhibition or prevention of cracks.** It has been observed that development of cracks in concrete is an inherent phenomenon. Concrete fails due to the formation and propagation of craeks. It has been discussed in detail in chapter 26. If the development and propagation of cracks is checked, the strength of concrete will increase. If 2 to 3% of fine aggregate is replaced by polythene or polystyrene 'Lenticules' pieces 0.025 mm thick and 3 to 4 mm in diameter, will result in the increase of concrete strength. The polythene pieces act to check the propagation of cracks without necessitating extra water for workability. Concrete cubes prepared by this method have shown strength upto 105 MPa.
5. **Sulpher filling or impregnation.** By impregnating low strength porous concrete by Sulpher, sufficiently high strength concrete has been produced. The process of impregnation is as follows:
   (*a*) The fresh concrete specimens are cured moist for 24 hours.
   (*b*) After moist curing they are dried at 120°C for 24 hours.
   (*c*) After drying the specimens are immersed in molten sulpher under vacuum for two hours.
   (*d*) After two hours of immersion, vacuum is released.
   (*e*) The specimens are further immersed in molten sulpher for 1/2 hour for further infiltration of sulpher. Sulpher impregnated concrete has been found to give strength upto 58 MPa. Refer chapter 24 also.
6. **Use of Cementitious aggregates.** The glassy slag clinker known as fondu is a cementitious material. When it is ground finely, it results in a kind of cement. When crushed coarsely it produces a kind of aggregate known as ALAG. Using ALAG as aggregate, concrete gives strength upto 125 MPa with water/cement ratio of 0.32.
7. **Seeding.** This process involves adding a small percentage of finely ground, fully hydrated portland cement to the fresh concrete mix. The Mechanism of developing high strength is difficult to explain. This method has not been found practical.

8.13. PRODUCTION OF ULTRA HIGH STRENGTH CONCRETE

The technological development has given impetus to the development of ultra high strength concrete.

Techniques of development of ultra high strength concrete

Following techniques may be used for the production of ultra high strength concrete:

1. Compaction by pressure
2. Helical binding
3. Polymerisation of concrete
4. Reactive powder concrete

1. Compaction by pressure. As already discussed, the cement paste derives strength due to the combined effect of friction and bond. In ceramic (clay) materials, grain size and porosity are the most important parameters which affect friction and bond, hence the strength. Attempts have been made to reduce the grain size and porosity by the application of very high pressure at room temperature as well as at higher temperatures.

Unusually high strength has been generated in materials by using 'hot pressing' techniques. The intermediate ranges of strengths have been developed by applying high pressure at room temperature to portland cement paste. At a temperature of 250°C, by subjecting a cement paste to a pressure of 357 MPa (3570 kg/cm^2). Compressive strengths as high as 680 MPa and indirect tensile strength of 66 MPa has been obtained. The water/cement ratio used was 0.093. It has also been observed that hot pressed materials are volume stable. The micro structure of such materials is very compact. The porosity of such materials was found about 1.8%,

2. Helical binding. In this method high tensile steel wires are binded externally over the concrete cylinders. This results in good strength. This is an indirect method of achieving ultra high strength in concrete.

3. Polymer Concrete. The conventional hardened concrete after a period of moist curing contains a considerable amount of free water in voids. The water filled voids form a significant component of the total volume of concrete ranging from 5% in dense concrete to 15% in gap graded concrete. We know that 1% voids reduce the strength of concrete by 5%. Researchers have observed that by reducing the grain size and porosity in concrete by any means, the high strength concrete may be obtained.

Thus in the case of polymer concrete, a monomer is impregnated into the pores of the hardened concrete. After impregnation of monomer it is polymerized either by thermal catalytic process or by radiation process. On polymerization the monomer expands and fills the voids fully and holds there firmly forming a solid material, resulting in the development of very high strength. Polymer concrete has been dis- cussed in detail in Chapter 24.

4. Reactive powder concrete. The concrete of 100 to 120 MPa strength has been used for construction of structural members and concrete with 250 to 300 MPa also has been used for non structural application such as flooring, safes and storage of nuclear wastes.

For the use of structural members, high ductility is needed along with high strength. Reactive powder concrete has been developed to meet both the requirements of strength and ductility. The strength of reactive powder concrete may vary from 200 MPa to 800 MPa with required ductility.

As we know the concrete is a heterogeneous material and the strength developed by cement paste is not fully retained when sand and aggregates are added. The Reactive powder concrete is made by using ground quartz less than 300 micron size, silica fume, synthesized precipitated silica, steel fibres about 10 mm in length and 180 micron in diameter in place of sand and aggregate *i.e.* the sand and coarse aggregate have totally been removed. Silica fume has been discussed in chapter 6 on Admixtures.

8.14. HIGH PERFORMANCE CONCRETE (HPC)

High performance terminology is a new coined term. A concrete mix which possesses the high workability, high strength, high modulus of elasticity, high density, low permeability and low resistance to chemical attack and high dimensional stability is called high *performance* concrete.

In normal concrete, relatively low strength and elastic modulus are due to the high heterogeneous nature of the structure of the material, partialarly the porous and weak transition zone, which exist at the cement paste aggregate interface. By densifying and strengthening the transition zone, many desirable properties can be improved many fold. A substantial reduction of the quantity of mixing water is the fundamental step for making high performance concrete (HPC). The reduction in water/cement ratio will result in high strength of concrete. But the reduction in water/cement ratio to less than 0.3, will greatly improve the qualities of transition zone to give inherent qualities expected of HPC.

To improve the qualities of transition zone, the use of silica fume has been found necessary. For the strength of concrete above 80 MPa (800 kg/cm^2) the use of silica fume as one of the ingredients has become necessary. The best quality fly ash may be used for other nominal benefits. Though these pozzolanic materials need more water, but their benefits will be more than their disadvantages. Thus the crux of the whole problem lies in using very low water/cement ratio consistent with high workability at the time of placing and compacting. NEVILE has suggested that the lowest water/cement ratio that could be used is 0.22.

Adoption of water/cement ratio in the range of 0.25 to 0.3 and getting high slump is possible only by the use of super-plasticizers. Thus in the production of high performance concrete (HPC) the use of appropriate super plasticizer is essential. The super plasticizer and cement should be compatible and should retain the slump and other properties for sufficiently long time till the placement and compaction of the concrete is over.

8.14.1. Aggregate for HPC

In normal concrete, the strength of aggregate particles usually is more than the strength of cement paste and thus the strength of aggregate plays a minor role. Any aggregate available at site may be used with little modification in its grading. However in case of High performance concrete the situation is altogether different. The bond between the hydrated cement paste and aggregate is so strong that significant stress transfer takes place across the transition zone. Due to the low water/cement ratio, the strength of cement paste is very high and some times even higher than the strength of the aggregate particles. The fractured surface of the HPC has shown that very often the fracture takes place through the aggregate pieces rather than cement paste, where as in normal concrete fracture takes place at the interface of cement paste and aggregate piece *i.e.* it fails in shear. Thus in many cases the compressive strength of the high performance concrete is limited on the basis of strength of aggregate particles.

8.13.2. Size of the aggregate for HPC

On the basis of practical experience it has been found that for a strength upto 100 MPa the maximum size of aggregate may be 20 mm. For concrete higher than 100 MPa the size of coarse aggregate should be limited to 10 to 12 mm only.

8.13.3. Shape of aggregate

Though crushed aggregate may be used but the aggregate should be cubic in shape, the flaky or elongated particles should be minimum.

In India High performance concrete of 60 MPa strength was used for the 1st time for the construction of containment dome at Kaiga and Rajasthan Atomic power projects.

QUESTIONS

1. Define water/cement ratio.
2. What is water/cement ratio law? Under what conditions this law is valid?
3. What are the various types of water in hydrated cement paste.
4. What is meant by non evaporable water?
5. What is the difference between the gel pores and capillary pores?
6. What is the minimum water/cement ratio for full hydration of cement?
7. Why porosity is important with regard to
   (*a*) Durability (*b*) Strength
8. Differentiate between the following:
   (*a*) Capillary porosity (*b*) gel porosity
   (*c*) Total porosity, and (*d*) Concrete porosity
9. What is effective water/cement ratio?
10. Discuss the effects of curing and age on strength of the concrete.
11. What factors affect the strength of concrete?
12. How different water/cement ratios affect the strength of concrete.

13. Define Gel/space ratio and also discuss its effect on the strength of the concrete.
14. Define High strength concrete.
15. Write short note on the method for the development of high strength concrete.
16. What is ultra high strength. How is it produced?
17. What is high performance concrete? Explain in brief.
18. What is polymer concrete? Explain in brief.

OBJECTIVE TYPE QUESTIONS

1. The main ingredients of a cement concrete are
   (*a*) Cement (*b*) Coarse aggregate
   (*c*) Fine aggregate (*d*) Water
   (*e*) Admixtures (*f*) All of the above
2. Which of the ingredient is inert ingradient of cement concrete
   (*a*) Water (*b*) cement
   (*c*) Aggregate (*d*) None of the above
3. Which of the following statement is false?
   (*a*) After curing normal concrete shrinks on drying
   (*b*) After curing normal concrete expands on drying
   (*c*) After curing normal concrete may expand or shrink depending upto the proportions of various ingredients
   (*d*) After curing normal concrete shrinks when still wet
   (*e*) After curing normal concrete neither expands nor shrinks
4. Which of the statement is true?
   (*a*) Cement concrete is an artificial stone in which larger particle voids are filled by smaller particles and voids of smaller particles are filled with cement paste
   (*b*) It is an artificial stone obtained by binding together particles of coarse and fine aggregate which are relatively inert.
   (*c*) It is the man made construction material made to meet the demand of any particular situation and most widely used
   (*d*) It is the material prepared from locally available materials to satisfy the required requirements
   (*e*) All of the above
5. Concrete can be specified as
   (*a*) By degree of control (*b*) By unit weight
   (*c*) Prescriptive specifications (*d*) By performance oriented specifications
6. The strength of concrete is influenced by
   (*a*) Type of testing machine (*b*) Rate of loading
   (*c*) Moisture conditions (*d*) Size of specimen
   (*e*) By all the above
7. To specify the concrete mix the most appropriate method is by the
   (*a*) Grade of concrete (*b*) Nominal mix ratio
   (*c*) Designed mix ratio (*d*) Degree of control
8. Which of the following statements is true?
   (*a*) The compressive strength of concrete decreases with entrained air
   (*b*) The compressive strength of concrete decreases with the increase of aggregate cement ratio
   (*c*) The compressive strength of concrete increases with the increase in the degree of compaction
   (*d*) All of the above
9. The strength of concrete depends upon
   (*a*) Concrete mix proportion (*b*) Degree of compaction
   (*c*) Type of cement (*d*) Curing temperature
   (*e*) All of the above
10. The stress-strain curve of concrete in compression is obtained by testing the cylindrical specimen under
    (*a*) Uniform rate of stress (*b*) Constant stress condition
    (*c*) Constant strain condition (*d*) Uniform rate of strain

11. The dynamic tests on concrete in comparison of static tests give
   (*a*) Lower value of poisson's ratio
   (*b*) Higher value of poisson's ratio
   (*c*) Same value of poisson's ratio
   (*d*) None of the above
12. The shrinkage in concrete is produced due to
   (*a*) Loss of water from the surface by evaporation
   (*b*) withdrawal of water stored in air voids of concrete
   (*c*) Hydration of cement
   (*d*) All the above
13. Which of the following statements is/are true?
   (*a*) The shrinkage of concrete increases with the increase in water/cement ratio
   (*b*) The shrinkage of concrete increases with the increase in cement content
   (*c*) The shrinkage of concrete increases with the decrease in humidity
   (*d*) The shrinkage of concrete increases with the decrease in the maximum size of aggregate
   (*e*) All of the above
14. Which of the following statements is false?
   (*a*) Permeability of concrete reduces with the strength of the cement paste
   (*b*) Permeability of concrete reduces with the decrease in porosity of concrete
   (*c*) Permeability of concrete reduces with the carbonation of concrete
   (*d*) None of the above
15. Which of the statements is false?
   (*a*) The thermal conductivity of concrete decreases with increase in water/cement ratio
   (*b*) The thermal conductivity of concrete decreases with the decrease in cement content
   (*c*) The thermal conductivity of concrete decreases with decrease in weight of concrete
   (*d*) Non of the above
16. Which of the following statements is correct?
   (*a*) The durability of concrete is due to its resistance to the internal disruptive forces
   (*b*) The durability of concrete is due to its resistance to chemical attack
   (*c*) The durability of concrete is due to its resistance to deterioration from atmospheric conditions
   (*d*) All the above
17. The inelastic behaviour of concrete is due to
   (*a*) The presence of macro and micro cracks
   (*b*) The shrinkage of concrete
   (*c*) The propagation of mortar and bond cracks
   (*d*) The use of aggregates
   (*e*) All the above
18. The stress-strain curve for the cement concrete is linear approximately upto
   (*a*) 75% of ultimate stress
   (*b*) 50% of ultimate stress
   (*c*) 25% of ultimate stress
   (*d*) 33.3% of ultimate stress
   (*e*) 62.5% of ultimate stress
19. The modulus of elasticity of concrete improves with
   (*a*) Decrease in curing period
   (*b*) Better compaction
   (*c*) High water/cement ratio
   (*d*) Age
   (*e*) None of the above
20. Which of the following statements are true?
   (*a*) The shrinkage of concrete can be reduced by using pre saturated aggregates
   (*b*) The shrinkage of concrete can be reduced by using low water/cement ratio
   (*c*) The shrinkage of concrete can be reduced by using water tight and non absorbent form work
   (*d*) All of the above
21. The strength of concrete depends upon
   (*a*) Water/cement ratio
   (*b*) Fineness of cement
   (*c*) Quality of coarse aggregate
   (*d*) Quality of fine aggregate
22. The thermal coefficient of expansion of concrete is
   (*a*) 3×10^{-4} per °C
   (*b*) 3×10^{-5} per °C
   (*c*) 3×10^{-6} per °C
   (*d*) 3×10^{-8} per °C
   (*e*) 3×10^{-3} per °C

23. 100% compressive strength in concrete may be developed in
    (a) 3 days
    (b) 7 days
    (c) 14 days
    (d) 28 days
    (e) 1 years
    (f) After 3 years
24. Which of the following statements is correct?
    (a) Creep in concrete is undesirable in prestresed concrete structures
    (b) Creep in concrete is undesirable in reinforced concrete columns
    (c) Creep in concrete is undesirable in continuous beams
    (d) All the above
25. Which of the following statements is true?
    (a) The strength of concrete is decreased by impact
    (b) The strength of concrete is decreased by fatigue
    (c) The strength of concrete is decreased by excessive vibration
    (d) All the above
26. The knowledge of flexural tensile strength is useful in the design of
    (a) Water retaining structures
    (b) Prestressed concrete structures
    (c) R.C.C. members
    (d) Pavement slabs and air field runways
27. The compressive strength of concrete is the most important property of conccrete as
    (a) It indicates the extent of voids in the concrete
    (b) It affects the permeability and durability of concrete
    (c) It depends upon the water/cement ratio
    (d) It is related to the structure of hardened cement pate and gives over all quality of concrete
28. The permissible stress for concrete subjected to fatigue should be
    (a) 30%
    (b) 50%
    (c) 80%
    (d) 95%
29. As per ISI, the maximum compressive strength of normal strength concrete should be
    (a) 10 MPa
    (b) 15 Mpa
    (c) 25 Mpa
    (d) 40 Mpa
    (e) 35 MPa
30. The tensile strength of concrete is about......% of compressive strength
    (a) 5%
    (b) 10%
    (c) 20%
    (d) 40%
    (e) 55%
31. For the determination of compressive strength of concrete generally cube of size... is used
    (a) 100 mm
    (b) 150 mm
    (c) 200 mm
    (d) 250 mm
    (e) 375 mm
32. As per Indian Standard specifications 456-2000 the concrete is designated into
    (a) 5 grades
    (b) 7 grades
    (c) 15 grades
    (d) 12 grades
33. Generally the porosity of concrete depends upon
    (a) Grading of aggregate
    (b) Quantity of mixing water
    (c) Degree of compaction
    (d) Cement content
    (e) All of the above
34. The concrete to be used near sea water, the mix proportion should not be leaner than
    (a) 1:3:6
    (b) 1:2:4
    (c) 1:2:3
    (d) 1:1:2
    (e) 1:1.5:3
35. For plain cement concrete exposed to sea waves the grade of concrete should not be lower than
    (a) M 10
    (b) M 15
    (c) M 20
    (d) M 25
    (e) 30 M
    (f) 40 m

36. Which of the statements are true?
   (*a*) The concrete in contact with alkaline water or alkaline soil should have high water/cement ratio
   (*b*) The concrete in contact with alkaline water or alkaline soil should use a rich mix
   (*c*) The concrete in contact with alkaline water or alkaline soil should have high alumina cement
   (*d*) The concrete in contact with alkaline water or alkaline soil should have low water/cement
   (*e*) The concrete in contact with alkaline water or soil should have higher percentage of fine aggregate
   (*f*) The high frost resistant concrete should be free from cracks
   (*g*) The high frost resistant concrete should be dense
   (*h*) The high frost resistant concrete should be steam cured
   (*i*) The high frost resistant concrete should be dense , steam cured and free from cracks
37. For determining the compressive strength of concrete the minimum number of cubes tested should be
   (*a*) 1 (*b*) 2
   (*c*) 3 (*d*) 5
   (*e*) 6 (*f*) 9
38. The unit weight of R.C.C generally is taken as
   (*a*) 18 kN/m^3 (1800 kg/m^3) (*b*) 22 kN/m^3 (2200 kg/m^3)
   (*c*) 25 kg/m^3 (2500 kg/m^3) (*d*) 24 kN/m^3 (2400 kg/m^3)
   (*e*) 26 kN/m^3 (2600 kg/m^3)
39. Generally the unit weight of plain concrete is taken as
   (*a*) 20 kN/m^3 (*b*) 22 kN/m^3
   (*c*) 25 kN/m^3 (*d*) 24 kN/m^3
40. Which of the following statements is true?
   (*a*) The common brick has the higher weight
   (*b*) Plain concrete has the highest weight
   (*c*) RCC has the highest weight
   (*d*) Plain concrete with brick aggregate has the highest weight
41. Which of the following statements is true?
   (*a*) Sulphuric acid does not react with concrete
   (*b*) Sewage water has no reaction with concrete
   (*c*) Vegetable oil has no reaction with concrete
   (*d*) Alcohol does not react with concrete
42. Which of the statements is false?
   (*a*) Algae present in concrete reduces it strength
   (*b*) Algae present in concrete causes large entrainment of air
   (*c*) Algae present in concrete reduces its bond strength
   (*d*) Algae present in concrete reduces its bond strength and causes large entrainment of air
   (e) All the above
43. The direct method of calculating tensile strength of concrete suffers from defects due to the
   (*a*) Stress concentration at the jaws
   (*b*) Difficulty in holding the specimen
   (*c*) Presence of ecentricity in application of load
   (*d*) All the above
44. For determining the tensile strength of concrete, the split test method is better than the direct tensile strength method due to
   (*a*) The split test gives more uniform results
   (*b*) In split test same moulds can be used for compression as well tensile test specimens
   (*c*) The split test gives results closer to the actual tensile strength of concrete
   (*d*) All the above
45. The 28 days compressive strength of concrete is...% of 365 days strength
   (*a*) 60% (*b*) 70%
   (*c*) 80% (*d*) 90%
46. The tensile strength of concrete is ... % of its compressive strength

(*a*) 20% (*b*) 10%
(*c*) 5% (*d*) 4%
(*e*) 3.5%

47. The cube strength of concrete is...% higher than its cylinder strength
(*a*) 10 to 15% (*b*) 15 to 20%
(*c*) 20 to 25% (*d*) 30 o 40%

48. The permissible diagonal tension strength of M 15 concrete is
(*a*) 2.5 MPa (*b*) 1.5 MPa
(*c*) 1.0 MPa (*d*) 0.5 MPa
(*e*) 0.75 MPa

49. The materials of a concrete mix may be expressed as
(*a*) Parts (by weight) of cement fine and coarse aggregate
(*b*) Cement aggregate ratio
(*c*) Cement factor
(*d*) Parts (by volume) of cement, fine and coarse aggregate
(*e*) Any of the above

50. Which of the following statement is false?
(*a*) Nominal mix is of a fixed proportions which ensure adequate strength
(*b*) Nominal mix may result in under or over rich mixes
(*c*) Nominal or standard mixes may be used for high quality concrete
(*d*) Mix design ensures a concrete of appropriate properties to be produced most economically
(*e*) Standard mixes are sets of proportions that can be used to produce the concrete of desired properties

Answers

1. (*f*)	11. (*b*)	21. (*a*)	31. (*b*)	41. (*d*)
2. (*c*)	12. (*d*)	22. (*a*)	32. (*c*)	42. (*e*)
3. (*e*)	13. (*e*)	23. (*e*)	33. (*e*)	43. (*d*)
4. (*e*)	14. (*d*)	24. (*a*)	34. (*b*)	44. (*d*)
5. (*d*)	15. (*d*)	25. (*d*)	35. (*d*)	45. (*c*)
6. (*e*)	16. (*d*)	26. (*d*)	36. (*c* to *i*)	46. (*b*)
7. (*a*)	17. (*c*)	27. (*d*)	37. (*c*)	47. (*c*)
8. (*d*)	18. (*b*)	28. (*b*)	38. (*d*)	48. (*d*)
9. (*e*)	19. (*d*)	29. (*d*)	39. (*c*)	49. (*e*)
10. (*d*)	20. (*d*)	30. (*b*)	40. (*c*)	50. (*c*)

9

Batching and Mixing of Concrete

9.1. BATCHING

The correct measurement of the various materials used in the concrete mix is called *batching*. It has been observed that batching errors arc partly responsible for the variation in the quality of concrete. This operation can be properly and better controlled than other factors responsible for the variation in the quality of concrete. It has been observed that poor batching is responsible for more variation than any other factor, but good control can reduce this part of variation to an insignificant amount. Thus batching operation is a very important operation.

9.2. TYPE OF BATCHING

Batching can be done in two ways as follows:

1. Volume batching   2. Weight batching

9.2.1. Volume batching. In this system of batching, the materials are measured by volume. The gauging of cement by volume is most inadvisable as it is difficult to secure accuracy in its measurement as the actual volume of a given weight of cement depends upon how it is filled into a gauge box and whether it is shaken down. The density of cement may vary from 1.12 gram/cm^3 if it is lightly poured into the container to 1.6 gram/cm^3 if tamped down sufficiently hard. Therefore it is convenient to use complete bags of cement in a concrete mix so that the batching, of cement on the site is unnecessary except where bulk cement is used. If a fraction of a bag of cement is required, then it should be weighed into a bucket suspended from an ordinary spring balance.

Aggregates can be gauged by volume and for this purpose wooden batch boxes called *farmas* are used. The size of farmas should be such as to measure the correct quantity of aggregates to be used with a whole bag of cement for the required mix. They should not be made so large as to be unwieldy.

Table 9.1. Batch volume of materials for various mixes

S. No.	*Proportion*	*Cement in kg*	*Sand litres*	*Coarse aggregate litre*
1.	1 : 1 : 2	50	35	70
2.	$1 : 1\frac{1}{2} : 3$	50	52.5	105
3.	1 : 2 : 2	50	70	70
4.	1 : 2 : 3	50	70	105
5.	$1 : 2\frac{1}{2} : 3\frac{1}{2}$	50	87.5	122.5
6.	1 : 2 : 4	50	70	140
7.	$1 : 2\frac{1}{2} : 5$	50	87.5	175
8.	1 : 3 : 5	50	105	175
9.	1 : 3 : 6	50	105	210

Each cement bag as delivered by the factories is packed to contain a net weight of 50 kg. As one litre of cement weight 1.44 kg. the volume of 50 kg cement will be $\frac{50}{1.44}$ = 34.72 lit., but for the sake of convenience the volume of 1 bag of cement containing 50 kg of cement is taken as 35 lit. Thus the farma should normally be made to have a volume of 35 lit., so that it may contain one full bag of cement. On this assumption, for various mixes quantities of materials may be taken.

The quantity of sand as indicated above is based on the assumption that the sand is in a saturated surface dry condition. If surface moisture is present, bulking of sand should be allowed as explained in chapter 4.

9.2.1.1. Size of farmas

The farma should be of convenient size, to measure in multiples of 35 lit. Tall and narrow farmas should be preferred than shallow and wide farmas. The general dimensions of farmas of different capacities are shown in Table 9.2.

Table 9.2. Sizes of farmas

S. No.	*Capacity in litres*	*Inside Measurement*		
		Length in cms.	*Breadth in cms.*	*Height in cms.*
1.	25	25	25	40
2.	30	25	25	48
3.	35	27	27	48
4.		40	35	25
5.	40	29	29	48
6.	45	30	30	50
7.	50	31	31	52

Out of the above dimensions concrete association of India has advocated the dimensions of farma as 40 cms long 35 cms wide and 25 cms deep. The farma is shown in Fig. 9.1.

Some authors have suggested the dimensions of gauge boxes as shown in Table 9.3 below. They kept the length and height of boxes same and varied width for various volumes.

Table 9.3. Volume of various gauge boxes

S. No.	*Volume inlitres*	*Length in cms*	*Height in cms*	*Width in cms*
1.	20	33.3	30	20
2.	25	33.3	30	25
3.	30	33.3	30	30
4.	35	33.3	30	35
5.	40	33.3	30	40
6.	45	33.3	30	45
7.	50	33.3	30	50

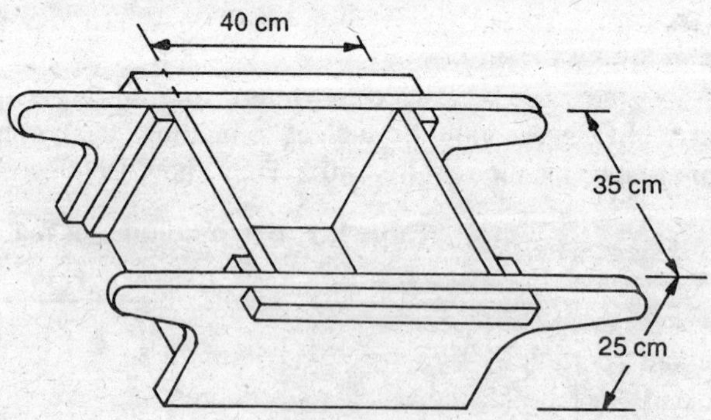

Fig. 9.1. Farma

The volume of each gauge should be written clearly with paint on the external face of the box.

The farma should be made of 3 cms thick prepared timber, so that it may give a good and strong farma. The joints should be tongued and grooved with the tongue on the inside of the box. This arrangement prevents dirt-getting due to the joint opening either due to shrinkage or rough handling. The faces of the joint should be painted with red lead in linseed oil before the farma is assembled. The inside face should be lined with sheet metal and the top edge of the box should be flush with sheet metal to keep a clean level edge for striking off. The handles should be shaped to provide an easy grip.

Measurement of water

Water usually measured by volume, provided the equipment is reliable, properly maintained and subject to calibration checks. The water contained in wet sand and coarse aggregate is difficult to measure accurately. The Value of this water can be assumed as suggested by IS 456-2000 shown in Table 9.4.

Surface moisture carried by aggregate

Surface moisture carried by aggregates is shown in Table 9.4 below as suggested by IS 456-2000.

Table 9.4. Approximate surface moisture of aggregates IS 456-2000

S. No.	*Aggregates*	*Approximate quantity of surface moisture*	
		Litre per m^3 of aggregate	*% of mass*
1.	Very wet sand	120	7.5
2.	Moderately wet sand	80	5.0
3.	Moist sand	40	2.5
4.	Moist gravel or crushed rock aggregate	20 – 40	1.25 – 2.5

9.2.2. Batching by weight

Now a days for the production of good concrete all materials are measured by weight. The mixes are incorporated with weight batching devices, such that the weight of any material placed in the loading skip is clearly shown on a dial gauge fitted in it. There are several forms of weigh batching equipment available covering a wide range of capacities to suit the jobs of different sizes. Fig 9.2 shows a concrete mixer with builtin weigh batching mechanism.

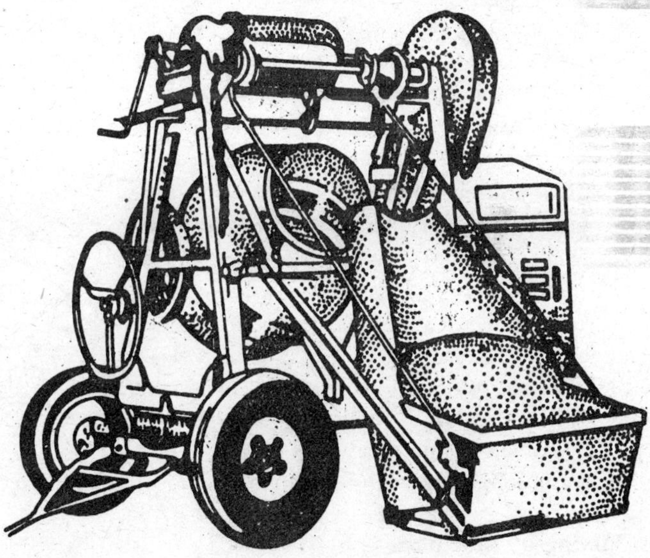

Fig. 9.2. Batching Mixer

9.3. MIXING OF CONCRETE

The object of mixing of concrete is to coat the surface of all aggregate particles with cement paste and to blend all ingredients of concrete into a uniform mass. Mixing of concrete can be done either by hand or by machines.

9.3.1. Hand mixing

Mixing of concrete by hand is less efficient than mixing by machines, but on small or unimportant works hand mixing is still practiced in India. For mixing concrete by hand, a water tight platform about 3.5 m long and at least 2 m wide should be provided. Concrete mixing by hand should never be done on ground, as earth and dirt dry grass, leaves etc. will mix with it. The mixing should always be done on a clean, and hard surface, such as concrete floor made by 1:3:6 or 1:4:8 mix or on a wooden floor or in a metal tray. The wooden platform 3.5 m long and 2.0 m wide is shown in Fig. 9.3. This platform is large enough to permit two men using shovels to work upon it at a time. The platform should be made of 3 to 5 cms thick planks, tongued and grooved so that the platform is rigid and joints water tight. A kerb on three sides should be provided to prevent water and cement draining away or material being showlled off the board.

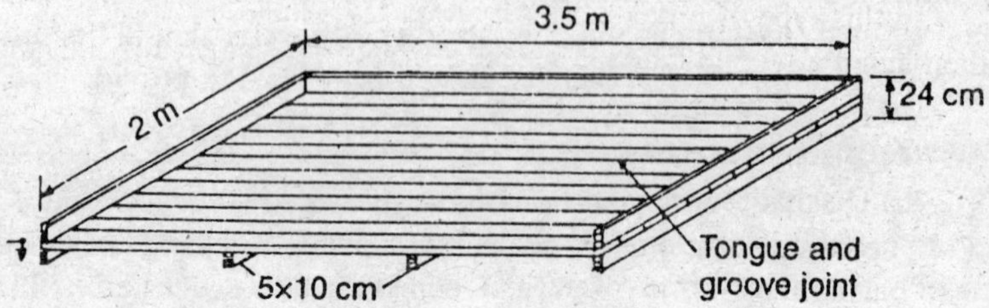

Fig. 9.3. Wooden platform

Operations

1. Spread out the measured quantity of sand (Fine aggregate) evenly on the mixing surface.
2. Dump the measured cement on the sand and distribute it evenly. In this case about 10% more cement is used than weight batching.
3. Mix sand and cement with powrah or shovel, turning the mixture over and over again till it is of even colour through out and free from streaks of brown and grey colour. Such streaks indicate non uniform mixture of sand and cement. The materials should be turned up side down at least three times. After mixing the sand and cement spread this mixture over the platform evenly once again.
4. On the top of this mixture, spread the measured quantity of coarse aggregate.
5. Mix again this mixture at least for three times by shoveling from the centre to the side, then back to the centre and again to the side. When it becomes a even mixture, make a heap of it with hollow at the centre.
6. In the hollow at the middle pour slowly about half to three quarter water of the total quantity of water required and mix it with the powrah. Add the remaining water slowly, turning the mixture over again until the colour and consistency are uniform throughout the pile.

For hand mixing, a steel mixing trough is a better arrangement than wooden platform, as it is easily portable from one job to another job. It also checks the loss of material while mixing. A steel mixing trough has proved economical than wooden platform due to its longer life. Fig 9.4 shows a steel trough.

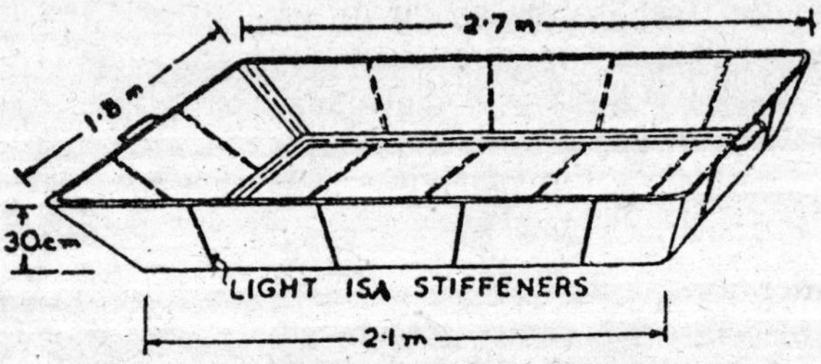

Fig. 9.4. Steel trough

9.3.2. Mixing by machines

Mixing of concrete by hand is expensive in labour in many countries, Thus mixing of concrete is done by machines. Concrete mixing by machines is more efficient and produces concrete of better quality at a faster rate and at less cost. As concrete mixers are manufactured in India itself, so concrete should be mixed by mixers.

9.4. TYPE OF MIXERS

Now a days concrete mixers of several types are available as follows:

1. Batch mixer   2. Continuous mixers

1. Batch mixer

In this type of mixers, after mixing one batch of materials, the mixed concrete has to be taken out and then again a second batch is put in. It has three distinct functions to perform.

(*a*) Filling material into the loading skip

(*b*) Discharging skip into mixing drum

(*c*) Discharging of concrete from the drum.

The completion of all these functions forms one cycle. In the field, usually concrete mixing is done with batch mixers of revolving drum type mixers. The batch mixers can further be sub divided as follows:

1. Tilting type mixers 2. Non tilting mixers
3. Open pan mixers.

1. Tilting type mixers. This class of mixers have a conical or bowl shaped drum with inside vanes, which revolve on an inclined axis. It is charged by means of loading skip, though the smaller size mixers are normally fed direct into the drum. Concrete is discharged by tilting the drum. Fig. 9.5 gives a diagrammatic sketch explaining its working. Fig 9.5 (*a*) shows filling material into loading skip; while Fig. 9.5 (*b*) shows discharging skip into mixing drum, while Fig. 9.5 (*c*) shows discharge of concrete from mixing drum.

(*a*) (*b*) (*c*)

Fig. 9.5. Tilting type mixers

The efficiency of the mixing operation depends on the details of design, but its discharge action is always good as all the concrete can be tipped out rapidly and in an unsegregated mass as soon as the drum is tilted. For this reason, tilting drum mixers are preferable for mixes of low workability and for those containing large size aggregate.

2. Non tilting mixers

In this class of mixers, the drum is cylindrical and always rotates about a horizontal axis i.e. its axis is always horizontal. In this case the material is charged by means of a cable operated loading skip or a charging hopper. Fig 9.6 shows a diagrammatic sketch of the non tilting type mixer. Fig 9.6 (*a*) shows filling material into loading skip, Fig 9.6 (*b*) shows discharging skip into mixing drum and Fig 9.6 (*c*) shows discharge of concrete. The discharge of concrete is obtained by either inserting a chute into the drum or by reversing the direction of rotation of the drum or by spiking of the drum.

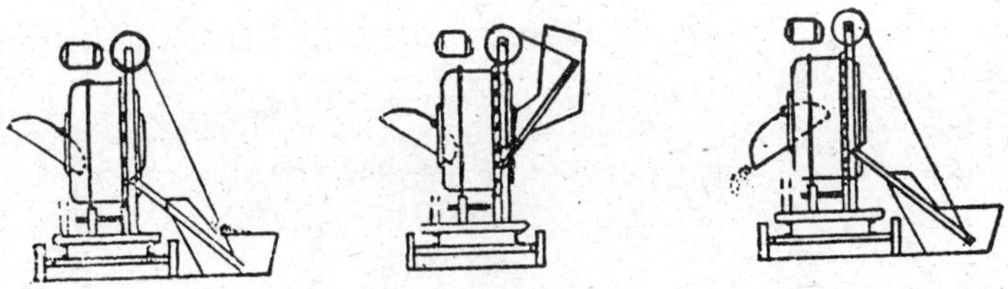

(*a*) (*b*) (*c*)

Fig. 9.6. Non tilting type mixers

Due to the slow rate of discharge concrete from non tilting type mixers, sometimes it is liable to segregation. In particular the large size of aggregate may tend to stay in the mixer so that the discharge starts as a mortar and ends as a collection of coated stones.

Pan mixers

This type of mixer is not mobile and is thus used either at a central mixing plant or at .large concrete project or at a precast factory or in a concrete laboratory. The mixer consists of a circular pan rotating about its vertical axis, with one or two star of paddles rotating about a vertical axis not coincident with the axis of the pan. Sometimes the pan is static and axis of the star travels along a circular path about the axis of the pan. In either case the relative movement between the paddles and the concrete is the same, and concrete, in every part is thoroughly mixed. Scraper blades prevent mortar sticking to the sides of the pan and the height of paddles can be adjusted to prevent a permanent coating of mortar forming on the bottom of the pan.

Pan mixers are efficient with stiff and cohessive mixes and thus are useful for precast factories. They are also suitable for mixing small quantities of concrete due to scrapping arrangements, smaller pan mixers of 40 lit capacity can be used in the laboratory. For discharge, such mixers have to be lifted physically, where as in big mixers there is one gate in the bottom covered with a gate, through which concrete is taken out.

Continuous mixers

These mixers do not require separate batching plant. They are designed to feed materials into the drum at rates related to the mix proportions required. The drum, which is mounted horizontally, consists of a long cylinder open at both ends and with internal blades of spiral shape so that they move the materials forward as the drum rotates. The materials are fed in by means of spiral conveyers and bucket elevators, the proportions are determined by the speed of the separate spirals. In case of continuous mixers, the proportions of materials is done on the basis of volume batching. Thus concrete obtained by the mixer has less strength than obtained from batch mixers. Further control oh mixing of ingredients in continuous mixer is also difficult. These mixers are used on big concrete projects such as construction of dam etc.

9.5. SIZE OF THE MIXER

The size of the mixer is described by the volume of concrete after compaction. Previously the volume of the unmixed ingredients in a loose state was also included in its description. The latter may be upto 50% greater than compacted volume. Mixers are made in a variety of sizes from 40 liters for laboratory use upto 13 m^3. Capacity upto 10% over load of the mixer, is considered harmless. The actual size depends upon the nature and size. of work. The capacity of mixers usually is given in cubic metres or litres in M.K.S units and in cubic feet in F.P.S. units. As the mixed concrete is more dense than its ingredients, for a particular quantity of concrete, the quantity of ingredients to be used is more by about 50%. Thus the capacity of mixers in M.K.S. units is described as 140/100, 200/140, 280/200, 400/280, and 600/400, which shows that to obtain 100 litre mixed concrete 140 litres ingredients should be Used. Numerator shows the quantity of unmixed ingredients while denominator shows the quantity of mixed concrete. Following Table 9.5 gives the capacity of mixers and their hourly output.

Table 9.5. Capacity of mixers and their hourly output

S. No.	*Capacity of mixer in M.K.S. units*	*Quantity of concrete prepared per hour*
1.	140/1000 litre	1890 litres
2.	200/140 litre	2646 litres
3.	280/200 litre	3780 litres
4.	400/280 litre	5670 litres
5.	600/400 litre	7560 litres

According to I.S. 1791-1961, the batch mixers are designated as follows:

Tilting drum type — 100 T, 140 T, 200 T

Non-tilting type — 140 NT, 200 NT, 280 NT, 400 NT and 800 NT etc.

The equivalent capacity in cubic feet is as follow:

F.P.S. units — $3\frac{1}{2}$, 5, 7, 10, 14, 28 ft.^{3}

100, 140, 200, 280, 400. 800 litres

The above figures are *nominal* mixed batched capacities. However Mixers can be used to mix 10% higher quantities. 200 litres capacity mixer is the most popular,size of the mixers. For any given size of mixer, it is necessary to know the number of 50 kg bags of cement which will produce a batch of concrete of given proportions. This information is given in Table 9.6 below.

Table 9.6. No. of cement bags per batch

Nominal proportion of mix by volume	*No. of 50 kg bags of cement to produce batch of concrete of suitable size for mixers of different capacities*				
	100 lit. $(5\frac{1}{2}/3\frac{1}{2})$	*200 lit. (10/7)*	*280 lit (14/10)*	*400 lit. (22/14)*	*800 lit. (45/28)*
1 : 1.5 : 3	0.75	1.5	2.5	3.5	6.5
1 : 2 : 3	0.75	1.5	2.0	3.0	6.0
1 : 2 : 4	0.5	1.0	1.5	2.5	5.5
1 : 2.5 : 5	0.5	1.0	1.5	2.0	4.5
1 : 3 : 5	0.5	1.0	1.5	2.0	4.0
1 : 3 : 6	0.5	0.75	1.0	1.5	3.0
1 : 4 : 8	—	0.5	0.75	1.5	3.0

9.6. MIXING TIME

On a site it is often a tendency to mix concrete as rapidly as possible, therefore it is important to know the minimum mixing time necessary to produce a concrete of uniform consistency and composition to give satisfactory strength. Actually the time of mixing of concrete varies with the size and type of mixer. Strictly speaking, it is not the mixing time but the number of revolutions of the mixer that is the criterion of adequate mixing. Generally about 20 revolutions are sufficient for adequate mixing. Since an optimum speed of rotation is recommended by the manufacturers of the mixer, hence the number of revolutions and time of mixing are inter dependent The variation in uniformity with mixing time based on Shalon's work is shown in Fig. 9.7. From the study of this figure, it will be seen that mixing for less than 1 minute to $1\frac{1}{4}$ minute produces an appreciable more variable concrete, but mixing beyond these values results in no significant improvement in uniformity. Thus mixing time of 2 minutes is quite reasanable.

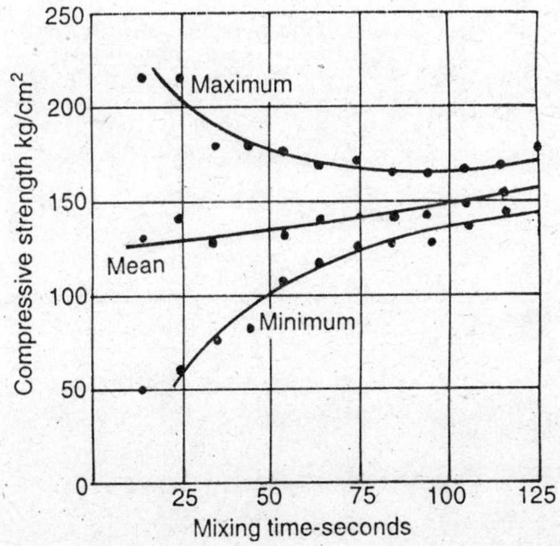

Fig. 9.7. Effect of mixing time on strength of concrete

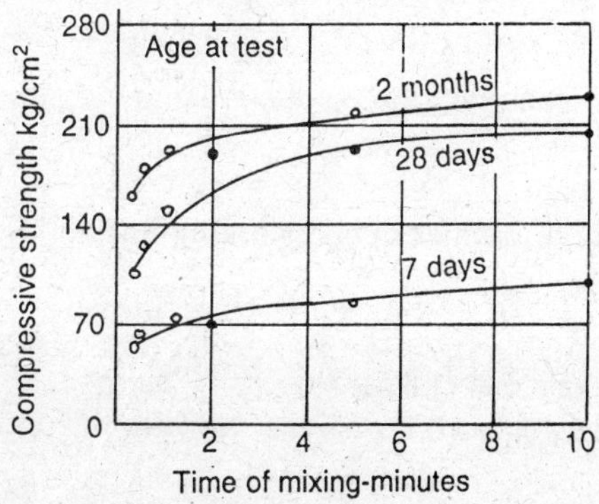

Fig. 9.8. Increase in strength with mixing time

The average strength of concrete also increases with an increase in mixing time as shown in Fig. 9.8 based on Abram's work. From the study of Fig. 9.8 it will be seen that the rate of increase of strength falls rapidly beyond about one minute mixing and the increase in strength is not large. Beyond 2 minutes mixing there is insignificant gain in strength, some times even a slight decrease in strength has been observed. Within the first minute, the influence of mixing time on strength is of considerable importance. Increasing the time of mixing from 30 seconds to 1 minute Shalon found significant increase in strength and for a given required strength a saving of 30 kg cement per cubic metre of concrete was possible. However mixing for prolonged period causes segregation. As mentioned above, the exact value of the minimum mixing time depends upon the type and size of the mixer. The values of mixing time as recommended by different Institutions and Bureaus are shown in Table 9.7. below.

Table 9.7. Mixing time

S. No.	*Capacity of mixer*		*Mixing time in minutes*		*As per I.S.*	
	m^3	*yd^3*	*Bureau of reclamation*	*American Concrete Institution and ASTM Standard*	*Capacity of mixer m^3*	*Time of mixing as per I.S. 4923 in minutes*
1.	0.8	1	1.5	1.0	upto 2 m^3	1.5
2.	1.5	2	1.5	1.25	upto 3 m^3	2.0
3.	2.3	3	2	1.5	upto 4 m^3	2.5
4.	3.1	4	2.5	1.75	—	—
5.	3.8	5	2.75	2.0	—	—
6.	4.6	6	3	2.25	—	—
7.	7.6	10	—	3.25	—	—

The mixing time is reckoned from the time when all the solid materials have been put in the mixer and all the water has been added not latter than one quarter of the mixing time has elapsed.

9.7. OUT PUT OF MIXER

The output of a concrete mixer depends upon the capacity of the mixer and the concrete mix adopted. However the output per hour is also affected by the length of mixing period and the time taken to charge and discharge the drum *i.e.* time of mixing cycle. The delays that arise due to one cause or the other even under normal circumstances invariably give an considerably less output than given by the manufacturers.

Let us take the case of 200 litre capacity mixer. The time taken in mixing one batch will be as follows:

Raising skip and loading ingredients into the drum = 0.5 mint.
Adding water and mixing in drum = 1.5 mint.
(During this time the skip is being lowered and recharged)
Discharging drum and completing loading of skip = 1.0 mint.
Total time = 3.0 mint.

No of batches in one working hour $= \frac{60}{3} = 20$ batches.

In a shift of 8 hours working, there will be only 7 hours of effective mixing time available.

So the batches produced in one day $= 20 \times 7 = 140$ batches.

If each batch represents 140 litre of wet concrete, then output per day

$= 140 \times 140 = 196000$ litres or 19.6 m^3 per day

For mixers having capacity more than 800 litres Orchard has suggested the output as

$= K \times$ nominal capacity of mixer

where,

$K = 0.65$ for tilting drum mixers, and

$K = 0.72$ for non-tilting mixers.

9.8. FEEDING THE INGREDIENTS

No general rules on the feeding of ingredients into the mixer can be given as they depend upon the properties of the mix and the mixer. Generally a small amount of water should be fed first, followed by all the solid materials, preferably fed uniformly and simultaneously into the mixer. If possible greater part of water should also be fed during the same time, remainder of the water may be added after the solids. I.S. 516-1959 has suggested the following sequence of feeding the ingredients.

1. Power operated mixer

(*a*) Water
(*b*) Half coarse aggregate
(*c*) Fine aggregate
(*d*) Cement
(*e*) Remaining aggregate

2. Hand Operated mixer

(*a*) Coarse aggregate
(*b*) Fine aggregate
(*c*) Cement
(*d*) Water

9.9. CHECKING OF MIXER

Before commencing operating mixer, following points should be attended.

1. The mixer should be placed on the firm and level ground.
2. The speed of the mixer should be kept 20 revolutions per minutes as given by manufacturers. The speed should be checked.
3. If the water is fed from tanks incorporated in the mixer, the water controlling device should be checked, so that correct amount of water may be added to the mix.
4. Inspect the engine, check oil, cooling water, petrol etc.
5. The engine should be allowed to run for few minutes to warm up.
6. Examine the mixer drum and blades and sec that they are clean and free from adhering lumps or concrete.
7. Also examine that all transporting machines are in working order.
8. While loading the skip, the ingredients should be put in the following order.

(*a*) Coarse aggregate (*b*) Fine aggregate (*c*) Cement.

While these materials are put into the drum, the reverse order will follow and the coarse aggregate will fall in the last. It will help to push any sand or cement which might have adhered to the mouth of the skip.

9.10. MAINTENANCE OF MIXER

1. Before closing down a shift for the day or in lunch break, the mixer should not be left loaded with concrete mix and the interior of the drum and blades should be flushed clean of all adhering mortar or concrete. If it is not cleaned, the age and efficiency of the mixer will be affected to a great extent. The quality of concrete also will be affected as the adhered part of mortar or concrete may mix with the green concrete which will affect its setting and strength. The cheapest and simplest method of cleaning the mixer is, that after emptying it, water, coarser pieces of coarse aggregate or brick bats are put in the drum and it is run for 10 revolutions and the water thrown out by emptying it. If need be, this process may be repeated.
2. The interior face of the drum of mixer, blades surface etc. should be greased or oiled.
3. The outer surface of the mixer should also be kept clean and free from adhering mortar or concrete.

4. If the mixer is run by a petrol engine, then the rope and belt should be checked, lest it may break and cause accident.
5. Wash the machine every day using a hose pipe and grease or oil all parts of the mixer.
6. When the mixer is working at one place for a long time, its wheel and axles should not be allowed to be burried into the accumulated materials.
7. To speed the discharge of adhering sand and cement, the loading skip should not be allowed hitting or hammering. It will shorten its life and impair its action.
8. Engine should be attended every day and the fuel and cooling water is replenished.

QUESTIONS

1. What do you under stand by batching of concrete ? How it affects the strength of concrete ?
2. In how many ways the concrete batching can be done? Explain fully. How the batching of ordinary concrete is done?
3. What are the advantages of batching by weight as compared to batching by volume ?
4. What types of concrete mixers are in common use ?
5. Explain the process of hand mixing of concrete.
6. How does the time of mixing affect the strength of concrete ?
7. What time of mixing is usually recommended ?
8. Write a short note on the maintenance of the mixer.
9. How the capacity of a batch mixer is designated ?

OBJECTIVE TYPE QUESTIONS

1. Which of the following statements is false?
   (*a*) The correct measurement of different concrete ingredients is called batching.
   (*b*) Poor batching is responsible for more variation in the quality of concrete than any other factor.
   (*c*) Batching has no role on the quality of concrete mix.
   (*d*) Good control can minimise to some extent the effect of poor batching.
2. Which of the following statements is false?
   (*a*) Batching operation is very important in the production of good concrete
   (*b*) Batching can be done by volume or weight basis.
   (*c*) In volume batching cement can be taken by volume and aggregate by weight.
   (*d*) Volume batching is superior to weight batching.
3. In volume batching the volume of one bag of cement of 50 kg is taken as
   (*a*) 37.5 litres (*b*) 33.2 litres
   (*c*) 35 litres (*d*) 40 litres
4. As per I.S. 456-2000 the surface moisture of very wet sand may be taken as % of the mass of sand
   (*a*) 10% (*b*) 15%
   (*c*) 18% (*d*) 7.5%
5. As per I.S. 456-2000 the surface moisture for moderatly wet sand may be taken % of the sand
   (*a*) 7.5% (*b*) 9.0%
   (*c*) 5.0% (*d*) 2%
6. As per IS 456-2000, the surface moisture of coarse aggregate may be taken % of gravel
   (*a*) 5.5% (*b*) 2.5%
   (*c*) 6.5% (*d*) 3.75%
7. Which one is not the object of mixing of concrete
   (*a*) To coat the surface of all aggregate particles with cement paste
   (*b*) To blend all particles of concrete into a uniform mass
   (*c*) To produce concrete of uniform colour and grading
   (*d*) To produce honey combed concrete
8. The choice of proper batching system depends upon

(*a*) Required production rate (*b*) Size of the job
(*c*) Availability of resources (*d*) Required standard of batching performance
(*e*) All the above

9. In weight batching the weight of surface moisture of coarse aggregate
   (*a*) Must be taken into account
   (*b*) It can be ignored
   (*c*) May or may not be taken into the account depending upon the size of job
   (*d*) It is taken into account by drying the aggregate
10. In the batching of materials, the ingredients should be measured upto a accuracy of
    (*a*) ± 1.5% (*b*) ± 2.5%
    (*c*) ± 3.0% (*d*) ± 5.0%
11. A mobile mixing plant is particularly useful
    (*a*) As it can also be used for carrying the materials
    (*b*) As it can be fixed close the site of concrete work
    (*c*) Where concrete is required to be laid over a larger area
    (*d*) It is not useful at all
12. Normally mixers are classified on the basis of
    (*a*) Number of drums
    (*b*) The capacity of batch handling
    (*c*) Total volume of concrete produced per day
    (*d*) No. of wheels provided in the mixer
    (*e*) Technique of discharging the mixed concrete.
13. The capacity of a concrete mixer is expressed in terms of
    (*a*) Volume of concrete mix produced per batch
    (*b*) Total volume of concrete produced per day
    (*c*) Weight of aggregate used per batch
    (*d*) Total volume of concrete handled per hour
14. Which of the following statements is false?
    (*a*) In volume batching it is advisable to set volume in terms of a full bag of cement
    (*b*) In volume batching allowance for moisture content for sand should be made
    (*c*) While filling the farma or box, no compaction should be allowed
    (*d*) Volume batching is adopted for small jobs
    (*e*) Non of the above
15. Which of the following statements is false?
    (*a*) The size of the mixer is designated by its handling capacity in litres
    (*b*) In the tilting type mixers the drum is tilted for discharging the concrete
    (*c*) The efficiency of the mixing operation depends upon the shape and design of vanes fixed in the drum.
    (*d*) A non tilting mixer rotates about a horizontal axis and can not be tilted.
    (*e*) Most of the mixers can be loaded upto 17% extra load than their capacity with out any loss of efficiency.
16. A pan mixer having a circular plan and rotating about a vertical axis is suitable as
    (*a*) A mobile mixer (*b*) A controled mixing plant
    (*c*) For ready made mixed concrete (*d*) For all the purposes
17. A mixer designated as 280 NT indicates that
    (*a*) Its nominal mix batch capacity is 280 litres
    (*b*) It is a non tilted type mixer
    (*c*) It is a non tilting type mixer requiring 280 revolution for proper mixing
    (*d*) All the above
18. Which of the following statements is correct?
    (*a*) Mixing time is the time required to produce a uniform concrete
    (*b*) It is reckoned from the time when all the solid ingredients have been put into the mixer.
    (*c*) It is inter dependent with the number of revolutions.
    (*d*) It may be ignored in favour of revolutions.

(*e*) All the above

19. As per IS 4923, the mixing time of a mix in a mixer upto 3 m^3 capacity should be
    (*a*) 60 seconds (*b*) 90 seconds
    (*c*) 120 seconds (*d*) 300 seconds
20. Which of the following statements is false?
    (*a*) The mixing time of concrete in a mixer varies with the size and type of mixer
    (*b*) For adequate mixing of concrete ingredients number of revolutions is the main criterion.
    (*c*) Number of revolution and time of mixing of a concrete mix are interdependent
    (*d*) Mixing time has no influence on the quality of concrete mix.
21. Which of the following statements is/are false?
    (*a*) A 400-280 T mixer indicates that 400 litres loose ingredients produce 280 litre mixed concrete
    (*b*) To produce 280 litres of concrete, the mixer needs 400 revolutions
    (*c*) The mixer is tilting type
    (*d*) It can be tilted upto 45° only
    (*e*) It can be revolved at 360° at its axis

Answers

1. (*c*)	6. (*b*)	11. (*c*)	16. (*b*)	21. (*b, d*)
2. (*c, d*)	7. (*d*)	12. (*e*)	17. (*a, b*)	
3. (*c*)	8. (*e*)	13. (*a*)	18. (*e*)	
4. (*d*)	9. (*a*)	14. (*e*)	19. (*c*)	
5. (*c*)	10. (*c*)	15. (*e*)	20. (*d*)	

10

Transportation and Placing of Concrete

10.1. INTRODUCTION

After mixing, concrete should be transported and placed at site as quickly as possible with out segregation, drying, etc. Hence transportation of fresh concrete is very important operation. Depending upon the type of work and equipment available various methods of transporting of concrete can be employed. The method selected should be suitable for use with the consistency of concrete employed.

It is important that the concrete be handled without segregation of the constituent materials. This condition may easily occur if special attention is not given to its prevention. Segregation occurs because concrete is not a homogenous combination, but a mixture of materials differing in size and specific gravity. Thus as soon as the concrete is discharged from the mixer, internal as well as external forces start acting to separate the dissimilar constituents. If over wet concrete is confined in restricting forms, the coarser and heavier particles tend to settle and finer and lighter materials tend to rise.

Thus the equipment for conveying concrete from mixer to form should be such as to result in uniform concrete of the desired consistency at the form. The method of conveying should not require wetter concrete than is required at form for placing nor it should produce segregation or excessive drying or stiffening etc.

To avoid segregation, when concrete is to be transferred from one conveyance to another, use of hoppers, baffles and short vertical drops should be used through a pipe to the centre of the receiving container as shown in Fig. 10.1. This belief is not correct that segregation produced during conveyance can be rectified by compaction. Segregation should be prevented rather than corrected after its occurrence. Fig. 10.1 shows correct and incorrect method of filling hoppers or buckets. Fig. 10.2 shows the control of separation of concrete at the end of conveyer belts, while Fig. 10.3 shows control of separation at the end of chutes. In this case a 60 cms long pipe is provided at the end of the chute. This Fig. 10.3 shows the correct and

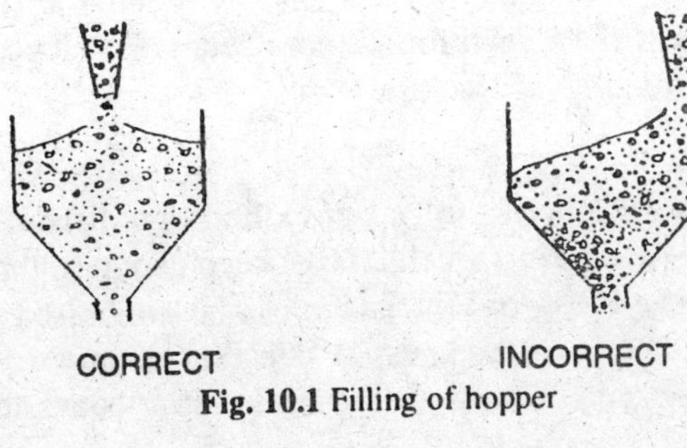

Fig. 10.1 Filling of hopper

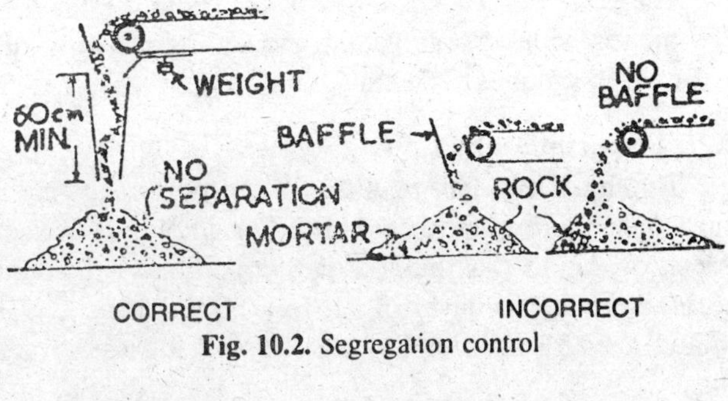

Fig. 10.2. Segregation control

incorrect methods of concrete discharge. Fig. 10.4 shows placing of concrete on a sloping surface. A baffle and drop at the end of chute will avoid separation and concrete remains on slope.

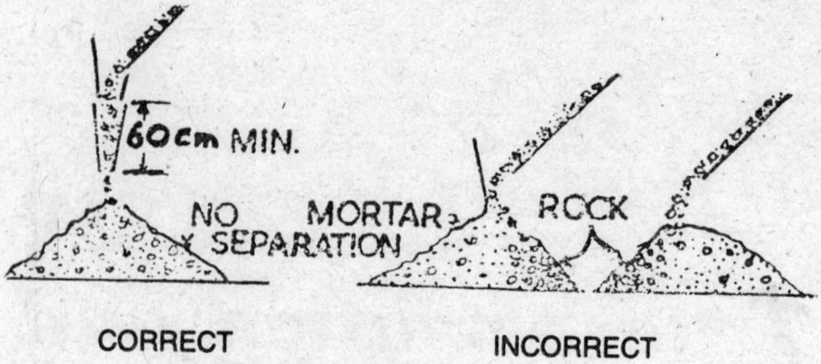

Fig. 10.3. Discharge of concrete

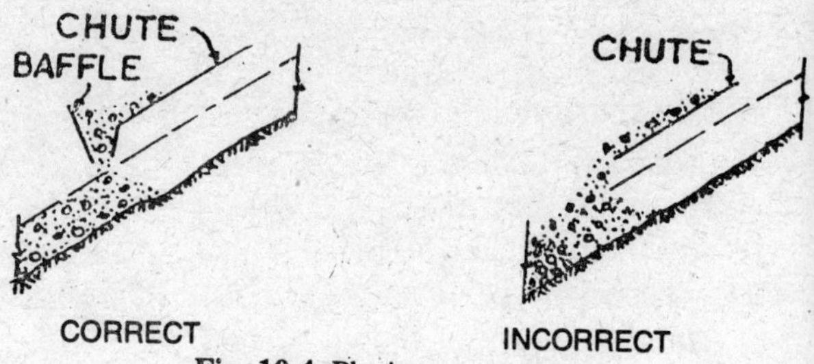

Fig. 10.4. Placing concrete

10.2. METHOD OF CONVEYANCE

For moving concrete from mixer to the form following methods may be employed.

1. Pan method
2. Wheel barrows
3. Dumpers
4. Lorries
5. Mono rail transporters
6. Hoists
7. Crane
8. Skips and buckets
9. Chutes
10. Conveyer belts
11. Pneumatic pressure equipment
12. Pumps.

1. Pan method

This method of concrete transportation can be employed for small jobs where quantity of concrete required is small and labour is available at cheap rates in abundance.

This method can also be employed at site where other modes of transportation is not feasible along narrow lanes. In this method labourer carry concrete on their head in iron pans. The main disadvantage of this method is that the progress of work is slow. It is costly also.

2. Transportation by wheel barrows

For small works, steel wheel barrows with pneumatic tyres can be used for moderate distances. The wheel barrows can be used on hard surface tracks. They can also be used where track can be prepared by laying planks. The capacity of a wheel barrow varies from 70 litres to 80 litres. However hand cart with two wheels having larger capacity can also be used, but pulling such carts in loose soils is difficult. In more uneven level areas concrete transported by these barrows are liable to segregation.

(2-b) Power barrows. The power driven wheel barrows can be used upto 350 meter distances on unlevelled surface. With the help of these barrows about 30 batches per hour can be lifted from the mixer. However in sandy soils these barrows can not be used.

3. Transportation by Dumpers and trucks

These are special types of trucks. These dumpers have been found suitable to transport concrete upto 350 metres without segregation and setting. The use of dumpers have been found more suitable on loose and uneven grounds. The capacity of a dumper is 2 to 3 m^3 while that of trucks is 4 m^3.

4. Transportation by tipping lorries

Tipping lorries can be used to transport concrete upto 5 km. Concrete to be transported to a distance more than 350 m should contain lesser amount of water, because there is likelihood of segregation in the transition due to shaking and bad condition of the road etc. The effect of segregation can be minimised by keeping the thicker layer of concrete in the lorry. Usually the height or thickness of concrete in the lorry should not be less than 40 cms. Tipping lorries are generally used for transporting ready made concrete discussed in the following paragraph in this Chapter. These lorries have arrangements for receiving, loading and discharging arrangements. With the help of these lorries the mix is discharged directly into the structure. These lorries are used for the transport of concrete for the construction of roads, air fields and pavements, dams, tunnels and canal lining etc.

5. Transportation by Monorail and Jubilee trucks

Monorail trucks are very convient for use with small and medium size mixing plants. Their main advantage is that they can be used across difficult and narrow sites with out requiring much space. The rail is readily fixed and can be moved to new positions as the job proceeds. Their main disadvantage is that they need a special type of rail line, which is very costly. However they can be used in all types of terrain.

Jubilee Trucks are special type of trucks which can be used to transport concrete through soft and difficult terrain with out much difficulty.

6. Transportation-by belt Conveyer

Belt conveyers are available in convenient forms which allow the movement of concrete easily to different parts at the site. This method is used when concrete is required to be transported continuously. This method is most suitable for concreting in hot-climate at a distance of 250 m to. 500 m from the mixing site. This method can also be used to carry concrete up slopes less than 30°. This method has proved very useful at places where other mode of transportation of concrete is not feasible.

Concrete to be transported by belt conveyer should not be very wet. The slump of the concrete should not be more than 9 cms in any case. However slump of 6 cms is quite sufficient.

The belt used has a rubber covering of 60 cms width. The speed of conveyer should not be more than 1 m per second. The line of conveys should not have any break in the plan. As stated above, the inclination of the conveyer should not be more than 30° in any case. However for different slumps, following inclinations have been suggested as a guide.

Table 10.1

S. No.	*Slump*	*Degrees of inclination*
1.	4 cm	12° – 18°
2.	4 – 6 cm	10° – 15°

Flat belts are used only upto 20 m distances. For larger distances trough shaped belts are used. While concrete is unloaded or transferred from one part of the conveyer to other, precaution to avoid segregation should be adopted as shown in Fig. 10.2.

7. Transport-by hoist

Now a days hoists are more frequently used to transport concrete at building sites upto a height of 150 m. The capacity of hoist usually adopted is 200 lit., 340 lit. or 510 lit. These hoist work at a speed of 75 meter per minute.

8. Transport-by crane

When cranes are used to transport concrete a suitable bucket or skip is required. One of the type of skip is known as *Lay back* skip. It is designed to fall on its back when lowered to the ground and it can be filled from a low level mixer discharge. When it is raised, it is pulled up right, and can discharge its contents through a gate at its lower end. For larger batches dump buckets arc used. Usually these buckets are cylindrical. Usually the capacity of such skips is about 115 lit. While using crane, care should be taken that concrete is not thrown from an excessive height, so that form work may not be damaged.

9. Transportation of concrete by elevating tower and chutes

This system of concrete transportation is suitable for large dams. In this system the concrete is filled at the head of deep chutes, by buckets in a central tower. From this point, concrete reaches at the required place through these chutes. The height of tower should not be higher than 170 m and the capacity of buckets should not be more than 1.3 m^3. Concrete to be used by this method should be sufficiently fluid. The slump of concrete should be more than 5.0 cms. For less fluid concrete, vibrators may be used on chutes to move the concrete. This method of concrete transportation has proved very useful when the strength of the concrete is not very important.

10. Transportation from chutes

Usually chutes are employed for transporting concrete from ground level to a lower level. The chute section should be lined with metal sheet and the slope of full length should be same. It should be not flatter than 1 vertical and 2.5 horizontal. The lay out of the chute should be such that concrete will be able to slide with out segregation as a compact mass.

Though this method is not good method for concrete transporting, yet it is adopted when the movement of labour can not be allowed due to lack of space or due to fear of disturbance to the reinforcement etc..

11. Transport of concrete by over head cable ways

In this system, concrete is transported by buckets by stretching cables on poles situated on the banks of the valley. This system is useful for large dams only.

With the help of this system, other construction material and equipment also can be transported. The capacity of buckets may be upto 6 m^3. The buckets arc open at the bottom with gates.

10.3. READY MIXED CONCRETE

Concrete available for placing from a central plant is known as *ready mixed concrete or pre mixed concrete.*

10.3.1. Advantages of ready mixed concrete

Following arc the advantages of ready mixed concrete:

1. This type of concrete is particularly useful on congested sites.
2. For road construction where little space is available for mixing plant and for stocking aggregate etc.
3. Ready mixed concrete can be made under better control than on site. Actually a factory type control on all operations is possible on the central mixing plant. This is the greatest advantage of ready mixed concrete.

   Ready-made concrete can be considered as a factory made product almost comparable with steel. Hence a great deal of uncertainty and variability associated with the production of concrete on many sites is removed.
4. The use of ready mixed concrete is advantageous when only small quantities of concrete is required or concrete is to be placed at intervals.

10.3.2. Disadvantages

The main disadvantage of ready mixed concrete is its high cost. It is costlier by about 10 to 15% than concrete mixed at site.

10.4. TYPE OF READY MIX CONCRETE

Ready mix concrete can be classified into two groups as follows:

1. Central mixed concrete
2. Transit mixed or truck mixed concrete.

1. Central mixed concrete. In this case the mixing is done at a central plant and the mixed concrete is transported in a special type of truck known as an *agitator truck.* The truck (agitator truck) revolves slowly while moving. The agitating container is conical in shape having smaller blades than mixer. The capacity of the container is 1.25 m^3 to 2.0 m^3. However the height of this container is more than a mixer. The container is put upright in the truck and to check the evaporation of water from the concrete an air tight stopper is placed on the top of the container.

The segregation and stiffencing of concrete is checked by revolving the container. The revolving of the container is also done by the engine of the truck. The rate of revolving of the container depends upon the speed of the lorry varying 2 to 6 revolutions per minutes. However 2 to 3 revolution per minute are quite sufficient.

10.4.1. Advantages of agitating trucks

1. To revolve the container, very less amount of power is needed.
2. During even in one hour journey, no ill effect on the properties of concrete is developed.

10.4.2. Disadvantage

The main disadvantage of this method is that these agitating trucks can not be used for any other purpose. Hence this method is uneconomical.

10.5. TRANSIT MIXED CONCRETE

In this method the materials are batched at a central plant and the dry mix is put in mixers kept in trucks. The mix is mixed either during transit to the site or immediately prior to the concrete being discharged at the site. The speed of rotation is between 4 to 16 revolutions per minute. ASTM has laid down the limit of 300 revolution for both agitating and mixing, and concrete must be laid within 90 minutes of mixing. The capacity of mixer may vary from 0.75 m^3 to 4.5 m^3.

10.5.1. Advantages

1. Transit mixing permits a longer haul and is less vulnerable in case of delay.
2. As the water is added to mix near the site of work, dislocation of the work does not take place
3. The discharge of concrete is done by reversing the direction of the revolving mixer rather than tipping the truck.
4. These mixers have a small revolving tubing, which can spread the concrete on a sufficient wide area. This operation makes the concrete spreading operation economical.

10.5.2. Disadvantages

1. Transportation by this method is limited to an area with in a radius of 9 to 15 km.
2. These trucks can be used only for this purpose.
3. The moist aggregate should not remain in contact with cement for more than 90 minutes.

Note. The agitating differs from mixing solely by the speed of rotation of the mixer. The agitating speed is between 2 and 6 revolutions per minute, where as mixing speed varies from 4 to 16 revolution per minute. It may be noted that the speed of mixing affects the rate of stiffening, while the total number of revolution controls the uniformity of mixing.

10.6. TRANSPORTATION OF CONCRETE BY PUMPS

Transport of concrete by means of pumps has been found very useful in the following circumstances.

1. At congested sites where mixing plant can not be taken close to the point of placing concrete.
2. At sites where storing of aggregate is not possible due to non availability of space.
3. Concrete by this method can be delivered to points over a wide area otherwise not easily accessible.
4. This mode of transportation has been found very useful for tunnel lining, large mass concrete structures, densely reinforced concrete structures, etc.
5. This method is more economical where large quantities of concrete is required.

Pumped concrete is free from segregation. Pumping delivers the concrete direct from the mixer to the form and thus avoids the double handling. Placing can proceed at the rate of the out put of the mixer and is not held back by the limitations of transporting and placing equipment etc.

Pumping of concrete is economical if the quantity of concrete required is more than about 1150 m^3 or uninterrupted supply of concrete is needed over a long period as at the beginning of each period of pumping, the pipes have to be lubricated by mortar (at the rate of about 0.25 m^3 per 1000 m length of 150 mm diameter pipe) and also at the end of the operation considerable effort is needed for cleaning the pipes.

10.6.1. Pumping system

The pumping system consists of the following components.

1. Hopper. Concrete mixed in the mixer is discharged into this hopper, from where it is discharged at the site by the pump through pipe Fig. 10.5.

2. Pump. Now a days several types of pumps such as direct acting, horizontal piston type with semi-rotary valves set etc. are available. In Fig. 10.5 single cylinder type reciprocating pump is shown. The pump is consisted of the following component parts.

(*a*) Inlet valve
(*b*) Outlet valve
(*c*) Piston
(*d*) Rubber cup
(*e*) Pipe.

10.6.2. Working

After mixing, the concrete is discharged into the hopper, and pump started. In the suction stroke, the inlet valve is open as shown in Fig. 10.5 (*a*) and delivery valve remains closed. During delivery stroke inlet valve closes and delivery valve opens as shown in Fig. 10.5 (*b*). As shown in the Fig., the diameter of the piston is some what less than the diameter of the cylinder. At the working end of the piston, rubber cups are attached, which check the wastage in the cylinder. At the other end, this piston works in bushes. These bushes are lubricated by the water flowing through empty space between the cylinder and the piston. This water also dissolves the cement paste leaking through rubber cups. Hence the danger of setting the cement

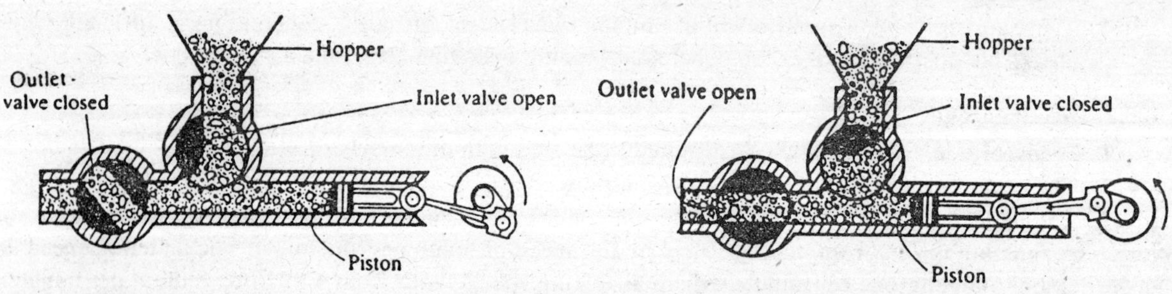

(*a*) Delivery stroke (*b*) Suction stroke

Fig. 10.5. Concrete pumping system

paste is reduced. In this way the pump is kept safe from damage. The whole assembly is set in such a way that every part of it can be opened and inspected as per need and the damaged part replaced.

10.6.3. Capacity

Usually concrete can be pumped along a straight and level pipe line for a distance of about 300 to 450 m and upto 40 m vertical height using a single pump. Any rise of 30 cms is equivalent to 2.4 m on the level ground and a right angled bend is equivalent to about 12 m. Hence for a bend of 90° a horizontal distance of 12 m and for $22\frac{1}{2}^\circ$ bend 3 m horizontal distance should be reduced. No sharp bends should be attached in a concrete pipe line. In between bends straight pipe should be attached.

Pipe line

Pipe lines for concrete are usually made of mild steel tubes in 3 m sections with special joints for quick assembly and release. Bends and short lengths are also available. The size of pipes varies from 11.25 cms to 20 cms inside diameter. The diameter of pipe should be at least three times the maximum size of aggregate used.

10.7. SQUEEZE TYPE CONCRETE PUMP

In recent times much improvements and refinements have been incorporated in the modern concrete pumps. During 1963 squeeze type concrete pump was developed in U.S.A. In this pump. Concrete placed in a collecting hopper is fed into the flexible pipe by rotating blades. The flexible pipe is connected to the pumping chamber. In the pumping chamber a vacuum of about 600 mm of mercury is created. This vacuum ensures the shape of the pipe cylindrical except when squeezed by the roller. This ensures the continuous flow of concrete. Two rotating rollers progressively squeeze the flexible pipe and move the concrete into the delivery pipe Fig. 10.6 shows the action of a squeeze pump. Often squeeze pumps are lorry mounted and concrete may be delivered through a folding boom.

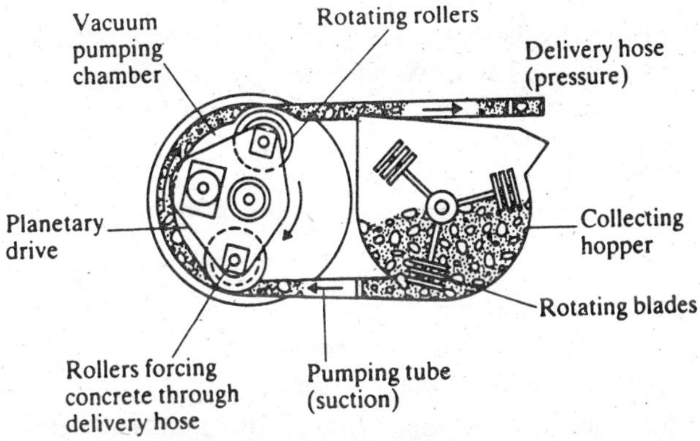

Fig. 10.6. Squeeze type pump

Most widely used modern pump is the hydraulic piston pump. Though the specifications of modern and original mechanically driven pumps differ, but the concept of working is the same. As stated earlier also a concrete pump consists of three parts namely

(*a*) Concrete receiving hopper (*b*) Value system
(*c*) Power transmitting system

10.8. TYPE OF MODERN CONCRETE PUMPS

There are three main type of concrete pumps. They are (1) Mobile, (2) Static or trailor, (3) Mortar or screed pump.

10.8.1. Type of Valves

The valve system is the most important part of any concrete pump. Following are the main type of valves.

(*a*) Squeeze type valves (*b*) Rotating or sliding gate valves
(*c*) Flapper valves (*d*) Hollow transfer tube valves
(*e*) Rock valves

Hollow transfer tube valves are most commonly used. Rock valve are also widely used valves.

Pipeline. Same as above.

10.8.2. Problems in pumping of concrete

The most common problem of pumping concrete is blockage. If the pump is mechanically sound, the failure of concrete to emerge at the end of the pipe line is called blockage. The increase in the pressure shown by the pressure gauge of the pump is the indication of the blockage of the pipe line. Most blockages take place or occur at the tapered sections of the pump end.

10.9. CAUSES OF BLOCKAGE

Generally blockages take place due to the following causes:

1. Un suitability of the concrete mix *i.e.* concrete mix is not designed properly.
2. Deficiencies in pipe line and joints.
3. Careless use of hose end.
4. Error of operator.

Some times use of admixtures, particularly accelerating admixture and high grade cement, high temperature may cause blockage. If continuous pumping is not done there are more chances of blockage.

If the pipe line is not cleaned properly after its previous use there are more chances of blockage. The use of un-cleaned, worn out hoses, too many and too sharp bends, use of worn out joints are also other causes of blockages.

Thus to avoid blockages, the hose must be well lubricated. Sufficient quantity of lubricating grout should be used to cover the entire length of pipe line before pumping concrete. The flexible rubber end hose should be handled with care. Careless handling may cause blockage.

10.9.1. Location of the blockage

The location of blockage can be determined by tapping the pipe line and observing the sound emitted from the pipe line.

10.9.2. Remedial measures of blockage

1. A minor blockage may be cleared by forward and reverse pumping. However excess pressure should not be applied blindly. It may agrivate the problem.
2. Blockage can be cleared by rodding or using sponge ball pushed by compressed air or water at high pressure.
3. Some times shortening the pipe line reduces pressure and on restarting the pumping, blockage is removed.

10.10. PROPERTIES OF THE CONCRETE TO BE PUMPED

Concrete to be pumped should meet the following specifications.

1. The Concrete should be neither too wet nor too dry. Usually the slump should vary between 5.7 cms to 10 cms. With a lower water content, the solid particles instead of moving longitudinally in a coherent mass in suspension exert pressure on the walls of the pipe. When the water content is in excess, segregation will take place. When the water content is at the correct or critical value, friction develops only at the surface of the pipe and in a thin 1 to 2.5 mm layer of the lubricating mortar. Thus all the concrete moves at the same velocity. For concrete to be pumped, a slightly higher cement content has been found useful as it allows the formation of lubricating film in the pipe. The magnitude of friction developed depends upon the consistency of the mix.
2. Cement/aggregate ratio should not be more than 1:6.
3. Water/cement ratio may range from 0.5 to 0.65.
4. A mix proportion of 1:2:4 has been found ideal for this concrete.
5. Well graded aggregate should be used for pumped concrete.
6. For pumped concrete light weight aggregate should not be used.
7. Usually 20 mm size aggregate should be used. For concrete with maximum size of coarse aggre-

gate of 20 mm, the optimum amount of fine aggregate should be between 35 to 40%; and the material finer than 300 micron should be between 15 to 20% and 3% passing through 150 micron sieve of weight of fine aggregate.

8. The quantity of fine particles *i.e.* cement and sand below 0.25 mm size *i.e.* particles below 300 micron should be between 350 to 400 kg/m^3.
9. The slump of pumpable concrete may be kept 7.5 cms to collapse range and diameter of pipe line should be 3 to 4 times the maximum size of aggregate. However concrete slump may vary from 4 cm to 10 cm and compacting factor 0.9 to 0.95.

10.11. SAFETY PRECAUTIONS DURING TRANSPORTATION OF CONCRETE

Usually following precautions should be adopted during transportation of concrete.

1. Places where lorries are to be discharged should have strong support for tipping the lorries.
2. No person should be allowed to stand at the place where the tipping lorry discharges concrete.
3. To avoid segregation, distance between the bottom of the skip to the top of surface where concrete is to be placed should not be more than one metre.
4. The distance between wagon being moved simultaneously by hand in one direction should not exceed 20 m on level surface and 30 m on slopes.
5. The whole system of pipe line should be checked by using hydraulic pressure 1.5 times the operating pressure before pumping the concrete. Generally water is used for this purpose.
6. The run of wheel barrow should be clean and at least 1.2 m wide.
7. While using hoist, the driver of the hoist should be in a position to see the place of charging and discharging the hoist.

10.12. PLACEMENT OF CONCRETE

The process of depositing the concrete in its required position is termed as *placement* of concrete.

When concrete is to be placed at a place it should be deposited as near as possible to its final position, so that when is it to be compacted it does not have to flow appreciably. Areas which will be in contact with concrete should be prepared well before placing concrete. Hence in order to get good finished surfaces, it is essential that surface where concrete is to be laid should be prepared carefully.

10.13. PREPARATION OF SURFACE BEFORE PLACING CONCRETE

In order to develop a proper and adequate bond between the base and the concrete placed, it is essential that the base is prepared well before placing the concrete. Before placing concrete different types of bases should be prepared as discussed below.

1. Natural soil. Before laying any concrete layer over a natural soil base, the soil should be properly compacted and leveled. After leveling the coarse grained soil should be made moist for a thickness of 30 cm and loamy and fine grained soils upto 15 cm thickness for 24 hours before laying the concrete layer. The moistening of soil is essential, to check absorption of water from concrete by the soil. However water should not be allowed to stand on the prepared surface.

2. In case of rocky bases. In this case the sides should be kept vertical. All loose particles should be removed and water sprinkled over the base and cleaned before placing the concrete. In this case also water should not be allowed to stand on the surface.

3. In case of brick soling and W.B.M. bases. The base should be made rough with the help of wire brush and cleaned. Loose particles and dust removed, water sprinkled and surface compacted before placing the concrete over it.

4. In case of hardened concrete base.

(*a*) *The difference in two operations is 4 hours.* The laitance on the surface of old concrete should be removed by rubbing it with wire brush and cleaned with water. All dust and rubbish should be removed by broom before laying the new layer of concrete.

(*b*) *Upto 48 hours.* The surface is rubbed with steel brush and washed with water and cleaned with the help of the broom. Now 1.5 cm thick layer of cement and sand mortar of similar composition as that of concrete is applied to the surface before new concrete is placed.

(*c*) *More than 48 hours old concrete.* In this case the hard surface is chiseled or sand blasted and cleaned as above. Now a slurry of neat cement is applied on the roughened surface and worked into the interstices after which 1.5 cm thick layer of cement sand mortar of the same composition as that of concrete should be applied before the slurry dries and then new concrete is placed immediately,

10.14. PLACING OF CONCRETE

Placing and compacting operations are the most critical field activities. Unless care is exercised in these operation, a very poor job may result even though concrete prepared is the best. To avoid segregation is most important, if it occurs remedial measures should be taken to eliminate it, so that homogeneous concrete is obtained.

When concrete is placed in deep forms, it is usually allowed to drop regardless of height. This results in segregation, damage to form and embedded fixtures.

Reinforcement and forms above the level of placement become coated with mortar which may dry before the concrete comes to that level. This condition should be avoided by dropping the concrete into an outside pocket and allowing it to flow over into the form without segregation. Fig. 10.7 shows correct and incorrect method of pouring concrete in deep forms.

In case of horizontal layers, it should be deposited close to its final location. In case of placing concrete in a slab, it should be dumped into face of previously placed concrete not away from the previously placed concrete. Fig. 10.8 shows a correct and incorrect method of placing concrete in slab with the help of buggies.

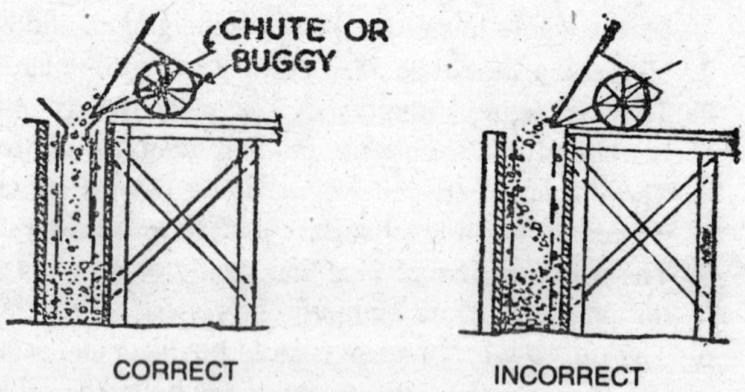

Fig. 10.7. Pouring of concrete

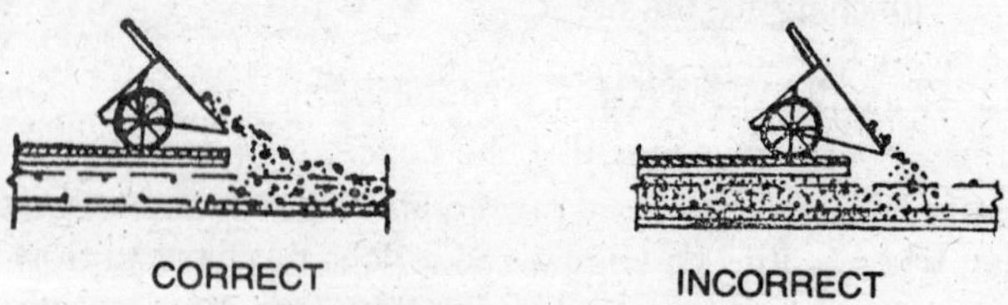

Fig. 10.8. Placing of concrete

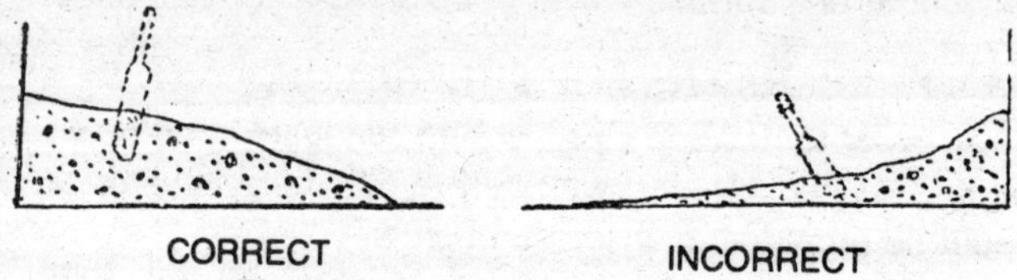

Fig. 10.9. Placing concrete on slopes

When concrete is to be placed on a slight slope, placing should begin at the lower end of the slope, permitting consolidation of the layer by vibration or any other suitable means. If placement is started at the top of the slope vibration tends to shift it down the slope. Fig. 10.9 shows a correct and incorrect method of placing concrete on a slope.

10.15. PRE-CAUTIONS TO BE TAKEN WHILE PLACING CONCRETE

Following precautions should be taken while placing concrete.

1. In case of reinforced concrete, thickness of concrete may vary from 15 cms to 30 cms. and 45 cms in case of mass concrete. Il should be laid in horizontal and uniform layers.
2. Concrete should not be thrown from a height of more than 1 m to prevent segregation.
3. No person should be allowed to walk over freshly laid concrete.
4. Placement of concrete should be discontinued during heavy downpour *i.e.* during heavy rain fall period.

5. Before placing new concrete, lataince over the old surface should be removed.
6. In order to prevent formation of irregular surface, concrete should be laid continuously.
7. The alignment of reinforcement and form work should not be disturbed.
8. In order to avoid sticking of concrete to surface of the form work, the internal faces of form work should be oiled or greased.
9. In R.C.C. slabs concreting should start from width wise from one end.
10. In order to produce better bond between concrete and reinforcement, grease, oil, dry cement etc. should be removed from the reinforcement.
11. While pouring concrete in deep forma, concrete should not be thrown From a height, but should be poured as shown in Fig. 10.6.

QUESTIONS

1. Write down the names of different methods of concrete transportation.
2. What precautions should be observed while transferring concrete from one vehicle to an other vehicle ?
3. What preliminary steps are necessary in preparing the following surfaces on which concrete is to be laid ?
   (*a*) Earth foundation (*b*) Rock foundation (*c*) W.B.M. surfaces.
4. What precautions should be adopted while placing concrete at site ?
5. What precautions should be taken while pouring concrete in
   (*a*) Deep form work (*b*) On sloping ground.
6. Write a note on pumped concrete.
7. Describe squeeze type concrete pump with a next sketch. Also discuss problems in pumping concrete by this pump.
8. Write down the properties of pumpable concrete.
9. Explain the causes of blockage of concrete pump and also suggest their remedial measures.

OBJECTIVE TYPE QUESTIONS

1. The freshly mixed concrete can be transported by
   (*a*) Wheel barrows (*b*) Tipping lorries
   (*c*) Agitator lorries or truck mixers (*d*) Dump buckets
   (*e*) Any of the above
2. The slump of pumpable concrete should be
   (*a*) 5.0 cm (*b*) 7.5 cm
   (*c*) 10.5 cm (*d*) 12.5 cm
3. The quantity of fine particles below 300 micron in a pumpable concrete should be
   (*a*) 250 to 300 kg/m^3 (*b*) 150 to 250 kg/m^3
   (*c*) 350 to 400 kg/m^3 (*d*) 450 to 500 kg/m^3
4. The ideal mix proportion for a pumpable concrete is
   (*a*) 1:2.5:3.5 (*b*) 1:2:4
   (*c*) 1:3:6 (*d*) 1:1.5:3.0
5. The water-cement ratio in a pumpable concrete should be
   (*a*) 0.35 to 0.4 (*b*) 0.45 to 0.55
   (*c*) 0.5 to 0.65 (*d*) 0.65 to 0.75
6. Which one of the following statements is false?
   (*a*) Usually 20 mm size aggregate is used in pumpable concrete
   (*b*) The fine particles passing through 300 micron should be 15 to 20% in the pumpable concrete
   (*c*) The light weight aggregate is the ideal one for a pumpable concrete
   (*d*) The diameter of the pipe line of a concrete pump should be 3 to 4 times of the maximum size of the concrete
7. Which of the following statements is correct?
   (*a*) The cement/aggregate ratio of a pumpable concrete should be more than 1:6

(*b*) The fine particles passing through 150 micron in a pumpable concrete should be more than 3.0%
(*c*) Concrete hauled by tipping lorries can be discharged on any soil
(*d*) The run of wheel barrow should be clean and at least 1.2 m wide

8. Which of the following statements is false?
(*a*) A 90° bend reduces the effective pumping distance by 12 m
(*b*) A 22.5° bend reduces the effective pumping distance by 3 m
(*c*) No sharp bend should be attached in a concrete pipe line.
(*d*) The provision of straight pipe line in between bends is not essential

9. Which of the statements is correct?
(*a*) Placing of concrete on a slight slope should be started from the top of the slope
(*b*) Placing of concrete on a slight slope should be started from the lower end of the slope
(*c*) In case of horizontal base concrete should be dumped away from the previously placed concrete
(*d*) While placing concrete in deep form, it can be dropped from any height

10. Which of the following statements is/are correct?
(*a*) Pumpable concrete is transported through completely filled delivery pipe line.
(*b*) The pumpable concrete should be very cohessive having a slump of about 75 mm
(*c*) The fine particles passing through 300 micron should not be less the 350 kg/m^3
(*d*) All the above

11. Which of the following statement is/are correct
(*a*) In the concrete pump delivery line the number of bends should be minimum
(*b*) The pipe should be cleaned immediately after use
(*c*) Before pumping concrete the pipe line should be lubricated with 1:3 cement sand mortar
(*d*) All are correct (*e*) Non of the above

12. Concrete pumped by a 60 H.P. pump can flow about
(*a*) 350 m (*b*) 400 m (*c*) 550 m (*d*) 250 m

13. Identify the correct statement
(*a*) Ready mixed concrete does not need control on its operations
(*b*) Ready mixed concrete is produced under site conditions
(*c*) The use of ready mixed concrete is advantageous when concrete is required in large quantities regularly
(*d*) Ready mixed concrete is weigh batched and mixed in a centrally located plant and transported in a agitator truck

14. When concrete partially is mixed at the control plant and the remaining mixing is completed during transportation is called
(*a*) Ready mixed concrete (*b*) Transit mixed concrete
(*c*) Shrink mixed concrete (*d*) Freshly mixed concrete

15. Which of the following statements is false?
(*a*) The delay in placing the concrete results in the gain of compressive strength of concrete provided it can still be compacted
(*b*) The effect of delayed placing of concrete varies with the rickness of the mix and initial slump
(*c*) It is taken into account by controlling the uniformity of concrete as delivered for placement
(*d*) Delay in placement has no effect on the properties of concrete

16. Which of the following statements is false?
(*a*) In the transit mixed concrete, the materials are batched at the control plant and the mix is mixed during transit
(*b*) The speed of rotation of the mixing should be between 4 to 16 revolution per minute
(*c*) The moist aggregate may remain in contact with cement for many hours with out causing any ill effect on the properties of concrete
(*d*) Concrete can be transported by this method with in a radius of 9 to 15 km

Answers

1. (*e*)	4. (*b*)	7. (*d*)	10. (*d*)	13. (*c, d*)	16. (*c*)
2. (*b*)	5. (*c*)	8. (*d*)	11. (*d*)	14. (*b*)	
3. (*c*)	6. (*c*)	9. (*b*)	12. (*b*)	15. (*d*)	

11

Compaction

11.1. INTRODUCTION

The process of compaction of concrete consists essentially of the elminiation of entrapped air from the concrete. The oldest means of achieving this aim is by punning with a rod, or by ramming or by vibrating. Thus the object of compacting concrete is to obtain a dense mass of concrete without voids, to get the concrete to surround all reinforcement and to fill all corners. Compaction of concrete influences the strength, durability, impermeability of concrete to a great extent. Each one percent less compaction reduces the strength of concrete by about 5% on an average. During the process of manufacture of concrete a considerable amount of air is entrapped forming voids in it.

11.2. VOIDS IN CONCRETE

Voids present in concrete in the form of small pores reduce the strength and density of concrete. Three kinds of voids may be present in the concrete as follows.

1. **Water voids.** These voids are present due to the water in excess of that needed for hydration.
2. **Air voids.** These are either due to insufficient compaction or due to deliberate entrainment of air in the mix. Concrete containing air voids left due to insufficient compaction of the freshly placed concrete lowers the strength very much. Experimental results have shown that 10% air voids left in concrete reduce its strength by more than 50%. Thus freshly laid concrete should be compacted sufficiently so that air voids are completely removed. Voids due to poor compaction can be seen readily when they are at the surface. The effect of air voids is shown in Fig. 11.1.

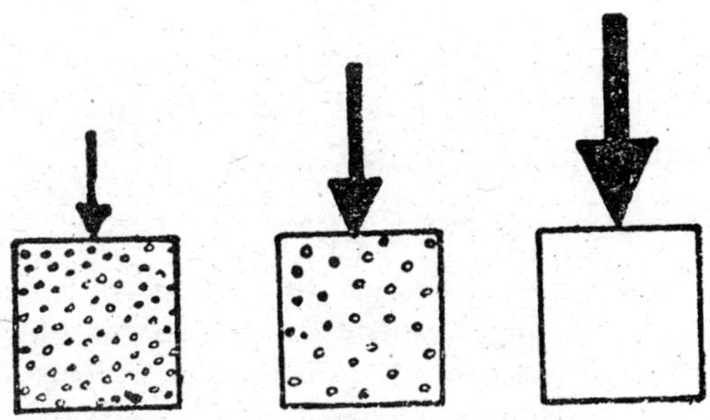

Fig. 11.1. Effect of amount of compaction on strength and density of concrete

Fig. 11.1 (*a*) shows the position of fresh uncompacted concrete having about 10% air voids. In this condition its compressive strength is found 122.5 kg/cm^2 and weight 2166 kg m^3. Fig. 11.1 (*b*) shows 5% air voids in the concrete, resulting its strength and weight as 190.5 kg/cm^2 and 2286 kg/m^3; while 11.1 (*c*) shows a fully compacted concrete having its strength and weight as 272.0 kg/cm^2 and 2410 kg/m^3 respectively. This shows the influence of air voids on the strength and weight of concrete. Honey-combed concrete does not develop good bond with reinforcement. Water may penetrate through these voids and corrode the steel.

11.3. METHODS OF COMPACTION

The method of compaction depends upon its workability, so that is can be fully compacted. In other words the required workability of concrete depends on how much it is to be compacted and by what method. It will also depend on the job condition. Usually following methods may be adopted for concrete compaction.

1. Hand Compaction or hand tamping
2. Mechanical compaction

1. Hand compaction. This method is adopted for members having reinforcement, pavements, narrow and deep members etc. Rammers and iron rods are used for this purpose. Mass concrete should be compacted in layers not more than 30 cms in thickness with templates or light rammers. For compacting reinforced concrete works iron rods are used. In this case the thickness of concrete layers should not be more than 15 cms. The most satisfactory method of compacting concrete properly is to consolidate each layer separately so that its top surface becomes level and fairly smooth before the next layer is placed.

When the rod is inserted vertically into a mass of workable concrete and moved up and down, it causes the concrete to be set in motion similar to that of the rod. This action is known is tamping or punning. When the concrete is set in motion in this way, the air bubbles present in the concrete come to the surface. Tamping should be carried out for each layer in such a way that concrete is filled in all the corners of the form work. While tamping is carried out, care should be taken that the rod should penetrate the full depth of the last layer placed and to some extent into the under lying layer to ensure proper bond between them. Secondly the reinforcement and form work should not be disturbed from their positions.

11.3.1. Tamping of road slabs

For compacting a concrete slab such as for roads, floors etc. a steel shod wooden tamping beam or screed is used as shown in Fig. 11.2. It can also ensure the correct level of the surface. The total length of the tamper should be 22.5 cms more than the width of the slab. For compacting the base coarse the tamper should be recessed near the ends by 2.5 cms as shown in Fig. 11.2.

The concrete is placed in the form, so that it is deeper than the side forms and the tamper is bumped up and down on the top surface of the concrete. By this actin concrete goes down to the level of the form. During tamping process, any low spots should be filled with concrete sprinkling from a shovel and tamped into the surface. A second run with the tamper is done with a to and fro motion to get the desired surface level.

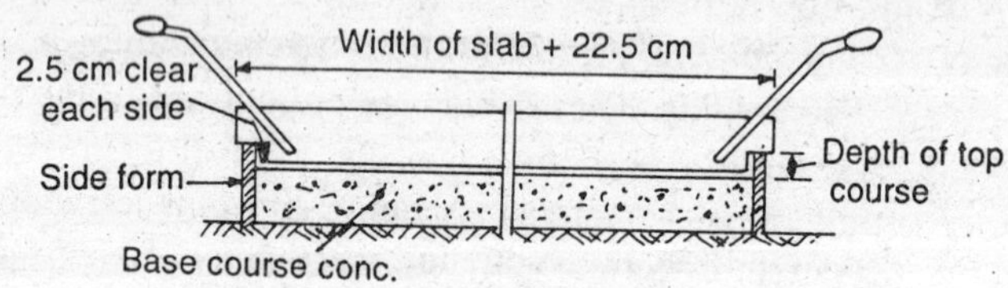

Fig. 11.2 Notched tamper

11.4. FINISHING CONCRETE SLABS

The operations adopted for obtaining a true, and uniform concrete surface are called finishing operations. A tamper usually leaves a slightly ridged surface. Thus it needs finishing. Actually the choice of concrete finish depends upon the use of the completed work.

11.4.1. Finishing operations

For finishing floors and slabs following operations are adopted:

1. Screeding
2. Floating
3. Troweling

1. Screeding. The levelling operation which removes bumps and hollows and gives a true and uniform concrete surface is known as *screeding.* For this purpose a straight edge is used. It is slightly longer than the section to be finished. The surface is struck off by moving the straight edge back and forth across the top of the surface. The straight edge is advanced forward a very little distance with each movement.

A small quantity of concrete mix should always be kept ahead of the straight edge to fill the voids and to maintain a plane surface. Screeds may be of roller type or vibrator type. A wooden screeding board's shown in Fig. 11.3.

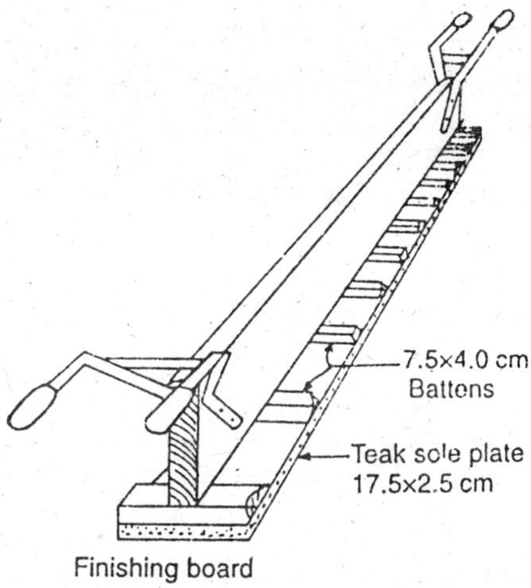

Fig. 11.3. Finishing Board

2. Floating. The operation of removing the irregularities from the surface of the concrete left after screening is known as *floating.* It helps in leveling the surface and compacting the concrete. Floating is done with the help of 1.5 m long and 20 cms wide wooden floats. To give ease in handling the float, a handle is provided at its centre. Finishing is done by moving the float forward and backward.

3. Troweling. The final operation of finishing is known as troweling. It is done where smooth surface is desired. Troweling should be done after the evaporation of water from the concrete surface. Spreading of dry cement on wet surface to absorb excess water should not be allowed as it is not a good practice, and will develop cracks and blistering.

11.5. TYPES OF SURFACE FINISH

According to the roughness of the surface, the surface finish can be classified as follows:

1. Tamped finish
2. Brush finish
3. Wooden float finish
4. Steel trowel finish

1. **Tamped finish.** As explained above.
2. **Brush finish.** Brush finish can only be done after the surface has been floated or belted. It is done with a bamboo broom brushed lightly across the slab after the concrete has set slightly. If a rougher surface is desired, further brushing may be done till the aggregate becomes exposed.
3. **Belt finish.** A belt finish is produced by using a strip of canvas about 15 cms wide and about 1.5 m longer than the width of slab. The belt is laid across the surface and drawn to and fro with rather long strokes and moved forward slowly in the direction of concreting.

11.6. SUITABILITY OF CONCRETE MIX

If concrete is to be compacted successfully by hand, then the concrete mix should be of proper proportions and required consistency. Concrete to be hand compacted should have following slumps as shown in Table 11.1.

Table 11.1.

S. No.	*Type of Job*	*Slump in cms*
1.	Heavily reinforced sections and works where compaction is difficult	10 to 15
2.	Normal reinforced concrete beams, slabs, columns, walls and footings	7.5 to 10
3.	Road slabs, mass concrete, foundations and walls.	2.5 to 7.5

If the concrete is highly deficient in fine aggregate or highly under sanded it may not be possible to compact it, however wet it is made or however much it is tamped. Such a mix would be very harsh and the mortar would tend to separate out from the coarse aggregate causing honeycombing even though thorough tamping may be applied to it.

On the other hand if the mix is over sanded, to make it workable larger amount of water is needed. In such cases excessive laintence would be formed on the surface after the concrete has been compacted. This laintence being a layer of slurry of cement and sand forms a weak and porous layer on the surface of the lift. Such layers often allow water to leak through construction joints of retaining walls and produce unsightly staining.

11.7. MECHANICAL COMPACTION

Mixes which are too stiff to consolidate by hand, they can be easily compacted by mechanical compaction. When a concrete mix is vibrated, it behaves as if it is very much wetter than it really is and will flow easily. This method of Compaction has proved very much effective than hand compaction.

In this case the concrete is compacted by vibration, during which the vibrator communicates rapid vibrations to the particles, increasing the fluidity of concrete. Due to vibration, the particles occupy a more stable position and the concrete fills all the space and the air present is forced out to the surface, resulting in dense and durable concrete The frequency, duration of vibration etc. depends on the conditions of vibration for compacting the mix, which have been discussed in the following paragraphs.

11.7.1. Advantages of Vibrated concrete

Following are the advantages of compaction by vibrations:

1. By the use of vibration, stiff mixes can be compacted easily.
2. For a given cement/aggregate ratio a much stronger and dense concrete can be produced.
3. Bond between reinforcement and concrete is improved.
4. Creep and shrinkage is reduced.
5. Laintence is also reduced to some extent.
6. Speed of placing concrete is increased.
7. Better finish is obtained.

11.8. TYPE OF VIBRATORS

Following three types of vibrators usually are used for concrete compaction:

1. **Internal vibrators.** These vibrator are inserted into the concrete and withdrawn after the compaction has been completed.
2. **External or Form vibrators.** These vibrators are clamped on the side of the form work.
3. **Surface vibrators.** These vibrators are placed on the top of the concrete surface and concrete compacted.

11.8.1. Internal Vibrator

It is also known as immersion, poker or needle vibrator. Usually it is considered to be the most effec- tive type of vibrator as it comes into intimate contact with the concrete. Though there are different kinds of internal vibrators, but they essentially consist of the following components.

1. A power unit 2. Flexible tube 3. Vibrating head

1. **Power unit.** It can be either a petrol engine or electric supply unit.
2. **Flexible tube.** It is a rubber tube having power connecting device at one end and vibrator head on the other end.
3. **Vibrator head.** It is a straight iron tube having eccentric weight fitted inside it. As the current passes through this tube, the vibratory action is caused by the rotation of the eccentrically weighted shaft at high

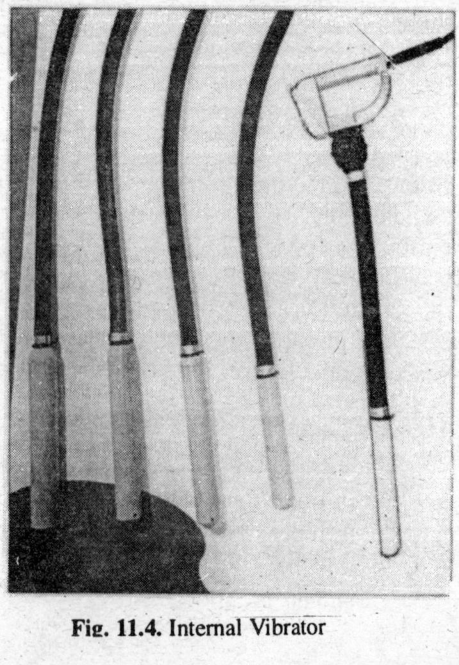

Fig. 11.4. Internal Vibrator

speed, usually over 7000 r.p.m. which are transmitted to the concrete particles. Fig. 11.4 shows an internal vibrator with an electric mortar.

The needle diameter may vary from 2.0 cms to 7.5 cms and length from 25 cms to 90 cms. The frequency of vibration may vary upto 12000 cycles per minute. The bigger needle is used in the construction of mass concrete works as dams.

The vibrating head is immersed in the fresh concrete and transmits vibrations to the concrete through the vibrator's body. The vibrating head should be immersed vertically in the concrete and should be kept inside the concrete. While running the vibrator, the bearings should be kept cool and breakdowns should be avoided. As the concrete consolidates, its surface level falls and the surface becomes smooth. Air bubbles may be seen breaking at the surface. When these bubbles cease to appear on the surface, the concrete may be assumed as compacted sufficiently.

The vibrator should be lowered or inserted vertically in the concrete. After the concrete is compacted, the vibrator should be withdrawn slowly at the rate of 7.5 to 8 cm/sec. as this speed will fill the hole caused due to withdrawal of vibrator without any air being entrapped. Now the vibrator is inserted at another point at a distance of 50 cm to 100 cm or 45 cm to 75 cm. However this distance depends on the shape of the form work and amount of reinforcement. This distance should be kept uniform. For concrete of workability of 0.78 to 0.85 compacting factor the vibrator should be spaced at points 35 to 90 cms apart.

The internal vibrator neither should be allowed to tough the inside face of the form work, as it may damage the surface nor the reinforcement as the displacement of reinforcement will upset all calculations.

The frequency of vibration varies from 3500 to 12000 cycles per minute. Frequency between 3500-5000 cycles per minute has been suggested as a desirable minimum, with an acceleration of not less than 4 g, but recent studies found favour for frequencies from 4000-7000 cycles per minute.

11.8.2. Time of Vibration

The time of compaction by the internal vibrator depends on the consistency of the mix. Usually from 5 to 30 seconds compaction is sufficient depending upon the consistency of the mix, but for some mixes upto 120 seconds compaction is required. The actual completion of compaction can be judged by the appearance of the surface of the concrete, which should neither contain excessive mortar nor it should be honey combed. Some researchers have correlated the time of compaction by internal vibrators with the consistency of the mix and the frequency of the vibrator. For complete compaction of concrete having 1.25 cm slump required 90 seconds vibration at 4000 r.p.m., 45 seconds at 5000 r.p.m. and 25 seconds at 6000 r.p.m.

When concrete is placed in layers the vibrator should be immersed through the entire depth of the freshly deposited concrete and into the layer below it, if this is still plastic or can be brought again into a plastic condition. In this way a plane of weakness at the junction of the two layers can be avoided. For layers more than 50 cms, the vibrator may not be fully effective in expelling air from the lower part of the layer. As stated above, the vibrator should remain vertical while in use. Fig. 11.5 shows a correct and incorrect position of the vibrators.

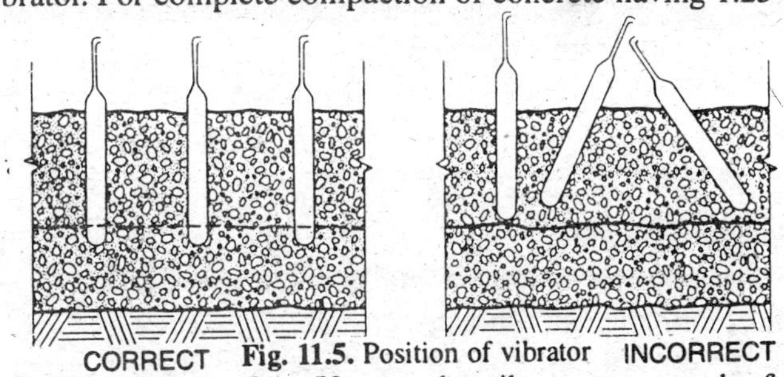

CORRECT **Fig. 11.5.** Position of vibrator INCORRECT

11.9. PRECAUTIONS TO BE OBSERVED WHILE USING INTERNAL VIBRATOR

While using internal vibrator, following precautions should be taken.

1. In order to prevent any leakage of mortar, the form work should be as tight as possible.
2. In order to avoid air being trapped, the thickness of the concrete lift should not be less than 15 cm.
3. For lifts more than 50 cm, internal vibrators should not be used, but upto 45 cm lift, the vibrator should be allowed to penetrate into the previously compacted concrete below to obtain a proper

bond between the two lifts or layers. If required the vibrating unit can be immersed completely upto the bottom of the form.

4. Vibrations should be controlled carefully by immersing the vibrator for 5 to 15 seconds at a point. The distance between two immersion points of the vibrator may vary from 45 to 75 cm or 50 to 100 cm.
5. The vibrator should be immersed vertically and should remain in vertical position throughout the operation at that point, otherwise the degree of compaction cannot be controlled well.
6. Vibrator should not be used to push concrete laterally in the form works as it will cause segregation of the concrete.
7. The vibrator should be withdrawn slowly usually 7.5 cm to 8.0 cm per second as at this speed of withdrawal, the hole left by vibrator will close fully without any air being trapped.
8. The vibrator should be immersed through the full depth of freshly laid concrete and into the layer below it if the concrete is still plastic or it can be brought into plastic state.
9. The vibrator neither should touch the inside of form work nor the reinforcement.
10. The vibrator should never be kept running for long when it is not in the concrete.
11. The tube should never be bent at an very sharp angle as it will produce unnecessary heavy strain on the internal flexible drive and the outer tube. The tube should be kept as straight as possible. Sharp bends should be avoided near the junction of the tube and the vibrating head.

Internal vibrators are made in sizes down to 20 mm diameter so that they can be used for heavily reinforced sections. This class of vibrators are found comparatively more efficient as all the work is done directly on the concrete. Though internal vibrators are usually constructed very strong and are capable being used under very rough conditions, however they cannot be expected to work continuously for an indefinite period of time without wearing.

The bearings inside the vibrating head are subject to severe wearing conditions and are likely to become over heated. This can be prevented by immersing the full length of vibrating head into the concrete.

11.10. FORM VIBRATOR OR EXTERNAL VIBRATORS

These vibrators are used for compacting concrete where internal vibrators can not be used such as for very heavily reinforced or very narrow sections or precast units etc. In such conditions vibration is applied through the form work by clamping these vibrators on the shuttering.

The vibrators are rigidly clamped to the form work resting on an elastic support, so that both the form and concrete are vibrated. In this case a considerable proportion of work done is consumed in vibrating the form work, resulting in low efficiency of the system. In order to check the leakage of cement mortar the form work should be strong and tight.

Principle of working

The principle of an external vibrator is same as that of an internal vibrator, but the frequency is usually between 3000 and 6000 cycles of vibration per minute. Bureau of reclamation has recommended at least 8000 cycles per minute.

When an external vibrator is used, concrete has to be placed in layers of suitable depth as air can not be expelled through a great thickness of concrete. The position of vibrator has to be changed as concreting progresses. They should not be placed more than 90 cms apart in any direction.

The vibrator shown in Fig. 11.6 consists of an electric motor with an unbalaced weight. This weight

Fig. 11.6. Form vibrator

causes the unit to vibrate when it is rotated by the motor. These vibrators should be fixed on the form work firmly and should not be placed more than 1 m apart.

11.10.1. Kango Hammer

It is another form of external vibrator. It is an electric hammer used on the out side of the vertical shuttering. This type of vibrator is useful for vibrating those parts of shuttering where it would be difficult to fix the ordinary clamp on the vibrator or where the vibrator is required to move continuously. Fig. 11.7 shows a kango hummer.

Fig. 11.7. Kango Hammer

11.10.2. Vibrating tables

These are also external vibrators and are suitable for pre cast concrete work. It provides a reliable means of compaction of precast concrete and has the advantage of offering uniform vibration.

11.10.3. Surface vibrators

These vibrators are used where a wide horizontal surface occurs such as in dams and very thick walls. Usually such vibrators are used for roads and floors. Though a large number of different types of surface vibrators exist, but pan type vibrator shown in Fig. 11.8 is generally used for floors and foundation works. It consists of a flat pan or tray with handles at each end and a vibrating unit mounted in the middle. The vibratory unit may have a petrol engine, or electric motor or may be pneumatic type. This type of vibrator is moved across the surface of the concrete by the handles.

11.10.4. Vibrating screeds

External vibrator type unit is often used for surface vibration by mounting it on a screed or tamper. Vibrating screeds may have more than one unit of such vibrators. Fig. 11.9 shows such a screed. These screeds can be used for compacting concrete layers not more than 20 cm in thickness.

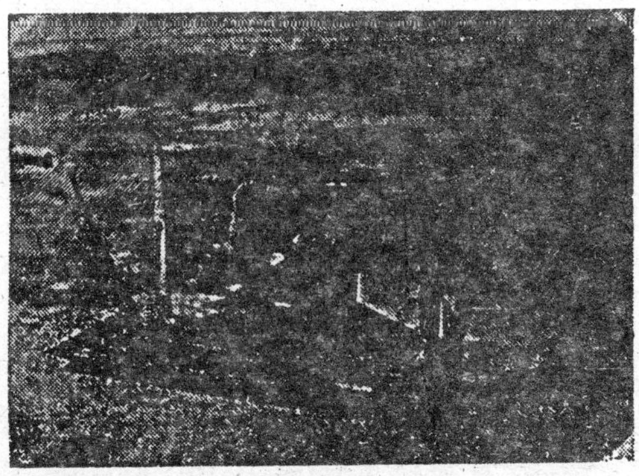

Fig. 11.8. Surface vibrator

11.10.5. Compaction by Pressure and Jolting

This method has proved very effective for compacting very dry concrete. This method is used for compacting hollow blocks, cavity blocks and solid concrete blocks. The stiff concrete is vibrated, pressed and also jolted. with the combined effect of vibration, pressure and jolt, the stiff concrete gets compacted to a dense form to give good strength and volume stability. By applying great pressure, concrete of low water/cement ratio can be compacted to yield very high strength.

11.10.6. Compaction by spinning

This is one of recent methods of compaction of concrete. This method of compaction is employed for the production of concrete pipes. When plastic concrete is spun at a very high speed, it gets compacted by the action of centrifugal force. Patented pipes as "Hume pipes", "Spun pipes" are compacted by this method. Refer chapter 23 also (Fero-cement).

11.10.7. Vibratory rollers

Compaction of very dry and lean concrete by vibratory rollers is one of the recent development. Concrete compacted by this method is known as Roller Compaction Concrete. This method of concrete compaction was developed in Japan and spread to USA and other countries mainly for the construction of dams and pavements. For compaction of dry lean concrete, heavy rollers which vibrate while rolling are used. Such roller compacted M_{10} grade concrete of 15 cms thickness has been successfully used as base course for Mumbai-Pune express highways and Delhi-Muthra highways. Refer chapter 24 also (Roller Compaction Concrete).

Fig. 11.9. Vibrating screed

11.11. SELECTION OF VIBRATORS FOR VARIOUS SITUATIONS

Actually the use of a certain type of vibrators depends upon the situation of work. Broadly following table 11.2 gives an indication of the use of the different vibrators.

Table 11.2.

S. No.	*Situation where a vibrator used*	*Type of vibrator*
1.	For foundation concrete, columns beams, large sections of mass concrete	Internal vibrator
2.	For deep beam sections, pre-cast concrete, tunnel lining, arches etc.	Form vibrator
3.	Road surfaces, floors of plain and, reinforced concrete	Surface vibrator

11.12. SUITABILITY OF MIX FOR COMPACTION WITH VIBRATOR

Concrete to be compacted by vibration, should be designed properly. The consistency of the concrete depends upon the conditions of placing, type of mix, and the efficiency of the vibrator. The slump of such concrete should not be more than 5 cm in any case, otherwise segregation of concrete will take place, which should never be allowed to occur. The value of slump and compacting factors for different works are shown in Table 11.3.

11.13. COMPARISION OF INTERNAL AND EXTERNAL VIBRATORS

1. Internal vibrators are more efficient as all the work is done directly on the concrete. They can be used for concrete layers upto 50 cm thickness.
2. Internal vibrators can be used even for heavily reinforced sections.
3. External vibrators are clamped rigidly to the form work, hence a considerable portion of the work done is wasted in vibrating form work.

4. Form work used for external vibrators should be very rigid and strong. This increases the cost of the form work.
5. By the use of external vibrator, excessive cement mortar comes to the surface of the concrete work. This surface being comparatively weak and less pervious, deteriorates very soon.

Table 11.3. Slump and Compacting Factor

S. No.	Placing condition	*Degree of workability*	*Average size of aggregate in mm*	*Compacting factors*	*Slump in mm*
1.	(*i*) Narrow sections requiring heavy vibration.	Very low	10 – 20	0.75 – 0.78	0 – 12
	(*ii*) Large sections which require normal vibration	Very low	40	0.78	0 – 25
2.	(*i*) Normal reinforced sections compacted by vibration	Low	10	0.83 – 0.85	0 – 6 6 – 25
	(*iii*) Heavy sections without reinforcement	Low	40	0.85	25 – 50
3.	(*i*) Normal reinforced sections compacted without vibration	Average	10 – 20	0.9 – 0.92	6 – 25 25 – 50
	(*ii*) Heavy reinforced section compacted without vibration	Average	40	0.92	50 – 100
4.	(*i*) Heavily reinforced sections compacted without vibration	High	10 – 20	0.92 – 0.95	25 – 100 50 – 100
	(*ii*) Normal sections not suitable to be compacted by vibration	High	40	0.95	100 – 175

11.14. OUTPUT OF IMMERSION VIBRATORS

For light vibrators having a centrifugal force of about 200 kg, the output of compacted concrete may be taken as 3 to 5 m^3 per hour depending upon the consistency of the mix and for heavy type vibrators having a centrifugal force of 450 kg, the output may be taken as 12 to 25 m^3 per hour.

QUESTIONS

1. What do you understand by compaction of concrete? What is the effect of compaction on the strength of concrete?
2. How you will ensure the full Compaction of concrete?
3. In how many ways compaction of concrete can be done? Why mechanical compaction is considered superior than hand compaction?
4. What precautions should be observed while compacting concrete with the help of internal vibrator?
5. Describe an internal vibrator. How it is used?
6. Compare the merits and demerits of internal and external vibrators.
7. How over compaction and under compaction affects the properties of concrete.
8. How the compaction of concrete roads is done?
9. What are the advantages of mechanical vibrated concrete over hand compacted concrete?

OBJECTIVE TYPE QUESTIONS

1. Which of the following statements is false?
   (*a*) Compaction of concrete increases the air contents in the concrete
   (*b*) Compaction of concrete increases the strength of the concrete
   (*c*) Compaction of the concrete increases the density of the concrete
   (*d*) Compaction of concrete decreases the air content in the concrete

2. Which of the following statements is correct?
   (*a*) Each 1% less compaction reduces the compressive strength of concrete by 15%
   (*b*) Each 1% less compaction reduces the compressive strength of concrete by 10.5%
   (*c*) Each 1% less compaction reduces the compressive strength of concrete by about 5%
   (*d*) All are correct
3. Which of the following statements is correct
   (*a*) Immersion vibrator should be inserted in concrete vertically
   (*b*) After compaction the rate of withdrawal of vibrator should be about 8 cm/sec.
   (*c*) The spacing of points of immersion of needle vibrator should be about 45 to 75 cm
   (*d*) The frequency of vibration by needle vibrator may be 4000 to 7000 cycles per minute
   (*e*) All are correct
4. Which of the following statements is false?
   (*a*) The time of compaction by the internal vibrator depends upon the consistency of the mix
   (*b*) The time of compaction by the internal vibrator depends upon the frequency of vibrator and consistency of concrete
   (*c*) The time of compaction by the internal vibrator dependents upon the strength and density of concrete
   (*d*) The vibrator should be immersed through the entire depth of the freshly laid layer and into the layer below it
5. The time of vibration of the needle vibrators usually varies as
   (*a*) 15 to 25 seconds (*b*) 30 to 40 seconds
   (*c*) 5 to 15 seconds (*d*) 1 to 2 hours
6. Which of the following statements is correct?
   (*a*) The immersion vibrator neither should touch the form work nor the reinforcement
   (*b*) The rate of with drawal of the vibrator should be about 8 cm/sec
   (*c*) The immersion vibrator should not be used to push the concrete laterally
   (*d*) The diameter of needle vibrator varies from 2.0 to 7.5 cm
   (*e*) All are correct
7. The length of needle vibrator varies
   (*a*) 100 to 125 cm (*b*) 25 to 90 cm
   (*c*) 120 to 150 cm (*d*) 10 to 20 cm
8. Which of the following statements is false?
   (*a*) Presence of even 5% voids in hardened concrete due to incomplete compaction reduces its strength by abut 35%
   (*b*) Compaction is accomplished by long external work
   (*c*) The process of uniform placement of concrete to get a homogeneous and dense mass of concrete is known as compaction
   (*d*) The process of moving concrete up and down with a spade is known as compaction
   (*e*) All of the above
9. Which of the following statements is false?
   (*a*) Compaction by mechanical vibration is suitable for all grades of concrete
   (*b*) Compaction by mechanical vibrations is suitable for all type of structural elements
   (*c*) Compaction by mechanical vibration is suitable for all mixes except very plastic mixs
   (*d*) Al the above
10. The acceleration produced on the particles during compaction of concrete by high frequency vibrations is of the order
    (*a*) 1 to 2 g (*b*) 4 to 7 g
    (*c*) 7 to 9 g (*d*) upto 1 g
11. Generally which type of vibrator is used for compaction of concrete
    (*a*) Needle vibrator (*b*) Form vibrator
    (*c*) Surface vibrator (*d*) Screed vibrator
12. For compacting thin R.C.C. slab which of the following vibrators is most suitable,
    (*a*) Vibrating table (*b*) Form vibrator
    (*c*) Surface vibrator (*d*) Immersion vibrator

13. Surface vibrator is effective when the thickness of concrete member is not more than
    (*a*) 90 mm (*b*) 150 mm
    (*c*) 120 mm (*d*) 450 mm
    (*e*) 200 mm
14. Which of the following statements is false?
    (*a*) Surface vibrator is most suitable for the compaction of raft footings
    (*b*) Surface vibrator is most suitable for the compaction of columns
    (*c*) Surface vibrator is most suitable for the compaction of road pavements
    (*d*) Surface vibrator is most suitable for the compaction of RCC slabs
15. While compacting concrete mixes by vibrators
    (*a*) Vibrations reduce entrained air
    (*b*) Vibrations spread concrete in the form
    (*c*) Vibration cause smaller particles to rise to the surface of the concrete to give better finish
    (*d*) Prolonged vibrations reduce chances of segregation
16. Rotational instability developed during compaction of concrete by the vibration technique is due to
    (*a*) Mix. being under sanded (*b*) Entrapped air
    (*c*) Mix. being over sanded (*d*) All of the above
17. Identify the false statement/statements
    (*a*) Punning with a rod is the modern method of compacting concrete.
    (*b*) Reinforced concrete layer more than 30 cms thick can be compacted by iron rod.
    (*c*) For heavily reinforced sections the slump of concrete should be 2.5 to 5 cm.
    (*d*) For mass concrete works and roads slabs the slump of concrete should be 10 to 15 cm.
    (*e*) All of the above
18. Identify the incorrect statement
    (*a*) Laitence on the surface of the concrete increases its abrasion resistance value
    (*b*) The creep and shrinkage of vibrated concrete are reduced
    (*c*) The bond strength of vibrated concrete is increased
    (*d*) For getting 0.78 to 0.85 compacting factor the spacing of penetration of vibrator should be between 35 to 90 cms.

Answers

1. (*a*)	4. (*c*)	7. (*b*)	10. (*b*)	13. (*e*)	16. (*c*)
2. (*c*)	5. (*c*)	8. (*e*)	11. (*a*)	14. (*b*)	17. (*e*)
3. (*e*)	6. (*e*)	9. (*d*)	12. (*c*)	15. (*a*)	18. (*a*)

12
Curing of Concrete

12.1. INTRODUCTION

We have already discussed that concrete derives its strength by the hydration of cement particles. The process of hydration is not a momentary action, it continues for long. Of course the rate of hydration is fast in the beginning, but its rate decreases as the time passes. It is observed that about 90% hydration is complete with in 28 days and the rest 10% hydration takes years together. The quantity of the product known as gel depends upon the degree of hydration. For hydration cement requires about 23% of water by weight of cement *i.e.* for hydration water/cement ratio of 0.23 is sufficient. 15% water by weight of cement is required for filling the voids in the gel pores. Thus a water/cement ratio of 0.38 is required to hydrate all particles of cement and also to occupy the space in the pores of the gel. Though theoretically a water/cement ratio of 0.38 would satisfy the requirement of water for hydration and no capillary cavities would be left, but practically a water/cement ratio of 0.5 will be required for complete hydration in a sealed container for keeping the desirable relative humidity level.

In the actual work, though higher water/cement is used, but the water used in the concrete evaporates leaving insufficient water in the concrete for the effective hydration to take place, particularly in the top layer. Thus to prevent the loss of water from surface of the concrete some measures must be taken by way of provision of impervious covering or by the application of curing compounds. Therefore curing can be considered as creation of favourable conditions during the early period for un interrupted hydration. The desirable conditions for hydration are:

1. Suitable temperature and 2. Sufficient moisture

Thus curing can be defined as the process of maintaining a satisfactory moisture content and a favourable temperature in concrete during the period immediately after the placement of concrete, so that hydration of cement may continue till the desired properties are developed sufficiently to meet the requirements of service.

It has been observed that the quality of concrete shows all round improvement with efficient un interrupted curing. If the curing is neglected in the early period of hydration, the quality of concrete will suffer a irreparable loss.

A concrete laid in the afternoon of a hot summer day in a dry climate will dry out quickly. The combined effect of hot sun and dry wind will produce a poorly hydrated cement concrete with inferior gel structure, which will not give the desired bond and strength. The quick surface drying of concrete results in the movement of moisture from the interior to the surface. This steep moisture gradient develops high internal stresses. These internal stresses also develop internal micro cracks in the semi plastic concrete.

During hydration, concrete generates a high quantity of heat of hydration. The generation of this heat is harmful for the stability of concrete. If the heat generated is removed by any means, the adverse effect of this heat can be minimised. This can be done by thorough curing.

12.2. OBJECT OF CURING

Following are the objects of curing.

1. The main object of curing is to keep the concrete saturated or as nearly saturated as possible, until the originally water filled space in the fresh cement paste has been filled to the desired extent by the product of hydration of cement.
2. To prevent the loss of water by evaporation and to maintain the process of hydration. In case of site concrete the active curing stops long before the maximum possible hydration has taken place. The influence of moist curing on the strength of concrete has been shown in Fig. 8.10.
3. To reduce the shrinkage of concrete.
4. To preserve the properties of concrete.

12.3. NECESSITY OF CURING

The necessity of curing arises from the fact that hydration of cement can take place only in water filled capillaries. For this reason, a loss of water by evaporation from the capillaries must be prevented. Further water lost internally by self desiccation has to be replaced by water from out side.

Water required for chemical reaction with cement *i.e.* for hydration is about 25 to 30% of the water added to the cement, rest of the water is used for providing workability and help to continue hydration. Thus hydration of sealed specimens can proceed only if the amount of water present in the paste is at least twice that of the water already combined. Self desiccation (drying up) is thus of importance in mixes with water/cement ratio less than 0.5. For higher water/cement ratios the rate of curing of sealed specimens is same as that of saturated specimen. It has been observed that only half the water present in the paste can be used for chemical combination, even if the total amount of water present is less than the water required for combination. This statement is important in view of the fact that formerly it was believed that a concrete mix containing water in excess of that required for the chemical reaction with cement, a small loss of water during hardening would not adversely affect the process of hardening and the gain in strength. Now it is known that hydration can take place only when the vapour pressure in the capillaries is sufficiently high, about 80% of saturation pressure. Hydration at a maximum rate can proceed only under conditions of saturation. From experiments it has been observed that below a vapour pressure of 0.8 of the saturations pressure, the degree of hydration is low and below 0.3 of the saturation pressure, hydration is negligible. For satisfactory development of strength it is not necessary that all cement should hydrate, the quality of concrete depends on *gel/space* ratio of the paste as discussed in chapter 8, page 196.

12.4. METHODS OF CURING

As the common object of all methods of curing is to prevent the loss of moisture from the exposed surface of concrete and to keep the surface continually damp, following methods may be adopted for achieving this objective.

Actually the method of curing depends upon the nature of work and atmospheric conditions. Usually following methods may be adopted.

1. Shading of concrete works.
2. Covering concrete surfaces with gunny bags or Hession, burlaps etc.
3. Sprinkling water on the concrete surface.
4. Ponding of concrete surface.
5. Membrane curing.
6. Steam curing.

1. Shading of concrete. This method is useful for large surfaces as roads. The object of this method is to protect the newly laid fresh concrete from direct sun rays and dry hot wind to avoid rapid drying and non uniform temperature development in the mass of concrete. This objective can be achieved by using canvas by stretching it over frames. In cold weather, these canvas prevent freezing of the concrete under frost condition.

2. Covering surfaces with gunny bags or burlaps etc. This method is widely used for structural concrete. In this method the concrete surface is covered with empty cement bags or burlaps etc. and water sprinkled at short intervals to keep them moist. The surface should not be allowed to dry even for a short duration. This method can be employed for horizontal as well as vertical components.

3. Sprinkling method. This is an excellent method of curing, provided sprinking of water could be done continuously. This method needs much more water for curing than any other method. This method is more suitable for floors. Intermittent sprinkling may cause formation of cracks, which is a very serious defect.

4. Ponding method. This method is useful for horizontal members only such as pavements, floors, slabs etc. In this case small dikes are formed of earth and water is filled in between the dikes. Water may be filled 2 or 3 times a day depending on the climatic conditions of the region. This method has been found more effective in neutralizing the heat of hydration than wet covering. Ponding method has been found to give more strength than wet covering method at all ages. From Fig. 12.1, it will be seen that with water/cement ratio of 0.32 the increase in compressive strength at 28 days is about 16%, at 3 days strength about 6% and at one day about 4 to 5%. With water/cement of 0.36 only 28 day strength is found about 6% more and water/cement ratio more than 0.4 shows no diference in compressive strength.

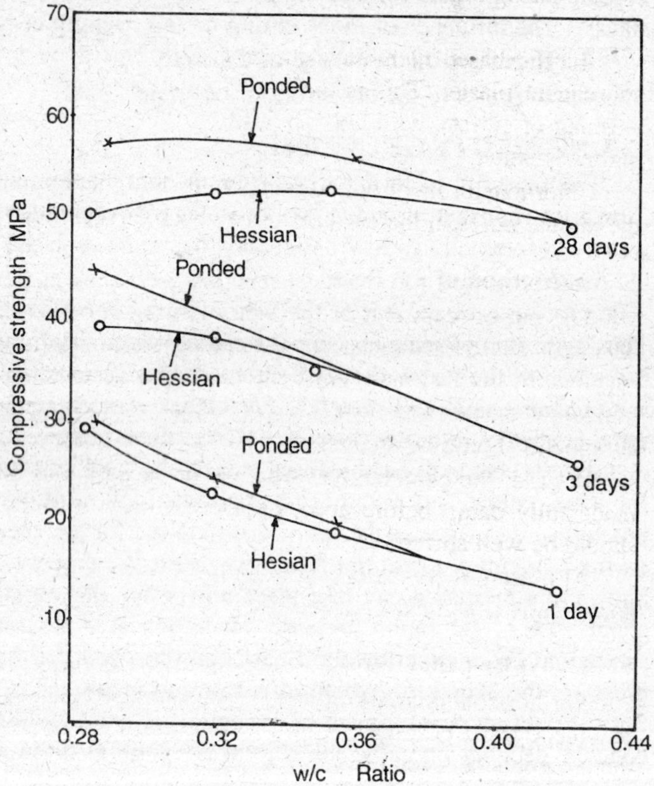

Fig. 12.1. Influence of curing conditions on strength of concrete

5. Membrane curing. This method is employed at places where water is scares. Chemical compounds or polythene sheets or water proof paper etc. are used for curing of concrete.

While using chemical membranes such as bitumen emulsion following precautions should be observed.

1. Such compounds should not be applied when there is free water on the concrete surface or after the concrete surface has dried out.
2. It should be applied after curing for 24 hours, the freshly laid concrete with moist gunny bags.

For this purpose bitumen emulsion, esphaltic and coal tar cut back can be used with advantage. However their use is restricted as the resulting surface is black, which absorbs excessive heat and the look also is not pleasing.

12.5. MEMBRANE CURING COMPOUNDS

To retard the loss of water from concrete during early period of setting and hardening liquid membrane forming curing compounds may be used. They are used not only for curing fresh concrete, but also for further curing after removal of form work. They can also be used for curing purposes after initial water curing for one or two days. The white pigmented curing compounds also reduce the temperature rise of concrete exposed to radiation from sun. Curing compounds may be made with the following bases.

1. Synthetic resin
2. Wax

3. Acrylic 4. Chlorinated rubber

Resin and wax based curing compounds seal the concrete surface effectively. However their efficiency reduces with time and after about 28 days they get disintegrated and peel off. After 28 days surface of concrete may be plastered. If plastering is required to be done earlier, the surface of the concrete should be washed off with hot water before plastering. The average efficiency of iesin and wax based membrane forming curing compounds may be taken as 80%, though it was found varying with time. In one study the typical curing efficiency was found 96% for 24 hours, 84% for 72 hours, 74% for 7 days and 65% for 14 days.

Acrylic based membrane forming curing compounds have been found to have better adhesion with subsequent plaster. This is their additional advantage. This membrane neither gets crumbled nor it need washing of surface with hot water. Due to the inherent property of acrylic emulsion, the bonding with the plaster is better.

Chlorinated rubber curing compounds not only form a thin film on the surface of concrete but also fill the minute pores in the surface of the concrete. Eventually the surface film wears out.

12.5.1. Method of application

The curing compounds may be applied by brush or spraying while the concrete is wet. In case of beams or columns the curing compound may be applied after the removal of form work. On horizontal surfaces the curing compound should be applied upon the complete disappearance of all bleeding water. In horizontal surfaces as that of roads and air field pavements, where texturing is required, the curing compound should be applied after texturing.

In case, the concrete has dried, the surface should be sprayed with water and thoroughly wetted and made fully damp before applying the curing compound. Before use the container of curing compound should be well stirred.

At present there is no Indian standard specification and code of Practice for membrane forming curing compounds and ASTM standards are followed.

12.5.2. Water proof paper or polythene sheet

For horizontal large surfaces polythene sheet or water proof paper can be used for curing concrete. The polythene sheet is spread over the surface as soon as possible without damage to the concrete surface and the lap joints between adjoining sheets lightly sealed. The polythene sheet or water proof paper serves dual purpose of preventing loss of water from the concrete and protecting the surface from damage. Care should be taken that the polythene or water proof paper is not torn. The surface should be inspected occasionally to ascertain that the surface is wet, if not, it should be rewetted and then resealed. This method has been found very economical and effective in regions where water is scarce.

12.6. MATURITY OF CONCRETE

The temperature during curing period also controls the rate of progress of the reactions of hydration and consequently affects the development of strength of concrete. The results of tests carried out on specimens cast, sealed and cured at a given temperature are shown in Fig. 12.2. This Fig. shows the ratio of strength of concrete cured at different temperatures to the 28 days strength of concrete cured at 70°F (21°C). The tempe-

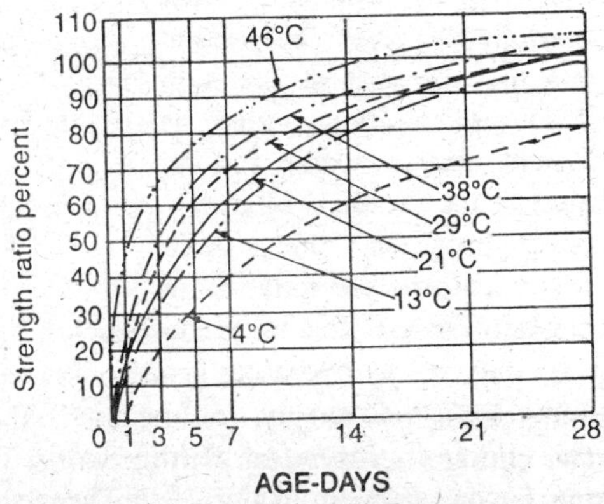

Fig. 12.2. Ratio of strength of concrete cured at different temperatures to the 28 day strength of concrete cured at 21°C (70°F)

ratures at which the specimens cast, sealed and cured are shown on the Fig. itself. From the Fig. 12.2, it will be seen that higher the curing temperature, higher the early strength, say upto 28 days. The effect of temperature at the time of setting is considered in the next article.

As the strength of concrete depends on both age and temperature, it can be said that the strength is a function of Σ (temperature × time interval). This summation is called *maturity*, and is measured in°C–hours (°F–hours) or °C–days (°F–day). The temperature can be reckoned between–12°C and – 10°C (11°F and 14°F). This is because at temperatures below the freezing point of water and down to about – 12°C (11°F) concrete shows a small increase in strength with time, but low temperature must not be applied until the concrete has set and gained sufficient strength to resist damage due to the action of frost. Please also see chapter 8.

Experiments have shown that the strength and maturity relation depends on the properties of cement used and on the general qualities of concrete and is valid for a limited range of temperature. The maturity rule applies fairly well when the initial temperature of concrete is between 16°C and 27°C (60 and 80°F) and no loss of moisture takes place due to drying during the period considered. Due to these limitations this rule could not be popular in actual practice.

12.7. INFLUENCE OF TEMPERATURE AT THE TIME OF SETTING ON THE STRENGTH OF CONCRETE

We have read that a rise in the curing temperature speeds up the chemical reactions of hydration and affects the early strength of concrete without any ill effect on the later strength. However a higher temperature during placing and setting, although increases the early strength, but affects adversely strength beyond about 7 days onwards. The explanation for this may be that a rapid initial hydration forms products of hydration of poorer physical structure, probably more porous, thus a large proportion of the pores always remain unfilled. From gel/space ratio rule this will lead to a lower strength compared with a less porous, though slowly hydrating paste in which a high gel/space ratio will eventually be reached. This adverse effect of high early temperature on the later strength of concrete has been explained by *Verbeck* and *Helmuth* as follows.

In their view the rapid initial rate of hydration at higher temperatures retard the subsequent hydration and produces a non uniform distribution of the products of hydration within the paste. The reason for this may be that at the high initial rate of hydration there is insufficient time available for the diffusion of the products of hydration away from the cement grain and for a uniform precipitation in the interstitial space. Thus as a consequence, a high concentration of the products of hydration is built-up in the vicinity of the hydrating grains. This retards the subsequent hydration of the grain and affects the long term strength adversely.

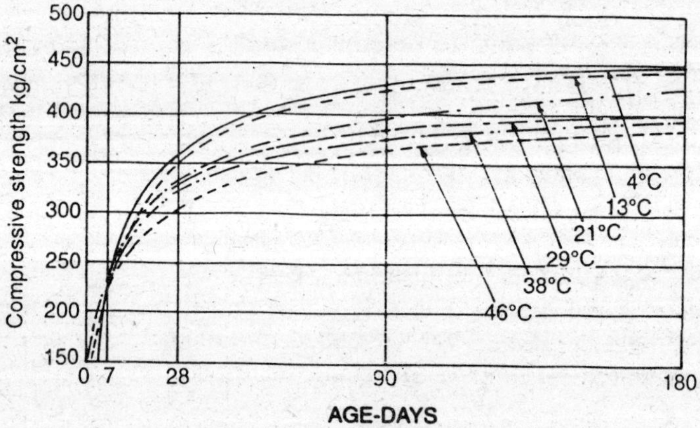

Fig. 12.3. Effect of temperature during the first two hours after casting on the development of strength

The effect of temperature during the first two hours after mixing on the development of strength of concrete has been shown in Fig. 12.3. The range of temperature varies from 40°F to 115°F (4°C to 46°C). Beyond the age of two hours all specimens were cured at 70°F (21°C). To prevent the movement of moisture, specimens were sealed. Specimens cured during first 24 hours at 36°F (2°C) and then at 64°F

(18°C) were found 10% stronger than those cured at 64°F (18°C) from the very beginning. Fig. 12.3 is based on *price's* results.

The temperature at the time of placing concrete also influences its strength. It has been observed that an increase of 9°F (5°C) decreases the strength by 19 kg/cm^2. The influence of curing temperature on strength of concrete tested after curing at 1 day and 28 days is shown in Fig. 8.13.

The temperature at the time of testing also has been found to influence the strength of concrete. Specimens cooled to 20°C (68°F) for two hours before testing showed no deleterious effect except temperature above 150°F or 65°C.

Specimens cast and stored at different temperatures for a period of 28 days and thereafter at 23°C, a higher temperature was found to result in a higher strength during the first few days after casting, but after 7 to 28 days situation changed radically as shown in Fig. 12.4. From the Fig. it will be seen that early high temperature leads to a lower strength for a given total maturity than when heating is delayed for a week or is absent totally. Specimens cured at temperatures between 4°C to 23°C for 28 days showed higher strength than those cured at 42 to 49°C. Even the concrete cast at 4°C (40°F) and stored at – 4°C (25°F) for 28 days and then at 23°C (73°F) was found stronger after 90 days from similar concrete stored at 23°C continuously Fig. 12.4.

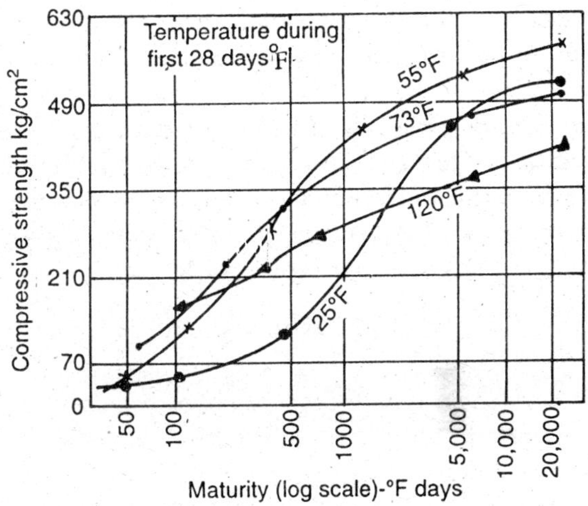

Fig. 12.4. Influence of the temperature during the first 28 days after casting on the strength

Klieger's tests have shown that there is an optimum temperature during the early life of concrete th: will lead to the highest strength at a desired age. Using ordinary portland cement for laboratory made concrete the optimum temperature has been found as 55°F (13°C). For rapid hardening cement it is 40°F (4°C). However beyond the initial period of setting and hardening the influence of temperature continues within limits *i.e.* higher temperature accelerates development of strength.

12.8. APPLICATION OF HEAT

The strength development of concrete is not only a function of time, but also that of temperature. When concrete is subjected to higher temperatures, the hydration process of cement accelerates, resulting in faster development of strength. To accelerate the hydration process of cement only dry heat can not

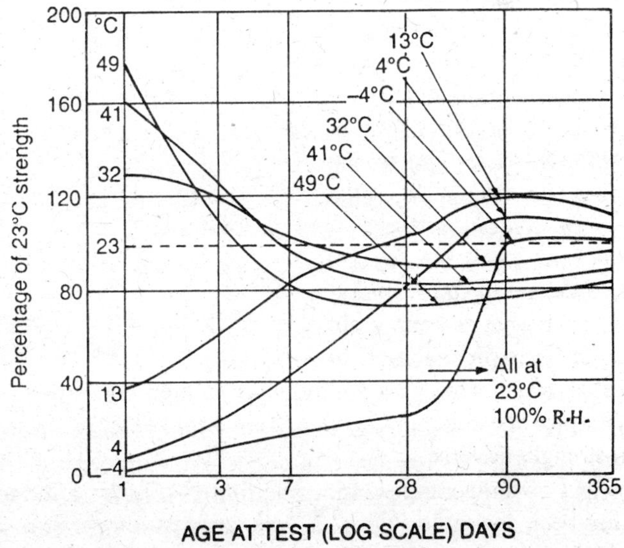

Fig. 12.5. Effect of temperature during the first 28 days on the strength of concrete (w/c ratio = 0.41, Air entrainment 4.5%)

be applied as the presence of moisture is also essential. Thus for applying higher temperature and maintaining required wetness to accelerate the hydration process, steam curing is the best solution.

12.8.1. Steam curing at atmospheric pressure

The main object of steam curing is to obtain a sufficiently high early strength of the concrete products so that they may be handled soon after their casting. Thus the advantages of steam curing are as follows:

1. Concrete members can be handled very soon after their casting.
2. Less space will be sufficient in the casting yard.
3. Higher out put is possible for a given capital out lay.
4. A less curing space will be sufficient.
5. The construction work can be started much earlier.
6. The completed work can be put to use at an early date.
7. The form work may be struck off at the early age and can be used else where.
8. Prestressing bed can be released early for further casting.

Thus the steam curing will not only give economical advantage but-also technical advantage in the matter of prefabrication of concrete members.

The main disadvantage of steam curing is the lower strength at the later age, but for many applications long term strength of concrete is not of much importance.

12.8.2. STEAM CURING AT ORDINARY PRESSURE

When steam curing is carried out at one atmospheric pressure *i.e.* the temperature is below 100°C, the process can be regarded as a special case of moist curing. Steam curing can be used successfully with different types of portland cements, but it should not be adopted with high alumina cement as it will have adverse effect on the strength of high alumina cement. Steam cured concrete of a low water/cement ratio has shown better results than a weaker mix.

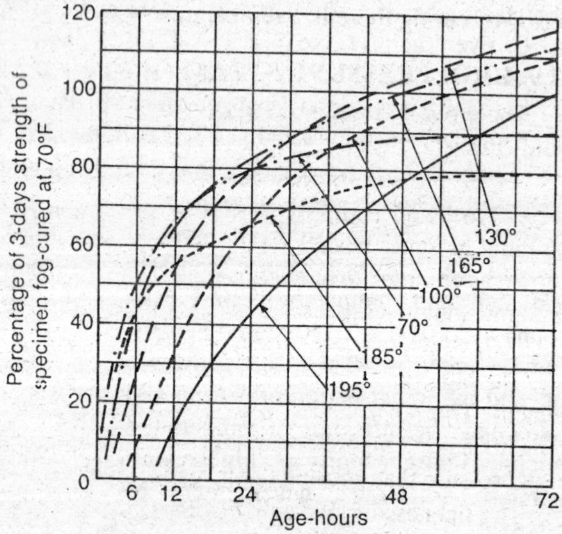

Fig. 12.6. Strength of concrete cured in steam at different temperature

Due to the nature of the operations involved in steam curing, the process usually is applied to pre cast units. Low pressure steam curing is applied in special built chambers or in tunnels through which the concrete members are transported on a conveyer belt. The chamber should be big enough to hold a days production. The door is closed and the steam is applied. Alternatively plastic covers or portable boxes are placed over the pre-cast units and steam is applied through flexible connections. Due to the accelerated hydration at high temperature of steam, the normal 28 days strength is developed in the concrete in about 3 days.

Due to the influence of temperature during the early stages of hardening on the later strength, a compromise between the temperatures giving a high early strength and a high late strength has to be made. Fig. 12.6 shows the typical values of strength of concrete cured with steam at different temperatures immediately after casting. From the Fig. 12.6, it will be seen that above 100°F curing temperature, lower the curing temperature higher the later strength. Raising the curing temperature from 130°F, the strength after 72 hours reduces by about 33%.

Thus the rate of increase in temperature at the commencement of steam curing is very important. It has been observed that if 120°F is reached in a period less than about 2 to 3 hours or 210°F in less than 6 to 7 hours *i.e.* if the rate of increase of temperature is between 40°F to 60°F per hour or 30°F to 35°F from the time of mixing, the gain in strength beyond the first few hours is affected adversely. Hence such a rapid rise in temperature should not be allowed. The effect of rapid rise in temperature is more pronounced in concrete with higher water/cement ratio and concrete with rapid hardening cement than ordinary portland cement. It has been observed that excessively rapid heating can cause a loss of strength at later ages about one-third compared with wet curing at room temperature. The retrogression of the strength of steam cured concrete is due to the pressure development in the air pores during heating as air has higher coefficient of thermal expansion than the surrounding solid material.

As the temperature at the time of setting has the greatest influence on the strength at later ages, delay in the application of steam curing has been found advantageous. From experiments it has been found that a delay of 2, 3 5 and 6 hours for 100, 130, 165 and 185°F temperature respectively will not have any adverse effect on the strength of concrete *i.e.* after sufficient delay, rapid heating has no adverse effect on the strength. If concrete is exposed to higher temperature with a smaller delay, the strength will be affected adversely. This effect is more serious for higher curing temperatures. A practical curing cycle may be adopted as, a delay of 3 to 5 hours, heating at the rate of 40°F to 60°F per hour upto a maximum temperature of 150°F to 180°F, then storage at the maximum temperature, followed by a period of "soaking" when no heat is added, but the concrete takes in the residual heat and moisture and finally cooling period. The total time should be about 18 hours.

It may be stated here that a longer period of curing at a lower temperature gives a higher optimum strength than a higher temperature applied for a shorter period. It has also been found that for any one period of curing there is a temperature which gives an optimum strength.

12.9. HIGH PRESSURE STEAM CURING (AUTO CLAVING)

The process is quite different both in the method of execution and in the nature of the resulting product from curing in steam at one atmospheric pressure.

As the pressure in this case is more than one atmosphere, the curing chamber used is of the pressure vessel type with a supply of wet steam. In this chamber arrangements for supply of excessive water is essential as super heated steam should not be allowed to come in contact with concrete. Such a vessel is known as an *autoclave*. High pressure steam curing can be applied to pre-cast products of ordinary as well as light weight concrete. The optimum curing temperature has been found experimentally as 350°F (177°C), which corresponds to a steam pressure of 8 kg/cm^2 above atmospheric pressure.

The high pressure steam curing has been found most effective when finely ground silica is added to the cement. The silica added reacts with the Ca $(OH)_2$ released on hydration of C_3S of the cement. Thus cements having higher percentage of C_3S have greater capacity for developing high strength when cured at high pressure than those having high content of C_2S.

The fineness of silica should be of the same order as that of the cement. The silica and cement should be intimately mixed before they are added to the mixer. Though the optimum amount of silica to be added depends on the mix proportions, but generally varies from 0.4 to 0.7 of the weight of cement. This amount makes the lime/silica ratio of the mixture very approximately 1. The high temperature during curing also affects the reactions of hydration of the cement itself.

The high temperature curing produces products of hydration as coarse and micro crystalline in character. The specific surface of high pressure steam cured paste is only about 5% that of cement paste cured at ordinary temperature. Hence not more than 5%, high pressure steam cured paste can be classified as gel. Followings are the advantages and disadvantages of high pressure steam curing.

1. With high pressure steam curing, compressive strength with in 24 hours can be obtained equal to that of 28 days normal cured concrete.

2. The high pressure steam curing improves the resistance of concrete to sulphates attack. The main reason for this is the formation of aluminates more stable in the presence of sulphates than those formed at lower temperatures. For this reason, cements with a high proportion of C_3A have shown greater resistance to sulphate attack than those having lower C_3A contents. Another reason for the improvement of sulphate resistance is due to the reduction in lime in the cement paste as a result of lime silica reaction. Further improvement in the sulphate resistance is due to the increased strength and impermeability of the steam cured concrete.
3. High pressure steam curing reduces drying shrinkage to about 1/2 to 1/6 of the concrete cured at normal temperature.
4. Moisture movement is also reduced.
5. Creep is also reduced significantly by high pressure steam curing.
6. High pressure steam curing reduces efflorescence, as no lime is left to be leached out.
7. High pressure steam curing also reduces the effect of freezing and thawing.
8. High pressure steam curing produces stable products and stabilizes unsound materials.

Disadvantages

1. High pressure steam curing reduces the bond strength of concrete with reinforcement by about 50% in comparison with ordinary curing.
2. High pressure steam curing makes the concrete brittle.
3. High pressure steam curing produces drier and light colour products than moist cured units.

The rate of heating during high pressure steam curing should not be too high as it will interfere with the setting and hardening process of concrete. A typical steaming cycle may consist of gradual increase in temperature of 360°F (182°C) which corresponds to a pressure of 10 kg/cm^2 over a period of 3 hours. The concrete is maintained at this temperature for 5 to 8 hours, and then the pressure is released within 20 to 30 minutes. Actual details of the steaming cycle depend on the plant used and the size of concrete members to be cured.

Steam curing should only be applied to concrete products made with portland cement. High alumina and super sulphated cement would be adversely affected by the high temperature.

12.10. PERIOD OF CURING

As per IS 456-1978, exposed surfaces of concrete should be kept continuously in a damp or wet condition by any method as discussed above at least for 7 days from the date of placing concrete as during this period abut 66% strength of the 28 days strength of concrete is developed. As explained earlier 92% hydration takes place during 28 days period if concrete is cured at 70°F and atleast 95% humidity is maintained. The strength at 28 days of such concrete is taken as standard. 70% strength is developed in about 10 days and 75% strength in 14 days. Hence the period of curing in the laboratory is recommended as 28 days and in the field at least 7 days. Further looking to the conditions and importance of work, Engineer incharge may fix the period of curing. The increase in strength of concrete with the period of curing has been found as follows:

Table 12.1

S. No.	*Period of curing*	*Strength in % of 28 days cured concrete*
1.	1 day	16.0
2.	3 day	40.0
3.	7 day	67.0
4.	28 day	100.0
5.	3 months	122.0
6.	6 months	146.0
7.	12 months	155.0

Further it has been observed that the strength of moist cured concrete increases by 50% over air exposed concrete for the entire period.

12.11. ELECTRICAL CURING

By this method the concrete can be cured by passing an alternating current through the concrete itself between two electrodes either embedded in or applied to the surface of concrete. While using this method care should be taken to prevent the moisture from going out leaving the concrete completely dry. This method is applicable mostly in very cold climatic regions and is not likely to find much of its use in ordinary climatic conditions due to economic considerations.

12.12. INFRA RED RADIATION CURING METHOD

This method of concrete curing is practised in very cold climatic regions in Russia. It is claimed that by this method much more rapid gain of strength can be obtained than with steam curing and that rapid initial temperature does not cause any decrease in the ultimate strength as in the case of steam curing at ordinary pressure. Usually this method is adopted for curing the hollow concrete products. The normal operative temperature is kept at about 194°F (90°C).

Maturity rule

As already explained the temperature effect on concrete is cumulative and can be expressed as the product of temperature and time, during which it prevails, known as maturity M. Thus maturity can be expressed as

$$M = \Sigma T \times \Delta t$$

where,

M = Maturity

T = Temperature measured from a datum of – 11°C. Thus for temp. of 30°, $T = 20 - (-11) = 41$°C.

Δt = Time interval (usually in days).

The maturity rule can be of practical use in estimating the strength of concrete. In SI units the relation between strength and maturity of concrete is as follows:

$$f_c = -33 + 21 \log M.$$

However this rule depends on the following factors:

(*a*) Cement actually used in the concrete work.

(*b*) W/c ratio.

(*c*) Whether any loss of water takes place during the curing period.

The harmful effect of an early high temperature vitiates the maturity rule. Hence for these reasons the maturity rule has not been widely accepted.

QUESTIONS

1. What is meant by curing? What are its objects?
2. What is the necessity of curing?
3. Enumerate different methods of curing and explain the procedure of curing where water is scarse.
4. How much water is required for reasonably complete hydration of the cement in a concrete mix?
5. How does the temperature at the time of setting affects the strength of concrete?
6. What is meant by curing of concrete? Why curing is important?
7. Name different methods of curing. Explain the procedure at one atmosphere pressure steam curing.
8. Discuss the advantages of membrane curing compared with water curing.
9. Compare the strength development of concrete stored moist from the time of demoulding at 24 hours at 5°C (41°F) and 40°C (104°F).

10. What is the effect of temperature during the first 24 hours on the 28 day strength of concrete?
11. What is meant by self desiccation and when does it occur?
12. Define maturity of concrete and also discuss the limitations on the prediction of concrete strength from its maturity?
13. Why does steam curing include a cooling period?
14. Describe steam curing at ordinary pressure.
15. Describe the procedure of auto claving.
16. Compare the mechanism of hydration at high temperature with that at normal temperature.
18. Discuss the advantages and disadvantages of steam curing of concrete.
18. Calculate the strength of concrete cured at 30°C (86°F) for 7 days. If the strength requirement is of 30 MPa, find out the temperature? [a = 18.6 MPa, b = 25°C]

OBJECTIVE TYPE QUESTIONS

1. Which of the following statements is false?
   (*a*) Curing of concrete provides adequate moisture with in concrete to ensure sufficient water for the continued hydration of cement.
   (*b*) Curing of concrete provides warm temperature which helps in the hydration of cement or chemical action of cement.
   (*c*) Curing of concrete governs the resultant micro structure of the hydrated cement.
   (*d*) None of the above
   (*e*) All the above
2. Ponding method of concrete curing gives more compressive strength than covered with burlap upto a water/cement ratio.
   (*a*) 0.55 (*b*) 0.62
   (*c*) 0.40 (*d*) 0.32
3. Which of the following methods is not used for curing
   (*a*) Chemical curing (*b*) Electrical curing
   (*c*) Mechanical curing (*d*) Membrane curing
   (*e*) Infra red curing
4. Which of the following statements is correct
   (*a*) Membrane curing of concrete is the process of providing plastic sheeting to the concrete as a protective cover
   (*b*) It is the process of membrane forming compound on the surface of the concrete
   (*c*) It is the process of spraying sodium silicate on the surface of the concrete
   (*d*) All the above
   (*e*) None of the above
5. Which of the following statements is correct?
   (*a*) Maturity of concrete is the 28 day compressive strength
   (*b*) It is 365 days compressive strength
   (*c*) It is percentage of 28 days strength of concrete cured at 18°C
   (*d*) It is the summation of product of curing period and temperature of curing
6. The standard moist curing of concrete for 7 days develops %. Compressive strength of 28 days strength
   (*a*) 60 to 70% (*b*) 75 to 80%
   (*c*) 82 to 90% (*d*) 90 to 95%
7. The standard moist curing of concrete for 14 days develops in % compressive strength of 28 days strength
   (*a*) 55 to 65% (*b*) 70 to 80%
   (*c*) 82 to 90% (*d*) 90 to 95%
8. Which of the following statements is false
   (*a*) Rubber latex emulsion can be used for membrane curing of concrete
   (*b*) Varnish can be used as concrete membrane curing
   (*c*) Cut backs or asphaltic emulsion can be used as concrete membrane curing
   (*d*) Sodium silicate solution can be used as concrete emulsion curing

(*e*) Emulsion of paraffin can be used as concrete membrane curing

9. Which of the following statements is false.
   (*a*) High alumina cement concrete can be steam cured with advantage
   (*b*) Steam curing can be used successfully with difference types of portland cements
   (*c*) Steam cured concrete of low water/cement ratio produces better strength than leaner mixes
   (*d*) Steam curing usually is applied to precast units.
10. Which of the following statement is correct?
    (*a*) By steam curing form work can be released at the early age and can be used else where
    (*b*) The pre stressed bed can be released early
    (*c*) Higher out put is possible for a given out lay
    (*d*) Less curing space will be sufficient
    (*e*) All of the above
11. Which of the following statements is correct?
    (*a*) Curing for a longer period at a lower temperature gives higher strength than higher temperature applied for shorter period
    (*b*) For any curing period, the curing temperature governs the strength development.
    (*c*) Early high temperature gives lower strength for a given total maturity
    (*d*) Temperature at the time of testing influences the strength of concrete
    (*e*) All of the above
12. Which of the following statements is false?
    (*a*) High pressure steam curing has been found more effective when finely ground silica is added to the cement
    (*b*) High pressure steam curing can not be applied to precast products of ordinary as well as light weight concrete
    (*c*) High pressure steam curing produces more strength of concrete when cement having higher percentage of C_3S is used than cements having high content of C_2S
    (*d*) Cements having high proportion of C_3A has greater resistance to sulphate attack than those having lower C_3A content
13. Which of the following statements is false?
    (*a*) High pressure steam curing reduces the moisture content
    (*b*) High pressure steam curing reduces the drying shrinkage to about 50 to 16% of the concrete cured at normal temperature
    (*c*) High pressure steam curing has no effect on the reduction of creep
    (*d*) By high pressure steam curing the compressive strength with in 24 hours can be obtained equal to 28 days normal cured concrete
14. Identify the wrong statement of the followings
    (*a*) High pressure steam curing increases the bond strength of concrete with reinforcement by about 50% in comparision with ordinary curing
    (*b*) High pressure steam curing produces drier and light colour products than moist curing
    (*c*) High pressure steam curing makes the concrete brittle
    (*d*) The strength of moist cured concrete increases by 50% over air exposed concrete for the entire period
15. Which of the statements is false?
    (*a*) Maturity strength of concrete depends on the type of cement actually used
    (*b*) Maturity strength of concrete depends on the w/c ratio of the mix
    (*c*) Maturity strength of concrete depends on whether any water loss has taken place during the curing period
    (*d*) None of the above

Answers

1. (*e*)	4. (*b*)	7. (*b*)	10. (*e*)	13. (*c*)
2. (*c*)	5. (*d*)	8. (*b*)	11. (*e*)	14. (*a*)
3. (*c*)	6. (*a*)	9. (*a*)	12. (*b*)	15. (*d*)

13

Other Strengths of Concrete

13.1. INTRODUCTION

In actual practice concrete is subjected to various types of loading other than static compression. In the design of concrete structures, it is assumed that concrete will not be subjected to tensile stresses, which will be borne by tensile steel. In the design only compressive strength of concrete is taken into account and its tensile strength is omitted being small. But later studies have shown that tensile stresses can not be avoided. These stresses are connected with shear and are generated by differential movements, such as shrinkage, which often result in cracking and reducing the durability of the structure. Thus it is important to know how the tensile strength is related to compressive strength.

Further in addition to tensile stresses, some structures are subjected to repeated loading. To assess the behaviour of the structure under repeated loading, the knowledge of fatigue strength is needed. The strength under impact of loading is also of interest. In other circumstances, as in concrete roads, the concrete surfaces are subjected to wear. Thus the resistance to wear is of importance.

Finally as the reinforced structural concrete contains steel reinforcement, the bond strength between the steel and concrete must be satisfactory to maintain the integrity of the structure. Thus in this chapter, tensile, Fatigue, Impact, Abrasion and Bond strengths of concrete will be discussed.

13.2. TENSILE STRENGTH OF CONCRETE

The actual tensile strength of cement paste or similar brittle material as that of stone is very much lower than the theoretical strength estimated on the basis of molecular cohesion of the atomic structure and calculated from the energy required to create the new surfaces by fracture of a perfectly homogeneous and flaw (fracture) less material. This theoretical strength has been found to be 1000 times higher than the actual measured strength.

This difference between the theoretical and actual strength can be explained by the presence of cracks in the concrete as accepted as a fact (postulated) by "GRIFFITH". These cracks lead to high stress concentration in the material under load so that a

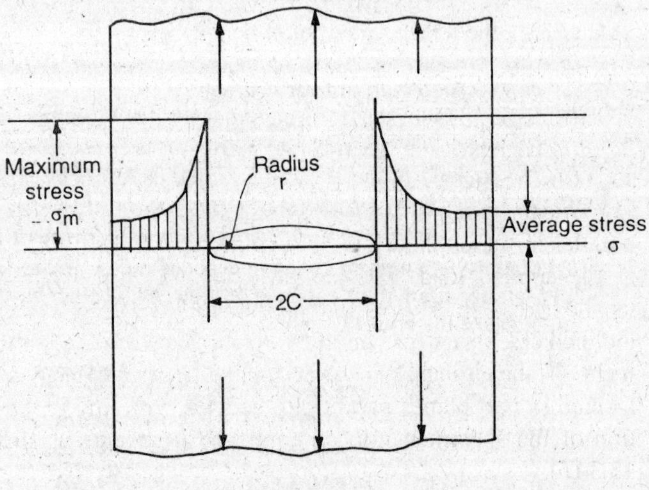

Fig. 13.1. Stress concentration at the tip of a crack in a brittle material under load

very high stress is reached in very small volumes of the specimen (at the edges or tips of the crack as shown in Fig. 13.1, resulting in localized microscopic fractures, while the average stress in the whole specimen is very low. Actually the flaws or cracks vary in size and only the few large cracks cause failure. The concentration of stress at the top edge, is infact three dimensional, but the greatest weakness is when the orientation of the crack is at right angle (normal) to the applied load as shown in Fig. 13.1. From the figure it will also be seen that maximum stress is higher, for the longer and sharper the crack *i.e.* the greater the value of c and smaller the value of 'r' then

$$\frac{\sigma_m}{\sigma} = 2\,(c/r)^{1/2} \qquad \ldots(13.1)$$

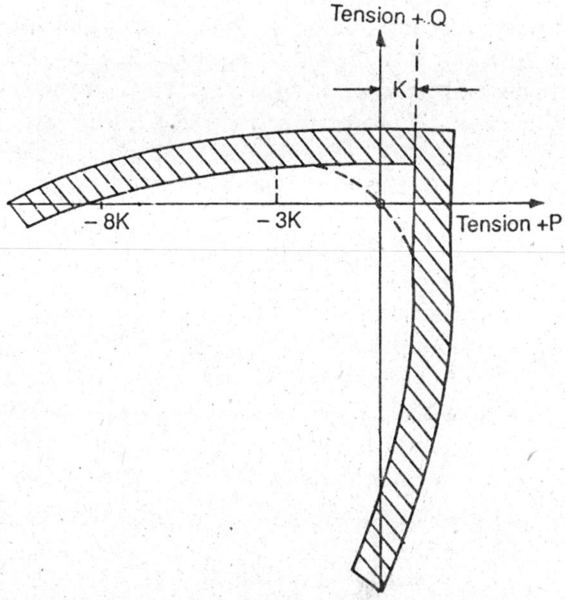

Fig. 13.2. Orowan's criteria of fracture under biaxial stress

It has been observed that when two unequal principal stresses are compressive, the stress along the edge of an internal flaw is tensile at some points so that fracture can take place The fracture criteria is represented graphically in Fig. 13.2 for a combination of two principal stresses P and Q, where K is the tensile strength in direct tension. Fracture occurs under a combination of P and Q such that the point representing the state of stress crosses the curve out wards on to the shaded side. From this Fig. 13.2 it can be seen that fracture may occur when uniaxial compression is applied. Infact this fact has been observed while testing concrete specimen in compression.

The nominal compressive strength is 8 K *i.e.* the eight times the tensile strength determined in a direct tension test. This figure is in good agreement with the observed values of the ratio of the compressive to tensile strengths of concrete.

13.3. FRACTURE PATTERN

The fracture pattern of concrete under different states of stress is shown in Fig. 13.3. Under uniaxial tension, fracture occurs more or less in a plane normal to the direction of the load as shown in Fig. 13.3 (*a*).

Under uniaxial compression the cracks are approximately parallel to the applied load, but some cracks are formed at an angle to the applied load. The parallel cracks are caused by a localized tensile stress in a direction normal to the compressive load. The inclined cracks are formed due to the collapse caused by the development of shear planes. Thus it should be noted that the cracks are formed in two planes parallel to the load, resulting in the disintegration of the specimen into column type fragments as shown in Fig. 13.3 (*b*).

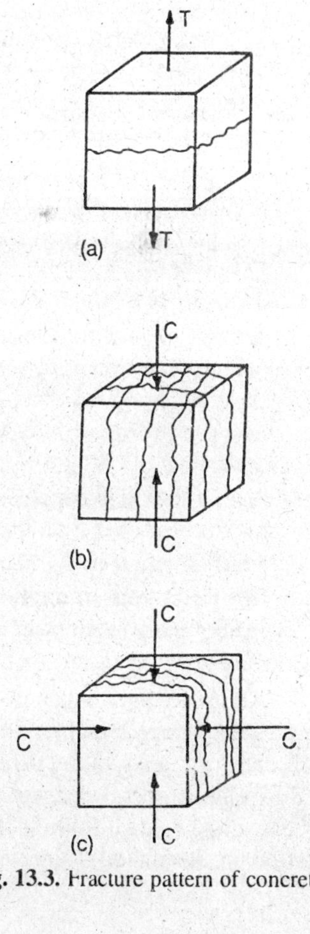

Fig. 13.3. Fracture pattern of concrete

Under biaxial compression the failure takes place in one plane, parallel to the applied load, resulting in the formation of slab type fragments as shown in Fig. 13.3 (*c*). Here it shall be noted that the fracture pattern of Fig. 13.3 are for direct stresses only. Thus there is no restraint from the platens of the testing machine, but in practice these platens introduce some lateral compression due to the friction between the specimen and steel platens. In case of ordinary testing machines it is difficult to eliminate this friction. However this effect can be minimised by keeping length/width ratio of the specimen greater than 2.0. This ratio ensures the elimination of platen restraint from the central portion of the specimen.

13.4. FACTORS AFFECTING RELATION OR RATIO OF TENSILE AND COMPRESSIVE STRENGTHS

Following factors affect the ratio of tensile and compressive strengths

1. **Properties of coarse aggregate.** The properties of coarse aggregate affect the cracking of concrete very much. It has been observed that vertical cracking in a specimen subjected to uniaxial compression starts under a load equal to 50 to 75% of the ultimate load. The stress at which the cracks form depends to a great extent on the properties of coarse aggregate. It has been observed that concrete made from smooth surfaced gravel cracks at much lower stress than concrete made with rough and angular crushed rock aggregate. This may be due to mechanical bond and shape of the coarse aggregate.

   Further it has been observed that the properties of coarse aggregate affect tensile strength or the cracking load in compression more than the compressive strength of concrete The influence of the type of coarse aggregate on the strength of concrete varies in magnitude and depends on the water/cement ratio of the mix. For water/cement ratio below 0.4, the use of crushed aggregate has resulted in increase in strength upto 38% than when gravel is used. With water/cement ratio above 0.5, the influence of water/cement ratio falls off and at 0.65 water/cement no difference in strength is observed. The properties of coarse aggregate have been found to have little effect on direct and splitting tensile strength, but flexural strength is found greater with the use of crushed and angular crushed rock aggregate than the rounded gravel.
2. **The properties of fine aggregate.** The properties of fine aggregate also influence the ratio of tensile to compressive strength of concrete.
3. The grading of aggregate also has been found to influence this ratio.
4. **Effect of moisture.** The moisture condition of concrete influences the relation between the flexural and compressive strength. If one concrete is cured continuously in water and the other is curved wet and then stored in dry environment and tested. It is found that the dry concrete gave greater compressive strength than the continuously wet cured concrete. The direct and splitting tensile strengths are not affected in similar manner. However flexural strength of drying concrete is found lower than that of wet concrete. This may be due to the development of shrinkage cracks in the concrete.
5. Age of the concrete at the time of testing. As stated earlier the increase in tensile strength after one month is slower than the compressive strength. Hence the age of specimen affects this ratio.
6. **Methods of testing.** Tensile strength is determined by the following methods:
   (*a*) Direct tension method
   (*b*) Splitting tension method
   (*c*) Flexural tension method

   All the three methods give different results. The lowest value is given by the direct tension method. Thus values are given in order as direct tension < splitting tension < Flexural tension.
7. **Size of specimen.** The smaller the size of test specimen, lesser volume of concrete is subjected to tensile stress, resulting in less chances of a weak element to be subjected to tensile stress and ultimately resulting in failure. On the other hand, larger the size of specimens, greater is the volume of concrete having greater chances of a weak element and ultimately resulting in failure.

Thus larger the specimen, greater the chances of failure. Seconally both the splitting and flexural test methods involve a non uniform stress distribution which reduces the propagation of a crack, resulting in delay of ultimate failure. On the other hand the stress distribution in the direct tension test is uniform, so that once a crack is formed, it can propagate quickly through out the section of the specimen.

8. **Effect of inadequate curing.** Tensile strength of concrete is found more sensitive to the inadequate curing than compressive strength. This may be due to the non uniform shrinkage of flexural test beams. As flexural test beams are very sensitive to shrinkage cracks and is very serious for the test.

13.5. DIFFICULTIES IN CARRYING OUT DIRECT TEST

To carry out the uniaxial tensile test is difficult due to the following problems:

1. **Problem of gripping the specimen.** Proper and satisfactory gripping equipment is not available to grip the test specimen *ie.* The gripping equipment should be such that the premature failure does not take place near the ends of the attachment. Generally there is a tendency of the specimen to break near the ends, which cause error in the results.
2. **Due to ecentricity in the applied load.** There should be no ecentricity in the applied load. However there is always some ecentricity present in the applied load system. The stresses are changed due to the ecentricity of loading, which may introduce major error on the stresses developed regardless of size and shape of the specimen. Therefore direct tensile test is not standardized and rarely used.

Thus due to these difficulties the tensile strength is determined by indirect methods as flexure test and splitting test. However these test methods give higher values of the tensile strength than the true tensile strength determined by uniaxial loading.

As stated above different test methods yield numerically different results in the following order.

(*a*) Direct or uniaxial tension yields the lowest value of tensile strength.

(*b*) Splitting tension test yields higher value than direct tension method, but lower than flexural tension test.

(*c*) Flexural tension test yields the greatest value of tensile strength of all the methods *i.e.* direct tension < splitting tension < flexural tension.

13.5.1. Reasons of Difference in Results

Following are the reasons for the difference in the value of tensile strength given by different methods.

1. With the usual size of the laboratory specimen, the volume of concrete subjected to tensile stress decreases in the same order as listed above *i.e.* area subjected in direct tension < splitting tension area < flexural tension area. Thus statistically there is a greater chance of a weak element in the larger volume than a smaller volume and thus more failure in larger volume.
2. Both the splitting and flexural test methods involve non uniform stress distribution which restrict the propagation of a crack and thus delay the ultimate failure. On the other hand in the direct test the stress distribution is

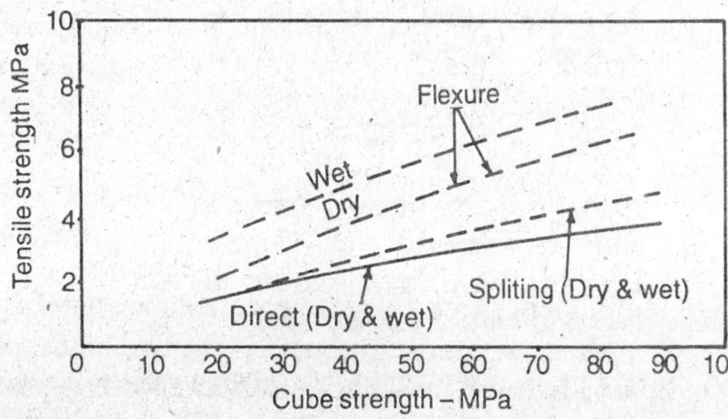

Fig. 13.4. Relation between tensile and compressive strength of concrete made with normal and light weight aggregate

uniform so that once a crack is formed, it may propagate quickly through the section of specimen. The relation between the compressive and tensile strength of concrete is shown in Fig. 13.4.

Methods of determination of tensile strength by spitting and flexural strength have been discussed in detail in chapter 19.

13.6. FLEXURE STRENGTH

When concrete subjected to bending, compressive as well tensile stresses are developed. In many cases direct shear stresses are also developed. The strength shown by the concrete against bending is known as flexure strength. The strength per unit area is known as flexure stress '*S*' and is given by the relation.

$$S = \frac{M \cdot y}{I}$$

where,

S = stress in the fibre farthest from the neutral axis

M = B.M. at the section

y = distance from neutral axis to farthest fibre

I = moment of inertia of the cross section

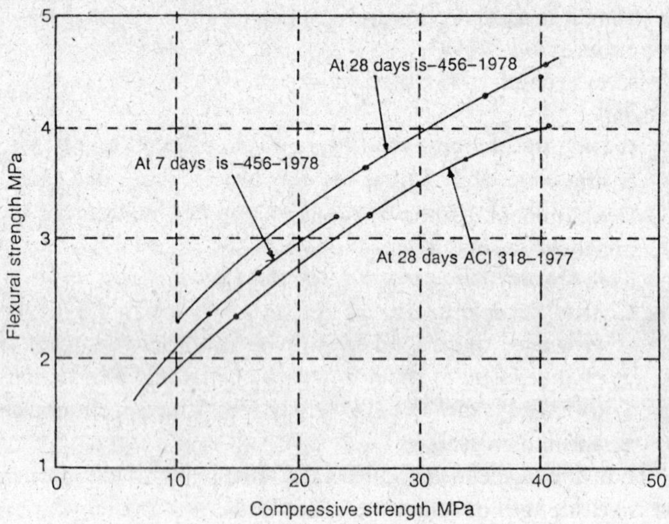

Fig. 13..5. Relation between flexural and compressive strength at various ages

The value of modulus of rupture depends upon the dimensions of the beam and on the arrangements of loading. Two systems of loading may be used as:

1. **Central point loading.** This loading system gives a triangular B.M. distribution, such that maximum stress occurs at one section of the beam only.
2. **Two point loading.** This loading system produces a constant B.M. between the load points. Now a days this method is taken as the standard method and central point method has been discontinued in many countries such as U.K. and U.S.A. etc. The relationship between flexural strength with compressive and tensile strengths have been shown in Fig. 13.5 and 13.6 respectively.

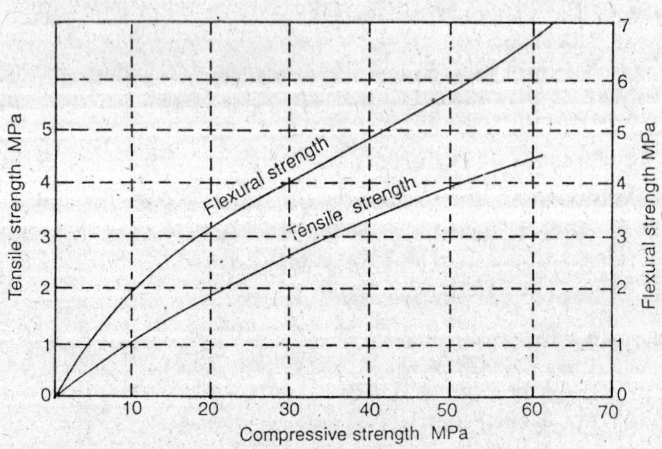

Fig. 13.6. Relation between flexural, compressive and tensile strength of concrete

13.7. RELATION BETWEEN COMPRESSIVE AND TENSILE STRENGTH OF CONCRETE

The theoritical compressive strength of concrete is eight times larger than its tensile strength. This implies a fixed relation between the compressive and tensile strength of concrete. Infact there is a close relation but not a direct proportionality. The ratio of tensile to compressive strength is lower for higher compressive strengths.

Experimental results also have shown that concrete in compression and tension (both direct tension and flexural tension) are closely related but the relationship is not of direct proportionality type. The ratio of tensile strength to compressive strength depends upon the strength of concrete. Thus higher the compressive strength, higher the tensile strength, but the rate of increase of tensile strength is of decreasing order. The tensile strength of concrete is more sensitive to improper curing than the compressive strength. This may be due to the following two reasons.

(*a*) Formation of inferior quality gel due to improper curing.

(*b*) Development of more shrinkage cracks due to improper curing. The use of pozzolanic materials have shown the increase in tensile strength.

The Central Road Research Institute Delhi has carried out extensive study for establishing the relation between tensile and compressive strength of concrete for the construction of concrete roads. Fig. 13.7.

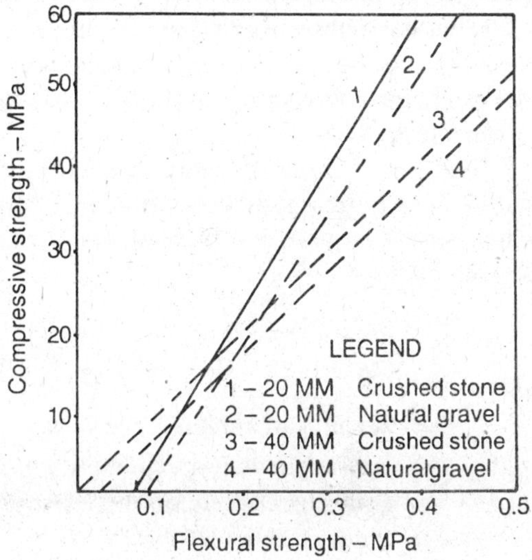

Fig. 13.7. **Relation between flexural and compressive strength**

On the basis of test data of the study, CRRI has suggested the following relation between flexural strength and compressive strength of concrete,

$$y = 11x - 3.4 \quad \text{...(13.1)}$$

where y is the compressive strength of concrete in MPa and x its flexural strength. This relation depends on the size of coarse aggregate. Fig. 13.7 shows the relation ship between compressive and flexural strength of concrete for various sizes of aggregates. The strength is found to vary with the nature and size of aggregate. The relation is reproduced below:

(*a*) For 20 mm crushed stone $y = 15.3 \times -9.0$

(*b*) For 20 mm Natural Graval $y = 14.3 \times -10.4$

(*c*) For 40 mm Crushed stone $y = 9.9 \times -5.5$

(*d*) For 40 mm Natural Graval $y = 9.8 \times -2.5$

The flexural strength of concrete was found to be 8 to 11% of the compressive strength of concrete of higher strength concrete of the order of 25 MPa (250 kg/cm^2) and 9 to 12.8% for concrete of strength less than 25 MPa (250 kg/cm^2) see Table 13.1.

Table 13.1. Flexural strength in % of compressive strength of concrete with different aggregates

S. No.	*Compressive strength in MPa*	*Flexural strength as percentage of compressive strength percent*			
		Gravel with max. size		*Crushed stone with max. size*	
		20 mm	*40 mm*	*20 mm*	*40 mm*
1.	49	8.7	—	7.7	—
2.	42	9.0	10.8	7.9	10.2
3.	35	9.3	10.9	8.2	10.3
4.	28	9.9	11.1	8.6	10.2
5.	21	10.8	11.3	9.3	10.3
6.	14	12.5	12.0	10.8	10.5
	Average	10.0	11.2	8.8	10.3

The ratio of flexural strength to compressive strength was found higher for 40 mm maximum size aggregate than that of 20 mm max. sized aggregate. In general the ratio was found slightly higher for natural gravel than for crushed stone.

It has been observed that the flexure strength or modulus of rupture is obtained much lower by two point method than central point loading as shown in Fig. 13.8.

The test can be performed as per IS 516-1959 or 1964 on a beam specimen of 10 × 10 × 50 cms within a span of 40 cms. The modulus of rupture is given by the relation.

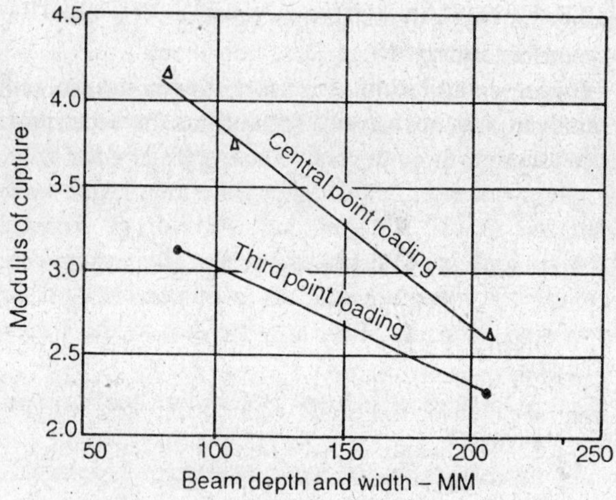

Fig. 13.8. Moduus of rupture of different sizes of beams subjected to central point and third point loading

$$fb = \frac{2p \times a}{bd^2}$$

where,

fb = modulus of rupture

p = load applied on specimen in kg.

a = distance between the crack and the nearest support

b = width of beam in cms

d = depth of specimen at failure point in cms

The value of modulus of rupture varies from 11% to 23% of the compressive strength of the same concrete. The average value may be assumed as 15% of the compressive strength. The use of angular aggregate or rough textured aggregate results in higher modulus of rupture than smooth textured aggregates. Thus the modulus of rupture is higher than direct tensile strengths for the same concrete due to the following reasons.

1. *Assumption of the shape of the stress block.* In the calculation of modulus of rupture, it is assumed that stress is proportional to the distance from the neutral axis of the beam, while the shape of the actual stress block under loads nearing failure is known to be non triangular, but parabolic. The modulus of rupture thus overestimates the tensile strength of concrete and gives a higher value than would be obtained in direct tensile test or splitting test.
2. The accidental eccentricity in a direct tensile test results in a lower apparent strength of the concrete.
3. Under direct tension the entire volume of specimen is subjected to the maximum stress, so that the probability of a weak element occurring is high.
4. The maximum fibre stress reached may be higher due to the fact that the propagation of a crack is blocked by less stressed material nearer to the neutral axis. However the actual values may vary depending on the properties of concrete. Relation between compressive, tensile strength and modulus of rupture is shown in Table 13.2 below.

Table 13.2. Showing variation in tensile strength obtained by different methods

S. No.	*Type of test*	*Mean strength in kg/cm²*	*Standard deviation in kg/cm²*	*Coefficient of variation*
1.	Direct tensile test	19.0	1.3	7
2.	Splitting test	27.9	1.4	5
3.	Modulus of rupture	41.7	2.5	6
4.	Compression cube test	412.3	14.3	3.5

13.8. CENTRAL POINT AND TWO OR THIRD POINT LOADING

The Central Road Research Institute Delhi has carried out extensitive study to find out the relation between central point loading and third point loading value of modulus of rupture. The ratio of span to depth of specimen was kept constant. On the basis of experimental data, they established the following relation.

$$x_1 = x_2 + 0.72$$

where,

x_1 = flexural strength of concrete in MPa under central point loading

x_2 = flexural strength of concrete in MPa under third point loading

During the study it was observed that central point loading gave higher average value of flexural strength than third point loading irrespective of the size of the specimen. The higher strength obtained in central point loading may be due to the following facts.

1. The beam is subjected to the maximum stress at the predetermined point not necessarily the weakest.
2. The span to depth ratio of specimen was kept 4. The alteration in this ratio was found to alter the flexural strength. The change in the span to depth ratio by 1% induced 3% change in the flexural strength when tested by third point loading and 2.5% change when tested by central point loading. With the increase in span to depth ratio, the flexural strength was found to decrease.
3. The rate of stress application was found to influence the flexural strength to a great extent. If the rate of application of stress is increased from the standard rate of application of 0.7 MPa per minute, the flexural strength was found to increase upto 25%. The increase was found more with the leaner mixes.

There are many empirical relations between the tensile and compressive strength of concrete.

One of the most common relation is given by the following relation

Tensile strength $= K$ (compressive strength)^n.

The value of K may be taken as 6.2 for gravel and 10.4 for crushed aggregate. The average value for both may be taken as 8.3 and the value of n may vary from 0.5 to 0.75.

The I.S. 456-2000 has suggested the following relation between the compressive strength and flexural strength of concrete.

Flexural strength $= 0.7\sqrt{f_{ck}}$

where f_{ck} is the compressive strength cylinder of concrete in MPa (N/mm^2).

The relationship between the compressive and tensile strengths of concrete suggested by Association of portland cement laboratories is shown in Table 13.3. below.

Table 13.3. Relation between compressive and tensile strength of concrete

S. No.	*Compressive strength of cylinders in MPa*	*Strength ratio*		
		Modulus of rupture by third point loading to compressive strength	*Direct tensile strength to compressive strength*	*Direct tensile strength to modulus of rupture*
1.	7	0.23	0.11	0.48
2.	14	0.19	0.10	0.53
3.	21	0.16	0.09	0.57
4.	28	0.15	0.09	0.59
5.	35	0.14	0.08	0.59
6.	42	0.13	0.08	0.60
7.	49	0.12	0.07	0.61
8.	56	0.12	0.07	0.62
9.	63	0.11	0.07	0.63

13.9. IMPACT STRENGTH

The impact force is the product of the mass of a body and its velocity. The necessity of the knowledge of impact force in practical life is felt in driving concrete piles and in the construction of foundations for machines which exert impulsive load and also in situations where accidental impact is possible as in the case of handling pre cast concrete members.

There is no unique relation between the impact strength and the static compressive strength of concrete. Thus to assess the impact strength, the principal criteria was considered as the ability of concrete specimen to withstand the repeated blows and to absorb energy. Thus the number of blows which the concrete can withstand (bear) before reaching the no rebound condition indicates a definite state of damage. Generally for a given type of aggregate, higher the compressive strength of the concrete, lower the energy absorbed per below before cracking, but greater the number of blows to reach no rebound condition. Thus the impact strength and the total energy absorbed by concrete increases with its static compressive strength and age. The relation between the strength of concrete and number of blows to no rebound condition is shown in Fig. 13.9.

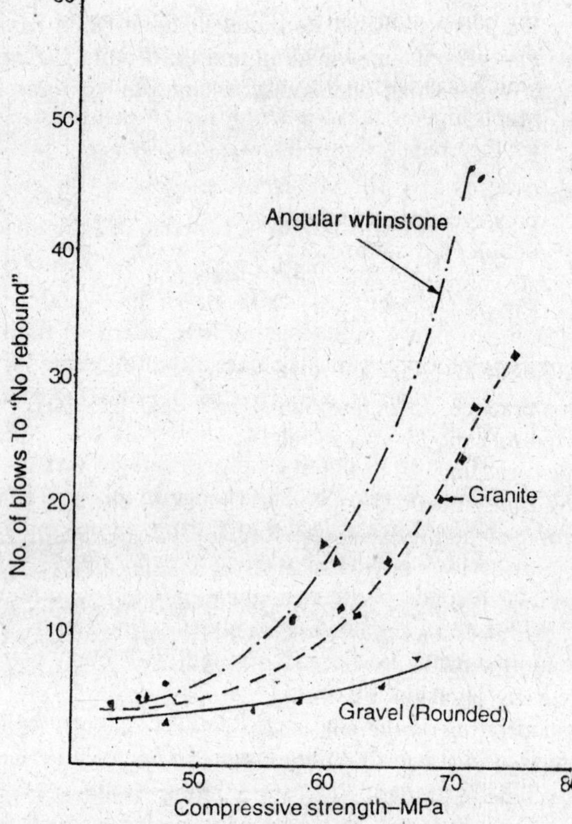

Fig. 13.9. Relation between compressive strength and No of blows to no rebound of concrete

13.9.1. Factors affecting the impact strength

It has been observed that the relation between the static compressive strength of concrete and its impact strength is affected by the following factors:

1. **Type of coarse aggregate.** The impact strength of concrete made with crushed rock aggregate with rough and angular surface is greater for the same strength made with natural gravel. This feature indicates that the impact strength of concrete is more closely related to its flexural strength than to its compressive strength. Thus the concrete made with natural gravel has low impact strength due to the weaker bond between the mortar and coarse aggregate.
2. **Storage condition of concrete.** The impact strength of moist or water stored concrete is lower than that of dry concrete, though water stored concrete can withstand more blows before cracking. Thus the compressive strength with out reference to storage conditions of concrete does not give an adequate indication of impact strength.
3. **Size of aggregate.** Concrete made with smaller maximum size aggregate gave significantly greater impact strength.
4. **Modulus of elasticity and poisson's ratio of aggregate.** The aggregate of low modulus of elasticity and low poisson's ratio gives greater impact strength than high modulus of elasticity and poisson's ratio aggregate.
5. **Cement content.** To get a concrete of satisfactory impact, strength, the cement content should be less than 400 kg/m^3.

6. **Effect of rate of loading.** Impact loading can be considered as the application of a uniform stress extremely rapidly, in which case strength measured will be much higher. It has been observed that if the rate of application of stress exceeds 5×10^6 MPa/s, the static compressive strength obtained is more than double the static compressive strength at normal rate of loading (0.25 MPa/sec.) Fig. 13.10.

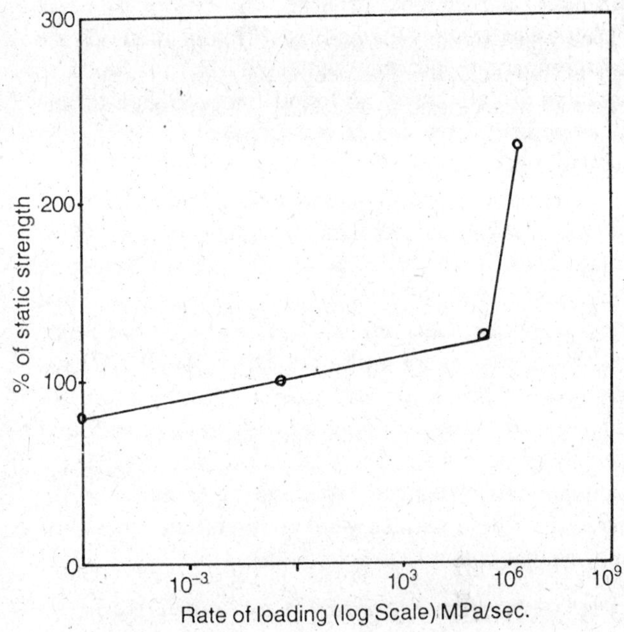

Fig. 13.10. Relation between compressive strength and rate of loading upto impact level

13.10. RESISTANCE TO ABRASION

In practice concrete surfaces can be subjected to various types of abrasive wear. For example scraping or sliding can cause wearing rubbing friction. In case of hydraulic structures, the action of abrasive solids as sand and other debris carried by water generally cause erosion of concrete. For these reasons it is desirable to know the resistance of concrete to abrasion. How ever it is difficult to assess the resistance of concrete to abrasion as the damaging action varies depending on the cause of wear. Thus no one test procedure is satisfactory for the evaluation of the resistance of concrete to the various conditions of the wear.

In all the tests, the depth of wear of a specimen is used as a measure of abrasion. ASTMC 779-89 has prescribed three test procedures for laboratory or field use. The tests are as follows:

1. The revolving disc test
2. Steel ball abrasion test
3. Dressing wheel test

1. **The revolving disc test.** The equipment consists of three flat surfaces which revolve along a circular path with a specified velocity of 0.2 Hertz (Hz), each plate also turn on its axis at 4.7 Hz. Silicon carbide is fed between the plates and the concrete as an abrasive material.
2. **Steel ball abrasion test.** In this method a load is applied to a rotating head. Steel balls are put in between the head and the concrete. During the test a circulating water jet is applied to remove the eroded material.
3. **The dressing wheel test.** In this method a modified drill press is used to apply the load to three sets of seven rotating wheels, which are in contact with concrete surface. The driving head is rotated for 30 minutes at a specified speed of 0.93 Hz. (One Hertz is equal to one cycle per second).

The above tests are useful for determining the resistance of concrete to heavy foot traffic, wheeled traffic and to the tyre chain and track vehicles. Generally speaking, the heavier the abrasion, the more useful the test in the order, revolving disc, dressing wheel and steel ball.

In case of flowing water, the erosion by the solids in water is measured by the method known as *shot blast method.* In this case 2000 pieces of steel shots of size of 850 micron are ejected or fired under an air pressure of 0.62 MPa from a 6.3 mm nozzle against a concrete specimen located at a distance of 102 mm.

The relation between the abrasion resistance and compressive strength obtained by the three methods prescribed by ASTM C-779-89 has been shown in Fig. 13.11. The results of all the three methods are quite different due to the arbitrary conditions of test. Though the values obtained by different methods are not comparable quantitatively, but the resistance to abrasion in all cases is found proportional to the water/cement ratio and thus related to the compressive strength.

Thus it can be concluded that the primary basis for the selection of abrasion resistant concrete is its compressive strength. The resistance to abrasion increases by the use of fairly lean mixes and crushed rock aggregate. Concrete which either does not bleed or bleeds only very little has been found to have stronger surface layer and thus is more resistant to abrasion. A delay in finishing the surface is found advantageous. Also for high abrasion resistance, adequate and prolonged moist curing is essential. In situations where surface wear is important the use of light weight concrete is not suitable.

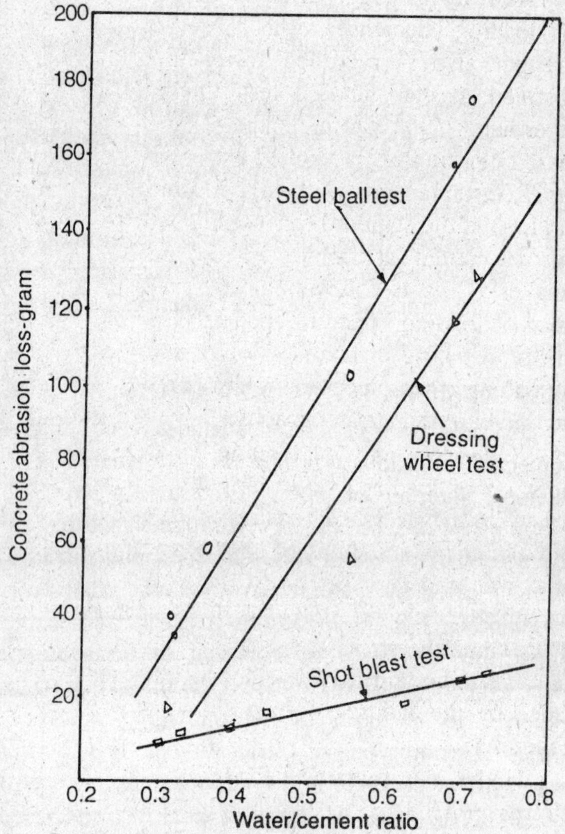

Fig. 13.11. Effect of w/c ratio on the abrasive strength of concrete

13.11. FATIGUE STRENGTH OF CONCRETE

The application of repeated load on a material develops fatigue in it. In practice many structures are repeatedly loaded. When a material fails under a number of repeated loads, each load being smaller than the static compressive strength of concrete, then the failure taken place is called fatigue failure. Concrete and steel both have a characteristic fatigue failure.

13.11.1. Type of fatigue failures

Generally there are two types of fatigue failure in concrete:

1. Simple fatigue failure
2. Static fatigue or creep rupture failure

1. **Simple fatigue failure.** In this type of failure the failure occurs under cyclic or repeated loading and is known simply as fatigue failure.
2. **Static failure.** In this case failure occurs under a sustained or slowly increasing load near or blow the strength under an increasing load, as in a standard test. This failure is known as static fatigue or creep rupture failure.

In both the cases a time dependent failure takes place only at stresses which are greater than a certain limiting value, but smaller than the short term static strength.

At this stage it will be appropriate to state that in the standard method of determining the compressive strength, the test is carried out in a short duration *i.e.* between 2 to 4 minutes. The duration of the test is important as the strength of concrete is dependent on the rate of loading. That is why the standard rate of loading has been prescribed by all standards. IS 516-1959 has prescribed the rate of loading on 150 mm cubes as 0.2 MPa/Second (140 kg/cm^2 per minute) and BS-1881 Part-116-1983 has prescribed this rate as 0.2 MPa to 0.4 MPa per second where as ASTM C 39-86 has prescribed the rate of loading as 0.15 to 0.34 MPa/see for 150 × 300 mm cylinders.

As shown in Fig. 13.12 as the rate of loading decreases, the observed strength also is recorded lower than obtained in the standard test. On the other hand if the rate of loading is increased *i.e.* the load is applied extremely rapid (instantaneously), a higher strength than at the standard test is obtained, but the strain at failure is recorded smaller. Thus it follows that at rapid rates of loading concrete appears more brittle in nature than under lower rates of loading when creep and micro cracking increase the strain capacity.

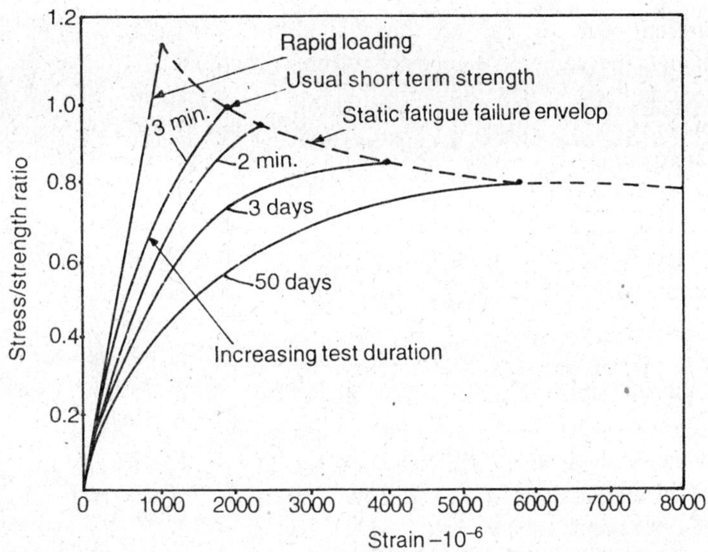

Fig. 13.12. Influence of test duration on strength capacity in compression

Under low rates of loading, (more duration of loading) static fatigue occurs when the stress exceeds about 70 to 80% of the short duration or standard test strength. This limiting (threshold) value represents the start of rapid development of micro cracks, which eventually link and cause failure. Thus when the stress exceeds the 70 to 80% of standard test strength called limiting value, concrete will fail after a certain period which is indicated by the failure envelop shown in Fig. 13.12.

Under the sustained load also, a similar Phenomenon takes place as shown in Fig. 13.13. In this case a certain load is applied fairly quickly and then kept constant. Above the same limiting value of 70 to 80% of the standard test (short term test) strength, the sustained load ultimately will result in failure. At the stresses below this limit, failure will not occur and the concrete will continue to creep.

Static fatigue also occur in tension at stresses greater then 70 to 80% of the short term strength. However the tensile strain capacity is much lower than compression strain capacity.

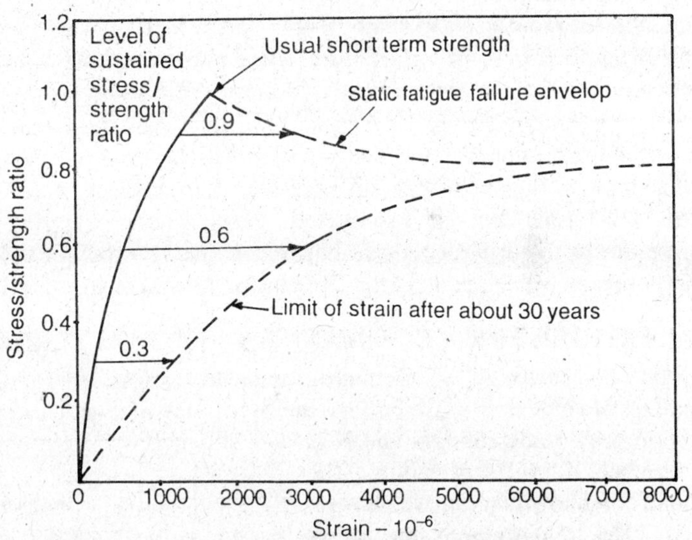

Fig. 13.13. Influence of sustained stress on strength and stress capacity of concrete in compression

13.12. BEHAVIOUR OF CONCRETE WHEN COMPRESSIVE STRESS VARIES

When the compressive stress alternates between zero and a certain fraction of short term static strength the behaviour of concrete is very significant. As the stress increases from zero to a certain value of about 20 MPa, the strain also increases. On decreasing the load though strain decreases, but not fully regains its original value, that is there is some residual strain. The stress and strain curve is shown in Fig. 13.14. This fig shows that there is a change in the shape of the stress strain curve under increasing and decreasing load as the number of load cycles increase. Initially the loading curve is concave towards the strain axis, then straight at about 675 cycles and eventually concave towards the stress axis. The extent of the latter concavity is reflected by an increase in the elastic strain and an decrease in the secant modulus of elasticity. This feature is an indication that how near the concrete is to failure by fatigue.

The area enclosed by two successive curves on loading and unloading is proportional to hysteresis (a continuous fig.) and represents the irreversible energy of deformation *i.e.* energy due to crack formation or irreversible creep. The area of the loop is affected by the rise of temperature of the specimen. It does not occur in specimens which do not fail in fatigue. On first loading to a high stress, the hysteresis is large, but then decreases as the number of cycles increases. When fatigue failure is about to occur, the area of loop increases and an extensive cracking takes place at the interfaces of the aggregate and cement paste. Thus consequently hysteresis and non elastic strain increase rapidly. As in static fatigue, the non elastic strain at fatigue failure and the strain capacity are much larger than in short term failure. The fatigue cracking is extensive and the observed strain at failure is much larger than the static failure. The non static strain increases with the number of cycles.

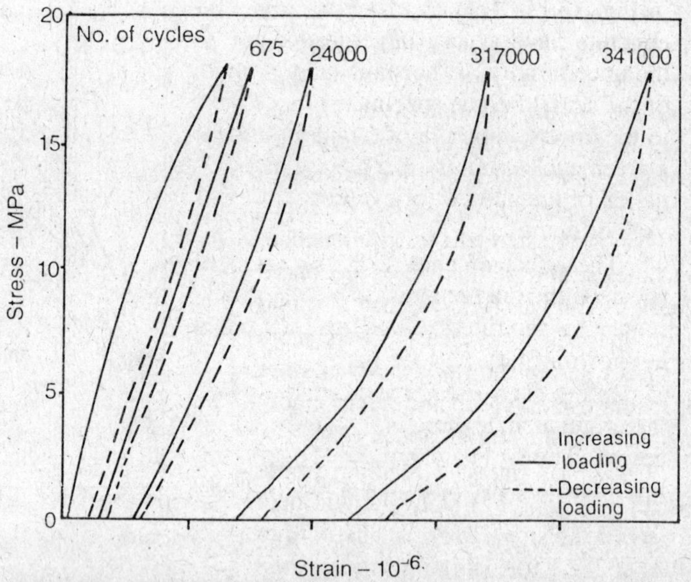

Fig. 13.14. Stress-strain relation under cyclic compressive loading

Cycling loading below the fatigue limit improves the fatigue strength of concrete. This shows that a concrete loaded a number of times below its fatigue limit will, when subsequently loaded above the fatigue limit exhibit, a higher fatigue strength than the concrete which had never been subjected to the initial cycles. The former concrete also exhibits a higher static strength by 5 to 15%. This increase in the concrete may be due to the densification of concrete caused by the initial low stress level cycling, as in the case of under moderate sustained loading. This property is akin to strain hardening in metals.

13.13. FATIGUE FOR A CONSTANT RANGE OF ALTERNATING STRESS

For a constant range of alternating stress, the fatigue strength decreases, as the number of cycles increases. This statement is illustrated by the S-N cures of Fig. 13.15. S is the ratio of the maximum stress to the short term static strength and N is the number of cycles at failure. The value of S is shown on *y* axis and N on *x*-axis. The maximum value of S below which no failure takes place is called as endurance limit. Mild steel has been found to have a endurance limit of about 0.5, which means that when S < 0.5 the value of N is infinity, where as concrete does not seem to have such limit. Thus it is necessary to define the fatigue strength of concrete by considering a very large number of cycles say one million (10^6) as shown

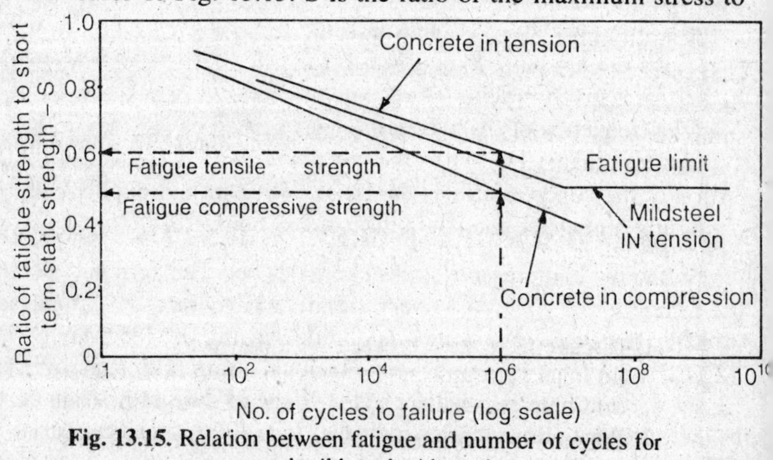

Fig. 13.15. Relation between fatigue and number of cycles for concrete and mild steel with a min stress

in Fig. 13.15. Actually the S-N curves for concrete have a very large scatter due to the uncertaintity of the short term strength of the actual fatigue specimen and also due to the uncertain nature of fatigue. Thus for a given cycle of stress, the precise determination of the number of cycles to failure is very difficult.

The effect of change in the range of stress on the fatigue strength, can be represented by modified (Good man) diagram as shown in Fig. 13.16.

In the diagram, a line passing through the origin at an angle of 45° to the x-axis is drawn. The ordinate measured from this line indicates the range of stress to cause failure after one million (10^6) cycles. For practical purposes, the lower load is the dead load and the upper load is the sum of dead and live load. Fig. 13.16 shows the fatigue strength for various combinations of compressive and tensile stresses. For example when the stress is 0.1 of the short term static strength, the corresponding maximum stress and the range of stress expressed as ratio of the short term static strength are as shown in Table 13.4.

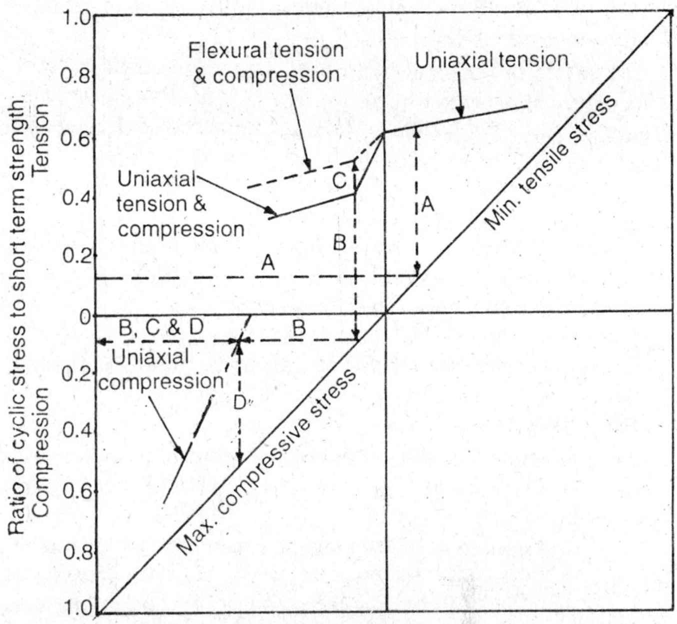

Fig. 13.16. Modified Goodman diagram for fatigue strength

Table 13.4.

S. No.	*Minimum stress and its mode*	*Symbol as shown in Fig.*	*Maximum stress 'S' and mode*	*Range of stress*
1.	uniaxial tension	A	0.6 uniaxial tension	0.5
2.	Uniaxial compression	B	0.4 uniaxial tension	0.5
3.	Flexural compression	C	0.5 flexural tension	0.6
4.	Uniaxial compression	D	0.5 uniaxial compression	0.4

From the above, it can be seen that highest range of stress is tolerable in flexure (c) when the minimum stress is compressive and the maximum stress is tensile. This combination is very important as it takes place in a pre-stressed concrete beam in practice.

As the strength of concrete increases with age, the fatigue strength also increases proportionately so that for a given number of cycles, fatigue occurs at the same fraction of the ultimate strength. A decrease in the frequency of the alternating load decreases the fatigue strength slightly, but only at a very low frequencies less than 1 Hz. when the creep per cycle is significant. It has been observed that the moisture condition of the concrete affects the fatigue strength marginally except in case of very dry concrete, which has a slightly higher fatigue strength than wet concrete.

QUESTIONS

1. Discuss the relation between the followings
   (*a*) Impact strength and compressive strength of concrete.
   (*b*) Compressive strength and tensile strength of concrete.
2. What precautions should be taken to ensure a good resistance of concrete to abrasion.

3. Describe the method to measure the resistance of concrete to abrasion.
4. Define the followings:
   (*a*) Fatigue (*b*) Endurance limit
   (*c*) Creep rupture (*d*) Hysteresis
5. What are the main factors which influence the fatigue strength of concrete.
6. Diffirentiate between the Fatigue and static fatigue.
7. For a given concrete, compare the direct tensile strength, flexural strength and splitting strength. Explain why these strengths are different.
8. How the type of aggregate influence the tensile strength of concrete?
9. Explain the effect of the followings on the concrete strength
   (*a*) Moisture condition of concrete
   (*b*) Rate of loading
   (*c*) How the loading of cycles affect the fatigue strength of concrete?

OBJECTIVE TYPE QUESTIONS

1. The tensile strength of concrete is... percent of its compressive strength.
   (*a*) 30% (*b*) 18%
   (*c*) 10% (*d*) 5%
2. Direct method of calculating the tensile strength of concrete is not suitable due to
   (*a*) Stress concentration at the jaws (*b*) Presence of ecentricity in the application of load
   (*c*) Difficulty in holding the specimen (*d*) All the above
3. The split tensile strength test is considered better than the direct tensile strength method due to
   (*a*) Splipt tensile strength test gives tensile strength values closer to the actual tensile strength test values.
   (*b*) Split tensile test gives more uniform results
   (*c*) Same moulds can be used for both compressive and tensile strength
   (*d*) All the above
4. Identify the correct statements of the following
   (*a*) Flexural beam test gives the highest value of tensile strength of concrete
   (*b*) Flexural beam test gives the lowest value of tensile strength of concrete
   (*c*) Flexural beam test is not related to tensile strength of concrete
   (*d*) Flexural beam test gives the abrasion value of concrete
5. Identify the correct statements of the followings:
   (*a*) Direct tensile test gives the lowest value of tensile strength of concrete
   (*b*) Direct tensile test gives the highest value of tensile strength of concrete
   (*c*) Direct tensile method is not standardized
   (*d*) All are correct
6. Identify the incorrect statements of the followings:
   (*a*) The tensile strength of concrete decreases with the increase in its compressive strength
   (*b*) The tensile strength of concrete increases with the increase in its compressive strength but the rate of increase in tensile strength is of decreasing order
   (*c*) The tensile strength is more sensitive to improper curing than compressive strength
   (*d*) Curing of concrete has no effect on its tensile strength
7. Identify the incorrect statement of the following:
   (*a*) The average value of modulus of rupture is about 15% of its compressive strength
   (*b*) Concrete made with the rough textured aggregate gives higher value of modulus of rupture
   (*c*) The modulus of rupture is higher than the direct tensile strength of concrete
   (*d*) The value of modulus of rupture is equal to the compression strength of concrete
8. Identify the incorrect statement of the following
   (*a*) The central point loading gives higher average value of modulus of rupture than two point loading
   (*b*) Same span to depth ratio does not alter the value of modulus of rupture
   (*c*) The alteration in span to depth ratio affects the value of modulus of rupture
   (*d*) The rate of stress application has no influence on the modulus of rupture
9. Identify the incorrect statements of the followings

(*a*) The moist concrete gives lower value of impact strength than dry concrete
(*b*) Higher the strength of concrete, greater the number of blows to reach the no rebound value
(*c*) For a given type of aggregate, the higher the value of concrete strength, lower is the energy absorbed per blow before cracking
(*d*) To get a concrete of satisfactory impact strength, the cement content in the concrete should be more than 400 kg/m^3
(*e*) Fatigue strength of concrete increases with age
(*f*) Fatigue strength of concrete decreases with age
(*g*) Moist condition of concrete affects the impact strength slightly
(*h*) The non static strain increases with the number of cycles

10. Identify the incorrect statement/statements
(*a*) Under uniaxial compression the cracks develop approximately parallel to the applied load
(*b*) Concrete made with smooth surfaced gravel cracks at much lower stress than concrete made with crushed aggregate
(*c*) Air dry concrete gives more strength than moist cured concrete
(*d*) The flexural strength of dry concrete is found lower than wet concrete
(*e*) None of above

11. The ratio of flexural to compressive strength of concrete of 250 kg/cm^2 and above varies as
(*a*) 3 to 7% (*b*) 8 to 11%
(*c*) 10 to 15% (*d*) 15 to 21%

12. The ratio of flexural to compressive strength of concrete of ordinary concrete having less than 250 kg/cm^2 strength varies as
(*a*) 5 to 10% (*b*) 11 to 16%
(*c*) 18 to 25% (*d*) 9 to 12.8%

13. The change in span to depth ratio of 1.0% induces change in flexural strength when tested by two point loading method
(*a*) 5% (*b*) 7.5%
(*c*) 9.5% (*d*) 3.0%

14. The increase in rate of loading of 0.7 MPa induces increase in flexural strength
(*a*) 20% (*b*) 25%
(*c*) 35% (*d*) 40%

15. To get a good impact strength concrete the cement content should not be less than
(*a*) 400 kg/m^3 (*b*) 500 kg/m^3
(*c*) 600 kg/m^3 (*d*) 800 kg/m^3

Answers

1. (*c*)	4. (*a*)	7. (*d*)	10. (*e*)	13. (*d*)
2. (*d*)	5. (*a, c*)	8. (*d*)	11. (*b*)	14. (*b*)
3. (*d*)	6. (*a, d*)	9. (*d, f*)	12. (*d*)	15. (*a*)

14

Properties of Hardened Concrete

14.1. INTRODUCTION

The knowledge of properties of hardened concrete is very important as these properties change continuously with time and ambient conditions. The important properties of hardened concrete are strength, elasticity, permeability, durability, creep and thermal properties etc. In this chapter strength of concrete has been dealt.

14.2. DEFINITION OF STRENGTH

The strength can be defined as the ability to resist force. With-regard to concrete for structural purposes it can be defined as the unit force required to cause rupture. Strength is a good index of most of the other properties of practical importance. In general stronger concretes are stiffer, more water tight and more resistant to weathering etc.

14.3. NATURE OF STRENGTH

Rupture of concrete may be caused by applied tensile stress, shearing stress or by compressive stress or a combination of two of the above stresses. Concrete being a brittle material is much weaker in tension and shear than compression and failures of concrete specimens under compressive load are essentially shear failures on oblique planes as shown in Fig. 14.1 (*a*). It is called as shear or cone failure. As the resistance to failure is due to both cohesion and internal friction, the angle of rupture is not 45° (plane of maximum shear stress), but is a function of the angle of internal friction. It can be shown mathematically that the angle φ which the plane of failure makes with the axis of loading is equal to $(45° - \varphi/2)$ as shown in Fig. 14.2 (*a*).

The angle of internal friction φ of concrete being of the order of 20°, the angle of inclination of the cone of failure in the conventional test specimen is approximately 35° as shown in Fig. 14.1 (*a*). Further the angle of the rupture may deviate from theoretical value due to the complex stress condition induced in the end conditions of the compression specimens. This deviation results from restraint to lateral expansion under the load caused by friction of the bearing plates on the end surfaces. When the

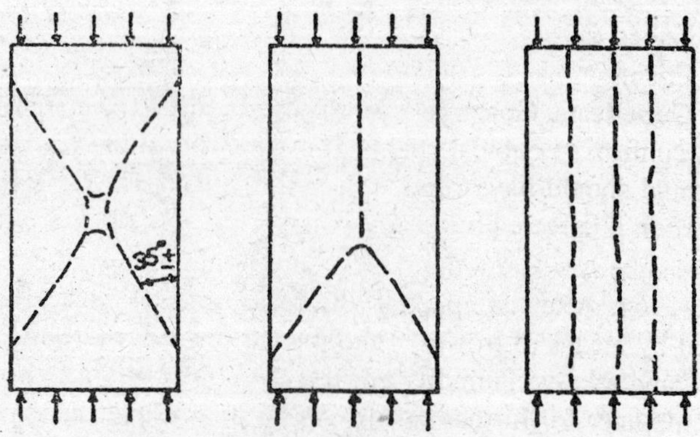

(*a*) (*b*) (*c*)

Fig. 14.1 Mode of rupture

strength of concrete is high and lateral expansion at the end bearing surfaces are relatively unrestrained, the specimen may separate into columnar fragments, known as a splitting or columnar fracture as shown in Fig. 14.1 (*c*). Usually failure occurs through a combination of shear and splitting as shown in Fig. 14.1 (*b*). Mostly concrete in structures is subjected to some combinations of compressive, tensile and shear stresses either directly or due to restraint of surrounding portions. The results of such combinations of stresses may be interpreted by mohar rupture diagrams as shown in Fig. 14.2 (*b*).

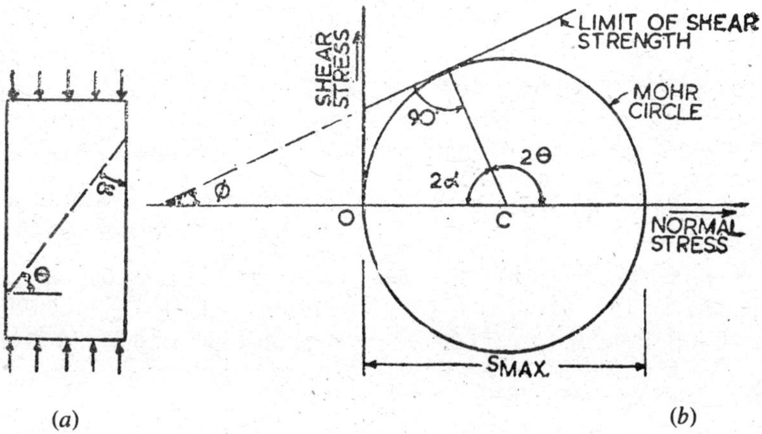

Fig. 14.2. Mohar rupture diagram

14.4. KIND OF STRENGTH

Strength may be classified as follows:

1. Compressive strength
2. Tensile strength
3. Shear strength
4. Bond strength
5. Flexure strength

1. COMPRESSIVE STRENGTH

For structural design the compressive strength is taken as the criterion of quality of concrete and the working stresses are prescribed as per codes in terms of percentages of the compressive strength as determined by standard tests.

Compressive Tests

To determine the compressive strength of concrete following three types of specimens can be used.

1. Cubes
2. Cylinders
3. Prisms

1. Cube tests. Generally specimens are cast in steel or cast iron moulds of 150 mm dimensions, which should confirm to cubical shape. The dimensions and planeness should be with in the limits of tolerance. The mould should have rigid connection with base. The rigid connection with base is essential when the compaction is effected by means of vibration. This reduces the leakage of mortar.

The cube is filled in three layers and compacted well either by vibration or standard tamping rod as per IS 516-1964. After compaction the top surface is made flush with edges of mould and the top surface finished by means of trowel. The finished surface is left undisturbed for 24 hours at a temperature of 66°F to 70°F and relative humidity not less than 90%. After 24 hours, the mould is stripped and the specimen is stored in water for further curing. As far as possible the curing temperature should be maintained at 66°F to 70°F, usually these specimens are cured upto 28 days. The test should be carried out as per IS 516-1964.

2. Cylinder test. The standard cylinder is 15 cms in diameter and 30 cms height and is cast in a mould generally made of cast-iron or steel, preferably with a clamped base. Cylinder specimens are made as cubes specimens, but are compacted in three layers by a 16 mm diameter rod having one end of bullet shape. The top surface of cylinder finished with a float is not smooth enough for testing and requires further preparation. To over come this difficulty caping of cylinders is done by cement paste or some other suitable material. Cylinders are used for the determination of compressive strength of concrete in United States, France, Canada, Australia and New Zealand, while cubes are used in U.K. Germany, India and Europe etc.

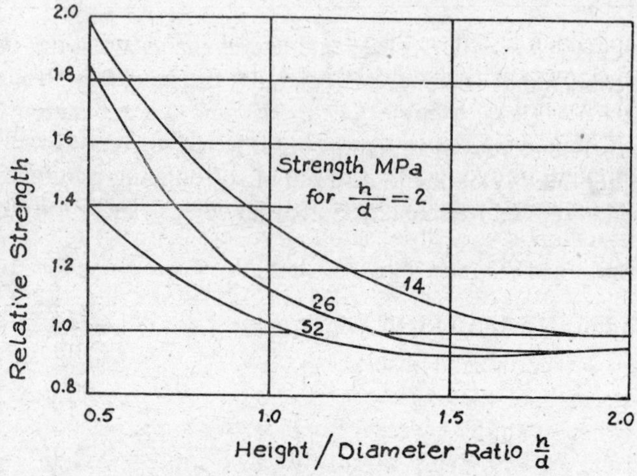

Fig. 14.3. Influence of height-diameter ratio on strength of cylinder of different strength concrete

The concrete strength is affected by the shape and size of the specimens, but high strength concretes is less affected than the low strength. Concrete Fig. 14.3 shows the influence of height/diameter ratio on the strength of cylinder for different strength of concrete as suggested by Murdok and Kesler.

14.5. FAILURE OF COMPRESSION SPECIMENS

Compression test develops a more complex system of stresses. The compression load develops the lateral expansion in the test specimen (cube or cylinder) due to the Poisson's ratio effect. The steel platens do not under go the same lateral expansion as that concrete goes. Thus the steel restrains the expansion tendency of the concrete in the lateral direction. This restraint induces a tangential force between the end surfaces of the concrete specimen and the adjacent steel platens of the testing machine. It has been observed that lateral strain developed in the steel plates is only 0.4 times of the lateral strain developed in the concrete. Thus the platens restrain the lateral expansion of the concrete in the part of the specimen near its ends. The degree of retraint exercised depends upon the friction actually developed. In case the friction is eliminated by the application of any suitable greasing material as grease, graphite, or paraffin wax to the bearing surfaces, the specimen shows a greater lateral expansion, and eventually gets split along its full length.

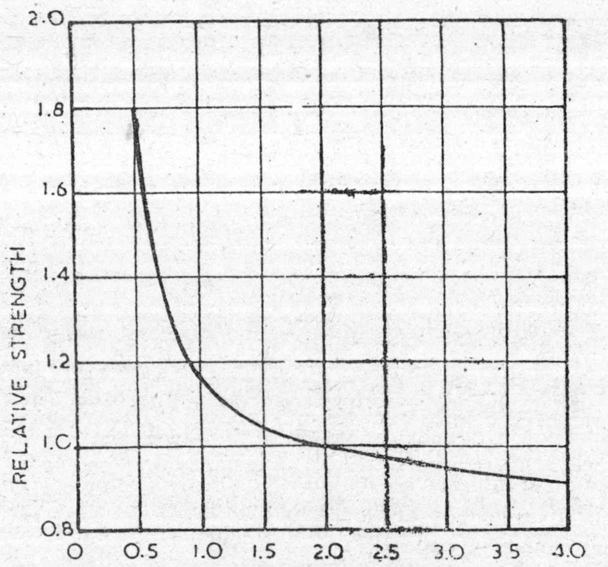

Fig. 14.4. General pattern of influence of H/D ratio on strength of cylinder

Under normal conditions of the test, the elements with in the specimen are subjected to shearing stresses as compressive stresses. The magnitude of shear stress decreases and the lateral expansion increases with the distance from the platens. Thus due to this restraint a cone of height of $\sqrt{3}/2\ d$ remain relatively undamaged in the specimen tested, where d is the lateral dimension of the specimen. However if the length of the specimen is longer than 1.7 *d*, a part of it will be free from the restraining effect of the platens. Thus the specimens with lengths less than 1.5 *d* show considerably higher strength than those with greater lengths as shown in Fig. 14.4.

Fig. 14.4 shows the general pattern of the influence of the height diameter ratio on the compressive strength of cylinder. For values of H/D ratio smaller than 1.5, the measured strength increases rapidly due to non restraining effects of the platens of the testing machine. For H/D between 1.5 to 4.0 strength variation is very little, and for H/D between 1.5 and 2.5 the variation of strength is within 5% of H/D ratio 2.0. For H/D ratio above 5, strength falls rapidly. Hence the choice of H/D ratio of 2 is suitable.

14.6. COMPARISON OF CUBE AND CYLINDER STRENGTHS

Experimental results have shown that there is no simple relation between the cylinder and cube strength of the same concrete. The ratio of cylinder/cube strength depends on the level of strength of concrete and is higher for high strength concrete. However for simplicity IS 516-1964 has suggested this ratio as 0.80. Table 14.1 below shows that this ratio varies from 0.77 to 0.96 in an irregular manner. The results are based on Evan's work. For 1000 kg/cm^2 strength concrete this ratio becomes 1.0.

Table 14.1. Strength of Cubes and Cylinders

S. No.	*Compressive strength*		*Ratio of cylinder/cube strength*	*Difference in cube and cylinder strength kg/cm^2*
	Cube strength kg/cm^2	*Cylinder strength kg/cm^2*		
1.	90.0	69.0	0.77	21.0
2.	152.0	117.0	0.77	35.0
3.	200.0	152.0	0.76	48.0
4.	248.0	200.0	0.81	48.0
5.	276.0	241.0	0.87	35.0
6.	290.0	262.0	0.91	28.0
7.	296.0	269.0	0.91	28.0
8.	358.0	317.0	0.89	41.0
9.	365.0	345.0	0.94	21.0
10.	421.0	365.0	0.87	55.0
11.	441.0	407.0	0.92	35.0
12.	483.0	441.0	0.91	41.0
13.	524.0	503.0	0.96	21.0

14.7. TENSILE STRENGTH

Concrete being a brittle material is not expected to resist direct tensile forces. However tension is of importance with regard to cracking, which is a tensile failure. Most of the cracking is due to the restraint of contraction induced by drying shrinkage or lowering of temperature. The tensile strength of concrete varies from 7% to 11% of the compressive strength but on average it is taken as 10% of compressive strength. Further it has been observed that higher the compressive strength, lower the relative tensile strength. The maximum tensile strength of concrete has been found of the order of 42.0 kg/cm^2. Some researchers have observed that the type of coarse aggregate has a greater relative effect on tensile strength than on compressive strength. Generally for concrete quality control, tensile test is never made. However to have an idea of tensile strength an indirect method known as splitting test is applied. (For details Please refer chapter 19, page 382).

14.8. SHEAR STRENGTH

Shear is the action of two equal and opposite parallel forces applied in planes a short distance apart.

Shear stress can not exist without accompanying tensile and compressive stresses. Pure shear can be applied only through torsion of a cylindrical specimen in which case the stresses are equal in primary shear. Secondary tension (maximum at 45° to shear) and secondary compression (maximum at 45° to shear, perpendicular to tension). As the concrete is weaker in tension than in shear, failure in tension invariably occurs in diagonal tension. Direct determination of shear is very difficult. Hence researchers have assumed the shear strength of concrete about 12% of the compressive strength. I.S. 456-1978 has suggested the values of shear as follows:

Table 14.2

Concrete compressive strength kg/cm²	150	200	250	300	350	400
Shear stress kg/cm²	16	18	19	22	23	25

Table 14.3. Permissible shear stress in concrete as per IS 456-2000

S. No.	$\frac{As \times 100}{b \times d}$	*Permissible shear stress in concrete N/mm² Grades of concrete*					
		M 15	M 20	M 25	M 30	M 35	M 40 and above
1.	≤ 0.15	0.18	0.18	0.19	0.20	0.20	0.20
2.	0.25	0.22	0.22	0.23	0.23	0.23	0.23
3.	0.50	0.29	0.30	0.31	0.31	0.31	0.32
4.	0.75	0.34	0.35	0.36	0.37	0.37	0.38
5.	1.00	0.37	0.39	0.40	0.41	0.42	0.42
6.	1.25	0.40	0.42	0.44	0.45	0.45	0.46
7.	1.50	0.42	0.45	0.46	0.48	0.49	0.49
8.	1.75	0.44	0.47	0.49	0.50	0.52	0.52
9.	2.00	0.44	0.49	0.51	0.53	0.54	0.55
10.	2.25	0.44	0.51	0.53	0.53	0.56	0.57
11.	2.50	0.44	0.51	0.55	0.57	0.58	0.60
12.	2.75	0.44	0.51	0.56	0.58	0.60	0.62
13.	3.00 and above	0.44	0.51	0.57	0.60	0.62	0.63

14.9. BOND STRENGTH

It can be definined as the resistance to slipping of the steel reinforcing bars which are embedded in concrete. This resistance is provided by the friction and adhesion between the concrete and steel friction between concrete and the lugs of deformed bars. It is also affected by the shrinkage of concrete relative to the steel. Bond involves not only the properties of concrete, but also mechanical properties of steel and its position in the concrete member. In general bond strength is approximately proportional to the compressive strength of concrete upto about 200 kg/cm². For higher strengths of concrete, the increase in bond strength becomes progressively smaller. In the initial stages of failure (slip) the bond strength depends on the magnitude and uniformity of lateral pressure that exists or may be developed between steel and surrounding concrete. Bond strength varies considerably with the type of cement, admixtures and water cement ratio *i.e.* on quality of paste. It is not affected by air entrainment.

Further it has been observed that bond strength increases with delayed vibration. It is higher for dry concrete than for wet concrete. It's value reduces at high temperatures. At 200°C to 300°C (400°F to 570°F) bond strength has been found 50% of the bond strength at room temperature. Bond strength is also reduced by alternations of wetting and drying, freezing and thawing etc. Its value usually is determined by pull out test. The bond strength for deformed bars may be taken 40% more than ordinary bars of the same diameter.

Bond strength is also a function of specific surface of gel. Cement having higher percentage of C_2S

will give higher surface of gel, giving higher bond strength. On the other hand cement having higher percentage of C_3S or concrete cured at higher temperature gives smaller value of specific surface of gel, resulting in lower bond strength. It has been observed that concrete cured at high pressure steam produces gel of about 1/20th specific surface of the gel surface produced at normal curing temperature. Thus the bond strength of high pressure steam cured concrete is lower. The values of bond strength are shown in Table 14.4. as suggested by IS 456-2000. All values are in N/mm^2.

Table 14.4. Permissible stress in concrete

S. No.	*Grade of concrete*	*Permissible stress in compression*		*Permissible stress in bond average for bars in tension*	
		Bending	*Direct*	*Plain bars*	*Deformaed brs*
1.	M 10	3.0	2.5	—	—
2.	M 15	5.0	4.0	0.6	0.84
3.	M 20	7.0	5.0	0.8	1.12
4.	M 25	8.5	6.0	0.9	1.26
5.	M 30	10.0	8.0	1.0	1.40
6.	M 35	11.5	9.0	1.1	1.50
7.	M 40	13.0	10.0	1.2	1.68
8.	M 45	14.5	11.0	1.3	1.82
9.	M 50	16.0	12.0	1.4	1.96

Note. for compression steel, bond stress may be increased by 25%.

14.10. FACTORS AFFECTING THE STRENGTH OF CONCRETE

Generally following factors affect the strength of concrete. Here these factors are discussed in brief.

1. Type of cement used
2. Type of aggregate
3. Richness of the mix
4. Age of concrete
5. Curing temperature
6. Temperature at the time of placing

1. Type of cement. Type of cement influences the strength development in concrete to a great extent depending upon its chemical composition and fineness of grinding. The percentage of C_3S in concrete is responsible for the higher strength development upto 28 days, while C_2S contributes to strength development after 28 days. In a well burnt modern cement clinker the C_3S content is about 45% and that of C_2S as 25%. Their sum in most of the cements varies form 70 to 80%. Thus in general the early strength say upto 28 days of portland cement will be higher with higher percentage of C_3S and after that percentage of C_2S will affect the strength development of concrete.

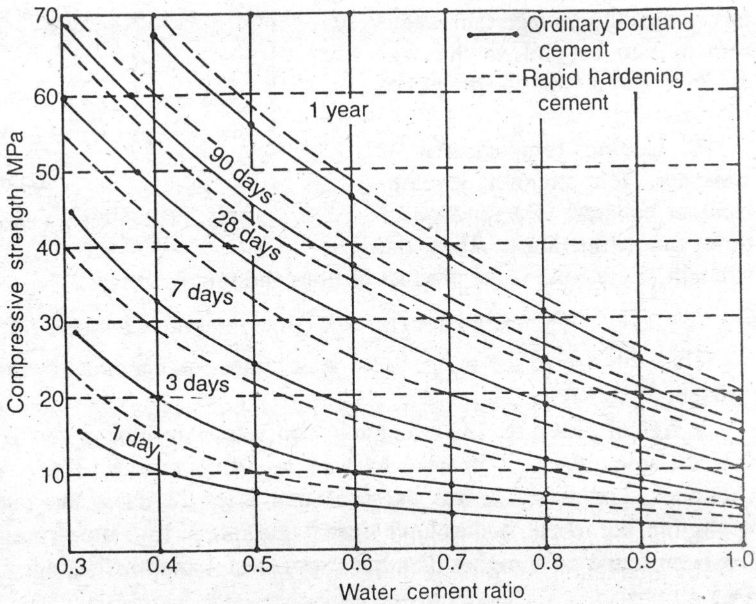

Fig. 14.5. Strength Development of Different cements

Further presence of alkalis in cement also affects concrete strength after 28 days to a great extent. The greater the amount of alkalis present, lower the gain in strength. Further the finer the cement, rapid and greater the strength development.

The effect of different type of cement and w/c ratio on compressive strength has been shown in Fig. 14.5.

2. Type of aggregate. Following characteristics of aggregate affect the strength of Concrete.

(*a*) *Shape and texture of particles.* Crushed rock aggregate with rough surface and angular particles develop about 15% higher strength in comparison of natural smooth surfaced gravel perhaps due to better bond between the aggregate and cement paste, other conditions being same.

(*b*) *Size of aggregate.* It has been observed that for structural concrete, the maximum size of aggregate upto 38 mm has produced highest strength after which strength started decling. It may be due to the fact that larger the aggregate size, the smaller the surface area to be wetted per unit weight of aggregate. Above 38.0 or 40 mm size aggregate the gain of water/cement is off set by the effect of lower bond area between aggregate and cement paste. Fig. 4.25.

(*c*) *Grading of aggregate.* A well graded aggregate will produce a denser concrete resulting in higher strength. The influence of type of aggregate on the strength varies in magnitude and depends upon the water/cement ratio of the mix. For water/cement ratio less than 0.4 the use of crushed aggregate has been found to give higher strength more than 38% than with the use of natural gravel.

3. Richness of the mix. For a particular workability, higher the cement content, lesser the amount of water required, resulting in higher strength. The richness of mix is useful upto a certain water/cement ratio, beyond which it will exhibit retrogression in strength of concrete. Fig. 14.6.

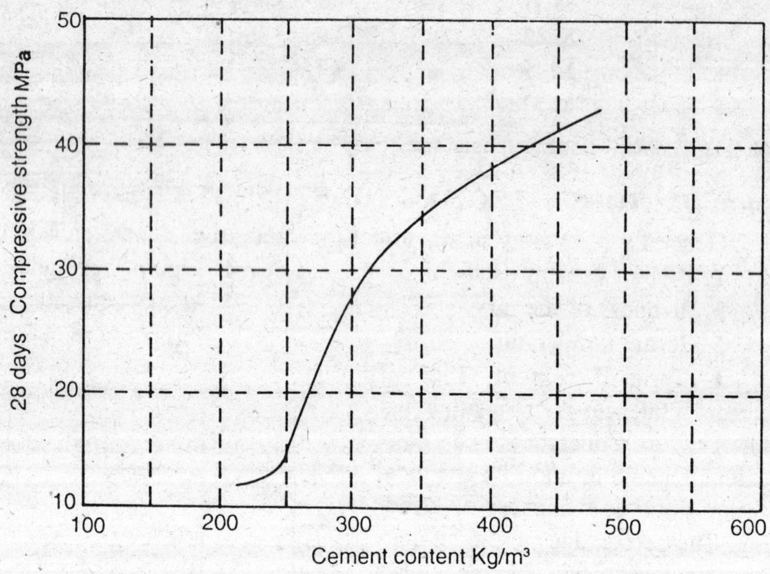

Fig. 14.6. Effect of richness of concrete on its strength

4. Curing temperature of concrete. The strength development of concrete is a function of time and temperature. Thus the strength of concrete is the product of time and temperature.

$$\therefore \quad \text{Concrete strength} = \Sigma\,(\text{time interval} \times \text{temperature})$$

Thus the rise in the temperature accelerates the chemical reaction of hydration and affects the early strength of concrete.

5. Age of concrete. The strength in concrete is developed due to the hydration of cement. As we know that different types of cement hydrate at different rate. Thus the strength development in concrete continues. Previously it was assumed that after 28 days, the rate of hydration is very small, nearly negligible, but recent studies have shown that rate of hydration continues upto 1 year. Strength after 1 year has been found 24% higher than the strength of 1 month. The age factor is shown in the following Table 14.5.

Table 14.5. Age factor for permissible stress in concrete as per British Code

Minimum age of member when full design load is applied in months	*Age factor for low strength concrete*	*Additional strength for high strength concrete MPa*
1	1.00	0
2	1.10	4.2
3	1.16	5.5
6	1.20	7.7
12	1.24	10.2

6. Effect of Compaction. It has been observed that each 1% of deficiency in compaction, results 5% reduction in compressive strength of concrete. The effect of compaction of concrete on its compressive strength is shown in Fig. 14.7.

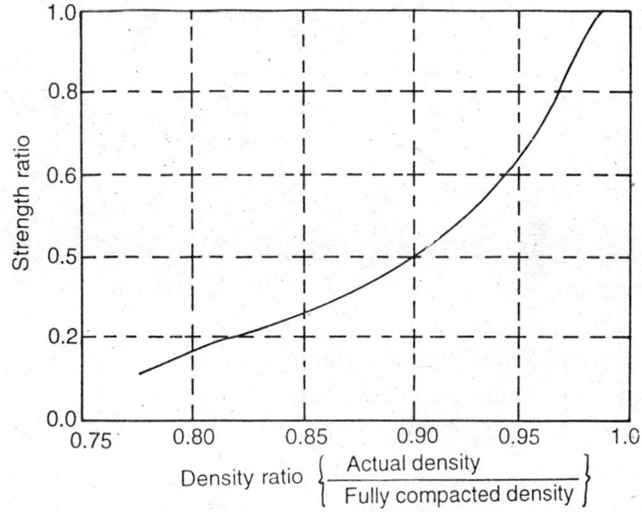

Fig. 14.7. Effect of compaction on strength of concrete

7. Aggregate-Cement ratio. The mix proportion has a marked influence on the compression strength of concrete. The effect of aggregate cement ratio with different workability in terms of compacting factor on its compressive strength is shown in Fig. 14.8.

8. Temperature at the time of placing. If the temperature is below 20°C the rate of hydration of cement will be very low resulting slow development of strength. On the other hand higher temperature during placing and setting will accelerate the process of hydration, but the quality of the gel formed will be poor, resulting in low strength.

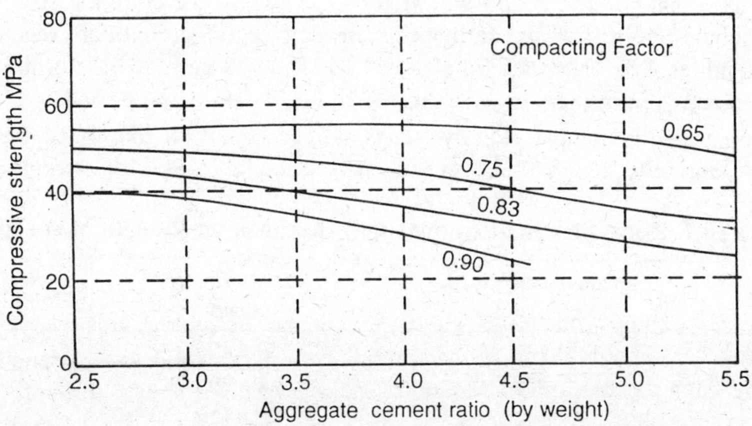

Fig. 14.8. Effect of aggregate/cement ratio on the compressive strength of concrete

9. Effects of loading conditions. Under sustained loading, the concrete will bear less stress than a load applied only for a few minutes. The effect of loading is shown in Table 14.6 below.

Table 14.6

S. No.	*Duration of load*				*Percentage of strength at standard test loading*
	Minutes	*Hours*	*Days*	*Year*	
1.	2	—	—	—	100
2.	10	—	—	—	95
3.	30	—	—	—	92
4.	60	1	—	—	90
5.		4	0.17	—	88
6.			100	—	78
7.			365	1	77
8.				3	73
9.				30	69

Note. This data is based on U.S.B.R. experiments.

14.4. FACTORS AFFECTING RESULTS OF STRENGTH TEST

Following factors have been found to influence the test results to a great extent.

1. Effect of size and shape of specimen
2. Effect of conditions of casting
3. Effect of moisture content of specimen
4. Effect of temperature of specimen
5. Effect of bearing conditions
6. Effect of rate of loading.

1. Effect of size and shape of specimen. As the concrete is composed of elements of variable strength, it is reasonable to assume that larger the volume of concrete subjected to stress the more likely it is to contain an element of a extreme low strength. Hence the measured strength of a specimen decreases with increase in its size.

From experimental results, cylinders of height equal to twice the diameter and cubes are taken as standard specimens. Such cylinders are neither so short that small variation in length affects the strength considerably nor so long that column action will affect its strength. The common size of cylinder is 15 × 30 cms and that of cube 15 cms. The standard specimen for flexural strength are rectangular beams with ratio of breadth to depth as 1.5. The standard size is 15 × 15 × 70 cms. If the normal maximum size of aggregate does not exceed 20 mm then 15 × 15 cms. × 50 cms beam may be used.

When a concrete is tested in compression by means of cylinders of the like shape, but of different sizes, it has been found that larger the specimen, lower the strength. In Table 14.7 the strength of various sizes of

Table 14.7. Effect of size of compression specimen on strength of concrete

Size of cylinder in cms	*Relative compressive strength %*	*Size of cylinder in cms*	*Relative compressive strength %*
5×10	109	30×60	91
7.5×15	106	45×90	86
15×30	100	60×120	84
20×40	96	90×180	82

cylinders relative to 15 × 30 cms cylinder expressed as percentage of 15 × 30 cms cylinder is shown. As the size of cylinder is increased above 45 × 90 cms., the variation in relative compressive strength is small. Experimental results also have shown that the decrease in strength with the increase in size of the specimen

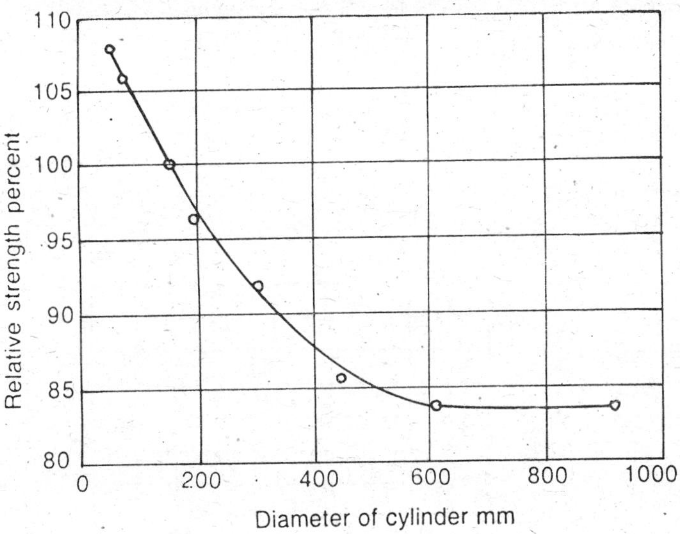

Fig. 14.9. Compressive strength of cylinders of different sizes

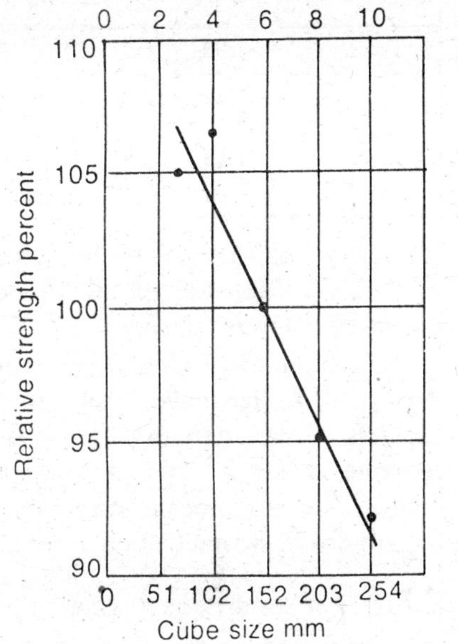

Fig. 14.10. Compressive strength of cubes of different sizes

is less pronounced in lean mixes than in rich mixes. For example the strength of 45 cms and 60 cms diameter cylinders relative to 15 diameter cms is 85% for rich mixes and 93% for lean mixes. Fig. 14.9. Fig. 14.10 shows the relation between mean strength of cylinder and cubes of different sizes.

Specimen size and aggregate size

The least dimension of test specimen should be appreciably larger than the largest size of the aggregate particles used in concrete. Generally the ratio of least dimension of test specimen and largest size of the aggregate should be between 3 and 4.

Effect of height to diameter ratio

Experiments conducted by U.S.B.R. have shown that the ratio of height to diameter of the specimen affects the compressive strength of concrete to a great extent. When cores or cylinders of non-standard shape are tested, the equivalent strength of standard shape (h/d = 2) can be computed approximately by multiplying the observed compressive strength by the corresponding factor given in the following Table 14.8.

Table 14.8. Effect of H/D ratio on compressive strength

Ratio of height to diameter of cylinder or core	*Strength correction factor*	*Ratio of height to diameter of cylinder or core*	*Strength correction factor*
2.00	1.00	1.10	0.90
1.75	0.98	1.00	0.85
1.50	0.96	0.75	0.70
1.25	0.94	0.50	0.50

The correction factors as recommended by ASTM standards C 42-77 and BS 1881 part-4, 1970 are shown in Table 14.9 below.

Table 14.9

Height to diameter ratio (H/D)	*Strength Correction factor*	
	ASTM C42 — 77	*BS 1881 — 1970*
2.00	1.00	1.00
1.75	0.98	0.98
1.50	0.96	0.96
1.25	0.93	0.94
1.00	0.87	0.92

As per I.S. 516-1959, this relation is shown in Fig. 14.11. The strength of 10 cm cube is 10% higher than 15 cms cube.

On the basis of their experimental results Murdock and Kesler have found that the correction depends on the strength of concrete. High strength concrete is less affected by variations in the proportions and shape of the specimens. It is of interest for low strength concrete only. (Fig. 14.3)

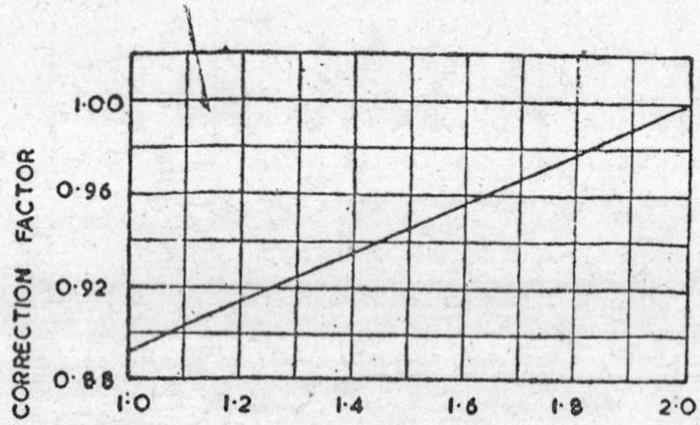

Fig. 14.11. Correction factor for H/D ratio of a core

2. Effect of conditions of casting

The method of moulding a specimen has been found to have an important effect on the indicated strength. The compaction of concrete influences the strength of the concrete. Each one percent less compaction results in the reduction of 5% strength that of fully compacted concrete. Use of card board cylinder mould resulted in 3 to 9% less strength than steel moulds due to relatively rough walls of card board moulds.

3. Effect of moisture content of specimen

Compression specimens tested in the air dry condition have been found to exhibit 20 to 40% higher strength than those of corresponding concrete tested in a saturated condition. This may be probably due to the following reasons.

(*a*) Greater density of dry paste.

(*b*) Development of initial tensile stresses in the paste due to localized restraint of paste shrinkage by pieces of aggregate.

(*c*) Development of hydrostatic pressure in saturated paste.

Thus a compressive specimen at the time of test should be saturated as saturation condition is uniform and can be achieved easily, where as dry condition is variable and indefinite. The cores taken from a structure are socked for 40 to 48 hours immediately prior to the compression test. However test specimens should be surface dry saturated.

With regard to the moisture content of flexure specimens at time of test, conflicting results have been reported by different researchers, due to non-uniformly drying of the specimens as it is very difficult to get uniform drying. Thus the modulus of rupture of concrete specimen which has been allowed to dry is lower than that of a similar saturated specimen. This difference is due to the tensile stresses induced by restraint and non-uniform shrinkage prior to the application of the load. The magnitude of the loss of strength depends on the rate at which moisture evaporates from the surface of the specimen.

Further the relative humidity also has a marked influence on the strength of concrete. It has been observed that when no moisture gradients are present, strength compressive or tensile decreases significantly with an increase in relative humidity, but extreme drying causes a drop in strength. If the relative humidity increase from 20% to 80% the flexure strength drops from 60 kg/cm^2 to about 48 kg/cm^2 *i.e.* about 20% loss.

4. Effect of temperature of specimen at test

The temperature of specimen at the time of test has a marked influence on the indicated strength of concrete. Temperature of specimen is quite distinct from curing temperature.

For compression some researcher at University of California have indicated that compressive strength at 25°F is 40% higher than that of the same concrete at 70°F and at 130°F is 15% lower than that of the corresponding specimen tested at 70°F. Flexure test of mortar at University of Texas has indicated that modulus of rupture at 40°F is 12% higher and at 100°F is 20% lower than that at 70°F. Thus on an average, a variation of 1°F to 4°F in testing temperature results in a difference of 1% in strength.

5. Effect of bearing conditions

It is important that concrete specimen should be loaded uniformly over the entire area, otherwise localised concentration of load will result failure by splitting the specimen rather than in compression or flexure. Thus in order to develop the full strength of the specimen following bearing conditions must exist.

1. The specimen should be accurately centred in the testing machine and the axis of the specimen should be vertical.
2. The bearing surfaces should be perpendicular to the axis of the specimen.
3. A spherical seated bearing block should be used and it should be accurately centered on the specimen with the centre of curvature of its spherical surface in the plane of contact with the specimen.
4. The bearing surface should be plane. The variation in the end surface of a cylinder from true plane even by 0.25 mm has resulted a reduction in strength by 35%. Hence bearing faces of testing specimen should be plane within 0.05 mm if they are not, then they should be capped. The bearing faces of testing machine should be plane within 0.025 mm of true plane. It has been observed that convex end surfaces cause greater reduction than concave faces. The reduction is high in high strength concrete.
5. If a capping material is used, it should have strength and elastic properties as near as possible to those of the specimen.

6. Effect of rate of loading

The rate of loading also affects the indicated strength of concrete. It has been observed that more rapid the static loading of concrete, higher the observed strength. As per I.S. 516, the standard rate of loading should be 140 kg/cm^2 per minute. If the rate of loading increased to 4200 kg/cm^2 per minute, then the observed strength will be about 12% higher than that obtained from the corresponding specimen at standard rate of loading.

On the contrary, if the rate of loading is reduced to 4.2 kg/cm^2 per minute, then the observed strength will be 12% lower than that obtained at standard loading. Further it has been found that concrete can withstand indefinitely stresses upto about 70% of the strength determined under standard loading. The increase in strength with more rapid loading is proportionately greater for leaner mixes. In a experiment on increasing the rate of loading to 50 times, the increase in indicated strength with given aggregate/cement ratio was found as given below in table 14.10.

Table 14.10. Effect of rate of loading

S. No.	*Aggregate/cement ratio*	*% increase in strength*
1.	3.0	17
2.	10.0	28
3.	14.0	31
4.	18.0	35

QUESTIONS

1. How does strength correlate with other properties of concrete? Why are strength tests made?
2. Explain the nature of compression failure of axially loaded concrete.
3. Explain the compression test on concrete. Compare cylinder and cube strength tests.
4. What percentage of compressive strength is taken to assess the tensile strength of concrete?
5. Define bond strength. On what factors the value of bond strength depends.
6. When concrete dries out, what is the immediate effect on strength? What happens on rewetting the specimens.
7. What factors affects the test results of concrete?
8. What variation in bearing condition of compression specimens are important?
9. What is the effect of rate of loading on the compressive strength of concrete?
10. Discuss the effects of different factors on the strength of concrete.

OBJECTIVE TYPE QUESTIONS

1. As per IS-516-1964 the cylinder/cube strength ratio is
   (*a*) 75% (*b*) 80%
   (*c*) 85% (*d*) 90%
2. Which of the following statements is correct?
   (*a*) The ratio of cylinder/cube strength depends on the level of concrete strength
   (*b*) The ratio of cylinder/cube strength is independent of the level of concrete strength
   (*c*) The ratio of cylinder/cube strength depend on the quantity of gypsum used in the cement
   (*d*) Ratio of the cylinder/cube strength is dependent on the setting time of concrete
3. Which of the following statements is false?
   (*a*) For normal concrete the cylinder/cube strength ratio varies for 0.77 to 0.96
   (*b*) For high strength concrete of about 1000 kg/cm^2, the cylinder/cube strength ratio is about unity
   (*c*) The cylinder/cube strength ratio is 1.0 for all types of concrete strengths
   (*d*) High strength concrete is less affected by the proportion of dimensions of the specimen than the low strength concrete
4. Identify the incorrect statements of the following
   (*a*) Compression test develops more complex system of stress in the test specimen
   (*b*) In the compression test the lateral expansion is developed in the test specimen due to the Poisson's ratio
   (*c*) The lateral expansion developed in steel platens is more than the lateral expansion in concrete
   (*d*) The lateral expansion developed in concrete is more than the lateral expansion developed in steel platens
5. The shear strength of concrete is taken percent of its compressive strength
   (*a*) 18% (*b*) 12%
   (*c*) 15% (*d*) 10%
6. Identify the incorrect statement of the followings
   (*a*) Bond strength is more affected by air entrainment
   (*b*) Bond strength decreases by alternete wetting and drying, freezing and thawing
   (*c*) Bond strength is developed due to the friction and adhesion between steel and concrete
   (*d*) Bond strength varies with the quality of the cement paste of the concrete
7. Identify the incorrect statement of the followings
   (*a*) The bond strength is affected by the shrinkage of concrete relative to the steel
   (*b*) The bond strength is proportional to the compressive strength of concrete upto about 200 kg/cm^2
   (*c*) Bond strength is lower for dry concrete than for moist concrete
   (*d*) Bond strength decreases with the rise of temperature
8. Identify the incorrect statements of the following
   (*a*) Bond strength is a function of the surface area of the gel
   (*b*) Bond strength is independent of mechanical properties of steel and its position in the concrete member
   (*c*) Bond strength increases with the increase of surface area of gel
   (*d*) Higher percentage of C_3S in cement reduces the bond strength

9. The increase in concrete strength after one year is... percent over 28 days strength
   (*a*) 35% (*b*) 28%
   (*c*) 24% (*d*) 18%
10. The strength of concrete loaded for 60 minutes is...percent of the concrete loaded for 2 minutes only
    (*a*) 80% (*b*) 69%
    (*c*) 78% (*d*) 90%
11. The strength of 30 × 60 cm cylinder is...percent of 15 × 30 cm cylinder
    (*a*) 100% (*b*) 91%
    (*c*) 84% (*d*) 82%
12. The ratio between the least dimension of the test specimen and the largest size of aggregate should be between
    (*a*) 3 to 4 (*b*) 5 to 7
    (*c*) 6.5 to 8.5 (*d*) 1.5 to 2.5
13. Identify the incorrect statement of the followings
    (*a*) Use of card board mould and steel mould give the same strength of the concrete cylinders cast in
    (*b*) Card board cylinder mould give 3 to 9% less strength of concrete than steel mould cylinders
    (*c*) Each one percent less compaction reduces the concrete strength by 5%
    (*d*) High strength concrete is less affected by proportion and shape of the specimen
14. Identify the incorrect statements of the followings
    (*a*) Air dry concrete specimen give 20 to 40% higher strength than the saturated concrete specimens
    (*b*) The modulus of rupture of dry concrete is more than the saturated concrete
    (*c*) The increase in relative humidity decreases the compressive as well tensile strength of concrete
    (*d*) The temperature of specimen at the time of testing has a marked influence on the strength of the concrete
15. Identify the incorrect statements of the followings
    (*a*) Higher the rate of static loading, higher the observed strength
    (*b*) The increase in strength due to rapid loading is more in leaner mixes
    (*c*) The bearing conditions of the testing machines have effect on the strength of the concrete
    (*d*) Rate of loading has no influence on the strength of concrete
16. Identify the correct statement/statements
    (*a*) Bond strength increases with delayed vibration
    (*b*) At a temperature of about 250°C bond strength is found 50% that of at room temperature
    (*c*) Bond strength reduces considerably for high pressure steam cured concrete
    (*d*) For higher strength concrete the value of bond strength decreases progressively
    (*e*) Failure of concrete in tension invariably occurs in diagonal tension
    (*f*) All are correct

Answers

1. (*b*)	5. (*b*)	9. (*c*)	13. (*a*)
2. (*a*)	6. (*a*)	10. (*d*)	14. (*b*)
3. (*c*)	7. (*c*)	11. (*b*)	15. (*d*)
4. (*c*)	8. (*b*)	12. (*a*)	16. (*f*)

15

Elasticity and Creep of Concrete

15.1. INTRODUCTION

In the theory of reinforced concrete, it s assumed that concrete is elastic, isotropic, homogeneous and obeys Hooke's law. Actually non of these assumptions is strictly true and concrete is not perfectly elastic material. By definition of elasticity, strain appears on the application of stress or force and disappears on removal of stress. If the stress-strain cure is straight as shown in Fig. 15.1 then the material is elastic. On the other hand if the curve is as shown in Fig. 15.2 then the material is not perfectly elastic. In case of concrete, it deforms on the application of load, but this deformation does not follow any set rule. The deformation of concrete depends upon the magnitude of the load, the rate of applying the load and the time elapsed after which the observations are recorded. Thus the deformation behaviour of concrete is quite complex.

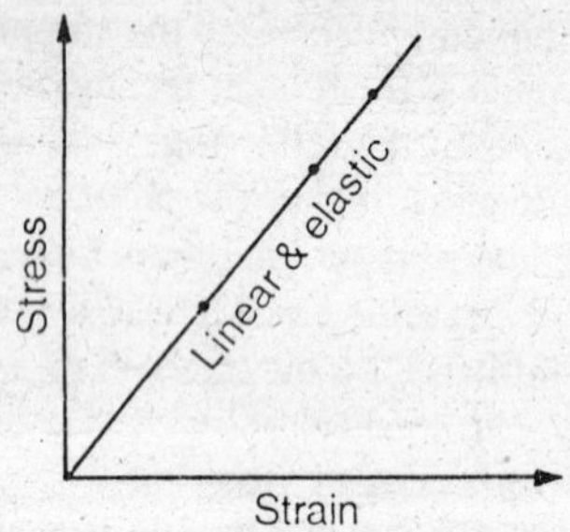

Fig. 15.1

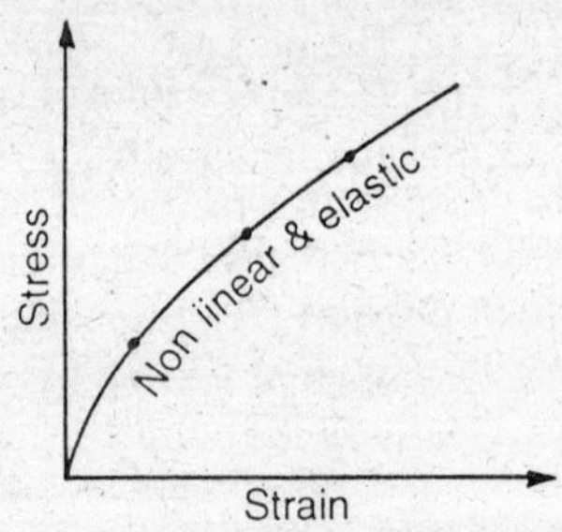

Fig. 15.2

Stress-Strain response

In order to calculate the deflection of structures and design of concrete members with respect to their sections, quantity of steel etc. the knowledge of deformation properties is necessary. At the time of design of a reinforced concrete structure, it is assumed that the bond between concrete and steel is perfect and the stress in steel is 'm' times the stress in concrete, where m is the ratio of modulus of elasticity of steel and concrete. This ratio is known as modular ratio. The accuracy of design will depend upon the value of modulus of elasticity of concrete, as the modulus of steel more or less is a definite quantity.

15.2. MODULUS OF ELASTICITY

It can be defined as the slope of the relation between the stress and strain. It can also be defined as the change of stress with respect to the elastic strain and may be computed by the following relation.

$$\text{Modulus of elasticity} = \frac{\text{unit stress}}{\text{unit strain}}$$

It is a measure of stiffness or resistance to deformation of a material. The terms elastic modulus or Young's modulus of elasticity can be applied strictly to linear relation ship *i.e.* straight part of stress strain curve. The magnitude of the observed strains and the curvature of the stress-strain relation depends on the rate of application of stress. When the load is applied extremely rapidly, the recorded strains are greatly reduced and the curvature of stress strain curve is reduced to a very small value. By slowing down the rate of loading *i.e.* by increasing the time of loading from 5 seconds to about 2 minutes, the increase in the strain is found to go up by 15%, but at normal rate of loading, normally 2 to 10 minutes time is required to test a specimen in an ordinary testing machine, the increase in strain is very small. Hence the degree of non linear behaviour is also very small.

15.2.1. Determination of modulus of elasticity

The modulus of elasticity is determined by subjecting a cylinder of 15 cm diameter and 30 cm length or 15 cm cube to uniaxial compression usually in U.T.M. (Universal testing machine) and measuring the strains or deformations by strain gauges or dial gauges fixed at certain gauge length. The value of strain is calculated by dividing the gauge readings by gauge length. The stress will be obtained by dividing the load by the area of cross-section of the specimen. A stress-strain curve is drawn with the halp of values of stress and strain obtained.

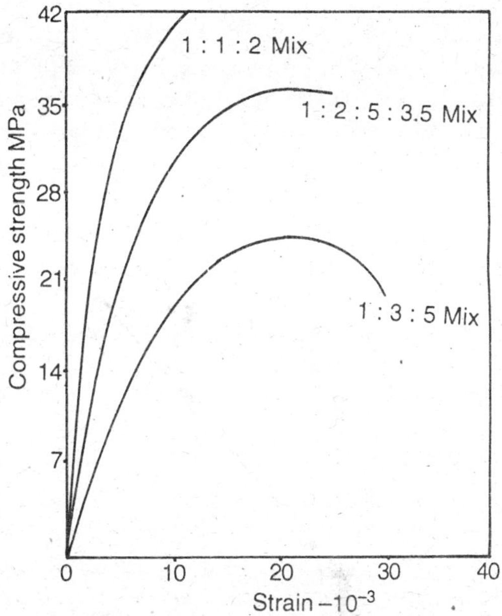

Fig. 15.3. Stress-Strain curves for different mixes

The modulus of elasticity so obtained from actual loading is called *static modulus of elasticity*. It has been observed that even under short term loading concrete does not behave as a elastic material. However upto about 10 to 15% of the ultimate strength of concrete, the stress-strain curve is not much curved and more accurate values of modulus of elasticity may be obtained. For higher stresses, the stress-strain curve will be more curved and will give inaccurate results. Stress-strain curve for various mix proportioned concrete are shown in Fig. 15.3. The modulus of elasticity of concrete may be measured in compression, tension or shear. The modulus of elasticity in tension is equal to the modulus of elasticity in compression.

Stress-strain relationship of aggregate and Cement Paste

The curve drawn between stress and strain of aggregate alone is found a fairly good straight line. Similarly the curve of stress-strain of cement paste alone shows a fairly good straight line. But the stress-strain curve of concrete, which is a combination of aggregate and cement paste gives a curved curve. Perhaps this is due to the development of fine or micro cracks at the interface of the aggregate and cement paste. This failure of bond at the interface increases at a faster rate than that due to applied stress. Thus the stress-strain curve continues to bend faster than the increase of stress. Stress-strain relation ship of aggregate, cement paste and concrete are shown in Fig. 15.4.

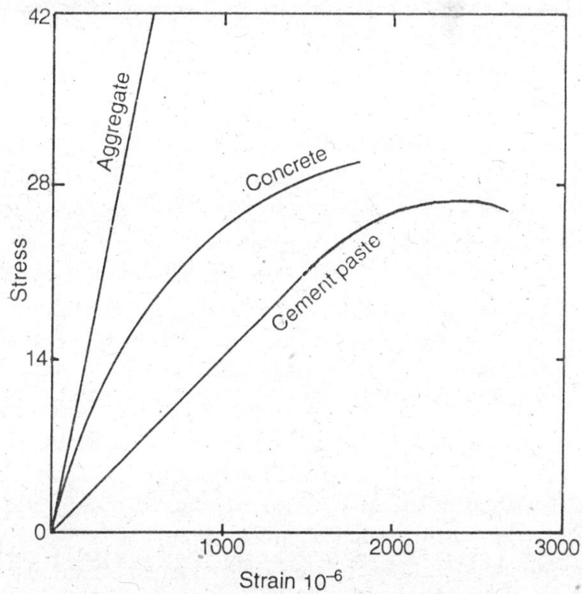

Fig. 15.4. Stress-strain curves for aggregate cement paste and concrete

15.4. MEASUREMENT OF STRAINS

The measurements of strains in concrete are not easy, but within limits it can be determined by Lamb's roller extensometer. In this method the extensometer is fixed on a 15 cms × 30 cms cylinder and placed in compression testing machine and loaded at a rate of 140 kg/cm^2 per minute. The load on cylinder increased till it reaches to 1/3rd of cube strength plus 7 kg/cm^2. Now this load is sustained for 1 minute. After sustained loading for one minute the load is released gradually at a rate of 1.5 kg/cm^2.

In the second operation, the reading of the extensometer is noted and it is again loaded till the load reaches to 1/3rd of the cube strength plus 1.5 kg/cm^2. The reading of extensometer is noted and the load released slowly till it reaches to a value of 1.5 kg/cm^2 on the cylinder specimen.

In the third cycle, the load from zero position to 1/3rd of the cube strength plus 1.5 kg/cm^2 is divided into 10 intervals. The cylinder is loaded with the standard rate and at the end of each interval the reading of extensometer noted. The difference between the strains of second and third observations should not be more than 5%. These strains are plotted against stress as shown in Fig. 15.5.

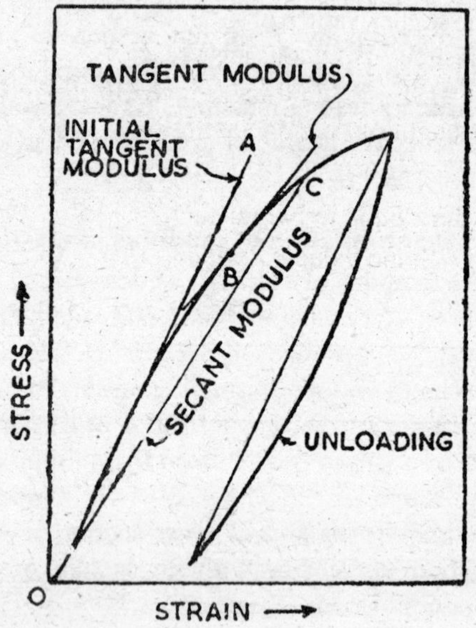

Fig. 15.5. Typical stress-strain curve for concrete

15.5. TYPES OF YOUNG MODULUS OF ELASTICITY

Elastic modulus of concrete can be classified into two main groups as

1. static modulus
2. dynamic modulus

1. Static elastic modulus. The strains obtained as above are plotted against stress and a curve is obtained as shown in Fig. 15.5. As concrete is an imperfect elastic material, stress strain diagram is a curved line. Hence three methods can be used to determine the modulus of elasticity.

(*a*) Initial tangent modulus
(*b*) Tangent modulus
(*c*) Secant modulus

(*a*) Initial tangent modulus. It is represented by the slope of a tangent to the stress-strain curve drawn passing through the origin. This modulus has significance only for low stresses and thus is of limited value and not easy to determine. It is represented by line OA in the Fig. 15.5.

(*b*) Tangent modulus. It is represented by the slope of the line drawn tangent to the stress-strain curve at any point on the curve, but this modulus applies only to very small changes in load above or below the load at which the tangent modulus is considered. Secondly it is difficult to determine tangent modulus with accuracy as the tangent to the curve is drawn by the eye judgment.

(*c*) Secant modulus. It is represented by the slope of a line drawn from the origin to any point C on the curve. This method is most practical and is in most general use as it represents the actual deformation at the selected point and no uncertainties are involved in its determination. Secant modulus is found to decrease with the increase in stress, hence stress at which it has been determined should be stated.

15.6. RELATION BETWEEN MODULUS OF ELASTICITY AND STRENGTH

It has been observed that for the same stress-strength ratio, the stronger the concrete, higher the strain.

On the contrary stronger the concrete higher the modulus of elasticity. This may be due to the fact that for stronger concretes its gel is also stronger, hence there is less strain for a given load. This lower strain gives the higher values of modulus of elasticity. In international system of units, (SI units) the unit of modulus of elasticity is GPa. (Gega Pascal)

ISI-456-2000 has suggested the relation between static modulus of elasticity *Ec* and the characteristic strength of concrete as follows:

$$E_e = 5000\sqrt{f_{ck}}$$

where *Ec* is in N/mm^2 units called (GPa), andf_{ck} concrete cylinder strength of 28 days.

Some values of modulus of elasticity are shown in Table 15.1.

Table 15.1. Modulus of elasticity of concrete of different strength

S. No.	*Average Compressive strength of works cube MPa*	*Modulus of elasticity GPa*
1.	21	21.4
2.	28	28.5
3.	35	32.1
4.	42	35.7
5.	56	42.9
6.	70	46.4

In SI units $E_e = 9.1\ (f_{ck})^{1/3}$ for concrete density 2320 kg/m^3.

Note: Actual measured values may differ ± 20% from the values obtained from the above relation.

15.7. FACTORS AFFECTING THE MODULUS OF ELASTICITY

Following factors affect the value of modulus of elasticity:

1. **Strength of concrete.** It is one of the most important factor which affects the modulus of elasticity. Higher strengths give higher value of modulus of elasticity.
2. **State of wetness of concrete.** The value of modulus of elasticity of wet specimen is found higher from 3 to 4 GPa (3.2 to 4.3 × 10^4 kg/cm^2) than dry specimen *i.e.* the modulus of elasticity of wet concrete is higher by 16.3% to 7.5 according to its compressive strength. Higher value 16.3% is observed for lower strength *i.e.* 21 MPa and 7.5% increase for 70 MPa strength, while the strength of wet concrete is found less than dry concrete. The strain of wet con- crete is found less than for dry concrete, hence the modulus of elasticity is higher for wet concrete than for dry concrete. The influence of moisture condition at the time of test for secant modulus at different ages is shown in Fig. 15.6.

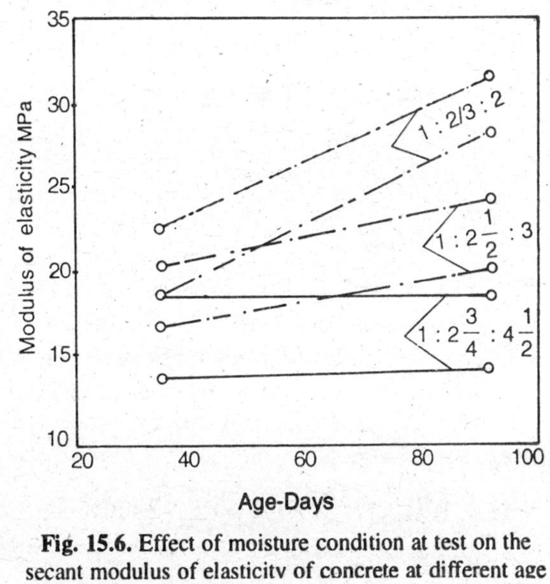

Fig. 15.6. Effect of moisture condition at test on the secant modulus of elasticitv of concrete at different age

3. **Properties of aggregate.** The modulus of aggregate and its volumetric proportion affect the modulus of elasticity of concrete as follows:
   (*a*) Higher the modulus of the aggregate, the higher the modulus of elasticity of con- crete. The modulus of aggregate is higher than the modulus of cement paste.

(*b*) The greater the volume of aggregate, the higher the modulus of elasticity of concrete. How ever strength of concrete is not affected much by these properties.

4. **The effect of age.** The modulus of elasticity of concrete increases more rapidly with age than the strength of concrete. Thus the relation between the modulus of elasticity of concrete and its strength depends on age.
5. **Mix proportion.** It has been observed that richer mixes have higher modulus of elasticity of concrete *i.e.* higher the amount of cement; higher the modulus of elasticity. The value of modulus of elasticity of concrete of mix proportion 1:1.67:2 is found 31.9 GPa while for a mix of 1:2.5:3 is 25 GPa for the same age and wet conditions. The relationship between modulus of elasticity, mix proportion and age is shown in Fig. 15.6.

The modulus of elasticity of light weight aggregate concrete usually varies from 40 to 80% of the modulus of normal weight concrete of the same strength, infact it is similar to that of cement paste.

Shape of stress-strain curve. The shape of stress-strain curve affects the static modulus of elasticity of concrete E_c, but not the dynamic modulus E_d hence the ratio of E_c and E_d is not fixed. The relation ship between the modulus of elasticity and strength is not much affected by the temperature upto 230°C as both these properties vary with temperature in the same way. Steam cured concrete has slightly lower modulus than water cured concrete of the same strength.

15.8. DYNAMIC MODULUS OF ELASTICITY

The value of modulus of elasticity E_c determined by actual loading of concrete is known as static modulus of elasticity. This method of testing is known as destructive method as the specimen is stressed or loaded till its failure. The static modulus of elasticity does not represent the true elastic behaviour of concrete due to the phenomenon of creep. At higher stresses the modulus of elasticity is affected more seriously.

Thus a non destructive method of testing known as dynamic method is adopted for determining the modulus of elasticity. In this case no stress is applied on the specimen. The modulus of elasticity is determined by subjecting the specimen to longitudinal vibration at their natural frequency, that is why this is known as dynamic modulus. In this method either the resonant frequency through a specimen of concrete or pulse velocity travelling through the concrete is measured. (Test details are given in chapter 19 on testing). From the known values of length of specimen, density of concrete and resonant frequency the value of dynamic modulus in S.I. units is determined from the relation.

$$Ed = K \cdot n^2 L^2 \rho$$

where,

Ed = dynamic modulus of elasticity
K = a constant
n = resonant frequency
L = length of specimen
ρ = density of concrete

If length of specimen is measured in mm and density ρ in kg/m^3 then

$$Ed = 4n^2 L^2 \rho \times 10^{-15} \text{ GPa}$$

The value of dynamic modulus of elasticity can also be determined from the relation

$$Ed = \rho v^2 \frac{(1+\mu)(1-2\mu)}{(1-\mu)}$$

where,

v = pulse velocity in mm/s
ρ density of concrete kg/m^3
μ = poisson's ratio.

The value of dynamic modulus of elasticity computed from ultrasonic pulse velocity method is some what higher than static modulus of elasticity as the creep remains un affected in dynamic modulus. Creep also does not significantly affect the initial tangent modulus. Thus the value of initial tangent modulus and dynamic modulus is approximately the same, but the value of dynamic modulus is appreciatly higher than secant modulus. The relation between static and dynamic modulic is given by the following relation in G.N/m^2.

$$Ec = 1.25\, Ed - 19 \qquad \ldots(i)$$

This relation is not applicable to very rich concrete with cement content more than 500 kg/m^3 and light weight concrete. For light weight concrete relation is

$$Ec = 1.04\, Ed - 4.1 \qquad \ldots(ii)$$

15.9. USE OF MODULUS OF ELASTICITY

Though concrete is not an elastic material in true sense, yet with in limits it is considered an elastic material. The modulus of elasticity of concrete is used in the calculations of structural deformations. In case of reinforced concrete structures it is used to determine the stresses developed in simple elements and also to determine the moments, deflections and stresses in more complicated structures. The dynamic modulus is used to determine the relative durability of concrete when exposed to severe climatic conditions as the dynamic modulus of concrete changes with the quality of concrete. This method is very useful to determine the quality of concrete, when it is subjected to alternate freezing and thawing.

5.10. POISSON'S RATIO

It is the ratio between lateral strain and longitudinal strain developed due to the application of axial compression. The sign of the strains is ignored. The axial contraction and lateral extension is of interest in the analysis of structures It is generally denoted by the letter μ. The value of poisson's ratio varies from 0.15 to 0.2 for normal weight and light weight concretes when determined from actual strain measurements as for determination of static modulus of elasticity.

Alternatively the poisson's ratio can be determined by measuring the ultrasonic pulse velocity and by finding the fundamental resonant frequency of longitudinal vibrations of a concrete beam specimen. The value of poisson's ratio may be determined from the following relation.

$$\left(\frac{v}{2\,nl}\right)^2 = \frac{1-\mu}{(1+\mu)(1-2\mu)}$$

where,

v = pulse velocity in mm/s

n = resonant frequency (Hz)

l = length of specimen in mm.

The value of poisson's ratio determined from dynamic method is found a little higher than the static method. This value ranges from 0.2 to 0.24.

15.11. CREEP

Creep can be defined as the increase in strain under a sustained constant stress, taking into account other time dependent deformations not associated with stress viz shrinkage, swelling and thermal deformations. Thus creep is reckoned from the initial elastic strain as given by secant modulus of elasticity at the age of loading. Although all materials undergo creep under certain conditions of loading to a greater or smaller extent, but the concrete creeps significantly at all stresses and for a long time. The creep of concrete has been found approximately a linear function of stress upto 30 to 40% of its strength. The order of magnitude of creep of concrete is much greater than that of other crystalline materials except for metals in the final stage of yielding prior to failure.

Thus it is a very important factor in the design of concrete structures as creep is several times larger than the strain on loading. If the sustained load is removed after some time, the strain decreases immediately by an amount equal to the elastic strain. Generally this strain is smaller than the initial elastic strain due to the increase in the modulus of elasticity with age. The instantaneously recovery is followed by a gradual decrease in strain called creep recovery as shown in Fig. 15.7. The shape of the creep recovery curve is similar to that of creep curve, but the rate of recovery is very fast, and its maximum value reaches more radically. The creep recovery is always smaller than the preceding creep, so that there is a residual deformation even after a period of one day under load. Hence creep is not a completely reversible phenomenon. Creep per unit stress is known as *specific creep*.

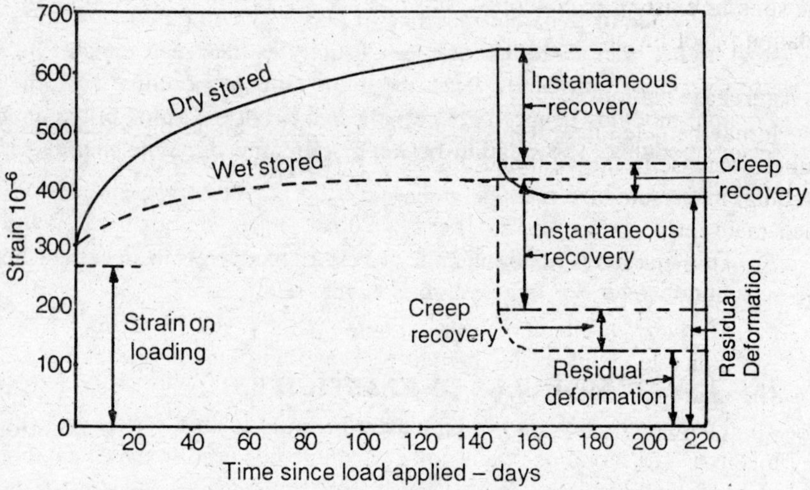

Fig. 15.7. Creep and creep recovery of concrete stored in water and air from the age of 28 days

Creep effects may also be seen from an other point of view. If a loaded concrete specimen is restrained so that it is subjected to a constant strain, creep will show itself as a progressive decrease in stress with time. This phenomenon is called relaxation and shown in Fig. 15.8.

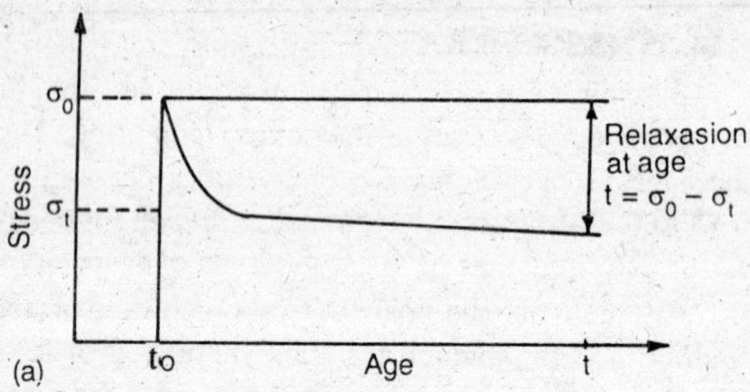

(a)

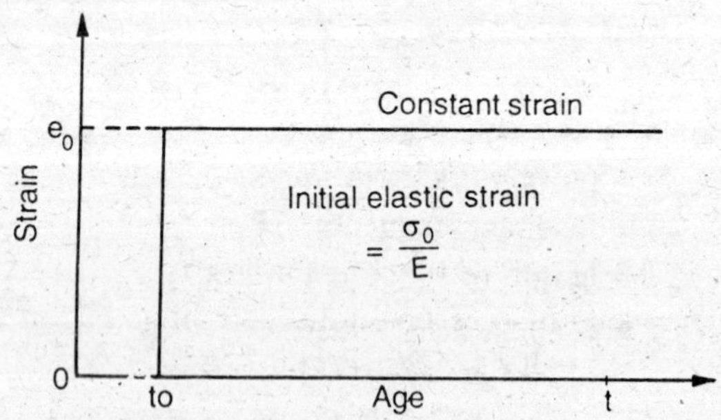

(*b*)

Fig. 15.8. Definition of relaxation for concrete initially subjected to stress σ_0

15.12. FACTORS INFLUENCING THE CREEP

Creep has been found to be affected by the following factors.

1. Cement paste in concrete *i.e.* aggregate/cement ratio.
2. Kind, size and grading of aggregate.
3. Water/cement ratio.
4. Composition and fineness of cement.
5. Age of concrete at the time of loading.
6. Intensity and duration of stress.
7. Moisture content of concrete.
8. Humidity of the ambient air.
9. Size of the specimen.
10. Temperature.

1. Cement paste

It should be noted that really it is the cement paste in concrete which undergoes creep. The role of aggregate in concrete is that of restraint. The usual normal weight aggregates are not liable to creep under the stresses existing in concrete. Thus creep is a function of the volumetric content of cement paste, but the relation is not linear.

2. Aggregate content

It may be noted that in the majority of the usual mixes the variation in the agg- regate content is small, but on increase in the volumetric content of aggregate from 65% to 75% can decrease creep by 10%. The grading, maximum size and shape of aggregate have been observed to affect the creep. It is believed that their main influence lies on the aggregate content provided concrete is fully compacted in all cases.

In fact there are certain physical properties of aggregate which influence the creep of concrete. They are as follows:

(*a*) *Modulus of elasticity of aggregate.* This is the most important factor, influencing the creep of concrete. Higher the modulus elasticity of aggregate, the greater the restraint offered by the aggregate to the potential creep of the cement paste *i.e.* lesser the creep Fig. 15.9.

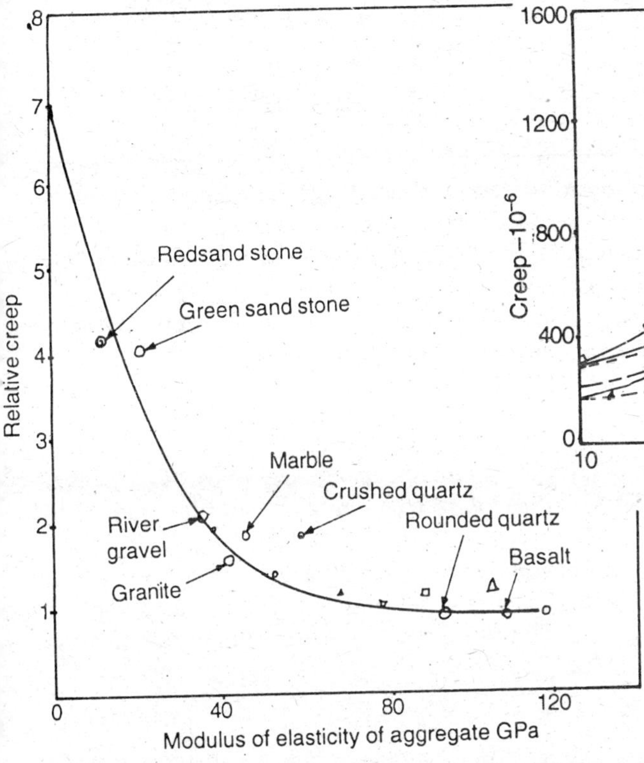

Fig. 15.9. Effect of modulus of elasticity of aggregate on relative creep of concrete

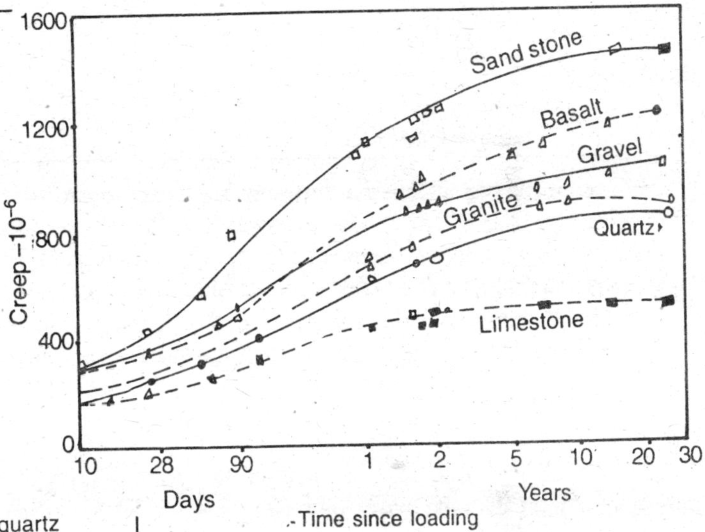

Fig. 15.10. Effect of quality of aggregate on the magnitude of creep of concrete

(*b*) *Quality of Aggregate.* The aggregate influences the creep of concrete through the restraining effect on the magnitude of the creep. The creeping of paste under load is restrained by the aggregates which do not creep. The stronger the aggregate, more is the restraining effect resulting in lesser magnitude of creep. The effect of the quality of aggregate on the magnitude of creep is shown in Fig. 15.10. After about 25 years, sand stone shows greatest creep while lime stone shows lowest creep.

(*c*) *Porosity of aggregate.* Porosity also has been found to influence the creep of concrete, but is not an independent factor to influence the creep of concrete. The porosity of aggregate plays an important role in the transfer of moisture with in the concrete, which is associated with the creep of concrete, as the transfer of moisture produces conditions of development of drying creep. Higher the porosity, lower the modulus of elasticity, hence higher the creep.

3. Effect of mineral composition of aggregate

Though it is not possible to make a general statement about the magnitude of creep of concrete made with different types of aggregates. However it has been observed that after 20 years' storage at a relative humidity of 50%, concrete made with sand stone aggregate showed creep more than twice that of concrete made with lime stone. The value of creep of different rocks is shown in Table 15.2 below.

Table 15.2. Creep of different aggregates after 20 years storage at 50% humidity

Type of aggregate	*Creep*
Sand stone	1500×10^{-6}
Basalt	1220×10^{-6}
Gravel	1100×10^{-6}
Granite	900×10^{-6}
Quartz	820×10^{-6}
Lime stone	600×10^{-6}

Even an greater difference between the creep strains of concrete made with different aggregates was discovered by RUSCH et al. He observed that after 18 months under load at a relative humidity of 65% the maximum creep was five times that of the minimum creep. The aggregates in the increasing order of creep are basalt, quartz, gravel, marble, granite and sand stone.

Grading, shape and the maximum size of aggregate have been found to affect the creep. The greater the maximum size of aggregate graded uniform from fine to coarse aggregate, the lesser the creep of concrete. This is true more specially for low water/cement ratio concrete.

4. Effect of light weight aggregate

The recent research has indicated that weight of aggregate has no effect on creep properties. The higher creep of concrete made with light weight aggregates is due to the lower modulus of elasticity of light weight aggregate.

As a general rule, it can be said that creep of structural quality light weight aggregate concrete is about the same as that of concrete made with normal aggregate. The elastic deformation of light weight aggregate concrete usually is larger than that of ordinary concrete. Thus the ratio of creep to elastic deformation is smaller for light weight aggregate concrete.

5. Effect of stress

In the direct stress tests on concrete a direct relation of proportionality between the creep and the applied load has been found to exist, but the upper limit is not certain. In terms of stress-strength ratio, an upper limit between 0.3 to 0.6 has been suggested.

In compression test of concrete specimen micro cracking takes place between the stress/strength ratio of 0.4 to 0.6, thus as cracking starts, the creep behaviour also starts changing. Thus it can be concluded that with in the range of working stresses, the proportionality between the creep and stress hold good.

Above the limit of proportionality, creep increases with the increase in stress at an increasing rate and above a certain stress/strength ratio, creep produces time failure. This stress/strength ratio exists in the region of 0.8 to 0.9 of the short term static strength.

6. Effect of strength of concrete on creep

It has been observed that the strength of concrete has a considerable effect on the creep with in a wide range. Creep has been found inversely proportional to the strength of the concrete at the time of application of load. The creep of concrete of different strengths is shown in Table 15.3 below. The linear function between the creep and stress/strength at different relative humidity is shown in Fig. 15.11.

Table 15.3. Creep of concrete of different strength

Compressive strength of concrete MPa	*Ultimate specific creep 10^{-6} MPa*	*Product of specific creep and strength 10^{-3}*
14	203	2.84
28	114	3.2
42	78	3.28
56	57	3.2

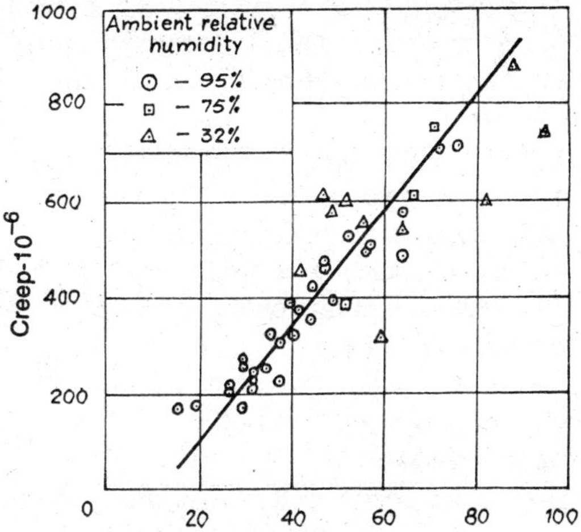

Fig. 15.11. Effect of relative humidity on creep of cement mortar

7. Effect of mix proportion

In the majority of practical mixes of similar workability, the variation of cement is very small. For example, consider normal weight aggregate concrete having aggregate/cement ratio as 9, 6 and 4.5 and the corresponding w/c ratio as 0.75, 0.55 and 0.4, by weight the cement paste content would be 24, 27 and 29% respectively. The difference in cement paste is not much. Hence the creep of these concretes also must not differ much, but infact this is not true as w/c ratio has most significant effect on creep.

We know that w/c ratio is the main factor which influence the porosity and strength. Thus lower the water/cement ratio, higher the strength. For a constant cement paste content, decrease in water/cement ratio results in decrease of creep or higher the water/cement ratio, higher the creep. Thus with in the wide range of mixes, creep is inversely proportional to the strength of concrete at the age of application of the load.

Effect of age at the time of loading

It has been observed that for a given type of concrete, the creep decreases as the age at the time of application of load increases as the strength increases with age Fig. 15.12.

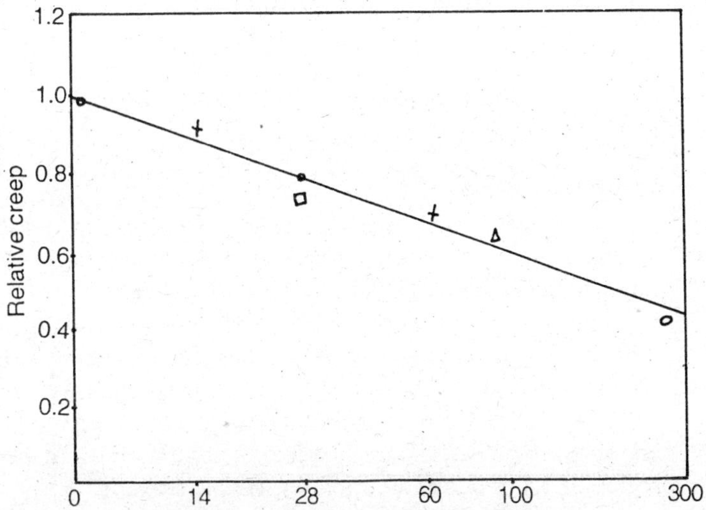

Fig. 15.12. Effect of age at the application of load on the creep of concrete

Effect of type of cement

The effect of type of cement on creep is not direct, but the type of cement affects the strength of concrete, hence creep is affected. On the basis of equality of the stress/strength ratio most portland cements lead sensibly to the same creep.

Effect of fineness of cement

Fineness of cement affects the strength development at early ages and thus influences the creep. It has been observed that the creep with finenest cement was greatest at first, but after 1000 days it became least due to the high gain of strength.

Effect of relative humidity of ambient air

It has been observed that for a given concrete, lower the relative humidity of surrounding air, higher the creep. The effect of relative humidity of 100,70 and 50% humidity on the deformation is shown in Fig. 15.13.

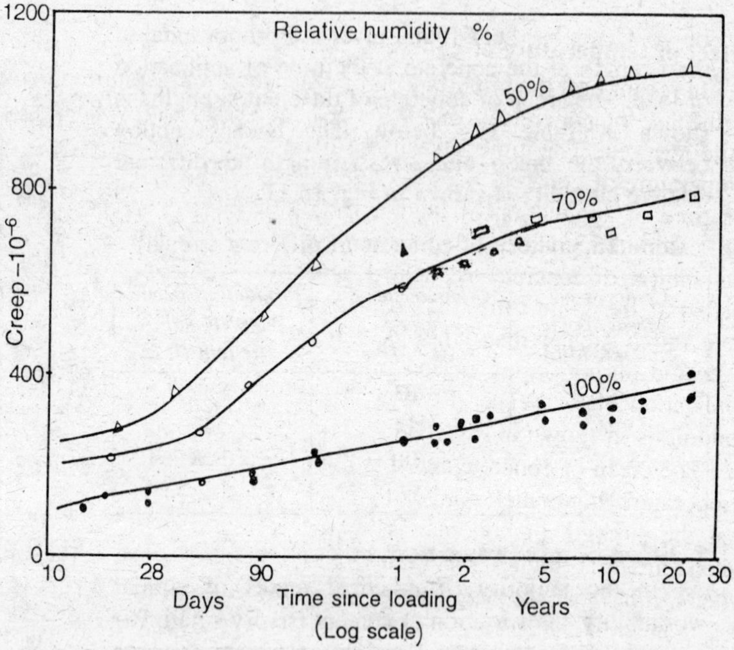

Fig. 15.13. Effect of relalive humidity on creep of concrete

Effect of alternate wetting and drying of concrete

It has been observed that alternate wetting and drying increases the magnitude of creep of concrete.

Effect of size of specimen

Creep has been found to decrease with the increase in the size of the specimen. This size effect is expressed in terms of the volume/surface ratio of concrete member as shown in Fig. 15.14.

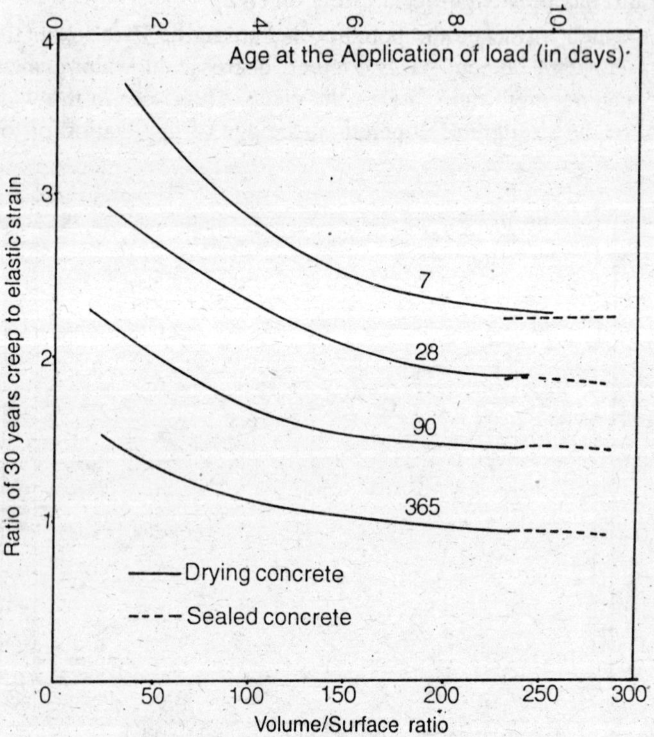

Fig. 15.14. Effect of volume/space ratio on the ratio of creep to elastic strain

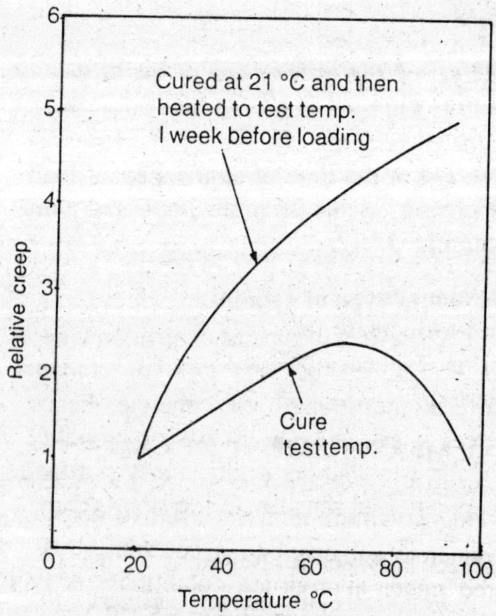

Fig. 15.15. Effect of temperature on creep of saturated concrete relative to creep at 21°C

Effect of temperature of concrete

In recent past the importance of influence of temperature on creep has assumed greater importance due to the use of concrete in nuclear pressure vessels as well as in other structures as bridges, multistory buildings etc. The time at which the temperature of concrete rises relative to the time of application of load, affects the creep-temperature relationship. If the saturated concrete is heated and loaded at the same time, the creep has been found greater than when concrete is heated during curing period prior to application of load. The effect of these conditions in shown in Fig. 15.15.

The creep of concrete cured at high temperature is smaller due to the fact that the strength of concrete is higher when cured at high temperature than when cured at normal temperature before heating and loading.

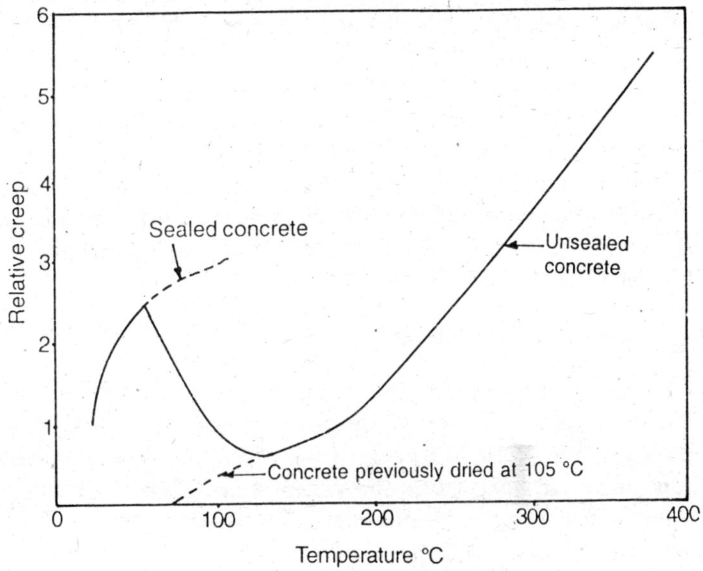

Fig. 15.16. Effect of temperature on creep of unsealed concrete relative to creep at 20°C

It has been observed if un sealed concrete is subjected to high temperature at the same time or just prior to the application of load a rapid increase in creep takes place as the temperature increases to about 50°C, then a decrease takes place in creep to a temperature of about 120°C and again creep increases upto at least 400°C as shown in Fig. 15.16. The initial increase in creep is due to the rapid expulsion of evaporable water. When all such water has been removed, creep is reduced greatly and becomes equal to that of pre dried concrete.

Fig. 15.17 shows the creep at low temperature as a proportion of creep at 20°C. At temperature below 20°C (68°F) creep decreases till the formation of ice which causes an increase in creep, but below the ice point creep decreases again.

Effect of admixtures and plasticizers

Admixtures and plasticizers have been found to increase the creep of concrete, but not in all cases, hence before use their effect should be tested.

15.13. MEASUREMENT OF CREEP

Usually creep is determined by measuring the change with time in the strain of a specimen of concrete subjected to a constant stress and stored under appropriate conditions. A typical testing device is shown in Fig. 15.18. The spring of the apparatus ensures that the load sensibly remains constant inspite of the contraction of the

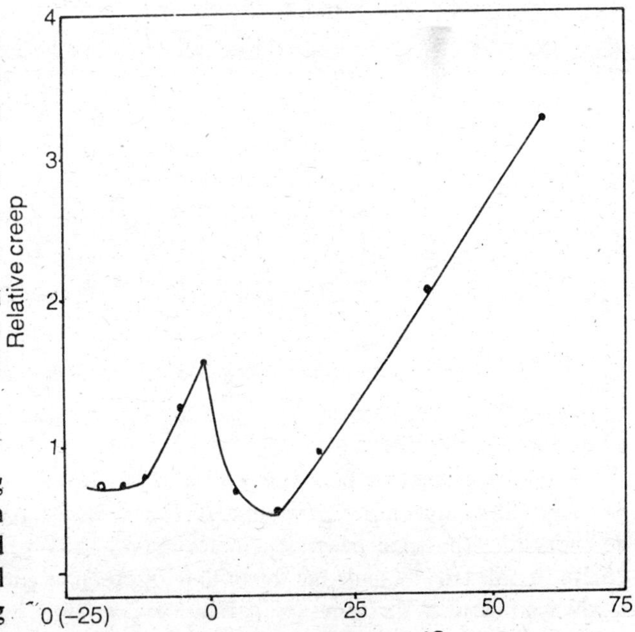

Fig. 15.17. Creep of sealed concrete at low temp relative to creep at 20°C

specimen with time. Under such conditions, creep continues for a long time, but the rate of creep decreases with time.

Under compressive stress the creep measurement is associated with shrinkage of concrete. To eliminate the effect of shrinkage and other autogenous volume charge, it is necessary to keep a companion specimen unloaded. While this correction qualitatively is correct, and gives usable results, but some researchers maintain that shrinkage and creep are not independent. At the same time they opine that shrinkage and creep are not additive as assumed in the test. Numerous mathematical formulae relating creep and time have been suggested. One of the most convenient relation is the hyperbolic expression suggested by Ross and Lorman. The Ross expression for specific creep C after time 't' under load is as follows:

$$C = \frac{t}{a + bt} \qquad \ldots(i)$$

where a and b are constants. If a graph is plotted between t and t/c, Taking t on × axis and t/c on y-axis, a straight line is obtained as shown in Fig. 15.19. The value of b is given by the slope and the intercept of t/c on y-axis gives the value of 'a'. Thus the values of constants a and b can be determined easily from the curve. Creep strain per unit stress is called specific creep.

The straight line should be so drawn that it passes through the points at later ages also. There may be some deviation from straight line during the early period after the application of load.

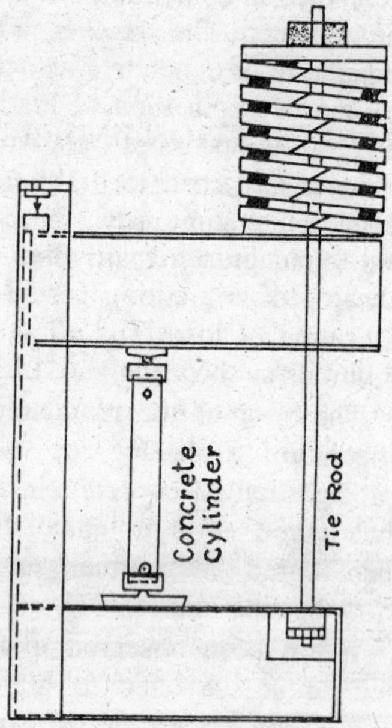

Fig. 15.18. Creep measuring device

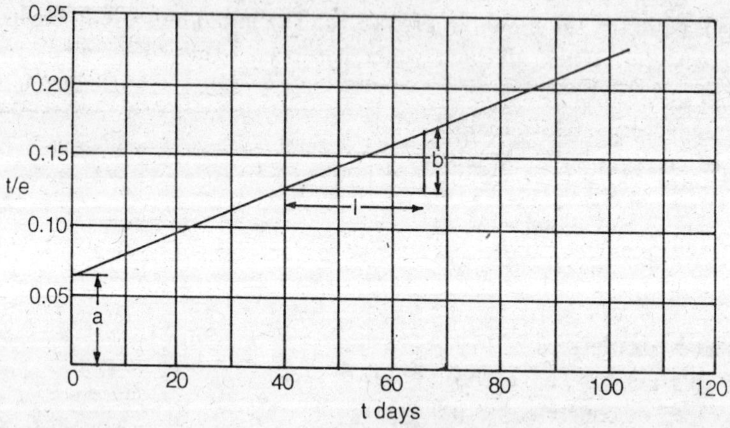

Fig. 15.19. Determination of creep constant according to Ross experiments

From the above relation (i), when the t is infinite, the ultimate creep at infinite time will be l/b, and when $t = a/b$, c will be $l/2 \cdot b$ *i.e.* it will be one half of the ultimate creep, obtained at time $t = a/b$.

If a loaded concrete member is kept in atmosphere and subjected to shrinkage, the deformation in the member will be developed from three different causes, namely elastic deformation, dry shrinkage and creep deformation. The time dependent deformation in concrete subjected to sustained load is shown in Fig. 15.20. In order to calculate the magnitude of creep in a member subjected to drying a companion specimen is always placed at the same temperature and relative humidity condition and the drying shrinkage of the un loaded specimen is determined. To find out the magnitude, of the creep the value of the drying shrinkage is subtracted from the total deformation of the loaded member. Knowing the instantaneous elastic deformation, the creep deformation can be calculated. For the sake of simplicity, it is assumed that shrinkage of concrete does not affect the creep in addition to load. In fact it should be remembered that in addition to the load, the shrinkage also has some influence on the magnitude of creep and creep on shrinkage.

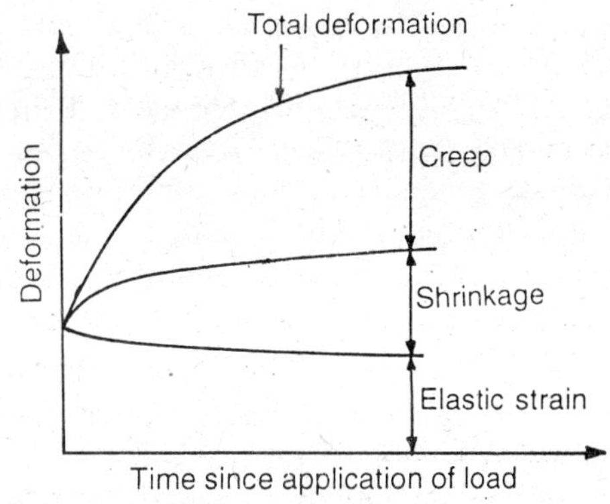

Fig. 15.20. Time dependent deformation in concrete subjected to a sustained load

15.14. HYDRATION UNDER SUSTAINED LOAD

Under sustained load the cement paste undergoes creep deformation continuously. If a concrete member is subjected to a drying condition, it will also undergo continuous shrinkage process. The migration of liquid from the gel pores due to creep may develop shrinkage to some extent. Thus it can be said that, the creep, the shrinkage and slip deformation cause deformation and fine or micro cracks at the discontinuities. Along with this phenomenon the process of hydration also goes on side by side producing more gel, which heals up the fine cracks produced by creep and shrinkage. This healing up of fine creaks by the delayed hydration process is also responsible for increasing the irrecoverable components of the deformation. Thus in actual practice, concrete structures are subjected to loading and drying and at the same time to some extent the delayed hydration also takes place. Under such complex situation the structure undergoes creep, drying shrinkage and also experiences micro cracks. Due to the progressive hydration the micro cracks formed due to any reason are healed up. This process is known as *hydration under sustained load.*

15.15. MAGNITUDE OF CREEP

Generally it is assumed that creep tends to a limiting value after an infinite time under load. But later studies have shown that the increase in creep beyond twenty 20 years under load is small and as a guide following values may be assumed.

1. From 18 to 35% (an average value of 26%) of the 20 year creep occurs in 2 weeks. Some authors have suggested 25% instead of 26%.
2. From 40 to 70% (an average value of 55%) of the 20 years creep occurs in 3 months. Some authors have suggested 50% instead of 55%.
3. From 64 to 83% (an average value 76%) of the 20 years creep occurs in 1 year. Some authors have suggested 75% instead 76%.

If creep after 1 year under load is taken as unity, then the average value of creep at later ages may be assumed as follows:

1.14 times after 2 years
1.20 times after 5 years
1.26 times after 10 years
1.33 times after 20 years
1.36 times after 30 years

These values show that ultimate creep is 1.36 times the one year creep. For calculation purposes, often it is assumed that ultimate creep is 4/3 times of 1 year creep. This estimated value is correct with in ± 15% for concretes loaded at early ages.

15.16. EFFECTS OF CREEP

The creep of concrete increases the deflection of reinforced beams and in some cases it may be a critical consideration in design. The deflection due to creep increases with time.

In reinforced concrete columns creep property of concrete has been found useful. Under load elastic deformation takes place immediately. Concrete creeps and deforms. It can not deform independent of steel reinforcement. There will be gradual transfer of stress from concrete to reinforcement. The creep results in a gradual transfer of load from concrete to reinforcement. Once the steel yields, any increase in load is taken by the concrete, so that the full strength of both steel and concrete is developed before the failure takes place. However in ecentrically loaded columns the creep increases the deformation, leading to buckling.

In case of statically indeterminate structures, column and beem junctions, creep may relieve the stress concentration induced by shrinkage, temperature changes or movements of support. In all concrete structures, creep reduces internal stresses due to non uniform or restrained shrinkage, so that there is a reduction in cracking. Thus creep is useful for concrete structures.

In case of mass concrete structures such as dams, creep is harmful and by itself may be a cause of cracking when the interior restrained concrete undergoes a cycle of temperature change due to the development of heat of hydration and subsequent cooling. An other example of adverse effects of creep is of tall buildings, in which case the differential creep between inner and outer columns may cause movements and cracking of partitions. Thus all precautions must be taken to reduce the differential movements.

Loss of prestress due to creep of concrete of prestressed concrete structures (beams), is well known and suitable provisions should be made to prevent the loss of pre stress in the design it self.

QUESTIONS

1. Define modulus of elasticity of concrete.
2. Define poisson's ratio of concrete. How does it vary with the increase in stress.
3. Differentiate between the static and dynamic modulus of concrete.
4. Define the following
   (*a*) Initial tangent modulus of elasticity
   (*b*) Tangent modulus of elasticity
   (*c*) Secant modulus of elasticity
5. What is the relation between the modulus of elasticity of concrete and its strength? How does it vary with age?
6. What is the effect of the properties of aggregate on the modulus of elasticity of concrete?
7. What is the significance of the shape of descending part of the stress strain curve of concrete?
8. Define creep of concrete.
9. How would you estimate the creep of concrete made with an unknown aggregate compared with a known mix?
10. Describe the role of aggregate on the creep of concrete.
11. Draw a stress-strain curve for concrete loaded at a constant rate of strain.
12. Discuss the main factors which affect the creep of concrete.
13. Compare the creep of mass concrete and concrete exposed to dry air.
14. Which modulus of elasticity would you use to determine the deformation of concrete to small variation in stress?
15. What is meant by specific creep of concrete?
16. Discuss the beneficial and harmful effects of creep of concrete.
17. Comment on the magnitude of concrete made with different cements.
18. Write a relation between static and dynamic modulic of concrete.

OBJECTIVE TYPE QUESTIONS

1. The stress and strain curve of concrete in compression is obtained by testing the cylinder specimen under.
   (*a*) Uniform rate of strain (*b*) Uniform rate of stress
   (*c*) Constant stress condition (*d*) Constant strain condition
2. The static test of concrete gives...than dynamic test
   (*a*) Lower values of Poisson's ratio (*b*) Higher value of Poisson's ratio
   (*c*) Equal values of Poisson's ratio (*d*) All of the above depending on the test condition

3. The inelastic behaviour of concrete is due to
   (*a*) Shrinkage in concrete
   (*b*) Presence of macro and micro cracks in concrete
   (*c*) Propagation of mortar and bond cracks
   (*d*) Use of coarse aggregate
4. The modulus of elasticity of concrete improves with
   (*a*) Shorter water curing period
   (*b*) High water-cement ratio
   (*c*) Age
   (*d*) Better compaction
5. Identify the false statement of the following
   (*a*) On applying load to the concrete its deformation follows an set rule
   (*b*) The deformation behaviour is quite complex
   (*c*) In the design of concrete structures the bond between steel and concrete is assumed perfect
   (*d*) Stress in steel is proportional to the modular ratio of steel and concrete
6. Identify the false statements of the following
   (*a*) Deformation of concrete depends on the magnitude of applied load
   (*b*) Deformation of concrete is independent of the time elesped after which the observation is recorded
   (*c*) The deformation of concrete depends on the rate of applying load
   (*d*) The accuracy of concrete design depends upon the value of modulus of elasticity of concrete
   (*e*) The modulus of elasticity of steel more or less is constant
7. Identify the false statement of the followings
   (*a*) Modulus of elasticity of a material is the measure of its stiffness or resistance to deformation
   (*b*) Modulus of elasticity of a material is not the measure of its stiffness
   (*c*) The term Young's modulus of elasticity can be applied strictly to a linear relationship of the stress-strain curve
   (*d*) The term elastic modulus can be applied to any part of the stress-strain curve
8. Identify the correct statement of the followings
   (*a*) The initial tangent modulus can be used for all stresses and very easy to calculate
   (*b*) Tangent modulus of concrete passes through the origin and easy to determine accurately and can be applied to all loads
   (*c*) Secant modulus passes through origin and any point on the curve. It is most practical and is in most general use.
   (*d*) The secant modulus increases with the increase in stress
9. Identify the true and false statements of the followings
   (*a*) Higher the strength of concrete, higher the value of its modulus of elasticity
   (*b*) Higher the strength of concrete, lower is modulus of elasticity
   (*c*) Leaner mix gives higher value of modulus of elasticity than rich mix
   (*d*) The strength of wet concrete is less than dry concrete
   (*e*) Higher the modulus of elasticity of aggregate, higher the modulus of elasticity of concrete
   (*f*) The modulus of elasticity of cement paste is higher than the modulus of elasticity of aggregate
   (*g*) The modulus of elasticity of concrete decreases more rapidly with age
   (*h*) Higher the cement content in concrete, higher its modulus of elasticity
   (*i*) Creep per unit stress is called specific creep
10. The creep in concrete is undesirable particularly in
   (*a*) Pre stressed concrete structures
   (*b*) R.C.C. columns
   (*c*) Continuous beams
   (*c*) Simply supported beams
11. Identify the true and false statements
   (*a*) Actually cement paste undergoes creep in concrete
   (*b*) Creep is a function of the volumetric content of cement paste, but the relation is not linear
   (*c*) Higher the modulus of elasticity of aggregate, higher the creep
   (*d*) The weight of aggregate has no effect on creep of concrete
   (*e*) Concrete made with light weight aggregate shows higher creep due to the lower modulus of elasticity of the light weight aggregate
12. Identify the true and false statements of the followings
   (*a*) The creep of structural quality light weight aggregate concrete is nearly same as that of normal weight aggregate concrete

(*b*) The elastic deformation of light weight aggregate concrete usually is lower than ordinary concrete
(*c*) The elastic deformation of light weight aggregate concrete usually is larger than ordinary concrete
(*d*) Lower the water-cement ratio, higher the creep
(*e*) Lower the water-cement ratio higher the strength
(*f*) Larger the size of specimen, higher the value of creep
(*g*) Creep decreases with the increase in size of the specimen

13. Identify the true and false statements of the followings
(*a*) The alternate wetting and drying has no influence on the value of creep
(*b*) Creep increases with the alternate wetting and drying
(*c*) Relative humidity of surrounding air has no effect on creep of concrete
(*d*) Lower the relative humidity of surrounding air, higher the creep
(*e*) Longer the age of concrete at the time of loading, lower the creep
14. Identify the true and false statements of the followings
(*a*) Better the quality of cement gel, lower the creep
(*b*) The strength of concrete increases with the age of gel
(*c*) Lower the age of gel, higher the strength of concrete
(*d*) The creep of fine cement increases at early age of concrete
(*e*) After about 3 years, the creep of concrete made with fine cement is least.
15. Identify the correct statement of the followings
(*a*) Type of cement has no direct effect on the creep of concrete
(*b*) Type of cement has direct effect on the creep of concrete
(*c*) Higher the relative humidity of the surrounding air, higher the creep
(*d*) Finer the cement, higher the creep of concrete at the later age of about 3 years
(*e*) Longer the age of concrete, higher the value of creep of concrete
16. By slow dowing the rate of loading by 1/24th of normal loading, the increase in strain is found
(*a*) 25% (*b*) 35%
(*c*) 45% (*d*) 15%
17. The modulus of elasticity of wet concrete of strength of the order of 21 MPa increases by about
(*a*) 16% (*b*) 21%
(*c*) 25% (*d*) 30%
18. The creep is a linear function of stress upto ...% of its strength
(*a*) 10 to 25% (*b*) 30 to 40%
(*c*) 35 to 45% (*d*) 40 to 50%

Answers

1. (*a*)	6. (*b*)	11. [False (*c*)]	16. (*d*)
2. (*b*)	7. (*b, d*)	12. [False (*b, d, f*)]	17. (*a*)
3. (*c*)	8. (*c*)	13. [False (*a, c*)]	18. (*b*)
4. (*c*)	9. [False, (*b, f, g*)]	14. [False (*c*)]	
5. (*a*)	10. (*a*)	15. [True (*a*)]	

16

Deformation And Cracking Independent of Load

16.1. INTRODUCTION

Concrete undergoes deformation due to the applied stress. But in addition to this, volume changes due to shrinkage, and temperature variations also take place. In practice these variations are of considerable importance as these movements partly or wholly are restrained and thus they introduce stress. These volume changes affect the long term strength and durability of concrete. Though shrinkage, swelling and thermal changes are categorised as independent of stress, but actually in practice it is not so simple. The restraint caused to the volume changes may induce tensile stresses in the concrete, which may result in the development of cracks in the concrete as concrete is very week in tension. Cracks in concrete must be avoided as far a possible. If it is not possible to avoid cracks, steps should be taken to control and minimise them as they affect the durability and structural integrity. Cracks are also aesthetically undesirable.

One of the most objectionable defects of concrete is the presence of cracks, more specially in floors and pavements. Shrinkage is one of the most important factors which contributes to the development of cracks in the floor and pavements. It is very difficult to produce a concrete which does not shrink and crack, however the magnitude of shrinkage may be reduced. Shrinkage is an inherent-property of concrete. It needs the understanding of factors which influence the shrinkage of concrete.

16.2. DEFINITION OF SHRINKAGE

Shrinkage may be defined as the volume charge in concrete due to loss of water or moisture due to evaporation or by hydration of cement or by carbonation. The reduction in volume *i.e.* volumetric strain is equal to 3 times the linear contraction. In practice the shrinkage is simply measured as linear strain. Its units are thus mm per mm, usually expressed in 10^{-6}.

16.3. CLASSIFICATION OF SHRINKAGE

Shrinkage can be classified into the following categories:

(*a*) Plastic shrinkage (*b*) Drying shrinkage

(*c*) Autogeneous shrinkage (*d*) Carbonation shrinkage

(*a*) **Plastic shrinkage.** Plastic shrinkage takes place, soon after the concrete is placed in the form work, while the concrete is still in plastic stage. The cement paste at this stage ungoes a volumetric contraction. The magnitude of this volumetric contraction is of the order of 1% of the absolute volume of the dry cement. The plastic shrinkage is caused by the loss of water by evaporation from the surface of concrete or by suction by dry concrete below. The contraction in volume induces tensile stress in the surface layers due to the restraint caused by non shrinking inner concrete. As the concrete is very weak in plastic state, plastic cracking takes place at the surface.

Plastic shrinkage is directly proportional to the loss of water *i.e.* plastic shrinkage is greater, the greater the rate of evaporation of water, which in turn depends upon the air temperature, the concrete temperature, relative humidity of the air and wind velocity etc. The rate of evaporation should not be greater than 0.5 kg/m^2 per hour of the exposed concrete surface to avoid plastic cracking of the surface. A complete prevention of evaporation from the concrete surface immediately after casting, reduces plastic shrinkage. As stated above, that the loss of water from the cement paste is responsible for the plastic shrinkage. The plastic shrinkage has been found greater, for the larger cement content in the mix and lower for larger aggregate content. The effect of cement aggregate ratio is shown in Fig. 16.1.

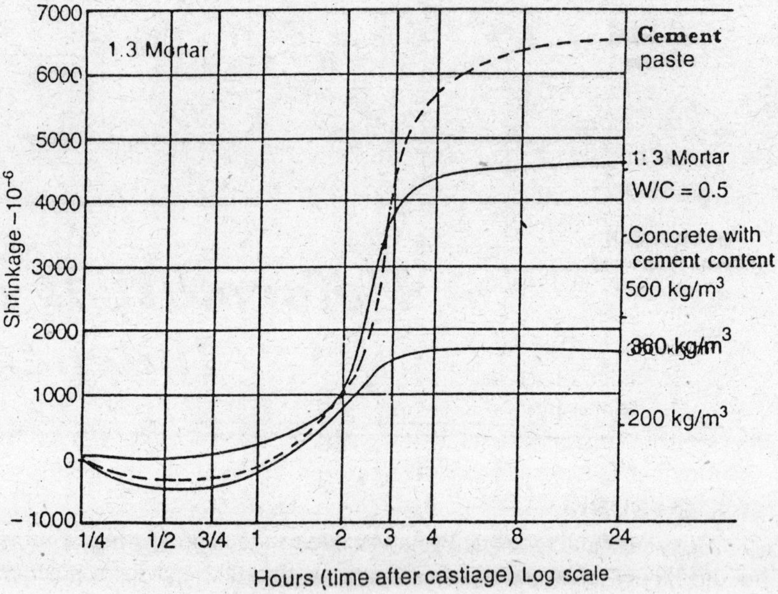

Fig. 16.1. Influence of cement content of the mix on the plastic shrinkage in air at 20°C

(*b*) Drying shrinkage. Withdrawal of water from hardened concrete stored in unsaturated air develops drying shrinkage. A part of this movement is irreversible. This part should be distinguished from the reversible part or moisture movement. In case of reversible moisture part, if the concrete allowed to dry in air of a given relative humidity is placed in water or at a higher humidity later on, the cement paste will absorb water and will swell. This phenomenon has been shown in Fig.

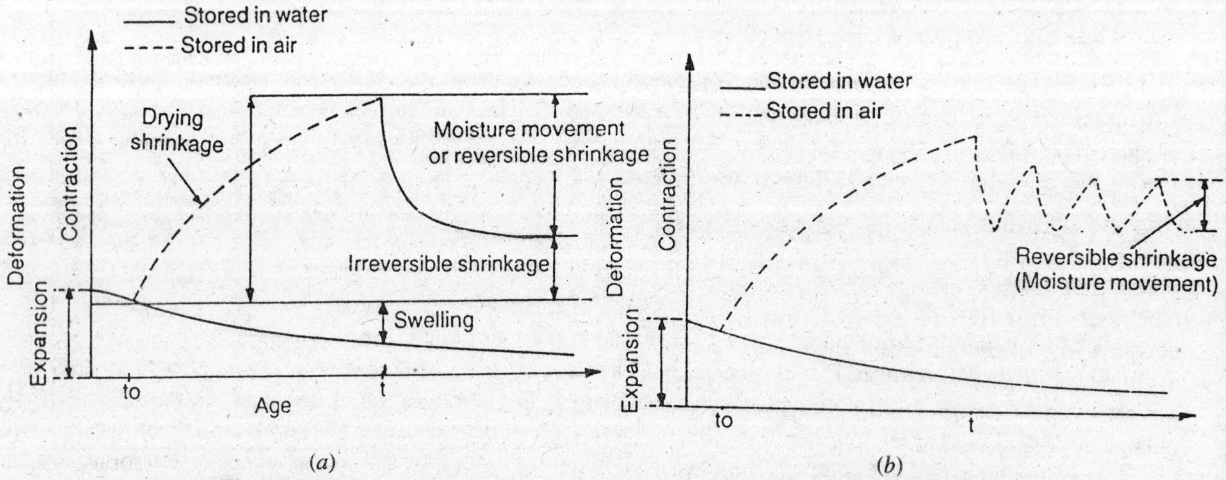

(*a*) (*b*)

Fig. 16.2. Moisture movement in concrete (a) Concrete dried from age t_0 till age t, (b) Concrete dried from age to until age t and then subjected cyclic drying and heatting

16.2 (*a*). The reversible moisture movement represents 40 to 70% of the drying shrinkage but it depends on the age before the start of first drying. If concrete is fully hydrated before exposing to drying, the reversible moisture movement will form the greater proportion of the drying shrinkage. On the other hand if drying is accompanied by extensive carbonation, the cement will not allow movement of moisture content and irreversible shrinkage will be larger. The process of swelling will be discussed later on. However not all the initial drying shrinkage is reco- vered even after a prolonged storage in water. For usual range of concrete, the pattern of moisture movement under alternating wetting and drying is a common occurrence in the practice. It has been shown in Fig. 16.2 (*b*). The magnitude of this cyclic moisture movement depends upon the duration of the wetting and drying periods, but drying is very much slower than wetting. Thus the influence of long dry weatherr can be reversed by a short period of rain. The movement of moisture also depends upon the following factors.

1. Range of relative humidity
2. Composition of the concrete
3. Degree of hydration at the time of intial drying

Concrete made with light weight aggregate has a higher moisture movement than normal weight aggregate concrete.

The irreversible part of shrinkage is associated with the formation of additional chemical and physical bond in the cement gel when adsorbed water has been removed. The phenomenon may be described as follows.

When concrete dries, first all the free water present in capillaries or pores evaporates and gets lost *i.e.* water present in concrete pores or capillaries which is not physically bound is lost. Thus under drying conditions, the gel water is lost progressively over a long time, as long as concrete is kept in drying conditions. This loss of free water does not cause any significant volumetric contraction of the cement paste. Due to the loss of free water, an internal relative humidity gradient is induced within the cement paste structure. As the time passes water molecules are transferred from the large surface area of calcium silicate hydrate into empty pores or capillaries and then out of the concrete. This phenomenon causes contraction in cement paste. This reduction or contraction in cement paste is not equal to the volume of water removed due to the internal restraint caused to contraction by the calcium silicate hydrate structure and also due to the negligible effect of free water loss on the change of volumetric contraction.

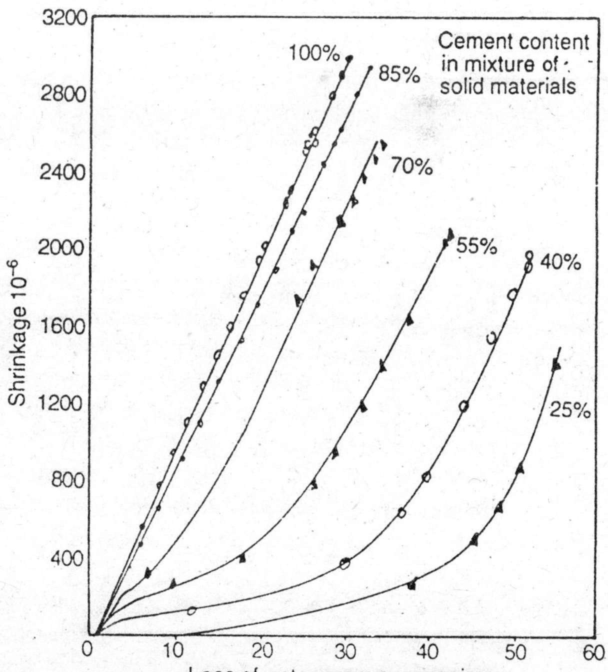

Fig. 16.3. Relation between shrinkage and loss of water from specimen

The loss of free water from the hardened concrete does not cause any appreciable change in volume. It is the loss of water held in gel pores that causes change in the volume of concrete. Fig. 16.3 shows the relationship between loss of moisture and shrinkage. Under drying conditions the gel water is lost progressively over a long time as long as the concrete is kept in drying conditions.

Theoretically it is estimated that the total linear change due to long time drying shrinkage is of the order of $10{,}000 \times 10^{-6}$, but actually this change has been observed upto 4,000 × 10^{-6}. Fig. 16.4 shows a typical apparatus for the measurement of shrinkage.

Further it has been observed that cement paste shrinks more than mortar and mortar shrinks more than concrete. Concrete made with smaller sized aggregate shrinks more than the concrete made with bigger size aggregate. The magnitude of drying shrinkage is also a function of the fineness of gel. The finer the gel, greater the shrinkage. As stated earlier, the high pressure steam cured concrete with low specific surface of gel, shrinks much less than that of normally cured concrete.

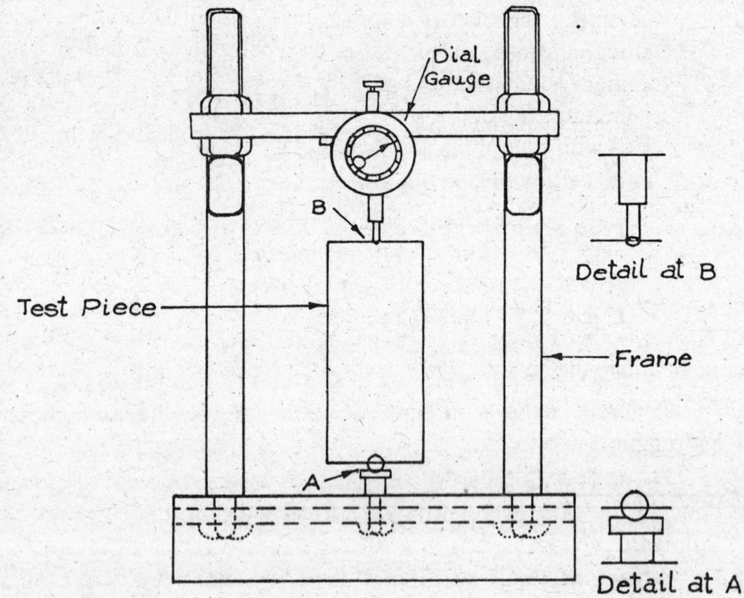

Fig. 16.4. Equipment for measurement for drying shrinkage

14.3.1. Magnitude of shrinkage

If no other reliable data is available, the magnitude of shrinkage can be estimated by the formula suggested by Schorer.

$$\varepsilon_s = 0.00125\,(0.90 - h) \qquad \ldots(16.1)$$

where,

ε_s = shrinkage strain

h = relative humidity expressed as a fraction. If the average humidity is 50%, then h = 0.50. If average humidity is 100%, then h = 1.0. In these conditions, shrinkage is given as

(*i*) If h = 0.5, then ε_s = 0.00125 (0.90 – 0.5) = 0.00125 × 0.4 = 0.0005

(*ii*) If h = 1.0, then ε_s = 0.00125 (0.9 – 1.0) = – 0.00125.

–ve sign indicates swelling.

The rate of shrinkage decreases with time. It has been observed that 14 to 34% of 20 years shrinkage takes place in two weeks time. Where as 40 to 70% in 3 months and 66 to 80% in one year.

(*c*) **Autogeneous shrinkage.** If no movement of water to or from the set paste of concrete is allowed, then the shrinkage developed is known as *autogeneous shrinkage*. This shrinkage is caused by the loss of water consumed or used up in the hydration of cement. Autogeneous shrinkage is not distinguished from shrinkage of hardened concrete due to the loss of water to the out side except for massive structures as interior of concrete dams. The magnitude of this shrinkage is very small of the order of 50 × 10^{-6} to 100 × 10^{-6}. Hence is not of much significance.

(*d*) **Carbonation shrinkage.** In addition to drying shrinkage, concrete also undergoes carbonation shrinkage. Many experimental data include both types of shrinkage, but their mechanism is different.

Carbonation is the reaction of carbon dioxide Co_2 present in the atmosphere, with the hydrated cement minerals in the presence of moisture. The action of Co_2 takes place even in small concentrations such as present in rural air, where the content of Co_2 is about 0.03% by volume. In an un ventilated laboratory the Co_2 content is about 0.1%, where as in the atmosphere of big cities, the carbon dioxide content exists about 0.3% and in exceptional cases it may go up to 1.0%. The rate of carbonation increases with the increase in the concentration of Co_2 especially at high water/cement ratio.

In the presence of mcisture, Co_2 forms carbonic acid, which reacts with $Ca(OH)_2$ to form calcium carbonate ($CaCo_3$). Other cement compounds are also decomposed, producing hydrated silica, alumina and ferric oxide The complete decomposition of calcium compounds in hydrated cement is chemically possible even at low pressure of Co_2 in normal atmosphere, but carbonation penetrates beyond the exposed surface of concrete extremely slowly. The simultaneous reaction of Co_2 with hydrated cement minerals in concrete induces contraction of concrete, which is known as *carbonation shrinkage.*

16.4. FACTORS AFFECTING THE RATE OF CARBONATION

The actual rate of carbonation depends on the permeability of concrete, its moisture content and on the content of Co_2, relative humidity of the ambient medium and size of the specimen , grade of concrete, depth of core, whether the concrete protected and time. As the permeability of concrete is governed by the water/cement ratio, the inadequately cured concrete will be more prone to carbonation *i.e.* the depth of carbonation of inadequately cured concrete will be more. The effect of following factors has been found more pronounced.

16.4.1. Effect of relative humidity

The highest rate of carbonation occurs at a relative humidity of 50 to 70%.

16.4.2. Effect of Time

The rate of carbonation depth is approximately proportional to the square root of time. It doubles between 1 and 4 years and then again doubles between 4 and 10 years. This process repeats upto about 5-years. However periodic wetting of concrete by rain slows down significantly the progress of carbonation.

16.4.3. Effect of w/c ratio

The depth of carbonation is directly proportional to the increase of water/cment ratio *i.e.* the depth of carbonation increases with the increase in water/cement ratio. It has been observed that depth of carbonation at w/c ratio 0.4 is half that of at w/c ratio 0.6 and at w/c 0.8, it is 50% higher than that at w/c ratio 0.6.

16.4.4. Effect of cement content

It has been observed that higher the cement content lessr the depth of carbonation. The depth of carbonation is found about 50% with cement content of 500 kg/m^3 of that having cement content of 310 kg/m^3. At cement content of 180 kg/m^3 it has been found twice that of at cement content of 310 kg/m^3. (Pl. also refer chapter 17).

The extent of carbonation can be determined easily by treating freshly broken surface with phenolphthalein. The portion containing free $Ca(OH)_2$ turn pink by soaking it in Phenolphthalein, where as carbonated portion remains unaffected.

16.5. EFFECTS OF CARBONATION

Following effects of carbonation are observed

1. Carbonation of concrete is accompanied by

(*a*) Increase in the weight of the concrete.

(*b*) Shrinkage in concrete known as carbonation shrinkage. Carbonation shrinkage most probably is caused due to the dissolving of crystals of $Ca(OH)_2$, while under a compressive stress imposed by the drying shrinkage and depositing $CaCo_3$ in the voids of cement paste. Thus the compressibility of cement paste is increased and the carbonation of the hydrates present in the gel does not contribute to the shrinkage.

(*c*) Carbonation results in increased strength.

(*d*) Carbonation results in reduced permeability. These changes possibly are due to the water released by carbonation, which promotes the process of hydration. The calcium carbonate produced reduces the voids with in the cement paste. This applies to concrete made with portland cement only. In case of super sulphated cement the strength of concrete decreases with carbonation. However this decrease in strength is not structurally significant.

(*e*) The most important effect of carbonation is the neutralization of alkaline nature of hydrated cement paste. The p_H value reduces from 12 to 8. This reduction in p_H value provides protection to steel from corrosion. However if full depth of reinforcement cover is carbonated and oxygen and moisture can penetrate into the concrete then corrosion and cracking of concrete may take place. This is a very significant development.

Fig. 16.5 shows the drying shrinkage of mortar specimen dried in Co_2 free air at different relative humidities and also the shrinkage after subsequent carbonation. It has been observed that carbonation increases shrinkage at intermediate humidities, but not at extreme limits of 100 and 25%. In the latter case there is no sufficient water present in the pores with in the cement paste for Co_2 to form carbonic acid. On the other hand at 100% humidity when the pores are full of water, the diffusion of carbon dioxide into paste will be very slow.

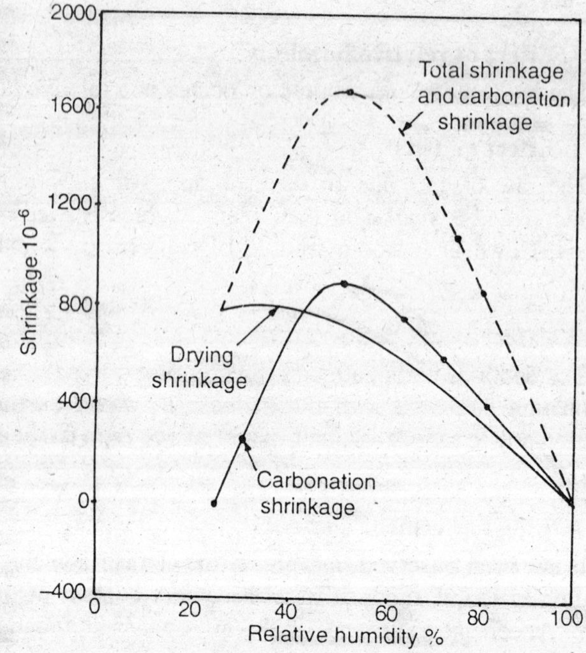

Fig. 16.5. Drying and carbonage shrinkage of mortar at different relative humidity

Thus carbonation is greater in concrete protected from direct rain, but exposed to moist air, then concrete periodically exposed fully to rain.

The sequence of drying and carbonation, greatly affects the total magnitude of shrinkage. Simultaneous drying and carbonation produces lower total shrinkage than when drying is followed by carbonation. Carbonation shrinkage of high pressure stean cured concrete is very small. Concrete subjected to alternate wetting and drying in air containing Co_2, carbonation shrinkage becomes progressively more apparent. The total shrinkage at any stage is greater than drying the concrete in Co_2 free air. Thus carbonation increases the magnitude of irreversible shrinkage and crazing of exposed concrete mass occur. However carbonation of concrete before exposure to alternate drying and wetting reduces moisture by about 50%.

16.4. SWELLING

Concrete or cement paste cured continuously in water from the time of casting exhibits an net increase in volume and its weight. This increase in volume due to continued hydration of cement is known as swelling. The swelling is due to the absorption of water by the cement gel. The water molecules act against the cohessive forces and tend to force the gel particles further apart with resultant swelling pressure.

16.5. FACTORS AFFECTING THE SHRINKAGE OF CONCRETE

Shrinkage of hardened concrete is influenced by various factors in a similar manner as that of creep under drying conditions. These factors are discussed below:

1. Aggregate, and its properties
2. Relative humidity
3. W/c ratio
4. Properties of cement
5. Entrained air
6. Curing storage condition
7. Size of specimen

1. Aggregate Content. The most-important influence on the shrinkage of concrete is exerted by the aggregate, which restraints the amount of shrinkage of the cement paste. For a constant w/c ratio and at a given degree of hydration, the ratio of shrinkage of concrete S_c to the shrinkage of neat paste Sp. depends on the aggregate content '*a*' in the concrete. This relation can be written as

$$S_c = S_p (1 - a)^n \qquad ...(1)$$

where,

a = relative volume concentration of aggregate in concrete

n = a constant, whose experimental value varies from 1.2 to 1.7.

There is some variation due to the relief of stress in the cement paste creep. Fig. 16.6 shows a typical relation and gives the value of n = 1.7, but the value of n depends on the modulus of elasticity and poisson's ratio of the aggregate and concrete. The volume of fractions will have some influence on the total shrinkage.

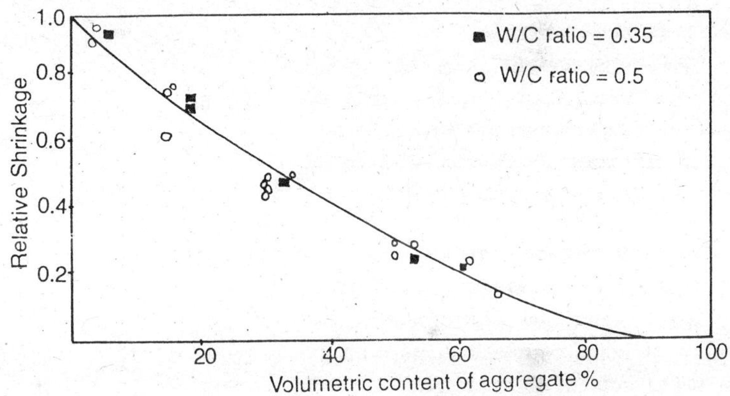

Fig. 16.6. Influence of volumetric content of aggregate in concrete

(a) **Max. size and grading of aggregate.** The maximum size and grading of aggregate directly do not have any influence on the magnitude of shrinkage of concrete with a given volume of aggregate and a given w/c ratio. But larger size aggregate permits the use of a leaner mix at a constant water/cement ratio. Thus the use of larger aggregate results in lower shri.ıkage. It has been observed that changing the maximum size of aggregate from 6.3 mm to 152 mm will raise the aggregate content from 60 to 80% of the total volume of concrete, resulting the decrease of shrinkage to 1/3rd of the original. Also it has been found that increase in the aggregate content from 71 to 74% has resulted in the reduction of shrinkage by 20% Fig. 16.6. The reduction in shrinkage by the addition of aggregate is due to internal cracking of the paste due to restraint of the aggregate. For aggregates upto the size of 6.3 mm the shrinkage has been observed uniform indicating that for these aggregates no internal cracking takes place.

(*b*) **Type of aggregate.** Type of aggregate or strictly speaking the modulus of elasticity of aggregate influences the shrinkage of concrete and determines the degree of restraint. The use of steel aggregate reduces the shrinkage to one third less and expanded shale one third more than normal or ordinary aggregate. The relation between the shrinkage and modulus of elasticity of concrete depends on the compressibility of the aggregate used. Even in ordinary range of ordinary aggregates there is a considerable variation in the shrinkage due to the variation of modulus of elasticity of aggregate as shown in Fig. 16.7. The aggregate in order of increasing shrinkage are as follows.

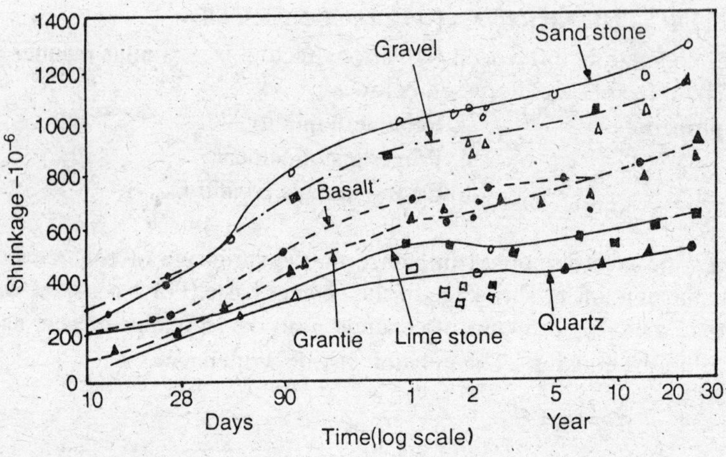

Fig. 16.7. Shrinkage of concrete with fixed mix proportion made with different aggregate modulus of elasticity

Sand stone has the highest shrinkage followed by gravel, then Basalt, Granite, lime stone and quartz.

Thus light weight concrete exhibits higher shrinkage than normal weight concrete. A charge in the modulus of elasticity of aggregate is reflected by a change in the value of n of equation 16.1.

2. Quality of cement paste

The quality of cement paste influences the magnitude of shrinkage. The quality of cement pate is dependent on the water cement ratio. Higher the w/c ratio, greater the shrinkage. Thus it can be said that for a given aggregate content the shrinkage of concrete is a function of the water-cement ratio. The effect of water-cement ratio on the shrinkage is shown in Fig. 16.8. The shrinkage of concrete made with different aggregate cement-ratio and water-cement ratio is shown in Table 16.1 below.

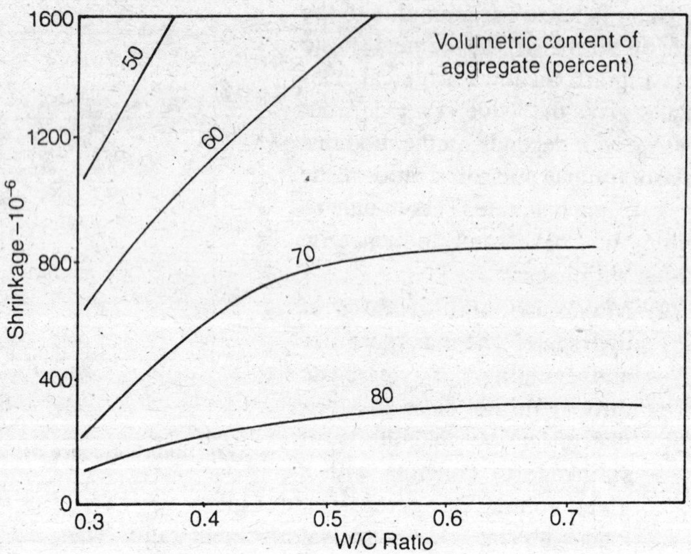

Fig. 16.8. Influence of water/cement ratio and aggregate content on shrinkage

Table 16.1. Typical values of shrinkage of concrete mortar after six month with different water cement and aggregate/cement ratio

Aggregate/Cement Ratio	*Water Cement ratio*			
	0.4	0.5	0.6	0.7
3	800×10^{-6}	1200×10^{-6}	—	—
4	550×10^{-6}	850×10^{-6}	1050×10^{-6}	—
5	400×10^{-6}	600×10^{-6}	750×10^{-6}	850×10^{-6}
6	300×10^{-6}	400×10^{-6}	550×10^{-6}	650×10^{-6}
7	200×10^{-6}	300×10^{-6}	400×10^{-6}	500×10^{-6}

3. Water Content

Though water is not believed to be a primary factor to influence the shrinkage, but the water content affects the water-cement ratio. Hence higher the amount of water, greater the shrinkage as higher the water-cement ratio, greater the shrinkage as shown in Fig. 16.8.

4. Properties of Cement

The properties of cement have little effect on the shrinkage of concrete. Latest studies have shown that fineness of cement have no influence on the shrinkage of concrete. However it increases the shrinkage of cement paste. Particles coarser than 75 micron hydrate comparatively little and have a restraining effect similar to aggregate.

5. Chemical composition of Cement

The chemical composition of cement has been observed as not having any effect on the shrinkage of concrete. However cement deficient in gypsum exhibits a greatly increased shrinkage. The range of gypsum contents which significantly affects the shrinkage is narrower than that affects the setting time.

6. Effect of high alumina cement

The shrinkage of concrete made with high alumina cement is of the same magnitude as that of concrete made with portland cement, but in case of high alumina cement shrinkage takes place much more rapidly than when portland cement is used.

7. Entertainment of air

Entertainment of air has been found to have no effect on shrinkage of concrete.

8. Effect of admixtures

Addition of calcium chloride increases the shrinkage of concrete generally between 10 to 50% due to the formation of finer gel and possibly due to greater carbonation of the more mature specimen with calcium chloride.

The effect of other admixtures on the increase in shrinkage of concrete is of varying amount, but the percentage influence on shrinkage is constant for a admixture, whatever the aggregate is used. The plasticizers which reduce the water-cement ratio of the concrete, their net effect on shrinkage is negligible.

9. Effect of curing and storage conditions

Shrinkage takes place for a long period. Some movements have been observed even after 28 years, but a part of long term shrinkage may be due to carbonation. The prolonged moist curing delays the development of shrinkage, but its effect on the magnitude of shrinkage is small and complex. In case of neat cement paste, the prolonged curing induces greater shrinkage. Further it has been observed that a well cured concrete shrinks more rapidly. In general it can be said that the length of the curing period is not an important factor in the shrinkage of concrete.

Mostly the magnitude of shrinkage is independent of the rate of drying except that transferring the concrete directly from water to a very low humidity, which can lead to fracture. Rapid drying does not allow a relief of stress by creep and may lead to more pronounced cracking.

10. Effect of relative humidity of the medium

The relative humidity of the medium surrounding the concrete greatly affects the magnitude of the shrinkage. If the concrete is placed in dry air, it shrinks, but if it is placed in water or air with 100% humidity it swells. This indicates that vapour pressure with in the cement paste is always less than the saturated vapour pressure. Thus the paste would be in hydrous equilibrium at some intermediate humidity.

If the concrete is placed in 100% humidity for any length of time, there will not be any shrinkage of concrete, instead the concrete will swell. A typical relationship between the shrinkage and time for which concrete is stored at relative humidities is shown in Fig. 16.9. The graph shows that shrinkage increases with time and also with the reduction in relative humidity, the rate of shrinkage decreases rapidly.

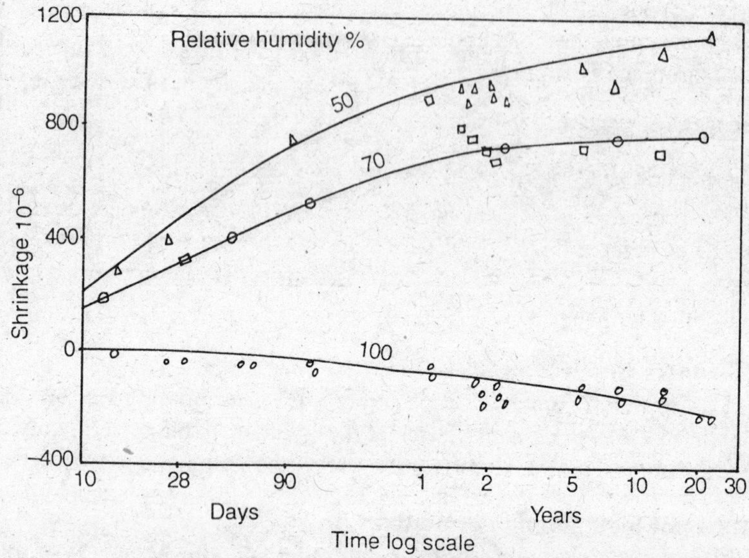

Fig. 16.9. Relation between shrinkage and time for concrete stored at different relative humidities

11. Effect of volume/surface ratio

Actual shrinkage of a given concrete member is affected by its size and shape. However the influence of shape has been observed as negligible. Thus shrinkage can be expressed as a function of the ratio of volume and exposed surface. The relation of volume/surface and shrinkage with time has been shown in Fig. 16.10. From this fig it will be seen that the relation between the logarithm of ultimate shrinkage and volume/space ratio is linear.

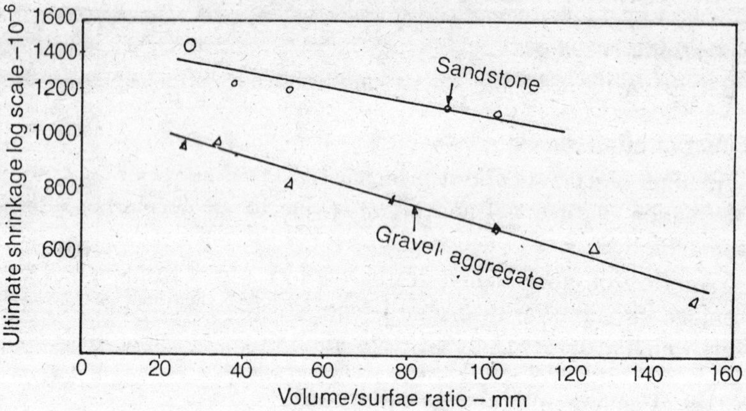

Fig. 16.10. Relation between ultimate shrinkage and vol/surface ratio

12. Effect of size and shape on shrinkage of concrete

As the drying takes place at the surface of the concrete the magnitude of shrinkage has been observed to vary considerably with the size and shape of the concrete specimen being a function of the surface/volume ratio. In case of small specimen the effect of carbonation is more pronounced. Thus in case of small specimens a part of the size effect may be due to carbonation. Hence for practical purposes the shrinkage can not be considered purely as an inherent property of concrete with out reference to the size of the concrete member.

Many researchers have indicated the influence of the size of the specimen on the shrinkage. It has been found that the observed shrinkage decreases with the increase in size of the specimen, but above some value, the size effect is small initially, but later on increases substantially as shown in Fig. 16.11. As stated above shrinkage is a function of surface/volume ratio of the specimen. The relation between the surface/volume ratio and the logarithm of shrinkage seems to be linear as shown in Fig. 16.10. Further the ratio of surface volume is linearly related to the logarithm of the time required for the half shrinkage to be achieved. This latter relation is applicable to concretes made with different aggregates so that while the magnitude of the shrinkage is affected by the type of aggregate used, the rate at which the final value of shrinkage is reached is not influenced.

Further on the basis of his work HOBBS says that theoretically shrinkage is indepent of the size of the concrete elements, but for realistic periods, it must be accepted that for larger sections or elements shrinkage is smaller.

13. Effect of Shape

The effect of shape is secondary. I shaped specimens have been found to exhibit 14% less shrinkage than cylindrical specimen of the same volume surface ratio. This difference is not significant for design purposes.

14. Effect of moisture movement

The rate of moisture movement under the given conditions of storage depends to a great extent on the size and shape of the concrete member. A large mass of concrete, is subjected to a greater variation of moisture content from point to point than a smaller specimen. These variations will produce a non uniform state of volume change with in the large mass. Under drying conditions shrinkage near the surface develops tensile stresses, which are in equilibrium with compressive stresses near the centre. These stresses may cause plastic yielding of the concrete, permanently elongating the tensile fibres and shortening the compressive fibres. Thus the maximum contraction of a large mass might be appreciably less than for a small specimen.

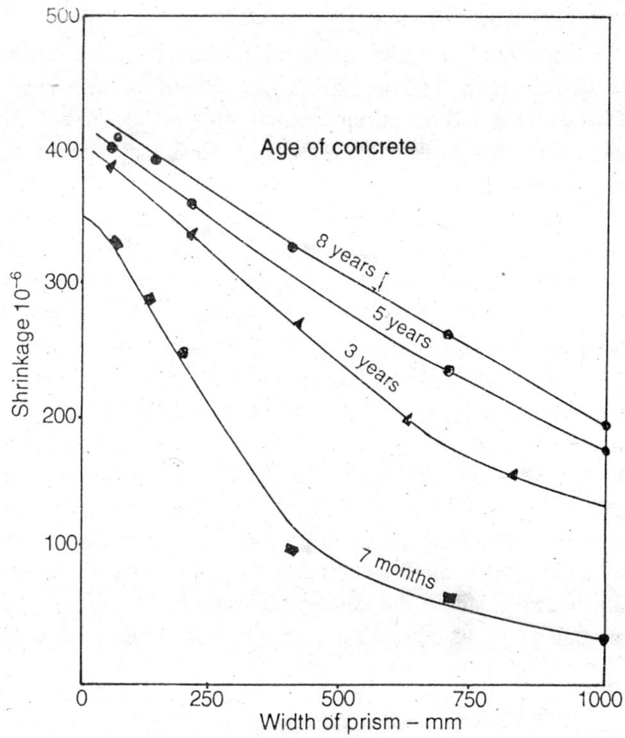

Fig. 16.11. Relation between axial shrinkage and width of concrete prism

In order to determine the loss of moisture at various distances from the exposed surface at 50% humidity Carlson carried out experiments and measured shrinkage distribution on a 60 cm long prism dried from one end only. During this study he found that the specimen was dry upto its middle point even after 600 days.

Next he carried out experiments on concrete slabs varying in thickness from 15 cm to 120 cm. He exposed these surfaces to dry air from both sides for drying and computed the drying distribution. During this study he observed that 15 cm thick slab took 12 months for 80% evaporation, 30 cm thick slab took 10 months for 40% evaporation and in 120 cm thick slab only about 10% evaporation took place during a period of about 12 months. Fig. 16.12.

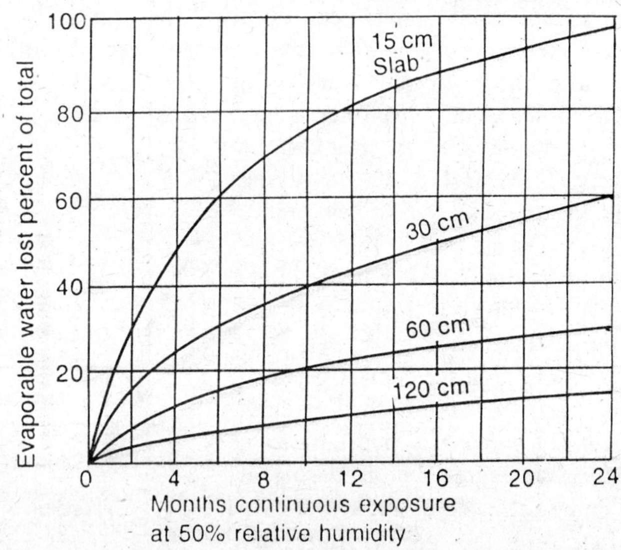

Fig. 16.12. Relation between evaporation of moisture and thickness of specimen

15. Effect of reinforcement

The reinforcement produces restraints on the movement of concrete, resulting less shrinkage than the plain concrete.

16.6. DIFFERENTIAL SHRINKAGE

In addition to internal restraint to shrinkage by aggregate and reinforcement, some restraint also is induced from non uniform shrinkage with in the concrete member itself. Moisture loss takes place at the surface of the concrete specimen, which is subject to differential shrinkage. This shrinkage is compensated by strain due to internal stresses. Tensile stresses occur near the surface and compressive stresses in the core. When drying takes place in an un symmetrical manner, warping of concrete takes place.

The progress of shrinkage extends gradually from the drying surface into the interior of the concrete extremely slowly. Complete dryness at a depth of 75 mm was observed after one month but it took 10 years to reach a depth of 600 mm. Results of L. Hermite are shown in Fig. 16.13. Ross found the difference in shrinkage of a mortar slab at the surface and at a depth of 150 mm as 470×10^{-6} after 200 days. If the modulus of elasticity of mortar is 21 GPa (3×10^6 PSI) the differential shrinkage would induce a stress of 10 MPa (1400 PSI). As the stress increases gradually it would be relieved by the creep, but even then surface cracking may occur. The increase in volume of aggregate would restrain the shrinkage considerably. Thus the advantage of using concrete rather the neat cement paste or mortar is clear.

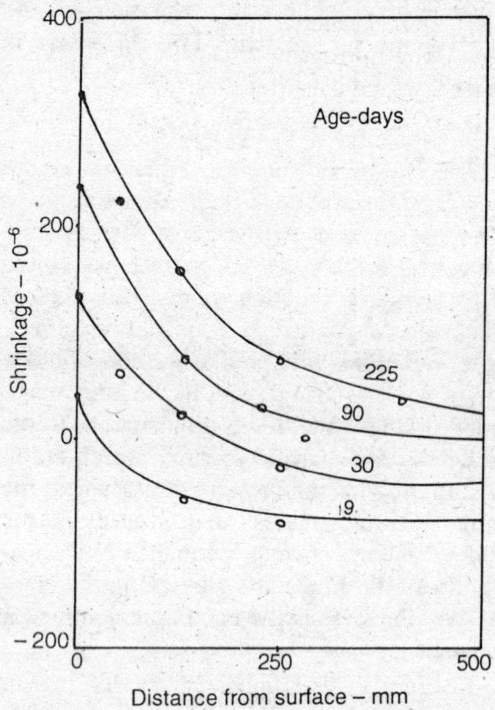

Fig. 16.13. Progress of shrinkage with time as a function of distance from drying surface

16.7. MOISTURE MOVEMENT

We know that when concrete is allowed to dry in air at a lower humidity it shrinks and when it is kept in 100% relative humidity or placed in water, it swells. Just as drying shrinkage is an ever continuing process, similarly swelling is also a continuing process if placed in water or 100% humidity conditions. If a concrete specimen is allowed to dry in air at a given humidity and subsequently placed in water it will swell. It has been observed that during this process all initial drying shrinkage does not recover fully even after a prolonged storage in water. For the usual range of concrete, the irreversible part of shrinkage is between 0.3 and 0.6 of the drying shrinkage, the lower value being more common. The absence of fully reversible behaviour may be due to the introduction of additional links with in the gel during the period of drying. During this period closer contact between the gel particles is established. In case, the cement paste has hydrated to a considerable degree, before drying, it will be less affected by the closer configuration of the gel in fully dry condition.

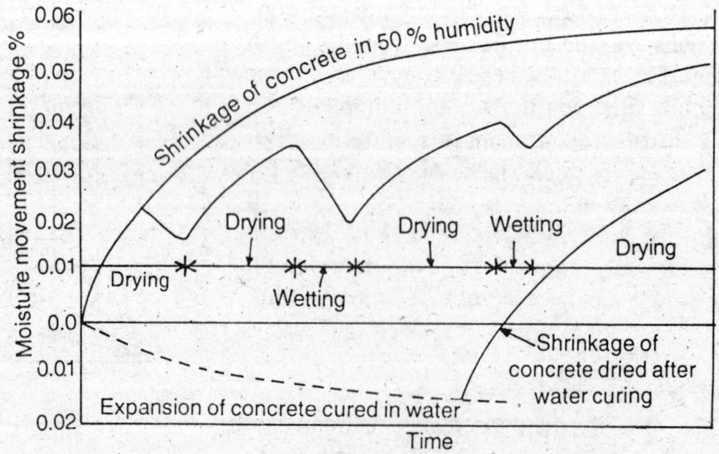

Fig. 16.14. Effect of wetting and drying on shrinkage

As drying shrinkage is due to the loss of adsorbed water around the gel particles, swelling is due to the adsorption of water by the cement gel.

The water molecules act against the cohesive force and push the gel particles away from each other, resulting in the swelling of concrete or paste. Further the ingress of water decreases the surface tension of the gel.

The property of swelling when placed in water or 100% humidity and shrinking when placed in dry conditions is known as *moisture movement* in concrete. Fig. 16.14 shows the typical moisture movement of 1:1. Cement mortar mix, stored alternatively in water and then dried in air at 50% relative humidity. The moisture movement in concrete induces compressive and tensile stresses alternately. These alternate compressive and tensile stresses may cause the fatigue in concrete which may reduce the durability of concrete. The typical values of moisture movement of concrete and cement mortar are shown in Table 16.2. Concrete dried at 50% relative humidity and immersed in water.

Table 16.2. Typical values of moisture movement

Net propertion by weight	*Moisture movement* 10^{-6}
neat cement paste	1000
1:1 mortar	400
1:2 mortar	300
1:3 mortar	200
1:2:4 concrete	300

16.8. THERMAL MOVEMENT

Cement concrete also has a positive coefficient of thermal expansion like other engineering materials. The value of coefficient of thermal expansion for concrete depends on the following factors.

1. Composition of concrete
2. Moisture condition of concrete at the time of temperature change

1. Influence of composition of concrete. The main constituents of concrete are cement paste and aggregate. The coefficient of thermal expansion for these two components are dissimilar. Thus the coefficient of thermal expansion of concrete is affected by these two values of thermal expansion and also the volumetric proportions of aggregate and cement paste and their elastic properties. The role of aggregate in thermal movement is similar to that in creep and shrinkage *i.e.* the aggregate restraints the thermal movement of the cement paste, which has highest thermal coefficient of expansion. Coefficient of thermal expansion may be defined as the change in unit length per degree change in temperature.

Let,

α_c = coefficient of thermal expansion of concrete

α_g = coefficient of thermal expansion of aggregate

α_p = coefficient of thermal expansion of cement paste

g = volumetric content of aggregate

then
$$\alpha_c = \alpha_p - \frac{2g(\alpha_p - \alpha_g)}{1 + \frac{K_p}{kg} + g\left(1 - \frac{K_p}{kg}\right)} \quad \ldots(i)$$

where,

$\frac{K_p}{kg}$ = stiffness ratio of cement paste to aggregate. This ratio is approximately equal to their moduli of elasticity ratio

The value of coefficient of thermal expansion of cement paste varies from 11×10^{-6} to 20×10^{-6} per °C depending upon the moisture condition. This dependence is due to the fact that thermal coefficient of expansion of cement consists of the following two components.

(*a*) **Kinetic or true thermal coefficient.** Which is caused by the molecular movement of the paste.

(*b*) **Hygrothermal expansion coefficient.** This expansion coefficient occurs due to an increase in the internal relative humidity (water vapour pressure) as the temperature increases, resulting expansion of the cement paste. No hygrothermal expansion is possible when the paste is totally dry or when it is fully saturated as in both these situations no increase in water vapour pressure is possible. However hygrothermal expansion occurs at some intermediate moisture content as shown in Fig. 16.15. It has been observed that for a green or young paste the maximum hygrothermal expansion takes place at 70% relative humidity. For an older paste the max hygrothermal expansion is smaller and occurs at a lower internal relative humidity. In concrete the hygrothermal expansion is also smaller.

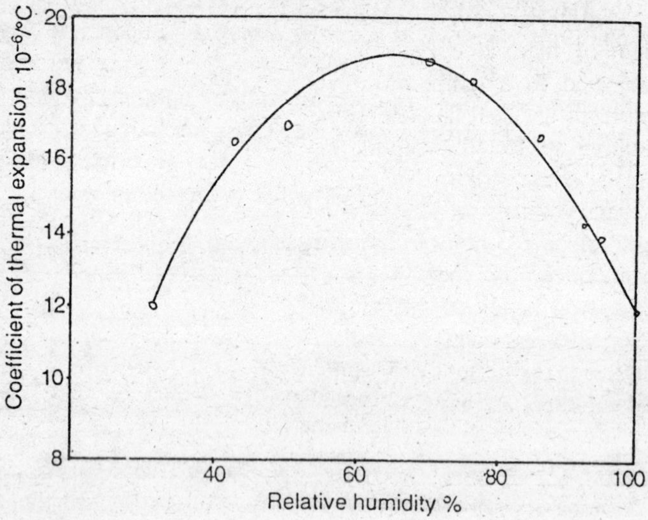

Fig. 16.15. Relation between ambient relative humidity and the linear coeff of thermal expansion of neat cement paste

The thermal coefficient of 1:6 concrete cured in air and at relative humidity of 64% and also for saturated concrete made with different types of aggregates is shown in Table 16.3.

Table 16.3. Coefficient of thermal expansion of 1:6 concrete made with different aggregates

Type of aggregate	*Linear coefficient of thermal expansion*		
	Air cured concrete 10^{-6} per °C	*Water cured concrete 10^{-6} per °C*	*Air and water cured concrete 10^{-6} per °C*
Gravel	13.1	12.2	11.7
Granite	9.5	8.6	7.7
Quartz	12.8	12.2	11.7
Dolerite	9.5	8.5	7.9
Sand stone	11.7	10.1	8.6
Lime stone	7.4	6.1	5.9
Portland stone	7.4	6.1	6.5
Blast furnance slag	10.6	9.2	8.8
Foamed slag	12.1	9.2	8.5

The value of coefficient of thermal expansion of aggregates vary from 5.0×10^{-6} to 12×10^{-6} per °C. Lime stone and Gabbros have low values where as gravel and quartzite have higher values of coefficient of thermal expansion.

The value of coefficient of thermal expansion near freezing temperature have been observed minimum. Further at temperatures lower than freezing point, the coefficient of thermal expansion is found higher again. Fig. 16.16 shows values of saturated concrete tested in saturated air.

In another case, concrete slightly dried after a period of initial curing and then stored and tested at 90% relative humidity, showed no decrease in the coefficient of thermal expansion shown by dotted curve in Fig. 16.16.

So far we have discussed the coefficient of thermal expansion of concrete subjected to a temperature variation of less than 65°C. It has been observed that concrete subjected to higher temperatures shows some what different values of thermal expansion due to presumably less moisture content in the concrete. The importance of coefficient of thermal expansion is felt at higher temperatures when dealing with fire hazzard. The values of coefficient of thermal expansion of concrete made with different types of aggregates at higher temperatures are shown in table 16.4.

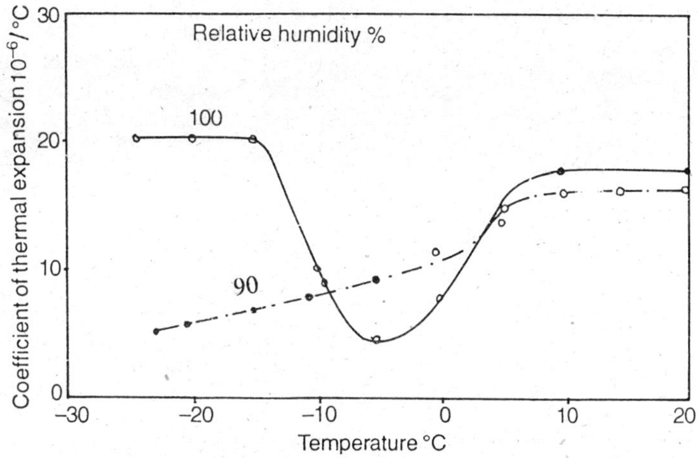

Fig. 16.16. Relation between linear thermal coeff. of expansion and temp of concrete

Table 16.4. Coefficient of thermal expansion at high temperatures

Curing condition	*W/c ratio*	*Cement content kg/m³*	*Type of aggregate*	*Linear Coefficient of expansion at the age*			
				28 days		*90 days*	
				Temp. below 260°C 10^{-6} per °C	Temp. above 430°C 10^{-6} per °C	Temp. below 260°C 10^{-6} per °C	Temp. above 430°C 10^{-6} per °C
Moist	0.4	435	Calcareous	7.6	20.3	6.5	11.2
	0.6	310	Gravel	12.8	20.5	8.4	22.5
	0.8	245		11.0	21.1	16.7	32.8
Air 50% relative humidity	0.4	435	Calcareous	7.7	18.9	12.2	20.7
	0.6	310	Gravel	7.7	21.1	8.8	20.2
	0.8	245		9.6	20.7	11.7	21.6
Moist Air	0.68	355	Expanded	6.1	7.5	—	—
	0.68	355	slag shale	4.7	9.7	5.0	8.8

16.9. EFFECT OF RESTRAINT AND CRACKING

In structural concrete the importance of shrinkage largely is related to cracking. We are concerned with the cracking tendency of the concrete as the initiation or start and absence of cracking depends not only on contraction but also its ability to expand, it strength and its degree of restraint to deformotion that may cause cracking. The restraint in the form of reinforcing bars or gradient of stress increases its ability to expand (extensibility) as it allows concrete to develop strain well beyond the corresponding maximum stress.

The high extensibility of concrete is generally desirable as it permits concrete to withstand the greater volume changes. The Bureau of Reclamation carried out some thermal cycle tests on concrete at a constant strain and found that tension developed on cooling it to the original temperature. The failing (tensile) stress was found lower in the concrete made with ordinary or modified cement than with low heat or portland pozzolana cement which could withstand a greater temperature drop before failure. The crack pattern developed when stress is relieved by creep is shown in Fig. 16.17. The cracking can be avoided only if the stress induced by the free shrinkage strain reduced by creep is smaller than the tensile strength of concrete.

The effects of restraint and cracking may also be explained as follows:

As the stress and strain occur together, any restraint of movement, introduces a stress corresponding to the restrained strain. If this stress and the restrained strain are allowed to develop to such an extent that they exceed the strength or strain capacity of concrete, then creeks will develop.

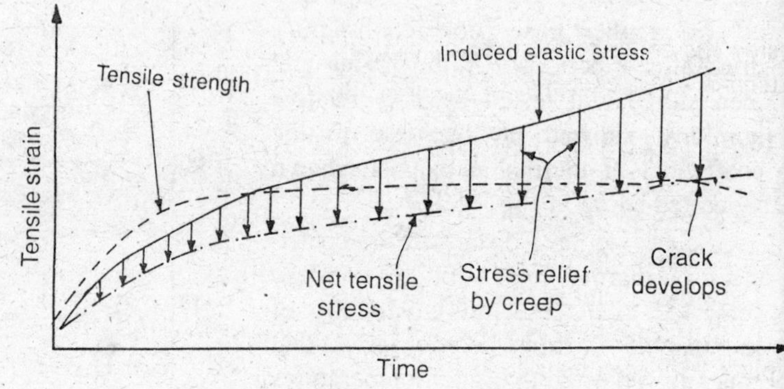

Fig. 16.17. Pattern of crack development

Restraint can induce both compression and tension, but in the majority of the cases, only tension causes problem. Restraints may be of the following two types.

1. External
2. Internal

1. **External restraint.** The external restraint exists when the movement in concrete member is fully or partly prevented by an external rigid or partly rigid adjacent member or foundations. The effect of external restraint can be explained by considering a section of a completely insulated concrete member whose ends are fully restrained This concrete section is subjected to a cycle of temperature *i.e.* the section is heated to a certain temperature and then cooled to its original temperature. As the temperature rises, and the concrete is prevented from expanding. In this condition the compressive stresses are developed in the concrete uniformly across the section. Usually these stresses are very small in comparison to the compressive strength of concrete.. More over these stresses partly are relieved by creep at early ages (discussed under the topic creep). When the temperature falls and concrete cools, it is also prevented from contracting, at first, any residual compressive stress is recovered and on further cooling tensile stress is developed. If these temperature changes take place slowly, the stress partly would be relieved by creep. In case concrete is more mature at this stage, the magnitude of creep would be smaller and the tensile stress will become much larger to reach the present tensile strength of the concrete, resulting in cracking across the section. If sufficient reinforcement is present in the concrete in such a condition, cracks will still develop in the concrete section, but they will be well evenly distributed and narrower in width while in case of un reinforced concretes cracks will be few but wider in width.

2. **Internal restraint.** This type of restraint exists when temperature and moisture gradients exist with in the concrete section. A combination of external and internal restraint is also possible.

   The internal restraint is an uninsulated concrete mass as a dam, in which heat develops due to the hydration of cement. The heat is dissipated from the surface of the concrete resulting a temperature gradient across the section. As no relative movement of any part of the concrete is possible, there is a restrained thermal strain. This thermal strain induces a stress.

Creeps contributes to thermal cracking with large, but slow temperature cycles due to the reduced effectiveness of stress relaxation by creep with time. However in other cases creep is beneficial in preventing cracking. For example if a thin concrete member is externally restrained, so that contraction due to shrinkage is prevented, the induced uniform elastic tensile stress is relieved by creep as shown in Fig. 16.17 above. The point where the tensile stress is relieved by creep, cracks will develop.

In case of thicker sections, with no external restraint, but having a moisture gradient, the shrinkage of the surface layer is restrained by the core of the section. In this case the compressive stress is developed in side the concrete member and tensile stress exists on its surface. Creep again relieves the stresses, but if tensile stress exceeds the current strength of the concrete, the shrinkage cracking will take place.

16.10. TYPES OF CRACKING

The intrinsic concrete cracks may be grouped as follows:

1. Plastic cracks
2. Early age thermal cracks
3. Dry shrinkage cracks

1. Plastic cracks. These cracks develop before the concrete has hardened *i.e.* between 1 to 8 hours of placement of concrete. As the evaporation of water takes place from the surface of the concrete, it contracts resulting inducement of tensile stresses in concrete causing cracks. These cracks are in the form of plastic shrinkage cracks and plastic settlement cracks. The plastic shrinkage cracks can be prevented by restricting the rate of evaporation of water from the surface to less than 0.5 kg/hour/m^2.

2. Plastic settlement cracks. These cracks develop due to the uneven settlement of concrete on bleeding due to the presence of obstructions. These obstructions may by in the form of reinforcing bars or un equal depth of concrete placed morolithically. The plastic settlement cracks may be reduced by using air entrainment admixtures as the air entrainment reduces bleeding of concrete. These cracks may also be eliminated by revibrating the concrete at a suitable time. Detailed discussion of cracks has been made in chapter 20. The cause and location of different type of cracks is shown in Table 16.5.

Table 16.5. Classification of intrinsic cracks

Type of cracks	*Location*			*Causes*		*Remedy Assuming Redesign impossible, and in all cases reduced restrainet*
		Most common	*Sub division*	*Primary*	*Secondary*	
Plastic settlement	(*i*) (*ii*) (*iii*)	Deep sections Top of columns Trough and waffle slabs	Over reinforcement Arching Change of depth	Excess bleeding	Rapid early drying Conditions	Reduce bleeding by air entrainment or by revibration
Plastic shrinkage	(*i*) (*ii*) (*iii*)	Roads and slabs R.C.C. slabs R.C.C. Slabs	Diagonal Random Over reinforcement	Rapid early drying Plus steel near surface	Low rate of bleeding	Improve early cusing
Early thermal contraction	(*i*) (*ii*)	Thick walls Thick slabs	External restraint Internal restraint	Excess heat generation Excess temp gradient	Rapid cooling	Reduce heat and or insulate
Long term drying Shrinkage		Thin slabs and walls	—	Inefficient joints	Excess shrinkage inefficient curing	Reduce water content and improve curing
Crazing	(*i*) (*ii*)	Fair faced concrete Slabs	Against form work Floated concrete	Impermeable form work Over trowelling	Rich mixes and poor curing	Improve curing and finishing
Corrosion of reinforcement		Columns and beans	Natural	Lack of cover	Poor quality of concrete	Causes listed should be removed
Alkali aggregate reaction		Damp locations	—	Reactive aggregate and high alkali cement	—	Causes listed should be removed

QUESTIONS

1. Discuss the influence of mix proportion of concrete on shrinkage.
2. Discuss the mechanism of drying shrinkage of concrete.
3. Compare the carbonation of concrete exposed to intermitent rain and protected from rain.
4. Discuss the main reactions in carbonation of concrete.
5. Discuss the factors affecting the shrinkage of concrete.
6. What is the effect of wind on fresh concrete.
7. How the restraint of movement of a member causes shrinkage cracks.
8. Discuss the influence of aggregate on the shrinkage of concrete made with a given cement paste.
9. Explain the term:
   (*a*) Autogeneous shrinkage (*b*) Carbonation shrinkage
   (*c*) Phenomenon of shrinkage of cement paste
10. Discuss the effects of carbonation. On which factor the rate of carbonation depends. Explain fully.
11. Discuss the type of restraints in concrete membrs and their effects.

OBJECTIVE TYPE QUESTIONS

1. The shrinkage in concrete develops due to
   (*a*) Loss of water by evaporation from the surface of concrete
   (*b*) Hydration of cement
   (*c*) Withdrawal of water stored in unsaturated air voids in concrete
   (*d*) All the above
   (*e*) None of the above
2. Shrinkage in concrete increases with
   (*a*) Decrease in humidity of the surroundings (*b*) Decrease in the maximum size of aggregate
   (*c*) Increase in cement content (*d*) Increase in water/cement ratio
   (*e*) All the above
3. Shrinkage of concrete can be reduced by
   (*a*) Using water tight and non absorbent form work (*b*) Using low water/cement ratio
   (*c*) Using pre saturated aggregate (*d*) All the above
   (*e*) Non of the above
4. Identify the false statement of the following
   (*a*) Plastic shrinkage is not affected by the loss of water by evaporation from the surface of concrete
   (*b*) Plastic shrinkage of concrete is caused by the suction of dry concrete below it
   (*c*) Drying shrinkage is developed due to withdrawal of water from hardened concrete stored in unsaturated air voids
   (*d*) Initial drying shrinkage is not recoverable even after a prolonged storage in water.
5. The rate of carbonation shrinkage depends
   (*a*) Moisture content of concrete (*b*) Permeability of concrete
   (*c*) Content of carbon dioxide (*d*) Relative humidity of the ambient medium
   (*e*) All the above
6. Identify the true and false statements of the followings
   (*a*) Carbonation of concrete increase its weight
   (*b*) Hydrates present in the gel contribute substantially to the shrinkage
   (*c*) Carbonation increase the strength of concrete
   (*d*) Carbonation does not increase the strength of concrete
   (*e*) Carbonation of concrete neutralize the alkaline nature of hydrated cement paste
7. Identify the false statements of the followings
   (*a*) Shrinkage of hydrated concrete is greatly affected by the aggregate content in the concrete
   (*b*) Concrete made with sand stone has the maximum shrinkage
   (*c*) Concrete made with lime stone has no effect on shrinkage
   (*d*) All aggregates have equal shrinkage

(*e*) Quality of cement paste has no influence in concrete shrinkage
(*f*) Water content in concrete has marked influence on shrinkage of concrete.

8. Identify the true and false statements of the followings
   (*a*) Fineness of cement has no influence on the shrinkage of the concrete
   (*b*) Greater the fineness of cement higher the shrinkage of concrete
   (*c*) Deficiency of gypsum in cement increases the shrinkage of concrete to a great extent
   (*d*) Deficiency of gypsum has no influence on the shrinkage of concrete
   (*e*) Entrainment of air has no influence on the shrinkage of concrete
   (*f*) Entrainment of air reduces the shrinkage of concrete to a great extent
   (*i*) Presence of chloride increases the shrinkage from 10 to 50%
   (*j*) Pressure of chloride has no effect on the shrinkage of concrete
9. Identify the true and false statements of the followings
   (*a*) The magnitude of shrinkage varies with the shape and size of concrete element
   (*b*) Size and shape of concrete element have no effect on the shrinkage of concrete
   (*c*) The shrinkage of concrete is a function of the ratio of its volume and exposed surface
   (*d*) The ratio of volume to its exposed surface has no effect on the shrinkage of concrete
   (*e*) Concrete placed in dry air shrinks while it is placed in 100% humid air it swells
   (*f*) Relative humidity of the surroundings has no effect on the shrinkage of concrete
   (*g*) The effect of prolonged curing on shrinkage of concrete is small but complex
   (*h*) Prolonged curing has no importance in the shrinkage of concrete
   (*i*) The presence of reinforcement reduces the shrinkage of concrete
   (*j*) The presence of reinforcement has no effect on the shrinkage of concrete
10. Identify the incorrect statement/statements of the following
   (*a*) The magnitude of volumetic contraction during plastic shrinkage is of the order of 1.0%
   (*b*) Concrete made with light-weight aggregate has higher moisture movement than normal weight aggregate concrete
   (*c*) Higher rate of carbonation takes place at relative humidity of 50 to 70%
   (*d*) Carbonation of concrete reduces its permeability
   (*e*) The effect of carbonation is greater on concrete protected from direct rain
   (*f*) The depth of carbonation is greater is a inadequately cured concrete
   (*g*) The depth of shrinkage is influenced by the quality of cement paste
   (*h*) The rate of evaporation of plastic concrete should be more than 0.5 kg/m^2 per hour of the exposed surface of concrete
   (*i*) The moisture movement in concrete is independent of degree of hydration at the line of initial drying and range of relative humidity

Answers

1. (*d*)
2. (*e*)
3. (*d*)
4. (*a*)
5. (*e*)
6. [False (*b*, *d*)]
7. (*c*, *d*, *e*, *f*)
8. [True (*a*, *c*, *e*, *i*)]
9. [False (*b*, *d*, *f*, *j*)]
10. [False (*h*,*i*)]

17

Durability And Permeability

17.1. INTRODUCTION

For a long time concrete was considered a very durable material requiring very little or no maintenance. The assumption proved largely true except when it is subjected to an severe or aggressive environment. Concrete structures have been built in highly polluted urban and industrial areas, harmful sub soil water in coastal areas and other hostile conditions where other materials of construction have not been found suitable or durable. In recent years the use of concrete has spread to highly harsh and hostile conditions. The premature failures of a number of structures in recent years has led to revise the impression that concrete is a very durable material.

Till 1930, the strength of concrete was considered the only factor at the time of mix design, ignoring all other factors including durability. But this conception was proved wrong when many concrete pavements failed due to frost attack. Though the compressive strength of concrete is a measure of durability to a great extent, but it is not entirely true that a strong concrete is always durable. For example a concrete of grade M_{20} or M_{25} is quite suitable for the construction of a structure in marine conditions, but environmental conditions may lead it disastrous failure. Thus now in addition to strength of concrete, exposure condition or environmental conditions have become an important factor for durability consideration. In the recent revision of IS-456-2000, the durability aspect has been given importance as that of codes of practice of other countries.

17.2. DEFINITION OF DURABILITY

The durability of cement concrete can be defined as its ability to resist weathering action, chemical attack, abrasion or any other process of deterioration. A durable concrete should maintain its original form and serviceability when exposed to adverse environment.

17.3. SIGNIFICANCE OF DURABILITY

It has been reported that in industrialized countries more than 40% of total resources of the building industry are spent on repairs and maintenance of concrete structures. In India also much money is spent on repair work. It is very unfortunate that not enough attention has been paid to durability aspect even in repair works.

Secondly in the present age all good and favorable sites of construction have been already used and the construction of concrete work has to be taken up in more hostile environments. Thirdly all good concrete materials are in short supply. Thus the construction of modern concrete structures assumes much more importance for durability than in the past. Due to these reasons in revised IS 456-2000, the approximate values for cement content, maximum w/c ratio, and minimum grade of concrete has been suggested for different exposure conditions. These recommendations have been given in Table 17.1 below.

Table 17.1. Minimum Cement Content, Max. w/c ratio and minimum grade of concrete for different conditions of exposure as per IS 456-2000

S. No.	*Exposure*	*Plain Concrete*			*Reinforced concrete*		
		Minimum cement content kg/m³	*Max. Free w/c ratio*	*Minimum grade of concrete*	*Minimum cement content kg/m³*	*Max. Free w/c ratio*	*Minimum grade of concrete*
1.	Mild	220	0.60	—	300	0.55	M20
2.	Moderate	240	0.60	M15	300	0.50	M25
3.	Severe	250	0.50	M20	320	0.45	M30
4.	Very severe	260	0.45	M20	340	0.45	M35
5.	Extreme	280	0.40	M25	360	0.40	M40

Note. 1. The minimum cement content and max. w/c ratio apply to 20 mm nominal maximum size of aggregate. For other sizes of aggregate suitable changes should be done as per Table 17.2 below.

2. Max. Cement Content. Cement content not including fly ash and ground granulated blast furnace slag in excess 450 kg/m^3 should not be used unless specified.

Table 17.2. Adjustment of minimum cement content for other aggregates than 20 mm size

S. No.	*Nominal max size of aggregate mm*	*Adjustment to minimum cement contents of table 17.1 kg/m³*
1.	10	+ 40
2.	20	0
3.	40	– 30

For general information and also to carry out the mix design based on British method, department of Environment method (DOE method) Table 17.3 and 17.4 are given below.

Table 17.3. Requirement of BS 8110 Part-I 1985 to ensure durability under specified conditions of exposure for R.C.C and Pre stressed concrete made with nominal weight aggregate

Condition of exposure	*Nominal cover to reinforcement in mm*				
Mild	25	20	20	20	20
Moderate	—	35	30	25	20
Severe	—	—	40	30	25
Very severe	—	—	50	40	30
Extreme	—	—	—	60	50
Max water/cementitious material ratio	0.65	0.60	0.55	0.50	0.45
Max. content of cementitious material in kg/m³	275	300	325	350	400
Minimum grade MPa	30	35	40	45	50

Note. 1. Grade is the characteristic cube strength.

2. The values given in table 17.3 are applicable when the max. size of aggregate is 20 mm. When the size of aggregate is 10 and 14 mm, the content of cementitious material should be increased by 40 kg/m^3 and 20 kg/m^3 respectively. Conversely when the max. size of aggregate is 40 mm, the content of cementitious material should be reduced by 30 kg/m^3. The least content of cementitious material in pre stressed concrete should be 300 kg/m^3.

3. For freezing and thawing exposure air entrainment should be adopted.

Table 17.4. Requirements to ensure durability for plain concrete as per B.S. 8110 Part-I 1985

Environment	*Exposure condition*	*Max. free water/cementitious material ratio*	*Min. cementitious material kg/m3 for nominal max. size agg.*				*Min. grade MPa*
			40 mm	20 mm	14 mm	10 mm	
Mild	Concrete surface protected against aggressive conditions or weather	0.80	150	180	200	220	20
Moderate	Concrete surface protected from severe rain while wet concrete subjected to condensation, concrete surfaces continously under water, concrete in contact with non aggressive solid	0.65	245	275	295	315	30
Severe	Concrete surfaces exposed to sevre rain, alternating wetting and drying, occasional freezing or sever condensation.	0.60	270	300	320	340	35
Very severe	Concrete surfaces exposed to sea water spray, deicing salts (directly or indirectly) corrosive fumes, or severe freezing conditions while wet.	0.55	295	325	345	365	35
Extreme	Concrete surfaces exposed to abrasive action *i.e.* sea water carrying solids or flowing water with $P_H \leq 4.5$ or vehicles and machinery.	0.50	320	350	370	390	45

Note. 1. Cementitious materials is inclusive of fly ash or slag.
2. Grade of concrete is the characteristic cube strength.
3. For very sever conditions only air entrained concrete should be used.

17.4. EFFECT OF W/C RATIO ON DURABILITY

W/c ratio has a great impact on the durability of the concrete. Higher w/c ratio is the main cause of volume change and higher permeability of concrete. The use of higher w/c ratio causes permeability, volume change, cracks, disintegration and finally the failure is a cyclic process in concrete. Thus from durability consideration, the use of lowest possible w/c ratio is the fundamental requirement to produce dense and impermeable concrete.

There is a tremendous difference in the micro structure of concrete made with low w/c ratio and high w/c ratio. The permeability of concrete made with low w/c ratio decreases to such a level that the concrete is impervious to water. The lower permeability of concrete does not mean that there is no inter connecting net work of capillaries in the concrete. These capillaries are so fine that water can not flow through them. When such concretes tested for chloride ions permeability test, it is observed that chloride ions diffuse in the concrete at a much lower rate 10 to 50 times slower than that of high w/c ratio concrete. Thus low w/c ratio concrete is less sensitive to carbonation, external chemical attack and other detrimental effects that make the concrete less durable. Further it has been observed that the corrosion of reinforcing steel can be checked by the use of low w/c ratio and provision of adequate cover, rather than using high w/c ratio and then protecting the steel by other means as by epoxy coating etc.

It is easy to propagate the virtues of low w/c ratio for alround durability of concrete, but in actual practice it was not possible to use w/c ratio less than 0.4 till the invension of super plasticizers. Now w/c as low as 0.25 or 0.2 can be used for producing flowing concrete.

In these low w/c ratio concretes there is not enough water available to fully hydrate all particles of cement. The water available can hydrate the surface particles only leaving plenty of particles unhydrated, which can play an important role as they keep strength in reserve. If due to any reason, environmental or structural, concrete gets cracked, the unhydrated particles start hydrating as soon as moisture or water starts penetrating through these cracks. Thus the unhydrated particles offer self healing potential to improve the durability of concrete.

17.5. CAUSES OF NON DURABILITY OF CONCRETE

The factors which cause non durability in concrete may be classified as internal causes and external or environmental causes. These causes may also be categorised as physical, mechanical and chemical.

1. **Physical causes.** These causes arise due to frost action discussed in chapter 18 and from differences in thermal properties of cement paste and aggregates discussed in chapter 4
2. **Mechanical causes.** These causes are developed mainly due to abrasion discussed in chapter 13.
3. **Chemical causes.** These causes are developed due to the chemical action between the seeping water through cracks or voids of concrete and cement paste. Thus these causes take place with in the body of the concrete. Hence the permeability of concrete is of paramount importance.

17.6. PERMEABILITY

Permeability of concrete can be defined as the ease with which the liquid or gases can travel through it. This property is important in relation to the water tightness of liquid retaining structures and to chemical attack.

17.6.1. Determination of permeability of concrete

Though no Bureau of standards as IS, B.S or ASTM has prescribed any test for permeability of concrete, but the permeability of concrete can be determined by means of a simple laboratory test. The results obtained by this test are mainly comparative. In such a test, the sides of the concrete specimen are sealed and water under pressure is applied to the top surface of the given thickness of the specimen. The test is allowed to get steady state conditions. In case of concrete usually it takes about 10 days to reach a steady state condition. After the steady state conditions have reached, the quantity of water flowing through the given thickness of the specimen in a given time is measured. The drop in the hydraulic head is given by the Darcey's relation as

$$\frac{1}{A} \cdot \frac{dq}{dt} = K \cdot \frac{\Delta h}{L} \quad \text{...(17.1)}$$

where,

$\frac{dq}{dt}$ = rate of flow of water

A = area of crosssection of the specimen

Δh = drop in the hydraulic head through the specimen

L = thickness of specimen

K = coefficient of permeability expressed in m/second.

Note. The water permeability is expressed as coefficient of permeability K

The permeability of concrete in air and other gases is important in the structures such as sewage tanks, gas purifiers and in pressure vessels in nuclear reactors, where as water permeability is important in the construction of hydraulic structures such as dams, water tanks etc.

Though for air or gases, permeability equation 17.1 also is applicable, but in case of air permeability the steady state condition is reached in hours only where as in case of water permeability it takes about 10 days. Further it has been observed that there is no unique relation between air and water permeabilities for any concrete, though they both mainly dependent on w/c ratio and the age of the concrete.

17.7. PERMEABILITY OF CEMENT PASTE

As we learnt in chapter 2, that cement paste consists of hydrates of various cement compounds as C_3S, C_2S, C_3A, C_4AF and Ca $(OH)_2$ and the gross volume available for these products of hydration is the sum of absolute volume of dry cement and the volume of the mix water. Thus the cement paste consists of gel of hydrates of cement compounds, $Ca(OH)_2$ and gel pores either are filled with water or remain empty. It has been found that gel has 28% pores or voids, but these pores are so small that hardly any water can pass through them under normal condition. The permeability of gel pores is found to be about 7×10^{-16} m/s, which is about 1/100th of the cement paste as a whole. Thus there is no contribution of gel pores to the permeability of cement paste.

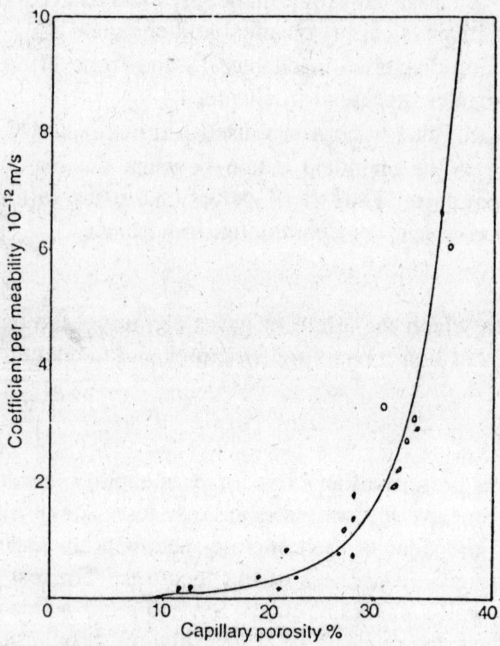

Fig. 17.1. Relation between permeability and capillary porosity of cement paste

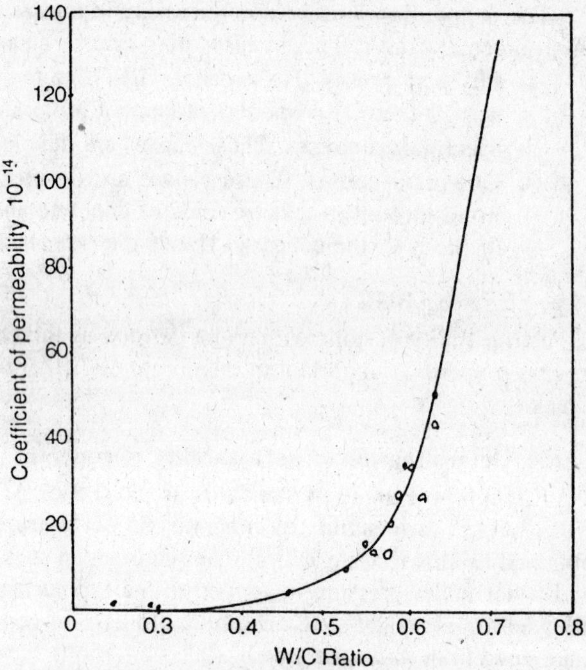

Fig. 17.2. Relation between permeability and w/c ratio for mature cement paste

The permeability of hydrated cement paste as a whole is greater due to the presence of larger capillary pores in the paste, which depend on the w/c ratio in the paste. Generally the w/c ratio is the main contributing factor to permeability. At low w/c ratio, not only the extent of capillary cavities is less, but the diameter of pores also is small. The pores or cavities formed at low w/c ratio get filled up in few days by the products of hydration of cement. Only very large cavities formed due to high water/cement ratio (usually more than 0.7) will not be filled up by the products of hydration, which are responsible for the high permeability of the paste. Thus the permeability

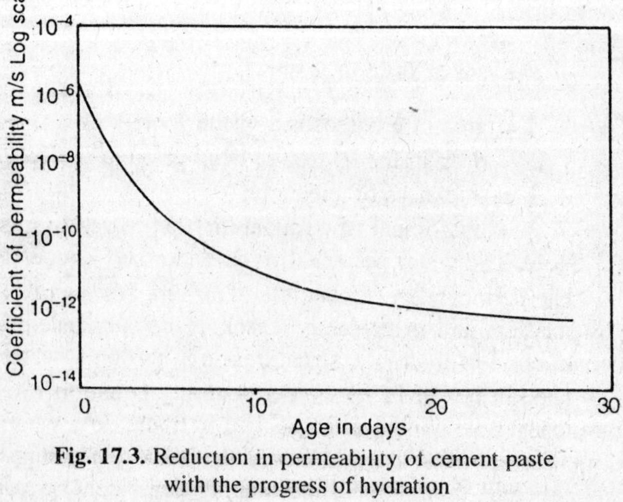

Fig. 17.3. Reduction in permeability of cement paste with the progress of hydration

of cement paste is a function of its porosity as shown in Fig. 17.1. The capillary porosity is governed by the w/c ratio and by the degree of hydration and the permeability of cement paste is also mainly dependent on these two parameters. A relation between the permeability and w/c ratio for mature cement paste (93% hydrated cement) has been shown in Fig. 17.2. From the study of Fig. 17.2, it will be seen that for a given degree of hydration permeability is lower for paste with lower w/c ratio, specially below w/c ratio 0.6 at which the capillaries become filled with hydrated, products of cement. From the Fig. 17.2, it will also be seen that as w/c ratio increases from 0.4 to 0.7 the coefficient of permeability increases more than 100 times. For a given w/c ratio, the permeability decreases with age as cement continues to hydrates and fills some of the original water pores as shown in Fig. 17.3. The reduction in permeability of cement paste is faster at lower w/c ratio. ACI standard 301-89 suggests that for water tight structural concrete w/c ratio not more than 0.48 for exposure to fresh water and not more than 0.44 for exposure to see water should be used. The value of max. permeability is often recommended as 1.5×10^{-11} m/s.

The influence of filling or segmentation of capillaries on permeability shows that the permeability is not a simple function of porosity. It has been observed that two bodies may have similar porosities, but different permeabilities. Infact one large passage connecting capillary pores will result in a large permeability, while the porosity will remain virtually unchanged.

Reduction in permeability of concrete paste with progress of hydration is shown in Table 17.5 below.

Table 17.5. Reduction in permeability of concrete paste with progress of hydration,

S. No.	*Age in days*	*Coefficient of permeability m/s*
1.	Fresh	2×10^{-6}
2.	5 days	4×10^{-10}
3.	6 days	1×10^{-10}
4.	8 days	4×10^{-11}
5.	13 adas	5×10^{-12}
6.	24 days	1×10^{-12}
7.	ultimate	6×10^{-13} (Calculated)

The permeability of cement paste with very low w/c ratio can be compared to the permeability of dense rock as shown in Table 17.6.

Table 17.6. Comparision of permeabilities of cement paste with dense rock

S. No.	*Type of rocks*	*Coefficient of permeability m/s*	*w/c ratio of mature paste of same permeability*
1.	Densetrap	2.47×10^{-14}	0.38
2.	Quartz cliorite	8.24×10^{-14}	0.42
3.	Marble	2.39×10^{-13}	0.48
4.	Marble	5.77×10^{-12}	0.66
5.	Granite	5.35×10^{-11}	0.70
6.	Sand stone	1.23×10^{-10}	0.71
7.	Granite	1.56×10^{-10}	0.71

From the above Table 17.6, it will be seen that cement paste even with high w/c ratio of 0.7 is quite impervious as that of Granite whose coefficient of permeability is 5.35×10^{-11} m/s. This value of coefficient of permeability is so small, that there is no possibility of any water to seep through it. But in actual practice, it is observed that mortars and concrete exhibit much higher values of permeability than shown in above Table 17.6. Definitely this is not due to the permeability of aggregate used in mortar or concrete. The aggregate is as impermeable as that of cement paste as can be seen from above table. In actual structures the higher permeability of mortar or concrete is due to the following reasons.

1. The development of fine or micro cracks due to thermal stresses and long term dry shrinkage.
2. Due to the development of large micro cracks in the transition zone.
3. Due to the development of cracks and volume change on account of various minor reasons.
4. Existence of entrapped air due to insufficient compaction.

17.8. PERMEABILITY OF CONCRETE

Theoritically by the introduction of coarse aggregate of low permeability into the cement paste it is expected that the permeability of concrete will be less as the permeability of coarse aggregate is low. Further the aggregates particles intercept the channels of flow and make it circuitous route. Thus concrete with the same w/c ratio and degree of compaction should give lower coefficient of permeability compared to cement paste. But in practice it has not been achieved. On the other hand the use of coarse aggregate especially large size aggregates have been found to increase the permeability of concrete considerably.

As explained above, the permeability of concrete in actual hydraulic structures has been found much higher than theoretical values. Table 17.7 shows the typical values of permeability of concrete used in dams in U.S.A.

Table 17.7. Typical values of permeability of concrete used in dams

Cement content in kg/m^3	*Water/cement ratio*	*Permeability 10^{-12} m/s*
156	0.69	8
151	0.74	24
138	0.75	35
223	0.46	28

It has been observed that the use of pozzolanic material in the optimum proportion reduces the permeability of concrete considerably due to the conversion of calcium hydroxide into cementitious material, which otherwise will leach out. High prssure steam cured concrete made with crushed silica decreases its permeability.

17.9. DEPTH OF PENETRATION OF MOISTURE

The depth *'d'* of moisture penetration in off shore concrete structures can be assumed as given by the following relation

$$d = \sqrt{2\,K\,h\,t} \qquad \text{...(17.2)}$$

where,

K = Coefficient of permeability
h = Head of water in metres
t = Time in years
d = Depth of penetration in mm

17.10. CHEMICAL ACTION

As discussed above, the durability of concrete is affected by physical, mechanical and chemical causes. The durability of concrete is most affected by chemical causes, which result in volume change, cracking of concrete and ultimately leading to deterioration of concrete. Now we shall discuss the effect of chemical causes on the durability of concrete. Under this head following effects will be discussed.

1. Sulphate attack
2. Acid attack
3. Sea water attack
4. Alkali aggregate reaction
5. Deicing salts effect
6. Carbonation etc.

17.10.1. Sulphate attack

Sulphates are chemical salts, which dissolve in water forming solution. Sulphates are found in most of the soils as calcium, potassium, sodium and magnesium sulphates. Out of these sulphates the solubility of calcium sulphate is low. Due to less solubility of calcium sulphate in water, ground contains less calcium sulphate than others. Ammonium sulphate usually is present in agricultural soil and water due to the use of fertilizers and in sewage and industrial effluents. Decay of organic matter in shallow lakes and marshy land often form hydrogen sulphide (H_2S) gas, having a very pungent smell. It can be transformed into sulphuric acid by bacterial action. Water used in concrete cooling towers also can be a source of sulphate attack on concrete. Thus natural as well as industrial water is a source of sulphate attack.

Solid sulphates do not react with concrete severely, but when in water solution they penetrate into the porous mass of concrete and react with the hydrated products of cement. Magnesium sulphate is more reactive and causes maximum damage to the concrete than others. Magnesium sulphate decomposes the hydrated calcium silicates as well as $Ca(OH)_2$ and hydrated tricalcium aluminate (C_3A). Eventually it forms hydrated magnesium silicate, which has no binding properties. The sulphate attack or reaction is indicated by the characteristic whitish appearance on the surface. Usually the sulphate attack starts at the edges and corners, and after wards cracks and spalling of concrete start. The reaction between the hydrated products of cement and water solution of sulphate causes increase in volume of cement paste in concrete or mortar. In the hardened concrete calcium aluminate hydrate (C_3A) can react with sulphate salt from out side through pores. The product of reaction is calcium sulpho aluminate, forming within frame work of hydrated cement paste. Due to this reaction the volume of solid phase increases upto 227%, causing gradual disintegration of concrete. The extent of sulphate attack depends on the concentration of sulphate solution and permeability of concrete.

The chemical equation of reaction of sulphates with hardened paste of cement is shown below

Reaction between sodium sulphate and calcium hydroxide

$$Na_2So_4 \cdot 10H_2O + Ca(OH)_2 \longrightarrow \frac{CaSo_4 \cdot 2\,H_2o}{\text{gypsum}} + 2\,NaOH + 8\,H_2O$$

(*ii*) Reaction with calcium aluminate hydrate

$$2(3CaO \cdot Al_2O_3 \cdot 12\,H_2O) + 3\,(Na_2So_4 10H_2O) \longrightarrow 3\,Cao \cdot Al_2O_3 \cdot 31\,CaSo_4 \cdot 3H_2o + 2\,Al(OH)_3 + 6\,NaOH + 17\,H_2o$$

Calcium sulphate reacts with only calcium aluminate producing calcium sulpho aluminate (3 CaO. Al_2O_3. $3CaSO_4.31H_2O$). This product calcium sulpho aluminate is called as *Ettringite*. Molecules of water may be 31 or 32.

The magnesium sulphate not only reacts with calcium hydroxide and hydrated calcium aluminate like other sulphates,. but also decomposes the hydrated calcium silicates completely and makes it breakable into pieces easily *i.e.* friable mass. Thus more harmful.

The rate of sulphate reaction (attack) increases with the strength of sulphate solution. A saturated solution of magnesium sulphate can cause serious damage to concrete of high w/c ratio with in a very short period where as concrete made with low w/c ratio can withstand the reaction of magnesium sulphate for 2 to 3 yeas. The strength of the solution is expressed as concentration, as the number of parts of mass of sulpher trioxide (SO_3) per million parts of water (PPM). 1000 ppm is considered as moderately severe and 2000 PPm very severe especially if magnesium sulphate is the prominent constituent.

Another factor which influence the rate of reaction is the speed of replenishment of sulphate consumed in the reaction. From this, it can be concluded that when concrete is subjected to pressure of sulphate containing water on one side, the rate of reaction is higher. Similarly alternate wetting and drying due to tidal variation or spraying causes rapid reaction or attack.

17.10.1.1. Methods of Controlling sulphate effects

For controlling the sulphate effects following measures may be adopted:

(*a*) **Use of sulphate resistant cement.** To control or resist the sulphate effect on concrete the most effective and efficient method is the use of low calcium aluminate (C_3A) cement. It has been discussed in detail in chapter 3. In general it can be said that 7% C_3A content is a rough division between cement of good and poor performance in sulphate waters.

(*b*) **Quality of Concrete.** A well designed, prepared dense and impermeable concrete exhibits better resistance to sulpher attack. Similarly a concrete prepared with small water-cement ratio exhibits a higher resistance to sulpher attack.

(*c*) **Use of air entrainment.** The use of air entrainment upto 6% of the mass of cement has been observed to have beneficial effect on the sulphate resisting qualities of concrete. This effect may be due to improvement of impermeability of concrete which controls the segregation, bleeding, and workability of concrete.

(*d*) **Use of Pozzolana.** Replacement a part of cement by some pozzolanic material reduces the sulphate attack. Mixing pozzolanic material into the concrete converts the leachable calcium hydroxide $Ca(OH)_2$ into insoluble non leachable cementitious product. The pozzolanic action improves the impermeability of concrete. The reduction in calcium hydroxide reduces the possibility of magnesium sulphate attack on concrete.

(*e*) **High pressure steam curing.** High pressure steam curing improves the resistance of concrete to sulphate attack. It is due to the fact that when high pressure steam curing is adopted, a certain percentage of cement is replaced by pozzolanic material which reacts with $Ca(OH)_2$ improving the sulphate resistance property of the concrete.

(*f*) **Use of high alumina cement.** The use of high alumina cement has been found to check the sulphate attack partly due to the absence of any free calcium hydroxide ($CaOH_2$) in the set concrete in contrast to portland cement. High alumina cement contains approximately 40% alumina. The high percentage of alumina when present in ordinary portland cement it is very susceptible to sulpher attack. But this high percentage of alumina present in high alumina cement behaves in a different way. The main reason of high resistance to sulpher attack is attributed to the formation of a thin protective film which checks the diffusion of sulphate ions into the interior of the concrete. It is observed that high alumina cement does not show higher resistance to sulphate attack at higher temperatures.

Miller and Manson on the basis of their research on the effect of sulphate on concrete for a period of about 25 years have concluded as follows:

(*a*) There is a definite correlation between the sulphate resistance of portland cement and the amount of tricalcium aluminate C_3A cement contained. High resistance has been observed in portland cement containing not more than 5.5% C_3A.

(*b*) Finer grinded cements showed no effect on sulphate attack.

(*c*) The resistance of different portland pozzolana cements varied very much.

(*d*) Four non portland types of calcium aluminate cements consistently showed a very high resistance to the sulphate bearing water. However there were indications that these cements are not completely stable at temperatures above 21°C to 38°C.

(*e*) Steam cured specimen at 100°C and more specially at 176°C were highly sulphate resistant. The degree of improvement was greater for those cements which were not highly sulphate resistant originally, that is those cements having relatively high C_3A.

(*f*) Out of the 40 admixtures tried, only few of them gave markedly improved resistance. The most effective were linseed, soyabean and tung oils.

When hardened portland cement is exposed to ground water containing sulphate compounds, it is necessary to limit the permeability of concrete, the use of high, resistant sulphate cement and higher quantity of cement content. IS 456-2000 has given recommendations for the type of cement, max free water-cement ratio and minimum cement content. These recommendations are reproduced in Table 17.8 below.

Table 17.8. Requirements for concrete exposed to sulphate attack as per IS 456-2000

S. No.	*Class*	*Concentration of sulphates Expressed as So_3 in soil*			*Type of Cement*	*Dense, fully compacted concrete made with 20 mm nominal size aggregate as per IS 383*	
		Total So_3 %	*So_3 in 2:1 water soil extract g/l*	*In ground water gram/lit g/l*		*Min. cement content kg/m^3*	*Max free w/c ratio*
1	2	3	4	5	6	7	8
(*i*)	1	Traces (< 0.2)	Less than 1.0	Less than 0.3	Ordinary portland cement or portland slag or portland pozzolana cement	280	0.55
(*ii*)	2	0.2 to 0.5	1.0 to 1.9	0.3 to 1.2	As above Super sulphated cement or sulphate resistant portland cement	330 310	0.50 0.50
(*iii*)	3	0.5 to 1.0	1.9 to 3.1	1.2 to 2.5	Super sulphated cement or sulphate resistant portland cement Portland pozzolana cement or portland slag cement	330 350	0.50 0.45
(*iv*)	4	1.0 to 2.0	3.1 to 5.0	2.5 to 5.0	Super sulphated or sulphate resistant portland cement	370	0.45
(*v*)	5	More than 2.0	More than 5.0	More than 5.0	Sulphate resistent portland cement or super sulphated cement with protective coating	400	0.40

Notes. 1. Cement content given in above table is irrespective of grades of cement.

2. Use of super sulphated cement is generally restricted where the prevailing temperature is above 40°C.
3. Super Sulphated cement gives an acceptable life provided that the concrete is dense and prepared with a w/c ratio of 0.4 or less, in mineral acids down to P_H 3.5.
4. The cement content given in this table are minimum recommended. For So_3 contents near the upper limit of any class, the cement content more than the values shown are recommended.
5. For severe conditions, such as thin sections under hydrostatic pressure on one side and sections partly immersed, the water cement ratio may further be reduced.
6. Portland slag cement conforming to IS 455 with slag content more than 50% exhibits better sulphate resisting properties.
7. Where chloride is encountered along with Sulphate in soil or ground water, ordinary portland cement with C_3A content from 5 to 8% shall be desirable to be used in concrete instead of sulphate resistant cement. Alternatively portland slag cement conforming to IS 455 having more than 50% slag or a blend of ordinary portland cement and slag cement may be used provided sufficient information is available on performance of such blended cements in these conditions.

17.10.2. Alkali-aggregate reaction

A chemical reaction between the active silica constituents of the aggregate and the alkalies of cement is known as alkali silica or alkali aggregate reaction. The reactive form of silica are opal (amorphous) chalcedony (cryptocrystalline fibrous) and tridymine (crystalline). These materials occur in several types of rocks as trap, andesites, rhyolites, siliceous lime stone, and certain types of sand stones. The reaction starts with the attack of (Na_2O and K_2O) on the reactive siliceous minerals in the aggregate by the alkaline hydroxide derived from the alkalies in the cement. As a result of this reaction an alkali silica gel of un limited swelling property is formed altering the borders of the aggregate. The gel is confined by the surrounding cement paste. The expansion of the gel produces internal pressure causing expansion of concrete. This expansion results in cracking and disruption of cement paste. The amount of swelling of gel depends upon the congenial condition of moisture and temperature in voids. The crack width may vary from 0.1 mm to 10 mm.

Till 1940, aggregate was considered as an inert material, but after the failure of concrete structures in 1940 due to alkali-aggregate reaction, now a days great emphasis is laid on aggregate alkali reaction test on aggregates to be used in large and important concrete constructions.

It is observed that alkali-silica or aggregate reaction can take place only at high concentration of 'OH' ions, *i.e.* at high P_H value in the pore water. The P_H value of pore water depends on the alkali content of cement. High alkali cement may have a P_H value of about 13.5 to 13.9 and the low alkali cement may have a P_H value of 12.7 to 13.1. Thus an increase of 1.0% in P_H value, represents a ten time increase in hydrogen ions concentration. Thus a low alkali cement which produces a low P_H value in pore water is safe against reactive aggregates.

Alkalis not only come from cement, but also come from sand containing sodium chlorides, admixture mixing water, sea water penetration, blast furnance slag, fly ash and deicing salts etc. getting into the concrete. Alkalis from all these sources must be included while finding the total alkalis expressed as sode equivalent in 1 m^3 of concrete if alkali reactive aggregate is used.

17.10.2.1. Soda Equivalent

The actual content of Na_2O plus 0.658 times K_2O content in cement is called soda equivalent. The minimum alkali content of the cement at which the expansive reaction may take place is 0.6% of the soda equivalent. B-S 5328 part-1 specifies a maximum of 3 kg of alkalies per cubic metre of concrete.

17.10.2.2. Factors which affect the rate of alkali-aggregate reaction

The reactivity of aggregate depends upon the following factors:

1. Size of the aggregate particles
2. Porosity of the aggregate particles
3. Alkali content in cement
4. Fineness of cement particles
5. Availability of non evaporable water in the paste
6. Alternate wetting and drying of concrete
7. Temperature in the range of 10 to 40°C accelerates the reaction.

17.10.2.3. Preventive measures

Following measures can be taken to reduce the alkali aggregate reaction

1. Addition of finely powdered silica to the concrete mix. The addition of reactive silica increases the surface area of the reactive aggregate. The increase in surface area of aggregates, increases the calcium hydroxide-alkali ratio of the solution at the boundaries of the reactive aggregate. Under such conditions a non expanding calcium alkali silicate gel or product is formed.
2. 20 gram of reactive silica should be added for each gram of alkali in excess of 0.5% of the mass of cement.

Practice followed in U.K. to minimise the risk of alkali-aggregate or silica reaction is as follows:

1. The contact of concrete from the external source of moisture should be cut off or prevented.
2. Portland cement with an alkali content not more than 0.6% expressed as Na_2o (This is the sum of the actual Na_2o content plus 0.658 times the K_2o) content of cement should be used.

3. A blend (mixture) of ordinary type portland cement and ground granulated blast furnance slag with a minimum of 50% slag should be used.
4. The mixture of ordinary portland cement and fly ash cement, with a min of 25% fly ash should be used provided that the alkali content of the concrete supplied by the portland cement component is less than 3.0 kg/m^3 of concrete. The alkali content of concrete can be calculated by multiplying the alkali content of portland cement (expressed as fraction) by the maximum expected portland cement content.
5. British standard 5328 part-I 1991 specifies that the alkali content of the concrete should be limited to 3.0 kg/m^3, which is now the alkali content of the composite cement (expressed as a fraction) times the maximum expected content of the cementitious materials.

17.10.3. Attack by sea water

In the present era, large number of concrete structures are constructed which are exposed to sea water either directly or indirectly. The coastal and off shore structures are exposed to simultaneous action of a number of physical as well as chemical deterioration processes. Concrete structures in sea water are subjected to freezing and thawing, abrasion by sand held in water and other floating bodies. The reinforcement of concrete is subjected to corrosion by the action of chlorine.

It has been observed that usually sea water contains 3.5% salts by weight of water. Abrahm on the basis of his research work stated that sea water having 3.5% salinity can be used for plain concrete if the aggregates are non alkali reactive. Sea water generally contains about 78% of sodium chloride and 15% magnesium sulphate and chloride. The ionic concentration of sodium and chloride are highest of the order of 11000 and 20,000 mg/litre respectively. The concentration of magnesium and sulphate is about 1400 and 2700 mg/litre respectively. The P_H value of sea water is found to vary from 7.5 to 8.4. The average value is taken as 8.2. Sea water also contains some amount of carbon dioxide Co_2.

As discussed under the topic sulphate attack, the magnesium sulphate reacts with free calcium hydroxide $Ca(OH)_2$ in set portland cement to form calcium sulphate, precipitating magnesium hydroxide, Magnesium sulphate, also reacts with the hydrated calcium aluminate to form calcium sulpho-aluminate. These reactions mainly are responsible for the chemical attack of concrete by sea water.

It has been observed that the deterioration of concrete in sea water is not caused by the expansion of concrete exposed to sulphate action, but due to the erosion or loss of constituents from the parent concrete mass with out causing undue expansion. It may be due to the fact that the presence of chlorides in sea water may have retarted the swelling or expansion of concrete in sulphate solution. Concrete is also found to have lost some amount of lime content due to leaching. Both calcium hydroxide and calcium sulphate are found more soluble in sea water, resulting in increased leaching out process. Thus in brief it can be said that concrete undergoes several reactions simultaneously when subjected to sea water. A less massive structure subjected to sea water shows the leaching effect more than expansion, where as massive structures as dock wall show both effects leaching as well as expansion. The rate of chemical attack is found to increase in temperate zones.

Further it has been observed that most sever attack of sea water on concrete takes place just above the high water level. The parts between the high and low water levels are less affected and the parts below low water level which remain constantly immersed in water are least affected. The disruption of concrete is caused by the crystallization of salts in the portion of concrete above high water level. In cold climatic regions the freezing of water in pores at spray level of concrete is responsible for causing non durability of concrete. Freezing may also take place between tidal variation levels.

In shallow waters, the sea water contains certain amount of sand and silt. The wave velocity causes abrasion of concrete. The impact and mechanical force of wave also contributes to the non durability of concrete.

17.10.3.1. Measures to minimise the sea water effects

Following measures may be adopted to minimise the effects of sea water on concrete.

1. Use of right type of cement with low C_3A content.
2. Use of rich concrete *i.e.* use of more cement in concrete with low water-cement ratio. The rich concrete with low w/c ratio makes concrete dense and impervious to the attack of sea water. It has very little capillary pores, which held no water to cause expansion either due to crystallization or freezing.
3. Provision of adequate cover to reinforcement.
4. Use of pozzolanic material.
5. Full compaction and good construction joints are necessary for the good durability of concrete in sea water.
6. For better durability, whereever possible high pressure steam cured prefabricated concrete elements should be used.

17.10.4. Acid attack

No portland cement is fully resistant to acid attack. In damp conditions sulpher dioxide (So_2) and carbon dioxide (Co_2) as well as some other fumes present in the atmospheric air form acids. These acids diffuse or penetrate into the concrete through porous structure of the concrete mass. These acids attack the calcium silicate hydrate (C-S-H) gel and calcium hydroxide $Ca(OH)_2$. $Ca(OH)_2$ is the most vulnerable part of the cement for the acid attack. This reaction makes the concrete very weak. Certain acids, such as oxalic and phosphoric acids are harmless, where as hydrochloric acid (HCl) is most reactive. Sulphuric acid (H_2So_4) is less reactive than (HCl). Silicious aggregates are more resistant to acid attack than calcarious aggregates. The acidic attack takes place in industries and some agricultural conditions such as floors of dairies.

In practice, the degree of acidic attack increases with the increase in acidity. Usually the acidic attack takes place when the P_H value is below about 6.5. At P_H value less than 4.5 the acidic attack is very severe. For P_H values between 3 and 6, the rate of acidic attack is proportional to the square root of time. This indicates that the rate of attack depends on the capacity of hydrogen ions to diffuse through the calcium silicate hydrates known as (C-S-H) gel after the calcium hydroxide $Ca(OH)_2$ has been dissolved and leached out.

If the concentration of free carbon dioxide in water is between 15 to 60 ppm, the concrete is attacked by this water. Pure water formed by melting of ice or by condensation and water with carbon dioxide with in excess of 60 ppm is found aggressive. The P_H value of such waters may be as low as 4.4.

The domestic sewage though alkaline in nature, causes deterioration of sewers, especially at higher temperatures, when sulpher compounds in the sewage are reduced by anaerobic bacteria to hydrogen sulphide H_2S. Though this gas is not destructive agent in nature by it self but when it is dissolved in moisture film on the exposed surface of the concrete, it undergoes oxidation forming sulphuric acid. The acidic attack takes place above the flow level of the sewage. The cement is gradually dissolved and progressive deterioration takes place. In this reaction of sulphuric acid, the calcium sulphate formed, reacts with the calcium aluminate in cement and forms calcium sulpho-aluminate, which on crystallization causes expansion and disruption of concrete.

The attack of calcium hydroxide $Ca(OH)_2$ can be reduced by the following measures.

1. By treating the surface with sodium silicate known as water glass. The sodium silicate when reacts with $Ca(OH)_2$, it forms calcium silicate in the pores.
2. Surface treatment with coal tar, rubber or bituminous paints, epoxy resins etc. has also been found useful.

17.10.5. Carbonation

Carbonation can be defined as the reaction of carbon dioxide CaO_2 with the hydrated cement. The carbon dioxide gas is present in the atmosphere with varying percentage from rural to urban and highly industrialized area. In rural area air, the amount of Co_2 is found 0.03% by volume, 0.1% or even more in urban areas and more than 0.3% in large and industrialized cities. In the presence of moisture carbon dioxide (Co_2) forms carbonic acid, which reacts with calcium hydroxide $Ca(OH)_2$ forming calcium carbonate ($CaCo_3$). In the process other cement compounds are also decomposed. The process of carbonation causes contraction in the concrete, resulting in a small shrinkage. This contraction is known as *carbonation shrinkage.*

The P_H value of pore water in the hardened concrete usually vary between 12.5 to 13.5 depending upon the alkali content in the cement. The high alkalinity of cement forms a thin protective layer around the steel reinforcement and protects it from the action of water and oxygen. As long as steel is in the high alkaline zone, it is not going to be corroded. Such condition is known as *passivation.*

In actual practice carbon dioxide present in atmosphere in smaller or greater concentration, diffuses or permeates into the concrete and reacts with calcium hydroxides, forming carbonates, and reducing the P_H value of pore water from about 13.0 to about 9.0. When all the calcium hydroxide $Ca(OH)_2$ has been carbonated, the P_H value reduces to about 8.3. In such a low P_H value the protective layer gets dissolved or destroyed and the steel is exposed to corrosion.

Carbonation proceeds from surface of the concrete inwards, but its rates of travel is very slow. The actual rate of carbonation depends on the following factors:

1. Permeability of the concrete
2. Its moisture content
3. Quantity of Co_2
4. Relative humidity of ambient medium
5. Grade of concrete
6. Depth of cover
7. Time
8. Whether the concrete is protected or unprotected

As the permeability of concrete is a function of w/c ratio and its curing, concrete with high w/c ratio and inadequately cured will have more carbonation, *i.e.* the depth of carbonation will be more.

It has been observed that if pores are filled with water, the rate of diffusion of Co_2 is very slow. But whatever amount of Co_2 is diffused, it is converted into dilute carbonic acid readily and the alkalinity of the concrete is reduced. On the other hand, if pores are dry, *i.e.* the relative humidity is low, the carbon dioxide remains unchanged in gaseous form and does not react with hydrated cement. The moisture penetration from external source is necessary for carbonation of concrete.

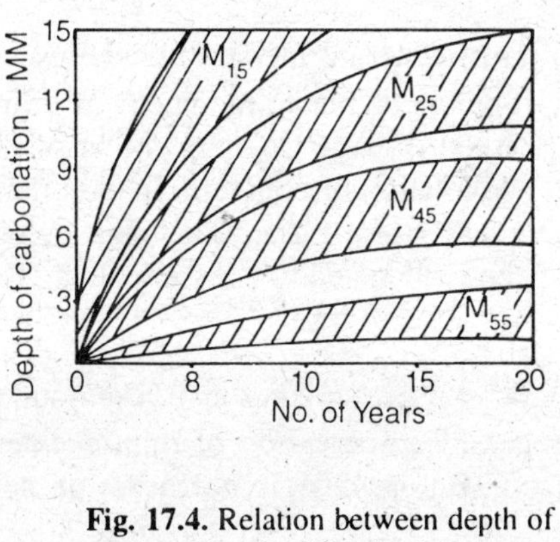

Fig. 17.4. Relation between depth of carbonation & strength of concrete

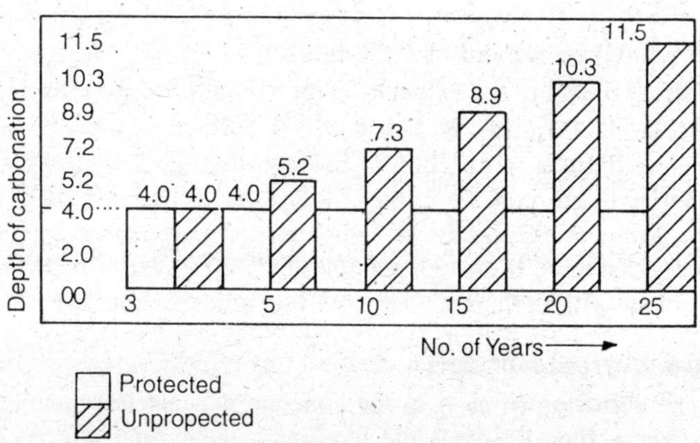

Fig. 17.5. Depth of carbonation of protected and unprotected concrete

The highest rate of carbonation takes place at a 50 to 70% relative humidity. The rate of carbonation depth is slower in case of stronger concrete as it is less permeable and much denser with low w/c ratio. Further the permeability of the skin concrete is much less for low w/c ratio and the diffusion of carbon dioxide takes place at a very slow rate than the more permeable concrete of high w/c ratio. Fig. 17.4 and Table 17.9 show the depth of carbonation of different grades of concrete.

Now it is well established that for longer durability of concrete it needs protection. The Long span bridge girders, industrial structures, fly-overs and chimney etc. need protective coating. It has been observed that in case of protective concrete the depth of carbonation remained constant at 4.0 mm from 3 years to 25 years age, where as in case of unprotective concrete the depth of carbonation continuously increased more or less at a constant rate from 4.0 mm to 11.5 mm in 3 years to 25 years age as shown in Fig. 17.5.

The depth of cover plays an important role in protecting the steel from carbonation. Table 17.10 shows the relation between w/c, depth of cover and time in years for carbonation to reach the reinforcement.

Table 17.9. Depth of carbonation with age and grade of concrete

Age in years	*Depth of carbonation in mm*	
	M_{20}	M_{40}
2	5.0	0.5
5	8.0	1.0
10	12.0	2.0
50	25.0	4.0

Table 17.10. Relation between, w/c, depth of cover and time in years for carbonation to reach the reinforcement

W/c ratio ↓ Grade of concrete →	*Depth of cover in mm*			
	15	20	25	30
0.45	100	100	100	100
0.50	56	99	100	100
0.55	27	49	76	100
0.60	16	29	45	65
0.65	13	23	36	52
0.70	11	19	30	43
		Time in years for carbonation		

17.10.5.1. Measurement of Carbonation

For establishing the extent of carbonation, following simple and most common method may be used.

Method. A freshly broken concrete surface is treated with a solution of phenolphthalein in dilute alcohol. If there is no reaction of calcium hydroxide $Ca(OH)_2$ with carbon dioxide Co_2, the colour of the concrete will turn pink *i.e.* if the colour turns to be pink, there is no carbonation of concrete. In case there is no charge in the colour of concrete, the carbonation of concrete has taken place. The pink colour indicates that there is enough amount of $Ca(OH)_2$, but it might have been carbonated to a lesser extent. The pink colour will be there even upto a P_H value of about 9.5.

17.10.6. Corrosion of steel

The corrosion of steel in the concrete is a electro-chemical process. The corrosion of reinforcement starts when chlorides reach the reinforcement through porous concrete. Before dealing corrosion of steel reinforcement, let us study the chloride attack first.

17.10.6.1. Chloride Attack

White dealing with the durability aspect of concrete, the chloride effect on concrete is the most important factor as it causes the corrosion of reinforcement of concrete. The statistical studies have shown that more than 40% structures have failed due to the corrosion of reinforcement steel.

Under the head carbonation we discussed that due to high alkaline nature of calcium hydroxide (P_H value about 13) in concrete a protective oxide film is formed around the surface of the reinforcement. This protection is called passivity. This protective passivity cover or layer may be destroyed due to the carbonation. This protective cover may also be destroyed or lost due to the presence of chlorides in the presence of oxygen and water. In reality the corrosive action of chloride is more serious than any other cause. Actually the sulphate attack destroys concrete where as chloride attacks the reinforcement. The volume of corroded reinforcement may go upto six times of its original volume causing cracks and spalling of concrete.

17.10.6.2. Source of chlorides

Chlorides may enter into the concrete from the following sources:

1. From cement of the concrete
2. Water mixed in concrete
3. Aggregates of the concrete
4. Admixtures added to the concrete
5. Chlorides may also enter by diffusion from atmosphere

Earlier Bureau of Indian Standards had recommended the maximum content of chloride in cement as 0.05%, but now it has been increased to 0.1%. The revised IS-456-2000 has specified the chloride content as chlorine (Cl), in concrete at the time of placing as shown Table 17.11.

Table 17.11. Limits of chloride content of concrete as per IS 456-2000

S. No.	*Use of concrete*	*Max. Total actual soluble chloride content in kg/m³*
1.	Concrete containing metal and steam cured at high temperature and prestressed concrete	0.4
2.	R.C.C. or plain concrete containing embeded metal (steel)	0.6
3.	Concrete not containing embeded metal or any material requiring protection from chlorides	3.0

The amount of chloride needed for starting or initiating the corrosion of reinforcement partly depends on the P_H value of the pore water in the concrete. At P_H value less than 11.5, the corrosion may develop even with out chlorides. At P_H value greater than 11.5, more amount of chloride is required for initiating corrosion.

Out of the total quantity of chloride present in concrete, partly is soluble and partly insoluble type of chloride. The insoluble chloride is chloro-aluminate. The soluble chloride is responsible for initiating corrosion of reinforcement. Table 17.12 below shows limiting chloride content corresponding to P_H value of concrete.

Table 17.12. Limiting chloride content showing corresponding value of P_H of concrete

S. No.	*Choride content in gram per litre*	*PPm*	*P_H value*
1.	6.7400	6740	13.5
2.	2.1300	2130	13.0
3.	0.6720	672	12.5

S. No.	*Choride content in gram per litre*	*PPm*	P_H *value*
4.	0.2130	213	12.0
5.	0.0670	67	11.5
6.	0.0213	21	11.0
7.	0.0021	2	10.0
8.	0.0002	0.2	9.02

17.10.6.3. Corrosion of reinforcement

Corrosion of steel is an electro chemical process, which usually takes place when two dis-similar metals are in electrical contact in the presence of moisture and oxygen. The same process takes place in the steel alone due to the difference in electro-chemical potential on the surface which forms anodic and cathodic regions, connected by the electrolyte in the form of the salt solution in the hydrated cement. The positively charged ferrous ions Fe^{++} at the anode pass into solution while negatively charged free electrons $\bar{e}$ pass along the steel into the cathode, where they are absorbed by the constituents of the electrolyte and combine with water and oxygen to form hydroxyl ions (OH^-). Then they combine with the ferrous ions to form ferric hydroxide. This hydroxide is converted to rust by further oxidation.

The reactions can be written as follows:

$$Fe \rightarrow Fe^{++} + 2\,\bar{e} \text{ (anodic reaction)}$$

$$4\,\bar{e} + O_2 + 2\,H_2O \rightarrow 4(OH) \text{ (cathodic reaction)}$$

$$Fe^{++} + 2(OH) \rightarrow Fe(OH)_2 \text{ (Ferrous hydroxide)}$$

$$4Fe(OH)_2 + 2H_2O + O_2 \rightarrow 4\,Fe(OH)_3 \text{ (Ferric hydroxide)}$$

From these equations it can be seen that oxygen is consumed, but water is regenerated and needed only for the process to continue.

Thus it can be noted that in a completely dry atmosphere no corrosion can take place, most probably below 40% relative humidity. It is also noticed that not much corrosion of reinforcement takes place if concrete is fully immersed in water except when water can entrain air. 70 to 80% relative humidity is most-conginial for the development of corrosion of reinforcement. At higher thar 80% relative humidity, the diffusion of oxygen is reduced considerably and atmospheric conditions along the steel are more uniform. It has also been observed that the products of corrosion occupy volúme about six times the original volume of steel depending upon the oxidation state.

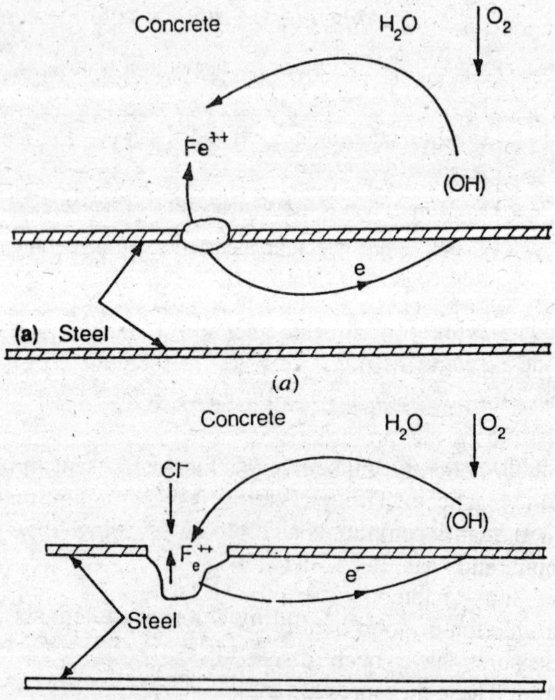

Fig. 17.6. (*a*) Electro chemical process, (*b*) Electro chemical corrosion in the presence of chloride

17.10.6.4. Reaction of chloride ions

Chloride ions present in the cement paste around the reinforcement react at anode sites as shown in Fig. 17.6 (*b*) The reaction forms hydrochloric acid (HCl), which destroys the passive protective layer formed around the steel. In this situation the surface of the steel acts as anode and the passive surface coating acts as cathode. The corrosion formed is in the form of a localized pitting as shown in Fig. 17.6.

The Chemical reaction may be as follows:

$$Fe^{++} + 2\,\overline{Cl} \rightarrow FeCl_2$$

$$FeCl_2 + 2\,H_2O \rightarrow Fe(OH)_2 + 2\,HCl$$

Thus $\overline{Cl}$ is regenerated. The other reactions, specially the cathodic reaction are same as in the absence of chlorides. It should be noted that rust contains no chloride, though ferric chloride is formed at an intermediate stage.

Due to the formation of hydrochloric acid in the pit, once it is formed, the pit remains active and increases in depth. The pitting corrosion takes place at a certain potential, called the process is started, the potential is higher in dry concrete than at high humidities. As soon as a pit forming processes started, the potential of the steel in its neighbourhood drops and no new pit is formed for some times. Eventually there may be large scale spread of the corrosion and general spread of corrosion may take place in the presence of large amount of chlorides.

It is important to remember that in the presence of chlorides as well as in their absence, the electro-chemical corrosion takes place only in the presence of water and oxygen. In this reaction only the oxygen is consumed. Even in the presence of large quantities of chlorides there is no corrosion of the dry concrete. It has been noticed that if the total chloride ions content is less than 0.4% by mass of cement, the corrosion of reinforcement is small in ordinary portland cement concrete. Only soluble chlorides are responsible for reinforcement corrosion. Dry chlorides have no effect on corrosion.

17.10.6.5. Effect of Corrosion

The increased volume of rust exerts pressure or thrust on the cover of the concrete, resulting in cracks, spalling or delamination as shown in Fig. 17.7.

17.10.6.6. Corrosion Control

The foremost corrosion control method is the production of good quality concrete and good construction practices. The production of good quality concrete is a very wide topic and has been discussed in previous chapters. Here other than production of good quality concrete measures have been discussed in brief. These measures are a follows:

1. Metallurgical methods
2. Use of corrosive preventive materials

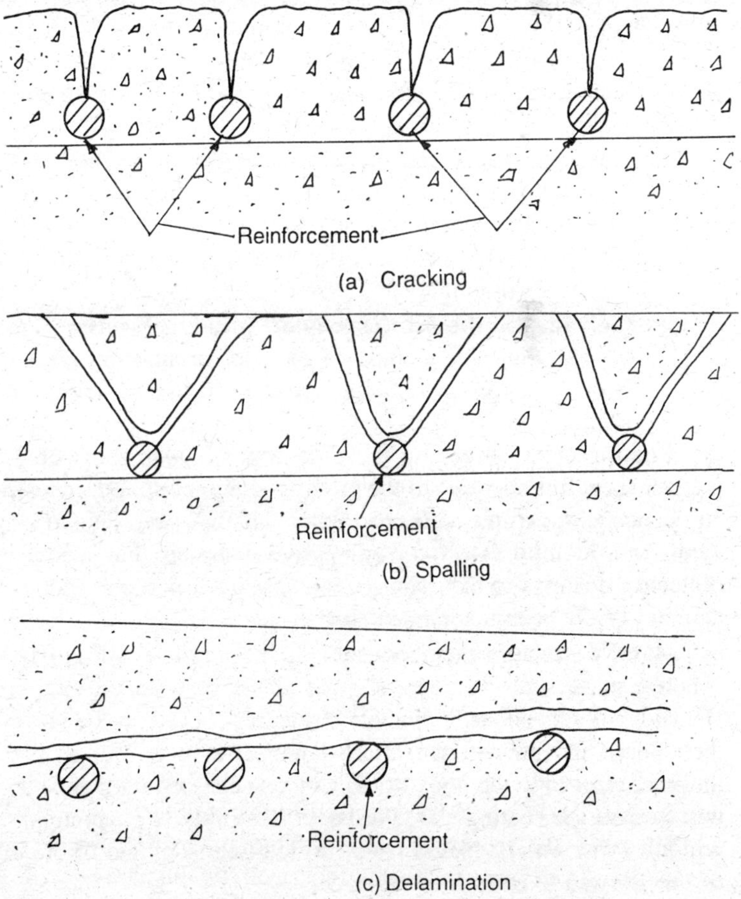

Fig. 17.7. Damage caused by corrosion to concrete

3. Coatings to reinforcement
4. Coatings to concrete
5. Cathodic protection
6. Design and detailing

1. Metallurgical Methods. To make the steel more corrosion resistant, its structure can be changed by metallurgical processes. This can be achieved by rapid quenching of the hot bars by series of water jets or keeping the hot steel bars for a short period in water bath. Many other methods may also be applied to improve the corrosion and other mechanical properties of the steel.

2. Use of corrosive preventive materials or inhibitors. Corrosion can be prevented or delayed by the use of certain corrosion preventive materials such as phosphates, nitrites, Benzonates etc. Out of the available materials, a admixture based on calcium nitrite is most widely used. It is added to the concrete during mixing process. The dosage of 10 to 30 litres per cubic metre of concrete has been found quite effective depending upon the quantity of chloride present in concrete.

As stated earlier, in the presence of high P_H in concrete, a protective layer of ferric oxide is formed around the steel which protects it from carbonation. However this protective layer also contains some ferrious oxide, which can start corroding steel when the chloride ions reach the steel. The nitrite ions present in corrosion preventing admixtures oxidise the ferrious oxide to ferric oxide, stabilizing the protective layer even in the presence of chlorides. However the concentration of nitrite must be sufficient to neutralize the diffusing chloride ions.

Calcium nitrite, a corrosion preventive material is available in liquid form containing about 30% calcium nitrite solids by weight. Higher the quantity of corrosion preventive material added to the solution, longer the period after which the corrosion of steel starts. For structures in chloride environment, the quantity of calcium nitrite in solution should not be less than 18 litres/m^3 of concrete. As in such situations the level of 7 kg chloride ions per cubic metre of concrete reaches during the service life of the structure.

(*a*) **Coating of reinforcement.** The object of coating a steel bar is to provide it a durable barrier against the aggressive materials such as chlorides or oxygen. The coatings should be strong enough to withstand the effects of pouring of concrete, its compaction and finishing and fabrication of reinforcement cage etc. A simple cement slurry coating is a cheep method for temporary protection against rusting of steel.

(*b*) **Galvanising the reinforcement.** In the galvanising process the steel bars are dipped in molten zinc. A thin zinc coating takes place around the steel. The zinc surface reacts with the calcium hydroxide present in the concrete to form a passive or protective layer and prevents corrosion of steel.

Coating of Concrete. In the past, concrete was considered a durable material by it self needing no maintenance. But now due to the environmental pollution, industrial fumes, contamination of ground water etc. concrete structures also need extra maintenance. The coating of concrete members not only protect them from harmful effects of aggressive materials, but it also gives it a aesthetic look. Now providing protective coatings to the major concrete structures such as long bridges, flyovers, industrial buildings and chimneys have been made mandatory.

Massive structure members such as bridge piers and girders are of considerable dimensions. Freshly concrete made such members contain plenty of water in the pores structure. It takes a long time to dry. Hence freshly made such concrete structures should not be coated with such materials which will seal off their pores and prevent the internal moisture to go out as per prevailing atmospheric conditions. The moisture trapped in the body of the concrete can do unimaginable harm to the durability of the concrete and will damage the coating also. For better durability of concrete, the protective coating should be such which will allow the water vapours from inside to out side and from out side to inside. But water as such should not be allowed to entre from out side.

Cathodic protection

In this method an electrode is embedded in the concrete above the reinforcement steel. A D.C. current is passed through this electrode. This electrode serves as anode and the reinforcement steel which is connected to the negative terminal of the D.C. source acts as cathode. In this process the external anode is subjected to corrosion and the cathodic reinforcement is protected from corrosion, hence the name cathodic protection.

This method of reinforcement steel protection is found very effective. It is well known and extensively used method for reinforcement corrosion prevention in advanced countries. In India it is not used due to its high cost and long term monitoring.

Design and detailing

The structural designer should take all necessary precautions in the designing and detailing with respect to spacing between reinforcement bars, to facilitate vibration of concrete for proper compaction, and give proper cover to reinforcement and to restrict the crack width etc.

Nominal Cover to reinforcement

The nominal cover is applicable to all reinforcement.

(*a*) *Columns.* In a column, for longitudinal reinforcement, the nominal cover should not be less than 40 mm or less than the diameter of the bar.

(*b*) In case of columns where minimum dimension is 200 mm or less, and the diameter of the reinforcing bar does not exceed 12 mm, the nominal cover of 25 mm should be provided.

(*c*) For footings a minimum cover of 50 mm should be provided.

The nominal cover to all reinforcements including stripes or links should be provided after taking into account the specified period of fire resistance upto 4 hours. The nominal cover suggested by IS 456-2000 is shown in table 17.13 below.

Table 17.13. Nominal cover to meet the durability requirements as per IS 456-2000

Exposure	*Nominal Cover to reinforcement in mm not less than*
Mild	20
Moderate	30
Severe	45
Very sevre	50
Extreme	75

17.10.7. Effect of deicing salts on concrete

The chemical salts used for removing or clearing the ice and snow from concrete roads in winter season of cold regions are known as deicing agents or salts. The use of these salts has been found to have adverse effect on concrete, probably by increasing the severity of the freezing and thawing cycles.

17.10.7.1. Salts used for deicing

Normally following salts can be used for deicing snow or ice

(*a*) Sodium chloride (NaCl) and calcium chloride ($CaCl_2$)

(*b*) Urea

(*c*) Ammonium salts

(*a*) **Sodium and Calcium chloride.** Normally sodium chloride or calcium chloride is used for deicing snow clearance on cement concrete roads. The repeated use of these salts with intervening periods of freezing or drying cause surface scaling of concrete roads.

(*b*) **Urea.** Some times urea is used as deicing salt. Though it has been found less deleterious (harmful), but it has been found less effective in removing ice.

(*c*) **Ammonium salts.** The use of these salts even in small concentration have been found very harmful. Thus their use as deicing salts is not recommended. In other words they should not be used as deicing salts.

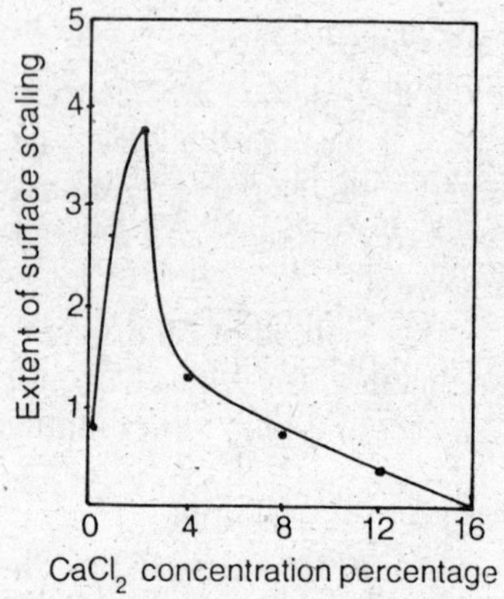

Fig. 17.8. Effect of concentration of $CaCl_2$ on concrete

The deicing salts produce osmotic pressure and cause movement of water towards the top layer of the slab where freezing takes place. Greatest damage has been observed to occur when concrete is exposed to relatively low concentration of salts (2 to 4% solution) as shown in Fig. 17.8. According to Verbeck and Klieger this action has been attributed as physical in nature and not as chemical. The repeated use of these salts cause surface scaling of the concrete roads resulting in severe damage to the surface. Fig. 17.8 shows the effect of calcium chloride concentration on scaling of an non air entrained concrete after 50 cycles of freezing and thawing with out removal of solution. The extent of surface scaling from 0 to 5.0 value shows no scaling, while 5 value indicates bad scaling.

17.10.7.2. Action of deicing salts

Mather has suggested the actin of deicers as follows:

According to Mather deicers increase the corrosion of steel of the concrete. The sequence of action is as follows. The deicer melts the ice or snow, which is usually ponded by the adjacent ice. The resulting liquid is absorbed. Due to the lower freezing point of this liquid, it remains in liquid state. As more and more ice melts, the melt water becomes diluted till its freezing point reaches near to the freezing point of water. This water then freezes. Thus freezing and thawing takes place as often as with out the use of deicers or even more often as possibly a insulating layer of ice has been destroyed. Thus it can be said that deicers increase the saturation and possibly increase the number of cycles of freezing and thawing. This action promotes the corrosion of steel. This argument supports the physical nature of the damage action of the deicers, which is independent of whether the deicer is organic or not or a salt or not. However there is a possibility of leaching of calcium hydroxide $Ca(OH)_2$, which has a greater solubility in the chloride solution than water. There is also possibility of formation of chloro-aluminates under wetting and drying conditions.

17.10.7.3. Measures to make concrete surface resistant to scaling

The concrete surface may be made more resistant to scaling by the following treatments

1. By air entrainment
2. By using rich mixes

Portland pozzolana cement has been found less resistant to deicing salts than ordinary portland cement.

The extent of damage of scaling by deicing salts has been found to be influenced by the procedure adopted. For example, the air drying of the concrete after wet curing but before to the exposure cycles (freezing and thawing) has been found to increase the resistance to surface scaling. However the drying out must be done before moist curing for sufficient duration to allow the cement paste to hydrate properly and extensively.

In case of air entrained concrete, the period of curing required for the development of high resistance to salt scaling is about the same as that necessary for the development of adequate strength of concrete to resist the applied loads.

The damage to the concrete would be severe if the deicing salts are applied with in a few weeks of placing of the concrete. However some protection can be obtained by sealing the concrete with linseed oil.

On the dry surface of the concrete a mixture of boiled linseed oil diluted in equal parts both Kerosene oil or mineral sprits can be applied in two coats on the surface of the concrete. Though the oil slows down the ingress of the deicer solution, but it does not seal the surface of the concrete. Hence the evaporation from the surface is not prevented.

The most severe damage to the concrete takes place when it is subjected to alternate freezing and thawing while the deicing solution remains on top of the concrete surface rather than being replaced by fresh water before each refreezing. On the other hand if the deicing solution is removed from the top surface of the concrete before the refreezing takes place, no scaling of the top surface of the concrete would take place even with non air entrained concrete.

17.10.7.4. Determination of resistance to Concrete scaling

The resistance of concrete to the scaling can be determined as follows:

The concrete specimen covered with deicing fluid is subjected to repeated cycles of freezing and thawing. The resistance to the scaling of the concrete is determined from the loss of weight, depth of spalling and the size of the spalled area. However no reliable data about the success of this test is available.

17.10.8. Frost resistant Concrete

1. Frost resistance concrete can be produced by the use of air entrainment in concrete as discussed in chapter 6 on admixtures.
2. Secondly the frost resistance of concrete can be increased by adopted mixes with low w/c ratios. The amount of water should be such that the paste can have only small capallaries and only little freezable water. However it is essential that substantial hydration of cement should take place before the exposure to the frost. Such concrete has less permeability and does not absorb water during wet weather.

QUESTIONS

1. Explain the effect of water-cement ratio and age on the permeability of concrete.
2. Explain the effects of silica contents in aggregates on the alkali silica reaction.
3. What are the consequences of sulphates in aggregates?
4. What is meant by ions concentration of chloride?
5. Why is the depth of cover to steel specified?
6. What are the necessary conditions for the alkali-silica reaction to take place?
7. Compare the permeability of steam cured and moist cured concrete.
8. Does the aggregate grading affect the permeability of concrete?
9. Explain the mechanism of sulphate attack of concrete.
10. What is the action of acids on concrete?
11. Why the permeability of concrete can not be predicted from its porosity?
12. Explain the effects of the followings on concrete
    (*a*) Sulphates in soil and ground water
    (*b*) Effect of sulphates on R.C.C.
    (*c*) Sewage attack
13. Which pores influence the permeability of concrete? Also state which pores have little influence on the permeability of concrete.
14. What is carbonation? Describe the corrosion of steel in concrete by it.
15. Describe the corrosion of steel in concrete containing calcium chloride.
16. Why the use of calcium chloride is undesirable in concrete?
17. Which cement minimises the sulphate effect and why?
18. What is the difference between the action of sulphate solution and sea water on concrete.
19. What measures are required to prevent the adverse effects of the sea water on R.C.C.

20. Why the permeability of concrete is important for the durability of concrete?
21. Compare alkali reactive siliceous aggregate and alkali carbonaceous aggregates.
22. What is meant by durability of concrete? For what purpose is the minimum cement content specified?
23. What cement should be used when aggregate is suspected to be alkali- reactive?
24. What is meant by alkali reactive aggregate?
25. How is the alkali reactivity is assessed?
26. Why it is important to know whether a given cement is ordinary portland cement or portland blast furnace cement.
27. Write a detailed note on the corrosion control.

OBJECTIVE TYPE QUESTIONS

1. The permeability of concrete reduces with the
   (*a*) Carbonation of concrete
   (*b*) The strength of cement paste
   (*c*) Decrease in the porosity of concrete
   (*d*) All the above
2. The durability of concrete is due to the resistance to
   (*a*) Chemical attack
   (*b*) Deterioration from environmental conditions
   (*c*) Internal disruptive forces
   (*d*) All the above
3. High frost resistance concrete should be
   (*a*) Free from cracks
   (*b*) Dense
   (*c*) Steam cured
   (*d*) Air entrained
   (*e*) All the above
4. Concrete to be used in contact with alkaline soil or alkaline water should have
   (*a*) High w/c ratio
   (*b*) Rich mix
   (*c*) High alumina content
   (*d*) Higher % of sand
   (*e*) Low w/c ratio
5. The porosity of concrete mainly depends upon
   (*a*) Grading of Aggregate
   (*b*) Cement content
   (*c*) Quantity of mixing water
   (*d*) Degree of compaction
   (*e*) All the above
6. Identify the incorrect statement of the followings
   (*a*) The durability of concrete is independent of its compressive strength
   (*b*) The compressive strength of concrete is a measure of durability of concrete to a great extent
   (*c*) Environmental conditions also have a great influence on the durability of concrete
   (*d*) In recent time more importance is given to durability aspect of concrete
7. Identify the false statement of the followings
   (*a*) Water/cement-ratio has no effect on the durability of concrete
   (*b*) Higher w/c ratio cause higher permeability and higher volume changes in concrete
   (*c*) To produce dense and impermeable concrete lowest possible w/c ratio should be used
   (*d*) Higher w/c ratio develop cracks in concrete finally disintegrates it
8. Identify the correct statement of the followings
   (*a*) The chloride ions diffuse at much lower rate in low w/c ratio concrete than that of high w/c ratio concrete
   (*b*) There is no difference in the micro structure of concrete made with low and high w/c ratio
   (*c*) The permeability of concrete increases if made with low w/c ratio
   (*d*) Use of low w/c ratio has not been found effective in controlling the corrosion of reinforcement of concrete
9. Identify the correct statements of the followings
   (*a*) The permeability of gel pores is about 1/100 the of cement paste as a whole
   (*b*) Gel pores have no contribution in the permeability of cement paste
   (*c*) W/c ratio is the main contributing factor to the permeability of concrete
   (*d*) Voids formed at high w/c ratio do not get filled by the products of hydration of concrete
   (*e*) All are correct
10. Identify the correct and false statements of the followings

(a) Magnesium sulphate is more reactive and causes maximum damage
(b) Dry sulphates react most violently and cause greater damage
(c) The solubility of calcium sulphate in ground water is highest. hence it causes greatest damage
(d) Ammonia sulphate is present in agricultural soils and water due to the use of fertilizers and sewage and industrial effluent
(e) The extent of sulphate attack depends upon the concentration of sulphate solution and permeability of concrete
(f) In hardened concrete calcium aluminate hydrate C_3A reacts with sulphate salts from outside through pores and the volume of the product increases upto about 225% causing disintegration of concrete

11. The sulphate attack can be controlled by
(a) Use of air entrainment
(b) High pressure steam curing
(c) Use of high alumina cement
(d) Use of pozzolana
(e) Use of sulphate resistant cement
(f) All are correct

12. The reaction between the active silica constituents of aggregate and alkalis of cement is called
(a) Alkali aggregate reaction
(b) Soda equivalent
(c) Flocculated reaction
(d) Carbonation reaction

13. The alkali-aggregate reaction is affected by
(a) Porosity of the aggregate particles
(b) Alkali content of cement
(c) Fineness of cement particles
(d) Size of aggregate particles
(e) All the above

14. Alkali-aggregate reaction can be prevented by
(a) By adding finely powdered silica to the concrete mix
(b) By cutting the contact of concrete from external source of moisture
(c) By reducing the alkali content of cement to less than 0.6% expressed as Na_2o
(d) By using a mixture of ordinary portland cement and ground granulated blast slag cement
(e) All the above are correct

15. The reaction of carbon dioxide with hydrated cement is known as
(a) Corrosion
(b) Silice-Alkali reaction
(c) Carbonatic reaction
(d) Unsoundness

16. Carbonation is the reaction between
(a) Hydrated cement and hydrogen peroxide H_2O_2
(b) Hydrated cement and carbon dioxide
(c) Hydrated cement and sulpher dioxide So_2
(d) Hydrated cement and calcium hydroxide

17. The rate of carbonation depends upon
(a) Relative humidity of ambient medium
(b) Quantity of carbon dioxide
(c) Permeability of concrete
(d) Moisture content of concrete
(e) Grade of concrete
(f) All the above

18. Identify the false statement of the following
(a) The depth of carbonation of protective concrete remains constant
(b) The depth of carbonation will be more of ill cured and high w/c ratio concrete
(c) Depth of carbonation of un protective concrete is independent of time
(d) The depth of carbonation of concrete is dependent on the depth of cover

19. Identify the correct statements of the followings
(a) Chloride attack on concrete is more serious than any other cause
(b) Sulphate reaction destroys concrete where as chloride reaction destroys reinforcement
(c) The volume of corroded reinforcement increases upto 6 lines of its original volume
(d) The chloride content in cement should not be more than 0.1%
(e) All the above are correct

20. Identify the false statement of the following
(a) Deterioration of concrete in sea water is caused due to expansion of concrete

(*b*) Deterioration of concrete in sea water is caused due to erosion of concrete mass
(*c*) Deterioration of concrete in sea water is caused due to leaching some lime content
(*d*) The most severe attack on concrete in sea water takes place just above the high water level

21. Sea water effects on concrete may be minimised
(*a*) By the use of cement with low C_3A content (*b*) By the use of Pozzolanic materials
(*c*) By the use of rich mix concrete (*d*) By providing adequate cover to reinforcement
(*e*) All are correct

22. To protect reinforcement from corrosion in moderate exposure condition the main cover should be
(*a*) 80 mm (*b*) 60 mm
(*c*) 30 mm (*d*) 25 mm

23. Identify the incorrect statement(s)
(*a*) Durability of concrete is its resistance to the deteriorating influences of both internal and external agencies
(*b*) Durability of concrete is not influenced by the permeability of concrete
(*c*) The gradual deterioration of concrete by chemically aggressive agents is called corrosion of concrete
(*d*) Corrosion of steel reinforcement causes internal stresses which promote destruction of concrete
(*e*) Micro cracks present at the aggregate cement interface do not affect durability of concrete as long as they are small in size and discontinuous

24. Identify the incorrect statement
(*a*) The principal form of destruction of concrete is decomposition due to leaching action
(*b*) The principal form of destruction of concrete is the chemical reaction between hardened cement constituent of concrete and chemicals of a solution
(*c*) Grinding action of sand storm
(*d*) Increase in the volume of solid phase due to crystallization with in the pore structure
(*e*) All the above

25. The deterioration of concrete can be prevented by
(*a*) Limiting w/c ratio
(*b*) Making a dense concrete
(*c*) Ensuring sufficient alkalinity to provide passive environment against corrosion of reinforcement
(*d*) Impregnating the pores of concrete with a suitable polymer
(*e*) All the above

26. Identify the incorrect statement(s)
(*a*) The corrosion of reinforcement can be prevented by the use of corrosion reducers or coating steel or concrete
(*b*) The corrosion of reinforcement can be prevented by the proper design of concrete for the intended environmental exposure
(*c*) Increase in thickness of concrete cover to reinforcement
(*d*) By the use of stainless steel
(*e*) By impregnating the pores of concrete by suitable polymer

27. The corrosion of embedded steel reinforcement is more rapid when the concrete member is immersed in
(*a*) Alkaline solution (*b*) Acidic solution
(*c*) Water with dissolved oxygen (*d*) Sea water
(*e*) Water with-chloride ion concentration

28. To reduce the corrosion of reinforcement, the chloride ions should be limited to its critical or threshold value (% by mass of cement)
(*a*) 0.5 (*b*) 0.1
(*c*) 0.15 (*d*) 0.2
(*e*) 0.25

29. Identify the incorrect statement(s)
(*a*) Structures immersed in water permanently show little corrosion of the reinforcement
(*b*) In regions of relative humidity of 50% or less the corrosive action on reinforcement is negligible
(*c*) The distress due to corrosive action may be in the form of deep pitting and a severe loss of cross section of reinforcement

(*d*) For pre stressed concrete the total amount of chloride ions should b limited to 0.1% by mass of cement
(*e*) For R.C.C. members completely immersed in sea water additional cover of 40 mm should be provided

30. Which of the following compounds may be used as iron corrosion reducer
(*a*) Fly ash (*b*) Molases
(*c*) Calcium shlphate (*d*) Calcium and sodium chloride
(*e*) Potassium dichromate, zinc and lead chromates

31. Identify the true and false statements
(*a*) Corrosion to steel does not take place at relative humidity less than 40%
(*b*) The product of corrosion occupy volume less than 4% times the original volume of steel
(*c*) For corrosion control a calcium nitrite based admixture is most widely used
(*d*) Rust contains large quantity of chloride
(*e*) In very severe conditions of exposure the cover to reinforcement should not be less than 50 mm
(*f*) Ammonium salts can be used for deicing with advantage
(*g*) In low w/c ratio concrete chloride ions diffuse at much lower rate then high w/c ratio concrete
(*h*) There is a unique relation between air and water permeabilities for any concrete
(*i*) Gel pores contribute much to the permeability of concrete
(*j*) The permeability of cement paste is governed by w/c ratio and degree of hydration
(*k*) The solubility of calcium sulphate is maximum
(*l*) Magnesium sulphate is least reactive of all sulphates

Answers

1. (*d*)
2. (*d*)
3. (*e*)
4. (*c*)
5. (*e*)
6. (*a*)
7. (*a*)
8. (*a*)
9. (*e*)
10. [False (*b*, *c*)]
11. (*f*)
12. (*a*)
13. (*e*)
14. (*e*)
15. (*c*)
16. (*b*)
17. (*f*)
18. (*c*)
19. (*e*)
20. (*a*)
21. (*e*)
22. (*c*)
23. (*b*)
24. (*c*)
25. (*e*)
26. (*d*)
27. (*b*)
28. (*c*)
29. (*d*)
30. (*e*)
31. [False, (*b, d, f, h, i, k, l*)

18

Concreting under Extreme Environmental Conditions

18.1. INTRODUCTION

When ever concrete is to be placed under extreme weather conditions or under water its performance is affected to a great extent if appropriate measures are not taken to control these conditions. Extreme weather conditions include situations where environmental temperature during the production, and placing of concrete and subsequent curing period are markedly different from those of normal conditions *i.e.* either the temperature is too low or too high. Under these conditions the properties and performance of concrete are affected to a great extent unless appropriate precautions are taken to safe guard against these factors.

In general an increase in temperature accelerates the rate of hydration resulting in the accelerated development of strength. This accelerated hydration of cement may result in the development of less uniform gel than that could be produced under normal conditions. On the other hand the decreased temperature retards the rate of hydration and the strength development, but improves the quality of gel resulting in a more orderly and compact gel.

The decrease in humidity, or increase in wind velocity or their combination further aggrevates the situation. This may cause rapid loss of water due to evaporation affecting the workability of fresh concrete. The rapid drying of concrete may develop plastic shrinkage and cracking. Due to evaporation, cooling of concrete may develop tensile stresses in it.

18.2. HOT WEATHER CONCRETING

Actually it is difficult to define the hot weather condition. However for the sake of convenience any operation of concreting done at a atmospheric temperature above 40°C (94°F) or when the temperature of concrete at the time of placement is expected to be above 40°C is considered as hot weather concreting. Concreting at a temperature above 40°C is not recommended with out proper precautions as specified in IS 7861 Part-III 1975.

The increase in the wind velocity further enhances the effect of high ambient temperature and reduced relative humidity. These are the most important climatic factors which affect the concreting in hot weather conditions.

18.3. PROBLEMS OF HOT WEATHER CONCRETING

At the temperature above 40°C, following special problems are encountered,

1. Rapid rate of hydration of cement, quick setting and early stiffening.
2. More plastic shrinkage.
3. Rapid evaporation of mixing water.

4. Less time for finishing.
5. Absorption of water from the concrete by the form work and subgrade.
6. Difficulty in un interrupted and continuous curing.
7. Difficulty in incorporation of air entrainment.

The effect of the above factors on the quality of concrete should be fully investigated and care should be taken to produce a strong and durable concrete.

1. **Rapid rate of hydration.** We have already discussed that the rate of hydration depends upon the temperature. Higher the temperature, higher the rate of hydration. At high ambient temperature the setting time of the cement is also reduced considerably. For proper setting of cement the temperature should be in the range of 27 ± 2°C. At a higher temperature, the setting time will be reduced resulting in early stiffening of the concrete, reducing the workability of concrete. The partially set concrete will have poor bond with the successive layers more than anticipated.

   It also has been discussed earlier that the gel structure and its quality formed at higher temperature in the early period of hydration is of poor quality. Concrete placed in hot weather no doubt will develop high early strength, but its long term strength will be less as shown in Fig. 8.14. This Fig. shows the effect of curing temperature on one day and 28 days compressive strength, which reduces about 40% due to curing at higher temperature. It has been observed that an increase of 11°C temperature of concrete resulted in about 25mm decrease in its slump.
2. **More plastic shrinkage.** In hot weather conditions, the rate of evaporation of water from the surface of the concrete will be faster than the rate of movement of water from the interior body of the concrete to the surface This will cause the setting up of moisture gradient, resulting in the formation of surface cracks. These surface cracks are known as plastic shrinkage cracks. The plastic shrinkage cracks are more pronounced where the exposed surface area is more than the depth of the concrete layer as in the case of roads, floors and pavement etc.
3. **Rapid evaporation of mixing water.** The hot weather condition normally is associated with the lower relative humidity. Due to the lower relative humidity, the water mixed in the concrete for the required workability will be lost soon turning the concrete unworkable. To compact such a concrete fully, enormous amount of compacting energy will be required. If it is not done, large voids will remain in the concrete, reducing it a very poor quality concrete, having all ill effects.
4. **Less finishing time.** In hot weather conditions, the finishing of the concrete must be done as early as possible after placing it in position. If it is not done due to quicker evaporation of water and faster stiffening, the quality of finishing will be of poor standard. Usually for finishing in such conditions extra fresh mortar has to be applied, resulting in poor performance of the concrete.
5. **Absorption of water by subgrade and form work.** In hot weather regions usually the subgrade is dry and absorptive. Thus the subgrade or the surface of form work has to be wetted before placing the concrete. If it is not done properly, the water will be absorbed by the subgrade and form work, leaving less water for proper hydration of cement. The concrete in contact with the subgrade and form work will be formed of poor quality. Thus the contact zone of concrete will be of poorer quality.
6. **Difficulty in curing.** In hot weather concreting early curing becomes necessary particularly if 53 grade cement is used. Hot weather needs a continuous curing. If there is any discontinuity in the curing, the concrete surface will dry up fast, resulting interruption in the continuous hydration. Once the interruption in curing takes place, the subsequent wetting will not contribute to the development of full strength. Continuous curing in hot weather costs more due to the high cost of water and labour.
7. **Difficulty in air entrainment.** Usually air entrained concrete is not used in hot-weather conditions. However, if used for better workability, the proportion of air entraining agent will be required more to compensate the loss of air entrainment due to higher temperature. The normal set

for standard temperature in respect of percent air entrainment do not apply for hot weather conditions.

8. **Conveyance of Concrete.** Conveyance of ready made concrete over a long distance is likely to pose a serious problem due to faster loss of slump. In such situations the transit mixer drum may be covered with insulating material.
9. **Use of curing compounds.** In hot weather concreting the use of curing compounds has not been found satisfactory as it leads to lower strengths than continuous water cured concrete strength. The reduction in strength is of the order of 30%.

18.4. REDUCTION IN RELATIVE HUMIDITY

The reduction in relative humidity has a marked influence on the strength of the concrete. It has been observed that specimens moulded and cured in air at 23°C and 60% relative humidity developed 73% strength of the specimens moist cured at 23°C for 28 days. The specimens moulded and cured in air at 38°C and 25% relative humidity attained only 62% strength of the moist cured specimens at 23°C for 28 days. The reduction of 35% in relatives humidity has been found to decrease the strengthly by about 11%.

Thus due to these difficulties concreting in important structures be stopped during hot periods. The temperature of concrete delivered at site in hot weather should be as low as possible at about 16°C (60°F). The upper limit of 29°C (85°F) should never be crossed.

18.5. TEMPERATURE OF FRESH CONCRETE

The temperature 'T' of freshly mixed concrete can be calculated easily from the temperatures of ingredients by the following relation.

$$T = \frac{0.22\,(T_a\,w_a + T_c\,w_e) + T_w\,w_w}{0.22\,(w_a + w_e) + w_w} \qquad \ldots(18.1)$$

where,

T_a = temperature of aggregate

T_c = temperature of cement

T_w = temperature of water

W_a = weight of aggregate

W_e = weight of cement

W_w = weight of water

The actual temperature of the concrete how ever has been found some what higher than given by the above relation (18.1) due to the mechanical work done in mixing and due to heat of wetting and hydration of cement etc. Experimentally it has been found that for a mix having aggregate/cement ratio of 5.6 and water/cement ratio as 0.5, a drop of 1°C or 1°F in the temperature of freshly mixed concrete can be obtained by lowering the temperature either of cement by 9°C (9°F) or of water by 3.6°C (3.6°F) or of aggregate by 1.6°C (1.6°F) respectively. The quantity of cement in a given mix being small, its temperature is not important. Though the use of hot cement is not detrimental to the strength, but cement at temperature about 75°C (170°F) should not be used. (The specific heat of common aggregate is 0.22, while that of water is 1.0 *i.e.* the specific heat of water is five times that of aggregate. Due this reason term 0.22 has been used in relation (18.1). Hence it is much easier to cool water than cement or aggregate.

18.6. RECOMMENDED PRACTICE AND PRECAUTIONS OF CONCRETING IN HOT WEATHER

To improve the quality of concrete, it is necessary that the temperature of the freshly mixed concrete should be as low as possible. It can be obtained by keeping the temperature of its ingredients as low as possible.

18.6.1. Aggregates

The temperature of aggregates can be minimised by adopting the following measures.

1. The aggregates should be stockpiled in shade.
2. The temperature of aggregates can be lowered by sprinkling water over them in stock pille. The evaporation of sprinkling water will cool the aggregates.
3. If possible aggregates may be cooled by spraying of cold air over them just before the batching.

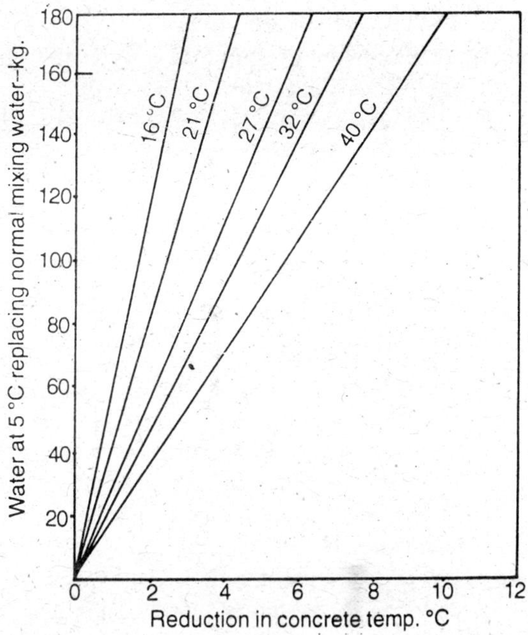

Fig. 18.1. Effect of cooled mixed water on concrete temperature

18.6.2. Mixing water

The temperature of the mixing water has the greatest effect on the temperature of the concrete as its specific heat is 1.0 while that of aggregate is 0.22 *i.e.* the specific heat of water is 5 times more that of aggregate. In practice it is easier to control the temperature of mixing water than other ingredients. The weight of water used in concrete is lesser than other ingredients.

18.6.3. Methods of lowering water temperature

The temperature of water may be lowered by the following methods.

1. The temperature of mixing water may be lowered by insulating or shading pipe line and tanks.
2. Use of cold mixing water will result in the good reduction of concrete temperature. As per IS 7861-1971, the effect of cold water at 5°C on the concrete temperature has been shown in Fig. 18.1.
3. If the ambient temperature is very high, the use of cold water will not be fully effective. In such situations ice may be used as a part of mixing water. Crushed ice may be put directly into the mixer. It should be ensured that ice is completely melted by the time mixing is complete. Fig. 18.2 shows the possible reduction of concrete temperature by the substitution of ice as part of mixing water.

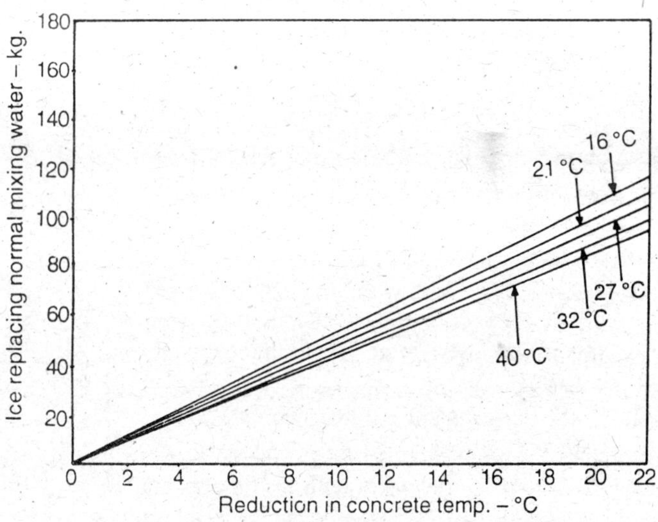

Fig. 18.2. Effect of ice in mixing water on concrete temperature

18.6.4. Production and Conveyance

1. To keep the temperature of concrete below 40°C at the time of placement, the temperature of aggregates, water and cement should be maintained as low as possible. At some locations

maximum placement temperature should be much lower than 40°C.

2. The required mixing time of concrete in hot weather should be minimum.
3. To reduce the length of delivery to the minimum, the concrete mixer must be positioned as near to the place of deposition as possible.
4. Cold water should be sprinked on subgrade, form work and reinforcement etc. before placing the concrete. The reinforcement projecting out of the concrete should be kept cool by any practical means or covered.
5. To reduce the time interval between successive layers or lifts, concrete should be placed comparatively in thin layers. However the thickness of concrete layer should not be so thin as to get dried up very soon.
6. After finishing the concrete surface it should be covered effectively to prevent the loss of moisture from the concrete.
7. Rapid hardening and drying of fresh concrete can be checked by protecting it from direct sun rays. In such situations, work should be started in the afternoon, so that the hydration of plastic concrete may take place during relatively cooler night. The temperature record of air, the concrete coming out from the mixer, the concrete placed and the temperature of the concrete during the early period of hydration should be maintained. It will help to regulate the temperature for future concreting. The concrete surface should not be allowed to become dry and at the same time water should not be applied before the final setting of concrete. The best practice is to cover the concrete with moist covering for 24 hours and then apply water by spray or ponding.
8. For curing, covering the top surface with gunny bags, or hessian cloth or with wet burlap is desirable. The gunny bags should be squeezed fully, so that water does not drip on the fresh concrete. Covering of finished floors with wet gunny bags may not be suitable, for flooring whose finishing is of primary importance. In such cases the use of moisture retaining materials has been found better as it has a definite cooling effect.
9. Wet-curing must commenced at the earliest possible time. If the concrete is effectively moist covered, the ponding may be commenced after 24 hours in case of floor, roof or pavements. Curing by ponding has been found better than covering with burlap, gunny bags as shown in Fig. 12.1. Sprinkling of water should not be applied till the concrete has set fully.
10. Surface sealing compounds should not be used as they loose some of their efficiency in hot weather. If they are to be used, they should be used after 24 hours of water curing.
11. Black surfaces should be white washed to reduce their heat absorbing capacity.
12. In massive structures such as dams, the temperature of hardened concrete can be controlled by circulating cold water or brine through copper pipes embedded in concrete at the pre determined distances or 1 m distance at the time of placing concrete.

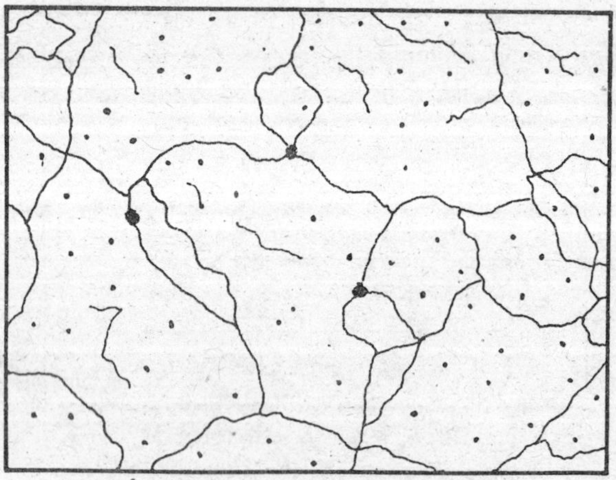

Cracks on concrete surface due to inadequate curing
Fig. 18.3. Cracks due to evaporation of moisture

13. Due to evaporation of water cracks will be developed on the surface of concrete as shown in Fig. 18.3.

18.6.5. Proportioning of Concrete mix

The mix should be so designed that it may contain minimum content of cement consistent with other functional requirements. As far a possible in hot weather concreting, cement of lower heat of hydration should be preferred to those having greater fineness and greater heat of hydration. In hot weather concreting use of water reducing or set retarding admixtures has been found useful. However accelerators should not be used.

18.7. PLACEMENT OF LARGE CONCRETE MASSES

When large volumes of plain (un reinforced) concrete is placed in position such as in gravity dams or spillways, the concrete is known as mass concrete. In mass concrete there is always a danger of thermal cracking due to restraint to contraction of concrete on cooling from a high temperature caused by the heat of hydration of cement. Such a cracking may take several weeks to develop. On the other hand there is a danger of early age thermal cracking in thinner sections, unless appropriately reinforced.

Thermal cracking takes place due to the variation in temperature. It should be clearly distinguished from plastic cracking. The plastic cracking occurs on or near the surface of concrete due to rapid evaporation of water from the concrete while it is still in a plastic state Fig. 18.3. Drying of concrete can also cause shrinkage cracking which normally takes place at a later stage than thermal cracking. The different types of cracking are discussed separately in chapter 26.

When a concrete mass is not insulated from the atmosphere, a temperature gradient exists with in the concrete due to the fact that its interior becomes hot due to the rise in temperature by the evaluation of heat of hydration, whilst the surface loses heat to the surrounding atmosphere. If the difference in temperature between the interior and the exterier is large enough, cracking will develop. During the period of rise in

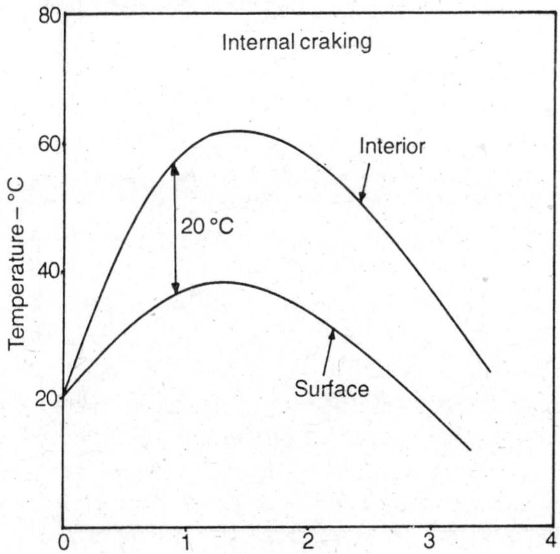

Fig. 18.4. Pattern of temperature change causing internal cracking

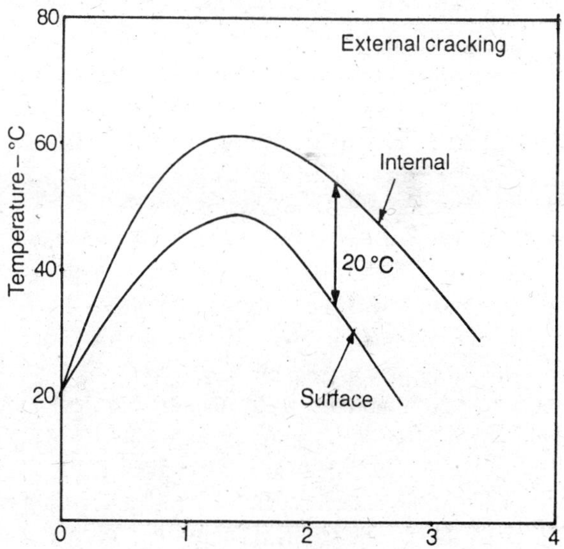

Fig. 18.5. Pattern of temperature change causing external cracking

temperature the cracks will develop in interior portion, as shown in Fig. 18.4 while in the course of cooling cracking will develop on surface as shown in Fig. 18.5. The cracking will develop if the temperature difference is more than 20°C. Cracks may also develop if concrete is placed against a cold surface. The interior is thus restrained from full thermal expansion and compressive stress is developed in the interior, which is balanced by tensile stress in the exterior. Though both stresses are relieved to some extent by the creep, but the tensile stress still may be sufficient to cause surface cracking. As the concrete starts cooling it contracts, the tensile stress in the exterior is relieved and if any surface crack closes, it renders the concrete harmless.

Since the interior wants to contract more than the exterior, the strain in the interior is restrained and tensile stress is developed, with a balancing compressive stress in the exterior. During this cooling phase, there is less relief of stress by creep than in the heating phase as the concrete is more mature. Thus the induced tensile stress caused by internal restraint on cooling may be large enough to cause cracking in the interior of concrete mass. Thus if cracking in concrete is to be avoided, the temperature differential or temperature gradient should be limited. According to Gibbon, limit to gradient should be about 20°C when gravel aggregate is used.

On the other hand if the entire mass of concrete is insulated from the out side air or earth so that the temperature is uniform through out. In this case cracking will take place only if the total mass is wholly or partly externally restrained from contracting during the cooling period. This form of restrained is known as *external restraint.* Thus to avoid cracking of concrete it is necessary to minimize the difference between the peak temperature of the concrete and the ambient temperature or to minimize the restraint. The tolerable temperature defferential or temperature gradient between the peak temperature and the final ambient temperature depends upon the type of aggregate used in concrete. if gravel aggregate is used, then tolerable temperature gradient should not be more than 20°C (36°F). In case certain lime stone aggregates are used, then it may be taken upto 40°C (72°F). In case light weight aggregates are used then it can be as high as 130°C (234°F).

18.8. MEASURES TO MINIMIZE THE TEMPERATURE DIFFERENCE OR GRADIENT

Several measures can be taken to minimize the temperature gradient as follows:

1. Cooling of the mix ingredients by any method given on page 356-57 so as to reduce the temperature of the fresh concrete to about 7°C (45°F). By this measure the difference between the peak temperature and ambient temperature on cooling will be reduced.
2. Cooling the surface of the concrete, but only for those sections whose thickness is less than 50 cm. For such sections steel form work may be used which offers little insulation. Thus cooling of the concrete surface reduces the temperature rise of the core without causing harmful temperature gradient inducing internal restraint.
3. Insulating of the entire surface of the concrete more than 50 cms in thickness including the upper surface. This can be achieved by using a suitable material for form work. In this way the temperature gradient may be minimized. Now the concrete will be allowed to expand and contract freely, provided there is no external restraint.
4. Selecting mix ingredients carefully.

The choice of the mix ingredients partly is dependent upon other factors also which influence cracking besides the temperature. A suitable aggregate can help to reduce the coefficient of thermal expansion of concrete and increase its tensile strain capacity. For example, concrete made with angular aggregate has a greater tensile strain capacity than concrete made with rounded aggregate. Similarly light weight aggregate leads to a greater tensile strain capacity than normal weight aggregate. However this advantage is reduced to some extent by the higher requirements of cement content when light weight aggregate is used for the same strength and workability.

The use of low heat cement, pozzolanic cement, part replacement of cement by pozzolanic materials, use of low cement content and of water reducing admixtures have been found beneficial in reducing the peak temperature. The choice of the type of cement is governed by the heat evolution characteristics which affect the temperature rise *i.e.* rate at which the heat is evolved and the total heat generated. The total heat generated is greater for higher cement content per unit volume of concrete. In small sections, the rate of heat evolution is more important with regard to temperature rise as the heat is dissipated steadily, where as in massive sections the temperature is more dependent on the total heat evolved due to greater self insulation.

Thus the temperature rise in concrete depends on a number of factors such as type and quantity of cement, size of the section, the insulating characteristics of the form work, and the placing temperature of the concrete, With respect to placing temperature of concrete it can be seen that higher the placing temperature, the faster the hydration of the cement and greater the rise of temperature.

In practice the lowest temperature rise may be obtained by blending the cement suitability. The best blending combinations of cements are given below in order of best performance.

1. Blend of sulphate resistant cement and ground granulated blast furnance slag cement.
2. Ordinary portland cement and slag cement.
3. Part replacement of portland cement by fly ash.

In case of massive sections, the quantity of cementitious materials *i.e.* cement plus slag or fly ash is governed more by impermeability and durability requirements (max. water/cement ratio) than by a specified 28 days compressive strength, which should not exceed 14 MPa (140 kg/cm^2). However in structural reinforced concrete, a higher early strength may be critical so that ordinary portland cement alone in larger quantities have to be used. Thus it is necessary to adopt alternative measures to minimise the ill effects of temperature rise.

The temperature rise may be controlled by measuring the temperature at several points by thermocouples. The insulation must control the loss of heat by evaporation, as well as by conduction and radiation. To control the heat loss by evaporation a plastic membrane or curing compound may be used, while the use of soft boards will insulate against the conduction and radiation loss. Plastic coated quilts have been found useful in all respects.

For minimizing the temperature gradient or temperature differential, the time of form work striking or removal is very important. For thin sections *i.e.* sections less than 50 cms in thickness, the early removal of form work is useful as it will allow the concrete surface to cool more rapidly. How ever for massive and isolated sections the insulation *i.e.* from work should remain in position till the whole section has cooled sufficiently, so that when the form work is removed finally, the drop in temperature does not exceed more than 10°C (50°F) for concrete made with flint gravel aggregate.

The reason for the lower values of tolerable gradient is that when the insulation is removed, the cooling of concrete surface is more rapid and the creep can not help in increasing the tensile strain capacity of the concrete. For this reason, the form work and insulation of large sections may have to remain in position for upto at least two weeks, before the concrete has cooled to a safe level of temperature. In case the section is subjected to external restraint, this measure will not be helpful in preventing the cracking of the concrete and other remedial measures have to be adopted.

Example 1. *Calculate the temperature of the fresh concrete from the following data neglecting the aggregate moisture.*

1. *Mix proportion* = *1:1.8:4.5*
2. *Water cement ratio* = *0.6*
3. *Cement content* = *300 kg/m^3*
4. *Temp. of cement* = *18°C*
5. *Temp. of water* = *20°C*
6. *Temp. of aggregate* = *30°C*

Solutions. From the given data,

Weight of cement = 300 kg/m^3

Weight of fine aggregate = 300 (1.8) = 540 kg

Weight of coarse aggregate = $300 \times 4.5 = 1350$ kg

Weight of water = $300 \times 0.6 = 180$ kg

∴ Let the temperature of resultant fresh concrete = T°C

(*a*) Temp. of water (given) = 20°C

(*b*) Temp. of cement = 18°C

(*c*) Temp. of aggregate = 30°C

∴ From equation 18.1

$$T = \frac{0.22\,(T_a\,w_a + T_c\,w_c) + T_w\,w_w}{0.22\,(w_a + w_c) + w_w}$$

$$= \frac{0.22\,(30 \times 1890 + 18 \times 300) + 20 \times 180}{0.22\,(1890 + 300) + 180}$$

$$= \frac{0.22\,(56700 + 5400) + 3600}{0.22\,(2190) + 180}$$

$$= \frac{0.22 \times 62100 + 3600}{481.8 + 180} = \frac{13662 + 3600}{661.8}$$

$$= \frac{17262}{6618} = \textbf{26.1°C Ans.}$$

Example 2. *For the concrete used in example 1, how much ice is required to reduce the temperature of the fresh concrete to 16°C. If the water/cement is to remain same, find also the amount of liquid water to be added to the concrete.*

Solution. If ice is added to the concrete then the equations 18.1

reduces to $$T = \frac{0.22\,(T_a\,w_a + T_c\,w_c) + T_w\,w_w - L\,w_i}{0.22\,(w_a + w_c) + w_w + w_i} \quad ...(18.2)$$

where L = ratio of latent heat of fusion of ice to the specific heat of water. It is taken equivalent to 80°C (144°F)

w_i = weight of ice

Here the temperature of fresh concrete is given as 16°C

then $$16 = \frac{0.22 \times (30 \times 1890 + 18\,(300) + 20\,(180 - w_i) - 80\,w_i}{481.8 + (180 - w_i) + w_i}$$

or $$16 = \frac{13662 + 3600 - 20\,w_i - 80\,w_i}{481.8 + 180 - w_i + w_i}$$

∴ $$= \frac{17262 - 100\,w_i}{481.8 + 180} = \frac{17262 - 100\,w_i}{661.8}$$

∴ $$16 = \frac{17262 - 100\,w_i}{661.8}$$

or $16 \times 661.8 = 17262 - 100\,w_i$

or $10588.8 - 17262 - 100\,w_i = 0$

or $-100\,w_i = -17262 + 10589.0$

$-100\,w_i = -6673$

or $w_i = 66.73 \text{ kg} \approx 67 \text{ kg}$

Thus ice = 67 kg

Water = 180 − 67 = **113 kg Ans.**

18.9. COLD WEATHER CONCRETING

Any concreting operation under taken at a temperature below 5°C is called cold weather concreting. Many codes do not advocate concreting operations at an atmospheric temperature below 5°C with out adopting special precautions. In India such areas are very small compared to fair weather regions. The production of concrete in cold weather presents peculiar problems such as delay in setting and hardening, damage to concrete in plastic stage when exposed to below freezing point due to the formation of ice crystals or lenses. Therefore it is essential that concrete temperature is maintained above 5°C, if possible at much higher temperature.

18.9.1. Effects of cold weather on concrete

(*a*) **Delay in setting and hardening.** As already discussed the rate of hydration of cement depends upon the temperature. If the temperature is low, concrete takes a long time to set and a longer time to harden. Thus the development of strength is very slow. The delay in setting time makes the concrete prone to frost attack and other disturbances. The delay in hardening period causes delay in the removal of form work, resulting in the slow rate of progress of the work. All these factors affect the economy of the work. Fig. 18.6 shows the effect of ambient temperature on setting time of concrete.

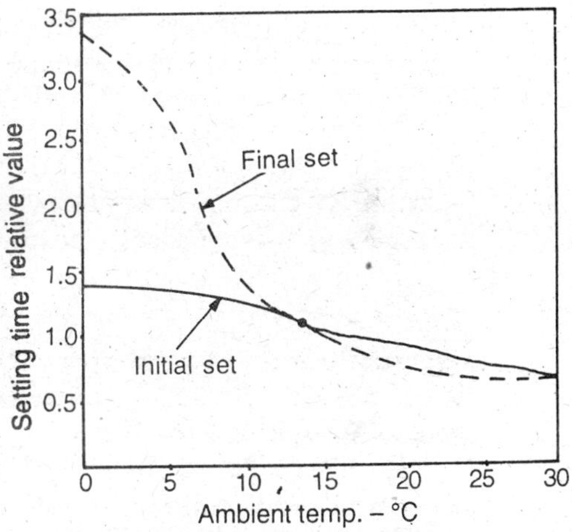

Fig. 18.6. Effect of ambient temperature on setting of concrete

(*b*) **Freezing of concrete at early age.** If the temperature falls down to below freezing point, the free water in the plastic concrete freezes. Freezing of water not only slow down or prevent the hydration of cement but also causes expansion in the concrete. Water on freezing expands in its volume causing expansion in the concrete. This expansion causes disruption, resulting irreparable loss in strength and quality of concrete.

(*c*) **Freezing and thawing.** In the cold weather regions, the fresh or hardened concrete may be subjected to freezing and thawing cycles due to varied climatic conditions. This alternate cycle of freezing and thawing adversely affects the durability of concrete and also exerts fatigue in the concrete.

18.10. CONDITIONS IN COLD WEATHER CONCRETING

In cold weather concreting following conditions may arise:

1. Low but above 0°C temperature at the time of concreting and hardening period.
2. Low temperature a the time of concreting, but below 0°C during hardening period.
3. Below 0°C temperature at the time of concreting and during hardening period.
4. Hardened concrete is subjected to alternate freezing and thawing.

To under stand the behaviour of concrete well and to take suitable action to neutralize the effects of such condition for the successful placing of concrete, it is necessary to deal effectively with the above four conditions.

1. Low temperature but above 0°C. We know that the strength of concrete is a function of time and temperature. From maturity concept, Maturity = Σ time × temperature. The low temperature, but always above freezing degree, develops no other bad effect in the concrete, except retarding the rate of hydration *i.e.* development of strength. Low temperature has no bad effect neither on fresh concrete nor on hardened concrete, but produces a high quality gel structure. It has been observed that the ultimate strength of concrete cured at 9°C (48°F) developed higher strength than that of the concrete cured at higher temperature. This may be due to the superiority of the gel structure on account of slow hydration. In this case no other precautions are necessary. It has only one draw back, that is the form work has to be removed after a long period due to the slow development of strength for stripping the form work. Thus putting the structure into service is delayed.

2. Temperature at the time of concreting low but below 0°C after concreting. In this situation following two cases may arise

(*a*) Temperature falls below 0°C when the concrete is still green.

(*b*) Temperature falls below 0°C after the concrete has attained sufficient strength or sufficiently hardened.

(*a*) It might have happened that at the time of mixing and placing the concrete, the ambient temperature was above freezing point, but the ambient and concrete temperature fell below freezing point before the concrete has attained sufficient strength. In such situations the free water still available in the concrete will freeze forming ice crystals in voids of the concrete. These ice crystals formed in the capillary cavities may cause capillary suction of water from the ground if it is saturated and become bigger. These ice crystals exert great pressure on the concrete and disintegrate it. Ice formation may also take place in the contact surface of aggregate and cement paste. After thawing these ice crystals will melt forming cavities. Thus the freezing of fresh concrete seriously damages the structural integrity of concrete and results in considerable loss of strength. In extreme cases it may result in forming a useless mass of concrete. Fig. 18.7 shows the increase in volume of concrete during prolonged freezing as a function of age when freezing starts. Maximum expansion takes place during 1st four hours. The decrease in the magnitude of expansion of concrete allowed to harden for about 24 hours is clearly seen. During this period concrete should be protected from frost.

The resistance to alternate freezing and thawing also depends on the age of the concrete when the first cycle of freezing and thawing occurred to the concrete. Fig. 18.8 shows the increase in volume with the number of cycles of freezing at different ages. This type of exposure has been found more severe than prolonged freezing with periods of thaw. Several such cycles can cause damage even to concrete cured at 20°C for 24 hours. However there is no direct relation between the frost resistance of young concrete and durability of mature concrete subjected to many cycles of freezing and thawing.

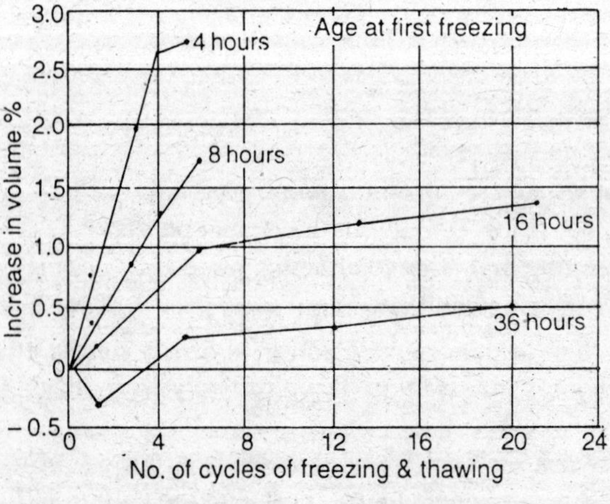

Fig. 18.7. Increase in vol. due to prolonged freezing

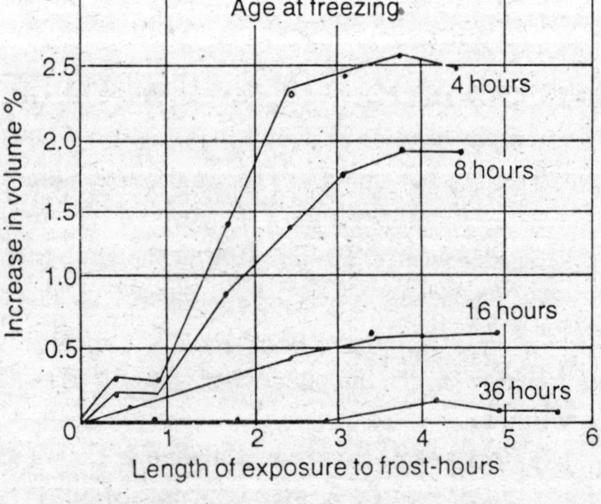

Fig. 18.8. Increase in vol. of concrete due to alternate freezing and thawing

(*b*) If the freezing takes place after the concrete has hardened sufficiently, there will not be much harm to the structural integrity of the concrete. At this stage, water mixed for making the concrete would have been lost either being used up in the hydration process or lost by evaporation. Due to the formation of cement gel, the capillary cavities of the concrete would have been reduced to a great extent. Thus very little free water would be available in the body of the concrete to freeze and damage the concrete. Therefore there is no immediate danger to the concrete.

(*c*) Temperature below 0°C at the time of concreting and during hardening period. While concreting when the temperature is below 0°C, certain precautions should be taken so that concrete does not get frozen.

18.11. MEASURES TO BE TAKEN TO AVOID FREEZING OF CONCRETE

Following measures suggested by IS 7861-Part-II 1981 should be adopted.

1. Preservation and utilization of heat of hydration

During the process of cement hydration, enormous amount of heat is generated. If this heat is preserved with in the body of the concrete for a duration equal to pre hardening period, it can offset the harmful effect of low temperature. The time interval after placing the concrete till it attains a certain amount of strength is known as *pre hardening period.* This period is shown in Table 18.1.

To conserve the heat, the concrete can be insulated by a membrane, saw dust, burlap or Hession cloth. In beams and columns the form work should not be stripped till the concrete has attained sufficient strength. Strength from 5 MPa to 14 MPa has been suggested but there is no reliable data available on the strength at which concrete can successfully resist temperature below freezing point. An alternative approach is to consider the minimum age of concrete stored at a given temperature when the exposure to frost will not cause damage (Table 18.1). In case of very low temperature the insulation of concrete should be efficient enough so that the surface temperature of concrete remains much higher than 0°C during the pre hardening period.

Table 18.1. Age of concrete at which exposure to frost does not damage the concrete

Type of Cement	*Water/Cement ratio*	*Age in hours at exposure when preceding curing temperature was*			
		5°C (41°F)	*10°C (50°F)*	*15°C (59°F)*	*20°C (68°F)*
Ordinary Portland Cement	0.4	35	25	15	12
	0.5	50	35	25	17
	0.6	70	45	35	25
Rapid hardening Portland cement	0.4	20	15	10	7
	0.5	30	20	15	10
	0.6	40	30	20	15

Table 18.2. Pre hardening period as per IS 7861 II-1979

Specified minimum strength at 28 days for ordinary portland cement MPa	*Requisite Prehardening period*			
	At any concrete temperature above freezing in units of maturity (°C hours)	*At stated concrete temperature in hours*		
		5°C (41°F)	*10°C (50°F)*	*20°C (68°F)*
M_{20}	1050	70	53	35
M_{25}	780	52	39	26
M_{30}	660	44	33	22
M_{40}	480	32	24	16

2. Selection of suitable type of cement

Certain type of cement hydrates fast producing much larger quantity of heat and developing early strength. Such cements contain higher percentage of tri calcium silicate (C_3S) and tri calcium aluminate (C_3A) and comparatively lower percentage of dicalcium silicate (C_2S). The prehardening period for such cement is about 40 to 50% of the normal portland cement. For low temperature concreting rapid hardening cement, and extra rapid hardening cements can be used. High alumina cement or mixture of portland and high alumina cement in certain proportions can also be used.

3. Pre heating of concrete ingredients (Materials)

Pre heating of the ingredients of concrete, is one of the very common methods employed to raise the temperature of the concrete at the time of casting in sub zero temperature concreting.

1. Heating of water. Heating of water is the easiest to be adopted. If the ambient temperature is not very low, heating of water alone will be sufficient in case cement and aggregates are not in frozen condition. While using hot water, it should be remembered that the temperature of the water should not exceed 60°C to 80°C (140°F to 180°F). Usually water should not be heated above 65°C (149 to 150°F) as

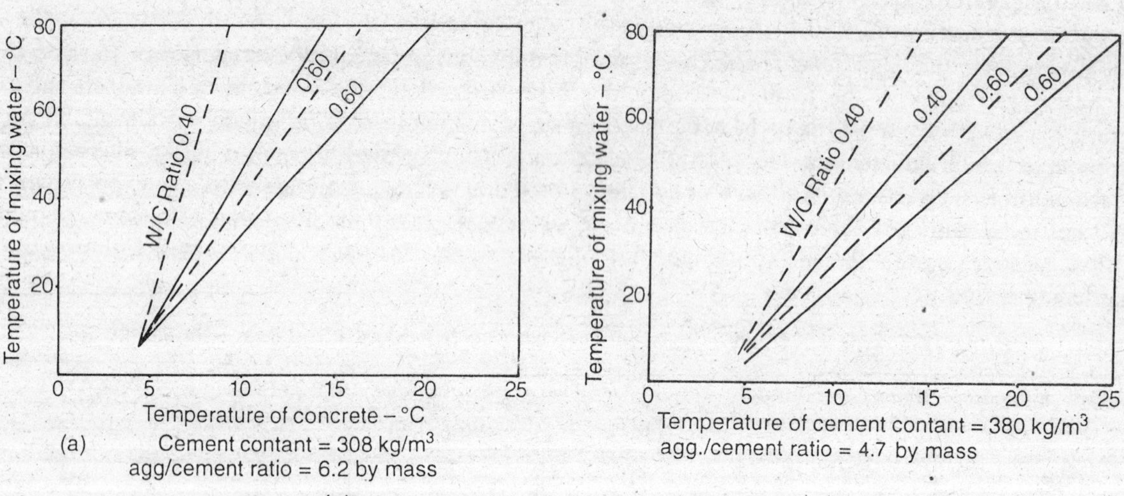

(*a*) (*b*)

Fig. 18.9. Required temp of mixing water to produce heated concrete

the flash set of cement will take place when hot water comes in contact with cement in the mixer. Therefore heated water should come in direct contact with the aggregate first and not the cement.

The Figs. 18.9 (*a*), (*b*) & (*c*) show the temperature to which the water should be heated to maintain the temperature of the resultant concrete for different aggregate/cement ratio and cement content. It will be seen from these Figs. that heating of water alone is sufficient, provided the aggregate is free from ice and the form work and top surface of concrete is properly insulated. In situations where the temperature is very low or good amount of heat is likely to be lost during transportation and placing, heating of water alone will

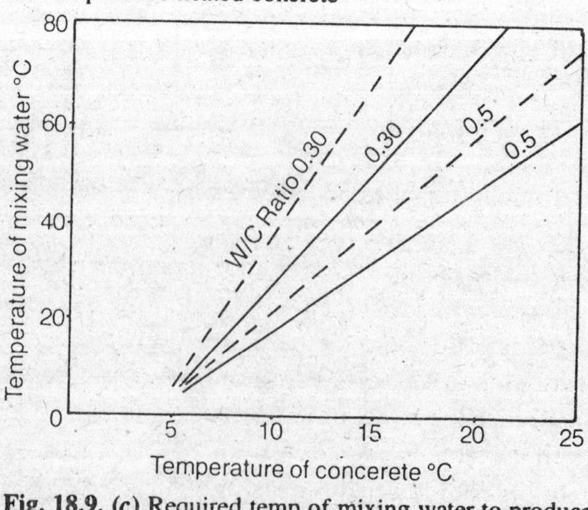

Fig. 18.9. (*c*) Required temp of mixing water to produce heated concrete

be inadequate to maintain the required temperature of the concrete. In such cases heating of aggregate also becomes necessary.

4. Aggregate Heating

Aggregate should never be heated directly as it will break during heating forming small pieces of coarse aggregate and disturbing its grading. The heating of aggregate preferably be done by passing steam through coils embedded under the stock piles. Heating of aggregate may also be done by injecting live steam into the stock piles or by hot air blowers, but these methods lead to a variable moisture content of the aggregate. Fine aggregate may also be heated on hot plates. Over heating of aggregate should be avoided. The aggregate should not be heated above 52°C (125°F).

5. Cement Heating

Cement should never be heated.

The temperature of mix ingredients must be controlled. In order to make sure that setting of concrete does not take place at too high a temperature, the temperature of the resulting concrete should be calculated in advance by equation 18.1 page 365. The temperature of resulting concrete should remain between 10°C (50°F) to 20°C (68°F) and during the period of 3 days after placement of concrete the temperature should not fall below about 10°C (50°F). However temperature upto 20°C to 21°C (68 to 70°F) and a longer period of controlled temperature is preferable. The curing period required before the concrete is exposed to frost is shown in Table 18.1. This period may also be calculated from Maturity equation given on page 363 The effects of high temperature during setting are discussed in chapter 12 on curing.

The pre hardening temperature of concrete may be maintained by electrical heating where ever economically feasible. For this purpose only low alternating current should be used. The evaporation of mixing water has to be restricted by covering the entire surface area effectively with vapour tight memberane.

The heating of concrete should be such that no part of it is heated excessively and the concrete does not dry out rapidly. Also no high concentration of carbon dioxide Co_2 in the atmosphere should take place. For these reasons the exhaust steam heating is the best.

In spite of all these precautions, the strength of electrical heated concrete is found about 80% of the normally cured concrete due to stresses developed during cooling of the heated concrete. Electrical heating is disadvantageous due to the high cost of installation, power consumption and loss of strength. However in Russia, Japan and Sweden electrical curing has been used quite extensively for protecting concrete from frost.

6. Use of accelerating admixtures

In cold weather concreting the use of accelerating admixtures has been widely adopted, which incidentally work as antifreezer. The most commonly used material is calcium chloride ($CaCl_2$). Some researchers do not permit the use of calcium chloride $CaCl_2$ more than 3.0% of the weight of cement due to developing of flash set and loss of long term strength. On the other hand others do not find any harm in the use of much higher quantity of calcium chloride where the temperature is very low.

However the use of calcium chloride may cause some increase in volume change, greater alkali aggregate reaction and lower resistance to sulphate attack.

It is reported that in Russia, Calcium, and sodium chlorides and potassium have been widely used for concreting at sub zero temperature. They have tried $CaCl_2$ as high as 20% by weight of mixing water in the construction of Gorky-Hydro Power Project. Russian practice is to use the combination of $CaCl_2$ and NaCl to neutralize the effect of temperature and also to give maximum benefits to the concrete at the plastic stage as well as hardened stage.

In order to lower the freezing point of the mixing water and to develop some strength, potash (K_2Co_3) has been tried in Russia. As potash accelerates setting of concrete, a retarder also has been used along with it. It is also has been reported that the use of potash neither adversely affects bond with steel nor it encourages corrosion of steel. Thus the use of potash in winter concreting has good potential.

Generally it is believed that the use of sodium chloride NaCl reduces the 28 days strength of concrete by 12%, though it accelerates the early strength. Therefore it has never been accepted as one of the standard accelerating agent.

All methods of winter concreting are based on maintaining positive temperature during the early age of concrete, till it develops strength which is not adversely affected by the freezing temperature.

The addition of $CaCl_2$ and NaCl regulate the freezing point of water in concrete and help to promote the continued hydration. $CaCl_2$ makes C_3A more active for accelerating the hydration. If NaCl alone is used more or less same condition will result as with $CaCl_2$ except that NaCl exhibits a better plasticizing properties. In case a combination of $CaCl_2$ and NaCl is used the concrete is found to develop quicker hardening property, much higher frost resistance property and also placeability characteristics. The suggested quanties of the salt mixture is shown in Table 18.3 below.

Table 18.3. Addition of the approximate quantity of NaCl and $CaCl_2$ in winter concreting

Open air temperature	*% contents of salts per degree fall of temp. by weight of mixing water*	*Quantity of NaCl and $CaCl_2$ by weight of mixing water*
From – 0°C to – 5°C	1.3	3% $caCl_2$ + 3.5 NaCl or 6.5% NaCl or 6.8 $CaCl_2$
From – 6°C to – 10°C	1.2	4% $CaCl_2$ + 8% NaCl or 12% NaCl or 6% $CaCl_2$ + 6% NaCl
From – 11°C to – 15°C	1.1	10% $CaCl_2$ + 6% NaCl or 8% $CaCl_2$ + 8% NaCl
From – 16°C to – 20°C	1.0	15% $CaCl_2$ + 5 NaCl or 10% $CaCl_2$ + 10 NaCl

It has been observed that if the concrete is well compacted, addition even of large quantity of salts result in very little corrosion of reinforcement. The corrosion problem becomes serious in the case of insufficient compaction and lack of cover to the reinforcing steel.

7. Use of air entrainment

Till recently it was considered that the durability of concrete depends only upon the compressive strength of concrete. But now it has been shown that even a weak concrete with air entrainment is more durable under freezing conditions than that of strong concrete with out air entrainment. The superiority of air entrained concrete over plain concrete is shown in Fig. 18.10.

Fig. 18.10 illustrates the influence of the w/c ratio on the frost resistance of concrete moist cured for 28 days. The quantity of entrained air of about 5% is sufficient. Generally it is observed that cement paste contains about 9% voids. Thus the thickness of cement paste between air bubbles should not be more than 0.25 mm. Fig. 18.11 illustrates the effect of w/c ratio on the frost resistance of

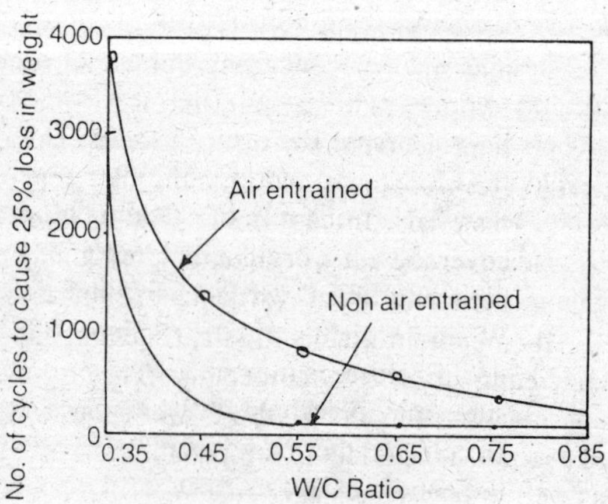

Fig. 18.10. Influence of w/c ratio on frost resistance of concrete

concrete moist cured for 14 days and then stored in air at 50% relative humidity for 76 days before exposure to freezing and thawing. In general it can be said that air entrainment increases the durability of concrete to the extent of about 3 to 7 times that of ordinary concrete.

8. Use of light weight aggregate in Cold weather concreting

In cold weather concreting light weight aggregate is advantageous as the light weight aggregate concrete has a lower thermal conductivity than normal concrete and thus acts as a self insulator. Light weight aggregate concrete has a low specific heat. Thus the heat of hydration of cement keeps this concrete more effectively against freezing than the normal weight aggregate concrete.

9. Reduction in water/cement ratio

The increase in cement content may generate more heat of hydration, resulting higher strength in concrete. Also by the use of air entrainment the water-cement ratio may be reduced which will produce greater resistance to freezing and thawing action. Thus it can be said that the use of air entraining admixtures in concrete is positively useful in increasing the durability of concrete in very cold regions.

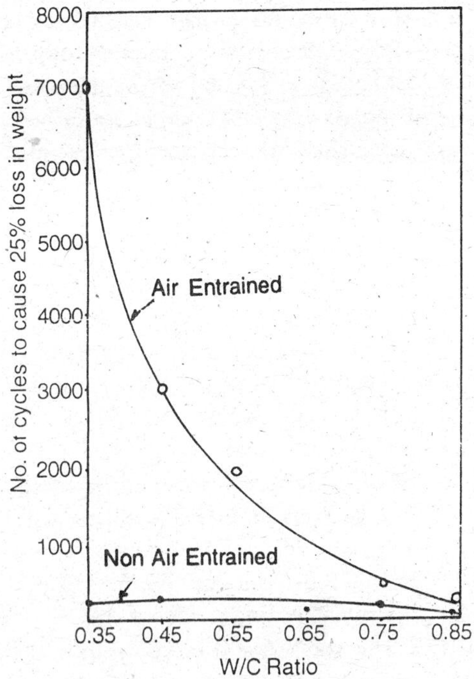

Fig. 18.11. Influence of w/c ratio on frost resistance moist cured for 14 days then at 50% humidity

18.12. SUMMERY OF PRECAUTIONS TO BE OBSERVED IN COLD WEATHER CONCRETING

1. Preparations for concreting in cold weather may be completed well in advance of severe conditions. To protect the mixing and batching plants from wind effects, wind breakers should be provided. To cover the surface of the concrete, tarpaulins, plastic sheets and other covering and insulating materials should be made available at the site. Steam generating plants and other necessary equipments should also be available at the site.
2. At the point of placing concrete the temperature of the concrete should not be less than 5°C. The concrete should be placed quickly and the top surface of the concrete be covered with an insulating material.
3. Before placing any concrete, all ice, snow and frost should be removed from the form work and reinforcement etc. and the temperature be raised as close as practicable to the temperature of the fresh concrete to be placed. No concrete should be placed on a frozen sub grade or on frozen materials. In case concrete is to be placed over an permanently frozen ground either it may be covered with a dry granular material for sufficient depth or the sub grade materials may be thawed upto a sufficient depth such that it will not freeze back upto the concrete.
4. When the air temperature is near or below freezing point, heated enclosures are commonly provided. Enclosures may be made of wood, canvas, fibre insulating boards, ply wood etc. These enclosures may be heated by steam, jet steam pipes and other types of heaters.
5. In cold weather concreting, in order to preserve the heat of hydration and protect it from freezing, the concrete surface should be covered as soon as the concrete is placed. The covering materials may be polythene plastic sheets, water proof paper, tarpaulins, sacks and clean straw blankets of about 5.0 cms thickness. Along with these materials air gap can also be provided as an insulation.

If possible insulating material may be placed against form work before concreting.

6. During placement of concrete, tarpaulin or any other readily movable coverings supported on form work should follow closely the placing of concrete, so that only a small area of finished surface is exposed to out side air These tarpaulins should be so used that hot air may be circulated freely on the surface. Layers of insulating materials may also be used for the protection of concrete against freezing action.
7. During freezing or near freezing conditions water curing is not necessary as loss of moisture from concrete due to evaporation of water will be greatly reduced in such cold conditions.
8. For concrete cast in insulated form work it is necessary to cover the member completely to retain the sufficient water in the concrete for hydration of cement. After removing the form work and insulation, the member immediately should be covered with plastic sheet or tarpaulin etc., properly lapped and made air tight. In no condition, the concrete released from insulated form work, be saturated with cold water. After discontinuing the protective measures the surface temperature of the concrete should be gradually adjusted to the air temperature.
9. Low pressure wet steam curing has been found best for heating the enclosures as well as for moist curing of concrete. Early curing with liquid membrane forming compounds may be followed with heated enclosures. It is better to cure first with steam curing during the initial period of protection and then using a curing compound after the protection has been removed and the air temperature is above freezing point.
10. Form work should not be removed till the concrete has achieved a strength of at least twice the stress to which the concrete may be subjected at the time of removal of form work. In the normal conditions, where ambient temperature does, not fall below 15°C and where ordinary portland cement is used and adequate curing is done, the removal of form work period shown in Table 18.4 may be adopted. It is a guide line. For lower temperatures and other cements it may be suitably modified.

Table 18.4. Recommended minimum time limits for striking form work as per IS 456-2000.

S. No.	*Type of form work*	*Minimum Period before striking form work*
1.	Vertical form work to columns, walls, beams	16-24 hours
2.	Sofit form work to slabs (Props to be refixed immediately after removal of form work	3 days
3.	Sofit-form work to beams (Props to be refixed immediately after removal of form work	7 days
4.	Props to slabs	
	Spanning upto 4.5 m	7 days
	Spanning over 4.5 m	14 days
5.	Props to beams and arches	
	Spanning upto 6.0 m	14 days
	Spanning over 6.0 m	21 days

11. In cold weather concreting form work other than steel provides better protection. The form work should not be removed until the end of minimum period or a little more.
12. During cold weather, the record of out side air temperature, temperature of concrete at the time of placing, and general weather, day, and time should be maintained.

18.13. UNDER WATER CONCRETING

Many a times concrete is required to be placed under water or in a trench filled with bentonite slurry. Special precautions need to be taken when ever concrete is to be placed under water.

18.13.1. Properties of Concrete

As per portland cement associations recommendations, concrete to be placed under water should possess the following qualities.

1. A richer mix than generally used for placing under normal conditions is required. At least 10% more cement than under normal conditions should be used. Usually 8 bags (150 kg each) *i.e.* 400 kg/cement per cubic metre of concrete is required. However the quantity of extra cement may vary according to the conditions of placing.

Aggregate. The proportion of fine and coarse aggregates should be so adjusted to produce the desired workability with a some what higher proportion of fine aggregate than used under normal conditions. The proportion of fine aggregate should be 45 to 50% of the total aggregate depending on the grading. In other words coarse aggregate neither should be less than 1.5 times nor more than 2.0 times of the fine aggregate. To produce a plastic and cohesive mixture the aggregate should contain sufficient fine material passing through 300 and 150 micron sieve.

As per ASTM standard specifications for concrete, aggregate not less than 10% of fine aggregate should pass through 300 micron sieve and not less than 2%, pass through 150 micron. The fine aggregate should meet the minimum requirement and some what higher percentage of fines would be better.

The maximum size of coarse aggregate should not be more the 40 mm. For most of the works the maximum size adopted is 20mm. The slump of the concrete should be high of the order of 15 to 20 cms.

Form work. The importance of form work in under water concreting is much more than normal concreting as the form work for under water concreting serves the following functions.

(*a*) It not only imparts the required shape to concrete but also protects the mix during its placement till it matures.

(*b*) It also protects the mix from direct action of current and waves.

(*c*) After placement it protects the concrete from the impact and abrasive action of water currents

Thus form work for under water concreting must be designed and prepared carefully keeping all aspects in view.

18.14. METHODS OF CONCRETING

Following methods can be adopted for placing concrete under water:

1. Placing of concrete in dewatered caissons or coffer dams
2. Tremie method
3. By drop bottom bucket method
4. By filling bags
5. Prepacked concrete or grouting

1. Placing of concrete in dewatered caissons or coffer dams

In this method same procedure is used as on dry conditions. In case concrete is to be placed under flowing water, then the velocity of flow should not be more then 5 cm/sec, so that mortar is not lost due to the following water. Dewatering by pumping should not be done while concreting is being placed or until 24 hours there after. Concrete should be placed continuously till it is brought upto the required height. While placing concrete, the top surface should be kept as nearly level as possible and formation of seams should be avoided.

2. Tremie method

Tremie is a French word, meaning hopper. Tremie is a water tight pipe. It is a composite metallic pipe having diameter varying from 20.0 to 25.0 cm capable of easy coupling for increase or decrease its length. A funnel shaped hopper is fitted to its upper end to facilitate pouring of concrete. The bottom end is closed with a loose plug as shown in Fig. 18.12. The valve at the discharge end is used to dewater the tremie and control the distribution of concrete. The tremie is supported on a working platform above water level and to facilitate the placing, it is built up in 1.0 m to 3.5 m section. The total length of the tremie pipe should be sufficient to allow a free flow of concrete upto the point of placement. The pipe should be strong enough to withstand the external pressure of water in which it is suspended and the partial vacuum pressure developed in side the pipe. A separate lifting device is provided for each tremie with its hopper at the upper end. Unless the lower end of the pipe is equipped with an approved automatic check valve, the upper end of the pipe should be plugged with a wadding of gunny sacking or any other approved material before delivering the concrete to the tremie pipe through the hopper, so that when the concrete is forced down from the hopper to the pipe, it will force the plug down the pipe and out of the bottom end establishing a continuous stream of concrete, and the water in the pipe if any is displaced by concrete.

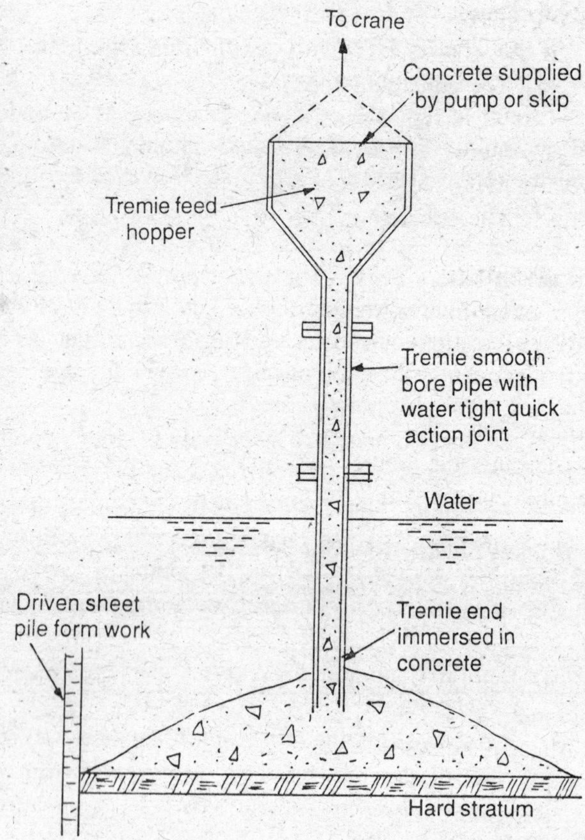

Fig. 18.12. Under water concreting by tremie method

Working Process

At the place of concreting, sheet piles form work is driven in side the water and the tremie pipe is lowered into position and the discharge end is kept as deeply submerged beneath the surface of freshly laid concrete as the head of concrete in tremie permits. The tremie pipe is lifted up and a slight jerk is given by a winch and pulley arrangement to discharge the concrete down. During concreting air and water must be excluded from the tremie by keeping the pipe full of concrete all the time.

As the concreting proceeds, the pipe should be raised slowly to have a uniform flow of concrete, and the concrete flows out wards. During concrete operation care should be taken to maintain the continuity of concreting with out breaking the seal provided by the concrete cover over the discharge end *i.e.* it should never be emptied. If this seal is required to be broken, the tremie should be lifted up and plugged before reconcreting is started. During all the time after starting placing concrete till the end of completion the lower end of tremie should remain below the top surface of plastic concrete. This will cause the concrete to build up from below instead of flowing out over the surface avoiding the formation of laitance layers. If the charge in the tremie is lost while depositing the concrete, the tremie should be raised above the concrete surface and unless sealed by a check value, it should be replugged at the top end as at the beginning, before refilling the depositing concrete. The tremie should never be moved laterally through the freshly placed concrete. For shifting the tremie to a new position it should be lifted vertically above the surface of concrete and shifted to its new position.

If the concrete is to be placed in large quantities, it is preferable to place concrete simultaneously and uniformly through a number of tremie pipes rather than sifting a single tremie pipe from one point to another point. The spacing between the tremies should be between 3.5 m to 5.0 m and the end tremies should be about 2.5 m away from the form work.

The risk of segregation and non uniform stiffening can be minimised by maintaining the concrete surface in form work as level as possible and by providing a continuous and rapid flow of concrete.

Advantages

If the work is executed properly, this method has the following advantages:

1. The concrete is not affected by the flowing water, except the top layer. The top layer may be cut off to remove the affected concrete at the end of the whole operation.
2. Under water concrete dos not need compaction as concrete automatically gets compacted by the hydrostatic pressure of water.
3. The concrete is of such a high consistency which normally does not require compaction.

Disadvantage

Concreting by tremie method requires high water/cement ratio for obtaining high consistency, which reduces the strength of concrete. But now, with the use of some plasticizer a concrete with as low w/c ratio as 0.3 or even less can be placed by tremie method.

Precautions

During the course of concreting no pumping of water should be done. If pumping is done simultaneously, it may suck the cement particles from the concrete.

3. Bucket placing method

In this method the concrete is deposited under water by a bottom opening bucket. The buckets usually are fitted with bottom roller or drop bottom gates as shown in Fig. 18.13. The gate opens freely outward when tripped. The bucket is filled completely with concrete and its top covered with a canvas cloth or gunny sack and lowered slowly to avoid back-wash or disturbance to concrete as the bucket is lowered into the water.

Some buckets are provided with a special base, which limits the disturbance to the concrete during discharge operation and also when the empty bucket is raised up from the freshly laid concrete. The bucket is lowered by a crane upto the bottom surface of the concrete and then opened either by a suitable arrangement from the top or by a diver. It is essential that the concrete be discharged directly on the surface on which it is to be deposited. The early discharge of bucket, by which the fresh concrete drops through water must be avoided.

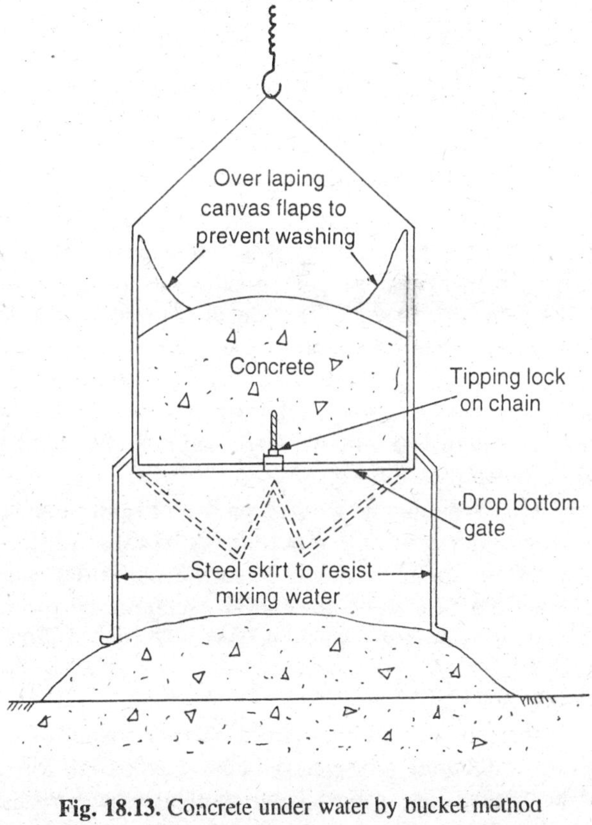

Fig. 18.13. Concrete under water by bucket method

Advantages

Following advantages of this method are observed:

1. The concreting can be carried out at the considerable depths below water surface.
2. Slightly stiffer concrete than tremie method can be used.

Disadvantages

The main disadvantage of this method is the difficulty in keeping the top surface of the placed concrete reasonably level.

4. Concrete filling in bags

In this method the jute sacks or coarse cloth bags of minimum capacity of 0.028 m^3 are filled about 2/3 with concrete and the spare part of the bag is turned down and tied securely. The bags are tied in such a way that they can be accommodated readily in a profile of the surface on which they are placed. The properly filled bags are lowered into the water and placed carefully in header and stretcher courses as in brick masonry construction with the help of divers so that the whole mass is interlocked.

Advantages

This method is found to have the following advantages:

1. Comparatively lean mixes may be used provided sufficient plasticity is retained.
2. No form work is necessary in this method.

Disadvantages

1. This method is slow and laborious as the accurate positioning of the bags in place can only be accomplished by the divers.
2. Voids in adjacent bags are difficult to fill.
3. There is little bonding other than developed by the mechanical interlock between bags.
4. The method comparatively is costly as more labour is involved in filling and tieing them.
5. This method is suitable for placing concrete in shallow water only.

5. Pre packed concrete or Grouting method

In this method a series of round cages are made of 50 mm mesh of 6 mm steel bars and extended upto the full height to be concreted. These cages are laid vertically over the full area to be concreted such that the distance between the centres of the cages and also to the faces of the concrete should not exceed one metre. The size of the stone aggregate neither be less than 50 mm nor more than 200 mm. This aggregate should be wetted before depositing it out side the steel cages over the full area and height to be concreted. While depositing the aggregate, care should be taken that no cage is displaced from its position.

After depositing the aggregate, the cement sand grout of 1:2 proportion and water/cement ratio not less than 0.6 and not more than 0.9 is prepared in a mechanical mixer. The maximum size of sand may be 5 mm and the cement sand proportion may vary from 1:1.5 to 1:4 depending upon the strength requirements and importance of the work. The prepared grout is sent down through 38 to 50 mm diameter pipe terminating into the steel cage about 50 mm above the bottom of the concrete bed. The pressure of the grout should be maintained at 2 kg/cm^2 to 3 kg/cm^2 (0.2 N/mm^2 0.3 N/mm^2) As the grouting proceeds, the pipe should be raised gradually upto a height of not more than 60 cms above the starting level. After this level, the pipe may be withdrawn from this cage and placed into the next cage. The procedure is repeated till all the cages are grouted upto this level.

After grouting the whole area for a height of about 60 cms, the same operation is repeated for the next layer of 60 cm and the procedure is repeated till the grouting is completed upto the desired height. The grout to be sent down should be sufficient to fill all the voids. The volume of voids may be assumed as 55% of the volume to be concreted or ascertained experimentally. As far as possible concrete should not be disturbed while it is deposited. This will minimise the formation of laitence.

Advantages

The following advantages have been observed:

1. Grouting or prepacked concrete exhibits lower drying shrinkage and higher durability.
2. It is more freezing and thawing resistant than ordinary concrete of the same proportions.

Disadvantage

The rate of development of strength is comparatively slow for the first two months, but the eventual strength is about the same as that of normal concrete.

Grouting method of concreting is very much suited for under ground construction and repair work of mass concrete structures such as dams, spillways etc.

The tremie method for under water concreting most commonly is used in U.S.A. and USSR, while in Holland where large volumes of concrete are placed under water, the usual method employed is that of placing by bucket method. The bag method almost is obsolete now. However it may be used for building up permanent under water form work.

QUESTIONS

1. What precautions would you adopt while concreting.
   (*a*) In hot weather (*b*) In cold weather
2. What are the causes of thermal cracking of concrete walls?
3. What are the thermal problems in
   (*a*) Mass concrete (*b*) Very large lifts or layer of reinforced concrete?
4. What are the physical changes in concrete subjected to one cycle of freezing?
5. Why some times insulation is used in placing large concrete pours or lifts?
6. What are the effects of hot weather on
   (*a*) Fresh concrete (*b*) Hardened concrete
7. What special measures are necessary for concreting in hot weather?
8. Two cements have the same total heat of hydration but their rate of heat development is different. Compare their performance in mass concrete.
9. Discuss the action of frost on fresh concrete.
10. For concreting in cold weather, what materials would you heat before putting them in the mixer? Explain with reasons. Are there any limitations on temperature?
11. What is the maximum rate of evaporation of water from a fresh concrete surface below which plastic cracking will not occur?
12. Should the concrete be placed in lifts (layers) or continuously? Explain with reasons.
13. When the ice be placed in the concrete mixer?
14. What measures you would take to minimise the temperature gradient.
15. Discuss the measures of temperature control in placing mass concrete.
16. How does the type of aggregate influence the thermal cracking of concrete.
17. Why is light weight aggregate superior to normal weight aggregate for reducing the thermal cracking.
18. What type of cement would you choose for the followings
    (*a*) Reinforced concrete (*b*) Mass concrete
19. How can the temperature of the concrete at the time of placing be raised and subsequently maintained?
20. Give a suitable range of temperature of the concrete at the time of placing to prevent it from frost damage.
21. Why is the size of section relevant to the minimum temperature at placing necessary to prevent frost damage at early age?
22. Discuss he influence of form work striking times on the risk of thermal cracking.
23. What should be the properties of concrete to be placed under water?
24. Describe fully the tremie method of under water concreting?
25. In which countries usually tremie method of under water concreting is used. Give its advantages and dis-advantages.
26. Describe with neat sketch the bucket method of under water concreting.
27. What is prepacked concrete? Discuss the procedure of placing prepacked concrete under water.

OBJECTIVE TYPE QUESTIONS

1. Identify the incorrect statement of the following
   (*a*) Concrete placement at 21°C temperature is called concreting in extreme conditions
   (*b*) Concrete placement at 40°C temperature is called concreting in extreme condition

(*c*) Concrete placement under water is called concreting under extreme condition
(*d*) Concrete placement at 50°C temperature is called concreting under extreme conditions

2. Tremic method is used for
(*a*) Dredging of sea
(*b*) Placing of concrete under water
(*c*) Grouting of fissured rocks
(*d*) Boring of soil

3. Concreting in hot weather results
(*a*) Reducing the handling time of fresh concrete
(*b*) Reducing the strength of hardened cement
(*c*) Increasing the tendency of cracking
(*d*) Makes it difficult to control air content
(*e*) All of the above

4. In hot weather concreting is recommended
(*a*) Use of cold mixing water
(*b*) Use of minimum cement content
(*c*) Use of low heat of hydration cement
(*d*) Use of water reducing admixtures
(*e*) Use of absolute minimum period between mixing and placement of concrete
(*f*) All of the above

5. Identify the false statements of the followings
(*a*) In hot weather concreting a part of mixing water may be replaced by ice
(*b*) In hot weather concreting ice cold water should be used
(*c*) In hot weather concreting refrigerated cooled cement should be used
(*d*) In hot weather concreting ice cold aggregate may be used

6. Identify the correct statement of the followings
(*a*) In hot weather concreting the finishing of the concrete should be carried as early as possible after placing the concrete
(*b*) In hot weather concreting compaction of concrete fully is no problem
(*c*) In hot weather concreting early curing of concrete is not necessary
(*d*) In hot weather concreting, concrete near the sub grade and form work is of the same quality as in the core

7. Identify the false statement of the followings
(*a*) In hot weather conditions the relative humidity of ambient air is low and the mixing water will be lost soon
(*b*) In hot weather concreting the plastic shrinkage in interior of the concrete is more than the surface
(*c*) In hot weather concreting the surface cracks developed are known as plastic shrinkage cracks
(*d*) In hot weather concreting early curing is necessary

8. Cold weather concreting is called when concrete is placed
(*a*) Between 21°C to 15°C
(*b*) Between 12°C to 8°C
(*c*) Below 5°C
(*d*) Between 40°C to 25°C

9. Cold weather concreting causes
(*a*) Delay in setting and hardening
(*b*) Freezing of concrete at early age
(*c*) Freezing and thawing
(*d*) All of the above

10. Identify the false statement of the following
(*a*) The time interval after placing the concrete till it attains a certain amount of strength is called pre hardening period
(*b*) To conserve heat the concrete can be insulted by a membrane
(*c*) Cement containing large quantities of C_3S and C_3A are usefull for cold weather concreting
(*d*) High alumina cement is not useful for cold weather concreting

11. Identify the correct statement of the followings
(*a*) For cold weather concreting mixing water can be heated upto 60°C
(*b*) For cold weather concreting mixing water can be heated upto 100°C
(*c*) The hot water can be mixed directly with the cement
(*d*) The hot water should come in contact with aggregate first than cement
(*e*) The aggregate can be heated directly with out any ill effect
(*f*) Aggregate should never be heated directly
(*g*) Cement should never be heated
(*h*) Calcium and sodium chlorides can be used as accelerating admixtures in cold weather concreting

12. Identify the correct and incorrect statements of the followings
    (*a*) Use of air entrainment has not been found useful in cold weather concreting
    (*b*) Use of air entrainment increases the durability of concrete
    (*c*) The use of light weight aggregate has not been found useful in cold water concreting
    (*d*) The use of light weight aggregate in cold weather concreting is more advantageous
    (*e*) Low water/cement ratio concrete is more resistant to freezing and thawing action
13. The properties of concrete to be placed under water should be
    (*a*) The slump of concrete should be 15 to 20 cms
    (*b*) The maximum size of coarse aggregate should be 20 mm
    (*c*) The cement content in concrete should not be the 400 kg/m^3
    (*d*) The amount of coarse aggregate neither should be less the 1.5 times nor more than 2 times of the fine aggregate
    (*e*) All of the above
14. In cold weather concreting the temperature of concrete during 3 days after placing should not fall below
    (*a*) 25°C (*b*) 15°C
    (*c*) 10°C (*d*) 0°C
15. The strength of electrical heated concrete is found......of normally cured concrete
    (*a*) 70% (*b*) 75%
    (*c*) 50% (*d*) 80%
16. In cold weather concreting entrainment of air increases the durability of concrete
    (*a*) 2 times (*b*) 3 to 7 times
    (*c*) 10 times (*d*) No effect
17. In cold climate the temperature of concrete at the point of placement should not be less than
    (*a*) 20°C (*b*) 15°C
    (*c*) 10°C (*d*) 5°C
18. The reduction of 35% in relative humidity decreases the strength of concrete by
    (*a*) 20% (*b*) 15%
    (*c*) 11% (*d*) 7%

Answers

1. (*a*)
2. (*b*)
3. (*e*)
4. (*f*)
5. (*c*)
6. (*a*)
7. (*b*)
8. (*c*)
9. (*d*)
10. (*d*)
11. [True (*a, d, f, g, h*)]
12. [False (*a, c*)]
13. (*e*)
14. (*c*)
15. (*d*)
16. (*b*)
17. (*d*)
18. (*c*)

19

Testing of Concrete

19.1. INTRODUCTION

We have seen that the properties of concrete are a function of time and ambient humidity. Thus it is not enough to know the properties of concrete and the selection of concrete mix that can give such properties, but it is also necessary that such properties develop in the concrete in the actual construction at site. Thus to ascertain that concrete has developed the desired properties, it has to be tested under specified or known conditions. Though there are many methods to test the properties of hardened concrete, but the most common of all tests on hardened concrete is the compressive strength test, partly because it is an easy test to perform and partly due to the fact that many desirable characteristics of concrete are qualitatively related to its strength; but mainly due to the basic importance of the compressive strength of concrete in construction.

19.2. CLASSIFICATION OF TESTS

The strength tests broadly can be classified into following two groups:

1. Mechanical test to destruction
2. Non destructive tests

1. The tests to destruction are in use for many years, but no universally accepted standard test has been devised. Different methods and techniques are used in different countries. Tests are made mainly for two objectives as quality control and
2. For compliance of specifications. Additional test may also be carried out for specific purposes as compressive strength tests to determine the strength of concrete at transfer of prestress or at the time of removing the form work, but the tests are not an end in themselves.

19.3. COMPRESSION TESTS

Compression test can be performed on the three types of test specimens, namely cubes, cylinders and prisms. Cubes of standard size of 150 mm are used in India U.K., Germany and many other countries of Europe. Cylinders are the standard specimens in U.S.A. France, Canada, Australia and New Zealand. In scandinavia tests are made both on cubes and cylinders. Usually cylinders of 150 × 300 mm size are used. Smaller test specimens may also be used but a ratio of the diameter of the specimen to maximum size of aggregate not less than 3 to 1 is maintained. In case of cubes minimum size of 150 × 150 × 150 mm should be used if the maximum size of aggregate is 20 mm. However a 100 × 100 × 100 mm cube may also be used.

19.4. MOULDS

Preferably metal moulds made of cast iron or steel should be used. The thickness of the mould should be enough to prevent any distortion. The tolerance between the opposite faces should be ± 0.2 mm. The angle between adjacent internal faces and between internal faces and top and bottom planes of the mould should be 90° ± 0.5°. The internal faces of the mould should be plane surfaces with a permissible variation of 0.03 mm. Each mould has a metal base plate having a plane surface.

While assembling the mould for use, the joints between all sections of the mould are thinly coated with mould oil and a similar coating of mould oil or grease is applied between the contact surface of the bottom of the mould and the base plate in order to ensure that no water goes out during filling it. To prevent adhesion of concrete, interior surfaces of the assembled mould are also thinly coated with mould oil.

The cylindrical mould is made of metal sheet of not less than 3 mm thickness. The internal mean diameter of the mould should be 150 ± 0.2 mm and in no direction the internal diameter should be less than 14.95 cms and not-more than 15.05 cms. The height should be 30 cm ± 0.1 mm.

A 16mm diameter and 60 cm long steel bar with a bullet point at one end is used as tamping rod.

19.5. PREPARATION OF SAMPLES

The mould is assembled, cleaned and oiled. The concrete is filled upto 1/3rd height of the mould. In case of 15 cm cube, each layer should be given at least 35 strokes and in case of 10 cm cube at least 25 strokes of the rod should be given. In case of cylindrical mould each layer should be given each layer of 10 cm at least 30 strokes. Each stroke should penetrate into the under lying layer and the bottom layer is roded through out its depth. If the voids are left by tamping rod, then sides of the mould are tapped to close the voids.

In case compaction is done by vibrations, then each layer should be vibrated either by means of electric or pneumatic hammer or vibrator or by a suitable vibrating table. Care should be taken that no segregation takes place in the mould which will result in low strength of the concrete.

19.5.1. Capping of specimen

Capping is applied to cylindrical specimens only, when the top end of the cylindrical specimen is not plane with in 0.05 mm. The capped surface should be nearly at right angle to the axis of the specimen. The planeness of the cap should be checked with the help of a straight edge and feeler gauge at three different diameters of the specimen. Caping can be done either on completion of casting or a few hours before testing of the specimen.

19.5.2. Materials of capping

Following materials are used for the capping:

1. Neat cement
2. Cement mortar
3. Hard plaster
4. Sulpher

1. Neat Cement. The test cylinders may be capped with a thin layer of stiff neat portland cement paste after the concrete has set in the mould, after about 4 hours of casting, so that concrete in the cylinder undergoes plastic shrinkage and subsides fully. The cap is formed either by a glass plate not less than 6.5 mm in thickness or a machined metal plate not less than 13 mm in thickness and having a minimum surface dimension at least 25 mm larger than the diameter of the mould. In order to prevent the tendency of the cap to shrink, cement for paste is mixed to a stiff paste for about 2 to 4 hours before it is to be used.

19.5.3. Curing

The test specimens are stored in place free from vibration in moist air of at least 90% relative humidity and at a temperature of 27 ± 2°C for 24 hours ± 1/2 hours from the time of addition of water to the dry ingredients. After this period, the specimens are marked and removed from the mould and immediately immersed in clean fresh water or saturated lime solution and kept there till taken out just prior to test. The specimens are not to be allowed to become dry at any time till they have been tested. The specimens prepared as above are known as laboratory prepared specimens. If the specimens are prepared in the field and cured under standard temperature and water, they are called standard specimens. If the specimens are prepared from the concrete to be filled in prototype structure and put along side it for curing then they are known as companion specimens.

19.6. FAILURE OF COMPRESSION SPECIMEN

1. Failure under uniaxial compression. Under uniaxial compression, the cracks developed are approximately parallel to the applied load, but some cracks are also formed at an angle to the applied load. The parallel cracks are caused by a localized tensile stress in a direction normal to the compressive load. The inclined cracks develop due to the collapse caused by the development of shear planes. The cracks are formed in two planes parallel to the load, such that the specimen disintegrates into column type fragments as shown in Fig. 13.3 (*b*).

Under biaxial compression, failure takes place in one plane parallel to the applied load and results in the formation of slab type fragments Fig. 13.3 (*c*).

Here it should be noted that the fracture pattern of Fig. 13.3 (*b*) and (*c*) is for direct stresses only. Thus there should be no restraint from the platens of the testing machine, while in practice thes platens of the machine introduce some lateral compression due to the friction generated between the steel platens and the concrete. In an ordinary machine, it is difficult to eliminate this friction. However its effect may be minimized by using a specimen whose length/diameter ratio is greater than 2.

2. Actual testing. The testing under uniaxial compression is the ideal mode of testing, but in actual compression testing more complex system of stresses is imposed. These stresses are imposed mainly due to the lateral forces developed between the end surfaces of the concrete specimen and the adjacent steel platens of the testing machine. These forces are induced due to the restraint of concrete, which tries to expand laterally (Poisson's effect). This expansion is restrained by the steel platens which are several times stiffer than concrete and have much smaller lateral expansion. The degree of platen restraint on the concrete section depends on the following two factors.

1. The friction developed at the interfaces of concrete and steel platens.
2. The distance from the end surfaces of the concrete.

Thus in addition to the imposed uniaxial compression, there is a lateral shearing stress also. The effect of this shearing stress is to increase the apparent compressive strength of concrete.

The influence of platen restraint can be seen by the typical failure modes of test cubes shown in Fig. 19.1. The effect of shear is always present, though the shear effect decreases to wards the centre of the cube. Thus the sides of the cube have nearly vertical cracks or completely disintegrate leaving a relatively undamaged central core (Fig. 19.1 (*a*)). This mode of failure takes place when the test is performed in a rigid testing machine. A less rigid machine can store more energy, resulting in a more explosive failure as shown in Fig. 19.1 (*b*). In this case, one face touching the platen cracks and disintegrates forming a cone or pyranid. Failures of other type than those shown in Fig. 19.1 (*a*) and (*b*) above are regarded as unsatisfactory and indicate a probable fault in the machine. Failure shown in Fig. 19.1 (*a*) is called non explosive while that of 19.1 (*b*) as explosive.

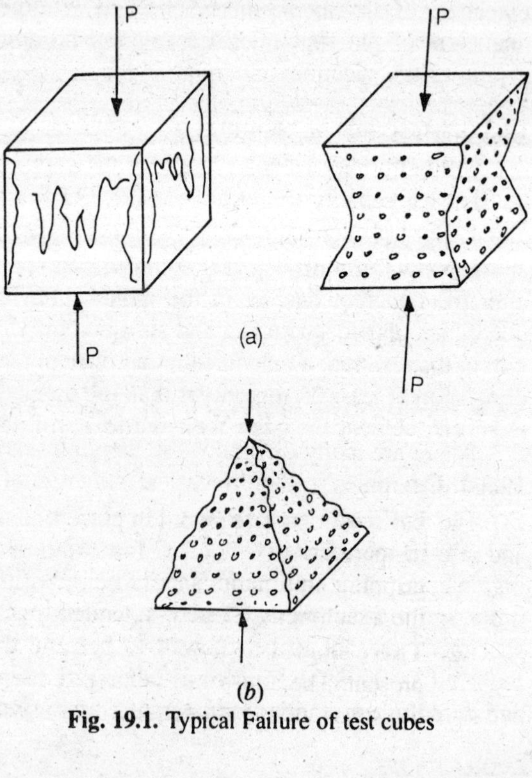

Fig. 19.1. Typical Failure of test cubes

If the ratio of height to width or height to diameter of the specimen increases, the influence of shear becomes smaller, so that the central part of the specimen may fail by lateral splitting. This situation arises in a standard cylinder test where the height/diameter ratio is 2. The possible modes of failures of cylinder test are shown in Fig. 19.2. Out of these failures the most usual failure is by spitting and shear as shown in Fig. 19.2 (*c*).

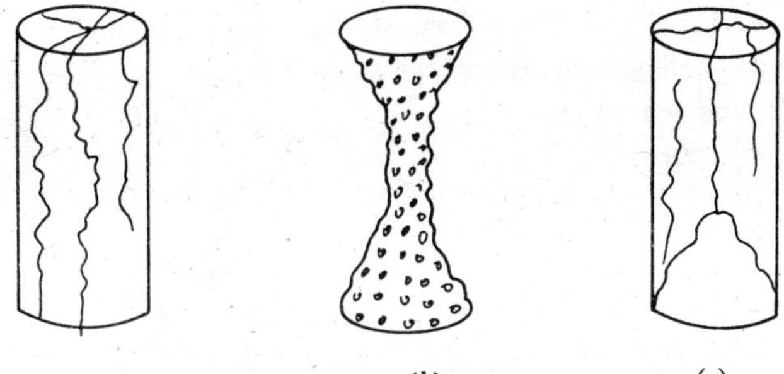

(*a*) (*b*) (*c*)

Fig. 19.2. Typical failure of test cylinder (*a*) shows splitting failure, (*b*) Shear (cone) and, (*c*) Splitting and shear

The compressive strength of concrete is determined by placing the specimen centrally in between the platens of the machine. The rate of loading as per IS 516, should be 0.233 MPa/second or 2.33 kg/cm^2 per second.

As the influence of platen restraint on the mode of failure is greater in a cube than in a standard cylinder, the cube strength approximately is taken as 1.25 times the cylinder strength, though it varies from 1.33 to 0.96 depending upon the strength of concrete and moisture condition of concrete at the time of testing. If the end friction is eliminated, the effect of height/diameter would disappear, which is very difficult to achieve in a routine test and is not feasible for the range of strength normally encountered. The general pattern of influence of height/diameter ratio on the apparent strength of cylinder is shown in Fig. 14.4.

19.6.1. Advantages of Cylinder as a test-specimen

Cylinders are believed to give a greater uniformity of results for nominally similar specimens due to the following reasons.

(*a*) The failure of cylinders is less affected by the end restraint of the specimen.

(*b*) The strength of cylinder is less influenced by the properties of aggregate used in the mix.

(*c*) The stress distribution over the cross section (horizontal planes) in cylinders is more uniform than on a specimen of square cross section.

For these reasons, the cylinder strength probably is closer to the true uniaxial compressive strength of concrete than cube strength. Further in structural compression members the situation is similar to that existing in a test cylinder. Thus the tests on cylinders are more realistic.

Further it may be noted that cube is loaded or tested on the surface at right angle to the axis of the cube as cast, where as cylinders are cast and tested in the same position. However the relation between the directions as cast and as tested have been found having no effect on the strength appreciably of cubes made with homogeneous and un segregated concrete.

(*b*) The strongest advantage in favour of cube is that it does not need capping. The capping procedure is expensive and time consuming. The capping material may also influence the strength of the specimen.

19.7. DETERMINATION OF TENSILE STRENGTH

There are many difficulties in the direct measurement of tensile strength of concrete. Following are the major difficulties in the direct determination of the tensile strength of concrete.

1. **Difficulty in gripping the specimen.** Proper and satisfactory gripping equipment is not available in the market which may assure uniform distribution of the pull applied to the concrete *i.e.* the gripping equipment should be such that the premature failure does not take place near the ends of the attachment. There is a tendency of the specimen to break near the edges or ends.
2. **There should be no eccentricity of the applied load.** However there is always some eccentricity present. The stresses are changed due to the eccentric loading which may introduce major error on the stress development regard less of size and shape of the specimen.

19.8. INDIRECT TENSION TEST METHODS

Under this category there are three tests as follows:

(*a*) Splitting tension test (*b*) Ring tension test

(*c*) Double punch test

However here only splitting tension test has been discussed.

19.8.1. Splitting tension test

This test was developed in Brazil in 1943. Some times this test is also called as Brazilian test. However at about the same period this test was also developed in Japan independently.

Test Procedure

Usually this test is carried out on cylindrical specimen by placing it horizontally between the platens or loading surfaces of the testing machine and the load is increased until failure of the specimen takes place by splitting in the plane containing the vertical diameter of the specimen.

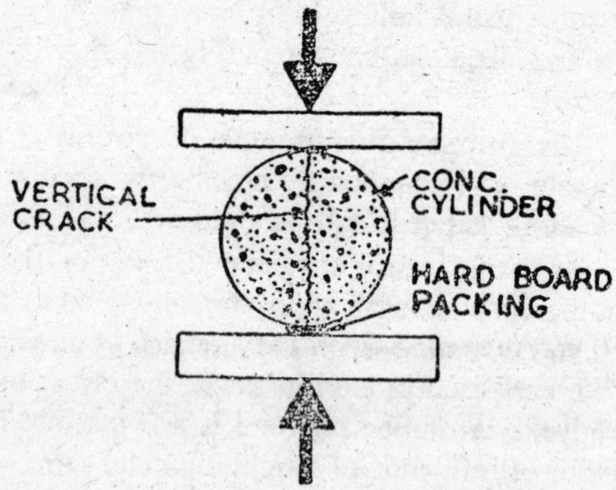

Fig. 19.3. Cylinder Splitting test

When the load is applied along the generatrix, then an element on the vertical diameter of the cylinder as shown in Fig. 19.3 is subjected to compressive stress, whose vertical and horizontal components are given as follows:

(*a*) Vertical component of compressive stress

$$= \frac{2P}{\pi LD}\left[\frac{D^2}{r(D-r)} - 1\right] \qquad ...(19.1)$$

(*b*) Horizontal component of compressive stress

$$= \frac{2D}{\pi LD} \qquad ...(19.2)$$

where,

P = compressive load applied to cylinder

L = Length of cylinder

r = Distance of the element centre from the top load

$(D\text{-}r)$ = distance of the element centre from the bottom load

D = diameter of the cylinder.

19.8.2. Horizontal tensile stress distribution

The loading condition produces a high compressive stress immediately below the two generators to which the load is applied and a larger portion corresponding to depth is subjected to a uniform tensile stress acting horizontally as shown in Fig. 19.4. It has been estimated that the compressive stress acts for about $\frac{1}{6}$th depth and the remaining 5/6th depth is subjected to tensile stress.

In practice to reduce the magnitude of the high compressive stresses near the points of application of the load, narrow packing of strips of suitable material such as plywood are placed between the surface of specimen and loading platens of the testing machine. The packing strips should be flexible enough to allow the load distribution over a reasonable area uniformly. To avoid large contact area the strip should be thin and narrow. Normally a plywood strip 3 mm thick, 25 mm wide and 300 mm long is sufficient. If this strip is not used, an 8% lower strength is recorded.

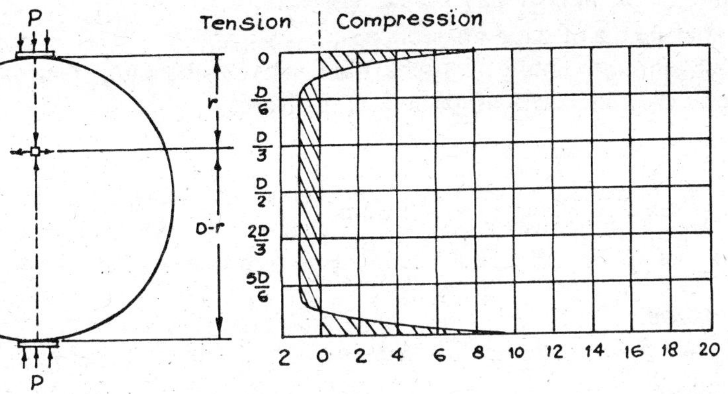

Fig. 19.4. Horizontal stress distribution in a cylinder in a splitting test loaded over a width $\frac{1}{12}$th of the cylinder

During the spitting test, the platens of the testing machine should not be allowed to rotate in a plane perpendicular to the axis of the cylinder, how ever a slight movement in the vertical plane containing the axis may be permitted to accommodate a possible non parallelism of the generators of the cylinder. This can be achieved by interposing a roller between one platen and the cylinder.

The load is applied at a constant rate of increase in tensile stress of 0.02 to 0.04 MPa according to BS 1881-Part-117-1983. The splitting strength can be calculated by the equation $f_{st} = \frac{2p}{\pi LD}$ as equation (*ii*) above.

19.8.3. Advantages of splitting test

The advantages of this method are as follows:

1. The test is simple to perform and it gives more uniform results than other tension tests.
2. In this test same type of specimen and same testing machine can be used as for the compression test.
3. Strength determined by splitting test in believed to be closer to the true tensile strength of concrete, than the modulus of rupture.
4. Splitting strength is 5 to 12% higher than the direct tensile strength.

However in case of cement mortar and light weight aggregate concrete, splitting test gives very low results.

19.9. FLEXURAL STRENGTH OF CONCRETE

In the flexure test, the theoretical maximum tensile stress reached in the bottom fibre of a test beam is known as the *modulus of rupture,* which is relevant to the design of highways and airfield pavements.

When concrete is subjected to bending, compressive as well as tensile stresses are developed. Some times direct shear stresses are also developed. The strength shown by the concrete against bending is known as *flexural strength.* The strength per unit area is called *flexural stress* and usually denoted by '*S*'. The value of flexural stress can be calculated by the following relation.

$$S = \frac{M \times Y}{I} \qquad \ldots(iii)$$

where,

S = stress in the farthest fibre from the neutral axis of the beam

M = bending moment at the section
Y = distance between neutral axis and farthest fibre
I = Moment of inertia of the cross section

The value of modulus of rupture (extreme fibre stress in bending) depends upon the size of the specimen (beam) and the arrangement of loading on the beam.

19.9.1. Size of specimen

The standard size of specimen is 15 × 15 × 70cms. Alternatively if the largest nominal size of aggregate does not exceed 20 mm the dimensions of the specimen may be 10 × 10 × 50 cms. IS 516-1964 has prescribed the size of specimen as 10 × 10 × 50 cms with in a span of 40 cms.

19.9.2. System of loading

For determining the flexural strength or modulus of rupture following two systems of loading of the specimen may be adopted:

1. **One point or central point loading.** In this system, the load is applied at the mid or central point of the test specimen, which gives a triangular B.M. distribution. The maximum fibre stress will be below the point of loading where the B.M. is maximum. Thus the maximum stress occurs at one section of the beam, not necessarily the weakest section of the beam.
2. **Two point loading** (at third point of span). This system of loading produces a constant bending moment between the load points, so that one third of the span is subjected to the maximum stress and thus in this region cracking is likely to take place. Now a days this system of loading is taken as the standard method of loading. In U.K. and U.S.A. also only this method is used. The system of two point loading is shown in Fig. 19.5. The test can be performed as per IS 516-1964 on a

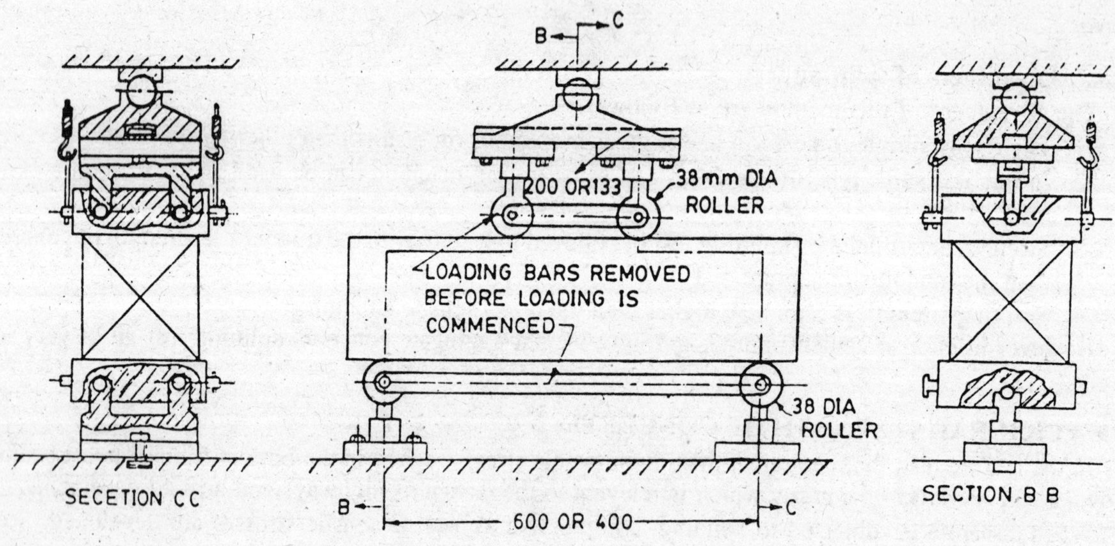

Fig. 19.5. Flexure test (Two point loading)

beam specimen of 10 × 10 × 50 cm with a span of 40 cm. The value of modulus of rupture is given by the relation.

$$f_b = \frac{3p \times a}{bd^2} \quad ...(19.3)$$

When the value of 'a' is less than 20 cm but greater than 17.0 cm for 15 × 15 × 70 cm specimen or less than 13.3 cms but greater than 11.0 cm for 10 × 10 × 50 cm specimen. In case 'a' is greater than 20 cm for 15 cm specimen or greater than 13.3 as for 10.0 cm specimen, then

$$fb = \frac{\rho \times l}{bd^2} \quad \ldots(19.4)$$

where,

fb = modulus of rupture
p = load applied on specimen in kg
b = width of beam in cms
d = depth of beam at failure point in cm
a = distance between the crack and nearest support
l = length of span in cm on which the specimen is supported.

On the basis of experiments, it has been observed that the variability of the results in two point loading system is less. The results of the flexural strength tested by central point loading and two point loading with a constant ratio of span to depth as 4, were analyzed statistically at Central Road Research Laboratory (Delhi) and the following general relation was obtained,

$$X_1 = X_2 + 0.72 \quad \ldots(19.5)$$

where,

X_1 = flexural strength of concrete in MPa under central point loading
X_2 = flexural strength of concrete in MPa under two point loading

It has been observed that test results under central point loading gave higher average values than the two point loading irrespective of the size of the specimen. The higher strengths obtained in central point loading may be due to the fact that the beam specimen is subjected to a maximum stress at predetermined section not necessarily the weakest. In the standard methods for determining the flexural strength of concrete, the span to depth ratio of the specimen was kept constant at 4. On the variation of span to depth ratio, the flexural strength also was found varying. 1% change in the span to depth ratio induced 3% and 2.5 variation in the strength when tested under two point loading and under one point loading respectively. With the increase in span to depth ratio, the flexural strength decreases.

19.10. RELATION SHIP BETWEEN TENSILE AND COMPRESSIVE STRENGTH

(Refer chapter 13)

The flexural strength of concrete for high strength concrete greater than 25 MPa has been found between 8 to 11% and for lower strength concrete less than 5 MPa as 9 to 12.5% of the compressive strength of concrete as shown in Table 19.1.

Table 19.1. Flexural strength expressed as percentage of compressive strength of concrete using gravel and crushed aggregate

Compressive strength in MPa	*Flexural strength as percentage of compressive strength*			
	Crushed stone aggregate with max. size		*Garvel aggregate with max. size*	
	20 mm	*40 mm*	*20 mm*	*40 mm*
49	7.7	—	8.7	—
42	7.9	10.2	9.0	10.8
35	8.2	10.3	9.3	10.9
28	8.6	10.2	9.9	11.1
21	9.3	10.3	10.8	11.3
14	10.8	10.5	12.5	12.0
Average	8.8	10.3	10.0	11.2

The Flexural to compressive strength ratio is found higher for concrete made with aggregate of 40 mm maximum size than that made with 20 mm maximum size aggregate. In general the ratio is found slightly higher in case of natural gravel than crushed stone aggregate.

19.11. EMPIRICAL RELATIONSHIP

Though there are numerous empirical relationship between the tensile and compressive strength of concrete. Here one of the general form is given as

$$\text{Tensile strength} = K\,(\text{compressive strength})^n \qquad \ldots(19.7)$$

where the value of K varies from 6.2 for gravel to 10.4 for crushed stone. The average value of K may be assumed as 8.3. The value of n varies from 0.5 to 0.75 (1/2 to 3/4).

Indian Standard IS 456-2000 has suggested the following relationship between the flexural strength and compressive strength of concrete.

$$\text{Flexural strength} = 0.7\sqrt{f_{ck}} \qquad \ldots(19.8)$$

where f_{ck} is the characteristic cylinder strength of concrete in N/mm^2 (MPa).

Portland Cement Laboratories Association has suggested the following relation between tensile and compressive strength of concrete as shown in Table 19.2.

Table 19.2. Relation between tensile and compressive strength of concrete

Compressive strength of concrete of cylinders in MPa	*Strength ratio*		
	Modulus of rupture under two point loading to compressive strength	*Direct tensile strength to compressive strength*	*Direct tensile strength to modulus of rupture*
7	0.23	0.11	0.48
14	0.19	0.10	0.53
21	0.16	0.09	0.57
28	0.15	0.09	0.59
35	0.14	0.08	0.59
42	0.13	0.08	0.60
49	0.12	0.07	0.61
56	0.12	0.07	0.62
63	0.11	0.07	0.63

19.12. PRE-PARATION OF TEST SPECIMEN AND TESTING

The standard sized beam specimens are prepared from the concrete mix to be tested. The mould should be of metal of sufficient thickness to prevent warping or spreading. The longer dimension of the mould should be horizontal.

The mould is cleaned, oiled from in side to prevent sticking of concrete with the mould side and placed in position on a horizontal surface. Concrete of specified proportions is prepared and filled in the mould and compacted preferably on a vibrating table. After compaction the specimen is levelled and covered with water soaked hessian. After 24 hours, the specimens are demoulded and immersed in water at a temperature of 27 ± 2°C.

At the age of testing, the specimens are taken out of the water, wipped and tested. In case the specimens are cast in the field and allowed to cure in atmospheric conditions, then the specimens should be immersed in water at a temperature of 27 ± 2°C for 48 hours before testing.

The specimens are tested in saturated surface dry condition. Before testing, the dimensions of each specimen should be noted. No surface preparation is required. The specimen is tested on the surface cast.

19.12.1. Testing Machine

Any reliable testing machine of sufficient capacity for the test and capable of applying the load at the specified rate may be used. When the high degree of accuracy is required, the permissible error should not be more than ± 0.5% of the applied load. For commercial type of testing the error should not be more than ± 1.5% of the applied load. The bed of the testing machine should have two steel rollers of 38 mm diameter, on which the specimen is to be supported. The distance between the rollers is 60 cm if the 15 × 15 × 70 cm beam is tested and 40 cm if 10 × 10 × 50 cm beam is to be tested.

The load is applied to the specimen through two similar rollers mounted at the third points of the supporting span that is spaced at 20 or 13.3 cms centre to centre. The load is equally divided between the two loading rollers. All the rollers are mounted in such a way that the load is applied axially and with out subjecting the specimen to any torsional stresses. Loading set-up is shown in Fig. 19.5.

19.12.2. Placing the Specimen in Testing Machine

The bearing surfaces of loading and supporting rollers are wiped clean of any dust. The contact surfaces of the specimen with the rollers are also cleaned. Now the specimen is placed in the machine in such way that the load is applied to the upper most surface as cast in the mould along the two lines spaced 20 or 13.3 cms apart. The axis of the specimen should be aligned with the axis of the loading device. In this case no packing is used in between the bearing surfaces of the rollers and specimens. The load is applied with out shock and jerk. The load is increases at about 0.7 kg/cm^2 per minute (0.007 MPa per minutes *i.e.* the rate of loading should be 400 kg/min. for thc 15 cms specimen and 180 kg/min. for 10.0 cms specimen. The load is increased till the specimen faids and the maximum load applied to the specimen at failure is noted. The appearance of the fractured faces of the concrete and any unusual features at the time of failure should be recorded.

19.13. CONCRETE CORE TESTS

The main purpose of determining the strength of concrete of standard specimens is to ensure that the potential strength of the concrete in the actual structure is satisfactory. If the strength of the standard compression test specimen is below the specified characteristic strength (minimum strength) value, then either the concrete in the actual structure is unsatisfactory or specimens are not truly representative of the concrete in the structure. The test specimens may not have been prepared correctly, nor handled properly or cured, or testing machine may be faulty etc. Thus the need of core test arises.

The examination and compression strength of testing cores, drilled from hardened concrete enable the visual inspection of interior regions of structural member along with estimation of actual strength of concrete. The cores are also frequently used to determine the water absorption, density, indirect tensile strength and also for chemical analysis.

19.13.1. Situations when core tests performed

The core tests are performed under the following situations:

(*a*) When the standard 28 days cube strength test gives lower strength than acceptable and the primary aim of the core test is to ascertain whether the structural element is of adequate strength.

(*b*) When it is required to estimate the load carrying capacity of the structure for its safety under change of loading contemplated for the structure.

(*c*) To detect the segregation, honey combing and to check the bond at construction joint or to verify the thickness of the pavement.

19.13.2. Location from where core is to be taken

The core should be drilled at the suspected part of the structure. The choice of core location primarily is governed by the basic purpose of the testing. For serviceability assessment, the core should normally be taken at the points where minimum strength and maximum stress coincide. In case of slender member core cutting may damage the future performance. Thus core should be taken at the nearest non critical locations. Some times aesthetic consideration concerning the appearance may also influence the choice of the location. For checking the specifications compliance, the cores should be taken avoiding the un representative concrete (normally occupying top 25% in case of columns, walls, deep beams and top thickness of slab). The reinforcement bars should be avoided as far as possible. In fact core test should be performed when other non destructive tests are not possible to perform.

19.13.3. Size of the Core

For compression testing, the standards specify that the diameter of the core should be at least three times the nominal maximum size of aggregate. It has been observed that as the ratio of aggregate size to core diameter increases, the accuracy of the results decreases. Further codes state that a minimum diameter of 100 mm of core should be used. In case of small sized members where large holes would damage the structure, smaller diameters are used. The choice of core diameter is also influenced by the length of the core specimen which can be obtained. Generally it has been accepted that the cores for compressive testing, the length/diameter ratio should be between 1.0 and 2.0. From economical considerations *i.e.* for reducing the drilling cost, damages and variability along the length etc. the core should be kept as small as possible. The length/dia ratio may be kept from 1.0 to .2. However to minimise the uncertaintity in relating the core strength to cylinder or cuble strength, the length/diameter ratio of the core should be close to 2.0.

19.13.4. Number of cores

As per code requirements the minimum number of standard cores should be 3 and non standard small sized cores should be 9.0.

19.13.5. Equipment

For drilling the cores, the portable rotary drill having cutting tool with diamond bits and water supply arrangement to lubricate the cutter is sufficient.

19.13.6. Testing

The cores obtained from drilling are trimmed and their ends either capped or grinded before visual examination, assessment of voids percentage and density. For trimming the core diamond saw is used. The core should have parallel ends, normal to the axis of the core. The ends of the core are capped with high alumina cement mortar to provide parallel end surfaces perpendicular to the axis of the core. The cap of the core end should be as thin as possible.

(*a*) **Visual examination.** The honey combing, cracks, aggregate distribution, drilling damages and other defects are easily seen on a dry surface. However for the assessment of type of aggregate, size and their characteristics, a wet surface is preferable. Voids between 0.5 to 3 mm are classified as small, 3 to 6 mm sized voids as medium and greater than 6 mm as large voids. When the voids are inter connected, they are called honey combing. The precise locations of the reinforcement present in the core must also be recorded.

(*b*) **Strength tests.** Following two types of strength tests are performed on the cores:

(*i*) *Compressive strength.* Before testing, the cores are capped and kept immersed in water at least for two days. At the time of test the cores are taken out and water on the surface is wipped out. Thus the cores are tested in saturated surface dry condition. The core is placed in the testing machine centrally and loaded at a rate of 0.2 MPa to 0.4 MPa per second and the mode of failure is noted. If the cap of any core cracks or get separated from the core, the result should be neglected.

(*ii*) *Tensile strength.* The tensile strength may be determined by the splitting test discussed earlier in this chapter on page 382.

19.13.7. Factors influencing the Core Compressive strength

Following factors are significant which influence the core compressive strength

1. Moisture and voids. The moisture condition of the core influences the measured strength. It has been observed that a saturated specimen has a value of 10 to 15% lower than comparable dry specimen. Thus while estimating the actual insitu concrete strength the relative moisture conditions of the core and the insitu concrete should be taken into consideration. Voids in the core concrete will reduce the measured strength. *Peterson* found that the ratio of core strength to standard cylinder strength at the same age is always less than 1.0, and decreases with the increase in the strength of cylinder. Upto cylinder strength of 20 MPa it is just less than 1 and 0.7 for 60 MPa strength.

2. Length/diameter ratio of core. It has been observed that as the *l/d* ratio increases, the measured strength decreases due to the effect of specimen shape and stress distribution during the test as shown in Fig. 14.4. For establishing a relation between core strength and standard cube strength, ratio of *l/d* = 2.0 is taken as the basis of computation.

3. Diameter of Core. The diameter of the core may influence the measured strength and variability. Measured concrete strength decreases with the increase in the size of specimen. This effect is significant. However this effect will be small for sizes above 100 mm, but for smaller sizes this effect is significant.

4. Position of cut out concrete in structure. Cores taken from near the top surface have usually lowest strength may it be a column, beam, or wall or slab. With the increase in depth below the top surface the strength increases, but at depths more than 300 mm, there is no further increase in strength. The difference may be 10 to 20%. In case of slabs, poor curing increases this difference.

5. Direction of drilling. Due to the layering effect, the measured strength of specimen drilled vertically relative to the direction of casting is likely to be greater than that for a horizontally drilled specimen from the same concrete. The average value of 8% of this difference has been reported in literature.

6. Effect of age. It has been observed that insitu, concrete gains little strength after 28 days. Tests on high strength concrete have shown that, though the core strength increases with age upto 1 year, but remains lower than the 28 days standard cylinder

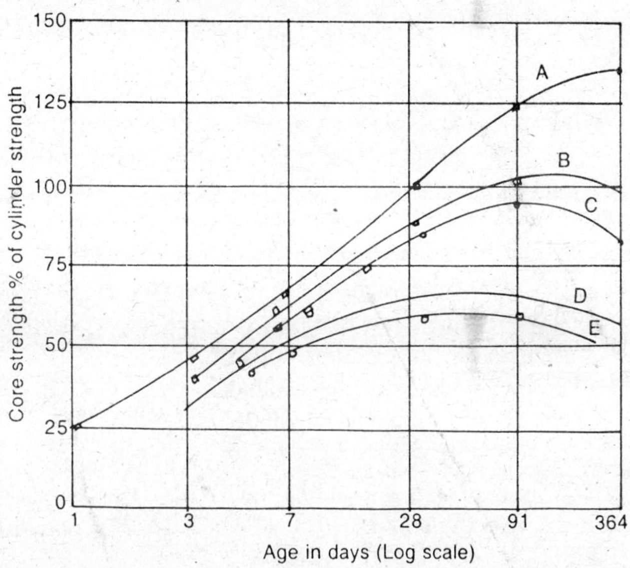

Fig. 19.6. Development of strength of core with age

Table 19.3. Development of Core strength with age

S. No.	*Age in days*	*Strength in MPa*		*Core strength as % strength of 28 days standard cylinder*
		Standard cylinder	*Core*	
1.	7	66.0	57.9	72%
2.	28	80.4	58.5	73%
3.	56	86.0	61.2	76%
4.	180	97.9	70.6	88%
5.	365	101.3	75.4	94%

strength as shown in Fig. 19.6 and Table 19.3. On the other hand Petersons has suggested the increase in core strength over that of 28 days cylinder strength as 10% after 3 months and 15% after 6 months. Thus the effect of age is not easy to discuss, but in the absence of definite moist curing, no increase in strength should be expected. Curve A of Fig. 19.6 shows the strength development of a standard cylinder. Curve B shows the strength of well cured slab core tested dry. Curve C shows strength development of well cured slab core tested wet. Curve D shows strength development of poorly cured slab, core tested dry and curve E shows strength development of poorly cured slab core tested wet.

19.13.8. Reinforcement

Due to the presence of reinforcement, the measured strength of concrete is found reduced upto 10%. Thus as far as possible reinforcement from the core must be avoided. In case the reinforcement is present in the core, the measured core strength should be corrected as follows:

$$\text{Corrected strength} = \text{Measured strength} \times \left[1 + 1.5\left(\frac{\phi_r, h}{\phi_c \times l}\right)\right]$$

where,

ϕ_r = diameter of reinforcement bar

ϕ_c = diameter of the core

h = distance of bar axis from the nearest end of core

l = uncapped length of core

In case core has mutiple bars, then

$$\text{Corrected strength} = \text{Measured strength} \times \left[1.0 + 1.5\left(\frac{\Sigma\,\phi_r \times h}{\phi_c \times l}\right)\right]$$

If the spacing of two bars is less than the diameter of the larger bar, then the bar with higher value of (ϕ_r, h) should be considered.

19.13.9. Estimation of cube strength from core strength

The equivalent cube strength can be estimated in two steps as follows:

1. To convert the core strength to an equivalent standard cylinder strength, a correction for the effect of length/diameter ratio is applied.
2. To convert the equivalent standard cylinder strength obtained in step (*i*) a proper relation ship between the strength of cylinder and cube is used. Generally the cube strength is taken as 1.25 times the cylinder strength for $l/d = 2.0 = \lambda$.

Taking into account the strength difference of 6% between a core with cut surface relative to cast cylinder and strength reduction of 15% for weaker top surface zone of a corresponding cast cylinder adopted by B.S. 1881, Part-120-1983.

(*i*) For vertical drilled core

$$\text{Estimated insitu cube strength} = \frac{2.3 f_c}{1.5 + 1/\lambda} \qquad \ldots(i)$$

(*ii*) For horizontal drilled core,

$$\text{Estimated insitu cube strength} = \frac{2.5 f_c}{1.5 + 1/\lambda} \qquad \ldots(ii)$$

where f_c is the measured strength.

However for the potential or target strength of a standard specimen made from a particular mix is about 30% higher than the actual fully compacted in situ strength. The potential strength is the strength equivalent to the 28 day strength of the standard test specimen. Then the expression for the cube strength is given as (*iii*) For vertical drilled core

$$\text{The Estimated potential cube strength} = \frac{3.0 f_c}{1.5 + 1/\lambda} \quad \ldots(iii)$$

(*iv*) For horizontal drilled core

$$\text{The Estimated potential cube strength} = \frac{3.25 f_c}{1.5 + 1/\lambda} \quad \ldots(iv)$$

IS 516-1959 describes the method of preparation of core after drilling and the procedure of test. According to IS 456-1978, the concrete in the member represented by the core test shall be considered acceptable if the average equivalent cube strength of the core is equal to at least 85% of the cube strength of the grade of concrete specified for the corresponding age, and no individual core has the strength less than 75%.

19.13.10. Disadvantages of Core method

Following are the disadvantages of core testing method:

1. The structural integrity of the concrete across the full cross section may be affected.
2. The ratio of length/diameter other than standard ratio 2.0 will have its effect on strength.
3. Capping of both ends of the core is also liable to affect the strength of concrete.
4. Existence of reinforcement will also have its effects on the strength of concrete.

Example 1. *A 55 mm non standard diameter core drilled vertically from a structure foundation contained one 20 mm diameter reinforcement bar normal to the core axis which was located 28 mm from one end. The core length after caping is 88 mm. The crushing load on the core length is 45 kN. Determine (a) the insitu cube strength and, (b) potential cube strength.*

Solution. As per B.S. 1881-Part-120-1983 insitu concrete strength is given as follows:

$$\text{Measured concrete core strength} = \frac{45 \times 10^3}{\pi/4\,(55)^2} = 18.94 \text{ MPa}$$

$$\text{Length to diameter ratio of the core} = \frac{88}{55} = \frac{8}{5} = 1.6$$

$$\therefore \text{ Estimated in situ concrete strength} = \frac{2.3 \times 18.94}{(1.5 + 1/1.6)} = \frac{2.3 \times 18.94}{1.5 + 0.625}$$

$$= \frac{2.3 \times 18.94}{2.125} = 20.5 \text{ MPa}$$

$$\text{Correction factor for reinforcement} = 1 + 1.5\left(\frac{20}{55} \times \frac{28}{88}\right)$$

$$= 1.0 + 0.174 = 1.174$$

$$\text{Corrected in situ concrete strength} = 20.5 \times 1.174$$

$$= 24.07 \text{ MPa}$$

Adding ± 12% for an individual result (2.8884) = 24.07 ± 2.89 MPa = 26.96 MPa

(*b*) Potential cube strength for vertical drilled core

$$\text{Estimated potential cube strength} = \frac{3.0 \times 18.94}{1.5 + 1/1.6} = \frac{56.82}{2.125}$$

$$= 26.74 \text{ MPa}$$

$$\text{Corrected for reinforcement, potential cube strength} = 26.74 \times 1.174$$

$$= 31.74 \text{ MPa}$$

19.14. ACCELERATED CURING TEST

Concrete mixes usually are designed for 7 and 28 days compressive strength. The concrete test results are available only on the expiry of 7 or 28 days period. During this period a considerable quantity of additional concrete may have been placed in the structure. At this late stage any remedial action, if the concrete is found too weak is impossible. If it is too strong then the mix was un economical. This is the main disadvantage of the standard compression test of concrete.

Thus it would be advantageous to be able to predict the 28 days strength with in few hours of casting, 8 hours period is found most suitable. Unfortunately, the 1 to 3 day strength of a given mix cured under normal conditions is not reliable in this respect as it is very sensitive to small variations in temperature during the first few hours of casting and to the fineness of cement. Thus the 28 day concrete strength after casting can be predicted by the accelerated curing methods.

19.14.1. Methods

ASTM C 684-89 has prescribed the following three methods of accelerated curing test for cylinders:

1. **Warm water method.** In this method, the cylinders after casting and finishing are immersed immediately in water at 35°C tempere in covered condition. After 24 hours of immersion, the cylinders are taken out, capped and tasted.
2. **Boiling water method.** In this method, the cast cylinders are cured for 23 hours in moist environment at 21°C and then immersed in boiling water for $3\frac{1}{2}$ hours. After curing in boiling water for $3\frac{1}{2}$ hours, specimens are taken out and allowed to cool for 1 hour. After cooling for 1 hour, specimens are capped and tested at the age of $28\frac{1}{2}$ hours.
3. **Autogeneous method.** In this method the specimens are cured by insulation for 48 hours, then capped and tested at the age of approximately 49 hours.

B.S. 1881 Part-112-1983 also gives following three methods. In this case in all the three methods the test cubes are cured in covered condition at temperatures of 35°C and 55°C and 82°C respectively.

1. **35°C temperature cured method.** In this method the cubes cast and immersed in covered condition in water at 35°C temperature after 15 minutes of casting. The specimens are cured at 35°C temperature for 24 hours. After this period the specimens are tested as usual.
2. **55°C temperature cured method.** In this method the specimens are allowed to remain undisturbed at 20°C for 1 hour after casting. Then the specimens are immersed in covered condition in water at 55°C and allowed to remain there for 20 hours. Then the specimens are allowed to cool in water at 20°C for 1 to 2 hours before testing.
3. **82°C temperature cured method.** In this method the specimens are allowed to remain un disturbed for at least 1 hour after casting. After this period the cubes are placed in a empty curing tank. Then the tank is filled with water at ambient temperature. Then the temperature of this water is raised to 82°C in a period of 2 hours. This temperature is maintained for further 14 hours. After this period, the water is discharged quickly and the cubes are tested with in 1 hour of discharge of water, while they are still hot.

The accelerated strength obtained by any of the above methods are all different and are lower than the 28 day strength of standard specimens. However for a given mix, the accelerated strength obtained by any method can be correlated with the standard specimen strength either at 7 days or 28 days.

19.15. INDIAN METHODS

The Indian Bureau of standards IS 9013-1978 has suggested the following two methods. Any of the two methods may be adopted for accelerated curing of concrete.

1. Warm water method. In this method the specimens are immersed in water for $1\frac{1}{2}$ to $3\frac{1}{2}$ hours after moulding.

Curing water temperature = 55 ± 1°C

Curing period = 20 hours ± 10 minutes

After the curing period, the specimen (cube) are demoulded and cooled at 27 ± 2°C for 1 hour before testing.

2. Boiling water curing method. In this method following procedure in adopted

Standard moist curing for 23 hour ± 15 minutes

Curing water temperature = 100° C

Curing period = $3\frac{1}{2}$ hours ± 5 minutes

Cooling period = 2 hours

The actual correction of accelerated test results at 28 day normally cured specimens depends upon the curing method, chemical composition of cement and mix proportions of concrete. It is recommended that relation between the two strengths should be established prior to placing concrete in the structure, so that accelerated test can be used as a rapid quality control test for detecting variations in the mix proportions. The relation suggested can be used to predict the 28 day compressive strength of the normally cured concrete with in ± 15% limits.

Fixed set method

In Canada, following relation between the accelerated strength R_a and 28 day cylinder strength R_{28} has been established, which is independent of type of cement, mix proportion, and type of admixtures etc.

$$\text{In MPa,} \quad R_{28} = \frac{180\, R_a}{80 + R_a} \qquad \ldots(1)$$

In this case, the accelerated curing of concrete is delayed till a fixed set has taken place. It is measured by the proctor needle penetration under load of 24 MPa. After a delay of 20 minutes, the moulded standard cylinder is placed in boiling water for 16 hours. After this period the specimen is demoulded and allowed to cool for 30 minutes. The cylinder is capped and tested after removal from boiling water.

Disadvantages of the method

Following are the disadvantages of this so called fixed set method:

(*a*) Time is wasted to ascertain the set of concrete.

(*b*) The erratic nature of the needle penetration test.

Thus it can be said that the standard compression test is really only a relative measure of the strength of concrete used in the structure. It can also be argued that there is no inherent superiority of the standard 28 days test over other tests. In fact there is a school of thought which argues that the accelerated strength test should be considered as a basis for acceptance of concrete, rather than nearly a means of predicting the 7 or 28 days strength.

19.16. BOND TO REINFORCEMENT

Determination of bond strength. Actually it is difficult to define bond strength. ASTM C 234-91 (a) has prescribed a method for the determination of the bond strength called *pull out test.* In this test a 19 mm (3/4") diameter deformed bar is embedded in a 150 mm cube. The bar is pulled out relative to the concrete till the bond fails or concrete splits or a minimum slip of 2.5 mm takes place at the loaded end of the bar. The bond strength then is taken as the load on the bar at failure divided by the nominal embedded surface area of the bar.

Surface protective treatment of reinforcement bars may reduce the bond strength due to the absence of rusted surface of the reinforcement, which enhances the bond strength. However the bond of galvanised reinforcement was found as good as that of ordinary steel bars and wires. The thickness of a galvanised coating usually varies from 0.03 mm to 0.1 mm. Due to this galvanised coating the steel is protected against corrosion even when cover to reinforcement is reduced upto 25% of the nominal value. With the galvanised coating the light weight aggregate concrete can be used with out increased cover. Fig. 19.7 shows relation between compressive and bond strength of plain and deformed bar.

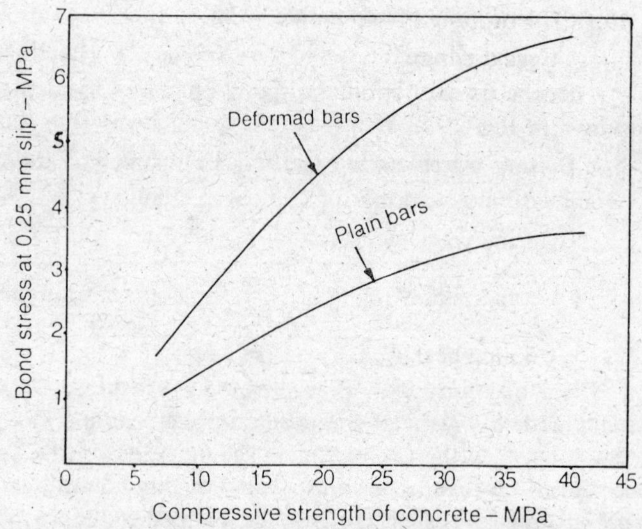

Fig. 19.7. Relation between bond stress and compressive strength of concrete

19.17. NON DESTRUCTIVE TESTING

Non destructive testing methods have been in use for the last about 40 to 50 years. During this period progress in this field has been made vary fast. Now it is considered that non destructive testing methods are a powerful means for evaluating the strength, durability and quality control of the existing concrete structures. In addition to above, the depth of cracks, micro cracks and progressive deterioration can also be studied by this method.

Though non destructive testing methods are relatively simple to perform, but the analysis and interpretation of these tests is tedious. Thus special knowledge is required to analyse the properties of hardened concrete. In the case of non destructive testing, the specimens are not loaded upto failure and the strength estimated can not be expected to yield absolute values of strength.

Thus these methods are used to measure some other properties of concrete from which its strength, durability and elastic parameters are estimated. Some of the such properties of concrete are hardness, resistance to penetration of projectiles, resonant frequency and its ability to allow ultrasonic pulse velocity to propagate through it. With the help of the electrical properties of concrete and its ability to absorb, scatter and transmit *x*-rays and Gamma-rays etc. moisture content, density, thickness and cement content of concrete can be estimated.

19.18. NON DESTRUCTIVE TESTING METHODS

Based upon the different properties of concrete, following non destructive methods have been developed.

1. Surface hardness test
2. Rebound test
3. Penetration and pull out tests
4. Dynamic or vibration tests
5. Combined method
6. Radio active and nuclear methods
7. Magnetic and electrical methods
8. Acoustic emission technique etc. Here some of the above methods have been discussed.

19.18.1. Surface hardness test

The hardness of the concrete surface usually is determined by the rebound hammer test. The rebound hammer test was developed in 1948 by a Swiss Engineer named Ernst Schmit. The weight of the hammer used is about 2 kg and its impact energy 2.2 N.m.

19.18.2. Equipment and its working

A typical rebound test hammer is shown in Fig. 19.8. All parts of the equipment are shown on the Fig.

It consists of a spring controlled hammer mass that slides on a plunger with in a tubular casing as shown in Fig. 19.8. When the plunger is pressed against the surface of the concrete, the mass rebounds

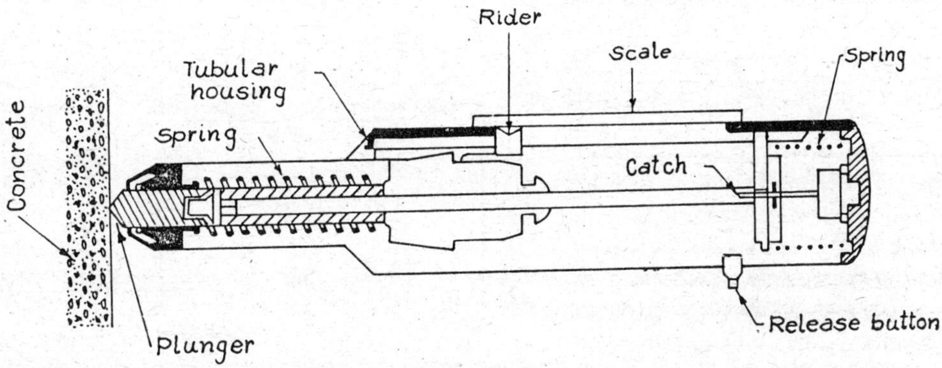

Fig. 19.8. Schmidt hardness tester hammer

from the plunger. It retracts against the force of the spring. This spring is automatically released when fully tensioned, causing the hammer mass to impact against the concrete through the plunger. When the spring controlled mass, rebounds it takes with it a rider which slides along a graduated scale and can be seen through a small window in the side of the casing. The rider can be held in any position on the scale by depressing the locking button to record the reading. The distance travelled by the mass is called the rebound number. It is indicated by the rider moving along a graduated scale.

The equipment can be operated vertically or horizontally. The plunger is pressed hard and steadily against the concrete surface to be tested at right angles, till the spring loaded mass is triggered off from its

(*a*) Instrument ready for test

(*b*) Body pushed towards test object

(*c*) Hammer is released

(*d*) Hammer rebounds

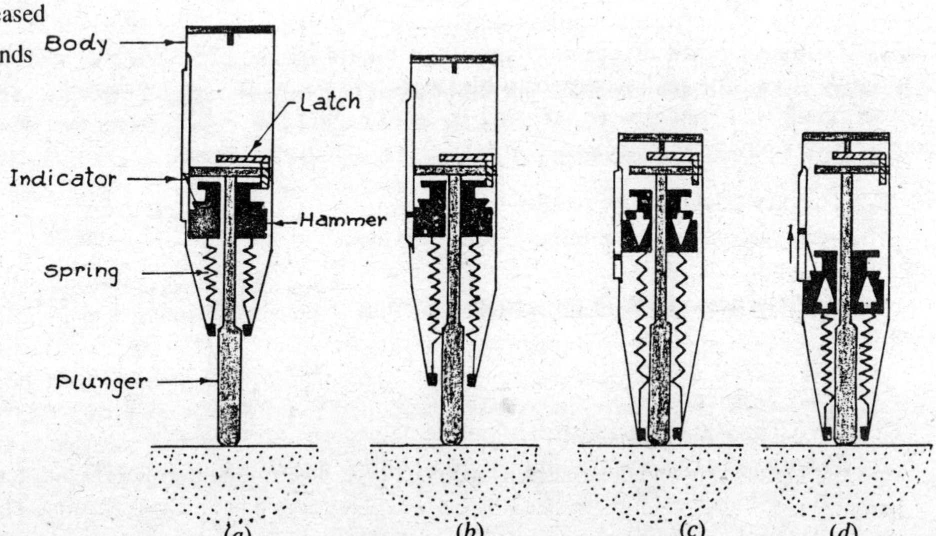

Fig. 19.9. Cross section of rebound hammer showing operating principle

locked position. After impact, the scale index is read while the hammer still is in the test position. The measurement of the distance taken is an arbitrary quantity, known as rebound number.

Each hammer varies considerably in performance. Thus it needs calibration for use on concrete made with the aggregates from the specific source, as the reading of the test is very sensitive to the local variations in the concrete, specially to the aggregate particles near the surface. The hammer may strike an aggregate particle, giving misleading result. Thus it is necessary to take several readings at each test location. B.S. 1881, Part 202 specifies 12 readings over an area of about 300 square mm. The surface should be smooth, clean and dry. The loose material from the surface must be removed. Fig. 19.9* shows the cross section of rebound hammer and its operating principle. Fig. 19.9 (*a*) shows the ready state of equipment for test, position (*b*) shows the body pushed towards the test object, position (*c*) shows the release of hammer and position (*d*) shows the hammer rebound.

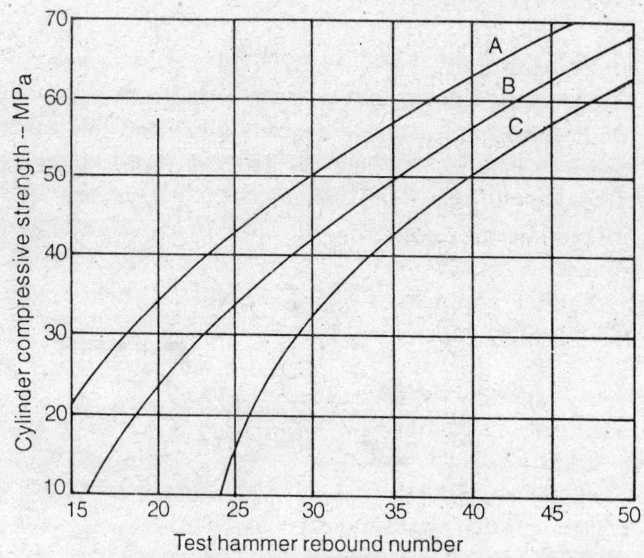

Fig. 19.10. Relation between rebound number and compressive strength of concrete

The test can be conducted horizontally, vertically upwards, or down wards or at any intermediate angle. At each angle the rebound number will be different for the same concrete. Thus separate calibration or correction charts for each condition should be prepared. Fig. 19.10 shows the relation ship between rebound number of test hammer and compressive strength of concrete curve A shows the relation between rebound number in vertically down impact and cylinder strength of concrete. Curve B shows relation of horizontal impact and curve C shows relation of vertically upward impact, while Fig. 19.11 shows the relationship between rebound number, angle and condition of moisture of test on compressive strength of concrete.

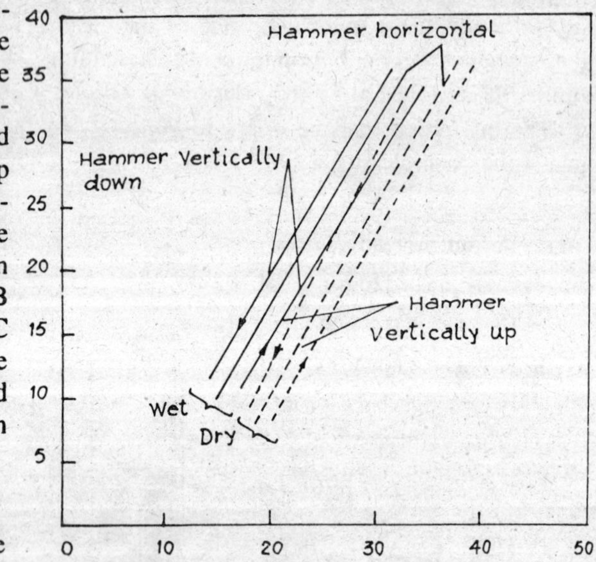

Fig. 19.11. Relation between rebound No., compressive strength, Diriction and moisture condition of specimen

19.18.3. Factors affecting the results

Following factors have been found affecting the results of the test:

(*a*) Mix characteristics. In this group following factors are covered:

(*i*) Type of cement

(*ii*) Cement content

(*iii*) Type and characteristics of coarse aggregate

(*b*) Member characteristics. In this group following factors are covered:

(*i*) Compaction of concrete

(*ii*) Age of concrete

*Courtesy M.S. Shetty

(*iii*) Internal moisture condition of concrete
(*iv*) Smoothness of surface under test
(*v*) Shape, size and rigidity of member
(*vi*) Temperature of concrete etc.

19.18.4. Relation between rebound number and strength of concrete

Experimental results have shown that there is a general correlation between the rebound number and compressive strength of concrete. However there is wide range of disagreement among the researchers regarding the accuracy of estimation of strength from rebound numbers. The variation in strength of a properly calibrated hammer has been observed between ± 15% and ± 20%.

19.18.5. Application of the test

International survey was conducted during 1965-1967 on the use of Schmitt rebound hammer. During this survey consensus emerged that this test is not fit to be used as acceptance test. However it is useful for the following applications

1. For checking uniformity of concrete quality
2. Approximate estimation of strength
3. Comparing a given concrete with a specified quality concrete

19.19. PENETRATION RESISTANCE TEST

During 1964-66, a technique or test was developed for concrete testing in the laboratory as well as insitu. Commercially this test is called as windsor probe test. The strength of the concrete is estimated from the depth of penetration of a metal rod driven by a standard charge of powder. The under lying principle is that for standard test conditions, the penetration is inversely proportional to the compressive strength of the concrete, but the relation depends upon the hardness of the aggregate. Thus the hardness of aggregate has to be determined on MOh's scale, which can be done with out any difficulty. Charts of strength versus depth of penetration are available for aggregates with hardness between 3 to 7 on Moh's scale. However in practice the penetration resistance should be correlated with the compressive strength of standard test specimen. Fig. 19.12 shows the relation between exposed probe length and 28 days compressive strength of concrete based on the work Arni H.T.

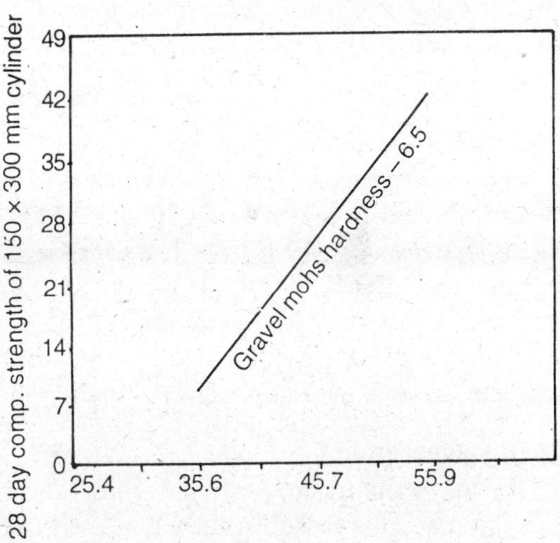

Fig. 19.12. Exposed probe length mm

Penetration resistance test basically measures the hardness of the surface like Schmidt hammer test. It also does not yield absolute values of strengths. However it is very usefull for determining the relative strength of concrete in the same structure or relative strength in different structures with out extensive calibration with specific concrete.

19.19.1. Test-Procedure

The probes are driven into the concrete in a set of three in close vicinity by firing a precision powder charge cardridge. The exposed depth is measured by calibrated depth gauge. The average of these depths is used in determining the strength. The penetration resistance test can be considered almost non destructive as the damage to the concrete made by 6.3 mm probe only locally and re testing in the vicinity is possible.

19.19.2. Advantages of penetration test

In this method the hardness of the concrete is measured upto about 6.3 mm depth of concrete and not just at the surface. In this case there is no extra cost of handling, storing, cutting or making good test pieces as in the core test method.

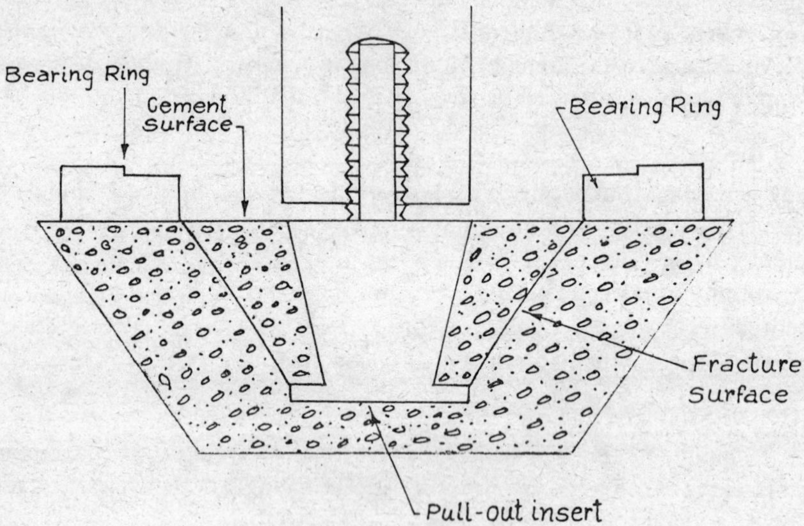

Fig. 19.13. Pull out test assembly

19.20. PULL OUT TEST

This test measures the force required to pull out a previously cast in steel rod with an embedded enlarged end as shown in Fig. 19.13. The test procedure has been described in ASTMC 900-87. However the reliability of the test has not yet been established. In Denmark this test has been successfully used. The stronger the concrete, more is the force required to pull out.

19.20.1. Operation

In the operation of test, the core of concrete is pulled out and the force required is related to the compressive strength of the parent concrete.

Due to the shape, the steel rod assembly is pulled out with a lump of concrete, approximately in the shape of a frustum of a cone. The pull out strength is calculated as the ratio of the pull out force to the idealized area of the frustum. Actually the concrete is subjected to tension and shear, but the calculated pull out strength approximately is taken as the shearing strength of the concrete.

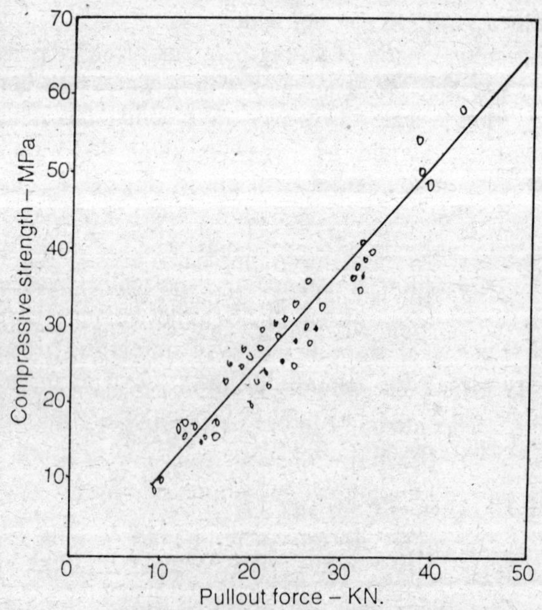

Fig. 19.14. Relation between compressive strength of cores and pull out force for actual structure

The ratio of the pull out strength and compressive strength decreases slightly with the increase in strength of concrete, but for a given strength it is independent of age. However the pull out force or strength correlates well with the compressive strength of core or standard cylinders for a wide range of curing conditions and ages. The typical test results are shown in Fig. 19.14. The ideal way to use pullout test in the field would be to incorporate assemblies in the structure. These assemblies can be pull out at any time, the need felt. It has been suggested that this test need not be carried out to completion. It may be sufficienet to apply a predetermined force to the embeded rod, if it does not pull out, the structure is assumed safe.

19.21. DYNAMIC OR VIBRATION METHODS

These methods are important non destructive methods used for testing concrete strength and other properties as well. The fundamental principle of working of these methods is the propagation of sound velocity through a solid material. A mathematical relationship could be established between the velocity of sound through the specimen and its resonant frequency. From these relation ship, the modulus of elasticity of the material is determined. For deriving these relationship the solid mediums are considered to be homogeneous, isotropic and perfectly elastic. However these relations are also applied to heterogeneous materials like concrete. The velocity of sound V in a solid material is a function of the square root of the ratio of its modulus of elasticity 'E' and its density ρ. Thus

$$V = f\left[\frac{gE}{\rho}\right]^{1/2}$$

where g is the acceleration due to gravity.

The velocity of sound in a solid material can be estimated by knowing the resonant frequency of the specimen or by noting the time of travel of short pulses of vibrations passing through the samples. In non destructive testing of concrete either resonance method or pulse velocity method may be adopted.

19.21.1. Resonant Frequency method

This method is based upon the determination of the fundamental resonant frequency of vibration of a specimen. The resonance is indicated by the point of maximum amplitude for the various driving frequencies generated. The resonant frequency method usually is used in the laboratory. The equipment used for the resonant frequency method usually is known as 'Sonometer'.

19.21.2. Use of Resonant frequency test

The resonant frequency test may be used for the following purposes:

1. For studying the deterioration effects of concrete subjected to repeated cycles of freezing and thawing.
2. To study the effects due to acidic and alkali reactions.
3. For determining the damage due to fire.
4. To calculate the dynamic Young's Modulus of elasticity of concrete, but the values obtained are some what higher than those obtained with standard static tests.

19.21.3. Pulse velocity method

This method can be sub divided into the following two groups:

1. **Mechanical sonic pulse method.** In this method the measurements of the time of travel of longitudinal or compressional waves generated by a single impact hammer blow or repeated blows are taken.
2. **Ultra sonic pulse velocity method.** In this method the measurements of the time of travel of electronically generated mechanical pulses through the concrete are taken. Out of the above two types of pulses, the ultra sonic velocity pulse method has become more popular through out the world.

1. Mechanical sonic pulse velocity method

In this method the pulses can be generated either by hammer blows or by the use of an electro acoustic transducer. For generating pulses electro acoustic transducers are preferred as they provide better control on the type and frequency of the pulses generated. Instrument used in this methods is called 'Soniscope'.

In this method when mechanical impulses are applied to a solid mass, three different kinds of waves are generated. Generally these waves are known as longitudinal waves, shear waves and surface waves. All these three waves travel with-different speeds. The speed of the longitudinal or compressional wave is twice that of the other two types, the shear and surface waves. The surface waves are the slowest of the three.

2. Ultra sonic pulse velocity method

The ultra sonic pulse velocity method basically consists of measuring the velocity of electronic pulse passing through the concrete from a transmitting transducer to a receiving transducer. Though a considerable degree of success has been achieved in the determination of the longitudinal wave velocity in concrete, but there is no unique relationship between the velocity and the strength of concrete. However under specific conditions the two quantities are directly related. The common factor is the density of concrete. A change in the density of the concrete results in a change of the velocity of the pulse.

The method is based on the principle that the pulse velocity passing through the concrete primarily is dependent upon the elastic properties of the material and is independent of the shape or its geometry. The pulse velocities range from about 3 to 5 km/sec. The pulse generator circuit consists of electronic circuit for generating pulses and a transducer for transforming these electronic pulses into mechanical energy having vibration frequencies in the range of 15 to 50 Khz. A typical test circuit is shown in Fig. 19.15. The pulses are generated at regular time interval between 10 to 50 seconds. The time of travel of the ultrasonic pulse passing through the concrete is measured accurately with an accuracy of ± 1%. The transit time is displayed either on an oscilloscope or read digitally. The path length between the transducers divided by the time of travel gives the average velocity of wave propagation. For use with concrete, transducers with natural frequencies between 20 and 200 KHz are most suitable.

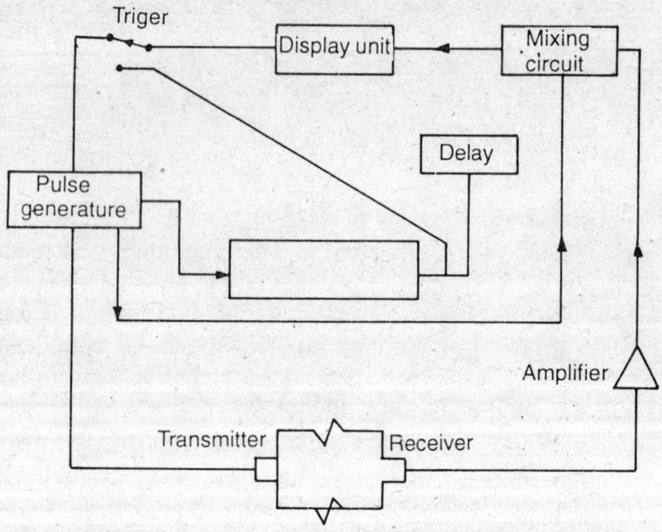

Fig. 19.15. Typical ultrasonic pulse velocity test circuit

Recently battery operated fully portable digitised units have been introduced for this purpose. This unit is called portable ultrasonic non destructive digital indicating tester. In short it is known as 'PUNDIT'. It weighs about 3 kg only.

19.21.4. Techniques for measuring pulse velocity through concrete

For transmitting pulse velocity through concrete following types of transducers have been found to be suitable.

1. Piezo-electric crystal transducer
2. Barium titanate

3. Lead Zirconate titanate transducer

Out of these transducers piezo-electrical crystal transducer is most popular.

The transducer is kept in contact with the concrete, so that the vibrations travel through it and picked up by an other transducer in contact with the opposite face of the specimen under test.

The transducers generate an electrical signal, which is fed through an amplifier to a plate of a cathode ray tube. A second plate supplies timing marks at fixed intervals. Thus from the measurement of displacement of the pulse signal and time of travel, the velocity of pulse may be calculate.

19.21.5. Arrangement of transducers

Transducers may be arranged on concrete surface in the following three ways as shown in Fig. 19.16.

1. On opposite face (direct transmission)
2. On adjacent face (Semi direct transmission)
3. On same face (Indirect transmission)

1. On opposite face. The arrangement of fixing the transducers on opposite sides has been found to be the best for the following reasons.

(*a*) The maximum pulse energy is transmitted at right angles to the face of the transmitter.

(*b*) The direct transmission method or opposite side arrangement is most reliable for the measurement of transit time.

(*c*) The path of pulse travel is clearly defined and can be measured accurately.

This approach is recommended for assessing the quality of concrete where ever possible.

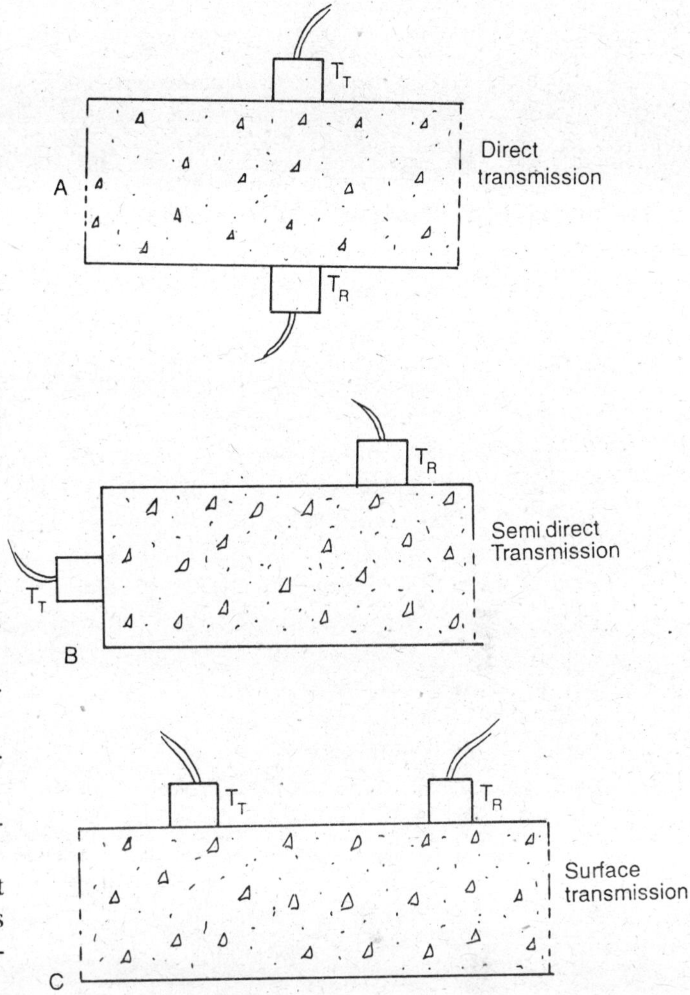

T_T = Transducer transmitter

T_R = Transducer receiver

Fig. 19.16. Typical arrangement of transducers

2. Semi direct or adjacent face method

This method can be used satisfactorily under the following conditions:

(*a*) If the path length is not large

(*b*) The angle between the transducers is not large

If these conditions are not met the clear signals will not be received due to the reduced or weak transmitted pulse.

3. Same face or indirect transmission method

In this case the pulse velocity is measured parallel to the surface of the concrete. In this case energy received is considerably low and the accuracy of readings is correspondingly decreased. In this case the properties of the surface layer only are known. It does not give any indication of strength of concrete at depth. Hence it is least satisfactory.

Transducers making point contact only with the surface of concrete are advantageous as no surface treatment is required, where as on a flat surface the good contact of transducers must be ensured over a considerable area. The probe transducers are more sensitive to operator pressure.

19.21.6. Factors affecting the value of pulse velocity

Following factors affect the value of pulse velocity:

1. **Smoothness of Contact surface under test.** There should be good acoustical contact between the concrete surface and the face of each transducer. Generally in normal testing, there is sufficient cast surface available for good contact. However in cases as the top surface of cylinder, it is desirable to smoothen the cylinder surface either by grinding or caping and holding the transducer tightly against the concrete surface. In addition a thin film of oil, soap etc. should be used.
2. **Length of path of pulse velocity.** As we know that concrete inherently is heterogeneous. Thus it is essential that path length of the pulse should be sufficiently long to avoid the introduction of any error due to its heterogeneity. In field work it does not pose any difficulty as the pulse velocity measurements generally are carried on thick structural concrete members, where the path length may be about 300 mm in case of columns and 23 meters in mass concrete as dams. However in the laboratory where small length specimens are used, the path length may affect the pulse velocity readings.
3. **Temperature of concrete.** It has been observed that variation in ambient temperature affects the pulse velocity in concrete significantly. The variation between 5°C to 30°C does not affect the pulse velocity significantly, but at temperatures between 30°C and 60°C an reduction of 5% in the pulse velocity has been reported. Probably this might have happened due to the development of micro cracking in the concrete.

Further it has been observed that below freezing temperature the pulse velocity increases due to the freezing of free water with in the concrete. At 4°C through the water saturated concrete an increase in pulse velocity up to 7.5% has been recorded. Corrections to be applied to pulse velocity due to change in temperature is shown in Table 19.4 below.

Table 19.4. Corrections to be applied to the measured pulse velocity due to change in temperature

Temperature in °C	*Correction to be applied in %*	
	Air dried concrete	*Water saturated concrete*
+ 60	+ 5.0	+ 4.0
+ 50	+ 3.5	+ 2.8
+ 40	+ 2.0	+ 1.7
+ 20	0.0	0.0
– 0	– 0.5	– 1.0
– 4 and below	– 1.5	– 7.5

4. **Moisture conditions of concrete.** It has been observed that in general the pulse velocity through concrete increases with the increase in moisture content of concrete. This effect is observed more in low strength concrete than high strength concrete. The difference may be from 10 to 15%. Thus it is considered that pulse velocity in saturated concrete is higher by about 2% than that of similar dry concrete and when water has frozen in concrete the pulse velocity increases by several percent.
5. **Presence of reinforcing steel.** It has been reported that pulse velocity in steel is 1.2 to 1.9 times

that of plain concrete. Thus the pulse velocity measured near the reinforcing steel bars may be high, not representing the true velocity of concrete. Thus the presence of steel bars in concrete affects the pulse velocity to a great extent. Therefore it is desirable to choose the pulse path that avoids the effects of reinforcing steel bars. When it is not possible to adopt such a path, suitable corrections are applied to the measured values of pulse velocity, taking into account the proximity of the pulse path to the reinforcing steel bars. The value of correction depends upon the quantity and orientation of the steel with respect to the pulse path of propagation, and the pulse velocity in the concrete.

(*a*) When the axis of reinforcement bars is perpendicular to the direction of propagation and the quantity of steel is small, the effect of reinforcement steel generally is small. The correction factor may be of the order of 1 to 4% depending upon the quality (strength) of surrounding concrete. The higher the quality of concrete lower the correction factor.

(*b*) When the reinforcement is parallel to the direction of propagation of the pulse velocity, it is difficult to avoid the effect of reinforcement steel. In this case the measured pulse velocity may be corrected, but the correction factors are not exact, but approximately. In case of two way reinforcement, it is almost impossible to make any reliable corrections.

6. The pulse velocity also depends upon the material and mix proportion of the concrete. The aggregates due to their density and modulus of elasticity affect the pulse velocity to a great extent.

19.21.7. Accuracy of Measurements

Generally the ultrasonic concrete tester measures the time of travel through small specimens with an accuracy of 0.1 microseconds. For the specimens of the same length, the accuracy of measurement for 'SONISCOPE' and 'PUNDIT' is of the order of 0.5 micro-seconds. Thus for laboratory studies under controlled conditions ultrasonic concrete tester is the ideal instrument. For field studies where the path lengths are longer Soniscope and 'Pundit' are the best equipments. The Pundit being lighter in weight about 3 kg only, is easy to carry along with.

19.21.8. Application or uses of pulse velocity methods

The pulse velocity methods have been used to evaluate the concrete structures and attempts have been made to correlate the pulse velocity with strength and other properties of concrete. Various uses of the pulse velocity methods are discussed below:

1. **Establishing the uniformity of concrete.** For this purpose, the ultrasonic concrete tester is an ideal tool for laboratory specimens and soniscope and Pundit are excellent tools for laboratory and field studies both.
2. **Establishing the acceptance criteria.** The high velocity value in concrete is an indication of good quality of concrete. Table 19.5 gives the pulse velocity rating as suggested by central water and power research station Khadakwasla and Table 19.6 gives the rating as suggested by Leslie and Cheesman.

Table 19.5. Quality criteria as suggested by central water and power research centre Khadakwasla (India)

Velocity in km/sec.	*Classification of quality*	*Overall in situ compressive strength in MPa*
4.0 and above	Very good	30 to 35
3.5 to 4.0	Good	25 to 30
3.0 to 3.5	Medium	20 to 25
3.0 and below	Poor	15 to 20

Table 19.6. Suggested pulse velocity for concrete by Leslie and Cheesman

Pulse velocity in m/sec	*General condition of concrete*
4575	Excellent
3660 — 4575	Good
3050 — 3660	Questionable
2135 — 3050	Poor
2135	Very poor

According to Jones, the lower limit for good quality concrete is between 4.1 and 4.7 km/seconds. If the pulse velocity is below 2.0 km/sec, the concrete quality is very poor.

19.21.9. Estimation of strength of concrete

There is no unique relationship between the pulse velocity and strength of concrete. It has been observed that there is a wide variation in the pulse velocity of concrete of a given quality. This variation of pulse velocity has been observed due to the influence of the coarse aggregate. Both the quantity and type of aggregate have been found to affect the pulse velocity. However for a constant water/cement ratio, the influence of the coarse aggregate on the strength of concrete comparatively has been observed small. Thus for different mix proportions, different relations between the pulse velocity and strength would be obtained as shown in Fig. 19.17. Jones has suggested that at a constant water/cement ratio, the higher the volume of aggregate, the higher the pulse velocity. Thus the estimated strength would be more. It has been found that for each 1% increase in volume of aggregate results 0.9 MPa increase in the strength of concrete.

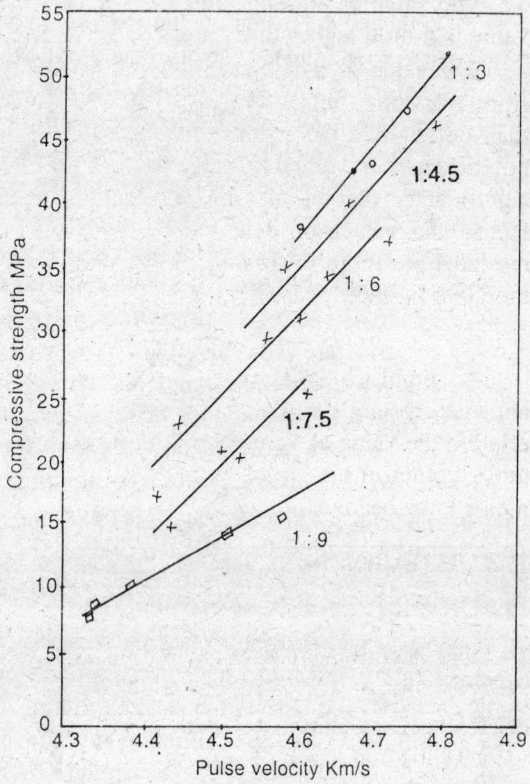

Fig. 19.17. Relation between pulse velocity and strength of concrete

19.21.10. Determination of pulse modulus of elasticity

By measuring the pulse velocity and knowing the poisson's ratio the dynamic modulus of elasticity can be determined by the following relation.

$$Ed = \rho v^2 \frac{(1+\mu)(1-2\mu)}{(1-\mu)} \qquad \ldots(i)$$

where,

v = pulse velocity

ρ = density of concrete

μ = poisson ratio

the value of Poisson ratio can be calculated from the following relation.

$$\left(\frac{v^2}{2\,nl}\right)^2 = \frac{(1-\mu)}{(1+\mu)(1-2\mu)} \qquad \ldots(ii)$$

where,

n = resonant frequency (Hz)

L = length of beam in mm

v = pulse velocity in mm/sec.

The value of poisson ratio varies from 0.2 to 0.24. This value is a little higher than found by static method.

The value of dynamic modulus of elasticity determined from ultrasonic pulse velocity method is some what higher than determined from static method as dynamic modulus is not affected by creep. Creep also is not found to affect significantly the initial tangent modulus in static method. Hence the values of dynamic modulus and initial tangent modulus are more or less equal. The relation between static modulus E_c and dynamic modulus E_d in GN/m^2 is.

$$E_c = 1.25\,E_d - 19 \qquad \ldots(iii)$$

An empirical relation ship between the pulse velocity and static young's modulus is shown in Fig. 19.18. From this relation the value of young's moduls many be determined for those points in the structure where pulse velocity measurements have been taken.

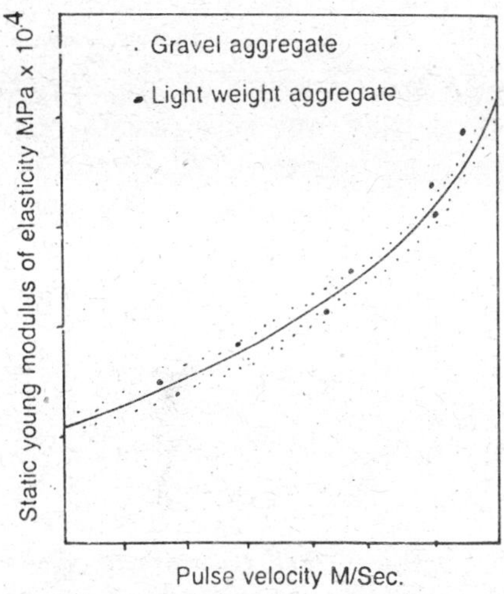

Fig. 19.18. Relation between pulse velocity and static young modulus of concrete

19.21.11. Estimation of setting characteristics of concrete

Soniscope has been used widely to determine the rate of setting of concrete.

19.21.12. Estimation of durability of concrete

The effects on durability of concrete of freezing and thawing of water, aggressive environmental effects such as sulphate and acidic effect etc. have been studied by many researchers using the pulse velocity method. Lack of compaction and change in water cement ratio can be detected by these studies.

19.21.3. Detection and measurement of cracks

The detection and measurement of cracks, and voids, deterioration due to frost or chemical action in massive concrete structures by the use of ultrasonic pulse technique is very important. The basic principle of crack detection is that if the depth and width of the crack is appreciable no signal will be received at the receiving transducer. If the depth of crack is small compared to the distance between the transducers, then the pulse will be deflected around the crack and the signals will be received by the transducer. However this increase in length will result in reduced pulse velocity in comparison with straight travel path. The difference in pulse velocity is used to estimate the path length. The difference between this path length and the straight path length will give double the crack depth in shown in Fig. 19.19.

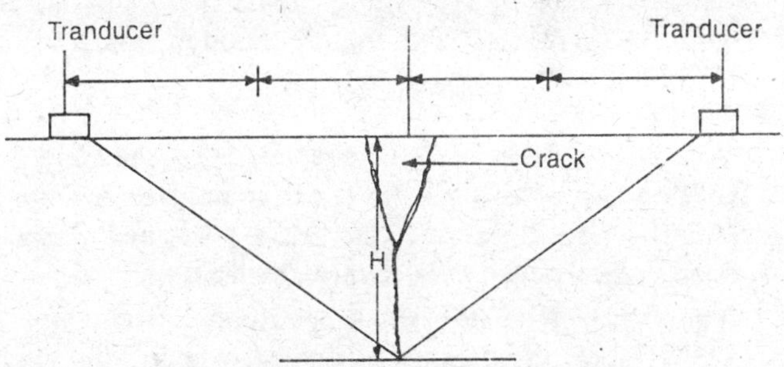

Fig. 19.19. Measurement of crack depth

19.21.14. Estimation of age of concrete

As shown in Fig. 19.20 the strength of concrete increases with the age of concrete, resulting the increase in pulse velocity. Fig. 19.20 shows the relation between age and pulse velocity for different w/c ratios.

19.21.15. Estimation of fire hazard

To estimate the hazard of fire, experiment were conducted on 88 × 102 × 406 mm prisms. The specemens were exposed to fire for 1 hour at temperatures ranging from 100°C to 1000°C. The specimens then were removed from furnance and allowed to cool to room temperature. Then velocity was measured by ultra sonic method and the specimens were tested for flexure strength. The percentage loss in pulse velocity was found more or less same as the loss in flexural strength of test prisms after exposure to fire.

The pulse velocity technique may also be used for the estimation of pavement concrete thickness. At the end it would be fair to add that the use of ultrasonic pulse measurement as a means of quality control on construction job is not practicable, as no satisfactory correlation exists between the variability of the compression test specimen and the variability of pulse measurements.

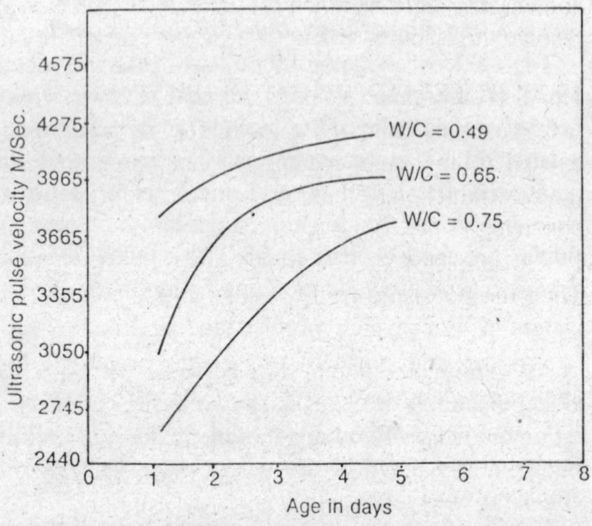

Fig. 19.20. Relation between age and pulse velocity of concrete

19.22. TESTS ON THE COMPOSITION OF HARDENED CONCRETE

Some times disputes arise about the quality of hardened concrete. The more pertinent question arises whether the cement content is there as specified. To resolve this dispute chemical and physical tests are carried out on a sample of hardened concrete.

19.22.1. Determination of cement content

ASTM Standard C 85-66 has prescribed a method for the determination of cement content in the hardened concrete. This method is based on the fact that silicates present in the portland cement are much more readily decomposed and are made soluble in dilute hydrochloric acid than the silica compounds normally contained in aggregates. Similarly the lime contained in cement is much more soluble than lime contained in aggregates, with the exception of lime stone aggregates.

Procedure

A representative sample of concrete is crushed and dehydrated at a temperature of 550°C for 3 hours. A small portion of this sample is taken and treated with 1:3 hydrochloric acid. By the chemical reaction with the hydro-chloric acid, the silica contained in the cement is liberated. The quantity of silica so liberated is determined by standard chemical methods.

The filtrate from the silica determination contains soluble calcium oxide from the aggregate and cement. Further calculations depend on whether the aggregate is largely siliceous or not. If the original aggregate is available its solubility should be tested.

From the contents of soluble silica and calcium oxide, the cement contents in the original volume of the sample can be calculated using the method given in ASTM standard C 85-66 (re approved in 1973). The results thus obtained are reliable and can be used to check the cement contents of different parts of a structure, when it is desired to check whether or not segregation of cement has taken place. However the accuracy of the test is lowest for lean mixes with low cement contents and often in this category of mixes the exact value of cement content is required. Further the test depends on the knowledge of the chemical composition of aggregate, which may not be available for testing. When large amounts of soluble silica and calcium oxide both are liberated from the aggregate, the method is not reliable.

More complex techniques are prescribed by B.S. 1881, part-6. 1971 for the determination of cement content. It should be noted that chemical tests are more expensive. Thus such tests should be used only to resolve the disputes and not as a means for quality control of concrete.

19.23. DETERMINATION OF ORIGINAL WATER/CEMENT RATIO

For the hardened concrete under test at present, the method for estimating the water/cement ratio that existed at the time of placing the concrete has been developed by Brown. In essence, the method involves the determination of the volume of the capillary pores and the weight of cement and combined water in the concrete.

A sample of the concrete is oven dried at 105°C and the air is removed from the pores under vacuum. Then the pores are refilled with carbon tetrachloride and the weight of sample is calculated. Thus the weight of water which originally occupied the pores can be determined.

As the voids formed by air entrainment are discontinuous, they remain filled with air at the time of applying vacuum and no water is absorbed in them. Thus the result is not affected by the air entrainment.

The sample now is broken up and the carbon tetrachloride is allowed to evaporate and the aggregate is separated and weighed. The loss on ignition and the carbon dioxide content of the remaining fine material are determined. From these two quantities the weight of combined water can be calculated.

The sum of the combined water and pore water gives the original amount of mixing water. The quantity of an hydrous cement can be determined either together with this method or by the method described in the last test. From these quantities of water and cement, the water/cement ratio can be determined with a accuracy of about 0.02 of the true value. The technique has been described into standard method B.S. 1881, Part-6-1971.

19.24. PHYSICAL METHOD

For determining the cement content, total aggregate content and fine/coarse aggregate ratio, Polivka carried out experiments on a sawn and varnished surface of a dried concrete specimen and developed a method known as 'point count method'. This method is based on the fact that the relative volumes of the constituents of a heterogeneous solid are directly proportional to (*i*) their relative areas in a plane section, and (*ii*) to the intercepts of these areas along a random line.

Further the frequency with which a constituent occurs at a given number of equally spaced points along a random line is a direct measure of the relative volume of that constituent in the solid. Thus a point count by means of a sterco microscope can rapidly give the volumetric proportions of a hardened concrete specimen.

The aggregate and voids containing evaporable water or air can be identified. The remainder material is assumed as the hydrated cement. To convert the quantity of this hydrated cement to the volume of unhydrated cement, the knowledge of the specific gravity of dry cement and the non evaporable water content of the hydrated cement is required.

The test determines the cement content of concrete with in 10% accuracy but the original water content or voids ratio can not be estimated by this method, as no distinction between the air and water voids has been made.

QUESTIONS

1. How is potential (fully compacted) concrete strength determined?
2. How is the actual strength of concrete determined?
3. What is the difference between the actual strength of concrete specimens and insitu strength?
4. What are the non destructive tests for determination of the strength of concrete.
5. Explain how the followings affect the strength of test specimen.
   (*a*) The incorrect curing of compression test specimen.
   (*b*) The incorrect making of compression test specimen.

(*c*) The deficient testing machine effect.

6. Why does a standard test specimen not give adequate information about the strength of concrete in a structure.
7. Why is the strength of test specimens subjected to accelerated curing different from strength of a similar standard test specimen.
8. Discuss the advantages and disadvantages of cube and cylinder shaped test specimens.
9. What is meant by non destructive methods of testing concrete.
10. Describe the following tests fully:
    (*a*) Schmidt hammer test
    (*b*) Pull out test
11. Suggest a non destructive test to investigate the followings
    (*a*) Suspected presence of voids and cracks in a large concrete dam.
    (*b*) To compare the quality of precast concrete floor units
12. Why does the core strength differ from the standard cube strength?
13. Describe the ultrasonic pulse velocity method for determining the strength of concrete.
14. Discuss the factors which affect the pulse velocity in concrete.
15. Discuss the possible reasons for the difference between the strength of test cylinders and cores from the same concrete.
16. Describe 'core' testing fully.
17. Discuss the advantages and disadvantages of the followings:
    (*a*) Pull out test
    (*b*) Windsor test
    (*c*) Ultrasonic pulse velocity test
18. Why are compressive test cylinders capped. Why cylinders are considered more appropriate test specimens to check the quality of concrete in a structure.
19. How does the strength of concrete core converted to the estimated strength of test cube.
20. Explain the difference in strength of large and small cylinders made from the same mix.
21. What is the purpose of determining the ultrasonic pulse velocity of concrete? Give its application also with suitable sketch where ever possible.

OBJECTIVE TYPE QUESTIONS

1. Identify the incorrect statement of the followings
    (*a*) The lateral expansion of concrete is much more than the plates of the testing machine
    (*b*) The lateral expansion of testing machine plates is several times more than the concrete
    (*c*) In uniaxial compressive testing more complex system of stresses is developed
    (*d*) Actually the uniaxial compression testing is the ideal
2. Identify the in correct statement of the followings
    (*a*) The shear effect developed during the compression testing is minimum at the centre of the specimen
    (*b*) The shear effect developed during the compression testing is minimum near the plantens of the testing machine
    (*c*) The influence of platen restraint on the mode of failure is more in a cube than in a standard cylinder
    (*d*) As the ratio of height/diameter increases the influence of shear decreases
3. Cylinder specimens are considered superior as test specimen due to
    (*a*) The failure of cylinders is less affected by the end restraint of the specimen
    (*b*) The strength of cylinder is less influenced by the properties of aggregate used in the mix
    (*c*) The stress distribution over the cylinder cross section is more uniform than on a specimen of square cross section
    (*d*) The strength of cylinder is more closer to the true uniaxial compressive strength of concrete
    (*e*) All the above
4. Identify the incorrect statement of the followings
    (*a*) The splitting tensile test is simple to perform and gives more uniform results than other methods
    (*b*) In this test same type of specimen and same machine can be used

(*c*) Tensile strength determined is closer to the true tensile strength
(*d*) This test gives 5 to 12% less tensile strength than the direct tensile test

5. Identify the correct statement of the followings
(*a*) Concrete core test gives better idea of tensile strength of concrete
(*b*) The size of aggregate used in the flexure test specimen has no influence on its strength
(*c*) The strength results obtained by one point loading method and two point loading method are same
(*d*) The tensile strength of concrete is more sensitive to improper curing than its compressive strength
6. The core testing of concrete should be performed
(*a*) When the primary aim of core testing is to ascertain the adequate strength of the structural member
(*b*) When it is required to detect the segregation and bleeding of the concrete
(*c*) When it is required to estimate the load carrying capacity of the structural member
(*d*) All the above
7. Identify the incorrect statement of the followings
(*a*) The core should be taken at the nearest non critical location
(*b*) The core should be taken at locations where minimum strength and maximum stress coincide
(*c*) The core should be taken occupying the top 25% portion in case of columns walls, deep beams and top thickness of slab
(*d*) The reinforcement of concrete should be avoided from the core
8. Identify the correct statements of the followings
(*a*) As per code the minimum number of standard cores should be 3
(*b*) For core drilling rotary drill having cutting tool with diamond bits and water supply arrangements is sufficient
(*c*) To minimise uncertaintily in correlating the core strength to cylinder or cube strength the ratio of height/diameter should be kept 2.0
(*d*) All the above
9. Identify the incorrect statements of the followings
(*a*) A saturated core has been found to have 10 to 15% less compressive strength than a dry core
(*b*) It has been observed that as the l/d ratio of the core increases, the measured strength also increases
(*c*) The measured strength of the core increases as its diameter increases
(*d*) The core drilled vertically has been found to have more strength than that taken horizontally
(*e*) The insitu concrete gains little strength after 28 days
10. The disadvantages of core testing are
(*a*) The structural integrity of concrete across the full cross section may be affected
(*b*) The length/diameter ratio other than 2.0 will have effect on the test results
(*c*) Capping of the specimen on both sides may affect the results
(*d*) Existence of reinforcement may affect the test results
(*e*) All the above
11. The results of rebound method of concrete testing are affected
(*a*) By the characteristics of mix *i.e.* type and content of cement
(*b*) Age of concrete
(*c*) Compaction of concrete (*d*) Smoothness of surface
(*e*) Temperature of concrete (*f*) All the above
12. The rebound test can be used
(*a*) To check the uniformity of concrete quality
(*b*) To estimate the approximate strength of concrete
(*c*) To compare a given concrete with a specified quality concrete
(*d*) All the above
13. The resonant frequency test can be used
(*a*) To study the deterioration effect of concrete subjected to repeated freezing and thawing
(*b*) To study the damage due to fire
(*c*) To study the effect of alkali and acidic reactions
(*d*) To determine the dynamic young's modulus of concrete
(*e*) All the above

14. The transducers may be arranged on concrete surface
    (*a*) On opposite faces (*b*) On adjacent faces
    (*c*) On the same face (*d*) All the above
15. Identify the correct statements of the followings
    (*a*) The value of pulse velocity is affected by the contact surface under test
    (*b*) The value of pulse velocity is affected by the path length of the velocity. The length should be sufficiently long
    (*c*) The variation of ambient temperature affects the pulse velocity of concrete
    (*d*) With the increase in moisture the pulse velocity increases
    (*e*) All the above
16. The pulse velocity of concrete is used
    (*a*) To establish the uniformity of concrete (*b*) To estimate the strength of concrete
    (*c*) To estimate the setting properties of concrete (*d*) To detect cracks and estimate its durability
    (*e*) To estimate the age of concrete (*f*) To estimate the fire hazards
    (*g*) All the above
17. The resonant frequency method is based on the assumption that
    (*a*) The modulus of elasticity of concrete improves with the quality of concrete
    (*b*) The resonant frequency of concrete is directly proportional to the square of its strength
    (*c*) The strength of concrete increases with its age
    (*d*) The pulse velocity depends primarily upon the mix proportion of the concrete and its materials
    (*e*) All of the above
18. The ultra sonic pulse velocity test is based on the assumption that
    (*a*) The frequency of the pulse is proportional to the compressive strength of concrete
    (*b*) The amplitude of the pulse is proportional to the compressive strength of concrete
    (*c*) The pulse velocity is reduced due to internal flaws
    (*d*) Time taken by a pulse passing through a mass is proportional to the modulus of elasticity of the concrete
19. The index of good quality of hardened concrete indicated, the pulse velocity is
    (*a*) Between 3.0 and 3.5 km/s (*b*) Above 3.5 km/s
    (*c*) Above 4.5 km/s (*d*) Below 3.0 km/s
20. The quality and strength of concrete in a structure can be estimated by
    (*a*) By the core test of concrete
    (*b*) By the pull out test of concrete
    (*c*) By the rebound hammer or schamidt hammer test
    (*d*) By the ultrasonic test
    (*e*) All the above
21. Identify the incorrect statement
    (*a*) The ultrasonic pulse velocity method can assess the quality of insitue fresh concrete
    (*b*) The velocity of ultra sonic pulse is about 2000 m/s at the time of setting of the fresh concrete
    (*c*) The accelerated strength of concrete are doubt full as far as 28 days potential strength is concerned
    (*d*) The maturity test gives valid results provided the initial temperature of concrete is in between 15°C and 26°C
    (*e*) All the above

Answers

1. (*b*)	6. (*d*)	11. (*f*)	16. (*g*)	21. (*c*)
2. (*b*)	7. (*c*)	12. (*d*)	17. (*a*)	
3. (*e*)	8. (*d*)	13. (*e*)	18. (*d*)	
4. (*d*)	9. (*b, c*)	14. (*d*)	19. (*b*)	
5. (*d*)	10. (*e*)	15. (*e*)	20. (*e*)	

20

Mix Design

20.1. INTRODUCTION

Cement concrete is a very useful constructional material whose properties can be modified readily at will. The desired properties of concrete can be obtained by using ingredients in a certain proportion. Thus determining the relative amount of materials is known as *mix design*. Hence mix design can be defined as the process of selecting suitable ingredients of concrete and determining their relative quantities for producing concrete of certain minimum properties as strength, durability and consistency etc. as economically as possible.

20.2. PURPOSE OF MIX DESIGN

From the definition of mix design, it can be seen that the purpose of mix design is two fold as follows:

1. To achieve the stipulated minimum strength and durability.
2. To make the concrete in the most economical way. Cost wise all concretes depend mainly on two factors (*a*) Cost of materials and (*b*) Cost of labour.

The cost of form work, batching, mixing, transporting, and curing etc. is nearly the same for good as well as bad concrete work.

Thus to achieve economy, the main attention should be directed to the cost of materials. As the cost of cement is many times more than other ingredients, thus the attention mainly should be directed to the use of as little amount of cement as possible consistent with the strength and durability. Mix proportions provided by the designs is called as *prescribed mix.*

20.3. OBJECTS OF MIX DESIGN

The object of mix design is to decide the proportions of materials which will produce concrete of required properties. The mix proportions should be selected in such a way that the resulting concrete is of desired workability while fresh and it could be placed and compacted easily for the intended purpose. The fresh concrete should be fluid enough to fill the form work and surround the reinforcement fully and the hardened concrete should develop required strength and durability.

20.4. FACTORS AFFECTING THE CHOICE OF MIX PROPORTION

According to IS 456-1978 and IS-1345-1980, the design of concrete should be based on the following factors:

1. Grade designation
2. Type of cement
3. Max. nominal size of aggregate
4. Grading of combined aggregates
5. Water-cement ratio
6. Workability
7. Durability
8. Quality control

1. Grade designation

Grade designation specifies the characteristic compressive strength of concrete. As per IS-456-1978, the characteristic compressive strength is that value of concrete stregnth below which not more than 5% of the test results are expected to fall. It is the major factor which influences the mix design. Depending upon the degree of control at site, the concrete mix should be designed for the mean compressive strength, which is a little higher than the characteristic strength.

2. Type of cement

The type of cement is important as the rate of strength development depends mainly on cement. The choice of the type of cement depends upon the requirements of its performance. When very high compressive strength is required, portland cement conforming to IS 8112-1976 is suitable. In case where an early strength is required, rapid hardening portland cement conforming to IS 8041-1978 and for mass concrete work, low heat portland cement conforming to IS 269-1979 is to be used.

3. Maximum nominal size of coarse aggregate

The maximum nominal size of coarse aggregate is determined by sieve analysis and is designated by the sieve size higher than the largest size on which 15% or more the aggregate is retained. It is governed by the size of the section and the spacing of the reinforcement. According to IS 456-1978 and IS 1345-1980, the max. size of the aggregate should be as follows:

(*a*) It should not be more than 1/4th of the minimum thickness of the member.

(*b*) It should be less by 5 mm than the minimum clear distance between the main reinforcement.

(*c*) It should be less by 5 mm than the minimum cover to the reinforcement.

(*d*) It should be less by 5 mm than the spacing between the prestressing cables.

For normal structural concrete work, the maximum size of 'aggregate may be used as 38 mm where as for high strength concrete it may be 10 mm to 20 mm.

4. Grading of Combined aggregate

In a concrete mix, the relative proportions of the fine and coarse aggregates is one of the important factor which affects the strength of the concrete. For dense concrete, it is essential that the fine and coarse aggregates be well graded. The locally available aggregates generally do not conform to the standard gradings. In such situations the aggregates should be combined in suitable proportions, so that the resulting grading is close to the desired grading. The aim of combining the aggregates is to obtain a grading close to the coarset grading of the standard grading curves, the most economical mix having the highest permissible aggregate cement ratio. The aggregates can be combined either by analytical calculations or graphically, using the method of Road Note 4. The recommended limits to the coarset and finest aggregate gradings as per IS-383-1963 are shown in Table 20.1.

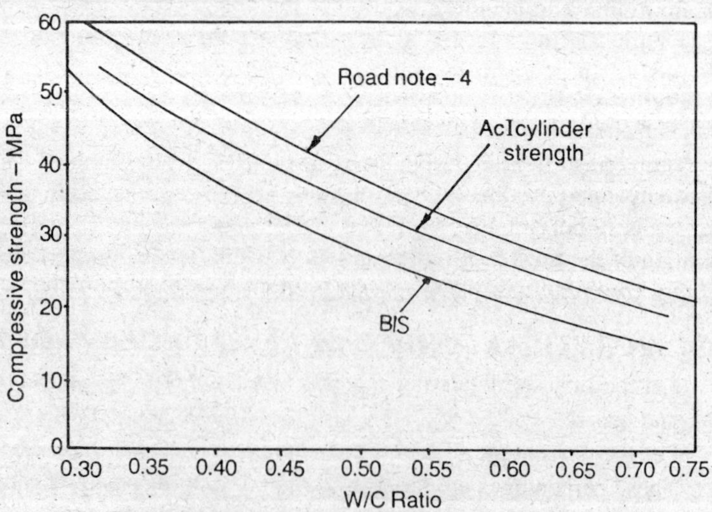

Fig. 20.1. General relation between w/c ratio and compressive strength of concrete

5. Water/Cement ratio

The compressive strength of

concrete at a given age under normal conditions of curing mainly depends upon water/cement ratio as discussed in chapter 7. Lower the water-cement ratio with in limits, greater the compressive strength and vice-versa. A number of relationships between compressive strength and water cement ratio are available, which are valid for a wide range of conditions. The generalized relationship between water-cement ratio and compressive strength of concrete is shown in Fig. 20.1. The method of design is shown later in this chapter.

6. Workability

For satisfactory placing and compacting of concrete the workability is controlled by many factors as shape and size of the section to be concreting, quantity and spacing of reinforcement, method of transportation, placing and compaction of concrete etc. The aim should be to have minimum possible workability consistent with satisfactory placing and compaction of concrete. The insufficient workability will result in incomplete compaction, resulting in less strength and durability.

There are various methods of determining the workability of concrete, but there is no rigid correlation between workabilities of concrete measured by different methods. Hence it is desirable to decide the test method before starting the concrete work. For comparable concretes workability measured by different methods is shown in Table 20.1.

Table 20.1. Recommended workability values

S. No.	*Degree of workability*	*Values of workabilities interms of*			
		Slump in mm	*Compacting factor*	*Vee Bee time in secs*	*Drop table revolutions*
1.	Extremely low (very stiff)	—	≤ 0.70*	30 — 20	96 — 48
2.	Very low (stiff)	0 — 25	0.75 — 0.80	20 — 10	48 — 24
3.	Low (stiff plastic)	25 — 50	0.80 — 0.85	10 — 5	24 — 12
4.	Medium (plastic)	50 — 75	0.85 — 0.92	5 — 2	12 — 6
5.	High (flowing)	75 — 150	> 0.92	2 — 0	6 — 0

* Compacting factor test is not used for concrete prepared with aggregate having nominal size of 40 mm and higher.

7. Durability

It can be defined as the resistance to internal and external deteriorating influences. The requirements of durability may be achieved by restricting the minimum cement content and minimum water-cement ratio as given in Table 20.2.

8. Quality Control

The strength of concrete is never constant. It varies from batch to batch. This variation may be due to the variation in the quality of constituent materials, variations in mix proportions, variation in the quality of batching and mixing equipment available, quality of workmanship and supervision etc. Controlling these factors is important to minimise the difference between the minimum strength and characteristic mean strength of the mix, thus reducing the cement content. The method of controlling these differences is called *quality control*. Quality control has been discussed fully in chapter 21.

20.4. ANALYTICAL METHOD OF CALCULATING % OF FINE AND COARSE AGGREGATE

Let the fine aggregate is designated as aggregate = I whose percentage is β
and coarse " " " " = II whose percentage is γ
Let the percentage of combined aggregate is α.

These percentages are taken, and mixed. Let these percentages pass through the sieve corresponding to the point on the standard grading curve taken as criterion *i.e.* the combined aggregate should be very approxi- mately near to this point.

Table 20.2. Mimimum Cement content kg/m^3 of portland cement to ensure durability under deicing

Exposure	*Plain concrete*				*Max free water cement ratio*	*R.C.C.*				*Water cement ratio*	*Pre stressed concrete*				*W/c ratio*
	Nominal size of aggregate in mm					*Nominal size of aggregate in mm*					*Nominal size of aggregate in mm*				
	40	20	12.5	10		40	20	12.5	10		40	20	12.5	10	
Mild. Completely protected against weather except for a brief period of exposure to normal weather conditions during construction.	200	220	260	270	0.70	220	250	280	290	0.65	300	300	300	300	0.65
Moderate. Sheltered from severe rain and freezing while saturated with water, Burried concrete under water continuously.	220	250	290	300	0.60	260	290	330	340	0.55	300	300	330	340	0.55
Severe. Exposed to sea water, moorland water alternate wetting and drying and freezing while wet subjected to condensation or corrosive fumes.	270	310	350	360	0.50	320	360	400	410	0.45	320	360	400	410	0.45
Subject to salt used for specified conditions of exposure. (deicing etc.)	240	280	370	330	0.55	260	290	330	340	0.55	300	300	330	340	0.55

Let x and y be the proportions of two aggregates in the combined state. Then to satisty the condition that α % of combined aggregate passes through the criterion point, then

$$\beta \cdot x + \gamma \cdot y = \alpha (x + y)$$

or

$$\beta \cdot x - \alpha \cdot x + \gamma \cdot y - \alpha \cdot y = 0$$

$$x(\beta - \alpha) + y(\gamma - \alpha) = 0$$

or

$$x(\beta - \alpha) = -y(\gamma - \alpha)$$

or

$$\frac{x}{y} = -\frac{(\gamma - \alpha)}{(\beta - \alpha)}$$

$$= \frac{(\alpha - \gamma)}{(\beta - \alpha)} = \frac{1}{K}$$

where.

$$K = \frac{(\beta - \alpha)}{(\alpha - \gamma)}$$

Thus $x : y$ = 1:K

The grading of the resultant combined aggregate is determined by first multiplying the grading of aggregate I and aggregate II by 1 and K respectively. The sum of corresponding products of the percentages passing the sieve sizes is divided by (1 + K) and the values are rounded off to the nearest percentage. The method is illustrated by the following example.

Example 1. *The gradings of fine and coarse aggregates available at a site are listed in columns 2 and 3 of table 20.3 below. These aggregates are to be combined in a suitable proportion to give the specified grading chosen from the standard curve which is listed in Column 4 of the same table 20.3*

Solution. Let one kg of the fine aggregate be combined to x kg of coarse aggregate to get the desired grading. Let percentage passing through 4.75 mm sieve is taken as the criterion. In the standard grading curve 44% of the total aggregate passes through the IS 4.75 mm sieve. Hence using the Table 20.3

Table 20.3.

IS sieve	*Percentage passing*		*Specified aggregate*	*Combined aggregate*	*Remark*
	Fine aggregate	*Coarse aggregate*			
1	2	3	4	5	6
40 mm	100	100	100	100	
20 mm	100	97	99	98.3	
10 mm	100	44	66	68.6	
4.75 mm	95	04	44	44.0	
2.36 mm	88	0	36	38.7	
1.18 mm	72	0	28	32.0	
600 micron	48	0	20	21.0	
300 micron	21	0	07	9.0	
150 micron	02	0	0	.01	

$$95(1) + 4(x) = 44(1 + x)$$

$$4x - 44x = 44 - 95$$

$$-40x = -51$$

or

$$x = \frac{51}{40} = \frac{5.1}{4} = 1.275$$

Thus the fine and coarse aggregates must be combined in the proportion of 1:1.275. The grading of resulting combined aggregate is obtained by multiplying column 2 and 3 of the above table 20.1, by 1 and

1.275 respectively and dividing the sum of these products by (1 + 1.275) = 2.275. The respective values obtained are put in columns 5 of the table 20.1 as shown. Comparing the results of combined aggregate grading with the standard specified grading, it will be seen that the percentage passing through 4.75 mm sieve is same and the other values are very close to the specified grading.

In this method the percentage passing through the criterion sieve must necessarily agree, where as others may not. If the variations are very small, they should be ignored and should be taken as such. In case the discrepancies are large the proportions may be changed by adopting an other criterion point. This method can also be used to combine more than two aggregate as illustrated by example 2.

Example 2. *The gradings of fine and coarse aggregate available at a site are listed in column b, c, & d respectively of the Table 20.4. These aggregates are to be combined to give the approximate grading values of the specified curve shown in Column (e) of the Table 20.4.*

Solution. Let 1 kg of fine aggregate is mixed with x kg of aggregate (1) and y kg with aggregate 2 listed in columns *b, c* and *d* respectively. As there are two unknown quantities, two criterion sieves have to be selected. Let the criterion sieve be 10 mm and 2.36 mm sieve. The specified grading is shown in Column (*e*) and the combined grading obtained is shown in Column (*f*)

Table 20.4

IS sieve	*Percentage passing*				
	Fine aggregate	*Coarse aggregate I*	*Coarse aggregate II*	*Specified grading*	*Combined grading*
a	*b*	c	*d*	e	*f*
20 mm	100	100	96	100	97.5
10 mm	100	92	19	50	50.0
4.75 mm	100	15	5	30	30.2
2.36 mm	86	3	0	22	22.0
1.18 mm	74	0	0	15	18.5
600 micron	52	0	0	10	13.0
300 micron	12	0	0	3	3.0
150 micon	03	0	0	0	0.75

$$1 \times 100 + 92x + 19y = 50(1 + x + y)$$
$$92x - 50x + 19y - 50y = 50 - 100$$
$$42x - 31y = -50 \qquad \ldots(i)$$

The combined aggregate passing through 2.36 sieve is 22%. Hence using table 2 we have.

$$1 \times 86 + 3(x) + 0(y) = 22(1 + x + y)$$
$$3x - 22x - 22y = 22 - 86$$
$$-19x - 22y = -64 \qquad \ldots(ii)$$

or
$$19x + 22y = 64 \qquad \ldots(iii)$$
$$42x - 31y = -50 \qquad \ldots(iv)$$

Solving equation (*i*) & (*ii*), $x = 0.5881$ and $y = 2.41$

$$\therefore \quad 1 + 0.5881 + 2.41 \approx 4.0$$

Hence the fine aggregate, coarse aggregate I and coarse aggregate II must be combined in the proportion of 1.0, 0.5881 and 2.41 respectively. The grading is shown in column (*f*) of the table 20.4. As the difference mainly is in sieve 1.18 mm and 600 micron, further approximation will not help. Hence it may be accepted. Similarly other sieve percentages are calculated as shown in column (*f*) of the Table 22.4.

Procedure

For getting each sieve grading, multiply column (*b*) by 1, column (*c*) by *x* and column (*d*) by *y* and add all the products and divide the product by the sum of $(1 + x + y)$. As for grading value for sieve 20 mm

$$(1 \times 100) + x(100) + y(96)$$

i.e.

$$(1 \times 100) + 0.588 \times 100 + 2.41 \times 96$$

$$= (100 + 58.81 + 231.36) = 3.998 = 97.5$$

2. Graphical method

It has been discussed later on page 434.

20.5. METHODS OF CONCRETE MIX DESIGN

There are various methods of mix design as follows:

1. Arbitrary method
2. Minimum void method
3. Maximum density method
4. Water-cement ratio method
5. Fineness modulus method
6. Standard deviation method
7. American method of mix design
8. Graphic or Road Note 4 method of mix design
9. Indian Road Congress IRC-44 method
10. High strength concrete mix design
12. Mix. design based on flexural strength
13. ACI committee 211-1 method
14. Department of Environment (DOE) mix design method
15. Mix design for pumpable concrete
16. Indian standard recommended (IS 10262-1982) method
17. Rapid method of mix design

Now a days out of the above methods following methods are commonly used:

1. ACI committee 211 method
2. DOE method
3. Indian Standard method
4. Rapid method of mix design

Before discussing the mix design let us look on the grades of concrete.

The mix should be designed to produce the grade of concrete having the required workability and characteristic strength not less than as given in Table 20.5.

Table 20.5. Grade of Concrete as per IS 456-2000

Groups	*S.I. units*		*M.K.S. units*		
	Grade designation	*Specified compressive strength at 28 days in N/mm²*	*Grade of concrete*	*Compressive strength of 15 cm cubes at 28 days after mixing kg/cm²*	
1	2	3	4	5	6
Ordinary concrete	M10	10	M100	135	100
	M15	15	M150	200	150
	M20	20	M200	260	200

Groups	*S.I. units*		*M.K.S. units*		
	Grade designation	*Specified compressive strength at 28 days in N/mm²*	*Grade of concrete*	*Compressive strength of 15 cm cubes at 28 days after mixing kg/cm²*	
1	2	3	4	5	6
Standard concrete	M25	25	M250	320	250
	M30	30	M300	380	300
	M35	35	M350	400	350
	M40	40	M400	500	400
	M45	45	M 450	—	—
	M50	50	M 500	—	—
	M55	55	M 550	—	—
High strength concrete	M60	60	M600	—	—
	M65	65	M650	—	—
	M70	70	M700	—	—
	M75	75	M750	—	—
	M80	80	M800	—	—

Note 1. Preliminary test. It is defined as the test conducted in a laboratory on the trial mix of concrete produced in the laboratory for designing a concrete mix before actual concreting at site to verify the strength of concrete and determining the adjustments required in the mix if needed. Thus a concrete for which mix is designed after carrying out priliminary test is called *controlled concrete;* and the concrete mixes adopted without carrying out priliminary tests is called *ordinary concrete.* For all important works controlled concrete should be used.

Works test

A test conducted eithr in the field or in a laboratory on the specimen made on actual site of works, out of concrete being used in the works is called *works tests.*

The 7 day strength may be adopted as given in Table 20.6

Table 20.6. Optional tests requirements of concrete

Grade of concrete	*Minimum compressive strength of 15 cm cubes at 7 days N/mm²*	*Modulus of rupture by beam test (Minimum)*	
		At 72 ± 2 hours N/mm²	*At 7 days N/mm²*
M10	7.0	1.2	1.7
M15	10.0	1.5	2.1
M20	13.5	1.7	2.4
M25	17.0	1.9	2.7
M30	20.0	2.1	3.0
M35	23.5	2.3	3.2
M40	27.0	2.5	3.4

Note 2. In international system of units (S.I. units) the units of force or pressure is Newton and denoted by 'N'. It can be defined as a force applied to a body having a mass of one kilogram gives an acceleration of one metre per second per second.

Thus $$1\,N = \frac{1\,kg}{g}$$

where $g = 9.806$

$$\therefore \quad 1\text{ kg} = 1g \times N = 9.806\text{ N}$$

$$\approx 10\text{ N}$$

$$\therefore \quad 1\,\text{kg/cm}^2 = \frac{10\text{ N}}{\text{cm}^2} = \frac{10\text{ N}}{100\text{mm}^2}$$

$$\text{or} \quad 1\text{ kg/cm}^2 = \frac{\text{N}}{10\text{ mm}^2}$$

$$\text{or} \quad 1\text{ kg/cm}^2 = 0.1\text{ N/mm}^2$$

(Hence the reader must familerise himself with the relation).

(*b*) **Nominal Mix concrete.** Where it is not practical to use controlled concrete, ordinary concrete of nominal mix is used. Nominal Mix grade for this concrete vary from M 5, M 7.5, M 10,M 15 & M 20 as per I.S. 456-1978, (M 50, M 75, M 100, M 150 and M 200). The proportions of these mixes are given in Table 20.7.

Table 20.7. Weight of combined aggregate for nominal mix concrete

Grade of concrete	*Total quantity of dry aggregate by mass per 50 kg of cement to be taken as the sum of the individual masses of fine and coarse aggregate in kg*	*Proportion of fine aggregate to coarse aggregate (by mass)*	*Quantity of water per 50 kg of cement mass in (litres)*
M5	800	Generally F:C::1:2 but subject to an upper limit of $1:1\frac{1}{2}$ and a lower limit of $1:2\frac{1}{2}$	60
M7.5	625		45
M10	480		34
M15	350		32
M20	250		30

Note 1. The proportion of fine to coarse aggregate should be adjusted from upper limit to lower limit progressively as the grading of the fine aggregate becomes finer and the maximum size of coarse aggregate becomes larger. Graded coarse aggregate should be used. For example, for an average grading of fine aggregate as of group II Table 4.3, Chapter 4, the proportions should be $1:1\frac{1}{2}$, 1:2, $1:2\frac{1}{2}$ for maximum size of aggregate 10 mm, 20 mm and 40 mm respectively.

2. It may be noted for general guidance that M 10, M 15, M 20 and M 25 of ordinary concrete correspond approximately to 1:3:6, 1:2:4, $1:1\frac{1}{2}:3$ and 1:1:2 nominal mixes of ordinary concrete.

3. M 5 and M 7.5 grades concrete may be used for lean concrete bases and simple foundations for masonry walls. These mixes need not to be designed. Grades of concrete lower than M 15 should not be used for reinforced concrete.

20.6. HISTORY OF PROPORTIONING CONCRETE MIXES

In the nineteenth century when concrete came into existance, it was used merely as covering material to steel to safeguard against the weathering effects. At that time, it was not supposed to take any stresses. The requirements of good concrete and factors influencing the properties of concrete were not known then. After World War I, more stress was laid on the use of cheap constructional materials. Therefore many researchers devoted themselves to investigate the different properties of concrete. In 1919 Duff Abram made a break through and put forward his water/cement ratio law, which proved very useful. Thus during the last eighty years or so concrete has become a indispensable constructional material and its use is increasing day by day.

The strength of concrete was supposed to increase with the increase of cement content and better compaction. The aggregate having least voids was considered better. The following three methods are based on the old concepts.

1. Arbitrary method
2. Minimum void method and
3. Maximum density method

1. Arbitrary method. This method is very simple and cheap, but not very accurate for producing high quality concrete. Due to its simplicity and cheapness it is still in use for ordinary concrete works.

To ensure that combined aggregate is dense and has least voids, the fine aggregate should be in sufficient quantity in the concrete. Hence the ratio of fine to coarse aggregate is kept from $1\frac{1}{2}$ to $2\frac{1}{2}$. In general, coarse aggregate is kept twice that of fine aggregate and measured by volume. The aggregates are supposed to be surface dry. If they are not surface dry, then the effect of bulking of sand, and surface moisture content of coarse aggregate should be taken into account. Bulking of sand and its measurement has been discussed in chapter 4. Suitable amount of water is mixed to give desired workability. Usually following grades are covered in this method as shown in Table 20.8.

Table 20.8. Grades of concrete used for different works

S. No.	*Grade of Concrete*	*Works for which concrete used*
1.	M5 (1:5:10)	These grades of concrete are used for lean concrete bases and simple foundations for masonry wokss.
2.	M7.5 (1:4:8)	These grades of concrete are used for lean concrete bases and simple foundations for masonry wokss.
3.	M10 (1:3:6)	Mass concrete works
4.	M 15 (1:2:4)	This concrete is quite suitable for reinforced concrete works as building structures. It can be used in beams, slabs and columns of buildings and for road works also.
5.	M20 ($1:1\frac{1}{2}:3$)	This concrete is used for hydraulic structures, piles, and columns.
6.	M25 (1:1:2)	This concrete is suitable for sections having refinforcement and thin sections *i.e.* where more fluid concrete is needed.

2. Minimum void method. This method aims at producing a mix having minimum voids, so that denset concrete may be obtained. This is achieved by mixing sufficient quantity of fine aggregate to fill all the voids of coarse aggregate. The cement is added in such quantities which could fill voids in fine aggregate. The voids of coarse aggregate and fine aggregate having been determined before hand. Then sufficient quantity of water is added to the mix to give the desired workability. The voids can be determined with the help of a graduated cylinder and water as follows:

1. Take the graduated cylinder and fill it with aggregate to a definite mark. Let the volume of aggregate be V_2.
2. Now empty the cylinder in such a way that there should be no loss of aggregate and fill water in the cylinder upto a definite mark; Let the volume of water be V_1.
3. Add the aggregate of volume V_2 in the water of the cylinder. Let the combined volume of water and aggregate be V.

$$\text{then void percent } p = \frac{V - V_1}{V_2} \times 100$$

This method has not proved practical, as on addition of fine aggregate and water the particles of coarse aggregate separate further apart, thereby increasing the voids originally determined.

3. Maximum density method. This methods is an improved form of minimum void method. Fuller improved the minimum void method by grading the coarse aggregate and proportioning aggregate and cement in such a way that the combined mixture gave maximum density concrete. An ideal curve of gradation was published and local available aggregate were made to conform to as near as possible to the ideal curve. It has been observed that the optimum percentage of fine aggregate, which requires minimum paste is practically always some what below the percentage of maximum density of mixed aggregate. The difference between the two percentages results from the separation of aggregate by paste. The amount of fine aggregate to be subtracted from the maximum density percentage to obtain the optimum percentage is usually 2 to 5% and in rare case it can go upto 8%. Thus 3% reduction can be adopted for all practical purposes without error.

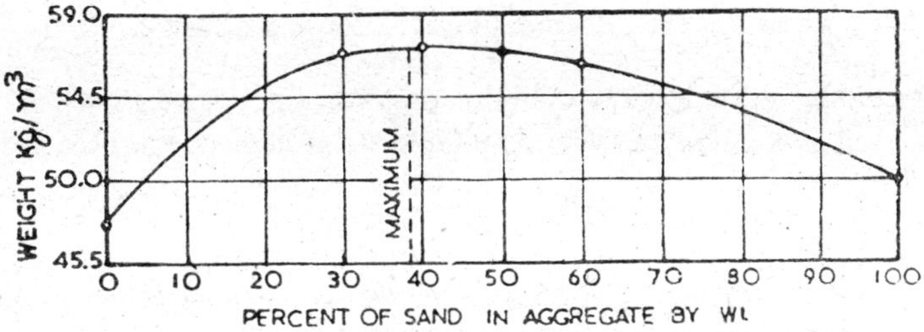

Fig. 20.2. % of sand and unit weight of mixed aggregate

The test can be carried out easily with the help of a container of known volume. The sand is taken (in 0, 30, 40, 50 and 100%) and mixed with coarse aggregate. The mixed aggregate is filled in thin layers and rodded gently and the weight of each proportion is taken and a curve is ploted between percentage of sand and unit weight of the mixed aggregate as shown in Fig. 20.2. From the graph the percentage of fine aggregate is calculated for the maximum unit weight. In the Fig. 20.2 the maximum weight of mixed aggregate occurs when percentage of fine aggregate is 38, but optimum percentage should be 38 – 3 = 35%.

For grading the material to obtain the maximum density he suggested the following empirical formula:

$$P = \left(\frac{d}{D}\right)^{1/2} \times 100 \qquad \text{...(20.1)}$$

where p is the percentage by weight of material finer than gauge 'd' and 'D' is the maximum size of coarse aggregate to be used. For example, if the maximum size of aggregate used in the mixture is 20 mm and 5 mm is the maximum size of fine aggregate, then the value of p for material finer than 5 mm is given as,

$$P = \left(\frac{5}{20}\right)^{1/2} \times 100 = 50\%$$

Thus 50 kg. of fine aggregate including cement have, to be mixed with 50 kg of coarse aggregate. If the ratio of cement and combined aggregate is 1:7 (usually this ratio may vary from 1:6 to 1:9), then the amount of cement in 100 kg total mix is $\frac{100}{8} = 12.5$ kg.

Thus weight of fine aggregate = 50 – 12.5 = 37.5 kg. Now if the densities of cement, fine aggregate and coarse aggregate are 1.44, 1.75 and 1.6 kg. per litre respectively, then volumes of cement, fine aggregate and coarse aggregate are $\frac{12.5}{1.44} = 8.7$ lit. $\frac{37.5}{1.75} = 21.3$ lit. $\frac{50}{1.60} = 31.25$ lit.

then ratios are $1:2\frac{1}{2}:3\frac{1}{2}$. The amount of water will be added to make the mix workable. Experiments though showed that this mix gave maximum density, but it could not be established to give the desired strength. This method could not be popular as the accuracy of grading is difficult to obtain in practice. Thus none of the above three methods could ensure the desired strength of concrete accurately.

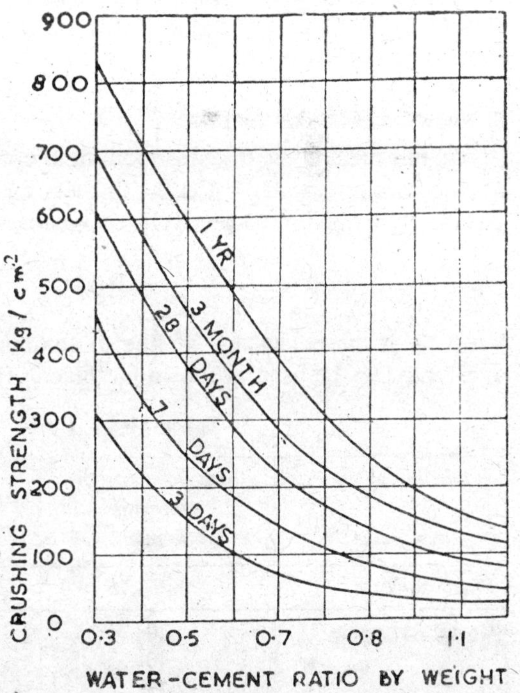

Fig. 20.3. Relation between w/c ratio and compressive strength of concrete

4. Water/Cement ratio method. On the basis of his extensive study Abram stated that with the given materials and conditions of test the ratio of quantity of mixing water to the quantity of cement alone determines the strength of concrete, so long as the mix is of workable plasticity. This is known as water/cement law. According of this law $P = \frac{984}{4^x}$ where x is water/cement ratio and P is the 28 day 15 × 30 cms cylinder strength. For designing a mix in practice, curves given in Fig. 20.3 can be used as a guide to select a suitable water/cement ratio for the compressive strength required of the mix. For exact values, strength and water/cement ratio suitably adjusted if needed. W/C ratios under different conditions of climate is shown in Table 20.9

Table 20.9. Maximum w/c ratios under different conditions of climate

Climate	*W/C ratio by volume*		
	Light structural members	*Hydraulic Structures*	*Heavy Sections such as dams, piers, foundations etc.*
Extreme Exposure to alternate wetting and drying, freezing and thawing for long period, sea water and sulphate water.	0.73	0.73	0.8
Severe Exposure to rain and snow, freezing and thawing, but not continuously.	0.8	0.8	0.9
Moderate Exposure to ordinary weather but not continuously in contact with water.	0.9	0.8	1.0
Protected Members protected against rain and frost, concrete below ground, but not subjected to harmful sub-soil water effects or freezing etc.	1.0	0.8	1.1

5. Fineness modulus method

In this method the fineness modulii of coarse, fine and combined aggregates are determined separately as discussed in Chapter 4. Let the fineness modulii of coarse aggregate, fine aggregate and combine aggregate be P_2, P_1 and P, respectively, then percentage of fine aggregate.

$$W = \frac{P_2 - P}{P_2 - P_1} \times 100$$

where W is the percentage of fine to combined aggregate of the mix. The fineness modulii of different aggregate may be used as shown in Table 20.10.

Table 20.10. Fineness modulus of deffirent aggregates

Type of aggregate	*Maximum size of aggregate in mm*	*Fineness madulii*		*Remark*
		Minimum	*Maximum*	
Fine Aggregate	5.0 to 4.75	2.0	3.5	
Coarse Aggregate	20	6.0	6.9	
	40	6.9	7.5	
	75	7.5	8.0	
	150	8.0	8.5	

Type of aggregate	*Maximum size of aggregate in mm*	*Fineness madulii*		*Remark*
		Minimum	*Maximum*	
Mixed Aggregate	20	4.7	5.1	
	25	5.0	5.5	
	32	5.2	5.7	
	40	5.4	5.9	
	75	5.8	6.3	
	150	6.5	7.0	

The ideal grading of the aggregate is shown in Table 20.11 but in practice it is difficult and costly to get such as grading.

Table 20.11. Ideal grading of aggregates

Maximum size of coarse aggregate	*Percentage passing the sieve*										
	150 mm	75 mm	40 mm	20 mm	10 mm	4.75 mm	2.36 mm	1.18 mm	600 micron	300 micron	150 micron
150 mm	100	70	50	36	25	18	12.5	9	6.25	4.5	3
75 mm	—	100	70	50	36	25	18	12.5	9	6.25	4.5
40 mm	—	—	100	70	50	36	25	13	12.5	9	6.25
20 mm	—		—	100	70	50	36	25	18	12.5	9

Quantity of water required in concrete mix

An approximate quantity of water required in the mix can be taken from the empirical relation given as

Quantity of water = 30% by weight of cement + 5% of combined aggregate by weight. Also the amount of water depending upon the maximum size of aggregate used in the concrete may be taken as shown below in Table 20.12.

Table 20.12. Amount of water in kg/m^3 to be used in the mix

1.	Size of coarse aggregate in mm	150	75	40	25	20
2.	Quantity of water in kg per m^3 concrete	144	164	180	192	200

20.7. SUMMERY OF THE PROCESS OF OLD MIX DESIGN METHODS

1. Choose a water/cement ratio for the required strength of concrete from the curve 20.3 or from table used for different climatic conditions given in chapter on workability or Table 20.8.
2. Determine the workability in terms of slump required for a particular job.
3. Determine the maximum size of aggregate that is available or to be used as per site conditions. Maximum possible size of aggregate should be used depending upon the size of the job as it will give least surface area to be wetted.
4. Mix fine and coarse aggregate in such a proportion that the combined aggregate either gives the grading as shown above in Table 20.11 or fineness modulus of Table 20.10 which needs optimum amount of fine aggregate.
5. The quantity of cement is obtained by the water/cement value to give the desired slump for the given water/cement ratio.
6. Determine the actual proportions by trial mix. The procedure is illustrated by the following example.

Example 3. *Design a concrete mix from the following data:*

1. *Required strength at 28 days* = *250 kg/cm²*
2. *Slump required* = *2.5 cm*
3. *Fineness modulii of coarse and fine aggregate* = *6.0 and 2.0 respectively*
4. *Maximum size of aggregate to be used* = *20 mm*
5. *Weight of coarse aggregate per cubic metre* = *1600 kg/m³*
6. *Weight of fine aggregate per cubic metre* = *1760 kg/m³*
7. *Weight of cement per cubic metre* = *1440 kg/m³*
8. *Voids in fine and coarse aggregate* = *40% in each*
9. *Voids in cement* = *50%*

Solution. From Fig. 20.3 the water/cement ratio for a given strength of 250 kg/cm² is given as 0.65. Hence for every bag of 50 kg cement, water should be used 32.5 kg.

From Table 20.10, the fineness modulus of combined aggregate varies from 4.7 to 5.2

The fineness modulus of fine aggregate has been given as 2.0 *i.e.* at the lower limit.

Hence fineness modulus of combined aggregate also has been taken at the lower limit as 4.7.

Then the ratio of fine aggregate to combined aggregate

$$\rho = \frac{6 - 4.7}{6.0 - 2.0} \times 100 = 32.5\%$$

i.e. 32.5 kg of fine aggregate is mixed in 67.5 kg of coarse aggregate.

Hence ratio of fine to coarse aggregate is 1:2 approximately.

Water. From Table 20.12, for 20 mm size aggregate the amount of water is 200 kg per cubic metre of concrete.

$$\text{For Water/cement 0.65 or cement used} = \frac{\text{water}}{0.65} = \frac{200}{0.65}$$

$$\therefore \quad \text{weight of cement used} = 307.7 \text{ kg or } \frac{307.7}{1440} \text{ cubic metre}$$

$$= 0.2137 \text{ m}^3 \text{ approximately}$$

$$\text{Solid volume of water} = \frac{200}{1000} = 0.2 \text{ m}^3$$

As the voids in cement are 50%, its solid volume

$$= \frac{0.2137}{2} = 0.10685 \text{ m}^3$$

$\therefore$ Total solids of fine and coarse aggregate in 1 m³ concrete

$$= (1 - 0.2 - 0.10685)$$

$$= 0.69315 \text{ m}^3$$

As the voids in fine and coarse aggregate are 40%, their solid matter is 60%

$\therefore$ Apparent volume of combined aggregates

$$= \frac{0.69315}{0.6} = 1.1563 \text{ m}^3$$

Out of this 1.1553 m³ combined aggregate, 1/3 is fine and 2/3 coarse aggregate.

Thus fine aggregate is 0.3851 m³ and coarse aggregate = 0.7702 m³

$\therefore$ Actual proportions are as follows:

Water	*Cement*	*Fine aggregate*	*Coarse aggregate*
32.5 kg pr bag of 50 kg cement, or	0.2137 m^3	0.3851 m^3	0.7702 m^3
200 kg per m^3	1	1.8	3.6

Note. Using the above quantity of water, the slump should be measured and water should be adjusted as per requirement of slump.

Table 20.13. Quantity of water for different slumps using different sizes of aggregate

Workability	*Slump in mm*	*Quantity of water per cubic metre of concrete for different sizes of aggregate*						
		10 mm	12 mm	20 mm	25 mm	40 mm	50 mm	80 mm
Low	25-50	250	235	220	210	195	180	170
Medium	75-100	270	250	240	230	210	200	190
High	150-175	290	270	250	240	225	210	200
Amount of entrapped air in percentage		3.0%	2.5%	2.0%	1.5%	1.0%	0.5%	0.3%

Table 20.14. Showing relations between water/cement ratio, 28 days and 7 days strength

Water/cement ratio	*Concrete 15 cm cube strength kg/cm²*	
	28 days	7 dyas
0.35	520	400
0.40	466	350
0.45	420	300
0.50	370	250
0.55	320	215
0.60	280	180
0.65	245	150
0.70	215	130
0.75	195	110
0.80	175	105

Table 20.15. Grading limits for aggregates and their fineness modulus

I.S. sieve	*Percentage passing*			
	Zone I	Zone II	Zone III	Zone IV
10 mm	100	100	100	100
4.75 mm	90 — 100	90 — 100	90 — 100	95 — 100
2.36 mm	60 — 95	75 — 100	85 — 100	95 — 100
1.18 mm	30 — 70	55 — 90	75 — 100	90 — 100
600 micron	15 — 34	35 — 59	60 — 79	80 — 100
300 micron	5 — 20	8 — 30	12 — 40	15 — 50
150 micron	0 — 10	0 — 10	0 — 10	0 — 15
Fineness modulus	4.0 — 2.71	3.37 — 2.1	2.78 — 1.71	2.25 —1.35

Table 20.16. Shows the proportion of fine to coarse aggregate for different size of aggregates

Coarse	*Fine aggregage*			
	Zone I	Zone II	Zone III	Zone IV
10 mm	1 : 1	1 : 1.5	1 : 2	1 : 3
20 mm	1 : 1.5	1 : 2	1 : 3	1 : 3.5
38 or 40 mm	1 : 2	1 : 2	1 : 3.5	—

Example 4. Prepare a concrete of M 150 grade in the field with the help of following data.

(*a*) *Maximum size of coarse aggregate to be used* = *20 mm*

(*b*) *Fineness modulus of coarse aggregate* = *6.8*

(*c*) *Fineness modulus of fine aggregate* = *1.7 – 2.75*

(*d*) *Workability* = *Low*

(*e*) *Slump* = *25 to 50 mm*

Solution. For good control as per IS 456-1978, to produce a M 150 grade concrete, for actual work, the mix should be designed for 200 kg/cm^2 strength of concrete.

For the given fineness modulus of fine aggregate, the sand falls in Zone III from Table 20.16. For maximum size of aggregate of 20 mm the ratio of fine aggregate to coarse aggregate is

F.A. : C.A. :: 1:3

From Table 20.7 for M 15 grade concrete the amount of combined aggregate required is 350 kg per bag of 50 kg of cement.

Thus proportions comes out as

Cement	Total aggregate	F.A. : C.A.	F.A. : C.A.	Water
50 kg	350 kg	1 : 3	87.5 lit : 262.5 lit	32 lit

Moisture content carried by fine and coarse aggregate as per IS 456-1978, (Table 4.12) is taken as 80 lit. and 40 lit. per cubic metre respectively.

then amount of water in fine aggregate = $\dfrac{80 \times 87.5}{1000} = 7.0$ kg.

amount of water in coarse aggregate = $\dfrac{40 \times 262.5}{1000} = 10.5$ kg.

$\therefore$ Total water present in aggregate = 17.5 kg.

Moisture in fine aggregate = 8%

From curve 4.8 for medium sand for 8%

moisture the percentage bulking of sand = 26%

then volume of fine aggregate = $\dfrac{126 \times 87.5}{100} = 110.25$ lit.

Hence proportions may be taken as,

Cement = 50 kg

Coarse aggregate = 262.5 lit.

Fine aggregate = 110.25 lit.

Water = 32 – 17.5 = 14.5 kg

New w/c ratio = **0.29 Ans.**

For actual design purposes following tables will prove useful

Table 20.17. Weight of dry aggregate per 100 kg of cement according to B.S. 5328-1976

28 days strength kg/cm^2	*Weight of aggregate (kg) for maximum size of aggregate in mm*							
	40		20		14		10	
	Slump in mm		*Slump in mm*		*Slump in mm*		*Slump in mm*	
	50 — 100	80 — 170	25 — 75	65 — 135	5 — 55	50 — 100	0 — 45	15 — 65
70	1080	920	900	780	×	×	×	×
100	900	800	770	690	×	×	×	×
150	790	690	680	580	×	×	×	×

28 days strength kg/cm²	*Weight of aggregate (kg) for maximum size of aggregate in mm*							
	40		20		14		10	
	Slump in mm		*Slump in mm*		*Slump in mm*		*Slump in mm*	
	50 — 100	80 — 170	25 — 75	65 — 135	5 — 55	50 — 100	0 — 45	15 — 65
200	660	600	600	530	560	470	510	420
250	560	510	510	460	490	410	450	370
300	510	460	460	400	410	360	380	320

Table 20.18. Percentage by weight of fine aggregate to total aggregate (B.S. 5328-1976)

Grade of concrete (28 days strength kg/cm²	*Grading zone of fine aggregate (1-4)*	*Percentage of fine aggregate for maximum size of coarse aggregate in mm*							
		40		20		14 (1/2")		10	
		Workability		*Workability*		*Workability*		*Workability*	
		Medium	*High*	*Medium*	*High*	*Medium*	*High*	*Medium*	*High*
70		30 — 40*		35 — 40*					
100									
150									
200	1	35	40	40	45	45	50	50	55
250	2	30	35	35	40	40	45	45	50
300	3	30	30	30	35	35	40	40	45
350	4	25	25	25	30	30	35	35	40

Note: * With sands at extremes of their grading or adjustment in the percentage of fine aggregate may be required. The lower values of percentage of fine aggregate applies to finer material such as for zone 4 sand and higher values to coarser sand such as zone 1 sand.

Table 20.19. Relation between water/cement ratio and compressive strength of concrete as per A.C.I. standard (2113-1875)

Compressive strength at 28 days			*Water/cement ratio (by weight)*	
kg/cm²	*MPa*	*P.S.I.*	*Non-air entrained concrete*	*Air entrained concrete*
480	48	7000	0.33	—
410	41	6000	0.41	0.32
340	34	5000	0.48	0.40
280	28	4000	0.57	0.48
210	21	3000	0.68	0.59
140	14	2000	0.82	0.74

Table 20.20. Minimum cement content of concrete with 20 mm aggregate (B.S. C.P. 110-1972)

Condition of exposure	*Minimum cement content for*					
	Plain concrete		*Reinforced concrete*		*Pre-stressed concrete*	
	kg/m³	lb/yd³	kg/m³	lb/yd3	kg/m3	lb/yd3
Non-corrosive	220	370	250	420	300	510
Sheltered from rain and freezing	250	420	290	490	300-	510
Exposed to alternating wetting and drying or freezing while wet or to sea water	310	530	360	610	360	610
Subject to deicing salt (Use of air entrained concrete)	280	470	290	490	300	510

20.8. AMERICAN METHOD OF MIX DESIGN

The American Concrete Institute (ACI) method is based on the fact that for a given maximum size of aggregate the water content in kilogram per cubic metre of concrete determines the workability of concrete mix, usually independent of the mix proportions. The relative water contents for various workabilities is given in Table 20.23. Table 20.24 gives the actual content of water for a reference (plastic) consistency of table 20.23 It is thus possible to start the mix design by selecting the water content from these tables. Further it is also assumed that the optimum ratio of bulk volume of coarse aggregate to the total volume of concrete depends only on the maximum size of aggregate and on the grading of fine aggregate. Table 20.25 gives the maximum bulk volume of coarse aggregate per unit volume of concrete For other consistency the values of Table 20.23 should be multiplied by a factor given in Table 20.26. The actual procedure is explained with the help of the following example.

Table 20.21. Aggregate/cement ratio by weight required to give the four degrees of workability with different gradings irregular aggregate (For 38.0 mm size grading)

Degree of workability →	*Very low*				*Low*				*Medium*				*High*			
Grading curve No. of Fig. →	1	2	3	4	1	2	3	4	1	2	3	4	1	2	3	4
W/C ratio by weight																
0.35	4.0	3.9	3.5	3.2	3.4	3.3	3.2	2.9	2.9	2.8	2.6	2.5	2.7	2.5	2.3	2.3
0.40	5.3	5.3	4.7	4.3	4.5	4.5	4.2	3.8	3.8	3.7	3.7	3.4	3.5	3.5	3.3	3.1
0.45	6.5	6.5	5.9	5.3	5.6	5.6	5.3	4.8	4.6	4.7	4.6	4.3	4.0	4.4	4.3	4.0
0.50	7.7	7.7	7.1	6.3	6.7	6.7	6.3	5.7	5.4	5.7	5.5	5.1	4.5	5.2	5.1	4.8
0.60	—	—	8.1	7.3	7.6	7.7	7.2	6.6	6.2	6.5	6.3	5.8	4.8	5.9	6.0	5.5
0.65			—	—	—	—	—	7.4	7.0	7.3	7.1	6.6	×		6.7	6.2
0.70								8.1	7.8	8.1	7.8	7.2	×		7.3	6.9
0.75												7.9	×		—	7.4
0.80													×		—	8.0

Note 1. These proportions are based on specific gravities of approximately 2.5 for coarse aggregate and 2.6 for fine aggregate.

2. × indicate that mix would segregate.

3. – indicate that the mix was out side the range tested.

Example 5. *Concrete of compressive strength of 350 kg/cm² (35 MPs) and 5 cms slump is required for a particular job, ordinary Portland cement being used. The maximum size of aggregate used is 38 mm ($1\frac{1}{2}$") its bulk density is 1600 kg/m³ and specific gravity 2.64. The fineness modulus of fine aggregate is 2.60 and its specific gravity 2.58. The absolute density in kg/m³ is 1000 times larger than the specific gravity.*

Procedure. *After fixing the maximum size and type of aggregate, the workability is determined with the help of water content obtained from given tables 20.23 and 20.24, and bulk volume of coarse aggregate from table 20.25. From given specific gravity of coarse aggregate, its absolute volume is determined. Now the water/cement ratio is chosen from strength as well as durability requirements and the quantity of cement is computed dividing water content by water/cement ratio. Thus the absolute volumes of water, coarse aggregate, are known. The absolute volume of fine aggregate can be determined by subtracting the above weights from the weight of concrete.*

Solution. For the required slump of 50 mm, the concrete is of stiff plastic degree. For this concrete

Table 20.22. Aggregate/cement ratio by weight to give different workability max size 19 mm rounded aggregate

Degree of workability →	*Very low*				*Low*				*Medium*				*High*			
Grading curve No. of Fig. →	1	2	3	4	1	2	3	4	1	2	3	4	1	2	3	4
W/C ratio by weight																
0.35	4.5	4.5	3.5	3.2	3.8	3.6	3.2	3.1	3.1	3.0	2.8	2.7	2.8	2.8	2.6	2.5
0.40	6.6	6.3	5.3	4.5	5.3	5.1	4.5	4.2	4.2	4.2	3.9	3.7	3.6	3.7	3.5	3.3
0.45	8.0	7.7	6.7	5.8	6.9	6.6	5.9	5.1	5.3	5.3	5.0	4.5	4.8	4.8	4.5	4.1
0.50	—	—	8.0	7.0	8.2	8.0	7.0	6.0	6.3	6.3	5.9	5.4	5.5	5.7	5.3	4.8
0.55	—	—	—	8.1	—	—	8.2	6.9	7.3	7.3	7.4	6.4	6.3	6.5	6.1	5.5
0.60	—	—	—	—	—	—	—	7.7	—		8.0	7.2	×	7.2	6.8	6.1
0.65			—	—	—	—	—	8.5	—			7.8	×	7.7	7.4	6.6
0.70				—			—	—	—				×	—	7.9	7.2
0.75													×	—	—	7.6

Note 1. The proportions are based on specific gravities of approximately 2.5 for coarse aggregate and 2.6 for fine aggregate.

2. × indicate that mix would segregate

3. – indicate that the mix was out side the range tested

having a maximum size of aggregate as 38 mm to 40 mm water content is taken from table 20.23 and 20.24 as $175 \times 0.92 = 161$ kg. per cubic metre of concrete.

Air entrainment is assumed as 1%. For this condition the water/cement ratio is taken from table 20.19 as 0.47 by extra polation.

$$\text{Hence cement content} = \frac{\text{Weigh of water}}{\text{Water/cement raito}} = \frac{161}{0.47}$$

$$= 342.55 \text{ kg.}$$

For a fineness modulus of 2.60 for fine aggregate (using the given fine aggregate) the bulk volume of coarse aggregate from table 20.25). is given as 0.73 m^3.

∴ Weight of coarse aggregate per cubic metre of concrete = $0.73 \times 1600 = 1168$ kg.

Hence absolute volumes of ingredients are calculated as follows:

1. Cement $= \dfrac{342.55}{3.15 \times 1000} = 0.1087 \text{ m}^3$

2. Water $= \dfrac{161}{1000} = 0.161 \text{ m}^3$

3. Coarse aggregate $= \dfrac{1168}{2.64 \times 1000} = 0.4424 \text{ m}^3$

4. Entrapped air 1% $= 0.01 \times 1 = 0.010 \text{ m}^3$

Total $= 0.7221 \text{ m}^3$

∴ Hence volume of fine aggregate required = $1 - 0.7221$

$= 0.2778 \text{ m}^3$

∴ Weight of fine aggregate $= 0.02779 \times 2.58 \times 1000 = 700.6$ kg.

Hence the weight of materials per cubic metre of concrete are:

1. Cement = 342.55 kg.
2. Water = 161.00 kg.
3. Fine aggregate = 700.6 kg.
4. Coarse aggregate = 1168.0 kg.

Total = 2372.55 kg.

Hence density of concrete = **2372.6 kg. Ans.**

20.9. VOLUME OF FULLY COMPACTED CONCRETE

The volume of fully compacted concrete can be calculated by using the so called absolute volume method, which assumes that the volume of compacted concrete is equal to the sum of absolute volume of all ingredients.

Generally the quantities of ingredients needed to produce 1 cubic metre of concrete are calculated by the following relation.

$$\frac{W}{1000} + \frac{C}{1000\,\rho_c} + \frac{A_1}{1000\,\rho_1} + \frac{A_2}{1000\,\rho_2} = 1$$

where,

W = weight of water used in the concrete
C = weight of cement used in the concrete
A_1 = weight of fine aggregate used in the concrete
A_2 = weight of coarse aggregate used in the concrete
ρ_c = specific gravity of cement (3.15)
ρ_1 = specific gravity of fine aggregate
ρ_2 = specific gravity of coarse aggregate

For comparing various mixes, it is some times convenient to convert the aggregate/cement ratio into the cement content or vice versa. Cement and Concrete Association of America has developed a chart, for this purpose. This chart has been reproduced below.

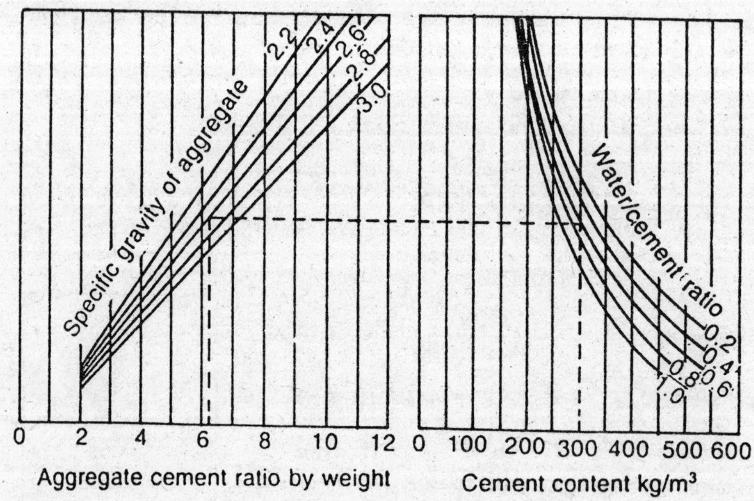

Fig. 20.4. Conversion chart for aggregate/cement ratio into cement content

Table 20.23. Relative mixing water required for different consistency of concrete

Description	*Consistency*			*Relative water content percent*
	Slump in mm	*VEE-BEE No. seconds*	*Compacting factor*	
Extremely dry	—	32 — 18	—	78
Very stiff	—	18 — 10	0.70	83
Stiff	0 — 30	10 — 5	0.75	88
Stiff Plastic	30 — 80	5 —3	0.85	92
Plastic (reference)	80 — 130	3 — 0	0.91	100
Fluid	130 — 180	—	0.95	106

Table 20.24. Approximate mixing water content for reference (plastic) mix of table 20.23 for different mix size aggregate

Maximum size of aggregate in mm	*Non air entrained water content*		*Entrained air percent*	*Air entrained water content*	
	kg/m³	*lbs/yd³*		*kg/m²*	*lbs/yd³*
10.0	225	385	3.0	200	340
12.5	215	365	2.5	190	325
20.0	200	340	2	180	305
25.0	195	325	2.5	175	295
40.0	175	300	1.0	160	275
50.0	170	285	0.5	155	265
75.0	160	265	0.3	150	250
150	140	230	0.2	135	220

Table 20.25. Bulk volume of coarse aggregate per unit vol. of concrete

Maximum size of Aggregate in mm	*Bulk volume of rodded coarse aggregate per unit volume of concrete for fineness modulus of sand of*			
	2.4	2.6	2.8	3.0
10.0	0.5	0.48	0.46	0.44
12.5	0.59	0.57	0.55	0.53
20.0	0.66	0.64	0.62	0.60
25.0	0.71	0.69	0.67	0.65
38.0 (40)	0.75	0.73	0.71	0.69
50.0	0.78	0.76	0.74	0.72
75.0	0.82	0.80	0.78	0.76
150.0	0.87	0.85	0.83	0.81

Table 20.26. Factor to be applied of the volume of coarse aggregate calculated from Table 20.23 for consistency other than plastic

Consistency	*Factor for maximum size of aggregate of*				
	10 mm	12.5 mm	20 mm	25 mm	40 mm
Extremely dry	1.90	1.70	1.45	1.40	1.30
Very stiff	1.60	1.45	1.30	1.25	1.25
Stiff	1.35	1.30	1.15	1.15	1.20
Stiff plastic	1.08	1.06	1.04	1.06	1.09
Plastic (reference)	1.00	1.00	1.00	1.00	1.00
Fluid	0.97	0.98	1.00	1.00	1.00

20.10. DESIGN OF MASS CONCRETE

Mass concrete for dams, spillways etc. can be designed easily with the help of concrete manual. The relevant tables have been reproduced below.

Table 20.27. Net water cement ratio for mass concrete

Location of concrete structure and degree of exposure	*Water-cement ratio by weight*	
	Severe climate, wide range of temp, long periods of freezing or frequent freezing and thawing	*Mild climate, rainy or arid, rarely snow or frost*
A. Concrete in portions of structures subject to exposure of extreme severity, such as the top 60 cms of wall, boxes, piers, and parapets. All of curbs, cills, ledges, copings, corners, and cornices, and concrete in the range of fluctuating water levels or spray, are parts of dams, spillways, Blow off boxes, tunnel inlets and outlets, tailrace walls, valve houses, canal structures and other concrete work.	0.45 ± 0.02	0.55 ± 0.02
B. Concrete in exposed structures and parts of structures where exposure is less severe than in A above, such as portions of tunnel lining and syphons, subject to freezing, the exterior of mass concrete, and the other exposed parts of structures not covered by A.	0.50 ± 0.02	0.50 ± 0.02
C. Concrete in structures or parts of structures to be covered with back fill, or to be continually submerged or otherwise protected from weather, such as cut off walls, foundations, and parts of structures, dams, trashracks, gate chambers, outlet works, and control houses. If severe exposure during construction appears likely to last several seasons reduce w/c ratio by 0.05 for parts most exposed.	0.58 ± 0.02	0.58 ± 0.02
D. Concrete that will be subject to attack by sulphate, alkalies in soils and ground waters, but will be placed during moderate weather.	—	0.50 ± 0.02
E. Concrete that will be subject to attack by sulphate, alkalies in soils and under ground waters, but will be placed during freezing weather, when Calcium Chloride would normally be used in mix. Do not mix $CaCl_2$, but decrease the W/C by 0.02%.	0.45 ± 0.02	—
F. Concrete deposited in water by tremie.	0.45 ± 0.02	0.45 ± 0.02
G. Canal lining	0.53 ± 0.02	0.53 ± 0.02
H. Concrete for interior of dams	Properties of this concrete will be governed by strength, thermal properties, and volume change requirements which will be established for each structure.	

Example 6. *For the construction of an spillway, design a concrete to give minimum strength of 211 kg/cm² (3000 P.S.I.) at 28 days using the following data.*

Data given

Compressive strength at 28 days = 211 kg/cm²

Specific gravity of coarse aggregate = 2.8

Specific gravity of fine aggregate = 2.65

Specific gravity of cement = 3.15

Table 20.28. Approximate water and air contents per cubic metre of concrete

Maximum size of coarse aggregate in mm	*Percent dry rodded unit weight of coarse aggregate per unit vol. of concrete*	*Air entrained concrete*			*Non-air entrained concrete*		
		Recommended air content percent	*Average water content kg/m*^{3}	*Sand percent of total aggregate by solid volume*	*Approximate air entrapped in percent*	*Average water content kg/m*^{3}	*Sand % of total aggregate by solid volume*
10	41	8	191.4	59	3.0	209.2	61
12.5	52	7	181.85	50	2.5	197.7	53
20	62	6	168.5	42	2.0	187.9	45
25	67	5	158.7	37	1.5	178.3	41
38 (40)	73	4.5	145.7	33	1.0	166.5	36
50	76	4	136.0	30	0.5	158.0	33
75	81	3.5	121.3	28	0.3	143.8	31
150	87	3.0	97.45	24	0.2	124.8	28

Table 20.29. Recommended slumps for various types of concrete construction

	Type of construction	*Max. slump in mm*
1.	Heavy mass construction	50
2.	Canal lining	75
3.	Slabs and tunnal inverts	50
4.	Tops of walls, piers, parapets and curbs	50
5.	Side walls and arch in tunnel lining	100
6.	Other structures	75

Slump of concrete = 75 mm
Maximum size of aggregate to be used = 75 mm
Permissible air to be entrapped = 3.5%

Solution. For mass concrete the average strength may be assumed at least 15% higher than minimum. Hence mix to be designed for $211 \times 1.15 = 243$ kg/cm^2 concrete.

From Table 20.28 per cubic metre of concrete. for a 75 mm maximum size aggregate and 3.5% air entrainment amount of water

$$= 121.3 \text{ kg.}$$

From Table 20.27 the water/cement ratio to be adopted for spillway is 0.5 ± 0.20.

Hence adopting water/cement ratio as 0.5, quantity of cement

$$= \frac{121.3}{0.5} = 242.6 \text{ kg.}$$

Solid volumes of ingredients

1. Solid volume of water $= \dfrac{121.3}{1000} = 0.1213 \text{ m}^3$

2. Solid volume of cement $= \dfrac{242.6}{3.15 \times 1000} = 0.0768 \text{ m}^3$

3. Air 3.5% $= 0.035 = 0.035 \text{ m}^3$

Total $= 0.2331$

Solid volume of aggregate $= 1 - 0.2331 = 0.7669 \text{ m}^3$

From Table 20.28 the percentage of sand = 28% of the combined aggregate

$\therefore$ Fine aggregate = 0.7669 × 0.28

= 0.214732 m^3

$\therefore$ Coarse aggregate = 0.5522 m^3

	Volume	*Weight*	
Water	= 0.1213 m^3	0.1213 × 1000	= 121.3 kg.
Cement	= 0.0768 m^3	0.07668 × 3.15 × 1000	= 241.9 kg.
F.A.	= 0.2147 m^3	0.2147 × 2.65 × 1000	= 569.0 kg.
C.A.	= 0.5522 m^3	0.5522 × 2.8 × 1000	= 1546.2 kg.
Air	= 0.035 m^3		
Total	= 1.000 m^3	Total weight	= 2478.4
		Density of concrete	= 2478.4 kg/m^3 **Ans**

20.11. GRAPHIC METHOD OF MIX DESIGN

This method has been developed by Road Research Laboratory, London and its detailed procedure has been explained in Road Note No. 4. Here this method is explained with the help of Fig. 20.5 and 20.6. The aggregates to be mixed together are seived and their percentage passing through standard seives for fine aggregate seive 4.75 mm, 2.36 mm, 1.18 mm, 600 micron, 300 micron and 150 micron are used. For coarse aggregate maximum size allowed, say 38 mm, 19 mm, 9.5 mm 4.75 mm, 2.36 mm seive used.

Procedure

1. The percentage passing through each seive of the coarse and fine aggregate or two fractions of coarse aggregate which are to be mixed to obtain the desired grading curve are noted along the two opposite vertical sides of a square from top to bottom as shown in Fig. 20.5. The points

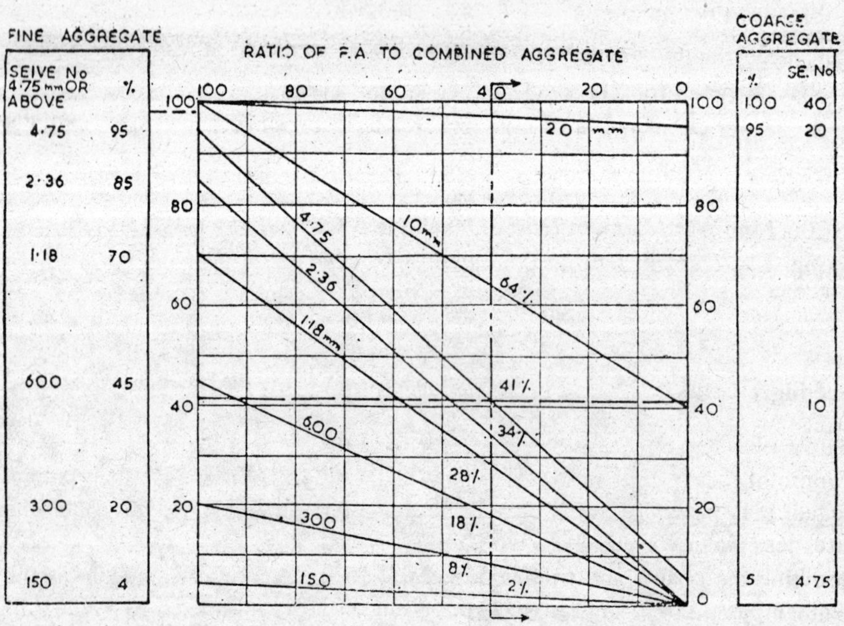

Fig. 20.5. Graphical method for combining the aggregates

corresponding to the same seive size are joined by the straight lines. If the seive size does not exist on any of the vertical axis, then the line should be joined to the 100% point on the left hand axis and 0% point on the right hand axis.

2. Now a vertical line is drawn through the point of inter section of the line joining the same seive size point and the horizontal line representing the correct percentage of aggregate smaller than the desired seive or the vertical line drawn from the appropriate point along the scale at the top of the diagram (this scale represents the ratio of fine to total aggregate) and the combined grading is given by the inter section of this line and the seive size lines joining the pairs of points. If two coarse aggregate are to be combined with a sand then the two C.A sizes to be combined using the % passing 20 mm sieve as a creterion. Its two sands are to be combined then 600 micron sieve should be taken as criterion.

Let us illustrate the procedure with the help of an example. Let the seive analysis of the material is given as shown in Table 20.30.

Table 20.30.

Sieve size	*Percentage passing*		
	Coarse		*Fine aggregate*
	19.1-4.75 mm	38.1-19.0 mm	
38.1 or 40 mm	100	100	100
19.1 or 20 mm	95	15	100
9.5 or 10 mm	35	10	100
4.75 mm	6	4	95
2.36 mm	0	0	85
1.18 mm	0	0	70
600 micron	0	0	45
300 micron	0	0	20
150 micron	0	0	4

I.S. 383-1970 has given the limits of grading for all in aggregate and the range is shown in the following Table 20.31.

Table 20.31.

I.S. sieve	*Percentage passing for all in aggregate of*	
	38.1 or 40 mm size	*19.1 or 20 mm size*
80 mm	100	—
38.1 or 40 mm	95 — 100	100
19.1 or 20 mm	45 — 75	95 — 100
4.75 mm	25 — 45	30 — 50
600 micron	8 — 30	10 — 35
150 micron	0 — 6	0 — 6

3. The graph of these limits is shown in Fig. 4.20 and 4.21. To choose the grading for the combined aggregate it is preferable to choose a grading which lies in good zone *i.e.* coarser grading as it requires less water for the given workability.
4. To combine the coarse and fine aggregates, 4.75 mm seive size is taken as the criterion. As the percentage passing 4.75 mm seive varies from 25-50%, it is taken as 41% taking 38.1 mm as the maximum aggregate size.

5. Now draw a horizontal line through 41% line parallel to x-axis.
6. Draw a vertical line through the point of inter-section of line joining the percentages of 4.75 mm line and horizontal line of 41% intersecting all lines as shown.
7. Measure the corresponding percentages indicated by these points of inter-section as shown in the Fig. 20.5. These will be the percentages of each fraction. These percentages are shown on the lines.
8. Now let us combine two fractions of coarse aggregate. In this case the percentage passing through 19.0 or (20) mm sieve size is taken as the criterion. The percentages passing each sieve are marked along the two opposite sides of the square as shown in Fig. 20.6 and the points corresponding to same sieve size are joined by straight lines. Fig. 20.6.

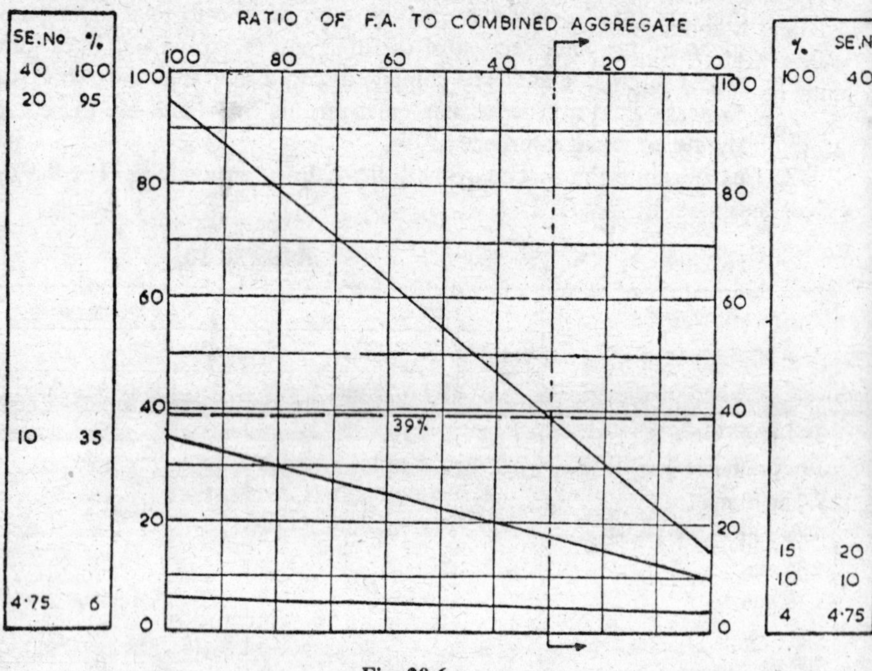

Fig. 20.6.

Now a vertical line is drawn through the point where the line joining the 19.0 mm value intersect the horizontal line representing the correct percentage of aggregate smaller than 19.0 mm as in our case say it is 39%.

20.12. MIX DESIGN BY INDIAN STANDARD METHOD

The bureau of Indian standards has recommended a procedure for mix design of concrete based on the experimental work carriedout in the national laboratories. The mix design procedure is given in IS-10262-1982. After that no revision has been done in this procedure, where as IS 456-1968 has been revised in 2000. Hence IS 10262-1982 needs revision as the strength of cement available in the country has improved significantly. Thus following changes need to be effected.

1. The 28 day strength of A, B, C, D, E & F category of cements needs to be revised.
2. The relation between the different strengths of cement and w/c ratio should be re-established.
3. The relation between 28 days compressive strength and w/c ratio should be extended upto a compressive strength of 80 MPa (800 kg/cm^2), if the graph is to be used for high strength concrete.
4. As per the revised IS 456-2000, the degree of workability is expressed in terms of slump in place of compacting factor. This change needs new values of sand and water content to be used for normal concrete upto 35 MPa and higher strength Concrete above 35 MPa.

However in the absence of any revision in IS 10262-1982, the existing procedure of IS 10262 is described below step wise.

The IS recommendations for mix design include the design for nominal concrete mixes (non air entrained) for both medium and high strength concrete. The method of mix design consists of determining the followings.

(*a*) Water content

(*b*) Percentage of fine aggregate corresponding to the maximum nominal size of aggregate for the reference value of workability

(*c*) Water-cement ratio

(*d*) Grading of fine aggregate.

The water content and percentage of fine aggregate is then adjusted for any difference in workability. Finally the mass of ingredients per unit volume of concrete is calculated by absolute volume method. This method is applicable to both ordinary portland and portland pozzolana cements. The final mix proportions selected after trial mixes, may need minor adjustment. In case of fly ash cement concrete, water content may be reduced by about 3 to 5% and proportion of fine aggregate may be reduced by 2 to 4%.

20.12.1. DATA REQUIRED FOR THE MIX DESIGN

For the mix design following data is required:

1. Characteristic (targeted) compressive strength at 28 days
2. Degree of workability (selection of water-cement ratio)
3. Estimation of entrapped air
4. Selection of water-cement and fine to total aggregate ratio.
5. Calculation of cement content.

1. Characteristic compressive strength at 28 days. The target mean compressive strength f_t at 28 days is given by the relation,

$$f_t = f_c + K.S. \quad \text{...}(i)$$

where f_t is the target mean strength at 28 days, f_c is the characteristic strength at 28 days. As per IS-456-2000 and IS-1343-1980, the characteristic strength of the concrete is that value of the concrete, below which not more than 5% results are expected to fall.

where,

S = standard deviation. For the initial value of mix design the value of standard deviation may be adopted from table 20.32 below.

K = a statistical coefficient known as tolerance factor or risk factor. The value of K may be adopted from table 20.33.

From table 20.33, the value of K is taken as 1.65, putting the value of K is equation (*i*) we get.

$$\therefore \quad f_t = f_c + 1.65\,S \quad \text{...}(ii)$$

Table 20.32. Value of standard deviation as suggested by IS 456-2000

Grade of Concrete	*Assumed standard deviation N/mm²*	*Remark*
M_{10} M_{15}	3.5 do	These values relate to the site control as below
M_{20} M_{25}	4.0 do	(*i*) Proper storage
M_{30} M_{35} M_{40} M_{45} M_{50}	5.0 do do do do	(*ii*) Weight batching of all materials (*iii*) Controlled addition of water (*iv*) Regular checking of all materials (*v*) Periodcal checking of workability and strength

2. Selection of water-cement ratio. Even when the water-cement ratio is fixed, the compressive strength of concrete is influenced by various factors such as type of cement and aggregate, maximum size of aggregate, surface texture of aggregate etc. Thus it is desirable to establish relation between the strength of concrete and free water/cement ratio for the materials to be used and site conditions. If it is not possible

Table 20.33. Values of tolerance factor

Tolerance level No. of samles	1 in 10	1 in 15	1 in 20	1 in 40	1 in 100
10	1.37	1.65	1.81	2.23	2.76
20	1.32	1.58	1.72	2.09	2.53
30	1.31	1.54	1.70	2.04	2.46
Infinite	1.28	1.50	1.64	1.96	2.33

Note. Under major concreting jobs, where large no. of samples are tested, the tolerance factor should be adopted corresponding to infinite no.

Table 20.34. Minimum Cement content, Max. w/c ratio, and minimum grade of concrete for different exposure with nominal weight aggregate of 20 mm nominal max. size as per IS 456-2000

S. No.	*Exposure*	*Plain concrete*			*Reinforced concrete*		
		Min. cement contents in kg/m³	*Max. Free w/c ratio*	*Min. grade of concrete*	*Min. cement contents in kg/m³*	*Max. Free w/c ratio*	*Min. grade of concrete*
1.	Mild	220	0.60	—	300	0.55	M_{20}
2.	Moderate	240	0.60	M_{15}	300	0.50	M_{25}
3.	Severe	250	0.50	M_{20}	320	0.45	M30
4.	Very severe	260	0.45	M_{20}	340	0.45	M35
5.	Extreme	280	0.40	M_{25}	360	0.40	M40

to establish such relation, then for the targeted strength of the concrete the free water/cement ratio may be obtained from the curve 20.7 given below.

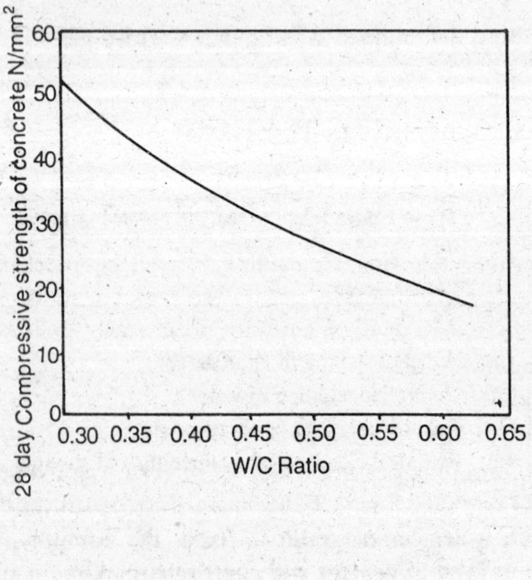

Fig. 20.7. General relation between free water/cement ratio and compressive strength of concrete

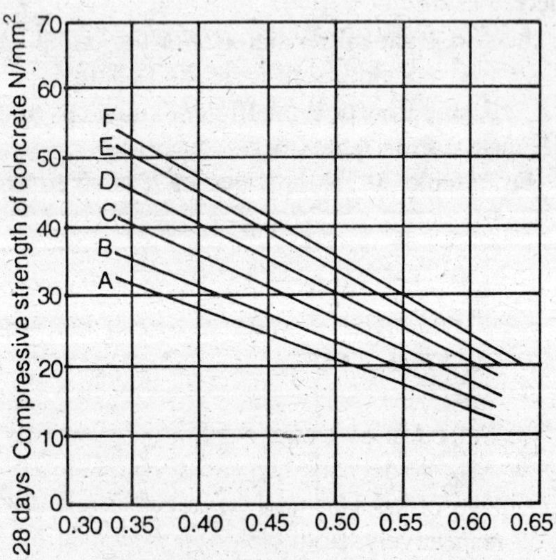

A = 31.9 – 36.8 N/mm²
B = 36.8 – 41.7 N/mm²
C = 41.7 – 46.6 N/mm²
D = 46.6 – 51.5 N/mm²
E = 51.5 – 56.4 N/mm²
F = 56.4 – 61.3 N/mm²

Fig. 20.8. Relation between free w/c ratio and concrete strength for different cement strength

In this method of mix design, the strength of cement has been incorporated. By incorporating the strength of cement, it is possible to effect economy in the concrete mix.

If the 28 days cement strength is known then for more accurate estimation of water/cement ratio curves shown in Fig. 20.8 can be used. How ever adoption of these curves will delay the work as for testing the 28 days strength; at least a delay of 28 days will be there in the whole process. To cut down this delay, accelerated strength tests may be adopted. Since 1982 the quality and strength of Indian Cement has improved considerably. Hence for determining the water/ cement ratio curve of Fig. 20.9 may be adopted in stead of Fig. 20.8. The curves of Fig. 20.9 are not a part of the IS recommended method. They are taken from practice in Germany and may be more useful for getting better results.

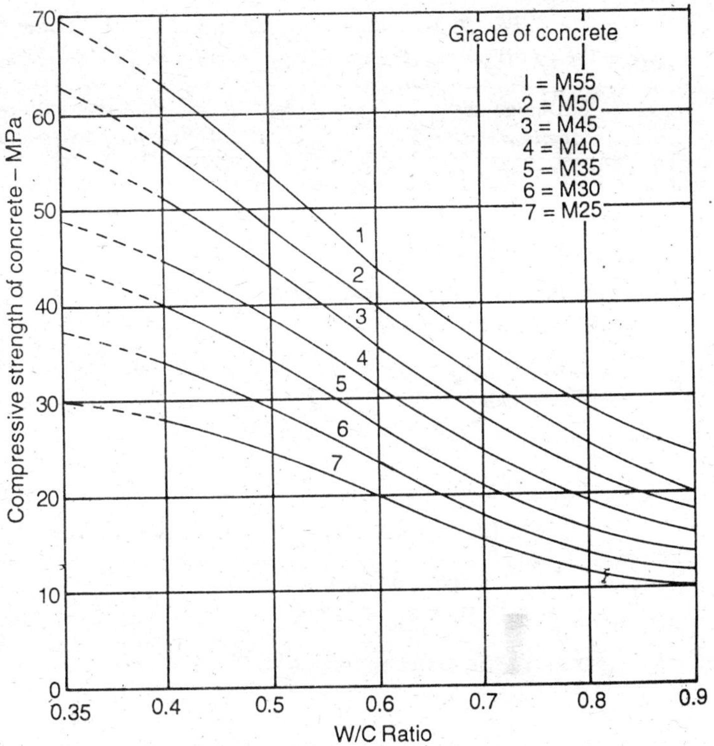

Fig. 20.9. Relation between w/c ratio and compressive strength used in Germany

The free water/cement ratio thus selected as discussed above, should also be checked from durability requirements as shown in Table 20.34, the lower value of the two should be adopted.

3. Estimation of entrapped air. The air content is estimated as shown in Table 20.35 for the nominal aggregate used.

Table 20.35. Approximate amount of entrapped air

Max. size of aggregate in mm	*Entrapped air as % of volume of concrete*
10	3.0
20	2.0
40	1.0

4. Selection of water content and fine to total aggregate ratio. For medium strength concrete *i.e.* below M_{35} grade concrete and high grade concrete *i.e.* higher than M_{35} grade, the water content and percentage of sand in total aggregate by absolute volume basis can be determined from table 20.36 and 20.37 respectively. Both tables are based on the following conditions.

(*a*) Crushed coarse aggregates conforms to IS 383-1970

(*b*) Fine aggregate consisting of natural sand conforms to the grading of zone II of IS 383-1970.

(*c*) Workability corresponding to slump of about 30 mm (compacting factor 0.80). The water/cement ratio of table 20.36 is 0.6 by mass and that of Table 20.37 as 0.35 by mass. For departure from above noted conditions, corrections have to be applied as suggested in table 20.38. Note. For relation between compacting factor and slump see Table 20.1 page 413.

Table 20.36. Approximate sand and water content per cubic metre of concrete w/c = 0.6, workability, C.F. = 0.8 and slump = 30 mm app., applicable for concrete upto grade M35

Maximum size of aggregate (mm)	*Water content including surface water per cubic metre of concrete in kg.*	*Sand as % of total aggregate by absolute volume*
10	200	40
20	186	35
40	165	30

Table 20.37. Approximate sand and water content per cubic metre of concrete, w/c ratio 0.35, workability slump about 30 mm, C.F. = 0.8. For concrete strength above 35 MPa or M35 grade

Max. size of aggregate in (mm)	*Water content including surface water per cubic metre of concrete in kg.*	*Sand as % of total aggregate by absolute volume*
10	200	28
20	180	25

Table 20.38. Adjustment in water content and sand percentage for other conditions

S. No.	*Change in conditions stipulated for tables*	*Adjustments required in*	
		Water content	*% sand in total aggregate*
1.	For sand conforming to grading zone I Zone III or Zone IV table 4 IS-383-1979	0	+ 1.5% for zone I – 1.5% for zone III – 3.0 for zone IV
2.	Increase or decrease in the value of compacting factor by 0.1	± 3.0%	0
3.	Each 0.5% increase or decrease in w/c ratio	0	± 1.0%
4.	For rounded aggregate	– 1.5 kg	— 7%

5. Calculation of cement content. The cement content per unit volume of concrete may be calculated from free water/cement ratio and the quantity of water per unit volume of concrete as

$$\text{Cement by mass} = \frac{\text{water content}}{\text{w/c ratio}}$$

The cement content so calculated should by checked for durability requirement Table 20.34. Greater of the two values should be adopted.

6. Calculation for aggregate content. Aggregate content may be calculated from the following relation.

$$V = \left[W + \frac{C}{S_c} + \frac{1}{P} \times \frac{f_a}{Sf_a} \right] \times \frac{1}{1000} \quad \ldots(1)$$

$$\text{Coarse aggregate} \quad C_a = \frac{1-P}{P} \times f_a \times \frac{S_{c_a}}{Sf_a} \quad \ldots(2)$$

where,

V = Absolute volume of fresh concrete, which is equal to vol. of concrete in m^3 minus the volume of entrapped air

W = mass of water (kg.) per m^3 of concrete

C = mass of cement (kg) per m^3 of concrete

S_c = specific gravity of cement

p = ratio of fine aggregate (F.A.) to total aggregate by absolute volume

f_a = total mass of F.A. (kg.) per m^3 of concrete

C_a = total mass of coarse aggregate (kg) per m^3 of concrete

Sf_a & S_{ca} = sp. gravities of fine and coarse aggregate respectively.

7. Actual quantities required for the mix. The mix. proportions calculated by the above noted method are based on the assumption that aggregates are saturated and surface dry. For any change than this conditions, *i.e.* when aggregates are moist or air dry or fully dry. Corrections in the quantity of mixing water as well as in aggregates have to be made.

8. The calculated mix proportion should be checked by trial batches. For each trial, the mix should be sufficient to prepare at least three 150 mm cubes and workability should be as per IS 1199-59. If any change is required to be done, it should be done as per table 20.38. The method is illustrated by following examples.

Example 8. (*a*) *Design stipulation (requirements)*

(*i*) *Characteristic compressive strength at 28 days in the field required = 25 MPa*

(*ii*) *Maximum size of crushed aggregate = 20 mm (angular)*

(*iii*) *Degree of workability = Medium, compacting factor 0.90 or slump 75 mm*

(*iv*) *Degree of quality control Good*

(*v*) *Type of exposure Mild*

(*vi*) *Grading zone of sand III (I.S. 385-1970)*

(*b*) *Characteristics of materials*

Cement

(*i*) *Type of cement Ordinary portland cement*

(*ii*) *Specific gravity 3.15*

(*iii*) *Bulk density of cement 1450 kg/m³*

(*iv*) *Compressive strength at 7 days Satisfies the requirements of IS 269-1989*

Aggregate	*Fine aggregate*	*Coarse aggregate*	*Remark*
Sp. gravity	2.60	2.75	C.A. Conforming to Table 2 IS-383-1970
Bulk density (kg/m³)	1700	1800	
Free moisture	1.5%	1.0%	
Fineness modulus	2.2	6.0	
Water absorption	2%	0.5%	

Sieve analysis of coarse aggregate is given below

Coarse aggregate

Sieve size in mm	*Fractions passing*		*% of different fractions*		*Conbined*	*Remark*
	I	II	I 60%	II 40%	100%	
20	100	100	60	40	10	Conform to Table 2 IS-383-1970
10	0	72.2	03	29.5	29.5	
4.75	—	8.7	—	4.7	4.7	
2.36						

(*c*) *Mix design. Target mean strength*

$f_t = f_c + K \cdot S$ The values of K and S are taken from tables 20.32 and 20.33

$= 25 + 1.6 \times 4 = 25 + 6.4 = 31.4$ Ma

(*d*) *Selection of water/cement ratio*

As the seven days strength is specified, use of Fig. 20.8 has been made.

For a targeted mean strength of 31.4 MPa, the w/c ratio is 0.48

This is lower than specified value of 0.55 for R.C.C. from durability consideration for mild exposure. Hence adopt w/c ratio as 0.48.

(*e*) *Selection of water and sand contents*

For 20 mm maximum aggregate size, sand conforming to the grading of zone II, from table 20.36, water content per cubic metre of concrete = 186 kg.

Sand content % of total aggregate = 35%

For change in w/c ratio, compacting factor, for sand belonging to zone III, following adjustments must be made as per table 20.38

S. No.	*Changes As per table 11.38*	*Percent adjustments required*	
		Water content	*Sand in total aggregate*
1.	For decrease in Water/Cement ratio by (0.60-0.48) *i.e.* 0.12	0	– 2.0
2.	For increase in compacting factor from 0.8 to 0.9 *i.e.* 0.10	+ 3.0	0
3.	For sand conforming to zone III of table 4, IS 383-1970	0	– 1.5
	Total change	+ 3.0	– 3.5%

Thus required sand as percentage of total aggregate by absolute value 35.0 – 3.5 = 31.5%

Required water content = 186 + 3% of 186 kg = 186.0 + 5.58 = 191.58 kg ≈ 191.6 kg.

(*f*) *Determination of cement content*

Water/cement ratio = (0.60 – 0.12) = 0.48

Amount of water = 191.6 kg

$$\text{Cement} = \frac{\text{Amount of water}}{\text{w/c ratio}} = \frac{191.6}{0.48}$$

$$= 399.2 \text{ kg/m}^3 \text{ app.}$$

Cement content from durability considerations from table 20.34 for mild exposure is adequate.

(*g*) *Determination of coarse and fine aggregate contents*

From table 20.35, for the specified maximum size of aggregate of 20 mm, the amount of entrapped air is 2%. Taking this into account and using equation no. 1 and 2 of page 440 we get.

Absolute volume of concrete = 1 – 0.02 = 0.98%

$$\therefore \quad 0.98 = \left[191.6 + \frac{3.992}{3.15} + \frac{1}{0.315} \times \frac{f_a}{2.6}\right] \times \frac{1}{1000}$$

$$= \left[191.6 + 126.73 + \frac{f_a}{0.819}\right] \times \frac{1}{1000}$$

$$\text{or} \quad 980 = \left[318.33 + \frac{f_a}{0.819}\right]$$

$$\text{or} \quad \frac{f_a}{0.819} = 980 - 318.33$$

$$= 661.67$$

$$\text{or} \quad f_a = 661.67 \times 0.819$$

$$= 542.57 \text{ kg. say } 543.0 \text{ kg.}$$

Coarse aggregate $C_a = \frac{1-0.315}{0.315} \times 543 \times \frac{2.6}{2.75}$

$= 1118$ kg.

Mix. Proportion is

Water	*Cement*	*Fine aggregate*	*Coarse aggregate*
191.6	399.0	543.0	1118
0.48	1	1.36	2.8

For 50 kg of cement, the quantities worked are as follows:

Cement = 50 kg

Fine aggregate = 68 kg

Coarse aggregate = 140 kg fraction I 60% = 84 kg

fraction II 40% = 56 kg

(*ii*) *Water*

1. For w/c ratio 0.48, water = 24 kg
2. Extra water for absorption by coarse aggregate 0.5% of mass = 0.70 litres.

(*iii*) *Quantity of water* to be deducted for moisture present in sand at 2% by mass = 1.38 litres

∴ Actual quantity of water to be added = 24 + 0.7 – 1.38 = 23.3 litres

Actual quantity of sand after adding water content = 68 + 1.38 = 69.38 kg.

Thus after allowing for free mass of moisture, sand quantity = 69.4 kg.

(*iv*) *Actual quantity of coarse aggregate*

Fraction (*i*) 84 – 0.42 = 83.68 kg

Fraction (*ii*) 56 – 0.28 = 55.72 kg.

Thus actual quantities of materials to be used are

Water = 23.3 litres

Cement = 50.0 kg

Sand = 69.9 kg

Coarse aggregate fraction I = 83.58 kg

Coarse aggregate fraction II = 55.72 kg. **Ans.**

20.13 AMRICAN CONCRETE INSTITUTE METHOD OF MIX DESIGN

Though ACI committee published its method of mix design in 1944 and almost all Indian multipurpose concrete dams have been designed using then prevalent ACI committee method of mix design. Since then many improvements have been incorporated in the original method. Here the latest method of concrete mix design based on ACI 211-1 of 1991 manual of concrete practice part-I recommendations is discussed. The ACI committee has assumed the following basic assumptions.

1. Fresh concrete of a given slump and containing a reasonably well graded aggregate of given maximum size will have practically a constant water content, regardless of variation in w/c ratio and cement content which are inter related over a considerable range of practical proportions.
2. The optimum dry rodded volume of coarse aggregate per unit volume of concrete depends on its maximum size and the fineness modulus of the fine aggregate as shown in table 20.39 regard less of shape of particles. The effect of angularity is reflected in the void contents. Thus angular coarse aggregates require more mortar than rounded aggregates.
3. Irrespective of methods of compaction, even after complete compaction is done, a definite

percentage of air remains in the concrete and is inversely proportional to the maximum size of the aggregate.

Procedure of mix design

For the design of the mix, following data is required

Data to be collected:

(*a*) Fineness modulus of selected fine aggregate.

(*b*) Unit weigh of dry selected fine aggregate.

(*c*) Specific gravity of coarse and fine aggregate in saturated, surface dry conditions.

(*d*) Absorption of coarse and fine aggregates.

(*e*) Specific gravity of cement.

Table 20.39. Dry Bulk valume of C.A. per unit of concrete as given by ACI (211-1-91)

Maximum size of aggregate (mm) ↓	*Bulk volume of dry rodded C.A. per unit vol. of concrete for fineness modulus of sand*			
F.M. →	2.4	2.6	2.8	3.0
10	0.5	0.48	0.46	0.44
12.5	0.59	0.57	0.55	0.53
20.0	0.66	0.64	0.62	0.60
25.0	0.71	0.69	0.67	0.65
40.0	0.75	0.73	0.71	0.69
50.0	0.78	0.76	0.74	0.72
70.0	0.82	0.80	0.78	0.76
150.0	0.87	0.85	0.83	0.81

Note. (*a*) The values given in the above table 20.39 are suitable for R.C.C. construction. For less workable concrete the values may be increased by 1.0%. For more workable concrete such as pumpable concrete the values may be reduced upto 1.0%.

(*b*) From specified minimum strength, estimate the average design strength either using standard deviation or using coefficient of variation.

(*c*) Find the w/c ratio for the given strength from the table 20.40 given below. Check the w/c from durability point of view from table 20.41. Adopt the lower of the two values.

Table 20.40. Relation between w/c ratio and average compressive strength of concrete according to ACI 211-1-91

Average compressive strength at 28 days MPa	*Effective w/c ratio by (mass)*	
	No. air	*Air entrained concrete*
45	0.38	—
40	0.43	—
35	0.48	0.40
30	0.55	0.46
25	0.62	0.53
20	0.70	0.63
15	0.80	0.71

Note. The values are measured on standard cylinders. The values given are for a max. size of aggregate of 20 and 25 mm and ordinary portland cement and for recommended percent of air entrained shown in Table 20.43.

Table 20.41. Requirements of ACI 318-89 for w/c ratio and strength for special exposure

S. No.	*Exposure condition*	*Max. w/c ratio for normal density aggregate concrete*	*Min. Design strength for low density aggregate concrete MPa*
1.	Concrete intended to be water tight (a) Exposed to fresh water (b) Exposed to sea or brackish water	 0.5 0.45	 25 30
2.	Concrete exposed to freezing and thawing in a moist condition (a) Thin sections, or guard rails, gutters and kerbs (b) Other elements (c) In the presence of deiceing chemicals	 0.45 0.50 0.45	 30 25 30
3.	For corrosion protection of R.C.C. exposed to deiceing salts, brackish water, sea water or spray from these sources.	0.40	33

(*d*) Decide max. size of aggregate to be used. Generally for R.C.C. works 20 mm and for prestressed concrete work 10 mm size aggregate is used.

(*e*) Decide workability in terms of slump for the job in hand from the following table 20.42.

Table 20.42. Recommended slump for various types of works as per ACI 211-1-91

S. No.	*Type of construction*	*Range of slump in mm*
1.	Reinforced foundation, walls and footings	20 — 80
2.	Plain footings, caissons and sub structure walls	20 — 80
3.	Beams and Reinforced walls	20 — 100
4.	Building columns	20 — 100
5.	Pavements and slabs	20 — 80
6.	Mass concrete	20 — 80

Note. For hand compaction the upper limit may be increasedly by 20 mm.

Table 20.43. Approximate requirement of mixing water and air content for different workabilities and nominal max. size of aggregate as per ACI 211-1-91

Workability	*Water content kg/m³ of concrete for indicated max. aggregate size*							
	10 mm	12.5 mm	20 mm	25 mm	40 mm	50 mm	70 mm	150 mm
Non air entrained concrete								
(*a*) Slump in mm 30-50	205	200	185	180	160	155	145	125
80-100	225	215	200	195	175	170	160	140
150-180	240	230	210	205	185	185	170	—
(*b*) Approximate entrained air content percent	3	2.5	2	1.5	1	0.5	0.3	0.2
Air entrained concrete								
Slump 30 — 50	180	175	165	160	145	140	135	120
80 — 100	200	190	180	175	160	155	150	135
150 — 180	215	205	190	185	170	165	160	—
Recommended average total air content percent								
(*a*) Mild exposure	4.5	4.0	3.5	3.0	2.5	2.0	1.5	1.0
(*b*) Moderate exposure	6.0	5.5	5.0	4.5	4.5	4.0	3.5	3.0
(*c*) Extreme exposure	7.5	7.0	6.0	6.0	5.5	5.0	4.5	4.0

Table 20.44. First estimate of density (unit weight) of fresh concrete as per ACI 211-1-91)

Max. size of aggregate size in mm	*First estimate of density of fresh concrete*	
	Non air entrained kg/m^3	*Air entrained kg/m^3*
10	2285	2190
12.5	2315	2235
20.0	2355	2280
25.0	2375	2315
40	2420	2355
50	2445	2375
70	2465	2400
150	2505	2435

(*f*) The total water required in concrete in kg/m^3 is read from above table 20.43 for the max. size of aggregate and the given slump. Table 20.43 gives the approximate amount of accidentally entrapped air.

(*g*) The cement content required is calculated by dividing the amount of water required by the w/c ratio.

(*h*) The bulk value of dry rodded coarse aggregate per unit volume of concrete is selected from table 20.39 for the particular max. size of coarse aggregate and fineness modulus of the fine aggregate.

(*i*) The weight of coarse aggregate per cubic metre of concrete is calculated by multiplying the bulk volume with bulk density.

(*j*) The solid volume of coarse aggregate in one cubic metre of concrete is calculated by knowing the specific gravity of coarse aggregate.

(*k*) Similarly the solid volume of cement, water and volume of air is calculated per cubic metre of concrete.

(*l*) The solid volume of sand is computed by subtracting the solid volume of cement, coarse aggregate, water and entrapped air from the total volume of concrete.

(*m*) The weight of fine aggregate is calculated by multiplying the solid volume of fine aggregate by specific gravity of fine aggregate.

Table 20.45 Required increase in strength (mean strength) for specified design strength when no tests records are available as per ACI 318-1989.

Table 20.45

S. No.	*Specified design strength MPa*	*Required increase in strength MPa*
1.	Less than 21	7
2.	21 to 35	8.5
3.	35 or more	10.0

The procedure of mix design by ACI 211-1-91 method is illustrated by the following example.

Example 9. *Design a concrete mix for the construction of an elevated water tank from the following data:*

(*a*) *The specified design strength of concrete is 35 MPa at 28 days of standard cylinders.*

(*b*) *The specific gravity of fine aggregate* = *2.65*

(*c*) *The specific gravity of coarse aggregate* = *2.75*

(*d*) *Max. size of C.A.* = *20 mm*

(*e*) *The dry rodded bulk density of C.A.* = *1600 kg/m^3*

(*f*) *Fine modulus of fine aggregate* = 2.8
(*g*) *Slump of concrete necessary* = 50 *mm*
(*h*) *Ordinary portland cement is used. Coarse aggregate is found to absorb upto 1% and free surface moisture in sand is found as 2%. Assume any data required.*

(*a*) **Design.** Assuming the risk factor K as 1.65 and standard deviation $S = 5$ on the basis that 5% of the results are allowed to fall below specified design strength.

∴ The mean strength in the field $f_m = f_{ck} + K.S.$

$$= 35 + 1.65 \times 5$$

$$= 35 + 8.25 = 43.25 \text{ MPa}$$

(*b*) **W/c ratio.** As ordinary portland cement is used, then from table 20.40, the w/c ratio comes as 0.41.

The w/c ratio obtained from strength point of view, is tobe checked against maximum w/c ratio given for specified exposure conditions as shown in table 20.41. The minimum value of these two w/c ratios is to be adopted.

From table 20.41, for water tight concrete, the water-cement ratio should be 0.50. Hence adopt w/c ratio as 0.41 obtained from strength Considerations. For a given slump of 50 mm and 20 mm maximum size of aggregate for non air entrained concrete from table 20.43,

water content = 185 kg/m^3. Also the approximate entrapped air is 2%.

(*c*) Quantity of cement $= \dfrac{\text{Amount of water}}{\text{w/c ratio}}$

$$= \frac{85}{0.41} = 453 \text{ kg/m}^3$$

(*d*) For maximum size of 20 mm of C.A. and fineness modulus of fine aggregate as 2.8, the dry bulk rodded bulk volume of C.A. is 0.62 per unit value of concrete from table 20.25.

(*e*) The weight of coarse aggregate = $0.62 \times 1600 = 992$ kg/m^3

(*f*) From table 20.44, the first estimated density of fresh concrete for 20 mm max. size of aggregate and for non air entrained air concrete = 2355 kg/m^3.

(*g*) The weight of all known ingredients of concrete are:

(*i*) Weight of water = 185 kg/m^3
(*ii*) Weight of cement = 453 kg/m^3
(*iii*) Weight of coarse aggregate = 992 kg/m^3
(*iv*) Weight of fine aggregate = 2355 – [185 + 453 + 992] = 725 kg/m^3.

The weight of fine aggregate may also be found from absolute volume method which is more accurate as follows:

Item No.	*Ingredient*	*Weight kg/m^3*	*Absolute value cm^3*
1.	Cement	453	$\frac{453}{3.15} \times 10^3 = 143.8 \times 10^3$
2.	Water	185	$\frac{185}{1} \times 10^3 = 185 \times 10^3$
3.	Coarse aggregate	992	$\frac{992.0}{2.75} \times 10^3 = 361 \times 10^3$
4.	Air	—	$\frac{2}{100} \times 10^6 = 20 \times 10^3$
		Total	$709.8 = 710.0 \times 10^3$ cm^3

Thus total absolute volume $= 710 \times 10^3$ cm^3

∴ Absolute volume of fine aggregate $= (1000 - 710) \times 10^3 = 290 \times 10^3$ cm^3 or 290 m^3

∴ Weight of fine aggregate = 290 × 1.65 = 768.5 kg/m^3

Hence adopt the higher value of the two *i.e.* 768.5 kg/m^3

(*i*) Estimated quantities of materials per cubic metre of concrete are

(*a*) Cement = 453 kg

(*b*) Fine aggregate = 768.5 kg

(*c*) Coarse aggregate = 992.0 kg

(*d*) Water = 185 kg

Thus the density of fresh concrete is 2398.5 say 2399 as against 2355 from table 20.44

(*j*) Proportions

C	F.A.	C.A.	Water
453	768.5	992	185
1	1.697	2.19	0.41

say 1:1.7:2.2 with w/c 0.41.

Weight of materials for one bag of cement mix in kg = 50:1.35:1.1:20.5

The above quanties are on the basis that F.A. and C.A. both are in saturated and surface dry state *i.e.* SSD condition.

(*k*) These proportions are to be adjusted to field conditions. F.A. has a surface moisture of 2%.

∴ total free surface moisture in F.A. = $\frac{2}{100} \times 768.5 = 15.37 = 15.37$ kg/m^3

∴ weight of F.A. in the field = 768.5 + 15.37 = 783.87 = 784.0 kg/m^3

Coarse aggregate absorbs 1% moisture = $\frac{992 \times 1}{100} = 9.92$ kg/m^3

weight of C.A. in the field = 992 — 9.92 = 982.08

say 982.0 kg/m^3

Taking into account the surface moisture of fine aggregate and absorption of coarse aggregate, quantity of water to be added in the concrete.

$$= 185 - 15.4 + 9.9 = 179.5 \text{ kg.}$$

say 180 kg.

(*l*) Quanties of materials to be used in the field

(*a*) Cement = 453 kg/m^3

(*b*) F.A. = 784 kg/m^3

(*c*) C.A. = 982.0 kg/m^3

(*d*) Water = 180 kg/m^3

Thus the field density of fresh concrete = 2399.0 kg/m^3.

(*m*) From the above proportion a trial mix may be prepared to study the properties of concrete such as workability, cohesiveness, finishing, 28 days strength and yield etc.

If the mix needs improvement, then suitable adjustments may be made or second trial of mix may be tried. If no improvement is observed, increase the quantity of water and cement. This will increase the yield. To keep the yield constant, reduce the quantities of C.A. & F.A. both correspondingly.

20.14. THE DEPARTMENT OF ENVIRONMENT'S DESIGN METHOD (DOE METHOD)

The DOE method of mix design is an improvement over Road Note No. 4 method. This (Road Note 4) method of concrete mix design or proportioning mainly is based on the extensive field and laboratory experiments carried out by Road Research laboratory U.K. The Road Note 4 method was published for the first time in 1950. This method of mix design was most popular and widely used upto 1970 all over the world. Most of the Indian Concrete roads and air fields were designed by this method, but it is obsolete now. Design by this method has been discussed on page 434.

The DOE method was first published in 1975 and revised in 1988. The DOE method of mix design is applicable to all types of concrete mixes including roads, while Road Note No. 4 was applicable to roads and air fields only. This method can also be used for concrete containing fly ash. DOE method is an standard method of mix design in U.K. now. This method used the relationship between water/cement ratio and compressive strength depending on the type of cement and aggregate used. The water contents required to give various levels of workability, as very low, low, medium and high expressed in term of slumps or Vee Bee time or compacting factor, are determined for the two types of aggregates as crushed aggregate and gravel. This method is suitable for mix design of normal concrete mixes having 28 days cube compressive strength upto 75 MPa for non air entrained concrete. The step by step procedure of mix design is given below.

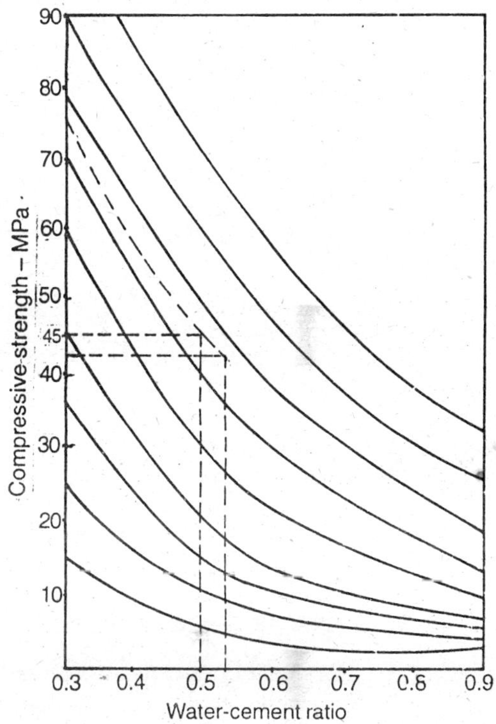

Fig. 20.10. Relation between compressive strength and free w/c ratio used in British mix design method

Procedure

Step 1. *Determine the target mean strength from the specified characteristic strength.*
Target mean strength = specified characteristic strength + standard deviation × Risk factor.
(Risk factor is taken on the assumption that 5% of results are allowed to fall below the specified characteristic strength).

Step 2. *Calculate the water/cement ratio* from Fig. 20.10. From table 20.46 the approximate compressive strength of concrete made with free water/cement ratio 0.5 is obtained.
From table 20.46, find out the 28 days strength for the type of cement and type of C.A. Now mark a point on the y-axis of the Fig. 20.10 equal to the compressive strength read from table 20.46, which is at w/c ratio 0.5. From this point draw a parallel dotted curve nearest to the point of intersection using this curve, read off the w/c ratio as against target mean strength. The method will be more clear from the example below.

Table 20.46. App. Compressive strength of concrete made with w/c 0.5 as per 1988 British Method.

S. No.	*Type of cement*	*Type of coarse aggregate C.A.*	*Compressive cube strength at the age in MPa*			
			3 days	7 days	28 days	91 days
1.	Ordinary portland cement (type I)	Un crushed	18 — 22	27 — 30	40 — 42	48 — 49
2.	Sulphate resisting cement (type V)	Crushed	23 — 27	33 — 36	47 — 49	55 — 56
3.	Rapid hardening portland cement (type III)	Un crushed	25 — 29	34 — 37	46 — 48	53 — 54
		crushed	30 — 34	40 — 43	53 — 55	60 — 61

Note. Higher value may be adopted

Step 3. *Determine the water content for the required workability,* taking into account the size of aggregate and its type from table 20.47 and 20.48

Table 20.47. App. Free water content required for various workability according to 1988 British Method

Aggregate		*Water content kg/m³ for slump*			
Max. size mm	*Type*	0 — 10 mm	10 — 30 mm	30 — 60 mm	60 — 180 mm
		Vee Bee secons > 12	6 — 12	3 — 6	0 — 3
10	Un crushed	150	180	205	225
	crushed	180	205	230	250
20	Un crushed	135	160	180	195
	crushed	170	190	210	225
30	Un crushed	115	140	160	175
	crushed	155	175	190	205

Table 20.48. Reduction in water content of table 21.47 when fly ash used.

% of fly ash in cementitious material	*Slump in mm Vee Bee seconds*	*Reduction in water content kg/m³*			
		0 — 10 > 12	10 — 30 6 — 12	30 — 60 3 — 6	60 — 180 0 — 3
10		5	5	5	10
20		10	10	10	15
30		15	15	20	20
40		20	20	25	25
50		25	25	30	30

Step 4. *Determination of cement content.* The amount of cement can be determined from the total water content and w/c ratio.

$$i.e.\ \text{Cement content} = \frac{\text{weight of water}}{\text{w/c ratio}}$$

The quantity of cement obtained by the above relation should be compared with the minimum cement content specified from durability considerations as given in Table 17.3 and 17.4. The higher of the two quantities should be adopted. If maximum cement content is specified, then the calculated cement content should be less than the specified maximum cement content.

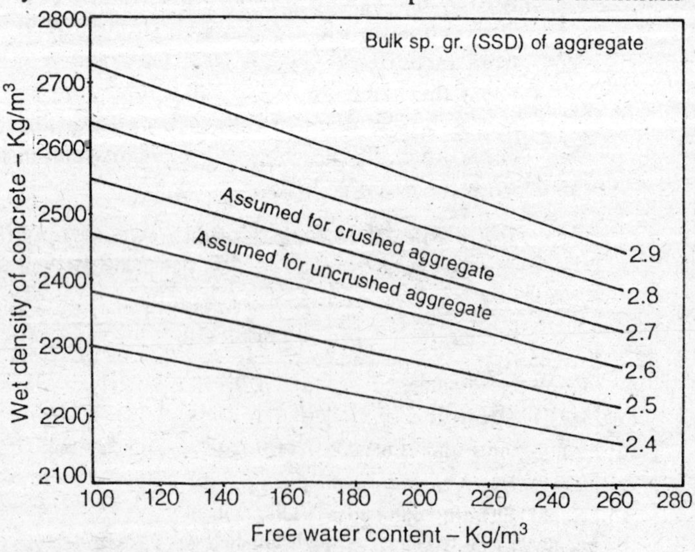

Fig. 20.11. Estimated wet density for fully compacted concrete

Step 5. *Determination of total aggregate content.* For determining the total aggregate content, the estimation of wet density of fully compacted concrete is required. This can be obtained from Fig. 20.11 for approximate water content and known specific gravity of aggregate. If the specific gravity of aggregate is not known its value for un crushed aggregate may be taken as 2.6 and 2.7 for crushed aggregate may be assumed as shown on curves A and B of the Fig. 20.11. The aggregate content is determined by subtracting the weights of cement and water content from the weight of fresh concrete read from the Fig. 20.11.

Step 6. *Determination of fine aggregate.* The proportion of fine aggregate in the total aggregate is determined from Fig. 20.12. Fig. 20.12 (*a*) is for 10 mm size, 20.12 (*b*) for 20 mm size, Fig. 20.12 (*c*) is for 40 mm size coarse aggregate. The parameters involved in Fig. 20.12 are max. size of aggregate, the water content, degree of workability and the percentage of fine aggregate passing through 600 micron sieve. Knowing the proportion of fine aggregate from Fig. 20.12, the weight of fine aggregate may be obtained by multiplying the total weight of aggregate by this proportion. Knowing the fine aggregate, the weight of coarse aggregate can be found. The coarse aggregate can further be divided into different fractions depending upon the shape of aggregate. Generally figures given in Table 20.49 may be adopted.

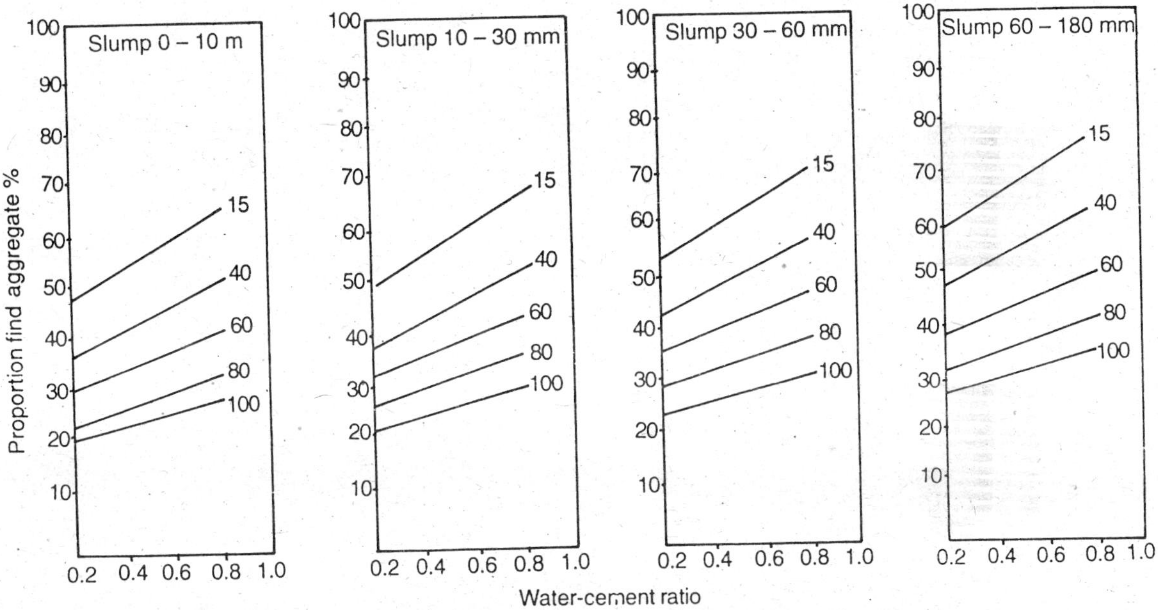

(*a*)

Fig 20.12. Recomended % of fine aggregate in total aggregate as a function of free w/c ratio for various workabilities and max. size of aggregate

Table 20.49. Proportions of coarse aggregate fractions as per 1988 British method

Total C.A.	5 — 10 mm	10 — 20 mm	20 — 40 mm
100	33	67	—
100	18	27	55

Note. 1. From the proportions so obtained trial mix may be prepared and samples should be prepared and tested to confirm its suitability for the proposed concrete structure.

2. If fly ash is used along with cement, then water content may be reduced as shown in Table 20.48.

Example 10. *Design a concrete mix for a targeted 28 days cube strength of 45 MPa from the following data:*

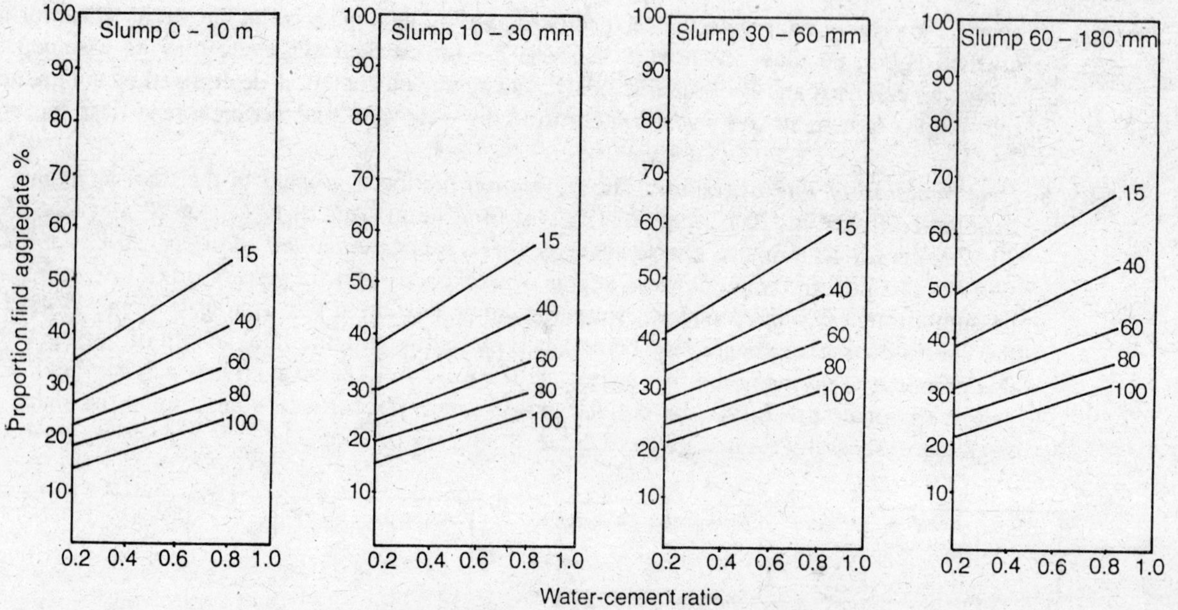

Fig 20.12. (*b*)

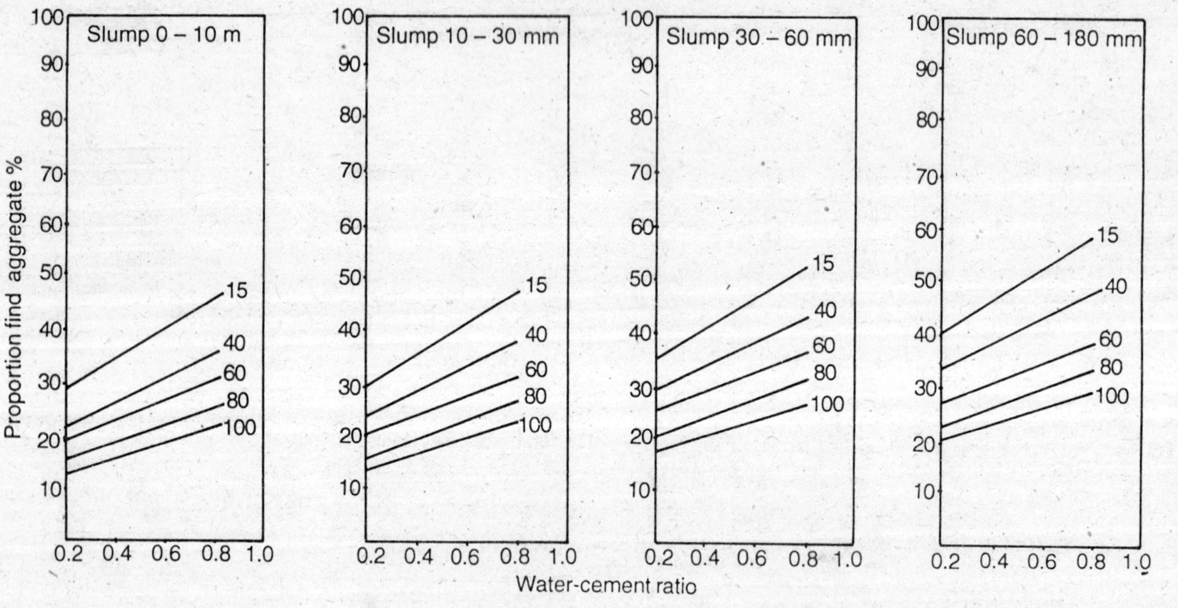

Fig 20.12. (*c*)

1. Max. size of uncrushed aggregate to be used = 20 mm
2. Low workability, slump = 10-30 mm
3. Specific gravity of aggregate = 2.65
4. The aggregate percentage passing 600 micron = 50%
5. Exposure to concrete is moderate
6. The cover to the reinforcement to be provided is 25 mm.

Design

Step 1. Determine the target strength from the relation.

Target strength = specified characteristic strength + standard deviation × Risk factor

In this case the target strength is directly given as 45 MPa at 28 days.

Step 2. Find out the water/cement ratio for targeted strength 45 MPa.

(*a*) For finding out the w/c ratio, refer to table 20.46. From this table for ordinary portland cement and uncrushed 20 mm aggregate the 28 days strength is 42 MPa.

(*b*) From Fig. 20.12 find the point of inter section of 42 MPa at 0.5 water/cement ratio. Through this point draw a doted line curve parallel to the neighboring curve. Now draw a strength line from the desired strength on *y*-axis, where this line cuts the curve, draw a perpendicular on *x*-axis which will give w/c ratio for the targeted strength *i.e.* 45 MPa.

From this curve for 45 MPa strength, the water/cement ratio comes out 0.54.

For uncrushed aggregate of 20 mm max. size aggregate approximate water content from table 20.47, is 160 kg/m^3.

For moderate exposure and 25 mm cover maximum w/c ratio from durability consideration is permitted as 0.5. Actually the lower value of the two should be adopted. Hence adopt w/c ratio as 0.5 water content for 10 to 30 mm slump from table 20.47 is 160 kg/m^3.

Cement content

From w/c ratio 0.5 and water content 160 kg,

$$\text{Cement content} = \frac{160}{0.5} = 320.4 \text{ kg.}$$

From Durability consideration, the quantity of cement should be used as 350 kg/m^3. Thus adopt greater cement content as 350 kg/m^3.

Determination of density of fresh concrete

From Fig. 20.11, for water content of 160 kg/m^3, 20 mm uncrushed, the wet density of concrete = 2490 kg/m^3

Determination of total weight of aggregate.

Total weight of aggregate = Total weight of concrete-weight of water-weight of cement.

$$= 2490 - 160 - 350$$

$$= 2490 - 510 = 2180 \text{ kg/m}^3$$

Fine aggregate from Fig. 20.12 (*b*) for slump 10-30 and aggregate passing through 600 micron as 50% for w/c ratio 0.5

F.A. = 27%

$$\therefore \text{ weight of fine aggregate} = \frac{2180 \times 27}{100} = 588.6 = 589 \text{ kg/m}^3$$

$$\text{weight of coarse aggregate} = 2180 - 5886 = 1591.4 \text{ kg/m}^3$$

Estimated quantities in kg/m^3 are

(*a*) Cement = 350 kg/m^3

(*b*) F.A. = 588.6 kg/m^3

(*c*) C.A. = 1591.4 kg/m^3

(*d*) Water = 160 kg/m^3

(*e*) Wet density = 2490 kg/m^3

From these quantities the trial mix is prepared, samples cast and tested at 28 days to judge the suitability of concrete for the desired work. If need arises, adjustment in quantities be made.

20.15. CONCRETE MIX DESIGN BY DOE METHOD USING FLY ASH

The use of fly ash as a part substitute of cement is fast gaining popularity through out the world. Thus one should be acquainted with the procedure of concrete mix design containing fly ash. The method of design of mix is illustrated by the following example.

Example 11. *Design a concrete mix using fly ash from the following data*

(*a*) *Characteristic 28 days mean strength* = *25 MPa*
(*b*) *Risk factor may be taken* = *1.65*
(*c*) *Standard deviation* = *5.0*
(*d*) *The max. size of coarse aggregate C.A.* = *20 mm*
(*e*) *40% F.A. passes through 600 micron sieve.*
(*f*) *Slump range* = *30-60 mm*
(*g*) *Cover to reinforcement* = *25 mm*
(*h*) *Specific gravity of F.A. and C.A.* = *2.6 and 2.7 respectively*
(*i*) *Percentage of fly ash to be used* = *30%*

Design Procedure

By DOE method of mix design using fly ash., Cement content is given by the relation

$$C = \frac{(100 - P)\,W}{(100 - 0.7\,P)\left(\dfrac{w}{C+0.3\,F}\right)}$$

where, F is the quantity of fly ash and it is given as

$$F = \frac{PC}{100 - P}$$

where, P is the percentage of fly ash in the total cementitious material

i.e. $$P = \frac{100\,F}{C + F}$$

W = Free water content

$\therefore \quad \dfrac{W}{C + 0.3\,F}$ is the free water Cementitious ratio for the design strength Fig. 20.12

Specified targeted strength $= 25 + 5 \times 1.65 = 25 + 8.25 \approx 33.25$ MPa

Taking 33 MPa as the target strength we proceed as follows:

From table 20.46 , for 0.50 w/c ratio (Here $\dfrac{W}{C+0.3\,F}$) , the 28 days compressive strength of concrete with ordinary cement is 42 MPa. For target mean strength of 33MPa, from Fig. 20.10, the value of free water $\dfrac{W}{C+0.3F}$ is 0.65.

Note. This value is not to be compared with maximum value from durability consideration of table 17.3 It is to be used for strength purpose only. From table 20.47, for crushed 20 mm max. size aggregate and 60 mm slump, the quantity of water is 210 kg/m^3.

In the present case, the fly ash used is 30%. Hence reduce water content as partable 20.48. From this table reduction for 30% fly ash is 20 kg/m^3.

Hence water content to be used = $210 - 20 = 190$ kg/m^3

Then cement content $$C = \frac{(100 - p)\,w}{(100 - 0.7\,p) \times \dfrac{w}{C + 0.65\,F}}$$

$$= \frac{(100 - 30)\,190}{(100 - 0.7 \times 30) \times w/c \text{ ratio}}$$

$$= \frac{70 \times 190}{(100 - 21) \times 0.65} = \frac{13300}{79 \times 0.65} = \frac{13300}{51.35}$$

$$= 259 \text{ kg/m}^3$$

Amount of fly ash $F = \frac{P \times C}{100 - P} = \frac{30 \times 259}{100 - 30} = \frac{30 \times 259}{70} = \frac{777}{7} = 111 \text{ kg/m}^3$

Hence total cementitious material content = $259 + 111.0 = 370 \text{ kg/m}^3$

$\therefore$ Free water/cement ratio $= \frac{190}{370} = 0.51$

From table 17.3 Cement content satisfy the durability requirements, but water/cementitious material ratio does not satisfy this durability condition. Hence adopt w/cementitious material ratio as 0.50 instead of 0.51.

Then water content $= 370 \times 0.5 = 185 \text{ kg/m}^3$

For water content of 185 kg/m^3, and average specific gravity of 2.65, the density of fresh concrete from Fig. 20.11 = 2420 kg/m^3

$\therefore$ Total weight of aggregate $= 2420 - (259 + 111 + 185)$

$$= 2420 - 555 = 1865 \text{ kg/m}^3$$

From Fig. 20.12 (*b*) for free water/cementitious material as 0.5 and for 40% F.A. passing through 600 micron sieve and for slump 30-60 mm is 38%.

$\therefore$ weight of F.A. $= \frac{38}{100} \times 1865 = 708.7$ kg. say 709 kg.

weight of C.A. $= 1865 - 709 = 1156$ kg.

Hence estimated quantities of materials on the basis of saturated surface dry condition are as follows:

Cement	= 259.00 kg
Fly ash	= 111.0 kg
Fine aggregate	= 709 kg
Coarse aggregate	= 1156 kg
Water	= 185 kg
Totals	= 2420 kg/m^3

The weight of aggregates may be adjusted according to free moisture content and absorption characteristics of the aggregates.

The trial mix may be prepared to determine its characteristic strength which should satisfy the desired requirements.

20.16. MIX DESIGN FOR PUMPABLE CONCRETE

Now a days in many situations, concrete is placed through pipes. Thus the Engineer incharage must be acquainted with the pumpable concrete. Pumpable concrete is not a special concrete, but a ordinary concrete which can be pushed through a pipe line is called a *pumpable concrete.* This concrete should be proportioned in such a way that its friction on the inner walls of thc pipe line does not increase to such a limit to prevent its movement at the pressure applied by the pump. This concrete should contain certain amount of fines (cement + fine aggregate) more than the ordinary concrete to offer lubrication on the inner walls of pipe line. The typical grading curves of pumpable concrete are shown in Fig. 20.13.

20.16.1. Requirements of mix design for pumpable concrete

The pumpable concrete should have;

(*a*) It should have minimum fine particles smaller than 0.25 mm in size (cement + fine aggregate), approximately 400 kg/m^3 of concrete for the max. size of 32 mm of coarse aggregate. In case of very angular and flaky aggregate, the quantity of fine aggregate may be increased by 10%.

(*b*) *Amount of cement.* This concrete must contain a minimum cement content of 240 kg/m^3 of concrete for max. size of 32 mm of coarse aggregate. In case the max. size of coarse aggregate is 16 mm, then quantity of cement should be increased by 10%.

(*c*) *Water/cement ratio.* The water/cement ratio of pumpable concrete may vary from 0.42 to 0.65.

(*d*) *Workability.* The slump may be between 75 mm to 150 mm.

(*e*) The grading curve of aggregate should be as shown in Fig. 20.13.

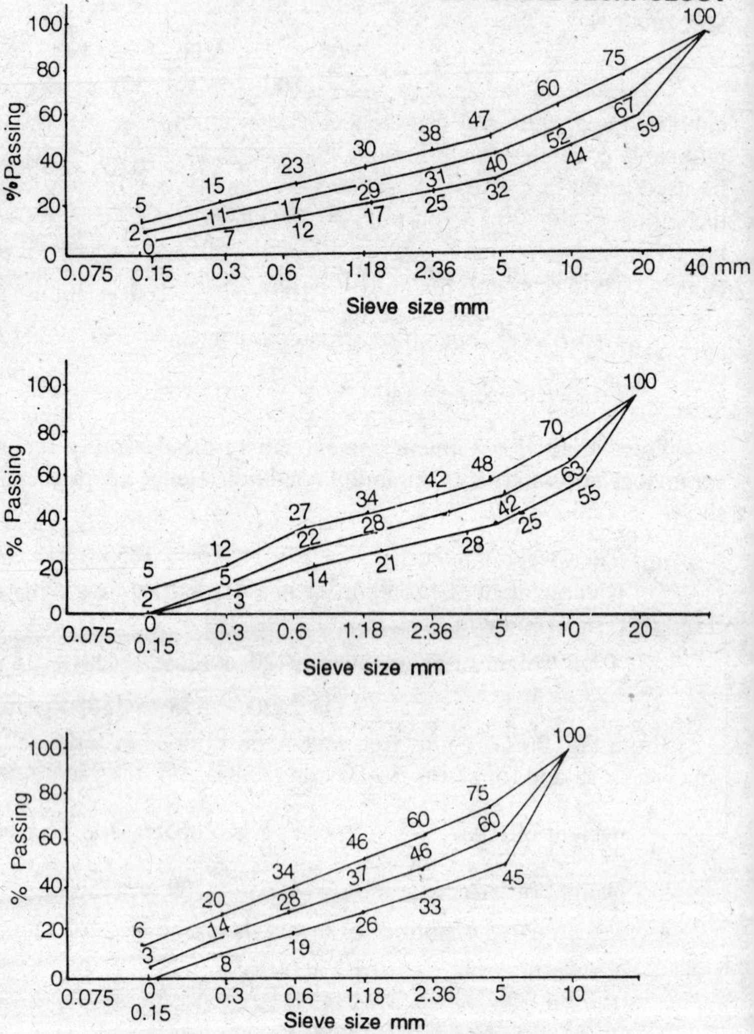

Fig. 20.13. Typical grading curves for pumpable mixes

For designing a pumpable concrete, it is essential to understand the action on the concrete when it is pumped through the pipe line.

The first requirement of the concrete is that under the pressure from the pump, the mix must neither bleed nor segregate. It must be able to bind all constituents of the mix together. The mix should be able to deform while flowing through the pipe line at tapered sections and bends. This property can be achieved by adding more fine particles. Thus the proportion of fines is of prime importance. For pumpable concrete the contents of fines (cement + fine aggregate) 350 kg/m^3 to 400 kg/m^3 are considered necessary. This amount of fines is also necessary for maintaining lubricating film around the concrete plug to reduce wear and tear of the whole system.

20.16.2. Blockage of pump system

Assuming the pump mechanically sound, there are following two reasons for the development of blockage in the pump.

1. Water is forced out of the mix. resulting bleeding and blockage by jamming.
2. The frictional resistance is too much due to the nature of ingredients of the mix.

The relationship between cement content, aggregate void contents and excessive friction on bleeding and segregation is illustrated by the following diagram 20.14.

To produce good quality pumpable concrete, a good grading of aggregate is necessary. Flaky and elongated aggregate will produce harsh concrete for the given cement content and water/cement ratio. For pumpable concrete typical grading curves are shown in Fig. 20.13. The grading curve of the aggregates to be used in the proposed mix should be parallel to the curves of Fig. 20.13, but not coarser than curve no. 2. The curve may be brought parallel by making adjustments in the proportions of F.A. and C.A.

It has been recommended that 10-20% of fine aggregate should pass through 300 micron sieve. Some times to safeguard against the under sanding 3-4% extra sand is added. The total content of fine aggregate in kg per cubic metre of concrete for various maximum size of coarse aggregate is shown in Table 20.50.

Table 20.50. Quantities of fines and size of coarse aggregate

Max. size of C.A. in mm	*Fines per cubic metre of concrete in kg*
8	525
16	450
32	400
64	325

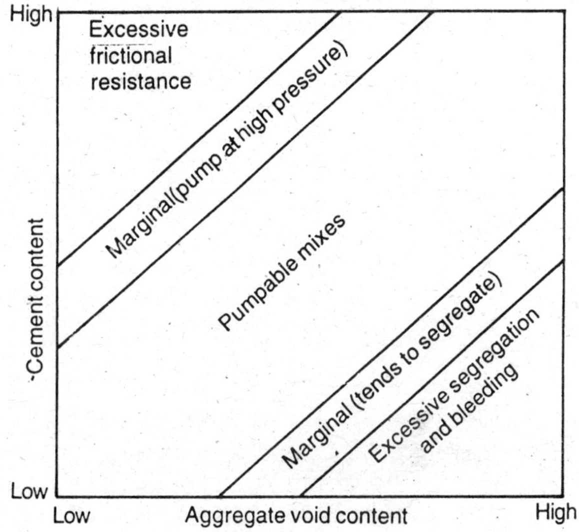

Fig. 20.14. Relation between cement content, aggregate void content and excessive friction on bleeding and segregation

Table 20.51. Limits of fines content (calculated on the basis of absolute density of cement equal to 3100 kg/m^3)

Free water content in l/m^3	*Fines solids kg/m^3*	
	Minimum	*Maximum*
150	260	365
160	280	390
170	295	415
180	315	440
190	330	465
200	350	490
210	365	515
220	385	540
230	400	565
240	420	590

Table 20.52. Mix proportion on saturated surface dry basis for 75-100 mm slump

Material	*Quantity in kg*
Fine aggregate	880
Coarse aggregate	930
Ordinary portland cement	310
Water	190
Total	2310

Table 20.53. Absolute density of materials

Material	*Density kg/m³*
Coarse aggregate (C.A.)	2550
Fine aggregate (F.A.)	2650
Ordinary portland cement	3100

Table 20.54. Aggregate gradings (For mix proportion of table 20.52)

Sieve size in mm	*Percentage passing*	
	Coarse aggregate	*Fine aggregate*
20	100	
14	60	
10	37	100
5	6	94
2.4	1	84
1.2		70
0.6		53
0.3		18
0.15		5

Table 20.55. Calculations of all in aggregate grading based on F.A. content of 880 kg and C.A. content of 930 kg and as per grading of Table 20.54.

Sieve size in mm	*Percentage passing*		
	C.A.	*F.A.*	*Combined grading*
20	51.5	48.5	100
14	31.0	48.5	79.5
10	19.0	48.5	67.5
5	3.0	45.5	48.5
2.4	0.5	41.0	41.5
1.2		34.0	34.0
0.6		25.5	25.5
0.3		9.0	9.0
0.15		2.5	2.5

Step by step design calculations for a pumpable concrete mix.

Step 1. Draw the grading curve of aggregate Fig. 20.15 shows a more acceptable grading curve for pumpable concrete using 20 mm max. size aggregate. The grading curve drawn should fall with in the curve of Fig. 20.15. If necessary redjustments in the proportions of coarse and fine aggregate may be made.

Step 2. The limits of fines contents should conform as given in Table 20.51.

Step 3. The mix proportions should be adopted on saturated surface dry condition as shown

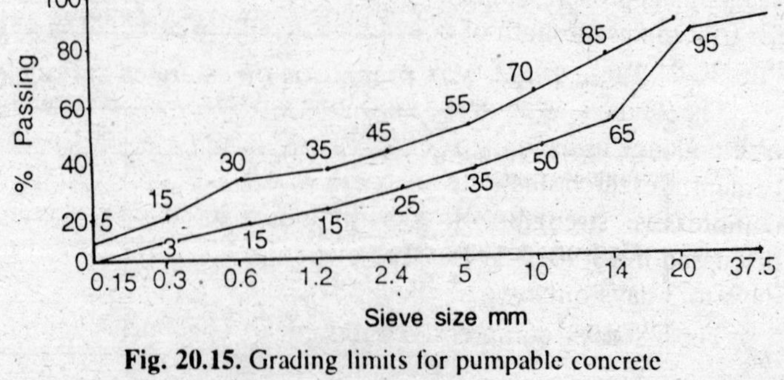

Fig. 20.15. Grading limits for pumpable concrete

in table 20.52 for a slump of 75 to 100 mm.

Step 4. The mix proportion of table 20.52 is based on the grading of aggregate shown in table 20.54.

Step 5. Absolute density of materials are taken as given in table 20.53.

Step 6. The calculations of combined aggregate grading based on the proportion given in table 20.52 is given in table 20.55. These combined grading limits should fall with in the limits given in table 20.53.

Step 7. Find out the fires contents.

Example 12. *Design a mix for pumpable concrete from the following data:*

1. *The max. size of coarse aggregate* = *20 mm.*
2. *The fine aggregate passes through the 300 micron or 0.3 mm* = *19%*
3. *Slump of concrete* = *75 to 100 mm*

Procedure

The proportions for 75-100 mm slump will be taken as given in table 20.52.

From the table 20.52,

Water = 190 kg or litres

Cement content = 310

Fine Aggregate = 880

We know that total fines less than 0.25 mm for pumpable concrete should be 350 to 400 kg per cubic metre of concrete.

As the fine aggregate passes 0.3 mm sieve is 19%, the sand particles passing through 0.25 mm sieve

$$= 19 \times \frac{25}{30} = 16\% \text{ app.}$$

$$\therefore \text{ Fine particles in sand} = \frac{16 \times 880}{100} = 140.8 = 141 \text{ kg.}$$

Cement content = 310

$\therefore$ Total fines = 310 + 141 = 451 kg.

From Table 20.51 for 190 kg water solid fines per m^3 of concrete should be 330 to 465 kg/m^3.

Hence total fines of 451 kg/m^3 as calculated are suitable.

From table 20.52, coarse aggregate = 930 kg.

Note. The crushed aggregate usually requires higher sand contents to achieve the required void content. Crushed fine aggregate contains a lot of dust passing through 0.150 mm sieve. The excess of dust particles should be avoided which may cause high pipe line friction and blockage.

20.17. RAPID METHOD OF MIX DESIGN

To estimate the preliminary water-cement ratio corresponding to the target mean strength a more realistic approach will be to correlate it with the 28 days compressive strength of cement. The characteristic strength is found to be better related to characteristic 28 days strength of cement rather than at earlier ages. Thus this approach will need 28 days for determining the characteristic strength of cement and next 28 days for trial mixes strength of concrete. The 28 day strength of cement can be taken as that given by curves of Fig. 20.8.

The 28 days or 56 days is too long a period for a contractor to wait for the results of the trial mix. There is a tendency to use mix directly without trying trial mixes. To reduce the time required for trial mixes, the cement Research Institute of India (CRI) has developed a method called rapid method, by which the compressive strengths of cement and concrete are obtained by using accelerated curing method as discussed in IS 9013-1978. This method reduces the period for finding the strength of trial mixes from 28 days to 3 days only.

The 28 days compressive strength of concrete is found to be statistically significantly related to its accelerated strength. Thus the trial mixes are correlated to the target mean accelerated strength rather than to the target mean 28 days strength, with the help of correlation between the two. A typical relation is shown in Fig. 20.16. This correlation is found to be independent of type or characteristics of cement used *i.e.* the correlation is not affected by the type of cement used, presumably due to the fact that they affect both the accelerated and normal 28 days strength of concrete in a proportionate manner, so that the effect is neutralised when their ratios are compared. More over for individual application such correlations can be established for the type of the materials and mix proportions to be used.

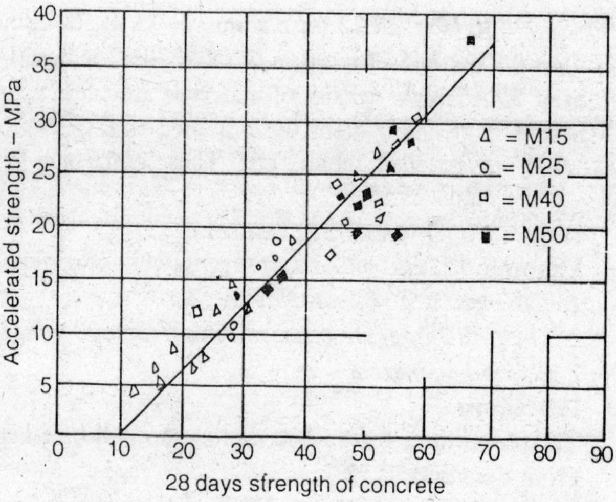

Fig. 20.16. Relation between accelerated and 28 day strength

On the other hand, results of accelerated compressive strength tests on standard cement mortar as per IS 4932-1968 have not been found reliable. This problem has been over come by testing cement also in a accelerated manner and determining its accelerated strength.

The reference concrete mix or accelerated strength of concrete mix has w/c ratio as 0.35 and workability very low with slump 0 to 10 or compacting factor 0.8 with the available cement *i.e.* (cement in hand).

The nominal maximum size of natural crushed aggregate should be 10 mm and fine aggregate should conform to zone II of table 4 of IS-383-1970. The typical composition of such as reference concrete mix per cubic metre of concrete is as follows:

Cement		= 570 kg
Fine aggregate		= 400 kg
Coarse aggregate		= 1178 kg
Water		= 200 kg
or Cement,	F.A.	C.A.
1 :	0.7 :	2.07
Water/cement ratio		= 0.35

Using the above proportions, 150 mm cube specimens of reference concrete are prepared with the available cement and cured by boiled water method. The accelerated strength is determined. Corresponding to this accelerated strength of the reference concrete, the water/cement ratio is determined from Fig. 20.17.

Using this water/cement ratio, the accelerated strength of the trial mix is compared with the characteristic target strength using the correlation between accelerated and normal 28 day strength of concrete.

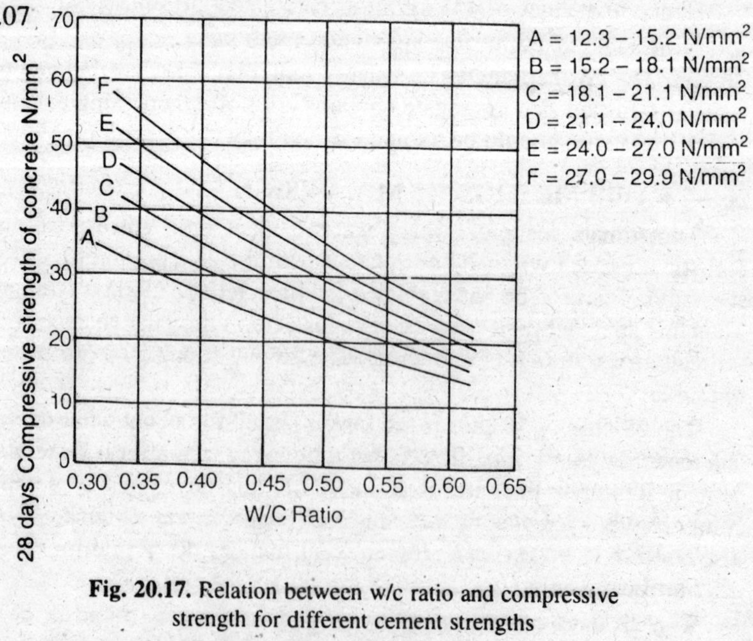

Fig. 20.17. Relation between w/c ratio and compressive strength for different cement strengths

Step by step procedure

1. The accelerated strength of standard or reference concrete is determined using the available cement. For determining the standard concrete strength 150 mm cubes are prepared from the above mentioned proportions and cured by boiling water method in accordance to IS 9013-1978.
2. For the required target mean strength of normal concrete, the water/cement ratio is determined by using the corresponding accelerated strength of standard concrete obtained in step (*i*).
3. The mix proportions are determined by any of the accepted methods of mix design and checked for workability of fresh concrete for the desired value.
4. W/c ratio for the required target strength of the mix is determined from Fig. 20.17.
5. The accelerated compressive strength of the trial mix is determined by preparing 150 mm cubes and curing by boiling water method as per IS 9013-1978.
6. The 28 day compressive strength of normal concrete is determined from the accelerated strength obtained in step (4) above by the following relations:

$$F_{28} = 8.25 + 1.64\, F_a \quad \text{...(1) For boiling water (100°C) curing}$$

$$F_{28} = 13 + F_a \quad \text{...(2) For warm water (55 ± 1°C) curing}$$

where,

F_{28} = 28 day compressive strength of normal concrete

F_a = Accelerated strength of concrete.

The curve is shown in Fig. 20.18

To Judge the suitability of the trial mix, the compressive strength, so obtained is compared with the target mean strength.

The accelerated curing method as per IS 9013-1978 is given below.

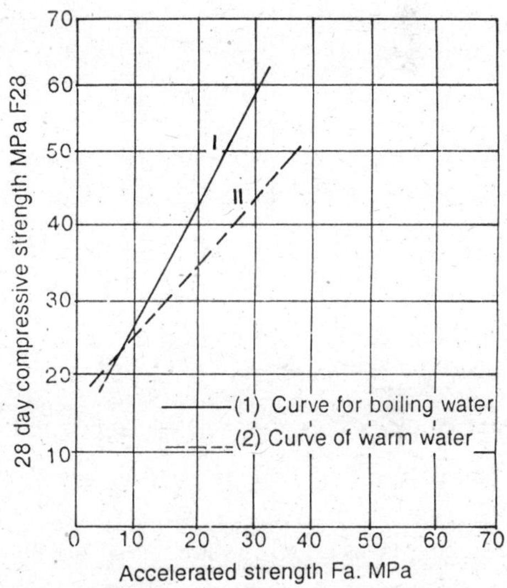

Fig. 20.18. Relation between accelerated and 28 days strength of concrete

1. Boiling water method

(*a*) Specimens are cured at 27 ± 2°C for 23 ± 1/4 hours under standard moist conditions.

(*b*) At the end of this period the specimens are cured in boiling water (100°C) for $3\frac{1}{2}$ hours ± 5 minutes.

(*c*) Specimens are cooled to a normal temperature of 27 ± 2°C in two hours time before testing.

2. Warm water methods

(*a*) $1\frac{1}{2}$ to $3\frac{1}{2}$ hours after casting, the specimens are immersed in water at a temperature of (55 ± 1°C) and cured for 20 hours ± 10 min.

(*b*) The specimen are demoulded and cooled at 27 ± 2°C for one hour before testing.

The average correlation is shown in Fig. 20.19 which is generally used for different concrete.

A correlation between 28 days strength and accelerated strength of cement is established as shown in Fig. 20.19 using all types of cements available in the country and different grades of concrete using boiling water curing method.

Example 13. *Design a mix for 28 days strength of 35 MPa if accelerated strength of standard concrete is 24.0 MPa.*

Solution. 1. Find out the w/c ratio from Fig. 20.17. From the curve *D*, for 28 days strength of 35 MPa, the w/c = 0.45.

2. From this w/c, find out the remaining proportions from any accepted method discussed earlier, and check the workability of fresh concrete for the desired value.
3. Find out the accelerated compressive strength of the trial mix.

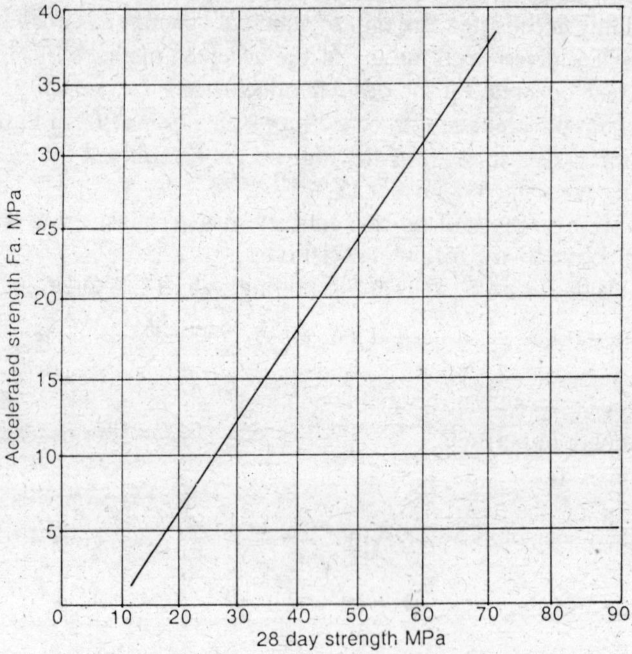

Fig. 20.19. General relation between accelerated and 28 days strength

4. Find out the 28 days compressive strength from the accelerated strength determined in step 3 by using the relation from Fig. 20.17 and compare it with the target strength.

20.17. FIELD ADJUSTMENT FOR WATER-CEMENT RATIO

In a concrete mix, if W, C, F_a and C_a are the required quantities of water, cement, fine aggregate and coarse aggregate, respectively to produce one cubic metre of fully compacted concrete. The volume of compacted concrete is equal to the sum of the absolute volumes of all ingredients.

Thus $$\frac{W}{1000} + \frac{C}{1000\, S_c} + \frac{F_a}{1000\, S_a} + \frac{C_a}{1000\, Sc_a} = 1.0 \qquad \ldots(1)$$

When the concrete has entrained air. Let its content be V percent of the volume of the concrete, the above equation (1) can be written as

$$\frac{W}{1000} + \frac{C}{1000\, S_c} + \frac{F_a}{1000\, S_a} + \frac{C_a}{1000\, Sc_a} = (1 - 0.01\, V) \qquad \ldots(2)$$

In case the specific gravities of fine and coarse aggregates are assumed equal say S_a, then for a given type of cement the above relation can be written as

$$\frac{W}{C} + \frac{1}{S_a}\left[\frac{F_a + C_a}{C}\right] = \frac{1000}{C} - \frac{1}{S_c} \qquad \ldots(3)$$

i.e. $$\text{(Water/ratio)} + \frac{\text{aggregate/cement ratio}}{\text{S}_\text{a}}$$

$$= \frac{1000}{C} - \frac{1}{S_c} \qquad \ldots(4)$$

The relation (4) can be used to convert-aggregate-cement ratio into cement content for a given water-cement ratio or vice versa from the curve of Fig. 20.20 produced by CRRI New Delhi.

If the aggregate contains free surface moisture whose water content is w percent of the mass of the saturated surface dry aggregate, then the masses of added water w and of wet aggregate must be adjusted.

The mass of free water is $C_c \left(\frac{W}{100}\right)$.

To obtain the mass of wet aggregate, the amount of free water is added to coarse aggregate. This comes as

$$C_a \left(\frac{W}{100}\right) + C_a = C_a \left(1 + \frac{W}{100}\right)$$

This amount of water should be subtracted from the water 'W' to be added to the concrete.

Central Road Research Laboratory (CRRI), New Delhi has developed curves as shown in Fig. 20.20 to adjust the water-cement ratio and aggregate cement ratio in the field *i.e.* at site to take care of the variation in the compressive strength of concrete due to the variation in the quality of cement obtained from different

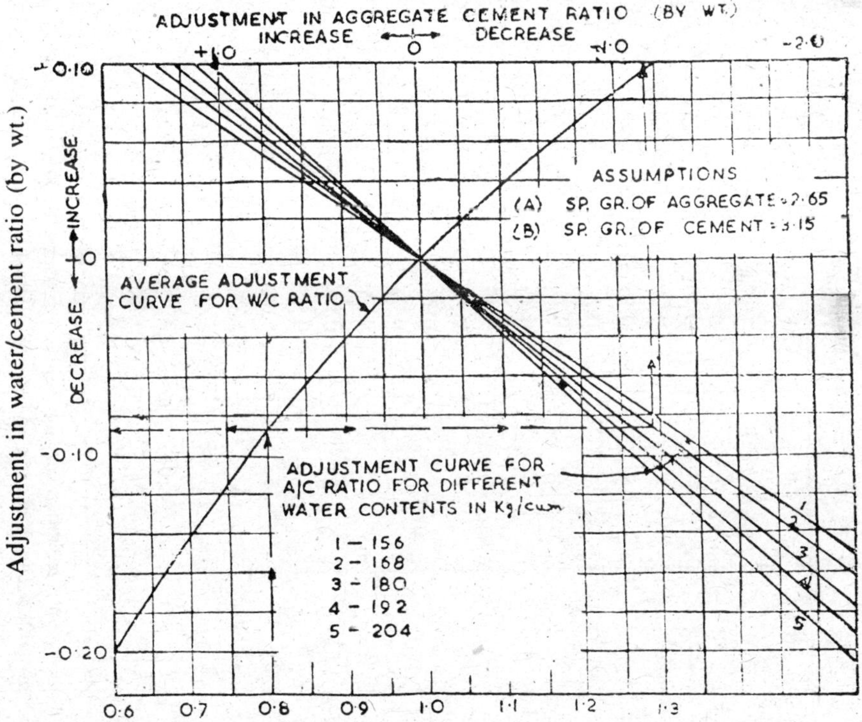

Fig. 20.20. Curve for field adjustment for w/c ratio

sources. If the source of supply of cement changes during the construction, the strength of concrete should be tested using the fresh cement, but keeping the w/c ratio and mix proportion same as before. If there is substantial difference say the new strength is 80% of the design strength, then as shown in Fig. 20.20 the w/c ratio should be reduced by 0.09% and aggregate cement ratio by 0.12%.

Table 20.56. Estimated quantities of materials required per cubic metre of compacted concrete or mortar

(Concrete Association of India)

Nominal mix			*Water*		*Cement*		*Sand litres*	*Broken stone litres*
Cement	*F.A.*	*C.A.*	*Water/cement ratio*	*Qt. per 50 kg bag of cement*	*By weight kg*	*By bags No.*		
1	1	×	0.25	12.5	1015	20.3	710	×
1	1.5	×	0.28	14.0	815	16.3	855	×
1	2.0	×	0.3	15.0	687	13.75	963	×
1	2.5	×	0.35	17.5	585	11.7	1023	×
1	3.0	×	0.40	20.0	505	10.1	1060	×
1	4.0	×	0.53	26.5	395	7.9	1106	×
1	6.0	×	0.70	35.0	285	5.7	1197	×
1	8.0	×	0.90	45.0	220	4.4	1232	×
1	1	2	0.30	15.0	560	11.2	392	784
1	2	2	0.42	21.0	430	8.6	602	662
1	1.5	3	0.42	21.0	395	7.9	414	828
1	1.67	3.33	0.48	24.0	363	7.25	419	838
1	2	3.0	0.50	25.0	385	7.7	539	808
1	2	3.5	0.53	26.5	330	6.6	462	808
1	2	4	0.55	27.5	310	6.2	434	968
1	2.5	3.5	0.57	28.5	305	6.1	534	748
1	2.5	4	0.60	30.0	285	5.7	499	798
1	3.0	4	0.65	32.5	265	5.3	556	742
1	2.5	5	0.65	32.5	255	5.1	446	892
1	3	5	0.69	34.5	240	4.8	504	840
1	3	6	0.75	37.5	215	4.3	452	904
1	4	8	0.95	47.5	165	3.3	462	924

Note. 1. This table is based on assumption that the voids in sand and broken stone are 40 and 45% respectively.

2. For gravel aggregate, decrease cement by 5% and increases sand by 2% and coarse aggregate in proportion to fine aggregate in the mix.

3. No allowance has been made for bulking and wastage.

Table 20.57. Estimated material required for concreting one square metre of surface

Nominal mix	*Material*	*Quantities for concrete thickness of*									
		10 cm	20 cm	30 cm	40 cm	50 cm	60 cm	70 cm	80 cm	90 cm	100 cm
1	2	3	4	5	6	7	8	9	10	11	12
1:1:2	C	56	112	168	224	280	336	392	448	504	650
	F.A.	39	78	117	157	196	235	274	314	353	392
	C.A.	78	157	235	314	392	470	549	626	715	784
1:1.5:3	C	39	79	118	158	197	237	277	316	356	395
	F.A.	41	82	124	165	207	248	289	331	372	414
	C.A.	83	166	249	332	414	497	580	662	745	828
1:1.67:3.33	C	36	73	109	146	182	219	256	292	328	363
	F.A.	42	84	126	168	209	251	293	335	377	419
	C.A.	84	168	251	335	419	503	586	670	754	838
1:2:3	C	38	77	115	154	192	231	270	308	347	385
	F.A.	54	108	162	216	270	324	378	431	485	539
	C.A.	81	162	242	323	404	485	566	646	727	808
1:2:4	C	31	62	93	124	155	186	217	248	279	310
	F.A.	43	87	130	174	217	260	304	347	390	434
	C.A.	87	174	260	347	434	521	608	695	782	868
1:2.5:5	C	26	51	77	102	128	153	179	204	230	255
	F.A.	45	89	134	179	223	268	312	357	402	446
	C.A.	89	178	268	357	446	535	625	714	803	892
1:3:5	C	24	48	72	96	120	144	168	192	216	240
	F.A.	50	101	151	202	252	302	353	403	454	504
	C.A.	84	168	252	336	420	504	588	672	756	840
1:3:6	C	22	43	64	86	108	129	151	172	194	215
	F.A.	45	90	136	181	226	272	317	362	407	452
	C.A.	90	181	271	362	452	542	633	723	813	904
1:4:8	C	17	33	49	66	82	99	106	132	149	165
	F.A.	46	92	139	185	231	278	324	370	416	462
	C.A.	92	277	277	370	462	554	646	739	831	924

C = Cement in kilogram, F.A. = Fine aggregate in litres, C.A. = Coarse aggregate in litres

Note. 1. For gravel aggregate decrease cement by 5% and increase sand by 2% and coarse aggregate in proportion to fine aggregate in the mix.

2. No allowance has been made for bulking and wastage.

QUESTIONS

1. Define a designed and prescribed mix.
2. Write a short note on the relation of maximum aggregate size and section of concrete member.
3. What is meant by free water/cement ratio?
4. How the moisture content of aggregate is calculated while calculating the batch quantities.
5. How the cost of labour is influenced by the workability of concrete?

6. What is the approximate relation between the entrapped air content and max. aggregate size?
7. What are the disadvantages of using too rich a mix?
8. Discuss the objects of mix design.
9. What information should be necessary before specifying the mix proportions.

OBJECTIVE TYPE QUESTIONS

1. Identify the correct statements of the followings
   (*a*) The determination of relative amounts of concrete ingredients is called mix design
   (*b*) Process of selection of suitable ingredients is called the mix design
   (*c*) Determining the relative properties of suitable ingredients is called the mix design
   (*d*) All the above
   (*e*) Non of the above
2. Identify the correct statements of the followings
   (*a*) The objective of mix design is to decide the proportions of material to produce concrete of required qualities
   (*b*) The objective of mix design is to decide the proportions of materials to produce concrete of any quality
   (*c*) The objective of mix design is to produce concrete of insufficient fluidity
   (*d*) The objective of mix design is the determination of water to be added in concrete
3. The choice of mix proportion is affected by
   (*a*) Workability of concrete (*b*) Type of cement
   (*c*) Maximum nominal size of coarse aggregate (*d*) Water/cement ratio
   (*e*) All the above
4. Identify the incorrect statement of the followings
   (*a*) The purpose of mix design is to obtain the concrete of desired strength and durability
   (*b*) The purpose of mix design is to produce concrete most economically
   (*c*) The cost of concrete depends on the cost of its ingredient materials
   (*d*) The cost of concrete is independent of the cost of labour
5. The proportions of materials in a concrete mix may be expressed as
   (*a*) Parts of cement, fine and coarse aggregate by volume
   (*b*) Parts of cement, fine and coarse aggregate by weight
   (*c*) Ratio of cement, by weight to sum of fine and coarse aggregate weight
   (*d*) By cement factor
   (*e*) By all the above
6. Identify the incorrect statement of the followings
   (*a*) Nominal mix of concrete is of the fixed proportions which ensure adequate strength
   (*b*) Nominal mixes may result in under or over rich mixes
   (*c*) Nominal or standard mixes may be used for high performance concrete
   (*d*) Mix design ensures the production of concrete of appropriate qualities most economically
7. The choice of mix proportions of a concrete is independent of
   (*a*) Maximum nominal size of aggregate (*b*) Minimum w/c ratio
   (*c*) Durability and quality control (*d*) Batching, mixing, placing and compaction
   (*e*) Grade designation
8. Identify the correct statement of the followings
   (*a*) The aim of mix design is to produce concrete of desired compressive strength, workability and durability
   (*b*) The compressive strength is dependent on w/c ratio
   (*c*) For the given aggregate, the workability of concrete is governed by its water content
   (*d*) Mix design is the basis of obtaining the optimum combination of ingredients
   (*e*) The final mix proportion is obtained on the basis of further trial mixes
   (*f*) All the above
9. The maximum nominal size of coarse aggregate is designated by the sieve size higher than the largest size on which the material retained is more than
   (*a*) 75% (*b*) 50%

(c) 25% (d) 15%

(e) 5% (f) None of the above

10. Identify the correct statement of the followings
    (a) The larger maximum size of coarse aggregate results in reduced workability
    (b) The larger maximum size of coarse aggregate is beneficial for high strength concrete
    (c) The larger maximum size of coarse aggregate requires a smaller quantity of cement for a particular w/c ratio
    (d) The larger maximum size of coarse aggregate reduces the stress concentration at the interface of aggregate and cement paste
11. Identify the correct statement of the followings
    (a) The compressive strength of air entrainment is approximately 80% that of non air entrant concrete
    (b) Grade designation gives the characteristic compressive strength requirements of concrete
    (c) The mix designed for a target mean compressive strength depends upon the degree of control
    (d) Durability of concrete means its resistance to the deteriorating influence of environment
    (e) The permeability of concrete paste increase exponentially with the increase in w/c ratio above 0.45%
    (f) All the above
12. Identify the true and false statements of the followings
    (a) W/c ratio of concrete is the ratio of volume of water to the volume of cement
    (b) W/c ratio of concrete is the ratio of volume of water to the weight of cement
    (c) W/c ratio of concrete is the ratio of weight of water to the weight of cement
    (d) W/c ratio of concrete is the ratio of weight of water to the volume of cement
    (e) W/c ratio of concrete is the ratio of weight of water required for chemical reaction to the weight of water required to wet the cement
    (f) Lower w/c ratio of concrete increases the compressive strength of concrete
    (g) The lower w/c ratio of concrete improves the frost resistance of concrete
    (h) Lower w/c ratio of concrete reduces its permeability
    (i) Lower w/c ratio of concrete reduces its shrinkage
13. Water in excess than required for chemical reaction results in
    (a) Development of segregation (b) Development of bleeding
    (c) Development of cracks (d) Development of honeycombing
    (e) Development of voids on drying
14. Identify the correct statement
    (a) Most of the methods of mix design are based on the w/c law as a criterion
    (b) Most of the methods of mix design are based on assumption that workability is solely dependent on the water content
    (c) Most of the methods of mix design are based on the assumption that durability is independent of cement content
    (d) Most of the methods of mix design are based on the principle that there is no air entrainment in the mix
15. For medium strength concrete the common method of mix design is
    (a) Trial and adjustment (b) DOE mix design
    (c) ACI mix design (d) IS method of mix design
    (e) All the above
16. Identify the correct statement of the followings
    (a) The trial and adjustment method aims to produce a concrete mix having minimum voids and maximum density
    (b) The trial and adjustment method requires sufficient quantity of cement to fill the voids in the mixed concrete
    (c) The trial and adjustment method indicates that the optimum percentage of sand is lower for lower w/c ratio
    (d) All the above
17. The DOE mix design method
    (a) Determines aggregate-cement ratio
    (b) Uses free water/cement ratio based on target mean compressive strength

(*c*) Uses free water content determined by the size and type of aggregate and level of workability
(*d*) All the above

18. Identify the correct statement of the followings
(*a*) The ACI method of mix proportioning takes into account the air content of concrete
(*b*) The ACI method of mix proportioning is suitable for normal and heavy weight concrete in the workability range of 25 to 100 mm slump
(*c*) The ACI method of mix proportioning can be used to produce concrete of targeted mean compressive strength upto 75 MPa
(*d*) The ACI method of mix proportion uses bulk volume of coarse aggregate estimated for maximum nominal size aggregate and fineness modulus of sand.
(*e*) All the above

19. Identify the incorrect statement of the followings
(*a*) ISI mix design method is suitable for medium and high strength concrete
(*b*) ISI mix design method is not suitable for medium and high strength concrete
(*c*) ISI mix design method requires data on the characteristic strength, degree of workability, maximum nominal size of aggregate and limitations of w/c ratio
(*d*) In ISI mix design method the calculations are based on the absolute volumes of ingredients

20. In a trial and adjustment concrete mix design method if the desired slump is not obtained, the adjustment in water content for each 10 mm difference in slump (in %) is
(*a*) 1.0 (*b*) 0.5%
(*c*) 5% (*d*) 7.5%
(*e*) 10%

21. For a constant combined aggregate-cement ratio, if the coarse aggregate is increased at the expense of fine aggregate, the total surface of the combined aggregate is
(*a*) Increased (*b*) Remains constant
(*c*) Decreased (*d*) Depends on other factors
(*e*) None of the above

22. In a concrete mix design for the adjustment of air entrainment by a amount of *e*, the reduction in water is done by *v*, then reduction in solid volume of sand will be
(*a*) $e - v/2$ (*b*) $\frac{1}{2(e+v)}$
(*c*) $e - v$ (*d*) $\frac{e}{2-v}$

23. Identify the correct statement of the following
(*a*) If the 1st trial mix gives more than 28 days design value then for next trial water content should be increased
(*b*) If the 1st trial mix gives more than 28 days design strength then for next trial water/cement ratio should be increased
(*c*) If the 1st trial mix gives more the 28 days design strength then for next trial proportion of sand should be increased
(*d*) If the 1st trial mix design gives more than 28 days design strength then for next trial curing period of concrete should be increased

24. If the water is added in a increasing amount to a fixed amount of dry mortar mix, then the volume of mortar
(*a*) Decreases (*b*) Increases
(*c*) No change takes place
(*d*) mortar increases proportionally more than the volume of water added
(*e*) Initially volume increases, then decreases to a minimum value

25. Identify the correct statement
(*a*) The minimum volume of water added to a mix then the volume of water is known as saturation water content
(*b*) The minimum volume of water added to a mix, then the volume of water known as basic water content
(*c*) The minimum volume of water added to a mix, then the volume of water is known as lowest water content

(*d*) The minimum volume of water added to a mix then the volume of water is known as hygroscopic water content

(*e*) The minimum volume of water added toe mix, then the volume of water is known as highest water content

26. The amount of water mixed in a mortar always should be
    (*a*) Equal to the basic water content
    (*b*) More than the basic water content
    (*c*) 50% of the basic water content
    (*d*) Less than the basic water content
27. For a mortar mix a water content of 1.25 means
    (*a*) 1.25 litres of water has been added per litre of mortar
    (*b*) 1.25 litres of water has been added per litre of cement
    (*c*) 25% more water has been added than the basic water content
    (*d*) 1 litre of water has been added to 1.25 litres of mortar
28. A nominal mix corresponding to M_{20} grade concrete mix is
    (*a*) 1:3:6
    (*b*) 1:2:4
    (*c*) $1:1\frac{1}{2}:3$
    (*d*) 1:1:2
29. The grade of concrete corresponding to a nominal mix proportion of 1:2:4 is
    (*a*) M_{25}
    (*b*) M_{20}
    (*c*) M_{15}
    (*d*) $M_{7.5}$
30. The grade of concrete corresponding to a nominal mix proportion of 1:3:6 is
    (*a*) M_{35}
    (*b*) M_{25}
    (*c*) M_{10}
    (*d*) $M_{7.5}$
31. As per IS 456-2000 total number of concrete grade is
    (*a*) 5
    (*b*) 10
    (*c*) 15
    (*d*) 20
32. The volume of sand per cubic metre of concrete of 1:2:4 proportion by volume would be approximately
    (*a*) 0.2 to 0.4
    (*b*) 0.4 to 0.6
    (*c*) 0.6 to 0.9
    (*d*) 0.8 to 1.0
    (*e*) Non of the above
33. In a 1:2:4 concrete the number of cement bags required would be
    (*a*) 5 to 6
    (*b*) 4 to 5
    (*c*) 3 to 4
    (*d*) 2 to 3
34. In beams and slabs generally the concrete of nominal mix is used is
    (*a*) 1:3:6
    (*b*) 1:2:4
    (*c*) $1:1\frac{1}{2}:3$
    (*d*) 1:1:2
35. For water retaining structures the nominal mix generally used is
    (*a*) 1:1:2
    (*b*) 1:2:4
    (*c*) 1:3:6
    (*d*) $1:1\frac{1}{2}:3$
36. To take care of individual samples, the laboratory design strength can be obtained by increasing the target strength by per cement
    (*a*) 0 – 5%
    (*b*) 5 to 10%
    (*c*) 10 to 15%
    (*d*) 15 to 20%
    (*e*) 20 to 25%
37. After moulding the trial mix test specimens should be placed at a temperature of
    (*a*) 12 ± 2°C
    (*b*) 15 ± 2°C
    (*c*) 25 ± 2°C
    (*d*) 27 ± 2°C
    (*e*) 35 ± 2°C
38. As per IS specifications concrete should be cured at a relative humidity of
    (*a*) 20%
    (*b*) 30%
    (*c*) 50%
    (*d*) 70%
    (*e*) 90%

39. Identify the correct statements of the followings
    (*a*) Bulking of sand always increases with the increase in the quantity of water
    (*b*) The effect of bulking of sand is not considered while batching by weight
    (*c*) For concrete foundations the mix proportion adopted is 1:2:4
    (*d*) Water content in ordinary concrete is 30% by weight of aggregate + 5% weight of cement
    (*e*) The joints in concrete should be provided along the line of minimum shear
    (*f*) Before laying the second lift of concrete, the surface of the old concrete should be treated with a rich cement mortar paste
    (*g*) The reinforcement of old concrete should extend into the new concrete laid

Answers

1. (*d*)	9. (*d*)	16. (*d*)	24. (*e*)	32. (*a*)
2. (*a*)	10. (*c*)	17. (*d*)	25. (*b*)	33. (*a*)
3. (*e*)	11. (*f*)	18. (*e*)	26. (*b*)	34. (*b*)
4. (*d*)	12. [False (*a, b, d, e*)]	19. (*b*)	27. (*c*)	35. (*d*)
5. (*e*)		20. (*a*)	28. (*c*)	36. (*c*)
6. (*c*)	13. (*e*)	21. (*c*)	29. (*c*)	37. (*d*)
7. (*d*)	14. (*b*)	22. (*c*)	30. (*d*)	38. (*e*)
8. (*f*)	15. (*e*)	23. (*b*)	31. (*c*)	39. (*b, e, f, g*)

21
Quality Control

21.1. INTRODUCTION

Generally at site concrete is produced in batches with the locally available materials of variable characteristics. Thus concrete of one batch is likely to be different from the other. The magnitude of this variation depends upon many factors as follows:

(*a*) Variation in the quality of the constituent materials.

(*b*) Variation in the mix. proportions due to batching.

(*c*) The quality of over all workmanship and supervision at site.

Further concrete has to go under a number of operations such as

(*i*) transportation, (*ii*) placing, (*iii*) compaction, (*iv*) curing etc. During all these operations considerable variation may develop partly due to the quality and efficiency of machinery and plants available and partly due to the difference in the efficiency of techniques used. Thus there is no single feature to define the quality of concrete. Under such conditions concrete generally is referred as good, fair or poor quality concrete. This interpretation is subjective. Thus it is necessary to define the quality of concrete in terms of desired performance characteristics, economics, safety and other such factors. Due to the large number of variables influencing the performance of concrete, quality control is essential. As the concrete serves the needs of safety and serviceability including durability, which vary from one situation and type of construction to another. Therefore uniform standards for general application to all the works are not practical.

Thus the aim of quality control is to reduce the above noted variations and produce uniform material of desired characteristics for the envisaged job. Therefore the quality control is a dynamic corporate programme to assure that all aspects of equipments, materials and workmanship are looked after well.

21.2. FACTORS CAUSING VARIATIONS IN THE QUALITY OF CONCRETE

The main factors which cause variations in the quality of concrete are as follows:

1. Personnel
2. Material
3. Equipment
4. Workmanship

1. Personnal

Personnal is the basic key for the successful execution of any plan or job. Therefore the basic requirement for the success of any quality control plan is the availability of trained and experienced personnel at all levels of concrete production and its execution. The designer must be well versed with the construction operations and the site engineer must be able to understand the statements of specifications fully and clearly. In quality control every thing cannot be specified and much depends on the skill and experience of the people involved in it.

2. Material

For producing concrete of uniform quality, its ingredients play a major role. Thus the ingredients used in concrete must be from the same source as far as possible, specially the cement. When ingredients from different sources are used, the strength and other qualities of the materials are likely to change. Thus the ingredients from different sources must be tested before use. The same type of cement from different sources and at different times from the same source exhibits variation in its properties, especially the compressive strength. Thus cement received from each source must be tested initially, once from each source of supply and after wards every two months as the variation in compressive strength is related to the composition of raw materials and the variation in the process of manufacturing. Cement should be protected from moisture. Set cement with hard lumps should be rejected.

3. Aggregates

The maximum size, moisture content, grading and shape of coarse aggregate are major source of variability in the concrete. Hence aggregates should be stock piled separately in single sizes. The graded aggregate should not be allowed to segregate.

Rule for grading of aggregate

1. For fine aggregate long and continuous gradings are preferable. The material passing through 300 micron (0.3 mm) sieve and 150 micron (0.15 mm) sieve should be minimum.
2. The gradings that are at the coarser end of the range are more suitable for rich mixes and those at finer end of the range are suitable for lean mixes.

Further size and grading of the coarse aggregate should be as discussed in detail in chapter 4 on aggregate.

4. Equipment

The equipment used for batching, mixing and compaction should be of the right type. The weight batchers should be checked frequently for their accuracy. Generally weight batching should be preferred than volume batching. If volume batching has to be adopted, the volume measures should be checked frequently for the weight volume ratio. Mixer's performance also should be checked to the requirements of the relevant standards. Concrete should be mixed for the stipulated time as under mixing and over mixing both effect the compressive strength of concrete and should be avoided. The vibrators should be of required frequency and amplitude.

The green concrete should be handled, transported and placed in such a manner that it does not segregate. The time interval between mixing and placing should be as minimum as possible. The targeted strength, impermeability and durability can be achieved only by thorough compaction. 1% voids left due to incomplete compaction will reduce the compressive strength by 5%.

21.3. FIELD CONTROL

It consists of inspection and testing. They play an vital role in the over all quality control plan. Inspection may be divided into the following two groups.

1. Quality control inspection
2. Acceptance inspection

1. Quality control inspection. For repeated type activities or operations an early inspection is important. After the plant is stabilized, occasional checks may be sufficient to ensure the continued satisfactory results. On the other hand for the activities or operations which are not of repetitive type more constant checks are necessary.

Apart from the tests of concrete material, concrete should be tested at the fresh or green and hardened stages. Tests in the green stage of concrete offer an opportunity for necessary corrective steps to be taken before it is too late. These tests include unit weight, air content and workability test. The accelerated strength tests from which a reliable idea of the 28 day strength can be obtained with in few hours are effective quality control tools.

2. Acceptance test. The tests whose results are at universal acceptance level are known as accepted tests. The 28 day concrete strength test is the only acceptance test on the basis of which the acceptance or rejection of concrete mix depends.

21.4. ADVANTAGES OF QUALITY CONTROL

Following are the advantages of quality control

1. Quality control is the rational use of available resources after testing their characteristics resulting in the reduction of material cost.
2. Quality control reduces the maintenance cost.
3. In the absence of quality control there is no guarantee that the weakness of a certain area can be compensated by over spending in other areas. For example the loss of strength due to incomplete compaction or in adequate curing of concrete can not be compensated by adding more cement in concrete at some other place.
4. In the absence of quality control at the site, the designer may be tempted to overdesign to minimise the risk. This will result in more cost.
5. Checks at every stage of production of concrete and rectifications of defects at the proper time will result in early completion of work reducing the delay and cost.

21.5. STATISTICAL QUALITY CONTROL

Cement concrete is a mixture of cement, aggregate, and water and thus have certain amount of variability in materials as well as in construction methods. This results in variation of concrete strength from batch to batch as well as in the same batch. To assess the strength of the final product is very difficult. To evaluate the strength of end product requires a very large number of destructive tests, which is very costly and time consuming. Thus we have to resort to sample tests. To adopt a very rigid criteria to reject a structure on the basis of a single or few standard samples will prove very costly. Thus to have a reasonable control on concrete work, the acceptance test basis of samples may be adopted, by ensuring that the probability of test result falling below the design strength is not more than a specified tolerance level.

The aim of quality control is to limit the variability of concrete as much as possible. Statistical quality control method provides a scientific approach to concrete designer to understand the realistic variability of materials. With the knowledge of variability of materials, he may lay down the design specifications with proper tolerance to provide for the unavoidable variations. The acceptance criteria is based on statistical evaluation of the test results of samples taken at random during the execution period of the work. For this purpose various statistical techniques are available.

The quality control of concrete will be of great importance on large contracts, where the specifications insist on certain minimum requirement. The efforts put in will be more than the benefits from the resulting savings in the over all concreting operations.

The control over the quality of concrete generally is carried out by testing 150 mm cubes or 150 × 300 mm cylinders prepared at site from the concrete used in the structure. These tests measure the potential strength of the concrete but do not indicate any variation in the

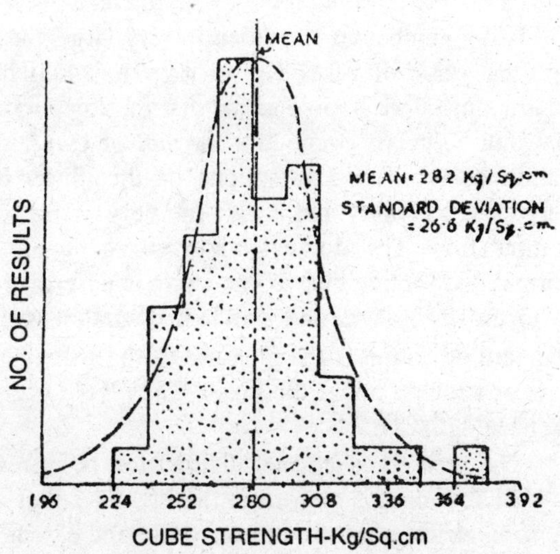

Fig. 21.1. A Histogram of strength values

compaction or curing conditions of the concrete in the structure. The compressive strength of tests cubes from random sampling of a mix show variations. These variations are inherent in the various operations involved in the preparation and testing of concrete. The variation is shown in Fig. 21.1. This Fig. has been drawn on the basis of table 21.1.

Table 21.1.

Range of variation in strength	*Frequency f*	*Mid value*	*Difference d*	$f \cdot d$	$f \cdot d^2$	*Remark*
371 — 378	4	374.5	– 56.0	– 224.0	12545	
378 — 385	3	381.5	– 49.0	– 147.0	07203	
385 — 392	7	388.5	– 42.0	– 294.0	12384	
392 — 399	1	395.5	– 35.0	– 35.0	01225	
399 — 406	4	402.5	– 28.0	– 112.0	03136	
406 — 413	2	409.5	– 21.0	– 42.0	00882	
413 — 420	5	416.5	– 14.0	– 70.0	00980	
420 — 427	6	423.5	– 7.0	– 42	00294	
427 — 434	4	430.5	0.0	00	000	
434 — 441	2	437.5	+ 7.0	+ 14.0	00098	
441 — 448	1	444.5	+ 14.0	+ 14.0	00196	
448 — 455	1	451.5	+ 21.0	+ 21.0	00441	
455 — 462	1	458.5	+ 28.0	+ 28.0	00784	
462 — 469	2	465.5	+ 35.0	+ 70.0	02450	
469 — 476	0	472.5	+ 42.0	+ 00.0	0000	
476 — 483	2	479.5	+ 49.0	+ 98.0	04802	
483 — 490	2	486.5	+ 56.0	+ 112.0	06272	
	N = 47			$\Sigma fd = -609$	$\Sigma fd^2 = 53691$	

In the Fig. 21.1, the strength interval is taken constant along the *x*-axis and no of specimens in each interval (called frequency, along *y*-axis. The figure obtained is called histogram. The area under the curve represents the total number of specimens to an appropriate scale.

If the number of specimen is very large and at the same time the size of the interval is decreased to a limiting value of zero. The histogram would become a continuous curve known as the distribution curve. Such a distribution curve is called a *Normal* or *Gaussian* distribution curve. The assumptions of this distribution are very close to reality and is an extremely useful tool in the computation. The doted smooth curve of Fig. 21.1 is normal distribution curve. The curve is described in terms of mean strength f_m and standard deviation σ or *S*. The standard deviation is the measure of the scatter or dispersion of strength about the mean. They have been defined on page 476-477.

The theoretical normal distribution is represented in Fig. 21.2. It can be seen from the Fig. 21.2 that the curve is symmetrical about the mean value and extends to plus and minus infinity. Actually in practice, very low and

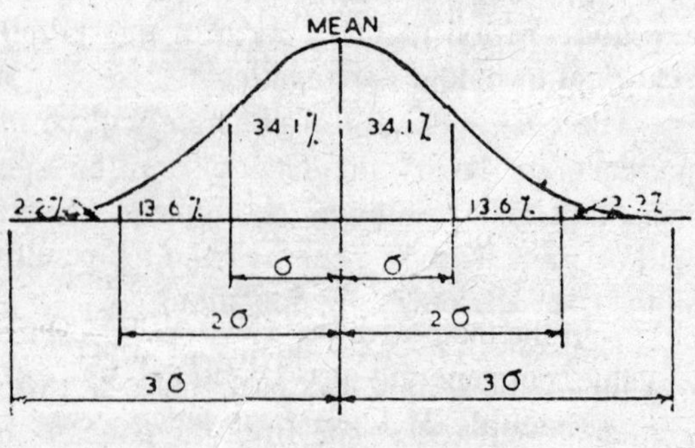

Fig. 21.2. Normal distribution curve

very high values of strength do not occur, but these extremes can be ignored as most of the area under the curve (99.6%) lies with in ± 3.0 S or σ. In practice this area can be taken to represent all the strength values of concrete. In other words, it can be said that the probability of a value of strength failing with in ± 3 S from the mean value is 99.6%. Similarly the probability of a value falling between any given limits about the mean value (f_m + $K.S.$) can be stated. The values of probability for various values of probability factor K together with the probability of falling a strength below ($f_m - KS$).

Table 21.2. Probability strength in the range $f_m + Ks$ and below $f_m - K.S.$ for normal distribution

Probability factor K	*Probability of strength in the rnage* $f_m + K.S.$ %	*Probability of strength below* $f_m - K.S.$ *(Risk factor) % Risk percent*
1.0	68.2	15.9 (1 in 6)
1.64	90.0	5.0 (1 in 20)
1.96	95.0	2.5 (1 in 40)
2.33	98.0	1.0 (1 in 100)
3.00	99.7	0.15 (1 in 700)

In the mix design the mean strength can be calculated by the following relation

$$f_m = f_{min.} + K.S. \quad \text{...(21.1)}$$

where $f_{min.}$ = minimum strength which is also known as specified characteristics strength or specified design strength.

The probability factor K usually is chosen as 1.64 or 2.33, *i.e.* there is a probability that 1 in 20 or 1 in 100 respectively of the strength values will fall below the minimum strength. The term K.S. is known as margin. In the calculation of the margin, the standard deviation 'S' or σ should be based on the results obtained using the same plant, materials and supervision. In the absence of such data, the value of S may be taken depending upon the number of available results 'n' and the characteristic strength f_{min} as follows:

If $n \leq 20$

then
$$S = 0.4 f_{min}, \text{ for } f_{min} \leq 20 \text{ MPa} \quad \text{...(21.2)}$$
$$S = 8 \text{ MPa for } f_{min} \geq 20 \text{ MPa}$$

(*ii*) If $n \geq 20$
$$S = 0.2 f_{min} \text{ for } f_{min} \leq 20 \text{ MPa}$$
$$S = 4 \text{ MPa for } f_{min} \geq 20 \text{ MPa} \quad \text{...(21.3)}$$

Note. The above values of standard deviation should be used till the sufficient data for the calculation of standard deviation is not available.

In the British method of mix design for air entrained concrete, it is assumed that a loss of 5.5% in compressive strength results for each 1% air entrained by volume in the mix. This reduction is compensated by aiming for a higher strength as

$$f_m = \frac{f_{min} + K.S.}{1 - 0.055\, a} \quad \text{...(21.4)}$$

where a is the percentage of air entrained.

Himsworth has suggested the value of coefficienet of probability K as shown in Table 21.3.

In the table 21.2 the value of K is shown as 1.64 if 5% results are allowed to fall below the minimum value, but generally it is taken as 1.65.

Example 21.1. *Find the mean strength of concrete for a over head tank concrete from the following data:*

1. *The characteristics strength of concrete* = *18 MPa*

Table 21.3. Value of K. Coefficient of probability
(Himsworth constants)

Percentage of results allowed to fall below the minimum	*Value of K*
0.1	3.09
0.6	2.50
1.0	2.53
2.5	1.96
6.6	1.5
16.0	1.0

2. *The number of test results available* = *75*
3. *Probability factor K* = *2.33.*

Solution.

$$f_m = f_{min} + K.S.$$

As the value of n is greater than 20, and f_{min} is less than 20 MPa, the standard deviation S is taken as

$$S = 0.2 \times f_{min} = 0.2 \times 18 = 3.6$$

Then
$$f_m = f_{min} + K.S.$$
$$= 18 + 2.33 \times 3.6 = 18 + 8.388 = 26.388 \text{ say}$$
$$= \mathbf{26.4 \text{ MPa Ans.}}$$

Example 2. *From the data of example 1, find the mean strength if air entrainment is 4%.*

Solution. From Eq. 21.4,

$$f_m = \frac{f_{min} + K.S.}{1 - 0.055 \times 4}$$

the value of $f_{min} + K.S.$ from example (1) is 26.4 MPa

the
$$f_m = \frac{26.4}{1 - 0.220} = \frac{26.4}{0.78} = \mathbf{33.85 \text{ MPa (app.) Ans.}}$$

21.6. COMMON TERMINOLOGIES

The terminologies used in the statistical quality control of concrete are as follows:

1. Mean strength
2. Standard deviation
3. Variance
4. Coefficient of variance

1. Mean strength. It is the average strength obtained by dividing the sum of all specimens (cubes) strength tested by the number of specimens

i.e.
$$\bar{x} = \frac{\Sigma x}{n}$$

where,

$\bar{x}$ = mean strength

Σx = sum of the strength of all specimens tested

n = number of specimens tested

2. Standard deviation. It is the root mean square deviations of all the results. This is denoted by σ or S. Numerically it is written as

$$\sigma = \sqrt{\frac{\Sigma (x - \bar{x})^2}{n - 1}}$$

where,

σ = standard deviation

n = number of specimens tested

x = particular value of strength

$\bar{x}$ = mean strength of specimens

The standard deviation increases with the increase in variability. The characteristics of normal distribution curve are fixed by the average value and the standard deviation, while the position of the curve along the y-axis is fixed by the mean value.

3. Variance. This is the measure of difference or variability from mean strength between any single observed data.

4. Coefficient of variation. This is an alternative method of expressing variation of results. It is non dimensional measure of variation. It is obtained by dividing the standard deviation by the arithmetic mean value. It is expressed as

$$v = \frac{\sigma}{\bar{x}} \times 100$$

where, v = coefficient of variation

21.7. MEAN STRENGTH

It is the average strength of a set of specimen tested. It is one of the most important properties of concrete. The mean compressive strength required at a specified period usually 28 days determines the nominal w/c ratio of the mix.

21.8. MINIMUM STRENGTH

All structural designs are based on the assumption of a certain minimum strength of concrete. The actual strength of concrete produced in a laboratory or at site is a variable quantity. Thus in the design of a concrete mix, the mean strength always is aimed higher than a certain minimum. Actually nc absolute minimum strength can be specified as from statistical point of view there is always a probability of a test result falling below a minimum however low it is set. To over come this difficulty, the IS 456-1978 introduced the concept of *characteristic strength.* The characteristic strength is that strength of the material (concrete) below which not more than 5% of the test results are expected to fall. Thus the probability factor is 5. The target mean strength may be obtained by the following relation.

$$f_t = f_{ck} + \sigma K \text{ or } (K.S.)$$

where, f_t = target mean strength

f_{ck} = characteristic strength

K = probability factor

σ or S = standard deviation

21.9. RELATION BETWEEN MEAN AND MINIMUM STRENGTH OF CONCRETE

The relation can be written as follows:

Mean strength = Minimum strength + standard deviation × Coefficient of probability or tolerance K.

Thus mean strength = Minimum strength + σK

The value of probility factor K may be taken from curve 21.3 or from table as shown in Table 21.2.

21.10. SAMPLING OF CONCRETE

1. Sampling procedure. To ensure that each concrete batch should have a reasonable chance of being tested, random sampling procedure should be adopted. Thus the sampling should be spread over the total period of concreting to cover all mixing units and all the batches.

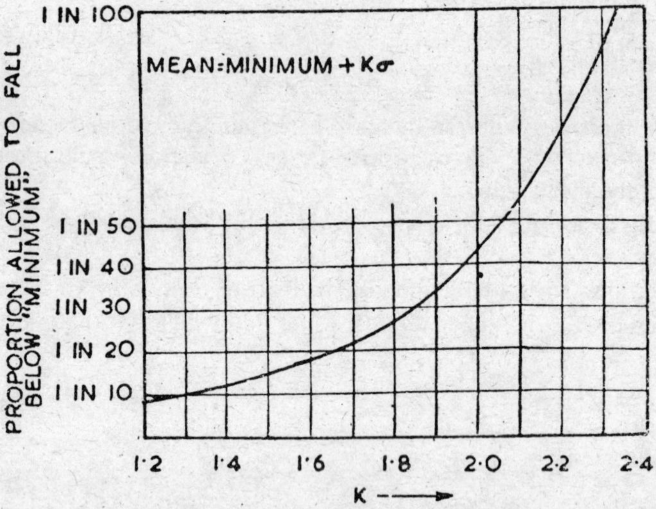

Fig. 21.3. Values of K for various tolerance

2. Frequency of sampling. The minimum frequency of sampling of concrete of all grades should be as follows as per IS 456-1978 shown in table 21.4.

Table 21.4. No. of samples to be taken

Quantity of concrete work in m^3	*No. of samples*
1 — 5	1
6 — 15	2
16 — 30	3
31 — 50	4
51 and above	4 plus one additional sample for each addional 50 m^3 concrete or part there of.

Note. At least one sample should be taken from each shift.

21.11. TEST SPECIMENS

Three specimens should be prepared from each sample to be tested at 28 days. Additional cube specimens may be prepared for determining the strength at 7 days or at the time of stripping the shuttering or to determine the duration of curing etc. The specimens should be tested as per Is 516-1959 or latest edition.

21.11.1. Test strength

The test strength of sample should be the average of the strength of three specimens. The individual variation in strength should not be more than 15% of the average strength.

21.11.2. Application

As stated above statistical methods may be used to analyse the variation in strength. The standard deviation and coefficient of variation are the most accepted methods. These are defined on page 476.

The procedure of the calculation of standard deviation and coefficient of variation is illustrated with the help of test results of a site-shown in Table 21.1.

Example 21.3. *With the data of table 21.1, calculate the value of standard deviation σ or S and coefficient of variation.*

Solution. From the data of table 21.1, the values of Σfd and Σfd^2 are as follows:

$$\Sigma fd = -609$$

and $$\Sigma fd^2 = 53691 \text{ and } N = 47$$

$\therefore$ Standard deviation $$\sigma^2 = \frac{\Sigma fd^2}{N} - \left(\frac{\Sigma fd}{N}\right)^2$$

$$= \frac{53691}{47} - \left(\frac{-609}{47}\right)^2$$

$$= 1142 - 168 = 974$$

or $$\sigma = 31.2$$

$\therefore$ Average strength $$= 430.5 - \frac{609}{47} = 417.5 \text{ app.}$$

Coefficient of variation $$= \frac{\text{standard deviation}}{\text{mean strength}} = \frac{31.2}{417.5}$$

$$= 0.075 \approx 7.5\% \text{ very good control}$$

According to U.S.B.R, the percentage of variation is given as follows:

Coefficient of variation %	*Degree of control*
20.0%	Very poor
15.0%	Fair
10%	Very good

IS 456-2000 has suggested values for standard deviation for different grades of concrete as shown in Table 21.5 below.

Table 12.5. Standard deviation for different grades of concrete as per IS-456-2000

Grade of Concrete	*Assummed standard deviation N/mm^2*
M_{10} M_{15}	3.5
M_{20} M_{25}	4.0
M_{30} M_{35} M_{40} M_{45} M_{50}	5.0

For different conditions of placing and degree of control typical values of standard deviation are shown in Table 21.6.

Example 4. *Determine the mean strength of concrete to be used in the construction of a spillway with the following data*

(*a*) *Minimum strength desired = 22.5 MPa*

(*b*) *Risk percentage = 16%*

Table 21.6. Typical values of standard deviation for different conditions of placing and mixing control

S. No.	*Placing and Mixing condition*	*Degree of control*	*Standard deviation MPa*
1.	Complete accurate grading, aggregate dried exact w/c ratio and controlled temperature and curing	Laboratory precision	1.3
2.	Weight batching of all materials, well grading of 3 sizes of coarse aggregate plus fine aggregate, controlled w/c. Allowance for moisture content of aggregate (surface plus adsorbed water) continued supervision	Excellent	2.8
3.	Weight batching of all materials, strict control of aggregate grading, control of w/c ratio allowance of moisture content, continud supervision	High	3.5
4.	Weight batching of all materials, control of aggregate grading, control of water added, frequent supervision	Very good	4.2
5.	Weighing of all materials, water content controlled by inspection of mix, periodic inspection of workability, use of two size of aggregate (Fine and coarses only intermittent supervision	Good	5.7
6.	Volume batching of all materials allowing for bulking of sand weight batching of cement, w/c ratio controlled by inspection of mix. intermittent supervision	Fair	6.5
7.	Volume batching of all materials, use of all in aggregate litle or no supervision	Poor	7.0
8.	Un controlled	Un controlled	8.5

Solution.

$$f_m = f_{\min} + K \cdot \sigma$$

The value of σ from table 21.5 is 4.0 and the value of K from table 21.2 is 1.0

Hence $$f_m = 22.5 + 4 \times 1.0$$
$$= 22.5 + 4 = \mathbf{26.5\ MPa\ Ans.}$$

21.12. ACCEPTANCE CRITERIA

Concrete is considered to comply the requirement of strength if it fulfills the following conditions as per Is 456-1978.

1. The test strength of every sample is not less than the characteristic value.

2. The strength of one or more samples may be less than the characteristic value but in each case it is not less than the greater value given by the following relations.

(*a*) Characteristic strength minus 1.35 times the standard deviation.

(*b*) 0.8 times the characteristic strength

(*c*) The average strength of the sample is not less than the characteristic strength plus

$$\left[1.65 - \frac{1.65}{\sqrt{\text{No. of samples}}}\right]$$ times the standard deviation.

Thus the compressive strength of any sample of concrete should not be less than the greater value given by relation (*a*) and (*c*) above.

1. Compliance

To obtain the 28 day specified strength with in the permissible range of limits is called the compliance of specification. According to BS 5328 1990, the compliance of the characteristic strength is based on groups of consecutive test results, as well as on single results. Each result is the average of two cubes, made in the specified manner from concrete which is sampled at a prescribed rate and normally tested at 28 days.

The compliance is assumed to be met, if both of the following requirements are satisfied.

1. The average strength determined from the first two, three or four consecutive test results or from any group of four consecutive results, complies with the results of the following table 21.7
2. No individual test result should fall short of the specified characteristic strength more than the value given in table 21.7.

Table 21.7. Compliance requirements for compressive strength as per B.S. 5328-Part-4-1990

Specified characteristic strength (grade) MPa	*Group of results MPa*	*Minimum value by which the mean strength of the group of test results should exceed the grade strength MPa*	*Max. value by batch any individual test result falls short of the grade strength MPa*
7.5 to 15	First 2	0	2
	First 3	1	2
	4*	2	2
20 and above	First 2	1	3
	First 3	2	3
	4*	3	3

4* Any consecutive four

2. Flexural strength

The compliance with respect to flexural strength of concrete is met when the following both conditions are satisfied:

1. The mean strength determined from any group of four consecutive test results exceeds the specified characteristic strength by at least 0.3 MPa (0.3 N/mm^2).
2. The strength determined from any test result is not less than the specified characteristic strength less then 0.3 MPa (0.3 N/mm^2).

21.13. ESTABLISHING THE COMPRESSIVE STRENGTH OF CONCRETE

Concrete is a very useful and faithful material. If due care is taken of all the ingredients and workmanship of the concrete structure, it generally does not fail to give the specified results. In case the test results obtained are unacceptable, then the strength can be established from the results of the following two tests:

1. Core test 2. Load test

1. Core test. The selection of point from where the core is to be taken depends upon the discretion of the inspecting authority or it can be decided from the cube testing register. The number of test specimens (cores) should not be less than three and they should represent the whole section of the doubtful concrete.

The core strength should be converted to equivalent cube strength. If the strength of equivalent cube obtained is at least 85% of the characteristic strength of the concrete grade, no strength of a individual core is obtained less than 75%, then strength of the concrete may be considered satisfactory.

In case such core tests are not possible or core test results are not found satisfactory then load test may be conducted. (Refer chapter 19)

1. Load tests for flexural members

To verify the performance of the structure *i.e.* the characteristic strength of the concrete, load tests may be carried out after the expiry of 28 days from the time of placing the concrete.

1. The structure should be subjected to a load equal to full dead load of the structure plus 1.25 times the live load for a period of 24 hours. After 24 hours the live load should be removed.
2. The deflection due to live (imposed) load should be recorded. If with in 24 hours of removal of live load, the structure does not recover at least 75% of the deflection under super impose load, the test should be repeated after 72 hours of the first test. If the recovery is less than 80% the structure should be rejected.
3. If the max. deflection in mm shown in 24 hours under load is less than $\frac{40\,l^2}{D}$, where l is the effective span in metres and D the over all depth of the section in mm, then it is not necessary to measure the recovery and the recovery criteria is not applicable.

2. Non destructive tests

Non destructive testing provides alternative method to core testing for the estimation of the strength of the concrete in the structure. It can also be used to supplement the data obtained from limited number of cores. Non destructive method of testing has been discussed in chapter 19.

3. Use of standard deviation or coefficient of variation

The use of standard deviation or coefficient of variation is based on the following argument. If the control over all materials and operations involved in the production of concrete including sampling and testing was perfect, then every result would be the same and would correspond to the mean value. In practice to have each operation fully perfect is impossible. The more uniform the operations, closer will be the result to the mean value. Hence lower will be the value of standard deviation. Thus the quality of concrete can be changed by standard deviation. At site it is observed that it is more difficult to achieve consistent results with high strength concrete and the value of standard deviation is higher for high strength concrete than medium or low strength concrete.

$$\text{Coefficient of variation} = \frac{\text{standard deviation}}{\text{mean strength}} = \text{a constant}$$

It is seen that with a constant coefficient of variation, the standard deviation increases with the strength and is larger for higher strength.

On the basis of their research work Murdock and Erntroy have shown that the coefficient of variation more nearly represent a particular standard of control at relatively low strengths, while standard deviation more nearly represent the standard of control at high strength. Thus Indian standard method has adopted the standard deviation method.

American Concrete Institute (ACI) has recommended following values of standard dviation for different. Control standards as shown in Tbale 21.8.

Table 21.8. Showing control standard and standard deviation

S. No.	*Control standard*	*Expacted standard deviation in MPa (N/mm^2)*	
		General construction	*Laboratory trial mixes*
1.	Excellent	< 3.0	< 1.5
2.	Very good	3.0 – 3.5	1.5
3.	Good	3.5 – 4.0	1.5 – 2.0
4.	Fair	4.0 – 5.0	2.0 – 2.5
5.	Poor	> 5	> 2.5 to 3.5

IS 456-1978 has suggested the following values of standard deviation for different grades of concrete

Table 21.9. Values of standard deviation for different grades of concrete

Grade of Concrete MPa	M_{10}	M_{15}	M_{20}	M_{25}	M_{30}	M_{35}	M_{40}
Assumed standard deviation MPa	2.3	3.5	4.6	5.3	6.0	6.3	6.6

Table 21.10. Suggested values of coefficient of variation for different grade of control

Degree of content	Well controlled as in lab	Excellent near that of lab	Excellant	Good	Fair	Fair (minus)	Bad
Coefficient of variation percent	5%	10%	12%	15%	18%	20%	25%

QUESTIONS

1. What is quality control of concrete?
2. Can quality assurance replace site supervision?
3. What is meant by characteristic strength of concrete?
4. What is the difference between the design strength and the mean strength of concrete?
5. If the specified characteristic strength is 15 MPa. Calculate the mean strength for 80 cubes results assuming the probability factor as 2.33. **[Ans.** 22.0 MPa]
6. Discuss the factors which cause variations in the quality of concrete.
7. How quality of concrete can be controlled in the field?
8. What is the aim of quality control of concrete and how it is achieved?
9. Define the following terms:
   (*a*) Standard deviation (*b*) Mean strength
   (*c*) Coefficient of variation (*d*) Minimum strength
   (*e*) Compliance and acceptance criteria.

OBJECTIVE TYPE QUESTIONS

1. Identify the correct statement
   (*a*) The quality control of concrete can be defined appropriately by the quality of overall workmanship and super vision of work at site
   (*b*) The quality control of concrete can be defined appropriately by the assurance that all aspects of materials, equipment and workmanship have been looked after well
   (*c*) The quality control of concrete can be defined appropriately by the conformity of specifications
   (*d*) The quality control of concrete can be defined appropriately by the assurance for the serviceability and safety of the structure
2. Quality control means
   (*a*) Adequate design at the minimum cost (*b*) Rational use of available resources
   (*c*) Completion of work at extra cost (*d*) None of the above
3. Quality control can be exercised by
   (*a*) Adequate compaction and curing
   (*b*) By motivating the workers to do every thing right from the first time
   (*c*) By the inspection and testing at all stages at the site
   (*d*) By resorting to the acceptance tests
4. Identifying the correct statements of the followings
   (*a*) The statistical quality control helps in narrowing down the tolerance limits of variability
   (*b*) The statistical quality control helps to ascertain the range of value that can be expected under existing conditions
   (*c*) The statistical quality control helps in taking into account the actual variability of concrete

(*d*) Larger the value of standard deviation, poorer will be the level of control
(*e*) Larger the value of standard deviation, better will be the level of control
(*f*) Larger the value of standard deviation, lower will be the variability

5. As per IS 546, 1978 concrete will be considered to satisfy the strength requirements if
   (*a*) The strength of sample is less than $f_{ck} - 1.35\ \sigma$
   (*b*) The test strength of every sample is not less than f_{ck}
   (*c*) Upto 5% samples have test strength less than f_{ck}
   (*d*) The test strength of sample may be upto 80% of f_{ck}
6. The target mean strength of concrete is given by the relation
   (*a*) $f_t = k \cdot f_{ck} + \sigma$ (*b*) $f_t = f_{ck} + K \cdot \sigma$
   (*c*) $f_t = f_{ck} + \sigma$ (*d*) $f_t = f_{ck} + K$
7. For weight batching well graded aggregate and excellent degree of control the value of standard deviation should be
   (*a*) 1.8 (*b*) 2.8
   (*c*) 3.5 (*d*) 5.7
   (*d*) 6.5
8. Which of the following statements is true
   (*a*) Statistical quality control helps in taking into account the actual variability of concrete.
   (*b*) Statistical quality control helps in narrowing down the tolerance limits of variability.
   (*c*) Statistical quality control helps to ascertain the range of values that can be expected under existing conditions.
   (*d*) All the above
9. Standard deviation is the measure of
   (*a*) Variability of test results
   (*b*) Spread of compressive strength test results about its mean strength
   (*c*) All the results falling out side or with in the certain range
   (*d*) All the above
10. For excellent control over the construction of a bridge the value of standard deviation should be
    (*a*) More 5.0 (*b*) Between 4 and 5
    (*c*) Between 3.5 and 4.0 (*d*) Less than 3.0
11. For excellent control on the construction of a building the value of coefficient of variation should be
    (*a*) 25% (*b*) 18%
    (*c*) 12% (*d*) 15%

Answers

1. (*b*)	4. (*c, d*)	7. (*b*)	10. (*d*)
2. (*b*)	5. (*b*)	8. (*a*)	11. (*c*)
3. (*c*)	6. (*b*)	9. (*d*)	

22

Light Weight Concrete

22.1. INTRODUCTION

The self weight of normal cement concrete varies from 2200 to 2600 kg/m^3. This is one of the main disadvantage of conventional cement concrete as this heavy weight of concrete makes it uneconomical structural material. To increase the efficiency of concrete as a structural material attempts have been made to reduce the weight of normal cement concrete. A cement concrete having self weight ranging from 300 kg/m^3 to 1850 kg/m^3 is called light weight concrete.

22.2. ADVANTAGES OF LIGHT WEIGHT CONCRETE

Following are the advantages of light-weight-concrete

1. Light weight concrete reduces the dead load of the structure.
2. It increases the progress of construction of the structure.
3. It lowers the haulage and handling charges.
4. The weight of structure on the foundation is an important factor in design, specially in the case of multi-story buildings and in weak soils. Heavier the dead load, deeper and thicker the foundations involving higher cost.
5. In framed structures, columns and beams have to carry loads of walls and floors. If walls and floor are made of light weight concrete, the foundations also will be lighter, resulting in considerable economy in the construction.
6. The thermal conductivity of light weight concrete is relatively low, which dampens the heat transfer from roof and walls, resulting lower inside temperature of the building. This lower temperature provides comfort to the inhabitants. The thermal conductivity improves with decrease in density.
7. In case of buildings where air conditioning is to be installed, the use of light weight concrete has been found advantageous from the point of view of thermal comfort and lower consumption of power.

22.3. CLASSIFICATION OF LIGHT WEIGHT CONCRETE

The light weight concrete can be classified into the following groups, depending on the method of production.

1. **Light weight aggregate concrete.** This type of concrete is produced by using porous light weight aggregate of low specific gravity usually less than 2.6.
2. **Aerated, cellular, foamed or gas concrete.** This type of concrete is produced by introducing larger voids with in the concrete or mortar. These voids should be clearly distinguished from the fine voids produced by air entrainment.

3. **No fines concrete.** This type of concrete is produced by omitting the fine aggregate from the mix, which results in the large number of interstitial voids. In this concrete normal weight coarse aggregate is used.

In essence, the decrease in density of the concrete in each method is obtained by the presence of voids either in the mortar or in the aggregate or in the interstices between the particles of coarse aggregate. The presence of voids reduces the strength of light weight concrete in comparision to normal weight concrete. As stated above in many applications high strength is not essential.

The light weight concrete provides good thermal insulation and has a satisfactory durability, but is not highly resistant to abrasion. Light weight concrete in general is more expensive than ordinary concrete. It requires more care in mixing, handling and placing than ordinary concrete.

The light weight concrete may also be classified according to its use as follows:

1. Structural light weight concrete
2. Masonry light weight concrete or non load bearing concrete
3. Insulating concrete

This classification of structural light weight concrete is based on a minimum strength.

1. **Structural light weight concrete.** The 28 day cylinder compressive strength of this concrete should not be less than 17 MPa. Its density should not exceed 1840 kg/m^3. Usually it should be between 1400 1800 kg/m^3.
2. **Masonry concrete.** The 28 day cylinder compressive strength of this concrete should be between 7 to 14 MPa. Its density should be between 500 to 800 kg/m^3.
3. **Insulating concrete.** Its coefficient of thermal conductivity should be below 0.3 J/m^{2}S°C/m. Its strength should be between 0.7 and 7 MPa and density generally lower than 800 kg/m^3.

In recent years light weight concrete has become more popular due to the manifold advantages it offers over the conventional concrete. A better understanding and development of modern technologies have also helped in the promotion and use of light weight concrete. The light weight structural concrete, is lighter than conventional concrete, but at the same time strong enough to be used for structural purposes. It combines the advantages of normal weight concrete and discards the disadvantages of normal concrete This type of light weight concrete has great future. Out of the main groups of light weight concrete the light weight aggregate concrete and aerated concrete are more often used than no fines concrete. Previously aerated concrete mainly was used for insulating purposes. Now a days it is also used for structural purposes

Table 22.1. Groups of light weight concrete

No fines concrete	*Light weight aggregate concrete*	*Aerated concrete*	
		Cheminical aerated (Gas forming)	*Foaming mixtures*
(*a*) Gravel	(*a*) Clinker	(*a*) Alluminium powder method	(*a*) Preformed foam
(*b*) Crushed stone	(*b*) Foamed slag	(*b*) Hydrogen peroxide method	(*b*) Air entrained foam
(*c*) Coarse clinker	(*c*) Expanded shale	(*c*) Bleaching powder methods	
(*d*) Sintered pulverised fuel ash	(*d*) Expanded clay		
(*e*) Expanded clay or shale	(e) Pumice		
(*f*) Expanded slate	(*f*) Expanded slate		
(*g*) Foamed slag	(*g*) Sintered pulverised fuel ash		
	(*h*) Exfoliated vermiculite		
	(*i*) Expanded perlite		
	(*j*) Organic aggregate		

along with steel reinforcement. The aerated concrete is more widely manufactured and used in Scandivian countries. In U.K. France, Germany and U.S. light weight aggregate concrete is widely manufactured and used due to the production of large scale artificial industrial light weight aggregate. Now a days considerable varieties of industrial light weight aggregates of varying properties are available by different trade names. Some of them are as follows:

(*a*) Aglite and Hadite (Expanded shale)

(*b*) Leca (Expanded clay)

(*c*) Lytag (Sintered pulverised fuel ash) etc.

The groups of light weight concrete are shown in Table 22.1.

22.4. TYPES OF LIGHT WEIGHT AGGREGATE

Light weight aggregates can be classified into the following two groups:

1. Natural light weight aggregate
2. Aftificial light weight aggregate

These aggregate are further classified as follows:

Natural light weight aggregate	**Artificial light weight aggregate**
1. Pumice	1. Artificial cinders
2. Diatomite	2. Coke breeze
3. Scoria	3. Foamed slag
4. Volcanic cinders	4. Bloated clay
5. Saw dust	5. Expanded shales and slate
6. Rice husk	6. Sintered fly ash
	7. Expanded perlite
	8. Thermocole beeds
	9. Exfoliated vermiculite

22.4.1. Natural Aggregate

They are not of uniform quality, and not found in many countries. As such they are not used universally for making light weight concrete. Out of all the natural light weight aggregate, only pumice is used widely.

1. Pumice

It is a rock of volcanic origin which occurs in many parts of the world. They are light in colour or nearly white. They are light in weight enough yet sufficient strong to be used as light weight aggregate. The light weight of these rocks is due to escaping of gas from the molten lava when erupted from beneath the earth's crest. It is of fairly even texture of inter connected cells. Chemically it is inert and has about 75% silica content.

Pumice is one of the oldest kinds of light weight aggregates which even has been used in Roman structures. It is mined, washed and used. To get the stronger aggregate, pumice may be heated to the beginning of fusion. The bulk density of pumice varies from 600 to 900 kg/m^3. Good variety pumice produces concrete with a density of 700 to 1400 kg/m^3. The insulating property of this concrete is very good, but it has high absorption and high shrinkage.

2. Diatomite

This is a hydrated amorphous silica derived from the remains of microscopic aquatic plants called diatoms. The deposits of this aquatic plants are formed under deep ocean bed. Later when the ocean bed is raised and became continent, the diatomaceous earth became available on land. In short diatomite is a semi consolidated sedimentary deposits formed in cold water environment. The average weight of pure diatomite is about 450 kg/m^3, where as the weight of impure diatomite is more than 450 kg/m^3.

3. Scoria

It is a hollow (vesicular) glassy rock of volcanic origin. Usually it is dark in colour and contains larger and irregularly shaped cells unconnected with each other.

4. Volcanic cinders

These are also of volcanic origin loose products resembling artificial cinder.

5. Saw dust

Saw dust has been used as a light weight aggregate in flooring and in the manufacture of precast products on a very small scale. A lot of difficulties have been experienced in the use of saw dust. The shrinkage and moisture movement is also very high of saw dust.

6. Rice husk

It has been used as light weight aggregate on a very limited scale.

22.4.2. Artificial Aggregates

The artificial aggregates are classified on the basis of raw materials used and the method of manufacture.

1. Aggregates classified on the basis of raw material are those aggregates which are produced by the application of heat. They are in order as expand clay, shale, slate, diatomaceous shale, perlite, obsidian and vermiculite.

2. The second category of aggregates are produced by the special cooling process through which an expansion of blast furnance slag is obtained.

3. Industrial cinders are categorised in the third group.

The materials which have partly fused particles arising from the combustion of coal are termed as cinder, clinker or Breeze. Now a days the use of these materials is diminishing due to the wider use of pulverised coal than lump coal. Cinder aggregates under go high dry shrinkage and moisture movement. The swelling or unsoundness of cinder or clinker often is due to the presence of excessive unbrunt coal particles. Some times the unburnt particles may be as much as 15 to 25%. These particles expand on wetting and contract on drying, which is responsible for the unsoundness of concrete made with cinder or clinker etc. Cinder aggregate has been used for producing building blocks for partition walls, for screeding over flat roofs and for plastering purposes etc.

Clinker aggregate

It is called cinder in U.S.A. It is made from well burnt residue of industrial high temperature furnaces, fused into lumps. The clinker should be free from harmful varieties of unburnt coal, which is a main source of unsoundness in the concrete made from this aggregate. B.S. 3799-1990 has laid down limits of loss on ignition and of soluble sulphate content in clinker aggregate to be used in plain concrete for general purposes and insitu interior concrete not normally exposed to damp conditions.

Iron or Pyrites in the clinker may result in staining of concrete surfaces. It should be removed. Unsoundness due to hard burnt lime can be avoided by allowing the clinker to stand wet for a period of several weeks. Due to wetness, the lime becomes slaked and there will be no expansion in the concrete.

When cinders are used as coarse as well as fine aggregate, the density of the concrete will be of the order of 1100 to 1400 kg/m^3. But in order to improve the workability of the mix, often natural sand is used as fine aggregate. In this case the density of the resulting concrete will vary from 1750 to 1850 kg/m^3.

Breeze

It is the name given to a material similar to clinker, but more lightly burnt and less well burnt. There is no clear cut dermarcation between breeze and clinker.

Expanded clay, shale, and slate. These are obtained by heating suitable raw materials in a rotary kiln to a temperature of 1000°C to 1200°C known as incipient or beginning to fusion temperature. At this temperature, the gases produced are entrapped in a viscous plastic mass, causing expansion of the material. This porous structure is retained on cooling. Thus the apparent specific gravity of the expanded material is lower than before burning. Generally the raw material is reduced to the desired size before heating, but crushing may also be applied after expansion.

Expansion of material may also be achieved by the use of sinter strand. In this case the moistened material is carried by travelling metal frame called grate having under burners such that heating gradually penetrates the full depth of the material bed. The viscosity of the material at this stage is such that the gases are entrapped into it and cause expansion of the material. The cooled mass either is crushed or material is broken into small pieces before heating as in the case of rotary kiln. The broken or pellitized material produces particles with a smooth shell of about 0.05 to 0.1 mm thick coating over the cellular interior. These particles are nearly spherical and have glazy surface. Due to this glazy surface they have lower water absorption than uncoated particles whose absorption ranges from 12 to 30%. Coated particles are easier to handle and mix. These coated particles produce concrete of higher workability, but their cost is more than the uncoated aggregate.

The density of expanded shale and clay aggregate made by the sinter strand method varies from 650 to 900kg/m^3 and when made in rotary kiln the density varies from 300 to 650 kg/m^3. Usually the density of concrete made from expanded shale and clay aggregate varies from 1400 to 1800 kg/m^3. The strength of concrete made from expanded clay or shale aggregate is higher than concrete made with other light weight aggregates.

Perlite

It is a glassy volcanic rock found in America, Italy and Ulster etc. When it is heated rapidly to a temperature of 900 to 1000°C, it expands due to the evolution of steam and forms a cellular material. The bulk density of this material is as low as 30 to 240 kg/m^3. The strength of concrete made with perlite aggregate is very low. Its shrinkage is very high as its modulus of elasticity is very low. Mainly it is used for insulation purposes. This concrete dries very soon and can be finished rapidiy. This is the main advan- tage of the concrete made with perlite aggregate.

Vermiculite

Raw vermiculite is a micaceous material, whose structure is laminar (made of layers) similar to mica. It is found in Africa and America. When heated with certain amount (percentage) of water to a temperature of 650 to 1000°C, it expands by delamination in the same way as that of slate or shale. This type of expansion is known as *Exfoliation*. The vermiculite expands many times of its original volume. Due to exfoliation of its thin layers it expands even upto 30 times of its original volume. The bulk density of exfoliated vermiculite varies from 60 to 130 kg/m^3. The strength of concrete made with vermiculite as aggregate is very low. The density of this concrete also is very low, but its shrinkage is very high. As the insulating properties of this concrete are very good, it is mainly used for insulating purposes. It is also used for insitu roof and floor screeds or for the manufacture of blocks, slabs, tiles, which are used for sound and heat insulation. The products of vermiculite concrete can be cut, sawn, screwed or nailed. The prefabricated panels of this concrete can be used for floor, wall and partition sound deadner. The hollow blocks of this concrete can be used for encasing steam or hot water pipe lines.

This concrete is non inflammable. Thus it can be used as a heat resistant material. The vermiculite mixed with gypsum is completely incombustible and it also possesses sound absorption and thermal insulation characteristics. Thus, it is used as heat resistant material.

Expanded or foamed slag

Expanded slag is one of the most important types of light weight aggregates. The blast furnance slag is a by-product of the manufacture of pig iron. The expanded or foamed slag is produced by rapidly quenching blast furnance slag. The quenching of slag can be done by the following two methods:

(*a*) Water jet process

(*b*) Machine process

(*a*) **Water jet process.** In this process a limited amount of water in the form of spray is made to come in contact with the molten slag as it is discharged from the furnance. By spaying the water, steam is generated. The slag hardens in a porous form. This steam is absorbed by the molten mass producing a porous, honeycombed material. This material resembles the pumice.

(*b*) **Machine process.** In this process, the molten slag is rapidly agitated with a controlled amount of water, the steam is entrapped in the molten mass of slag. There is some gas formation also due to the chemical reactions of some of the slag constituents with water vapour. Such a product is also called expanded or foamed slag.

In case the cooling is done with a large excess of water, granulated slag is formed, which is used in the manufacture of blast furnance slag cement.

The strength and texture of foamed slag depends upon the chemical composition and the method of production. In general the structure is similar to that of natural pumice. The expanded slag must be.

1. Free from excess of sulphate
2. Free from volatile impurities such as coal
3. Free from contamination of heavy impurities

The bulk density of expanded slag varies from 300 to 1100 kg/m^3 depending upon the details of cooling process and to some extent on the particle size and grading. Concrete made with expanded slag has a density of 950 to 1750 kg/m^3.

In India expanded or foamed slag is manufactured in many steel mills and industries have come up near the steel mills to manufacture ready made building blocks and partition wall panels. Such prefabricated products are lighter in weight. Hence their cost of cartage or transportation is cheaper. Expanded slag can also be used for the manufacture of R.C.C. lintels and other structural members. By controlling the density, foamed slag can be used for load bearing walls and also for the production of structural light weight concrete.

Swelled or bloated clay

When certain variety of glass and shale are heated to a temperature of beginning of fusion or melting gases are formed with in the mass at this temperature. Due to the formation of gases the heated materials swell or, expand many times more than their original volumes and cellular structure is formed. The expansion of materials is known as bloating. The cellular structure so formed is retained on cooling. The product so formed is known as light weight aggregate and is used for the production of light weight aggregate concrete.

In western countries bloated clay products have been produced by different techniques and are available in the marked by different trade names as Haydite, Rocklite, Leca, Aglite, Gravelite, etc. In India Central Building Research Institute of India has developed a technique for the manufacture of bloated clay for structural use. The experimental building constructed at CBRI using bloated clay as structural light weight aggregate has given good performance.

Sintered fly ash

Fly ash is the finely divided residue from thermal power plants and railway locomotives, obtained from burning of powdered coal. These particles are glassy spherical. If these small particles of fly ash are heated further, they combine forming small porous nodules or pellets, which have considerable strength.

A limited quantity of water is added to the fly ash and their pellets are made. After making pellets, they are burnt or heated to a temperature of 1000°C to 1200°C. This sintering process is similar to that adopted in the manufacture of portland cement. The fly ash may contain certain unburnt coal. The quantity of unburnt coal may vary from 2 to 15% or more depending upon the efficiency of burning. While sintering the fly ash, the aim should be to make use of the fuel present in the fly ash and no extra fuel should be used. This process improves the quality of sintered fly ash. Sintered fly ash is one of the most important type of structural light weight aggregate. In U.K. it is sold by the trade name 'Lytag'. It has low drying shrinkage and high strength/density ratio. As the light weight aggregates are factory made under strict control conditions, they are less variable than many natural aggregates. The physical properties of light weight aggregate are shown in Table 22.2.

Table 22.2. Physical properties of light weight aggregates

Type of aggregate	*Particle shape and surface texture*	*Density kg/m³*	*Bulk density kg/m³*	*24 hour water absorption capacity %*	*Typical concrete*	
					Compressive strength MPa	*Unit weight kg/m³*
A. Aggregate for high strength concrete f_{ck} > 15 MPa						
Expanded clay	Rounded and slightly rough particles	Coarse 600 to 1600 fine 1300 to 1800	300 to 900	5 to 30	10 to 60	1000 to 1700
Expanded shale and slate	Often angular and slighly rounded, smooth surface	Coarse 800 to 1400 Fine 1600 to 1900	400-1200	5 to 15	20 to 50	1300 to 1600
Fly ash	Similar to expanded clay	1300 to 2100	600 to 1100	20	30 to 60	1500 to 1600
Foamed blast	Irregular, angular	1000 to 2200	400 to 1100	10 to 15	10 to 45	1800 to 2000
Furnance slag	Particles with rough and opened pore surface					
Sintered colliery waste	Angular with opene pored surface	1000 to 1900	500 to 1000	15	10 to 40	1400 to 1600
B. Agg. for medium strength 3.5 to 15 MPa						
Pumice	Rounded particles with open textured but smooth surface	550 to 1650	350 to 650	50	5 to 15	1200 to 1600
C. Agg. for low strength (0.5 to 3.5 MPa)						
Perlite	Rounded and angular shape and rough surface	100 to 400	40 to 200	—	1.2 to 3.0	400 to 500
Vermiculite	Cubical	100 to 400	60 to 200	—	1.2 to 3.0	300 to 700

22.5. LIGHT WEIGHT AGGREGATE CONCRETE

Often the light weight concrete is made by using the light weight aggregate. As already discussed, the different light weight aggregates have different densities. Hence light weight concrete made using different types of light weight aggregate will have different densities. Concrete produced by using expanded perlite or vermiculite will have a low density of the order of 300 kg/m³, where as by the use of expanded slag, Sintered fly ash or bloated clay etc. a concrete having density as high as 1900 kg/m³ can be obtained. The

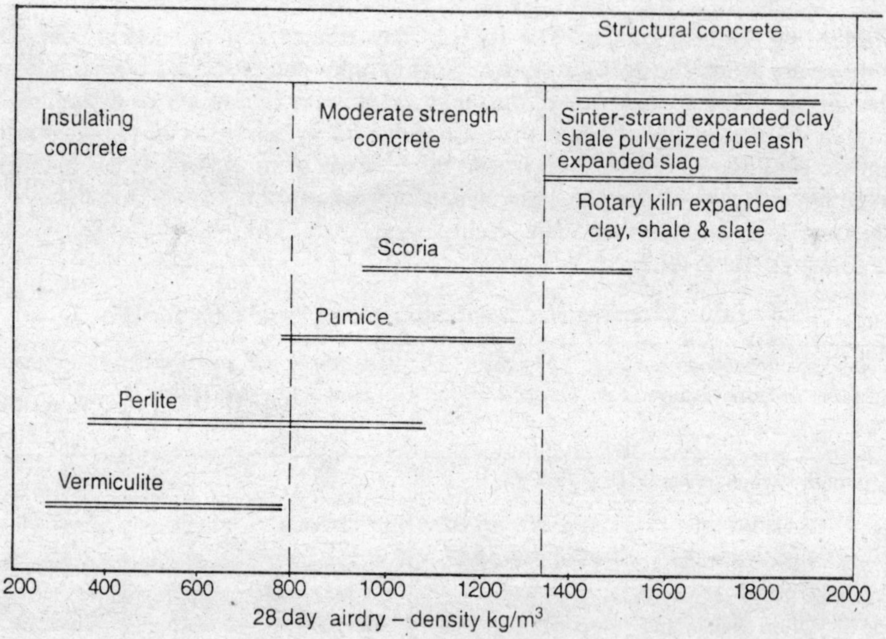

Fig. 22.1. Typical ranges of densities of concrete made with various light weight aggregates

strength of light weight concrete varies from 0.3 N/mm^2 to 40 N/mm^2. In the production of such concrete, cement content varying from 200 kg/m^3 to about 500 kg/m^3 may be used. Typical ranges of densities of different light weight concrete are shown in Fig. 22.1.

The strength of light weight concrete depends on the density of aggregate. Less porous aggregate, which is heavier in weight produces stronger concrete particularly with higher cement content. The grading of aggregate, w/c ratio, and degree of compaction also affects the strength of concrete.

Table 22.3. Typical properties of light weight concrete

Type of concrete	*Bulk density of aggregate kg/m^3*	*Mix. proportion by vol. cement: aggregate*	*Dry density of concrete kg/m^3*	*Compressive strength MPa*	*Dry shrinkage of concrete 10^{-6}*	*Thermal conductivity J/m^2 S°C/m*
Foamed slag	Fine 900 Coarse 650	1:8 1:6 1:3.5	1700 1850 2100	7 21 41	400 500 600	0.45 0.69 0.76
Rotary kiln expanded clay	F. 700 C. 400	1:11 1:6 1:5 1:4	650-1100 1100 1200 1300	3-4 14 17 19	— 550 600 700	0.17 0.31 0.38 0.40
Rotory kiln expanded clay with natural sand	C. 400	1:5	1350-1500	17	—	0.57
Sinter-strand expanded clay	F. 1050 C. 650	1:5 1:4	1500 1600	24 31	600 700	0.55 0.61
Rotary kiln expanded slate	F. 950 C. 700	1:6 1:4.5	1700 1750	28 35	400 450	0.61 0.69

Type of concrete	*Bulk density of aggregate kg/m³*	*Mix. proportion by vol. cement: aggregate*	*Dry density of concrete kg/m³*	*Compressive strength MPa*	*Dry shrinkage of concrete 10⁻⁶*	*Thermal conductivity J/m² S°C/m*
Sintered pulverized fuel ash	F. 1050 C. 800	1:5.9 1:5.3 1:4.5 1:3.1	1490 1500 1540 1570	20 25 30 40	300 300 350 400	— — — —
Sintered pulverized fuel ash with natural sand	Coarse 800	1:6.1 1:5.5 1:5.0 1:3.6	1670 1700 1750 1790	20 25 30 40	300 300 350 400	— — — —
Pumice	500-800	1:6 1:4 1:2	1200 1250 1450	14 19 29	1200 1000 —	0.14
Exfoliated vermiculite	65-130	1:6	300-500	2	3000	0.10
Perlite	95-130	1:6	—	—	2000	0.03

Table 22.4. Typical Properties of common light weight concrete

S. No.	*Type of concrete*	*Bulk density of aggregate kg/m³*	*Dry density of concrete kg/m³*	*28 days compressive strength in MPa*	*Drying shrinkage 10⁻⁶*	*Thermal conductivity J/m²S°C/m*
1.	Pumice	500-800	1200	15	1200	0.14
2.	Perlite	40-200	400-500	1.2-3.0	2000	0.05
3.	Vermiculite	60-200	300-700	0.3-3.0	3000	0.10
4.	Cellular (Fly ash)	950 F. 1000	750 900	3.0 6.0	700 —	0.19 0.22
5.	Autoclaved aerated	—	800	4.0	800	0.25
6.	Sintered fly ash	F. 1050 C. 800	1500 1540	25 30	300 350	— —
7.	Sentered fly ash with natural sand	C. 800	1700	25	300	—

22.6. STRUCTURAL LIGHT WEIGHT CONCRETE

It is a concrete light in weight and sufficiently strong when used with steel reinforcement. Thus it is going to be more acceptable and economical material of construction than conventional concrete.

The 28 day compressive strength of structural light weight aggregate concrete is more than 17 MPa and air dried unit weight is not more than 1850 kg/m³. This concrete may consist either entirely of light weight aggregate or a combination of light weight and normal weight aggregate. For practical considerations, the common practice of producing structural light weight Concrete is to use normal sand as fine aggregate and light weight coarse aggregate of maximum size 19 mm. Concrete made with normal sand and light weight aggregate is known as *sanded light weight concrete* in contrast to "all light weight concrete."

22.6.1. Workability

Workability of light weight aggregate concrete needs special attention, as for equal workability light weight aggregate concrete gives a lower slump and a lower compacting factor than the normal weight aggregate concrete as work done by gravity is smaller in case of light weight aggregate concrete. On the other hand if a higher workability is kept, there will be a higher tendency of segregation. In case of higher slump and over vibrations, the mortar goes down and aggregate tends to float, which is a reverse phenomenon that of normal weight aggregate concrete. In such conditions the finishing operations of deck slab and floors will be difficult. To over come this difficulty, usually the maximum slump is restricted to 100 mm. Due to the porous nature of light weight aggregates they have high and rapid water absorption. If the aggregate is dry at the time of mixing, it will absorb water rapidly and the workability decreases quickly. This problem can be over come by mixing the aggregate with at least one half of the mixing water before adding cement to it. However this procedure will increase the density and decrease its thermal insulation.

The light weight aggregate mixes tend to be harsh, which can be reduced by air entrainment. Air entrainment reduces water requirements and also the tendency of segregation and bleeding. The usual total amount of air content by volume is 4 to 8% for 20 mm maximum size of aggregate and 5 to 9% for 10 mm maximum size of aggregate.

Light weight aggregate concrete exhibits higher moisture movement than the normal weight concrete. The wet concrete swells more while dry concrete shrinks more. Due to the higher drying shrinkage and lower tensile strength, the light weight aggregate concrete develops shrinkage cracks. The coefficients of thermal expansion of light weight aggregate concrete is much lower than ordinary concrete. Typical values are shown in in Table 22.5.

Table 22.5. Coefficient of thermal expansion of light weight aggregate concrete

S. No.	*Concrete with the light weight aggregate*	*Linear coeff. of thermal expansion determined over a range of −22°C 52°C in 10^{-6} per °C*
1.	Cinders	About 3.8
2.	Expanded shale	6.5 to 8.1
3.	Expanded slag	7.0 to 11.2
4.	Perlite	7.6 to 11.0
5.	Vermiculite	8.3 to 14.2
6.	Pumice	9.4 to 10.8

22.7. CHARACTERISTICS OF LIGHT-WEIGHT CONCRETE

Following are the important characteristics of light weight concrete:

1. **Low density.** The density of this concrete varies from 300 to 1200 kg/m^3. The lightest variety is suitable for insulation purposes while the heavier variety is used for structural purposes. The low density of cellular concrete makes it suitable for precast roofing and floor units. These units being lighter are easy to handle and transport from factory to the site.
2. **High strength.** The compressive strength of cellular concrete is high in relation to its density. The compressive strength of such concrete has been found to increase with the increase in its density. The tensile strength of cellular concrete is about 15 to 20% of its compressive strength. The strength to mass ratio of cellular concrete is much higher than normal concrete. Thus the weight of roof slab and floor of the cellular concrete are about 25% of the normal reinforced concrete.
3. **Durability.** Aerated concrete is slightly alkaline. Due to its porosity and low alkalinity it does not provide any protection to the steel reinforcement as provided by the dense compacted concrete. Thus the reinforcement used in cellular concrete needs special treatment for the protection against corrosion.
4. **Thermal insulation.** The insulation value of light weight concrete is about 3 to 4 times more than that of bricks and about 10 times that of concrete. The degree of insulation of 20 cm thick wall of aerated concrete of density of 800 kg/m^3 is the same as that of 40 cm thick brick wall of 1600 kg/m^3 density.
5. **Fire resistance.** The fire resistance properties of light weight concrete are excellent. Its low

thermal conductivity makes it suitable for the protection of other structures from the effect of fire.

6. **Sound insulation.** The sound insulation of cellular concrete is not as good as that of dense concrete.
7. **Shrinkage.** The shrinkage of light weight concrete is small. The autoclaving of cellular concrete reduces its dry shrinkage to 1/5th *i.e.* 20% of that occurring during air curing.
8. **Repairability.** The light weight concrete products can be easily cut, drilled, nailed and sawn. This property makes the construction easier. The local repair of the structure can be attended as and when required with out affecting the rest of the structure.
9. **Speed of construction.** By adopting prefabrication of units, the structure can be designed on the concept of modular coordination, which ensures a faster rate of construction.
10. **Economy.** Due to the high ratio of strength to mass and light weight of cellular concrete products, their use results in lesser consumption of steel. Composite floor construction using precast un reinforced cellular concrete blocks and reinforced concrete grid beams results in appreciable saving in the consumption of cement and steel. This reduces the cost of construction of roofs and floors considerably. Using this type of construction a saving of about 15-20% can be effected in the construction of roofs and floors in comparison to conventional construction.
11. **Quality control.** With the use of light weight concrete products a better quality control can be exercised as these units are factory made.

22.8. OTHER PROPERTIES OF LIGHT WEIGHT AGGREGATE CONCRETE

Followings are some of the other properties of light weight aggregate concrete as compared to normal weight concrete.

1. For the same strength, the modulus of elasticity of light weight concrete is lower by 25 to 50% than normal concrete. Hence its deflections are greater.
2. Its resistance to freezing and thawing is greater than normal weight Concrete due to the greater porosity of light weight aggregate, provided the aggregate is not saturated before mixing.
3. Its fire resistance is greater as light weight aggregate have a lesser tendency to spall. Thus concrete suffers a lesser loss of strength due to rise in temperature.
4. It is easy to cut to fix desired attachments.
5. For the same compressive strength its shear strength is lower by 15 to 25% and bond strength is lower by 20 to 50%. Thus in the design of reinforced concrete beams these differences have to be taken into account.
6. The tensile strain capacity of light weight aggregate is greater than normal weight aggregate. Thus the tensile strain capacity of light weight aggregate concrete is about 50% greater than normal weight concrete. Hence the ability to withstand restraint to movement *i.e.* due to internal temperature gradient is greater for light weight concrete.
7. For the same strength the creep of light weight aggregate concrete is about the same as that of normal weight concrete.

22.9. APPLICATIONS OF LIGHT WEIGHT CONCRETE

Light weight concrete can be used as follows:

1. As Load bearing masonry walls using cellular concrete blocks.
2. As precast floor and roof panels in all types of buildings.
3. As partition walls in all types of buildings as residential, industrial and institutional buildings.
4. As insulating materials to exterior walls in all types of buildings, specially in office and industrial buildings.
5. As a filler in the form of precast reinforced wall panels in multistoryed buildings.
6. As precast composite floor or wall panels etc.

22.10. MIX PROPORTION OF LIGHT WEIGHT CONCRETE

The water/cement ratio has the same influence on the strength of light weight aggregate concrete as that on normal aggregate concrete. Hence theoretically same procedure may be adopted for mix design as in the case of normal weight aggregate concrete. But in the absence of accurate values of absorption, specific gravity and free moisture content in the aggregate makes it difficult to apply the water/cement ratio law accurately for the mix proportion of light weight aggregate concrete.

Light weight aggregate produced artificially usually is bone dry If it is saturated before mixing, the strength of the concrete will be lower by 5 to 10% than, dry aggregate is used for the same cement content and workability. In case of bone dry aggregate, some of the mixing water is absorbed after mixing, but before setting, reducing the effective water/cement ratio. The density of concrete made with saturated aggregate is higher, but the resistance to freezing and thawing is reduced. On the other hand if the aggregate with high absorption is used with out pre soaking, it will be difficult to obtain workable and cohesive mix. In general, aggregate with more than 10% absorption should be pre soaked and air entrainment should be done.

Thus the light weight concrete mix design usually is established by trial mixes. The proportion of fine to coarse aggregate and water and cement requirements are estimated on the previous experience with a particular aggregate. The different degrees of absorption by different light weight aggregates is one of the main difficulty in the design of mix proportions.

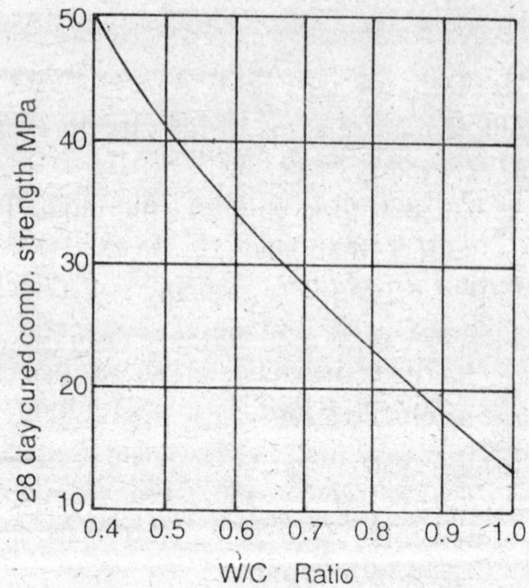

Fig. 22.2. Typical relationship between w/c ratio and comp. strength of light weight aggregate concrete

There are several methods to determine the aggregate content. Here the use of effective water/cement ratio for the calculation of aggregate content has been discussed. The method described here is based on the well known British mix design method. The steps involved to obtain the mix proportion for the stipulated 28 day strength are as follows:

Step 1. The target mean strength of the concrete is determined from the characteristic strength, coefficient of probability and standard deviation as $f_t = f_{ck} + K.S.$

Step 2. The required water/cement ratio for the required target strength is determined from the curve of Fig. 22.2

Step 3. For the water-cement ratio obtained in step 2, the aggregate-cement ratio (by volume), cement content in kg/m^3 and optimum percentage of fine aggregate for desired workability are selected from table 22.6 given below.

Step 4. To obtain the effective free water content for the mix, the water content is adjusted for water absorption and the moisture content of aggregates.

Step 5. For the data, obtained as above, a trial mix is prepared and water content is adjusted to maintain the desired workability. The density of fresh wet compacted concrete is calculated and cement content checked. If the cement content and density are not found correct, minor adjustment may be made either by adding or subtracting some quantity of cement and adding or subtracting some volume of fine aggregate as follows:

Volume of fresh concrete = Absolute volume of ingredients

i.e. 1000 litres

$$= \frac{\text{weight of cement}}{\text{density of cement}} + \frac{\text{weight of fine aggregate}}{\text{density of fine aggregate (Saturated surface dry)}}$$

$$+ \frac{\text{weight of coarse aggregate}}{\text{saturated surface dry density of coarse aggregate}} + \text{air} + \text{free water}$$

Table 22.6. Variation of cement content aggregate cement ratio, fine aggregate content with water-cement ratio for light weight aggregate concrete

Water cement ratio	*Degree of workability*						*Remarks*
	Medium compacting factor = 0.9 slump 15-75 mm			*High compacting factor 0.95 slump = 75 – 100 mm*			
	Cement kg/m³	*Aggregate cement ratio*	*F.A. %*	*Cement kg/m³*	*Aggregate cement ratio*	*F.A. %*	
0.40	525	3.0	28	591	2.65	27	
0.45	468	3.5	30	533	3.03	28	
0.50	419	4.04	32	474	3.50	30	
0.55	372	4.63	35	425	4.01	32	
0.60	332	5.35	40	383	4.55	34	
0.65	293	6.05	49	342	5.23	38	
0.70	260	6.83	58	306	5.99	44	
0.75	230	8.02	69	273	6.75	53	

Example 1. *Design a light weight aggregate concrete mix, with the following data:*

(*i*) *28 day characteristic strength = 20 MPa*

(*ii*) *Degree of workability desired = 0.95 C-F, slump (75-100 mm)*

(*iii*) *Degree of control at site = good*

(*iv*) *Unit weight of cement, F.A., C.A. = 1425 kg/m³, 1100 kg/m³ and 850 kg/m³ respectively*

(*v*) *The moisture content of fine and coarse aggregate by mass = 10 and 6% respectively*

(*vi*) *Short term absorption of F.A. & C.A. by mass = 5 and 11% respectively.*

Solution *Procedure*

(*i*) Target mean strength $f_t = 20 + 1.65 \times 6 = 20 + 9.90 \approx 30$ MPa

(*ii*) Water-cement ratio for 30 MPa strength from curve of Fig. 22.2 = 0.67

(*iii*) From table 22.6

Aggregate-cement ratio by inter pollution = 5.53

Fine aggregate percent = 40.25 ≈ 40%

Cement content by inter polation = 327.6 ≈ 328 kg/m³.

(*iv*) Dry volume per cubic metre of concrete—

(*a*) Cement $= \dfrac{328}{1425} = 0.23 \text{ m}^3$

Total Aggregate $= 5.53 \times 0.23 = 1.272 \text{ m}^3$

Fine aggregate = 40% of 1.272 = 0.51 m³

∴ Coarse aggregate $= 1.272 - 0.51 = 0.762 \text{ m}^3$

(*v*) Batch masses of ingredients for 1 m³ concrete in kg.

Ingradients	Water	Cement	F.A.	C.A.
	0.67 × 328	328	0.51 × 1100	0.762 × 850
Apparent masses	220.0	328	561.0	648.0
Adjustment for moisture content	– 56.1		10% of 561	6% of 698
	– 38.9		+ 56.1	+ 38.88
	– 95.0			

Absorption of aggregate

F.A. = 5% of 561 + = 28.05 kg

Coarse = 11% of 648 + = 71.28 kg

99.33 kg

∴ Corrected dry batch masses = 220 + 99.33 – 95.01 = 4.33 + 220 = 224.33

	Water	Cement	F.A.	C.A.
	224.33	328	561	648
mix proportion	0.68	1	1.7	1.98
	0.68	1	1.7	2.0

22.11. AERATED CONCRETE

It is one of the light weight concrete. It is a mixture of water, cement and finely crushed sand. Aerated concrete is obtained by introducing gas bubbles into the plastic mix of cement and sand mortar. The product obtained is cellular in structure containing voids of size 0.1 to 1 mm similar to sponge rubber. The skin of cells or voids must be able to withstand mixing and compaction pressure. This resulting concrete is known as aerated or cellular concrete, but strictly speaking, the use of word concrete is not appropriate as no coarse aggregate is used in it.

22.12. METHODS OF PRODUCTION OF AERATED CONCRETE

There are two basic methods of producing aerated concrete. An appropriate name is given to each product.

1. Gas concrete. It is obtained by a chemical reaction generating a gas in the fresh mortar. When this mortar sets, it contains a large number of gas bubbles. The consistency of the mortar should be such that the gas produced may expand it, but gas should not excape from it *i.e.* the consistency of mortar should be correct. The speed of gas evolution, consistency of mortar and its setting time should match with each other.

For generating gas, finally divided aluminum powder is most commonly used. The proportion of aluminum powder may be 0.2% of the mass of the cement. The reaction between this active powder and calcium hydroxide or alkalis, librates hydrogen bubbles. Powdered zinc or aluminum alloy can also be used. Some times hydrogen peroxide is used to produce oxygen bubbles.

2. Foamed Concrete. It is produced by adding a foaming agent in the mix which introduces and stabilizes the air bubbles during mixing at high speed. The foaming agent usually used is some form of hydrolyzed protein or resin soap. In some processes a stable pre formed foam is added to the mortar during mixing in a ordinary mixer.

The aerated concrete may be made with out sand, but such concrete can only be used for non structural purposes such as for heat insulation. The density of aerated concrete produced with out sand varies from 200 to 300 kg/m^3. When the aerated concrete is produced by a mixture of cement and very fine sand, the density of the usual mixes varies from 500 to 1100 kg/m^3. In the case of other light weight concretes, the strength of aerated concrete varies with the density. The thermal conductivity of aerated concrete also varies with its density.

According to HOFF, the strength of cellular concrete can be expressed as a function of void contents taken as the sum of the induced voids and volume of evaporated water.

The strength of a concrete having density of 500 kg/m^3 is found in the range of 3 to 4 MPa (30 to 40 kg/cm^2 and thermal conductivity of about 0.1 J/m^{2}S°C/m and for a concrete with a density of 1400 kg/m^3, the corresponding values of strength and thermal conductivity would be approximately 12 to 14 MPa and 0.4 J/m^{2}S°C/m. By comparison the conductivity of ordinary concrete has been found about 10 times more than that of cellular concrete. Further it should be noted that thermal conductivity increases linearly with the moisture content. At 20% moisture content the conductivity is found almost double of that when the moisture content is zero.

The modulus of elasticity of aerated concrete usually varies between 1.7 and 3.5 GPa (0.25 to 0.5 $\times 10^6$ PSi). It's creep expressed on the basis of stress/strength ratio, (creep per unit of stress) is found to be the same as that of ordinary concrete. However on the basis of equal stress, the specific creep of aerated concrete is found higher in comparison with ordinary concrete.

The thermal movements, shrinkage and moisture movements of aerated concrete have been found higher in comparision with light weight aggregate concrete of the same strength. But these can be reduced by auto claving *i.e.* high steam curing. Autoclaving also improves the strength of the aerated concrete.

The permeability of high pressure steam cured aerated concrete decreases with the increase in its moisture content, but even when the concrete is dry, the permeability at low pressure is negligible. The relation between the wet density and compressive strength of aerated concrete is shown in Fig. 22.3 Fig. 22.4 shows the relation of dry density and autoclaved high pressure steam cured concrete. Flowing aerated concrete can be obtained by using a super plasticizer.

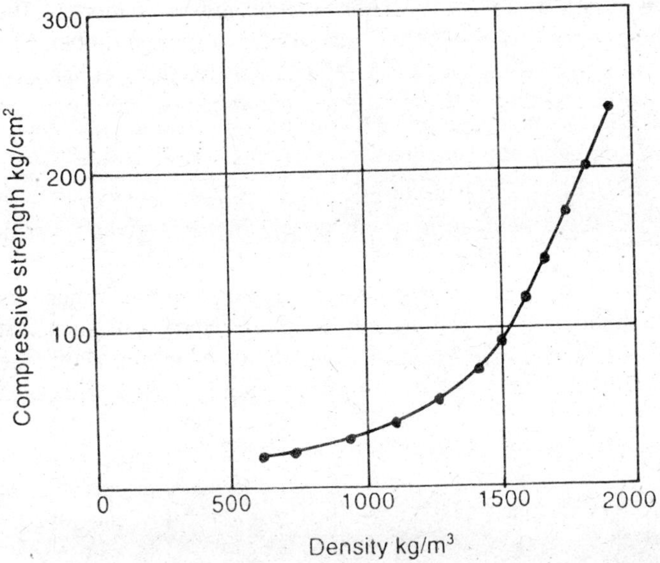

Fig. 22.3. Relation between comp. strength and wet. density of aerated concrete

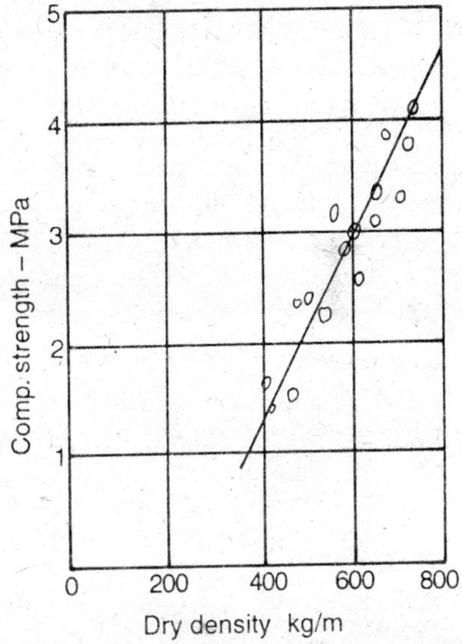

Fig. 22.4. Relation between strength and density of high pressure steam cured aerated concrete

22.13. USES OF AERATED CONCRETE

The aerated concrete usually is used for the following purposes:

1. Due to its low thermal conductivity and weight, mostly it is used for heat insulation purposes.
2. As it offers better fire resistance than ordinary concrete, it is used for fire proofing.
3. Structurally aerated concrete is used mostly in the form of precast members or autoclaved blocks. It can also be used for floor construction in place of hollow tile floor.
4. Recently it has been used for light insulation.

22.14. PROPERTIES OF AERATED CONCRETE

Aerated Concrete has the following properties.

1. It can be sawn, cut, nailed. It can hold nails.
2. It is quite durable.
3. The rate of water penetration through aerated concrete is low.
4. It has better resistance to frost.
5. Its water absorption is high. Hence untreated aerated concrete should not be exposed to aggressive atmosphere.

22.15. NO FINES CONCRETE

As the name suggests, this concrete does not contain fine aggregate (sand). This concrete usually is an agglomeration (*i.e.* group of particle not arranged in any particular order *i.e.* it is made of nominally one size coarse aggregate particles. Each particle has a cement paste coating of about 1.3 mm thickness around it. Thus large pores exist with in the body of the concrete which are responsible for its low strength. How ever due to large size of pores or voids no capillary movement of water takes place as in the case of aerated concrete. Hence the rate of penetration of water in no fines concrete is low.

For a given type of aggregate, the density of no fines concrete depends mainly on the grading of the aggregate. With one size aggregate, the density is about 10% lower than when a well graded aggregate of the same specific gravity is used. The usual size of aggregate used in no fines concrete is 10 to 20 mm. However 5% over size and 10% under size is permissible, but no material should be smaller than 5 mm. A no fines concrete having a low density of the order of 640 kg/m^3 can be produced by using light weight aggregate. When normal aggregate is used, its density may vary from 1600 to 2000 kg/m^3. Sharp edged aggregate should not be used, the sharp edges will be crushed under load.

22.16. MIX PROPORTION

Generally no fines concrete is produced with a cement aggregate ratio of 1:6 to 1:10, but practical mixes vary rather widely. The variation of cement aggregate ratio for lean mixes is from 1:10 to 1:20. The corresponding cement contents are 130 kg/m^3 to 70 kg/m^3. Where as in case of normal concrete made with well graded aggregate the water/cement ratio is the controlling factor for the strength development. In case of no fines concrete there is a narrow optimum value of the w/c ratio for any given aggregate. A higher water-cement ratio than the optimum would make the cement paste drain away from the aggregate particles, while with too little water-cement ratio the paste would not be sufficient adhesive. The optimum water-cement-ratio varies between 0.38 and 0.52 depending upon the cement-content necessary for sufficient coating of aggregate. Actually the strength of no fines concrete is governed by water-cement ratio, cement aggregate ratio and unit weight of concrete. The relation between compressive strength, W/C ratio and A/C ratio is shown in Fig. 22.5.

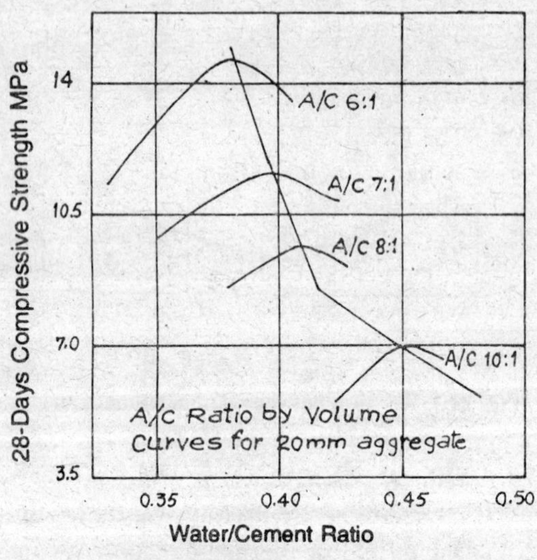

Fig. 22.5. Relation between comp-strength, w/c and A/c ratio for no fines concrete

The compressive strength of no fines concrete generally varies between 1.4 MPa to 14 MPa depending mainly on its density, which is governed by the cement content in the concretes shown in Table 22.7 below.

Table 22.7. Typical data for 10 mm to 20 mm no fines concrete

Aggregate/Cement ratio by vol.	*W/c ratio by mass*	*Density kg/m^3*	*28 day comprssive strength MPa*
6	0.38	2020	14
7	0.40	1970	12
8	0.41	1940	10
10	0.45	1870	7

The actual strength of no fines concrete should be determined by tests. The increase in strength with age is similar as that of ordinary concrete.

No fines concrete develops very little cohesion. Hence form work should not be removed till it has developed sufficient strength to hold the materials together. Moist curing is important, especially in windy or in a dry climate as it has very small thickness of cement paste.

22.17. PROPERTIES OF NO FINES CONCRETE

Following are the properties of no fines concrete:

1. No fines concrete compacts very little. Hence the vibration should be applied for a very short period otherwise the cement paste would run off.
   (*b*) Roding is not recommended.
2. There is no workability test for no fines concrete. The visual check for ensuring even coating of aggregate particles with cement paste is sufficient.
3. As no fines concrete segregates, it can be dropped from a considerable height and placed in high lifts.
4. The modulus of rupture of no fines concrete is about 30% of its compressive strength. This proportion is higher than the normal weight concrete.
5. The shrinkage of no fines concrete is much lower than that of normal weight concrete as the contraction is restrained by the large volume of aggregate relative to the paste. However the initial rate of shrinkage is higher as large surface area of the cement paste is exposed to the air. After one month drying, the value of shrinkage is between 120×10^{-6} to 200×10^{-6}. No fines concrete made with river bed gravel showed a drying shrinkage of the order of 200×10^{-6}, which is about 50% of the conventional concrete. In case of no fines concrete 50 to 80% of the total shrinkage takes place with in about 10 days where as in the case of conventional concrete the drying shrinkage with in 10 days is about 20 to 30% only.
6. The thermal movement of no fines concrete is about 70% of that of normal weight concrete. The actual value of coefficient of thermal expansion depends on the type of aggregate used.
7. The thermal conductivity of no fines concrete is low. For light weight aggregate it is found as 0.22 $J/m^2 S°C/m$ and 0.81 $J/m^2 S°C/m$ for normal weight concrete. However the high moisture content of the concrete increases the thermal conductivity appreciably.
8. No fines concrete is highly resistant to frost due to the absence of capillaries in it, provided the pores are not saturated. In case, the pores are saturated, freezing would cause a rapid disintegration. High absorption upto 12% by mass makes no fines concrete un suitable for use in foundations and in situations where it may be in contact with water.
9. To reduce the permeability to air, the external walls of the no fines concrete should be plastered or rendered on both sides. Painting and rendering reduces the sound absorbing properties of no fines concrete, so that where the accoustic properties are considered more important, one side of the wall should not be rendered.
10. Its cost is low as the cement content is as low as 70 to 130 kg/m^3.
11. Typical values of modulus of elasticity of no fines concrete are shown in the following Table 22.8.

Table 22.8. Showing modulus of elasticity of no fines concrete of various strength

Compressive strength MPa	*Modulus of elasticity*	
	GPa	*PSi* $\times 10^6$
4.8	10.3	1.5
3.4	9.0	1.3
2.4	6.9	1.0

22.18. USES OF NO FINES CONCRETE

1. No fines concrete normally is not used in reinforced concrete. However if it is essential to use no

fines concrete in reinforced concrete, then the reinforcement has to be coated with a thin layer of about 3 mm of cement paste to improve its bond and prevent corrosion. Shot creating may be applied for coating the reinforcement.

2. In spite of its lower weight and strength it can be used for even of many storyed buildings.

QUESTIONS

1. Discuss the use of no fines concrete.
2. Discuss the properties of insulating concrete.
3. What is the difference between the light weight concrete and light weight aggregate concrete?
4. Discuss structural light weight concrete.
5. What are the main differences between light weight and normal weight concretes?
6. What happens when alluminium powder is added to the mix.
7. Compare the following properties of light weight concrete with normal weight concrete.
   (*a*) Modulus of elasticity (*b*) Shrinkage
   (*c*) Creep
8. Discuss the effect of density and moisture content on thermal conductivity of concrete.
9. Discuss aerated concrete and no fines concrete in detail.
10. Discuss the properties of aerated concrete.
11. Discuss the properties of no fines concrete.
12. Discuss the uses of aerated and no fines concrete.

OBJECTIVE TYPE QUESTIONS

1. Identify the true and false statements of the followings
   (*a*) Light weight concrete can increase the efficiency of concrete as a structural material.
   (*b*) The density of light weight concrete varies from 300 to 1850 kg/m^3
   (*c*) The light weight concrete reduces the dead load of the structure
   (*d*) The use of light weight concrete increases the progress of construction
   (*e*) The use of light weight concrete reduces the handling and transport cost of the material
   (*f*) Light weight concrete has good sound insulation.
2. The light weight concrete may be produced by
   (*a*) Incorporating air in its composition (*b*) Using light weight aggregate
   (*c*) Omitting sand fraction from the aggregate (*d*) Forming air voids in cement slurry
   (*e*) Any of the above
3. Identify the in correct statement of the followings
   (*a*) Light weight concrete has high thermal insulation
   (*b*) Light weight concrete has excellent fire resistance
   (*c*) Light weight concrete has low drying shrinkage
   (*d*) Light weight concrete has high sound insulation
4. Light weight aggregate is produced by
   (*a*) Sintering (pulverising) fly ash (*b*) Expanding clay by heating *i.e.* bloating clay
   (*c*) Using blast-furnace slag (*d*) By exfoliation of vermiculite
   (*e*) Any of the above
5. Light weight concrete is used for
   (*a*) Improving thermal insulation
   (*b*) To reduce the dead load of the structure
   (*c*) For construction of non bearing and partition walls etc.
   (*d*) As filler in wall panels of multistory buildings (*e*) Any of the above
6. Aerated concrete is produced by the addition
   (*a*) Sodium silicate (*b*) Zinc sulphate
   (*c*) Aluminimum powder (*d*) Copper sulphate
   (*e*) Non of the above

7. Identify the incorrect statement of the followings
   (*a*) As the density of aerated concrete increases its strength decreases
   (*b*) Aerated concrete has high thermal insulation property
   (*c*) Aerated concrete has high sound insulation property
   (*d*) The density of aerated concrete varies from 300 kg/m^3 to 800 kg/m^3
   (*e*) The lower grade aerated concrete is used for insulated purposes
8. Identify the incorrect statement of the followings
   (*a*) The aggregate/cement ratio of no fines concrete varies from 6:1 to 10:1
   (*b*) The aggregate/cement ratio of no fines concrete varies from 3:1 to 5:1
   (*c*) The water/cement ratio of no fines concrete varies from 0.38 to 0.52
   (*d*) The water/cement ratio of no fines concrete varies from 0.45 to 0.75
   (*e*) The consistency of no fines concrete can be measured either from slump or compacting factor method accurately
   (*f*) The density of no fines concrete made with light weight aggregate is about 360 kg/m^3
   (*g*) The drying shrinkage of no fines concrete is equal to normal concrete
   (*h*) The drying shrinkage of no fines concrete is about 50% of normal conventional concrete
   (*i*) The rate of drying shrinkage of no fines concrete is about 2.5 times that of normal concrete
9. In the production of aerated concrete, the amount of aluminum powder is percent of cement
   (*a*) 1.5% (*b*) 1.8% (*c*) 0.5% (*d*) 0.2%
10. Identify the incorrect statements
    (*a*) The thermal conductivity and weight of aerated concrete is more
    (*b*) The thermal conductivity and weight of aerated concrete is low hence it is used for thermal insulation
    (*c*) Aerated concrete is not durable
    (*d*) Aerated concrete is quite durable
    (*e*) Resistance to frost of aerated concrete is not good
    (*f*) Resistance to frost of aerated concrete is quite good
    (*g*) The fire resistance of aerated concrete is better than ordinary concrete, hence used for fire protection
    (*h*) The water absorption of aerated concrete is low
11. Identify the correct statement(s)
    (*a*) No fines concrete is not suitable for RCC works
    (*b*) The strength and weight of no fires concrete are high
    (*c*) The cement/aggregate ratio of no fines concrete vary from 1:10 to 1:20
    (*d*) No fines concrete compacts well. Hence any amount of vibration may be applied
    (*e*) The workability of no fines concrete can be tested by any method available for testing ordinary concrete
    (*f*) There is no workability test for no fines concrete
    (*g*) No fines concrete segregates very much, hence it should not be dropped from much height
    (*h*) No fines concrete segregates very little, hence it can be dropped from a considerable height
12. Identity the correct statement(s)
    (*a*) The modulus of rupture of no fines concrete is about 30% of its compressive strength
    (*b*) The frost resistance of no fines concrete is very high
    (*c*) The thermal movement of no fines concrete is about 70% of that of normal concrete
    (*d*) The shrinkage of no fines concrete is much lower than the normal weight concrete
    (*e*) Thermal conductivity of no fines concrete low

Answers

1. [False (*f*)]	4. (*e*)	7. (*a, c*)	10. (*a, c, e, h*)
2. (*e*)	5. (*e*)	8. (*b, d, e, g*)	11. (*a, c, f, h*)
3. (*d*)	6. (*c*)	9. (*d*)	12. All are correct

23

Nuclear Energy Shield, Ferro Cement And Sulpher Concrete

23.1. INTRODUCTION

Present era is the era of technological advancement. Due to the development of nuclear energy much advancement has been made in the field of science and technology. Though the development of nuclear energy has changed the pace of development in all sphere of life, but at the same time it has created some problems of safety for the perssonel working on it. Thus it is essential that protection against nuclear hazards should be provided to them. High density concrete has been found a very effective material to check nuclear energy hazards. It is also called *nuclear energy shield.*

In this chapter along with nuclear shield sulpher concrete and Fero-cement have been discussed.

23.2. HIGH DENSITY CONCRETE

As the name suggests, the density of this concrete varies from 3360 kg/m^3 to 3840 kg/m^3, where as the density of normal concrete is of the order of 2400 kg/m^3. The density of light weight concrete is about 1900 kg/m^3 and that of normal concrete about 2400 kg/m^3. Thus the density of high density concrete is about 50% more than the density of conventional concrete. However this concrete can be produced of density upto 5200 kg/m^3 using iron as both fine and coarse aggregate.

With the advent of the nuclear energy, there is a considerable demand of the concrete technologists in the market. Due to the use of nuclear energy producing reactors, large scale production of penetrating radiation and radio active materials also has taken place. Thus all nuclear energy producing units such as nuclear reactors, particle accelerator, industrial radiography, *x*-ray and gamma ray therapy units require nuclear shielding material for the protection of the operating perssonnel against the biological hazards such as radiation. The normal as well as high density concrete is effective and economical for the construction of permanent shield against radiation.

23.3. TYPES OF RADIATION AND THEIR HAZARDS

The radiation can be classified into two groups as follows. These radiations are considered in the design of biological shields.

1. Electro-magnetic waves
2. Nuclear particles

1. **Electro-magnetic waves.** These waves are of high frequency and have high energy. These waves are known as *X* and gamma rays. These are the only electro-magnetic waves which need shields for the protection of personnel. Though they are similar to high rays, but possess higher energy and greater penetrating power. *X* and gamma rays are identical, but their source of production are

different. Both these rays have high penetration power, but they can be adequately absorbed by an appropriate thickness of concrete shield.

2. **Nuclear particles.** Nuclear particles consist of nuclei of atoms or their fragments. These fragments are known as neutrons, protons, alpha and beta particles. Except neutrons all the other particles possess an electric charge. On the other hand neutrons are un charged and remain un affected by electric field, until they interact by collision with a nucleus. They have no definite range and some of them may penetrate any shield.

Alpha, beta and proton particles carry electrical charge, which interact with electric field, surrounding the atom of the shielding material and lose their energy considerably. Generally these particles do not create a separate shielding problem, though accelerated protons at high energy levels may require heavy shielding comparable to that required for neutrons.

Thus *X* and gamma rays, and neutrons need protection shield. As stated above *X* and gamma rays are similar except in energy and origin. The biological hazards of radiation arise from the fact that the radiation interact with human tissues. In the process of interaction some of the energy of the human tissues is lost. The energy loss is sufficient to ionize the atoms of the cells, up setting the delicate chemical balance and causing the death of cells. If enough cells are affected, the organism dies. Thus the radiation must be reduced or weakend sufficiently, so that the remainder or left out radiation may not cause permanent damage to the persons exposed to it.

Apart from biological hazards, a very high temperature is also generated by the nuclear reaction. Thus the shielding is necessary to protect the electronic and other sensitive equipment in the vicinity.

23.4. SHIELDING ABILITY OF CONCRETE

Due to the following characteristics, concrete has been found an excellent shielding material

1. It has sufficient capacity to absorb the radiation both of neutron and gamma rays, reducing the radiation to a very weak state.
2. It has good mechanical properties as strength and durability.
3. When green, it can be moulded into any shape. Thus the ease of construction makes concrete a specially suitable material for radiation shielding.
4. Its initial and maintenance cost is also relatively low.

23.4.1. Disadvantages

Its disadvantages are as follows:

1. As the sections of the structure are heavy, they need more space. Thus the use of concrete as shielding against radiation needs more space.
2. The weight of shielding concrete is very high in the range of 3360 to 3840 kg/m^3.

23.5. AGGREGATES TO BE USED IN SHIELDING CONCRETE

For making shielding concrete heavy weight aggregate having a specific gravity between 3.5 to 4.0 is needed. There are many aggregates whose specific gravity is more than 3.5 for making a heavy weight concrete. Some of natural commercially used aggregates are as follows:

1. Barite
2. Magnetite
3. Ilmenite
4. Limonite
5. Hematite etc.

Barite is the most common natural aggregate having a specific gravity of 4.1 with a 95% purity. Steel and iron aggregates in the form of shots and punching scrap for use as a heavy weight aggregate are also available in the market. They are known as *artificial aggregate.*

While selecting the aggregate to be used, the availability of the aggregate locally and their physical properties should be considered. In general the heavy weight aggregate should be strong, clean, inert and relatively free from deleterious materials which might impair the strength of concrete. The capacity of various heavy aggregates to absorb gamma rays is directly proportional to their density. Also the heavier elements are more effective in absorbing fast neutrons by inelastic collisions than the lighter one. Therefore as heavy aggregate as possible should be used for the construction of shield.

However, density is not the only factor to be considered in the selection of a aggregate for neutron concrete shield. The desired increase in hydrogen content required to slow down the fast neutrons, can be accomplished by the use of hydrous ores. These materials contain a high percentage of water of hydration. On heating the concrete, some of this fixed water in the aggregate may be lost. Lemonite and goethite are reliable sources of hydrogen as long as shield temperature does not exceed 200°C, where as serpentine is good upto 400°C. The physical properties of high density aggregate are shown in Table 23.1 below.

Table 23.1. Physical properties of high density aggregate concrete

Aggregate	*Limonite*	*Limonite + magnetite*	*Barite*		*Magnetite*	*Iron limonite*
Placement	*Conventional*	*Pre packed*	*Conventiond*	*Pre packed*	*Conventional*	*Pre packed*
Density (kg/m^3)	2960	3360	3620	3680	3580	4370
Compressive strength MPa	42.0	33.0	44.0	24.0	41.0	23.0
Modulus of elasticity GPa	32.0	36.0	31.0	26.0	31.0	39.0
Shrinkage %	0.021	0.023	0.029	0.029	0.018	0.013

23.6. REQUIREMENTS OF RADIATION SHIELDING CONCRETE

The important requirements of radiation shielding concrete are as follows:

1. High density of the concrete. The higher the density of the concrete, higher the absorption of radiation. The radiation shielding quality of concrete can be increased by increasing its density.
2. The other important requirement of radiation shielding concrete is its structural strength even at high temperature.

Thus to produce high density and high strength concrete, it is necessary to control the water/cement ratio very strictly. Appropriate admixture and proper vibrators for good compaction should be employed. After that good quality control should be followed.

High density concrete used for shielding differs from normal weight concrete in the following respects.

High density concrete should contain sufficient material of light atomic weight, which produces hydrogen. Some times in high density concrete serpentine aggregates are used due to their ability to retain water of crystallisation at high temperatures which assure a source of hydrogen. The availability of water of crystallisation in all heavy weight aggregate is not necessary.

High density concrete may contain high content of cement and may exhibit increased creep and shrinkage. Due to the high density of aggregate, it has a tendency of segregation. Coarse aggregate used may be of only high density mineral aggregate, or a mixture of mineral aggregate and steel particles or only steel particles. Experiments have shown that if only smooth cubical pieces of steel or iron ore are used as coarse aggregate, the compressive strength will not be more than 21 MPa, regardless of the water/cement ratio or grout mixture ratio. If sheared reinforcing bars are used as aggregate along with good grout, normal strength will be obtained. The grout used in high density pre placed aggregate concrete should be some what richer than that used in normal density pre placed concrete. High modulus of elasticity, low thermal expansion, and low elastic and creep deformation are the ideal properties for both high density and normal concrete.

23.7. PROPERTIES OF HIGH DENSITY CONCRETE

Following properties of high density concrete have been observed:

1. The strength of this concrete measured on standard cylinders has been found 42 MPa at 28 days for a water/cement ratio 0.58 and 24 MPa at water/cement ratio 0.9.
2. The density of this concrete for a mix of 1:4.6:6.4 with water/cement ratio of 0.58 has been found as 3700 kg/m^3.
3. The coefficient of thermal expansion of barite concrete measured in the range of temperature of 4°C to 38°C is found about twice that of normal concrete.
4. The modulus of elasticity and poisson's ratio of high density concrete and normal concrete are approximately the same.
5. Shrinkage of high density concrete is about 1/4 to 1/3 of the normal concrete.
6. Thermal conductivity, diffusivity etc. of high strength concrete are considerably lower than corresponding values for normal aggregate concrete.
7. Concrete made with barite aggregate does not stand well to weathering.
8. Fine barite aggregate delay the setting and hardening process of the concrete, hence trial mixes are advisable.
9. No entrained air should be permitted in this concrete. However use of de-entraing agent is suggested.

23.8. SULPHER CONCRETE (SC)

In recent years, there is enoromous increase in the production of sulpher, especially in Canada. In Canada there is a problem to consume the large quantity of sulpher produced. This situation has led to use the sulpher as a low cost construction material for producing sulpher concrete and sulpher infiltrated concrete.

Sulpher concrete consists of sulpher, fine and coarse aggregate only. It contain neither cement nor water. It attains high strength at early age of the order of 35 MPa in 8 hours.

23.9. MIX PROPORTION

For optimum strength and workability the typical mix proportions are as 20% sulpher, 32% fine aggregate and 48% coarse aggregate and 5% silica flour, which comes as 1:1.6:2.4. The ratio of fine to coarse aggregate comes as 1:1.5. The grading of the aggregate should be as to give a minimum void content. When a comparison of 1:1.6:2.4 sulpher concrete made with conventional portland cement concrete of equal strength having proportions as 1:1.8:2.6 with water/cement ratio as 0.41, showed that sulpher concrete gained strength very rapidly and reached its ultimate strength in 6 to 8 hours under normal ambient temperature and humidity conditions where as normal portland cement concrete attained its ultimate strength in about 1 year time.

23.10. METHOD OF PRODUCTION

Either of the following two methods may be adopted for the production of sulpher concrete.

1. **Method No. 1.** In this method the powdered sulpher and aggregates are mixed in a conventional mixer provided with a heater. With the help of this heater, the temperative of the mix is raised rapidly to a temperature of 140°C. At this temperature the ingredients of the mix form a uniform mixture, which can be cast into moulds.
2. **Method No. 2.** In this method the coarse aggregate is preheated slowly to a temperature of about 180°C and then this aggregate is fed into a tilting drum mixer. Now a sufficient quantity of sulpher is put into the drum to coat the coarse aggregate. Then the fine aggregate is added followed by the remaining sulpher. At this stage a workability agent such as silica flour is also added and the mixture is cast into the moulds or form. To allow for the contraction of sulpher on cooling in the

mould or form, a little extra mixture is filled. After cooling the surplus concrete is removed by sawing.

23.11. PROPERTIES OF SULPHER CONCRETE

The physical and mechanical properties of sulpher concrete are as follows based on the work of Shri V.M. Malhotra.

Property	Range
Compressive strength MPa (145 PSi)	28 — 70
Direct tensile strength MPa	3 — 8
Modulus of rupture MPa	3 — 10
Modulus of elasticity GPa (10^6PSi)	20 — 45
Coefficient of thermal expansion 10^{-6} per °C (10^{-6} per °F)	8 — 35
Thermal conductivity J/m^{2}S°C/m	0.4 — 2.0
Water absorption percent	0 — 1.5

Note: 145 lbs/inch^2 = 1 N/mm^2 (1 MPa)
1 GPa = (10^4 MPa)

23.12. ADVANTAGES OF SULPHER CONCRETE

Following advantages have been observed of sulpher concrete

1. As compared with portland cement concrete, sulpher concrete gains strength very rapidly and attains about 90% of its ultimate strength in 6 to 8 hours under normal temperature and humidity conditions.
2. Sulpher concrete made with crushed aggregate gives much higher strength than made with natural gravel.
3. The strength values obtained from large specimens have been found lower. The decrease probably may be due to combined effect of specimen size and lower rate of cooling while in mould. This aspect of sulpher concrete can pose a serious problem for thick structural members.

These advantages make the sulpher concrete suitable for use in pre cast units for out door applications and its chemical durability makes it suitable for industrial plant use.

Disadvantages

It has the following disadvantages:

1. It has a low melting point of 119°C with a consequential loss of strength.
2. It is vulnerable to combustion and produces toxic gases.
3. It creeps more than portland cement concrete.
4. It has poor resistance to freezing and thawing.
5. It produces corrosive effect on reinforcing steel under wet or humid conditions.
6. It is very brittle.

These disadvantages make the sulpher concrete unsuitable for most structural applications.

23.13. SULPHER INFILTRATED CONCRETE (SIC)

Sulpher infiltrated concrete was developed as an economical alternative to polymer impregnated concrete (PIC) to be used for higher strength and durable precast elements. Sulpher is considerably cheaper than polymers and the technique of impregnation is more simple. These factors result in cost benefits.

23.14. PRODUCTION OF SULPHER INFILTRATED CONCRETE (SIC)

The concrete to be infiltrated should be produced using normal aggregates with aggregate/cement ratios between 3:1 to 5:1. The water/cement ratio should be high between 0.7 and 0.8. The size of coarse aggregate should be 10 mm and below. It should be well graded. The fine aggregate should be of good quality. Sulpher also should be of high purity of 99.9%.

23.14.1. Infiltration Procedure

Procedure A. After moist curing of elements for 24 hours at about 23°C, they are dried at 121°C to 125°C for an other 24 hours. After drying, the specimens are immersed in molten sulpher at 121°C under vaccum for 3 hours. The specimens are removed from container, wiped clean of sulpher and allowed to cool to room temperature for one hour and weighed to determine the weight of sulpher infiltrated in concrete.

The period of immersion depends upon the type and size of the member. For lean concrete the period of immersion is 2 hours under vacuum. After this period the vacuum is released and the specimens are soaked for an additional half an hour in the molten sulpher under atmospheric pressure. After this period the elements are removed from the molten sulpher wiped clean and allowed to cool. It is weighed to determine the weight of sulpher infiltrated in concrete.

In case of low water/cement ratio concretes which are relatively dense, external pressure is applied after the release of vacuum to force sulpher into the concrete. The above procedure may be modified to suit the individual job conditions. However following points should be kept in mind.

1. For concretes with a water/cement ratio of the order 0.65, the one day old elements must be handled with care to avoid damage.
2. The drying temperature should be kept as high as possible, but not exceeding 150°C, as the higher temperature may damage the gel structure of the young hydrated cement paste. The period of drying will depend on the type and size of the element.
3. The period of vacuum (evacuation time) appears to be less critical than the immersion time in molten sulpher after evacuation. For concretes with water/cement ratio of about 0.55 increased immersion time is essential to achieve full infiltration.

Procedures B. In this case, the dried concrete specimen is placed in an air tight container and subjected to vacuum pressure of 2 mm of mercury for 2 hours. After releasing the vacuum, the specimens are soaked in the molten sulpher at atmospheric pressure for an other half an hour. The specimen is taken out, wiped clean, cooled to room temperature for about an hour. The specimen is weighed and the weight of sulpher impregnated in concrete is determined.

The specimens made by both the procedures are tested in compression and tension by splitting method. From the results it has been observed that:

1. The compressive strength of sulpher infiltrated specimens (cubes and cylinders) is enormously higher than the strength of plain moist cured specimens. It is found that with water/cement ratio 0.7, the increase in compressive strength of cubes prepared by procedure B is found about 7 times higher. With the use of 0.8 water/cement ratio, cubes prepared by procedure B gave about 10 times higher strength.
2. Similarly specimens prepared by procedure B gave more than 4 times increase in splitting tensile strength.
3. The elastic properties of sulpher infiltrated concrete improved by 100%.
4. Sulpher infiltrated concrete showed a very high resistance to freezing and thawing. The sulpher infiltrated concrete was found in good condition even after 1230 cycles when prepared by procedure B, while plain moist cured concrete disintegrated after about 40 cycles. Concrete made with procedure A, deteriorated after about 480 cycles.

The improvement in the strength of sulpher impregnated concrete may be due to the fact that randomly distributed pores in the body of the concrete have regions of stress concentration when loaded externally. The impregnation of these porous bodies by some material would modify the stress concentration. The extent of modification will depend how well the impregnant has penetrated into the smaller pores. The test results of specimens prepared by both procedures are shown below in Table 23.2

Table 23.2. Typical values of compressive strength of 5 cm cubes moist cured and sulpher infiltrated cubes

Duration of moist curing hours	*Duration of drying in hours*	*Age at test in hours*	*Strength moist cured cubes MPa*	*Compressive strength of sulpher infiltrated cubes*			
				Procedure A		*Procedure B*	
				Sulpher infiltrated %	*Strength MPa*	*Sulpher infiltrated %*	*Strength MPa*
24	24	54	13.6	9.1	68.0	12.6	108.5

Details of mix

Water/cement ratio = 0.70

Aggregate/cement ratio = 8.5:1

Ratio of C.A. to F.A. = 1:1

Table 23.3. Typical values of compressive and splitting tensile strength 7.5 × 15 cms moist cured and sulpher infiltrated cylinders

Duration of moist curing hours	*Duration of drying in hours*	*Age at test in hour*	*Compression Strength of moist cured cylinders in MPa*	*Sulpher infiltrated cylinders using procedure B only*			
				Tensile strength in MPa	*Sulpher loading %*	*Compression strength MPa*	*Splitting tensile strength MPa*
24	24	54	9.0	1.9	12.4	72.0	10.5

Note. Mix proportion same as above.

23.15. USE OF SULPHER INFILTRATED CONCRETE

The techniques of production of this concrete are simple, inexpensive and effective. The attainment of strength in about 2 days makes this process all the more attractive.

As the high strength of concrete can be achieved in a very short interval of time, the sulpher infiltrated concrete can be used for the manufacture of precast roofing elements, fencing posts, sewer pipes and railway sleepers. It can also be used in industry, where high corrosion resistant concrete is required. However this method can not be employed conveniently to cast insitu concrete. Further it has been observed that the sulpher infiltrated pre cast concrete units are cheaper than normal concrete. The added cost of sulpher and process may be offset by the savings in the concrete.

23.16. DURABILITY OF SIC

1. The performance of the sulpher infiltrated concrete generally has been found satisfactory against freezing and thawing, sea water attack, wetting and drying conditions.
2. It is more durable than conventional concrete in high concentrations of H_2SO_4 and HCl.
3. The strength properties are not significantly affected when exposed to short term temperatures upto 100°C. At these temperatures it shows certain amount of ductility before failure.
4. The increase in abrasion resistance depends on the sulpher loading in the concrete. The sulpher filling of the pores of the concrete provides an un interrupted path for heat flow resulting in increased thermal conductivity over that of normal dry concrete.
5. This concrete provides a corrosive protection cover to the embedded steel. The sulpher loading required for a given corrosive protection depends upon the water/cement ratio used in the concrete. Higher the water/cement ratio, higher the sulpher loading required. The minimum sulpher loading for 0.7 water/cement ratio is 10% and for 0.4 water/cement ratio 5% sulpher loading is sufficient.
6. When left in stagnant water for a long time, slight leaching of sulpher has been observed and the concrete showed undesirable expansion followed by cracks.

23.17. FERRO-CEMENT

Essentially ferro cement is a form of reinforced concrete, but it differs from the conventional type of reinforced concrete. The reinforcement used in it consists of closely spaced, multiple layers of wire mesh or fine rods completely surrounded by cement mortar. Ferro cement is much thinner than reinforced concrete and the mesh may be formed in any shape with out a conventional form. Then it can be plastered or mortared by any method.

In 1940, Mr. P.L. Nervi an Italian engineer and architect developed this material, known as Ferro cement. It consists of closely spaced wire meshes which are impregnated with rich cement mortar mix. Though this material is of recent origin, but have been used in may countries notably in China, New Zealand and U.K. There is a growing awareness of the advantages of this technique of construction all over the world. It is well known that conventional reinforced concrete elements are heavy, brittle, develop cracks and can not be repaired satisfactorily, if damaged. The reinforcement is also liable to be corroded. These disadvantages make the normal reinforced concrete un suitable for certain type of works. Due to these shortcomings of normal reinforced concrete, Ferro cement can be considered as one of its substitute in many situations.

In case of ferro cement, the mortar provides the mass and the wire mesh imparts tensile strength and ductility to the material. In terms of structural behaviour ferro cement exhibits very high tensile strength weight ratio and superior cracking performance. The distribution of small diameter wire mesh reinforcement over the entire surface provides a very high resistance against cracking. Also many other engineering properties such as toughness, fatigue-resistance, impermeability etc. are considerably improved by the use of ferro cement.

23.18. MATERIAL USED

In ferro cement production following materials are used:

Cement mortar matrix. The ferro cement consists of a rich cement mortar matrix of 10 to 60 mm thickness with a reinforcement volume of 5 to 8% in the form of one or more layers of very thin mesh and a skeleton reinforcement consisting of mild steel bars or welded mesh.

Cement. The choice of cement depends on the service conditions. The cement should be fresh, of uniform consistency and free of lumps and foreign matter.

Sand or fine aggregate. Sand is an inert material. It occupies 60, to 75% volume in the ferro cement mortar. To impart good properties to the mortar, sand should be hard, strong, non porous and chemically inert. It should be free from silt, clay and other organic impurities. The maximum particle size should be 2.36 mm. The particles larger than 2.36 mm if present in sufficient quantity, may cause the mortar porous. If particles less than 1.18 mm are present in large quantity, will require more water for the required workability, affecting the strength and impermeability very adversely. Thus the sand should be of grading zones II and III with particles greater than 2.36 mm and smaller than 1.18 mm removed. Use of fine sand in ferro cement is not recommended.

Water/cement. As it governs the strength and workability of the mortar, it depends upon the maximum grain size, the fineness modulus and the grading of the sand. Generally water/cement ratio by mass may vary between 0.35 to 0.60. In order to reduce permeability, water/cement ratio should be kept below 0.40. The moisture content of the aggregate should be taken into account in the calculations of required water.

The amount of water many be reduced by the use of appropriate admixtures.

Cement/sand ratio

Cement sand ratio may be kept 1:2 or 1:3. The slump of fresh mortar should not exceed 50 mm For most works the strength of moist cured cubes should be about 350 MPa.

The matrix constitute about 95% of the ferro cement and governs the behaviour of the final product. Thus proper selection of constituent materials, their mixing and placing is important. The total volume of cement and fines should be about 300 cm^3 per litre of mortar. A change in the amount of cement must be accompanied by a corresponding change in the fines.

Thickness of elements

The thickness of ferro cement elements usually is of the order of 2 to 3 cms with 2 to 3 mm external cover to reinforcement.

Reinforcement

The reinforcement used in ferro cement is of two types:

(*a*) **Skeleton steel.** The skeleton steel frame is made conforming exactly to the geometry and shape of the structure. This is used for holding the wire mesh in position and shape of the structure. The diameter of the steel rods may vary from 3 to 8 mm and spaced at 70 to 100 mm apart. It may be tied reinforcement or welded wire fabric. The welded wire fabric is made from 3 to 4 mm diameter wires welded at 80 to 100 mm centre to centre. These skeleton frames are used for cylindrical or other surfaces where these meshes can be bent easily. In case where higher stresses may occur, mild steel bars are used as skeleton steel. The spacing of transverse and longitudinal steel bars depends upon the type and shape of the structure. In case of boat hulls a spacing of 75 to 100 mm is adequate, where as in water tanks, bins etc. the spacing may vary between 200 to 300 mm. The bars may be tied with the binding wires, they may also be welded. The reinforcement should be free from dust, loose rust, coating of paints, oil etc.

(*b*) **Wire mesh.** The wire mesh consists of galvanized wire of 0.5 to 1.5 mm diameter spaced at 6 to 20 mm centre to centre. The wire mesh may be of the shape as square woven wire mesh or welded wire mesh, expanded metal or Hexagonal wire mesh etc. Generally square woven meshes consisting of 1.0 to 1.5 mm diameter wires spaced about 12 mm are preferable. The minimum yield strength of plain wires used in fabric should be 415 MPa and 500 MPa for deformed wires. The steel content may vary between 300 kg to 500 kg per cubic metre of mortar.

23.19. CONSTRUCTION OF FERRO CEMENT MEMBERS

The construction of ferro cement may be divided into four phases as:

1. Fabrication of skeleton frame system 2. Fixing of bars and mesh
3. Application of mortar and 4. Curing

The quality of mortar and its application is the most critical phase. Mortar can be applied by the following four methods.

1. Hand plastering 2. Semi mechanised process
3. By centrifuging 4. Guniting

In ferro cement construction no form work is required as in conventional reinforced concrete. So it is more suitable for structures with curved surfaces as shells and other free form shapes.

First the skeleton frame is made using small diameter steel rods bent to the required shape, generally cylindrical in shape. Usually this frame provides rigidity to the whole structure before impregnation or plastering. Placing of mortar is known *impregnation of mesh with matrix*.

The required number of wire mesh layers are fixed on both sides of the skeleton frame. First external mesh layers are fixed and tied to the frame bars. The mesh should be fixed by staggering the hold positions in such a way that the effective hold size is reduced. Between two mesh layers space of 1 to 3 mm should be left. When ever two pieces of the mesh are to be joined, a minimum overlap of 80 mm should be provided and tied at a interval of 80 to 100 mm centre to centre.

23.20. PREPARATION OF THE MIX

The required quantities of specified quality cement and good graded sand of 2.36 to 1.18 mm particle size, water proofing and anti shrinkage compounds are weighed accurately and mixed dry. The liquid additives are added to the mixing water in the required quantity.

Now about half of the mixing water is put into the mixer and then the dry mixed ingredients of the mix are charged into the mixer and mixed for about $1\frac{1}{2}$ minutes. Then the remaining mixing water is added gradually while the mixing is continued. Generally the total mixing time should not exceed 3 minutes.

The cement sand (aggregate) ratio may be kept 1:2 or 1:3. Some authors have suggested this ratio as 1:1.75 to 1:2.5 by mass. The water/cement ratio may be adopted between 0.35 to 0.4 depending upon the workability. The quantity of mix of a batch should be such which could be used with in 1 hour of mixing, so that mortar could be placed before it starts setting.

23.21. PLACING OR IMPREGNATION OPERATION BY HAND

It is the most critical operation in ferro cement casting. If the mortar impregnation is not proper, the quality of the structure will not be good and it will not give desired performance.

A sufficient quantity of mortar is dashed from out side through the layers against a G-1 sheet held on the other side. The flexible G-1 sheet is moved around and the mortar is dashed from the out side. The process is continued till the whole structure is built up. During process of putting the mortar, it should be ensured that no voids are left in the body of the structure. It can be ensured by using a wooden hammer of about 100 mm diameter with 150 mm long wooden handle. The mild hammer blows are given over the temporarily held form to remove the voids. This will give sufficient vibrations for compacting the mortar. The whole thickness is build up gradually in two or three consecutive dashing of mortar and then both internal and external surfaces are made smooth.

Shells and boat hulls like structures are built by the technique known as two operation mortar impregnation. In this system, first the out side mesh is plastered and the inner layer is left exposed. The excess mortar is scrapped by trowel and wire brushes. The mortar is left for setting till it attains sufficient strength for carrying the load from the inside during the application of a second layer of mortar. Before applying the second layer, a fine cement slurry is sprayed over the entire inner surface.

In structures where many layers are used as reinforcement and thickness is more than 20 mm, in such cases it is desirable to do the casting in three layers. The middle or core layer is applied first covering the skeleton steel and one layer of wire mesh. This core provides a firm surface for mortar application on its top and bottom. The core is cured at least for 3 days before the other two layers of mortar are applied. For getting the good bond, between old and new mortar cement slurry should be sprayed over the middle layer.

For thin cylindrical units of about 1 m diameter, 6 mm diameter steel rods at a spacing of 15 cm be used for making a cage of cylindrical shape and then woven or chicken mesh can be tied to the mesh and impregnated or plastered. In such type of construction, the use of chicken mesh is not advisable as it is very flexible and plastering over it may not be satisfactory.

In this method the control of thickness is difficult and the minimum thickness of the section works out to be more than 20 mm. The greater thickness not only makes it uneconomical, but also some technical advantages are lost. The strength obtained by hand plastering or impregnation is lower compared to other methods due to poor compaction of mortar by this method. The units cast by this method may be used for pipes, storage structures and gas holder units etc. This method of casting is suitable of units of shapes for which making of mould is difficult. This method can also be applied for making cylindrical shaped units of size approximately 60 cms in diameter or above.

B. Semi mechanised process

A semi mechanised process for making ferro cement cylindrical units has been developed by Structural Engineering Research Centre (SERC) Roorkee. In this process a central cylindrical mould is used. Over this central mould one layer of wire mesh is wound. Over this layer a 4 mm diameter wire is tied at a spacing of 150 mm in both directions. One layer of chicken mesh is wound over this wire layer. This forms the complete wire mesh system of reinforcement.

Now the cement sand mix prepared is impregnated or plastered layer by layer. Due to the tightly wound mesh around the form work, the thickness of the unit is reduced. With this system, units upto one cm thickness can be cast containing two layers of wire mesh in that thickness *i.e.* with in 1 cm thickness. This system is called semi mechanised as the mould can be rotated to facilitate dashing of mortar.

Advantage of Semi mechanised method

Following advantages have been observed of this method:

1. In this method better compaction can be obtained by means of a straight edge pressed against the inner mould.
2. The uniformity of thickness is better in this method than hand plastering.
3. The wire mesh can be wound tightly over the mould and also can be tightened during the casting operation. This helps in avoiding unevenness of thickness and looseness in the mesh.
4. This system does not need any sophisticated equipment and electricity.
5. Local, un skilled people can handle this process.
6. This process can be adopted easily in rural areas.
7. The cylindrical units of size upto 1.0 m or above can be cast by this process.

C. Centrifuging method

For the fabrication of concrete cylindrical units, generally centrifuging process is adopted. The first crack strength of ferro cement has been observed higher in comparison of normal reinforced concrete. Thus the pipe thickness can be reduced, resulting in lesser dead weight. In the existing centrifuging process, the mild steel reinforcement cage has been replaced by wire mesh layers cage. The trial casting at SERC Roorkee has shown that this method can be adopted for casting ferro cement units. Due to good compaction, ferro cement pipes cast by centrifuging process can be used as high pressure pipes.

D. Guniting

The process of guiniting can be adopted for applying the mortar to the wire mesh system. This process seems to be suitable for mass production of ferro cement prefabricated units. A continuous process of layer guniting with an interval of about, an hour will yield good results. If the process is applied properly by an experienced gun man can produce good compacted and uniform surface.

23.22. PROPERTIES OF FERRO CEMENT

1. Compressive strength. The behaviour of thin ferro cement element under compression primarily is controlled by the properties of cement mortar matrix. Its compressive strength varies from 27.5 to 60 MPa.

2. Tensile strength. The tensile strength of ferro cement depends mainly on the volume of reinforcement in the direction of force and the tensile strength of the mesh. The ultimate tensile strength is 34.5 MPa and allowable tensile stress is taken as 10.0 MPa The tensile behaviour may be divided into three groups.

1. Pre cracking stage
2. Post cracking stage
3. Post yielding stage

A ferro cement member subjected to increasing tensile stresses behaves like a liner elastic material till the development of first crack in the matrix. Once the cracks are developed, the material enters the stage, of *multiple cracking* and this stage continues upto the point where wire mesh starts to yield. In this stage number of cracks go on increasing with the increase in tensile stress with out any significant increase in the width of the crack. With the yield of reinforcement, the mortar enters the stage of *crack widening*. At this stage the number of cracks remain constant, but the width of crack go on increasing. The behaviour mainly is controlled by the reinforcement bars.

Fatigue strength

The fatigue behaviour of ferro cement flexural elements is governed by the tensile fatigue properties of mesh like reinforced and pre stressed concrete beams. The fatigue strength of ferro cement is poor under cyclic loading.

Impact strength

The impact strength of ferro cement has been found to increase linearly with the increase of specific surface (volume fraction) and ultimate strength of mesh reinforcement. Further for the same reinforcement fraction, the element having welded wire mesh reinforcement showed highest impact strength while chicken nesh reinforced section showed lowest impact strength. The impact strength of woven mesh reinforced ferro cement is found higher than chicken wire mesh and lower than welded wire mesh reinforced elements.

23.23. Application of ferro cement

Due to the very high percentage of well distributed and continuously running steel reinforcement, the ferro cement behaves like steel plates. Its cracking resistance, ductility, impact and fatigue resistances are higher than that of normal concrete. The impermeability of ferro cement product is far superior than ordinary R.C.C. products. Due to these properties the ferro cement can be used for the following purposes.

1. Ferro cement can be used successfully for casting domestic over head tanks. These tanks being light and flexible can be transported and hoisted with out difficulty. The inlet and out let connections also can be done easily with the help of modern adhesives like "m seal". These tanks will be cheaper than any other type of material tanks.
2. These tank units can also be modified into silos for storing grains in villages. These tanks will help in preserving grains from moisture effect and rodents.
3. Similar ferro cement tanks can be used in villages as gas holding units in 'Gobbar gas' plants. With some modifications ferro cement tanks can also be used as septic tanks.
4. Due to the favourable properties of ferro cement, this material has been widely used for boat building in U.K., U.S. and New Zealand. It has been reported that 14 m long ferro cement boat weighs only 10% more than the wooden boats. Ferro-cement boats are found 300% cheaper than fibre reinforced concrete boats, 200% cheaper than steel boats and 35% cheaper than timber boats.
5. The cost of ferro cement is only about 10% of the cost of cast iron. Thus the use of ferro cement manhole covers is becoming very popular, where these manhole covers are not subjected to heavy vehicular traffic.
5. Ferro cement is becoming more popular material for pre fabricated roof units. The folded plates of ferro cement being light can be advantageously used as prefabricated roof units. A 3 cm thick ferro cement folded plate with two layers of chicken wire mesh can be used safely over a span of 3.5 m. It can also be used for prefabricated channel units for roof construction.
7. Ferro cement being a light material, considerable reduction in self weight of structure and foundation cost can be reduced to a great extent. A 30% reduction in dead weight on supporting structure, 15% saving in steel consumption and 10% saving in roof cost has been observed in USSR by the use of ferro cement.
8. Ferro cement is found most suitable material for the production of pressure pipes. It is much lighter than normal RCC pipes.
9. Ferro cement also is found suitable for casting curved benches for parks, gardens, and open cinema theatre. It can also be used to cast tree guards. They can be cast in two parts to facilitate their removal at a later data.

23.24. ADVANTAGES OF FERRO CEMENT

Following are the advantages of the ferro cement:

1. The construction technique of ferro cement is simple. It does not require skilled labour.
2. Complete or partial elimination of form work is possible.

3. Ferro cement construction is easily amenable to repairs in case of local damage due to abnormal loads as impact load.

Summery of composition and properties of Commonly used ferro cement are shown in Table 23.4 below

Table 23.4. Normal range of composition and properties of ferro cement

S. No.	*Parameters*	*Range*
1.	**Wire mesh**	
	(*a*) Type of mesh	Welded wire or square woven or chicken wire mesh or galvanized wire mesh or expanded metal
	(*b*) Diameter of wiere	Diameter of wire may be between 0.5 to 1.5 mm
	(*c*) Size of mesh opening	It may be between 5 to 25 mm
	(*d*) Distance between mesh layers	The distance between two layers should be greater than 2 mm
	(*e*) Volume fraction of reinforcement	Upto 8% in both directions corresponding to 650 kg/m^3 of concrete
	(*f*) Specific surface of rainforcement	Upto 4 cm^2/cm^3 in both directions
2.	**Skeleton reinforcement**	
	(*a*) Type	Rods, strands, wires or wire fabrics
	(*b*) Diameter	3 to 10 mm
	(*c*) Grid size	50 to 100 mm
3.	**Mortar composition**	
	(*a*) Portland cement	Any type depending on application
	(*b*) Cement sand ratio	1:2 to 1:3 or 1:1.75 to 1:2.5
	(*c*) Water/cement ratio	It may range from 0.35 to 0.6, but normally a w/c ratio of 0.35 to 0.4 is used
	(*d*) Fine aggregate	Fine sand all passing IS 4.75 mm sieve and 5% by mass passing through IS 1.18 mm sieve. Thus the sand of continuous grading curve between 1.18 mm and 2.36 mm size should be used.
4.	**Matrix Properties**	
	(*a*) Thickness	The mortar thickness may be between 10 to 60 mm but normally it should be between 20 to 30 mm
	(*b*) Cover to reinforcement	1.5 to 5 mm
	(*c*) Compressive strength	27.5 to 60 MPa
	(*d*) Ultimate tensile strength	34.5 MPa
	(*e*) Allowable tensile stress	10.0 MPa
	(*f*) Modulus of rupture	55.0 MPa

QUESTIONS

1. Define high density concrete.
2. Why a high density concrete is called nuclear energy shield?
3. Explain in brief different types of nuclear radiation and their hazards.
4. Discuss the characteristics of an nuclear shielding concrete. Also state its disadvantages.
5. Discuss various types of aggregates used for high density concrete.
6. Discuss the physical properties of high density aggregate concrete.
7. What are the important requirements of radiation shielding concrete.
8. Explain the properties of the high density concrete.
9. What is an sulpher concrete? What are its advantages and disadvantages?

10. What is the difference between sulpher concrete and sulpher infiltrated concrete?
11. What is meant by ferro cement? Explain fully.
12. Explain the methods of production of sulpher concrete.
13. Generally what mix proportions are used for the production of sulpher concrete.
14. State the properties of sulpher concrete.
15. Discuss the method of production of infiltrated sulpher concrete.
16. Discuss the uses of sulpher infiltrated concrete.
17. Discuss the different method of construction of a ferro cement member.
18. Discuss the followings:
    (*a*) Properties of ferro cement
    (*b*) Application of ferro cement

OBJECTIVE TYPE QUESTIONS

1. The unit weight of high density concrete is
   (*a*) 1350 kg/m^3 to 1860 kg/m^3 (*b*) 350 kg/m^3 to 800 kg/m^3
   (*c*) 2300 kg/m^3 to 2400 kg/m^3 (*d*) 3360 kg/m^3 to 3840 kg/m^3
2. The high density concrete can be produced having density upto...
   (*a*) 4250 kg/m^3 (*b*) 4500 kg/m^3
   (*c*) 4880 kg/m^3 (*d*) 5280 kg/m^3
3. The density of aggregate to be used in high density concrete should be
   (*a*) 1.75 to 2.5 (*b*) 2.6 to 3.0
   (*c*) More than 3.5 (*d*) Less than 1.5
4. Aggregate for high density concrete can be obtained from
   (*a*) Barites (*b*) Magnetite
   (*c*) Limonite (*d*) Hematite
   (*e*) Any of them
5. Identify the incorrect statements of the followings
   (*a*) High density concrete is used for radiation shielding
   (*b*) The radiation shielding quality of concrete can be achieved by increasing its density
   (*c*) For radiation shielding quality of concrete its high structural strength at high temperature is essential
   (*d*) For radiation shielding quality of concrete its high structural strength at high temperature is not essential
6. The most appropriate use of high density concrete is
   (*a*) In the construction of hydraulic structures
   (*b*) In the construction of mass concrete structures like gravity dams
   (*c*) In the construction of radiation shielding
   (*d*) In the construction of thin structural members
7. Identify the correct statement/statements of the followings
   (*a*) High density concrete has higher tendency of segregation
   (*b*) For concreting high density concrete pre placed aggregate method has been found most effective
   (*c*) For the production of high density concrete the use of sheared reinforcing bars as coarse aggregate has been found more effective than smooth cubical pieces of iron or steel
   (*d*) High density concrete contains high cement content
   (*e*) All the above
8. Identify the incorrect statement of the followings
   (*a*) For the construction of neutron concrete shield only high density aggregate is sufficient
   (*b*) For the construction of neutron concrete shield limonite and geothite are reliable aggregates upto 200°C
   (*c*) For the construction of neutron concrete shield limonite and geothite are not reliable aggregates upto 200°C
   (*d*) For the construction of neutron concrete shield serpentine is good upto 400°C
   (*e*) All heavy weight aggregates have the ability to retain water of crystallisation at high temperature
   (*f*) For the construction of neutron concrete shield the use of high density and hydrous ore is necessary
9. For the production of high density concrete the ideal properties are...
   (*a*) High modulus of elasticity (*b*) Low thermal expansion

(*c*) Low elastic and creep deformation (*d*) High percentage of water of hydration
(*e*) All of the above

10. The shrinkage percentage of high density concrete is
(*a*) 0.013 to 0.029 (*b*) 0.03 to 0.039
(*c*) 0.041 to 0.051 (*d*) 0.055 to 0.075
11. The constituents of sulpher concrete are except
(*a*) Sulpher (*b*) Fine aggregate
(*c*) Coarse aggregate (*d*) Cement
(*e*) Water
12. The ratio of fine to coarse aggregate in sulpher concrete is
(*a*) 1:1.5 (*b*) 1:2.5
(*c*) 1:3 (*d*) 1:3.5
13. In sulpher concrete, the percentage of sulpher usually is kept
(*a*) 50% (*b*) 55%
(*c*) 35% (*d*) 20%
14. Identify the incorrect statements
(*a*) Under normal temperature and humidity conditions the sulpher concrete attains about 90% of the ultimate strength in 6 to 8 hours
(*b*) The strength of sulpher concrete made with crushed aggregate is higher than that made with natural gravel
(*c*) The cement content in sulpher concrete is of the order of 450 kg/m^3
(*d*) Sulpher concrete is very brittle
(*e*) The creep of sulpher concrete is much less than portland cement concrete
15. Identify the incorrect statement/(s)
(*a*) The sulpher concrete has poor resistance to freezing and thawing
(*b*) The sulpher concrete has corrosive effect in reinforcement in wet conditions
(*c*) The quantity of water in sulpher concrete is of the order 220 lit/m^3
(*d*) The compressive strength of sulpher concrete varies from 28 to 70 MPa
16. Identify the true and false statements
(*a*) The techniques of production of sulpher infiltrated concrete are simple in expensive, and effective
(*b*) It is more durable than cement concrete in situations where concentration of H_2So_4 and HCl is high
(*c*) The sulpher infiltrated concrete provides corrosive resistant cover to reinforcement
(*d*) Cement is not used in sulpher infiltrated concrete
(*e*) The sulpher infiltrated concrete can not be used for the manufacture of precast roofing elements, sewer pipes and railway sleepers
(*f*) High strength in sulpher infiltrated concrete is developed after a long period of curing
17. Identify the correct statements of the followings
(*a*) Sand occupies 60 to 75% volume in ferro-cement mortar
(*b*) Water/cement ratio in ferro-cement should be between 0.35 to 0.4
(*c*) The ratio of cement and sand may be 1:2 to 1:3
(*d*) The volume of reinforcement in ferro-cement may vary 5 to 8%
(*e*) All the above
(*f*) Non of the above

Answers

1. (*d*)	6. (*c*)	11. (*d, e*)	16. True (*a, b, c*)
2. (*d*)	7. (*e*)	12. (*a*)	17. (*e*)
3. (*c*)	8. (*a, c, e*)	13. (*d*)	
4. (*e*)	9. (*e*)	14. (*c, e*)	
5. (*d*)	10. (*a*)	15. (*c*)	

24
Special Concretes

24.1. INTRODUCTION

There are many types of concrete, which have been developed for special purposes. To improve the particular properties of a special concrete in general the cement based matrix is modified in some way or the other to improve particular properties. Some of the concretes are of very recent origin. In this chapter some of these concretes will be discussed in brief to familiarize the reader with the new materials.

24.2. POLYMER CONCRETE COMPOSITES

Before discussing the various types of polymer concrete composites, it will be proper to define certain terms used in polymer concrete.

(*a*) **Monomer.** A monomer is an organic molecule which is capable of combining chemically with similar or different kind of molecules to form a high molecular weight material called polymer.

(*b*) **Polymer.** A polymer is consisted of numerous monomers which are linked together in a chain like structure.

(*c*) **Polymerization.** The chemical process which causes these linkages is known as *polymerization.*

24.3. CLASSIFICATION OF POLYMERS

Polymers can be classified into the following two categories:

1. Thermoplastics
2. Thermoset

1. **Thermoplastic polymers.** These polymers have long, linear and parallel chains which do not have cross links. These polymers exhibit reversibility on heating and cooling *i.e.* they are reversible on heating and cooling.
2. **Thermoset.** These polymers have randomly oriented chains which are cross linked. These polymers are not reversible on heating and cooling *i.e.* they are not reversible with the changes in the temperature. However thermoplastic can be converted into thermosets by the use of cross linking agents.

In general polymers are chemically inert materials and have higher tensile and compressive strength than conventional concrete. However polymers have been found to have higher creep and lower modulus of elasticity than conventional concrete. The polymers may be degraded by heat, oxidizing agents, ultra violet light. Chemicals and micro-organisms and certain organic solvents may also cause stress cracking. Many of these disadvantages may be over come by choosing suitable polymers and adding certain substances to the polymers.

24.4. FORMS OF WATER PRESENT IN CONCRETE

It has already been discussed that water in concrete takes one of the following three forms:

1. **Combined water.** This water combines chemically or physically with the products of hydration and is held very firmly. In a fully hydrated cement the amount of combined water is about 23% of the mass of dry cement.
2. **Gel water.** The hydrated cement or cement gel consists of solid products of hydration plus the water which is held physically or adsorbed on the large surface area of the hydrates and is called *gel water.* This is located in gel pores. The volume of this gel water is about 28% of the cement gel.
3. **Capillary water.** The solid products of hydration occupy a volume less than the sum of absolute volume of the original dry cement and the combined water by about 18.5%. This residual space for a fully hydrated cement, with no excess water, required for the hydration is known as *capillary pores.* Water present in these pores is called *capillary water.*

24.5. VOLUME OF PORES

The porosity depends upon water/cement ratio and on the degree of hydration. For a w/c ratio of 0.6, the total volume of pores varies from 47 to 60% of the total volume of the cement paste depending upon the degree of hydration.

Many researchers have conceived that reduction in porosity results in increase of the strength of concrete. Thus to reduce the porosity, concrete compaction by vibration, pressure application, etc. have been practiced. Though all methods of concrete compaction have proved helpful to a great extent, but non of these methods could really reduce the water voids and the inherent porosity of gel which is estimated to be about 28%. The impregnation of monomer and its subsequent polymerization is the latest technique adopted to reduce the inherent porosity of concrete gel to improve its strength and other properties. The constant efforts of researchers to improve and develop the properties of concrete have resulted in the development of a new type of concrete known as *polymer concrete.* The Pioneering work for the development of polymer concrete has been carried out by united states Bureau of Reclamation (USBR).

The development of polymer concrete composite material is to produce a new material by combining the old technology of cement concrete with the modern technology of polymer chemistry.

24.6. CLASSIFICATION OF POLYMER CONCRETE

Polymer Concrete may be classified into the following four groups:

1. Polymer Cement Concrete (PCC)
2. Polymer Concrete (PC)
3. Partially impregnated and surface coated polymer concrete.
4. Polymer Impregnated Concrete (PIC)

24.6.1. Polymer Cement concrete (PCC)

Polymer cement concrete can be prepared by mixing cement, aggregates, water and monomers as usual in ordinary concrete. The plastic mixture is cast in moulds, cured, dried and polymerized. Following monomers may be used in Polymer Cement Concrete (PCC)

(*a*) Epoxy-styrene
(*b*) Polyster-styrene
(*c*) Furans
(*d*) Vinylidene chloride

However polymer cement concrete produced in this way has shown a very modest improvement in strength and durability. RUSSIAN authors have reported recently that a superior polymer cement concrete can be produced by using Furfuryl alcohol and Aniline hydrochloride in the wet mix. This product has been found specially dense, non shrinking and high resistant to corrosion, low permeability, high resistant to vibrations and axial extension etc. Where as U.S. researchers have found that the use of epoxy resin has produced polymer cement concrete having some superior characteristics over ordinary concrete. The PCC using polymer latex has given a tensile strength of 5.8 MPa with w/c ratio of 0.25 compared with control specimen of 4.4 MPa. The increase in tensile strength is very modest.

Uses

Polymer cement concrete can be used for flooring in deck steel over bridges, food processing and chemical industries, wear resistant floors etc. It is also useful for repair of sea defence structures due to early development of strength.

24.6.2. Polymer Concrete (PC)

It is a composite in which cement water matrix of cement concrete is replaced by a polymer binder. The main technique in producing polymer concrete is to minimise the volume of voids in the aggregate mass, so that minimum quantity of binder polymer is needed to bind the aggregates. This can be achieved by properly grading and mixing the aggregates to obtain the maximum density and minimum volumes of voids.

The graded aggregates are prepacked in a form and vibrated. After this, the monomer is diffused through the aggregates and polymerisation is initiated by chemical or radiation process. To improve the bond between the monomer and aggregates a adhesive agent is added to the monomer. In case polyester resins are used then no polymerisation is needed.

Polyester resin concrete with binder content varying from 20 to 25% have shown tensile strength in the range of 9 to 10 MPa at 7 days. The compressive strength of P.C. has been found of the order of 140 MPa with a short curing period.

24.6.2.1. Necessity for developing the polymer concrete

The most important reason for the development of polymer concrete is to over come the short comings of the conventional concrete under the following situations.

1. On curing the alkaline portland cement concrete forms internal voids. In these voids water can be entrapped, which on freezing expands, resulting cracks in concrete.
2. The alkaline portland cement concrete is easily attacked by chemically aggressive (reactive) material, which causes rapid deterioration of the concrete.
3. The polymer concrete can be made compact with minimum voids and hydrophobic (water reppelant) and resistant to chemical attack.

However polymer concrete suffers from certain short comings. Its main short coming is its brittleness. It has been found that the tensile strength and toughness of polymer concrete can be increased by the dispersion of fibre reinforcement. The use of fibrous polyester concrete (FPC) in the compressive region of reinforced concrete beams provides a high strength and ductile concrete at reasonable cost. Also the polyester concretes is visco elastic in nature and will fail under sustained compressive loading stress at 50% higher than the ultimate stress. Thus the polyester concrete can be used for structures with a high ratio of live load to dead load and for composite structures in which polymer concrete may relax during long term loading.

24.6.3. Partially impregnated and surface coated (SC) concrete

In situations where in addition to strength increase, the major requirement is the surface resistance to chemical and mechanical attack, the partial impregnation may be sufficient. Partial impregnation has been found quite effective in the increase of the strength of the original concrete.

The partially impregnated concrete can be produced by soaking the initially dried spacimens in liquid monomer like methyl methacrylate and then sealing them by keeping under hot water at 70°C to prevent or minimise the loss due to evaporation. The polymerisation can be done by using thermal catalytic method. Benzoyal Peroxide is added as a catalyst to the monomer. The depth of penetration of the monomer depends upon the following factors.

1. Pore structure of hardened and dried concrete
2. The viscosity of the monomer
3. The duration of soaking of specimens in the monomer

24.6.3.1. Use of partially impregnated and surface coated concrete

The main use of this concrete has been done in improving the durability of concrete where the abrasive wear, freezing and thawing, spalling and corrosion of reinforcement are the main cause of deterioration as in bridge decks. Bridge deck deterioration is a major problem every where. Excellent penetration can be achieved by ponding the monomer on the concrete surface. While monomer is ponded on the surface due care should be taken to prevent the evaporation of monomer. By soaking a 5 cms thick slab for 25 hours with Methyl methacrylate (MMA), the polymer was found to penetrate upto 2.5 cm depth *i.e.* upto 50% depth of the slab. By surface treating and partial impregnation of the concrete surface, its tensile and compressive strength, modulus of elasticity and resistance to acid attack can be increased significantly.

24.6.3.2. Application of monomers in the field

The application of monomers in the field like bridge decks, impregnation is more difficult than laboratory application and poses more problems. A typical procedure for surface treatment in the field may be adopted as follows:

1. First dry the surface for several days with-electric heating blanket.
2. After drying the surface, remove the heating blanket and cover the slab with over dried light weight aggregate at the rate of 0.64 m^3 per 100 square metre of surface.
3. Initially apply monomer system at the rate of 2.0 to 3.0 litre per square metre of surface.
4. To retard the evaporation of monomer cover the surface with polythene.
5. To prevent the temperature rise, which may initiate the polymerisation prematurely, shade the surface. Premature polymerisation will reduce the penetration of monomer into the concrete.
6. To keep the aggregates moist for the minimum soak time of 8 hours, additional monomer should be added into the concrete.
7. Now apply heat to polymerise the monomer. For this purpose steam, hot water or heating blanket may be used.

24.6.3.3. Monomer system to be used for the above purpose

Following monomer system is suggested for this purpose

(*a*) Methylmethacrylate (MMA), 1% Benzoyl Peroxide (BP), 10% Trimetholpropanetrimethacrylate (TMPTMA). It acts as cross linking agent which helps in polymerisation at low temperature of 52°C and BP acts as catalyst.

(*b*) Isodecyl metha crylate (IDMA), 1% BP, 10% TMPTMA

(*c*) Isobutyl metha crylate (IBMA), 1% BP, 10% TMPTMA

24.6.4. Polymer impregnated concrete

It is one of the widely used polymer composite. It is nothing but a conventional pre cast concrete, cured and dried in oven or by dielectric heating from which the air in open cells is removed by vacuum process. Then a low viscosity liquid monomer or pre polymer partially or fully is impregnated or diffused into the pore system of the hardened cement composites or cement concrete and then polymerised using radiation or by the application of heat or by chemical initiation. The partial or surface impregnation improves the durability and chemical resistance, but the over all improvement in the structural properties is modest. On the other hand in depth or full impregnation improves structural properties considerably.

As stated above, hardened concrete, after a period of moist curing contains a considerable amount of free water in voids. The water filled voids form a significant component of the total volume of concrete ranging from 5% in dense concrete to 15% in gap graded concrete. In polymer impregnated concrete these water filled voids are filled with polymers. The air and moisture in voids affect the monomer loading.

24.6.4.1. Process of impregnation

1. Concrete specimens of well designed and adequately moist cured of optimum strength, are taken.
2. The moisture of the specimens is removed by drying the concrete by heating at a temperature of 120°C to 150°C. The small specimens can be heated in a air oven. For large cast insitu surfaces a thick blanket of sand usually 10 mm thick can be used to check a steep thermal gradient. Infra-red heaters may also be used. To expel the large part of the free water in the concrete about 6 to 8 hour heating is required.
3. To avoid flammability, the concrete surface is cooled to safe levels (about 35°C).
4. The air from the dry concrete specimens is removed by vacuum process. The degree of vaccum and its duration have been found to have a significant influence on the quantity of monomer that can be impregnated *i.e.* on the depth of impregnation.
5. To achieve the desired depth of penetration of the monomer, the specimens can be soaked in the monomer. The soaking duration in the monomer depends on the viscosity of monomer, characteristics of concrete and preparation of specimens prior to soaking. The soaking duration for the desired depth of penetration can be reduced by exerting external pressure by the use of nitrogen gas. Generally air is used for this purpose.
6. To prevent the evaporation of the monomer, the surface should be covered with a plastic sheet.
7. Now the polymerization of the monomer is initiated. Polymerization can be effected by thermal catalytic technique or by ionizing radiation. For polymerization by thermal catalytic technique the catalyzed monomer is heated to a temperature between 60°C to 150°C depending upon the type of monomer. The heating can be done under water or by low pressure steam injection or by infra red heaters or in an air oven. The duration of heating may vary from 2 to 6 hours depending upon the polymer used.

The heating decomposes the catalyst and initiates the polymerization reaction. This reaction is called a *thermal catalytic reaction.* When monomer has penetrated into the concrete, polymerization can also be initiated using ionizing radiation such as gamma rays. Fully polymerized or cross linked polymers become solids and occupy the full volume in which they have been impregnated. At the impregnation stage, the polymer has to be in a pre polymer liquid form, which is generally called *monomer.* The state of polymerization of monomers or of prepolymer resins is brought about also by adding initiators and cross linking agents.

24.6.4.2. Polymers Used for Impregnation

Broadly following polymers are used for impregnation:

1. **Thermoplastics.** Usually these polymers soften between 100°C to 150°C called glass transition temperature. Thus the advantage of using thermoplastic impregnated concrete is lost at such temperatures. Thermoplastic monomers have low viscosity and can penetrate well into the hardened concrete and fill large part of the pores Their polymerization is achieved by addition reactions not leading to low molecular weight byproducts.
2. **Thermosetting resins.** These polymers are more viscous and difficult to impregnate into the concrete. They can withstand higher temperatures with out softening. But the condensation reactions which occur may lead to the formation of low molecular weight byproducts, which would occupy some of the space.

Thus it is necessary that a monomer or its polymer should be chemically compatible with the compounds of cement and the constituents of hydrated cement paste to prevent their adverse effects.

Monomers/resins used for polymer impregnated concrete are as follows:

1. Styrene
2. Methyl methacrylate (MMA)
3. Butylacrylate
4. Acrilonitrite

5. Epoxies and their copolymer combinations
6. Polyster

The amount of monomer that can be loaded into the concrete specimen depends on the amount of water and air voids that occupy the total void space.

24.7. USE OF POLYMER IMPREGNATED CONCRETE

The polymer impregnated concrete can be used as follows:

1. **Surface impregnation of Bridge decks.** The impregnation of bridge decks renders them impervious to the intrusion of moisture, deicing chemicals and chloride ions etc.
2. **Application in Irrigation structures.** The effect of cavitation and erosion in dams and other hydraulic structures is catastrophic. Conventional repairs of such damages are very expensive and time consuming, resulting in huge losses due to loss of benefits from irrigation, flood control and power generation. In such situations the polymer impregnated treatment may prove to be cost effective. The concrete may be removed from the damaged portion and the damaged area patched up, dried and treated by impregnation.
3. **Use as structural members.** Polymer-impregnated concrete has a bright future to be used as a structural material. Polymer-impregnated pre-stressed concrete beams have shown remarkable high performance over conventional concrete. The maximum tendon force in case of impregnated concrete could be upto 4 times that of ordinary concrete. The creep deflection was found of the order of 1/9 to 1/16 that of static deflection. The shear strength also improved by the same factor as that of compressive strength. The compressive strength of PIC being of the order of 100 to 140 MPa, it can be used for heavier loads and longer span bridges and pre fabricated sections.
4. **Marine and under water applications.** Greatly improved structural properties and low water absorption and permeability make the polymer impregnated concrete an excellent material for marine and under water application such as sea floor structures, desalination plants etc. It has also been observed that even partial impregnation of concrete piles in sea water reduced the corrosion of reinforcing bars by 24 times *i.e.* by the use of partial impregnation reinforcement corrosion reduced to 1/24 that of ordinary R.C.C. work. The materials to be used in the construction of flash distilation plants (vessels) have to withstand the corrosive effects of distilled water, brine and vapours at a temperature upto 143°C. The carbon steel vessels used at present for desalination are costly and deteriorate after prolonged use. The use of PIC will prove economical over the conventional carbon steel vessels.
5. **Nuclear power plants.** To meet the power requirement demand for industrial purposes, most of the countries have resorted to nuclear power genration. For the generation of nuclear power, pressure vessels are required to withstand the high temperature and at the same time to be able to provide shield against radiation. To avoid radiation hazards nuclear power generation also needs the containment of spent fuel rods which remain radio active for a long time. The present high density concrete shield is not very effective. PIC having high strength and durability coupled with high impermeability can be used to solve these problems.
6. **Sewage disposal works.** Sewer pipes when buried under sulphate infested soils deteriorate due to the attack of effluents. The sewage treatment works made of concrete are also attacked severly from corrosive gases. Polymer impregnated concrete being highly resistant to shalphate and acids may prove to be a most suitable material for this purpose.
7. **Impregnation of Ferro cement products.** Ferro cement products being thin, generally 1 to 4 cms thick are liable to corrode. The impregnation of polymer will improve the functional efficiency of ferrocement products.
8. **Water proofing of structures.** Seepage and leakage of water through structural elements such as roof and slabs is a perpetual problem and has not been fully solved by the use of conventional water profing methods. The use of polymer impregnated mortar may solve this problem.

9. **Industrial use.** To withstand the chemical attack generally concrete has been used for flooring in dairy farm product buildings, tanneries and chemical factories etc. The performance of conventional concrete has not been found very satisfactory. It is hoped that polymer impregnated concrete will provide durable flooring in such situations.

24.8. PROPERTIES OF POLYMER IMPREGNATED CONCRETE (PIC)

1. **Compressive strength.** Loading with a 6.4% polymer and using methylemethacrylate as monomer, compressive strength was found of the order of 144 MPa using radiation technique of polymerisation. When the thermal catalytic process of polymerisation was applied on the same type of specimen, they gave compressives strength as 130 MPa where as control (un impregnated) specimens gave compressive strength of 38 MPa only.

Styrene impregnated specimens also showed similar trend, but with some what lower strength. The polymerisation by radiation method produced concrete of higher strength than that produced by thermal catalytic method.

Perlite lightweight aggregate concrete impregnated with MMA and polyester styrene also have shown considerable increase in compressive strength. However MMA impregnated specimens gave higher strength than polyester styrene impregnated specimens. The average compressive strength of a 1:8 mix non air entrained perlite concrete specimens impregnated with MMA was of the order of 56 MPa for polymer loading 6.3% where as un impregnated (controlled) specimens gave only compressive strength as 1.2 MPa.

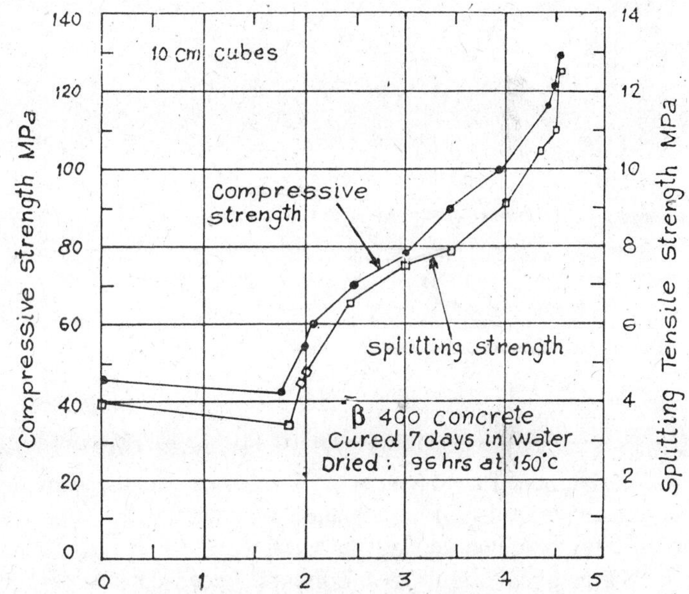

Fig. 24.1. The strength of 10 cms cubes as a function of polymer loading

2. **Tensile strength.** The increase in tensile strength of a PIC has been found as high as 3.9 times that of control (un impregnated) specimens for a polymer loading of 6.4%. MMA *i.e.* the tensile strength of impregnated concrete was of the order of 11.7 MPa as compared to the strength of un impregnated (control). Specimen of 3 MPa using radiation process of polyrisation. Thermal catalytically initiated polyrisation produced concrete of 3.6 times that of control (un impregnated) specimen and 7.3% less than radiation polymerisation process. The relation between polymer loading and compressive and tensile strength has been shown in Fig. 24.1.

Flexure strength. Polymer impregnated concrete with polymer loading of 5.6% MMA and polymerised by radiation showed flexural strength of the order of 18.8 MPA while control concrete showed flexural strength as 5.2 MPA *i.e.* the flexural strength of PIC was found 3.6 times more than un impregnated concrete.

Polymer Concrete (PC) .The polyester resin concrete has been found to produce flexural strength of the order of 15 MPa at 7 days.

Creep. The compressive creep deformation of MMA and styrene impregnated concretes have been observed to be in the opposite direction of the applied load *i.e.* negative creep. During loading application after initial movement these concretes expand under sustained compression.

Shrinkage due polymerisation. The shrinkage takes place through two stages of impregnation treatment *i,e,* (*a*) through initial drying, (*b*) through polymerisation. Shrinkage through polymerisation is peculiar to PIC. It is several times higher than the normal drying shrinkage.

Durability. The durability of PIC (polymer impregnated concrete) has been found much higher than un impregnated concrete due to the saturation of the hydrated cement with corrosion resistant polymer.

Freezing and thawing resistance. Polymer impregnated concrete has shown excellent resistance to freezing and thawing. MMA impregnated and radiation polymerised concrete withstood 8110 cycles of freezing and thawing where as un impregnated concrete withstood only 740 cycles. Partially impregnated concrete withstood 2310 cycles.

Resistance to sulphate attack. Keeping a failure criteria of 0.5% expansion, the improvement in the sulphate resistance in polymer impregnated concrete has been found at least 200% and 89% in partially impregnated concrete.

Acid resistance. In PIC concrete the acid resistance has been found to improve by 1200% when exposed to 15% HCl for 1395 days compared to un impregnated concrete. 15% sulphuric acid and 5% hydrochloric acid effect on PIC has been shown in Fig. 24.2.

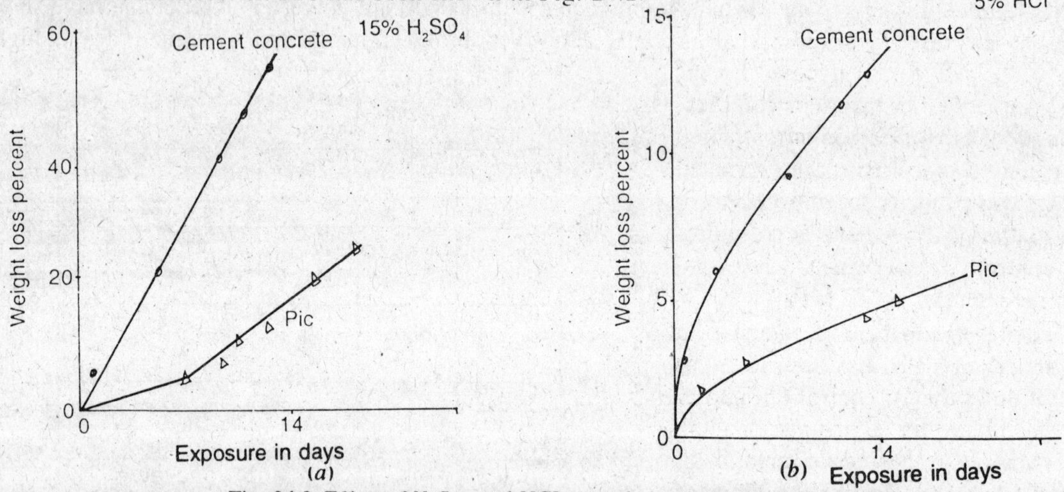

Fig. 24.2. Effect of H_2So_4 and HCL on polymer impregnated concrete

Resistance of abrasion. A 5.5% MMA impregnated concrete has been found 50 to 89% more resistant to abrasion than the un impregnated concrete. Surface impregnated concrete slab surfaces have shown 20 to 50% improvement in abrasion resistance.

Water absorption. 5.9% Polymer loaded concrete has shown a maximum reduction of 95% water absorption.

Coefficient of thermal expansion. 5.5% MMA impregnated and radiation polymerised concrete has a coefficient of thermal expansion of 5.63×10^{-6} and styrene impregnated concrete 5.10×10^{-6} where as the coeff of thermal expansion of un impregnated concrete is 4.02×10^{-6}. Hence the coeff of thermal expansion of polymer impregnated concrete is higher than un impregnated concrete.

24.8.1. Stress-Strain relationship

The flexural strength of polymer impregnated concrete has been found about 3.6 times higher than un impregnated concrete due its higher modulus of elasticity. The stress-strain relationship of PIC has been found nearly linear upto failure. There is little departure from the linearity upto 90% ultimate strength. The stress-strain curve for MMA impregnated concrete, MMA and Butyla Crylate (BA) and Cement concrete stress-strain relationship is shown in Fig. 24.3 (*a*), where as Fig. 24.3 (*b*) shows the stress-strain relationship for polymer concrete (PC) for the same polymers (MMA and MMa-BA).

The stress-strain curve for styrene TMPTMA impregnated concrete also showed the same characteristics as that of MMA impregnated concrete. The modulus of elasticity for MMA impregnated concrete

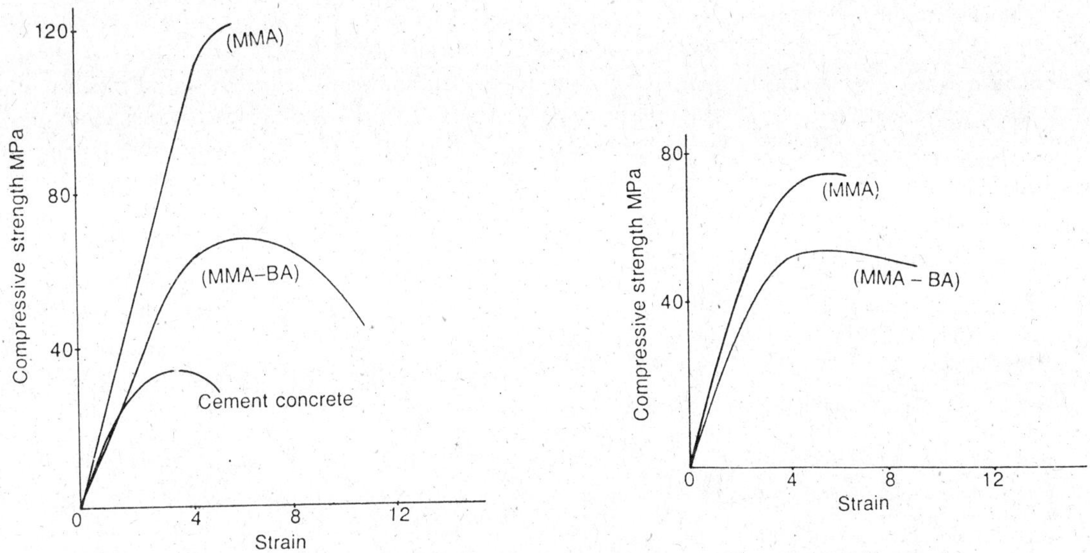

(*a*) Polymer impregnated concrets (*b*) Polymer concrete

Fig. 24.3. Stress-strain relationship for polymer concrete

was found as 49 GPa where as for un impregnated concrete it was observed as 27 GPa. Thus the modulus of elasticity increased by 1.8 times of the MMA impregnated concrete.

Table 24.1. Properties of polymer loaded concrete based on the work Meyer steinberg

S. No.	*Type of concrete*	*Polymer loading weight % (MMA)*	*Density gms/cc*	*Compressive strength MPa*	*Strength weight ratio*	*Durability*	*Benefit/ cost index*
1.	Conventional control concrete	0.0	2.40	35.3	33	Poor	1.0
2.	Surface coateal (SC) paint or over lay	0.0	2.40	35.3	33	Limited	1.1
3.	Coating in depth (CID)	1.0	2.40	42.3	40	Good	1.3
4.	Polymer cement concrete (PPC)	35.0	2.08	52.8	58	Fair	0.4
5.	Polymer impregnated concrete PIC						
	Standard aggregate						
	(*a*) Undried-dipped	2.0	2.45	70.5	49	Fair	1.4
	(*b*) Dried evacuated filled	6.0	2.55	141.0	126	Very good	2.0
	(*c*) High silica, steam cured	8.0	2.55	268.0	240	Very good	3.0
	Light weight aggregate						
	(*a*) Structural light weight concrete	15.0	2.08	176.0	193	Very good	2.5
	(*b*) Insulated light weight concrete	65	0.96	35.3	84	Very good	2.5
6.	Polymer concrete (PC) cement less	6.0	2.40	141.0	133	Excellent	4.0

Table 24.2. Typical mechanical properties of PIC based on work of (V.M. Malhotra)

S. No.	*Monomer used*	*Polymer loading % by mass*	*Compressive strength MPa*	*Tensile strength MPa*	*Flexural strength MPa*	*Modulus of elasticity GPa (10^6PSi)*
1.	Un impregnated	0	35	2	4	19 (2.7×10^6 PSi)
2.	MMA	4.6 – 6.7	142	11	18	44 (6.4×10^6 PSi)
3.	MMA + 10% TMPTMA	5.5 – 7.6	151	11	15	43 (6.2×10^6 PSi)
4.	Styrene	4.2 – 6.0	99	8	16	44 (6.4×10^6 PSi)

S. No.	Monomer used	Polymer loading % by mass	Compressive strength MPa	Tensile strength MPa	Flexural strength MPa	Modulus of elasticity GPa (10^6PSi)
5.	Acrylonitrile	3.2 – 6.0	99	7	10	41 (5.9×10^6 PSi)
6.	Chlorostyrene	4.9 – 6.9	113	8	17	39 (5.6×10^6 PSi)
7.	10% polyster + 90% styrene*	6.3 – 7.4	144	11	23	46 (6.7×10^6 PSi)
8.	Vinyl chloride	3.0 – 5.0	72	5	—	29 (4.2×10^6 PSi)
9.	Vinlidence chloride	1.5 – 2.8	47	3	—	21 (3.0×10^6 PSi)
10.	T-Butyl-styrene	5.3 – 6.0	127	10	—	45 (6.5×10^6 PSi)
11.	60% styrene* + 40% MPTMA	5.9 – 7.3	120	6	—	44 (64×10^6 PSi)

*Concrete dried at 105°C over night radiation polymerisation

Table 24.3. Typical mechanical properties of polymer concrete based (on work of V.M. Malhotra)

S. No.	Polymer-Monomer	Polymer/aggregate ratio	Density	Compressive strength MPa	Tensile strangth MPa	Flexural strength MPa	Modulus of elasticity GPa
1.	Polyster	1:10	2400	117	13	37	32
2.	Polyster	1:9	2330	69	—	17	28
3.	Polyster styrene	1:4	—	82	—	—	—
4.	Epoxy + 40% Dibutyl phthalate	1:1*	1650	50	130	—	2
5.	Expoxy + Polyaminoamide	1:9	2280	65	—	23	32
6.	Exoxy-polyamide	1:9	2000	95	—	33	—
7.	Exoxy-furan	1:1*	1700	65	7	0.1	—
8.	NMA-TMPTMA	1:15	2400	137	10	22	35

*Polymer Mortar

24.9. ROLLER COMPACTED CONCRETE

Roller compacted concrete, abrriviated as R.C.C. is of recent origion. It is also known as lean rolled concrete. Roller compacted concrete is almost a dry concrete having no slump. This concrete is consolidated by vibratory rollers. The applications of this concrete are mainly in the construction of dams, rapid placement of single layer paving for highways and runways and also for multi layer placement for foundations.

Mix

The cement content of this concrete varies from 60 to 360 kg/m^3 of concrete. To minimize the heat of hydration in massive concrete placements, and also to minimize cracking, the cement content should be kept as low as possible and the maximum possible size of aggregate should be used. The use of minimum quantity of cement and large size aggregate will help in controlling the segregation of the concrete. The use of pozzolana often has been found very economical than cement alone. The use of pozzolana is also advantageous in reducing the heat of hydration. In some cases high value fly ash has been added to the extent of 60 to 80% of the volume of cementitious materials in the construction of dams.

The mixture of cementitious material, aggregate and water is mixed in a conventional batch mixer or in any other suitable mixer.

Placement

To allow complete compaction, the roller compacted concrete is placed in thin layers. The optimum layer thickness should be between 20 to 30 cms. To ensure adequate bond between the new and old layer called as cold joint, segregation of concrete must be avoided. To achieve this objective a high plasticity bedding mix must be used at the start of the placement. The concrete can also be used for continuous placement without cold joints. The compressive strength of roller compacted concrete of the order of 7 MPa to 30 MPa has been obtained.

For effective compaction, the roller compacted concrete must be dry enough to support the mass of the vibrating equipment, but wet enough to allow the cement paste to be evenly distributed through out the mass during the mixing and consolidation processes.

The first Roller compacted concrete dam was started in Japan during 1978 and was completed in 1980. Since then many other dams were built by this technique in different parts of the world. By the end of 1985, seven Roller compacted concrete dams were completed and by the end of 1992 the number of such dams rose to 96 in 18 different countries, mainly in Japan, U.S.A. and spain etc.

In India though no dam has been built by this techniques but the technique has been used in the road construction. The roller compacted concrete has been used as a base concrete in the construction of Delhi-Mathura Concrete road Project. Similarly RCC (Roller Compacted Concrete) has also been used as a base course concrete in Pune-Mumbai express high way construction. In both the projects the roller compacted concrete is called as "Dry lean concrete". The thickness of the concrete was kept 15 cm and the grade of concrete was M_{10}. The concrete was thoroughly compacted by vibratory rollers, over which pavement quality concrete of grade M_{40} was placed. The thickness of pavement layer was kept as 35 cm.

24.10. FIBRE REINFORCED CONCRETE

As discussed earlier, plain concrete has a very low tensile strength, limited ductility and little resistance to cracking. Internal micro-cracks are inherently present in the concrete. The poor tensile strength of concrete is due to the development of such micro-cracks. These micro-cracks eventually lead to brittle fracture of the concrete. Thus the purpose of reinforcing the cement based matrix with steal or fibres is to increase the tensile strength by delaying the growth of cracks and to increase the toughness by transmitting stress across a cracked section so that much larger deformation is possible beyond the peak stress than with out fibre reinforcement.

Thus fibre reinforced concrete may be defined as concrete made with hydraulic cement, containing fine or coarse and fine both aggregate and discontinuous discrete fibres. The fibre reinforced concrete generally has higher cement content, and higher fine aggregate content and smaller size of coarse aggregate in comparison with conventional concrete.

In plain concrete and similar brittle materials micro cracks (structural cracks) develop even before applying load. These cracks develop due to drying shrinkage or volume changes. The initial width of these cracks is very small and seldom exceeds a few microns, but their other dimensions may be much higher.

After loading, these micro cracks propagate and open up. Due to the stress concentration, additional cracks form in place of these minor cracks. These structural cracks spread very slowly due to the resistance at inter surface of cement paste and bigger aggregate particles and changes of direction bypassing the more resistant particles in matrix. Actually the main cause of development of such micro cracks is of inelastic deformations in concrete.

24.10.1. Fibres used

The fibres can be classified into two groups as follows:

1. Natural materials as asbestos, cellulose, sisal.
2. Artificial manufactured products as steel, glass, carbon and polymer etc.

Each type of fibre has its own characteristic properties and limitations. Hence all of them can not be used effectively and economically.

Quantity of fibres

The quantity of fibres used in fibre reinforced concrete is small usually 1 to 5% by volume.

24.10.2. Properties of fibres

To make the fibres effective as reinforcement, the tensile strength, modulus of elasticity and the elongation of fibres at failure should be substantially higher than the corresponding properties of the matrix. The typical properties of some fibres are shown in the following Table 24.1.

Table 24.4. Properties of fibres

S. No.	*Type of fibre*	*Specific gravity*	*Tensile strength MPa*	*Modulus of elasticity GPa*	*Elongation at failure %*	*Poisson's ratio*
1.	Crysotile asbestos	2.55	3.0 to 4.5	164	3.0	0.30
2.	Alkali resistant glass	2.71	2.0 to 2.8	80.0	2 to 3.0	0.22
3.	Steel	7.84	1.0 to 3.2	200.0	3.0 to 4.0	0.30
4.	Carbon	1.74-1.99	1.4 to 3.2	250 to 450	0.4 to 1.0	0.2 to 0.4
5.	Poly propylene	0.91	780-850	8	8	0.29 to 0.46
6.	Kevlar	1.45	3.6	65 to 130	2 to 4	0.32
7.	Nylon	1.1	4.2	78 to 85	16 to 20	—
8.	Rayon	1.5	7.3	42 to 63	10 to 25	—

Further the creep of fibres used as reinforcement should be very low. Their Poisson's ratio should be similar as that of the matrix. Some other significant characteristics of the fibres are as follows:

1. *Aspect ratio.* It is the ratio of length to mean diameter of the fibre. The stress bearing capacity of fibre depends upon its aspect ratio. Typical aspect ratio varies from 30 to 150.
2. Shape
3. Surface texture
4. Length and
5. Structure

It has been observed that aspect ratio influences the properties and behaviour of the composite to a great extent. The increase in aspect ratio upto 75, increases the ultimate strength of concrete linearly and relative toughness, but beyond this value of aspect ratio both ultimate strength and relative toughness decrease. Table 24.5. Shows the effect of aspect ratio on strength and toughness.

Table 24.5. Effect of aspect ratio on strength and relative toughness

S. No.	*Type of Concrete*	*Aspect Ratio*	*Relative strength*	*Relative toughness*
1.	Plain concrete with	0	1.0	1.0
2.	Randomly dispersed fibres	25	1.5	2.0
3.	do	50	1.6	8.0
4.	do	75	1.7	10.5
5.		100	1.5	8.5

24.10.3. Description of different fibres used

1. Steel fibre. It is the most commonly used fibre. Generally round fibres of diameter ranging from 0.25 to 0.75 mm are used. The steel fibre is likely to get rusted and lose some of its strength. However rusting takes only at the surface. A significant improvement in impact, fatigue and flexural strength of concrete has been observed by the use of steel fibre. It has been used extensively in various types of structures, specially for over lays of roads, air field pavements, bridge decks etc. It has also been used successfully for the construction of thin shells and plates.

2. Asbestos. It is a natural fibre and has proved to be the most successful of all fibres as it can be mixed with portland cement. The tensile strength of asbastos has been found varying between 560 to 980 N/mm^2.

The flexural strength of the composite product known as asbestos cement has been found considerably higher than the portland cement paste.

3. Polypropylene and nylon fibres. These fibres possess very high tensile strength. These fibres are found useful to increase the impact strength of the composite. They have low modulus of elasticity and higher elongation, which do not contribute to its flexural strength.

4. Glass fibre. It has been introduced recently for the production of fibre concrete. It has been found to have very high tensile strength varying from 1020 to 4080 N/mm^2. Originally glass fibre used along with portland cement was found to be affected by alkaline nature of cement. Thus a alkali resistant glass fibre has been developed. The trade name of this glass fibre is "CEMFILL". Concrete made with alkali resistant glass fibre showed considerable improvement in its durability in comparison to the conventional E, glass fibre.

5. Carbon fibres. Perhaps the carbon fibres possess very high tensile strength and Young's modulus. Their tensile strength has been observed of the order of 2110 to 2815 N/mm^2. The concrete made with carbon fibre as reinforcement showed very high flexural strength and modulus of elasticity. It has been found quite durable. It can be used for the construction of protective covering panels and shells. It has bright future.

24.10.4. Factors affecting the properties of fibre reinforced concrete

As stated above the fibre reinforced concrete is a composite material consisted of fibres in cement matrix either in the orderly manner or randomly distributed manner. Thus its properties would depend upon the efficient transfer of stress between the fibres and the matrix, which is dependent on the following factors.

1. Type of fibre and its geometry
2. Fibre content
3. Orientation and distribution of the fibre
4. Mixing and compaction of concrete
5. Amount, shape and size of aggregate. These factors are discussed briefly below.

1. For effective and efficient transfer of stress, the modulus of elasticity of the matrix must be much lower than that of fibre used. The fibres of low modulus of elasticity as polypropylene and nylon impart greater degree of toughness and resistance to impact as they have the capacity of absorption of large amount of energy, but they do not contribute to the improvement of strength. On the other hand, high modulus fibres as steel, glass and carbon contribute more to the improvement of strength and stiffness of concrete.

The interfacial bond between the matrix and the fibres also determine the effectiveness of transfer of stress from the matrix to the fibre. For improving the tensile strength of the composite a good bond is essential. The interfacial bond could be improved by providing larger area of contact, improving the degree of gripping and frictional properties by treating the steel fibres with acetone or sodium hydroxide.

Volume of fibres

Usually the quantity of fibres is used between 1 to 5% by volume. The strength of the composite largely depends on the quantity of fibres used in it. The effect of volume between 0

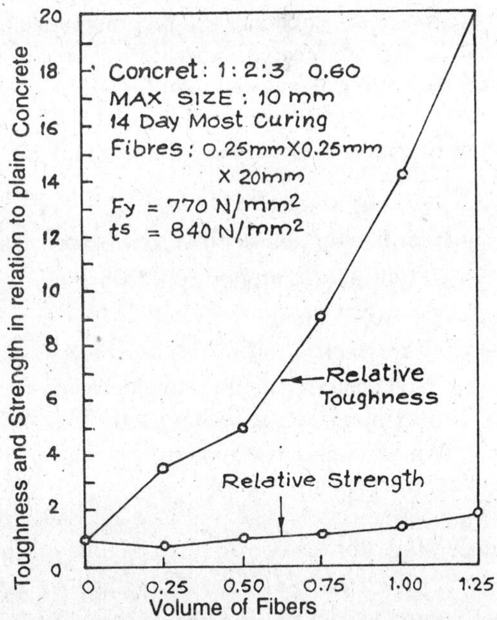

Fig. 24.4. Effect of Fibre volume on flexure strength

to 1.25% by volume on strength and toughness of fibre reinforced composite is shown in Fig. 24.4. The effect on the toughness is more than on strength. From Fig. 24.5 it can be seen that the increase in tensile strength and toughness of the composite is liner with the increase in volume of fibres upto 1.5%. The use of higher percentage of fibre is likely to cause segregation and harshness of concrete and mortar.

2. Aspect ratio of the fibre. Discussed on page 530.

3. Orientation of fibres. It has been observed that the orientation of the fibre relative to the plane of crack in concrete influences the reinforcing capacity of the fibre. The maximum benefit occurs when the fibre is unidirectional and parallel to the tensile stress. Experiments have shown that the fibres aligned parallel to the applied load offered more tensile strength and toughness than randomly or perpendicular distributed fibres.

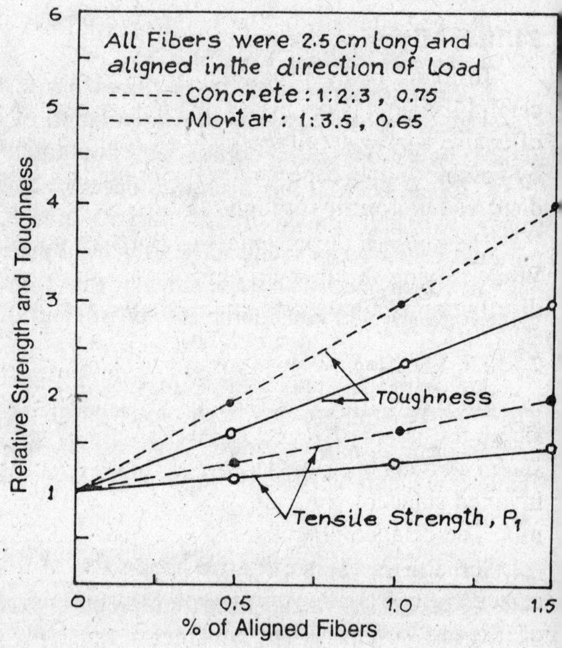

Fig. 24.5. Effect of Fibre volume on tensile and toughness

4. Workability and Compaction of Concrete. The addition of fibres decreases the workability of the concrete considerably. The workability of fibre reinforced concrete decreases with the increase in fibre content and its aspect ratio. The decrease in workability effects the consolidation of concrete to a great extent. Even prolonged external vibration has no effect at this low workability. The fibre volume at which this situation arises depends upon the aspect ratio of the fibre *i.e.* on its length and diameter.

An other effect of low workability is non uniform distribution of fibres The workability can be increased by increasing the water-cement ratio or by the use of some water reducing admixtures.

5. Size of the Coarse aggregate. In order to avoid appreciable reduction in the strength of the composite, many researchers have recommended the maximum size of coarse aggregate as 10 mm. In fact fibres also act as aggregate. Though the geometry (shape) of fibres is simple, but their influence on the properties of the fresh concrete is complex. The inner particle friction between fibres and between aggregates and fibres controls the orientation and distribution of the fibres and thus the properties of the composite. The use of friction reducing admixtures and admixtures which can improve the cohesiveness of the mix will be useful.

24.10.5. Proportion of fibre reinforced Concrete

A typical mix proportion of fibre reinforced concrete is shown below:

Cement content	325 to 550 kg/m^3
Water-cement ratio	0.4 to 0.6
Percentage of fine to total aggregate	50 to 100%
Maximum size of aggregate	10 mm
Air entrainment (Content)	6 to 9%
Fibre content	0.5 to 2.5% by volume of mix
Steel fibre 1%, 78 kg/m^3	
Glass fibre 1% .25 kg/m^3	
Nynol 1% 11 kg/m^3	
Fibre aspect ratio	50 to 100

24.10.6. Mixing of the mix

To avoid balling (bundling) of fibres, segregation and difficulty in mixing the materials uniformly careful handling is necessary. Increase in the aspect ratio, volume percentage of fibres and size and quantity of coarse aggregate all intensify the balling tendency and difficulties. A steel fibre content more than 2% by volume and an aspect ratio more than 100% is difficult to mix. It is important to note that the fibres are dispersed uniformly through out the mix.

The uniform dispersement of fibres can be achieved by the addition of fibres before the water is added. While mixing in laboratory mixer, the addition of fibres through a wire mesh basket, will help the even distribution of fibres. For the use in the field some other suitable method may be adopted.

24.10.7. Methods of determining workability

For determining the workability of fibre concrete usual methods are slump and Vee Bee methods, but slump test is not always a good indicator of workability. For this reason a new method known as *inverted slump test* has been developed to find the workability of fibrous mixes. The time taken for loosely filled inverted standard cone into a standard container by internal vibration is the measure of the fluidity of the mix. The detailed procedure is described in ACI 544-2R-89.

Some researchers have suggested cone penetration test for measuring the workability of fibre reinforced concrete. They have reported that the depth of penetration in mm of a metallic cone with an apex angle of 30° and weight of 40N has been found to give representative workability for normal range mixes. The depth of penetration for normal range of mixes has been found to vary from 30 mm to 50 mm.

24.10.8. Factors affecting workability

Aspect ratio and fibre volume concentration predominantly affect the workability of fibre reinforced concrete. A minimum fibre volume concentration is known as critical concentration and is needed to increase its strength. The critical concentration is inversely propertional to the aspect ratio. For aspect ratio $l/d = 100$, a volume concontration of 0.5% for flexural strengthening and 1.7% for tensile strengthening is required.

24.10.9. Properties of fibrous Concrete

Following properties of fibrous concrete have been observed.

1. It has increased static and dynamic strength.
2. It has higher energy absorbing characteristics.
3. It has better fatigue strength.
4. It has better isotropic properties than normal reinforced concrete due to uniform disperson of fibres through out the concrete.

24.10.10. Application or uses of fibre concrete

There are many uses of fibrous concrete as follows:

1. The glass fibre reinforced concrete is used for precast, flat or shaped decorative panels and facings for architectural and outer coverings known as cladding.
2. The asbestos cement is cheaper and is used for the production of flat and corrugated sheets. The asbestos cement is fire resistant also. Thus it has been widely used for covering the cheap houses. Garagges, fire resistant panels and pipes etc.
3. *Polypropylene fibre concrete.* The modulus of elasticity of polypropylene fibres is low under normal rate of loading but it increases subsequently under impact loading. Thus this concrete is used for making casing for conventionally driven reinforced concrete piles.
4. *Steel and glass fibre concrete.* As the flexural, fatigue and impact strength of these fibres is good, they are used as the overlays (bases) to concrete pavements and airfield pavements. Steel fibre can

also be used in shot crete. However the steel fibres may get corroded especially near or at the surface exposed to weather. Other general uses of fibre reinforced concrete products are permanent and reusable form works and protection and strengthening of the skin of concrete members. In general it can be said that fibre reinforced concrete can be used for all types of works as road pavements, floorings, bridge decks, canal lining, beams, boats, roof and wall panels, manhole covers etc. It is resistant to cavitation or erosion effect, hance used in hydraulic structures.

24.11. SAW DUST CONCRETE

Sometimes in partition walls and some types of roofs, nailing properties of the concrete are essential. Nailing is that property of the material by virtue of which nails can be driven in it and are firmly held. This type of concrete can be obtained by using saw dust as aggregate.

Saw dust concrete consists roughly equal parts by volume of portland cement, sand and saw dust with water sufficient to give a slump of 25 to 50 mm i.e. cement to saw dust may be 1:2 to 1:3 by vol. Such a concrete bonds well with ordinary concrete and is a good insulator. The saw dust should be clean and without a large amount of bark.

In order to avoid adverse effect on setting, hydration, and rotting of saw dust and to reduce moisture movement, chemical treatment of saw dust is advisable. To offset the delay in setting and hardening addition of about 5% calcium hydroxide has been found effective. The density of saw dust concrete varies from 652 to 1600 kg/m^3. As the properties of this concrete depend on the quality of saw dust, use of trial mix is recommended. The size of saw dust may vary from 1.18 mm to 6.3 mm. Saw dust concrete can be used in the manufacture of precast concrete products, joint less flooring and roofing tiles etc.

24.12. PREPLACED AGGREGATE CONCRETE

This type of concrete is produced in two operations. In the first operation, coarse aggregate is placed in the form and compacted by form vibrators. In the second operation the voids from 30 to 35% of the over all volume to be concreted are filled with cement mortar. Preplaced aggregate concrete is also known as *prepacked concrete* or *intrusion concrete* or *grouted concrete.*

Aggregate used. In this concrete, usually gap graded aggregate is used. Typical gradings of coarse and fine aggregates are shown in Table 24.6 and 24.7 respectively. The coarse aggregate must be free from dust and dirt as these will impair the bond between cement paste and aggregate. The coarse aggregate should also be thoroughly wetted or inundated before the mortar is intruded, but water should not be allowed to stand for long.

Table 24.6. Typical grading for coarse aggregate

Seive size in mm	150	75	38	19	13
Cumulative % passing	100	67	40	6	1
	—	100	62	4	1
	—	100	97	9	1

Table 24.7. Typical grading for fine aggregate

Sieve size in mm	2.36 mm	1.18 mm	600 micron	300 micron	150 micron
Cumulative % passing	100	98	72	34	11

Mortar

Mortar may consist two parts of portland cement, one part of very finely divided and highly active pozzolana, and three to four parts of fine sand with sufficient water to form fluid mixture. Pozzolana is added to improve fluidity of the mortar. It also reduces bleeding and segregation of the mortar. An intrusion aid is also added to improve the fluidity of the mortar and to hold the solid constituents in suspension and delaying the stiffening of the mortar. The mortar is made of a thick cream consistency.

The mortar is pumped under pressure through about 35 mm diameter perforated or slotted pipe spaced at 2.0 m apart starting from the bottom of the mass. These pipes are gradually withdrawn after the grouting is complete.

Preplaced concrete is economical in cement as about 120 kg/m^3 to 150 kg/m^3 of cement is used, but the strength obtained is low of the order of 200 kg/cm^2 only due to high water/cement ratio.

Advantages

Following are the advantages and disadvantages of preplaced concrete.

1. Preplaced concrete can be placed in locations which are not easily accessible for ordinary concreting.
2. It can be placed in sections containing a large number of embedded items such as in nuclear shields.
3. Segregation of heavy and coarse aggregate is eliminated.
4. Pumping over long distances is possible.
5. Under water construction is also possible by its use.
6. It's drying shrinkage is lower than that of ordinary concrete.
7. It's use is preferable in mass concrete construction where temperature has to be controlled.
8. It is also used to provide an exposed aggregate finish.

Disadvantages

1. It develops shrinkage cracks.
2. It needs special skill and experience in application, hence costly.

24.13. VACCUM-PROCESSED CONCRETE

The problem of obtaining high workability with a minimum water/cement ratio is solved by the use of vaccum processing of freshly placed concrete. In this method a part of water mixed with concrete for suitable workability is sucked back by the pump after the concrete is laid in position. This concrete is known as *vaccum concrete.*

Procedure. A mix with suitable workability is placed in the forms in the usual manner. As fresh concrete contains a continuous system of water filled channels, the application of a vaccum to the surface of the concrete results in a large amount of water being extracted from a certain depth of concrete. Thus the final water/cement ratio before setting is reduced, which controls the strength. The magnitude of the decrease in the water cement ratio is shown in Table 24.8.

Table 24.8.

Water/cement ratio		*Compressive strength*	
Before processing	*After processing*	*Before processing in kg/cm^2*	*After processing in kg/cm^2*
0.74	0.68	177	230
0.71	0.59	150	223
0.65	0.57	206	270
0.60	0.55	297	328

Effect of vaccum processing

It has following effects:

1. The final strength of concrete increases by about 25% and 28 days strength is reached in 8 to 9 days.
2. The permeability of concrete decreases sufficiently.
3. It gives high density concrete.

4. The increase in bond strength of concrete is found about 20%. It's modulus of elasticity is always higher.
5. The over all durability of concrete is increased.
6. Coarser grading of aggregate yields more water than finer grading *i.e.* more water is extracted.

However, some of the water extracted leaves behind voids, so that full theoretical advantage of water removal may not be achieved in practice. The increase in strength on vaccum treatment is proportional to the amount of water removed upto a critical value, beyond which there is no significant increase. Thus prolonged vaccum treatment is not useful. The critical value depends on the thickness of concrete and on the mix proportions. It has been observed that the strength of vaccum processed concrete broadly follows the usual dependence on the final water/cement ratio as shown in Fig. 24.6.

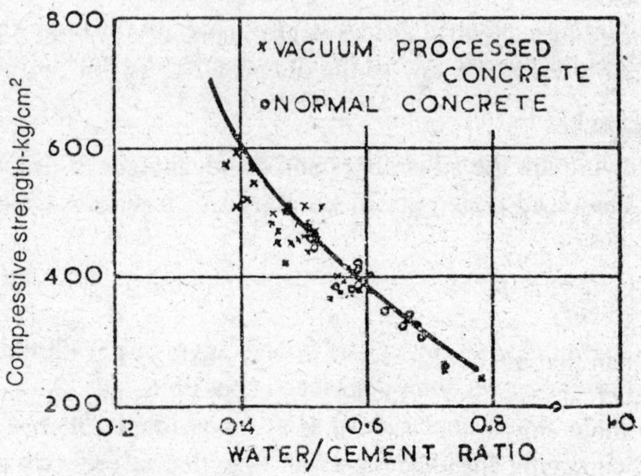

Fig. 24.6. Relation between compressive strength and w/c ratio on vaccum processed concrete

Procedure of applying vaccum

The vaccum is applied through porous mats connected to a vaccum pump. The mats consist of an air tight cover, usually made of plywood, with a vaccum chamber formed by expanded metal. This is faced with a fine wire gauge covered by muslin which prevents the removal of cement particles along with water. Fig. 24.7 shows a cross section of a vaccum mat. The mat can be placed on the top of the concrete surface immediately after finishing it and also be incorporated inside the faces of the forms.

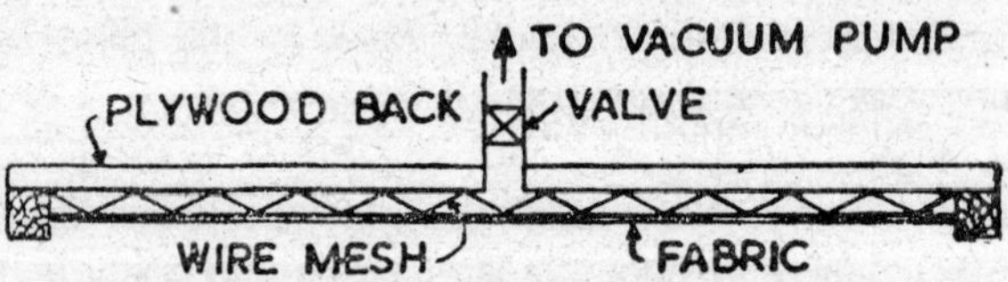

Fig. 24.7. Cross section of vaccum mat

Vaccum is created by a vaccum pump, the capacity of which is governed by the perimeter of the mat and not on its area. The magnitude of pressure usually ranges between 40 cms to 65 cms of mercury. This vaccum reduces the water content upto 20% over a depth of 15 cms to 30 cms. The reduction is greater nearer to the mat and usually the suction is assumed to be effective upto 15 cms to 20 cms depth only. Thus for a concrete section mat about 30 cms thick vaccum should be applied from two opposite sides. The withdrawal of water produces settlement of the concrete to the extent of about 3% of the depth over which the suction acts. The rate of withdrawal of water falls with time. Duration of processing of 15 to 25 minutes has been found most economical and effective. Beyond 30 minutes very little reduction in water content has been observed.

The formation of voids can be checked, if in addition to vaccum processing, intermittent vibration is also applied. By the application of vibration higher degree of consolidation is achieved and the amount of water withdrawn is almost double.

Advantages

1. Vaccum processed concrete stiffens very rapidly, hence the form work can be removed after 30 minutes of casting even on columns about 4.5 m high. It is of considerable economic value as the form work can be reused at frequent interval.

2. The surface of vaccum processed concrete is entirely free from pitting and the uppermost 1 mm surface is highly resistant to abrasion. This property is very useful in the construction of concrete work where the concrete surface is in constant contact with flowing water at a high velocity.
3. Vaccum proceed concrete bonds well with the old concrete hence it can be used for resurfacing road slabs and for other repair work.

Disadvantages

Its main disadvantage is its high initial cost.

24.14. SHOT CRETE OR GUNITING

The procedure of applying cement mortar or concrete through a hose and pneumatically projected at high velocity on the back up surface is known as *shot creating* or *guniting* and the mortar or concrete is known as *shot crete* or *gunite.* The technique of depositing very thin layers of mortars in each pass of the nozzle than that available with the shot creat is known as *guniting.* This is the difference between guiniting and shot create. The force of the jet impacting on the surface compacts the material such that it can support itself without sagging or sloughing even on a vertical face or overhead. In general terms it may be called sprayed concrete. The shot crete has no different properties than that of conventionally placed concrete of similar proportions; it is the method of placing that imparts some significant advantages to it in some of its applications. However considerable skill and experience is required in the application of shot crete. Thus the quality of shot crete depends to a large extent on the performance of the operator.

Uses

Shot crate usually is used in the following situations.

1. For the construction of thin, lightly reinforced sections such as curtain walls.
2. For the construction of shell or folded plate roofs.
3. For tunnel lining and for protective covering of soft rocks.
4. For pre-stressed tanks.
5. For repairing of deteriorated concrete and for stabilizing of rock slopes.
6. For encasing steel for fire proofing.
7. For repair or laying new canal and reservoir lining.
8. It can also be applied to a surface covered by running water, in such cases an accelerator producing flash set such as washing soda should be used. Though it adversely affects its strength, but makes repair work possible.
9. For repairing of old buildings.

Advantages

Shot crete has been found to have following advantages and disadvantages.

1. The shot crete layer can be made very strong by applying pneumatic pressure.
2. 3 cms to 5 cms thickness of short crete lining is sufficient.
3. Shot crete lining does not need expansion and construction joints.
4. Short crete can be applied even on uneven base successfully.
5. Shot crete can be used for repair of disintegrated and leaking lining etc.
6. Shot crete can be applied at least from a distance of 1 m, hence it is very useful to apply lining while tunneling.

Disadvantages

1. The success of shot crete depends on the performance of the operator.
2. The cost of construction of shot crete is more than ordinary concrete of same proportion and same thickness.

3. It is less durable than ordinary lining of the same thickness.
4. Shot crete lining in canals is damaged very soon due to settlement, shrinkage and hydrostatic pressure etc.
5. To obtain perfect bond with the base is impossible.

Equipment

One of the type of guniting equipment known as cement gum is shown in Fig. 24.8. It consist of two compression chambers one above the other. The upper chamber serves as feeding hopper for the lower chamber which is under constant pressure, while the upper chamber is alternately under pressure and free of pressure. By suitable valves the pressure in the upper chamber can be increased to that, in the lower chamber and the connecting gate opened, and the dry mortar then flows into the lower chamber. The connecting gate is then closed, the upper chamber opened up and refilled. In this way cycle is repeated. The delivery of material from the lower chamber to the hose is regulated by a feed wheel driven by an air motor. A separate hose carries water to the water ring in the nozzle where radial sprays wet the cement sand mixture. In the Fig. 24.8 H is the upper chamber and L lower chamber K and J are bell values, where M and N are gear wheel and small opening respectively.

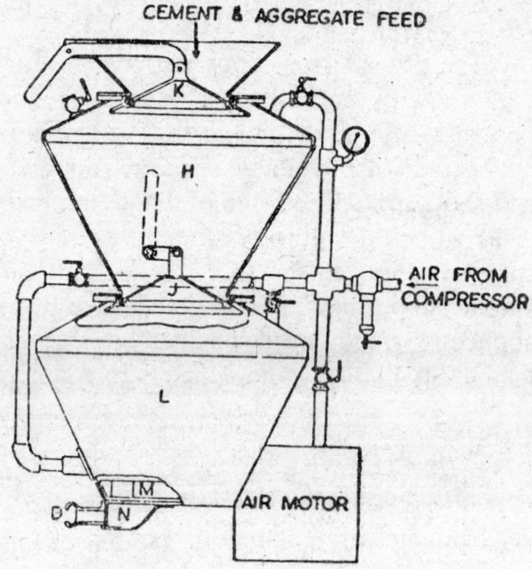

Fig. 24.8. Shot crete equipment

Preparation of base

All surfaces to be guniting should be cleaned thoroughly to obtain a good bond. Any loose or weak material should be removed by chipping, followed by sand blasting. Sand blasting can be done with the cement gun equipment using a sand blast nozzle and a low feed rate for the sand. In order to reduce the shrinkage stresses, the base which has dried, should be moistened thoroughly for a few hours before carrying out the guniting operation. Any absorptive surface to be gunited should be moistened to retard any excessive withdrawal of water from the shot crete, but excessive water should be avoided.

Grading of sand

The grading of sand to be used in guniting is very important. If the sand is very fine, it will produce a weak layer subject to excessive shrinkage, if too coarse, the amount of rebound will be excessive and a rough textured surface will be obtained. The maximum size of sand particle may be 6 mm and the fineness modulus may vary from 2.5 to 3.3. The following grading is found most suitable.

Table 24.

S. No.	*Size*	*Commulative %*	
		Passing	*Retained*
1.	4.75	100 — 95	0 — 5
2.	1.18 mm	80 — 44	20 — 56
3.	300 micron	30 — 10	70 — 90
4.	150 micron	2 — 0	98 — 100

The sand should have a moisture content between 3 to 6% for satisfactory operating of the equipment, but in no case it should exceed 8%. A 4% moisture content is found to give best results. If the sand is too dry it will not flow uniformly, but will come out in brusts and dry patches will result. If too wet it will clogg the equipment. Dry sand will give more rebound.

Rebound

The material which bounces back from the working face is known as *rebound*. It is largely the coarser particles of sand which rebound. The amount of rebound depends upon the following factors.

1. Rebound is greater when guniting is done on vertical or on over hanging surfaces than level or sloping surfaces.
2. Greater the nozzle velocity, more the rebound.
3. Lower the water/cement ratio, greater the rebound.

The amount of rebound varies from 20% to 40% of the material handled. The approximate value of rebound is 5 to 15% for horizontal surfaces, 15 to 35% for sloping and vertical surfaces and 25 to 40% for over head surfaces and corners.

Mix proportion

Mortar mixes having one part of cement and 4 to 4.5 part of moist sand by weight are found quite satisfactory. In general richer mixes shrink more and high shrinkage may destroy the bond with the base. For this reason richer mixes should be avoided. The usual water/cement ratio varies from 0.35 to 0.5 or 14 litres of water per 50 kg of cement is sufficient. The 7 day strength of 1:3 mix can be of the order of 70 MPa.

Mixing and placing

Before putting the dry materials into the cement gun, the sand and cement should be mixed thoroughly for $1\frac{1}{2}$ minutes till the homogeneous mixture of one colour is obtained. Any mixed material not used within 45 minutes of mixing should be rejected.

For placing the mortar, the hose length should be kept as small as possible as long hose requires greater pressures for air and water. Though hose length upto 110 m have been used but preferably they should not be longer than 30 to 45 m. For the shorter lengths the air pressure should be about 3.5 kg/cm^2 at the nozzle and the water pressure at the nozzle should be 4.2 kg/cm^2. Both air and water pressure should not be more than 5.25 kg/cm^2 for a long hose. Though the volume of air required depends upon the size of the nozzle and air pressure, but, for an average work using 3 cm diameter nozzle about 7.25 cubic metre air per minute is required.

Operation

The line diagram of a cement gun is shown in Fig. 24.9. After filling sand cement mix in vessel C, air at a pressure of 2.2 kg/cm^2 to 3.5 kg/cm^2 is sent from compressor A to vessel C through moisture extractor B. At B the the moisture in air is absorbed and dry air reaches in the vessel C. This air pushes the cement-sand mixture through pipe D and ejects it through nozzle E. as shown in Fig. 24.9. Through another pipe, air is sent from compressor A at a pressure of 3.0 to 4.6 kg/cm^2 to water tank F. From this tank air is delivered through pipe G and ejected at E. Pressures are controlled at E.

While guniting, the nozzle should be held normal to the surface and about 1 to 1.5 m from it. In order to obtain a uniform layer, it should be kept moving. In case for thicker layer, it should be provided in layers not thicker than about 2.5 cm using stiffer mix as thicker layer tends to slough from vertical and over head surfaces. Successive layers should be applied before the first layers have dried. All rebound material

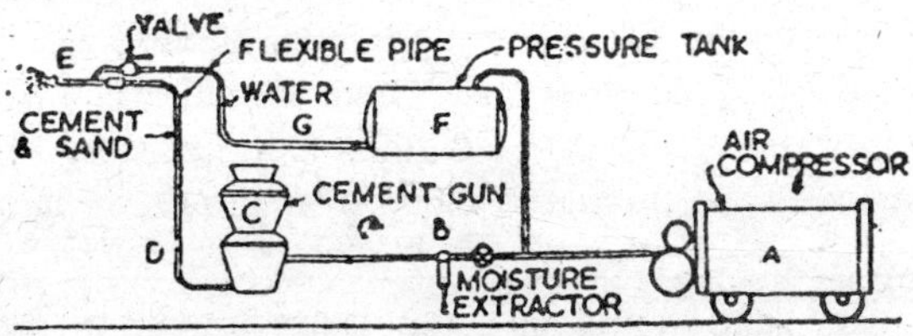

Fig. 24.9. General Arrangement for shotcreting

should be removed carefully, as there is a tendency for the rebound material to collect in the forms or to coat the surface of completed work. Wooden templates should be used at corners, edges and on surfaces where it is necessary to obtain true lines and proper thickness.

If a smooth surface is desired, steel troweling can be done, but it should be done at least after 1 hour of placing the mix. The process of guniting should be suspended when wind is blowing as it will not be possible to maintain the consistency of the mix.

Curing. The completed work should be protected from direct sun rays at least for 3 days and should be moist cured for at least 14 days.

24.15. COLCRETE

It is grouted concrete obtained by penetrating or injecting the colgrout into the voids of preplaced coarse aggregates. Colgrount is the colloidal mix of cement, sand and water in requisite proportions produced by high speed mixing in a mixer known as *colcrete mixer.* Colcrete mixer is a double drum concrete mixer. The proportioning of the ingredients can be done either by weight or by volume. The cement and water is mixed in the first drum of the mixer and the water/cement slurry produced in this drum is transferred into the second drum and sand is added to produce the cement, sand and water grout. The mixing cycle in each drum may be kept 1.5 minutes or more till a suitable grout is obtained.

14.15.1. Advantages of colcrete

In ordinary 1:2:4 mix, the surface area of coarse aggregate per cubic metre of concrete is found of the order of 68800 square metres. To wet and activate this area with a relatively small amount of water of a particular water cement ratio concrete in a short mixing period presents great difficulty. Cement particles tend to adhere closely which entraped air. Thus mixing of conventional concrete remains imperfect. To over come this difficulty the constituents of the concrete are passed through a colloidal mill, where each solid particle surface is brought in contact with the liquid.

14.15.2. Colcrete process

After cleaning the surface and form work, a layer of big size boulders is placed in the form section and the voids of bolders are packed by graded stones of diminishing sizes, the minimum size being 40 mm. The minimum size of 40 mm is chosen to enable the concrete grout to penetrate into the voids. Again a layer of big size boulders is spread and voids filled with graded diminishing size stone pieces. The height of each layer may vary from 22.5 cms to 30 cms. The process is repeated till the height of the lift is reached. Voids in the packed aggregate may vary from 33% to 40%.

Mixing of Colgrout

The colgrout is mixed in double drum colcrete mixers to form colloidal grout of suitable consistency. The cement and water is mixed in the first drum of the mixer and water cement slurry produced is transferred to the second drum where sand is added to produce cement-sand grout. The mixing time in each drum of 1.5 minute is found sufficient.

Grout pipes of 7.5 cms to 10 cms in diameter can be used They may be inserted either at the time of packing boulders or inserted after the packing into the holes left for this purpose. The pipes are spaced at about 2 metres centre to centre and the grout is injected at a velocity of about 30 cms per second. The pipes are taken from the bottom of the lift and are raised by about 5 to 10 cms before grout to clear the outlets. The grouting should be done continuously and its fluidity should be maintained during the period of injection in the grout pipe. Grout should not be allowed to form air locks by flowing along surface of low penetration resistance, as along flat surfaces. After the grout has come to the surface, grout pipes are removed and surface leveled off by gravity *grouting of the surface.*

Characteristics of Colgrout

1. The cement is thoroughly mixed with other constituents of the mix as each particle of the cement

in the mix is completely wetted by the high speed shearing action of the mixer.

2. The colgrout has colloidal characteristics, resulting in the maximum gel formation of the cement. This prevents aggregation of sand resulting in the reduction of bleeding to a minimum.
3. As colgrout is quite fluid and stable, it can be pumped to considerable distances to the point of placement. It does not need any admixture, however for special purposes these may be used by high speed mixing.
4. The breaking up of aggregations and separations of the smaller particles of cement is achieved by high speed mixing, which results in greater fluidity.
5. Colgrout normally is composed of same ingredients of cement and sand in the proportion of 1 part of cement and upto 4 part of sand.

QUESTIONS

1. Describe the effects of incorporating fibres in concrete.
2. Discuss the significance of the modulus of elasticity of fibres incorporated in concrete.
3. Describe the roller compacted concrete.
4. Write the uses of glass fibre reinforced concrete.
5. Differentiate between the sulpher concrete and sulpher infiltrated concrete.
6. State the advantages and disadvantages of sulpher concrete.
7. What is ferro cement? Explain.
8. What is inverted slump test? Explain.
9. Discuss the uses of ferro cement.
10. What is meant by polymer impregnated concrete? Explain.
11. Under what conditions the polymer impregnated concrete is used? Explain.
12. What are the effects of incorporating the fibres in concrete.
13. Describe the polymer concrete.
14. What is the difference between the thermoset and thermoplastics polymers?
15. Discuss the polymer portland cement concrete.

15. What is pre packed concrete? Write down its advantages and disadvantages.
17. What is shotcrete? Write down its uses, advantages and disadvantages.
18. Write notes on the followings:
    (*a*) Guniting (*b*) Colcrete
    (*c*) Vaccum processed concrete

OBJECTIVE TYPE QUESTIONS

1. Polymer impregnated concrete is produced by
   (*a*) Incorporating a polymeric material into concrete during the mixing state
   (*b*) Impregnating low viscosity prepolymers into the pores system of hardened concrete and polymerising it by heating
   (*c*) Replacing the cement water matrix in cement concrete by prepolymer and polymerising it
   (*d*) Any of the above processes
2. The surface polymer impregnation of bridge deck concrete improves mainly its
   (*a*) Structural properties (*b*) Chemical resistance and durability
   (*c*) Riding surface of concrete (*d*) All of the above
3. Monomer loading is affected by the
   (*a*) Degree of vaccum applied and its duration (*b*) Amount of air in voids
   (*c*) Extent of moisture in concrete (*d*) All the above
4. The polymerisation by heating the catalyzed monomer to the required level can be done by
   (*a*) Low pressure steam injection (*b*) Infra red heaters
   (*c*) Heating in an air oven (*d*) Heating under water
   (*e*) Any of the above

5. Identify the incorrect statements
   (*a*) Thermoplastic resins are more viscous and difficult to impregnate into concrete but can with stand higher temperature with out softening
   (*b*) Heating decomposes the polymer before polymerizing by cross linking
   (*c*) Thermoplastic monomers loose their effectiveness at high temperature
   (*d*) All the above
6. The use of polymer impregnation for the repair of damaged concrete structures has been found as
   (*a*) Suitable for restoration and preservation of stone monuments
   (*b*) Cost effective for normal structures
   (*c*) Suitable for strengthening piles in sea water
   (*d*) All the above
7. The polymerization of polymer concrete can be achieved by
   (*a*) Radiation
   (*b*) Catalyst promoter reaction
   (*c*) Thermal catalytic reaction
   (*d*) Any of the above
8. Polymer concrete can be used for
   (*a*) For the manufacture of electrical transmission poles
   (*b*) Treating sluiceways and stilling basins of the dams
   (*c*) For over lays
   (*d*) For rapid repair of damaged air filed pavements and industrial structures
   (*e*) All the above
9. Polymer modified concrete
   (*a*) Its processing process is simplest
   (*b*) It is least expensive
   (*c*) It constitutes an inter penetrating matrix that binds the aggregate
   (*d*) It is obtained by incorporating a polymeric material into concrete during the mixing stage
   (*e*) All the above
10. Fibre reinforce concrete has
   (*a*) Superior crack resistance and improved ductility
   (*b*) Has high impact resistance and toughness
   (*c*) It can be used for tunnel linning and hydraulic structures
   (*d*) It can be used for air port run ways, precast products, blast and impact resistant structures
   (*e*) For improved bond indented and band fibres can be used
   (*f*) It is more vulnerable to corrosion damage than conventional steel reinforced concrete
   (*g*) All the above
11. Identify the false statements
   (*a*) The workability of fresh fibre concrete is high
   (*b*) The workability of fresh fibre concrete is low
   (*c*) The fibre reinforced concrete is more cohesive and less prone to segregation
   (*d*) The fibre reinforced concrete is less cohesive and more prone to segregation
   (*e*) High modulus fibres improve flexural and impact resistance simultaneously
   (*f*) Low modulus fibres improve the impact resistance of the concrete
   (*g*) Low modulus fibres have no effect on the impact resistance of concrete
12. Identify the incorrect statements
   (*a*) The ratio of diameter of fibre to its length is called aspect ratio
   (*b*) The improvement in structural performance of fibre reinforced concrete depends on strength characteristics of fibres, volume of fibres, shape and aspect ratio of fibres
   (*c*) The ultimate strain of steel fibres reinforced concrete is 20 to 50 times that of plain concrete
   (*d*) By adding 4% steel fibres, the flexural strength increases by 2.5 times the strength of un reinforced composite
13. Identify the incorrect statements
   (*a*) With the use of vegetable fibres long term durability is doubt full
   (*b*) Organic fibres may decay

(*c*) Asbestos fibres cause health hazards
(*d*) Carbon fibres are very expensive and more vulnerable to damage than glass fibres
(*e*) Glass fibres are chemically stable in cement paste matrix.

14. The performance of hardened fibre reinforced concrete basically depend upon
(*a*) Critical concentration of fibres (*b*) Aspect ratio
(*c*) Specific surface of fibre (*d*) All the above

15. The highest improvement in the impact strength is given by
(*a*) Glass fibres (*b*) Carbon fibres
(*c*) Asbestos fibres (*d*) Vegetable fibres

16. The fundamental requirements of fibre concrete is
(*a*) The mix should have sufficient paste to coat the fibres and aggregate
(*b*) Uniform distribution of fibres through out the mix
(*c*) The mix should have optimum content of fibres for workability
(*d*) All the above

17. Identify the incorrect statements
(*a*) W/c ratios of 0.45 to 0.6 are associated with steel fibres reinforced concrete
(*b*) Steel fibre reinforced concrete contains cement contents of 300 to 500 kg/m^3
(*c*) The aspect ratio of steel fibres range from 10 to 100
(*d*) The fibre content in steel fibre reinforced concrete varies from 1.0 to 2.5%
(*e*) The fine to total aggregate ratio in steel fibre reinforced concrete varies from 0.5 to 1.0

18. Fibrous ferro cement
(*a*) Panels can with stand very high stresses compared to that of conventional ferro cement
(*b*) Has improved toughness and impact resistance than conventional ferro cement
(*c*) Fibrous ferro cement can be obtained by adding short fibres to plain mortar matrix of ferro cement
(*d*) All of the above

19. Shot crete is
(*a*) Very useful for restoration and repair of fire damaged concrete structures
(*b*) Used for stabilization of rock slope and tunnel invert etc.
(*c*) Generally economical than conventional concrete
(*d*) It is a very thin concrete layer deposited by injecting it with high velocity on the prepared surface
(*e*) All the above

20. Shot crete differs from conventional concrete in
(*a*) Materials, proportion and void system (*b*) Nature of failure
(*c*) Compaction (*d*) Application procedure
(*e*) All the above

21. Identify the incorrect statements
(*a*) If less amount of water is added to the mortar, more material will rebound from the surface
(*b*) If more water is added to the mortar, the shot crete will slough if jetted on to the vertical surface
(*c*) The w/c ratio of shot-crete should be between 0.45 to 0.6
(*d*) Dry mix process is preferred in case of light weight concrete
(*e*) In the wet mix process all the ingredients are mixed before entering the chamber of delivery equipment

22. Shot cretes suffers due to
(*a*) High cost of shot crete and wastage due to rebound
(*b*) Spalling of shot crete due to corrosion of reinforcement
(*c*) Peeling of un sound shot crete due to failure of bond due to inadequate surface preparation
(*d*) Necessity of cleaning and hauling the rebound material to the approved waste area
(*e*) Environment problems due to dust problem
(*f*) All the above

23. Special shot-crete can be obtained
(*a*) By using calcium aluminate C_3A cement (hydraulic cement) as binding material
(*b*) By using air entraining cements
(*c*) By adding upto 2% steel fibres by volume

(*d*) Any of the above

24. While using shot crete for repairing damaged concrete it is essential that
    (*a*) Shot crete is applied on the moist surface
    (*b*) The fresh layer should be applied before the initial set of the previous layer
    (*c*) At the perimeter of the cavity the square shoulders should be provided
    (*d*) All unsound material should be removed
25. Identify the correct statements
    (*a*) Guniting is a technique of depositing very thin layers of mortar in each pass of nozzle than that available with the shot-crete
    (*b*) In cuniting mix of 1:3 to 1:4.5 with w/c ratio of about 0.3 may be adopted.
    (*c*) In guniting careful and skilful handling of nozzle is essential for high quality finish work
    (*d*) Guniting reduces the permeability and increases the resistance to chemical and weathering effects
    (*e*) All are correct
26. Identify the incorrect statements
    (*a*) Roller compacted concrete is known as lean rolled concrete
    (*b*) Roller compacted concrete is almost dry having no slump
    (*c*) Roller compacted concrete mainly is used in the construction of dams
    (*d*) Roller compacted concrete mainly is used for thin structural members
27. Identify the incorrect statements
    (*a*) The cement content in roller compacted concrete varies from 450 to 550 kg/m^3
    (*b*) The cement content in roller compacted concrete varies from 60 to 360 kg
    (*c*) The bond between new and old layer is also called cold joint
    (*d*) The compressive strength of roller compacted concrete varies from 7 to 30 MPa
    (*e*) Roller compacted concrete is consolidated by internal vibrators
28. Identify the incorrect statements
    (*a*) Pre placed and prepacked concretes are two kinds of concretes
    (*b*) The voids in the prepleced concrete are of the order of 30 to 35%
    (*c*) In preplaced concrete the cement content is 120 to 150 kg/m^3
    (*d*) The segregation of preplaced concrete is very high
    (*e*) There is no segregation in the preplaced concrete
29. Identify the incorrect statements
    (*a*) The permeability of vaccum processed concrete is very high
    (*b*) The modulus of elasticity of vaccum processed concrete is always higher
    (*c*) The final strength of vaccum processed concrete decreases by 25%
    (*d*) The over all durability of vaccum precessed concrete is higher
    (*e*) Vaccum processed concrete bonds well with the old concrete
30. Identify the correct statements
    (*a*) Saw dust concrete is vibrated by internal needle vibrators
    (*b*) Preplaced concrete is vibrated by internal needle vibratos
    (*c*) To fill the voids of aggregates of preplaced concrete, cement sand mixture is spread over the aggregates and then water is sprinkled over it
    (*d*) Under water construction is not possible with preplaced concrete
    (*e*) Vaccum processing is applied to increase the w/c ratio of the concrete
    (*f*) Vaccum processed concrete stiffens very rapidly hence form work may be removed after 30 minutes

Answers

1. (*b*)	7. (*d*)	13. (*e*)	19. (*e*)	25. (*e*)
2. (*b*)	8. (*e*)	14. (*c*)	20. (*e*)	26. (*d*)
3. (*d*)	9. (*e*)	15. (*a*)	21. (*c*)	27. (*a, e*)
4. (*e*)	10. (*g*)	16. (*d*)	22. (*f*)	28. (*a, d*)
5. (*b*)	11. (*a, d, g*)	17. (*e*)	23. (*d*)	29. (*a, c*)
6. (*a*)	12. (*a*)	18. (*d*)	24. (*d*)	30. (*f*)

25

From Work

25.1. INTRODUCTION

The temporary construction used as a mould for the structure in which concrete is placed and allowed to harden in the desired shape is known as *form work* or *shuttering*. The average cost of the form work is about 33 to 40% of the cost of the whole job. Hence the careful and economic design of the form work is essential. More over the appearance of the finished surface of concrete and progress of work are largely dependent on the use of properly constructed form work.

25.2. REQUIREMENTS OF FORM WORK

The main object of the form work is to give the necessary shape to the concrete and to support it while it is setting and hardening. In order to obtain these objectives, a from work should meet the following requirements.

1. **It must be true to grade and alignment.** The surface of the shuttering in contact with the concrete must be true to grade and alignment, so that the desired type of surface finish may be obtained.
2. **It must be strong enough.** The mould or shuttering has to bear the weight of concrete, and any other loading of man and machinery etc. Thus it should be strong enough to resist all these loads without undue distortion or deflection.
3. **It must be sufficiently durable.** During the process of hardening of concrete in the mould, it may absorb some moisture and may alter its shape. If so happens, the resulting surface will be unsightly. Hence the mould must be sufficiently durable.
4. **It should have tight joints.** During compaction, specially while compaction is provided by vibration, the cement mortar may leak out through joints, if they are not sufficiently tight. Hence to prevent the leakage of mortar, the joints should be tight enough, otherwise honeycombing will be developed near the leaking joints.
5. **It must be easy to handle.** It must be made up of sections which can be handled readily by the available means and which can be erected and assembled quickly.
6. **It must be easy to stripe.** It must be constructed in such a way that it can be stripped easily in the correct sequence without damage to the concrete.
7. **No nails etc. should protrude from it.** In case no plastering is to be done on the concrete, the shuttering should not be allowed to protrude any nail or wire etc. from it, as they will produce unpleasing surface.

25.3. PLANNING AND ORGANISING FOR FORM WORK

When the use of shuttering is decided, the economics of different types of form work should be considered in relation to the basic requirements as noted above. The economics will include the initial cost of material, speed of assembling and striking and the amount of repeated use which can be made of the form work.

25.4. MATERIALS USED FOR FORM WORK

For the construction of form work, following materials may be used.

1. Timber 2. Steel

1. Timber used for form work

Timber has been used for shuttering or form work ever since the reinforced concrete is used as a construction material. Timber used for shuttering should possess the following properties.

1. It should be soft, as they are easy to plane and work with.
2. Coarse grained knotty timber should not be used, as nailing is difficult in the region of knots. Also coarse grained timber will show its grains on the finished surface of the concrete.
3. It should not be hard, as it is costly and difficult to work. They develop cracks on nailing.
4. As shuttering undergoes a great deal of wetting and drying under rough conditions, hence timber used for shuttering should be partially seasoned. Kiln seasoned or fully dry timber is usually too dry and is liable to swell by absorbing moisture from concrete when used for form work. On the other hand, too green a timber will shrink excessively, particularly in hot weather. Good quality timber is preferable. It must retain its shape under very rough conditions of drying and wetting. Timber used for form work should be planed smooth on all four surfaces, but for props, joists, however can be rough sawn.

25.5. SHEETING OR SHEATHING

It is that part of form work which comes into contact with the concrete face. It usually consists of 12.5 cm to 22.5 cm wide boards. The thickness of planks may vary from 2.5 cm to 5.0 cm depending on the load it is required to carry. Tongued and grooved boarding is very suitable for sheeting as it provides a smooth surface with good leak proof joints when new. However, this may give trouble after being used for several times. In certain cases thick plywood is very suitable as sheathing material, provided it is bonded with a water proof glue. Plywood can be obtained with a hard plastic face which provides a very smooth and durable surface. Though this form of sheeting is expensive than other forms of boarding, but it can be used for many more repetitions and also reduces the number of joints in the form work.

25.5.1. Absorptive form lining

Absorptive form lining is used as a means of removing excess water from the concrete surfaces for eliminating sand streaks and surface voids and at the same time for producing an attractive surface finish. The absorptive material generally is 12.5 mm thick and is fastened inside the regular forms. Special care should be exercised to keep the lining dry and undamaged before and during placement and compaction of concrete. As the lining tends to adhere to the concrete, hence it should be stripped within 36 hours after placing the concrete. This lining has been found to increase the relative durability of concrete.

25.5.2. Advantages of timber shuttering

Following are the advantages of timber shuttering:

1. Timber is very suitable material for form work due to its adaptability and ease in manufacture.
2. It is a good heat insulator and helps to protect the concrete from hot sun and cold wind.
3. It's initial cost is less.

25.5.3. Disadvantages

1. Its life is short. It can not be reused for a large number of times.

2. It requires constant maintenance. Hence its maintenance cost is more.

2. Steel form work

Steel form work has the following advantages and disadvantages.

Advantages

1. It is more suitable for standard size units as for precast units where large number of uses are required.
2. It's life is much longer than timber form work.
3. It can be assembled easily within a short period.
4. It gives a better smooth surface of concrete.
5. It can be stripped easily within no time.

Disadvantages

1. It's initial cost is high.
2. It does not provide the concrete with the same degree of protection from frost or hot sun shine as timber form work. Hence in extreme hot climate, extra protection against frost or sun shine is required.

25.6. DESIGN LOAD

In the construction of floors and roofs, the form work has to bear the weight of wet concrete, live load due to labour and impact due to pouring of concrete besides its own weight. For the design of planks and joists in bending and shear, a live load including the impact may be taken as 370 kg/m^2. The surfaces of the form work should be given a camber such that after deflection due to weight of concrete and reinforcement the surface of form work should remain horizontal. The sheathing with a full live load of 370 kg/m^2 should not deflect more than 0.25 cms and the joists with 200 kg/m^2 of live load should not deflect more than 0.25 cms.

25.7. PRESSURE ON FORM WORK OF COLUMNS AND WALLS

In the design of form work for columns or walls, the hydrostatic pressure of concrete should also be taken into account. This pressure depends on the following factors.

The greatest load to be carried by a form work is generally due to the weight of concrete. Thus the form work under the sofit of beams and slabs will carry a direct weight of the concrete. The weight of dense concrete may be assumed as 2300 kg/m^3. Hence the pressure per unit area (1 m^2) on the sofit will be 2300 kg per metre height of concrete.

The vertical sides of shuttering specially of deep beams or columns or walls are also acted upon by the pressure due to freshly placed concrete. This pressure is affected by the following factors.

1. Rate of placing of concrete and its rate of hardening.
2. Method of consolidation of concrete whether by hand or by vibration. Vibrated concrete exerts greater pressure than hand compacted concrete.
3. Consistency and proportions of the mix. (*i.e.* amount of water in the mix.)
4. Temperature of the concrete, lower the temperature, higher the pressure. Degree of arching action of aggregate also affects pressure distribution.
5. Size and shape of form work.
6. Size and spacing of reinforcing steel.
7. Amount of shrinkage occurring during setting.
8. Rigidity of form work.

1. Rate of placing of concrete. It has been observed that for each rate of placing, the pressure reaches a maximum at some depth and then decreases at even greater depths. The decrease is probably due to the initial setting and stiffening of concrete. It is also influenced by compaction of concrete, friction against the form and arching action within the concrete. Column forms are filed so rapidly that the concrete behaves as a fluid during the entire placement period.

2. Method of Consolidation. The use of vibration for compaction causes greater fluidity of the concrete than the hand compaction. Thus vibration compaction develops greater pressure on the forms. This is because, as the fluidity is retained while vibration is in progress, the full hydrostatic head of the concrete under vibration is effective in producing lateral pressure. This pressure can be calculated by considering the height of concrete of a fluid having the same weight per cubic meter as that of concrete.

3. Temperature of concrete. The temperature of the concrete influences the maximum intensity of lateral pressure. It is due to the fact that at low temperatures the stiffening of the concrete is delayed and the concrete remains fluid for longer periods and for greater depths of placement. It has been observed that concrete placed at 50°F develops maximum pressure about 30% greater than concrete at 70°F.

The evaluation of effect of other factors is difficult, hence their influence is neglected being small.

On the basis of his experimental data, *Rodin* has suggested the pressure distribution as shown in Fig. 25.1. The value of maximum pressure can be computed in M.K.S. units as follows:

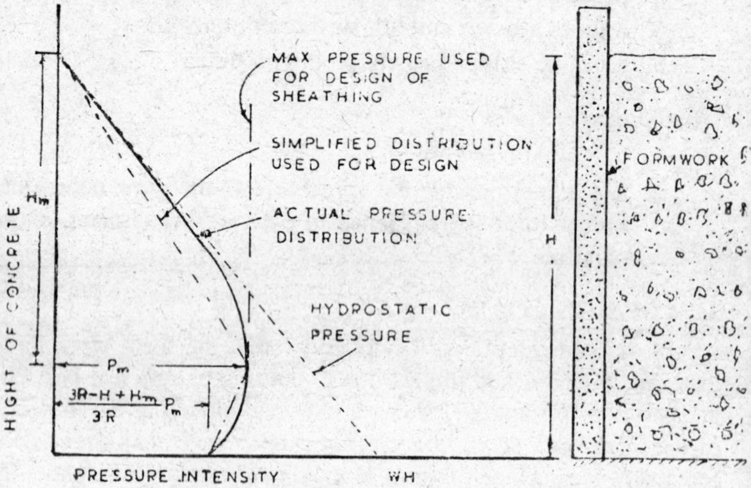

Fig. 25.1. Pressure distribution of concrete on form work

$$Pm = 2880\ R^{1/3} \text{ for hand placed concrete}$$

$$Pm = 3900\ R^{1/3} \text{ for internally vibrated concrete}$$

$$Hm = 1.09\ R^{1/3} \text{ Height of max pressure from the top of concrete}$$

where,

Pm = Maximum pressure in kg/m^2.

R = Rate of placing concrete in metre per hour.

These results are based for concrete having a slump of 15 cms at a temperature of 70°F. If external vibrators are used, the concrete may be vibrated at any depth. In that case the full hydrostatic pressure is taken.

then $Pm = WH$ (W = weight of concrete. Here it is taken as 2400 kg/m^3.)

ACI formula for pressure

For wall forms with R not exceeding 2 m per hour.

$$Pm = 0.73 + \frac{144R}{(1.8T + 32)}$$

Max. allowable $P = \dfrac{10t}{m^2}$ or 2.4 H. whichever is less (*ii*) When $R > 2$ m.

$$Pm = 0.73 + \frac{212}{(1.8\,T + 32)} + \frac{45R}{(1.8\,T + 32)}$$

Max. allowable pressure same as above

(*iii*) For column form,

$$Pm = 0.73 + \frac{144R}{(1.8\,T + 32)}$$

Max. allowable pressure = 15t/m^2 or 2.4 H, whichever is less.

where,

Pm = Max. lateral pressure t/m^2. (tonnes/m^2)

R = Rate of concrete placement in meter per hour.

T = Temp. of concrete.

H = Max. height of fresh concrete in the form.

t = Weight in tonnes

Russian Formula

$$Pm = 1100\,H$$

where,

H = height of layer in metre not to exceed 4V.

V = Rate of pouring in meres (pour/hour)

This formula is derived from the theory of cohesionless material as $P = \gamma H \tan^2 (45° - \varphi/2)$ putting $\gamma = 2500$ kg/m^3.

$$\phi = 23° \text{ for concrete}$$

$$P = 2500\,H \tan^2\left(45° - \frac{23°}{2}\right) = 1100\,H$$

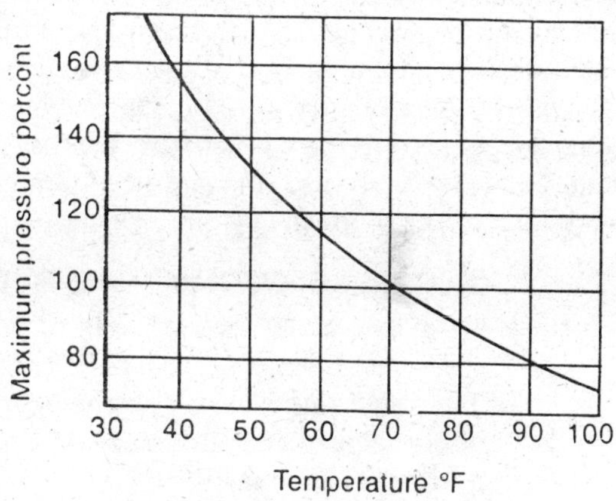

Fig. 25.2. Effect of temperature on maximum pressure on form work

The effect of temperature on the maximum concrete pressure on form work is shown in Fig. 25.2.

25.8. TOLERANCES IN FORM WORK

The form work should be constructed as per design to the shape lines and dimensions as shown on the drawings. However tolerances can be allowed as given below as per I.S. 456-1978.

Table 25.1

1.	Deviation from specified dimensions of cross section of columns and beams	– 6 mm + 12 mm
2.	Deviation from dimensions of footings (tolerance apply to concrete dimensions only)	
	(*a*) Dimensions in plan	– 12 mm + 50 mm
	(*b*) Ecentricity	0.02 times the width of the footing in the direction of deviation but not more than 50 mm
	(*c*) Thickness	± 0.05 times the specified thickness

According to Dr. Jaikishan and Dr. O.P. Jain a pressure equivalent caused by a liquid having density 2300 kg/m^3 for heights of concrete from 1.5 m to 6 m may be taken as 1200 kg/m^3. For intermediate heights of concrete poured with 1/2 to 3/4 metre an hour, the corresponding weight for the whole mass may be interpolated between 2300 kg/m^3 and 1200 kg/m^3 assuming the variation as a straight line law. As a guide line following values may be assumed as shown in table 25.2.

Table 25.2

S. No.	*Depth of Concrete in m*	*Unit-weight of fluid exerting pressure equivalent to that of concrete*
1.	1.5	2300 kg/m^3
2.	1.8	2230 kg/m^3
3.	2.1	2150 kg/m^3
4.	2.4	2080 kg/m^3
5.	2.7	2010 kg/m^3
6.	3.0	1930 kg/m^3

25.9. CLEANING AND TREATMENT OF FORMS

Before placing the concrete in the form, all rubbish, particularly chippings, and saw dust etc. should be removed carefully and the surface of the form work in contact with concrete should be cleaned and wetted or treated with mould oil etc., but care should be taken that oil does not come in contact with reinforcement nor it should stain the surface of the concrete nor it should have any adverse effect on its hardening. Steel surfaces require a heavier oil than that used for timber. If wetting of timber is not done before placing concrete, the boards will soak water from concrete and swell, resulting in uneven and bulging surface of concrete. Secondly the boards may not be so firmly attached to the concrete that at the time of stripping form work, the surface of green concrete will be pulled off resulting in unsighty surface of the concrete work.

25.10. POINTS TO BE KEPT IN MIND BEFORE PLACING CONCRETE IN FORM WORK

Following points should be kept in mind while placing concrete in the form work.

1. The geometric dimensions should be checked carefully with steel rule or steel tape. The accuracy of horizontal surfaces may be checked by spirit level and verticality by plumb bob.
2. In order to control the seepage of cement mortar through joints all openings more than 2 mm should be filled up properly.
3. The form work should be free from dust or any kind of rubbish.
4. In order to check the absorption of water by form work from green concrete, the form work either should be well wetted or oiled properly. It will give smooth surface of the concrete work.
5. The nails etc. should not protrude from the form work. It should be checked and any nails or timber piece found protruding, should be removed and mould should be repaired suitably.
6. The alignment of the form work should be checked carefully and it should not be disturbed during concreting operations.

25.11. TIME OF STRIPPING OF FORM WORK

As per I.S. 456-2000, forms should not be struck until the concrete has attained a strength at least twice

Table 25.3. Stripping time of form work as per IS-456-2000

S. No.	*Structures*	*Duration of stripping of form work*
1.	Walls, columns and vertical faces of all structural members	24 hours to 48 hour as may be decided by the engineer incharge
2.	Slabs (props left under)	3 days
3.	Beam sofit (props left under)	7 days
4.	Removal of props under slabs	
	(*a*) Spanning upto 4.5 m	7 days
	(*b*) Spanning over 4.5 m	14 days
5.	Removal of props under beams and arches	
	(*a*) Spanning upto 6 m	14 days
	(*b*) Spanning over 6 m	21 days

Note. The props left under, their sizes and disposal should be such as to be able to carry safely full dead load of slab, beam or arch as the case may be together with any live loa' likely to occur during curing or further construction.

the stresses to which the concrete may be subjected at the time of removal of the form work. The strength referred to shall be that of the concrete using the same cement and aggregates,, with the same proportions and cured under the conditions of temperature and moisture similar to those existing at work. In special circumstances the strength development of concrete can be assessed by placing companion cubes near the structures and curing under the same conditions as that of the structure. Where ever possible, form work should be left longer as it will help the curing of the concrete. In normal circumstances and where ordinary portland cement is used, and temperature does not fall below 15°C, forms should generally be removed after the expiry shown in table 25.3.

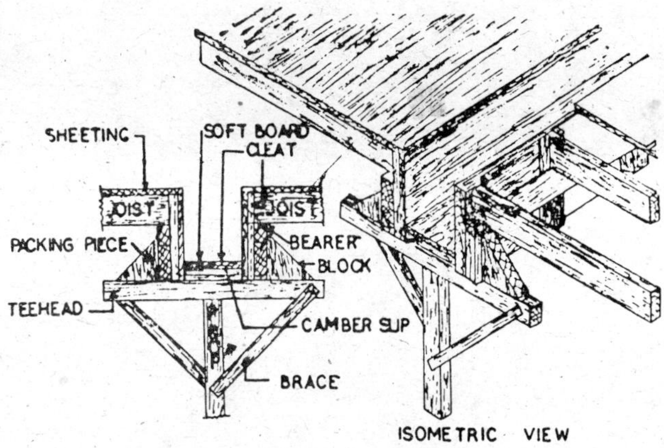

Fig. 25.3. Sectional elevation and view showing form work for a beam and slab construction

For other cements the stripping time recommended for ordinary portland cement may be suitably modified.

Thus at the end it can be said that form work must be sufficiently strong to resist all vertical and horizontal loads acting on it and have water tight joints to prevent leakage of cement mortar. It should retain its

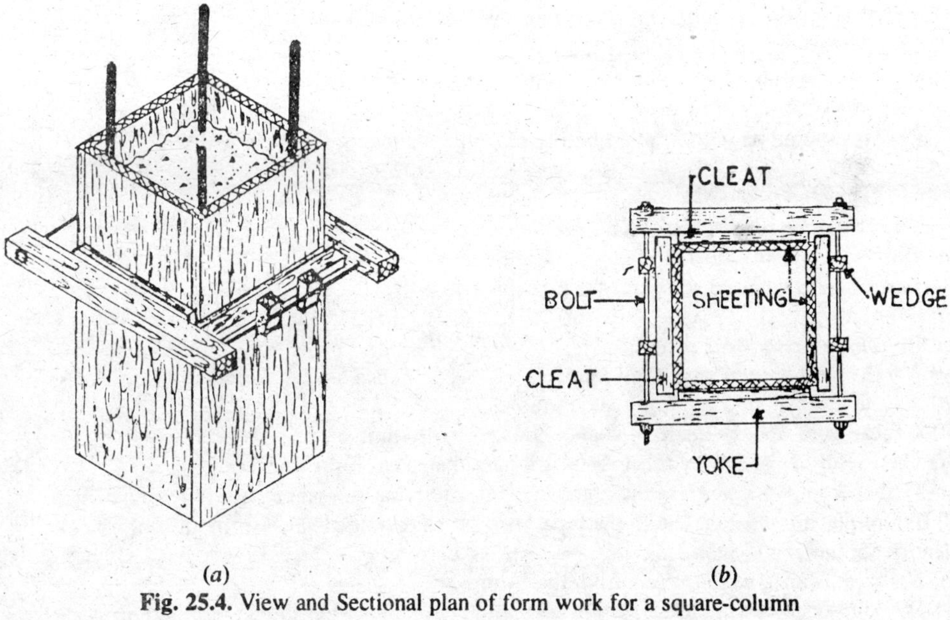

(*a*) (*b*)

Fig. 25.4. View and Sectional plan of form work for a square-column

proper shape, if once it deforms during placement of concrete, it will be impossible to pull it back to its original position. Fig. 25.3 shows a sectional elevation and view of the form work for a beam and slab construction Fig. 25.4, 25.5, 25.6 show view and sectional plan of form work for a square column, circular column and hexagonal column respectively.

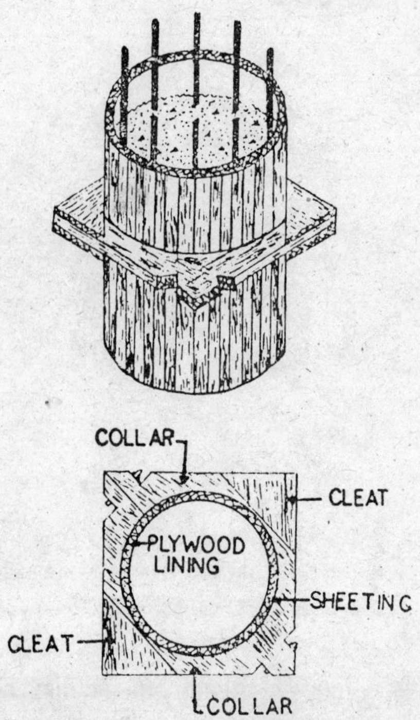

Fig. 25.5. View and sectional plan of form work for a circular column

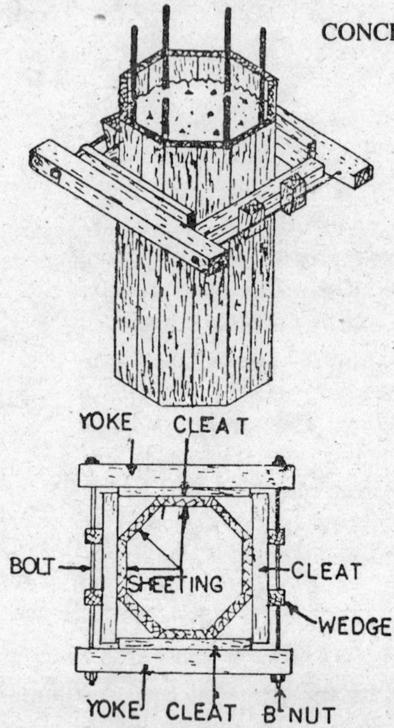

Fig. 25.6. View and sectional plan of form work for a hexagonal column

QUESTIONS

1. List the requirements of concrete form work.
2. What factors influence the lateral pressure exerted by the concrete?
3. Why is it necessary to oil an timber form work?
4. Compare and contrast timber and steel form work used for concrete work.
5. List the time of stripping of form work for various works as per I.S. 456-2000.
6. What points should be kept in mind before placing concrete in the form work?

OBJECTIVE TYPE QUESTIONS

1. Form work can be made of material except
   (*a*) Timber (*b*) Steel (*c*) Card board
2. The cost of form work comes percent of the total cost
   (*a*) 60% (*b*) 50% (*c*) 75% (*d*) 33 to 40%
3. Identify the incorrect statements
   (*a*) A form work should have tight joints
   (*b*) A form work should be strong and durable
   (*c*) A form work may be made of coarse grained knotty timber
   (*d*) The useful life of timber form work is longer than steel form work
   (*e*) Timber from work protects the green concrete from hot sun and cold wind
   (*f*) Before placing the concrete in the form work, it should be cleaned from all rubbish
4. Identify the incorrect statements
   (*a*) Nails etc. should not protrude from the form work
   (*b*) The joint openings in timber form work more than 2 mm wide should be filled properly to check leakage of cement mortar
   (*c*) The alignment of form work should not be disturbed during concreting
   (*d*) Timber form work gives better smooth surface than steel form work
   (*e*) The cost of steel form work is less than timber form work

Answers

1. (*c*) 2. (*d*) 3. (*c, d*) 4. (*d, e*)

26

Cracks in Concrete structures And their prevention

26.1. INTRODUCTION

Though concrete relatively is a durable building material, yet it may suffer or develop damages during its life duc to many reasons. Concrete suffers from damages during its production or during its service conditions requiring inmediate attention. The causes of damages many be as (*i*) Applied and environmental loads exceeding the designed loads, (*ii*) Accidents and subsidence etc. Some times damages in a structure are caused by poor construction practices, error in design and detailing and construction over loads. The other causes may be drying shrinkage, thermal stress, chemical reactions, weathering, and reinforcement corrosion etc.

The damages in plastic or green concrete may develop due to plastic shrinkage and settlement cracking. Some times on removing or stripping off the forms many surface defects such as *ridges, bulges, bolt-holes, honey combing etc.*, are noticed in the fresh concrete members. Such defects can be avoided to a great extent by using water tight and rigid form work in such a way that form work may be removed with out the use of crow bar or tools. In addition to these defects, blow holes are developed during the concreting operation due to improper design of form work. These holes are developed in the surface of concrete by water bubbles and trapped air against the face of the form work. These defects can be reduced by adopting form work slightly water absorbent and giving adequate compaction to the concrete. In case smooth surface is required or blow holes are vary large, then these holes may be filled with 1:1 or 1:2 cement sand mortar. The sand used should be sieved through 300 or 600 micron sieve depending upon the smoothness of surface desired. Preferably crushed lime stone dust should be used in place of sand. The mortar should be rubbed over the affected area with a rubber face float and finally it should be rubbed with a smooth stone for a smooth finish.

The honeycombing consisting of groups of inter connected deep holes indicate the inadequate compaction or loss of matrix through joints of form work or between previously cast surface and form work. In such cases, the affected area is cut by saw to a depth of about 5 cms. The unsound material is chipped out upto the solid concrete. The surface is cleaned, washed and dried. After preparing the surface a bonding coat of neat cement is applied to all exposed surfaces and new concrete is filled and compacted.

The repair of projections and bulges can be done by chipping off the concrete from the surface and then rubbing it with a grinding stone. The scouring of a vertical surface of a hardened concrete indicates a sign of excessive wet or harsh concrete. usually it is a superficial defect. If it is un usually deep and cover to reinforcement is small, then measures to rectify it may be the same as that suggested for filling the blow holes. The finishing repair should be carried as soon as possible after removing the form work and concrete becomes too hard. In order to develop a good bond between the parent concrete and repaired work, the repair should be carried out with in 24 hours of removing the form work.

If repair is not carried out properly, the newly placed concrete becomes loose and ineffective with the passage of time and finally gets detached from the parent concrete. The darker colour of the repaired patches can be corrected by adding 10 to 20% white cement in the mortar if the surface is of importance. Defects developing during construction are shown in Table 26.1.

Table 26.1. Summary of defects developed during construction

S. No.	*Symptoms*	*Cause*	*Preventive measures*	*Remark*
1.	Voids in concrete	**Honeycombing:** Inadequate compaction, loss of cement paste or grout	(*i*) Improve compaction (*ii*) Reduce max size of aggregate (*iii*) Prevent leakage of paste or grout	(*i*) Inject good resin mix (*ii*) Cut and repair
2.	Blow holes in form faces of concrete	Air or water trapped against form work. Inadequate compaction, unsuitable mix design, use of undesirable release agents	Improve compaction, change mix design, use of absorbent form work and appropriate release agent	Fill with polymer modified fine mortar
3.	**Cracks.** In horizontal surface as concrete stiffens or soon after that	Plastic shrinkage, rapid drying of surface	1. Use air entrainment 2. Shelter during placing concrete	Seal or paint by brushing by cement or low viscosity polymer
4.	Cracks from above reinforcement or in deep lifts	Plastic settlement, concrete continues to settle after starting to stiffen	Change mix design, use air entrainment	Recompact concrete of upper part while still plastic. Seal cracks after concrete has hardened
5.	Cracks in thick sections developing as concrete cools	Check thermal contraction	Delay cooling till concrete has gained strength. Restraint to contraction should be minimised.	Seal cracks
6.	Erosion of vertical surfaces	Scouring, water moving upwards against form face	1. Reduce water content 2. Mix design should be more cohesive	Apply polymer modified fine mortar
7.	Colour variations	Variation in mix proportions, curing conditions, materials characteristics of form face, vibration, leakage of water from form work	Prevent leakage from form work. Ensure uniformity of all relevent factors.	Adopt surface coating
8.	Powdery formed surface	Surface retardation caused by sugers present in certain timbers	Change form material. Seal surface of form work. Before other applications apply lime wash to form face.	Generally no treatment required.
9.	Rust strains	1. Pyrites in aggregates 2. Rain streaking from unprotactive steel 3. Rubbish in form work 4. Ends of wire ties turned out.	Avoid contaminated aggregates. Protect exposed steel, clean form thoroughly. Turn ends of ties inwards	Clean with dilute acid or sodium citrate or sodium surface coating

S. No.	Symptoms	Cause	Preventive measures	Remark
10.	Plucked surface	Careless removal of form work. Insufficient release agent	More care in removing form work and more care in application of release agent	Patch as for spalled concrete or rub in fine mortar
11.	Lack of cover to reinforcement	Displacement of reinforcement during placement of concrete or reinforcement fixed badly. Inadequate tolerance in detailing	Provide better support to reinforcement. More acurate steel fixing. Greater tolerance in detailing.	1. Apply protective coat. 2. Apply polymer modified cement and sand rendering

26.2. CRACKING OF CONCRETE STRUCTURES

Cracking is the most common indication of the defects in a concrete structure. It may affect appearance only or may indicate significant defect or lack of durability. Cracks may represent the extent of the damage or they may point to problems of greater magnitude. Cracks may cause corrosion of reinforcement due to entry of moisture and oxygen.

Cracks in a structure broadly may be classified into two groups as *superficial* and *structural cracks*. The structural cracks may further be divided into two categories as (*i*) *Active* and, (*ii*) *Dormant*. An active crack is that in which a movement is observed to continue, where as in a dormant crack no movement occurs.

26.3. ASSESSMENT OF CRACKS

For the assessment of the cracks following information will be useful:

1. Pattern of cracks
2. Type of crack, whether it is active or dormant.
3. Whether the crack is old or new
4. Whether it appears on the opposite face of the member
5. Type of foundation used, soil condition, sign of movement of ground, if any
6. Observations on the similar structures in the vicinity
7. Study of method of construction, test results of the site, specifications etc.
8. Weather in which the structure has been constructed.

Thus the cracking is a complex phenomenon and before any repair work is taken in hand the cause of damage must be identified clearly after careful investigations.

26.4. TYPE OF CRACKING

The cracking of concrete may be divided into the following categories:

1. Cracking of plastic concrete
2. Cracking of hardened concrete
3. Thermal cracking
4. Cracking due to chemical reaction
5. Cracking due to weathering
6. Cracking due to corrosion of reinforcement
7. Cracking due to poor construction practices
8. Cracking due to construction over loads
9. Cracking due to error in design and detailing
10. Cracks due to externally applied loads

1. Cracking of plastic concrete. The cracking of plastic concrete takes place when the exposed surfaces of freshly placed concrete are subjected to a very rapid loss of moisture due to low humidity, high temperature or wind. Due to this rapid loss of moisture, the surface of the concrete shrinks. Tensile stresses develop in the weak, stiffening plastic concrete due to the restraint developed by the surface below the drying layer of concrete. These tensile stresses cause shallow, short and discontinuous cracks running in all directions. Some times these cracks extend upto the free edge. In un reinforced concrete slabs they are seen to develop diagonally. The presence of reinforcement may change the direction of cracks. Fig. 26.1.

Fig. 26.1. Plastic shrinkage over reinforced slab

The plastic shrinkage generally takes place before the final finishing prior the curing starts. These cracks at the surface often are wide enough. On large surface areas and elements and on horizontal surfaces as slabs or floor they extend from few centimeters to many metres. These plastic shrinkage cracks may extend the full depth of elevated thin structural elements.

Control of plastic shrinkage cracks

The plastic shrinkage cracks can be controlled by reducing the relative volume charge between the fresh surface and the surface below it by preventing the rapid loss of moisture due to dry winds and hot weather. The rapid moisture loss can be controlled by saturating the the air above the concrete surface by fog nozzles and covering the concrete surface by plastic sheets at the time of placing and finishing the concrete. The surface temperature may also be reduced by using sun shades and wind velocity can be reduced by providing wind breakers. Further the concrete work may be done in the night or in the afternoon. Further flat work may be scheduled after the completion of vertical members or walls. After the formation of cracks the best remedial measure is to seal them to prevent the entry of water into them. The sealing may be done by brushing with cement paste or low viscous polymers.

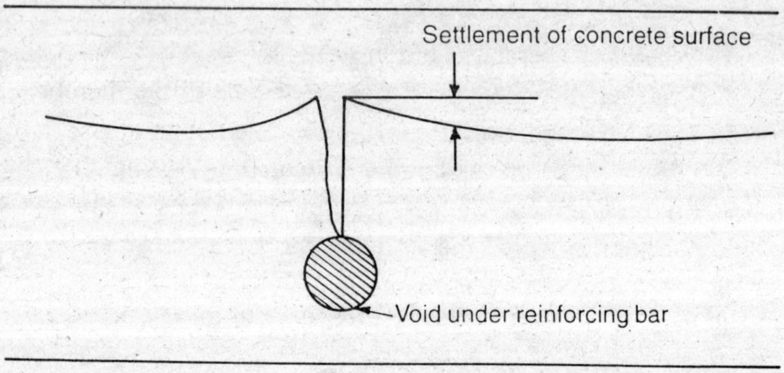

Fig. 26.2. Typical plastic settlement crack over reinforcing bar

2. Settlement Cracks

These cracks develop due to the settlement of concrete after placement, vibration and finishing. The green concrete has a tendency to settle especially in deep sections after it has started stiffening. If during this interval the fresh concrete is restrained by the previously laid concrete or reinforcing steel or form work, tie bolts, these restraints may cause cracks or voids near the restraining element as shown in Fig. 26.2.

Factors effecting the settlement cracks

The cracks developed due to the presence of reinforcing steel is affected by the following factors. The settlement cracking increases

1. With increase in the size of reinforcement steel bar
2. Increase in slump, *i.e.* the greater the slump, higher the cracking
3. By the decrease in cover thickness, lesser the cover thickness, greater the cracks
4. Insufficient compaction increases the settlement cracking many folds
5. Highly flexible form or leading base also increases settlement cracking.

Remedial Measures

The settlement cracking may be checked by adopting the following measures:

1. The concrete should be poured in small thickness and each layer is properly compacted before laying the next layer.
2. The use of minimum w/c ratio should be adopted *i.e.* the slump should be as low as practically possible.
3. The thickness of concrete cover over reinforcement should be adequate.
4. There should be adequate time interval between the placement and final finishing of concrete.

Cracking of hardened Concrete

The volume changes due to moisture movement is the inherent characteristic of the concrete. Upto 1% shrinkage of volume of cement paste has been observed due to loss of moisture from it. However the internal restraint provided by the aggregate reduces the magnitude of this volume change to about 0.05%. On the other hand an increase in moisture content tends to increase its volume. If these volume changes are restrained by the sub grade or by an other part of the structure then the tensile stresses are developed.

When the tensile stresses exceed the concrete tensile strength, then concrete cracks. The cracks may propagate at much lower stresses than are required to cause crack initiation. On walls and slabs the surface cracking occurs due to drying shrinkage when there is higher water content in concrete of surface layers than the interior concrete. The surface cracking appears in the form of a series of shallow closely spaced fine cracks.

In case of massive concrete elements, the tensile stresses are developed due to the differential shrinkage between the surface and interior of the concrete. Due to the quick evaporation of moisture from the outer surface of the concrete, the surface shrinkage is more and causes the cracks to develop. In due course of time these cracks penetrate deeper into the interior concrete.

Factors effecting the extent of cracking

The extent of shrinkage cracking depends upon the following factors:

1. Degree of restraint
2. Modulus of elasticity of concrete
3. Amount of shrinkage
4. Amount of creep

The extent of drying shrinkage is mainly influenced by the amount and type of coarse aggregate and the amount of water content in the concrete. The shrinkage is found to decrease with the increase in the amount of aggregate and reduction in the water content. Further higher the stiffness of the aggregate, lower the shrinkage of the concrete. Thus the concrete made with granite or basalt aggregate showed 50% shrinkage than that of the concrete made with sand stone aggregate. Thus the drying shrinkage can be reduced by using the maximum practical amount of aggregate and lowest amount of usable water in the concrete mix.

Prevention of shrinkage cracking

The shrinkage cracking can be controlled by the following methods:

1. By providing properly spaced construction joints
2. By providing proper steel detailing
3. By the use of shrinkage compensating cement

Cracking due to Chemical reactions

Cement is the most important constituent of the concrete. Cement usually is alkaline. When water is added to the mix, it turn out to be a strongly caustic solution due to solubility of alkalis from cement. This caustic liquid attacks reactive silica to form alkali-silica gel of unlimited swelling type. This silica gel grows in size. The continuous growth of silica gel exerts excessive pressure and causes cracking. In case of hardened concrete the alkalis of cement react with acidic compounds in the presence of moisture. Due to these reactions the concrete matrix becomes weak and its constituents leach out. In the case of hardened concrete the silica contained in aggregates and alkalis from cement react to form a swelling silica gel and draws water from other portions of the concrete. This causes local expansion accompanied by tensile stresses. If these tensile stresses are large, they deteriorate the whole structure.

Preventive measures

Following measures may be taken to control the silica-alkali reaction

1. Use of low alkali-cement
2. Proper selection of aggregate having low quantity of silica
3. Use of pozzolana

Symptoms of silica-alkali reaction

Generally following symptoms have been observed:

1. Development of map cracking of concrete
2. Leaching out gel from cracks (Fig. 26.3)

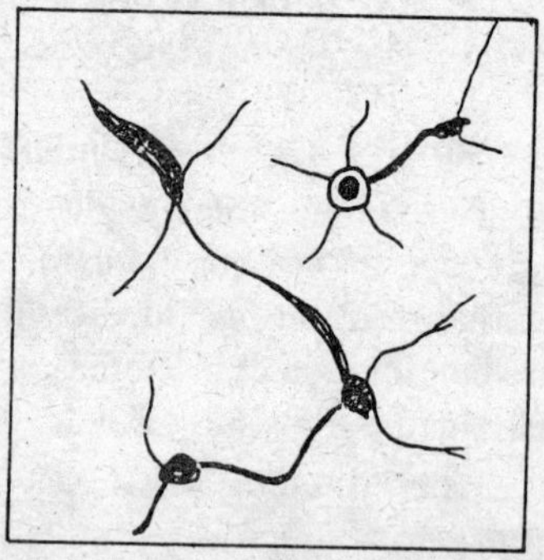

Fig. 26.3. Alkali aggregate reaction (unstressed) cracks

Alkali-Carbonate reaction

This reaction takes place between certain lime stone aggregate and cement as lime stone contains more silica. The reaction forms silica alkali gel. The layers of this gel occur between the aggregate particles and the surrounding cement paste. As discussed above, this gel also forms the map cracking

Preventive measures

The problem may be minimised by adopting following precautions:

1. A voiding reactive aggregate
2. Use of low alkali cement
3. Use of smaller size aggregate

Sulphate effect

When sulphate bearing water comes in contact with the concrete, the sulphate penetrates into the hydrated paste of cement and reacts with the hydrated calcium aluminate of cement and forms calcium sulphominate, which subsequently increases to a very large volume. The increase in volume causes high local tensile stresses resulting in the deterioration of the concrete as shown in Fig. 26.4. The use of pozzolana cement resists the sulphate attack better.

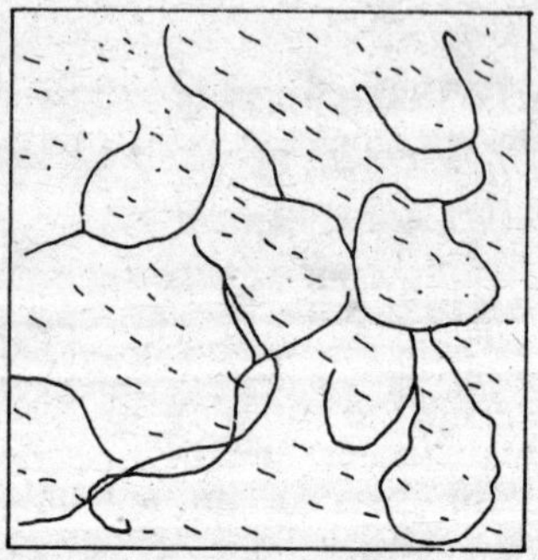

Fig. 26.4. Sulphate attack cracks

Effect of Carbon dioxide

When carbon dioxide from the air reacts with the calcium hydroxide ($CaOH_2$) of the hydrated cement paste, it forms calcium carbonate, which occupies smaller volume than the calcium hydroxide, resulting in the so called carbonation shrinkage. The development of carbonation shrinkage may result in significant surface grazing. This situation is serious on freshly placed concrete surfaces kept warm during winter season by improperly vented combustion heaters.

Cracking due to weathering

Following environmental factors cause cracking of concrete:

1. Freezing and thawing
2. Wetting and drying
3. Heating and cooling

1. Freezing and thawing. The greatest damage to concrete is caused by freezing and thawing in all parts of the world except tropical regions. It is the most common weather related physical deterioration. In the hardened concrete there are various explanations for the frost damage as follows:

(*a*) The empty space available in the concrete is insufficient to accommodate the additional solid produced due to the freezing of free water held in concrete. The ice formed due to freezing of free water exerts pressure resulting in cracking of concrete. The damage is related to the degree of saturation.

(*b*) During depressing point of freezing. Capillary water from the concrete comes out on the surface forming ice lenses parallel to the surface of the concrete. This ice lense forming exerts pressure resulting in cracking of concrete.

(*c*) When the moisture present with in the capillaries of the concrete freezes developes water pressure there, resulting in cracking of the concrete. Similarly if the aggregates used are saturated above the critical degree of saturation, the expansion of absorbed water during freezing may cause the cracking of the concrete.

Remedial measures

Following remedial measures may be taken against freezing damage:

1. Use of lowest practical water-cement ratio and total water content.
2. Adequate air entrainment has been found effective to control the freezing damage.
3. Use of durable aggregate also is useful to check the freezing effect.
4. Adequate curing of concrete prior to exposure to freezing conditions is also important.

Effect of wetting and drying, heating and cooling etc.

When volume changes due to these effects are excessive, cracks may develop resulting in the disintegration of concrete. The fire and frost-actions also damage the concrete. The damage due to fire and frost appears in the form of general spalling and flacking of concrete from the surface. With the increase in temperature above about 300°C concrete gradually loses strength. If the aggregates used in the concrete have high coefficient of thermal expansion, the damage will be greater.

Cracking due to corrosion of reinforcement

It is the most common and frequent cause for the deterioration of reinforced concrete structures. Though the corrosion of reinforcement has been discussed fully in chapter 17, however the salient features of this aspect have been given here for ready reference.

1. When reinforcing steel comes in contact with moisture, it reacts with the oxygen of the moisture forming iron oxide and hydroxide. The volume of these oxides is much greater than the volume of the original metallic iron. This increase in volume causes high radial bursting stresses around the reinforcing bars, resulting in local radial cracks. These splitting cracks may propagate along the bars resulting in the formation of longitudinal cracks parallel to bars or spalling of concrete as shown in Fig. 26.5. These cracks provide easy passage to moisture, air or oxygen, fumes containing chlorides etc. helping to corrosion to continue and causing further cracking of concrete.

Fig. 26.5. Reinforcement corrosion crack

As discussed earlier, reinforcing steel usually does not corrode in the concrete due to the formation of a tightly adhering protective oxide coating in a highly alkaline environment. This phenomenon is called passive protection.

If this passivity of steel is destroyed either by reducing the alkalinity of the concrete by the reaction of carbon dioxide with alkalis of cement or by the reaction of aggressive chloride ions reaction, the reinforcing bars will corrode. In case the concrete has low permeability, then transverse cracks usually do not contribute to the continuation of corrosion of reinforcement. If the combined density and concrete cover thickness is sufficient to restrict the flow of moisture or air, corrosion either will cease or will slow down.

Preventive measures

Reinforcement corrosion can be checked by adopting following measures:

1. To keep the permeability of concrete as low as possible, is the best control measure against corrosion induced splitting.
2. To keep the protective cover to reinforcement of sufficient thickness.
3. In very severe exposure conditions, protected coated reinforcement or sealers or over lays on concrete and corrosion retarding admixtures may be adopted.

Cracking due to faulty construction practices

In concrete structures cracking also results due to faulty practices adopted during the construction period, such as:

1. **Adding more water than specified to improve workability.** It will not only reduce the strength, but will also increase the ultimate drying shrinkage and settlement of the concrete.
2. **Early termination of curing.** It will result in the inducement of increased shrinkage in concrete when it has developed low strength. Incomplete hydration of cement due to inadequate supply of moisture or drying will not only reduce the long term strength, but also the durability of the structure.
3. **In adequate compaction or lack of support of form.** Inadequate compaction will reduce the strength. It has been observed that 1% deficiency in compaction will result in 5% decrease in strength. Further these factors will result in settlement cracks before it has developed sufficient strength to support its own weight.
4. **Improper location of construction joints.** Construction joints not provided at the proper place will result in cracking at the planes of weakness. See table 26.1.

Cracking due to over loads during construction

The loads induced in the structure during construction may be far more severe than those experienced in service. These conditions may occur at the early ages, when the concrete is most susceptible to damage and often results in permanent cracks.

A common error is observed when the precast members are not properly supported during transportation and erection. The use of arbitrary or convenient lifting points may cause severe damage. If a heavy or big element lowered too fast, and then stopped suddenly has significant momentum, which is translated into an impact load while stopped. This impact load may be many times more than the dead weight of the element.

Placing of equipment and storage of materials during construction may result in more severe loading condition than any load for which the structure has been designed. The damage from such construction over loads can be prevented if the designer provides information regarding the damages of such loads.

Cracking due to error in design and detailing

The design and detailing errors that may cause unacceptable cracking are as follows:

1. Improper selection and/or detailing of reinforcement.
2. Use of poorly detailed re-entrant corners in walls, precast members and slabs.
3. Restraint of members subjected to volume changes due to variations in temperature and moisture.
4. Lack of adequate contraction joints.
5. Improper design of foundations results in differential settlement within the structure.

6. *Re-entrant corners.* These corners provide a location for stress concentration and thus are main locations for initial cracks, as in the case of window and door openings in concrete walls and beams.

To keep the inevitable cracks narrow and to prevent them from further propagating, provision of additional properly anchored diagonal reinforcement is necessary. An inadequate amount of reinforcement may result in excessive cracking. A common mistake observed is to lightly reinforce an non structural member or element and tying it with the rest of the structure in such a way that it is required to carry a major portion of the load once the structure begins to deform. The non structural element will carry a load in proportion to its stiffness. As this element is not detailed to act structurally, unsightly cracking may result even though the safety of the structure is not threatened. The restrained members subjected to volume changes usually develop cracks. A wall, slab or a beam restrained against shortening even if pre-stressed, can easily develop tensile stresses sufficient to cause cracking. Beams should be free to move.

The improper design of the foundation may result in excessive differential movement with in a structure. If the differential movement is relatively small, the cracking problem may be only visual in nature. In case there is a major differential settlement, the structure may not be able to redistribute the load rapidly and a failure may occur. However in R.C.C. structures creep allows some redistribution of load.

The structures in which cracking may cause major problem of serviceability need special care in the design and detailing. These structures also need continuous inspection during all phases of construction.

26.5. THERMAL CRACKING

Thermal cracking is associated with thermal shrinkage and volume changes in the concrete. Before discussing the thermal cracking, it is essential to know the thermal properties of concrete. The study of thermal properties of concrete is an important aspect while dealing the thermal cracking and the durability of concrete. The important thermal properties of concrete are as follows:

1. Thermal conductivity
2. Thermal diffusivity
3. Specific heat
4. Coefficient of thermal expansion

1. Thermal Conductivity. This is the measure of the ability of a material to conduct heat through it. Thermal conductivity is measured in joules per second per square metre of area of the body, when the temperature difference is 1°C per metre thickness of the body. The conductivity of concrete depends upon the following factors:

(*a*) Type of aggregate
(*b*) Moisture content
(*c*) Density
(*d*) Temperature of concrete

When the concrete is saturated, the value of thermal conductivity ranges between about 1.4 to 3.4 $J/m^2.S°C/m$. The wet density of concrete made with different aggregates varies from 2240 to 1590. The Higher the density of concrete, higher the value of concrete thermal conductivity. Typical values of thermal conductivity are shown in Table 26.2 below.

Table 26.2. Typical values of thermal Conductivity of Concrete made with different aggregates

S. No.	*Type of aggregate*	*Wet density of concrete kg/m^3*	*Conductivity J/m^2 S°C/m*
1.	Quartzite	2440	3.5
2.	Dolomite	2500	3.3
3.	Lime stone	2450	3.2
4.	Sand stone	2400	2.9
5.	Granite	2420	2.6
6.	Basalt	2520	2.0
7.	Baryte	3040	2.0
8.	Expanded shale	1590	0.8

2. Thermal diffusivity. It represents the rate of change of temperature with in the concrete mass. It is related with the thermal conductivity by the following relation.

$$\text{Diffusivity} = \frac{\text{Thermal conductivity}}{\text{Specific heat} \times \text{density of concrete}} = \frac{\text{Conductivity}}{\text{C} \times \text{P}}$$

The range of diffusivity of concrete is between 0.002 to 0.006 m^2/h.

3. Specific heat. It is the quantity of heat required to raise the temperature of a unit mass of a material by one degree centigrade. The value of sp. heat for concrete varies in between 840 to 1170 J per kg per degree centigrade of temperature.

4. Coefficient of thermal expansion. It is defined as the change in unit length per degree of temperature. In concrete it depends upon the mix proportion. The value of coefficient of thermal expansion of hydrated cement paste varies between 11×10^{-6} to 20×10^{-6} per °C and for aggregates it varies between 5×10^{-6} and 12×10^{-6} per °C. It has been observed that lime stones and Gabbros have low values of coefficient of thermal expansion while Gravel and Quartzite have high values. Thus the kind and content of aggregate influences the value of coefficient of thermal expansion of concrete. The average value of coefficient of thermal expansion for concrete may be assumed as 10×10^{-6} per °C.

26.6. THERMAL EXPANSION AND SHRINKAGE

We have learnt that due to the development of heat of hydration the temperature of concrete increases. The thermal changes due to heat of hydration will be important only for few days in normal structures but for mass concrete work, it may last for long. The temperature difference with in a concrete structure results in differential volume change. When the tensile strain due to differential volume change exceeds the tensile strain capacity of the concrete, it develops cracks. The temperature differentials associated with the heat of hydration affect the mass concrete such as dams, piers, large column etc., where as temperature differentials due to changes in the ambient temperature can affect any structure as bridges decks, air field pavements, roads, etc. These structures are subjected to diurnal or seasonal changes of temperature. In certain parts and cities of India, the change of ambient temperature in day and night is as high as 30°C and the actual change in temperature of concrete surface is much higher than 30°C. The seasonal changes may be as high as 40°C.

The libration of heat of hydration of cement makes the internal temperature of concrete to rise during the initial period of curing so that it is slightly warmer than its surroundings. As the concrete cools, it will try to contract. Any restraint on the free contraction during cooling will result in the development of tensile stresses which are proportional to the temperature change, coefficient of thermal expansion, degree of restraint, and modulus of elasticity. The more massive the structure, the greater is the potential for temperature differential and degree of restraint.

Similarly the change in diurnal or seasonal temperatures as mentioned above makes the concrete to expand and contract. As the structures are not free to expand or contract due to restraint at support in case of roof slabs or bridge girders and sub grade reaction in case of air field pavement etc., a considerable tensile stress more than the tensile strength of concrete will be developed, resulting cracking of concrete. An idea of the tensile stress that could be developed due to the temperature variation can be have from the following example.

Example 1. *Calculate the tensile stress developed in the concrete having the characteristic compressive strength as 36 MPa. Use standard formulae.*

Solution. From Is 456-2000, modulus of elasticity of concrete is given by the relation

$$\text{Modulus of elasticity} = 5000\sqrt{fc}\ \text{N/mm}^2$$

$$= 5000 \times \sqrt{36} = 30{,}000\ \text{N/mm}^2 = 3.0 \times 10^4\ \text{N/mm}^2$$

$$\text{Flexural strength} = 0.7\sqrt{f_c}\ \text{N/mm}^2$$

$$= 0.7 \times 6 = 4.2\ \text{N/mm}^2$$

Assuming coefficient of thermal expansion of concrete as 10×10^{-6} per °C and diurnal variation in temperature as 25°C

i.e. The thermal shrinkage strain $= 25 \times 10 \times 10^{-6}$

$= 250 \times 10^{-6}$

On the basis of his experimental work, *Lowe* has suggested that cracks are developed in concrete at a differential strain of 200×10^{-6}. In the present case the differential strain is 250×10^{-6}, which will cause vary high degree of micro cracking in the concrete.

$$\text{Further modulus of elasticity} = \frac{\text{Stress}}{\text{Strain}}$$

$$\therefore \quad 3.0 \times 10^4 = \frac{\text{stress}}{250 \times 10^{-6}}$$

$$\text{Tensile stress} = 3.0 \times 10^4 \times 250 \times 10^{-6}$$

$$= 7.5 \text{ N/mm}^2$$

The tensile strength of concrete is 3.5 N/mm^2. Thus a tensile stress of 7.5 N/mm^2 which is more than the double of the tensile strength of concrete. Thus this stress is sure to cause high degree of micro cracks in the concrete. In case of stronger concrete with higher values of modulus of elasticity and higher degree of variation of temperatures, the tensile stress will be much more. However the concrete of higher compressive strength will have higher tensile strength to with stand the higher tensile stresses. But due to the lower value of creep of high strength concrete, the relaxation in the stress will be smaller. Thus the stronger concrete will crack more than the weaker concrete from this consideration. However cracking of concrete is a complex phenomenon.

26.7. MICRO-CRACKING

Very fine cracks are known as micro cracks. Investigations have shown that very fine cracks in the concrete exist at the interface between the coarse aggregate and cement paste even prior to the application of load on the concrete. These cracks remain stable upto about 30% or more of the ultimate load and then start to increase in length, width and number. The over all stress under which these cracks develop is sensitive to the water cement ratio of the paste. At this stage the propagation of cracks is slow. At 70 to 90% of the ultimate strength, these cracks open through the mortar (Cement paste and fine aggregate). These cracks pass over (bridge) the bond cracks and a continuous crack pattern is formed. This stage of cracking is known as the *fast crack propagation stage.* If the load remained sustained, failure may take place with time.

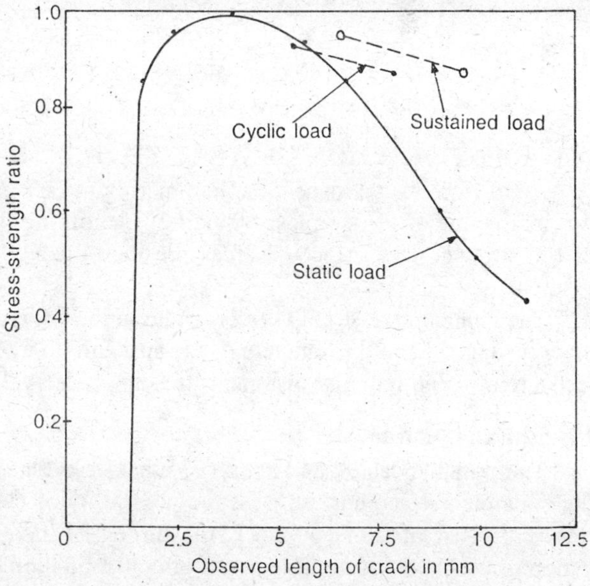

Fig. 26.6. Length of micro cracking

The results of length measurement of cracks are shown in Fig. 26.6. From the figure, it can be seen that there is very little increase in the total length between the beginning of loading and a stress of about 0.85 of the prism strength (10 cm × 10 cm × 300 prism). A further increase in stress resulted large increase in the total length of the crack. At a stress/strength ratio of about 0.95 (determined on prism) not only the interface cracks but mortar cracks were also observed. The orientation of many cracks was seen roughly parallel to the applied load. On the descending part of the stress/strength curve, the rate of increase in the crack length and width was found large.

26.7.1. Crack Width

It has been observed that crack widths at surface of the concrete play an important role in the durability of concrete structures. The design Engineer should under stand this fact and give serious thought to it while designing the structure. IS-456-2000 has specified the crack width as follows:

1. In general the width of surface crack should not exceed 0.3 mm in members, where cracking is not harmful and does not have any serious adverse effect upon the preservation of reinforcing steel nor upon the durability of concrete.
2. Cracking in tensile zones of members is harmful either due to exposure to the effects of the weather or continuously exposed to moisture or in contact with soil or ground water. In such situations the maximum upper limit of crack width is suggested as 0.2 mm.
3. For aggressive environment such as severe category of exposed conditions, the surface width of cracks should not in general exceed 0.1 mm.

Some specifications, limit the crack widths at the points near the main reinforcement instead of the surface. International pre-stressing Federation has recommended the maximum crack width at the main reinforcement to be 0.004 times the normal cover thickness. If the thickness of the normal cover is taken as 50 mm, then the crack width near the main reinforcement comes to be $0.004 \times 50 = 0.2$ mm. Crack formation in concrete due to different reasons is shown in the following Table 26.3, page 565.

26.8. EVALUATION OF CRACKS

Before starting repair of cracked structure, the knowledge of location and extent of cracking is essential for the effective and proper repair. The objectives of repair are restoration and enhancement of durability of structural strength, functional requirements and aesthetics. Following are the purposes of the crack evaluation.

1. To identify the cause of cracking
2. To asses the safety and serviceability of the structure
3. To establish the extent of cracking
4. To establish the likely extent of future deterioration
5. To study the feasibility of various remedial measures
6. To make the final assessment of serviceability after repairs

26.9. IDENTIFICATION OF WEAK SPOTS

Apart from visual inspection, hammering the surface with a light hammer and listening the sound from the area is one of the simplest method of identifying the the weak spot as dull sound indicates hollowness of the surface. The suspected areas are then opened up by chipping the weak concrete for further assessment.

The comparative strength of concrete in the structure can be assessed by non destructive tests and tests on cores taken from the concrete of the structure to a reasonable accuracy. Commonly used non destructive tests are rebound hammer test and ultrasonic pulse velocity test.

Visual Examination

The possible causes and nature of cracks can be ascertained by visual examination. The appearance of the concrete surface may suggest the possibility of chemical attack by the general softening and leaching matrix. In case of sulphate attack, the surface of the concrete becomes white. The rust stains are the indication of corrosion of reinforcement or contamination of aggregate with iron pyrites. The discolouration or presence of dirt on the broken surface of the cracked concrete gives an indication that the crack is quite old.

Table 26.3. Types and Causes of cracks in concrete

- Cracks in Concrete
  - Before hardening
    - Drying
      - Plastic shrinkage
      - Settlement
      - Bleeding
      - Delayed curing
    - Constructional
      - Form work movement
      - Excessive vibrations
      - Sub grade settlement
      - Finishing
    - Early frost damage
  - After hardening
    - Unsound materials
      - Cement
      - Aggregate
      - Excess silt, dust and mud etc.
    - Long term drying shrinkage
    - Thermal
      - Heat of hydration
      - External temperature
      - Joints in concrete
      - Elevated temperature
      - Freezing and thawing
    - Moisture movements
    - Transition zone
    - Biological
    - Structural design deficiencies
    - Chemical
      - Sulphate attack
      - Alkali-aggregate reaction
      - Acid attack
      - Sea water
      - Carbonation
      - Chloride attack
    - Corrosion of reinforcement

The general flaking of the exposed surface of the concrete suggests frost damage. The colour of concrete damaged in fire hazzard indicates the maximum temperature reached.

The crack pattern is also useful in evaluating the cracks. A mesh pattern suggests the drying shrinkage cracking and surfacing crazing may indicates either frost attack or alkali-aggregate reaction cracking. Generally it is frost attack. The cracks caused by unidirectional bending will be the widest in the zone of maximum tensile stress and will tapper along their length, while cracks caused by direct tension will be roughly of uniform width.

The width and location of cracks should be noted on the sketch of the structure. Crack width may be measured to an accuracy of 0.025 mm with the help of a small hand held microscope. It has a scale on the lens which is held close to the surface to be viewed. Location of spalling, exposed reinforcement, rust staining and surface deterioration etc. should be noted on the sketch.

Non destructive testing

Non destructive test may be used for determining accurate and reliable information about the presence of internal cracks and voids, depth of penetration of cracks which are visible on the surface. By tapping the surface with an ordinary light hammer, often useful information may be obtained. A dull sound indicates the separation of concrete due to fire or otherwise. it also indicates the presence of cracks below the surface.

The most common technique to detect the crack using ultrasonic non destructive test equipment is through transmission testing using. **Soniscope.** The method consists of transmitting a mechanical pulse to one face of the concrete member and receiving it at the opposite face, and calculating the pulse velocity from the time taken by the pulse to pass through the member and the distance between the transmitting and receiving transducers. If there is internal crack, the pulse will travel at the corner or edge of the crack, increasing the path length of the pulse. The increase in path length of the signal as it passes around the end of the crack, there will be a significant change in the pulse velocity. Generally higher the pulse velocity, better the quality and durability of the concrete.

If the signal is displaced on the oscilloscope, the internal discontinuities can also be detected by weakening or reducing the strength of the signal.

If no signal arrives at the receiving transducers, it indicates an significant internal discontinuity, such as void or crack. The extent of the discontinuity can be assessed by taking readings at a series of positions on the member. The result of ultrasonic testing should be interpreted continuously. Generally with fully saturatured cracks the ultra- sonic testing will be ineffective. The arrangement of the test is shown in Fig. 26.7.

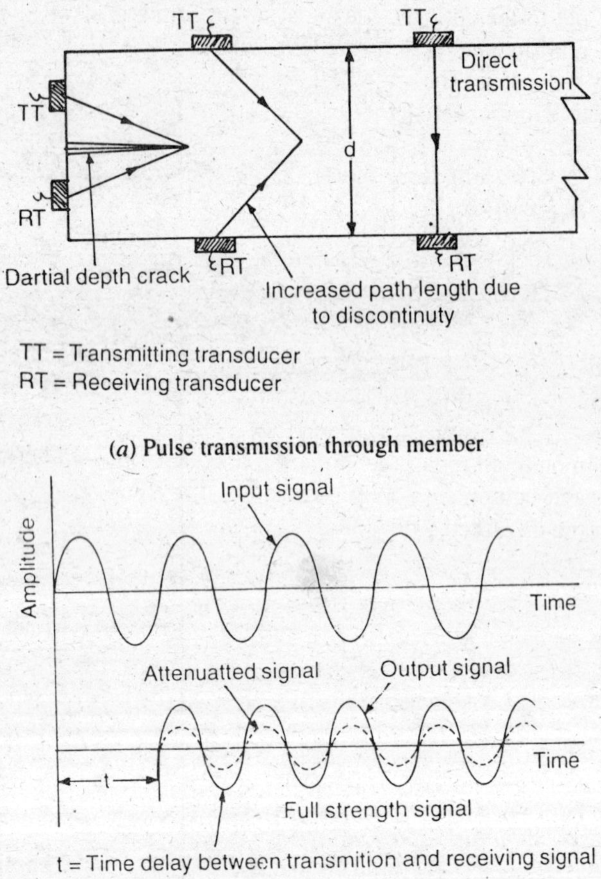

(*a*) Pulse transmission through member

(*b*) Oscilloscopie signal

Fig. 26.7. Ultrasonic testing

26.10. SELECTION OF REPAIR PROCEDURE

The repair of concrete structures may vary to a great extent, giving it just a superficial treatment to the total replacement. By proper investigations using the well designed equipment, tools and materials a number of structures have been reinnovated economically, which were though damaged beyond repairs. An appropriate repair method can be selected depending upon the cause, extent of damage, importance of the structural member and its location. The success of the repair will depend upon the proper choice of the method. The procedure should be selected to accomplish one or more of the following objectives.

1. To improve its durability
2. To improve the appearance of concrete surface
3. To increase its functional performance
4. To increase the stiffness of the member
5. To increase the load carrying capacity of the structure
6. To increase the water tightness of the structure
7. To protect the reinforcement from corrosive material etc.

Depending upon the extent and nature of the damage, one or more methods may be adopted for example to increase the tensile strength of the cracked member, epoxy grout can be used along with additional reinforcement. If further cracking is not anticipated, then epoxy injection can be used to restore flexural stiffness of the member. In water retaining structures cracks likely to cause leakage should be repaired unless the leakage is insignificant. When the appearance of the cracks becomes un acceptable, they should be repaired.

The long term success of the repair procedure mainly depends upon the nature of cracks as well as their cause. If the cracks are developed due to the continuing settlement of the foundation, repair will not be effective till the settlement problem is tackled.

26.11. TREATMENT OF CRACKS

The treatment of Concrete structures is carried out in the following two stages:

1. Preparation of surface for repairs
2. Application of repair material

1. Preparation of surface. Before the execution of any repair, one of the essential requirements common to all repair techniques is to remove the damaged or deteriorated concrete with the help of proper tools and equipments. While removing the damaged portion, care should be taken that no damage is caused to the un affected portion. For preparing the surface for repair following steps are adopted.

(*a*) Complete removal of damaged portion.

(*b*) Under cutting alongwith the formation of smooth edges.

(*c*) Removal of the cracks from the surface.

(*d*) Formation of well defined cavity with rounded inside corners. The incorrect and correct cavity of damaged area is shown in Fig. 26.8 (*a*) & (*b*) respectively.

(*e*) Providing rough and uniform surface for repair.

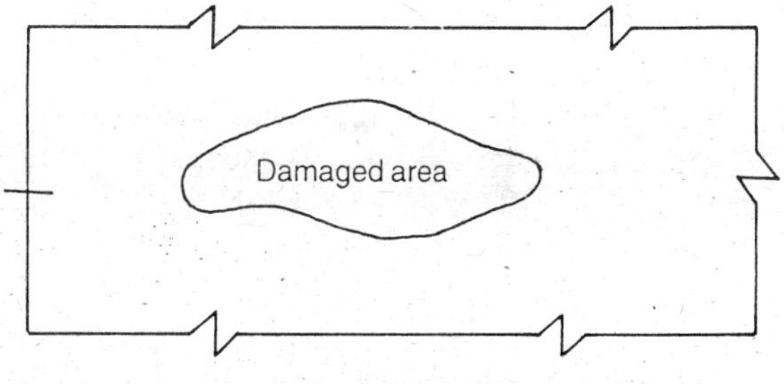

(*a*) Plan of damaged area

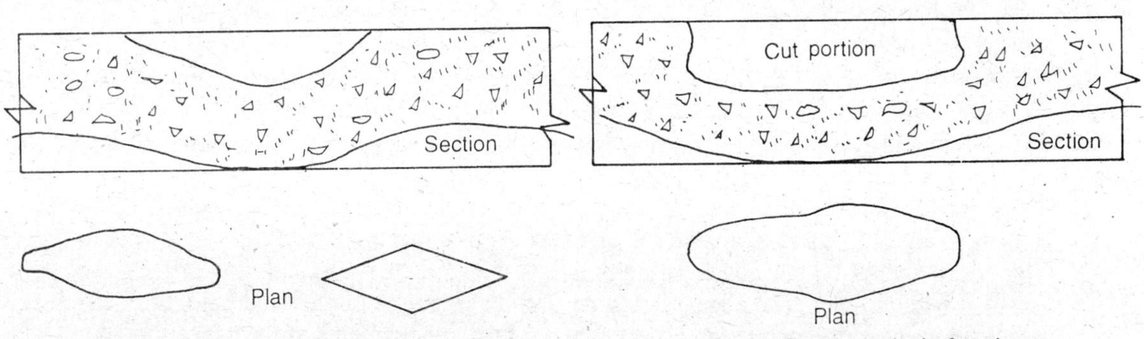

(*b*) Incorrect method of cutting damaged part (*c*) Correct method of cutting

Fig. 26.8. Preparation of surfaces by cutting out the damaged portion

The surface so prepared should be clean, dry, strong and free of laitance.

(*a*) *A clean surface* means that there should be no foreign matter such as loose particles, dirt, grease or oil, paints, resin etc. on it.

(*b*) *Dry surface* means that no free water should be there on the surface.

(*c*) *Free of laitance*. Laitance is the very thin layer or skin of high water cement ratio gel which appears on the surface during concrete compaction. The laitance is quite weak and has poor adhesion with the parent concrete. Thus it should be removed before laying the repair material on the surface. Strong concrete below the surface refers to the ability of concrete to resist fractures due to the stresses developed on it by the repair material etc.

Dust and other foreign matter present on the surface of the concrete usually can be removed by wire brushing. If this method is not found satisfactory, then grinding, sand or steel blasting and scarifying may be adopted, as these are the commonly adopted methods for dust-removing.

For cleaning a concrete surface, the sand or steel shot blasting is the most effective method. In some cases, low pressure water jet blasting has been found most effective. The presence of oily substance on the surface of concrete can be detected by sprinkling water on the surface. If the water stands in droplets with out spreading out immediately, it indicates the presence of oily substance on the surface, which will interfere with the bonding of repair materials.

The grease, oil and animal fats etc. can be removed by scrubbing the surface with caustic-soda solution, detergents or trisodium phosphate. The process is known as *chemical cleaning*. During the washing procedure, a vigorous scrubbing action should be carried out with a stiff broom. To remove all traces of loosened oil and as well as the cleaning solution, the surface should be washed off thoroughly with a pressure hose.

If on scrapping the surface with a knife blade, fine powdery substance is observed on the surface, it indicates the presence of laitance on the surface, which may be removed by acid etching. In case acid etching method is adopted, then the surface should be pre-cleaned by removing any build up of oil, grease, dirt etc. In case presence of chlorides in concrete is not objectionable, a 10% solution of HCl acid in water should be applied in the ratio 1:15 litre/m^2 of the surface. A stiff broom or brush should be used to spread and vigorously scrub the acid solution uniformly on the surface. After the subsidence of foaming action, the surface should be washed off thoroughly with water and still scrubbing it with stiff broom. This is necessary to remove the salts which might have been formed by the reaction of the acid with the cement. The presence of acid after washing should be checked with the litmus paper. When the presence of chloride is objectionable, a 15% solution of phosphoric acid can be used. The presence of acids from other sources may also be ascertained by placing a litmus paper in a thin film of water on the surface of concrete. A P_H value below 4 indicates the high value of acidity of the concrete for the successful application of repair.

26.11.1. Repair Procedures

The repair of damaged or cracked structure may be classified into two categories:

1. Ordinary procedures 2. Special procedures

1. Ordinary Procedures. The fine or superficial cracks are rectified by treating the surface with soft distempers, white wash or silicate cement paints etc. The methods and materials for the repair of patches of damaged concrete in the structure are discussed below. The repair can be carried out in four steps as follows:

(*i*) **Preparation of surface.** The cracked and damaged areas are cut out from the solid concrete. The area to be cut out should be marked with a saw cut to a depth of about 5 mm to show neat edges. The edges should be cut out as straight as possible and right angle to the surface with corners rounded with in holes. The edges should be slightly under cut to provided keys at the edges of the patch. To prevent the edges from breaking under load, the thickness of the edges should not be less than 25 mm. All the loose and unsound concrete is removed. All the loose material should be cleaned and the surface should be washed off before actual patching work is started. Excess water from the cavity should be removed. To obtain a good bond, the surface of concrete should be coated with a thin layer of neat cement grout before placing patching concrete.

If the reinforcement has been corroded then the concrete should be removed from the considerable area to ensure that all corroded areas are exposed for cleaning with ease. Carbonated or chloride contaminated concrete in contact with reinforcement should be removed and in its place fresh concrete or impermeable resin compound is placed. After cleaning the reinforcement corrosion, controlling or inhibiting chemicals such as phosphates may be applied on the exposed surface of the reinforcement. In case of cement based repairs, a slurry coating of polymer latex and cement can be used. Rasin based coatings are suitable for both cement based and resin based repair materials.

(*ii*) **Selection of materials.** The repair materials should be selected in such a way that the mechanical properties of the repair materials should be similar to those of structure being repaired. The cement based repairs can provide fire resistance while resins soften at relatively low temperature. For conventional repairs, the cement based materials to be used for patch work, may either be mortar or concrete depending upon the extent of repair.

(*iii*) **Application of materials.** Generally following methods may be used for filling the materials:

1. Dry packing
2. Concrete replacement
3. Mortar replacement
4. Grouting
5. Large volume prepacking of concrete
6. Guniting or shot creting

After preparing the surface, a bonding coat should be applied to all the cleaned exposed surfaces. It should be done with minimum delay. The bonding coat may be of cement slurry or an equal amount of cement and sand mixed with water to a fluid paste consistency. Adequate preparation of surface and good work manship are the ingredients of efficient and economical repairs.

1. Dry packing. In this method the low water content mortar is placed on the prepared surface. To produce an intimate contact between the mortar and the existing surface, the mortar is well rammed. Due to the low water cement ratio of the paste, the shrinkage of the mortar is less and it provides a durable, strong and water tight patch.

For repair work, usually cement and sand mortar in the proportion of about 1:2.5 or 1:3 is used. Usually sand passing 1.18 mm IS sieve is used. However coarse concreting sand may also be used, but for a smooth finish of the surface and for the final layer finer sand should be used. The first layer of repair material should be applied immediately after the application of bonding coat, while latter is still wet. Provision of some mechanical anchorage for the patch work should be provided. It may be done by providing dowels drilled and grouted into the surrounding concrete. The water content of the mix should be chosen carefully as excess water will increase the shrinkage, which may loosen the replaced material, where as less water will not make a strong and sound solid pack. The water content in the mix should be such that the mortar could be moulded into a ball by hand, and at the same time it does not exclude water, but leave the hand damp only.

To minimise the shrinkage in place, the mortar should be left for 30 minutes after adding water and then remixed before it is used. The repair material should be filled in place properly and well compacted. The thickness of the compacted layer should be of about 10 mm. The next layer normally should be applied after the preceeding layer has developed sufficient strength to support the next layer. In order to obtain a good bond, the preceding layer should be scratched before placing the next layer. Each layer is compacted well over its entire surface with the help of 200 mm to 300 mm long hard wood stick and upto 25 mm diameter with a hammer. The last overflowing layer should be struck flush with the surface. There should be no time lags between the layers. In case there is an delay between the layers, a fresh bonding coat should be applied when the work is resumed. The mortar may be finished by placing a flat hard wood against the mortar and strike it several times with a hammer. The patch work is cured by covering it with a absorbent material that keeps it damp, preferably it may be covered with polythene sheets sealed at edges. Shading from sun should be done. After the completion of the whole patch work curing membranes may be sprayed.

For the repair of inactive or dormant cracks, the portion of the crack adjacent to the surface is widened to form a slot of 25mm wide and 25mm deep with a power driven sawtooth bit. The base of the slot should be slightly greater than the surface width. Now the slot is thoroughly cleaned and dried. After the slot is dry, the bonding coat is applied prior to placing the repair material. After finishing the surface it should be moist cured by tieing with wet burlap along the length of the crack.

2. Concrete replacement. Generally this method is used for large and deep patches as encountered in the repair of old and deteriorated portions of concrete structures where concrete is to be replaced to a minimum depth of about 15 cm. Usually this method is adopted for the repair of walls, piers, Kerbs, parapets and for refacing walls and relining channels. This method particularly has been found suitable for situations where the hole extends through out the concrete section or where the surface area of the hole is at least 900cm^2 or 0.09 m^2 with a minimum depth of 10 cms for plain concrete and incase of RCC the minimum area of the hole should be 450 cm^2 or 0.045m^2 with a depth a little more than reinforcing steel bars.

Procedure. As in other cases of repairs, the defective concrete is removed upto the sound surface and reinforcement is cleaned. In case, if it is not possible to place the repair material immediately, then a protective coating to reinforcement must be applied to protect it from corrosion.

In case of plain concrete, the defective area is prepared as explained above. In case of RCC a minimum clearance of about 25mm around the each exposed reinforcing bar should be provided. In case of wall repairs, the top of the hole should be cut to a fairly horizontal line with a 1 to 3 upward slope from back toward the face to prevent the formation of air pockets at the top during vibration. The bottom and sides of the hole should be cut sharp and approximately square as shown in Fig. 26.9. All interior corners should be rounded to a minimum radius of 25mm. For repairing the wall for more than 0.5m, the back form work is built in one piece and the front form work is made in horizontal sections to place concrete conveniently in about 30cm deep layers or lifts. All joints of the form work should be mortar tight. Before placing the front sections of the form work for each lift, the surface of old concrete should be coated with cement grout of the same water-cement ratio as that for the mortar in the replacement concrete. To reduce the shrinkage, there should be a minimum interval of time of 30 minutes between the placement of two layers or lifts. The mix proportion and water-cement ratio of the replacement concrete should be the same as used in the structure. The water content should be used as low as possible. If possible, compaction of the repaired material should be done by internal vibration. In case external vibration is used, then care should be taken that the seals between the form work and the existing concrete are not damaged. The stripping period of the form work may vary from 20 to 48 hours depending upon the location and extent of repair.

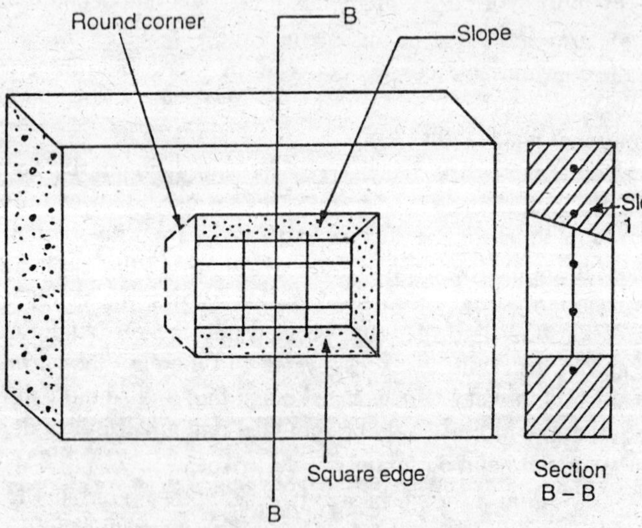

Fig. 26.9. Repair by concrete replacement method

3. Mortar replacement. This method is useful for cavities too wide for dry pack and two shallow for concrete replacement. Generally this method is used for shallow depressions not deeper than the thickness of side concrete to the nearest reinforcement bar near the surface. For replacement of deteriorated concrete this method is useful only for small patches. The mortar replacement can be done by hand or by using a small pressure gun.

It is preferable to pre-shrink the repair mortar by mixing it to a plastic consistency as long in advance as cement permits. The pre shrinking time ranges from 60 to 120 minutes. For hand placing the mortar should be of the same proportion as that of the mix of the structure. In case of pressure gun the mortar should have a cement sand proportion of 1:4.

In case the hole to be repaired is deeper than 25mm, then the mortar should be laid in layers not exceeding 15mm in thickness to avoid sagging and loss in the bond. The subsequent layers may be applied at an interval of 30 minutes or more. The final layer should be placed slightly overflowing the hole and struck off level with the surface.

4. Grouting. The deep and wide cracks may be repaired by filling them with either neat cement grout or cement sand grout depending upon the width of the crack. The cement sand ratio may be kept 1:4. The water-cement ratio should be kept as low as practicable to maximise the strength and minimise the shrinkage. The water reducing agents may also be added to improve the properties of the grout.

Procedure. The surface along the crack is cleaned first and then built up grout ports in the form of nipples or seals are provided at intervals. Afterwards, the crack is sealed between the ports with a cement paint etc. Before applying the grout, the seal is tested. After seal testing, the whole area is filled with grout mortar. After the crack is filled up, the pressure should be maintained for several minutes to ensure good penetration. This method particularly is useful for the repair of wide cracks in concrete walls and gravity dams etc.

For narrow cracks in concrete, chemical grouts consisting of solutions of two or more chemicals that can combine to form gel and a solid precipitate can be used advantageously. The chemical grouts are also useful in moist conditions and provide wide limits of control of gel time.

5. Large volume pre packed concrete. This method of repair is used for the repair of old works and usually is adopted in situations where placing of concrete by conventional methods is difficult. This method is used advantageously for the repair of larger jobs, under water placement, repair of tunnel lining, resurfacing of dams, spillways, retaining walls, piers etc.

Procedure. Clean and well graded coarse aggregate is filled in the form work placed against the surface to be repaired. The aggregate is well compacted in the form work and wetted after compacting it. Now the grout of designed proportion of cement, fine sand and some pozzolanic material is pumped into the voids of the compacted mass of aggregate. The water content should be as low as practicable for the desired fluidity. Some admixtures to the mixing water may be added to increase the fluidity of grout and to control early stiffening of the grout and mixing water. The form work must be a closed type, open only at the top to avoid trapping of air pockets. The form work may be of

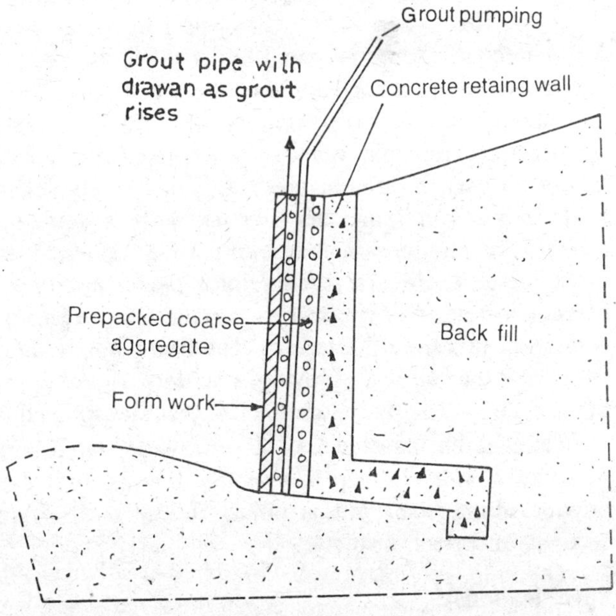

Fig. 26.10. Pre packed concrete repair of a retaining wall

conventional rigid type that either encloses the member to be repaired or is sealed to it at its edges. To monitor the progress of aggregate grouting, some times transparent pannels are provided. The grout lines are attached to inlets or injection points fixed to the form. The pumping of grout should be started from the lowest point as shown in Fig. 26.10 and proceed upwards in order to prevent the formation of the air pockets. In case complete filling from bottom requires very high injection pressure, more than one injection point. may be built into the form work at different levels. The spacing between grout lines should not be more then 1.5 m centre to centre and the grout level in the mass of aggregate should increase uniformly, as determined by the observations of grout levels in the grout pipes. In the grout pipes above the level of the out lets a positive head of at least 1 to 2 m should be maintained. The injection of the grout should be smooth, uninterrupted operation. After the forms have been filled, positive head should be maintained till the grout has set.

Shot Creting or guniting

As explained in chapter 24 it is a mortar or concrete conveyed through pressure hose and applied pneumatically at high velocity on the surface. The application of this material has been found useful in several major repair works due to ease with which it can be applied on vertical, horizontal or over head surfaces. Mostly it is used for tunnel lining and for protective covering of soft rocks, for repair or laying new canal and reservoir lining, for stabilizing of rock slopes and repair of old and damaged concrete work.

The objective of this type of repair is to replace the lost or removed concrete and to increase the effective cover to the steel reinforcement or to protect against the future damage by adding additional concrete.

Preparation of the surface

All the damaged or affected concrete should be removed upto the sound and strong surface. The undamaged surface also must be prepared by thoroughly roughening it, to remove all original cement laitance surface deposits and impurities. For the development of good bond, the prepared surface must be rough, sound and homogeneous.

When a large portion of the structure is defective, the whole of the accessible external surface should be encased with a specified minimum thickness of sprayed concrete, which should be brought out to uniform profile and eyeable lines by additional infilling of the area from where damaged concrete has been removed. This can be achieved by applying sprayed concrete over the areas of un damaged concrete also. The surface should be prepared as discussed above.

In case sprayed concrete is with out polymer admixtures, generally a welded steel fabric or steel fibres are incorporated in it to minimize the risk of developing cracks of sufficient size, which may allow penetration of air and water. The incorporation of steel fabric encourages the development of a large number of very fine and insignificant cracks. A typical fabric for this purpose may be in the form of a mesh made of 3 to 4 mm diameter high tensile bars welded at a spacing of 75 to 100 mm. With the use of such a fabric the minimum thickness of sprayed concrete should be 50 mm which will provide adequate cover to the fabric it self. The fabric reinforcement should be securely fixed by nails driven into the plugs set in parent concrete and bent over to grip the reinforcement. The spacers should be fixed to hold the reinforcement at 12 mm from the surface. The fixing points should be close enough so that the mesh does not bulge out during the concrete spraying. The thickness of sprayed concrete may be reduced if non corroding steel fabric is used. The minimum thickness of the sprayed concrete may vary from 30 mm to 50 mm.

Holes or chases of at least 20 mm wide and 20 mm deep should be cut at the perimeter of the area to be sprayed with the help of pneumatic tools. Into these holes the edges of the steel fabric will tuck to provide sound finish at that point. To check the correct thickness light timber profiles should be fixed securely at correct positions.

Specifications

The maximum size of aggregate to be used in sprayed concrete should be 10 mm. It should be clean and well graded from 10 mm to 1.18 mm *i.e.* fines but there should be no excess of fine particles. It should be free from dust, silt and clay. The typical cement aggregate ratio may vary from 1:3.5 to 1:4. The strength of concrete at 28 days should be about 30 MPa. Where ever possible the construction joints should be formed at a slope, not at right angle as in the case of cast concrete. Normally the face of the sprayed concrete is carried forward at a slope to form the construction joint sloping. To get a good bond at the joint the interface of the joint must be cleaned of rebound, overshoot and laitance etc.

In case defects are in isolated areas, patch repair may be carried out, but the repair should extend at least upto 300 mm on the sound concrete at the perimeter of the defective area and should terminate in chases. Rectangular patches are preferable to irregular shapes.

The spraying should be carried out with the nozzle held at right angles to the interface and at such a distance that the concrete compacts effectively. Usually 1 m distance from the face is sufficient. To form an even layer on the surface the nozzle should be fanned from side to side and up and down. If there is any unevenness in the spray of material, the nozzle should be turned away from the work till the spray becomes even again. The thickness of layer at a time should not be more than about 50 mm on vertical surfaces and 25mm on over head surfaces. The surface of each layer may be slightly trimmed with the edge of a steel float and must be wetted again once set before applying the next layer.

Curing

The curing of sprayed concrete is more important even than that of conventional cast concrete as water loss in thinner sections may take place easily and can cause more serious adverse effects on its properties. The curing may be done by fine water spray, by tieing wetted hession etc. Curing compounds may also be used.

Curing of repair work. The curing of patch material needs much more care than that of a complete structure due to the tendency of old concrete to absorb moisture from the replacement material. Same curing methods may be adopted as used for curing of conventional concrete.

26.12. SPECIAL PROCEDURES

The Polymers are of recent origion. They have been introduced recently in concrete technology for multipurpose applications in the repair and maintenance of concrete buildings and other structures. For concrete repairs mainly following two different types of polymers are used. Polymers are natural or artificial compounds made from large sized molecules.

(*a*) Polymers used as modifiers for cementitious systems

(*b*) Reactive thermosetting resins.

For the repair of active as well as dormant cracks, epoxy (a resin) mortars consisting of an epoxy, hardener, and sand have been found effective to seal the cracks. The epoxy resins and polymer possess excellent adhesive and sealing properties, but the cost of this type of repair is very high.

(*a*) Polymer modified Cementitious system

Normally polymers used as admixtures for cementitious systems are latex (a milky white disperson in water). These polymers are used to gauge the cementitious mortar as a whole or as a partial replacement of mixing water. The polymer latex forms a network of polymer strands inter penetrating the cement matrix and improves the structural properties and reduces permeability of the mortar. Such mortars provide the same alkaline passivation protection to steel as the conventional materials do. These mortars can be placed in a single layer of 12 to 16mm thickness and provide adequate protective cover.

26.12.1. Functions of Polymer latex

The functions of the polymer latex are as follows:

(*i*) It acts as a water reducing plasticizer.

(*ii*) It provides a good bond between repair mortar and concrete surface to be repaired.

(*iii*) It improves the tensile and flexural strength of the mortar.

(*iv*) It reduces the permeability of repair mortar to water.

26.12.2. Modifiers for Cementitious systems

Following type of polymer latexes have been used as modifiers for cementitious systems:

(*a*) Poly vinyl acetate (PVAC).

(*b*) Styrene butadiene rubber (SBR).

(*c*) Polyvinyldiene dichloride (PVDC).

(*d*) Acrylics and modified acrylics.

Generally styrene acrylics, polyvinyl dichloride (PVDC) are not recommended for repair mortars for RCC works. Polyvinyl acetate (PVAC) latexes are widely used as general purpose bonding aids and admixtures for building industry for interior applications. In concrete repair mortars styrene butadiene rubber (SBR) acrylic and modified acrylic latexes most commonly are used as admixtures.

26.12.3. Resin based materials

The resin mortars are used for repair in locations where the area to be repaired comparatively is less and the cover is less than 12 mm. In case of resin mortars the protection of reinforcement depends upon the total permeability of the cover. In this case the surface of the reinforcement should be prepared to a very high standard. The resin mortars are made with reactive resins and carefully graded aggregates.

Usually in concrete repair works epoxy resin mortars are used. The polymer and acrylic resin based mortars are used for small area repairs where very rapid development of strength is required. In most of the repair situations the polymer based repair material is bonded directly to the concrete or other cementitious materials. Thus it is important that the mechanical and physical properties of polymer repair mortar and concrete should be similar. The polymer bonding aids may assist in achieving a reliable bond between green un cured concrete and cured concrete.

26.12.4. Polymer based repairs

The polymer concrete includes composites prepared by one of the following methods:

(*a*) Polymer impregnated concrete (PIC)

(*b*) Polymer cement concrete (PCC)

(*c*) Polymer concrete

These materials have been discussed in detail in chapter 24 under polymer Concrete. However crack repair technique is discussed in the following paragraphs.

26.13. CONCRETE REPAIR BY POLYMER IMPREGNATION

In this system of repair, the damaged concrete surface is cleaned thoroughly and dried. After cleaning and drying the cracked concrete surface is flooded with a monomer, which is then polymerized in place, filling and structurally repairing the crack.

A monomer system is a liquid consisting of small organic molecules capable of combining to form a solid plastic. The monomer system used for impregnation or injecting into the concrete contains a catalyst or initiator and the basic monomer. They also contain a cross linking agent. On heating the monomers they join together. The process of joining together is known as polymerization. After polymerization the product on cooling becomes tough, strong and durable, plastic that greatly enhances a number of properties of the concrete.

Monomers do not mix with water. They have varying degree of toxicity, flammability and volatility. These are low viscosity fluids which are soaked into the dry concrete filling the cracks in the same way as water. However if the cracks contain moisture, the monomer will not be soaked into the concrete at each crack face, resulting in un satisfactory repair. Further if a volatile monomer evaporates before the polymerization, the repair will be ineffective.

26.13.1. Repair of fractured elements

For repairing fractured elements, polymer impregnation method may be used. In this case the fracture is dried first, then it is temporarily encased in a water tight sheet metal. Now the fracture is soaked with monomer and polymerized. On polymerization of the monomer the fractured element becomes a solid mass with enhanced strength and properties. Large voids in compression zones may be filled with fine and coarse aggregates before flooding them with monomers, providing a polymer concrete repair.

26.13.2. Treatment of Concrete surfaces with large number of cracks

In this situation vaccum impregnation may be used.

Process. The part of the structure to be repaired is enclosed with in an air tight plastic cover and then the air from all cracks with in the cover is sucked by applying vaccum. After exhausting the air from all cracks, the monomer or resin grout is forced under one atmospheric pressure in cracks and pores of the concrete surface. On completion of impregnation, the cover is removed before the impregnant hardens. The selection of appropriate impregnant and degree of vaccum depends on experience. This process is extensively used to reduce the permeability of weak concrete or masonry. This process may also be used to improve the abrasive resistance of industrial concrete floor slabs. However polymer impregnation has not been found successful for the repair of fine cracks.

26.14. RESIN BASED REPAIRS

In reinforced concrete cracks wider than approximately 0.3 mm, require sealing to check the entry of moisture, oxygen and other harmful gases etc. The choice of the method and materials, will depend upon the cause of cracking, and whether there is a need of permanent structural filling of cracks to carryout any other required strengthening. For restoring the structure to its original strength, the use of low viscosity expoxy resin has been found very effective. With epoxy resin system it is possible to fill completely cracks finer than 5 mm by using pressure injection technique. However work should be carried out skillfully to avoid the blowing off the surface seals due to back pressure that may develop in case of very fine cracks. To fill the fine cracks fully sustained pressure for several minutes may be required.

Generally the resin and hardener are in liquid form and each by itself is stable for an indefinite period. On mixing these substances together, a chemical reaction takes place and their liquid system is converted to a tough plastic solid at ambient temperature. They develop excellent strength and adhesive properties. They are resistant to many chemicals. They have been found to possess good chemical and physical stability. They harden rapidly and resist water penetration. Thus they provide durability and resistance to cracking. Resin mortars may be obtained by adding coarse sand as filler.

The epoxy based compounds are invariably formulated with plasticizers, extenders, dilutents and fillers to produce a large number of products having a wide range of properties. The excellent adhesion characteristics, fast setting properties, high strength and chemical stability has led their extensive use in the concrete construction.

26.15. GENERAL USE OF EPOXIES

In concrete construction, epoxies have been used for the following purposes:

(*a*) For providing skid resistant overlays and wearing surfaces on concrete floors.

(*b*) As water proof membrane.

(*c*) Most extensively used in the repair of potholes.

(*d*) To seal cracks in the structural members.

The clean and dry surface is painted with epoxy compounds before placing the repair materials. The cracks may be sealed with epoxy compounds, epoxy mortar or a portland cement mortar after priming the surface with epoxy compound. For early and quick use polymer or resin overlays may be constructed. They can be put to early use due to faster curing. As they are joint less, they are more hygienic and chemical resistant.

Materials. Epoxy, polyester and acrylic resins as a class are known as thermosetting materials due to the fact that on curing their molecular chains are locked together permanently. These materials do not melt on heating like thermoplastic materials. These materials loose strength with the increase in the temperature. Generally they are supplied as two or three component system as resin, hardener and filler.

26.16. CLASSIFICATION OF RESINS

Broadly resins are classified as follows:

(*a*) Epoxy resins

(*b*) Un saturated reactive polyester resins

(*c*) Un saturated acrylic resins.

Acrylic resin system form high strength materials. They are based on monomers of very low viscosity or blend of monomers and methyl-methacrylate monomers.

Polyester and acrylic resins contain volatile constituents which are inflammable. Most acrylic resins are highly inflammable with a flash point below 10°C. Their vapours also cause toxic reaction.

26.17. PROPERTIES OF COMMONLY USED RESINS

Epoxy resins. Following are the properties of epoxy resins:

(*i*) Their strength is very high

(*ii*) Their bonding characteristics are good.

(*iii*) They have high impact resistance

(*iv*) They have high chemical resistance

They may be used to provide a non slippery finish

(*b*) Polymer resins. These resins have a better resistance to heat and thus can be laid over wider temperature range. They are mixed with cement and fine hard aggregate and can be laid in thickness upto 15 mm.

(*c*) Polyvinyl acetate (PVAC). When this mortar overlays are laid over the existing concrete, they are used as bonding aid. The liquid can be applied directly on a clean, sound surface and allowed to dry. The slight re-emulsification of the film on being re wetted by the application of fresh mortar topping provides a good bond.

(*d*) Natural rubber latex. This admixture has excellent adhesive properties, but difficult to mix with ordinary portland cement. Generally it is used with less alkaline high alumina cement for patch work or for laying floors on which vinyl tiles are to be laid.

(*e*) Styrene-butadiene rubber (SBR). It is an good and effective alternative to polyvinyl acetate (PVAC). It is highly water resistant. However the dried film does not develop good bond on re wetting. Thus it will act as a debonding layer if allowed to dry out. Hence the mortar mix should be applied while the tack coat of SBR is still wet.

(*f*) Acrylic resins. These admixtures when mixed with mortars develop excellent water resistance and improved bond strength. With this type of resins seamless, non dusting thin floor over lays can be readily produced.

(*g*) Styrene acrylic resins. A mixture of tough styrene with acrylic resin using 1:3 cement sand mortar can be used to produce hard wearing floor overlays at a moderate cost.

26.17.1. Repair procedure

(*a*) Use of resin mortar. The surface preparation requirements are same as that for cement based repairs. The constituents of resin based material must be mixed together thoroughly in mechanical mixers or stirrers. Most of the failures of the resin based repairs have been repeated due to either inadequate mixing or improper proportioning. For smaller repair works to get proper proportioning, the constituents normally are available in pre batched packs.

After the preparation of surface, a primer or tack coat of un filled resin is applied to the freshly exposed surface of concrete and reinforcement. In general one coat is sufficient, but if the sub strata is porous two coats will be needed. In case two coats are applied, the second coat should be applied while the first coat still is tacky.

The patching material should be applied while the primer is sill tacky and each successive layer should be applied before the previous layer has cured too much. The resin based materials cure or harden by chemical reaction, which starts as soon as constituent materials are mixed. Thus they have little pot life *i.e.* mixing period is very short. Hence the quantity of materials to be mixed in any one batch should be pre-calculated so that it could be used before it becomes too stiff. The resin based patches should be well compacted so that they become impermeable.

While using resins and hardners, normal safety measures must be observed, that is gloves should be worn and splashes should be washed off the skin, but solvents should not be used for this purpose Adequate ventilation should be provided and smoking, eating and drinking should be prohibited during the application of resin based materials.

(*b*) Resin injections. The polymer injection under pressure will ensure that the sealing material or sealent penetrates to the full depth of the crack.

Procedure. The injection holes are drilled at close intervals along the length of the crack and the epoxy is injected under pressure in each hole in turn till the injection material starts to flow out of the next hole. The hole which is injected is then sealed off and the next hole is treated.

Precautions. Before injecting the epoxy, it should be ensured that the crack at surface is sealed between the holes with rapid curing resin.

26.18. REPAIR OF CRACKS IN MASSIVE STRUCTURES

In this case a series of holes usually 20 mm in diameter and 20 mm deep spaced at 150 to 200 mm interval intercepting the crack at a number of points are drilled and then epoxy injection is injected in these holes to seal the crack. The method has been used successfully in the repair of cracks in dams, piers, buildings and other such structures. However unless cause of cracks is removed, cracks may reoccur again some where in the structure. This method has not been found effective if the cracks are constantly leaking and can not be dried out. Epoxy injecting is a highly specialised job, which requires a high degree of skill for satisfactory execution of the work.

Steps involved in Epoxy injection

Following steps are involved in the Epoxy injection.

1. Preparation of the surface. The cracks are cleaned by removing all dirt, oil and grease, fine particles of concrete etc.. These elements may prevent the penetration of epoxy and development of the bond between the filling material and the surface of the cracks. The contaminents should preferably be removed by flushing the surface with water or solvent. The solvent is then blown out using compressed air or by air drying.

To check the leaking out of epoxy before it has gelled or cured, the surface cracks should be sealed. The surface can be sealed by brushing an epoxy along the surface of the cracks and allowing it to harden. If extremely high pressure is needed for injecting the epoxy, then epoxy injection should be sent through a V shaped grove of 12 mm depth and 20 mm width. After filling the epoxy in the grove it should be struck off flush with the surface.

2. Installation of entry ports or device. The entry port or nipple is an opening to allow the injection of a adhesive directly into the crack with out leaking. The spacing of injection ports depends upon many factors such as depth and width of cracks, the variation in crack width with its depth, viscosity of epoxy, injection pressure etc. The choice of spacing actually depends on experience.

In case of V shaped groove of the cracks, a hole of 20 mm diameter upto a depth of 12 to 25 mm below the top of the V grooved section should be drilled into the crack and A tire valve stern is bonded with an epoxy adhesive in the hole. In case of other shaped cracks than V shaped groove, the entry port is provided by bonding a fitting having a hat shaped cross section with an opening at top to fill the adhesive. This fitting is kept flush with the concrete face over the crack.

3. Mixing of the epoxy. The mixing can be done either by batch or continuous method. In batch mixing the adhesive components are premixed in specified proportions with a mechanical stirrer in quantities which can be used prior to the commancement of the curing of the material. With the curing of the material the pressure injection becomes more difficult. In the continuous mixing system the two liquid adhesive components pass through metering and driving pumps prior to passing through an automatic mixing head. The continuous mixing system allows the use of fast setting adhesives that have short working life.

4. Injection of epoxy. In its simplest form, the injection equipment is consisted of a reservoir or funnel attached to a long flexible tube. This system provides a gravity head to the flowing material. For small quantities of repair materials, usually the small hand held guns are the most economical. A steady pressure can be maintained by these small guns which reduces the chances of damage to the surface seal.

For big jobs often power driven pumps are used for injection. Pressure to be applied for injecting the material should be selected carefully. The use of excessive pressure may multiply the cracks causing additional damage. As stated earlier also the injection pressures governed by the depth and width of the cracks, the viscosity of resins and seldom exceeds 0.1 MPa. Fine cracks preferably be injected under low pressure in order to allow the material to be drawn into the concrete by capillary actin. To increase the injection pressure during the course of work the common practice is to over come the increased resistance against flow as crack is filled with material. For relatively wider cracks gravity head of few centimeters may be enough.

In case of vertical and inclined surfaces, the injection process should start by injecting epoxy into the entry port at the lowest level until the epoxy level reaches the entry port above. Then the injection tube is removed and the lower entry port is capped. For forcing the epoxy into fine hair line cracks, a pressure upto 0.7 MPa can be applied on the port from which the injection tube has been removed for a period of 1 to 10 minutes using an inert gas. The process is repeated at the successively higher ports until the cracks have been fully filled and all ports capped.

For horizontal cracks, the injection should start from one end of the crack to the other in the same manner. If the pressure maintained remains constant, it indicates that the crack is full. In case pressure does not remain constant, it indicates that the epoxy is still flowing into un filled portions or leaking out of the crack.

5. Removal of surface seal. After curing of the injected epoxy, the surface seal may be removed either by grinding or by other suitable means. Fittings and holes at the entry ports should be painted with an epoxy patching compound.

6. Health and safety precautions. The epoxy materials are toxic and skin irritants. Hence their skin contact, inhalation of their vapours and ingestion must always be avoided. Following precautions must be observed.

(*a*) Full face should be covered and goggles should be used during all the mixing and blending operations.

(*b*) Rubber gloves, polythene or protective overall should be used.

(*c*) For the protection of skin, skin cream may be used.

(*d*) Adequate fire protection should be provided.

26.19. COMMON TYPES OF REPAIRS

1. Sealing of cracks. Every concrete structure has joints and cracks, hence joints and crack sealars are very important in concrete structures. The crack sealers should ensure the structural integrity and serviceability. They should also provide protection from penetration or ingress of harmful liquids and gases.

Method of sealing. For sealing the crack, it should be enlarged along its length on the exposed surface. The process of doing the enlargement of the crack is known as chasing or routing the crack. After doing the enlargement of the crack, it is sealed with a suitable joint sealer as shown in Fig. 26.11.

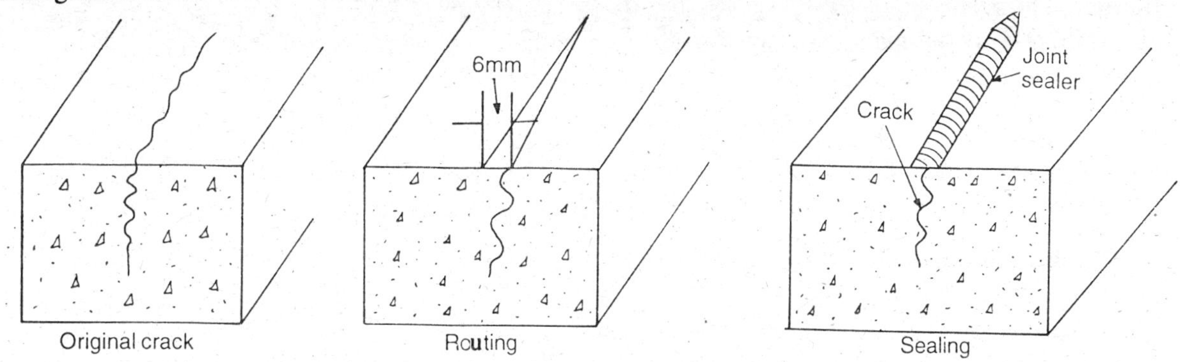

Fig. 26.11. Crack repair by routing and sealing

Non routing operation may affect the permanency of the repair. The routing operation consists of cutting a sufficiently large groove to receive the sealer on the surface. The groove may be cut by a concrete saw or hand tools. The minimum surface width of routing of 6 mm is sufficient as repair of narrower grooves is difficult. The surface of the routed joint should be cleaned with air jet and allowed to dry before placing the sealer or sealant.

26.20. FUNCTIONS OF THE SEALANT

Following are the functions of the sealant or sealar.

1. To prevent water from leaking to reinforcement.
2. To prevent the development of hydrostatic pressure with in the joint.
3. To check the development of stains on the surface of the concrete.
4. To prevents the development of moisture problems on the far side of the member.

Often epoxy compounds are used as sealant material. When appearance is not important and water tightness of the joint is not required, hot poured joint sealants are used. Urethanes which remains flexible over a wide range of temperature, have been used successfully for sealing the cracks upto 20 mm in width and of considerable depth.

26.20.1. Flexible scaling

For repairing an active crack, it is necessary to provide for its continuing movement *i.e.* its movement is not checked. This can be achieved by following the crack along its length, the process is known as to rout or chase the crack. The surface of the crack is prepared as discussed above and it is filled with a suitable field moulded flexible sealant. The strain capacity of the sealant should

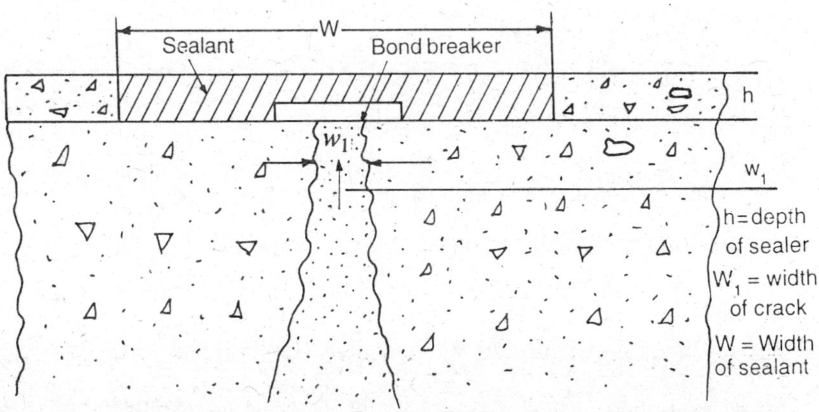

Fig. 26.12. Repair of an active crack by flexible sealing

be of the same order as that of the crack material. A wide crack spreads movement over a greater width so that the resulting strain is compatible with sealant to be used. The sealant must adhere to the sides of the chase or rout, but it should not be bonded from its bottom, so that the movement in the crack spreads over the full width of the chase. This can be achieved by providing a bond breaker or debonding strip of a material such as polythene or pressure sensitive tape at the bottom of the chase before applying the sealant. This debonding strip does not bond the sealant during or before the cure or hardening of the sealant and allows the sealant to change its shape with out stress concentration at the bottom. A sectional view of a typical movement joint or flexible sealing is shown in Fig. 26.12. With an increase in chase width, the crack movement which induces tension or shear in sealant will exert considerably reduced stress on the adhesive interface with the concrete, enabling the face seal to cope with the extensive movements.

26.20.2. Providing additional steel

The cracked reinforced concrete elements, usually bridge decks can be repaired successfully by using epoxy injection and reinforcement bars. The procedure is as follows:

(*a*) 1st the crack is sealed by epoxy injection as discussed earlier.

(*b*) After sealing the crack, holes of 20 mm diameter are drilled at 45° to the element surface and crossing the crack plane approximately at right angle as shown in Fig. 26.13.

(*c*) 12 to 16 mm diameter reinforcing bars are placed in the drilled holes. These bars should extend at least 50 cms on each side of the crack. The spacing of these bars may be adopted as per need or as per design.

(*d*) The holes and crack plane is filled with an epoxy injection under low pressure varying from 0.35 to 0.55 MPa. The epoxy bonds the bars to the sides of the hole and fills the crack plane. In this way the cracked concrete surface becomes to a monolithic form.

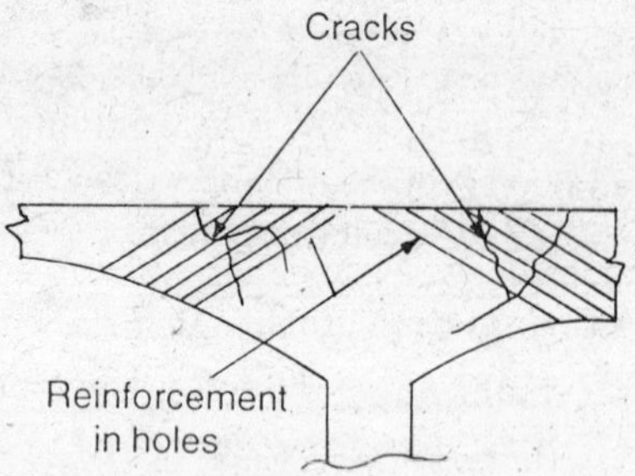

Fig. 26.13. Repair by providing additional steel

For a successful repair, an elastic exterior crack sealant is required. For this purpose gel type epoxy crack sealants have been found usefull. These sealants should be applied in a uniform layer of 1.5 to 2.5mm thickness extending upto approximately 20 mm on each side of the crack.

For local strengthening, resin bonding of flat steel plates to the external surface of the critical structural member of the bridge or building has been found most practical and economical.

26.20.3. Stitching of cracks

Stitching of cracks process is used when the tensile strength of the member is to be restored across the major cracks. Stitching does not close the crack, it only prevents it from further spreading. Stitching tends to stiffen the structure which may concentrate the over all structural restraint, developing cracks in concrete some where else. Thus it is necessary that the adjacent section to the stitching should be strengthened by using external reinforcement embedded in a suitable overlay.

Procedure of stitching

A stitching dog is a U shaped metal unit with short legs. The procedure is as follows:

(*a*) The holes are drilled on both sides of the crack in a staggered way.

(*b*) The holes are fully cleaned by air jet or otherwise.

(*c*) Now the stitching dogs are placed in the holes, so prepared across the crack as shown in Fig. 26.14.

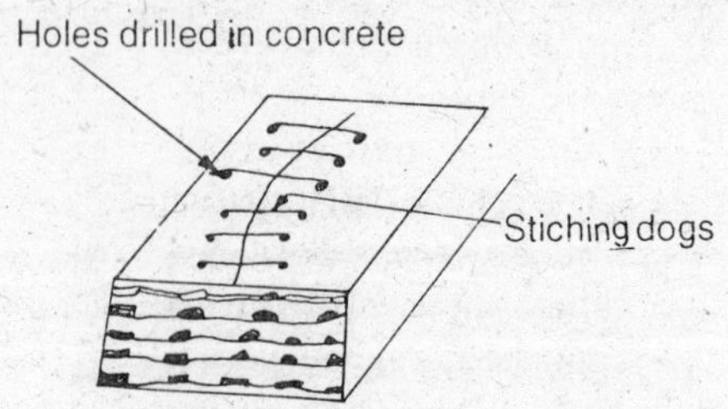

Fig. 26.14. Repair by stiching the cracks

(*d*) The holes with stitching dogs are filled with either non shrinkable grout or with an epoxy resin based bonding system.

The stitching dog should be variable in length and orientation or both.

It should be so located that the tension transmitted across the crack is not concentrated to a single plane with in the section, but spreads over a large area. The spacing of stitching dogs near the ends of the crack should be reduced.

In case of bending members, the stitching should be done on the tension face where the movement is taking place. In case the member is under axial tension then the stitching dogs should be placed symmetrically even if demolition or excavation has to be resorted to gain access to opposite side of the section.

In this case the stitching dogs should be relatively thin and long. These dogs can not take much compressive force. In case the crack has a tendency to close as well as to open or spread, the dogs must be strengthened by encasement in an overlay. In case of water retaining structures, the cracks first be made water tight before starting the stitching. The remedial measures for repairing the structural cracking of a slab and beam are shown in Fig. 26.15. Fig. 26.15 (*a*) shows the method of repair the cracking in slab while Fig. 16.15 (*b*) shows the method of correction of cracking beam.

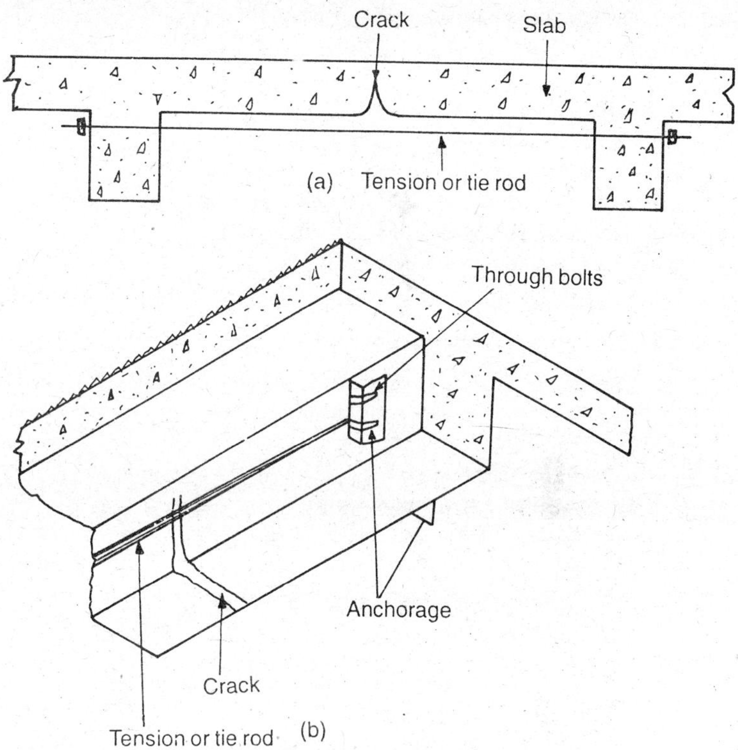

Fig. 26.15. Repair of flexural cracks in slab and beam

26.20.4. Repair by Jacketing

This method of repair is useful for the compression member as columns and piles, piers etc. In this case a durable material is fastened over the existing concrete and the gap is filled with a grout. The grout filled provides the needed performance characteristics. Thus jacketing restores or increases the section of an existing member by encasement in a new concrete. This technique is applicable to protect the member against further deterioration as well as for strengthening it. In either case the concrete section is increased beyond the designed value to allow for some future deterioration.

QUESTIONS

1. Concrete is a durable construction material, yet it develops damages. Comment.
2. State the defects developed in concrete during its construction period.
3. Define cracks in concrete and give their classification.
4. How the assessment of cracks is made.
5. Name different types of cracks and discuss plastic cracks fully.
6. Discuss cracks due to chemical reactions. Also suggest their preventive measures.

8. Give different causes of development of cracks in concrete.
9. Define the following terms:
   (*a*) Thermal conductivity
   (*b*) Specific heat
   (*c*) Coefficient of thermal expansion
10. Why the evaluation of cracks is essential before carrying out repair work.
11. On what factors the method of repair depends.
12. Write a note on the preparation of surface for carrying out- cracks treatment.
13. Discuss concrete replacement method of repair.
14. Discuss the pre-packed concrete method of repair.
15. Discuss fully shot creating method of repair of works.
16. What is polymer latex? State its functions.
17. Discuss resin based repairs fully.
18. Discuss the procedure of repair of concrete floor slab system with sketch.

OBJECTIVE TYPE QUESTIONS

1. The danger or distress in concrete structure may develop due to
   (*a*) Errors in the design and detailing
   (*b*) Poor construction practices
   (*c*) Thermal and shrinkage stresses
   (*d*) Corrosion of the reinforcement
   (*e*) All the above
2. Blow holes are developed due to
   (*a*) Excess of water content
   (*b*) Improper design of form work
   (*c*) Lack of compaction
   (*d*) Inadequate workability
3. The repair of projections, bulges, bolt holes, etc. should be done with in days of stripping off the form work
   (*a*) 24 hours
   (*b*) 3 days
   (*c*) 7 days
   (*d*) 21 days
4. In a concrete structure the most common symptom is
   (*a*) Surface crazing
   (*b*) Cracking of concrete
   (*c*) Scaling of concrete
   (*d*) Spalling of concrete
5. Cracking in plastic concrete is developed due to
   (*a*) Local restraint to the settlement of concrete
   (*b*) Due to highly flexible or leaking form
   (*c*) Relative volume changes between surface and interior concrete by very rapid loss of moisture due to low humidity, high wind or high temperature
   (*d*) Any of the above
6. Identify the incorrect statement
   (*a*) Cracks may point to problems of greater magnitude or may represent total damage
   (*b*) The cracking in concrete structure is not a cause to blame the designer or builder
   (*c*) A crack where continuous movement is observed is known as dormant crack
   (*d*) Cracks in concrete members usually develop due to incompatible dimensional (volume) changes
7. Cracking of plastic concrete can be checked by
   (*a*) Using concrete of lowest possible slump
   (*b*) Giving adequate vibrations and by proper form design
   (*c*) Providing sufficient time interval between placement of various elements of the concrete
   (*d*) Covering the surface by plastic sheets between the final finishing operations
   (*e*) All the above
8. Identify the incorrect statement
   (*a*) Cracking in structural concrete due to weathering can be controlled by using lowest practical content of water
   (*b*) Cracking in structural concrete due to weathering can be controlled by using lowest practical w/c ratio
   (*c*) Cracking in structural concrete due to weathering can be controlled by the use of non air entrained concrete

(*d*) Cracking in structural concrete due to weathering can be controlled by reducing temperature difference with in a concrete structure

9. Cracking due to corrosion of reinforcement is characterized by
   (*a*) Spalling and splitting of concrete in a definite pattern
   (*b*) By exposed reinforcement
   (*c*) By longitudinal cracks parallel to the bar or spalling of concrete
   (*d*) By rust staining
   (*e*) By all the above
10. The size of micro cracks in concrete is
   (*a*) 0.01 to 0.05 mm (*b*) 0.05 to 0.1 mm
   (*c*) 0.1 to 0.3 mm (*d*) 0.3 to 0.5
11. Before starting the repair work of the cracks, diagnosis is made to determine the
   (*a*) Location and extent of cracking (*b*) Causes of cracking
   (*c*) Suitability of various remedial measures (*d*) Likely extent of further deterioration
   (*e*) All the above
12. The weak spots in a concrete member can be identified by
   (*a*) Tapping the surface and listening the sound for hollow areas
   (*b*) By opening up the suspected weak portion
   (*c*) By observing exposed reinforcement, spalled area, surface deterioration and rust staining
   (*d*) By non destructive tests
   (*e*) By all the above
13. The selection of repair technique is based on the following objectives
   (*a*) To restore load carrying capacity
   (*b*) To improve the functional requirements
   (*c*) To improve the durability
   (*d*) To check the access of the corrosive agents to reinforcement
   (*e*) All the above
14. The preparation of surface for repair consists of
   (*a*) Complete removad of unsound material
   (*b*) Removing cracks from the surface
   (*c*) Under cutting with formation of smooth edges
   (*d*) Providing rough but uniform surface
   (*e*) All the above
15. The best way of removing laitance from the surface of concrete is
   (*a*) By sand blasting only (*b*) Grinding, scarifying and sand blasting
   (*c*) Acid etching (*d*) Cleaning with caustic soda solution or detergents
   (*e*) Any of the above
16. The repair of large and deep patches of deteriorated concrete in a structure, the material filling is done by
   (*a*) Dry packing (*b*) Mortar replacement method
   (*c*) Concrete replacement method (*d*) Pre packed concrete
   (*e*) Grouting
17. Deepand wide cracks in concrete members can be repaired by
   (*a*) Guniting or shot creting (*b*) Grouting
   (*c*) Epoxy injection (*d*) Mortar replacement method
   (*e*) Any of the above
18. Epoxy injection technique is used for
   (*a*) Sealing narrow cracks in structural members (*b*) Scaling actively leaking cracks
   (*c*) Repairing hydraulic structures (*d*) Any of the above
19. For sealing cracks in concrete structures by epoxy, the minimum width of routing should be
   (*a*) 3 mm (*b*) 6 mm
   (*c*) 9 mm (*d*) 15 mm
   (*e*) 20 mm

20. Identify the incorrect statement
    (*a*) The stitching of cracks is adopted to re-establish the tensile strength across major cracks
    (*b*) The stitching of cracks is adopted to prevent the crack from further propagation
    (*c*) The stitching of cracks is adopted to stiffen the structure
    (*d*) The stitching of cracks is adopted to strengthen the cracks which have a tendency to close as well as to open
21. Sulphur impregnated concrete can be used
    (*a*) As a practical and inexpansive substitute of polymer impregnated concrete
    (*b*) For repairing fractured members
    (*c*) For repairing slab and decks containing fine dormant cracks
    (*d*) As a practical substitute of polymer modified cement concrete over lays
22. Identify the correct statement
    (*a*) For polymer concrete usually methyl methacrylate is used
    (*b*) For polymer concrete latexes of styrene butadiene acrylic is used
    (*c*) For polymer concrete usually 99.9% pure sulphur is used
    (*d*) Non of the above
23. Jacketing
    (*a*) Is the process of fastening a durable material over concrete surface and filling the gap with-grout
    (*b*) It increases the section of an existing member by encasement a new concrete
    (*c*) It is used for compression members as columns and piers
    (*d*) It can be used advantageously for repairing the deteriorated concrete columns along with collars
    (*e*) All the above
24. Autogeneous healing
    (*a*) It can not take place in continuous saturation
    (*b*) It is natural process of crack repair developing in the presence of moisture
    (*c*) It is particularly affective in cycles of drying and remoisturing
    (*d*) All the above
25. Identify the incorrect statement
    (*a*) the choice of under water repair is influenced by the available method of access
    (*b*) The placement method and form work adopted must be able to minimize the mixing of water to the repair material
    (*c*) The under water repair and supervision is not difficult and costly
    (*d*) The under water repair requires adequate preparation and special technique

Answers

1. (*e*)	6. (*c*)	11. (*e*)	16. (*c*)	21. (*a*)
2. (*b*)	7. (*e*)	12. (*e*)	17. (*b*)	22. (*a*)
3. (*a*)	8. (*c*)	13. (*e*)	18. (*a*)	23. (*e*)
4. (*b*)	9. (*e*)	14. (*e*)	19. (*b*)	24. (*b*)
5. (*d*)	10. (*c*)	15. (*c*)	20. (*c*)	25. (*c*)

27

Joints, Repairs And Maintenance of Concrete

27.1. INTRODUCTION

It is seldom possible to cast all concrete needed in a structure without interruption. From safety and durability considerations masonry and concrete structure should not be raised more than 1.5m at a time *i.e.* in one day in one lift. Hence some kind of joint has to be provided. This kind of joint is known as construction joint. Construction joints are a source of weakness in the structure. Hence efforts should be made to obtain good bond at these joints. To avoid trouble arising from bad construction joints, it is essential to have knowledge how and where to construct a construction joint.

Further due to the variation in environmental conditions, the properties of concrete are affected to a great extent. The rise and fall in temperature causes expansion and contraction respectively in concrete. To safe guard against these ill effects there is need for the provision of joints in the concrete. The drying shrinkage causes cracks in concrete. The ingress of moisture, water vapors and atmospheric gases such as carbon dioxide, oxygen, sulpher dioxide etc. cause deterioration of concrete structures which need repair and periodic maintenance. In this chapter joints, repairs and maintenance techniques have been discussed.

27.2. TYPE OF JOINTS

Broadly joints can be classified in the following four categories:

(*i*) Construction joints
(*ii*) Expansion joints
(*iii*) Contraction or dummy or control joints
(*iv*) Isolated joints

27.3. CONSTRUCTION JOINTS

These are temporary joints left between subsequent concreting operations. The position of construction joints should be preplanned before starting the concreting. Till such locations the concrete must be placed in one operation. The joint should be located at such places where the concrete is least vulnerable to maximum bending moment and maximum shear force.

All care exercised in producing and compacting concrete to ensure good quality concrete is wasted if construction joints are not provided properly. The extent of trouble likely to arise from the bad construction joints depends to a great deal on the type of structure. A water retaining structure may be more seriously damaged by leakage of water through joints than earth retaining structures. The leakage of water leaches out material at the joint, resulting in widening the joint and becomes serious as the structure becomes older. The leaching salts are deposited on the joint surface making it unsightly.

27.4. CAUSES OF DEVELOPMENT OF DEFECTS

The defects in construction joints may be due to the following probable reasons:

1. The joint is made either vertical or horizontal as an inclined joint is very weak and generally flakes off. In a vertical joint proper stop end board must be used. If no stop board is used the concrete near the joint will be honeycombed and form a place of weakness as shown in Fig. 27.1, Fig. 27.1 shows a correct and incorrect position of joint.
2. The concrete may not have been properly spread and compacted to form a smooth horizontal surface.
3. Due to badly fixed shuttering causing a lip to form on the surface. This may happen if the shuttering is not properly clamped to the lower portion in case of a vertical structure as a wall or column. The loss of mortar also causes honeycombing near the joint as shown in Fig. 27.2.

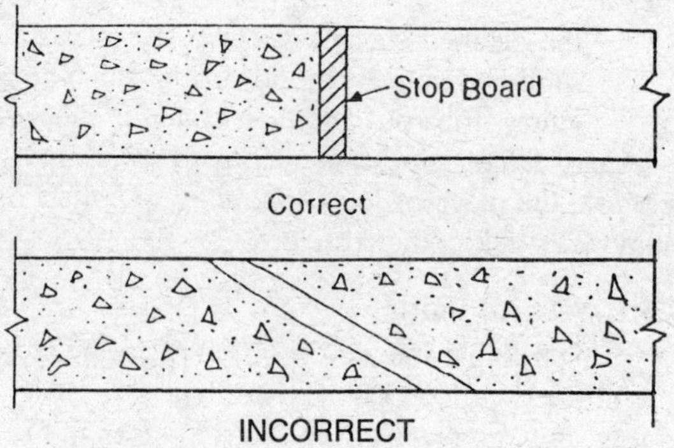

Fig. 27.1. Correct and incorrect position of joint

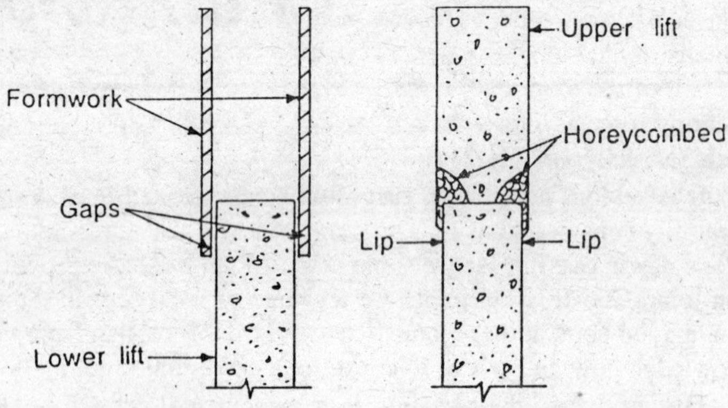

Form work in position for upper lift CORRECT

Upper lift placed and form work removed INCORRECT

Fig. 27.2. Fixing of shuttering

27.5. CORRECT POSITION OF JOINTS

In order to avoid defects in construction joints, the general principle is that the position of construction joints should be decided in advance so that they occurs at suitable place of minimum shear and should not be left to chance. For proper transmission of stresses across the joints, it is necessary to extend the reinforcement of the old concrete into the new concrete. Shear keys should also be provided as shown in Fig. 27.3.

At the joints before adding new concrete, the surface of old concrete should be treated as follows:

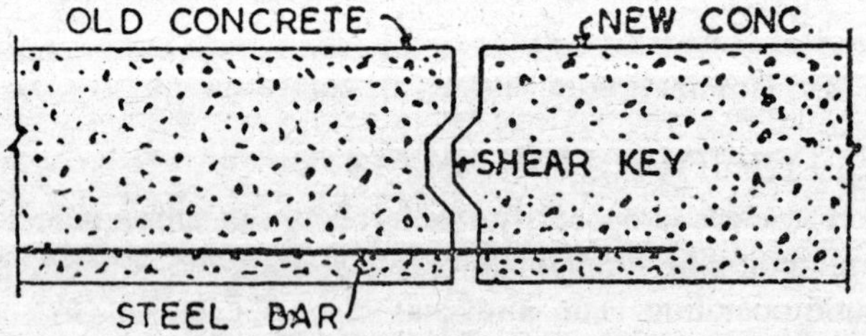

Fig. 27.3. Provision of shear key

(*a*) If the second layer is to be added with in 4 hours after the laying of first layer, the laitence on the surface of the old concrete should be rubbed with a wire brush and cleaned with water before the new concrete is poured, but no water should be allowed to stand over the surface.

(*b*) If the second layer is to be added with in 48 hours after the first layer, then the surface is rubbed with a wire brush and clêaned with water as above and a 1.5 cm layer of cement mortar of the same composition as that of concrete should be applied over the cleaned surface before the new concrete is placed.

(*c*) If the second layer is to be added after 48 hours after the first layer or on old concrete, a layer of new concrete is to be added. In this case the laitence is removed either by sand blasting or by chiselling and the surface is cleaned with water. Then a slurry of neat cement should be applied on the cleaned surface and worked into interstices with broom, after which a 1.5 cm thick layer of sand and cement mortar of the same composition as that of concrete should be applied before the slurry dries out and then concrete placed immediately.

Apart from appearance consideration of the work, the place of joint should be such that it may not weaken the structure.

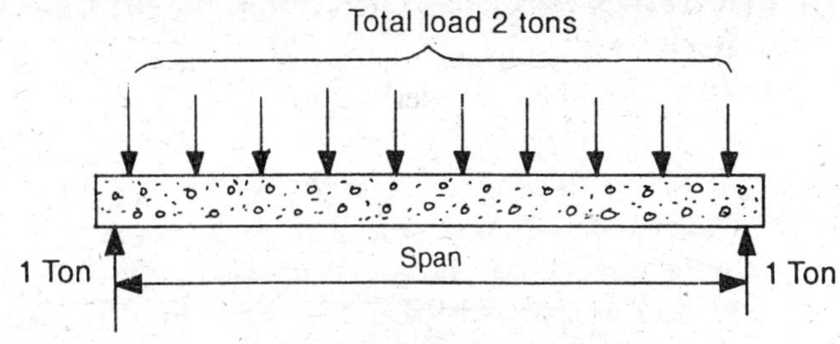

Fig. 27.4

27.5.1. Vertical joints

Vertical joints reduce the "shear" strength of reinforced concrete beams and slabs considerably, but practically have no effect on the bending strength, if made properly. This can be illustrated with the help of Fig. 27.4 and 27.5. Fig. 27.4 shows a beam loaded with a uniformly distributed load of 2 tonne. The up ward reaction at each support is of one tonne as each support shares the half of the total load. Due to this up ward force there is a tendency of the beam to break due to vertical shearing force as shown in Fig. 27.5. Thus if a vertical joint is placed near the supports, the beam is likely to fail as shown in Fig. 27.5. However at the centre of the beam, there is no such tendency of shearing. This is shown in Fig. 27.6 which is a diagram of half the beam with the same distributed load.

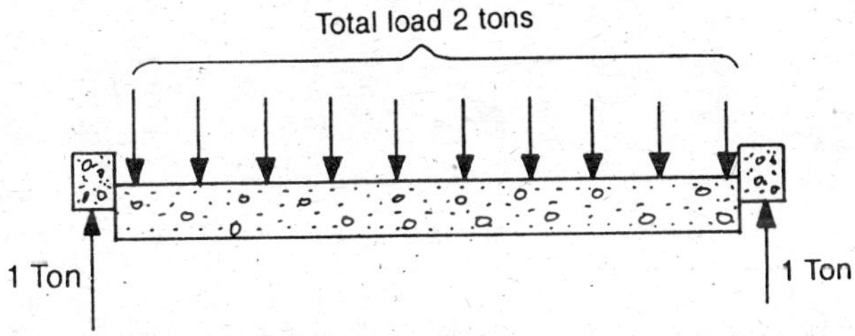

Fig. 27.5

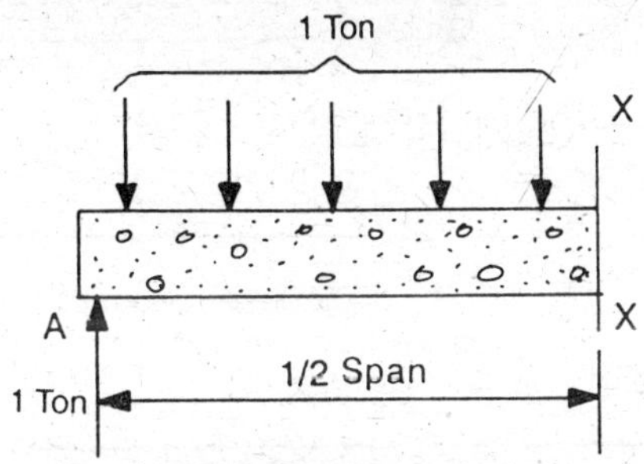

Fig. 27.6

In this case the up ward force at A is fully balanced by the down ward weight acting over the half span of the beam, thus there is no tendency for the beam to slide up or down at section xx.

27.6. BENDING STRENGTH

Bending is a condition set up in a beam by the loading and its effect is measured by the magnitude of its bending moment. B.M. is the tendency which the applied forces have for causing rotation of a section of the beam. In Fig. 27.6 the force of one tonne at A exerts a clock wise B.M. on the section xx (B.M. = force × lever arm). In this case lever arm is half the span. The distributed load on the beam also exert a turning effect on the section xx, but of opposite nature. In this case the B.M. is anti clockwise and half in magnitude of the first. The lever arm in this case being 1/4 of the span. The net B.M. tries to rotate the section xx in clock wise direction, but the reinforcement and concrete are able to resist this rotation. The stresses developed in concrete beam section under such conditions are shown in Fig. 27.7.

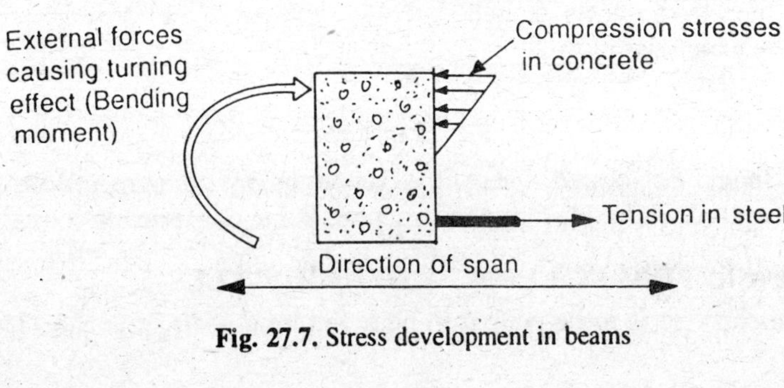

Fig. 27.7. Stress development in beams

From Fig. 27.7 it will be seen that compression as well as tension stresses developed in the beam act at right angles to the cross section of the beam and if a vertical plane of weakness such as construction joint exists there, it will not affect the bending strength of the section appreciably.

27.7. LOCATION OF CONSTRUCTION JOINTS

(*a*) **Walls and columns.** In case of walls and columns the construction joints should be horizontal. They should be provided at floor level, sofit level of lintels and sill level of windows. They should not be provided at the corners, as it would be difficult to tie the corners. In columns the concrete should be filled to the level. Preferably few cm below the junction of beam.

(*b*) **Beam and slab.** In case of a beam the bending stresses act at right angle to the section *i.e.* they act in the direction of the span and do not affect the bending strength of the section appreciably. The vertical joints reduce the shear strength of the RCC beam or slab. Thus the best location for the construction joint in beams and slabs is where the shear stress is least. In most cases of beams and slabs this condition will be satisfied if the joint is made at the extreme position of the middle third of the span. In case of short span slabs it can be made at the centre of the span.

2. If it is unavoidable to provide a construction joint at the junction of a beam and slab, then special arrangement should be made using shear reinforcement or providing a suitable key to increase the shear strength of the joint.

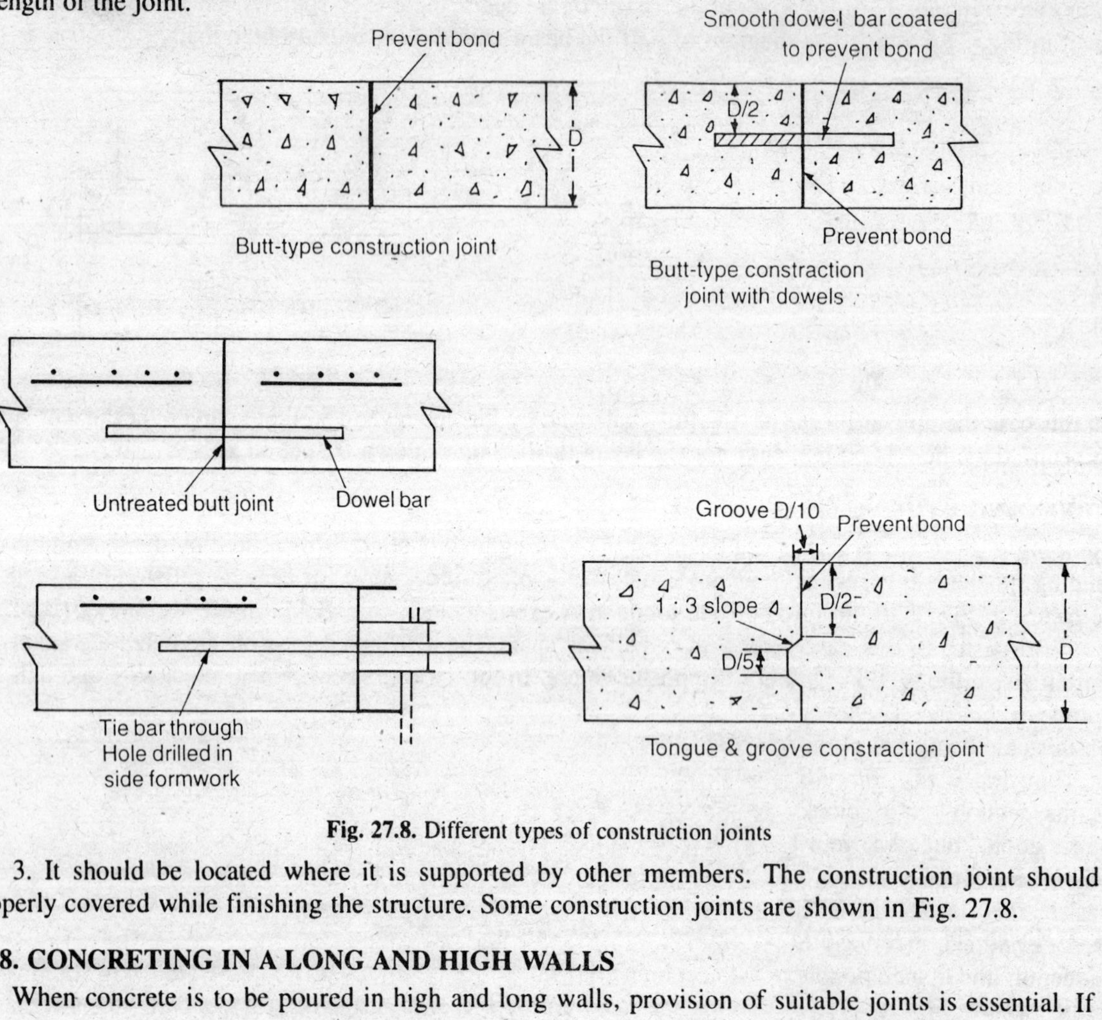

Fig. 27.8. Different types of construction joints

3. It should be located where it is supported by other members. The construction joint should be properly covered while finishing the structure. Some construction joints are shown in Fig. 27.8.

27.8. CONCRETING IN A LONG AND HIGH WALLS

When concrete is to be poured in high and long walls, provision of suitable joints is essential. If the wall is not required to be water proof, then ordinary horizontal and vertical joints may be provided. In case, walls are to be made water proof, special care has to be taken. For vertical joints it is essential to provide a proper stop end board with a water stop as shown in Fig. 27.9. Fig. 27.9 (*a*) shows concreting in first portion with vertical stop board, while Fig. 27.9 (*b*) shows concrete in second portion after the stop board is removed and water seal stretched.

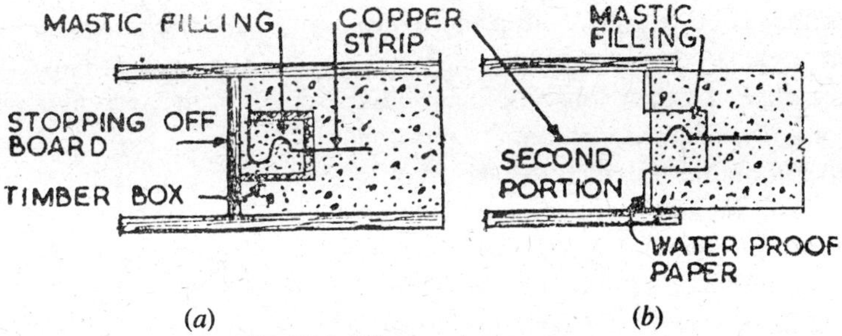

Fig. 27.9. Water seal arrangement

27.9. HORIZONTAL JOINT

In case of horizontal joints, keys should be provided as shown in Fig. 27.10. In this case the wooden pieces are inserted in the first layer of concrete as shown in Fig. 27.10 and they are removed before the new concrete is poured.

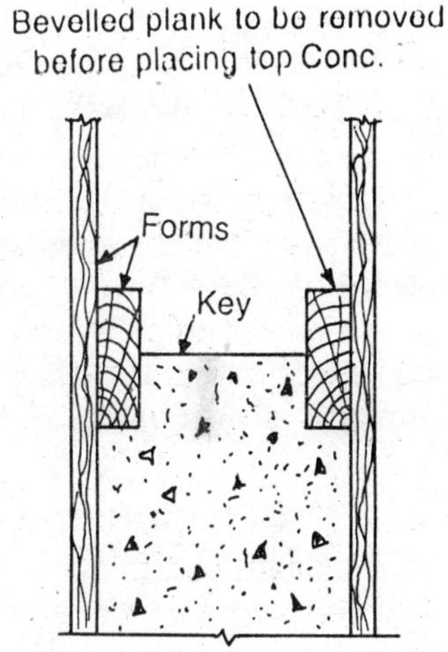

Fig. 27.10. Keys for horizontal joints

27.10. JOINING COLUMNS IN MULTISTORED BUILDINGS

In this case dowels must be left in the lower columns which connect them to the upper columns. The floor slab in such cases is concreted over the lower columns at least 48 hours after placing concrete in the column. If this time is not given, the column concrete may shrink leaving a gap between the floor concrete and it self.

27.11. JOINT IN WATER RESERVOIR AND TANK WALLS

These structures require special care and treatment as these are subjected to large heads of water causing seepage. These joints should be made water proof. To make them water proof, a copper strip is inserted across the joint as shown in Fig. 27.9. The strip is kept loose by providing a loop at its centre and thus it can provide for the movement of the wall. The loop is enclosed by a soft mastic around it so as to enable it to move freely. The loop is kept towards the water surface of the wall. It is unusual that the walls of the tank are made monolithic and in one operation with the wall base. The floor slab is laid separately and a proper joint is given between it and the wall base as shown in Fig. 27.11.

While laying wall base a step is made to receive the floor base. After this concrete has hardened the floor slab is laid and a water proof paper is put on the step before concreting. The tappered stop boards as shown in Fig. 27.11 should not be taken out till the concrete in the floor slab has hardened. Now this joint is filled with a plastic material which may remain plastic at all temperatures and whether dry or wet. Fig. 27.12 shows different types of water stops.

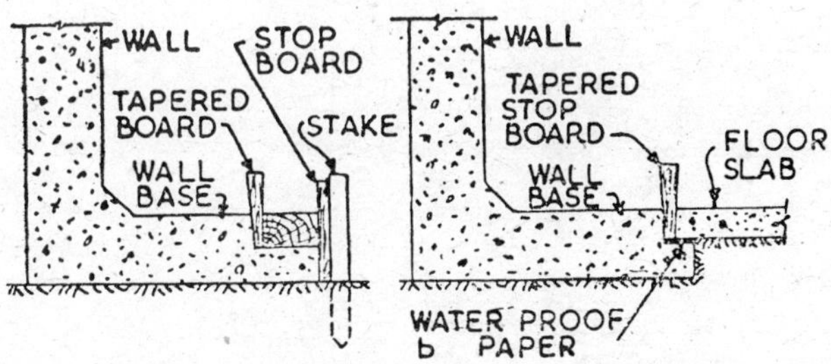

Fig. 27.11. Joints in water retaining structures

27.12. JOINTS IN CONCRETE FLOORS AND PAVEMENTS

Generally the concrete pavements and industrial floors are constructed in alternate bays to minimize the early shrinkage of concrete. To allow the maximum possible shrinkage in the concrete, the alternate bays should be concreted after the maximum possible time interval.

In case of dimensional roof slabs and in other special conditions expansion joints should be provided to take care of the expansion and contraction of the concrete. In pavements proper joints are provided to take care of the cracks developed due to thermal expansion and contraction, due to variation in temperature and long term dry shrinkage.

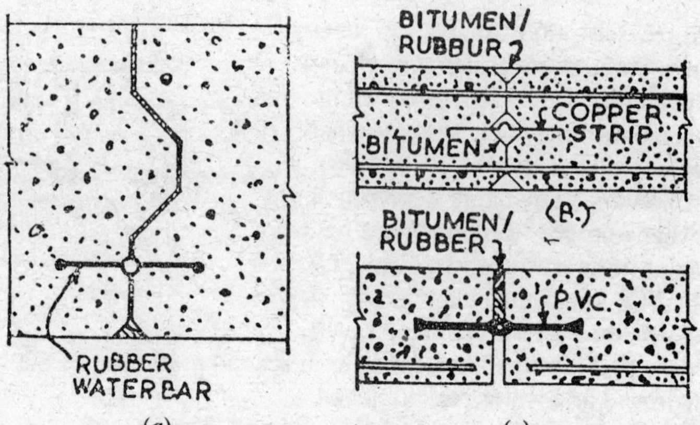

Fig. 27.12 (*a*) Joint for mass concrete water, retaining structure, (*b*) Joint for R.C.C. water retaining structure

27.13. JOINTS IN ROAD SURFACES

In case of concrete roads, the area is divided into panels and each panel is cast separately from the other. In the joints between these panels some plastic material as felt, bitumen or cork is filled. This allows free movement of each panel and saves it from cracking. The edges of each panel are prevented from damage by filling enough bitumen in the joints as shown in Fig. 27.13. In case of roads, having heavy traffic, the edges are further reinforced by providing iron angles built in the slab during concreting as shown in Fig. 27.14. The angles are fixed into concrete by means of 7 mm hook bolts.

27.14. JOINTS IN BUILDINGS

In buildings, vertical and horizontal joints in walls can be given more conveniently at off

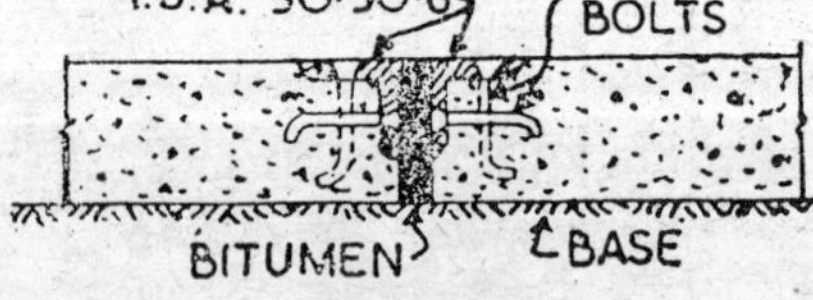

Fig. 27.13. Joint in road surfaces

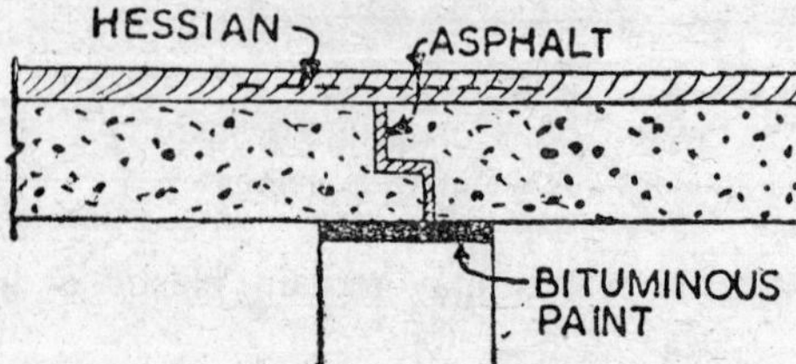

Fig. 27.14

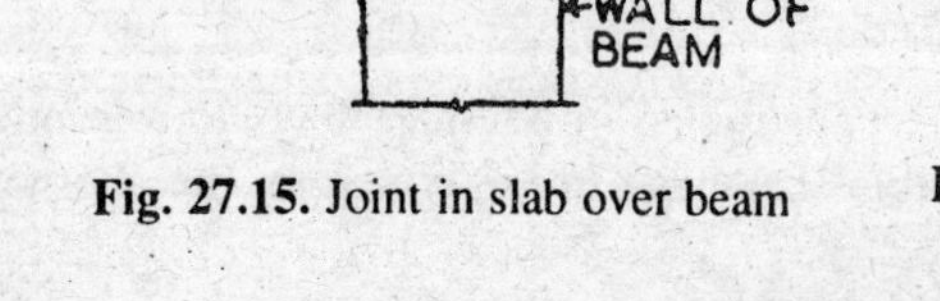

Fig. 27.15. Joint in slab over beam

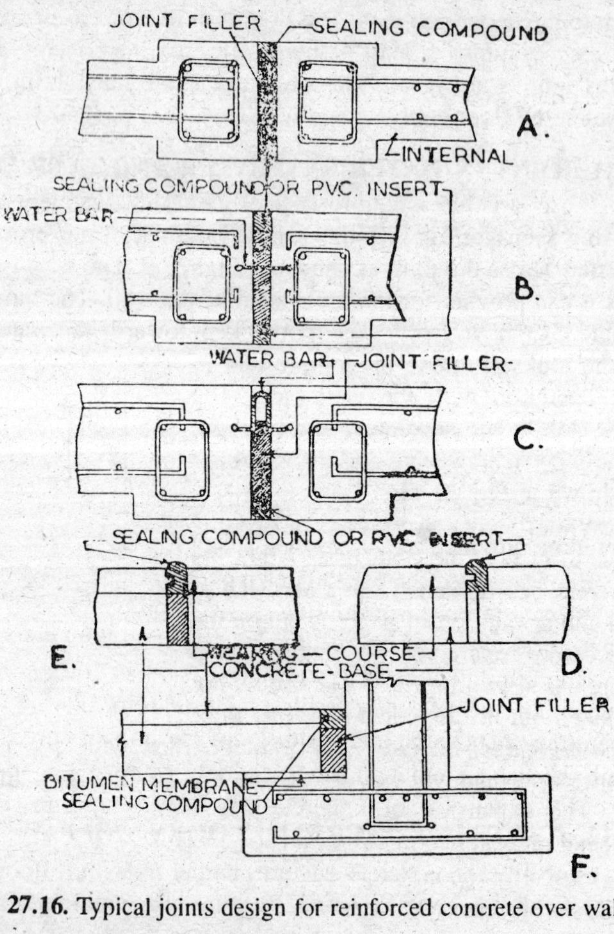

Fig. 27.16. Typical joints design for reinforced concrete over wall

sets, recesses, floor lines etc. The expansion joint in a roof slab must be water tight and as well capable to allow free movement to the roof. It is always given over a wall or beam as shown in Fig. 27.15. A bitumen paint is very essential between the slab and the wall or beam under it to ensure free movement of the slab. The joint can either be vertical or made in the form of a step to eliminate further possibility of water leaking through it. Asphalt is filled in the joint. In order to prevent cracking of asphalt over the joint, a piece of hessian is placed over the joint and covered with asphalt as shown in Fig. 27.15. This reinforces the asphalt and keeps it separate from the slab, by which the flexibility is increased. Fig. 27.16 and 27.17 show details of joints over wall and beams.

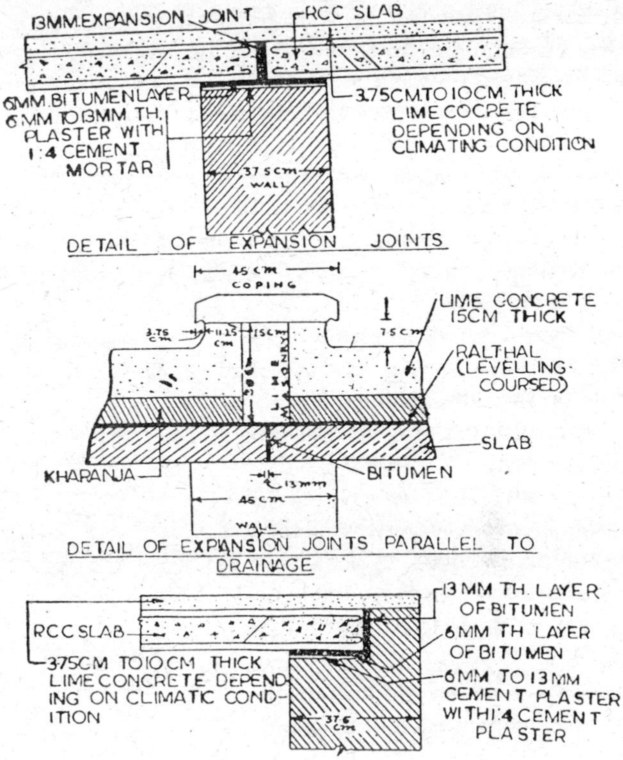

Fig. 27.17. Detail of bearing of RCC slab over wall

27.15. EXPANSION JOINTS

In concrete, volume change takes place due to many reasons. Thus to safe guard against this volume change certain provision such as provision of joints must be made to relieve the stresses produced in the concrete. Expansion is a function of length. Concrete is very sensitive to change of temperature and expands if the temperature rises and contracts if it falls. The expansion of concrete causes compressive stresses and contraction causes tensile stresses in the concrete. Some movements are also caused by the deflection of supports as well as shrinkage of concrete. If the concrete members are not allowed free movement, then internal stress will be developed in the structure and may prove disastrous to the safety of the structure. Thus it is essential that there should be some provision for the free movement of the structure.

A long building experiences large expansion. It is estimated that a 60 m long building with a variation of temperature of 50°F or 10°C may undergo an expansion of 2.5 cms. Thus buildings, more than 45m long should be provided one or two expansion joints.

Roof is one of the building elements which is subjected to maximum temperature variations. The roof is subjected to expansion during the day and contraction during the night or from season to season. This expansion and contraction causes pushing or pulling to the supporting load bearing walls. Thus serious cracks develop in the masonry walls supporting the slab. Therefore to prevent the pushing and pulling of the wall, the slab should be made to slide over the wall.

The expansion of concrete has been found to depend on water/cement ratio of the concrete. For a 30 m long 1:2:4 concrete structure the expansion for different water-cement ratio is found as shown in Table 27.1.

Table 27.1. Concrete expansion

Water-Cement ratio	*Amount of expansion in cms*
0.3	0.4
0.6	1.25
0.7	2.4

27.15.1. Spacing of expansion joints

The spacing of expansion joints is kept according to the amount of expansion. For a 60 m long concrete structure for a variation of 50°F in temperature the expansion will be about 2.5cm with the value of coefficient of thermal expansion as 6.0×10^{-6} for plain concrete and 6.5×10^{-6} for reinforced concrete. According to some researchers the amount of expansion varies from 0.6 to 2.5 cm for a variation of 50°F temperature. Thus the width of the joint should not be more than 1.25 cm. On this basis the spacing of the expansion joints may be kept upto 35 m. As per I.S. 456-1978 any structure more than 45m longer should not be constructed without one or more expansion joints. From practical consideration the spacing between expansion joints may be kept between 18 to 20 m. However from the recent studies, it has been observed that actually concrete does not expand to the extent indicated by simple analytical calculations due to the frictional resistance offered by the sub grade. Hence spacing between expansion joints may be kept much larger than in the past.

Further joint spacing is also affected by the season of the construction. For structures constructed in summer expansion joint spacing may be kept more than for structures constructed in winter. The joint spacing should be such that total expansion for summer constructed structures should not be greater than 1.25 cm and 2.5 cm for winter constructed structures. Apart from above intervals, expansion joints also should be provided at locations where the structure changes its direction as L, T and U shape portions of the structure.

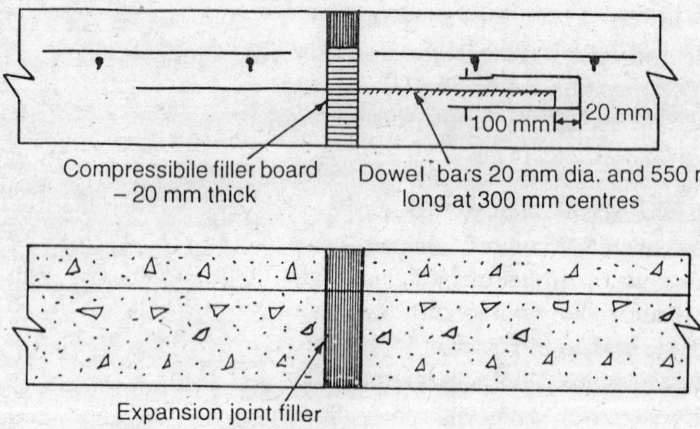

Fig. 27.18. Expansion joints

Following points should be kept in mind to make the expansion joints more effective.

1. Adjacent to the expansion joint the structures preferably should be supported on separate walls or columns, but not necessarily on separate foundations.
2. Reinforcement should not extend across the expansion joint.
3. The break between the sections should be complete.

I.S.-456-2000 has given the following recommendations on the construction of expansion joints.

As the decision on the location, spacing and nature of expansion joints depends on many factors hence the provision of expansion joint in R.C.C. structures should be left to the discretion of the designer of the R.C.C. structure. However for general guidance it has been recommended that structures longer than 45 m in length should be provided one or more than one expansion joints.

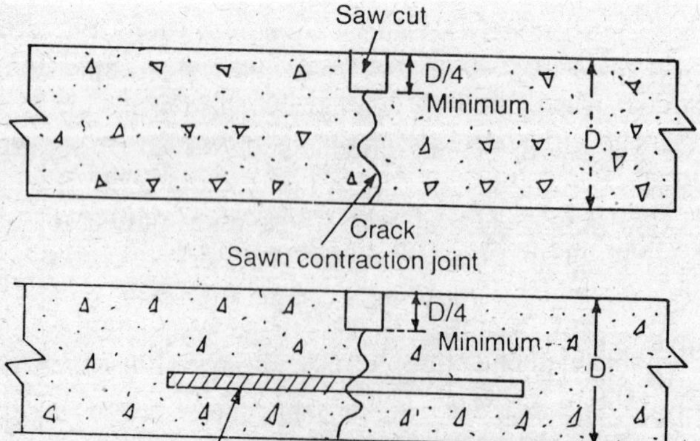

Fig. 27.19. Contraction joints

27.16. CONTRACTION JOINTS

Concrete contracts or shrinks due to plastic and dry shrinkage. Stresses in concrete are developed when shrinkage is restrained, resulting in developing the cracks. To avoid the formation of these cracks, contraction joints are provided. Contraction joints are also called as *control joints* or dummy joints. Contraction joints can be avoided by providing sufficient reinforcement in the structural element to take up the shrinkage stresses. Contraction joints generally are provided in un reinforced concrete pavements and floors. The spacing between the contraction joints may vary from 5 to 10 metres.

Contraction joints are made at the time of placing concrete by embedding a timber batton or plate of sufficient depth and thickness. This timbei is removed when the concrete has hardened. Some times steel plates of sufficient depth and thickness may be embedded into the concrete instead of timber plates and removed when the concrete has hardened. The recent practice of providing contraction joints is to cut a groove in the concrete of stipulated depth and width with the help of a sawing machine. Normally sawing is done with in about 24 hours of finishing the surface. If the saw cut is done after seven days or more, the depth of cut should be kept as 1/3 of the thickness of the slab. The minimum width of 3 to 4 mm is sufficient. Wider widths of cuts are unnecessary and un economical as their cutting and sealing cost will be higher. The groove or cut should be filled with suitable joint sealing compound to improve the riding quality of the pavement. It will also protect the edges of the concrete and prevent water from seeping into the base. The depth of joint should be about 1/4 the thickness of the slab as shown in Fig. 27.19.

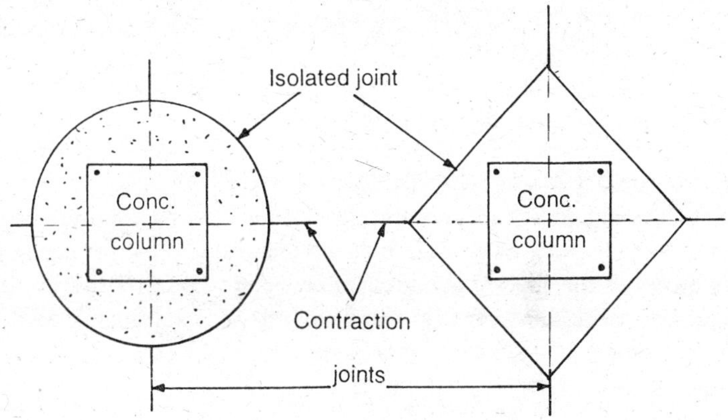

Fig. 27.20. Isolated Joints around column

In residential building flooring the conventional contraction joints are avoided by casting the slab in alternate bays to allow for the total plastic shrinkage and for maximum extent of drying shrinkage. To create discontinuity between the adjacent bays and to prevent the development of continuous cracks, usually glass or aluminium strip is placed in between the bays.

27.17 ISOLATION JOINTS

As the name suggests, this type of joint is provided where the concrete floor meets the permanent structural elements such as walls, columns, foundations etc. The depth of the isolation joint is kept equal to full depth of the concrete floor and its width of 10 to 12 mm is sufficient.

To avoid ingress of moisture or other undesirable elements, these joints should be filled with resilient materials and topped with joint filling compounds as shown in Fig. 27.20. A typical layout on ground of joints for concrete floor is shown in Fig. 27.21.

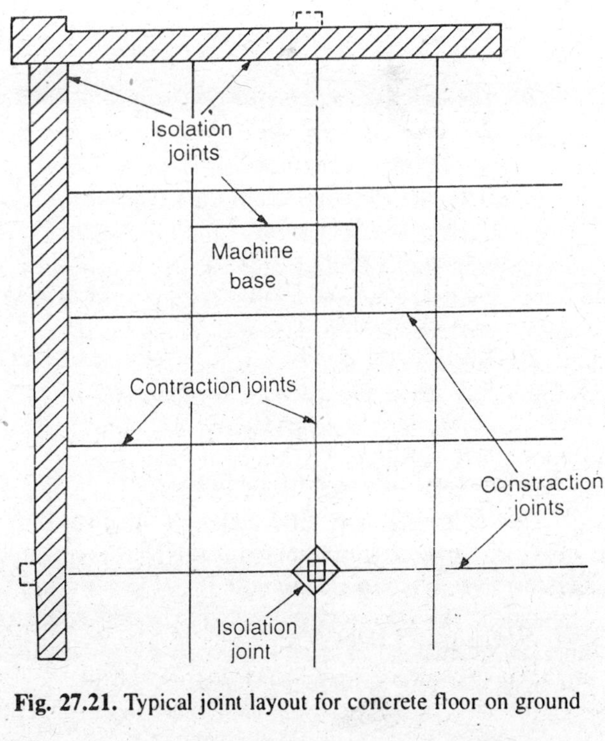

Fig. 27.21. Typical joint layout for concrete floor on ground

27.18. REPAIR AND MAINTENANCE OF CONCRETE WORKS

The process of preserving and keeping the concrete surface in good conditions is known as repair and maintenance of concrete. The concrete work may fail due to the following reasons.

1. Faulty mix design
2. Faulty workmanship
3. Unfavourable weather conditions
4. Developments of cracks due to variation in temperature or otherwise.

27.19. METHODS OF REPAIRING NEW AND OLD CONCRETE WORKS

For repairing concrete works following methods may be adopted:

1. By the use of expanding cement.
2. By dry pack method.
3. By replacement of concrete.
4. By replacement of mortar etc.

1. By the use of expanding cement method

This method is specially useful for hydraulic structures. If small holes or cracks have developed in the structure, the hole or crack is cleaned and either concrete made of expanding cement or cement sand mortar is filled in the place. This cement expands upto 1% of its volume and fills space tight against the old surface, resulting water tight joint or repaired surface. It takes about 15 days for full expansion. Further development of shrinkage cracks in concrete can be eliminated by using a small quantity of expanding cement.

2. By dry pack method

This method is suitable for very small holes usually not deeper than 2.5 cms. The holes are made sharp and square on the surface and the interior portion is roughened and cleaned thoroughly and the dry pack material paste is filled. The step wise procedure may be adopted as follows:

(*a*) The hole is prepared well by roughening the interior of the hole and cleaning it by blowing compressed air or by any suitable means.

(*b*) The hole is washed with the help of a water jet.

(*c*) The hole is allowed to dry. Over this dry surface a thin layer of cement sand mixture in the proportion of 1:1 is spread.

(*d*) Before the cement grout layer dries out, the dry packed material is put into the hole. The dry pack material is consisted of 1 part of cement and 2½ part of sand. Water should be added in very small quantity to avoid shrinkage.

(*e*) Now the dry packed material is compacted well so that the compacted layer does not exceed 1 cms in thickness in any case.

(*f*) To make the good bond with the succeeding layer, the upper surface of the layer is made rough.

(*g*) The above procedure is repeated till the hole is filled fully and the last layer is finished to match the surrounding surface.

3. Replacement of concrete method

This method is used for holes 15 cms deep or more in old concrete. The hole is prepared by cutting it square at surface and the bottom and sides should be cut as sharp as possible. At least of 2.5 cms clearance must be available around the hole for proper working. Hence no reinforcement bars should be left partially embedded. The water/cement ratio of the new concrete should be kept same as that of old concrete as it will provide better bond. The shuttering or form work should be removed after 48 hours as during this period concrete will gain sufficient strength.

Procedure

1. The hole is prepared by cutting to proper size and roughened.
2. The hole is washed with a jet of water and allowed to dry.
3. A layer of sand and cement mixture is spread over the hole and form work adjusted.
4. Now the concrete is filled and compacted properly.

4. Mortar replacement method or pneumatically placed mortar

This method is used for repairing holes of moderate depths between 2.5 cms to 10 cms. In this method a slurry of sand cement with sufficient water is shot into the hole under pressure through nozzle. The nozzle can be kept at least 1 m away from the defective surface. The hole should be cleaned and washed thoroughly before injecting the mortar. Usually the thickness of layer should not exceed 1.5 cms, but if required the thickness may be increased by applying successive layers at an interval of 45 to 60 minutes.

Advantages of pneumatically placed mortar

Following advantages of this method have been observed.

1. Ease of placement of mortar
2. Minimum need of form work
3. It gives high strength and longer durability

5. Pre packed Concrete

This method is specially useful for the repair of tunnel lining, dams and bridges, under water construction of bridge piers, dry docks etc. In this method the aggregate coarser than 6 mm is filled in the form and a grout mix consisting of 1 part of cement; 1/2 part of finely divided active silicious material, and 1/2 part of fine sand is pumped into the aggregate to fill the voids there. The resulting concrete is strong with practically no shrinkage as the coarse aggregate particles are in direct contact with each other. Due to this fact this system has proved to be an ideal one for patch work in hardened concrete.

27.20. FORMATION OF CRACK

The development of hair cracks on the surfaces of concrete works is a common feature. The development of these hair cracks is also called as *crazing*. Though these cracks do not affect the strength of the structure, but give unsightly look. These cracks may develop due to the following reasons.

(*a*) Due to un equal settlement or shrinkage
(*b*) Expansion and contraction due to variation in temperature
(*c*) Due to chemical action
(*d*) Expansion and contraction due to moisture movement
(*e*) Use of more amount of cement
(*f*) Use of excessive amount of water
(*g*) Due to insufficient curing etc.

27.20.1. Corrective Measures for cracks

Following measures may be adopted to rectify the cracking.

1. The fresh concrete should have low water/cement ratio to reduce shrinkage and well compacted to prevent settlement due to shrinkage.
2. The aggregates used should be well graded to give high quality concrete.
3. In order to avoid formation of hair cracks, dry cement should not be allowed to be sprinkled over the wet surface to absorb bleeding water, but finishing operation should be delayed till the evaporation of waters is complete.
4. The curing of concrete should be allowed for a sufficient time.

5. In order to avoid absorption of moisture from the concrete by the surface over which concrete is to be placed, the surface should be made sufficiently moist. This will avoid drying shrinkage.
6. Form work used should be sufficient strong.

27.21. TYPICAL REPAIRS OF CONCRETE STRUCTURES

Beams, slabs and columns are the most important components of the concrete structures. Due to the large number of cracks or damages observed in these components of the structures, the repair and rehabilitation of such members assumes greater importance. Techniques of repairs for Beams, slabs and columns are discussed in the following sections.

1. Repair of concrete floor and slab system

For the change of occupancy or to increase the life span of concrete slab system, generally their repair or renovation and upgradation is needed. Provision of services below the floor surface may also require the replacement of floor surface. These may require complete structural upgradation or the repair of visual damage only or provision of a thin surface topping to existing concrete to produce a wearing surface having a good resistance to abrasion and wear.

Before carrying out the repair of the concrete floor slabs, the causes of damage must be investigated and specifications of the repair must be drawn keeping in mind the future use of the floor. The floor should be surveyed for the defects and the existing levels of the floor should be recorded with respect to a known datum. The existing services in the floors should also be plotted and tested for their satisfactory condition. In many cases only the bonding coat may be sufficient while in other cases the topping over the whole area may be required. Before carrying out the repair operation, the damaged area and the joints should be repaired, otherwise these defects may reflect up through the new topping.

Under certain circumstances, the slabs in concrete structures may deteriorate in selective locations exposing the reinforcement. Scaling may occur due to an inadequate internal air void system in the concrete. Considerable scaling may also occur in the presence of moisture and also due to freezing and thawing in cold regions. The surface delamination of concrete in the slab may also occur due to the corrosion of reinforcement. The delamination of concrete above and around the reinforcement indicates deterioration which is dangerous for the long term structural integrity. To reduce the further corrosion of embedded reinforcement, repair should be done to prevent the moisture infiltration into the concrete.

For a large extensively damaged slab system, the use of a thin methyl methacrylate polymer concrete over lay has proved very useful, as usually polymer concrete does not absorb moisture.

Preparation of surface

Each repair area should be marked or delineated by a saw cut 3 mm wide and 6 mm deep groove around its perimeter upto at least 100 mm out side of the damaged area as shown in Fig. 27.22. The entire area in-between this boundary should be scarified by suitable machine or by hand to remove the concrete upto a level below the damage to get a sound and clean concrete suitable for repair. After the scarification of the damaged area, the delaminated surface should be located by using a small chipping gun.

The reinforcement in the delamination area should be exposed and chipping continued till all concrete with in 12 mm of the entire exposed portion of reinforcing bars is removed. To ensure that all delaminated unsound concrete has been removed, the prepared surface should be resounded again. To remove all corrosion by-products from the reinforcement, it should be sand blasted. Finally the entire repair area should be blown off with the compressed air to remove any loose corrosion particles, concrete, blasting sand and dust etc.

In case of cement sand mortar repair, the prepared surface of reinforcement is coated with a cement paste layer. This cement paste layer will provide additional protection to the reinforcement. After the coated surface has dried or cured, the area to be repaired is kept thoroughly wet for 24 hours if possible. Before filling the cementitious material consisting of 1:3 cement sand mortar of suitable workability by hand, all water from the surface should be wipped off or removed. For small repair works, the proprietary materials may be used which are carefully batched and their quality controlled. Due to the higher workability of the repair mix they should be only hand tempted.

For other cement sand mixes vibrating hammer with square plate bottom are often used, but for a large area a short beam fitted with form vibrator may be used for compaction. The repair is finished off with hand trowel. It should be allowed to cure for 7 days by covering it with polythene sheets.

For high quality local repairs, dry cementitious mortar materials along with a polymer as styrene butadiene, rubber latex etc. can be used.

Procedure. The exposed surfaces of concrete and reinforcement are coated with a primer compatible with the repair material system. The primer can be applied by rolling it on the surface with a paint roller and allowed to cure. The primer coat on the reinforcement provides it an additional protection against corrosion. After the primed surface has cured adequately, it becomes impervious to moisture and could remain protected from environmental effects.

In case of deep sections, an initial bedding layer of polymer concrete is placed around the exposed reinforcement to ensure that the exposed reinforcement is fully surrounded or encapsulated by the polymer concrete. In deeply removed areas the polymer concrete is spaded beneath the reinforcing bars to remove the air pockets. Then the chipped areas are back filled with sand loaded polymer concrete. Over the exposed reinforcement a thin coat of neat polymer concrete followed by a 6 mm of polymer concrete layer is applied.

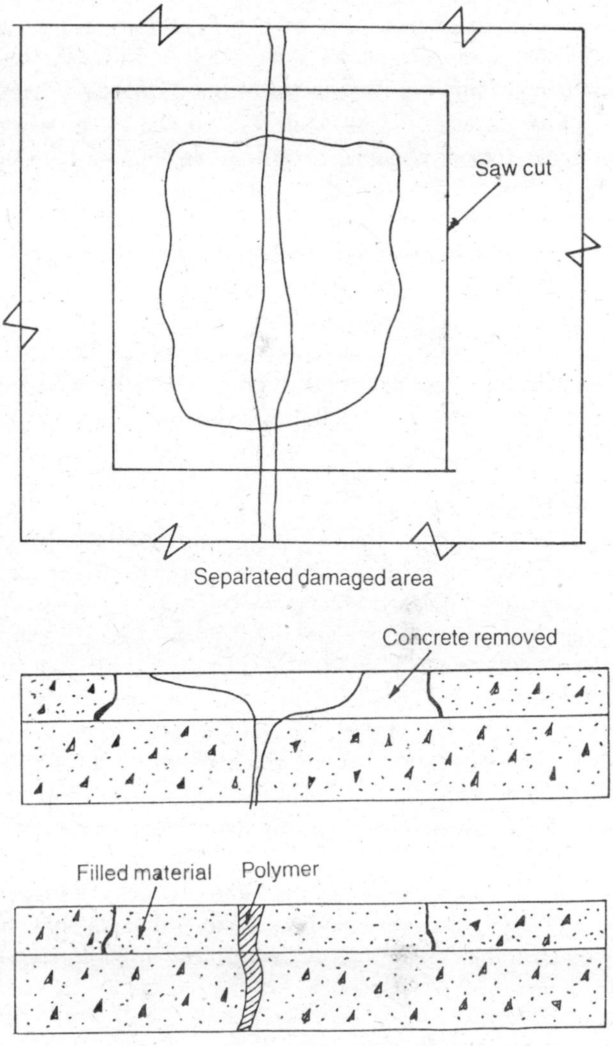

Fig. 27.22. Repair of damaged area of a concrete slab

Before applying the second layer of polymer concrete to build up the cover thickness in the area over the reinforcement, the first applied material should be allowed to cure. To provide a minimum thickness of 6 mm polymer concrete over the entire repair area, a final layer of polymer concrete is applied. Over the exposed reinforcement a minimum 12 mm polymer cover is desirable.

After curing the final layer of polymer concrete, the joint between the repair material and unrepaired concrete should be sealed with the same primer as placed on original prepared concrete surface.

In deeper patches, to control the shrinkage, the material should be applied in layers. At higher temperature above 21°C, the rapid evaporation of polymer liquid reduces the working time available before the material gains the initial set. Thus placing, screeding and troweling must be done quickly. In such situations working at night or early in the morning gives a better control for reducing ambient temperature.

27.22. OVER LAYS AND SURFACE TREATMENTS

In active or dormant cracks in structural and pavement slabs both can be repaired by laying bonded overlay or topping. Mostly cracks developed due to variation in loading, moisture and temperature are subjected to movement. These cracks will reflect through any bonded overlays and the crack repair will be ineffective. However drying shrinkage cracks can be repaired effectively by the use of overlays.

Fine dormant cracks of decks and slabs can be repaired by the use of overlay of polymer modified portland cement concrete or mortar. In highway bridge a minimum thickness of 40 mm of the overlay should be used..For such repairs polymers such as latexes of styrene, butadiene acrylic, non reemulsifiable polyvinyl acetate and certain water compatible epoxy resin system can be used. The minimum quantity of resin solids should be 15% by mass of the portland cement.

Procedure. Before applying an topping or overlay, the old floor slab should be shot blasted to make it rough to develop good bond between the old surface and topping. After shot blasting the surface should be well cleaned and saturated with clear water. The localized depressions or damages should be repaired before applying cementitious topping. Usually two types of toppings may be used, namely bonded or un bonded toppings. The thickness of the topping is governed by the strength and thickness of the old floor slab.

Bonded toppings

These toppings require bonding aids such as resins, polymers and cementitious grout. A cementitious grout of creamy consistency can be applied by brush on the floor slab immediately before placing the topping mix. The proportion of mix of 1:1:2 by mass of cement sand and 10 mm coarse aggregate has been found quite adequate for topping. The sand used should be medium grade (zone II) and the coarse aggregate should be clean and hard. Generally granite aggregates are used. In addition to granite, flint or quartzite gravel, ballast and hard lime stone can also be used. The quantity of water to be added should be minimum to attain full compaction. The topping mix should be laid in 20 to 40 mm thick layers in bays such that the construction joints of old floor must reflect up through the topping.

The mix should be compacted on the old floor and troweled level at the intervals while topping is hardening. After final trowelling the topping should be left for curing by covering it with polythene for at least 7 days.

In case of polymer modified portland cement topping, a bond coat consisting of broomed latex mortar or an epoxy adhesive should be applied immediately before placing the topping. The polymer modified topping should be mixed, placed and finished rapidly with in 15 minutes in warm weather. 24 hours curing of such toppings is sufficient.

Unbonded toppings

This is an additional slab laid over the old floor slab, hence no surface preparation is required. However the construction joints in the old floor must be reflected through the new slab. As a damp proof membrane properly lapped polythene sheets are laid over the base slab. Concrete of M30 grade having a cement content of 350 kg/m^3 should be placed and compacted. The concrete should be laid in bays of sizes upto 15 m^2. The thickness of concrete layer may be 100 mm. Before hardening of this concrete a high strength topping of 10 to 15 mm thickness should be placed over it and compacted on the surface. The mix of the topping may be as discussed above. The trowelling during the hardening and curing should be done as in the case of bonded topping.

Reconstruction of slabs

In case of broken slabs, it is preferable to reconstruct it afresh. In case of ground floor slabs, the sub grade should be inspected, compacted and brought to correct level by using lean concrete about 150 mm thick or well graded crushed rock material. A polythene sheet should be placed over the top of the sub base to act as a damp proof layer before concreting. The concrete should be fully compacted with any suitable method, finished and cured for at least 7 days by covering it with polythene sheet. It should not be loaded for 28 days.

Repair of beams

In case of extensively damaged beams additional reinforcement at the bottom of the beam together with the new stirrups should be provided. The stirrups either can be anchored by expanding bolts set in the sides of the beam below the slab sofit or may be taken right round the beam through the holes drilled in the slab. To provide a good bond between the old and new concrete the old surface should be roughened. The new concrete may be placed by guniting. If required shear connectors may also be provided by expanding bolts etc.

27.23. SURFACE COATINGS

A layer of material which adheres to the surface and forms a continuous membrane or film is known as coating. Generally coatings adhere to the concrete and form membrane after their application. Concrete basically is a permeable or porous material. The porosity of concrete is developed due to the evaporation of about 60% water added to it for workability. After placing the concrete it retains about 25% water as water of crystallization and 15% water as gel water during its curing period. The evaporation of water forms capillary pores which allow ingress or diffusion of carbon dioxide and other gases into the concrete. These gases and carbon dioxide dissolve in the pore water to form acidic solution, which further react with the ingredients of concrete and damage it. The porosity of concrete also allows ingress of water containing harmful reagents in solution, which are a potential source of damage to the concrete.

Concrete is strongly alkaline and is susceptible to attack from acidic reagents. Thus for the protection of the structural concrete, coatings of suitable materials are applied. Different types of coatings are described below.

27.24. TYPES OF COATINGS

1. **Anti carbonation coatings.** The coatings applied to the concrete surface to check the process of carbonation are called anti-carbonation coatings. The carbonation is the process in which carbon dioxide reacts with pore water forming carbonic acid, which reacts with calcium hydroxide and forms Calcium carbonate $CaCo_3$. In the process other cement compounds are also decomposed damaging the concrete. The anti carbonation coatings are based on chlorinated rubber, polyurethane resin or acrylic emulsions. These coatings may be effectively used to resist carbonation and general atmospheric deterioration of reinforced concrete. In situations where the spalling and corrosion are more wide spread, the use of anti carbonation coatings have not been found satisfactory.
2. **Coatings to resist the acidic effects.** In industrial areas, the concrete structures occasionally are subjected to abnormally acidic environment due to the release of sulpher dioxide from steel plants, oil refineries and power stations etc. into the atmosphere. These gases readily dissolve in atmospheric moisture and rain water forming sulphurous acids. Concrete in constant contact with such waters disintegrates easily. Thus to protect the concrete from such environment, coatings of highly chemical resistant materials should be provided. Under most circumstances two parts of polyurethane coating has been found most suitable.
3. **Coatings to protect cracked concrete.** The very fine cracks not considered structurally significant may be protected by applying coatings over the cracks locally. These are known as conventional coatings. The coatings should have flexibility and ability to bridge the cracks. Epoxy polyurethane and high build polyurethane formulations have been found very successful to protect the cracked concrete.

27.25. LEAK SEALING

The leakage of water in concrete structures is a inevitable source of damage to the reinforcement. The construction joints, shrinkage and restraint cracks form the leak paths. The amount of leaking water vary from damp patches to running leaks. In case of damp patches the water evaporates from the patches so formed and in case of running leaks, pool of water is formed on undrained surfaces. Honeycombed concrete, expansion and contraction joints are also the common routes for heavy leakage. Damp patches may also be formed due to the passage of water through voids formed due to plastic settlement along the reinforcing bars.

In case of water retaining structures, the extent of leakage may be determined by monitoring the loss of water from the structure. According to B.S. 5337 the structure may be taken as water tight if total drop in surface level does not exceed about 1.5 mm in 24 hours.

For effective leak sealing it is essential to identify the sources and routes of leakage. Due consideration must be given to the likely cause of leakage and the behaviour of the structure during the service period.

27.26. TECHNIQUES OF LEAK SEALING

Leak scaling is very expensive, it should be taken up when it is necessary. Leak sealing methods may be classified as follows:

1. Conventional leak sealing methods
2. Leak sealing by injection method

1. Conventional methods. Minor sources of leakage may dry up by *autogeneous healing*, which is the accumulation of calcium salts along the path of leak. The accumulation of salts will obstruct the passage of water and reduce the leakage to negligible proportions. After identifying the leak spots, the remedial measure may involve the local or total surface seal in the form of a coating system. Following sequence of action may be adopted.

(*a*) Surface preparation

(*b*) Filling of surface dents or depressions etc. known as imperfections of surface with-resin based grouts

(*c*) Application of primer

(*d*) Finally application of two coats of high build paint.

Procedure. The suspected joints and random shrinkage cracks are filled with the injection of a low viscosity resin. Short patches of honeycombed concrete should be filled with a resin based mortar of putty. Laitance and surface contaminants should be removed by sand blasting and power wire brush. Thus the prepatory work is quite extensive.

The movement joints, as expansion and contraction joints may be sealed by filling a resin into them. On hardening or curing this resin will form a flexible sealant. The concrete joints must be thoroughly prepared and cleaned before the application of the sealant. If required an appropriate primer or bonding coat should also be applied.

2. Injection sealing. From pressure and liquid flow considerations the simplest and most cost effective way is to seal the leakage from the water retaining side of the structure. In case it is not possible to reach the wet side, the leakage can be tackled from the dry side which is considerably more difficult than wet side. To seal the leakage successfully, the water passage must be filled with grout (sealant) completely. As the working time of the typical repair material is very short the velocity of flow of the material should be kept very high to fill the water passage fully.

To seal the leakage, the first basic requirement is to restrict or confine the water flow to a tube through which the sealant may be introduced. Once the flow of water has been controlled, the connection between the tube and concrete must be made strong enough to withstand the injection pressure. During injection process, the concrete may be over stressed, hence it is preferable to maintain low pressure. The grout may be injected by the following two methods.

(*a*) Direct method (*b*) Indirect method

(*a*) Direct method. In this method the grout or material is injected against or up the pressure gradient from the down stream side. The direct methods are very slow as the grout or sealant is pumped very slowly through very narrow passages against pressure and the pressure can not be maintained for long enough to achieve complete penetration. In many cases water may find another finer path way leading from the same source.

(*b*) **Indirect method.** In this case the grout or sealant is introduced on the pressure side so that the path ways are filled under the acting hydrostatic head. By this method the work of sealing the leakage can be completed quickly as surface seals are not required and mechanical anchorages may be used.

27.27. UNDER WATER REPAIRS

For under water repairs, same methods may be adopted as for above water *i.e.* dry repairs with modifications as per need. However the materials used in dry repair *i.e.* above water repair are often unsuitable for under water repairs.

To decide the use of material and technique for under water repairs laboratory trials should be carried out. Laboratory trials should also be carried out to identify the possible problem areas and to ensure smooth site operations. As usual, before undertaking the repair work, the damaged area should be cleaned of marine contaminants. This will help in detailed inspection for assessing the extent of damage. In case of smaller areas this can be done by using mechanical wire brushes, needle guns or scabbling tools etc. In case of larger areas a high pressure air jet may be used. After cleaning the surface the extent of cracked and spalling concrete should be ascertained either with the help of divers or remote operated vehicles to photograph the area.

27.27.1. Special features

The special features of under water repairs are as follows:

1. The under water repairs are more complex and highly costly. Hence the repair operations should be as simple as possible. The choice of technique depends on the available mode of access to the damaged area.
2. The adequate preparation of the damaged area may need special technique to be adopted.
3. The repair materials must be compatible with under water use both during placing and curing. Cementitious materials have been found to be better suited for under water repair.
4. Form work and placement method adopted should be such that the mixing of repair material with the water should be minimum.
5. The supervision of under water repair is costly and difficult.

27.28. STEPS INVOLVED IN UNDER WATER REPAIR

Following steps are involved in under water repair

1. Preparation of the damaged area

The preparation of surface consists of removal of cracked or badly damaged concrete and cutting of distorted reinforcement. The damaged concrete may be removed by any of the following methods.

(*a*) **By the use of high pressure water jetting.** In this method water jet with a pressure between 200 to 1000 atmosphere is directed on the concrete surface to remove the hardened cement paste mortar from the spaces between the aggregates. In this process the reinforcement is itself cleaned and can be used in repair. If the reinforcement is also to be cut, then an abrasive slurry is injected into the cutting jet.

(*b*) **By the use of splitting technique.** In this case the damaged concrete can be cut by inserting the hydraulic expanding cylinders into pre drilled holes and then increasing the pressure in these cylinders till the splitting of the concrete.

(*c*) **By the use of expanding cement.** In this case the expansive cement is mixed with water to form a cement paste. This cement poste is filled into plastic bags. In turn these plastic bags are deposited in the pre drilled holes in the structure. The expansion of the cement during the next 12 to 24 hours generates stresses of the order of approximately 30 MPa, which is quite sufficient to split the concrete.

(*d*) **By the use of soft explosion.** In this case the pressurized carbon dioxide cartridges are placed in pre drilled holes. The cutting dust and earth is filled in the holes and rammed with wooden tools to make it water tight. The pressure is then released by electrically detonating a small initiating charge in each cartridge producing comparatively a gentle explosion, which results in controlled splitting of concrete by cracks formed between the prepared holes.

(*e*) **By the use of diamond tipped saw.** This method is useful for minor works only as for core cutting. In this case a hydraulically powered diamond tipped saw and drill is used for cutting the concrete under water. The reaction force to the tools can be provided by strut or strap arrangement bolted to the structure.

(*f*) **Cutting of steel.** For cutting the steel under water usually following methods are adopted
(*i*) oxygen fuel gas cutting (*ii*) oxy-arc cutting
(*iii*) mechanical cutting

After the removal of damaged concrete, all distorted or broken steel has to be removed and replaced before restoring the cover. The reinforcing bars are replaced with new lengths, joined either by couplers or lapped with the existing bars. Immediately before replacing the damaged concrete, the surface must be flushed with clean water to remove any microbiological growth which may reduce the bond significantly between the repair material and the surface.

2. Application of materials

(*a*) **Placement of mortar.** For the prevention of future deterioration or in case of minor damages cementitious or resin based materials may be filled into the defects or cracks. This patch work is suitable only for small volumes. To reduce wash out of cement from conventional cementitious grouts and mortars adhesive admixtures should be used. The high performance mortars mixed above water can be poured by free fall through water to fill the form work. Normally the mixes are formulated to be self levelling to ensure good compaction without vibration. These mixes can be laid in thickness varying from 20 mm to 150 mm. To safeguard against wave actin damage on vertical faces the repair may be carried out using either form work and a free flowing grout or a hard epoxy putty.

The normal epoxy or polyester resin mortars are totally un suitable for under water use. For under water use special formulations have been developed. Normally these are free flowing. Hence they can be poured through water into the form work directly. For vertical face works, special types of under water grade epoxy putty has been developed.

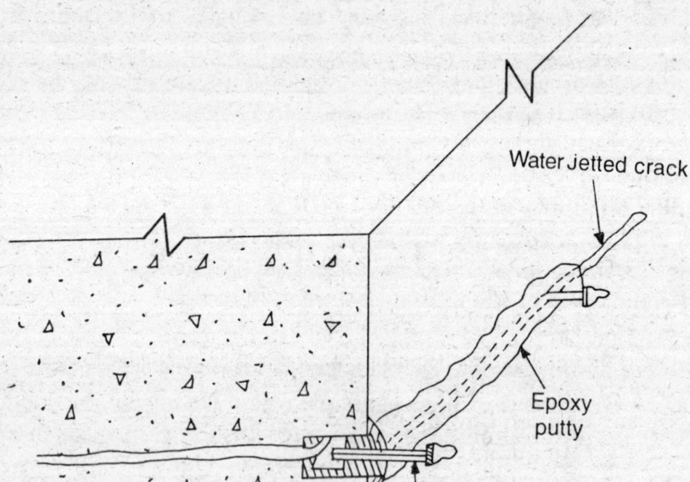

Fig. 27.23. Under water crack injection arrangement

(*b*) **Grout injection into the crack.** The general principles for injecting grouts into the cracks are the same as that for above water injecting. But due to the risk of washout cementitious material, generally non conventional epoxy resin injections are preferred. As shown in Fig. 27.23 epoxy putty is used to seal the cracks between injection points. The epoxy resins must be of low viscosity solvent free under water grade so that water in cracks may be replaced by a structural material. For small repair work, the hand held cartridge injection gun may be used satisfactorily.

(*c*) **Large scale repair.** For placement of bulk repair material under water, following requisites are necessary:

(*i*) The form work complete with inlet pipes and external vibrators should be easy to erect.

(*ii*) The existing structure should be able to tolerate the vibration.

(*iii*) To ensure an leak tight joint, flexible seals should be used.

(*iv*) For vertical repairs, to secure the form work with the concrete, a positive attachment of steel straps or rock bolts fixed into the hole drilled in concrete as shown in **Fig.** 27.24 should be used.

(*v*) In between the concrete face and form work a thick layer of compressible gasket as neoprene rubber should be used to form an final seal.

(*vi*) Finally the gaps due to unexpected variations in levels should be sealed.

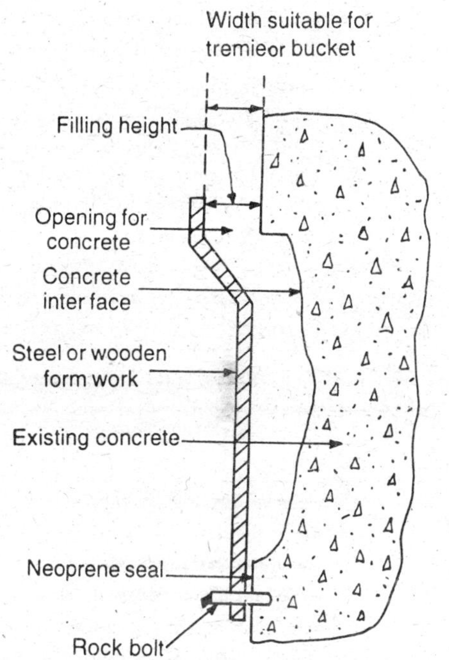

Fig. 27.24. Form work details for under water repair

Mix Design

For under water repair, certain modifications in the mix design may be done depending upon the nature of work. On the basis of experience, the concrete mix proportion should be selected to give the desired strength having slightly more sand in the mix *i.e.* the mix should have more fine aggregate. To have a provision for washout of cement, the cement content is increased by 25% of the designed quantity of the mix. Lean mixes having cement less than 350 kg/m^3 have not be found suitable for under water repairs. Round river gravels and well washed marine dredged aggregates have been found quite suitable for tremie and pump placing methods of concrete.

For heavily reinforced concrete for small repairs to obtain necessary flow characteristics super plasticizing admixtures should be used in the mix.

27.29. PLACEMENT METHODS

For under water repairs, the method of placement of concrete should be selected in such a way that the contact area between the concrete and water is minimum to prevent turbulence. The concrete may be placed by any of the following methods.

1. By tremie pipe method
2. By skip *i.e.* Bottom opening bucket
3. By pumping
4. Pre packed aggregate method. These methods have been discussed fully in chapter 18. Concreting under water.

The pre packed aggregate concrete method of placement has been found ideally suitable for under water or tidal works where access condition are limited or conventional concrete may be washed out by fast flowing water.

27.30. FIRE DAMAGED STRUCTURES

The damage caused to a reinforced concrete structure by fire may be classified into the following two categories:

1. **Completely destroyed or burnt.** In this case whole of the damaged portion has to be replaced during restoration operation of the structure.
2. **Slightly damaged or deformed.** In this case only the repair and finishing of the damaged portion is sufficient.

The extent of damage caused to a R.C.C. structure during a fire depends on the duration of the fire and the temperature the structure experienced during the fire. High temperature during a fire reduces the strength of reinforced concrete structures due to the following causes.

(*a*) The change in the strength and deformability of materials.

(*b*) Reduction in cross-sectional dimensions of the structural members.

(*c*) Weakening of bond between the reinforcement and the concrete, which determines the structural action under the load.

Normally the maximum temperature reached during a fire is estimated indirectly *i.e.* from the melting of metallic or other non combustible articles. From statistics available on the damaged R.C.C. structures by fire, the duration and maximum temperature reached during the fire are shown in the following Table 27.1.

Table 27.1. Showing duration of fire and range of temperature reached

S. No.	*Type of structure*	*Duration of fire in hours*	*Range of temperature reached in °C*
1.	Residential and administrative buildings	1 to 2 hours	1000 to 1100°C
2.	Theaters and departmental stores	more than 2 to 3 hours	1100 to 1200°C
3.	Industrial building and ware houses where considerable quantities of solid and liquid combustible quantities are stored	more than 2 hours	1300°C

Thus the duration of fire and the maximum temperature reached vary over a wide range. Temperatures of 1000 to 1100°C in fires lasting from 1 to 2 hours have been observed more frequently than 1300°C.

An accurate estimation of the performance characteristics of structures damaged in a fire helps in taking effective measures of restoration. The performance characteristics take into account the physico-chemical and mechanical properties of the materials burnt and that of heated concete. There is an accumulation of irreversible damages of mechanical and physico-chemical factors. Under mechanical factors, creep, cracking, shrinkage and plastic deformations may be classified, while under physico-chemical factors corrosion, absorption and degradation etc. may be classified. These informations enhance the reliability of estimation of residual load carrying capacity of the structural members, resulting in a considerable saving in the cost of restoration of the structure. However from this information the determination of the physico-chemical characteristics of materials and geometric dimensions of the structure is difficult.

The strength and stiffness of concrete and steel decreases as the temperature of the member increases and dimensional changes take place. The changes in strength and stiffness of the concrete are influenced by the constituent elements of the concrete *i.e.* the type of cement and aggregate and water content. The cracks or spalling develops in beams, columns and slabs due to the development of stresses caused by thermal strains. The development of cracks and spalling decreases the area available to resist the applied loads or forces. The behaviour of different structural elements damaged in fire is discussed below.

27.30.1. Axially Loaded Columns

Normally the failure of axially loaded columns takes place at mid height due to brittleness. The failure occurs due to the disintegration of concrete in the whole section accompanied by buckling of longitudinal bars. Due to the fire, a large variation in temperature between the concrete of periphery and centre of the section takes place. The range of this temperature variation has been found 800°C or even more. This variation in temperature causes variation in the strength of concrete. The strength of concrete varies along the cross section. The central portion of the section keeps its original value of strength while it reduces to zero at the peripherical surface.

The temperature at which the crushing strength of the concrete is reduced to 50% of its initial value is known as *critical temperature.* The value of critical temperature depends upon the nature or type of aggregate used in the concrete. The value of critical temperature for concrete made with sand stone or granite aggregates is 550°C and for concrete made with lime stone is 700°C.

It has been observed that quartz, granites and gravels expand steadily upto about 573°C. At this temperature they go a sudden expansion of 0.85%. This expansion develops a disruptive action on the stability of concrete. At this temperature the fire resisting properties of the concrete are least if the quartz is the principal dominant mineral in the aggregate.

Amongst the igneous rock aggregate, the best fire resistant aggregates are dolerites and basalts. The lime stone expands steadily upto a temperature of about 900°C and then begins to contract due to decomposition and librates carbon dioxides. As the decomposition of lime stone takes place at a very high temperature of 900°C, the dense lime stone aggregate has been found a good fire resistant aggregate. The blast furnace slag aggregate is regarded as the best fire resistant aggregate. Broken brick aggregate also has been found as a good fire resistant aggregate. On the basis of extensive research work, it has been found that even the best fire resistant concrete will fail if it is exposed to a temperature more than 900°C for a considerable period. The serious reduction in strength takes place at a temperature of about 600°C. Upto a temperature of about 300°C Concrete does not show apprecial loss in strength, but at about 500°C the 50% strength of concrete is lost.

Due to the non uniformity of temperature in the cross-section, the hottest layers of concrete and main reinforcement bars near the surface of the column are separated due to the thermal creep and loss of strength and also due to the contraction in concrete. This results in increased stresses in the centre of the section where the moderately hot concrete retains its strength and elasticity. The complete failure of column takes place when the stresses in the central portion of the cross-section become equal to the initial prism strength of the concrete and deformation approaches its limiting value of 0.0025 to 0.0030.

27.31. REHABILATION OF FIRE DAMAGED ELEMENTS

1. **Ecentrically loaded columns.** The failure of ecentrically loaded columns takes place when the reinforcement bars in tension heat up. In such cases the fire resistance of the structural elements can be increased by increasing the thickness of the protective cover to the reinforcement.
2. **R.C.C. slabs.** The behaviour of R.C.C. slabs exposed to fire is governed by the temperature of bottom reinforcement and heat transmission in concrete. The reinforcing bars are assumed to retain 50% of their original strength. The carrying capacity of slabs can be .ncreased by increasing their thickness.
3. **R.C.C. Beams.** Due to heating up, the bond between the transverse reinforcement and concrete is weakend considerably. The weakening of bond between the concrete and transverse reinforcement reduces the residual shear load carrying capacity to a great extent. The depth and width of the beam can be increased. The required increase in the dimensions of beam, longitudinal and transverse reinforcements should be calculated by taking into account the change in compressive strength of concrete and modulii of elasticity of concrete and steel.
4. **Axially loaded columns.** The carrying capacity of axially loaded columns depends upon the cross section of the column, coefficient of change in strength of concrete due to high temperature and corresponding critical temperature. The carrying capacity can be restored by increasing the cross section with suitable increase in the longitudinal reinforcement.

For restoring the damaged structure the reinforcing bars can be anchored conveniently into the existing concrete walls and foundations by drilling hole in the concrete some what larger than the diameter of the bar and epoxy gel coated bar is set into the hole.

In case of slabs also, the epoxy coated reinforcement may be used, but the thickness of epoxy coating should not be more than 0.25 mm.

QUESTIONS

1. Discuss the different types of joints.
2. Discuss the procedure of concreting in long and high walls with emphasis on the provision of joints.
3. Discuss fully how a joint in water reservoir or tank wall can be provided.
4. Discuss the correct location for construction joints.
5. Explain expansion joints with reference to their spacing and effectiveness.
6. What is a contraction joint? How they are provided.
7. Discuss the salient features of repair of concrete floor slab system.
8. Write short notes on the followings:
   (*a*) Anti carbonation coatings (*b*) Anti acidic coatings
   (*c*) Leak sealing (*d*) Fire damage of concrete structures
9. Discuss in detail the under water repairs of concrete with neat sketch where ever possible.
10. Give the classifications of joints. Give the correct location of construction joints.
11. Why and where expansion joints are provided?
12. Write a short note on repair of concrete structures.
13. What is crazing? What corrective measures can be taken to control it.
14. Write a note on expansion joints.
15. Enumerate the suitable locations of construction joints.

OBJECTIVE TYPE QUESTIONS

1. In concrete structures joints may be provided of the type
   (*a*) Construction joint (*b*) Contraction joint
   (*c*) Expansion joint (*d*) Isolation joint
   (*e*) All of the above
2. The deliberately provided joints in concrete structures are known as
   (*a*) Construction joints (*b*) Expansion joints
   (*c*) Isolation joints (*d*) Leakage joint
3. Identify the correct statements
   (*a*) The construction joint should be provided where the shear force is maximum
   (*b*) The construction joint should be provided where the shear force is minimum
   (*c*) The construction joint should be provided where the bond strength is maximum
   (*d*) Any where is the section
4. Identify the incorrect statements
   (*a*) Vertical joints reduce the shear strength considerably
   (*b*) The best location of providing construction joint in the concrete slab and beams is the middle third of the span
   (*c*) The construction joint should be provided at the support of the beam and slab
   (*d*) In water retaining structures a copper strip should be provided across the joint at its centre with a loop
   (*e*) The loop should be free to move and provided towards the water surface of the wall
   (*f*) The loop should be enclosed in soft mastic material to allow its free movement
   (*g*) The floor slab of water retaining structure should be monolitic with its walls
5. Identify the incorrect statements
   (*a*) Concrete expansion is a function of its w/c ratio
   (*b*) Higher the w/c ratio, higher the expansion of the concrete
   (*c*) Higher the w/c ratio, lower the expansion of the concrete

(*d*) The spacing of expansion joints should be about 20 m

6. Identify the correct statements
   (*a*) The expansion joints should be provided where the structure changes its direction
   (*b*) The expansion joint spacing for summer constructed structures should be such that total expansion is not greater than 1.25 cm and 2.5 cms winter constructed structures
   (*c*) As per IS 456-1978 any concrete structure longer than 45 m in lengtn should be provided with 1 to 2 expansion joint
   (*d*) The reinforcement should not extend across the expansion joint
   (*e*) All the above
7. Identify the incorrect statements
   (*a*) Contraction joint is provided to avoid the development of shrinkage cracks
   (*b*) Contraction joints are also known as control joint or dummy joint
   (*c*) Contraction joints are usually provided in the reinforced concrete floors and pavements
   (*d*) The spacing of contraction joint may vary from 5 to 10 m
   (*e*) The contraction joints may be provided after setting the concrete
   (*f*) Isolation joints may be provided where the concrete floor meets the permanent structural elements as walls, column etc.
8. The technique of epoxy injection is used for
   (*a*) Sealing actively leaking cracks
   (*b*) Sealing narrow cracks in structural members
   (*c*) Repairing hydraulic structures
   (*d*) All the above
9. For scaling the cracks in concrete structures by using epoxy, the minimum width of routing should be
   (*a*) 20 mm
   (*b*) 15 mm
   (*c*) 9 mm
   (*d*) 6 mm
   (*e*) 3 mm
10. The bonded over lays of polymer modified portland cement concrete or mortar
    (*a*) Should have minimum thickness of 75 mm
    (*b*) Should be cured for 72 hours
    (*c*) Can be used for repairing slabs and decks containing fine dormant cracks
    (*d*) Should be mixed, placed and finished with in 30 minutes
11. Polymer impregnation of concrete is not effective in the following cases except
    (*a*) When cracks contain moisture
    (*b*) When creaks are dry
    (*c*) When cracks are fine
    (*d*) When volatite monomer evaporates
12. The best fire resistant aggregate is
    (*a*) Sand stone
    (*b*) Lime stone
    (*c*) Brick aggregate
    (*d*) Blast furnace aggregate
13. 50% strength of concrete is lost at the temperature of
    (*a*) 350°C
    (*b*) 500°C
    (*c*) 950°C
    (*d*) 750°C

Answers

1. (*e*)	4. (*c*, *g*)	7. (*c*, *e*)	10. (*c*)	13. (*b*)
2. (*b*)	5. (*c*)	8. (*b*)	11. (*b*)	
3. (*b*)	6. (*e*)	9. (*d*)	12. (*d*)	

28

Rheology of Concrete

28.1. INTRODUCTION

Rheology is the science of the flow and deformation of the materials. It is concerned with the relationship between stress-strain, rate of strain and time. The term Rheology deals with the materials whose flow properties are more complicated than those of simple fluids as liquids and gases. The Rheological principles and techniques applied to concrete include the deformation of hardened concrete, handling and placing of freshly mixed concrete and the behavior of its constituents parts, namely cement paste and slurries.

The Rheology of fresh concrete like workability includes the parameters of stability, mobility and compactibility, which are necessary to determine the suitability of any concrete mix. The line diagram of Rheology of fresh concrete is shown in Fig. 28.1. For defining the Rheological properties of fresh concrete, the above parameters are defined in terms of forces involved in the transmission of mechanical stresses on the concrete. During handling and placing of fresh concrete, it is subjected to normal and shearing forces.

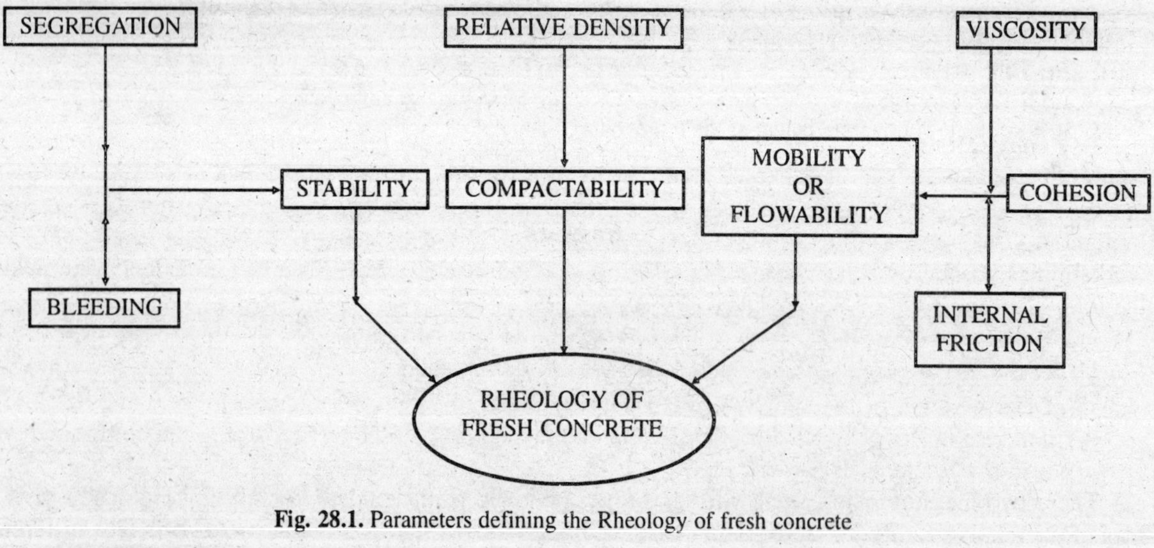

Fig. 28.1. Parameters defining the Rheology of fresh concrete

28.2. DEFINITIONS

1. Stability. It can be defined as a condition in which the aggregate particles are held in a homogeneous dispersion by matrix and random sampling have shown the same particle size distribution during transportation, placing and compaction. The stability of concrete is measured by the characteristics of its segregation and bleeding.

2. Segregation. It is defined as the mixture's instability caused by the weak matrix that can not hold the individual aggregate particles in homogeneous dispersion. The resistance to segregation depends upon the cohesion between the particles of the mix. Segregation in concrete may occur in wet as well as dry consistencies.

3. Segregation in wet mix. Segregation in wet mix may occurs, when water content in the mix is such that the paste is unable to hold the aggregate particles in the distributed position during the transportation, placement and compaction of the concrete.

4. Dry segregation. Dry segregation occurs when the concrete is of low water-cement ratio which results in crumbly mix during handling. If concrete is vibrated then crumbly mixes often have been found satisfactory as during vibration the matrix becomes fluid momentarily and develops shear resistance and cohesion.

5. Bleeding. It occurs when the mortar is unstable and releases free water. Bleeding should be controlled and reduced to a minimum.

6. Mobility. Mobility of fresh concrete can be defined as its ability to flow under mechanical stresses. The flow is restricted by cohesive, viscous and frictional forces. The cohesive force is developed due to adhesion between the matrix and aggregate particles. It provides *tensile strength* to fresh concrete that resists segregation. The viscosity of the matrix contributes to the ease with which the aggregate particles can move and rearrange themselves with in the matrix. At low stresses no flow takes place and the mix behaves as a solid of extremely high viscosity. As the stresses increase, the viscosity gradually decreases and the bond strength between particles becomes insufficient to prevent the flow and the concrete behaves like a liquid. The *internal friction* develops when a mixture is displaced and the aggregate particles translate and rotate. The resistance to deformation depends on the following factors.

1. Shape and texture of aggregate
2. Type of cement used
3. Richness of the mix
4. Water-cement ratio of the mix etc.

Thus the angle of internal friction plays an important role in the mobility of a concrete mixture. The mobility of a concrete mix may be determined by the laboratory triaxial compression test. At the construction site the relative mobility characteristics may be determined by the Vee Bee flow test in conjunction with compacting factor test.

7. Compactibility. It is a measure of the ease with-which the fresh concrete can be compacted. By compection the entrapped air is expelled and the aggregate particles are repositioned in a dense mass with out causing segregation. Compactibility is measured by the *compacting factor test.* This test has some limitations. The cohessive mix sticks in the hoppers of the test apparatus and mixes with low or very low workabilities produce results with wide variations. The compacting factor test can be extended by taking the following two additional measurements.

1. Determination of the density of the concrete in its loose un compacted state by filling the cylinder of the test apparatus with a hand scoop with out compaction.
2. Determination of the density of mechanically vibrated concrete sample from the same batch. The concrete is loosely placed in three layers into the cylinder of the test apparatus and compacted with a 25 mm diameter needle vibrator.

These two measurements along with the values obtained from standard compacting factor test give an idea of the relative ease with which a mix changes from its loose state to the compacted one. The difference between the actually compacted state and theoretical maximum compaction gives an relative measure of void content of concrete. Thus an indication of the durability, permeability and relative strength of hardened concrete is obtained.

Thus the knowledge of rheological properties of concrete is useful in selecting concrete mixes that can be efficiently compacted in the form. The normal prevellent methods of measurement of workability tests as slump, compacting factor, Vee Bee and other tests are of limited scope as they measure only one parameter. Hence these tests are known as single point tests.

28.3. REPRESENTATION OF RHEOLOGICAL BEHAVIOR

The ideal liquids which obey the Newtons law of viscous flow, (Shear stress being proportional to the rate of shear strain) are called *Newtonian liquids.* The constant of proportionality may be used as a physical constant characteristic of the materials. The flow behaviour of fresh concrete does not follow this law. The ratio of shear stress to shear rate is not constant, but depends upon the shear rate at which it is measured and it may also depend on the shear history of the concrete sample investigated.

At low shear rates which are important in practice, the rheological behaviour of concrete can be represented by a straight line which does not pass through the origin, *i.e.* which has an intercept on the stress axis. This intercept indicates the minimum value of stress below which no flow takes place. This straight line is of the form $Y = mx + c$.

The fact that concrete can stand in a pile (as in the case of slump test) suggests that for a flow to develop some minimum stress is necessary. This minimum stress is known as *yield stress* and denoted by the symbol τ_0. Thus the flow equation of concrete as suggested by Bingham can be written as

$$\tau = \mu \gamma + \tau_0 \qquad \ldots(1)$$

where,

τ = shear stress

μ = a constant, having dimensions of viscosity and called plastic viscosity

τ_0 = value of yield stress

γ = Rate of shear stress

The constants μ and τ are the parameters characterizing the flow properties of the material. Thus Bingham model distinguishes between the shear stress of the material expressed in terms of its cohesion, plastic viscosity and the rate at which the shear load is applied. At least two points are required to establish a straight line. Thus the workability of concrete can not be defined by the single point tests that determine only one parameter, *i.e.* provide only one single point. Thus to have a better understanding of concrete rheology some other tests have to be conducted in combination of the above test. For example to measure mobility and compactibility Vee Bee test can be used with compacting factor. To over come this shortcoming of Bingham model, *Tattersal* measured mobility characteristics by a single test method which provided two or more than two points (shear conditions). The procedure is based on determining the power required to mix concrete at different speeds and then calculating the torque by dividing the power by the speed. He suggested the following relation between the torque and mixing speed.

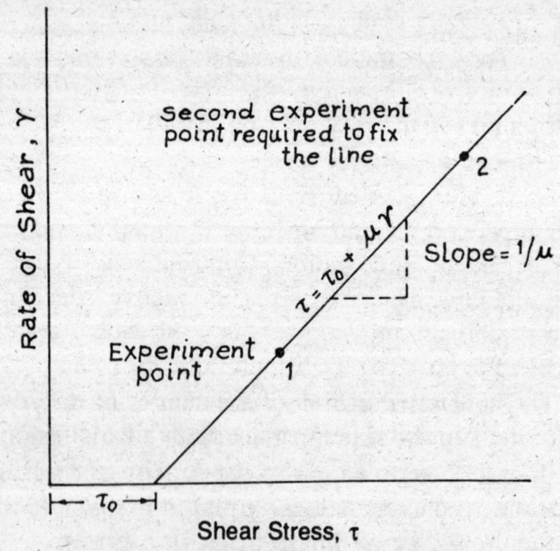

Fig. 28.2. Bingham model

$$T = g + hN \qquad \ldots(2)$$

where,

T = Torque measured

N = No. of r.p.m.

g and h are constants proportional to the cohesion and plastic viscosity respectively of the mixture.

It has been observed that two mixtures which have identical values of g and h will also have identical values for consistency, Vee Bee time or degree and compacting factor. On the other hand if the values of g and h of the two mixture differ, then the two mixture may have similarity in one of the three standard tests namely consistency, Vee Bee time and compacting factor, but will behave differently in the other two.

It has been observed that concrete behaviour departs from the Bingham model significantly at least in one of the following respects.

1. The flow curve is not linear except over a very limited range of shear rates.
2. The yield stress is not well defined.

In case the flow curve is concave up wards *i.e.* its slope increases with shear rates. It shows that the sharing forces are destroying some structures that existed in the unstressed material. The progress of destruction of structure has been found greater for the higher rates of shear. If the rate of shear is increased gradually, a curve ABC is obtained as shown in Fig. 28.3. If reaching at point C, the rate of shear is decreased steadily to zero the descending curve obtained does not coincide with the up curve. If the point C represents the break down in the structure under shear and the process of structural break down immediately and instantaneously is reversed, the decrease in shear rate from D will result in the progressive built up of the structure to the same level as it had on the up curve at the start, but time is required to rebuild the structure of the material. Thus as the rate of shear is decreased, the shear stress at any particular rate of shear on the down curve will be less than the shear at the same rate on the up curve. Therefore the up and down curves will not be coincident and a hysteresis loop will be formed. The Bingham model can be applied to the fresh concrete under practical situations provided the limits are recognized.

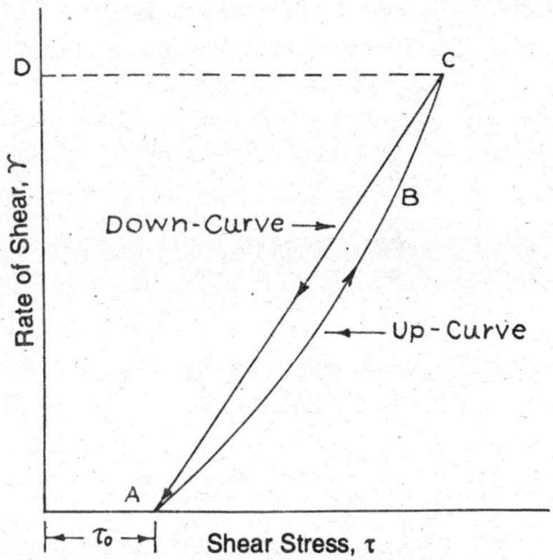

Fig. 28.3. Deformation curve for fresh concrete

28.4. FACTORS AFFECTING THE RHEOLOGICAL PROPERTIES OF CONCRETE

Similar to workability, the rheological properties of fresh concrete are affected by the mix proportions, namely the amount of each constituent, properties of the ingredients, the amount of mixing, the presence of admixtures, and the time elapsed after mixing. Though these factors have been discussed in chapter 7, (properties of fresh concrete), but here these factors are discussed in relation to their influence on the flow properties of concrete.

(*a*) Mix Proportion

The concrete mix is proportioned to provide workability needed during placement and compaction to assure the stipulated performance characteristics of the hardened concrete.

In case there is an excess amount of coarse aggregate in a concrete mix, it will be deficient in mortar to fill the void system, resulting in a loss of mobility and cohesion. Such a mix is known as a harsh mix and requires more efforts to place and compact it. The harshness in the mix may also be developed by a low air content. An increased air entrainment may reduce the excessive use of fine aggregate. On the other hand an excessive amount of entrained air or fine aggregate in concrete will increase the cohesion to such an extent that will make the concrete difficult to move *i.e.* its mobility will decrease. The more amount of fine aggregate in a concrete mix increases the surface area of the particles which requires more amount of paste to coat the surface of the particles to have the same mobility. This high amount of cement paste results in higher drying shrinkage and cracking.

In practice usually concrete mixes are proportioned with an excess amount of fine aggregate and higher cement content than needed for a concrete of optimum fine aggregate content.

The higher cement content makes the concrete slow moving and sticky, especially in the normal range of slump for cast insitu concrete. Further the higher cement content and lower water-cement ratio reduces the workability of rich mixes from that measured immediately after mixing.

(b) Consistency

The consistency of concrete is an indicator of the relative water content in the concrete mix. It is measured with the help of the slump test. The increase in slump or water content above that required to get a workable mix produces greater fluidity and decreased internal friction. The decrease in cohesion of the mix increases the potential for segregation and increased bleeding. Thus more amount of water content, than that needed to produce a workable mix will not improve the rheological properties of concrete. Contrary to this, too low of water content or slump will reduce the mobility and compactibility of concrete which will cause difficulties in placing and compacting the concrete. It has been observed that as far as rheological properties of concrete are concerned an increase of one percent of air entrainment is equivalent to an increase of water content by 3% or 1% of fine aggregate. On the other hand an excessively dry mix may result loss of cohesion and may cause an increased dry segregation.

(c) Hardening and stiffening

The rate of hardening of concrete increases with the use of rapid hardening cement, cement deficient in gypsum and the accelerating admixtures. The increased rate of hardening of concrete reduces its mobility. The porous and dry aggregate reduce the workability of the concrete by absorbing water from the concrete mix. The workability also reduces if the surface area of aggregate particles to be wetted is increased.

(d) Aggregate shape and texture

The rough and highly angular aggregate particles produce higher percentage of voids which need more paste to fill these voids. Thus there is need for more fine aggregate and water content in the mix. Similarly angular fine aggregate will increase the internal friction in the concrete mix requiring more water content than needed when well rounded natural sand is used. Thus the shape and texture of aggregate influences the rheology of the concrete to a great extent.

(e) Aggregate grading

As stated earlier also, a well graded aggregate gives a good workability. Gap grading or a change in the size distribution of aggregate may cause appreciable effect on the workability and void system of the concrete mix. These effects have been found more in the fine aggregate than coarse aggregate. The water requirement in the mix increases with the decrease in the size of fine aggregate particles, resulting in increasingly sticky concrete. On the other hand as the size of fine aggregate particles increases *i.e.* fine aggregate becomes coarser, the cohesion of the concrete reduces resulting in harsh concrete mix and the tendency of bleeding increases. Thus to maintain the workability of the concrete mix adjustments in the grading of fine aggregate becomes necessary due to the above noted changes.

(f) Maximum size of aggregate

An increase in the maximum size of aggregate will reduce the surface area of the aggregate particles to be wetted resulting in the reduction in the cement content necessary for a constant water-cement ratio.

(g) Admixtures

The rheology of concrete has been found to be effected by the following admixtures.

(*a*) Plasticizers and super plasticizers
(*b*) Air entraining agents
(*c*) Accelerators and retarderss

These admixtures are used in the following three ways.

(*i*) To give the same workability with less water content, resulting in higher strength

(*ii*) To give the same workability and strength with reduced cement content. However the cement content should be sufficient from workability considerations.

(*iii*) To give increased workability with the same long term strength and durability.

Plasticizers based on lingosulphonate salt (0.15%) have been found to reduce water content by 10% with out any adverse effect on the properties of concrete. Super plasticizers have made it possible to produce flowing or self levelling concrete which can be compacted with minimum effort into the corners of the form work and around the congested reinforcement. For a self levelling concrete the maximum yield value may be kept as 350 Pa. Such a concrete can be obtained by the use of synthetic naphthalene or metamine resins or ultra pure lignosulphate. However concrete with very high workabilities are likely to segregate.

The water-cement system constitute a system of particles suspended in a high electrolyte concentration bringing the particles close enough to stick together. This phenomenon is known as *flocculation*. The presence of plasticizers modify the condition in the water-cement suspension to prevent the formation of flocculated structure by altering the inter particle repulsion/attraction.

The plasticizers or super plasticizers interact with cement particles forming a membrane of absorbed charged molecules around each particle. These charged molecules physically prevent the particles to come so closer to each other to stick and the flocculation of particles is prevented. Thus the membrane forms an electrostatic or steric barrier for the particles to come closer to have contact. The attraction between the particles can be reduced to zero by increasing the thickness of this membrane. The mechanism of deflocculation or dispersion of cement particles reduces the yield. In addition of attractive forces, repulsive electrical forces are also developed between particles due to the absorption of ionized compounds which increase the plastic viscosity through the operation of secondary electro-viscous effect. Thus the admixtures prevent close contact between the cement particles by a combination of electrostatic or steric repulsion, weakening the structure which can be formed at rest and reducing the yield value. Beyond an optimum value, the increase in the concentration of plasticizer does not decrease the yield rate appreciably. However with the increase in cement content of the mix, reduction of yield value increases. The value of plastic viscosity increases if the sand content in the mix is low and decreases with higher sand content. It is due to the fact that when concrete with low sand content flows, it is the floccuted cement in the mix that separates the coarse particles. In case the cement is deflocculated then these coarse particles come closer and touch each other developing a greater resistance to the flow of concrete, resulting an increase in the plastic viscosity of the concrete even though cement paste is reduced. On the other hand concrete with more sand content needs less cement to fill the voids in the coarse aggregate as sand present in the concrete will fill these voids.

(*h*) Air entraining agents

The air entraining agents produce spherical bubbles of 10 to 250 micron in diameter by modifying the surface tension of the aqueous phase in the mix. Most commonly materials used as air entraing agents are sodium olerate, sodium caprate, alkyle sulphate and pemric acid salts etc. The air bubbles are produced by these compounds which have negatively charged head group as ($-Coo^-$, So_3^{2-}, So_4^{2-}) which is hydrophilic (water attracting) and a non polar tail which is hydrophobic (water repelling). Thus the air bubbles generated have an apparent negative charge which form bridges between cement particles resulting in increased yield value. These air bubbles act as ball bearings allowing large particles to slide over each other more easily, decreasing the plastic viscosity. The rheological properties of the concrete are changed very significantly by the air entrained agents.

The air entrainment increases the cohesion and reduces the tendency of bleeding in the mix. It has been observed that 4 to 6% air entrainment by volume increases the cohesion of the mix and sand content may be reduced by about 5%.

(*i*) Accelerators and retarders

The accelerators will reduce and the retarders will extend the workability time for a given mix. The time of retention of improved workability is critical for the concrete where it is to be transported before placement. The reduction in workability is similar to the stiffening of concrete due to slow chemical reaction during the induction period. The addition of admixtures change the nature of membrane formed around the cement particles and the composition of aqueous solution resulting the change in the rate of stiffening. This effect especially has been observed when super plasticizers are used.

A retarder plasticizer reduces the workability loss and increases the retention time due to slowing down the setting of cement. Super Plasticizers have been found to effect much improvements in workability with out using retarders which are essential with conventional plasticizers.

28.5. RHEOLOGY OF HARDENED CONCRETE

The rheology of hardened concrete like creep illustrates the mechanical behaviour of an ideal elastic, viscous and plastic component.

The gradual increase in strain with time, with out the increase in stress is due to creep. Thus creep can be defined as the increase in strain under sustained stress. Under sustained stress with time, the gel, the adsorbed water layer, the water held in the gel pores and capillary pores yields, flows and readjust themselves. This behaviour is known as creep in concrete. Creep in concrete is considered to be an isolated rheological phenomenon and this is associated with the gel structure of cement paste. Thus cement paste plays a dominant role in the deformation of concrete.

28.5.1. Rheological representation of creep

The mechanical behaviour of hardened cement paste which exhibits both elastic and inelastic components of deformation under load can be expressed in rheological terms. Thus the rheological approach illustrates the mechanical behaviour of an ideal elastic, viscous and plastic components. The rheology of creep can be expressed in macroscopic and microscopic state.

28.5.2. Macroscopic rheological approach

In case of macroscopic approach the structure of cement paste can be represented as a continuous solid

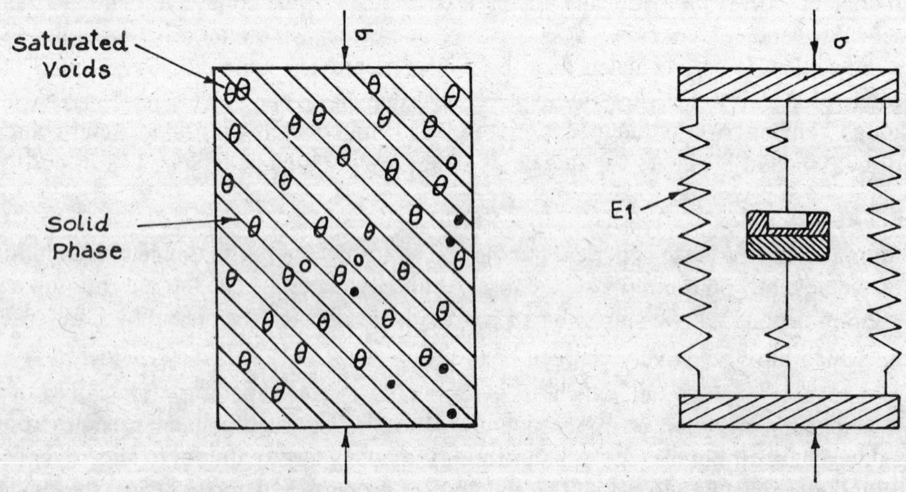

(*a*) Structural Model (*b*) Rheological Model

Fig. 28.4. Macroscopic representation of deformational belaviour of hardened cement paste

phase having saturated voids of various sizes in a wide range. A macroscopic representation of deformational behaviour of hardened paste is shown in Fig. 28.4 (*a*). From this model time dependent volume changes can be demonstrated as long as the isotropic stresses are applied through the solid phase and the drainage of the liquid can take places as suggested by ORI.ISHAI.

The corresponding rheological model is shown in Fig. 28.4 (*b*). This model consists of a spring device representing the elastic mass around a central viscous desh-pot representing the confined liquid. With the help of this model the deformational behaviour of cement paste can be demonstrated.

28.5.3. Microscopic Rheological approach

In case of an microscopic approach the structure of cement gel can be represented as an anisotropic crystal clusters randomly oriented in a solid matrix as shown in Fig. 28.5. The application of a macroscopic shear stress to the anisotropic system results in an irrecoverable volumetric contraction of the spaces in some of the clusters as shown in Fig. 28.5 (*a*) and a separation in other clusters as shown in Fig. 28.5 (*b*). Only few *i.e.* a fraction of elements are subjected to pure shear as shown in Fig. 28.5 (*c*). On removing the load, there is a visco-elastic recovery, but due to some deviatory stress component, certain local irrecoverable volume changes remain.

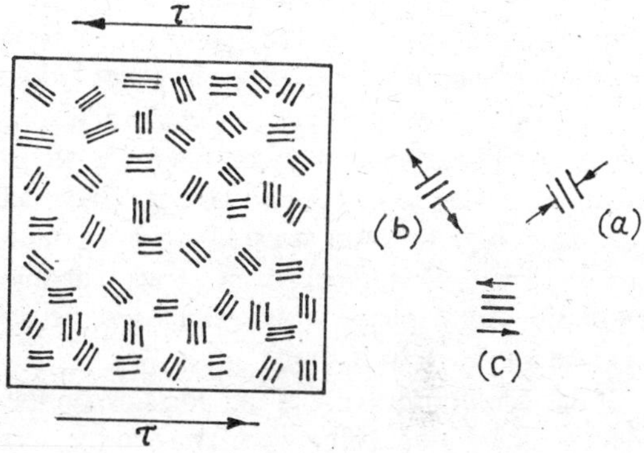

Fig. 28.5. Microscopic representation of deformational behaviour of anisotropic crystal cluster

Further Fig. 28.6 shows the sub microscopic models. They represent metastable crystaline gel consisting of two sheet like crystals separated by a layer of water. Three basically different mechanism of deformation can be possible.

1. There may be compressive stresses normal to contact layer as shown in Fig. 28.6 (*a*).
2. Tensile stresses normal to the contact layer Fig. 28.6 (*b*).
3. Shear stresses parallel to the contact layer Fig. 28.6 (*c*)

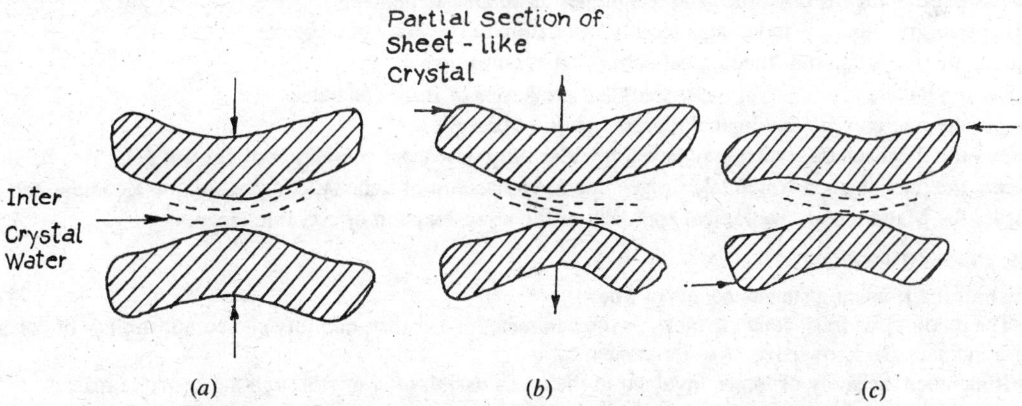

Fig. 28.6. Sub microscopic model representing three basic mechanical state

In case (1) the liquid is compressed and squeezed out laterally. This results in the reduction of the inter crystalline space. The rate of liquid movement is slow and decreases with the narrowing of space which tends towards a limit equal to a monomolecular compressed water layer. The main cause of time dependent irrecoverable changes in the cement gel is the squeezing out of liquid against the strong frictional forces.

In mechanism (2) visco-elastic elongation takes place at faster rate than in the compression. How ever this elongation is restrained by the solid matrix and delayed. Complete recovery may take a long time after the removal of the load.

Mechanism (3) according to Troxell, the shear stress results in water layers.

Below the elastic limit of the material, due to complex system of applied loading, various combinations of the above noted basic mechanism of deformation may take place. On the basis of the available experimental evidence, it can be assumed that the long term deformation mechanism in cement gel is, that is involved in narrowing the intercrystalline spaces. This is reflected in the slow and decreasing rate of time dependent deformation as well as in the irrecoverable components of the deformation which increase with loading time.

The time dependent deformation behaviour of loaded and unloaded hardened cement paste shows a distinct similarity between creep and its recovery, shrinkage and swelling. All these process are governed by the movement of various types of water held in the cement paste. Further it can be explained as follows:

The most common type of loading is uniaxial compression. The application of uniaxial loading develops an instantaneous elastic response of both the solid and liquid systems. The external load applied is distributed between these two phases. Under sustained loading the compressed liquid starts to diffuse and moves from high to lower stressed areas. Under uniform pressure movement of water takes place out wards from the body. This mechanism is accompanied by the transfer of load from the liquid phase to the surrounding solid phase which increases the stress acting on the solid matrix gradually resulting in an increased elastic deformation.

It has been observed that the pressure on the capillary water gradually disappears after several days of under sustained load, being transferred to the surrounding gel. Similarly after some weeks of sustained load the pressure on the gel pore water disappears. However the pressure on inter and intra crystalline adsorbed water continues to act during the entire period of loading, though the magnitude of pressure decreases gradually. Thus it can be said that the ultimate deformation of the hardened cement paste is the elastic response of its solid matrix, which behaves as if the spaces with in it were quite empty (the space with in the matrix filled with unstable gel).

QUESTIONS

1. Define rheology of a material.
2. Discuss the rheological principles and techniques as applied to concrete.
3. Define stability, mobility and compactibility in relation to rheology of concrete.
4. Explain the presentation of rheological behaviour of concrete.
5. discuss the factors which affect the rheological properties of fresh concrete.
6. Discuss the microscopic rheological representation of creep.
7. Discuss the mechanisms which may develop under sub microscopic condition of cement gel.
8. Discuss the phenomenon which takes place due to application of uniaxial compression on a cement gel.
9. Discuss the Macroscopic rheological approach of the representation of concrete creep.

OBJECTIVE TYPE QUESTIONS

1. Which of the following statements is not true?
   (*a*) The rheology of fresh concrete includes the parameter of stability, mobility and compactibility of concrete
   (*b*) It includes the knowledge of water-cement ratio
   (*c*) It includes the study of forces involved in the transmission of stress through the concrete mass.
   (*d*) It includes the deformation curve of fresh concrete.
2. The conventional workability tests as slump test, compacting factor test, Vee Bee test and remoulding tests are called as single point tests due to
   (*a*) They can be conducted at one place only
   (*b*) They measure only one parameter of the workability
   (*c*) Each of them gives complete information about the workability
   (*d*) All of them are correct

3. The flow or rheological equation of fresh concrete is expressed by
   (*a*) Lechatelier's model (*b*) Nevile model
   (*c*) Newton's model (*d*) Bingham model
4. Rheological properties of concrete are independent of
   (*a*) Type of mixer (*b*) Water content
   (*c*) Aggregate shape, texture and grading (*d*) Type of cement
   (*d*) Temperature
5. The flow properties of concrete are mainly dependent on
   (*a*) Water/cement ratio
   (*b*) Richness of the mix
   (*c*) Shape and texture of aggregate
   (*d*) Fineness modulus and grading of aggregates
   (*e*) Factors affecting the resistance to deformation
6. Which of the following is correct?
   (*a*) Combination of compacting factor and Vee Bee time tests gives better understanding of rheology of concrete
   (*b*) Combination of slump and compacting factor gives better under standing of rheology of concrete.
   (*c*) Combination of slump and Vee Bee tests gives better under standing of rheology of concrete
   (*d*) Combination of remoulding and compacting factor gives better under standing of rheology of concrete

Answers

1. (*b*) 2. (*b*) 3. (*d*) 4. (*a*) 5. (*e*) 6. (*a*)

Laboratory Testing

Experiment 1. *To verify the purity of cement in the field.*

Theory. Though cement is manufactured in factories under controlled conditions, but there are possibilities of its adulteration during transportation and storage. The adulteration in cement may be detected by the following test.

Apparatus. Following apparatus is required.

(*a*) One stove

(*b*) One steel plate

(*c*) Test tube or glass tumbler

Procedure

Visual Inspection

1. The bright grey colour indicates the freshness and purity of cement.
2. Rub the cement between the fore finger and thumb, the grity touch will indicate the adulteration with sand while greasy touch will indicate pure cement.
3. Take a sample of about 100 grams of cement and put it on a steel plate and heat it on a stove thoroughly for about 20 minutes. The change of colour of the sample is an indication of adulteration. In case of pure or genuine cement there should be no change in the colour.
4. In case, cement is suspected to be adulterated with flyash (coal ash), then take a small quantity of cement and put it in a glass tumbler and add water till the tumbler is half full with water.
   (*b*) Shake the tumbler or container thoroughly and allow it to settle for a few minutes.
   (*c*) Cement particles being heavier will settle down and ash particles either will float on the surface or held in suspension. The amount of these particles will give an idea about the extent of adulteration.

Experiment 2. *To verify the quality of cement in the field by verifying the following:*

(*a*) Setting and hardening action.

(*b*) Soundness of cement

Theory. Same as above.

Apparatus. 1. Stove, 2. Enameled trays, 3. Measuring steel rule.

A. Setting and hardening action

Procedure

1. Take a suitable sample of the cement to be tested and put it into the enameled tray and add 28% water of the weight of cement and mix well. Out of this paste prepare three small pats each 75 mm × 75 mm × 25 mm in size.

2. Prepare similar number of pats with good quality cement.
3. Cover all the pats with wet cloth for 24 hours.
4. After 24 hours, try to make thumb nail impression on the pats taken from both sets of pats. Good quality cement pats will not show the nail impression, that is it will resit this impression.
5. If the cement does not resist the impression, then continue the curing of the pats upto 48 hours. After 48 hours of curing, try to break the pat with the pressure of the thumb. Bad quality cement pat will break easily under the pressure of the thumb and this cement should be tested in the laboratory.
6. If after 48 hours, pats show improvement in hardening, but do not attain hardness comparable with good quality cement, a third trial should be made after 72 hours of curing.
7. If the only defect in the cement under test is its slow setting quality, then it will become as strong as good quality cement after this period and no further testing is required.

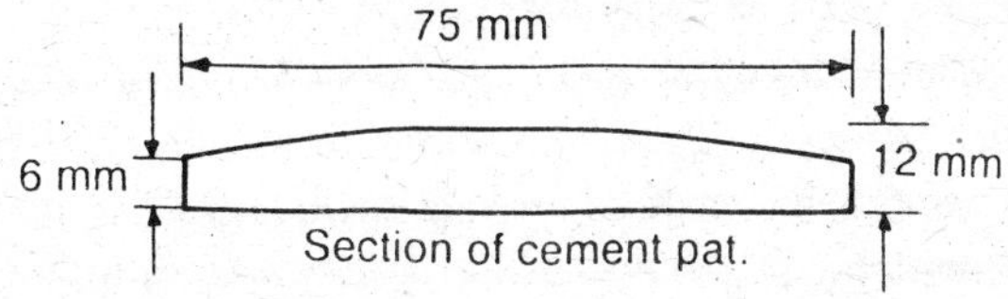

B. Ascertaining Soundness of Cement

Make a pat of cement 15 mm thick and 75 mm in diameter, cure this pat for 24 hours with moist cloth and then boil it in water for 6 hours and observe the surface of this pat. Section of pat is shown in Fig. 1.

1. If the surface does not develop cracks after boiling, then the cement is sound, Fig. 1 (I).
2. If the surface develops a crack patterns as shown in Fig. 1 (III) then the cement is unsound.
3. Contraction cracks as shown in Fig. 1 (II) are few and well defined and start from edge to edge. These cracks do not indicate anything wrong with the cement. hence they should be clearly distinguished from unsound cement cracks.

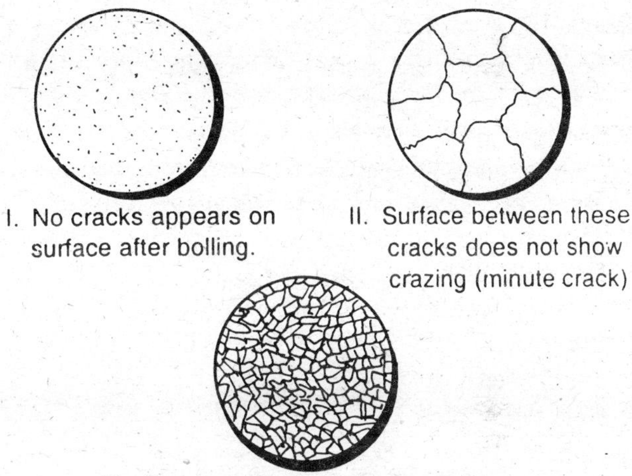

Fig. 1. Field test for soundness of cement

Experiment 3. *To determine the fineness of cement by sieving.*

Theory. A certain fineness of cement particles is essential, as the reaction of water with cement always starts at the surface of the particles. Larger the surface area available for reaction, greater is the hydration of cement. Thus rapid development of strength requires greater degree of fineness. However too much fineness also is undesirable due to the high cost of grinding, quick deterioration when exposed to air and more shrinkage of fine cement etc.

Apparatus. Usually following apparatus is required.

1. Weighing balance of 200 gram capacity.
2. I.S. test sieve No. 9 (90 microns).
3. Trowel
4. Tray 30 cms × 30 cms
5. One brush with about 25 cms long handle.

Procedure

1. Weigh 100 grams cement accurately and put it on a standard I.S. sieve No. 9 (90 microns sieve).
2. Break lumps of cement if any in the sample with thumb and fingers. In no case it should be rubed on the sieve.
3. Holding the sieve in both hands, sieve it continuously for 15 minutes giving a gentle wrist motion or on a mechanical sieve shaker. However care should be taken that no cement spills.
4. After sieving for 15 minutes, weigh the residue left on the sieve. This residue should not be more than 10% of the weight of sample for ordinary portland cement and 5% for rapid hardening cement.

Precautions

1. Sieving must be done continuously.
2. Weighing should be done carefully. Weighing machine should be checked before use.
3. After sieving, cement from the bottom surface of the sieve should be removed gently.
4. At the end, sieve should be cleaned carefully with the help of the brush.

Experiment 4. *To determine the percentage of water for normal consistency for a given sample of cement.*

Theory. The normal consistency of a cement paste can be defined as the percentage of water by weight of cement, which produces a consistency which permits a plunger of 10 mm diameter to penetrate to a depth 5 mm to 7 mm above the bottom of the vicat's mould.

Apparatus. Following apparatus is needed for this experiment.

1. Vicat's apparatus with plunger of 10 mm diameter. (Ref. Fig. 2.13, page 29).
2. Weighing balance of 1 kg capacity with weights
3. Trowel
4. Enamel trough
5. Standard spatula
6. Stop watch
7. Thermometer 50°C range
8. Non porous plate.

Procedure

1. Weight 400 grams cement accurately and put it in a enameled trough.
2. To start with, add about 25% clean water by weight of cement and mix it carefully by a spatula. The time of gauging should not be less than 3 minute and not more than 5 minute. The gauging time shall be counted from the time of adding water to the dry cement till commencing to fill in the mould.
3. Resting the vicat mould on non porous plate, fill it with the cement paste.
4. Make the surface of the cement paste level with the top of the mould with a trowel weighing about 250 grams. To expel the entrapped air, mould should be gently shaken or given jerk.
5. Place this mould together with the non porous plate under the rod, bearing the plunger. Adjust the indicator at zero mark, when the plunger touches the surface of the test block. (cement paste in the mould).
6. Release the plunger quickly and allow it to penetrate into the paste and note its depth of penetration.
7. Prepare other trial pastes with varying percentages of water and test as discussed above untill the needle penetrates 5 mm to 7 mm above the bottom of the mould.
8. Express this amount of water as a percentage by weight of the dry cement.

Observations

(*i*) Date of test ______________

(*ii*) Temperature (*a*) Cement __________°C

(*b*) Water __________°C

(*c*) Room __________°C

(*d*) Quantity of cement used = W_1

S. No.	*Quantity of water added W*	*Percentage by weight of dry cement*	*Time of gauging in minutes*	*Penetration from the bottom of the mould in mm*	*% of water required to prepare cement paste of standard consistency (P)*
1.					
2.					
3.					
4.					
5.					

Calculation $P = \frac{W}{W_1} \times 100$

Precautions

1. For gauging of cement clean appliances should be used.
2. Temperature of cement, water and room at the time of test should be 27 ± 2°C.
3. While filling mould no pressure should be exerted.

Experiment 5. *To determine the initial and final setting time of cement.*

Theory. When water is mixed with cement to form a paste, a reaction starts. This reaction is known as hydration. Due to this reaction the mixture of cement and water starts changing from a fluid state to a solid state and is called *setting.* It should not be confused with hardening which is the second stage of hydration. In the first few minutes, the setting action is more predominant and after some time hardening action becomes rapid.

Initial setting time. It is defined as the period elapsing between the time water added to the cement and the time when the 1 mm square section needle fails to penetrate into the test block to a depth of about 5 mm from the bottom of the mould.

Final setting time. This can be defined as the period elapsing between the time water added to the cement and when 1 mm square section needle makes an impression on the test block, but 5 mm attachment fails to make any impression on the test block.

Apparatus

1. Vacat's apparatus with mould and non porous plates, needle etc. as shown in Fig. 2.13, page 29.
2. Weighing balance of 1 kg. capacity with weight box.
3. Trowel.
4. Enamel trough.
5. Standard spatula.
6. Stop watch.

7. Thermometer °C (0-100°C)
8. Measuring cylinder—500cc. capacity.

Procedure

1. Weigh about 400 grams of neat cement accurately and put it into the enamel trough.
2. Add 0.85 times water required for standard consistency and prepare the cement paste.
3. Start stop watch as soon as water is added to the cement.
4. Resting the vicat's mould on the non porous plate, fill it with the neat cement paste prepared. The gauging time should not be less than 3 minutes and not more than 5 minutes.
5. After filling the mould completely, smooth off the surface of the paste and make it level with the top of the mould.
6. Now put the whole assembly (mould with cement paste and plate etc.) on the base plate of the apparatus.
7. Place the needle in the rod and lower it gently till it comes in contact with the surface of the test block and release it quickly, allowing it to penetrate into the block and note the penetration after every two minutes and rotate the mould, so that needle may not penetrate at one place only.
8. Repeat the procedure till the needle fails to penetrate into the test block to about 5 to 7 mm from the bottom of the mould. Stop the stop watch. The reading of the stop watch in seconds is the initial setting time.

Observation

(*a*) Sample prepared (*i*) Date..............................

(*ii*) ....Hours........Minutes

(*b*) Temperature (*i*) Cement ....°C

(*ii*) Water ....°C

(*iii*) Room ....°C

(*c*) Quantity of cement (C).........g.

(*d*) Water added for standard consistency (P)

(*e*) Water to be added..........$0.85\ P \times C$

Sample No.......

S. No.	*Time at which water is first added* (T_1)	*Time at which penetration readings taken*	*Remark*
1.			
2.			
3.			
4.			

(*f*) Time when needle fails to penetrate about 5 mm to 7 mm. from the bottom of the mould (T_2)

(*g*) Time at which water is first added T_1

(*h*) Initial Setting Time ($T_2 - T_1$)

Final Setting Time

Procedure. Steps from 1 to 8 are same as above.

1. Now replace the 1 mm square needle (*c*) of the vicat's apparatus by the needle with an annular attachment (F).

2. Repeat step 7 a number of times till the needle makes an impression on the cement paste block, while the attachment (F) fails to do go.
3. The time between the moment water is added to the cement and the moment needle only makes the impression is called the final setting time for the cement under test.

Observation

(*a*) Time when the needle makes an impression, but the attachment fails to do so, T_3

(*b*) Final setting time, $(T_3 - T_1)$

Precautions

1. Needle must be cleaned each time before use.
2. After recording the penetration of the needle, the mould should be shifted (change its position) so that penetration of needle may not take place at the same place.
3. The accuracy of the stop watch should be checked.
4. For gauging cement clean appliances should be used.
5. The test block should be kept in 90% relative humidity at 27 ± 2°C and away from draught.

Experiment 6. *To verify the soundness of a given sample of cement.*

Theory. The presence of free lime (CaO) and magnesia (MgO) react with water very slowly and increase in volume considerably. If these two substances are present in cement, they may cause large changes in the volume of concrete after it has hardened and may cause its disintegration. Thus the cement is called unsound if the percentage of free lime and magnesia exceeds 3% and 6% respectively as laid down by I.S.I. The unsoundness can be detected by Le Chatelier apparatus.

Apparatus required.

1. Le Chatelier apparatus. (Fig. 2.15, page 33)
2. Two number of glass sheets.
3. Trowel.
4. Measuring cylinder.
5. Stove or water bath with electric heating arrangements.
6. Enamel tray.
7. Thermometer.
8. Stop watch.
9. Weighing balance and weight-box.

Procedure

1. Weigh 100 grams of cement carefully and add 0.78 times the water needed for preparing a paste of standard consistency and make a good paste.
2. Place the mould on a glass plate and fill it with the cement paste formed as in (1) above.
3. Cover the mould with another glass plate.
4. Place a small weight on the cover plate and immediately immerse the whole assembly in water at a temperature of 27°C to 32°C and keep it there for 24 hours.
5. At the end of 24 hours, measure the distance between the indicator points. This distance should be measured to an accuracy of a mm.
6. Submerge the whole assembly again in water at 27°C to 32°C and heat it at such a rate that water may start boiling with in 25 minutes to 30 minutes and keep it in boiling water for three hours.
7. After three hours remove the assembly from the water, and allow it to cool and measure the distance between the indicator points.

8. The difference between the two readings of distances between the indicator points is a measure of expansion of cement.

Observations

1. Weight of cement (C) = gram
2. Water required for normal consistency (P) = gram
3. Water added to cement sample ($P \times C$) = gram
4. Time at which sample is put in water at 27°C to 32°C = T_1
5. Time when water brought to boiling point = T_2
6. Distance between the pointer ends at 27°C to 32°C before heating = d_1
7. Time of heating = $(T_2 - T_1) = T$
8. Distance between the pointer ends after heating = d_2 mm

Difference = $(d_2 - d_1)$

Precautions

1. All measurements should be done very accurately.
2. While filling the mould, the edges of split mould should be kept together gently. A fine thread may be tied around the mould.
3. Water should be brought to boiling gradually during the specified time.
4. The indicator arms of the apparatus should not be pressed.

Experiment 7. *To determine the compressive strength of cement.*

Theory. The compressive strength test is the final check on the quality of cement. The compressive strength of cement is measured by determining the strength of 7.06 cm length cubes made of cement and standard sand mortar of 1:3 proportion by weight.

Apparatus

1. Cube moulds of 7.06 cm length.
2. Cube vibration machine.
3. Trowel.
4. Enamel trough.
5. Measuring cylinder of 100 c.c.
6. Balance
7. Thermometer.
8. Non-porous plate.

Procedure

1. For each cube weigh and mix materials separately. For each cube material required is as follows:
   (*a*) Cement 185 gram
   (*b*) Standard sand 535 gram
   (*c*) Water, $P_n/4 + 3.0\%$ of combined weight of cement and sand.
2. Weigh the cement and standard sand accurately and place them on a non-porous plate.
3. Mix the cement and sand dry with the trowel for one minute and then add water and mix till the colour of the mixture is uniform.
4. Gauging time should not be less than 3 minutes and not more than 4 minutes.
5. Clean the interior surface of the mould and oil or grease lightly.
6. Place the prepared mould on the vibrating machine and firmly hold it in position by means of suitable clamps.

7. Attach a suitable hopper at the top of the mould to facilitate filling the mould. The hopper should not be removed till the vibration is over.
8. After mixing, put the full mass of the mix as prepared above in (3) in the hopper and compact the same fully by vibration for a period of abut 2 minute at a frequency of 1200 ± 400 vibration per minutes.
9. Keep the cube at 27°C ± 2°C and at 90% relative humidity for 24 hours after vibration.
10. At the end of the 24 hours, remove the mould and put the specimen immediately in clean and fresh water at 27°C ± 2°C for curing and keep them there till required for testing. The specimen should not be allowed to dry up before testing.

Testing

1. The cubes as prepared above are tested at the following ages.
   (*a*) At 3 days and 7 days for ordinary portland cement.
   (*b*) At 1 day and 3 days for rapid hardening portland cement.
2. Place the specimen in the testing machine centrally on the faces other than cast faces.
3. Apply the load uniformly at a rate of 140 kg/cm^2 per minute.

Observations

1. Sample Prepared on (*a*) Date ....
   (*b*) Time ....hrs........min.......
2. Temperature (*a*) Room ....°C
   (*b*) Water ....°C

S. No.	*Items*	*Samples*		
		I	II	III
1.	Weight of cement = grams			
2.	Weight of standard sand = grams			
3.	Weight of water = grams			
4.	Size of specimen = L .... cm = B .... cm = H .... cm			
5.	Area of specimen face = cm^2			
6.	Load at failre of specimen = p kg.			
7.	Age at the time of testing = days			
8.	Compressive strength at the age of test = kg/cm^2			
9.	Average compressive strength = kg/cm^2			

Precautions

1. All appliances used should be clean.
2. The mixing time should not be more than 4 minutes.
3. The mould should be cleaned before use and oiled.
4. The load on the specimen should be applied uniformly and gradually.
5. The specimen should be immediately tested after taking out from the curing water. The excess water should be wiped out by jute or cloth.

Experiment 8. *To determine the fine silt in the aggregate.*

Theory. The fine material such as clay and silt are harmful for concrete. These fine materials may form coatings on the surface of coarse aggregate and prevent good bond between aggregate and cement paste. If present in loose form, they require more water to wet their surface as their surface areas is more per unit weight. The increase in water results in increased water- cement ratio, which reduces the strength of concrete.

The size of silt particles varies between 0.002 mm and 0.06 mm while those of clay below 0.002 mm.

Thus tests should be performed to determined the quantity of silt and clay before using the fine aggregate.

The field test to determine the quantity of silt and clay is accurate, if the percentage of silt and clay is limited to 6% by volume. In case this percentage is more than 6%, then more accurate test as per I.S. 2386 part II 1963 should be carried.

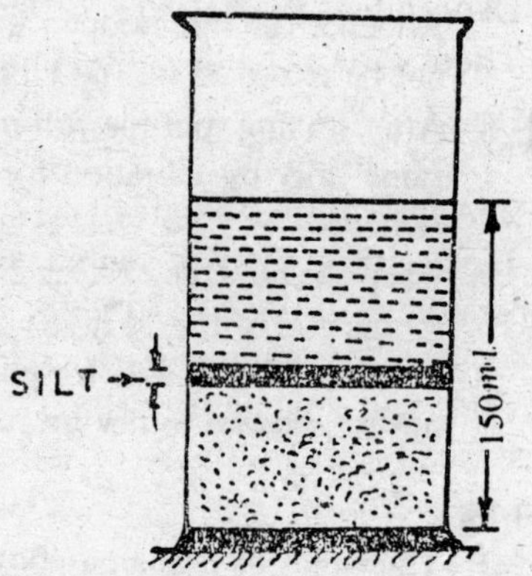

Fig. 2. Measuring cylinder showing silt in fine aggregate

Apparatus. Measuring cylinder of 250 ml (c.c.) capacity.

Procedure

1. Fill the measuring jar with 1% solution of common salt upto about 50 ml mark.
2. Add sand to be tested in jar, till the level of common salt solution reaches 100 ml mark.
3. Add more solution of above concentration in the jar till the level reaches 150 ml mark.
4. Now cover the jar tightly with palm and shake the mixture of sand and common salt solution by turning up side down repeatedly.
5. Allow the mixture to stand in the jar for 3 hours and note the level of silt and sand. Silt being lighter than sand will form upper layer.
6. Measure the thickness of silt layer and calculate its percentage.
7. Repeat the above procedure and take three readings and obtain their mean value.

Observation

S. No.	*Items*	*Samples*		
		I	II	III
1.	Volume of sample = V_1 ml			
2.	Volume of silt after 3 hours = V_2 ml			
3.	Percentage of silt by volume = $\left(\frac{V_2}{V_1} \times 100\right)$			
4.	Average value %			

Precautions

1. The sample of fine aggregate should be taken carefully.
2. The 1% solution of common salt should be prepared by dissoluing 10 gram of common salt in 1 lit. of water.
3. The mixture of sand and 1% solution should be shaken vigorously.

Experiment 9. *To determine the specific gravity and water absorption of aggregates.*

Theory. As per I.S. 2386-Part-III-1963, specific gravity of aggregates can be divided into two categories as follows:

1. Specific gravity
2. Apparent specific gravity

1. Specific gravity. It can be defined as the ratio of the weight of aggregate dried and maintained at a temperature of 100°C to 110°C for 24 ± ½ hour to the weight of equal volume of water displaced by saturated surface dry aggregate. The volume of water displaced is equal to the volume of solid matter of the aggregate and volume of all pores both permeable and impermeable. Specific gravity calculated on this basis usually is used in the calculation of absolute volumes of concrete and its yield. Majority of aggregates have specific gravity value between 2.6 to 2.9. Values lower than 2.6, necessarily do not mean that the aggregate is of poor quality. Normally lower limit has been laid down for specific gravity.

2. Apparent specific gravity. It can be defined as the ratio of the weight of aggregate dried and maintained at a temperature of 100°C to 110°C for 24 ± ½ hours to the weight of equal volume of water displaced by the dry aggregate. In this case, the volume of water displaced is equal to the water displaced by solid matter and only impermeable pores.

Water absorption. It can be defined as the difference in weight between the saturated surface dry aggregate and dry aggregate. It is expressed as the percentage of dry weight of aggregate. Its knowledge is very important. If the aggregate absorbs water which neither wets the surface of aggregate nor it takes part in chemical reaction, the workability of the concrete will be reduced, resulting in lower strength.

Apparatus

1. Balance or scale of capacity not less than 3 kg. and having sensitivity of 0.5 gram.
2. *Oven.* A well ventilated oven fitted with devices to maintain a temperature at 100°C to 110°C.
3. A wide mouthed glass vessel such as jar of about 1.5 litre capacity with flat ground lip and a plane ground disc of plate glass to cover it air tight.
4. *Cloth.* Two pieces of soft and absorbent clothes of size 75 cms × 45 cms.
5. *Tray.* A shallow tray not less than 325 cm^2 in surface area.
6. *Container.* An air tight container having a capacity to take the sample.
7. *Wire basket.* Basket of not more than 6.3 mm mesh.

Procedure

1. Take about 2 kg. of aggregate sample and screen it on a 10 mm I.S. sieve.
2. Wash the sample thoroughly to remove fine particles of dust and drain it.
3. Place the sample in wire basket and immerse it in distilled water at a temperature of 22°C to 32°C for 24 ± ½ hours.
4. Soon after immersion and at the end of soaking period, rotate the vessel rapidly in clock wise and anti clock wise direction to remove the entrapped air or bubbles on the surface of the aggregate.
5. Now over fill the vessel by adding more distilled water and slide the plate glass disc cover over the mouth to ensure that no air is trapped in the vessel.
6. Dry the vessel from the out side and weigh it. Let the weight of the vessel be W_1.
7. Now empty the vessel and fill it with distilled water and slide the disc in position as above.
8. Again dry the vessel from out side and weigh it. let the weight of the vessel be W_2.
9. Place the aggregate on a dry cloth and dry its surface gently with the cloth. When the first cloth becomes wet and absorbs no further moisture, transfer the aggregate to the second cloth and spread it in a thin layer in such a way that no stone remains one above the other. Leave the aggregate exposed to atmosphere away from direct sun rays for not less than 10 minutes or untill it appears

to be completely surface dry. The aggregate is turned over at least once during this drying period. A gentle current of unheated air may be passed after first 10 minutes to accelerase the drying of difficult particles of the sample.

10. Weigh the aggregate again. Let the weight be W_3.
11. Now place the aggregate in a shallow tray and put it into the oven at a temperature of 100°C to 110°C for 24 ± ½ hours.
12. After 24 hours, take the aggregate out of the oven and air cool it in a air tight container and weigh again. Let the weight of the aggregate be W_4.
13. Repeat the experiment with three different samples.

Observations

S. No.	*Description*	*Sample*		
		I	II	III
1.	Weight of vessel + wt. of sample + water $= W_1$ gms			
2.	Weight of vessel + water $= W_2$ gms.			
3.	Weight of saturated and surface dry sample $= W_3$ gms.			
4.	Weight of oven dried sample $= W_4$ gms.			
5.	Specific gravity $= \frac{W_4}{W_3 - (W_1 - W_2)}$			
6.	Apparant specific gravity $= \frac{W_4}{W_4 - (W_1 - W_2)}$			
7.	Water absorption $= \frac{W_3 - W_4}{W_4} \times 100\%$			

Precautions

1. The aggregate should be thoroughly washed to remove dust.
2. For soaking the aggregate distilled water should be used.
3. The glass disc should be slided over the mouth of the vessel in such a way that no air is trapped in the vessel.
4. The difference in temperature of water in the vessel during first and second weighing should not exceed 2°C.

Experiment 10. *To determine the specific gravity and water absorption when the aggregate is smaller than 10 mm. (Pycno-meter method).*

Theory. Same as for exp. No. 9.

Apparatus

1. Balance
2. Oven
3. Vessel Pycno-meter as shown in Fig. 3
4. Air drier
5. A tray not less than 325 cm^2 in arca.
6. An air tight container large enough to take up the sample.
7. Filter paper and funnel.

Procedure

1. Take a sample of one kg. if the aggregate is in between 10 mm to 4.75 mm and 500 grams if the aggregate is finer than 4.75 mm and place it in a tray and cover it with distilled water at a temperature of 22°C to 32°C.
2. Remove the entrapped air or bubbles on the surface of the aggregate soon after immersion in the distilled water by agitating the aggregate gently with a rod. Keep the sample immersed in the distilled water for 24 ± ½ hours.
3. Drain off the water from the sample carefully by decantation through a filter paper and any material retained is returned to the sample.
4. To evaporate the surface moisture the aggregate including any solid matter retained on the filtre paper is exposed to a gentle current of warm air. To ensure uniform drying it is stirred frequently till no free surface moisture is seen.

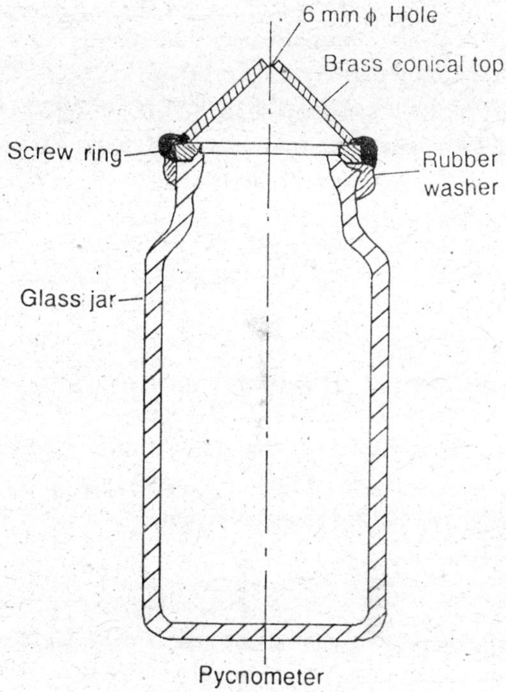

Fig. 3. Pycnometre

5. Weigh the saturated and surface dry sample. Let the weight be W_1.
6. The aggregate is placed in Pycno-meter and filled with distilled water.
7. Remove any entrapped air by rotating the Pycnomter on its side. During this operation the hole in the apex of the cone should be covered with finger.
8. Dry the Pycnometer on the out side and weigh it. Let the weight of sample + water be W_2.
9. Dry the contents of the Pycnomter in the tray. While transferring the contents, care should be taken that no aggregate particle falls out side.
10. Refill the Pycnometer with distilled water to the same level as before. Dry it from the out side and weigh it. Let the weight be W_3.
11. Remove the water from the sample by decantation and dry the sample in the oven at 100°C to 110°C for 24 ± ½ hour. Cool and weigh it. Let the weight be W_4.

Observations

S. No.	*Description*	*Sample*		
		I	II	III
1.	Weight of sample taken $= W_1$ gms			
2.	Weight of saturated and surface dry sample $= W_1$ gms.			
3.	Weight of Pycnometer + sample + water $= W_2$ gms.			
4.	Weight of Pycnometer + water $= W_3$ gms.			
5.	Weight of oven dry aggregate $= W_4$ gms.			

S. No.	*Description*	*Sample*		
		I	II	III
5.	Specific gravity $= \dfrac{W_4}{W_3 - (W_2 - W_3)}$			
7.	Apparant specific gravity $= \dfrac{W_4}{W_4 - (W_2 - W_3)}$			
8.	Water absorption $= \dfrac{W_1 - W_4}{W_4} \times 100\%$			

Experiment 11. *To determine the bulk density and voids of aggregates of the given type of aggregates as per I.S. 2316-Part-III-1963.*.

(*a*) 20 mm graded and angular type aggregate.

(*b*) 20 mm single size and angular type aggregate.

(*c*) 20 mm graded round aggregate.

(*d*) Fine aggregate.

Theory

Bulk density. It can be defined as the weight of material required to fill a container of unit volume. This unit volume consists of solid material plus the volume of voids and usually is expressed as kg/lit. The value of bulk density of aggregate depends upon the amount of effort made to fill the container as densely as possible, its shape, specific gravity and grading of aggregate etc. More graded the aggregate, greater the bulk density. Angular and flaky shape of the aggregate reduce the bulk density. Thus the bulk density of rodded and loose material will differ.

The knowledge of bulk density helps in the conversion of the aggregate quantity by weight to quantity by volume, which is helpful in weigh batching and volume batching of the material.

For batching purposes, if materials are measured, the bulk density of the loose material should be calculated. On the other hand if the bulk density test is carried out to detect change in grading and shape of the aggregate, then rodded bulk density test should be carried out to compare the results.

If bulk density test is carried out frequently on the site, the appreciable change in the volume of the bulk density helps in detecting change in the grading or shape or the aggregate and enables to maintain better quality control at site.

Apparatus

1. A balance having a sensitively of 0.5% of the weight to be weighed.
2. Cylindrical metal measures of 3, 15 and 30 litres capacity according to maximum size of coarsest particle of the aggregate as follows:

Size of aggregate	*Size of measure*
(*a*) 4.75 mm and below	3 litres
(*b*) 4.75 mm to 40 mm	15 litres
(*c*) over 40 mm	30 litres

3. Tamping rod 16 mm dia and 60 cm long with one end rounded.
4. Container, trough, steel rule and measuring cylinder 250 ml capacity.

Procedure

(*a*) For rodded weight.

Condition of the specimen

1. For determining the bulk density, aggregate with the given percentage of moisture may be used.
2. For determining voids, the material should be dry, while noting observations, condition of material should be mentioned.
3. Select the cylindrical metal measure according to the size of aggregate.
4. Fill the measure up to about 1/3 rd full with the thoroughly mixed aggregate.
5. Tamp the aggregate with 25 strokes of the rounded end of the tamping rod.
6. Now fill the measure upto 2/3rd of its height with the remaining aggregate and tamp the aggregate with 25 strokes with the tamping rod as before.
7. Now fill the cylinder measure to over flowing and tamp it 25 times as before.
8. Struck off the surplus aggregate by using the tamping rod as straight edge.
9. Weigh the measure with aggregate. The net weight of the aggregate in the measure will give the bulk density in kg/lit.

(*b*) Loose weight

1. Select the cylindrical metal measure according to size of the aggregate.
2. Fill the measure to its capacity *i.e.* to its over flowing condition by a scoop or shovel.
3. The surface of the aggregate is levelled using the tamping rod as a straight edge.
4. Weigh the measure with aggregate and find out the net weight of aggregate.
5. The bulk density is calculated in kg/lit.

Observation

Condition of aggregate. Air dry/surface dry/moist

S. No.	*Description*	*Samples*		
		I	II	III
1.	Capacity of the measure $= V$ litres			
2.	Weight of the measure $= w_1$ kg.			
3.	Weight of the measure + compacted aggregate $= w_2$ kg			
4.	Weight of the measure + lose aggregate $= w_3$ kg			
5.	(*i*) Then, rodded bulk density $\gamma_R = \frac{w_2 - w_1}{V}$ kg/lit. (*ii*) Loose of voids $\gamma_L = \frac{w_3 - w_1}{V}$ kg/lit. % of voids $= \frac{G_s - \gamma}{G_s} \times 100\%$ where G_s = sp gravity. γ = bulk density			

Precautions

1. Weighing should be done very carefully.
2. While filling measure, the aggregate should be discharged from a height not exceeding 5 cm above the top of the measure to avoid any segregation of the aggregate particles.

Experiment 12. *To determine the surface moisture in a given sample of fine aggregate by displacement method (IS 2386-Part-III-1963).*

Theory. If all the pores in the aggregate are filled with water, but its surface is dry and contains no free moisture, then it is called as saturated and surface dry aggregate. In this condition the aggregate neither absorbs water nor does it give out water.

Surface moisture is expressed in terms of weight of saturated surface dry aggregate as well as in terms of wet aggregate.

Fine aggregate when exposed to rain, collects large amount of moisture on the surface and retains this moisture for a long period. Fine aggregate received fresh from river bed also contains considerable amount of moisture. Further if fine aggregate is required to be washed before use it retains moisture. This moisture always adds to the water to be used in concrete mix and increases water/cement ratio resulting in reduced compressive strength of concrete. Thus it is essential to know the surface moisture content of fine aggregate to fix the correct water/cement ratio. Thus actual water to be added in the mix shall be the water calculated from water/cement ratio minus the free moisture content of the fine aggregate.

Apparatus

1. A balance having capacity of 2 kg or more and sensive to 0.5 g.
2. Flask of glass graduated upto 0.5 ml or less. The capacity of flask should be 2 to 3 times the loose volume of the sample.

Procedure

1. Take the representative sample of the fine aggregate and weigh it. Let the weight be W_1 gram. The weight of sample should not be less than 200 gram. Larger sample gives more accurate results.
2. Fill the container upto the mark with water and again weigh it. Let this weight be W_2 grams.
3. Empty the container and add some water sufficient to cover the sample.
4. Put the sample in the container and remove the entrained air, by giving rapid clock wise and anti-clockwise rotation to the container.
5. Fill the container with water upto the original mark and weigh again. Let this weight be W.

Observations

S. No.	*Description*	*Samples*		
		I	II	III
1.	Weight of sample $= W_1$ grams			
2.	Weight of container + water filled upto the mark $= W_2$ grams			
3.	Weight of container + water upto the mark + sample $= W$ grams			
4.	Weight of water displaced by the sample $V_s = W_2 + W_1 - W$			
5.	Dry volume $V_d = \frac{W_1}{\text{Sp. gr. of sample}}$, where V_d is the volume of sample on saturated and surface dry basis.			
6.	Then % surface moisture in terms of weight of saturated and surface dry aggregate, $P_1 = \frac{V_s - V_d}{W - V_s} \times 100\%$			
7.	Percentage surface moisture in terms of weight of wet aggreate $P_2 = \frac{V_s - V_d}{W_1 - V_d} \times 100\%$			

Precautions

1. The weight of the sample should not be less than 200 grams.
2. Weighing should be done accurately.
3. Air entertained if any, should be removed carefully.

Experiment 13. *To determine the moisture content in fine aggregate by frying pan method.*

Theory. Same as for displacement method.

Apparatus

1. A balance of 2 kg. capacity.
2. Thermostatically controlled heater.
3. A tray 60 cms × 30 cms in size.

Procedure

1. Take about one kg of representative sample of fine aggregate and weigh it. Let the weight be W_1 grams.
2. Put the aggregate in the tray and dry the aggregate over a source of heat. While heating, care should be taken not to over dry the aggregate.
3. Weigh the dry aggregate. Let the weight be W_2 grams.

Observations

S. No.	*Description*	*Samples*		
		I	II	III
1.	Weight of wet sample $= W_1$ g.			
2.	Weight of dry sample $= W_2$ g.			
3.	Loss of weight $= (W_1 - W_2)$ g.			
4.	% moisture in terms of dry aggregate $P_1 = \frac{W_1 - W_2}{W_2} \times 100\%$			
5.	% moisture in terms of wet aggregate $P_2 = \frac{W_1 - W_2}{W_1} \times 100\%$			

Precautions

1. Weighing should be done very carefully and accurate.
2. Sample should not be over dried. It should be heated to the free flowing condition *i.e.* if the sand is put into a pile by means of a conical mould, on removing the mould, sand should slump freely.
3. The brownish tinge acquired by the sand is an indication of over heating of sand.

Experiment 14. *To determine the bulking of fine aggregate. (I.S. 2386-Part-III-1963).*

Theory. Bulking is defined as the increase in volume of a given volume of sand due to the presence of surface moisture. The increase is caused by the film of surface water covering each particle of sand and pushing them apart due to surface tension. Bulking of sand varies with the fineness of sand. Fine sand bulks about 40%, medium sand to 25% to 29% and coarse sand to about 18%.

With the moisture content of 5 to 6%, the increase in the volume of sand varies from 20 to 40% depending upon the fineness of sand. Beyond this percentage of moisture content, bulking tends to decrease with further addition of water. The volume of fully saturated sand is approximately the same as that of dry sand measured in loose condition.

When the batching of aggregate is done by volume, bulking results in smaller weight of sand occupying the fixed volume of measuring box. The concrete mix thus becomes deficient in sand which causes following defects in the concrete.

1. Sand deficient mix causes segregation of concrete.
2. Sand deficient mix results in honeycombed concrete. The strength and impermeability of such concrete reduces to a great extent.
3. The yield of such concrete is also reduced.

Thus, while adding fine aggregate to the concrete mix by volume, the bulking of sand should be checked carefully and the required volume of sand should be proportionately increased according to bulking of sand.

Apparatus

1. A container of suitable size.
2. Steel rule.
3. Steel rod 6 mm in diameter.
4. 250 ml capacity measuring cylinder.

Procedure

Method I

1. Take a suitable container, preferably a cylindrical container and fill it about 2/3rd full with the sand in loose state *i.e.* sand should not be compacted in any way.
2. Smooth and level off the top of the sand with the steel rule and push this steel rule in the centre of the surface to the bottom of the container vertically and note its height. Let this height of sand be h cms.
3. Empty the sand out of the container into another container.
4. Fill the container with water to 1/4th to 1/3rd volume occupied by sand.
5. Put back about half the sand in the container having water and stir with 6 mm steel rod so that its volume reduces to minimum.
6. Add the remaining sand and stir or rod it in the same way as in 5 above.
7. Smooth and level off the surface of the sand and measures its depth by pushing the steel rule at the middle by pushing the rule vertically down to the bottom. Let this height be h_1.

then bulking of sand % $= \dfrac{h - h_1}{h_1} \times 100\%$

Observations

S. No.	*Description*		*Samples*		
			I	II	III
1.	Height of loose sand	h cms			
2.	Height of sa..urated sand	h_1 cm			
3.	Percentage bulking $= \dfrac{h-h_1}{h_1} \times 100\%$				

Method II

1. Take the 250 ml capacity measuring cylinder and pour damp sand into it. Consolidate the sand by shaking the cylinder until it reaches 200 ml mark.

2. Take the sand out.
3. Put some water into the measuring cylinder and add the sand taken out in step N. 2 and stir it well.
4. The surface of sand in the cylinder will be at a lower mark than original. Let the surface of sand be at y ml mark.

then percentage bulking $= \dfrac{200 - y}{y} \times 100\%$

Precautions

1. The top surfaces of sand should be properly levelled smooth at the time of measuring the height.
2. The height of sand should be measured accurately.
3. No sand should be lost while transferring it from one container to the other container.

Experiment 15. *To determine particle size distribution of fine, coarse and all in aggregate by sieve analysis.*

Theory

Coarse aggregate. The aggregate particles retained on 4.75 mm I.S. sieve is called *coarse aggregate.*

Fine aggregate. Aggregate particles passing through 4.75 mm I.S. sieve and retained on 75 micron sieve is called *fine aggregate.*

All in aggregate. The combination of coarse and fine aggregate is known as *all in aggregate.*

Single size aggregate. In this type of aggregate, the size of particles belongs to one or two consecutive sieve sizes only.

Graded aggregate. Aggregate containing particles of all sizes in suitable proportions is known as graded aggregate. The main advantage of this aggregate is that it has minimum voids and improves workability of concrete mix considerably. Aggregate having one sized particles considerably larger than the other sizes makes the concrete harsh (deficient in fine particles) and does not give good surface finish when worked with trowel.

Thus by sieve analysis, the proportions of different sizes of particles in each aggregate can be determined. The results of sieve analysis of each aggregate are calculated in terms of percentage of total aggregate passing through each size of sieve. To get an visual grasp of the grading, the results of each type of aggregate can be plotted on a graph with percentage passing on y-axis as ordinates and sieve aperture on x-axis as abscissa on logarithmic scale. Though there is no ideal grading, yet limits are placed on grading, upper limit for finer grading and lower limit for coarser grading. Higher the percentage passing, finer the grading and greater the water requirement for a fixed water/cement ratio, resulting in poor quality concrete. Lower the percentage passing, coarser the grading and greater the tendency to segregate. Thus the most suitable grading is that which gives minimum number of fines, but sufficient to give the necessary cohesiveness to the mix.

Appratus

1. A set of I.S. test sieves as given in table 4.17, page 95.
2. A balance of 10 kg capacity.
3. Brushes.

Procedure

1. Take the representative sample and make it air dry either by drying it at room temperature or heating it at a temperature of 100°C to 110°C.
2. Weigh the dried sample.
3. Place the weighed sample on the specified set of sieves with the largest sieve at the top according to the maximum size of the aggregate and sieve it successively on each sieve of the set.

4. Shake each sieve separately over a tray untill not more than a trace passes, but in no case less than for 2 minutes.
5. At the end of the sieving, clean the material sticking to 75 micron and 150 micron sieves at their bottoms by light brushing.
6. After the completion of the sieving, weigh the material retained on each sieve together with any material cleaned from the mesh.
7. Find the percentage of each weight retained on different sieves in terms of the total sample.
8. Calculate cumulative percentage retained on each sieve.
9. Calculate cumulative percentage passing on each sieve.
10. Draw a graph for each aggregate and compare the curves.

Precautions

1. Take the sample in specified quantity according to the maximum size of aggregate.
2. The aggregate sample should be air dried before weighing and sieving as wet sample will clog the sieve.
3. Before sieving, finer sieves should be cleaned gently with brush.
4. Sieves should not be surcharged. For coarse aggregate to be sieved through 40 mm sieve the weight of sample should not be more than 1 kg and for fine aggregate to be sieved through 20 mm sieve the weight of the sample should not be more than 500 grams.
5. Sieving should be done in such a way that each particle gets sufficient chance of passing through the sieve opening.
6. Weighing of material should be done carefully.

(*a*) Observation—Sieve analysis results for coarse aggregate—

I.S. Sieve size	*Weight of aggregate retained sample size*			*Total weight*						
	I	II	III	*Sum*	*Average sum*	*Percent retained*	*Cummulative percent retained*	*Percent passing*	*Cummulative % passing*	*Remark*
80 mm										Graded coarse aggregate
63 mm										
40 mm										
20 mm										
16 mm										
10 mm										
4.75										
2.36										
80 mm										Single size coarse aggregate
63 mm										
40 mm										
20 mm										
16 mm										
10 mm										
4.75										
2.36										

(*b*) Sieve analysis results for fine aggregate—

I.S. Sieve size	*Weight of aggregate retained sample size*			*Total weight*						
	I	II	III	*Sum*	*Average sum*	*Percent retained*	*Cummulative percent retained*	*Percent passing*	*Cummulative % passing*	*Remark*
10 mm										
4.75 mm										
2.36 mm										
1.18 mm										
600 micron										
300 micron										
150 micron										
75 micron										

(*c*) Sieve analysis results for all in aggregate—

I.S. Sieve size	*Weight of aggregate retained sample size*			*Total weight*						
	I	II	III	*Sum*	*Average sum*	*Percent retained*	*Cummulative percent retained*	*Percent passing*	*Cummulative % passing*	*Remark*
80 mm										
63 mm										
40 mm										
20 mm										
16 mm										
10 mm										
4.75 mm										
2.36 mm										
1.18 mm										
600 micron										
300 micron										
150 micron										
75 micron										

Experiment 16. *To determine the fineness modulus of aggregate.*

Theory. *Fineness modulus* of aggregate is an index number which gives an idea about the coarseness or fineness of an aggregate. It can be written as F.M.

Fineness modulus of an aggregate is approximately proportional of the average size of particles in the aggregate. In other words, coarser the aggregate, higher the fineness modulus. The maximum value of fineness of coarse aggregate is found to be 8.0 and for coarse sand 3.5. As stated on page 106, the fineness modulus for fine aggregate varies from 2.0 to 3.5, for coarse aggregatefrom 5.5 to 8.0 and for all in aggregate 3.5 to 6.5.

Fineness modulus is determined by adding the cumulative percentage of material retained on each sieve and dividing the sum of cumulative percentage of material retained on each sieve by 100.

Apparatus

1. Set of sieves
2. A balance having a capacity of 10 kg.
3. A tray.

Procedure

Take a suitable sample of aggregate and put it on the specified sieve as follows:

For coarse aggregate 80 mm, 40 mm, 20 mm, 10 mm, 4.75 mm, 2.36 mm, 1.18 mm, 600 micron, 300 micron, 150 micron.

The aggregate is sieved as for sieve analysis, and the weight retained on each sieve is found. From the value of weights retained, cumulative percentage of weight retained on each sieve is calculated. After the lowest sieve, the percentage retained should be taken as explained by the following example.

Very fine or very coarse sand is objectionable for concrete mix because the very fine sand makes the mix uneconomic as finer the sand, greater the amount of water needed for a definite workability producing low strength concrete. On the other hand coarse sand produces harsh and unworkable mix. Thus the fineness modulus of sand should not be less than 2.5 and more than 3.5 for producing good quality concrete.

Observations:

Sample wt = 10 kg Sample weight 1 kg

I.S. Sieve sizes	*Coarse aggregate*			*Fine aggregate*		
	weight retained on each sieve in kg.	*cumulative weigh retained in kg.*	*cummulative % of weight retained*	*weight retained on each sieve in gram*	*cumulative weigh retained in gram*	*cummulative % of weight retained*
80 mm	0	0	0	—	—	—
40 mm	1.2	1.2	12.0	—	—	—
20 mm	4.0	5.2	52.0	—	—	—
10 mm	3.0	8.2	82.0	—	—	—
4.75 mm	1.8	10.0	100.0	20	20	2.0
2.36 mm	—	—	100.0	90	110	11.0
1.18 mm	—	—	100.0	200	310	31.0
600 micron	—	—	100.0	250	560	56.0
300 micron	—	—	100.0	350	910	91.0
150 micron	—	—	100.0	90	1000	100.0
Total	10 kg.	—	746.00	1.0 kg.		291

$$\text{Fineness modulus for coarse aggregate} = \frac{746}{100} = 7.46$$

$$\text{Fineness modulus for fine aggregate} = \frac{291}{100} = 2.91$$

Experiment 17. *To determine the flakiness index and elongation index of coarse aggregate (I.S. 2386-Part-I-1963).*

Theory. Flaky particles. A particle of aggregate is said to be flaky if its least dimension is less than 0.6 times of its mean dimension. Flakiness index is the weight of flaky particles measured as percentage of the total weight of the sample. Flakeness index more than 35 to 40% is undesirable.

Elongated particle. A particle is said to be elongated if its length is greater than 1.8 times its means dimension. Elongated index is the weight of elongated particles measured as percentage of the total weight of the sample. For this no limit has been laid.

The flaky or elongated particles are not desirable as their large number creates more voids, requiring more fine materials and also more water for the same workability. These particles tend to be oriented in one plane, causing laminations, and affect the durability of concrete adversely. Their combined value should not be more than 40 to 45% of the weight of aggregate.

Procedure (For Flakiness index)

1. Take sufficient quantity of aggregate to provide at least 200 pieces of any fraction to be tested.
2. Sieve the sample through sieves as shown in observations table.
3. Separate particles retained on the prescribed sieves.
4. Try to pass each aggregate particle through the corresponding slot of thickness gauge Fig. 4. The aggregate piece passing through 50 mm and retained on 40 mm sieve, should only be passed through $\left(\frac{50+40}{2}\right) \times 0.6 = 27.0$ mm slot. If the aggregate passes through this 27.0 mm slot; then the aggregate piece is flaky.
5. Weigh all the pieces which pass through this slot.
6. Calculate the flakiness index

$$= \frac{\text{Wt. of material passing through the thickness gauge}}{\text{Total weight of sample}} \times 100$$

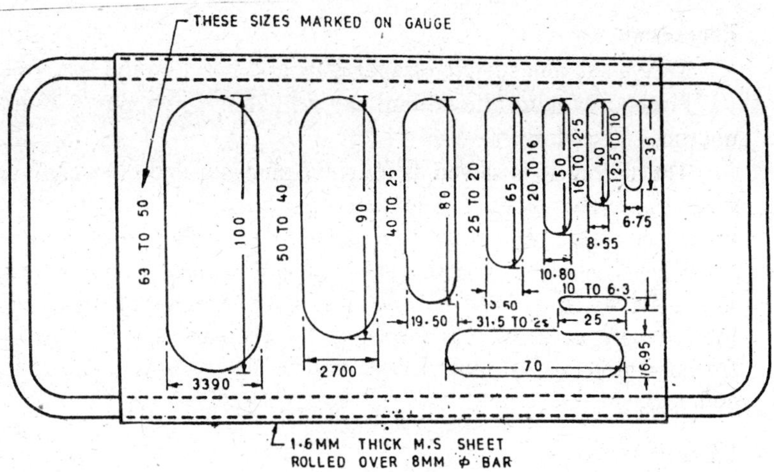

Fig. 4. Thickness Gauge

For elongation index

1. Sieve the sample through I.S., sieve as specified in observation table.
2. Separate aggregate pieces retained on sieves.
3. Try to pass each aggregate piece through the corres-ponding slot of length gauge (Fig. 5). If the length of the particle is $\left(\frac{50+40}{2}\right) \times 1.8 = 81$ mm, it is said to have retained on the length gauge.
4. Weigh all such pieces
5. Calculate the elongation index as follows—

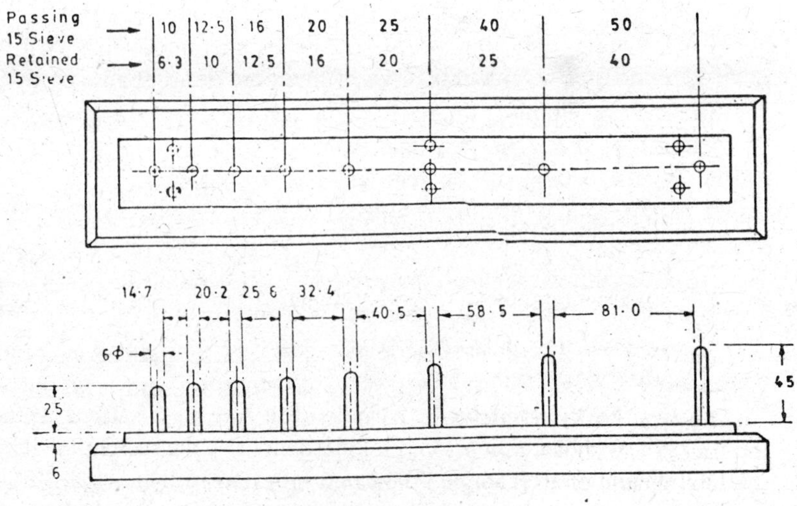

Fig. 5. Length Gauge

$$= \frac{\text{Weight of material retained on the length gauge}}{} \times 100$$

Observations

Size of aggregate		Corresponding thickness gauge col $\left(\frac{I+II}{2}\right) \times 0.6$ mm	Weight of aggregate passing through thickness gauge W_2	Corresponding length gauge col $\left(\frac{I+II}{2}\right) \times 1.8$ mm	Weight of aggregate retained on length gauge W_2
Passing through I.S. sieve mm	*Retained on I.S. sieve mm*				
63 mm	50	33.9		101.7	
50 mm	40	27.0		81.0	
40 mm	31.5	19.5		58.5	
31.5 mm	25.0	16.95		50.85	
25 mm	20	13.50		40.5	
20 mm	16	10.80		32.4	
16 mm	12.5	8.55		25.6	
12.5 mm	10.0	6.75		20.2	
10.0 mm	6.3	4.89		14.7	

Note. Suppose the aggregate particle passes through 50 mm sieved and retained on 40 mm sieve, then

$$\text{thickness gauge} = \left(\frac{50 + 40}{2}\right) \times 0.6 = 27.0 \text{ mm}$$

$$\text{length gauge} = \left(\frac{50 + 40}{2}\right) \times 1.8 = 81 \text{ mm}$$

Experiment 18. *To determine the workability of concrete mix.*

Theory. The ease in transportation, placement, compaction, finishing, and resistance to segregation of concrete mix is known as workability. In more scientific terms it can be defined as the property of concrete which determines the amount of useful internal work necessary to produce full compaction. Though the definition is quite easy, but its correct determination is quite difficult. However some tests have been devised to measure workability. Two of them are described in the following paragraphs.

Slump test. Slump is the measure of subsidence of the concrete pile formed in a mould of the shape of frustum of cone. The decrease in height of the slumped concrete is called slump. slump can be divided into three categories as follows:

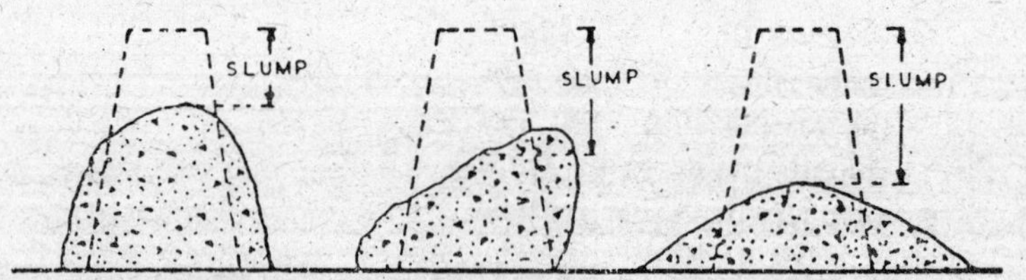

(*a*) TRUE SLUMP (*b*) SHEAR SLUMP (*c*) COLLAPSE SLUMP

Fig. 6. Various types of slumps

1. True slump. If the concrete slumps evenly all-round as shown in Fig. 6 (*a*) then it is called true slump. Actually this slump is aimed to be determined.
2. Shear slump. If instead of slumping evenly all-round, one half of the core slides down as inclined plane, then it is called shear slump. It is difficult to measure. Usually it occurs in harsh mixes. Fig. 6 (*b*).
3. Collapse slump. In this case concrete slides as soon as cone is removed and it is difficult to measure. It occurs in very wet mixes. Concrete giving shear or collapse slump is considered unsatisfactory for placing. Fig. 6 (*c*) above.

This test being very easy to perform, hence it is very suitable for field work. A particular amount of slump is required for different types of concrete work. Once the slump is decided for a particular work, it is easy to obtain concrete of that workability.

This test is very useful to check the day to day or hour to hour variation in the ingredients of the concrete mix used for a particular job on the site. Increase in slump indicates that either the moisture content in aggregate has changed unexpectedly or grading of aggregate has changed. Low value of slump indicates that mix is unworkable.

Cohessive mix. A good cohesive mix subsides without the coarse aggregate tending to fall out of the mix.

Harsh mix. A mix deficient in fine aggregate or sand is said to be a harsh mix. It gives honey combed surface and its yield is also less. A harsh mix does not give smooth finish to the surface even with trowelling under pressure, while adequately sanded mix gives smooth finish with normal trowelling.

Over sanded mix. It gives smooth finish with even light trowelling.

Apparatus

1. A mould in the form of frustum of cone (Fig. 7.2, page 165).
2. Tamping rod, 60 cms long and 1.6 in diameter, rounded at one end.
3. Trowel.
4. Trough.
5. G.I. plain sheets.
7. Steel rule.

Procedure

1. Clean the internal surface of the mould thoroughly by removing set concrete, dust or moisture etc. and apply a light film of oil or grease.
2. Place the mould on a smooth horizontal, rigid and non absorbent surface, or on a carefully levelled metal plate or masonry platform.
3. Hold the mould in position firmly.
4. Fill the concrete in the mould upto 1/4th of its height and tamp it with the tamping rod by giving 25 strokes uniformly spread over the full surface of the concrete, while tamping, care should be taken that pointed end is thrushed into the concrete.
5. After compacting first layer, fill concrete by quarter height and again tamp. Similarly other layers are tamped.
6. After tamping the top layer, struck off extra concrete by a trowel or tamping rod and level it with the top of the mould. That is the mould is exactly filled.
7. Raise the mould up vertically carefully. On raising the mould the concrete will subside.
8. Measure the height of the subsided concrete heap by steel rule immediately after removing the mould.
9. The difference between the original height and subsided heap of concrete will give the value of slump. The procedure is repeated for three times and their mean value is taken.
10. Compare the value of slump so obtained with the standard value. If they compare well, then workability of the mix is satisfactory for that particular job otherwise change water content; and repeat the procedure, till desired slump is obtained.

Higher value of slump is desirable when the compaction of the concrete is to be done manually or sections are small or heavily reinforced or size of the aggregate is greater. Standard values of slumps for different type of works are shown in Table 7.2, page 166.

Observations

Particulars	*Cement*	*Total aggregate*	*F.A.:C.A.*	*F.A.*	*C.A.*	*Water added*	*W/C ratio*	*Slump*	*Workability*
1. Initial proportions by vol. per bag of cement									
2. Laboratory trial batched per 3 kg of cement by volume.									
Proportion by weight (Multiply by bulk density)									

I. Trial
II. Trial
III. Trial

Note. From above table the effect of water/cement ratio on slump can also be verified when F.A.C.A.; cement and aggregate ratios are kept constant.

Experiment 19. *To determine the workability of concrete by compacting factor method.*

Theory. In drier mixes, slump test does not give slump and to detect the change in workability a more sensitive method is necessary. The compacting factor test works on the principle of determining the degree of compaction achieved by a standard amount of work by allowing the concrete to fall through a standard height. The compacting factor gives an idea of the degree of compaction. Thus *compacting factor can be defined as the ratio of the density actually achieved in the test to the density of fully compacted concrete.* Therefore compacting factor method of determining of workability of concrete is more rational method than slump test method. Compacting factor method is more suitable for dry mixes with low slump. It is more useful in laboratory testing, but if possible it could be used at site also.

Apparatus

1. Compacting factor apparatus as I.S. 1199-1959 (reference Fig. 7.6 page 168).
2. Two trowels.
3. Hand scoop.
4. Tamping rod.
5. Platform weighting machine.

Procedure

1. Clean the inner surface of the apparatus including cylinder and apply light film of oil or grease.
2. Cover the lower hopper and cylinder with a iron sheet to avoid falling of concrete into them while filling the upper hopper with concrete.
3. Close the trap doors of upper and lower hoppers carefully.
4. Now place the sample of concrete gently in the upper hopper with a hand scoop and fill the upper hopper upto its brim.
5. Remove the covering sheet from the lower hopper and open the trap door of the upper hopper, so that concrete falls into the lower hopper.
6. Remove the covering sheet from cylinder and open the trap door of the lower hopper, so that the concrete falls into the cylinder.

7. If the concrete sticks to the sides of the hopper, it may be pushed gently with the help of rod from the top.
8. Remove the excess concrete remaining above the level of the top of cylinder with the help of two trowels.
9. Clean the out side of the cylinder.
10. Weigh the cylinder alongwith concrete and find out the weight of concrete.
11. Compact the concrete in the cylinder by vibration and fill it fully with the compacted concrete or empty the cylinder and fill it in layers approximately 5 cms in thickness and vibrate fully to obtain full compaction.
12. Clean the outside of the cylinder and weigh it. Find out the weight of compacted concrete. Weight of empty cylinder being known.
13. Then compacting factor

$$= \frac{\text{Weight of un compacted concrete of cylinder}}{\text{Weight of fully compacted concrete in the cylinder}}$$

Observation

S. No.	*Description*		*Samples*		
			I	II	III
1.	Weight of cylinder	$= W_1$ kg.			
2.	Weight of cylinder + concrete falling through standard height	$= W_2$ kg.			
3.	Weight of concrete $= (W_2 - W_1)$	$= W_3$ kg.			
4.	Weight of cylinder + Fully compacted concrete	$= W_4$ kg.			
5.	Weight of fully compacted concrete $= (W_4 - W_1)$	$= W_5$ kg.			
6.	Then compacting factor $= \frac{(W_2 - W_1)}{(W_4 - W_1)}$	$= \frac{W_4}{W_5}$			

Bibliography

1. D.F. Orchard: Concrete Technology, John Willy & Sons, ING, New York-I.G.
2. A.M. Neville: Properties of Concrete, Practice, Pitman, U.K.
3. R.H. Elvery, Concrete Practice Vol. I & II, ASIA Publishing House.
4. Concrete Association of India, Concrete worker's is Guide, A.C.C.
5. Dr. Jai Krishna and Dr. O.P. Jain, Plain and Reinforced Concrete, Nemchand Jain, Roorkee.
6. George Earl Troxell, Composition & Properties of Concrete, Magra-Hill Book Company.
7. I.S.I., Indian Standards, I.S.I. New Delhi.
8. Kulkarmi P.D. & Mittal L.N.: Laboratory Manual for Concrete, TTTI Chandigarh.
9. A.M. Neville & J.J. Brooks: Concrete Technology, Addison Wesley Longman, INC.
10. M.L. Gambhir: Concrete Technology, Tata-Magra Hill, Publishing Company Ltd, New Delhi.
11. M.S. Shetty: Concrete Technology Theory and Practice, S-Chand and Company, New Delhi.
12. V.K. Mehrotra: Roller Compacted Concrete Dams (Planning Design and Construction), Standard Publishers Distributors, Delhi.
13. Satish Chandra: Waste Materials Used in Concrete Manufacturing, Standard Publishers Distributors, Delhi.
14. Satish Chandra: Lightweight Aggregate Concrete, Science, Technology and Applications, Standard Publishers Distributors, Delhi.
15. S. Popovics: Concrete Materials Properties, Specifications & Testing, Standard Publishers Distributors, Delhi.
16. Ramachandran: Concrete Admixtures Handbook, (Properties, Science & Technology), Standard Publishers Distributors, Delhi.
17. C.B. Kukreja: Material Testing Laboratory Manual, Standard Publishers Distributors, Delhi.

Index

A

B

C

D

P

Q

R